A GLOSSARY OF OLD SYRIAN
VOLUME 2

LANGUAGES OF THE ANCIENT NEAR EAST

GONZALO RUBIO, *Pennsylvania State University*
Editor-in-Chief

Editorial Board

JAMES P. ALLEN	*Brown University*
AARON BUTTS	*Catholic University of America*
GENE B. GRAGG	*The Oriental Institute, University of Chicago*
REBECCA HASSELBACH-ANDEE	*The Oriental Institute, University of Chicago*
ANTONIO LOPRIENO	*Jacobs University Bremen*
H. CRAIG MELCHERT	*University of California, Los Angeles*
PIOTR MICHALOWSKI	*University of Michigan*
P. OKTOR SKJÆRVØ	*Harvard University*
CHRISTOPHER WOODS	*University of Pennsylvania*

1. *A Grammar of the Hittite Language*, by Harry A. Hoffner Jr. and H. Craig Melchert
   Part 1: *Reference Grammar*
   Part 2: *Tutorial*
2. *The Akkadian Verb and Its Semitic Background*, by N. J. C. Kouwenberg
3. *Most Probably: Epistemic Modality in Old Babylonian*, by Nathan Wasserman
4. *Conditional Structures in Mesopotamian Old Babylonian*, by Eran Cohen
5. *Mood and Modality in Hurrian*, by Dennis R. M. Campbell
6. *The Verb in the Amarna Letters from Canaan*, by Krzysztof J. Baranowski
7. *Grammar of the Ancient Egyptian Pyramid Texts*, Volume 1: *Unis*, by James P. Allen

8/1. *A Glossary of Old Syrian*, Volume 1: *ʔ–ḳ*, by Joaquín Sanmartín
8/2. *A Glossary of Old Syrian*, Volume 2: *l–z*, by Joaquín Sanmartín

9. *Middle Egyptian*, by Peter Beylage
10. *Classical Ethiopic: A Grammar of Gəʿəz*, by Josef Tropper and Rebecca Hasselbach-Andee
11. *Rethinking the Origins: Ancient Egyptian and Afroasiatic*, edited by María Victoria Almansa-Villatoro and Silvia Štubňová Nigrelli
12. *Motion, Voice, and Mood in the Semitic Verb*, by Ambjörn Sjörs

A Glossary of Old Syrian

Volume 2: *l–z*

Joaquín Sanmartín

Eisenbrauns | University Park, PA

Library of Congress Cataloging-in-Publication Data

Names: Sanmartín, Joaquín, author.
Title: A glossary of old Syrian / Joaquín Sanmartín.
Other titles: Languages of the ancient Near East.
Description: University Park, Pennsylvania : Eisenbrauns, [2024]– | Series: Languages of the ancient Near East | Includes bibliographical references and indexes.
Summary: "A lexicographical index of the linguistic continuum of local dialects spoken in both the Syrian-Levantine (coastal Mediterranean) and Syrian-Mesopotamian (continental-Euphratian) areas during the Bronze Age"—Provided by publisher.
Identifiers: LCCN 2018038068 | ISBN 9781646022809 (cloth : alk. paper)
Subjects: LCSH: Semitic languages—Dialects—Syria—Glossaries, vocabularies, etc. | Syria—Languages—Dialects—Glossaries, vocabularies, etc.
Classification: LCC PJ3079.S26 2018 | DDC 492/.1—dc23
LC record available at https://lccn.loc.gov/2018038068

Printed in the United States of America
Published by The Pennsylvania State University Press,
University Park, PA 16802-1003

Eisenbrauns is an imprint of The Pennsylvania State University Press.

The Pennsylvania State University Press is a member of the Association of University Presses.

It is the policy of The Pennsylvania State University Press to use acid-free paper. Publications on uncoated stock satisfy the minimum requirements of American National Standard for Information Sciences—Permanence of Paper for Printed Library Material, ANSI Z39.48–1992.

Contents

List of sigla and bibliographical abbreviations vii
A. Sigla vii
B. Bibliographical abbreviations ix

Preliminary remarks xiii

Glossary
l 1
m 21
n 65
p 118
r 147
s (s^3) and S 181
ṣ 212
s^1 (š) 227
s^2 (ś) 270
ṣ́ 283
t 289
ṭ 306
θ (ṯ) 314
θ̣ (ẓ) 332
w 336
y 368
z 381

Indexes 389
A. Verbal roots 391
B. Nominal bases, syllabic notations 410
C. Nominal bases, alphabetic tradition 481

List of sigla and bibliographical abbreviations

A. Sigla

|x-x-x| (n)	Etymon, e.g., **|ʔ-b-r| (1)**, always untranslated. Nominal bases and verbal roots are both considered morphological concretions of an abstract etymon
= , *xx*= , =*xx*	The sign '=' functions as an equalizer if there is a space between the sign and the two equalized terms, as in "*malku* = *šarru*." Otherwise (i.e., *immediately* attached before or after a segment or placed between segments) it merely marks a graphemic or morphemic boundary, as in *a-bi*=, =*a-bu*, |yustaʔaxxað=|, |ʔad=u=ni=ʔil=a|, etc.
xxx, **|C-C-C|**	Transcription / normalization of lexemic bases (nouns: **xxx**, e.g., syllabic **ʔab**, alphabet. **åb**) and verbal roots: **|C-C-C|**, e.g., **|ʔ-b-r|**; usually translated
xx-xx-xx	Transliteration (e.g. *a-ia-*(*a-*)*bu*/*bi*)
→	first-degree bibliographical reference
A4	MBab. Alalakh
A7	OBab. Alalakh
abs.	absolute state
accus.	accusative
adj.	adjective, adjectival
ad loc.	ad locum
advb.	adverb(ial)
Af.	Afʕel. See C
Akk.	Akkadian (AHw and CAD)
Amh.	Amharic
Amm.	Ammonite
Arab.	Arabic (mainly Lane AEL, Wehr(-Cowan) DMWA)
Aram.	Aramean (mainly Hoftijzer / Jongeling DNWSI, Levy WTM, Sokoloff DJPA)
Ass., **ASS**	Assyrian, Assyria (source)
Bab, **B**	Babylonian, Babylon (source)
C	Causative stem. See Afʕel, H, Hof., Š
c.	common gender
CAram.	Common Aramaic
cf.	*confer*, compare
ChrAram.	Christian Palestinian Aramaic
cj.	conjecture, conjectural
Cpass.	Causative stem, passive
CSem.	Common Semitic
cstr.	construct state
Ct	Causative stem with -*t*-infix
ctx.	context [bkn: broken; frg.: fragmentary]
CTX	free, default context (No lexical list, no PN or DN)
D	Triconsonantal verbal stem with long second radical. See Paʕʕel, Piʕʕel
dat.	dative
DemAram.	Aramaic in Demotic Script (R. Steiner / A. Mosak Moshavi, in: Hoftijzer / Jongeling DNWSI 1285ff.)
denom.	denomination, denominated
desig.	designation, designating
DN(N)	divine name(s), theonym(s), epithet(s)
Dpass.	D passive. See Pu.
du.	Dual
EA	El Amarna (letters)
EA-Akk.	Akkadian (documented in the texts) from El Amarna

EB	Ebla (source)
Eg., **EG**	Egyptian, Egypt (source)
e.g.	*exempli gratia*, for example
elem.	element, segment
EM	Emar (source)
emph.	emphatic
encl.	enclitic
esp.	especially
Eth.	Ethiopic (mainly GəՙəZ, according to Leslau CDG; Tigre and Tgrinya). See also Amh.
etym.	etymology
EUPH	Euphratian (source, mainly Mari)
f(f.)	and following
fem.	feminine
fn.	footnote
G	Basic / ground verbal stem
genit.	genitive
GN	gentilic
Gpass.	G passive
Gr.	Greek
Gt	-*t*-infixed verbal stem G
H	Hifՙil / Haqtal. See C
Hb.	Hebrew
Hof.	Hofՙal
Hurr.	Hurrian
ibid.	*ibidem,* in the same place
IE	Indo-European
inf.	infinitive
JAram.	Jewish Aramaic
L	Stem with lengthened second radical (biconsonantal verbs)
Late	first millennium
Lex.	lexeme (mostly Arabic) known exclusively from lexicographic works
LL	lexical list
loc.cit.	*loco citato*, in the place cited.
Mand.	Mandaean
Mas.	Masoretic (Hebrew)
masc.	masculine
MAss.	Middle Assyrian
MBab.	Middle Babylonian
MBQ	Tall Munbaqa (Ekalte; source)
MN	month name
Mng	meaning
MSArab.	Modern South Arabian (Mehri, Ḥarsūsi, Baṭḥari, Ǧibbali, Soqoṭri)
MŠ	Malku-Šarru (source)
Myc.	Mycenaean
N	*n*-prefixed verbal stem / naqtal
NAss.	Neo-Assyrian
NBab.	Neo-Babylonian
NHb.	Mishnaic / Medieval and Late Hebrew
no.	number
nom.	nominative
NP	noun phrase
NWSem.	Northwest Semitic
OAkk.	Old Akkadian
OAss.	Old Assyrian
OBab.	Old Babylonian
obl.	oblique

op.cit.	*opere citato*, in the work cited
OSArab.	Old South Arabic
Pa.	Paʕʕel. See D
pass.	passive
Ph.	Phoenician (Hoftijzer / Jongeling DNWSI)
Pi.	Piʕʕel. See D
Pilp.	Pilpel. See R
pl.	plural
pl.t.	*plurale tantum*, plural only
PN(N)	personal name(s), anthroponym(s)
prefc.	prefix conjugation
ptc.	participle
Pu.	Puʕʕal. See Dpass.
Pun.	Punic (Hoftijzer / Jongeling DNWSI)
Q	Qaṭna (source)
R	reduplicated verbal biconsonantal stem. See Pilpel
R	Tall al-Rimah (source)
Rdg	reading
RS-Akk.	Akkadian (documented in the texts) from Ras Shamra
Š	š-prefixed verbal stem. See C
Sam.	Samaritan Aramaic
SBab	Standard Babylonian
sg.	singular
Soq.	Soqotri
Št	verbal stem with š-prefix and -t-infix / šataqtal. See Ct
stat.	stative
suff.	(with) suffix, suffixed
suffc.	suffix conjugation
Syr.	Syriac (Brockelmann / Sokoloff SL)
TA	Taanakh (source)
TN	place name, toponym
TU	Tall Biʕa (Tuttul, source)
U3	Ur III
UGA	Ugaritic in the alphabetic tradition
UGS	Syllabic notations in Ras Shamra texts
unc.	uncertain
unkn.	unknown
var., vars.	variant, variants
vb.	verb(al)
VP	verbal phrase
WSem.	West Semitic

B. Bibliographical abbreviations

Periodicals and series are cited as a rule according to the *Keilschriftbibliographie* (Or[NS]), AHw, CAD, and DUL (see below).

AAA	*Asia Anteriore Antica. Journal of Ancient Near Eastern Cultures* (Florence)
AbB	Altbabylonische Briefe in Umschrift und Übersetzung (Leiden)
ACF	*Annuaire du Collège de France* (Paris)
ActaSum	*Acta Sumerologica* (Hiroshima)
Aḫituv Toponyms	S. Aḫituv, *Canaanite Toponyms in Ancient Egyptian Documents* (Jerusalem 1984)
AHw	W. von Soden, *Akkadisches Handwörterbuch*, 3 vols. (Wiesbaden 1965–1981)
AION	*Annali dell'Istituto Universitario Orientale di Napoli* (Naples)
ALASP	*Abhandlungen zur Literatur Alt-Syrien-Palästinas* (Münster)

ANET(Suppl)	J. B. Pritchard, ed., *Ancient Near Eastern Texts Relating to the Old Testament* (Princeton, 1955) J. B. Pritchard, ed., *The Ancient Near East. Supplementary Texts and Pictures Relating to the Old Testament* (Princeton, 1969).
AOAT	Alter Orient und Altes Testament (Münster; Kevelaer / Neukirchen-Vluyn)
AoF	*Altorientalische Forschungen* (Berlin)
AOS	American Oriental Society: Papers Presented at the Annual Meetings.
Archi Ebla	A. Archi, *Ebla and its Archives: Texts, History, and Society* (Berlin 2015)
ARCHIBAB	Archives Babyloniennes (XX–XVIIe siècles av. J.-C.), http://www.archibab.fr/ (Paris)
ARES	Archivi reali di Ebla, Studi (Rome)
ARET	Archivi reali di Ebla, Testi (Rome)
ARM(T)	Archives royales de Mari (Textes) (Paris)
Arnaud Emar	D. Arnaud, *Recherches au pays d'Aštata: Emar 6*; vols. 1–2, *Textes sumériens et accadiens: Planches*; vol. 3, *Textes sumériens et accadiens. Texte*; vol. 4, *Textes de la bibliothèque: Transcriptions et traductions* (Paris, 1985–1987)
AULS	F. Renfroe, *Arabic-Ugaritic Lexical Studies* (Münster, 1992)
AuOr	*Aula Orientalis* (Sabadell / Barcelona)
AuOrS	Aula Orientalis Supplementa (Sabadell / Barcelona).
BaE	L. Cagni, ed., *Il bilinguismo a Ebla: Atti del convegno internazionale (Napoli, 19–22 aprile 1982)* (Naples, 1984)
BAH	Bibliothèque archéologique et historique, Institut français d'archéologie de Beyrouth (Paris)
BaM	*Baghdader Mitteilungen* (Berlin)
Barth Pronominalbildung	J. Barth, *Die Pronominalbildung in den semitischen Sprachen* (Leipzig, 1913)
Barth Studien	J. Barth, *Etymologische Studien zum semitischen, insbesondere zum hebräischen Lexicon* (Leipzig, 1893)
BBVO	Berliner Beiträge zum Vorderen Orient Texte (Berlin)
Benz PNPPI	F. L. Benz, *Personal Names in the Phoenician and Punic Inscriptions* (Rome, 1972)
Bordreuil / Pardee ManUg	P. Bordreuil and D. Pardee, *A Manual of Ugaritic*, Linguistic Studies in Ancient West Semitic 3 (Winona Lake, 2009)
Borger MZL	R. Borger, *Mesopotamisches Zeichenlexikon: Zweite, revidierte und aktualisierte Auflage* (Münster, 2010)
Bourguignon Emprunts	A. Bourguignon, "Les emprunts sémitiques en grec ancien. Étude méthodologique et exemples mycéniens" (PhD diss., Free University of Brussels, 2011–2012)
Brockelmann / Sokoloff SL	C. Brockelmann and M. Sokoloff, *A Syriac Lexicon* (Winona Lake / Piscataway, 2009)
Brockelmann GVG	C. Brockelmann, *Grundriss der vergleichenden Grammatik der semitischen Sprachen in zwei Bänden* (Hildesheim, 1961)
BSA	*Bulletin of Sumerian Agriculture* (Cambridge)
BSOAS	*Bulletin of the School of Oriental and African Studies* (London)
BuB	Babel und Bibel (Winona Lake)
Buccellati Amorites	G. Buccellati, *The Amorites of the Ur III Period* (Naples, 1966)
Buck ADU	M. E. Buck, *The Amorite Dynasty of Ugarit: Historical Implications of Linguistic and Archaeological Parallels* (Leiden, 2019)
BZAW	Beiheft zur Zeitschrift für die alttestamentliche Wissenschaft (Berlin)
CAD	*The Assyrian Dictionary of the Oriental Institute of the University of Chicago* (Chicago, 1956–2010)
Catagnoti Eblaite	A. Catagnoti, "Eblaite," in *A Companion to Ancient Near Eastern Languages*, ed. R. Hasselbach-Andee (Hoboken, 2020), 149–61
Chadwick DMG	J. Chadwick and M. Ventris, *Documents in Mycenaean Greek*, 2nd ed. (Cambridge, 1973)

CHD	*The Hittite Dictionary of the Oriental Institute of the University of Chicago* (Chicago, 1989)
ChS I	*Corpus der hurritischen Sprachdenkmäler*, part 1, *Die Texte aus Boğazköy*, ed. V. Haas et al., 10 vols. (Rome, 1984–2005)
Cohen Calendars	M. F. Cohen, *The Cultic Calendars of the Ancient Near East* (Bethesda, 1993)
Cohen DRS	D. Cohen with the collaboration of F. Bron and A. Lonnet, *Dictionnaire des racines sémitiques* (Leuven, 1994–1999)
Cohen SSCE	Y. Cohen, *The Scribes and Scholars of the City of Emar in the Late Bronze Age* (Winona Lake, 2009)
Conti Problemi e metodi	G. Conti, "Problemi e metodi nella ricostruzione di una lingua "morta": il caso dell'eblaita," in *Grammatica e lessico delle lingue "morte"*, ed. U. Rapallo and G. Garbugino (Genova, 1998)
CS 1, 2, 3	W. W. Hallo and K. Lawson Younger Jr., eds., *The Context of Scripture*, vol. 1, *Canonical Compositions from the Biblical World* (Leiden, 1997); vol. 2, *Monumental Inscriptions from the Biblical World* (Leiden, 2000); vol. 3, *Archival Documents from the Biblical World* (Leiden, 2003)
CunMon	Cuneiform Monographs (Groningen)
CUSAS	Cornell University Studies in Assyriology and Sumerology (Philadelphia)
Dalley / Walker / Hawkins Tell Rimah	S. Dalley, C. B. F. Walker, and J. D. Hawkins, *The Old Babylonian Tablets from Tell al-Rimah* (London, 1976)
De Boer Amorites	R. de Boer, "Amorites in the Early Old Babylonian Period" (PhD diss., Leiden University, 2014)
Del Olmo CR	G. del Olmo Lete, *Canaanite Religion According to the Liturgical Texts of Ugarit*, 2nd ed. (Münster, 2014)
Diakonoff HU	I. M. Diakonoff, *Hurrisch und Urartäisch* (Munich, 1971)
DOSA	J. C. Biella, *Dictionary of Old South Arabic: Sabaean Dialect* (Chico, 1982)
DUL	G. del Olmo Lete and J. Sanmartín, *A Dictionary of the Ugaritic Language in the Alphabetical Tradition*, trans. and ed. W. G. E. Watson, 3rd rev. ed. (Leiden, 2015)
^{2}DUL	G. del Olmo Lete and J. Sanmartín, *A Dictionary of the Ugaritic Language in the Alphabetical Tradition*, trans. and ed. W. G. E. Watson, 2nd rev. ed. (Leiden, 2004)
Dupont-Sommer Warka	A. Dupont-Sommer, "La Tablette cunéiforme araméenne de Warka," *RA* 39 (1942–1945): 35–62
Durand REA	J.-M. Durand, "La religion à l'époque amorrite d'après les archives de Mari," in *Mythologie et religion des Sémites Occidentaux*, ed. G. del Olmo Lete, vol. 1, *Ebla et Mari*, OLA 162.1 (Leuven, 2008), 163–722
Eblaitica	*Eblaitica: Essays on the Ebla Archives and Eblaite Language*, 4 vols., Publications of the Center for Ebla Research at New York University (Winona Lake, 1987–2002)
EDA	L. Cagni, ed., *Ebla 1975–1985: Dieci anni di studi linguistici e filologici. Atti del Convegno Internazionale (Napoli, 9-11 ottobre 1985)* (Naples, 1987)
EI	*Eretz Israel* (Jerusalem)
Erman / Grapow WäS	A. Erman and H. Grapow, *Wörterbuch der ägyptischen Sprache*, 7 vols. (Berlin, 1926–1963)
EV	"Extracts from the Vocabulary of Ebla," in MEE 4. See VE.
Feliu Dagan	L. Feliu, *The God Dagan in Bronze Age Syria* (Leiden, 2003)
Fleming Democracy	D. E. Fleming, *Democracy's Ancient Ancestors: Mari and Early Collective Governance* (Cambridge, 2004)
Fleming Installation	D. E. Fleming, *The Installation of Baal's High Priestesses at Emar* (Atlanta, 1992)
FM	Florilegium Marianum (Mémoires de NABU) (Paris)
FO	*Folia Orientalia* (Krakow)

Fronzaroli ProsEbl B	A. Archi, A. Catagnoti, P.Corò, and P. Fronzaroli, *The Prosopography of Ebla: B* (web publication 2008; revised 2011), http://www.sagas.unifi.it/upload/sub/eblaweb/dbase_prosopografia/b.pdf.
Fronzaroli ProsEbl G	A. Archi, A. Catagnoti, P.Corò, and P. Fronzaroli, *The Prosopography of Ebla: G* (web publication 2008; revised 2011), http://www.sagas.unifi.it/upload/sub/eblaweb/dbase_prosopografia/g.pdf.
Fronzaroli ProsEbl K	A. Archi, A. Catagnoti, P.Corò, and P. Fronzaroli, *The Prosopography of Ebla: K* (web publication 2008; revised 2011), http://www.sagas.unifi.it/upload/sub/eblaweb/dbase_prosopografia/k.pdf.
Fronzaroli Studi	P. Fronzaroli, *Studi sul lessico comune semitico. Rendiconti dell'Academia Nazionale dei Lincei*, Series 7, 19 vols. (Rome, 1964–)
Fs. Beek	J. D. Seger, ed., *Retrieving the Past: Essays on Archaeological Research and Methodology in Honor of G. W. Van Beek* (Winona Lake, 1996)
Fs. Birot	J.-M. Durand and J. R. Kupper, *Miscellanea babylonica: Mélanges offerts à M. Birot* (Paris, 1986)
Fs. Bittel	R. M. Boehmer and H. Hauptmann, eds., *Beiträge zur Altertumskunde Kleinasiens: Festschrift für K. Bittel*, vol. 1, *Text* (Mainz, 1983)
Fs. Borger	S. Maul, ed., *Eine Festschrift für R. Borger zu seinem 65. Geburtstag. Tikip santakki mala bašmu* (Groningen, 1998)
Fs. Buccellati	S. Valentini and G. Guarducci, eds., *Between Syria and the Highlands: Studies in Honor of G. Buccellati and M. Kelly-Buccellati* (Rome, 2019)
Fs. Carter	Y. L. Arbeitman, ed., *The Asia Minor Connexion: Studies on the Pre-Greek Languages in Memory of C. Carter* (Leuven, 2000)
Fs. Charpin	G. Chambon, M. Guichard, and A.-I. Langlois, eds., *De l'argile au numérique: Mélanges assyriologiques en l'honneur de Dominique Charpin* (Paris, 2019)
Fs. Cohen	J. Lentin and A. Lonnet, eds., *Mélanges David Cohen: Études sur le langage, les langues, les dialectes, les littératures, offertes par ses élèves, ses collègues, ses amis, présentées à l'occasion de son quatre-vingtième anniversaire* (Paris, 2003)
Fs. De Meyer	H. Gasche, M. Tanret, C. Janssen, and A. Degraeve, eds., *Cinquante-deux reflexions sur le Proche-Orient ancien offertes en hommage à Leon De Meyer*, Mesopotamian History and Environment Occasional Publications 2 (Leuven, 1994)
Fs. Finet	M. Lebeau and P. Talon, eds., *Reflets des deux fleuves: Mélanges A. Finet*, Accadica Supplements 6 (Leuven, 1989)
Fs. Fronzaroli	P. Marrassini, ed., *Semitic and Assyriological Studies Presented to P. Fronzaroli by Pupils and Colleagues* (Wiesbaden, 2003)
Fs. Garelli	D. Charpin and F. Joannès, *Marchands, diplomates et empereurs. Études sur la civilisation mésopotamienne offertes à P. Garelli* (Paris, 1991)
Fs. Graziani	N. Borrelli, ed., *Ana šulmāni: Ancient Near Eastern Studies in Honour of Simonetta Graziani* (Naples, 2022)
Fs. Groneberg	D. Shehata, F. Weiershäuser, and K. Zand, eds., *Von Göttern und Menschen: Beiträge zu Literatur und Geschichte des Alten Orients. Fs. für B. Groneberg* (Leiden, 2010)
Fs. Haas	T. Richter, D. Prechel, and J. Klinger, eds., *Kulturgeschichten: Altorientalistische Studien für V. Haas zum 65. Geburtstag* (Saarbrücken, 2001)
Fs. Hallo	M. Cohen, D. C. Snell, and D. B. Weisberg, eds., *The Tablet and the Scroll: Near Eastern Studies in Honor of W. H. Hallo* (Bethesda, 1993)
Fs. Huehnergard	R. Hasselbach and N. Pat-El, eds., *Language and Nature: Papers Presented to J. Huehnergard on the Occasion of his 60th Birthday* (Chicago, 2012)

Fs. Kienast	G. Selz, ed., *Festschrift für B. Kienast zu seinem 70. Geburtstage dargebracht von Freunden, Schülern und Kollegen* (Münster, 2003)
Fs. Kupper	Ö. Tunca, ed., *De la Babylonie à la Syrie, en passant par Mari: Mélanges offerts à Monsieur J.-R. Kupper à l'occasion de son 70e anniversaire, Textes* (Liège 1990)
Fs. Lambdin	D. M. Colomb and S. T. Hollis, *"Working With No Data": Semitic and Egyptian Studies Presented to Th.O. Lambdin* (Winona Lake, 1987)
Fs. Leslau	A. S. Kaye, *Semitic Studies in Honor of W. Leslau* (Wiesbaden, 1991)
Fs. Limet	Ö. Tunca and D. Deheselle, eds., *Tablettes et images aux pays de Sumer et d'Akkad: Mélanges offerts à Monsieur H. Limet* (Liège, 1996)
Fs. Loewenstamm	Y. Avishur and J. Blau, eds., *Studies in Bible and Ancient Near East Presented to S. E. Loewenstamm on His Seventieth Birthday* (Jerusalem, 1978)
Fs. Matthiae	M. G. Biga, D. Charpin, and J.-M. Durand, with L. Marti, eds., "Recueil d'études historiques, philologiques et épigraphiques en l'honneur de P. Matthiae," special issue, *RA* 106 (2012)
Fs. Muraoka	M. F. J. Baasten and W. T. van Peursen, eds., *Hamlet on a Hill. Semitic and Greek Studies Presented to Professor T. Muraoka on the Occasion of his Sixty-Fifth Birthday*, OLA 118 (Leuven, 2003)
Fs. Oelsner	J. Marzahn and H. Neumann, eds., *Assyriologica et Semitica: Festschrift für J. Oelsner anlässlich seines 65. Geburtstages am 18. Februar 1997* (Münster, 2000)
Fs. Pennachietti	G. Borbone, A. Mengozzi, and M. Tosco, *Linguistic and Oriental Studies in Honour of F. A. Pennachietti* (Wiesbaden, 2006)
Fs. Perrot	F. Vallat, ed., *Contribution à l'histoire de l'Iran: Mélanges offerts à J. Perrot* (Paris, 1990)
Fs. Pettinato	H. Waetzoldt, ed., *Von Sumer nach Ebla und zurück: Festschrift G. Pettinato* (Heidelberg, 2004)
Fs. Postgate	Y. Heffron, A. Stone, and M. Worthington, eds., *At the Dawn of History: Ancient Near Eastern Studies in Honour of J. N. Postgate*, 2 vols. (Winona Lake, 2017)
Fs. Renger	B. Böck, E. Cancik-Kirschbaum, and T. Richter, eds., *Minuscula Mesopotamica: Festschrift für J. Renger* (Münster, 1999)
Fs. Richter	W. Gross, H. Irsigler, and T. Seidl, eds., *Text, Methode und Grammatik. Festschrift Wolfgang Richter zum 65. Geburtstag* (St. Ottilien, 1991)
Fs. Röllig	B. Pongratz-Leisten, H. Kühne, and P. Xella, eds., *Ana šadî labnāni lū allik: Beiträge zu altorientalischen und mittelmeerischen Kulturen. Festschrift für W. Röllig* (Neukirchen-Vluyn, 1997)
Fs. Sanmartín	G. del Olmo Lete, L. Feliu, and A. Millet, eds., *Šapal tibnim mû illak: Studies Presented to Joaquín Sanmartín on the Occasion of his 65th Birthday* (Barcelona, 2006)
Fs. Scandone Matthiae	A. Vacca, S. Pizzimenti, and M. G. Micale, eds., *A Oriente del Delta: Scritti sull'Egitto ed il Vicino Oriente antico in onore di Gabriella Scandone Matthiae* (Rome, 2018)
Fs. Sommerfeld / Krebernik	I. Arkhipov, L. Kogan, and N. Koslova, *The Third Millennium. Studies in Early Mesopotamia and Syria in Honor of W. Sommerfeld and M. Krebernik* (Leiden, 2020)
Fs. Veenhof	W. H. van Soldt and J. G. Dercksen, eds., *Veenhof Anniversary Volume: Studies Presented to Klaas R. Veenhof on the Occasion of his Sixty-Fifth Birthday*, PHIHANS 89 (Leiden, 2001)
Fs. vSoden	M. Dietrich and O. Loretz, eds., *Vom Alten Orient zum Alten Testament: Festschrift für W. Freiherr von Soden zum 85. Geburtstag* (Neukirchen-Vluyn, 1995)
Fs. Watson	G. del Olmo Lete, J. Vidal, and N. Wyatt, eds., *The Perfumes of Seven Tamarisks: Studies in Honour of Wilfred G. E. Watson* (Münster, 2012)

Fs. Wilcke	W. Sallaberger, K. Volk, and A. Zgoll, eds., *Literatur, Politik und Recht in Mesopotamien: Festschrift für Claus Wilcke*, Orientalia Biblica et Christiana 14 (Wiesbaden, 2003)
Gantzert ELT	M. Gantzert, "The Emar Lexical Texts, Parts I–IV" (PhD Diss., University of Leiden, 2011)
Gelb / Steinkeller / Whiting Ancient Kudurrus	I. J. Gelb, P. Steinkeller, and R. M. Whiting, *Earliest Land Tenure Systems in the Near East: Ancient Kudurrus*, Oriental Institute Publications 104 (Chicago, 1991)
Gelb CAAA	I. J. Gelb, *Computer-Aided Analysis of Amorite* (Chicago, 1980)
Gelb Lingua	I. J. Gelb, *La lingua degli amoriti, Rendiconti dell'Accademia Nazionale dei Lincei 8/13* (Rome, 1958)
Gelb MAD 1 / 2 / 3	I. J. Gelb, *Materials for the Assyrian Dictionary*, vol. 1, *Sargonic Texts from the Diyala Region*, 2nd ed. (Chicago, 1961); vol. 2, *Old Akkadian Writing and Grammar*, 2nd ed. (Chicago, 1961); vol. 3, *Glossary of Old Akkadian* (Chicago, 1957)
Gelb Proto-Akkadian	I. J. Gelb, *Sequential Reconstruction of Proto-Akkadian* (Chicago, 1969)
Gelb TI	I. J. Gelb, "Thoughts about Ibla: A Preliminary Evaluation," *Syro-Mesopotamian Studies* 1.1 (1977): 3–30
Giacumakis AkkAl	G. Giacumakis, *The Akkadian of Alalaḫ* (The Hague, 1970)
Gladius	*Gladius: Estudios sobre armas antiguas, armamento, arte militar y vida cultural en Oriente y Occidente* (Madrid)
Golinets Onomastikon 2	V. Golinets, *Das amurritische Onomastikon der altbabylonischen Zeit*, vol. 2, *Verbalmorphologie des Amurritischen und Glossar der Verbalwurzeln* (Münster, 2018)
Gröndahl PTU	F. Gröndahl, *Die Personennamen der Texte aus Ugarit* (Rome, 1967)
Haas Hurrriter	V. Haas, ed., *Hurriter und Hurritisch*, Xenia: Konstanzer althistorische Vorträge und Forschungen 21 (Konstanz, 1988)
HALOT	*The Hebrew and Aramaic Lexicon of the Old Testament*, rev. trans. by M. E. J. Richardson, 5 vols. (Leiden, 1994–2000)
Hannig WbÄgD	R. Hannig, *Grosses Handwörterbuch Ägyptisch-Deutsch* (Mainz, 2009)
Hasselbach SargAkk	R. Hasselbach, *Sargonic Akkadian: A Historical and Comparative Study of the Syllabic Texts* (Wiesbaden, 2006)
HdO	Handbuch der Orientalistik (Leiden)
Helck Beziehungen	W. Helck, *Die Beziehungen Ägyptens zu Vorderasien im 3. und 2. Jahrtausend v. Chr.*, 2nd ed. (Wiesbaden, 1971). References are to chapter 36: "Asiatische Fremdworte im Ägyptischen," 505–27
Hess APN	R. S. Hess, *Amarna Personal Names* (Winona Lake, 1993)
Hoch SWET	J. E. Hoch, *Semitic Words in Egyptian Texts of the New Kingdom and the Third Intermediate Period* (Princeton, 1994). Cited by page and paragraph
Hoftijzer / Jongeling DNWSI	J. Hoftijzer and K. Jongeling, *Dictionary of the North-West Semitic Inscriptions*, 2 parts (Leiden, 1995)
Horowitz / Oshima CunCan	W. Horowitz, T. Oshima, and S. Sanders, *Cuneiform in Canaan: Cuneiform: Sources from the Land of Israel in Ancient Times* (Jerusalem, 2006)
Hrůša MŠ	I. Hrůša, *Die akkadische Synonymenliste malku = šarru: Eine Textedition mit Übersetzung und Kommentar* (Münster, 2010)
HSAO	Heidelberger Studien zum Alten Orient (Wiesbaden / Heidelberg; see also WGE)
HSS	Harvard Semitic Studies (Atlanta, Winona Lake, etc.)
Huehnergard AkkUg	J. Huehnergard, *The Akkadian of Ugarit* (Atlanta, 1989)
Huehnergard UVST / ²UVST	J. Huehnergard, *Ugaritic Vocabulary in Syllabic Transcription* (Atlanta, 1987) / 2nd ed. (2008)
Huffmon APNMT	H. B. Huffmon, *Amorite Personal Names in the Mari Texts: Structural and Lexical Study* (Baltimore, 1965)
IOS	*Israel Oriental Studies* (Jerusalem)
Ismail WTL	F. Ismail, "Altbabylonische Wirtschaftsurkunden aus Tall Leilān (Syrien)" (PhD diss., University Tübingen, 1991)

Ismail, etc., Tell Beydar	F. Ismail, W. Sallaberger, P. Talon, and K. Van Lerberghe, *Administrative Documents from Tell Beydar. Seasons 1993–1995*, Subartu 2 (Turnhout, 1996)
Izre'el AmAkk	S. Izre'el, *Amurru Akkadian: A Linguistic Study*, 2 vols. (Atlanta, 1991)
Izre'el AmScholT	S. Izre'el, *The Amarna Scholarly Tablets* (Groningen, 1997)
Kaskal	*Kaskal: Rivista di storia, ambienti e culture del Vicino Oriente antico* (Florence)
Kilani VGW	M. Kilani, *Vocalisation in Group Writing: A New Proposal* (Hamburg, 2019)
Kloekhorst EDHIL	A. Kloekhorst, *Etymological Dictionary of the Hittite Inherited Lexicon* (Leiden, 2008)
Kogan Classification	L. Kogan, *Genealogical Classification of Semitic: The Lexical Isoglosses* (Boston, 2015)
Krebernik Beschwörungen	M. Krebernik, *Die Beschwörungen aus Fara und Ebla: Untersuchungen zur ältesten keilschriftlichen Beschwörungsliteratur* (Hildesheim, 1984)
Krebernik PET	M. Krebernik, *Die Personennamen der Ebla-Texte* (Berlin, 1988)
Krebernik Tall Bi`a	M. Krebernik, *Ausgrabungen in Tall Bi`a / Tuttul*, vol. 2, *Die altorientalischen Schriftfunde* (Saarbrücken, 2001)
Kronasser EHS	H. Kronasser, *Etymologie der hethitischen Sprache* (Heidelberg, 1966)
Ktema	*Ktema: Civilisations de l'Orient, de la Grèce et de Rome Antiques* (Strasbourg)
KTT	Keilschrifttext aus Tuttul. See Krebernik Tall Bi`a.
KTU	M. Dietrich, O. Loretz, and J. Sanmartín, *The Cuneiform Alphabetic Texts from Ugarit, Ras Ibn Hani and Other Places*, 3rd enlarged ed. (Münster, 2013)
Lackenbacher TAU	S. Lackenbacher, *Textes Akkadiens d'Ugarit: Textes provenant des vingt-cinq premières campagnes* (Paris, 2002)
Lalies	*Lalies: Actes des sessions de linguistique et de littérature* (Paris)
Lane AEL	E. W. Lane, *Arabic-English Lexicon*, 2 vols. (Cambridge, 1984)
LAPO	Littératures anciennes du Proche Orient (Paris)
Laroche DLL	E. Laroche, *Dictionnaire de la langue louvite* (Paris, 1959)
Laroche GLH	E. Laroche, *Glossaire de la langue hourrite* (Paris, 1980)
Lauinger STOBA	J. Lauinger, *Following the Man of Yamhad: Settlement and Territory at Old Babylonian Alalah* (Leiden, 2015)
LEbla	L. Cagni, ed., *La lingua di Ebla: Atti del convegno internazionale (Napoli, 21–23 aprile 1980)* (Naples, 1981)
Leslau CDG	W. Leslau, *Comparative Dictionary of Ge'ez* (Wiesbaden, 1987)
Levy WTM	J. Levy, *Neuhebräisches und Chaldäisches Wörterbuch über die Talmudim und Midraschim*, 2nd ed. (Leipzig, 1924)
Lieberman SLOBA	S. Lieberman, *The Sumerian Loanwords in Old-Babylonian Accadian* (Missoula, 1977)
MAARAV	*MAARAV: A Journal for the Study of the Northwest Semitic Languages and Literatures* (Los Angeles)
Mander Dieux	P. Mander, "Les dieux et le culte à Ebla," in *Mythologie et religion des Sémites Occidentaux*, ed. G. del Olmo Lete, vol. 1, *Ebla et Mari*, OLA 162.1 (Leuven, 2008), 1–160
Marchesi A'aly Inscriptions	G. Marchesi, "Appendix 5: Inscriptions from the Royal Mounds of A'ali (Bahrain) and Related Texts," in *The Royal Mounds of A'ali in Bahrain: The Emergence of Kingship in Early Dilmun*, ed. S. T. Laursen (Aarhus, 2017), 425–37
MariRe	G. D. Young, ed., *Mari in Retrospect: Fifty Years of Mari and Mari Studies* (Winona Lake, 1992)
Masson Emprunts	O. Masson, *Recherches sur les plus anciens emprunts sémitiques en grec* (Paris, 1967)
Mayer Ekalte	W. Mayer, *Ausgrabungen in Tall Munbaqa Ekalte*, vol. 2, *Die Texte* (Stuttgart, 2001)
MEE	Materiali epigrafici di Ebla (Naples, Rome). See also MVS.
MemNABU	Mémoires de NABU. See FM.

Memoriae Diakonoff	L. Kogan, N. Koslova, S. Loesov, and S. Tischenko, eds., *Memoriae Igor M. Diakonoff*, BuB 2 (Winona Lake, 2005)
Memorial Kutscher	A. Rainey, ed., *Kinattūtu ša dārâti: R. Kutscher Memorial Volume* (Tel Aviv, 1993)
Memorial Marrassini	A. Baussi, A. Gori, and G. Lusini, eds., *Linguistic, Oriental and Ethiopian Studies in Memory of P. Marrassini* (Wiesbaden, 2014)
Miglio Tribe and State	A. Miglio, *Tribe and State: The Dynamics of International Politics and the Reign of Zimri-Lim* (Piscataway, 2014)
Militarev / Kogan SED 1, SED 2	A. Militarev and L. Kogan, *Semitic Etymological Dictionary*, vol. 1, *Anatomy of Man and Animals* (Münster, 2000); vol. 2, *Animal Names* (Münster, 2005)
Miralles Marzeah	L. Miralles, *Marzeah y thíasos: Una institución convivial en el Oriente Próximo Antiguo y en el Mediterráneo* (Madrid, 2007)
MisEb	P. Fronzaroli, ed., *Miscellanea eblaitica* (Florence, 1988–).See QuSe
Moran AmL	W. L. Moran, *The Amarna Letters* (Baltimore, 1992)
Moran AmSt	W. L. Moran, *Amarna Studies: Collected Writings*. ed. J. Huehnergard and S. Izre'el (Winona Lake, 2003)
Moscati Grammar	S. Moscati, ed., *An Introduction to the Comparative Grammar of the Semitic Languages: Phonology and Morphology* (Wiesbaden, 1969)
MROA I, II 1/2	G. del Olmo Lete, ed., *Mitología y religión del Oriente Antiguo*, 2 vols. (Barcelona, 1993, 1995)
MSL	*Materialien zum sumerischen Lexikon* (Rome, 1937)
Muchiki Egyptian	Y. Muchiki, *Egyptian Proper Names and Loanwords in North-West Semitic* (Atlanta, 1999)
MVN	Materiali per il Vocabolario Neosumerico, Multigrafica editrice (Rome)
MVS	Materiali per il Vocabolario Sumerico (Rome). See MEE
NABU	Nouvelles assyriologiques brèves et utilitaires (Paris)
Neu Das Hurritische	E. Neu, *Das Hurritische: Eine altorientalische Sprache in neuem Licht* (Mainz, 1988)
Noth Personennamen	M. Noth, *Die israelitischen Personennamen im Rahmen der gemeinsemitischen Namengebung* (Stuttgart, 1928)
NuzHur	Studies on the Civilization and Culture of Nuzi and the Hurrians (Winona Lake, Bethesda)
OBO	Orbis Biblicus et Orientalis (Fribourg)
OLA	Orientalia Lovaniensia Analecta (Leuven)
OMA	Orient et Méditerranée: Archéologie (Paris)
Or(NS)	*Orientalia* (Nova Series) (Rome)
OrAn	*Oriens Antiquus* (Rome)
Orel / Stolbova HSED	V. E. Orel and O. V. Stolbova, *Hamito-Semitic Etymological Dictionary: Materials for a Reconstruction*, HdO 1.18 (Leiden, 1995)
Orient	*Orient: Reports of the Society for Near Eastern Studies in Japan* (Tokyo)
Pagan ARES 3	J. M. Pagan, *A Morphological and Lexical Study of Personal Names in the Ebla Texts*, ARES 3 (Rome, 1998)
Pentiuc Vocabulary	E. J. Pentiuc, *West Semitic Vocabulary in the Akkadian Texts from Emar* (Winona Lake, 2001)
Pettinato Culto	G. Pettinato, *Culto ufficiale ad Ebla durante il regno di Ibbi-Sipiš* (Rome, 1979)
Pettinato Rituale	G. Pettinato, *Il rituale per la successione al trono ad Ebla* (Rome, 1992)
Pettinato TIE	G. Pettinato and F. D'Agostino, *Thesaurus inscriptionum eblaicarum*. vol. A/2 (áb-az) (Rome, 1997)
PIHANS	Publications de l'Institut historique-archéologique néerlandais de Stamboul (Leiden)
Pokorny IEW	J. Pokorny, *Indogermanisches etymologisches Wörterbuch*, 2 vols. (Bern / München, 1959–1969)
PPG	J. Friedrich and W. Röllig, *Phönizisch-Punische Grammatik, 3. Auflage*, reworked by M. G. Amadasi Guzzo with the collaboration of W. R. Mayer (Rome, 1999)

Proceedings 33ᵉ RAI	J.-M. Durand, ed., *La Femme dans le Proche-Orient antique: Compte rendu de la XXXIIIe Rencontre Assyriologique Internationale, (Paris, 7–10 juillet 1986)* (Paris, 1987)
Proceedings 44ᵉ RAI	L. Milano, S. de Martino, F. M Fales, and G. B. Lanfranchi, eds., *Landscapes, Territories, Frontiers and Horizons in the Ancient Near East. Papers Presented to the XLIV Rencontre Assyriologique Internationale*, 2 vols. (Padova, 1999)
Proceedings 46ᵉ RAI	C. Nicolle, *Nomades et sédentaires dans le Proche-Orient ancien. Compte rendu de la XLVIe Rencontre Assyriologique Internationale* (Paris, 2004)
Proceedings 53ᵉ RAI	L. Kogan, N. Koslova, S. Loesov, and S. Tischchenko, eds., *Language in the Ancient Near East: Proceedings of the 53e Rencontre Assyriologique Internationale*, 2 vols. in 3 parts (Winona Lake, 2010)
Proceedings 54ᵉ RAI	G. Wilhelm, ed., *Organization, Representation, and Symbols of Power in the Ancient Near East. Proceedings of the 54th Rencontre Assyriologique Internationale* (Winona Lake, 2012)
PRU	*Le palais royal d'Ugarit* (Paris)
Pruzsinszky PTEm	R. Pruzsinszky, *Die Personennamen der Texte aus Emar* (Bethesda, 2003)
QDLF	*Quaderni del Dipartimento di Linguistica* (Florence)
QuSe	*Quaderni di Semitistica* (Florence)
RA	*Revue d'assyriologie et d'archéologie orientale* (Paris)
Rainey CAT	A. F. Rainey, *Canaanite in the Amarna Tablets: A Linguistic Analysis of the Mixed Dialect Used by Scribes from Canaan*, 4 vols., HdO 1.25 (Leiden, 1996)
Rainey EAC	A. F. Rainey, *The El-Amarna Correspondence*, 2 vols., HdO 1.110 (Leiden, 2015)
Rainey EAT	A. F. Rainey, *El Amarna Tablets*, 2nd ed. (Kevelaer / Neukirchen-Vluyn, 1978)
RGTC	Répertoire Géographique des Textes Cunéiformes / Beihefte zum Tübinger Atlas des Vorderen Orients (Wiesbaden)
RHA	*Revue Hittite et Asianique* (Paris)
RHR	*Revue de l'histoire des religions* (Paris)
Richter / Lange Idadda	T. Richter and S. Lange with a contribution by P. Pfälzner, *Das Archiv des Idadda*, Qaṭna Studien 3 (Wiesbaden, 2012)
Richter BGH	T. Richter, *Bibliographisches Glossar des Hurrischen* (Wiesbaden, 2012)
RlA	*Reallexikon der Assyriologie und Vorderasiatischen Archäologie*, (Berlin, 1932–)
RSO	*Rivista degli studi orientali* (Rome)
RSOu	*Ras Shamra-Ougarit: Publications de la Mission Française Archéologique de Ras Shamra-Ougarit* (Paris, 1983–)
SANER	Studies in Ancient Near Eastern Records (Boston)
SAOC	Studies in Ancient Oriental Civilization (Chicago)
Saporetti OnomMAss 1	C. Saporetti, *Onomastica Medio-Asira*, vol. 1 (Rome, 1970)
Sasson MilitEstabl	J. M. Sasson, *The Military Establishment at Mari* (Rome, 1969)
SCCNH	Studies on the Civilization and Culture of Nuzi and the Hurrians (Bethesda)
Schneider APÄQ	T. Schneider, *Asiatische Personennamen in ägyptischen Quellen des Neuen Reiches* (Freiburg, 1992)
SD	A. F. L. Beeston, M. A. Ghul, W. W. Müller, and J. Ryckmans, *Sabaic Dictionary (English-French-Arabic)* (Louvain-la Neuve / Beyrouth, 1982)
SEL	*Studi epigrafici e linguistici sul Vicino Oriente antico* (Verona)
Sivan / Cochavi-Rainey WSVES	D. Sivan and Z. Cochavi-Rainey, *West Semitic Vocabulary in Egyptian Script of the 14th to the 10th Centuries BC*, Beer-Sheva 6 (Beer-Sheva, 1992)
Sivan GAGl	D. Sivan, *Grammatical Analysis and Glossary of the Northwest Semitic Vocables in Akkadian Texts of the 15th–13th c. B.C. from Canaan and Syria* (Kevelaer / Neukirchen-Vluyn, 1984)

Sjörs NegSem	A. Sjörs, *Historical Aspects of Standard Negation in Semitic* (Leiden, 2018)
SLE	P. Fronzaroli, ed., *Studies on the Language of Ebla*, QuSe 13 (Florence, 1984)
SMEA	*Studi Micenei ed Egeo-Anatolici* (Rome)
Sokoloff DJPA	M. Sokoloff, *A Dictionary of the Jewish Palestinian Aramaic of the Byzantine Period* (Ramat Gan, 1990)
Stamm ANG	J. J. Stamm, *Die akkadische Namengebung* (Leipzig, 1939; repr., Darmstadt, 1968)
Stark PNPI	J. K. Stark, *Personal Names in Palmyrene Inscriptions* (Oxford, 1971)
StEb	*Studi Eblaiti* (Rome)
StMes	*Studia Mesopotamica: Jahrbuch für altorientalische Geschichte und Kultur* (Münster)
Streck Amorite	M. P. Streck, "Amorite," in *The Semitic Languages: An International Handbook*, ed. S. Weninger, Handbücher zur Sprach- und Kommunikationswissenschaft 36 (Berlin, 2011), 452–59
Streck Onomastikon 1	M. P. Streck, *Das amurritische Onomastikon der altbabylonischen Zeit*, vol. 1 (Münster, 2000)
Studia Eblaitica	P. Matthiae, ed., *Studia Eblaitica: Studies on the Archaeology, History, and Philology of Ancient Syria* (Wiesbaden, 2015)
Study ANE	J. S. Cooper and G. M. Schwartz, *The Study of the Ancient Near East in the Twenty-First Century*, The W. F. Albright Centennial Conference (Winona Lake, 1996)
Système palatial	J.-M. Durand, "L'organisation de l'espace dans le Palais de Mari: Le témoignage des textes," in *Le système palatial en Orient, en Grèce et à Rome*, ed. E. Lévy (Leiden, 1987), 39–110.
Takács EDE 1–3	G. Takács, *Etymological Dictionary of Egyptian*, 3 vols. (Leiden, 1999, 2001, 2008)
Tallqvist ANG	K. N. Tallqvist, *Assyrian Personal Names* (Helsinki, 1914)
Textile terminologies	C. Michel and M.-L. Nosch, eds., *Textile Terminologies in the Ancient Near East and Mediterranean from the Third to the First Millennia BC*, Ancient Textiles Series 8 (Oxford, 2010)
THeth	*Texte der Hethiter*
TIE	*Thesaurus Inscriptionum Eblaicarum*, ed. G. Pettinato and F. D'Agostino, 2 vols. (Rome, 1995–1996)
Tischler HethEtymGl	J. Tischler, *Hethitisches etymologisches Glossar* (Innsbruck, 1983–)
Tonietti PrepEb	M. V. Tonietti, *Aspetti del sistema preposizionale dell'eblaita* (Venice, 2012)
Topoi Suppl 2	D. Parayre, ed., *Les animaux et les hommes dans le monde syro-mésopotamien aux époques historiques*, Topoi Orient Occident Supplement 2 (Lyon, 2000)
Tropper KWU	J. Tropper, *Kleines Wörterbuch des Ugaritischen* (Wiesbaden, 2008)
Tropper UG	J. Tropper. *Ugaritische Grammatik: Zweite, stark überarbeitete Auflage* (Münster, 2012)
UBL	Ugaritisch-Biblische Literatur (Münster)
Ug	*Ugaritica* (Paris)
VE	"Vocabulary of Ebla," reconstructed in MEE 4. See EV
Vita Ejército	J.-P. Vita, *El ejército de Ugarit* (Madrid, 1995)
VO	*Vicino Oriente* (Rome)
vSoden GaG	W. von Soden with W. R. Mayer, *Grundriss der akkadischen Grammatik*, 3rd ed. (Rome, 1995)
vSoldt SAU	W. H. van Soldt, *Studies in the Akkadian of Ugarit* (Kevelaer / Neukirchen-Vluyn, 1991)
vSoldt Topography	W. H. van Soldt, *The Topography of the City-State of Ugarit* (Münster, 2005)
Vycichl DEC	W. Vycichl, *Dictionnaire étymologique copte* (Leuven, 2001)
Watson LSU	W. G. E. Watson, *Lexical Studies in Ugaritic*, AuOrS 19 (Barcelona, 2007).

Wehr(-Cowan) DMWA	H. Wehr, *A Dictionary of Modern Written Arabic*, ed. J. Milton Cowan, 3rd ed. (Wiesbaden, 1971)
Westenholz Emar Tablets	J. G. Westenholz, with J. Ikeda, Sh. Izre'el, M. Sigrist, I. Singer, and M. Yamada, *Cuneiform Inscriptions in the Collection of the Bible Lands Museum Jerusalem: The Emar Tablets* (Groningen, 2000)
Westenholz Legends	J. G. Westenholz, *Legends of the Kings of Akkade* (Winona Lake, 1997)
WGE	H. Waetzold and H. Hauptman, eds., *Wirtschaft und Gesellschaft von Ebla: Akten der Internationalen Tagung Heidelberg 4.–7. November 1986* (Heidelberg, 1988)
Wilhelm AdS	G. Wilhelm, *Das Archiv des Šilwa-Teššup* (Wiesbaden 1980–)
Wilhelm KlBHurr	G. Wilhelm, *Kleine Beiträge zum Hurrischen* (Wiesbaden, 2018)
Wiseman AT	D. J. Wiseman, *The Alalakh Tablets* (London, 1953)
WO	*Die Welt des Orients* (Göttingen)
WVDOG	Wissenschaftliche Veröffentlichungen der Deutschen Orient-Gesellschaft (Wiesbaden)
YNER	Yale Near Eastern Researches (New Haven)
ZA	*Zeitschrift für Assyriologie und Vorderasiatische Archäologie* (Berlin)
Zadok PSC	R. Zadok, "A Prosography and Ethno-Linguistic Characterization of Southern Canaan in the Second Millennium BCE," *Michmanim* 9 (1996): 97–145
Zamora Vid	J-Á. Zamora, *La vid y el vino en Ugarit* (Madrid, 2000)

Preliminary remarks

After the publication of the first volume (ʔ–ḳ) in 2019, this second volume (l–z) brings *A Glossary of Old Syrian* (GlOS) to completion. The linguistic approaches and the methodological criteria remain unchanged.

Due to the peculiarities of the lexical material, which in this section embodies a large number of sibilants and interdental phonemes, I have thought it appropriate to make liberal use of macrographemes for some transcriptions, thus obviating the oscillations that are evident in transliterating the various syllabaries.

In syllabic contexts, especially those prior to MBab., the macrographeme *S* may occasionally accommodate the CSem. phonemes $|s^1|$, $|s^2|$, and $|\theta|$. In alphabetic contexts, *S* usually replaces the *s̀* / *ś* notations of the various Ugaritological schools.

As in volume 1, the repertoires of lexical isoglosses scrupulously conform to the usual spellings given in the respective dictionaries and lexicographic collections. With regard to Hebrew, I have resorted to the macrographeme *Š̌* in cases where the Masoretic (Aramaizing) tradition postulates a phoneme *ś* that, in my opinion, was absent in preexilic times.

I am over again very much obliged to Prof. Dr. Gonzalo Rubio, LANE Editor-in-Chief, to my former publisher Jim Eisenbraun, and to the staff of The Pennsylvania State University Press for their patience and support in editing and publishing volume 2 of *A Glossary of Old Syrian*. I also thank the anonymous reviewers who have had the diligence and patience to read the first drafts, and whose welcome comments have prevented the occasional slip-up. Of course, any mistakes are entirely my own responsibility.

May I remind the reader that this work is a mere collection of data; it is not intended as a thesaurus. As a last remark, let me recall the old Tao (*The Book of Chuang Tzu*): "There is what is, and there is what is not, and it is not easy to say whether what is not, is not; or whether what is, is."

Glossary

l

|l| (1)	
|l| (2)	
|l| (3)	
|l-ʔ-k|	
|l-ʔ-m| (1)	
|l-ʔ-m| (2)	
|l-ʔ-w/y| (1)	Cf. **|l-w-y|**
|l-ʔ-w/y| (2)	Cf. **|l-ḫ-ḫ|**
|l-ʔ-y| (3)	
|l-b-ʔ|	
|l-b-b|	
|l-b-x|	Cf. **|s^1-b-ħ|**
|l-b-n| (1)	
|l-b-n| (2)	
|l-b-s^1|	
|l-D-n|	
|l-g-g|	
|l-g-m|	
|l-ħ-ħ|	Cf. **|l-ʔ-y/w| (2)**, **|l-ħ-y| (2)**, **|s^1-l-ħ| (2)**
|l-ħ-k|	
|l-ħ-m| (1)	
|l-ħ-m| (2)	
|l-ħ-m| (3)	
|l-ħ-n|	
|l-ħ-r|	See **|r-x-l|**
|l-ħ-y| (1)	
|l-ħ-y| (2)	Cf. **|l-ʔ-y/w| (2)**
|l-x-s^1|	
|l-ḳ-ħ|	
|l-ḳ-ḳ|	
|l-ḳ-ṭ|	
|l-l-ʔ|	
|l-l-x|	
|l-l-l|	
|l-m-d|	
|l-p-ḳ|	
|l-p-t|	
|l-r-m-n|	
|l-s-m|	
|l-ṣ-b|	
|l-s^1-n|	
|l-t-H|	
|l-ṭ-p|	
|l-ṭ-s^1|	
|l-w-ħ|	
|l-w-r|	
|l-w-S|	
|l-w-ṭ|	
|l-w/y-θ|	
|l-w-y|	Cf. **|l-ʔ-w/y| (1)**
|l-w-z|	
|l-y-l(-y)|	
|l-y-θ̣|	

|l| (1)

Sem.: *l* (*lᵉ*, Hb.) "to(wards), on, at, in, according to, away from"; *l* (Ph., Aram., Syr.), *ly*/*i* (Pun.) "to, for";[1] *li* (Ar.) "for, at, by", *la* (Eth.) "to(wards), for, according to". See also *lmh* (*lām*(*m*)*āh*, *lāmeh*, Hb.; Aram., Syr.) "why?"; *limā* (Ar.) id.; *lmh* (*lam*(*m*)*āh*, Hb.; Aram., Syr.) "why?"; *lmn*(*ʔ*), *lmwn* (Syr.) id.; *limā*(*ḏā*) (Ar.) id.

---

[1] Akk. *la* "from" and *la=pāni* "in front of" are Aram. loans.

la (A), li (A), lu (A) "to, for"

•LL: **UGS** [MU] = *a-na* = *i-di-da* = *le-e* (|li=|, pronounced [ē]) in this context → Sivan GaGl 241; Huehnergard UVST 142; vSoldt SAU 304; Tropper UG 172, 187.
•ONOM: **EB** Cf. *a-da-(a-)ad*, *a-da-a-du*, *la-da-ad*, *la-ti-(a-)ad* → Pagan ARES 3 256, 276, 345.
U3 Unc. rdg *lá-ni*(!)-DINGIR → Buccellati Amorites 164f.[2]
EUPH Passim; see e.g. *la-na-su-ú(-um)*, *la-ka-zu-bu-um*, *la-na-^{d}da-gan*; *la-ka-*DINGIR, *la-a-ka-mi-*AN, *la-ka-a-ma*, *la-na-^{d}*IM, *la-na-*DINGIR, *lá-ni-*DINGIR, *la-ra-^{d}sin*, *la-ú-la-a-da*, *la-ad-ni-ia*, *la-aḫ-ra-bu*, *la-am-ra-tum*, *la-(a-)ia-si-im*, *la-ka-me-et*, *la-ṣa-pa-tim*, *la-ḫu-ka-bi*, *a-šu-ub-la-*DINGIR, *i-la-la-ka*, *ni-iq-mi-la-na-si*, *ṣí-id-qú-la-na-si*, *ab-di-la-i-la*, *a-ḫu-um-la-a-bi*, *^{d}na-bu-la-a-bu*; *li-ya*, *li-ia-*EL, *li-ia-zi-it-ru-ú*, *su-ma-li-ka*, *su-mu-li-el*, *su-ma-ia-li-ia*, *a-šu-ub-li-el*; cf. *ia-um-lu-ḫu*, *^{d}da-du-um-lu-ú*[3] → Huffmon APNMT 222; 224; Gelb Lingua 163, CAAA 23, 144f.; Zadok Fs. Hallo 325.
EM Cf. *da-gal-li* |dagan=lī|, *da-gal-li-a-bi* → Pruzsinszky PTEm 79, 137 [275f.].

l (A) "to, for; from"

•CTX: **UGA** *l*, *ly* → Tropper UG 758ff.; DUL 471ff.: *l* (I).

lama "why?" (?)

•ONOM: **EUPH** Cf. unc. *la-ma-la-*DINGIR, *la-ma-a-da-e*, l*a-ma-a-te*,-*la-ma-i-la*, *la-ma-du-du* → Huffmon APNMT 103f.; Gelb Lingua 163; CAAA 24, 144 (altern.: 'Lama' DN).[4]

lami "why?" (?)

•ONOM: **EM** Cf. *la-mi-ba-aʔ-la*, *la-mi-^{d}*KUR → Pruzsinszky PTEm 217f. [589].

lm "why?"[5]

•CTX: **UGA** → Tropper UG 754; DUL 494.

|l| (2)

Sem. negative functor: *lʔ* (*loʔ* Hb.) "no, not"; *l*, *lʔ*, *lʔw*, *lh*, *lw*, *lwʔ* (Aram., *lw* Syr.) id.; *lā* (Akk., Ar.) id.

lā "no, not"

•CTX: **EB** *la*, *a-* before verbal forms with prefix |yi=|: |lā=yi=| → Tonietti QuSe 25 321f.; Catagnoti QuSe 29 46f., 104f., 205.[6]
EA Cf. *la*, *la-a*, *la-a-mi* → Rainey CAT 3 206f., 209ff.
UGS Cf. *la*, *la-a* → Nougayrol Ugaritica 5 257 (no. RS 20.163 v. 2', 3', 5, 7'; Huehnergard UVST 141).[7]
•LL: **UGS** NU/NA = *la-a* = *ma-nu-ku* = *la-a* → Sivan GaGl 240; Huehnergard UVST 141; vSoldt SAU 304 (71), BiOr 47 731.
•ONOM: **EB** No clear examples found.
EUPH No clear examples found.

l (B) "no, not"

•CTX: **UGA** → Tropper UG 814ff.; DUL 478ff.: *l* (II); Sjörs NegSem 116ff., 120ff., 124ff., 128ff., 131ff.
•ONOM: **UGA** No clear examples found.

---

[2] For the altern. rdg *dug$_4$-ga*(!)-DINGIR see op.cit. 46.
[3] For *^{d}a-mu-um-lu-ú* read *^{d}a-mu-um-*KU*-ú*; Durand MARI 1 99.
[4] According to Durand REA 651f. the DN **Lama should be read *labaʔ*.
[5] Elem. *l* (A)=*m*(*h*); see below under *m*(*h*) (|m| 2).
[6] Cf. Ebl. *i-si-a-ma-ma* |lēslamma|, ARET 13 1 r. V 7, from Mari; Catagnoti QuSe 29 45: "esso non fu consegnato".
[7] See Huehnergard AkkUg 239.

|l| (3)

Sem. emphatic functor: 'asseverative' "yes, truly, indeed!"; optionally prefixed for emphasis to attributes ('precative'): *l* (*l*^{e}, Hb. '*lamed emphaticum*', 'vocative *lamed*'); *lw* (Aram., asseverative); *l* (Aram., Ph. precative); *l*(*y*) (Pun. asseverative); *la* (Ar. intensifying; *la*, *la ya* 'vocative'); *l*(*i*) (Ar. precative); *lū* (Akk. asseverative), *lu*, *li*, *la* (Akk. precative); *la* (Eth. precative).

la (B), li (B), lu (B), lū "yes, truly, indeed; let it be, let me, you, him; may"

●CTX: **EB** *a-* |la| before verbal forms with prefix |yi=|: |la=y=|; *lu* |lū| before prefix |yu=|: |lu=yu=|→ Catagnoti QuSe 29 44f., 105f., 205f.
EA *lu-ú*, *li-i*(C=) (asseverative, optative, injunctive) → Rainey CAT 3 193ff.
●LL: **EB** Cf. unc. NU.UŠ = *lu-wu-um*, *a-wu-um* → Krebernik ZA 73 23f. fn. 78, 45.
●ONOM: **EB** Unc. *a-*, *la-*; cf. *a-ga-ma-al*$_6$, *la-ga-ma-al*$_6$, *a-mu-da*/*du* → Gelb Lingua 33; Archi QuSe 13 234; Catagnoti QuSe 15 256f.: "(egli è) veramente ND"; altern. from |l (2)| "no, not" in Pagan ARES 3 277: |(l)ā=gamāl| "merciless", 280: |yamūt=| "he died". See further: *a- du-du*, *ʔa*$_5$*-du-ud*, *a-ʔà-na-ad*, *a-da-bù*, *a-za-la-il*, *á-da-mi-gú*, *la-wa-ki-lu*, *lu-gi-na-šu* → Pagan ARES 3 256, 272f., 276f., 284f., 345f.[8]
U3 *la-a-ba*, *la-a-nu-um*, *la-da-bu-um*, *la-ḫi-a-nu-um*,[9] *la-šu-il* → Buccellati Amorites 163ff.
EUPH Passim, e.g.: *la-ḫi-a-du*, *la-ḫi-ṣa-du-uq*, *la-aḫ-wi-ba-lu*, *la-wi-la-*AN/^{d}IM, *la-wi-la-*^{d}*da-gan*, *la-aḫ-su-di-*DINGIR, *la-ḫa-at-na-a-mu-ud*, *la-a-mu-ri-im,la-ki-in-a-du*, *la-aḫ-su-di-ìl*, *la-aḫ-wi-ḫa-am-mu*, *la-aḫ-wi-*^{d}IŠKUR, *la-aḫ-wi-na-ti-nu(-ú)*, *la-ar-mu-lu-uk*, *la-ar-na-ap-su*, *la-ir-mu-lu-uk*, *la-di-in-*^{d}IŠKUR, *la-di-in-ìl*, *la-ḫu-un-ìl*, *la-ri-im-ḫa-mu*, *la-ri-im-na-ar*, *la-di-nu-um*, *la-a-mu-ri-im*, *la-mu-ra*, *la-na-su-ú(-um)*, *la-aḫ-si-ru-um*, *la-aḫ-wi-a-du*, *la-wi-*DINGIR, *la-aḫ-wi-ba-aḫ-lu*, *la-am-ṣi-um*, *la-ia-si-i-im*; *ša-du-ul-la-mar-ṣú-um*, *a-šu-ub-la-*AN, *bu-nu-la-šar*, *su-mu-la-*DINGIR/*el*, *ás-du-um-la-a-bu-um*, *a-ia-la-su-mu-ú*, *ya-ar-sa-ab-la-el*, *ṣú-ri-la-ri-im*, *a-kun-la-i-la,-ia-ar-sa-ap-la-i-la*; *li-zi-aš-du-um*, *li-tu-ur-a-li*, *iš-ḫi-li-el*, *mi-il-ki-li-el*, *a-šu-ub-li-el*, *su-mu-li-el*, *su-mu-li-zi*; *lu-ḫa-a-a-sa-mu-um* → Gelb Lingua 156f.; CAAA 24, 140ff.; Huffmon APNMT 223; Zadok Fs. Hallo 325; Streck Onomastikon 1 165 § 2.29, 304 § 3.70.[10]
A7 → Arnaud AuOr 16 173: often in PNN before the subject (*=la=ʔadd*, *=la=ʕamm*, etc.) and before the attribute (*la=ʔaḫī-*, *l=-kīn-*, etc.).
EM *la-na-ša*, *la-ar-i-la*, *la-ti-iʔ-ša*; *lu-a-da*, *lu-da-li*; cf. unc. *lu-ú-ad-*KUR → Pruzsinszky PTEm 141 (fn. 710) [597f.], 218 [590f.].

la (C) "oh!" (?)

●ONOM: **EUPH** Unc.; cf. among others: *la-a-mu-ri-im*, *la-la-bu-*[*um*] → Gelb CAAA 141; Huehnergard JAOS 103 581.[11]

---

[8] For the writings *la*(*-a*) see Krebernik PET 94: negation; |l-ʔ-y| "to be mighty"; affirmative / vocative. See also Tonietti NABU 2011/4.
[9] l|a=ʔax=ī=ʕanum| "Truly Anum is my brother", see |ʔ-x| (1); altern.: |la=ʔaxī=ʕanum| "may I live, oh Anum"; see |ħw/yw/y| (1).
[10] For the elem. *=lu-ú* in PNN from Mari see Huffmon APNMT 244 (unc.), and Zadok WeOr 9 36 f. 4 (unlikely).
[11] "O (god) Amurru"; "o Lion". Altern. Huehnergard loc.cit. "for Amurru", "for the Lion"; regarding the first name *la-a-mu-ri-im* see also Streck apud Tropper UG 315: |la=(y)aʔmur=im| "(GN) möge (den Namensträger freundlich) ansehen".

l (C) “yes, truly, indeed” — •CTX: **UGA** *l* → Tropper UG 810; DUL 481ff.: *l* (III); Sjörs NegSem 113f.

l (D) “oh!” — •CTX: **UGA** *l* → Tropper UG 804ff.; DUL 481: *l* (IV).

|l-ʔ-k| — Sem.: *mlʔk* (*malʔak*, Hb.; Ph., Aram.) “messenger, angel”, *mlʔkh* (*mᵉlākāh*, Hb.) “trade, mission”, *mlʔk(ʔ)* (Aram., Syr.) “messenger, angel”, *mlʔkh* (Aram.) “mission”, *mlʔkw(tʔ)* (Syr.) “mission”; *ʔalʔak*, *ʔalāk* (Ar.) “to send”, *malʔāk*, “messenger”; *laʔaka* (Eth.) “to send”, *malʔak* “messenger, angel”, *mal(ə)ʔəkt* “letter, message”.

|l-ʔ-k| “to send” — •CTX: **UGA** G suffc. *lỉk*, *lỉkt*; prefc. *ỉlảk*, *tlảk*, *tlảkn*, *ylảk*; suff. *ỉlảkk*, *tlảkn*; imp. *lảk*; inf. *lảk*, suff. *lảkm*; Gpass. *lủk*; D prefc. *tlỉk*; suff. *tlỉkn* → DUL 482f.
•ONOM: Cf. unc. *la-ga-a-gú* → Pagan ARES 3 136, 345.[12]

mālak “messenger” (?) — •CTX: **B** (I am sending you PN) *ma-la-ki* (OBab. letter) → AHw p. 1573; CAD M/1 159; Zadok Fs. Hallo 325; Streck Onomastikon 1 104 § 1.95.

mlảk “messenger” — •CTX: **UGA** Sg. *mlảk*; suff. *mlảkk*; pl. / du. *mlảkm*, cstr. *mlảk* → DUL 540.

mlảkt “message” — •CTX: **UGA** Sg. *mlảkt*; suff. *mlảkty*, *mlảktk*, *mlảkth* → DUL 540.

|l-ʔ-m| (1) — Sem.: *l(ʔ)wm*, *lʔmym* (*lᵉʔōm*, *lᵉʔummîm*, Hb.) “nation, people, tribe”. See further *lʔm* (JAram.) “nation”, *tlym(ʔ)* “(twin) brother”; *līm(u)* (Akk.) “(big quantity >) thousand”, *līmu(m)*, *limmum* “(representative of the clan >) eponym(ate)”. See further: *lāʔama* (Ar.) “to agree”, *ʔiltaʔama* “to fit together”, *liʔm* “peace, concord”.[13]
Non-Sem.: Cf. **lumum=* (West Chadic) “in quantity”, **lum=* (East Cushitic) “big”.[14]

liʔm, **līm** “people, tribe; DN” — •CTX: **EB** Cf. 2 *li-im*, (pl. redupl.) *li-im-li-im* → Bonechi MARI 8 477f. (with fn. 8.: “clans”); Fronzaroli ARET 13 23, 279; Catagnoti QuSe 29 7, 99, 117, 206.[15]
EUPH *li-mi*, *li-mi-ia*, *li-im-ka* → Marello MemNABU 1 115, 119 fn. 2; Fleming Amurru 3 199ff.; Zadok Fs. Hallo 325; Durand LAPO 16 146, 148 fn. f; Amurru 3 176; FM 8 no. 31:22; Streck Onomastikon 1 102f. § 1.95.
EM *li-im*, cf. *ᵈli-iʔ-mi* (DN?) → Pentiuc Vocabulary 110f.; Ikeda BiOr 60 274.
EA Cf. rdg *li-mì-ma* |limīma| < |liʔmīma| (EA 195:13) → Moran AmL 273 fn. 2.[16]
•LL: **MŠ** *li-i-mu* = MIN (: ERIM, *ṣābu*; // *ni-i-rù*, *um-ma-nu*); *li-i-mu* = MIN (: *ki-im-tu*) → Hrůša MŠ 433 (exp. I 89ff.; 442 (exp. I 318).[17]

---

[12] |laʔka=DN| “send, DN!”; altern. |raḥḳa=DN| “DN is distant”; see |r-ḥ-ḳ|.
[13] Sjöberg Fs. Pettinato 275, Fs. Wilcke 252, read |laʔammu| (with reference to Arab. *lʔm*) in EB (LL) MÍ.DU₁₁.GA = *la-a-mu-mu* (VE 1208), against Civil BaE 89; Krebernik ZA 73 11; Fronzaroli StEb 7 179, all: *rʔm* (Akk.) “to love”. The marginal position of the Arab. verbal root in Semitic makes Sjöberg’s proposal unlikely.
[14] Orel / Stolbova HSED 366f. no. 1692: **lüm=* “big, many”.
[15] Passim *li-im* “thousand” as in Akk.
[16] Diff. rdg Sivan GaGl 131, 241; Rainey CAT I 167; EAC 1533: *le-lá-ma* “evening”.

●ONOM: **EB** Passim (=)*li-im* see e.g. *a-li-im*, *a-ba/*ba_4*-li-im*, *iš-má-li-im*, *i-bí-ni-li-im*, *ib-ḫur-li-im*, *ig-rí-iš-li-im*, *a/i-ga-li-im*, *a/i-mi-iš-li-im*, *a-bur·-li-im*, *a-gur-li-im*, *en-ar/àr-li-im*, *en-ga-li-im*, *da-ḫír-li-im*, *a-ḫír-li-im*, *dal-da-li-im*, *gul/gur-li-im*, $iš_{11}$*-gur-li-im*, $iš_{11}$*-gi-li-im*, *il-gú-uš-li-im*, $iš_{11}$*-ar-li-im*, *gi-(a-)li-im*, *ki-li-im*, ru_{12}*-zi-li-im*, *si-ti-li-im* → Krebernik PET 95, 290; ARES 1 45; Bonechi MARI 8 478ff.; SEL 8 77; Pagan ARES 3 222f 8, and passim.
U3 *ià-ši-im-li-im* → Buccellati Amorites 153; Gelb CAAA 24, 146.
EUPH Seldom =*lim: ia-ku-un-*^{d}*lim*, *ri-ip-i-lim*, *ia-mu-ut-li-mu*; passim =*li-im*; see e.g. *ia-ak-ba-ar-li-im*, *ia-ḫa-ad-li-im*, *ia-aḫ-ta-aq-li-im*, *ia-ti-iq-li-im*, *i-ṣí-li-im*, *ia-nu-ud-li-im*, *ri-ip-i-li-im*, *ia-ap-ḫu-ur-li-im*, *ia-du-ur-li-im*, *ia-šu-ub-li-im*, *ia-aḫ-du-un-li-im*, *ia-ḫi-il-li-im*; *ba-aḫ-di-li-im*, *qar-ni-li-im*, *ri-ip-i-li-im*, *iš-ḫi-li-im*, *sa-am-si-li-im*, *ta-aḫ-*ti_4*-li-im*, *bi-na-li-im* → Huffmon APNMT 226f.; Gelb CAAA 24, 145f.; Durand REA 693f.; Zadok Fs. Hallo 325f.; Streck Onomastikon 1 235 § 2.147 fn. 2, 323 § 5.10.
EM *a-bi-li-mu*, AD-*li-mu*, *a-bi-li-iḫ/iʔ-mu*, ^{d}*lim-a-bi*, *li-im-šar-ra*, *li-mì-šar-ra*, *li*-LUGAL, *li-mi*-LUGAL, *li*(?)-*im-da* (Dagān), *li-mi/mì-da*(*-a*), *li-*(*iʔ-*)*mi-*^{d}KUR/*da-gan* → Pruzsinszky PTEm 184 [49ff., 593f., 595]; Streck AfO 51 309f.

luʔm "people, tribe" — ●ONOM: **EB** Cf. unc. *lu-ma-ar*, *lu-ma*-NI → Krebernik PET 95; Bonechi MARI 8 523 fn. 334.[18]
EUPH Cf. *a-bu-um-lu-mu*, *a-ḫu-um-lu-*(*ú-*)*mu*, *ḫa-du-*(*un*)*-lu-mu*, *ia-aḫ-du*(*-un*)*-lu-mu* → Bonechi MARI 8 523 fn. 334; Durand REA 694.

lỉm "people, tribe" — ●CTX: **UGA** Sg. abs. *lỉm*, suff. *lỉmm*; pl. *lỉmm* → DUL 483f. *lỉm* (I, II).
●ONOM: **UGA** *yrgblỉm* → DUL 963.

limm "people, tribe" — ●ONOM: **EB** Cf. unc. *li-ma-da-gan* → Pagan ARES 3 222f., 346.[19]
EUPH *i-da-lim-ma* → Gelb CAAA 24, 145; Streck Onomastikon 1 235 § 2.147 n. 2, 283 § 3.43 n. 1.
Q Cf. *na-ap-lim-ma* → Gelb CAAA 24, 146.
A7 *ab-bi-lim-ma*, *li-ma-a-du* → Wiseman AT 141; Gelb CAAA 24, 145; Arnaud AuOr 158.
A4 Cf. *at-ti-li-ma* → Gelb CAAA 24, 146.

|l-ʔ-m| (2)

Sem. etym. unc.: Cf. *laʔuma* (Arab.) "to be ignoble, lowly", *luʔm* "ignoble, low".

laʔum "low, mean" (?) — ●ONOM: **U3** Cf. unc. *la-ù-ma-nu-um* → Zadok Fs. Hallo 326 (listed under L-W/Y-M).

|l-ʔ-w/y| (1)

Cf. |**l-w-y**|

Sem.: *leʔû*(*m*) (Akk.) "to be able, to win", *lēʔû*(*m*), *lāʔium*, *lēyûm* "powerful", *teleʔû*, fem. *telē/ītu*(*m*), *taliyatu* "very competent".

---

[17] See MŠ III 61: [*līmu*] = [ummānu]; Hrůša MŠ 363.
[18] Diff. Pagan ARES 3 245, 346: *lamm*=, *lumm*= "sapling".
[19] |limma=dagān| "DN is Līm" (?); altern. |rīma=DN| "DN is love"; Pagan ARES 3 346.

|l-ʔ-w/y| (A) "to be able, (to show oneself) to be powerful"	•CTX: **UGA** G suffc. *lảt*; prefc. suff. *tlủản* (or rdg *tlủn*!*n* / *tlủn*), *nlỉym*; imp. *lỉ* → DUL 484f. •ONOM: **EB G** prefc. |yilʔā=DN| cf. *íl-a-da-mu*, *íl-a-i-sar*, *íl-a-ma-lik*, *íl-a-sar*; |yilʔē(=DN)| cf. *íl-e*, *íl-e-da-mu*, *íl-e-i-sar* → Krebernik PET 47, 94; Pagan ARES 3 136f., 334f. **U3** Cf. *ià-li-e* |yalʔē| → Buccellati Amorites 151; Gelb CAAA 23, 144; Streck Onomastikon 1 179 § 2.58 n. 1; Golinets Onomastikon 2 505. **EUPH** G prefc. *el-i-*^{d}*da-gan*, *il-a-*^{d}IM, *i-le-e-*^{d}IM, *i-il-ḫi-*^{d}*da-gan*; *ia-al-e*, *ia-al-e-*^{d}*da-gan*, *ia-al-e-pa-aḫ*, *ia-al-*^{d}*da-gan*, *ia-al-a-*^{d}IM, *ia-al-(e-)ú-mu*, *ia-al-yu-(ú-)mu*, *an-nu-ta-al-e*, ^{d}*ma-ma-ta-al-e*, EŠ$_{4}$.DAR*-ta-al-e*, *be-li-ta-li-iḫ* → Huffmon APNMT 224f., Gelb Lingua 162; CAAA 23, 144; Zadok Fs. Hallo 326; Streck Onomastikon 1 232f. § 2.144 n. 1; Golinets Onomastikon 2 310f., 314, 403. **TU** *ia-al-a-*^{d}IM, *il-e-*^{d}*da-gan*, *íl-e-li-im* → Krebernik Tall Bi`a 218, 220; Golinets Onomastikon 2 310f., 403. **A4** *i-la-du* → Wiseman AT 137; Gelb CAAA 591 (2527); Golinets Onomastikon 2 311. **EG** Cf. unc. *y:-rw-r-y*$_{2}$*-y*, *b-ʕ-ʕ-:r-r-y*^{F} → Schneider APÄQ 36 no. 54, 87 no. 166.
lả "power, strength"	•CTX: **UGA** → DUL 482.
lản "power, strength"	•CTX: **UGA** Suff. *lảnk*, *lảnh* → DUL 484.
laʔiy "powerful"	•ONOM:[20] **EB** |laʔā| *la-a-iš*$_{11}$*-lu*, *la-a-iš*$_{11}$*-ru*$_{12}$, *la-a-mu-du*, *la-a-sar*, *la-a-zi-kir*;|laʔ(ā)| *la-ì-la-mu*, *la-mu-du*; |laʔ(ī)| *i-bí-la*;[21] |(l)aʔā| *a-a-iš-lu/ru*$_{12}$; |(la)ʔā| *a-iš-lu*, *a-mu-dum*, *a-zi-kir* → Pagan ARES 3 136f., 273, 279f., 285f., 320, 344f.; Catagnoti QuSe 15 250. **EUPH** *la-i-im*, *la-i-yu-um*, *la-i-ia*, *la-i-yu-um*, *la-i-tum*, *la-i-ia-tum*, *i-la-la-e/i*, ^{d}*da-gan-la-i*, *la-ú-um*,[22] *i-la-la-aḫ* → Huffmon APNMT 224; Gelb CAAA 23, 143; Zadok Fs. Hallo 326; Golinets Onomastikon 2 318, 403. **A7** *la-ú-*^{d}IM, *la-ú-la-a-da* → Wiseman AT 141; Arnaud AuOr 16 163, Streck Onomastikon 1 271 § 3.19; Golinets Onomastikon 2 317, 403. **TU** *a-bu-la-ú* → Krebernik Tall Bi`a 208; Golinets Onomastikon 2 318, 403. **EM** *la-uʔ*, *ba-bu-la-ú*, ^{d}*ra-ša-ap-la-i*, ^{d}UTU*-la-i* → Pruzsinszky PTEm 173 [591], 200 [174], 201 [695, 736]. **UGS** *la-e-ia-a*, *la-i-ia*, *la-i-ia-ya* → Huffmon APNMT 225; Gröndahl PTU 154; Sivan GaGl 241; DUL 485: *lʔi*.
liʔy "power"	•ONOM: **EUPH** *li-i-um*, *li-ú-um*, *li-i-*^{d}*da-gan* → Gelb CAAA 23, 146.
lỉy "powerful"	•ONOM: **UGA** *lỉy* → DUL 485.
ảliy(n) "the most powerful"	•CTX: **UGA** → DUL 51: *ảliy*, *ảliyn*.

[20] The EA PN *le-e-ia* (Hess APN 104, 207) is probl. Egyptian.

[21] \|yibbiʔ=laʔ(ī)\| "the powerful one called"; altern. \|yibbiʔ=raʕ\| "the friend called", Pagan ARES 3 320.

[22] Listed under LAWUJ with *la-i-im* (gen.) and *la-e-em* (acc.). See \|l-w-y\|, and further: *la-wi-la-ti*, Zadok Fs. Hallo 326: L-ʔ-Y, L-W/Y-Y.

ålit "the most powerful" (fem.)	•ONOM: **UGA** DN → DUL 51.
talʔiy "victor"	•ONOM: **EM** Cf. ^{d}IŠKUR-*ta-li*, ^{d}IŠKUR-*ta-li-i*, ^{d}U-*ta-li-i* → Pruzsinszky PTEm 193 [207], diff.: "vermag, kann".
tilʔā "victory"	•ONOM: **EM** ^{d}EN-*ti-il-a* → Pruzsinszky PTEm [218].
tlỉyt "victory"	•CTX: **UGA** → DUL 856.

|l-ʔ-w/y| (2) Cf. **|l-ħ-ħ|**	Sem.: *lʔy* (JAram., Syr.) "to toil, be tired; to labour, weaken"; cf. *tlʔh* (*t*^{e}*lāʔāh*, Hb.) "tribulation, hardship"; see further *laʔy* (Ar.) "slowness, tardiness"; *laʔû*(*m*) (Akk.) "small child, baby(ish)". Probl. related to *lakû*(*m*) (Akk.) "weak, suckling".
|l-ʔ-w/y| **(B)** "to be drained, weaken"	•CTX: **UGA** G prefc. suff. *tlů* → DUL 485. •ONOM: **EUPH** Cf. unc. *la-ḫi-ia-tim* → Zadok Fs. Hall 326: listed under L-Ḥ-Y "to languish, faint".
laʔay "suckling" (?)	•ONOM: **EM** Cf. unc. *la-ḫé-ia* → Pruzsinszky PTEm 87 fn. 176 [584].

|l-ʔ-y| (3)	Culture word, Sem.: *liʔum*, *lû*(*m*) (Akk.) "bull"; *lītu*(*m*), *littu* "cow"; *laʔan* "bull" (Arab.), *lāʔa* "gazelle, antelope", redupl. *luʔluʔa* "wild cow"; see also: *léʔ*, *ləháytən* (OSArab.) "cow(s)"; *ʔélheh* (MSArab.) "cow". Non-Sem.: **laʔ=* (West Chadic) "cow"; **la/uw=* (Agaw) "cow, cattle"; **loʔ/w=* (East Cushitic) "cattle".[23]
luʔy "bull" (?)	•ONOM: **U3** Unc.; cf. *lú-a-nu-um* → Buccellati Amorites 165f.[24]
liʔyan "head of large cattle"	•LL: **EB** ALIM = *lí-a-núm*, *lí-a-nu-um* → Pettinato MEE 4 282 (VE 731); Civil BaE 90; Militarev / Kogan SED 2 191; Bonechi QDLF 16 50 fn. 70.
liʔyatt "cow"	•LL: **EB** ALIM.SAL = *lí-a-tum* → Pettinato MEE 4 282 (VE 732); Militarev / Kogan SED 2 191.

|l-b-ʔ|	Culture word, Sem.: *lbʔ* (pl. *l*^{e}*bāʔim*, Hb.) "lion", *lbyʔ* (*lābîʔ*, *l*^{e}*bîyāʔ*) "lioness"; *lbʔ* (Aram.) "lion"; *lābu*(*m*), *labʔum*, *labbu* (Akk.) "lion", *lābatu*(*m*), *labbatu* "lioness"; *labʔa*, *labāʔa*, *labuʔa* (Arab.) "lioness"; (OSArab.)*lbʔ* "lion". Non-Sem.: Cf. *ȝby* (Eg.) "panther"; see further: **lVbVʔ=Vr=* (West Chadic) "wild cat";**ʔa=lib=ar* (Central Chadic) "lion"; **lub=ak=* (Saho-Afrar) "lion"; *lib=aḥ=* (Lowland East Cushitic) "lion".[25]
labʔ, **labw** "lion; DN"	•CTX: **EUPH** *la-ab-i*, *la-ab-i-im* → Durand MARI 7 50f. •LL: **EB** PIRIG = *bar-ga-um* / *ab-ba-um* |labʔ/wʔ=| → Pettinato MEE 4 96 V 4; Civil BaE 90; Sanmartín AuOr 9 1991 192f.

---

[23] Orel / Stolbova HSED 354 no. 1632: **laʔ=*, **law=* "cattle".

[24] See further Huffmon APNMT 224: *luʔu*, unc. The Ebl. PNN with the elem. =DIB-*ù* (Pagan ARES 3 223: =*luʔ-ù*) are out of the question.

[25] Orel / Stolbova HSED 355 no. 355: **labiʔ=* / **libaʔ=* "lion".

•ONOM: **U3** *la-ba-um* → Owen JCS 33 257.[26]
EUPH *la-bi-sa-ma, a-pil-la-bi, ša-du-ul-la-bi*; *ša-du-um-la-bu-a* → Huffmon APNMT 225; Gelb 24, 144; Durand REA 651.[27]
R *la-bu-a*/ḪA-*nu* → Dalley / Walker / Hawkins Tell Rimah 261; Zadok Fs. Hallo 326.
Q Cf. *la-ab-bu* ZABAR → Richter / Lange Idadda 84f.: "bronzenes Löwengefäss".
EM *la-bu-*^{d}KUR, *la-ab-ú-* ^{d}KUR → Pruzsinszky PTEm 196: [583].
EA *la-ab-a-ia*/*ya* → Sivan GAGl 240; Moran AmL 382; Hess APN 102, 207; vSoldt Fs. Huehnergard 443f.
UGS *la-ab-ʔi-ya* → Sivan GAGl 240; Huehnergard UVST 245.

lbỉ "lion; DN" •CTX: **UGA** Sg. suff. *lbỉm* → DUL 486.
•ONOM: **UGA** *ʕmlbỉ* → DUL 161; *lbỉy* → 486; *šmlbỉ* → 814.

labʔa, **labwa** "lioness; DN" •ONOM: **EUPH** *am-ti-la-ba, ḫa-am-mu-la-ba-a, i-din-*^{d}*la-ba, iš-ḫi-*^{d}*la-ba, sa-mu-*^{d}*la-ba, su-mu-la-ba, ša-du-um*/*un-la-ba, ša-du-la-ba* → Huffmon APNMT 225; Gelb 24, 144; Durand REA 651; Golinets BuB 9 70; Knudsen JCS 34 15.[28]

labaya "lioness" •CTX: **EG** *r-ba-ya* → Hoch SWET 202 no. 273.[29]

lbỉt "lioness; DN" •ONOM: **UGA** → DUL 139: *ʕbdlbỉt.*

|l-b-b|

Primary noun, Sem.: *lb*, *lbb* (*lēb*, *lᵉbab*, Hb) "heart, entrails, mind"; *lb* (Ph., Pun.) id.; *lb*(*ʔ*), *lbb*(*ʔ*) (Aram., Syr.) id.; *libbu*(*m*) (Akk.) id.; *lubb* (Arab.) id.; *lb*, *lbb* (OSArab.) id.; *ḥelbēb*, *ḥewbēb*, *ʔélbeb* (MSArab.)id.; *ləbb* (Eth.) id.
Non-Sem: *ỉb* (Eg.) "heart"; **lVb=ak* (Agaw) id; **lVb=* (West Chadic) "lungs"; **(HV=)lib* (Central Chadic) "belly, stomach"; **lib=* (Omotic) "heart"; **lib=* (Rift) "chest"; **lub=* (East Chadic) "heart"; **lub=* (Saho-Afar) id.; **la*/*ub=* (Lowland East Cushitic) id.

libb "heart" •LL:[30]
•ONOM: **EUPH** Cf. *i-nu-uḫ-li-bi, i-túr-li-ib-bi* → Gelb CAAA 24, 146; Zadok Fs. Hallo 326.
EM Cf. *lìb-ba*/*bi, a-ḫi-lìb-bi, i-túr-*ŠÀ → Pruzsinszky PTEm 87, 115, 216 [89, 536, 592]; Tropper BiOr 62 67.

lb "heart" •CTX: **UGA** Sg. *lb*, suff. *lbk*, *lby* → DUL 485f.

|l-b-x|
Cf. |s^1-b-ħ|

Sem.: Cf. *lubūḫa* (Arab.) "to be fleshy, corpulent, fat", *labīh* "fleshy, plump, fat".

---

[26] Cf. unc. *lu-bu-e-el*, *lù-bu*-DINGIR; Buccellati Amorites 166 (|lubʔ=u=ʔel|, questionable). Diff. Gelb CAAA 23 (LʔʔP), LUʔP, LUʔUP (147).
[27] For *ša-du-ul-la-bi* and *ša-du-um-la-bu-a* see also Sasson UF 6 384; Streck Onomastikon 1 260 § 3.7: Hurr.?
[28] For *ša-du-um*/*un-la-ba* and *ša-du-la-ba* see also Sasson UF 6 384; Streck Onomastikon 1 260 § 3.7: Hurr.?
[29] Kilani VGW 121f.: |rvb'o:y(v)|.
[30] For EB ŠÀ.TAR.SUR = *dal-da-li-bù* see Conti QuSe 17 164: |taltar(r)ibu(m), tas^{1}tar(r)ibu(m)|, and below: |s^1-r-b|.

|l-b-x| "to be fleshy, corpulent, fat" — •LL: **EB** Cf. ŠÀ.KAL = *tal-ta-bí-ḫum* → Sjöberg Fs. Pettinato 265.[31]

|l-b-n| (1)

Sem.: *lbn* (*lābān*, Hb.; Pun. also =*labon*), "white", *lbn* (also Aram =*libnā* in *puruḫlibnu*; JAram.) "white poplar; whiteness; storax", *lbnh* (*l^{e}bōnāh*, Hb.) "frankincense", (*l^{e}bānāh*, Hb.) "full moon"; *lbnt* (Edom.) "incense altar"; *lubān* (Arab.) "frankincense"; *lbn* (OSArab.) "a kind of incense burner". See further: *laban* (Arab.) "milk", *labanī* "milky", *labbān* "milkman".

labn (A), laban "white; a lunar deity"

•LL: **UGS** [BABBAR] = [*peṣû*] = [...] = *la-ba-nu* → Sivan GAGl 240; Huehnergard UVST 142; vSoldt SAU 304 (73).
•ONOM: **EB** *la-ba-na-AN* |laban=ān|? → Krebernik PET 240; Pagan ARES 3 137, 345.
U3 *la-ba*-NE-*rí-iš* → Zadok Fs. Hallo 326.
EUPH *la-ab-nu-um, la-ba-an, iš-ḫi-la-ba-an, šu-la-ba-an, za-aḫ-la-ba-an/nu*,[32] *ḫi-it-làl-^{d}la-ba-an, su-mu-la-ba-an, la-pa-na-i-la* → Gelb CAAA 24, 144; Zadok Fs. Hallo 326; Durand REA 676.
UGS : *la-ab-na-a, l*[*a*(?)]-*ab-nu* → Gröndahl PTU 154; Sivan GAGl 240.[33]

labn (B) "a kind of incense burner" (?) — •CTX: **Q** *la-ab-nu* → Richter / Lange Idadda 94.[34]

labbin "pallid, albino" (?) — •ONOM: **A7** *la-ab-bi-na* → Wiseman AT 141; Gelb CAAA 24, 144.

lbn "white" — •CTX: **UGA** Pl. *lbnm* → DUL 486: *lbn* (I).
•ONOM: **UGA** → DUL 487: *lbn* (II).[35]

|l-b-n| (2)

Sem.: *lbn* (Hb.) "to make bricks", *lbnh* (*l^{e}bēnāh*) "sun baked brick"; *lbn* (JAram.) "to work in bricks", *lbnh, lbnt?* "brick" (Aram.); *labānu*(*m*) "to spread, stroke" (Ass. "to brick over; cover with brickwork"), *labnu*(*m*) (Ass.) "(spread) flat, moulded", *libittu*(*m*) "mudbrick(s)"; *labbana* (Arab.) "to make bricks", *libn, labin* "adobes", *labbān* "brickmaker".

|l-b-n| "to make bricks" — •CTX: **UGA** D prefc. *tlbn* → DUL 486.

labbān "brickmaker" — •CTX: **UGS** LÚ *la-ba*(?)-*nu* → Sivan GAGl 240, UF 21 1989 361; Huehnergard UVST 142.

labitt "brick" — •CTX: **EA** SIG$_4$(-*tu*) : *la-bi-tu* → CAD L 176; Sivan GAGl 240; Izre'el Orient 38 87f.

---

[31] Cf. diff. Conti QuSe 17 166: |tas^{1}tab(b)iḫum| (Hb., Aram. *šbḥ* < *šbḫ* "lodare; crescere in valore"). According to Sjöberg, ŠÀ.KAL = *tal-ta-bí-ḫum*(LUM) and ŠÀ.KAL (ša-ga-ga) = *ʔà-la-lum* might be two different lexical entries.
[32] Durand MARI 8 632 fn. 422; former reading: *a-ḫi-la-ba-an*, Gelb CAAA 144.
[33] Passim in TN Lebanon; Belmonte RGTC 12/2 174: *Labnānu, Labʔānu*; see further *Lab(i)nūma*; Belmonte RGTC 12/2 173; *Lubānu*, Belmonte RGTC 12/2 177.
[34] With a diff. translation: "ein Gegenstand" (flache Schüssel?), loc.cit.
[35] See also the TNN *lbnn*, DUL 487: *lbnn* (I); *lbnm* → DUL 487; the GN *lbny* → DUL 488: *lbny* (I), and the PN *lbny*, DUL 488: *lbny* (II).

libatt, **libitt** "brick"	•LL: **EB** SIG$_4$.DÚR.GAR = *li-ba-tum*; [SIG4.DÚR.GAR] = *li-bí-tum* → Krebernik ZA 73 6; Gordon Eblaitica 1 20f.; Conti QuSe 17 87.
lbnt "brick"	•CTX: **UGA** → DUL 487f.
malbatt "brick mould"	•LL: **EB** GIŠ.SIG$_4$.DÚR = *ma-ba-du*, *ma-ba-a-tum*, *ma-ba-tum* → Conti QuSe 17 142; Sjöberg Fs. Oelsner 411 fn. 8.
nalbatt "frame (for gems)"	•CTX: **EUPH** Pl. *na-al-ba-na-tim* → Durand MARI 7 380f.

|l-b-s^1|	Sem.: *lbš* (Hb., Aram., Syr.) "to put on a garment, to clothe oneself with something", *lbwš* (*lābûš*, Hb.) "garment", *lbš*, *lbwš*(*?/h/t?*) (Aram., Syr.) "dressing, garment", *mlbš*(*?*) (*malbûš*, Hb., JAram.) "robe, garment";. *labāšu*(*m*) (Akk.) "to put on clothing", *lubūšu*(*m*) "clothing, wardrobe", *libšu*(*m*), *lubšu*, *lubāšu*(*m*), *nalbašu*(*m*) "(a fine) cloak, coat"; *labisa* (Arab.) "to put on, wear", *libās*, *labūs*, *libs*, *malbas*, "clothing, dress"; *lbs* (OSArab.) "to put on, wear", *lībes* (MSArab.) id, *labs* "clothing, dress"; *labsa* (Eth.) "to clothe oneself, put on", *ləbs*, "clothes, garment", *malbas*, *malbast* "clothing, garment".
|**l-b-s^1**| "to clothe oneself, wear"	•CTX: **EB** D prefc. *du-a-ba-áš* → Fronzaroli QuSe 15 15, ARET 11 143, 179; Catagnoti QuSe 29 206. **EG** Cf. *r*(*u_2*)*-bi-ša* (|labis^{1}a| ?; Eg. stative) → Hoch SWET 203 no. 275: "to wear a cuirass". **UGA** G prefc. *ylbš*, *tlbš*; suffc. *lbs*; act. / pass. ptc. *lbš*, fem. *lbšt*; C suffc. with suff. *šlbšn* → DUL 488: |*l-b-š*|.
labīs^{1}a "cuirass, leather armour"	•CTX: **EG** *ra-bi-ša-ya* → Hoch SWET 202f. no. 274.[36]
lbs^1 "clothing; sails"	•CTX: **UGA** Sg. *lbš*; pl. *lbšm*; cstr. *lbš*; du. *lbšm*. → DUL 488f. *lbš*.
lps^1 "cloak, outer garment"	•CTX: **UGA** → DUL 496: *lpš*.
malbas^1 "cloak"	•CTX: **EA** GADA.MEŠ *: ma-al-ba-ši* → Hoftijzer / Jongeling DNWSI 630; AHw 724; CAD M/1 162; Sivan GAGl 243; Rainey EAT 80; Izre'el Orient 38 73.
mlbs^1 "cloak, luxurious cape"	•CTX: **UGA** Sg. *mlbš*, suff. *mlbšh* → DUL 541: *mlbš*.
mulabbiSt "female housekeeper, attendant"	•CTX: **EB** *mu-a-bí-iš-tum* → Fronzaroli NABU 1991/49; QuSe 15 14, ARET 11 161; Krebernik PIHANS 106 90; Pasquali QuSe 23 27, 65, Textile terminologies 187; Catagnoti QuSe 29 206.

|l-D-n|	Culture word, Sem.: *lṭ* (*loṭ*, Hb.) "laudanum resin"; *ldn*(*?*) (JAram., Syr.) id.; *ladinnu*, *ladnu*, *ladunu* (Akk.) id.; *lādan*, *lāḏan*, *lāḏana*, *lawdanūn* (Arab.) id.; *ldn* (OSArab.) id.; *lōzan* (Eth.) id. Non-Sem.: *lá/ēdanon* (Gr.) "laudanum resin".[37]

[36] Sivan / Cochavi-Rainey WSVES 83: *la-bi-šá-ya* "armour"; Helck Beziehungen no. 150.

[37] Masson Emprunts 55 fn. 3.

lōdan "laudanum resin"	•CTX: **EG** *ru$_2$-d-n-nu*, *ra-d-n-ya* → Hoch SWET 212 no. 288.
|l-g-g|	Culture word, Sem.: *l(w)g* (*log*, pl. *lôggîm*, Hb.; Aram., JAram.) "small liquid measure"; see further: *lgh*, *lgtʔ* (Syr.) "wooden bowl", *lgwnh*, *lgwntʔ* (Syr.) "pitcher".
lg "measure of capacity for liquids, jar"	•CTX: **UGA** Pl. *lgm* → DUL 489: *lg* (I). •ONOM: **UGA** Unc. cf. *lg* → DUL 490: *lg* (II); unc. cf. *lgn* → DUL 490.
|l-g-m|	Culture word, Sem.: Cf. *lgm(ʔ)* (Syr.) "rein, bridle, bit", *lgm* (D) "to chew"; *liǧām* (Arab.) "bridle, reins", *ʔalǧama* "to bridle, rein in"; *ləgwām* (Eth.) "bridle, rein", *lag^{w}ama* "to rein, bridle".
talgim "harness(ing)" (?)	•LL: **UGS** Cf. [DÍM (for DIM) = *riksu* = *x-x*[ ] = *tal-gi-mu* → Huehnergard NABU 2019/46.[38]
|l-ħ-ħ| Cf. **|l-ʔ-y/w| (2)**, **|l-ħ-y| (2)**, **|s^1-l-ħ| (2)**	Sem.: Cf. Hb. *lḥ* (*laḥ*, Hb.) ""still moist, fresh", (*lē^{a}ḥ*), Hb.) "freshness, vital force"; *lḥlḥ* (JAram.) "to moisten", *lḥ* (Syr.) "moisture", *lyḥh* (JAram.) "moisture"; *laḥiḥa* (Arab.) "to shed tears (the eyes)", *ʔalaḥḥa* "to rain"; *laḥḥa* (Eth.) "to be humid". Non-Sem.: Cf. *ywḥ* (Eg.) "to moisten".[39]
|l-ħ-ħ| "to moisten"	•CTX: **UGA** G prefc. *tlḥn*, *ylḥn* → DUL 491: */l-ḥ(-ḥ)/*. •ONOM: **EUPH** Cf. unc. *la-ḫa-ta-an* → Zadok Fs. Hallo 326.
laħ "young shoot"	•LL: **MŠ** *la-a-ḫu* = *pe-er-ḫu* → AHw 528; CAD L 45; Hrůša MŠ 436 exp. III 232. •ONOM: **EUPH** Cf. unc. *la-ḫi-ia-tim* → Zadok Fs. Hallo 326: listed under L-Ḥ-Y.
|l-ħ-k|	Sem.: *lḥk* (Hb.) "to eat up"; (JAram., Syr.) *lḥk* "to lick"; (Akk.) *lêku(m)* id.; (Arab.) *laḥika* id. Non-Sem.: Cf. **lVḳ=* "to lick".[40]
|l-ħ-k| "to lick"	•CTX: **UGA** G prefc. *tlḥk* → DUL 491: */l-ḥ-k/*.
|l-ħ-m| (1)	Sem.:. *lḥm* (Hb.) "to eat with someone", (Ph.) "to eat, devour", *lḥm* (*leḥem*, Hb.; Pun., Palm.) "grain, bread, food"; *lḥm(ʔ)* (Aram., JAram., Syr.) "bread; food,

[38] For the previous rdg *rig(i)m* "word" ([GIM / BAN? = …] = *x-x-*[ ] = *ri-gi-mu*) see Laroche UF 11 479; Huehnergard UVST 50, 177, 193; ^{2}UVST 398; vSoldt SAU 307 (132: \|rig(i)mu\|).
[39] Watson UF 40 554.
[40] Orel / Stolbova 368 no. 1697.

meal"; *lêmu*(*m*), la*ʔāmum* (Akk.) "to take food or drink"; *laḥama* (Arab.) "to feed on meat", *laḥm* "meat".
Non-Sem.: *laHam= (West Chadic) "meat".[41]

|l-ħ-m| **(A)** "to eat" — •CTX: **UGA** G prefc. *ỉlḥm*, *tlḥm*, *nlḥm*, suff. *tlḥmn*; suffc. *lḥm*; imp. *lḥm*; inf. *lḥm*, suff. *lḥmm*; D prefc. *ylḥm*; C prefc. *tšlḥm*, *yšlḥm*; suff. *yšlḥmnh*; impv. *šlḥm* → DUL 491f.: */l-ḥ-m/* (I).

lħm "grain; bread; food, meat" — •CTX: **UGA** sg. *lḥm*; suff. *lḥmy*, *lḥmk*, *lḥmh* → DUL 492: *lḥm*.

s¹lħmt "provisions, victuals" — •CTX: **UGA** → DUL 805*: šlḥmt.*

|l-ħ-m| (2)

Sem.: *lḥm* (Hb.) G/N "to fight"; *hltḥm* (Gt Moab.) "to make war", *talāḥama*, *ʔiltāhama* (Arab.) "to join in battle" / "to fight in close combat".

|l-ħ-m| **(B)** "to fight" — •CTX: **UGA** G prefc. *ylḥm*, suff. *ỉlḥmn*; suffc. *lḥmt* → DUL 492: */l-ḥ-m/* (II).[42]

|l-ħ-m| (3)

Sem.: Cf. *lḥm* (Syr.) "to be fitting; to join"; *laḥama* (Arab.) "to stick, consolidate"; *läḥama* (Tigre) "to hold together".

laħam "suitable, fitting" (?) — •LL: **UGS** [TE = *simtu*(?)] = *ḫa-aḫ-li* = *la-ḫa-m*[*u*(?)] → Huehnergard UVST 142.[43]

laħim "squeezed, put close together" — •LL: **EB** NÍG.LU = *la-i-mu* / *a-i-mu* → Conti QuSe 17 69; Catagnoti QuSe 29 58, 122, 206.

tilħamt "tangle" — •CTX: **EB** *ti-ʔà-ma-du* → Catagnoti QuSe 29 67, 232.
•LL: **EB** NÌ.LU.LU = *ti-ʔà-ma-tum* → Conti QuSe 17 69; Catagnoti QuSe 29 67, 232.

|l-ħ-n|

Sem.: Cf. *laḥina* (Arab.) "to be intelligent".

|l-ħ-n| "to be intelligent" — •ONOM: **UGA** *ylḥn* → DUL 949. Also as element of the composite DN *ydʕ ylḥn*.

|l-ħ-r|

See **|r-x-l|**

|l-ħ-y| (1)

Primary noun, Sem.: *lḥy* (*leḥî*, Hb; JAram.) "chin, jawbone; side"; *lētu*(*m*), *lītu* (Akk.) "cheek, side";[44] *laḥy* (Arab.) "jawbone", *liḥya* "beard"; *leḥyīt*, *məźḥét*,

---

[41] Orel / Stolbova HSED 356 no. 1642: **laḥam*= "meat, food". Probl. an innovation; see Arab. *laḥm* "meat".
[42] For the PN UGA *ỉltḥm*, UGS *iltaḥ*(*i*)*mu* see |*t-H-m*| "to plan, intend, decree", *DaHm* "decree, message (GlOS Part One: |*D-H-m*| (1)), and cf. Gzella BiOr 64 548f.
[43] For the variant rdg EB *a-a-mu-mu* (= TE.ME; Huehnergard UVST 81 fn. 33) see *ʔayyam* "someone" (|ʔ-y-y| (1), GlOS Part One).
[44] Cf. Nuzi-Akk. and SBab. *laḫû*.

	málḥeh (MSArab.) “beard, chin, jaw”; *maltāḥt* (Eth.) “cheek, jaw”; *läḥe* (Tigre) id.
lħ (A) “cheek, jaw”	•CTX: **UGA** Du. *lḥm*; pl. *lḥt* → DUL 490: *lḥ* (I).

|l-ħ-y| (2) Cf. **|l-ʔ-y/w| (2)**	Sem.: *lḥy* (Aram., Syr.) “to destroy, delete, expel”; *laḥā* (Arab.) “to insult, abuse, revile, *laḥw/y* “insult, abuse. Cf. *lḥy* (*l*^{e}*ḥî*, Hb.) “curse”; (Aram.) “bad, wicked”.
|l-ħ-y| “to revile, verbally abuse”	•CTX: **EG** *n-ra-ḥa* |laħâ| → Hoch SWET 186f. no. 251. •ONOM: **EUPH** Cf. unc. *la-ḫi-ia-tim* → Zadok Fs. Hallo 326.
laħiy “deceitful”	•CTX: **EUPH** *a-wa-tum la-ḫi-tu* → ARMT 13 172 (144: 31f).

|l-x-s^1|	Sem.: *lḥš* (*yitlaḥaš*, Hb.; Aram., JAram., Syr. G) “to whisper”, *lḥš* (*laḥaš*, Hb.) “whisper, incantation”, *mlḥš* (*m*^{e}*laḥ*^{a}*šîm*, Hb. ptc. D) “magician”; *lḥšt* (Ph.) incantation, spell; *lḥš(?)*, *lḥšh* (JAram., Syr.) “whisper, incantation”; *laḫāšu(m)* (Akk.) “to murmur prayers”, *liḫšu* “whisper”, *mulaḫḫišu* “whisperer”.[45] Non-Sem.: Cf. m u š l a ḫ (Sum.) “snake charmer” (> Akk. *mušla(la)ḫḫu*).
laxxāS “whisperer, chatterer”	•LL: **EB** INIM.SI$_{11}$ = *a-ḫa-su-um* → Bonechi QDLF 16 86; cf. Conti QuSe 17 98. •ONOM: **EUPH** Cf. fem. *la-ḫe-èš-tum* → Zadok Fs. Hallo 326.
lxs^{1}t “chatter, whisper, murmur”	•CTX: **UGA** → DUL 493: *lḫšt*.
mlxs^1 “conjuror, snake charmer”	•CTX: **UGA** → DUL 543: *mlḫš*.

|l-ḳ-ħ|	Sem.: *lqḥ* (Hb.) “to take”, *mlqḥym* (du. *melqāḥayim*) “tongs”, *mlqwḥym* (du. *malqôḥayim*) “gums”; *lqḥ* (Ph., Pun., Aram.) “to take”; *leqû(m)*, *laqû(m)* (Akk.) id.; *laqaḥa* (Arab.) “to conceive”; *lqḥ* (OSArab.) “to take”; (MSArab.) “to conceive”; *laqqəḥa* (Eth.) “to lend”.
|l-ḳ-ħ| “to take, grasp; to receive, accept”	•CTX: **EB** Gt prefc. *a-a-da-ga-si* |la=yiltaḳḳaħ=si| (durative, suff.) → Fronzaroli ARET 11 137, 179; SEL 12 62; Catagnoti QuSe 29 143, 206. **EA** G suffc. [*la-*]*qa-ḫu*; Gpass. suffc. *la-qí-*[*ḫ*]*u* → AHw 537; CAD L 100; Sivan GAGl 241; Rainey CAT 2 290, 296, 298, 304; Izre’el Orient 38 71. **UGA** G prefc. *yqḥ*, *tqḥ*, *iqḥ*, *tqḥn*, *yqḥnn*; suffc. *lqḥ*, *lqḥt*; imp. *qḥ*, *qḥn*, suff. *qḥny*; inf. *lqḥ*; Gpass. *yqḥ*; N suffc. *ylqḥ*(?), *nlqḥt* → DUL 496-499: */l-q-ḥ/*. •ONOM: **EM** Cf. *la-qi/qì* → Pruzsinszky PTEm 173 [590].
maḳḳaħ “tong(s)”	•CTX: **UGS** Du. cstr. 1 *ma-qa-ḫa* |maḳḳaħā| → AHw 607; CAD M/1 253; Sivan GAGl 244; Huehnergard UVST 143; vSoldt SAU 305 (88).
mḳħ “tong(s)”	•CTX: **UGA** Du. *mqḥm* → DUL 560: *mqḥ*; Del Olmo AuOr 37 290.

[45] Cf. *mušla(la)ḫḫu* (Akk.) “snake charmer”.

|l-ḳ-ḳ|	Sem.: *lqq* (Hb.) "to lick up, lap"; *laqlaqa* (Tigre) id.; cf. *laqqa* (Arab.) "to strike with the hand".
|l-ḳ-ḳ| "to lick up, lap"	•ONOM: **EUPH** Cf. *la-qì-qù-um* → Zadok Fs. Hallo 326.

|l-ḳ-ṭ|	Sem.: *lqṭ* (Hb., Aram., Syr.): "to gather out", *lqṭ* (*leqeṭ*, Hb.) "remnants", *ylqwṭ* (*yilqûṭ*) "pouch", *lqṭ(?)* (JAram., Syr.) "gleaning, collection"; *laqātu(m)* (Akk.): "to gather out", *liqtu(m)* "gathered material, selection"; *laqaṭa* (Ar.): "to gather out, collect, pick out", *luqṭa* "gleanings", *ʔiltiqāṭ* "collection, gleaning".
|l-ḳ-ṭ| "to gather out, collect, pick out"	•LL: **EB** ŠE Ú.RI.GA = *a-ga-tum* → Krebernik ZA 73 13; Conti QuSe 17 112. •ONOM: **EUPH** *ia-al-gu-tum* → Golinets Onomastikon 2 109, 403.
|l-ḳ-θ̣| "to gather out, collect, pick out" (?)	•CTX: **UGA** Unc., G inf. (?) *lqẓ* → DUL 499.[46]
liḳṭ "harvesting, gathering"	•LL: **EB** ŠE Ú.RI.RI.GA = *li-gi-tum* → Krebernik ZA 73 13; Conti QuSe 17 112. •ONOM: **EUPH** *li-iq-t/ṭim* → Zadok Fs. Hallo 326.
ỉlḳṣ "exquisite" (?)	•CTX: **UGA** Unc., pl. *ỉlqṣm* → DUL 61: *ỉlqṣm*, said of a "gem"(?). Probl. a borrowing with D > S shift.

|l-l-ʔ|	Culture word, Sem.: *laliu(m)*, *laliʔu*, *lalāʔu(m)* (Akk.) "kid, goat";[47] *lúloh* (MSArab.) "sheep". Non-Sem.: **lal=* (East Chadic) "she-goat, cattle".[48]
lall, lala(?), lali(?) "suckling (lamb or kid)"	•ONOM: **EB** Cf. *la-li*, *la-lu*, *la-lum* → Pagan ARES 3 222, 345.[49] **EUPH** Cf. *la-lum*, *la-lu-um*, *la-la-i-im*, *la-la-a-num*, fem. *la-la-a-tum*, *la-la-ḫa-tum* → Gelb CAAA 144; Durand MARI 8 665; Millet Albà TopoiSuppl 2 478f.; Kogan AuOr 21 254. **UGS** Cf. DUMU *la-li-i*[→ Gröndahl PTU 12, 28, 155.
llủ "suckling (lamb or kid)"	•CTX: **UGA** Sg. *llủ*, *llỉ*, *llả*; pl. *llỉm* → DUL 494.
llỉt "young sheep or kid"	•ONOM: **UGA** → DUL 494.

|l-l-x|	Culture word, etym. unc. Cf. *Lullu* (TN), *Lulaḫḫi* (a group).[50] Non-Sem.: Cf. *lulaḫḫi* (Hurr.) "foreign, alien".[51]

---

[46] Rdg and ctx. unc.; altern. rdg (G prefc.) *l* <*y*>*kẓ*. For Ug. *θ̣* instead of etym. *ṭ* see Tropper UG 113f.

[47] Notice further *lilu* "a kind of sheep" (Mari); Bottéro ARM 7 143: *li-lum*(!), 250; CAD L 190; AHw vacat.

[48] Orel / Stolbova HSED 357 no. 1647: **lal=* "goat, cattle".

[49] |laliʔ| "kid"; altern. |lalī| "desire" (cf. Akk. *lalû(m)* "plenty, exuberance; desire, longing (for))".

[50] Laroche GLH 160f.

llx "an element of the shabrack" (?)	•CTX: **UGA** Pl. suff. *llḫhm* → Loretz AOAT 386 112; Richter BGH 531; DUL 494: *llḫ*.
|l-l-l|	Onomatopoeia: Sem.: *lll* (Syr.) "to speak foolish", *ll* "foolish"; *lillu*(*m*) (Akk.) "idiot"
lill "light, weak"	•CTX: **EUPH** KAŠ *li-lum* → Limet ARMT 19, 23.
|l-m-d|	Sem.: *lmd (Hb. D)* "to teach", (Syr. G) "to adhere to", *lmd* (*limmud*, Hb.) "taught, trained"; *tlmyd* (*talmîd*, Hb.) "pupil", *tlmyd(?)* (JAram) "student, scholar"; *tlmd* (Syr.) "to teach"; *lamādu*(*m*) (Akk.) "to become aware, informed", *lamdu* "experienced", *lummudu*, *lammudu* "taught", *talmēdum*, *talmīdu(m)* "apprentice"; *lamada* (Arab.) "to bow (before, to); *lamada* "be accustomed to, be familiar with" (Eth.), *talmid* "disciple".
|l-m-d| "to learn, become aware, informed"	•CTX: **EB** G prefc. (precat.) *lu-ma-du-ma* |lū=yilmadū=ma| → Catagnoti QuSe 29 134, 206. **UGA** D prefc. with suff. *ảlmdk*. *ylmdnn*; suffc. *lmd* → DUL 495: "to teach, train".
lmd "trained, pupil, apprentice"	•CTX: **UGA** Sg. *lmd*; pl. abs. *lmdm*, cstr. *lmd*, suff. *lmdhm* → DUL 495.
lmdt "female apprentice"	•CTX: **UGA** Sg. suff. *lmdth* → DUL 495.
tlmd "trained, one being tamed"	•CTX: **UGA** Du. *tlmdm* → DUL 857.
|l-p-ḳ|	Sem.: *lafaqa* (Arab.) "to join and sew together".
|l-p-ḳ| "to join and sew together" (?)	•LL: **EB** Cf. AD.MIN*tenû* = *lu-bù-ga* → Sjöberg Fs. Wilcke 264: noun Du., exact mng unknown. See also Conti / Bonechi NABU 1992/10.
|l-p-t|	Sem.: *lpt* (Hb.) "to touch and hold"; *lapātu*(*m*) "(Akk.) "to touch, take hold of"; *lafata* (Arab.) "to turn, bend".
|l-p-t| "to play, strike"	•CTX: **EB** G prefc. *i-a-ba-ad* |yilappat| (durative) → Fronzaroli QuSe 15 13, ARET 11 153, 179; Catagnoti QuSe 29 131, 206.
|l-r-m-n|	Culture word, Sem.: *lurmûm*, *lurimāʔu*, *lurinnu*, *lurīnu*, *nurmû* (Akk.) "pomegranate (fruit and tree)";[52] *rmwn* (*rimôn*, Hb.) id.; *rmn*, *rwmn*(*?*) (Aram., Syr.) id.; *rummān* (Arab.) id.; romān (Eth.) id.
lrmn "pomegranate"	•CTX: **UGA** Pl. *lrmnm* → DUL 499.

---

[51] Richter BGH 236.

[52] See also *armannu*(*m*), *arwānum* (Akk.), usually "apricot"(?) but probl. "pomegranate", and Eg. *alhammān* "pomegranate" (also an ornament; Hoch SWET 24f. no. 12).

nurmān "bead (in the shape of a pomegranate)"	•CTX: **Q** *nu-úr-ma-nu* → Bottéro RA 44 120; AHw 804: *nurmânu*; CAD N/2 344f.: *nurmânu*.

|l-s-m|	Sem.: *lasāmu*(*m*) "to run, serve as a runner" (Akk.), *lasmu*(*m*) "speedy", *lāsimu*(*m*) "swift; runner, courier", *lismu*(*m*) "running, race".
|l-s-m| "to run, hurry"	•CTX: **UGA** G prefc. *tslmn* → DUL 499.
lsm "swift, steed (horses)"	•CTX: **UGA** Pl. *lsmm* → DUL 499f.
lsmt "haste, alacrity"	•CTX: **UGA** → DUL 500.
mlsm "chariot runner"	•CTX: **UGA** → DUL 551; Tropper UG 563.[53]
malsam "running, course"	•LL: **UGS** KAR = *la-sà-mu* = *i-z*[*u*]*-ri* = *ma-al-sà-mu* → Huehnergard UVST 82, 143; vSoldt SAU 305.
malsamūt "running, course"	•LL: **EM** (177', Ashkelon version) [U$_4$ KAŠ$_4$.ŠE = *ūm lismi* = *yōmu ma-a*]*l-sà-mu-ti* → Huehnergard / vSoldt IEJ 49 191; Horowitz / Oshima CunCan 42f.[54]
tuttaSSil "to act as messenger" (?)	•LL: **EB** Unc. KAS$_4$.KAS$_4$ = *du-da-zi-lum* (VE 980; nomen actionis < |m-s-l|, metath. of |l-s-m| ?) → Fronzaroli QuSe 13 139; questionable, other derivations are possible.

|l-ṣ-b|	Etym. unc. Cf. *balāṣu* (Akk.) "to stare".[55]
lṣb "brow" (?)	•CTX: **UGA** → DUL 500 (questionable).

|l-s^1-n|	Primary noun, Sem.: *lšwn* (*lāšôn*, Hb.) "tongue, word, language"; *lasoun* (Ph.) id.; *lšn*(*?*) (Aram., Syr.)id., *lšn* (denom. JAram. D/C, Syr. D) "to speak, slander"; *lišānu*(*m*) (Akk.) "tongue, word, language"; *lisān* (Arab.) id.; *ls^{1}n* (OSArab.) id.; *əwšēn, lēšen, léšin, lšín*, etc. (MSArab.) id.; *ləssan* (Eth.) id. Non-Sem.: *ns* (Eg.) "tongue"; **les* (Copt.) "tongue"; **ḫa=lis=um* (West Chadic) "tongue"id.; **ʔV=lyas=* (Central Chadic)id.; **lyas=* (East Chadic)id.; **mi=las=* (Omotic) id.[56]
|l-s^1-n| "to slander"	•CTX: **UGA** G/D Prefc. *tlšn* → DUL 501: */l-š-n/*.
las^{1}ān "tongue"	•CTX: **UGS** Cf. [*l*]*a-ša-na-ia* → Huehnergard UVST 143.[57] •LL: **UGS** Ú EME.UR.GI$_7$ = *la-ša-nu* UR.GI$_7$.MEŠ (name of a plant) → Huehnergard UVST 143.

[53] Tropper UG loc.cit.: |mulassim=| "die, welche (die Streitwagen) schnell laufen lassen", D ptc.
[54] See Gantzert ELT 2 37 (1111d, 1216).
[55] Further references to *blṭ* (Syr. Gt) "to have a bulging eye", *liṣb* (Arab.) "defile, gorge", etc., are unlikely for phonological and / or semantic reasons. Militarev / Kogan SED 1 vacat.
[56] Orel / Stolbova HSED 361 no. 1666: **les=* "tongue".
[57] Nougayrol Ug 5 257: [*l*]*a ša-na-ia* (153 v. 4'), but see also fn. 1 with reference to *lšn*.

liSān "tongue"	•LL: **EB** EME.LÁ = *a-a-gú(-um) li-sa-nu* |ʕaHāḳu(m) lisānu(m)| / *ba-ti-mu-um li-sa-nu* |pādimu(m) lisānu(m)|; KA.NU(nundum$_x$)-maḫ = *li-sa-ne-lum/lu-um* |lisān=ʔilim| → Krebernik ZA 72 208, 215; 73 7f.; Fronzaroli VO 7 15; Conti QuSe 17 94; Catagnoti QuSe 29 144, 206; Bonechi / Catagnoti Fs. Sommerfeld / Krebernik 164, 174.
ls¹n "tongue"	•CTX: **UGA** Sg. *lšn*, suff. *lšn*[*y*], *lšnh*, *lšnk*, pl. *lšnm* → DUL 501.

|l-t-H|	Culture word, Sem. etym. unc: Cf. *latāku*(*m*) "to test", *litiktu*(*m*) "test; a measuring vessel"; *ltk* (*lētek*, Hb.; JAram., Syr.) "a measurement of capacity"; *ltk* (Syr.) "fitting, coinciding"; see further: *letû*(*m*) (Akk.) "to split";[58] cf. *ladaġa* (Arab.) "to bite, sting".
ltħ "a dry measure"	•CTX: **UGA** Sg. *ltḥ*, var. *ltḫ* → DUL 501f.: *ltḥ* (I).[59] •ONOM: **UGA** Cf. unc. *ltḫ* → DUL 502: *ltḫ* (II).[60]
mltħ "a measure of capacity and area"	•CTX: **UGA** Sg. *mltḥ*, du. *mltḥm* → DUL 552: *mltḥ* (fraction or multiple of the *ltḥ* (?)).

|l-ṭ-p|	Sem.: *laṭafa* (Arab.) "to be friendly, kind, merciful", *laṭufa* "to be thin, soft, fine", *laṭīf* "gentle, gracious, mild".
laṭap "gentle, kind, fine"	•ONOM: **EUPH** *la-ṭà-pa-a*, *la-ṭà-pa-an* → Tropper / Hayajneh Or 72 163; Zadok Fs. Hallo 326.
laṭup "gentle, kind, fine"	•ONOM: **EUPH** *la-ṭú-pu-um* → Tropper / Hayajneh Or 72 163.
lṭpn "gentle, kind, fine	•CTX: **UGA** Sg. *lṭpn*, var. *lẓpn* → DUL 502: "Benevolent", epithet of the god El.

|l-ṭ-s¹|	Sem.: *lṭš* (Hb.) "to sharpen"; (JAram., Syr.) "to sharpen, polish, wipe"; *laṭasa*, *laṭaša* (Arab.) "to strike, hit".
|l-ṭ-s¹| "to sharpen"	•CTX: **UGA** Gpass. ptc. fem. *lṭšt* → DUL 502: /*l-ṭ-š*/.
talṭas¹ "sharpness" (?)	•ONOM: **EG** Cf. *t-:r-t-ꜣ-šꜣ* → Schneider APÄQ 239 no. 511.

|l-w-ħ|	Primary noun, Sem.: *lwḥ* (*lûaḥ*, Hb.) "tablet"; *lḥ* (Pun.) id.; *lwḥ(?)* (Aram., Nab., Syr.) id.; *lēʔu*(*m*) (Akk.) id.; *lawḥ* (Ar., Eth.) id., *luḫ* (Eth.) "plank".
lēH "plaque"	•CTX: **EA** Cf. 9 *le-e-ḫu* → CAD L 156: *lēʔu* a.1' (EA 14 II 2; list of gifts from Egypt).[61]
lħ (B) "missive, message"	•CTX: **UGA** pl. (?) *lḥt* → DUL 490: *lḥ* (II).

[58] Unc. *a-na la-ta-i-šu* (PRU 6 10:11), AHw 1571.
[59] See especially Tropper UG 123, 372f.; Gsella BiOr 64 549.
[60] The PN *la-te-ḫu* is probl. unrelated and remains unexplained; see Gröndahl PTU 306.
[61] AHw 457 and Rainey EAC 116 (among many others) read *le-e-ʔu*[5], but see Borger AOAT 305 276f. (no. 132: ḪU).

|l-w-r|

Sem.: Cf. *lawara* (Eth.) "to perforate".

lūr "nail"

•CTX: **EB** Cf. GIŠ *lu-lum* → Pasquali QuSe 23 150ff.
EUPH GIŠ *lu-ru* → Pasquali QuSe 23 151.
•LL: **EB** Cf. GIŠ.TE = *lu-ru*$_{12}$*-um* → Pasquali QuSe 23 151.

|l-w-S|

Sem.: *lwš* (Hb., Aram.) "to knead"; *lâšu* (Akk.) "to knead" id., *līšu*, *lēšu* "dough"; *lāṯa* (*lawṯ*, Arab.) "fold, twist"; *lws*, *losa*, *lośa* (Eth.) id.[62]

|**l-w-s**^{1}| "to knead, soil, plaster"

•CTX: **UGA** G prefc. suff. *ylšn* → DUL 500f.: /*l-š*/.

liliS "dough" (?)

•LL: **EB** Cf. NINDA.GÚG.GÚG = *li-li-šu* → Sjöberg Fs. Pettinato 258.

ủlθ "a tool for moulding or mixing clay"

•CTX: **UGA** → DUL 65: *ủlṯ*.

|l-w-ṭ|

Sem.: Cf. *lwṭ* (Hb.) "to wrap (up)"; *lâṭu*(*m*) (Akk.) "to confine, keep in check"; *lāṭa* (*lawṭ*, Arab.) "to plaster, polish; to hide, conceal".

|**l-w-ṭ**| "to cover, conceal, control" (?)

•LL: **EB** Cf. AN.SI.GAR = *la-ʔa*$_5$(NI)*-tum* → Sjöberg Fs. Renger 521
•ONOM: **EB** Unc., cf. elem. *lu-du*= in *lu-du-du-na* |luṭṭu(?)=dunna|, *lu-du-ma-nu* |=manū|, *lu-du-ù-na* |=ʔūna| → Pagan ARES 3 137, 346.
EG Cf. *r-t:*$_2^F$ → Schneider APÄQ 160 no. 338.

|l-w/y-θ|

Primary word, Sem.:. *lyš* (*layiš*, Hb) "lion" (cf. PN *lwš*, Qere *layiš*); *lyt*(*ʔ*) (JAram.) id.; *layṯ* (Arab.) id., *ʔalyaṯ* "brave, courageous", *layyaṯa*, *luyyiṯa* "to be brave, behave like a lion".

lawθ "brave, lion" (?)

•ONOM: **U3** *la-ù-ša* → Owen JCS 33 257; Zadok Fs. Hallo 326.

|l-w-y|
Cf. **|l-ʔ-w/y| (1)**

Sem.: *lwh* (Hb.) "to accompany"; *lwyh* (*liwyāh*) "wreath", *lwytn*, "Leviathan"; *lwy* (Aram., Syr.) "to accompany", *lwyh*, *lwytʔ* (Syr.) "retinue, procession"; *lawā* (Arab.) "to turn, twist", *liwan* "curvature"; *lewō* (MSArab.) "to bend", *látwi* "to come together"; l*awû*(*m*), *lawāʔum*, *lamû*, *labāʔu*, *labû* (Akk.) "to surround, besiege, move in a circle", *lawītum* "encirclement", *liwītum* "circumference", *lamutānu*, *lautānu* "slave(s), retainer(s)", *nalbân* "all around"; *lawaya* (Eth.) "to twist, wind".

---

[62] Arab. *lāta* "to soak in water or in fat" seems unrelated for phonological reasons.

|l-w-y| "to surround, accompany"	•CTX: **EB** G inf. *a-wa-um* |lawāy=|; D suffc. *lu-wu-a*, *lu-wu* |luwwuy|, *lu-a* |lūy|, *lu-wu-a-ad* |luwwuyat| → Rubio PIHANS 106 123 fn. 40; Catagnoti QuSe 29 161, 165, 206. **UGS**[63] •ONOM: **EB** |yilbay=|: *íl-ba*, *íl-ba-um*, passim with DNN: *íl-ba-da-ar*, *íl-ba-da-mu*, *íl-ba-da-si-nu*, *íl-ba-gú-nu*, *íl-ba-i-sa*, *íl-ba-ma-lik*, *íl-ba-sa/sá-mu*, *íl-ba-sum*, *íl-ba-šu*, *íl-ba-šum*, *íl-ba-zi-kir*, *íl-ba*$_4$*-ma-lik*,[64] *íl-ba*$_4$*-sá-mu*; |talway=| passim with DNN: *da-a-ì*(NI)*-lu*, *da-a-bù-lum*, *da-a-šum/zu-um*, *da-a-zi-kir*, *da-a-zu-um*; unc. |tilbay=(?)|: *dùl*(DÙL)*-wa-ga-ba-al*$_6$, |talbay=| *dùl*(SÚR)*-ba-ma-lik* → Krebernik PET 49, 53, 155, 171, 220f.; Pagan ARES 3 137, 296, 304, 335. Diff. Catagnoti / Fronzaroli ARET 16 158: **rby* "essere grande".
lāwiy "one who encircles"	•ONOM: **EB** Cf. *la-wi*, *a-dar-la-wi* |lāwiy| → Krebernik PET 241; Pagan ARES 3 137, 277, 345. **EUPH** *la-wi-na-*^{d}IM, *la-wi-la-ti*, *la-wi-li-ia* → Zadok Fs. Hallo 326.
lawuy "companion, one who surrounds"	•LL: **EB** Cf. KU.LI = *la-ù-um* → Sjöberg Fs. Renger 541.[65] •ONOM: **EUPH** *la-wu-*(*la-*)^{d}IM, *la-wu-*(*la-*)DINGIR → Gelb CAAA 23, 143f.
ltn "the wound, coiled one"	•ONOM: **UGA** Name of a mythical monster → Tropper KWU 66: |lôtānu|; UG 272: "die Gewundene"; DUL 502: *ltn* (I). See also DUL 502: *ltn* (II), PN.
lwn(y) "follower, mate" (?)	•CTX: **UGA** → DUL 503.
lyt "retinue" (?)	•CTX: **UGA** → DUL 503.

|l-w-z|	Primary noun, Sem.: lwz (*lûz*, Hb.) "almond tree"; *lwz(ʔ)* (JAram., Syr.) "almond"; *lawz* (Arab.) "almond(s), almond-tree", *lawza* "almond"; *lawz* (Eth.) "almond".
lūz "almond-tree"	•LL: **EB** GIŠ.ŠIM GAM.GAM = *lu-zu-um*, *lu-zú* → Zurro AuOr 1 266; Conti QuSe 17 124. •ONOM: **EG** Cf. unc. TN *nuḏ-na* (|luzina| pl. with nunation ?) → Hoch SWET 199 no. 268.

|l-y-l(-y)|	Primary noun, Sem.: *lyl(h)* (*layil*, *laylāh*, Hb.) "night"; *ll* (Ph.) id.; *llh* (Moab.) id.; *lyly(ʔ/h)* (Aram., Syr., Nab.) id.; *līlum* (Akk.) "night", *līliātum* (Akk.) "evening"; *layl*, *layla* (Arab.) "nighttime, night, evening"; *lly* (OSArab.) id.; *laylət*, *leylat*, *līlət* (MSArab.) id.; *lelit* (Eth.) id.; denom. *lyn* (Hb.) "to spend the night, stay overnight".[66]
|l-y-n| "to sleep, stay the night"	•CTX: **UGA** G prefc. *yln* → DUL 496.

[63] According to Tropper there is a |l-w-y|(?) C "umwinden, umhüllen" (*ảšlw*, UG 590, 671, KWU 66, unc.) but see below |s^{1}-l-w| "to rest".

[64] For the rdg *ba*$_4$ (GÁ) see Rubio PIHANS 106 113; Catagnoti QuSe 29 19.

[65] Cf. diff. Krebernik ZA 73 38: |raʕum(?)| "Freund"; Catagnoti / Fronzaroli ARET 16 247.

[66] For Ph. see Tropper ALASP 6 39ff. (Zincirli rdg *ytlk*(!)*n*).

lēl "night"	•CTX: **EA** GI_6-*ša* : *l*[*e-l*]*a*, *le-l*[*a*] → CAD L 184; Rainey EAT 79; Sivan GAGl 131, 241; Izre'el Orient 38 89.[67] •ONOM: **EUPH** *le-e-lum*, *li-li-a-nu-um*, *li-li-mi-il-ki* → Zadok Fs. Hallo 326.
ll "night, nightfall"	•CTX: **UGA** Sg. *ll*, suff. *llm* → DUL 493: *ll* (I).

|l-y-θ̣|	Sem.: Cf. *lyṣ* (Hb.) "to speak boastfully", *lṣ* (*lēṣ*) "scoffer", *lṣṣym* (G ptc. pl. *loṣ*[e]*ṣîm*) "scoffers"; see also *mlṣ* (Ph., Pun.) "interpreter".
|**l-y-ṣ**| "to speak loudly" (?)	•ONOM: **UGA** Cf. *lṣn* → DUL 500; *mlṣ* → DUL 551.
lθ̣t "scorn" (?)	•CTX: **UGA** Sg. suff. *lẓtm* → DUL 503: *lẓt*.

[67] In EA 195:13 read *li-mì-ma* "peoples" with Moran AmL 273, Rainey EAC, for wrong *le-lá-ma* (Sivan GAGl 131, 241; Rainey CAT I 167: "evening").

m

|m| (1)
|m| (2)
|m-ʔ| (1)
|m-ʔ| (2) Cf. **|m-ʔ-d|**
|m-ʔ-d| Cf. **|m-ʔ| (2)**
|m-ʔ-S|
|m-ʔ-t| (1)
|m-ʔ-t| (2) See **|m-ʔ| (2)**
|m-ʕ|
|m-ʕ-d|
|m-ʕ-y| (1)
|m-ʕ-y| (2)
|m-d-d| (1) Cf. **|y-d-d|**
|m-d(-d/w)| (2)
|m-d-l(-l)|
|m-d-r|
|m-D(-w)|
|m-ð-r| See **|m-S-r|**
|m-g-g|
|m-g-n|
|m-g-r|
|m-ɣ-m-ɣ|
|m-ɣ-y| See **|m-θ̣-ʔ/y|**
|m-h-r| (1) Cf. **|m-x-r|**
|m-h-r| (2)
|m-h-r| (3)
|m-ħ-l| Cf. **|ħ-w-l|**
|m-ħ-w/y|
|m-x-x|
|m-x-r| Cf. **|m-h-r| (1)**
|m-x-ṣ| See **|m-x-ṣ́|**
|m-x-s^{1}| See **|m-x-ṣ́|**
|m-x-ṣ́|
|m-x-w|
|m-k|
|m-k(-k)|
|m-k-r|
|m-k-s|
|m-k-w/y|
|m-ḳ-ḳ|
|m-ḳ-l|
|m-ḳ-s^{1}|
|m-ḳ-ṭ|
|m-l-ʔ|
|m-l-g|
|m-l-ħ|
|m-l-x| (1)
|m-l-x| (2)
|m-l-k|
|m-l-ḳ|
|m-l-l|
|m-l-ṭ| Cf. **|p-l-ṭ|**
|m-m-m| (1)
|m-m-m| (2)
|m-n-ʕ|
|m-n-d|
|m-n-d-n|
|m-n-ħ|
|m-n(-n)| (1)
|m-n(-n)| (2)
|m-n-w/y| (1)
|m-n-w/y| (2)
|m-r-ʔ| (1)
|m-r-ʔ| (2)
|m-r-d|
|m-r-d-D|
|m-r-ħ| See **|r-m-ħ|**
|m-r-x|
|m-r-x-S|
|m-r-ḳ| (1)
|m-r-ḳ| (2)
|m-r-m-x(-x)|
|m-r(-r)| (1)
|m-r(-r)| (2)
|m-r(-r)| (3)
|m-r-r| (4)
|m-r-S|
|m-r-s^{1}|
|m-r-ṣ́|
|m-r-ṭ|
|m-r-y|
|m-r-y-n|

|m-S-G| See |m-s¹-k| (1)
|m-S-H|
|m-s-k|
|m-S-r| (1)
|m-s-r| (2)
|m-S-S/w/y| (1)
|m-S(-S)| (2)
|m-S-S-w|
|m-S-ṭ|
|m-S-w|
|m-ṣ-d|
|m-ṣ-x| See |m-x-ṣ̂|
|m-ṣ-r| See |m-S-r|
|m-ṣ-ṣ|
|m-s¹-ħ|
|m-s¹-x| (1)
m-s¹-x| (2)
|m-s¹-k| (1)
|m-s¹-k| (2)
|m-s¹-l| (1)
|m-s¹-l| (2)
|m-s¹-r|
|m-s¹-y|
|m-s²-w/y|
|m-t|
|m-t-ʕ|
|m-t-ħ|
|m-t-ḳ|
|m-t-n| (1)
|m-t-n| (2)
|m-t-r|
|m-ṭ–r|
|m-ṭ-y|
|m-θ|
|m-θ-l|
|m-θ-y|
|m-θ̣-ʔ/y|
|m-w-g|
|m-w-ḳ|
|m-w-n| (1)
|m-w/y-n| (2)
|m-w-s¹|
|m-w-t|
|m-y-ʕ|
|m-y-n| See |m-w/y-n| (2)
|m-z-ʕ|
|m-z-g|
|m-z-l|
|m-z-r|
|m-z-y/z|

|m| (1) Sem.: Optional prosodic reinforcer of single words and / or sentence connective bound morph without own lexical value. Cf. *=m*, *=mw* (=[*V*]*m*, *=mô*, Hb.; optional, prosodic reinforcement of all sort of morphemes; mainly a mere stylistic device); *=m* (Aram.; optional prosodic reinforcement with prepositions and conjunctions and, seldom, adverbs); *=ma* (Akk.; marker of nominal sentences, prosodic reinforcement, sentence connective), *mi* (in citation of direct speech); *=mma* (Arab.), *=mā* (*mā az-zāʔida*, with prepositions:); *=m*, *=mw(y)* (OSArab.; optional morph, no lexical mng); *=mma* (Eth.; emphasis of all sort of morphemes).[68]

[68] For a lexical and grammatical survey see Del Olmo Lete AuOr 26 30ff. ("Language distribution").

=ma optional prosodic reinforcer

●CTX: **EB** *=ma* → Catagnoti QuSe 29 106f., 207.
Q *=ma* → Richter / Lange Idadda 77: cf. *ṭá-ta-ma.*
EM *=ma* → Seminara MEE / MVS 6 521f.
EA *=ma*; passim with verbs, nouns, pronouns, rare with adverbs → Moran JCS 4 172; Izre'el AmAkk 326ff.; Rainey CAT 3 227ff.
UGS *=ma* → Huehnergard AkkUg 203ff., 281; Izre'el AmAkk 326ff.[69]
●LL: **MŠ** Cf. *al-ma* = *áš-šu* → Hrůša MŠ 368 (III 126).
●ONOM: **EB** Passim; cf. among many others: *ʔa*$_5$*-za-ma*, *a-dam-ma*, *a-na-ma-dar*, *bu-ma-ì*, *da-da-ma-lum*, *i-zi ma*, *i-ti-ma-il*, *mu-ti-ma*, *sar-ì-lum-ma*, *sar-ma-ì*, *si-na-ma-gú-ma* → Fronzaroli ARES 1 13; Krebernik PET 95; Pagan ARES 3 83, 257, 272, 276f., 282, 293, 297, 326f., 353, 362, 364.
EUPH Passim; cf. among many others: *a-ḫu-um-ma*-DINGIR, *a-ḫu-um-ma-da-ri*, *a-na-ku-i-la-ma*, *a-na-ku*-DINGIR-*lam-ma*, *am-ta-i-la-ma*, *da-du-ma*(-^{d}*da-gan*), *da-ga-am-ma-ìl*, *i-da-lim-ma*, *iš-ḫi-lu-ma*, *ka-a-li-i-lu-ma*, *bi-ni-ma-ḫu-um*, *bi-in-ma-a-ḫi-im*, *bi-nu-ma-*^{d}*da-gan*, *bu-nu-ma*-DINGIR, *bi-nu-ti-ma-i-la*, DINGIR-*ma-a-bi*, *ḫa-ab-du-ma-*^{d}*da-gan*, *ḫa-ab-di*-DINGIR-*ma*, *mi-il-ku-ma-il*, *mu-ut-ḫa-li-ma*, *mu-tum*-DINGIR, *mu-tu-ma*-DINGIR, *mu-tum-ma-el*, *mu-ti-qa-mu-ma*-DINGIR, *pu-ma-el*, *qa-mu-ma-a-ḫi*, *qa-mu-ma-a-ḫu-um*, *ra-ma-ma-el*, *sa-mi-ma-ia-si-im*, *šu-uḫ-ma-ba-il*, *ta-nu-uḫ-ma-il*, *zi-im-ri-i-lu-ma*, *zu-sa-mi-ma*, *zu-ú-ma-a-bi* → Huffmon APNMT 118f., 228; Gelb Lingua 163f., CAAA 24, 148ff.; Zadok Fs. Hallo 326; Streck Onomastikon 1 141 § 1.123a, 165 § 2.29, 170 § 2.28, 261 § 3.7 fn. 1, 276f. § 3.27f., 279 § 3.34, 280 § 3.40, 304 § 3.70 fn. 1.
A7 *ab-bi-lim-ma*, *am-mi-ta-ku-um-ma*, *a-na-i-lim-ma*, *i-ri-iš-ma-*(*a*-)*bi*, *ir-šu-ma-bi* → Wiseman AT 125, 127, 138f.; Gelb CAAA 24, 148ff.
Q *na-ap-lim-ma* → Gelb CAAA 24, 150.
A4 *a-bi-ma*, *bi-ni-ma*(-DINGIR), *mil-kum-ma*-DINGIR, *mi-il-ku-ma* → Wiseman AT 126, 131, 142; Gelb CAAA 24, 148ff.; Streck Onomastikon 1 276f. § 3.27.[70]
EM Cf. *ib-bi-ma*, DINGIR-*lum-ma-a-ḫu*, *a-ḫu-ma*, *i-la-am-ma*, DINGIR-*lum-ma*, ^{d}IM-*ma* → Pruzsinszky PTEm 83 [431], 116 [107], 118 [190], 124 [481], 143, 196 [461].[71]
EA *bá-a-lu-ú-ma* → Sivan GAGl 208; Hess APN 49f.
UGS Passim, cf. among others: *am-mu-ma-ya*, ^{d}IM-*ma-ṣí-ri*, DINGIR-*ma-ra-kub* → Gröndahl PTU 45, 53, 56, 97, 115, 109, 179, 183, 326, 330.[72]

=me, **=mi** optional prosodic reinforcer

●CTX: **EA** Passim *=mi*, *=me* (rdg *mì*?), with nouns, pronouns, verbs, adverbs, prepositions, interrogatives, etc. → Moran JCS 4 172; Izre'el AmAkk 330ff.; Rainey CAT 3 234ff.
UGS *=me*, *=mi* → Huehnergard AkkUg 209f.; vSoldt SAU 470; Izre'el AmAkk 330ff.[73]

---

[69] For UGS *šanâm*(*ma*) "secondly" in correlation with *ištēn*(*šu*) "firstly") see Huehnergard AkkUg 200; vSoldt SAU 411f. It is probl. a frozen form in analogy to others like *kīam*, *kannam*(*ma*), *ayya*/*ikâm*(*ma*), *kannam*(*ma*), *urra*(*m*) *šēra*(*m*), etc. (Huehnergard AkkUg 293ff.). The orig. accusative suffix *=am* / *=a*(*m*/*n*) with adverbial function is widely attested in Semitic: Ebla (see Catagnoti QuSe 29 91), Arab., Eth., Hb.

[70] PNN ending with the suffix *=mu* (e.g. *aš-ta-ar-mu*, Wiseman AT 130) are probl. hypocoristic.

[71] Note that the suffix *=ma* could be an abbreviation of *ma*(*lik*); cf. DINGIR-*lu*$_4$*-ma-lik* (Pruzsinszky PTEm 124 [480]), DINGIR-*ma-li-ki* (ibid. 124 [476]); ^{d}*da-gan-ma* / ^{d}*da-gan-ma-lik* (ibid. 121 fn. 521 [277f.], 124 fn. 561 [278f.]).

[72] The affixes *=ma*/*mi*/*mu=* form hypocoristic PNN in combination with *=*(*a*/*u*)*nu* (e.g. *ia-ri-ḫi-ma-nu*, *a-bi-ma-nu*/*na*/*ni*; Gröndahl PTU 53, 87, 145).

[73] UGS *mā* as marker of the spoken word is an Assyrianism; vSoldt SAU 470 fn. 264.

•ONOM: **EB** Cf. *bù-du-mi, ḫu-zi-mi, sar-mi-lu* → Pagan ARES 3 83, 257, 293, 320, 363.
U3 *pu-me-il* → Buccellati Amorites 177, 200.
EUPH Passim; cf. among many others: *a-bi-mi-ki*-DINGIR, *ba-la-mi-na-am-ḫu*, ba-ni-me-el, *bu-nu-um-e-lu-um, ia-aq-rum*-DINGIR, *mu-tum-(e-)el, mu-ti-me-el, mu-tu-me-el, ra-bi-mi-il/lum, su-mu-me-el, sa-am-mi-a-ta-ar, si-im-me-a-tar, š/sa-ma-me-el* → Huffmon APNMT 118f., 228; Gelb CAAA 25, 155f.
Streck Onomastikon 1 160 § 2.20, 165 § 2.29, 168 § 2.34, 171 § 2.39, 261 § 3.7 fn. 1, 275 § 3.24, 304 § 3.70 fn. 1
EM Cf. *a-ḫa-(am-)mi* → Pruzsinszky PTEm 143 [78].
EA Cf. *ba-lum-me-e* → Hess APN 52.
UGS Cf. DUMU-*aš-tar-mi* → Gröndahl PTU 34, 53, 113.[74]

=m optional prosodic reinforcer
•CTX: **UGA** *=m* → Tropper UG 825ff., DUL 504ff.: *-m* (I), *-m* (II).
•ONOM: **UGA** *=m* → Gröndahl PTU 25, 53.[75]

|m| (2)

Sem.: |mV=| in two apophonic variants |ma/i=| for animate and inanimate subjects, often expanded with the deictic morphs. The resulting morphemes form the bases of interrogative and indefinite pronouns. Animate set: see (Hb.) *my* (*mî*) "who?"; *mn* (*man*, Aram., Syr.) "who?; whoever"; *mannu(m)* (Akk) "who?", *mamma, mamman* "someone, anyone", *mannummê, mannumma* "who(so)ever"; *man* (Arab.) "who?; whoever"; *mn* (OSArab.) "who?; whoever"; *mōn* (MSArab.) "who"; *mannu* (Eth.) "who?". Inanimate set: *mh* (*māh*, Hb.) "what?", *mdwʕ* (*maddûᵃʕ*) "why?"; *mʔ, mh* (*mā*, Aram., Syr) "what?", *md(ʕ)m, mydy* "something"; *mā, mah, mahmā* (Arab.) "what?"; *mīnum* (Akk.) "what?", *mimma* "something, anything", *mīnummê* "whatever, all, each (of)", *minde/a* "perhaps"; *mi, mənt* (Eth.) "what?".

mah "what, how?"
•LL: **MŠ** *al-ma = áš-šu* |ʔal=mā| → Hrůša MŠ 368 (III 126), 534, 544: "because".[76]
•ONOM: **EB** Cf. *ma-ʔà, ma-ʔà-ma-lik*; unc. *má-da-mu* (= *ma-a-da-mu* ?),[77] *má-du-du* → Krebernik PET 96; Pagan ARES 3 251, 347.[78]
EUPH *ma-a-la-na-di-ta-na, ma-a-ra-su-um* → Gelb Lingua 148, CAAA 24, 148.

m(h) "what?; anything"
•CTX: **UGA** *m, mh* → Tropper UG 239f.; DUL 528.

lm "why?"[79]
•CTX: **UGA** → Tropper UG 754; DUL 494.

mdʕ (A) "why?"[80]
•CTX: **UGA** → Tropper UG 754; DUL 519.

mhk(m) "anything, whatever it may be; nothing"
•CTX: **UGA** *mhk, mhkm* → Tropper UG 243; DUL 529.

---

[74] Many PNN ending with the suffix *=mi* are hipocoristic in the genitive (e.g. *ia-qar-mi, ia-tar-mu/mi*; Gröndahl PTU 53, 145, 148, 337f.).
[75] Passim hypocoristic suffix in one-word PNN; Gröndahl PTU 53.
[76] See Hb. *ʕl mh* (*ʕal meh*) "on what account?"; JAram., Syr. *ʕl mʔ, ʕl mnʔ, ʔmʔy* "why?".
[77] Krebernik PET 249.
[78] Cf. ibid. 138 under *mʔʔ* (?) "to praise / adore" (hence |maʔ=| "sovereign").
[79] Elem. *l* (A)=*m*(*h*); see under *l* (1).
[80] Elems *m*(*h*)=|w-d-ʕ|; cf. Hb. *mdwʕ*.

mk (B) "behold!" (?)[81] •CTX: **UGA** → DUL 536: *mk* (II).

man(n) (A) "who?" •CTX: **EB** *ma-nu*, (accus.) *ma-na* → Catagnoti / Fronzaroli ARET 16 121, 252; Catagnoti QuSe 29 88f., 209.
EA *ma-an-nu*; (gen.) *ma-ni*, *ma-an-ni* → AHw 603: *mannu(m)*; CAD M/1 214f.: *mannu*; Rainey EAT 81: *mannu*; Rainey CAT 1 103f.
•ONOM: **EB** |ma(n)| passim; cf. among others: *ma-ʔà-mu*, *ma-ʔà-ù*, *ma-a-ḫu*, *ma-aš-da-su*, *ma-ì-lum*, *ma-ì-a*, *ma-ba-ni*, *ma-ba-*ru_{12}, *ma-*bu_{14}*-u*/*úr*; |manna|: cf. *ma-na*, *ma-na-ʔà-ù*, *ma-na-a-a-mu*, *ma-na-ku-tu*; |mannu|: *ma-nu-gi-MUL*; |mannum|: *ma-nu-um*, *ma*/*má-núm* → Krebernik PET 33, 96; Pagan ARES 3 252, 347ff.
U3 Cf. *ma-na-nu-um* → Buccellati Amorites 168; Gelb CAAA 24, 153.
EUPH *ma-na-ta-an*, *ma-an-na*/*ni-ia*, *ma-na-ba-la*, *ma-an-ba-al-ti*-DINGIR, *ma-na-bi-iḫ-di-im*, *ma-(an-)na-ba-al-ti*-DINGIR, *ma-na-ba-al*/*aš-te-el*, *ma-na-ta-ri*; *ma-nu-sa-ma*, *ka-ak-ka-ma-an-nu* → Huffmon APNMT 231f.; Gelb Lingua 153, CAAA 7, 12, 24, 153.

man(n) (B) "what?" •CTX: **EA** (accus.) *ma-an-nu*; *ma-an-na*; (genit.) UGU *ma-an-ni*, *ma-ni* (adverbial), UGU *ša* [*m*]*a-an-ni* → AHw 603: *māni*; CAD M/1 212f.: *manni*; Rainey EAT 81, CAT 1 111f.

man(n) (C) "how many?" •CTX: **EA** *ma-ni* (UD.KÁM.MEŠ(-*ti*)) → AHw 603: *māni*; CAD 211: *mani*; Rainey CAT 1 112f.

man(n) (D) "someone, anyone" (?) •CTX: **EA** Unc. rdg [*m*]*a-am-ma* → Moran AmL 210 fn. 5 "anything"; Rainey CAT 1 114; EAC 667: rdg [*k*]*i*(!)*-am-ma* "thus" (?).

mn (A) "what?" •CTX: **UGA** *mn*, *mnm* → Tropper UG 240f.; DUL 553: *mn* (I), 1.

mn (B) "who(so)ever" (?) •CTX: **UGA** → Tropper UG 239; DUL 533: *mn* (I), 2.

mndʕ "perhaps"[82] •CTX: **UGA** → DUL 554f.

mnk (A) "whoever, anyone"[83] •CTX: **UGA** *mnk*, *mnkm* → DUL 556.

mnk (B) "whatever, anything"[84] •CTX: **UGA** *mnk* → DUL 556.

mnm (A) "any(body), whoever" •CTX: **UGA** → Tropper UG 242f.; DUL 556f.: *mnm*, b.

mnm (B) "any(thing), whatever" •CTX: **UGA** → Tropper UG 243; DUL 556f.: *mnm*, a.

manman "anyone, someone" •ONOM: **EB** Cf. unc. *ma-an-ma-an-ne-iš*, *ma-na-ma-ne-su* → Krebernik PET 31, 245f.; Pagan ARES 3 251f., 347f.

mnmn "anyone, someone" •CTX: **UGA** → Tropper UG 242; DUL 557.

---

[81] Probl. *m(h)*=*k* (A).
[82] Probl. *mn* (A)=|w-d-ʕ|.
[83] Probl. *mn* (A)=*k* (A).
[84] Probl. *mn* (B)=*k* (A).

mannumma "whoever"
•CTX: **EB** *ma-nu-ma*, (accus.) *ma-na-ma* → Fronzaroli StEbl 5 100f., ARET 13 282; Catagnoti QuSe 29 89f., 209.

mati "when?"[85]
•CTX: **EA** *ma-ti-mi*, *a-di ma-ti* → Rainey CAT 3 115.
•ONOM: **EB** Unc. cf. *ì-ma-ti*, *ì-má-ti*, *sa-da-ma-ti* → Pagan ARES 3 257, 329, 360.

min (A) "who?"
•CTX: **EA** *mi-nu* → Rainey CAT 1 105f.[86]

min (B) "what?, why?"
•CTX: **EB** (accus.) *mi-na*, (dat.) *me*/*mi-ne-iš*, (du. obl.) *me*/*mi-na-a* → Fronzaroli StEbl 5 99, ARET 13 283; Catagnoti / Fronzaroli ARET 16 28, 254; Catagnoti QuSe 29 89, 211f.
EA (accus.) *mi-na*, *mi-na-am*, *mi-na-am-mi*; (genit.) *a-na mi-ni* / *mi*-NIM(*ni*$_7$?); (adverb.) *mi-nu-um*, *mi-nu-mi* → AHw 655f.: *mīnu*(*m*) I; CAD M/2 89ff: *mīnu*; Rainey CAT 1 109ff.
•ONOM: **EB** |mi(n)|: *mi*-DINGIR, *mi-da-mu*, *mi-da-šè*, *mi*-^{d}*ku-ra*, *mi*-^{d}*da-gan*; |min|: *mi-na-núm*; |mina|: *mi-na-ì*, *mi-na-du*, *mi-na-il*, *mìn-na-il*; |minu|: *me*/*mi-nu*-^{d}*ku-ra*; |minum|: *mi-núm* → Pagan ARES 3 252f., 350f.[87]

min (C) "whatever, everything, anything"
•CTX: **EA** *mi-mu*, *mi-im-mu*; (accus.) *mi*/*mì-ma*, *mim-ma*, *mi-im-ma*, *mi-am-ma*; (genit. / accus.) *mi-im-mi*/*mì* → Rainey CAT 1 114ff.

minmiy(at) "everything, assets"
•CTX: **EA** *mi-mu*, *mi-im-mu*, suff: *mi-mu-šu*; (genit.) *mi-im-mi*(MEŠ/ḪÁ)), *mi*/*mì-im-me*, *mi*/*mì-im-mì*, *mi-im-mé*/*mi-ia*; (accus.) *mi-im-ma*(MEŠ), *mi-am-ma*, suff. *mi-im-ma-šu*, *mi-am-mi-šu*; cstr. *mi-im*, *mim-me* → Rainey CAT 1 119ff.
•ONOM: **EB** Cf. *mi-mi-du* |mimmīt=|, *mi-mi-a-du* |mimmiyat=| → Pagan ARES 3 253, 351.[88]

mīnumma "whatever, everything, anything"
•CTX: **EB** *me*/*mi-nu-ma*, (genit.) *me*/*mi-ne-ma*, (accus.) *me-na-ma* → Fronzaroli ARET 13 284; Catagnoti / Fronzaroli ARET 16 254f.; Catagnoti QuSe 29 34f., 89f., 212.
•LL: **EB** NÌ.NAM = *me-na-ma-ma* → Conti QuSe 17 76; Catagnoti QuSe 29 90, 212.

miy "who?"
•CTX: **EA** (|miya| absolitive case?) *mi-ia*, *mi-ia-mi*/*mì*, *mi-ia-ti* → AHw 651: *mīja*; CAD M/2 62f.: *mija*; Rainey EAT 82; Sivan GAGl 248; Rainey CAT 1 50, 69, 106ff.; Izre'el Orient 38 90.
•ONOM: **EB** *mi-ga*, *me*/*mi-ga-ì*, *mi-ga-lum*, *mi-ga*-DINGIR, *mi-ga-il*,[89] *mi-gi-il* → Gelb TI 21; Krebernik PET 33, 97; Pagan ARES 3 253, 350f.
EUPH MIM(*mí*)-*ma-ḫir-sù*; *me*/*mi-ia-mu-ta*, *mi-ia-na-su* → Gelb TI 11; Zadok Fs. Hallo 317.
EA Unc. cf. MI-*ya* → Moran AmL 383; Hess APN 114: either WS or Hurrian for *Ziliya*.

my (A) "who?"
•CTX: **UGA** → DUL 598f.: *my* (I), 1.
•ONOM: **UGA** *mảd* → DUL 506; *mảdt* → DUL 507: *mảdt* (II); *mảḫbt* → DUL 507. Cf. *myn* → DUL 599.

my (B) "what?"[90]
•CTX: **UGA** → DUL 598f.: *my* (I), 2.

---

[85] Probl. |ma(h)=ti / tay (encl.)|. For a comparative approach see Tropper UG 836. Cf. Hb. *mty* (*mātay*), *ʔmty*, *ʔymty*, *ʔymt* (Aram., JAram., Syr.) "when, whenever, when?"; Arab. *matā* (*mty*) "where?; *māʔəze* "when" CDG 324; Akk. *mati* "when?"; cf. Ph. *mtm* "always" (?).

[86] According to AHw and CAD: *min* (B) "what?, why?" below.

[87] Cf. unc. *mi*-KUM-^{d}*ku-ra* (var. *ma*-KUM-^{d}*ku-ra*); Krebernik PET 246, 251; Pagan ARES 3 142 (*mwk*? "to be low / depressed / poor", with listing and discussion of other proposals).

[88] The altern. connection with Akk. *memītu* (LL) "term for a girl" (Pagan ARES 3 225, 351) seems unlikely.

[89] For *mi-gi*-NE (Pagan ARES 3 351: *li*$_9$) see vSoden HSAO 2 332; Krebernik AfO 32 57 fn. 11. Dombrowski ZDMG 138 217 reads *ṣil*=.

[90] Probl. *m*(*h*)=(encl.)*y*; see Tropper UG 239.

|m-ʔ| (1)

Primary noun, Sem.: *mym* (*mayim*, pl. Hb.) "water, liquid, juice"; *mym* (pl. Ph.) id.; *myyn*, *myʔ* (pl. Aram., Syr.) id.; *myʔ* (pl. Nab.) id.; *mn* (pl. Palm.) id.; *mû*, *māʔū*, *māmū*, *māwū* (Akk.) id.; *māʔ* (Arab.) id.; *mw* (OSArab.) id.; *ḥe-mōh*, *ḥe-myōh* (MSArab.) id.; *māy* (Eth.) id.
Non-Sem.: *mw* (Eg.) "water"; **mV=* (Berber) id.; **maʔ=* (West Chadic) id.; **maʔ=* / **maw=* (Central Chadic) "river, water, dew".[91]

maʔw, māw, māy "water, liquid, juice"

•CTX: **EB** Pl. *mu-ù* |mūʔū| < |māʔw=ū| → Fronzaroli ARET 13 62, 285, 315.
EA Pl. A.MEŠ *mé-e-ma*, A.MEŠ : *mé-ma*, A : *mé-ma* |mēm=| < |māy=im=| → CAD M/II 17; Sivan GAGl 14 n. 3, 246; Rainey CAT 1 36, 145; Izre'el Orient 38 76f.
•LL: **EB** Pl. A.ŠU.LUḪ = *ma-wu i-da-a*, *ma-*u_9 *i-da*; A.UD = *ma-wu ʔà-mu-tum*; A.BAL = *ma-wu mu-da-bar-si-ù-tum*;[92] A.GA.DU = *ma-wu ʔà*$_5$*-dar-tim*;[93] A.TUKU = *ʔà*$_5$*-a-ù ma-a*, *a-a-ù mi*[94] → Krebernik ZA 73, 1983, 23 (616), 24 (619), 25 (637, 640a); Fronzaroli QuSe 13 145; Fales QuSe 13 180f.; Conti QuSe 17 170f., 172; Bonechi Proceedings 44 RAI 2 100f.; Catagnoti QuSe 29 24, 62, 108, 120, 211.
Aphek [...A.]MEŠ = *ma-wu* = *mu-mi* (pl.|mū=mi| < |māy=ū=(encl.)mi|) → Sivan GAGl 14 n. 4; 246; Horowitz / Oshima CunCan 32 (:Aphek 3: Tel Aphek 8151:1).
•ONOM: **EB** *ma-*u_9*-um* → Pagan ARES 3 223, 349.

my (C) "water, liquid, juice"

•CTX: **UGA** Sg genit. *my* (|māyi| < |māʔi|), (accus.) *mh* (|māha| < |māʔa|); pl. obl. *mym* (|māy=im=|), *mm* (|mēm=|), suff. *mmh* → Tropper KWU 83, UG 163f.; DUL 529: *mh/y*.

maʔit "irrigated land, fertile land"

•CTX: **EM** ZAG-*šu ma-i-tu*$_4$: *ma-ak-ri-tu*$_4$ → Dietrich / Loretz UF 33 194ff.; Tsukimoto ASJ 12 200; Watson NABU 2002/9.

mỉyt "irrigated land, fertile land"

•CTX: **UGA** Sg. *mỉyt*, (miswriting: *mhyt*) → Dietrich / Loretz UF 33 194ff.; DUL 513: *mỉyt*, cf. 531: *mhyt*.

|m-ʔ| (2)
Cf. **|m-ʔ-d|**

Primary noun, Sem.: *mʔh* (*mēʔāh*, Hb.) "(one) hundred"; *mʔh* (Aram., Syr., Palm.) id.; *mʔt* (Ph. Pun.) id.; *meʔatu*(m), *mât*, *mē*, *mētu*(*m*) (Akk.) id.; *miʔa* (Arab.) id.; *mʔt* (OSArab.); *myīt* / *mī* (MSArab.) id.; *məʔət* (Eth.) id.

miʔat "hundred"

•CTX: **EB** Passim. *mi-ad* → Catagnoti QuSe 29 117, 211.[95]

miʔt "hundred"

•CTX: **UGS** Du. cstr. |miʔtē| 2 *me-te* KÙ.BABBAR → Sivan GAGl 247; Huehnergard UVST 144.

mỉt "hundred"

•CTX: **UGA** Sg. *mỉt*; pl. *mảt*, suff. *mảtm*; du. *mỉtm* → DUL 509ff.

|m-ʔ-d|
Cf. **|m-ʔ| (2)**

Sem.: *mʔd* (*m*^{e}*ʔod*, Hb.) "might; in abundance, very much"; *mâdu*(*m*), *maʔādu*, *miādu*(*m*) (Akk.) "to be or become much, numerous", *mādu*(*m*) "many, numerous, much", *mādūtu* "numerousness"; *ʔimtaʔada* (Arab.) "to acquire".

---

[91] Orel / Stolbova HSED 368f. no. 1699: *maʔ= "water".

[92] Fales QuSe 13 181: "waters which break through" < |p-r-s| "to break through"; but see Krebernik ZA 73 25 (640a): Pl. ptc. Nt(n?) B-L-Ś-H; cf. under 640b: A.BAL(!) (KUL) = *ma-ba-lum*, and Hb. *mbwl* "flood" (< |y-b-l|). See also: Bonechi Bonechi Proceedings 44 RAI 2 100: A.BAL = *mawü multaparšiḫūtum* "cascade".

[93] Bonechi Proceedings 44 RAI 2 101: *māwū hadartim*, *hadrum*, **hdr* "bouillonner".

[94] Bonechi Proceedings 44 RAI 2 101: *ḥawāyu māwī*, *ḥawāyu mī* "réservoir d'eau", **ḥwy*.

[95] Cf. unc. *ma-i*-AD (Edzard ARET 2 132; Catagnoti QuSe 29 211: *ma-i-at* "100.000": |mayyāt|, a comparative form ("Steigerungsform") of |miʔat / miʔāt| "100"; see *maʔid* under |m-ʔ-d|.

|m-ʔ-d| "to be numerous, plentiful"	•CTX: **EB** G prefc. *i-ma-ì-du* → Catagnoti QuSe 29 150, 207. **UGA** G suffc. *mảd*; D prefc. *ảmid*, *ymỉd* → DUL 506. •ONOM: **EUPH** Most items in Gelb CAAA 318 (MʔD) are dubious; see also here under |m-ʕ-d|.[96]
maʔd "(in) abundance"	•CTX: **EB** *ma-da a ma-da-ma* "more and more", *ma-ti-iš* "much" → Catagnoti / Fronzaroli ARET 16 30, 251; Catagnoti QuSe 29 117, 207. •LL: **UGS** [MAḪ = *mādu* / *maʔdu* =]-*ši* = *ma-a-du-ma* → Sivan GAGl 241; Huehnergard UVST 87, 144; vSoldt SAU 304 (75). •ONOM: **EB** Cf. unc. *da-zi-ma-du*, *da-zi-ma-ad-um*, *da-zi-ma-ad*, *ma-da-da-mu*, *má-da-du-ra* → Krebernik PET 96; Pagan ARES 3 138, 299, 347, 349. **EUPH** Cf. unc. *ì-lí-ma-di-a-aḫ*, *ì-lí-ma-da-ḫi/ḫa*, *ì-lí-mi-di-aḫ* → Gelb CAAA 318; Knudsen JCS 34 15.
maʔid "abundant, great; 100.000"	•CTX: **EB** Cf. unc. *ma-i*-AD → Edzard ARET 2 132: *ma-i-at* "100.000";[97] Archi / Biga ARET 3 367; cf. *ma-i*-[AD], Waetzoldt MEE/MVS 12 no. 42 v? 1, 1. Pseudo-Sumerogram; exact rdg and interpretation dubious. •LL: **EB** Cf. unc. *ma-i*-AD, *ma-i-ḫu*-AD, *ma-<i?>ḫu*-AD → Krebernik ZA 73 44: Pseudo-Sumerograms; rdg dubious. See also Bonechi Studia Eblaitica 7 33ff. •ONOM: **EB** Cf. unc. *gú-ma-ì-du*, ^{d}*ku-ra-ma-i-da* → Pagan ARES 3 138, 314, 344.
mỉ/ủd "abundance"	•CTX: **UGA** Sg. *mỉd*, *mủd*; suff. *mỉdy*; var. *mủid* → DUL 506f.
mảdt "great quantity, many people, a crowd"	•CTX: **UGA** Sg. suff. *mảdtn* → DUL 507: *mảdt* (I).

|m-ʔ-S|	Sem.: Cf. *mʔs* (Hb.) "to refuse, reject"; *mʔs* (JAram.) "to reject, find repulsive"; *mêšu(m)* (Akk.) "to disregard, scorn"; *maʔasa*, *maʔsa* (Arab.) "to get annoyed, get angry, get cross (with)".
|m-ʔ-S| "to forgive" (?)	•ONOM: **EB** Cf. *a-mi-iš-li-im*, *i-mi-iš-li-im* → Krebernik PET 54; Pagan ARES 3 139, 280, 323.

|m-ʔ-t| (1)	Sem. etym. unknown; single isogloss *mātu(m)* (Akk.) "land, country".
māt "land, country"	•CTX: **EB** Du. obl. *ma-da-a* |mātay(n)| → Fronzaroli ARET 13 42, 281; Catagnoti QuSe 29 111, 210.[98] •ONOM: **U3** *ku-na-ma-tum* → Gelb CAAA 25, 151. **EUPH** Cf. *ia-un-ma-tum*, *da-nu-ma-tum*, *ki-ni-iš-ma-tum*, *ši-i-ma-tum*, *ta-ku-un-ma-tum*, *ta-dur-ma-tum*, *ta-tu-ur-ma-tum*, *ta-ri-iš-ma-tum* → Gelb CAAA 25, 151; Streck Onomastikon 1 260 § 3.7, 313 § 4.6, 354 § 5.85. **A7** *be-el-ti-ma-ti*, *i-ri-ma-tu*, *ta-kum-ma-ti* → Wiseman AT 131, 138, 149; Gelb CAAA 25, 151.

\|m-ʔ-t\| (2)
See **\|m-ʔ\| (2)**

[96] For the rdg *ia-am-i-id-*^{d}*ad-mi* (cf. Gelb CAAA 147: MʔID) see Streck Onomastikon 1 359, who prefers *ia-qar*(!) DUMU *da-ad-mi*.

[97] Edzard loc.cit.; Catagnoti QuSe 29 211: \|mayyāt\|, a comparative form (Edzard: "Steigerungsform") of \|miʔat / miʔāt\| "100"; see *miʔat*, under \|m-ʔ\|.

[98] Diff. Archi Fs. Garelli 222 fn. 42: "quand?" (\|matay\|).

|m-ʕ|	Etym. unc.; probl. onomatopoeic shout or cry "please!" indicating a wish, desire, request, as for instance in baby talk. [99]
mʕ "please!"	•CTX: **UGA** → DUL 513f.: *mʕ* (I).[100]

|m-ʕ-d|	Sem.: Cf. *mʕd* (elem. in OSArab. PNN) "hardness, firmness".
maʕd "hardness, firmness"	•ONOM: **U3** Cf. *ma-aḫ-da-nu-um* → Buccellati Amorites 166f. **EUPH** Cf. *ma-di-ia*, *ma-di-ia-ma*, *ma-di-ia-tum*, DINGIR-*ma-di*, *ì-lí-ma-di* → Streck Onomastikon 1 272f. § 3.19 fn. 1.

|m-ʕ-y| (1)	Primary noun, Sem.: Cf. *mʕh* (*māʕāh*, Hb.) "grain"; *maʕw* "ripening date". See further: *mʕh* (Nab., Syr.), *mʕyn* (Palm. pl.) "a weight, a certain coin".
mʕt "kernel" (?)	•CTX: **UGA** → Pardee AuOr 20 175f.; Bordreuil-Pardee RSOu 18 112; Tropper KWU 68.

|m-ʕ-y| (2)	Primary noun, Sem.: Cf. *mʕh* (*mēʕeh*, Hb.) "entrails, intestines"; *mʕyn*, *mʕyʔ* (pl. Aram., Syr.) "intestines, viscera, innards; belly, loins"; *maʕy*, *miʕān*, *miʕāʔ* (Arab.) "intestine".[101]
mmʕ "gore, innards"	•CTX: **UGA** *mmʕm* (Pl. tantum) → DUL 552f.
mʕmʕ "intestinal disease" (?)	•CTX: **UGA** → De Moor / Spronk UF 16 244, 249: name of a demon?[102]

|m-d-d| (1) Cf. **|y-d-d|**	Sem.: *mdd* (Hb.) "to measure", *mdh* (*middāh*) "length, measurement", *mdd* (Pun.) "to measure", mdt (Ph., Pun.) "measure"; (Akk.) madādu(m) "to measure (out)", *mādidu* "measuring official", *middatu*(*m*) "measure"; *madda* (Arab.) "to extend, stretch, lay out", *madd* "extension", *mudd* "measure", *madad* "support, reinforcement"; *mdd* (OSArab.) "period of time"; *madada* (Eth.) "spread, level".
|m-d-d| "to measure, stretch"	•ONOM: **A4** Cf. unc. *ma-di-ia* → Wiseman PN AT 141; Sivan GAGl 246. **UGA** Cf. unc. *ỉlmd* → DUL 55; *ymd* → DUL 952.
md (C) "duration; during"	•CTX: **UGA** → DUL 519: *md* (III).
madid "a vessel"	•CTX: **EG** *ma$_2$-di-di*, *m-du-du*, *ma-di-d(i)* → Hoch SWET 177 no. 238.[103]
maddat "measurement"	•CTX: **UGS** *: ma-ad-da-tù*[104] → Huehnergard UVST 145.

[99] Cf. diff. Tropper UG 813, who suggests a connection with Eth. *mʕʕ* "to be angry, rage, enraged".

[100] DUL 514: *mʕ* (II) should be deleted and considered another instance of the precative particle *mʕ* (I); see among others Renfroe AULS 128.

[101] Cf. Arab. *naʕāma* "brain membrana"; Militarev / Kogan SED 167 no 185: dissim. < **maʕāmat*.

[102] UGA *mʕmʕ*, attested once in bkn and unc. ctx., is most probably an allomorphism of *mmʕ*. The mng "convulsion" (?), DUL 515, is etymologically questionable and seems contextually unnecessary. According to De Moor / Spronk, loc.cit., the disease called *mʕmʕ* is also the name of the demon invoked in the UGS PN *ma-ma-a*-DINGIR (*maʕmaʕ=ʔilu*).

[103] Sivan / Cochavi-Rainey WSVES 82: *má-di-di* "vessel"; also Helck Beziehungen no. 133.

[104] Note the gloss mark.

mddt (B) "dispenser, distributor"	•CTX: **UGA** Pl. *mddt* → DUL 521: *mddt* (II).[105]
|m-d(-d/w)| (2)	Culture word, Sem.: *md* (*mad* Hb.) "gown, robe", by-form *mdw* (*mādû*) "robe";[106] *md(?)* (JAram.) "priest's cloak". See also *mudûm* (túg mu.du₈.um, OAkk.) "a garment".[107]
md (A) "cape, covering"	•CTX: **UGA** Sg. suff. *mdy*, *mdk*, *mdh*; pl. (?) suff. *mdth* → DUL *md* (I): 518.
|m-d-l(-l)|	Culture word, Sem.: Cf. *naddullu*, *nattullu* (MBab.) "part of harness". Non-Sem.: *NAM-TÚL-LUM* (Akkadogram in Hitt.) "part of harness, halter".
|m-d-l| "to bridle" (?)	•CTX: **UGA** G/D prefc. *tmdln*; imp. *mdl* → DUL 521: /m-d-l/.[108]
mdl "a part of harness, halter" (?)	•CTX: **UGA** Sg. *mdl*, suff. *mdlk*, *mdlh* → Good UF 16 81; Watson LSU 50ff.; DUL 521f.: *mdl* (I), *mdl* (II).
nadall, nadull "part of harness, halter" (?)	•CTX: **EB** *na-da-lum* → Conti QuSe 19 31; Sjöberg Fs. Renger 521f. **EUPH** *na-du-[l]u* → Talon ARM 24 107 (192:2). **EA** 2 *na-at-tu[l]-la-a-tum ša* KUŠ → Adler AOAT 201 310 (22 I 21). **KAMID EL-LOZ** KUŠ *a-ši-tu qadu na-tu-la-te* → Wilhelm ZA 63 71, 74 (Kl 72.600:19); Görg ZA 76 308.
|m-d-r|	Primary noun, Sem.: *mdr(?)* (Syr.) "soil, clay, dust", denom. *mdr* (Syr. C) "to rot"; *midru(m)* (Akk.) "a type of land", *midirtu* "garden plot"; *madar* (Arab.) "clods of earth, mud"; *mdr* (OSArab.) "earth, soil"; *mədr* (Eth.) "earth, soil, field".
madar "field"	•CTX: **EM** *ma-da-ri-ia* → Zadok AION 51 117; Pentiuc Vocabulary 117f.
|m-D(-w)|	Sem. etym. unc. (Eg. loanword?): Cf. *mṭh* (*maṭṭeh*, Hb) "stick, staff". Probl. unrelated: *mwṭ* (*môṭ*, Hb.) "pole";. *miṭṭu(m)*, *mī/ēṭu* (Akk.) "a divine weapon". Non-Sem.: Cf. *mdw* (Eg.) "stick".[109]
mad "stick" (?)	•LL: **EB** Cf. GIŠ.RU = *ma-du-um* → Fales WGE 207.[110]
mṭ "rod, staff, riding crop"	•CTX: **UGA** Sg. cstr. *mṭ*, suff. *mṭm* → DUL 594.
|m-ð-r| See **|m-S-r|**	

[105] For UGA *mddt* (A) "beloved, friend" see below under |y-d-d|.
[106] See also *mdwh* (*madweh*).
[107] CAD M/2 168; cf. Durand MARI 6 661, with some reservations.
[108] Probl. denom. of UGA *mdl* below.
[109] Cf. Orel / Stolbova HSED 391 no. 1807: **muṭ*= "stick"; see also Takács EDE 1 246.
[110] See also Fales loc.cit. fn. 22 for EB LL GIŠ.ḪÚBxKASKAL = *mu-du*, *mu-du-um*, *ma-du-um*.

|m-g-g|	Sem.: *mg* (Hb.) “garrison, troops, army” (*rab māg* “commander”); *mgʔ* (Aram.) id. (*rb mgʔ* “commander”); *muggu*, *mungu* (Akk.) “garrison, troops, army” (*rab muggi* “commander”).[111] Non-Sem.: *m(ʕ)gꜣ* (Eg.) “ein (fremder) Soldat”.
|m-g-g| “to fight, battle”	•CTX: **EA** G suffc. *ma-a-ga-mi*, *ma-an-ga-am-mi* (EA 362: 13, 15), *man-ga* (EA106:15) → Kottsieper UF 20 125ff.[112] •ONOM: **EG** Cf. *b-ʕ-:r-w-t-:r-m-g-w*, *m-g-ꜣ-y-ꜣ* → Schneider APÄQ 85 no. 159, 135 no. 288.[113]
|m-g-n|	Culture word with various Semitizations: *mgn* (Hb., Pun., Palm.) “gift”, denom. *mgn* (Hb. D) “to give as a gift”, (Ph. D) “to offer”; *mgn* (Aram., Syr.) “gratis”, denom. *mgn* (JAram. D) “to hand over”; *mag/kannu*, *magānu* (Akk.) “gift”; *maǧǧān* (Arab.) “free (of charge), gratuitous”; *mangana* (Eth.) “gratis”. Non-Sem.: Hurr. **makānn*= “gift, present”.[114]
|m-g-n| “to regale, welcome”	•CTX: **UGA** D prefc. *nmgn*, suff. *nmgnkm*, *tmgnn*; suffc. *mgntm* → DUL 525.
makānn “gift, present”	•CTX: **A4** Cf. *ma*-QA-*na* → Giacumakis AkkAl 86. •ONOM: **A4** *a-ri-ma-gan* → Wiseman AT 129; Sivan GaGl 247. **UGS** DUMU *ma-ga-ni* → Gröndahl PTU 156; Sivan GAGl 247.
makannūt “gift, present”	•CTX: **A4** Cf. *ma*-GA-*nu-ti* → Giacumakis AkkAl 86.
mgn (A) “gift, present”	•CTX: **UGA** Sg. *mgn*, suff. *mgnk* → DUL 525: *mgn* (I). •ONOM: **UGA** *bn mgn* → DUL 526: *mgn* (III).
|m-g-r|	Sem.: Cf. *mgr* (D, Hb.) “to throw down upon”, *mgwr* (*māgôr*) “grain pit”, *mgwrh* (*mᵉgûrāh*) “grain pit, storage room”, *mmgwrh* (*mammᵉgûrāh*) “grain-silo”; *mgr* (Syr.) “to fall”, (Aram. D) “to throw down”.
tamgur, tumgur “granary”	•LL: **EB** ŠE.DUB = *d*[*u*]*-mu-gú-lum*, *dam-gú-lu-um*, *dam-g*[*ú-lum*] → Conti QuSe 17 37, 39, 176.
|m-ɣ-m-ɣ|	Culture word, Sem.: Cf. *memī/ētu* (Akk. LL) “a plant”.
mɣmɣ “a medicinal plant”	•CTX: **UGA** → DUL 526f.: *mġmġ*.
|m-ɣ-y| See |**m-θ̣-ʔ/y**|	

[111] Kottsieper UF 20 125ff.

[112] For an altern. explanation *mangag* “distress, anxiety” (Akk. *magāgu*(*m*) ?) see Gianto StPohl 15 44f. n. 7; Moran AmL 360f. n. 3; Rainey EAC 1234f., 1627. See further, and unlikely: Thureau-Dangin RA 19 92; AHw 15, CAD A/1 141: *agāmi* advb. “today”.

[113] See also *watar* “excellent, outstanding” (|w-t-r|).

[114] Dietrich / Mayer AOAT 382 250. Cf. Diakonoff Orientalia 41 114 fn 90; Laroche GLH 164.

|m-h-r| (1) Cf. **|m-x-r|**	Sem.: *mhr* (Hb. D) "to hasten", *mhyr* (*māhîr*) "skilful, experienced", *mhrh* (*m^{e}hērāh*) "haste"; *mhryt* (Palm.) "freely"; *mhr* (Syr. D) "to instruct"; *mhyr* (Aram., Syr.) "skilled", *mhyrʔt* (Syr.) "promptly, skilfully"; *mahara* (Arab.) "to be skillful", *māhir* "skilful, dexterous", *mahāra* "skilfulness, dexterity"; *tmhrt* (OSArab.) "elite corps"; *mahara* (Eth.) "to teach, instruct, train", *məhur* "trained, instructed".
mahar, **mahir**, **mehir**, **mihr** "warrior; skilled, trained personal"	•CTX: **EG** *ma*$_{(4)}$*-ha–r*, *ma*$_{4}$*-h-ri*, *ma*$_{4}$*-h-rin* → Hoch SWET 147ff. no. 190.[115] •ONOM: **U3** Cf. *ma-aḫ-ra-nu-um* → Huffmon APNMT 229f.; Buccellati Amorites 167; Wilcke WO 5 28; Gelb CAAA 25, 151.[116] **EUPH** Cf. *ia-si-im-ma-har*, *ma-ḫi-ra*, *ma-ḫi-ra-nim*; *me-eḫ-ri-*^{d}IM → Huffmon APNMT 229f.; Gelb CAAA 25, 151, 156; Durand REA 654 (DN). **EA** Cf. IM-*me-ḫe-er*, IM-*me-ḫér*, *ba-lu-mé-*<*ḫe*>*-er*[117] → Sivan GAGl 246; vSoldt BiOr 46 647; Hess APN 50ff., 208. **UGS** Cf. PN ÌR-*me-ri*, ÌR-*mi-ir* (GaGl 246; Rainey IOS 3 46; vSoldt BiOr 46 647.[118] **EG** *ma-ha-r-ya*, *ma-ha-r-ya-*{*t*}, *ma-ha-r-*{*t*}, *ma-ha-r-i̇-*{*t*} → Hoch SWET 140ff. no. 190.
mhr (A) "(trained) soldier, warrior"	•CTX: **UGA** Sg. *mhr*, suff. *mhrk*, *mhrh*; pl. *mhrm* → DUL 529: *mhr* (I). •ONOM: **UGA** *i̇lmhr* → DUL 55; *ʕbdmhr* → DUL 139f.; *mhrʕm* → DUL 531; *mhrn* → DUL 531.
mhr (B) "warrior strength"	•CTX: **UGA** Sg. suff. *mhrh* → DUL 530: *mhr* (II).[119]

|m-h-r| (2)	Primary noun, Sem.: *mhr* (*mōhar*, Hb.) "bride-money"; *mhr*(*?*) (Aram., Syr.) id.; *mahr* (Arab.)id., denom. *mahra*, *ʔamhara* "to provide with a dowry"; *mhrt* (OSArab.) "property, gift, possessions", *mhr* (denom. C) "to fix a date of payment"; *máher*, *mɛ́hər*, *mēhar* (MSArab.) "bride-money".
mhr (C) "dowry, bride-price"	•CTX: **UGA** Sg. suff. *mhry*, *mhrk*, *mhrh* → DUL 530: *mhr* (III).

|m-h-r| (3)	Primary noun, Sem.: *mwhr*(*?*) (Syr.) "horse's foal"; *mūru*(*m*) (Akk.) "young animal, young bull, foal"; *muhr* (Arab.) "foal, cub, first born animal"; *mhrt* (OSArab.) "filly".
muhr "foal, colt"	•ONOM: **EB** *mu-lu*, *mu-rí*, *mu-ra*, *mu-rí-a*, *mu-lu-wa-du*; fem. *mu-lu-du* |muhrt=| → Pagan ARES 3 225, 352.[120] **U3** Cf. unc. *mu-ra-nu-um* → Buccellati Amorites 174f.; Gelb CAAA 158. **EUPH** *mu-ru-*^{d}*da-gan* → Gelb CAAA 158; Durand MARI 8 643 fn. 589, 666; Golinets BuB 9 73.

115 Sivan / Cochavi-Rainey WSVES 81: *ma-ha-r* "warrior"; Helck Beziehungen no. 103.

116 Cf. Pun. PNN *Maarba*, *Maarbal*, *Maharbal*; Benz PNPPI 340f.

117 EA 260:2; read *Balu Mir* by Moran (AmL 381: "The Lord is Mir"; and cf. Hess APN 239. See also IM.UR.SAG; Moran AmL 381: "Baʕlu [Hadda] is a warrior" (?).

118 See Huehnergard AkkUg 410: DINGIR.UR.SAG, NWSem. *mih(ī)r* (UGA *i̇lmhr*) and Ug.-Akk. ÌR.UR.SAG (UGA *ʕbdmhr*). Diff.: Gröndahl PTU 159: MR I mesop. Wettergott Mer. Cf. Pun. PNN *MERBALON*, *MERBALOS*; Benz PNPPI 340f.

119 Tropper KWU 70: mng unc.

120 Note also *mu-rí-iš* \|muhriš\| "like a foal"; altern. \|muhri=s(u)\| "his foal".

muhrat, muhrut "young female animal"	•ONOM: **EUPH** *mu-uḫ-ra-tum* → Gelb CAAA 158.
mr (D) "young of an animal, cub" (?)	•CTX: **UGA** Pl. *mrm* → DUL 562f.: *mr* (VI).
|m-ħ-l| Cf. |ħ-w-l|	Sem.: Cf. *mḥwl* (*māḥôl*), *mḥlh* (*m*^{e}*ḥolāh*) "dance in a ring", *mḥlt* (*māḥ*^{a}*lat*) "a musical term"; *muḥalli* (Arab.) "musician"; *māḥəlet* (Eth.) "song". See further: *mēlulu*(*m*) (Akk.) "to play", *mēlultu*(*m*) "game, play".
maħħāl "dancer"	•LL: **EB** NE.DI = *ma-ʔà-lu-um*, *ma-ʔa*$_{5}$*-lum*, *ma-ʔa*$_{5}$*-lu-um* → Conti QuSe 17 201ff.; Bonechi QDLF 16 87; see also Catagnoti QuSe 16 181f.
|m-ħ-w/y|	Sem.: *mḥh* (Hb.) "to wipe clean, wipe out, efface, annihilate"; *mḥy* (Ph., JAram.) id.;[121] *maḥā* (Arab.) "to efface, erase"; *maḥawa* (Eth.) "to uproot, pluck out".
|**m-ħ-y**| "to clean, wipe, erase"	•CTX: **UGA** G impv. *mḥy*; Gpass. prefc. *ymḥ*; N prefc. *ymḥ*, suffc. *nmḥt* (unc.) → Tropper UG 663f.; DUL 532: /*m-ḥ*(*-w:y*)/.
|m-x-x|	Primary noun, Sem.: *muḫḫu*(*m*) (Akk.) "skull, top of the head"; *muḫḫ* (Arab.) "brain, marrow"; reduced bases: *mḥ* (*mo*^{a}*ḥ*, Hb.) "bone-marrow"; *mwḥ*(?) (JAram., Syr.) "brain, skull, marrow". Denom. *maḫḫaḫa* (Arab.) "to suck out marrow", *ʔamaḫḫa* "to have much marrow, be fat". See further *mḥ* (*mē*^{a}*ḥ*, Hb.) "fatling sheep"; *mḥ* (Pun.) "fat, rich".
muxx "top, skull"	•LL: **EB** SAGxNI = *mu-ḫu* SAG, SAGxNI.SÙ = *mu-ḫu-um* → Krebernik ZA 73 12; Fronzaroli StEb 7 173, QuSe 13 146; Bonechi / Catagnoti Fs. Sommerfeld / Krebernik 179.
mx "marrow, brains"	•CTX: **UGA** → DUL 533: *mḫ*.[122]
|m-x-r| Cf. **|m-h-r| (1)**	Sem.: *mḥyr* (*m*^{e}*ḥîr*, Hb.) "purchase price"; *maḫāru*(*m*) (Akk.) "to face, confront; oppose; receive", *māḫiru*(*m*) "opponent, antagonist, recipient", *maḫīru*(*m*), *makīrum* "exchange rate, market price", *rab maḫīri* "market overseer", *māḫirānu* "the one who received, recipient", *namḫaru* "a vesser, container"; *mxr* (OSArab.) "to face towards, oppose, fight".
|**m-x-r**| "to approach; to receive; to fight, struggle"	•CTX: **EB** G prefc. *i-ḫu-ma* |yimxur=|, [*a*]*-ḫu-lu* |la= yimxur=|; suffc. *ma-ḫi-la* |maxir|, *ma-ḫa-ra* |maxrā| → Fronzaroli StEb 7 170, ARET 11 158, ARET 13 13, 269, 315; Catagnoti / Fronzaroli ARET 16 109, 212; Catagnoti QuSe 29 125, 127, 130, 207f. **EUPH** G inf. cf. *i-na ma-ḫi-rim* → Durand, ARM 26/1, 196 fn. c. **EM** G pass. ptc. *ma-ḫi-ir*, unc. D prefc. *um*-ḪÍR*-ru-ni* → Westenholz Emar Tablets 13: Durand NABU 2013/07. •LL: **EB** GABA.RU = *ma-ḫa-lum*/*lu-um* → Krebernik ZA 73 35; Fronzaroli StEb 7 170, QuSe 13 145; Catagnoti QuSe 29 138, 208.[123] •ONOM: **EUPH** Cf. *im-ḫu-ur-a-šar* → Durand REA 654 (DN). **A7** Cf. *ta-am-ḫu-ra*-(...DN?) → Arnaud AuOr 16 175.

[121] Cf. *mwḥ* (JAram. Gt) "to be dissolved";

[122] For DUL 533f.: /*m-ḫ*/ "to feel exuberant" (denom. ?, bkn ctx.; Tropper KWU 71: mng unc.) see more likely \|m-x-w\|, below.

māxir, **maxxār** "recipient, buyer; opponent, rival"	•CTX: **EG** *ma-ḫ-r* → Hoch SWET 150f. no. 194.[124] •LL: **EB** SANGA.GAR = *ma-ḫi-lum* → Conti QuSe 17 89; Bonechi QDLF 16 82. •ONOM: **EB** Cf. SAL(*mám*??)-*ma-hir* |man(??)=māxir| → Pagan ARES 3 139, 350. **EUPH** MIM(*mí*)-*ma-ḫir-sù* → Gelb TI 11.
maxir "basket, box"	•CTX: **EG** *ma-ḫi-ru*$_2$, metath. *ma-r-ḫ* → Hoch SWET 151 no. 195.[125]
mxr (A) "price, commercial value"	•CTX: **UGA** Sg. suff. *mḫrk*?, *mḫrhn* → DUL 533f.: *mḫr* (I).
mxr (B) "tax collector"	•CTX: **UGA** → DUL 534: *mḫr* (II).
maxārt "wooden front part" (?)	•LL: **EB** Cf. GIŠ.GABA = *ma-ḫa-tum* → Conti QuSe 17 127; Sjöberg Fs. Pettinato 262.
maxirat "bag"	•CTX: **EG** *ma*$_2$-*ḫi-ra-ta* → Hoch SWET 151f. no. 196.
tamxīr "presentation, offering"	•ONOM: **EUPH**, **R** UDU.ḪI.A *ta-am-ḫi-ra-am*; cf. MN ITI *tám-ḫi-ri-im* → AHw 1314; CAD T 117.[126]

|m-x-ṣ|

See |**m-x-ṣ̂**|

|m-x-s¹|

See |**m-x-ṣ̂**|

## |m-x-ṣ̂|	Sem.: *mḥṣ* (Hb.) "to smash"; *mḥʔ*, *mḥy* (Aram., Syr.) "to strike", (JAram.) *mḥy*(*ʔ*) "weaver"; *maḫāṣu*(*m*) (Akk.) "to hit, wound", *māḫiṣu*(*m*) "weaver"; *mḫḍ* (OSArab.) "to smite, defeat". See further *maḫaḍa* (Arab.) "to churn, beat and agitate"; *maḥaṣa* (Arab.) "to stamp (when dying)"; *meḥaḍ* (MSArab.) "weaver"; *maḥaṣa* (Eth.) "to smite, cut, destroy".
|**m-x-ṣ̂**| "to hit, beat"	•CTX: **EA** G prefc. (representing D?) suff. *yi-ma-ḫa-aš-ši*, *ti-ma-ḫa-ṣa-na-*[*ni*], *ti-ma-ḫa-ṣú-ka*, *ti*$_7$-*ma-ḫa-ṣú-nu*; suffc. suff. *ma-aḫ-ṣú-ú* |maxṣ̂ū=hū|, pass. *mi-ḫi-ṣa*; bkn ctx. *ma-aḫ-ṣú- ni*$_7$[127] → Sivan GAGl 138, 247; Rainey EAT 80; Rainey CAT 1 77, 92, 2 55; EAC 1569; Izre'el Orient 38 82, 84, 91, 93. •LL: **EB** ŠU.ŠU.RA = *ma-ḫa-zi i-da* |maxaṣ̂ yiday(n)|; TÙN.BAR = *ma-ḫu-zú*, *ma-ḫu-zu-um* |maxxuṣ̂um| → Krebernik ZA 73 20, 29 (760); Saporetti BaE 403f.; Fronzaroli QuSe 13 145; Fales QuSe 13 179.
|**m-x-ṣ**| "to hit, beat"	•CTX: **UGA** G prefc. *ỉmḫṣ*, *ảmḫṣ*, *tmḫṣ*, *ymḫṣ*, suff. *ỉmḫṣh*, *tmḫṣh*, *ymḫṣk*; suffc. *mḫṣt*; act. ptc. *mḫṣ*, pl. *mḫṣm*, suff. *mḫṣy*; inf. *mḫṣ*; Gt prefc. *ỉmtḫṣ*, *tmtḫṣ*, suff. *tmtḫṣn* → DUL 534f.: /*m-ḫ-ṣ*/.

[123] Note GIŠ.SUBUR(LAK-39) = *su-mu-ḫu-lum*/*lu-um* → Bonechi QuSe 19 141: *šumḫurum* "the pulled one, the towed one" (mng a cart).
[124] Sivan / Cochavi-Rainey WSVES 81: *ma-ḫ*( )*r* / *ma-ḫar* "price"; Helck Beziehungen no. 108.
[125] Sivan / Cochavi-Rainey WSVES 81: *ma-ḫi-ru* "basket"; Helck Beziehungen no. 109; Kilani VGW 120: |mvḫ₂'i:/u:rv|.
[126] Diff. Durand REA 654: "lutte".
[127] Perhaps with acc. suff 1 c. sg.; see Rainey EAT 80.

|m-x-s^1| "to hit, beat"	•CTX: **UGA** G suffc. *mḫšt* → DUL 536: */m-ḫ-š/*.[128]
|m-ṣ-x| "to hit, beat; weave" (?)	•CTX: **UGA** G prefc. *ymṣḫ*, suff. *åmṣḫnn*; N prefc. suff. *ymṣḫn* → Renfroe AULS 132.[129]
māxiš, māxiṣ "weaver"	•CTX: **A7** → LÚ.MEŠ *ma-ḫi-ṣí*(!) → Wiseman AT 158; AHw 584; CAD M/1 102; Giacumakis AkkAl 86. **A4** LÚ.MEŠ *ma-ḫi-iṣ* → CAD M/1 102; Giacumakis AkkAl 86. **UGS** LÚ *ma-ḫi-ṣu* → Huehnergard UVST 146, ^{2}UVST 393; vSoldt SAU 305 (77).
mixiṣ "a striking instrument"	•CTX: **UGS** [URUDU.MEŠ] *me-ḫi-*[*ṣ*]*u-ma* MEŠ → Sivan GAGl 247; Huehnergard UVST 146.
mxṣ (A) "weaver"	•CTX: **UGA** Sg. *mḫṣ*, pl. *mḫṣm* → DUL 535: *mḫṣ* (I).
mxṣ (B) "a striking instrument"	•CTX: **UGA** → DUL 535f.: *mḫṣ* (II).
tmtxṣ "fight"	•CTX: **UGA** Sg. suff. *tmtḫṣh* → DUL 859: *tmtḫṣ*.

|m-x-w|	Sem.: Cf. *maḫû*(*m*) (Akk) "to rave", *maḫḫû*(*m*), *muḫḫû*(*m*) "ecstatic".
|m-x-w/y| "to be frenzied, violently agitated"	•CTX: **UGA** G suffc. *mḫ*, imp. or inf. *mḫ*.[130]
muxxuw "ecstatic"	•ONOM: **EB** Cf. *mu-ḫu*, fem. *mu-ḫu-da* |muxxūta| → Pagan ARES 3 139, 352.[131]

|m-k|	Loanword. Non-Sem.: *mk* (Eg.) "a special quality of linen; byssus ?".
mik "a special quality of linen; byssus ?"	•CTX: **UGS** *ša me-ku* → Lackenbacher / Malbran-Labat RSOu 23 86.[132]

|m-k(-k)|	Sem.: *mwk* (Hb., JAram.) "to come down; to lie down", *mkk* "to lower, sink"; *mkk* (JAram., Syr.) "to be low", *mk*(*ʔ*) "nether region", (JAram.) *mwk*(*ʔ*) (Mand.) "low area, bedding".
|m-k(-k)| "to fall, be cast down"	•CTX: **UGA** G prefc. *tmk*, *ymk* → DUL 536f.
mk (A) "depressed place, bog"	•CTX: **UGA** → DUL 536: *mk* (I).

|m-k-r|	Sem.: *mkr* (Hb.) "to sell", *mkr* (meker) "purchase price, trade", (*makkār*) "merchant"; *mkr* (Pun.) "to sell; merchant"; (Aram.) "to acquire property for a price, buy", *mwkrw* "price", *mkyrh*, *mkyrtʔ* (JAram.) "sale"; *makāru*(*m*) (Akk.)

128 Secondary phonetic modification / allomorph of |m-x-ṣ|; Held JAOS 79 173, Tropper UG 105.
129 Diff. DUL 578: */m-ṣ-ḫ/* (wrongly: */m-ṣ-ḥ/*) "to pull"; Tropper KWU 80: G "zu Boden reissen", N "aneinander zerren".
130 Note DUL 532f. */m-ḫ/* "to feel exuberant" (?) by metonym. seman. shift denom. < *mḫ*; but see *mx* "marrow, brains" under |m-x-x|.
131 Altern. *mu-ḫu* |muxx=| "skull", Pagan ARES 3 225; unlikely.
132 Also in Bogh.; see CAD M/2 66: *miku*.

	"to do business", *mākirum* (OAss.) "trader",[133] cf. *tamkāru(m)*, *damk/gāru* "merchant, businessman"; *makkara* (Arab.) "to hoard (grain)"; *mkr* (OSArab.) "merchant, tradesman".
|m-k-r| "to trade, sell"	•CTX: **UGS** G inf. / verbal noun *a-na ma-ka-ri* → Huehnergard UVST 146f.; Tropper UG 481. **UGA** N prefc. *tmkrn* → DUL 537.
mākir "merchant"	•CTX: **EG** Pl *mak-ru$_2$-ʔu* |mākiruyu| → Hoch SWET 169 no. 223.[134]
mkr (A) "merchant, commercial agent, runner"	•CTX: **UGA** Sg. *mkr*, suff. *mkry*, *mkrn*, pl. abs. *mkrm*, cstr. *mkr*; du. (?) *mkrm* → DUL 537f.
mkr (B) "sale, trade good, merchandise"	•CTX: **UGA** Sg. *mkr* → Tropper KWU 72 (on KTU 4.808:1: "Verkauf" od. "Verkaufsware" |ma/ikr=|; DUL 538 under *mkr* "merchant").

|m-k-s|	Sem.: *makāsu(m)* (Akk.) "to levy customs or rental dues".
|m-k-s| "to put a tax"	•CTX: **UGS** G prefc. *i-ma-ak-ka-su* → Lackenbacher / Malbran-Labat RSOu 23 86 (irregular vocalism).

|m-k-w/y|	Sem.: Cf. *mikûm* (Akk.) "seductive (feminine) charm(s)".
mikiyt "seductive woman"	•CTX: **EA** Cf. 10 MI.MES *: mi-ki-tu* → AHw 652: *mikûm*; CAD M/2 66: *mikû*; Loretz / Mayer UF 6 493; Moran AmL 135f. fn. 2; Rainey CAT 1 186.

|m-ḳ-ḳ|	Sem.: *mqq* (Hb. N) "to rot; to melt, dissolve".
|m-ḳ-ḳ| "to melt, dissolve" (?)	•LL: **EB** Cf. GÍN.IR = *ma-gu* → Conti QuSe 17 187.

|m-ḳ-l|	Culture word, Sem.: *mql* (*maqqēl*, Hb.; pl. *maqᵉlôt*) "rod, branch, staff".
maḳḳīl "rod, branch, staff"	•CTX: **EG**: *ma$_2$-qi$_2$-ra*, *ma-qi$_2$-n-t*, *ma-gi$_2$-w-t*, *ma-gi$_2$-ʔ-t*, *ma-gi$_2$-t* → Hoch SWET 166 no. 217.[135]

|m-ḳ-s¹|	Culture word; Sem.: Cf. *mqšh* (*miqšāh*, Hb.) "wrought metal, hammered work". See further: *qšh* (Hb.) "to be heavy, hard"; *qšy* (Aram.) "to be difficult"; *qasā* (Arab.) "to be hard".
|m-ḳ-s¹| "to emboss, hammer" (?)	•CTX: **EG** Cf. *ma-ga-sa*, metath. *ma-sa-qa* (stative |maqas¹a| → Hoch SWET 172f. no. 229.

[133] On the non-existent *makkārum* (AHw 589; CAD M/1 131; Durand MARI 5 669f.) see Veenhof NABU 1992/5.
[134] Sivan / Cochavi-Rainey WSVES 82: *mak-rú-ʔu* "merchant"; Helck Beziehungen no. 128; Kilani VGW 77: \|mvk(v)r'U'\|.
[135] Sivan / Cochavi-Rainey WSVES 82: *ma-qa-la* "staff"; Helck Beziehungen no. 125.

|m-ḳ-ṭ| Sem.: *maqātu*(*m*) (Akk.) “to fall”, *miqtu*(m) “fall” (also name of a demon); *maqqaṭa* (Arab.) “to knock down, pull down”, *muqṭ* “trap, snare”; *mqṭt* (OSArab.) “setting of a heavenly body”.

|m-ḳ-ṭ| “to fall, go down” •CTX: **EB** G prefc. *a-gu-du*, *la-mu-gu-du* |lu=(ʔa)mḳuṭ=|; Ct prefc. *ti-iš-da-<ma->ga-ad* |tiStamaḳḳaṭ| (?) → Fronzaroli ARET 13 18 (|tiStaḳḳat|), 301, 315; Catagnoti QuSe 29 46, 67, 127, 134, 145, 209.
•ONOM: **EUPH** Cf. *ia-am-qu-du*, *i-am-ku-du*; (Gt) *ia-am-da-ga-ad*, *ia-am-ta-qa-aq-ta-am* → Gelb CAAA 25, 153, 157; Golinets Onomastikon 2 188f., 407f., 488.

miḳiṭ “the Fall (DN)” •ONOM: **EUPH** Cf. *la-šu-mi-gi/ki-it* → Gelb CAAA 25, 157.

|m-l-ʔ| Sem.: *mlʔ* (Hb., Ph.) “to be full, fill up”, *mlʔ* (*mālēʔ*, Hb.) “full”, *ml*(*w*)*ʔ* (*melōʔ*) “fullness”, *mlwʔ* (*millôʔ*) “terraced structure”, *mlʔh* (*m*^{e}*leʔāh*) “the whole harvest”; *mlʔ*, *mly* (Aram., Syr.) “to be filled, to fill up”, *mly* (Aram., Syr.) “full”,[136] *mlʔ*(*ʔ*) (JAram., Syr.) “fullness”, *mlwʔ*(*ʔ*) (JAram., Syr.) “fullness, complete amount”, *mwly*(*ʔ*) (Syr.) “completion”, *mly*, *mlytʔ* (JAram., Syr.) “fullness”, *mlʔ* (Hatra) “filled terrace”, *mlwtʔ* (Syr.) “pitcher”, *mlwytʔ* (JAram.) “place for drawing water”; *malû*(*m*) (Akk.) “to be full, fill up”, *malû*(*m*), *malʔum*, “full”, *malû*(*m*) “abundance, fullness”, *mīlu*(*m*) “high water, fullness”, *malâtu* “the entire offerings (for a period)”, *malītu* “a ritual vessel”, *tamlīu* “filling, terrace”; *malaʔa* (Arab.) “to fill, fill up”, *maliʔa* “to be(come) filled”, *malīʔ* “filled”, *milʔ* “filling”; *mlʔ* (OSArab.) “to fill”, “fullness, duration of time”, *tmlʔ* “fill of a wall”; *méleʔ*, *mīleʔ* (MSArab.) “to be full”, *melō* “to fill”; *malʔa* (Eth.) “to fill, fill up”, *məluʔ* “full”, *məlʔ* “fullness”.

|m-l-ʔ| “to be full” •CTX: **EB** G prefc. *du-ma-lá* → Fronzaroli ARET 13 73, 255; Catagnoti QuSe 29 152, 208.
UGA G prefc. *ymlủ*, suffc. *mlả*, *mlảt*; D prefc. *ymlủ*, *nmlủ*, suff. *tmlảh*, suffc. *mlả*; imp. (?) *mlỉ*; act. ptc. fem. pl. *mmlảt* → DUL 539.
•ONOM: **EUPH** *a-am-li*-DINGIR → Gelb CAAA 25, 157; Zadok OLA 28 130; Streck Onomastikon 1 237f. fn. 1; Golinets Onomastikon 2 176, 404.[137]

maliʔ “full” •LL: **EB** AB.SI = *ma-li-um* → Krebernik ZA 73 36; Catagnoti QuSe 29 47, 120, 208.

mlủ “fill, full measure” •CTX: **UGA** Sg. *mlủ*, suff. *mlủn* → DUL 539f.

mlảt “fullness” •CTX: **UGA** → DUL 540f.

mlỉt “fullness, plenty” •CTX: **UGA** → DUL 541.[138]

malīt “artificial terrace” (?) •CTX: **EM** *ma-li-tu/tu*$_4$*/ti* → Pentiuc Vocabulary 120f.; Ikeda BiOr 60 271: glottal stop not represented.

maluyanita “a vessel” •CTX: **EG** Cf. *ma-ru*$_2$*-ya-ni-ta* → Hoch SWET 137 no. 176.

|m-l-g| Culture word, Sem.: *mulūgu*, *mulūgūtu* (Nuzi-Akk.) “a type of dowry”; *mlwgʔ* (JAram., Mand.) “trousseau”.

---

136 Warka *ma-li-e*, Hoftijzer / Jongeling DNWSI 628: *mlʔ*$_4$.
137 Cf. unc.: *a-lam-ma-li-a-at*, *ti-im-lu-ú*, Zadok Fs. Hallo 326.
138 Altern. adj. fem. “full”; Tropper KWU 72, UG 437.

mlg "(a type of) trousseau, dowry"	•ONOM: **UGA** Cf. DN *mlghy* → DUL 541f.

|m-l-ħ|	Primary noun, Sem.: *mlḥ* (*melaḥ*, Hb.) "salt"; *mlḥ(ʔ)* (Aram., Syr.)) "salt"; *milʔu* (Akk.) "saltpetre"; *milḥ* (Arab.) "salt; wit, esprit"; *malḥ* (Eth.) "salt; taste, judgement". Denom. verbs with further derivations: *mlḥ* (Hb.) "to salt"; (JAram., Syr.) id., (Syr.) "to become salty"; *mlyḥ* (Palm.) "salty"; *malaḥa* (Arab.) "to salt", *maluḥa, ʔamlaḥa* "to be(come) salty", *maluḥa* "to be beautiful, handsome, good", *malīḥ* "salty, pleasant"; *malləḥa* (Eth.) "to season with salt, make tasty".
milħ, **malīħ** "salt / salty (land)"	•ONOM: **EG** Elem. in TN *ma-ri-ḥa* → Hoch SWET 139f. no. 180.
mōliħ "salt worker"	•CTX: **EG** Pl. *mu$_2$-ra-ḥ-mu$_4$* |mōliħimū| → Hoch SWET 140 no. 181.[139]
mlħt "salt"	•CTX: **UGA** → DUL 542f.: *mlḥt*.[140]

|m-l-x| (1)	Sem.: *mlḥ* (Hb. N) "to be torn to pieces"; *malāḫu(m)* (Akk.) "to tear out"; *malaḫa, ʔimtalaḫa* (Arab.) "to pull out, tear out; to draw"; *melōx* (MSArab.) "to pull down"; *malḫa* (Eth.) "to tear out". See further: *mlg* (JAram., Syr.) "to pluck out".
|**m-l-x**| "to tear out"	•CTX: **EB** G pass. ptc. *ma-i-ḫum* |malix=| → Fronzaroli ZA 88 232f.; Catagnoti QuSe 29 17, 38, 122, 208. •LL: **EB** Cf. unc. SAGxTAG4 = *ma-al$_6$-a-tum* |malaxtum| (?) → Conti QuSe 17 110.[141]
|**m-l-ħ**| "to pull out, draw"	•CTX: **UGA** G pass. ptc. *mlḥt* → Tropper KWU 73: *mlḥ**, UG 122, 476.[142]

|m-l-x| (2)	Culture word, Sem.: *mlḥ* (*mallāḥ*, Hb.) "seaman, sailor"; *mlḥ(ʔ)* (Aram., Syr.) id., > *mallāḥ* (Arab.) id. Compare *malāḫu(m)* (Akk.) id. Non-Sem.: malaḫ (Sum.) "sailor".
mallāx "sailor"	•LL: **EB** MÁ.LAḪ$_5$ = *ma-la-ḫu-um* → Fronzaroli StEb 7 170; QuSe 13 145.

|m-l-k|	Primary noun, Sem.: *mlk* (*melek*, suff. *malk=*, Hb.) "king, ruler", *mlkh* (*malkāh*) "wife of the king, queen"; *mlk* (Ph., Pun., Moab., Ammon., Edom., Nab., Palm., Hatra) "king", *mlkt* (Ph., Pun., Nab., Palm.) "queen"; *mlk(ʔ)* (Aram., Syr.) "king", *mlkh, mlktʔ* "queen"; *malku(m), maliku(m)* (Akk.) "prince, king",[143] *malkatu(m)* "queen"; *malik* (Arab.) "king, ruler", *malika* "queen"; *mlk* (OSArab.) "king", *mlkt* "queen". Denom. verbs and other derivations: *mlk* (Hb.) "to be the

[139] Sivan / Cochavi-Rainey WSVES 80: *mu-la-ḥ* "salt worker"; Helck Beziehungen no. 99.
[140] For further instances of the basis in bkn and unc. contexts see DUL 542: *mlḥ* (I) "beauty" (?), and DUL 542: *mlḥ* "salt" (?). Cf. Watson Historiae 17 15ff.
[141] Cf. diff. rdg *ma-al-a-tum*, Krebernik ZA 73 46f.: \|marʔatum\| "daughter" (cf. \|m-r-ʔ\| (1)); Civil AuOr 2 293; Sjöberg Fs. Kienast 543f.: "unkempt hair" (Akk. *malû*).
[142] Tropper loc.cit.: "Mit gezücktem Dolch" (*b ḥrb mlḥt*), with Ug. *ḥ* against etym. \|x\| (*ḫ*); diff.: DUL 543 "knife with salt", under *mlḥt* "salt" (below: \|m-l-ħ\|).
[143] Hasselbach SargAkk 188: *ma-al-kum* "governor". WSem.? Cf. Kogan Classification 91f.; Hrůša MŠ 196.

king, rule", *mlkwt* (*malkût*), *mmlkh* (*mamlākāh*), *mmlkwt* (*mamlakût*) "kingship, royal dominion"; *mlk* (Aram., Syr.) "to reign", *mlwkh*, *mlwkt?* (Aram.) "kingship"; *malikūtu*(*m*), *malkūtu* (Akk.) "rule, government"; *malaka* (Arab.) "to exercise authority, possess, own"; *mulk* "kingship, reign; property, domain", *milk* "property, possessions", *mālik* "reigning, owning, the possessor of command", *malakūt* "realm, kingdom", *mallāk* "owner", *malīk* "king", *malīka* "queen", *mamlaka* "kingdom"; *hmlk* (OSArab. C) "to cause to possess", *mlk* "kingship; property", *mlyk* "royal", *mlkt* "queen"; *amlōk*, *s^1emlōk* (MSArab.) "to give a man legal possession of a wife"; *malaka* (Eth.) "to own property, dominate", *malāki* "master, ruler", *məlkat* "domination", *məlkot* "ownership", *ʔamlāk* "Lord, God".[144]
Non-Sem.: Cf. **mulVk=* (West Chadic) "stranger"; **mulak=* (Central Chadic) id.[145]

|m-l-k| "to settle, rule, give advice"

•CTX: **EB** G prefc. *ne-mi-ga-am$_6$* |nimlikam|, imp. *mi-ga-am$_6$* |milikam|, *me-li-ga-A* |milkay=|, inf. *ma-a-ga* |malāka(m)|; D inf. suff. *ma-lu-gi-iš* |malluk=is|; Ct inf. *su-da$_5$-lik* |sutamlik| → Tonietti MARI 8 237; Catagnoti QuSe 29 7, 47f. fn. 192, 31, 113, 139, 145, 208.[146]
EM D inf. *ma-al-lu-ki/u* |malluk=| → Pentiuc Vocabulary 115; Ikeda BiOr 60 269.
UGS G prefc. *i-ma-li-ik* → Sivan GAGl 248; Huehnergard UVST 147; vSoldt SAU 454: *malāku* UGU.
UGA G prefc. *ymlk*, *åmlk*; suffc. *mlkt*; act. ptc. *mlk*; D prefc. *åm*{.}*lkn*; *nmlk* → DUL 543f.: /*m-l-k*/.
•ONOM: **EUPH** *ia-am-li-ka-an*, *ia-am-lik-*^{d}IM, *ia-am-lik-*DINGIR, *a-am-lik-*DINGIR, *ia-am-li-ik-*DINGIR, *ii-im-lik-*DINGIR, *ì-lí-a-am-lik*, *la-am-lik* → Huffmon APNMT 230; Gelb 25, 152; Streck Onomastikon 1 177 § 2.56, 297 § 3.56b fn. 3, 346 § 5.64; vSoldt Fs. Muraoka 467; Golinets Onomastikon 2 24, 28, 59f., 109, 127, 167, 404ff., 491.
EM Cf. G prefc. *am-la-ki* → Pruzsinszky PTEm 154 fn. 62 [130].[147]
UGS ^{d}IM-*ma-lak*(?) → Gröndahl PTU 157f.; Sivan GAGl 248; vSoldt Fs. Muraoka 457.
UGA *ymlk* → DUL 952.

malk (A) "ruler; (the) king; DN"

•CTX: **EB** *ma-lik* (st. cstr.) → Archi MARI 5 37; Fronzaroli StEb 5 72; QuSe 13 145; Biga / Milano ARET 4 310.[148]
•LL: **UGS** [EN] = [*ša*]*r-ru* = *i-wi-ir-ni* = *ma-al-ku* → Sivan GAGl 243; Huehnergard UVST 147; vSoldt SAU 305 (78). Pl. ^{d}*ma-lik* MEŠ |ma/ālikūma| (= alph. *mlkm*) → Huehnergard UVST 147; vSoldt SAU 305 (79).
MŠ *ma-al-ku* = *šar-ru*, *ma-al-ka-tu$_4$* = *šar-ra-tu$_4$* → Hrůša MŠ 300, and see MŠ 196.
•ONOM: **EB** Writing =*ma-lik*(UR) passim (Sem. logogram), e.g. *a-ib-ma-lik*, *a-ma-ma-lik*, *a-si-ma-lik*, *a-šu-ur-ma-lik*, *bar-za-ma-lik*, *bíl-ma-lik*, *bù-da-ma-lik*, *da-am$_6$-ma-lik*, *dar-am$_6$-ma-lik*, *da-ḫir-ma-lik*, *du-bu-ḫu-ma-lik*, *dur-ma-lik*, *en-bù-ma-lik*, *en-na-ma-lik*, *gi-la-ma-lik*, *gi-ra-ma-lik*, *gú-na-ma-lik*, *i-da-ma-lik*, *i-ib-ma-lik*, *ì-lum-ma-lik*, *i-rí-ig-ma-lik*, *i-šar-ma-lik*, *i-ti-ma-lik*, *i-zi-ma-lik*, *ib-*

[144] The East Semitic lexical peculiarity *malāku*(*m*) (Akk.) "to discuss, advise" is ultimately related to *mal*(*i*)*k* "ruler, king".
[145] Cf. Orel / Stolbova HSED 388 no. 1791: **mulak=* / **mulik=* "stranger, chief".
[146] For verbal nouns (theme D) see below: *mullukt*, *tumtallik*.
[147] The instances *im-lik*=DN could be Akk.; see Pruzsinszky PTEm 84 fn. 137 [482ff.]; vSoldt Fs. Muraoka 455: "Dagan provides counsel".
[148] For the writings *me-*Gum (*me-*Kum, < |ma(l)k=um / me(l)k=um| see Tonietti MARI 8 234ff.; Matthiae Fs. Fronzaroli 391f.

du-ma-lik, ib-ḫur-ma-lik, ig-bú-ul-ma-lik, iḫ-ra-ma-lik, íl-a-ma-lik, íl-ba-ma-lik, in-ma-lik, ìr-am$_{6}$*-ma-lik, ìr-da-ma-lik, ìr-kab-ma-lik, iš*$_{11/12}$*-a-ma-lik, kún-ma-lik, kùn-ma-lik, lu-la-ma-lik,* PUZUR$_{4}$*-ra-ma-lik, rí-dam-ma-lik, rí-ì-ma-lik, ru*$_{12}$*-zi-ma-lik, si-na-ma-lik, si-ti-ma-lik, šu-ma-lik, šum-ma-lik, zé-ma-lik, zi-mi-na-ma-lik*, etc.[149] Other writings: *=ma-gú* |malku(m)|: *en-na-ma-gú, si-na-ma-gú(-ma), iš*$_{11}$*-ma-gú;*[150] reduced *=ma*: *a-*DUM*-ma*, *=ma-li: bar-za-ma-li* → Pomponio / Xella AOAT 245 458ff.; Archi ARES 1 215f.; Krebernik PET 97; Tonietti MARI 8 238; Renger ARES 1 168ff.; Bonechi MARI 8 478 fn. 7, 484; Pagan ARES 3 139f.; Catagnoti QuSe 29 7.

A4 DINGIR*-ma-al-ki, bi-it-ta-mal-ki* → Wiseman AT 131, 137; Gelb CAAA 25, 152; Sivan GAGl 242; Arnaud AuOr 16 156; Streck Onomastikon 1 305 § 3.71; vSoldt Fs. Muraoka 642.

EM *ma-al-ku-*^{d}*da-gan* → Pruzsinszky PTEm 126 [605]; vSoldt Fs. Muraoka 452, 470.

EG |malk=|, |milk=|, elem. in PN and TN *ma-r-ka-ya, ma-ra-ka, ma*$_{3}$*-ra-ku, ma-r-ku-{k}, ma-ru*$_{2}$*-ka-ʔu, h-ma*$_{4}$*-ru*$_{2}$*-k* (with article: *h*C= |ham=|) → Hoch SWET 144f. no. 187.[151]

malk (B), malāk "ruling, guideline, decision, advice"

•CTX: **EB** *ma-a-ki* |malākī| or |malkī| (?) → Renger ARES 1 168ff.; Fronzaroli ARET 13 20, 281; Archi PIHANS 106 104.

•ONOM: **EUPH** Cf. *ma-la-ak-*DINGIR, *ma-la-ak-ì-lí, ma-la-ku-il,* ^{d}*da-gan-ma-la-ku,* ^{d}*iš-ḫa-ra-ma-ka-ki, mu-tu-ma-la-ka* → Huffmon APNMT 230f.; Gelb CAAA 25, 152.[152]

milk (A) "ruling, guideline, decision, advice"

•CTX: **EB** *mi-a-gú* |milk=u(m)|, suff. *mi-gú-na* |milik=nay(n)| → Tonietti MARI 8 237 fn. 115; Catagnoti QuSe 29 74, 211.

•ONOM: **U3** *mi-il-ga-nu-um, mi-il-ki-lí-il* → Buccellati Amorites 172f.; Gelb CAAA 25, 156.

EUPH passim; cf. e.g. *mi-il-ku-iš*$_{8}$*-tár, ka-ak-ka-mil-ki, li-li-mi-il-ki, mi-il-ki-ia, me-il-ku, mi-il-ki-im, mi-il-ka-tum, mi-il-ku-ma, mi-il-ku-nim, mi-il-ka-*^{d}IM, *mil-ki-e-ra-aḫ, mil-ki-ba-al, mil-ki-*^{d}*da-gan, mi-il-ki-*DINGIR, *mi-il-ki-lu/lum, mi-el-ki-i-la, mi-il-ki-lu-i-la, mi-il-ku-ma, mi-il-ku-ma-il/*DINGIR, *mi-il-ku-da-nu-um,* DINGIR*-mi-il-kum, ì-lí-mil-ku,* EŠ$_{4}$-DAR*-me-il-ki, ki-mi-il-ki-el, la-i-la-mi-il-ki, ì-lí-mi-il-ka-ia* → Gelb CAAA 25, 156f.; Zadok Fs. Hallo 326; Streck Onomastikon 1 165 § 2.29, 238 § 2.152, 276 § 3.27, 279 § 3.34, 308 § 3.77, 344 § 5.59; Golinets Onomastikon 2 404ff.

EA *mi-ìl-ki-lí, mil-ki-lu*$_{(4)}$*/li/lì* (cf. *mil-ki-*DINGIR)[153] → Sivan GAGl 247; Hess APN 18f., 86f., 112f. 208, 239; vSoldt Fs. Muraoka 463ff., 470.

UGS *mi-il-ka-a, mi-il-ka-ia, mi-il-ki-*SUM, *mil-ku-*SIG$_{5}$*(-ú), mi-il-ki-i-in-a-dal* (altern. rdg *mi-il-ki-i-in-a-ri*, Hurr.), *mi-il-ki-lu* → vSoldt Fs. Muraoka 458, 470

[149] For the instances see http://virgo.unive.it/eblaonline/cgi-bin/search_tabwindow.cgi, search string: *ma-lik* (2188 results).

[150] Diff. Pagan ARES 3 307: |ḫinnam=ʔAgū| "(have) mercy, DN!", |ši=naʕmaq=u| "she is wisdom|.

[151] Sivan / Cochavi-Rainey WSVES 80: *ma-l-kú / mi-l-kú* "gift"; Helck Beziehungen no. 101, from Hb. *mlk* "Königs(gabe)".

[152] For other (questionable) explanations (G suffc.; noun *malak* "König") see Golinets Onomastikon 2 405f. with fn. 1040.

[153] "My advice is Ilu", etc.; altern. "Milku (DN) is god".

milk (B) "ruler; (the) king; DN"

•CTX: **EA** *mil-ka* (333:21) → Izre'el Orient 38 88.
•ONOM: **A4** *mi-il-ki-ta-ga*, *mi-il-ku-ma*, *mi-il-kum-ma*-DINGIR; *i-li-mi-il-ki* → Wiseman AT 137, 142; Gelb CAAA 25, 156f.; Sivan GAGl 247; Arnaud AuOr 16 158; vSoldt Fs. Muraoka 462f.
EA *a-bi-mil-ki* (cf. *a-bu*-LUGAL, *ia-bi*-LUGAL),[154] NIN-*mi-il-ki* (cf. NIN-LUGAL), *i-li-mil-ku* (cf. DINGIR-LUGAL), *mi-il-ki-lí*, *mil-ki-lum*/*lim*/li, *mil-ki*-DINGIR → Sivan GAGl 247; Hess APN 18f., 86f., 112f. 208, 239; vSoldt Fs. Muraoka 463ff.[155]
UGS DINGIR-*mil-ku* (cf. DINGIR-LUGAL)[156] → vSoldt Fs. Muraoka 458ff.
EG See *malk* (A) "king, ruler; DN".

mulk "government, royal authority"

•CTX: **EA** *mu-ul-ka* (333:20) → CAD M/2 188; Sivan GAGl 249; Rainey EAT 82, CAT 2 154, 175; Izre'el Orient 38 88.

mal(i)k "ruler, king; dead king(s); DN"

•CTX: **EUPH** (offerings) *a-na ma-li-ki*, *a-na ma-li-kim*, *ša ma-li-ki* → Tsukimoto AOAT 216 65ff.; Jacquet FM 6 51ff.; 12 94, and passim ibid.; Archi StEb 5 201ff.; Charpin RA 84 90.
•LL: **EB** NAM.EN = *ma-li-gú-um* → Krebernik ZA 73 38.[157]
MŠ *ma-li-ku* = vacat / MIN (: *šar-ru*) → Hrůša MŠ 300, and see MŠ 196.
•ONOM: **EB** See above *malk* (A).
EUPH passim; cf. *ma-li-ki*, *ma-li-ka*(*-tum*), ^{d}IM-*ma-lik*, ^{d}*a-mu-un-ma-li-ki*, *an-nu-ma-lik*, ^{d}*da-gan-ma-lik*, ^{d}EN.ZU-*ma-lik*, ^{d}*ka-mi-iš-ma-li-ki*, ^{d}*na-bu-ú*/*um-ma-lik*, *sa-am-si-ma-lik*, *ma-li-ik-*^{d}*da-gan*, *ma-lik-e-lim*, *ma-lik-ʔà-a*, *ma-lik*-AN; DN as elem. in PNN, passim; cf. *li-bur-*^{d}*ma-lik*, *ia-du-ur-ma-lik*, *ia-ku-un-ma-lik*, *i-túr-ma-lik*, *a-ḫi-*(*e-*)*ma-lik*, *a-mi-ma-lik*, *ab-du-ma-lik*, *ab-du-ma-li-ki*, *da-du-ma-lik*, *ḫa-ab-du-ma-li-ki*, *ḫa-lí-ma-lik*, *ḫa-ri-ma-li-ki*, *ḫi-ib-rum*(!)*-ma-lik*, *ì-lí-*$^{(d)}$*ma-lik*, *ia-ki-in-*^{d}*ma-lik*, *ia-ri-im-ma-lik*, *mu-tu-ma-lik*, *na-ap-si-ma-lik*, *la-aḫ-wi-ma-li-ku*, *ri-ip-a-ma-lik* → Huffmon APNMT 230f.; Gelb CAAA 25, 152; vSoldt Fs. Muraoka 466f.; Durand SEL 8 84, REA 676f.; cf. Golinets Onomastikon 2 131ff., 406.[158]
A7 *ma-li-ki*,[159] *ad-du-ma-lik*, *an-du-ma-lik*, *ia-tar-ma-lik*, *e-wi-ma-lik* → Wiseman AT 134; Gelb CAAA 25, 152; cf. Golinets Onomastikon 2 131ff., 406.
A4 *bi-it-ta-mal-ki*, DINGIR-*ma-lik*, DINGIR *ma-al-ki* → Wiseman AT 133, 137; Sivan GAGl 243; Arnaud AuOr 16 162; vSoldt Fs. Muraoka 642f.
EM, MBQ *a-bi-ma-lik*, *a-ḫi-ma-lik*, *ab-da-ma-lik*, ÌR-*ma-lik*, $^{(d)}$EN-*ma-lik*, ^{d}IŠKUR- / ^{d}U- / *ba-aḫ-la-ma-lik*, NIN-*ma-lik*, ^{d}*da-gan-* /^{d}KUR-$^{(d)}$*ma-lik*, DINGIR-*ma-li-ki*, DINGIR-*lu*$_{4}$*-ma-lik*, ^{d}*iš-rù-ma*, ^{d}*iš-ru-ma-lik*, *ma-lik*, *še-um-ma-lik* → vSoldt Fs. Muraoka 450ff.; Pruzsinszky PTEm 88 [605], 118 [181], 181 [14], 118 [191ff.], 121 [278f.], 124 [476, 480], 125 fn. 568, 129 [751].
UGS *a-bi-ma-al-ku*, *a-bi-ma-li-ki*, NE-^{d}*ma-lik* 459; cf. *a-bi*-LUGAL, *a-ḫa-tu*$_{4}$/*ti*-LUGAL, *a-ḫi*-LUGAL, *ia-du*-LUGAL, *ia-pa*-LUGAL, *ia-ri*-LUGAL, *qu-ú*-LUGAL → vSoldt Fs. Muraoka 456f., 459.

---

154 For the spelling *ia-bi=* see Moran AmL 240 fn. 1 (EA 153).
155 For IŠ-*ku-ru* in EA 83:53, 84:43 (read IŠ-*kur-r*[*u*], against Hess APN 91f.: ^{I}*iš-kur*), 85:85, and 86:25 (*škr* "to become drunk"), see instead Moran AmL 383: *Milk=uru* (WSem. "Milku is the light", with IŠ(*mil*).
156 For DINGIR-*mu-lik*, DINGIR-(*lì-*)*mu-lik* see below: *muluk*.
157 Diff. Fronzaroli QuSe 13 145; StEb 1 6: "kingship".
158 See Streck Onomastikon 1 104 § 1.95: Akk. *māliku*(*m*) "counselor"; Golinets Onomastikon 2 131ff.: "ratend, der Ratender", etc. Cf. unc. *ma-li-kum*, Buccellati Amorites 111, 167: "counselor" or "prince". See also MN ITI *ma-al-ka-nim*, passim; Limet ARM 11f.; Zadok Fs. Hallo 326.
159 Wiseman AT 131: wrong rdg *Ba-li-ki*.

muluk "(defunct) member of the royal family; DN"	•ONOM: **EUPH** DN as elem. in PNN, passim; cf. *ba-aḫ-li-mu-luk, ia-ri-im-mu-lu-uk, a-bi-mu-lu-ki, i-tar-mu-lu-uk, la-ar-mu-lu-uk* → Gelb CAAA 25, 158; Zadok Fs. Hallo 326; Durand REA 677. **UGS** Cf. unc. DINGIR(*-lì*)*-mu-lik* → vSoldt Fs. Muraoka 457.[160]
mālik "councellor"	•CTX: **EA** LÚ.MEŠ MAŠKIM : *ma-lik* MEŠ → Gianto SEL 12 69f.
mallak "king-size (ration)"	•CTX: **EUPH** *ma-la-kum ša* GU_4 → Durand ARM 21 67ff.
mlk (A) "king; dead king(s); DN"	•CTX: **UGA** Sg. *mlk, mlkỉ*, suff. *mlkn*, pl. *mlkm* → DUL 544-548: *mlk* (I).[161] •ONOM: **UGA** *mlk* → DUL 549: *mlk* (IV); *mlkbn* → DUL 549; *mlknʕm* → DUL 549; *mlkrpỉ* → DUL 549; *mlkytn* → DUL 551; *mlkyy* → DUL 551; *ảbmlk* → DUL 10; *ả/ỉḫmlk* → DUL 37; *ảḫtmlk* → DUL 40; *ỉlmlk* → DUL 55f.; *ʕbdmlk* → DUL 140; *ʕdmlk* → DUL 146; *kṯrmlk* → DUL 468; *pmlk* → DUL 663; *qnmlk* → 695; *šmmlk* → DUL 815; *špšmlk* → DUL 825; *ybnmlk* → DUL 938; *ypʕmlk* → DUL 959. See vSoldt Fs. Muraoka 456f., 459.
mlk (B) "ruling, guideline, decision, advice"	•ONOM: **UGA** *mlkršp* → DUL 549; *mlkym* → DUL 550. See vSoldt Fs. Muraoka 458, 461.
mlk (C) "kingdom"	•CTX: **UGA** Sg. *mlk*, suff. *mlkk, mlkh* → DUL 548: *mlk* (II).
malkat "queen"	•CTX: **EB** passim *ma-lik-tum* (Sem. logogram) → Fronzaroli StEb 1 5; Grégoire LdE 386; Mander HSAO 2 261ff.; Bonechi MARI 8 478 fn. 7; Catagnoti QuSe 29 7, 208; Pasquali NABU 2014/36.[162]
malika, malikat, malikt "queen, princess; DN"	•ONOM: **EUPH** *ma-li-ka, ma-li-ka-tum, ši-ma-li-ik-ti* → Gelb CAAA 25, 152. **EM** DÙG.GA*-ma-lik-ti* → Pruzsinszky PTEm 130 [795]; vSoldt Fs. Muraoka 453.
milikt "ruling, guideline, decision, advice"	•ONOM: **EB** *mi-la*(*-ga*)*-ti, mi-li-ga-ti, mi-li-gi-du, mi-li-gi-ti* → Pagan ARES 3 139, 351.
mullukt "enthronement"	•CTX: **EB** *mu-lu-ga-da-sum* |mulluktaSum| → Catagnoti QuSe 29 31, 208.
mlkt "queen"	•CTX: **UGA** → DUL 549f.
mumtalk, muttalk "judicious"	•CTX: **EUPH** LÚ.MEŠ *mu-ut-ta-al-ku, mu-um-tal-kim* → Eidem FM 55 fn. b.
namlakt "realm, territory"	•CTX: **EUPH** Pl. *nam-la-ka-at, nam-la-ka-ti-šu* → AHw 728; CAD N/1 233; Moran Biblica 50 41; Zadok Fs. Hallo 326; Charpin ARM 26/2 166; Charpin / Ziegler FM 5 37; Birot ARM 27 42; Kupper ARM 28 86.
tuttallik "exertion of kingship"	•LL: **EB** NAM.NAM.EN = *du-da-li-gú-um, du-da*<*-li-*>*gú-um* |tumtallik=| → Krebernik ZA 73 38 (1089); Fronzaroli QuSe 13 139; Conti QuSe 17 37; Catagnoti QuSe 29 144, 208.

|m-l-ḳ|	Sem.: *mlq* (Hb., JAram.) "to pinch off, nip off"; *ʔimtalaqa* (Arab.) "to pull, tear out"; *malaqa* (Eth.) "to cut, pluck, break off".
|m-l-ḳ| "to uproot, tear off"	•LL: **EB** $SI.UR_4$ = = *me-a-gu-um* → Conti QuSe 19 33f.; Pasquali Textile terminologies 174.

160 Probl. epenthesis of *Mulk* (< *\|Muluk\|), another variant of the DNN *Mal*(*i*)*k*, *Milk*, etc.; see Durand REA 677.

161 See also *blmlk* "commoner", GlOS 1 119: \|b-l-y\| (2).

162 For DINGIR.DINGIR *ma-lik-tum-ma-lik-tum* "reines décédées et divinisées après leur mort".

|m-l-l|	Sem. etym. unc. Cf. *mll* (Hb.) "to give a sign (with the fingers)", *mlylwt* (*m^{e}lîlôt*) "ears of corn for rubbing" (also JAram. *mlylh*); *mll* (MHb.) "to rub between the fingers".
|m-l-l| "to rub with the fingers, caress" (?)	•CTX: **UGA** G prefc. *ymll* (!) → DUL 551. •ONOM: **UGA** Cf. *mlʕn* → DUL 441, Sem. PN but probl. unrelated.
mll "waste, scraps" (?)	•CTX: **UGA** Unc. (bkn ctx.) → DUL 551.

|m-l-ṭ| Cf. **|p-l-ṭ|**	Sem.: *mlṭ* (Hb. D) "to save, rescue".
|m-l-ṭ| "to save, rescue"	•ONOM: **EG** Cf. *m-rw-ty-t* → Schneider APÄQ 131 no. 280.
namlaṭ "refuge, shelter"	•ONOM: **EUPH** Cf. TN *nam-la-ṭa* → Zadok Fs. Hallo 326.

|m-m-m| (1)	Culture word, Sem.: *mammû(m)* (Akk.) "frost, ice", *mammītu(m)* "a winter month". Non-Sem.: m a b i (Sum.) "frost".
mm "winter" (?)	•CTX: **UGA** → DUL 552: *mm* (I): *zt mm* "winter olives". Unc.; see there for other proposals.

|m-m-m| (2)	Onomatopoeia; Sem.: *mummu* (Akk.) "roar". Non-Sem.: m u m u n (Sum.) "noise".
mumm "cry (of joy)"	•LL: **EB** GÙ.ḪÚL = *mu-mu* → Conti QuSe 17 97; Sjöberg Fs. Renger 524.

|m-n-ʕ|	Sem.: Cf. *manaʕa* (Arab) "to stop, hinder, hold back", *manuʕa* "to be strongly fortified, impregnable", *manʕ* "closure, hindering", *manʕa* "resistance, insuperability".
manʕat "fortress" (?)	•CTX: **EG** Cf. unc. *ma-n-ʕa-ta* (|manʕata|, or else |maʕanta| with metathesis| ?) → Hoch SWET 127 no. 163: "property, estate".

|m-n-d|	Culture word, Sem.: *mundu(m)*, *muddu*(m), *mindu* (Akk.) "a type of flour".
mndɣ "a type of flour"	•CTX: **UGA** → DUL 555: *mndġ*.

|m-n-d-n|	Culture word, Sem.: *mindinu(m)*, *midinu(m)* (Akk.) "tiger / cheetah".
mudan "an animal (tiger / cheetah ?)"	•LL: **EB** Cf. MUN.TI.NÚM = *mu-da-núm*, *mu-da*-NE-*núm* → Civil BaE 92f.: Sjöberg WO 27 11 (altern. rdg; *mu-da-bí-lum* "an insect"(?)).

|m-n-ħ|	Primary noun, Sem.: *mnḥh* (*minḥāh*, Hb.) "gift, present, tribute"; *mnḥt* (Ph., Pun.) "offering made to the gods"; *mnḥ* (Hatra) "offering, gift"; *mnḥh*, *mnḥtʔ* (Aram.) "meal offering"; *minḥa* (Arab.) "act of kindness, gift, present, remuneration, loan". Denom. *manaḥa* (Arab.) "to grant, give, award".
|**m-n-ħ**| "to deliver"	•CTX: **UGA** G suffc. *mnḥ*; pass. ptc. fem. *mnḥt* → DUL 555: /*m-n-ḥ*/.
mnħ "delivery, contribution, tribute"	•CTX: **UGA** → DUL 555: *mnḥ*.
manħat "gift, tribute"	•CTX: **EG** *man-ḥ-ta*, *man-ḥ-{t}-ta* → Hoch SWET 128 no. 165.[163]
mnħt "tribute"	•CTX: **UGA** → DUL 556: *mnḥt*.
mnħy "offering"	•CTX: **UGA** Sg. suff. *mnḥyk* → DUL 556: *mnḥy*.

|m-n(-n)| (1)	Culture word, Sem.: *mnyn(ʔ)* (Syr.) "weevil, horse fly"; *mūnu* (Akk.) "caterpillar"; *minana* (Arab.) "spider". Non-Sem.: **mVm=* (Berb.) "flea's eggs"; **min*(*n*)= (Cushitic) "tapeworm".[164]
mun "caterpillar"	•LL: **EB** *mu-núm* (in monol. list) → Sjöberg WO 27 22.

|m-n(-n)| (2)	Culture word. Non-Sem.: *maṇí=* (Vedic) "necklace".
maninn "a necklace"	•CTX: **Q** *ma-ni-in-nu*, *ma-ni-na* → Bottéro RA 44 120. **EA** *ma-ni-in-nu*, *ma-ni-in-na* → AHw 603: *maninnu*; CAD M/1 211f.: *maninnu*. **A4** *ma-ni-in-ni* → AHw 603: *maninnu*; CAD M/1 211f.: *maninnu*.

|m-n-w/y| (1)	Sem.: *mnh* (Hb. G) "to count", (D) "to apportion, allot", mnh (māneh) "mina", mnh (mānāh) "share, portion, fate"; *mnʔ* (Pun. unc.) "to count" (?); *mny* (Aram., Syr). "to count" (D) "to appoint, assign", *mnh*, *mnʔ*, *mnyʔ* (Aram., Syr.) "mina", *mnh*, *mntʔ* "part, portion", *mnh* (Syr.) "computation", *mnyn(ʔ)* (Aram., Syr.) "number, amount"; *mnh* (Palm.) "share, portion", *mnyn* (pl. Palm., Hatra) "mina"; *manû*(*m*) (Akk.) "to count, calculate, recite", *manû*(*m*) "mina", *mīnu*(*m*) "number", *minītu*(*m*), *mi*/*aniātum* "measure, dimension; limbs", *minûtu*(*m*) "count(ing), number; recitation", *munūtu*(*m*) "account, accounting"; *manan* (Arab.) "mina". Strong lexicalized basis in cstr. st. **mīn=* "number, amount" > prep. *mn* (*min*, Hb.) "away from, out of, since"; *mn* (Ph., *MIN*, *MON* Pun., Moab.) "from"; *mn*, *mi-in*(=) (Aram., Syr.) "from"; *min* (Arab.) "of, at, on, from, since"; *mn* (OSArab.) "from"; *men* (MSArab.) "from"; *ʔəm*(*ənna*) (Eth.) "from". Cf. further: *manā mānā* (Arab.) "to pay, reward", *manan*, *manīya* "destiny, lot". Non-Sem.: m a n a (Sum.) "mina"; *mnâ* (Gr.) id.
|**m-n-w/y**| **(A)** "to measure, count; deliver"	•CTX: **EB** G inf. cstr. *ma-na-ì* |manāʔi| → Fronzaroli ARET 13 173, 282; Fronzaroli / Catagnoti Fs. Pennachietti 297; Catagnoti QuSe 29 163, 209.

[163] Sivan / Cochavi-Rainey WSVES 80: *min-ḫi-tá* "gift"; Helck Beziehungen no. 91.
[164] Orel / Stolbova HSED 384 no. 1771: **min=* "worm".

	•ONOM: **EUPH** Unc. *ma-nu-um, la-ma-nu-um, ma-nu-tum, ma-nu-a-tum*; cf. *ma-am-nu-um* → Gelb CAAA 25, 153; Zadok Fs. Hallo 326 (See under |m-n-w/y| (2)). **A4** *ia-am-nu* → Dietrich / Loretz ZA 60 102 17:8; Sivan GAGl 248. **EG** Cf. *ʕ-n-ty-mn-ty, m-n:-n-ȝ* → Schneider APÄQ 73 no. 132, 126 no. 269-270.
min (D) "in, at, on"	•CTX: **EB** *mi-in* → Fronzaroli QuSe 15 8 (9); Tonietti QuSe 19 87ff., 93ff.; Catagnoti QuSe 29 97, 102, 112, 211.
minū "from"	•CTX: **EB** *mi-nu* → Archi Eblaitica 4 13f., PIHANS 106 100; Baldacci WO 16 16ff.; Fronzaroli QuSe 15 8 (9); ARET 11 160, ARET 13 283f.; Tonietti QuSe 19 83f.; QuSe 25 328f.; Catagnoti QuSe 29 97, 35, 97, 212.
manū "mina"	•CTX: **EG** *man-nu*$_2$ → Hoch SWET 127 no. 162.[165]
mn (C) "mina"	•CTX: **UGA** → DUL 554: *mn* (III).
mināt "portion, member"	•ONOM: **EM** Cf. *mi-na-tu*$_4$ → Pruzsinszky PTEm 89 [632].
mnt (A) "portion, ration; piece, member"	•CTX: **UGA** Suff. *mnty, mnth, mntk* → DUL 558: *mnt* (I) a; Tropper KWU 75: *mnt*$_1$.
mnt (B) "enumeration, list; spell, incantation"	•CTX: **UGA** Sg. *mnt*, suff. *mnty, mnthn* → DUL 558: *mnt* (I) b, c; Tropper KWU 75: *mnt*$_2$.

|m-n-w/y| (2)	Sem.: *manāʔum, menû(m), manû(m)* (Akk.) "to love", *minûtum* "desire, love"; *tamannā* (Arab.) "to wish, desire", *munya* "wish, desire"; *emtōni, metōni* (MSArab.) "to wish, desire"; *mny, tamannaya* (Eth.) id.
|m-n-w/y| (B) "to love"	•ONOM: **U3** *ma-na-um* → Buccellati Amorites 168; Gelb CAAA 25, 153; Wilcke WO 5 30f. **EUPH** *ma-na-wa* → Gelb CAAA 25, 153. **UGA** Cf. unc. *mn* → DUL 554: *mn* (V); *mnỉpʕl* → DUL 554; *mny* → DUL 559; *mnyn* → 559; *mnyy* → DUL 559.
maniy "(the) beloved; DN"	•ONOM: **EB** Cf. *má-ni, ma-ni-a, en-na-ma-ni, en-ma-nu, iš*$_{11}$*-ma-ni, lu-du-ma-nu, ma-ne-a-du, ma-ni-lu/lum, bíl-za-ma-ni, šar-ma-ni, ù-a-má-ne, zi-la-ma-ne, zu-ma-ne/ni* → Krebernik PET 96; Pagan ARES 3 140, 292, 306f., 342, 346, 348, 362, 371, 387, 389. **U3** *ma-ni-um, ma-ni-il* → Buccellati Amorites 168f.; Gelb CAAA 25, 153. **EUPH** *ma-ni-el* → Gelb CAAA 25, 153. **A7** Cf. *ma*(?)*-ni-*^{d}*da-gan* → Gelb CAAA 25, 153.
meny "(the) love; DN" (?)	•ONOM: **EB** *mi-ne, ù-na-mi-ne, a-ga-me/mi-nu, al*$_6$*-mi-nu, ti-ša-mi-nu, be-li-me-ni* → Krebernik PET 97; Catagnoti MARI 8 591; Pagan ARES 3 140, 277, 286, 351, 371f. **EUPH** *me-ni-tum* → Huffmon APNMT 231; Gelb CAAA 25, 155. **UGS** Unc. *ad-du-mi-nu* → Huffmon APNMT 231; Gröndahl PTU 159.[166]

|m-r-ʔ| (1)	Primary noun, Sem.: *mrʔ, mry(ʔ)* (Aram., Nab., Palm., Hatra, Syr.) "master", (Syr.) *myrʔ* "the Lord, God", *mrh, mrt, mrtʔ* (Palm., JAram., Hatra, Syr.) "mistress"; *marʔ, mirʔ, murʔ, imruʔ, imraʔ* (Arab.) "man", *marʔa, imraʔa* "woman", *murūʔa* "manhood, manliness comprising all knightly virtues";

[165] Sivan / Cochavi-Rainey WSVES 80: *min-nu*^{nù} "mina"; Helck Beziehungen no. 87.

[166] With a diff. derivation from |m-n-w/y| (1), unlikely.

	māru(m), *marʔu(m)*, *merʔum*, *mēru* (Akk.) "son, boy", *mārtu(m)*, *marʔatum*, *merʔa/etum* "daughter, girl". Non-Sem.: *mrw* (Eg.) "people"; **maʔar* (Chadic) "boy: uncle".[167]
marʔ, mār (the) master; DN"	•LL: **EB**.[168] •ONOM: **EB**[169] Cf. *en-mar*, *en-mar-ru*$_{12}$, *gi-ti-ma-ar*, *ma-la-gú-bí*(NE), *ma-la-ḫu*,[170] *ma-li-ì-a*, *ma-li-ì-lu*, *ma-ra-ì*, *ma-ra*-DINGIR(AN), *ma-rí-lum*, *mar-ga*, *mar-a*[171] → Pagan ARES 3 224, 306, 313, 348ff. **EUPH** *i-ṣi-ma-ri-e*; cf. unc. *ma-ru-ia-tum*, *ma-ri-a-nu-um*[172] → Gelb CAAA 25, 154.
murʔ (A) "a kind of cavalier or knight"	•CTX: **UGS** Sg. / pl. cstr. nom. / obl. LÚ(.MEŠ) *mur-u/ú/i*; pl. abs. LÚ(.MEŠ) *mur-ú-ma* |murʔūma| → Sivan GAGl 249; Huehnergard UVST 148f.; vSoldt SAU 305 (89).
maruʔ "a military position (involving horses)"	•CTX: **EG** *ma-ru*$_2$*-ʔu*, *ma-ru*$_2$*-ʔa*, *ma-r-ru*$_2$. → Hoch SWET 132ff. no. 173.[173] •ONOM: **EG**: *ma*$_4$*-ru*$_2$ → Hoch SWET 132ff. no. 173.
mr (A) "son"	•CTX: **UGA** Sg. cstr. *mr* → DUL 562: *mr* (V); Akkadianism.
mrů (A) "a kind of cavalier or knight"	•CTX: **UGA** Sg. *mrů*, *mri̊*; pl. *mrům*, *mri̊m*; cstr. *mrů*, *mri̊* → Richter BGH 533; DUL 564: *mrů* (III).
marʔiy "a regal garment" (?)	•CTX: **EB** Cf. pl. *ma-rí-a-tum/ti* TÚG.NU.TAG → Bonechi RA 110 66; Pasquali NABU 2018/58.

|m-r-ʔ| (2)	Sem.: *mrʔ* (Hb.) "to feed on the fat of the land, graze", *mryʔ* (*m^{e}rîʔ*) "fatted steer"; *mārû(m)*, *marāʔum* (Akk.) "to fatten", *marû(m)*, *marʔu(m)* "fattened", *mārû(m)* "animal fattener"; cf. *maraʔa*, *mariʔa*, *maruʔa* (Arab.) "to be(come) wholesome (food)", *marīʔ* "healthful".
|m-r-ʔ| "to fatten"	•CTX: **UGA** G prefc. *ymrů* → DUL 563.
marīʔ "fattened, fatling, dense"	•CTX: **EUPH** Cf. Ì *ma-ri-i* → Reculeau, NABU 2001/18. **UGS** *ma-ru-u* → Sivan GAGl 244. •ONOM: **EUPH** *ma-ru-li-el*, cf. unc. *ma-ru-ia-tum*, *ma-ri-a-nu-um*[174] → Gelb CAAA 25, 154. **UGS** Unc. *a-ḫa-ma-ra-nu* → Gröndahl PTU 304.[175]
murʔ (B) "a container for (fat) ointments"	•CTX: **EB** *mu-rúm*, *mu-lum* → Fronzaroli Fs. Limet 58; Pasquali QuSe 23 171.
mrů (B) "fattened, fatling"	•CTX: **UGA** Sg. *mri̊*, *mrå*, *mr{i̊}å*; fem. *mråt* (?); du. *mri̊m*; pl. cstr. *mri̊*, suff. *mri̊h*, *mrik* → 563: *mrů* (I).
mrů (C) "animal fattener"	•CTX: **UGA** Sg. *mri̊*; pl. *mrům* → DUL 564: *mrů* (II).

[167] Orel / Stolbova HSED 377 no. 1740: **mar= / maraʔ=* "man".

[168] For EB SAGxTAG$_4$ = *ma-al*$_6$*-a-tum* see Conti QuSe 17 110 \|malaxtum\| (\|m-l-x\|); diff. Krebernik ZA 73 46f. \|marʔatum\| "daughter".

[169] For an altern. explanation "(the) strong (one); DN" see *marr* under \|m-r-r\| (2).

[170] Altern. *malaḫḫu* "sailor" (Pagan ARES 348); unlikely.

[171] Altern. (Akk.) "the son".

[172] See altern. *maruʔ* "fattened" under \|m-r-ʔ\| (2).

[173] Sivan / Cochavi-Rainey WSVES 80: *ma-rú-ʔe* "groom, squire"; Helck Beziehungen 95.

[174] See altern. *marʔ*, *mār* "(the) master; DN" under \|m-r-ʔ\| (1).

[175] Cf. Gelb MAD 3 182: *marānum*. Diff.: Sivan GAGl 244: MARRU "strong, mighty".

|m-r-d|	Sem.: *mrd* (Hb.) "to rise in revolt, rebel", *mrd* (*mered*) "rebellion", *mrdwt* (*mardût*) id.;[176] *mrd* (Aram., Syr.) "to rebel", *mrd* (Aram., JAram.) "rebellious", *mryd* (Syr.) id., *mrd(?)* (JAram., Syr.) "rebellion", *mrwdw(t?)* (Syr.) "resistance".
mard "bold, audacious"	•ONOM: **EUPH** *ma-ar-du, ma-ar-da-at* → Zadok Fs. Hallo 326; Streck Onomastikon 1 105 § 1.95.
murd "resistance"	•ONOM: **EUPH** *mu-ut-mu-ur-di* → Zadok Fs. Hallo 326.
ʔamrad "very bold, audacious"	•ONOM: **EG** Cf. *pꜣ-y:-m-rw-d, pꜣ-y:-m-r-d* → Schneider APÄQ 104 no. 211.

|m-r-d-D|	Culture word, etym. unc.; Sem.: *mardatu(m), mardutu* (Akk.) "rug, tapestry".[177] Non-Sem.: **mardade=* "kind of rug or tapestry" (Hurr.); **mardado=ɣl=* (Hurr.) "rug maker".[178]
mardad, mardat, mardet "rug, tapestry"	•CTX: **EUPH** Passim; cf. (TÚG) *mar-da-at*, (TÚG) *mar-da-tum* → AHw 611; CAD M/1 277f.; Durand ARM 30 61ff. **Q** TÚG *: mar-da-du, mar-da-ti-šu, mar-da-te-na* → Richter / Langhe Idadda 83, 85, 193; Vita / Watson NABU 2016/60. **UGS** TÚG *m]ar-de₄-tu* → Huehnergard UVST 177 (? RDY).
mardadoɣl "rug maker"	•CTX: **Q** *mar-da-du-ḫu-ul-la* → Richter AoF 32 39; Richter / Langhe Idadda 91. **A4** LÚ.(MEŠ) *mar-dá-tu-ḫu-li* → AHw 611: CAD M/1 278; Dietrich / Loretz WO 3 192; Giacumakis AkkAl 87; Mayer UF 9 189; Richter AoF 32 39f.
mrdt "rug, tapestry"	•CTX: **UGA** Sg. *mrdt*, pl. *mrdt* → DUL 566.

|m-r-ħ|
See |**r-m-ħ**|

|m-r-x|	Sem.: *mrḥ* (Hb.) "to spread on (ointment)"; (JAram.) "to smooth (with plaster)"; *maraḫa* (Arab.) "to oil, anoint".
|**m-r-x**| "to be coated"	•CTX: **UGA** Ct suffc. *šmrḫt* → DUL 567f.: /*m-r-ḫ*/.

|m-r-x-S|	Culture word, Sem. etym. unknown.[179]
marxaS (A), marxuS "a stone (alabastron)"	•**CTX**: **TU** *ma-ar-ḫa-šu-um* → Krebernik Tall Bi`a 55f. (54:15). **EM** NA₄ *mar-ḫu-šú* → Arnaud Emar 6.3 277 (282:24). **UGS** NA₄ *mar-ḫa-šu* → AHw 611:*marḫu/ašu(m)*; CAD M/1 280f.: *marḫušu*.[180]

[176] Cf. PNN *mrd* (*mered*, Hb.): "audax; audacity"; *mrd* (Palm.): id.

[177] See Mayer UF 9 178ff. for Nuzi-Akk., MAss. and NAss. instances.

[178] Laroche GLH 168; Dietrich / Loretz WO 3 192; AHw 611; CAD M/1 278; Richter AoF 32 39ff., BGH 246 (*mardade*, Qatna: 'Hurrizität nicht sicher').

[179] Despite Hb. *mrḥšt* (*marḥešet*, Hb.) "baking pan" no clear semantic relation can be established to *rḥš* (Aram., Syr.) "to creep"; *raḫāšu(m)* (Akk.) "to move" (?); *taraḫḫaš, ʔirtaḫaš* (Arab.) "to get disturbed, upset". Cf. Mari-Akk. GIŠ *mar-ḫu-še*, Eidem FM (Mém. NABU 1) 53 [A.55]: 15 "bois-*m*.", and GU₄ *i-na mar-ḫa-ši-im*, Durand ARM 21 15:12 / 16:14'. *Marḫašu* probl. denotes several items considered original from or typical of the Iranian countries Marḫuš and / or Marḫasi (Durand LAPO 16 76, 79 fn. g; lexical sections of AHw 611:*marḫu/ašu(m)*; CAD M/1 280f.: **marḫašû, marḫušu*).

[180] Read NA₄ *mar-ḫa-lì* in EA 25 I 52.

marxaS (B), marxiS (A) "a dagger, slice"

•CTX: **EUPH** *ma-ar-ḫa-šu*(*m*), (GÍR) *mar-ḫa-šu*(*m*), GÍR *mar-ḫi-šum* → Durand LAPO 16 413; Arkhipov ARM 32 114f.

marxaSt, marxiS (B) "an utensil; spade"

•CTX: **EB** *mar-ḫa-sa-da* → Lahlouh / Catagnoti ARET 12 562; Pasquali Or 83 271.
UGS Cf. *mar-ḫi-iš* → Huehnergard UVST 163 (?ʕŠY), 179 (?RḪŠ).
•LL: **EB** GIŠ.MAR.ḪAŠ.RU.URUDU = *mar-ḫaš-tum*, *mar-ḫa-iš*$_{11}$*-tum*, *mar-ḫa-áš-tum* → Conti QuSe 17 14, 139; Pasquali Or 83 274.

|m-r-ḳ| (1)

Primary noun, Sem.: *māraq* (Hb.) "broth"; *maraq* (Arab.) id.; *maraq* (Eth.) id.

marḳ "broth"

•LL: **EB** A.AKA = *mar-gúm*, *ma-la-gu-um* → Conti QuSe 17 167; Catagnoti QuSe 29 29, 210.

|m-r-ḳ| (2)

Sem.: Cf. *maraqa* (Arab.) "to go or pass through; to pierce, penetrate".

tamriḳ "crossing, passing" (?)

•LL: **EB** ZÀḪ (A.ḪA) = *dam-rí-gu* → Conti QuSe 17 39, 169.[181]

|m-r-m-x(-x)|

Culture word, Sem.: *marmaḫḫu*(*m*) (Akk.) "a fruit tree".

marmax(x) "a fruit tree"

•CTX: **EUPH** Du. GIŠ *mar-ma-ḫe-en* → Durand NABU 1989/26.

|m-r(-r)| (1)

Sem.: *marra* (Arab.) "to pass through, go, walk". See further: *mwr* (Hb. N, C) "to (ex)change"; (Syr.) "to exchange valuables, to buy".

|m-r(-r)| (A) "to go away, leave; to travel through; to desist"

•CTX: **EA** G prefc. *im-ru-ur-mi* (Akkadianized form); C prefc. *yu-ša-am-ri-ir*, *tu-ša-am-ri-ru*, imp. *šu-um-*[*ri-ir*][182] → AHw 609 (III ug. Fw.), CAD M/1 268; Sivan GAGl 180, 249, Moran AmL 148, 176; Rainey CAT 1 159.
UGS G pref. cf. *i-mar-ru-ur* → Sivan GAGl 249.
UGA G prefc. *amr*, *tmr*; suffc. (?) *mrr*; imp. *mr* → DUL 569: /*m-r*(*-r*)/ (I).

s^{1}mrr (A) "expulsion, repelling" (?)

•CTX: **UGA** → Tropper KWU 121, UG 601, 679. Diff. DUL 818: *šmrr* "poisoning, poison"; see |m-r-r| (2).

|m-r(-r)| (2)

Sem.: *mrr* (Hb.): "to be bitter, hard, painful", *mr* (*mar*) "bitter(ness)", *m*(*w*)*r* (*mor*, *môr*) "myrrh", *mrh* (*morāh*) "bitterness, sorrow", *mrr* (*māror*) "bitter", *mrrh* (*m*^{e}*rērāh*, *m*^{e}*rorāh*) "gall-bladder, bile, poison", *mmr* (*memer*) "bitterness"; *mrr* (Aram., Syr.) "to be bitter", *mrmr* (Syr.) "to make bitter", exacerbate", *mi-ir-ra-ʔ* (Warka-Aram.) "poison", (JAram., Syr.) *mrr*(*ʔ*) "bitterness, gall, poison", *mryr* (Aram., Syr.) "bitter", *mrrh*, *mrrtʔ* "gall-bladder", *mwr*(*ʔ*) (JAram., Syr.) "myrrh"; *marāru(m)* (Akk.): "to be bitter, to prevail", *marru*(*m*) "bitter", *martu*(*m*) "gall (bladder), bile", *murru* "bitterness; myrrh", *marmar*(*r*)*u* "strong";

---

[181] Altern. rdg A.KU6 = *dam-rí-gu*; cf. Sjöberg Fs. Wilcke 257: "broth" and see here |m-r-ḳ| (1). See also Bonechi JNES 79 330 fn. 38.

[182] EA 185:74. Diff. Moran AmL 266f. n. 11: "*he will make (him) fl*[*ee*] from him", syntax ("converted perfect"?) and meaning (banishment?) uncertain; Rainey EAC "he caused apostasy from him".

marra, marāra, ʔamarr (Arab.): "to be bitter", *marrara* "to make bitter", *ʔamarra* "to fight"; *ʔistamarra* "to become strong, firm", *mirra* "strength vigor", *mirra, marāra* "gall, bile", *murr* "myrrh, bitter", *marīr* "strong", *marāra* "bitterness, gall-bladder"; *mrrt* (OSArab.) "myrrh"; *mer* (MSArab.) "bowel", *merrét, merrāt* "bile, gall; strength"; *mrr, marara, marra* (Eth.) "to be bitter, embittered", *marir* "bitter, ferocious", *mərur* "bitter", *mərar, mərrat* "bitterness, rancor".
Non-Sem.: *ʕmȝ* (Eg.): "to be sour"; **mar* (West Chadic): "sour";[183] *mýrra* (Gr.) "myrrh".

|m-r(-r)| (B) "to strengthen, fortify"
•CTX: **EUPH** D prefc. *i nu-ma-ri-ir* → Lackenbacher NABU 1987/82; ARM 26/2 419f. (483: 25); Zadok Fs. Hallo 326; Durand MARI 7 53f.; Streck Onomastikon 1 106 § 1.95.
EM D prefc. *ú-ma-ri-ir* → Pentiuc p. 188; Ikeda BiOr 60 269.[184]
UGA G prefc. *åmr, tmr*; *ymr*, suff. *åmrkm, tmrn, tmrnn, ymrm*; N ptc. *nmrrt*; R prefc. *åmrmrn* → DUL 569f.: /m-r(-r)/ (II).
•ONOM: **EUPH** Cf. unc. *ma-ra-rum/ru-um* → Gelb CAAA 153 (unexplained);[185] further: IA-*ma-ra*, IA-*ma-rum* |yimar(r)=| (?) → Gelb CAAA 72.[186]
UGS Cf. *ma-ar-ka-bu*-TI(*dì*?) → Gröndahl PTU 148, 159f.[187]
UGA *ymrm*[188], *ymrn* → DUL 954.
EG Cf. *m-:r-rw-y* → Schneider APÄQ 130 no. 277.

marr (A) "strong, valiant, hero"
•ONOM: **EB**[189] *gi-ti-ma-ar, en-mar-ru*₁₂, *ma-la-gú-bí*(NE), *ma-la-ḫu*,[190] *ma-li-ì-a, ma-li-ì-lu, ma-ra-ì, ma-ra*-DINGIR(AN), *ma-rí-lum, mar-ga, mar-a*,[191] *mar-la-a-ḫu* → Pagan ARES 140, 313, 348ff.
A4 *ma-ri-ia, ma-ri-a-at-ti, ša-di-ma-ra* → Dietrich / Loretz ZA 60 94 8:40; 96 9:26; 99 13:9; Sivan GaGl 244.[192]
UGS *a-ḫa-ma-ra-nu* → Sivan GAGl 244.

murr "bitter(ness); myrrh"
•CTX: **EA** ŠIM.ZAR.MEŠ *: mu-ur-ra* → AHw 676; CAD M/2 221; Sivan GAGl 250.
•LL: **EB** ŠE.MUNU₄ = *mu-ru*₁₂*-um, mu-ru*₁₂ → Conti QuSe 17 178.[193]

mr (B) "bitter; strong; valiant"
•CTX: **UGA** Sg. *mr*, suff. *mrm* → DUL 562: *mr* (II), (IV).
•ONOM: **UGA** Cf. *mrådn* → DUL 564, *mrʕm* → DUL 565, *mrnn* → DUL 569, *mršp* → DUL 571.

mr (C) "myrrh; bitterness"
•CTX: **UGA** Sg. *mr*, pl. *mrm* → DUL 561f.: *mr* (I), (III).

mrrt "myrrh; bile (?)"
•CTX: **UGA** → DUL 570: *mrrt* (I), (II).
•ONOM: **UGA** Unc. elem. of the mythical TN *mrrt tġll bnr* → DUL 570f.: *mrrt* (III).[194]

---

[183] Orel / Stolbova 376 no. 1734: **mar=* "to be sour".
[184] WSem. lexeme with Akk. Morphology.
[185] Cf. Zadok OLA 28 97: Hb. PN *mᵉrārî.*
[186] Gelb CAAA 14: ʔ?MR, verb, B: *yaʔmr*, 72: stem *ʔmar*. For Hb. PN *ymrh* (*Yimrāʰ*) see Zadok OLA 28 130. IA-*ma-rum* could also be understood as |yamma=rūm(imp.)|.
[187] Unless Akk. *mār* cstr. st. "son of". Diff. Sivan GAGl 244: MARKABU.
[188] Or |yammu=rām| (adj., stat.), |yamma=rūm| (imp.)?
[189] Altern. explanations: *marʔ, mār* "(the) master; DN" under |m-r-ʔ| (1).
[190] Altern. *malaḫḫu* "sailor" (Pagan ARES 348); unlikely.
[191] Altern. "the son" (Akk.).
[192] Connections with |m-r-ʔ| (2) "to fatten" or Akk. *māru(m)* (cf. |m-r-ʔ| (1)) "son" are also possible for these spellings.
[193] Perhaps: "un tipo di malto amaro".

marmarr "very strong"	•CTX: **EB** *mar-ma-ru*$_{12}$*-lum* → Fronzaroli ARET 13 109, 282, 315; Catagnoti QuSe 29 91, 114, 209. •LL: **EB** Cf. Ú.KISAL = *mar-mar*-LUM → Conti QuSe 17 115.[195]
s^{1}mrr (B) "poisoning, poison" (?)	•CTX: **UGA** → DUL 818: *šmrr*. Diff. Tropper KWU 121, UG 601, 679: "Verjagung, Vertreibung" (?); see |m-r(r)| (1).
tamrir "bitter (cosmetic oil)"	•CTX: **EUPH** Ì *tam-ri-ru* → AHw 1316; CAD T 146; Joannès MARI 7 253.

|m-r(-r)| (3)	Culture word, Sem.: Cf. *marratu*(*m*) (Akk.) "a chain" (?).
marat "kind of chain" (?)	•CTX: **EB** *ma-ra-tum, ma-la-tum* → Pasquali QuSe 23 167f.

|m-r-r| (4)	Culture word, Sem.: *mr*(*?*) (JAram., Syr.) "a type of hoe"; *marru*(*m*) (Akk.) "shovel, spade"; *marr* (Arab.) "(iron) shovel". Non-Sem.: mar (Sum.) "shovel"; *mr* (Eg.) "to dig".
marr (B) "a trade"	•CTX: **EB** Cf. *mar-rúm, mar-lum* → Lahlouh / Catagnoti ARET 12 562; Pasquali Or 83 274.

|m-r-S| Cf. **|s-r-θ|**,	Sem.: *mrs* (JAram., Syr.) "to crush, stir, steep", (Syr. D) "to macerate", *mwrs*(*?*) (Syr.) "maceration", *marāsu* (Akk.) "to mix, mash", *mersu*(*m*), *mirsu*(*m*) "(a cake) ingredients: dates, sesame, oil, etc."; *marasa* (Arab.) "to soak, macerate", *maraṯa* "to moisten, dampen"; *marasa* (Eth.) "to moisten, steep".
merīθu "steep, mixed drink"	•CTX: **EG** *mer-su*$_2$ → Hoch SWET 140f. no. 183.[196]
mrθ (A) "steep, mixed drink"	•CTX: **UGA** → DUL 571f.: *mrṯ* (I).

|m-r-s^1|	Culture word, Sem.: *maršu*(*m*), *marašu* (Akk.) "leather strap".
marS, maraS "lace, string"	•CTX: **EB** *mar-šum, ma-ra-šum* → Pasquali QuSe 23 166.

|m-r-ṣ|	Sem.: *mrṣ* (Hb.) "to be bad, painful"; *mrʕ* (Aram., Syr.) "to be sick", *mrwʕ*(*t?*), *mwrʕn*(*?*) (Syr.) "sickness"; *marāṣu*(*m*) (Akk.) "to fall ill, become arduous; care for, be concerned", *marṣu*(*m*) "sick, troublesome", *murṣu*(*m*) "illness, sorrow, distress"; *mariḍa* (Arab.) "to become diseased, sick", *maraḍ* "sickness", *marīḍ* "sick, unwell, indisposed"; *mrḍ* (OSArab.) "suffer from disease", *mrḍ* "sickness".

194 As for Ug. *ảmr* / KUR(.MEŠ) *a-mur-ri* (TN) and *ảmrr* (DN) see DUL 69f.: *ảmr* (III), and 70f.: *ảmrr*. For the TN "Amurru" cf. further Streck Onomastikon 1 26 § 1.8.

195 Sjöberg Fs. Kienast 545f.: the mng of *mar-mar*-LUM is still unknown.

196 Delete the reference (loc.cit. fn. 57) to Akk. *mêrištum* "must"; see CAD Š/3 421: "supplies".

|m-r-ş| "to be worried, concerned"

•ONOM: **EUPH** *ia-em-ri-ṣum, ia-am-ra-aṣ, a-am-ra-zum, ia-am-ra-aṣ-*DINGIR, *ia-am-ra-zi-*DINGIR, *ia-am-ru-uṣ-*DINGIR, *ia-am-ru-iṣ-*DINGIR, *i-ia-am-ru-uṣ-zi-i-lu-um, yu-um-ra-aṣ-*DINGIR, *yu-um-ra-zi-*DINGIR → Gelb CAAA 25, 157; Zadok Fs. Hallo 326; Streck Onomastikon 1 155 § 2.7 fn. 3, 168 § 2.35 fn. 2, 199 § 2.95, 203 § 2.95, 229 § 2.138238 § 2.153; Golinets Onomastikon 2 40, 51, 109f., 408.
R *yu-um-ra-aṣ-*DINGIR → Gelb CAAA 25, 157; Dalley / Walker / Hawkins Tell Rimah 260; Golinets Onomastikon 2 110, 408.

|m-r-ṣ| "to fall ill"

•CTX: **UGA** G suffc. *mrṣ*, inf. → DUL 571: */m-r-ṣ/*.

maraş, maruş "worried, angry; the angry one (also as DN)"

•ONOM: **EB** *mar-za-ì* → Pagan ARES 3 141, 350.
U3 *ma-ra-zum* → Buccellati Amorites 169; Gelb CAAA 25, 153; Wilcke WO 5 28; Streck Onomastikon 1 203 § 2.95; Golinets Onomastikon 2 150, 408.
EUPH *ma-ar-za-ia, ma-ra-su-um, a-ḫi-ma-ra-aṣ/uṣ,* ⁽ᵈ⁾*ḫa-li-ma-ra-aṣ, a-bi-ma-ra-aṣ, a-da/ta-ma-ra-aṣ, i-da-ma-ra-aṣ, bi-ni-ma-ra-aṣ, bi-ni-ma-ra-zi, bu-ni-ma-ra-aṣ, zi-ik-ru-ma-ra-az, mar-za-tum, ma-ar-za-ta, um-mi-mar-ṣa-at, ia-tum-mar-za, i-ia-tum-ma-ar-za-at, ki-ma-ru-uṣ, ia-ḫa-ad-ma-ra-aṣ, ki-il-a-ma-ra-aṣ, ki-la-ma-ra-aṣ, ki-na-ma-ra-ṣu* → Huffmon APNMT 233; Gelb CAAA 25, 153; Streck Onomastikon 1 141 § 1.123a, 162 § 2.22, 171 § 2.38, 179 § 2.59, 191 § 2.88 fn. 3, 197 § 2.95, 203 § 2.95, 220 § 2.119, 267 § 3.14, 271 § 3.18, 354 § 5.83, 360 Suppl.; Golinets Onomastikon 2 142, 149f., 408.

mrş "illness"

•CTX: **UGA** → DUL 571.

|m-r-ṭ|

Sem.: Cf. *mrṭ* (Hb.) "to pull out hair"; *mrṭ* (Aram., Syr.) "to pluck out", *mrṭ* (JAram.) "baldness", (Syr.) "goat hair; feather", *mrṭwn(?)* "little feather"; *marāṭu* (Akk.) "to scratch, scrape off"; *maraṭa* (Arab.) "to tear out, pull out", *marīṭ* "hairless"; *maraṭa* (Eth.) "to uproot, pull out". See further: *mlṭ* (*hitmalleṭ*, Hb.) "to be bald"; *malaṭa* (Arab.) "to shave".

|m-r-ṭ| "to be plucked out, be bald" (?)

•ONOM: **UGA** Cf. *mrṭn* → DUL 571.

|m-r-z-ħ|

Culture word, Sem.: *mrzḥ* (*marzēᵃḥ*, Hb.) "cultic celebration"; *mrzḥ* (Ph., Nab., Palm.) "religious feast", *mrzḥw, mrzḥwtʔ* (Palm.) "presidency of the *m.*"; *mrzḥ(?)* (JAram.) "funerary banqueting society".

marza/iħ "cultic association, (cultic) banquet"

•CTX: **EB** Cf. UGULA *mar-za-*u_9, LÚ *mar-za-*u_9, *mar-za-*u_9 EN → Edzard ARET 2 133; Archi ARET 1 31 (3 v. 3); Waetzoldt MEE 12 37 v XIV 30; Archi NABU 2005/41; Miralles Marzeah 51ff.[197]
EM LÚ.MEŠ *mar(!)-za-ḫu* → Fleming Installation 269; Pentiuc Vocabulary 124f.
UGS Cf. (É) LÚ.MEŠ *mar-za-i(-ma)*, LÚ.MEŠ *mar-zi-i*, LÚ.MES *mar-zi-ḫi* → AHw 617: *marzaʔu*; CAD M/I 321: *marziʔu* (*marzaʔu, marziḫu*); Sivan GAGl 245; Huehnergard UVST 178, 272; vSoldt SAU 305 (90); Tropper UG 171, 176.
•ONOM: **EM** Elem. |marzaħān| in MN ITI *mar-za-ḫa-ni* |marzaħān| → Pentiuc Vocabulary 124f.

mrzħ "cultic association, (cultic) banquet"

•CTX: **UGA** Sg. *mzrḥ*, suff. *mzrḥh* → DUL 574: *mrzḥ*.

mrzʕy "divine or cultic title"

•CTX: **UGA** → DUL 573f.

---

[197] PN according to Pagan ARES 3 168f. (unlikely).

|m-r-y|

Sem.: Cf. *mry* (Syr. D) "to embitter", (C) "to rebel, provoke", *mry* (JAram.) "rebellion", *mwrwn* "rebellious person"; *mārā* (Arab.) "to wrangle, dispute, contest", *mi/urya, mirāʔ* "quarrel, dispute".

mumrāt "rebellion"

•LL: **EB** ŠU.NI.RU = *mu-mu-la-tum, mu-mu-ra-tum* → Sjöberg Fs. Wilcke 256.

|m-r-y-n|

Culture word, Sem.: *mariyannu* (Nuzi-, Bogh. Akk.)[198] "a caste of warriors (chariot drivers)".
Non-Sem. **márya=* (Old Indo-Aryan) "(young) man";[199] *marianni, mariyanni* (Hurr.) "elite class of chariot drivers".[200]

maryann "knight titular of a war-chariot"

•CTX: **A4** cf. *ma-ri-ia-nu, ma-ri-i-an-nu, ma-ri-ia-an-nu, ma-ri-ia-an-ni, ma-ri-ia-an-na, ma-ri-ia-ni-na* → Wiseman AT 162; Dietrich /Loretz WO 89f., 93; Giacumakis AkkAl 87; Illingworth Iraq 50 104; Zeeb AOAT 282 22ff., 473; vDassow UF 34 842ff., 879, SCCNH 18 268ff.; Niedorf AOAT 352 18f., 130ff., 220ff. and passim; Wilhelm KlBHurr 137; Yamada NABU 2014/92.
Q *ma-ri-ia-an-ni*, LÚ.MEŠ *mar-ia-ni-na*, LÚ.MEŠ *ma-ri-ia-nu*, LÚ.MEŠ *ma-ri-ia-an-nu* → Richter / Lange Idadda 184.
EM LÚ *mar-ia-an-nu*, LÚ *mar-ia-nu-ut-ti* → Pentiuc Vocabulary 123f.; Pruzsinszky PTEm 10 fn. 51.
UGS *mar-ia-nu*, LÚ(.MEŠ) *mar-ia-nu*, LÚ.MEŠ *mar-ia-ne*, LÚ.MEŠ *mar-ia-an-ni*, LÚ *mar-ia-nu-ma*, LÚ.MEŠ *mar-ia-ni-ma*,[201] LÚ.MEŠ *mar-ia-nu-ka*, LÚ.MEŠ *mar-ia-nu-ti* → Sivan GAGl 245; Huehnergard UVST 149, 256, 296; vSoldt BiOr 46 648, SAU 427; DUL 572f.: *mryn* (I).
EG *m(a)-ra-ya-na, ma*$_{3/4}$*-ra-ya-na, ma*$_{3}$*-ra-ya-n, ma—r-ya-na* → Hoch SWET 135ff. no. 175.[202]
•ONOM: **R** *ma-ri-an-nu/ni* → Saporetti OnomMAss 1 317.
UGS *mar-ia-nu, ma-ri-ia/ya-na* → Gröndahl PTU 29, 160; DUL 573: *mryn* (II).

mryn "knight titular of a war-chariot"

•CTX: **UGA** Sg. *mryn*; pl. *mrynm* → DUL 572f.: *mryn* (I).
•ONOM: **UGA** *mryn* → Richter BGH 533f.; DUL 573f.: *mryn* (II).

|m-S-G|
See **|m-s**[1]**-k| (1)**

|m-S-H|

Culture word, only WSem. attestations; probl. Hurr.

maSH "a kind of bead or ring"

•CTX: **EA** *ma-áš-ḫu* → AHw 625; CAD M/1 365; Moran AmL 42 fn. 9; Rainey EAC 1350.
Q *ma-aš-ḫu* → AHw 625; CAD M/1 365; Richter / Langhe Idadda 170.[203]
A4 *ma-áš-ḫé* → AHw 625; CAD M/1 365; Giacumakis AkkAl 88.

---

198 See in addition Alalaḫ, Emar, Ugarit: *maryann*, below.
199 Pokorny IEW 738f.
200 Laroche GLH 168. For the LÚ *mariyannū* in Hitt. sources (Masat Höyük) see R.H. Beal, The organisation of the Hittite military (T Heth 20), 1992, 182f. See Richter BGH 244ff.; Wilhelm KlBHurr 136ff.
201 KTU 4.69 I (r.e.) 29; see Roche PIHANS 114 112 fn. 43; Loretz AOAT 386 84f., 88.
202 Sivan / Cochavi-Rainey WSVES 80: *ma-r-ya-na* "chariot warrior"; Helck Beziehungen no. 96.
203 TT 62 21; wrong rdg *maš-ḫu* 184.

|m-s-k| Cf. **|m-z-g|**	Sem.: *msk* (Hb.) "to mix, reconstitute", *msk* (*mesek*) "spiced drink", *mmsk* (*mimsak*) "jug of spiced wine".
|m-s-k| "to mix, combine"	•CTX: **UGA** G prefc. *ymsk* → DUL 575.
msk "mixture, mixed wine"	•CTX: **UGA** Sg. *msk*, *mẓ*$_2$*k* (allomorph); suff. *mskh* → DUL 575.
mskt "mixture, emulsion"	•CTX: **UGA** → DUL 575.
mmskn "earthenware bowl, jug"	•CTX: **UGA** → DUL 553.

|m-S-r| (1)	Culture word, Sem.: Cf. *namṣāru(m)* (Akk.) "a sword".[204]
mamṣar "knife, sword"	•CTX: **UGS** 2 URUDU *ma-am-ṣa-ar bu-li* → Sivan GAGl 243; Huehnergard UVST 148; vSoldt SAU 305 (81); Tropper UG 173.
maðarāna "a weapon" (?)	•CTX: **EG** Cf. *m-ḏa-ra-na*$_2$ → Hoch SWET 178 no. 241.
mðrn "(broad)sword"	•CTX: **UGA** Sg. *mḏrn*, pl. *mḏrnm* → Richter BGH 532; DUL 524: *mḏrn*; Del Olmo AuOr 37 291.

|m-s-r| (2)	Sem.: *msr* (JAram., Syr.) "to deliver; to appoint, entrust"; (Hb. N) "to be picked out"; *māsara* (Eth.) "to cause someone to grasp".
|m-s-r| "to deliver up"	•ONOM: **EUPH** Cf. G prefc. *im-sú-rum*, C prefc. (?) *ia-am-zi-ru* → Gelb CAAA 25, 157; Zadok Fs. Hallo 326.

|m-S-S/w/y| (1)	Sem.: *mss* (Hb. N) "to melt"; *msms* (JAram.) "to dissolve"; *mašša* (Arab.) "to macerate, soak in water". See further: *msh* (Hb. C) "to cause to melt"; *msy* (JAram., Syr.) "to melt"; *masā* (*masy*, Arab.) "to emaciate", *masawa*, *maswa* (Eth.) "to melt".
|m-s-S| "to liquefy, dissolve"	•CTX: **UGA** Gpass / N prefc. *ymsś*, tD suffc. suff. (?) *tmsm* → Tropper UG 42, 48, 103, 537; DUL 576: */m-s-s(/ś)/*.
mss "sap, juice" (?)	•CTX: **UGA** → DUL 576.
ms^{1}ms^1 "marsh" (?)	•CTX: **UGA** → Renfroe ALASP 5 132f.; DUL 585: *mšmš*.

|m-S(-S)| (2)	Culture word, Sem: *ms* (*mas*, Hb.) "forced labour, corvée, conscription".[205]
maS(S) "corvée worker"	•CTX: **A7** LÚ.MEŠ *ma-si/zi* → AHw 619; CAD M/1 327; Sivan GAGl 245. **EA** LÚ.MEŠ *ma-as-sà* MEŠ → AHw 619; CAD M/1 327; Sivan GAGl 245; Rainey EAT 81, CAT 1 16f.

---

204 Western diffusion through Hurrian. No obvious connection with Akk. *maṣāru(m)*, mng unc. "to stride about" (?).

205 Note that Eth. *mənśāʔ* "gift" is not to be compared with with Hb. *mas* "forced labour" (Leslau CDG 404; against HALOT 603).

|m-S-S-w|	Culture word, Sem.: Cf. *massû(m)* (Akk.) "leader, expert". Non-Sem.: m a s s u (Sum.) "leader, expert".
mswn "a high official, leader, expert" (?)	•CTX: **UGA** Sg. *mswn*, suff. *mswnh* → DUL 576f.
|m-S-ṭ|	Sem.: *muštu, multu, mušdu* (Akk.) "comb"; *mušṭ* (Arab., probl. a loan) "comb", *mašaṭa, maššaṭa* "to comb". See also *mašadu(m)* (Akk.) "to comb (cloth, wool)",[206] *mušāṭu(m)* "hair combings".
muSṭ "comb"	•CTX: **EUPH** GIŠ *mu-uš-ṭum, mu -uš-ṭà-tim* → Arkhipov ARM 32 137.
muSāṭ "comb"	•LL: **EB** GIŠ.ZUM = *mu-sa-tum* → Sjöberg Fs. Pettinato 276; Pasquali Or 83 274.
muSṭāt "comb"	•CTX: **EG** *ma-ša-di-di-t, ma-ša-di* (pl.?) → Hoch SWET 164f. no. 212: |muštāta|.[207]
|m-S-w|	Culture word. No adequate isoglosses traced.
maSwat, maSuwt "a type of tree or wood"	•CTX: **UGS** Cf. GIŠ *ma-ás-wa-tu*, pl. GIŠ.MEŠ *: ma-ás-wa-tu*, GIŠ.MEŠ *: ma-sa-wa-tu* → Huehnergard UVST 147f., ^{2}UVST 393; vSoldt SAU 305: "cypress" (?).[208] •LL: **EB** Cf. Ú.KUR = *ma-su-tum, ma-sa-tù-um* → Sjöberg Fs. Kienast 545; see also Catagnoti Fs. Scandone Matthiae 140.
|m-ṣ-d|	Primary noun, Sem.: Hb. *mṣwd(h)* (*māṣôd, m^{e}ṣûdāh*, Hb.) "mountain stronghold";[209] *mṣd(?), mṣdh, mṣdt?, mṣwdh* (JAram.) "fortress, fortified position"; *maṣād* (Arab.) "refuge, shelter; summit, top".
mṣd (A) "large fortified tower" (?)	•CTX: **UGA** sg. suff. *mṣdh* → DUL 578: *mṣd* (II). •ONOM: **UGA** Cf. TN *mṣd* → DUL 578: *mṣd* (III).
|m-ṣ-x| See **|m-x-ṣ|**	
|m-ṣ-r| See **|m-S-r|**	
|m-ṣ-ṣ|	Sem.: *mṣṣ* (Hb., JAram., Syr.) "to slurp, lap; to suck"; *maṣṣa* (Arab., Eth.) "to suck, suckle". See further: *myṣ* (*mîṣ*, Hb.) "pressing", *mwṣ* (JAram.) "to suck", *mṣy* (Syr.) "to squeeze, suck".
mṣṣ "one who sucks"	•CTX: **UGA** → DUL 582.

[206] Only LL and OAss. with this meaning.
[207] Sivan / Cochavi-Rainey WSVES 81: *ma-šá-di* "to hollow"; Helck Beziehungen no. 123; Kilani VGW 121: \|mvšd'o:dv\|.
[208] Huehnergard UVST 148 accepts with some reserves a connection with Syriac *msutā* "cypress".
[209] Together with TN *mṣd*.

|m-s^1-ħ|	Sem.: *mšḥ* (Hb.) "to smear, anoint", mšḥh (*mašḥāh, mišḥāh*) "anointing", *mšyḥ* (*māšîḥ*) "anointed"; *mšḥ* (Pun.) "to anoint"; *mšḥ* (Aram., Syr.) "to anoint", *mšḥ(ʔ)* "oil", *mšyḥ(ʔ)* "anointed one"; *muššuʔu* (Akk.) "to rub", *muššuʔtu* "ointment", *masaḥa* (Arab.) "to rub, anoint", *masḥa* "rubbing, anointing"; *masḥa, massəḥa, maśḥa* (Eth.) "to anoint", *məsuḥ, mas/śiḥ* "anointed".
|**m-S-ħ**| "to rub, anoint, oil"	•CTX: **EB** G suffc. du. *ma-zi-ʔà* |maSiħay| → Fronzaroli ARET 11 160; Catagnoti QuSe 29 125, 156, 210: "essi (du.) sono lavati"; cf. Krebernik PIHANS 106 88: "rub, wash!".[210] **UGA** G prefc. *ymšḥ*, suff. *ymšḥhm* → DUL 582: */m-š-ḥ/*. •ONOM: **EUPH** G pref. *ia-am-sa-aḫ, ia-am-sa-ḫi-il* |yamSaħ|; cf. unc. (N?) *na-am-si-e-*^{d}IM → Gelb CAAA 25, 325; Zadok Fs. Hallo 326.
maSħ "anointed"	•ONOM: **EUPH** *ma-aš-ḫu-um, ma-aš-ha-tum* → Gelb CAAA 25, 154.
maSīħ "anointed"	•ONOM: **EUPH** Cf. *ma-si-ḫu-um, ma-si-ḫa-an* → Huffmon APNMT 232; Gelb CAAA 25, 154.
muSāħ "anointed"	•ONOM: **EUPH** *mu-sa-ḫu-um, mu-sa-aḫ-ḫu-um* → Gelb CAAA 25, 158.
ms^{1}ħt "anointing"	•CTX: **UGA** → DUL 582f.: *mšḥt*.

|m-s^1-x| (1)	Sem.: *mšḥ* (JAram., Syr.) "to measure", *mšḥh, mšḥtʔ* (Aram.) "measurement, size", *mwšḥ(ʔ)* (Syr.) "measuring"; *mašāḫu(m)* (Akk.) "to measure", *mašīḫu* "a measure of capacity".
mas^{1}ix "amphora"	•CTX: **EG** *ma-s(a)-ḫi*, pl.? *ma-sa-ḫi-ta* → Hoch SWET 152f no. 198f.[211]

|m-s^1-x| (2)	Sem.: Cf. *mašaḫu* "to flash, shine, glow", *mišḫu* "flash, illumination".
mas^{1}x "a bead" (?)	•CTX: **Q** *ma-aš-ḫu* → Bottéro RA 44 120; AHw 625: *mašḫu(m)* II, 2; CAD M/1 365: *mašḫu* A. **A4** *ma-áš-ḫé* → AHw 625: *mašḫu(m)*, 2; CAD M/1 365: *mašḫu* A. **EA** *ma-áš/aš-ḫu* → AHw 625: *mašḫu(m)*, 2; CAD M/1 365: *mašḫu* A.

|m-s^1-k| (1)	Primary noun, Sem.: *mšk* (*mesek*, Hb.) "leather pouch"; *mšk(ʔ)* (Aram., Syr.) "skin, leather"; *mašku(m)* (Akk.) "skin, hide"; cf. *maska* (pl. *musuk*, Arab.) "newly skinned hide". Non-Sem.: *msk3* (*msq*, Eg.) "skin, leather".
msg "skin, leather" (?)	•CTX: **UGA** Sg. *msg*, pl. *msgm* → DUL 574.

|m-s^1-k| (2)	Sem.: *mšk* (Hb.) "to seize, carry off"; *mšk* (JAram.) "to pull, carry along, attract"; *masaka* (Arab.) "to grab, grasp"; *masaka* (Eth). "to drag, draw".
|**m-s^1-k**| "to adhere, give support" (?)	•CTX: **EM** G prefc. *ti-im-ša-ak* → Pentiuc Vocabulary181f.
|**m-θ-k**| "to carry, take"	•CTX: **UGA** G suffc. / ptc. sg. *mṯkt* → Tropper UG 109; DUL 596: */m-ṯ-k/*.

---

[210] Unless from |m-s^2-ʔ|; see above.
[211] Cf. Sivan / Cochavi-Rainey WSVES 81: *ma-šá-ḫi / ma-šá-ḫi-tá* "a vessel".

|m-s^1-l| (1)	Sem.: *mšl* (Hb., Ph., Pun., Aram.) "to rule, reign".
|m-s^1-l| "to rule, reign"	•ONOM: **EG** Cf. *y-m-sw-r* (*ya-ma$_4$-su$_3$-ra*) |yams^{1}ul=| → Schneider APÄQ 55 no. 96; Hoch SWET 53 no. 53.

|m-s^1-l| (2)	Culture word; only WSem. attestations.
maSSilāt "a tapestry or embroidered shawl" (?)	•CTX: **EUPH** *ma-si-la-tum*, *mas-si-latum*, *ma-ás-si-la-tum* (pl.t. |maSSilāt=| ?) → Durand ARM 30 65f.
ms^{1}lt (A) "garment or harness"	•CTX: **UGA** Sg. *mšlt*, pl. *mšlt* → DUL 584: *mšlt* (I).

|m-s^1-r|	Sem.: Cf. *mašāru(m)* (Akk.) "to drag (across the ground)".
|m-s^1-r| "to set a vehicle in motion, to drive it" (?)	•CTX: **UGA** C imp. *šmšr* → DUL 585f.: /*m-š-r*/.

|m-s^1-y|	Primary noun, Sem.: *mūšu(m)* (Akk.) "night", *mušītu(m)* id.; *ʔmš* (*ʔemeš*, *ʔomeš*, Hb.) "last night"; *masāʔ* (Arab.) "evening, night", *massā* "to wish a good evening", *ʔamsā* "to enter into evening"; *məset*, *məsyat* (Eth.) "evening, twilight", *masya* "to become evening".
|m-S-y| "to become evening, get dark"	•LL: **EB** GU$_6$.AN = *ma-sa-a-um* (G inf. |maSāy=|) → Conti QuSe 17 195f.
mīSy "night"	•LL: **EB** GI$_6$.AN = *me-su*; GI$_6$.AN = KI.A.NA = *me-šum*; GI$_6$.SÁ = *ba-na me-si-im* |baynay mīsim| → Fronzaroli QuSe 13 147; Conti QuSe 17 196; Krebernik PIHANS 106 88, 92; Catagnoti QuSe 29 212. **EA** Cf. GI$_6$-*ša* : *l*[*e-e*]*l* (243:13; read *mi-ša* in CAD M/2 130, *mīšu* B; AHw *vacat*) → Moran AmL 297 fn. 1 ad loc.; Rainey CAT 1 167, 3 1; EAC ad loc.
mūSy "night"	•CTX: **EB** *mu-si-im* → Archi / Biga ARET 3 374; Fronzaroli StEb 7 175, ARET 11 162, 180. •LL: **EB** GI$_6$.AN = *mu-šum* → Fronzaroli QuSe 13 147; Conti QuSe 17 195f.; Krebernik PIHANS 106 88, 92; Catagnoti QuSe 29 212. •ONOM: **EB** Cf. GIBIL-*mu-su* |bil=mūsu|, altern.|ḫadaθa=mūsu|, *iš$_{11}$-mu-si* |yiθ=musī| → Pagan ARES 3 225f., 292, 313, 342.
ʔamSay "the evening before" (?)	•CTX: **EB** Cf. *am-sa-a* → Fronzaroli QuSe 15 18; ARET 11 47, 139; SEL 12 63.

|m-s^2-w/y|	Sem.: *mesû(m)*, *masāʔum* (Akk.) "to wash, clean(se), purify".
|m-s^2-w/y| "to wash, clean(se), purify"	•CTX: **A7** *ú-ul me-ši*, *i-ma-aš-ši* → CAD M /2 30ff.; Giacumakis AkkAl 88. **UGS** *i-ma-aš-ši* → CAD M /2 30ff.; Huehnergard AkkUg 111; vSoldt AkkUg 434 fn. 81. •ONOM: **EUPH** Cf. *ia-am-si*-DINGIR, *yi-im-si*-DINGIR → Huffmon APNMT 232; Gelb CAAA 25, 157.

|m-t|

Primary noun, Sem: *mt* (pl. *m^{e}tîm*, Hb.) "men, people"; *mutu*(*m*) (Akk.) "husband, man, warrior", *mutūtu*(*m*) status of a husband, manliness, bravery"; *mət* (Eth.) "husband".

mit "man, husband, hero; DN"
mut "man, husband, hero; DN"

●ONOM: **EB** Cf. *mi-ti*, *mi-ti-šè-lu*; *me-ti-iš* → Pagan ARES 3 226, 350f.
EUPH Cf. *la-ka-me-et*, *i-mu-ut-ki-me-et*, *i-mu-ut-ki-ma-me-et* → Zadok Fs. Hallo 326f.[212]
●LL: **MŠ** *mu-tu*$_{4}$ = MIN (: *eṭ-lu*, I 169), *mu-tu* = MIN (: *zi-ka-ru*, exp. I 65), *mu-tu* = MIN (: *qar-ra-du*, exp. I 108) → Hrůša MŠ 312, 432, 434
●ONOM: **EB** Passim; for the different spellings (*mut*, *mutu*, *mutum*, *muti*, *muta*) see: *en-ga-mu-ud/du*, *ga-la-mu-ud*, *i-ti-mu-ud*, *i-ti-mu-ud-il*, *i-u*$_{9}$*-mu-ud*, *ib-u*$_{9}$*-mu-ud/du*, *i-bù-mu-du* |ʕibʔu=Mut(u)|,[213] *iš*$_{11}$*-rí-mu-ud*, *si-la-mu-ud* |s^{1}īra=Mut|,[214] *mu-ti*, *mu-ti-ḫa-lam*, *mu-ti-iš-ma-a*, *mu-ti-ma*; *a-mu-da*, *a-mu-ti*, *a-mu-du*(*m*) |(*la*)*ʔā=Mutu/i/a*|,[215] *la-mu-du*, *la-a-mu-du*, *ba-la-mu-du*, *si-mu-du*, *si-na-mu-du* → Krebernik PET 97; Catagnoti QuSe 15 234ff.; Pomponio UF 15 152; Pagan ARES 3 226, 280f., 286f., 290, 306, 309, 326f., 333, 342, 353, 363f.
U3 *mu-da-nu-um*, *i-wi-mu-ti* → Buccellati Amorites 160, 174; Gelb CAAA 26, 158, 160.
EUPH Passim; cf. *mu-ti-lum*, *mu-ta-num*, *mu-ta-nu-um*, *bi-mu-ti-ma-i-la*; for the different spellings (mut, mutu, mutum, miti, mute, muta) see among others: *mu-ta-ad-di*, *mu-tu-ad-ki*, *mu-ut-an-nu*, *mu-tu-a-bi-iḫ*, *mu-tum-a-bi-iḫ*, *mu-tu-a-bi-ḫi-im*, *mu-tu-am-na-nu-um*, *mu-ut-a-ri-ra*, *mu-tu-an-zu*(*!*)*-ú*, *mu-ta-a-pu-uḫ*, *mu-tu-ar-ra-ap-ḫi-im*, *mu-ut-áš-di*(*-im*), *mu-tu-aš-di*, *mu-ut-*$^{(d)}$*aš-kur*, *mu-tu-aš-kur*(*-ra*), *mu-tu-ba-lu-ú*, *mu-te-ba-al*, *mu-ut-bi-si-ir*, *mu-tu-bi-si-ir*, *mu-ut-*^{d}*da-gan*, *mu-tu-*^{d}*da-gan*, *mu-tu-um-*DINGIR, *mu-ut-dìr-ra*, *mu-ut-*É.GAL*-lim*, *mu-tu-*É.GAL*-lim*, *mu-tum-e-el*, *mu-tum-e-lum*, *mu-tu-e-ra-aḫ*, *mu-ti-a-ra-ah*, *mu-ti-e-ra-aḫ*, *mu-te-e-ra-aḫ*, *mu-tu-e-šu-uḫ*, *mu-ut-ga-bi-id*, *mu-ut-ḫa-ar-ra*, *mu-ut-ḫa-at-ta*, *mu-ti-ḫa-ad-ki-im*, *mu-ut-ḫa-bu-ur*, *mu-ut-ḫa-li*, *mu-tu-ḫa-li*, *mu-ut-ḫa-la-mi*, *mu-ti-ar-ra-ap-ḫé*, *mu-ut-ḫa-zu*(!)*-ra*, *mu-ut-*(*ḫa-*)*ak-ka*, *mu-ut-ḫa-li*, *mu-ut-ḫa-ma-nim*, *mu-ut-ḫa-na*, *mu-ut-*^{d}*ḫa-na-at*, *mu-tu-ḫa-na-at*, *mu-ut-ḫa-at-ki-im*, *mu-tu-ḫa-ad-ki-im*, *mu-ut-*(*ḫa-*)*ap-ki*, *mu-ut-ḫa-za-ri*, *mu-tu-a-za-ra*, *mu-ut-a-za-ri-im*, *mu-ut-ḫu-bur/bu-ur*, *mu-ut-ḫu-mu-zi*(*-im*), *mu-tu-ḫur-ra*, *mu-ti-ḫu-ur-ša-na/ni*, *mu-tu-*^{d}IM, *mu-ti-*^{d}IM, *mu-te-*^{d}IM, *mu-ta-*^{d}IM, *mu-ti-ma-*^{d}IM, *mu-tu-ia-an*, *mu-ut-ia-li-iḫ*, *mu-ut-ia-mi-ìš*, *mu-tum-ya-ri-iq*, *mu-ta*(*-ia*)*-šu-uḫ*, *mu-tu-i-la*, *mu-ut-ti-iu-um*, *mu-ut-ka-zi-e*, *mu-ti-ka-ṣi-e*, *mu-tu-ku-bi*, *mu-tu-ku-um-ri*, *mu-tu-ma/mi-*DINGIR, *mu-ti-*

---

212 For an altern. analysis see Durand REA 670: "Il (le roi) est mort de sa (belle) mort". See |m-w-t|.
213 "Burden of Mut" (ʕ-b-ʔ|); altern. |yipʕu=Mut| "splendour of Mut", see |y-p-ʕ|.
214 "Flesh of Mut" (s^{1}-ʔ-r|); altern. |s^{1}īra=Mut| "song of Mut", see |s^{1}-y-r|;
215 "Mut is powerful"; altern. |yamūt=a| "he died", see |m-w-t|. Cf. *am*$_{6}$*-mu-ti/du/dum* (unc.),

mi-DINGIR, *mu-tu-ma-ku-ú, mu-ti-me-el, mu-tu-me/mi-el, mu-tum-ma/me-el, mu-ti-ma-ku-ú, mu-tu-ma-la-ak/ka, mu-tu-ma-lik, mu-ti-ma-ki-im, mu-tu-ma-ta-ki-im, mu-tu-me-er, mu-ut-mu-ur-di, mu-ut-na-ḫa-lim, mu-tu-na-ri, mu-ut-na-ri-im, mu-ut-na-wa-ar, mu-tu-nu-ma-ḫa-a, mu-tum-ni-ša, mu-ut-qa-zi-im, mu-ut-ra-bi, mu-ut-ra-ma, mu-ut-ra-me-e/im, mu-ti-ra-me-e, mu-tu-ra-ma/me/mi-e, mu-ut-ra-ap-ši-im, mu-ut-sa-am-si, mu-tu-sa-am-si, mu-ut-sa-ap-ḫi, mu-tu-su-mi-im, mu-ut-ša-ki-im, mu-ut-sa-lim, mu-ta-ta-ki-in mu-ta-tar(-um), mu-ta-zi, mu-tu-ti/tu-zi, mu-tu-wa-an, mu-tu-ya-ma; ḫa-ia-mu-ti, di-wi-ir-mu-ti, di-bi-ir-a-mu-ti, me-ia-mu-ta, mi-ia-mu-du* → Huffmon APNMT 234f.; Gelb CAAA 26, 158ff.; Durand SEL 8 81ff.; Streck Onomastikon 1 291 § 3.53, 294ff. §§ 3.56, 320 § 5.6, 342 §§ 5.55f., Suppl. 360f.

A7 *mu-ti-ia, mu-ta-ni, mu-ut-ḫa-la-ab, mu-ut-ḫa-su-um, mu-ti-*^{d}UTU → Gelb CAAA 26, 158f.; Sivan GAGl 250; Streck Onomastikon 1 294ff. §§ 3.56.

A4 Cf. DUMU-*mu-ta, mu-ú-ta* → Sivan GAGl 250.

EM *mu-ti/tù, mu-ú-ta/tù/*tu_4, *mu-ut-ra-mì* → Pruzsinszky PTEm 174 [638f.], 201 [636].

EA *mu-ut-ba-aḫ-lù, mu-ut-*^{d}IM(*-me*) → Sivan GAGl 250; Hess APN 114f., 208, 236; Moran AmL 383.

TA *mu-ut*[-^{d}IŠKUR(?)] → Sivan GaGl 250; Horowitz / Oshima CunCan 149.

UGS *mu-ut-*^{d}U → Gröndahl PTU 162f.; Sivan GAGl 250.

mt (A) "man, husband, hero"
•CTX: **UGA** Sg. *mt*, pl. cstr. *mt*, du. *mtm* → DUL 590f.: *mt* (III).
•ONOM: **UGA** *mt* → DUL 591: *mt* (V); *mtbʕl* → DUL 591; *mty* → DUL 594.

tmtt "group of men, team, crew"
•CTX: **UGA** → DUL 859.

|m-t-ʕ|

Sem.: Cf. *mataʕa* (Arab.) "to take away", *ʔamtaʕa* "to do without, dispense with"; *mtʕ* (OSArab.) "to save, protect"; *mūta* (MSArab.) "to make a clean getaway", *həmtɛ* "to help someone to get clean away"; *mtʕ* (Aram.) "to rescue".

|m-t-ʕ| "to take away; to help, rescue"
•CTX: **UGA** G prefc. *tmtʕ* → DUL 591.[216]
•ONOM: **EUPH** Cf. *ia-ma-(at-)ti*-DINGIR → Huffmon APNMT 235; Gelb CAAA 25, 154.

mātiʕ "helper, saviour"
•ONOM: **EB** *ma-ti-ḫu* → Pagan ARES 3 141f, 349.
EUPH *ma-ti*-DINGIR, *ma-ti-ia-li, ma-ti-ia-tu-ú* → Gelb CAAA 25, 154.

matāʕ "salvation, rescue"
•ONOM: **EUPH** *ma-ta-a-ki-el* → Gelb CAAA 25, 154.

|m-t-ħ|

Sem.: *mtḥ* (Hb.) "to spread, stretch out", *mtḥt* (read cstr. *mitḥat*) "outspreading"; *mtḥ* (JAram., Syr.) "to stretch, pull, extend", *mtḥ(ʔ)* (Syr.) "extent, cord, line, extension", *mtḥh, mtḥtʔ* (JAram.) "stretching"; *matāḫu(m)* (Akk.) "to lift"; *mataḥa* (Arab.) "to draw (water from a well)", *mattāḥ* "long".

|m-t-ħ| "to erect"
•LL: **EB** KUR.PAD.NA.RÚ = *ma-da-ù zi-ga-na-tim* |matāħ sikkannātim|, var. = *ma-da-*u_9 NA_4.NA_4 → Conti QuSe 17 91; Catagnoti QuSe 29 112, 115, 210.

mataħ "unit of measurement: length, stretch"
•CTX: **EM** *ma-ta-ḫu* → Pentiuc Vocabulary 123.

mtħ "unit of measurement; length, stretch"
•CTX: **UGA** Cstr. sg. / pl. *mtḥ* → 591f.: *mtḥ*.

---

[216] Diff. Tropper UG 521, KWU 84: altern. Gt |m-w/y-ʕ| "in Wasser einweichen", cf. Arab. *my/wʕ*, Eth. *mwʕ*. See also Watson UF 39 678.

|m-t-ḳ|	Sem.: *mtq* (Hb.) "to be(come) sweet", *mtwq* (*mātôq*) "sweet", *mtq* (*mātēq*, *moteq*) "sweetness; *mtq* (JAram. D) "to sweeten", *mtyq* "sweet"; *matāqu*(*m*) (Akk.) "to be(come) sweet", *matqu*(*m*) "sweet", *mutqu* "sweet thing, sweetness", *mutqû*, *mutāqu*(*m*) confectionery, sweetmeat", *mutqītu* (?) "a sweet bread"; *tamaṭṭaqa* (Arab.) "to taste repeatedly", *maṭqa* "sweetness"; (MSArab.) *maṭḳ* "sweet"; *mataqa* (Eth.) "to be sweet", *mətuq* "sweet", *mətqat* "sweetness", *məṭuq* "sweetness". Non-Sem.: *mittakaimi*= (later: *mi*(*n*)*tgaimi*=, *mi*(*n*)*tagami*= (Luw. ptc. in Hitt. context) "sweetened, sweet".[217]
mtḳ "sweet"	•CTX: **UGA** Du. fem. *mtqtm* → DUL 593: *mtq*.
mtḳt "cake" (?)	•CTX: **UGA** → DUL 593: *mtqt*.
tamtuḳ "sweetness"	•LL: **EB** NÌ.KI = *da-ma-du-gu-um*, *da-ma-du-gu* → Krebernik ZA 73 2; Conti QuSe 17 30, 40, 66f.

|m-t-n| (1)	Primary noun, Sem.: *mtnym* (*motnayim*, Hb. du. t.) "hips and loins"; *mtnyn*, *mtnyʔ* (JAram. pl.t.) "loins"; *mtnn*, *mtntʔ* (Syr. pl.t.) "loins, ribs or side"; *matnu*(*m*) (Akk.) "sinew, tendon, string"; *matn* (Arab.) "half or side of the back, rear part"; *moten*, *mōtən*, *mətūn* (MSArab.) "flesh of back"; *matn* (Eth.) "sinew, nerve, muscle".
matn "tendon"	•LL: **EB** SA.ŠU = *ma-da-nu* → Fronzaroli QuSe 13 144, StEb 7 172; Conti QuSE 17 117; Bonechi / Catagnoti Fs. Sommerfeld / Krebernik 175.
mtn (A) "tendon, loin"	•CTX: **UGA** Du. *mtnm* → DUL 592: *mtn* (I).
mtnt "loin"	•CTX: **UGA** → DUL 593 (cultic terminology).

|m-t-n| (2)	Sem. etym. unc. Cf. *mtn* (JAram.) "to be slow, await".
|m-t-n| "to wait" (?)	•CTX: **UGA** G prefc. *tmtn* → DUL 592.

|m-t-r|	Sem.: *btr* (Hb.) "to cut in pieces", *matara* (Arab.) "to cut", *batara* "to cut (off)"; *matara* (Eth.) "to cut".
s^1mtr "cutting"	•CTX: **UGA** → DUL 819: *šmtr* (I). •ONOM: **UGA** Cf. unc. *šmtr* → DUL 819: *šmtr* (II).

|m-ṭ–r|	Primary noun, Sem.: *mṭr* (*māṭar*, Hb.) "rain", *mṭr* (C) "to let rain fall, cause to rain"; *mṭr*(*ʔ*) (Aram., Syr.) "rain", *mṭr* (C) "to cause to rain", *mmṭrn*(*ʔ*) "one that rains"; *miṭirtu*, *miṭru*, *miṭratu* (Akk.) "watercourse"; *maṭar* (Arab.) "rain", *maṭara* "to rain", *ʔamṭara* "to cause to rain", *mimṭar*(*a*) "raincoat"; *mṭrn* (OSArab.) "field watered by rain"; *meṭṭāreh* (MSArab.) "canvas water-bottle".
|m-ṭ-r| "to rain"	•CTX: **UGA** G prefc. *tmṭr*, suff. *tmṭrn*, Cptc. *mšmṭr* (see below) → DUL 595. •ONOM: **EUPH** *ia-am-ta-ru-um* → Gelb CAAA 26, 157.
maṭar "rain; DN"	•ONOM: **EUPH** Cf. *ma-ta-rum*, DINGIR-*ma-tar*, *ì-lí-ma-tar*/*ta-ar* → Huffmon APNMT 183; Gelb CAAA 26, 154f.; Durand REA 654.[218]
mṭr "rain"	•CTX: **UGA** Sg. *mṭr*, suff. *mṭrh* → DUL 595.

[217] See Rabin Orientalia 32 130.
[218] For the DN Madar see *madār* (\|d-w-r\|); diff.: Gelb CAAA 26, 154f.: MAṬAR "to rain".

mθ̣r "rain"	•CTX: **UGA** Sg. suff. *mẓrn* → Tropper UG 113; DUL 601: *mẓr*.
maṭart "rain"	•CTX: **EUPH** Pl. *i-na ma-ṭà-ra-tim* → Durand AuOr 17/18 192f.
mṭrt "rain"	•CTX: **UGA** Sg. suff. *mṭrtk* → DUL 595.
mmṭr "portico, porch" (?)	•CTX: **UGA** → DUL 553.
ms¹mṭr "rainmaker; DN"	•CTX: **UGA** → 585: *mšmṭr* (ptc. C |m-ṭ-r|; see above).

|m-ṭ-y|	Sem.: *maṭû(m)*, *maṭaʔu(m)* (Akk.) "to be(come) little, less, be in short supply".
|m-ṭ-y| "to be scarce, lacking, be in short supply"	•CTX: **EB** G suffc. *ma-ti-ma* |maṭiy=ma|, prefc. *am₆-da-ga* |ʔamṭay=ka|, *a-i-mu-du* |la=yimaṭṭayu| → Catagnoti / Fronzaroli ARET 16 73, 75, 214; Catagnoti QuSe 29 21, 51, 67, 80, 125, 137, 164, 210.

|m-θ|	Culture word. Non-Sem.: Cf. *ms* (usually pl. *msw*, Eg.) "kind".
mθ "infant, baby boy"	•CTX: **UGA** → DUL 595f.: *mṯ* (I). •ONOM: **UGA** Cf. unc. *mṯ* → DUL 596: *mṯ* (II).
mθt "damsel, young lady"	•CTX: **UGA** → DUL 598: *mṯt*.

|m-θ-l|	Sem.: *mšl* (Hb.) "to show a parable"; *mtl* (JAram., Syr.) "to compare"; *mašālu(m)* (Akk.) "to equal", *mušalu(m)* "metal mirror", *tamšīlu(m)* "likeness"; *maṯala* (Arab.) "to ressemble", *tamṯīl* "likening"; *mṯl* (OSArab.) "to conform; be similar"; *masala*, *masla* (Eth.) "to be like", *tamaslo(t)* "model".
miθil "mirror"	•CTX: **Q** *mi-ši-il up-un* → Richter / Langhe Idadda 83, 85: "Handspiegel". **EA** Cf. unc. *mé-še-li* → CAD M/2 257: *mušalu* A 1.d.[219]
tamθāl "(fabric) similar (to linen)"	•CTX: **EB** *dam-ša-lu*(-TÚG), AKTUM-TÚG *dam-ša-lu* → Pasquali QuSe 19 222; QuSe 23 49 fn. 215.
tmθl "equal amount, equivalent"	•CTX: **UGA** → DUL 859f.: *tmṯl*.

|m-θ-y|	Culture word; Hitt. loan. Non-Sem.: TÚG *massiya=* (Hitt.) "a garment, kind of shawl, sash" (?).[220]
maθθiyann "a garment, kind of shawl, sash"	•CTX: **UGS** TÚG *ma-ši-ya-an-nu*, TÚG *: ma-aš-ši-ia-an-na* → CAD M/1 389; Sivan GAGl 246; vSoldt UF 22 336 fn. 111.
mθyn "a garment, kind of shawl, sash"	•CTX: **UGA** → 598: *mṯyn*.

[219] EA 356:51 (Adapa): *ta-am-ta i-na mé-še-li in-ši-il-ma* "the sea was like a mirror"; diff. Izre'el AmScholT 46, 48f.: "He sliced the sea in its midst" (from Akk. *mišlu(m)*).
[220] Tischler HethEtymGl L/M 159f.

|m-θ̣-ʔ/y|

Sem.: *mṣʔ* (Hb., Ph.) "to reach, meet; to find"; *mṭy* (Aram., Syr.) "to come, reach, happen", *mṣy* (JAram., Syr.) "to be able, find"; *maṣû(m)*, *maṣāʔum* (Akk.) "to correspond, be equal, comply"; *maḍā* (Arab.) "to pass, happen, proceed, advance, go away"; *mẓʔ* (OSArab.) "to go proceed"; (MSArab.) *míð̣i* "to reach"; *mẓʔ* "to enter"; *maṣʔa* (Eth.) "to come, happen to, occur".

|**m-θ̣-ʔ**| "to meet, run into, find; to be successful"

•CTX: **UGA** G prefc. *ymẓả*, suffc. suff. *mẓảh* → DUL 600: /*m-ẓ-ʔ*/.
•ONOM: **EUPH** *e-im-zu-um*, *ie-e-im-zu-um*, *e-im-ṣi-um*, *ia-am-zi-um*, *ia-am-zi-ú/yu-um*, *ia-am-zu-(ú-)um*, *ia-am-zi*-DINGIR, *ie-e-em-zi*-DINGIR, *ia-am-ṣi-ad-nu*, *ia-am-zi-ad-nu-ú*, *ia-am-zi-ḫa-ad-nu(-ú)*, *ia-am-zu-ad-nu-ú*, *ia-am-zi-bu-ne-ne*, *yi-im-si*-DINGIR, *ia-am-zu-ma-lik* → Huffmon APNMT 232f.; Gelb CAAA 25, 157; ARM 23 627; Zadok Fs. Hallo 326 (M-Ṣ-Y); Streck Onomastikon 1 181 § 2.65 fn. 1, 2; Golinets Onomastikon 2 176ff., 408f.
TU *e-em-ṣí-ú-um*, *i-im.ṣí-um* → Krebernik Tall Bi`a 213, 216; Golinets Onomastikon 2 178, 408f.

|**m-ɣ-y**| "to come, arrive"

•CTX: **UGA** G prefc. *ảmġy*, *tmġ*, *tmġyn*, *ymġy*, *ymġ*, suff. *tmġyy*, *ymġyk*, *ymġyn*, *tmġyn*; suffc. *mġt*, *mġy*, *mġyt*, *mġny*; imp. *mġ*; inf. *mġy*, suff. *mġyy*, *mġyh* → Tropper UG 95; Kogan Classification 255; DUL 527f.: /m-ġ-y/.
•ONOM: **UGS** Cf. DUMU *ia-am-ḫa-na* → Gröndahl PTU 156; Sivan GAGl 247.
UGA Cf. *bn mġln* → Gröndahl PTU 156; Coogan Or 44 197; DUL 526: *mġln*.

maθ̣iy "successful"

•ONOM: **EUPH** *ma-zi-ú-um*, *ma-zi-a-tum*, *é-a-ma-zi*, *zi-id-kum-ma-zi* → Gelb CAAA 25, 154; Golinets Onomastikon 2 186, 408f.

|m-w-g|

Sem.: Cf. *mwg* (Hb. D) "to soften"; *mgmg* (JAram.) "to cause to flow"; *māǧa* (*mwǧ*) (Arab.) "to heave, swell, surge", *tamāwaǧa* "to flow, flood, surge", *mawǧa* "wave"; see further. *mogad*, *mawgad* (Eth.) "wave, flood".

maḳīḳ "soft, moist soil"

•CTX: **EG** Cf. *ma-qi-qu*$_2$, *ma*$_2$*-qi*$_2$*-qa*, *ma*$_2$*-qi*$_2$*-qa-t* → Hoch SWET 168 no. 221.

|m-w-ḳ|

Sem.: *muqqu(m)* (Akk.) "to weary, tire, be slack", *muqqu(m)* "weakened, wearied"; see further: *myq* (Syr. D) "to deride"; *mawāqa*, *muʔūq*, *mawqa* (Arab.) "to be stupid, dumb, foolish", *mūq* "stupidity"

māḳ "slack, frailty" (?)

•LL: **EB** Cf. Unc. GÍN.IR = *ma-gu*, *si-tum* → Conti QuSe 17 187.

muḳḳ "slow, slack"

•ONOM: **EB** Cf. *mu-ga*, *mu-gú* → Pagan ARES 3 138 (*mʔq* ?), 352.

|m-w-n| (1)

Sem.: *mânu* (Akk.) "to supply (with food)"; *māna* (*mawn*), *mawwana* (Arab.) "to provision, supply with provisions".

mawn "supply, stock"

•CTX: **EB** *ma-na* |mawn=a|, *ma-na-a* |mawn=nay(n)|, cstr. *mu-nu* |mūn| → Fronzaroli ARET 13 113, 282; Catagnoti / Fronzaroli ARET 16 52, 252; Catagnoti QuSe 29 44, 74, 118, 211.

|m-w/y-n| (2)

Sem.: Cf. *myn* (cstr. *mînô*, *mînēhû*, Hb.) "kind, type, species", *tmwnh* (*t*ᵉ*mûnāh*) "form, manifestation"; *myn(ʔ)* (JAram.) "kind, type, species"; (Palm., Syr.) "nation, people".

mn (D) "species (of animal)"

•CTX: **UGA** Pl. *mnm* → DUL 554: *mn* (II).

---

tmn, tmnt "frame, form"

•CTX: **UGA** Sg. *tmn*, *tmnt* (pl.?) → DUL 858: *tmn* (I), *tmnt*.
•ONOM: **UGA** Unc. *tmn* → DUL 858: *tmn* (II); unc. *tmnn* → DUL 858.

|m-w-s^1|

Sem., with some reduplicated and quadriconsonantal by-forms: Cf. *mwš* (Hb.) "to handle, touch, feel". See also: *mšš* (Hb.) "to feel, touch"; *mšš* (JAram., Syr.) "to feel, grope", *mšmš* id.; *massa* (Arab.) "to touch"; *mašāšu*(*m*) (Akk.) "to wipe off, clean"; *marsasa* (Eth.) "to grope for".

|m-w-s^1| "to feel, look over" (?)

•ONOM: **EUPH** Cf. *mu-uš-na-a-du*, *ia-*(*a-*)*mu-ši-*DINGIR → Gelb CAAA 26, 147; Zadok Fs. Hallo 327.

|m-w-t|

Sem.: *mwt* (Hb.) "to die", *mwt* (*māwet*) "death, dying"; *mwt* (Aram., Syr.) "to die", *mwt*(*?*) "death", *myt* "dead"; *mt*, *myt* (Pun., Amm., Nab., Palm.) "to die", *mwt* (Nab., Palm., Hatra) "death"; *mâtu*(*m*) (Akk.) "to die", *mītu*(*m*), *mētu*(*m*) "dead", *mūtu*(*m*) "death"; *mwt* (OSArab.) "to die"; *mōt* (MSArab.) "to die", *mawt* "death", *mōyət* "dead"; *māta* (Arab.) "to die", *mawt* "death", *mayyit* "dead"; *mota* (Eth.) "to die", *məwwə*/*ut* "dead, deceased", *mot* "death, destruction".

|m-w-t| "to die"

•CTX: **EB** G prefc. UG$_7$ *i-mu* |yimūt=| (incomplete spelling) → Fronzaroli ARET 13 63, 270.
EA C prefc. *ti-mi-tu-na-nu* (|timītūna=ni| < |tumītūna=nu| < |tuhamītūna=nu| "you put us to death" → Sivan GAGl 175f., 250; Rainey CAT 2 46 190; Tropper AfO 44/45 140; Moran AmL 295; Izre'el Orient 38 87. Cf. unc. *ma-at-ti* (G suffc.?) → Finkelstein EI 9 33f; Rainey CAT 1 62, CAT 2 286, 364; see Moran AmL 330 n. 20 and 333 n. 7 for other proposals.
UGA G prefc. *åmt*, *åmtn*, *tmtn*, *ymt*, suff. *ymtm*, *ymtn*, suffc. *mt*, *mtt*, inf. suff. *mtm*, ptc. *mt* (see below: *mt* (B)) → DUL 588f.
•LL: **EB** Cf. AL$_6$.UG$_7$ = *a-li a-mu-tù* → Hecker BaE 209.[221]
•ONOM: **EB** *a-mu-da*/*du*/*dum* |yamūt=|, *i-mu-da-mu*, *i-mu-ud-da-mu* |yimūt=|; *da-mu-dum* |tamūt=|, *da-mu-da-mu* → Pagan ARES 3 142, 280, 298, 300, 323.
U3 *a-bí-a-mu-ti*, *ià-a-mu-tum*[222] → Buccellati Amorites 127; Gelb CAAA 26, 147f.; Wilcke WO 5 25f.; Golinets Onomastikon 2 282, 409ff.
EUPH Passim; see *ia-mu-ut-da-du*, *ia-mu-ut-di-rum*, *ia-mu-ut-ḫa-ma-ad*/*di*, *ia-mu-ut-ku-lu-up*, *ia-mu-ut-ku-ru-up*, *ia-mu-ut-li-mu*/*im*, *ia-mu-ut-mé-rum*, *i-mu-ut-ki-me-et*, *i-mu-ut-ki-ma-me-et*,[223] *ia-mu-ut-ṣa-bu-um*, *ia-mu-ta-nu*, *a-bi-ia-mu-ta*, *ì-lí-ia-mu-ut*, *ip-ti-ia-mu-ta*, *su-mu-ia-mu-ut-ba-la*/*lim*, *su-mu-e-mu-ut-ba-la*, *su-mu-ia-mu-tu-ba-la*, *tu-up-ti-ia-mu-ta*, *la-ḫa-ad-na-a-mu-ut*; elem. in TN *ia-mu-ut-ba- al*/*lu*/*li*/*lim*;[224] unc. *a*/*am-mu-ut-pa-*DINGIR, *a-mu-ut-bi-*DINGIR, *a-mu-ut-bi-i-la* → Huffmon APNMT 229; Gelb CAAA 26 147f.; Zadok Fs. Hallo 327; Streck Onomastikon 1 180 § 2.63; Golinets Onomastikon 2 282ff., 409ff., 497f.
A7 *ia-mu-ut-ni-ri* → Wiseman AT 136; Gelb CAAA 26, 148; Arnaud AuOr 16 175; Streck Onomastikon 1 191 § 2.88; Golinets Onomastikon 2 282, 409ff.
EM DINGIR-*lì-ia-mu-ut*, *ì-li*/*lí-ia-mu-ut*; unc. *ia-mu-ut-ḫa*, *i-mu-ut-tá-ba-ri* → Pruzsinszky PTEm 210 [419], 214f. [474f., 488].
UGS *ia-mu-ut-šar-ri* → Malbran-Labat RSOu 7 5:4; Huehnergard Syria 74 214.
UGA *ymtd*/*šr* → DUL 954.

---

221 Perhaps "wo/wann ich sterbe". See also Fronzaroli ARET 13 63.
222 Diff. Buccellati Amorites 149: from |x-m-ṭ|; unlikely.
223 |=kī(ma)=mit| "as a hero"; see Zadok Fs. Hallo 326f. and here: |m-t|.

mawt, mōt "death"	•CTX: **EB** É *ma-tim* / *ma-dim* / *ma-ti* |bayt mawtim| "(casa della) morte" → Catagnoti QuSe 29 109, 221. **EA** BA.UG$_7$: *mu-tu-mi* → Rainey CAT 1, 36, CAT 2 254, CAT 3 203; Gianto SEL 12 68f.
muwāt "dying" (?)	•ONOM: **EB** *mu-wa*(PI)*-da* → Pagan ARES 3 142, 353.
miyt "dead, mortal"	•CTX: **EM** Pl. *mi-ti*, *mì-ti$_7$* → Pentiuc Vocabulary 125f.; Ikeda BiOr 60 269, 271.
mt (B) "dead; mortal"	•CTX: **UGA** Sg. *mt*, pl. *mtm* → DUL 589: *mt* (I).
mt (C) "death"	•CTX: **UGA** Sg. *mt*, suff. *mtm*, *mtk*, *mth*, *mth<m>* → DUL 589f.: *mt* (II).
blmt "immortality"	•CTX: **UGA** Sg. *blmt*, suff. *blmtk* → DUL 220: compound noun *bl=mt*; see *bl* (A) (|*b-l-y*| (2)); *mt* (C), above.
s^{1}ħlmmt "Mortality Shore" (?)	•ONOM: **UGA** → DUL 800: *šḫlmmt*; TN; mythical place of the divine dead, antechamber to the underworld (see |s^1-ħ-l| (1)).
|m-y-ʕ|	Sem.: Cf. *māʕa* (*myʕ*, Arab.) "to flow (liquid)", *mayyaʕa* "to melt, liquefy", *ʔamāʕa* "to make flow"; *myʕ*, *meʕa* (Eth.) "to become water, melt", *maʕawa* "to be humid, wet", *məhwa* "to melt, be liquified".
|**m-y-ʕ**| "to soak in water" (?)	•CTX: **UGA** Cf. *tmtʕ* (Gt prefc. ?) → Watson UF 39 2007 678; Tropper KWU 84.[225]
|m-y-n| See |**m-w/y-n**| **(2)**	
|m-z-ʕ|	Sem: *mazaʕa* (Arab.) "to tear, rip", *mazzaʕa* "to tear to pieces".
|**m-z-ʕ**| "to tear to pieces"	•CTX: **UGA** G / tD (?) prefc. *tmzʕ* → DUL 599.
|m-z-g| Cf. |**m-s-k**|	Sem.: *mzg* (Aram., Syr.), *ma-zi-ga-ʔ* (Warka-Aram.) "to mix (liquids)", *mzg(ʔ)* (JAram., Syr.) "drinking, drink", *mmzg* (Syr.) "tempered, mixed"; *mzg* (*mezeg*, Hb.) "mixed, spiced wine"; *mazağa* (Arab.) "to mix", *mazğ*, *mizāğ* "mixture". See also: *mašağa* (Arab.) "to mix", *mašağ*, *mašiğ*, *mašīğ* "mixed".
|**m-z-g**| "to mix drinks"	•ONOM: **EUPH** Cf. *ma-zi-gu-um* → Zadok Fs. Hallo 327.
|m-z-l|	Sem. etym. unc.; probl. by-form of |ʔ-z-l|. Cf. *ʔzl* (Hb.) "to go away, disappear"; *ʔzl* (Aram., Syr.) "to go".
|**m-z-l**| "to go, travel, run"	•CTX: **UGA** G prefc. *ymzl*, inf. *mzl* → DUL 599.[226] •LL: **EB** KAS$_4$.KAS$_4$ = *du-da-zi-lu-um*, *du-da-zi-lum* |tuttazzil= < tumtazzil=| (?) → Pettinato LdE 256 fn. 55; Fales SEL 1 23ff.; Fronzaroli QuSe 13 139: "to act as messenger"(?); Catagnoti QuSe 29 123, 139, 145, 188: "to travel"(?).[227]

224 TN *Yamūt-Baʕl*, passim, with several variants (*ie-e-mu-ut-ba-lum*, *e-mu-ut-ba-a-lum*, *e-mu-ut-ba-la*, *ia-mu-ut-ba-la-i*, *ia-mu-ut-ba-a-lum*, etc.); Gelb CAAA 26, 147f.; Golinets Onomastikon 2 37, 39, 280ff.

225 Diff. see DUL 591: /m-t-ʕ/ G "to remove, shed", said of clothing (?) (Arab. *mataʕa*, "to take away").

mazzāl "courier, messenger"	•CTX: **EB** *ma-za-lum* → Pettinato MEE 3 183 fn. 13; Fales SEL 1 23ff.; Arcari BaE 323f.; Waetzoldt BaE 430f.; Lahlouh / Catagnoti ARET 12 565; Pomponio ARET 15 450; Bonechi QDLF 16 85 n. 7.[228]
|m-z-r|	Sem.: Cf. *mzr* (Hb.) "to spread"; (NHb.) "to spin, twist yarn"; (Syr.) "to stretch"; *mazārum* (Akk.) "to treat fibers in a certain way, twist, weave; to make them into yarn, cord, felt", *māziru* (Akk. Nuzi) "maker of yarn, cord, felt" (?),[229] *mizru* "fibers treated in a certain way; kind of twisted material, felt" (?); see further: *mazara, mazzara* (Arab.) "to stretch out, inflate".
mazr "yarn, cord, felt" (?)	•CTX: **EUPH** *ma-az-ra-tum* → AHw 637; Durand MARI 6 661, ARM 30 143. **UGS** 2 TÚG.MEŠ (ÉŠ) *ma-za-r*[*u*]-*ma* MEŠ; [TÚG.MEŠ (ÉŠ) *mu-r*]*u-ú ma-az-ru*-[*tu*]; cf. in frg. ctx. 2 *ma-za-r*[→ Durand MARI 6 661, ARM 30 143.[230]
mazzār "spinner, maker of yarn, cord, felt" (?)	•CTX: **EB** LÚ *ma-za-lum* → Pasquali QuSe 19 255f., Textile terminologies 174.[231]
|m-z-y/z|	Sem.: Cf. *mzh* (*māzeh*, Hb.) "weakened". See also *mazza* (Arab.) "to suck"; further *mazāʔu*(*m*), *mazû* (Akk.) "to press, squeeze".
|m-z-y/z| "to be weak; to suck" (?)	•ONOM: **EG** Cf. *m-ṯꜣ* → Schneider APÄQ 139 no. 295.

[226] Diff. Tropper UG 165, KWU 84: "hinken, hinterhergehen, auf der Spur folgen"; metath. of *zml* "hinken" (Arab.).

[227] Catagnoti loc.cit. normalizes |tuʔtazzil=| (from |ʔ-z-l|). For the optional assimilation of preconsonantal |m| in Ebla see Conti QuSe 17 37f.; Catagnoti QuSe 29 66f. See also Fronzaroli ARET 13 275.

[228] Altern. see *maθθār* "guardian", |n-θ-r|. See further *ma-za-um*, and Archi NABU 2005/40.

[229] AHw 1574; diff. Durand ARM 30 143: *mazīru* "a kind of yarn".

[230] Diff. Huehnergard UVST 105: *maʔzar* (?), from *ʔzr* (unlikely); cf. also Sivan GAGl 242 (MAZRU "girdle").

[231] Cf. Fronzaroli StEb 1 84: |maẓẓar=um|.

n

|n| (1)
|n| (2)
|n-ʔ|
|n-ʔ-d| (1)
|n-ʔ-d| (2)
|n-ʔ-m|
|n-ʔ-ṣ|
|n-ʔ(-t)|
|n-ʕ-l|
|n-ʕ-m| Cf. **|n-ħ-m|**
|n-ʕ-r| (1)
|n-ʕ-r| (2)
|n-ʕ-r| (3)
|n-b| (1)
|n-b| (2)
|n-b-ʔ|
|n-b-ʕ|
|n-b-b|
|n-b-x|
|n-b-k|
|n-B-l| (1)
|n-b-l| (2)
|n-b-l| (3)
|n-b-r|
|n-B-S|
|n-b-ṭ|
|n-d|
|n-d-ʔ|
|n-d-b| Cf. **|n-ṭ-p|**
|n-d-d| (1)
|n-d-d| (2)
|n-d-ħ|
|n-d-n| See **|n/w/y-D-n|**
|n/w/y-D-n|
|n-d-p|
|n-d-y| Cf. **|w-d-y|**
|n-ð-r| Cf. **|ʔ-d-r|**, **|d-r-r|**
|n-g-ʕ| (1)
|n-g-ʕ| (2)
|n-g-b| (1)
|n-g-b| (2)
|n-G-d|
|n-g-h|
|n-g-ħ|
|n-G-p|
|n-g-r|
|n-g-s^1| Cf. **|n-g-θ|**
|n-g-s^2|
|n-g-θ|
|n-g-w/y|
|n-g-z|
|n-ɣ-ṣ|
|n-H-B|
|n-h-d|
|n-h-ḳ|
|n-h-l| (1)
|n-h-l| (2)
|n-h-r| (1)
|n-h-r| (2) Cf. **|n-w-r|**
|n-H-S| See **|n-ħ-S|**
|n-ħ-b|
|n-ħ(-ħ)|
|n-ħ-l|
|n-ħ-m| Cf. **|n-ʕ-m|**
|n-ħ-r|
|n-ħ-S| See **|n-H-S|**
|n-ħ-s^1| (1)
|n-ħ-s^1| (2)
|n-ħ-t|
|n-ħ-w/y|
|n-x-l|
|n-x-r|
|n-x-s|
|n-x-s^1|
|n-k-h|
|n-k-l| (1)
|n-k-l| (2)
|n-k-m|
|n-k-p|
|n-k-r|
|n-k-S| (1)
|n-k-s| (2)
|n-k-t|
|n-k-θ| Cf. **|n-θ-k|**
|n-k-y|
|n-ḳ-b|
|n-ḳ-d|
|n-ḳ-ð|
|n-ḳ-h|
|n-ḳ-ḳ|
|n-ḳ-l|
|n-ḳ-m|
|n-ḳ-p|

|n-ḳ-r|
|n-ḳ-y| (1)
|n-ḳ-y| (2)
|n-m-ḳ|
|n-m-l| (1)
|n-m-l| (2)
|n-m-r| (1)
|n-m-r| (2) See |**n-w-r**|
|n-m-s^1| (1)
|n-m-s^1| (2)
|n-m-y|
|n-m-z| See |**n-z-m**|
|n-n-ʔ|
|n-p-x|
|n-p-ḳ| See |**p-w-ḳ**|, |**y-p-ḳ**|
|n-p-l| (1)
|n-p-l| (2)
|n-p-p|
|n-p-r| (1)
|n-p-r| (2)
|n-p-S|
|n-p-ṣ| (1)
|n-p-y| (1)
|n-p-y| (2)
|n-S-ʕ/x|
|n-S-G| Cf. |**n-s-k**|, |**n-θ-ḳ**|
|n-S-x| See |**n-S-ʕ/x**|
|n-s-k| Cf. ||**n-t-k**|, |**n-θ-ḳ**|
|n-s-ḳ|
|n-s-s|
|n-s-y| (1)
|n-s-y| (2)
|n-ṣ-b| Cf. |**w-ṣ-b**|
|n-ṣ-ħ (1)|
|n-ṣ-ħ| (2)
|n-ṣ-ḳ| See |**y-ṣ-k**|
|n-ṣ-l|
|n-ṣ-p|
|n-ṣ-r|
|n-ṣ-ṣ|
|n-s^1-B| (1)
|n-s^1-b| (2)
|n-s^1-g| See |**n-S-G**|
|n-s^1-ḳ| (1)
|n-s^1-ḳ| (2)
|n-s^1-r| (1)
|n-s^1-r| (2)
|n-s^1-y| (1)
|n-s^1-y| (2)
|n-s^2-ʔ|
|n-s^2-r|
|n-ṣ̂-m|
|n-ṣ̂-ṣ̂|
|n-t-b| (1)
|n-t-b| (2)
|n-t-k| See |**s^1-t-k**|, cf. |**n-s-k**|
|n-t-n| See |**n/w/y-D-n**|
|n-t-r| See |**t-r-r**|, |**t-w-r**|
|n-ṭ-ʕ|
|n-ṭ-l|
|n-ṭ-p| Cf. |**n-d-b**|
|n-ṭ-ṭ|
|n-ṭ-y|
|n-θ-k| Cf. |**n-k-θ**|
|n-θ-ḳ| Cf. |**n-s-k**|
|n-θ̣-r|
|n-w-ʕ|
|n-w/y-b| (1)
|n-w/y-b| (2)
|n-w-d|
|n-w-ħ| Cf. |**(ʔ-)n-H**|
|n-w-x|
|n-w-ḳ|
|n-w-l|
|n-w-m|
|n-w-p|
|n-w-r|
|n-w-s|
|n-w-ṣ|
|n-w-y|
|n-y-l|
|n-y-r|
|n-z-ḳ|
|n-z-l|
|n-z-m|

|n| (1)	Morpheme with highlighting / euphonic function. Cf. Hb. *nʔ* (*nāʔ*) emphatic ("surely").[232]
=na (A), =ni (A) highlighting and euphonic enclitic (≈ "yea")	•CTX: **EUPH** *a-li-na, a-li-na-ma* → Streck Onomastikon 1 106 § 1.95. •ONOM: **EUPH** Cf. *a-an-na-ba-al, la-aḫ-wi-na-ti-nu*(*-ú*), *la-wi-na-*dIM, *mu-uš-na-a-du, nu-uḫ-mu-na-*^{d}IM,[233] *su-um-na-ia-tar, šu-ub-na-il*; *=ni* with vowel assim.: *šu-ba-ni-*DINGIR, *ši-ma-aḫ-ni-*DINGIR, *a-sa-ak-ni-el, ta-aḫ-ti-in-ìl, ḫa-qú-ub-ni-ìl, ia-aḫ-zi-ir-ni-il, na-aḫ-ni-ìl* → Huffmon APNMT 236; Gelb CAAA 529; Zadok Fs. Hallo 327; Streck Onomastikon 1 106 § 1.95, 305f. § 3.70 fn. 6.
=n (A) highlighting and euphonic enclitic (≈ "yea")	•CTX: **UGA** *=n*; *=ny*; *=nh* → DUL 602f.: *-n* (I).[234]

|n| (2)	Sem. formative elem. in first person pronouns: sg. c. accus. |=ni=ya|, pl. c. |=nā|. Suffixed forms: Hb.: *=ny* (*nî*, 1 sg. c. accus.), *=nū* (1 pl. c.); Aram., Syr.: *=n* (1 sg. c. accus.; 1 pl. c.); Akk. *=ni* (1 sg. c. accus.), *=a*(*m*), *=ni*(*m*) (1 sg. c. dat.), *=niāti* (1 pl. c. accus.), *=niāši*(*m*) (1 pl. c. dat.); Arab. *=nī* (1 sg. c. accus.), *=nā* (1 pl. c.); Eth. *=nī* (1 sg. c. accus.), *=na* (1 pl. c.). Indep. forms: cf. Akk. *nû*(*m*) "our", "*niāti* (1 pl. obl. c.), *niāšim* (1 pl. dat. c.).
=ni (B) "me, to me" (?)[235]	•ONOM: **EB** Cf. unc. *en-na-ni-il, i-bi-ni-li-im* → Archi StEb 2 38f.; Pagan ARES 3 254; Catagnoti QuSe 29 79.[236]
=n(y) "my; me"[237]	•CTX: **UGA** *=n, =ny* → Tropper UG 214, 219f.: *n* expanded by-form of |=ī| (|=nī|); DUL 603: *-n* (II). •ONOM: **UGA** Cf. *ìlḥbn* → Gröndahl PTU 162; DUL 53.
=na (B), =nā "our"[238]	•ONOM: **EB** → Pagan ARES 3 263f. **EUPH** Passim; cf. *sa-am-su-na, sa-am-su-i-lu-na, iš-ḫi-lu-na, la-na-*^{d}*da-gan, na-ap-su-na-i-la, nu-uḫ-mi-na-i-la, su-mu-na-a-bi, su-um-na-*^{d}IM → Gelb Lingua 152; Huffmon APNMT 235f.; CAAA 528f.; Zadok Fs. Hallo 327. **A7** *sa-am-su-na-ba-la* → Wiseman AT 145; Gelb CAAA 115 **UGS** LUGAL EN-*na-a* → Huehnergard ^{2}UVST 393; Tropper UG 214, 224; Márquez UF 32 370.
=ni (C) "our"[239]	•ONOM: **EB** → Pagan ARES 3 253f.; cf. Archi StEb 2 38f. **U3** *a-du-ni-la, lá-ni-*DINGIR → Buccellati Amorites 131, 164f.; Gelb CAAA 529. **EUPH** Passim; cf. *i-lu-ni, a-du-ni-a-bi-ia, su-mu-la-ni, si-ma-aḫ-la-ni, su-mu-ni* → Gelb Lingua 152, CAAA 529. **A7** *i-la-a-ni* → Wiseman AT 137; Gelb CAAA 529.
=nu "our; us"[240]	•CTX: **EB** *=nu* → Fronzaroli StEb 5 96; Catagnoti QuSe 29 72, 79, 217. **EA** SAG.DU-*nu* : *ru-šu-nu, i-na bi*$_{4}$*-ri-nu* → Rainey CAT 1 85, 92, 164, 174. •ONOM: **EB** → Pagan ARES 3 253f.

232 For a comparative overview see Gzella BiOr 64 552.

233 Durand RA 82 108ff. (A.1610+: 40; LAPO 17 266f.).

234 |=na| (?). For an etym. connection with the so-called energic verbal forms ending in *=n*, *=nn* (|=an(na)|) see Tropper UG 497f., 823.

235 Suff. pronoun accus. 1 sg. c.

236 Diff, rdg: *i-bí-id*$_{x}$*-li-im*, Bonechi RA 91 34.

237 Suff. pronoun genit. / accus. 1 sg. c.

238 Suff. pronoun genit. 1 pl. c.

239 Suff. pronoun genit. 1 pl. c.

240 Suff. pronoun genit. / accus. 1 pl. c., and accus. 1 sg. c.; see also Catagnoti Eblaite 156.

=n (B), =ny= "our; us"[241]	•CTX: **UGA** *=n, =ny=* → Tropper UG 214, 224f.; DUL 603 *-n* (III). •ONOM: **UGA** Cf. *ảbn, ỉbn* → Gröndahl 162f.; DUL 11: *ả/ỉbn*; *ảḫn, ủḫn* → Gröndahl PTU 162f.; DUL 37: *ả/ỉḫn(y), ủḫn*; *hyảbn* → Gröndahl PTU 163; DUL 345f.; *mlkbn* → Gröndahl PTU 163; DUL 549; *mġln* → Gröndahl PTU 162; DUL 526; *ṯbln* → Gröndahl PTU 162; DUL 884.
=nay(n), =ney(n), =nē(n) "of both of us; both of us"[242]	•CTX: **EB** *=na-a, =ne-a, =na, =ne* → Fronzaroli MAARAV 5/6 119; Archi PIHANS 106 100; Catagnoti QuSe 29 72ff., 219. •ONOM: **EUPH** Cf. *=ni-a, =ni-e* in: *su-mu-la-ni-a, ì-lí-iš-ma-ni-a, si-ma-aḫ-la-ni-e, si-ma-aḫ-i-la-a-ni-e, su-ma-ḫa-la-ni-e*, etc. → Gelb CAAA 529; Streck Onomastikon 1 168f. § 2.35 fn. 4.
=ny "of both of us; both of us"[243]	•CTX: **UGA** → Tropper UG 227; DUL 644 *-ny*. •ONOM: **UGA** Cf. unc. *ảḫny, ỉḫny* → Gröndahl PTU 166; DUL 37: *ả/ỉḫn(y)*.
nāʔ, niāʔa "our, belonging to us"[244]	•CTX: **EB** *ne-a-a, ni-a-a* → Catagnoti QuSe 29 25, 88, 217. •ONOM: **EB** Cf. unc. *gi-na-a* |kī(n)=naʔa| (var. *gi-na-ù*), *na-a-li-im, ḫa-ra-na-ù, ti-da-na-ù* → Pagan ARES 3 253, 312, 317, 353, 369.
niāSi "to us"[245]	•CTX: **EB** *ne-a-si* → Catagnoti QuSe 29 71, 217.
=niāti "to us"[246]	•CTX: **EB** *=ne-a-ti* → Catagnoti QuSe 29 72, 81, 217.
niāti "our; to us"[247]	•CTX: **EB** *ne-a-ti* → Catagnoti QuSe 29 71, 217.
niāʔūti "our"[248]	•CTX: **EB** *na-a-ù-ti* → Catagnoti QuSe 29 88, 217.

|n-ʔ|	Culture word. No obvious connection with *nētu* (Akk.) "a wooden object"; *nêʔu(m)* (Akk.), *naʔāʔum* (OAkk.) "to turn back"; *ʔanʔā, ʔināʔ* (Arab.) "to remove, move away".
niʔt "axe, hatchet"	•CTX: **EB** *ne-a-tum, ni-a-ti-ga* → Fronzaroli ARET 13 126, 287; Archi NABU 2005/69; Pasquali QuSe 23 172, Or 83 274. Cf. *ni-ti* → Archi ARET 7 231; Bonechi QDLF 9 277f.: "blade" (?). **EUPH** *pa-aš ni-tim, pa-šu (...) ni-tim* → Durand MARI 3 279; Archi NABU 2005/69; Arkhipov ARM 32 140f. **UGS** *ni-it, ni-iʔ-tu*, pl. *ni-ʔa-tu* → Sivan GAGl 253; Huehnergard UVST 150, ²UVST 394; vSoldt SAU 305 (94).
nỉt "axe, hatchet"	•CTX: **UGA** Sg. *nỉt*; du. *nỉtm* → DUL 604; Watson Fs. Postgate 707; Del Olmo AuOr 37 290.

|n-ʔ-d| (1)	Primary noun, Sem.: *nʔd* (*noʔd*) (Hb.) "leather bottle"; *nwd(?)* (JAram.) "skin bag"; *nādu(m)* (Akk.) "(water-)skin"; *ḥə-nīd/-nōd* (MSArab.) "water-skin".
nảd "(little) bag"	•CTX: **UGA** → DUL 603.

|n-ʔ-d| (2)	Sem.: *nâdu(m), naʔādu* (Akk.) "to praise, celebrate"; *nʔd* (OSArab.) "excellence"; *nəʔda* (Eth.) "to praise, extol", *nəʔud* "praised, glorified".

[241] Suff. pronoun genit. / accus. 1 pl. c.
[242] Suff. pronoun genit. / accus. 1 du. c.
[243] Suff. pronoun genit. / accus. 1 du c.
[244] Indep. possessive pronoun nomin. obl. 1 c.
[245] Indep. pronoun dat. pl. (OAkk. loan?).
[246] Suff. pronoun dat. 1 pl. c. (OAkk. loan?).
[247] Indep. pronoun obl. 1 pl. c. (OAkk. loan?).
[248] Indep. possessive pronoun obl. 1 pl. c.

naʔd "exalted"	•ONOM: **EB** *a-bí-na-du*, *a-mi-na-du*, *ḫu-ra-na-dum*, *na-da-iš* |naʔda=YiS(ru)|, *zi-bí-na-du* → Catagnoti QuSe 15 260; Pagan ARES 3 142, 274, 280, 319, 353, 385.
|n-ʔ-m|	Sem.: *naʔāmu*(*m*) (Akk.) "to advance boldly".
|n-ʔ-m| "to advance"	•CTX: **EB** G prefc. *na-a-ma* |ninʔam=ma| → Fronzaroli ARET 13 139, 286; Catagnoti QuSe 29 52, 60, 129, 146, 212.
|n-ʔ-ṣ|	Sem.: *nʔṣ* (Hb.) "to spurn"; *nâṣu*(m), *naʔāṣu* (Akk.) "to despise, scorn".
|n-ʔ-ṣ| "to despise, insult"	•CTX: **EA** G prefc. *ia-an-aṣ-ni* → Rainey CAT 2 72. **UGA** G prefc. suff. *ynảṣn*, act. ptc. *niṣ*, suff. *niṣy*, *niṣk*, *niṣh* → DUL 603f.
|n-ʔ(-t)|	Sem. etym. unc. Cf. *nʔh* (Hb.) "to be pleasing, delightful", *nʔwh* (*nāʔweh*) "beautiful, suitable"; *naʔata*, *naʔt*, *naʔit* (Arab.) "to moan"; *nāʔa*, *nayʔa* (Arab.) "to be uncooked", *nīʔ*, *niyy* "raw"; *nyʔ*, *neʔa* (Eth.) "to be ready to be cooked", *nāʔt* "unleavened bread".
nảt "a type of sacrifice"	•CTX: **UGA** → DUL 604: "lament" (?), altern. "sacrifice of unleavened bread".
|n-ʕ-l|	Sem.: *nʕl* (Hb.) "to secure (a door with straps)", *mnʕl* (*minʕāl*) "bolt", *mnʕwl* (*manʕûl*) "bar, bolt".
maʕʕalt "bolt"	•LL: **UGS** D[UR = *markassu*(?) = ...]-*a*(?) = *ma-a-al-*tu_4 → Huehnergard UVST 79, 153; Tropper UG 144, 279.
|n-ʕ-m| Cf. **|n-ħ-m|**	Sem.: *nʕm* (Hb.) "to be lovely, pleasant", *nʕm* (*noʕam*) "kindness", *nʕym* (*nāʕîm*) "pleasant, lovely, delightful", *mnʕmym* (pl.t. *manʕammîm*) "delicacies"; *nʕm* (Pun.) "good, fortune; agreeable, favourable"; *nʕm* (JAram. C)[249] "to be lovely, pleasant", *nʕym* "pleasant"; *naʕama*, *naʕima* (Arab.) "to become plentiful and easy; to be good, pleasant, be happy, pleased", *naʕam* "gazing livestock", *naʕma* "life of ease", *nāʕim* "soft, tender", *naʕīm* "amenity, comfort", *niʕma* "blessing, benefaction, grace", *nuʕmā* "happiness", *nuʕūma* "softness, tenderness", *manāʕim* "favours, blessings"; *nʿm* (OSArab.) "to please, be favourable, prosperous"; *nʕmtm* "prosperity, success"; *náʔmēt* (MSArab.) "well-being", *nəʔáym* "soft, smooth".
|n-ʕ-m| "to be large, rich" **naʕm** "pleasure, fortune, prosperity, grace"	•CTX: **EUPH** G suffc. *na-aḫ-mu* → Streck Onomastikon 1 107 § 1.95. •ONOM: **EG** Cf. *bʕl-m-n-ʕ-m* → Schneider APÄQ 85 no. 160. •CTX: **EB** *na-mi* |naʕm=ī| → Fronzaroli ARET 13 176, 286. **EUPH** *na-aḫ-mu-um* → Zadok Fs. Hallo 327; Durand LAPO 3 218 a.; Streck Onomastikon 1 107 § 1.95, 322 § 5.8 fn. 3. •ONOM: **EB** *na-ma-nu*, *na-me*/*mi*, *na-ma-da-mu*, *na-ma-ha-*al_6 → Pagan ARES 3 142f., 354. **EUPH** Passim; cf. *na-aḫ-mi*(*-im*), *na-aḫ-ma-nu*, *na-aḫ-mi-ia*, *na-ma-el*, na-*aḫ-mi-e-ra-aḫ*, *na-ah-mi-as-du*, *na-aḫ-mu-um-*^{d}*da-gan*, *na-aḫ-me-*^{d}*da-gan*; *a-ḫa-ta-na-aḫ-mi*, *a-bi-na-aḫ-mi*, *um-mi-na-aḫ-me*, ^{d}*iš-ḫa-ra-na-aḫ-me*, ^{d}*da-gan-na-aḫ-*

[249] Only marginal attestations, probl. Hb. loan.

	mi, ka-ak-ka-na-aḫ-mi, bi-na-aḫ-ne-el → Huffmon APNMT 238; Gelb CAAA 26, 161. **A7** *a-bi-na-aḫ-mi, na-mi-a-nim, na-mi-da-ka, na-(aḫ-)mi-*^{d}*da-gan, um-mi-na-mi* → Wiseman AT 142, 150; Gelb CAAA 26, 161; Sivan GAGl 250; Arnaud AuOr 156; Streck Onomastikon 1 322 § 5.8 fn. 3. **EM** *na-aḫ-mu, na-aḫ-mi-*DINGIR, *na-aʔ-[ma]-*^{d}KUR, *na-aḫ-mi-*KUR, *na-aʔ-mi-ša-da, na-aḫ-mi-ša-la-mu*; cf. SIG$_5$-*ma-at-*DINGIR-*lì*[250] → Arnaud SEL 8 32; Pruzsinszky PTEm 174 [646], 197 [645], 197 [644], 197 [646], 197 [645f.], 201 [645].
niʕm "pleasure, fortune, prosperity, grace; DN"	•ONOM: **EUPH** Passim; cf. *ni-iḫ-mu-um, ni-iḫ-ma-tum, ḫa-lu-ni-ḫi-im, a-bi-ni-ḫi-im, ì-lí-ne-ḫi-im, ḫa-am-mu-ni-ḫi-im, áš-di-ni-ḫi-im, mu-ta-ni-ḫi-im, zi-bi-ni-ḫi-im*; *ni-ḫi-ma, ni-ḫi-ma-tum* → Huffmon APNMT 238f.; Gelb CAAA 26, 165; Durand REA 683, 688. **A7** *ni-ma-a-du* → Wiseman AT 143; Gelb CAAA 26, 165; Arnaud AuOr 16 158; Streck Onomastikon 1 324 § 5.13 fn. 1.
nuʕm "pleasure, fortune, prosperity, grace; DN"	•ONOM: **EB** *en-nu-mu, a-da-nu-mi* → Pagan ARES 3 142f., 279, 307. **EUPH** Passim; cf. *nu-uḫ-ma-an, nu-uḫ-mi-a-bi, nu-uḫ-mi-*DINGIR, *nu-uḫ-mi-ì-lí, nu-uḫ-me-e-ba-al, nu-uḫ-mu -na-*^{d}IM,[251] *nu-uḫ-mi-*^{d}*da-gan, nu-uḫ-mi-li-im, nu-uḫ-mu-ba-a-tim*; *ḫa-ka-nu-uḫ-mu* → Huffmon APNMT 238; Gelb CAAA 26, 167; Zadok Fs. Hallo 327; Streck Onomastikon 1 325 § 5.16 fn. 2. **UGS** *nu-ma-re-ša-ip, nu-ú-ma-ya(-nu), nu-uʔ-me, nu-me-nu* → Gröndahl PTU 163; Sivan GAGl 255; Huehnergard UVST 254, AkkUg 400; vSoldt SAU 30, 331 n. 159.; see DUL 606: *nʕmn* (II); 607: *nʕmy* (II).
naʕam "pleasure, fortune, prosperity, grace"	•ONOM: **EB** *na-am*$_6$, *na-a-ma, na-am*$_6$*-da-mu, na-am*$_6$*-ḫa-al*$_6$, *=ha-lu, =hal*!(AN)*:lu, na-am*$_6$-Ì.GIŠ,[252] *bur-na-ḫa-am*$_6$ → Pagan ARES 3 142f., 296, 353.
naʕim "pleasant; the Gracious One (DN)"	•CTX: **EG** *n-ʕ-mu, na-ʕa-ma*$_4$, *na-ʕ-ma*$_4$*-na* → Hoch SWET 181f. no. 244: |naʕimu ?/ naʕmu ?|. •ONOM: **EB** *a-bù-na-im, a-ḫu-na-im, a-ḫum-na-im* (DNN?), *su-na-ì/im-ma-du, zú-na-ì-ma-du*; probl. DN: *bu/bù-da-na-im, gi-da-na-im, i-ib-na-im,*[253] *ìr-am*$_6$*-na-im, rí-ì-na-im, ru*$_{12}$*-zi-na-im* → Krebernik PET 98; Pagan ARES 3 142f., 275, 278f., 365, 389; 293, 311, 323, 337, 359f. **EUPH** *na-i-mu, na-ḫi-mi(-im), na-ḫi-mu-um* → Gelb CAAA 26, 161. **EG** See above: CTX.
nuʕām "pleasant, lovely, delightful"	•ONOM: **EUPH** *nu-ha-ma, ì-lí-nu-ḫa-am* → Huffmon APNMT 239; Gelb CAAA 26, 167; Zadok Fs. Hallo 327; Streck Onomastikon 1 332 § 5.33 fn. 3. **EM** *nu-a-me* → Pruzsinszky PTEm 175 [653].
nʕm (A) "pleasant, gracious"	•CTX: **UGA** Sg. *nʕm*, fem. *nʕmt*, pl. masc. *nʕmm* → DUL 605: *nʕm* (I); 606: *nʕmt* (I). •ONOM: **UGA** Cf. *ảdnnʕm* → DUL 20f.; *mlknʕm* → DUL 549.
nʕm (B) "pleasure, fortune, grace; DN"	•CTX: **UGA** Sg. *nʕm*, suff. *nʕmh*, suff. *nʕmm*, *nʕmn* → DUL 605f.: *nʕm* (II). •ONOM: **UGA** Cf. *nʕmn* → DUL 606: *nʕmn* (II); *nʕmy* → 607 *nʕmy* (II); *nʕmyn* → DUL 607.
nʕmn "handsome, pleasant, gracious"	•CTX: **UGA** → DUL 606: *nʕmn* (I).
naʕmūt "fortune, goodness, grace"	•ONOM: **EB** *na-mu-ud, na-mu-du* → Pagan ARES 3 142f., 354.

[250] Akk./ WSem. hybrid (?) \|naʕmī=māt=ʔilʔ\|.
[251] Durand RA 82 108ff. (A.1610+: 40; LAPO 17 266f.).
[252] \|naʕam=šammun=i\| "grace of the fat one".
[253] \|yiʔhib=naʔim\| "DN loved"; altern. \|yīhib=naʔim\| "DN gave"; see \|w-h-b\|.

nʕmt "fortune, goodness, grace"	•CTX: **UGA** → DUL 606f.: *nʕmt* (II).
nʕmy "fortune, goodness, grace"	•CTX: **UGA** DUL 607: *nʕmy* (I).
menʕim "loveliness, delightfulness, grace"	•ONOM: **EUPH** *me-en-ḫi-mu-um, me-en-ḫi-ma, me-en-ḫi-ma-tum* → Gelb CAAA 26, 160 (under NḤIM); Zadok Fs. Hallo 327; Streck Onomastikon 1 338 § 5.47, 360 (Suppl.).

|n-ʕ-r| (1)	Primary noun, Sem.: *nʕr* (*naʕar*, Hb.) "boy; servant", *nʕr*(*h*) (*naʕ^{a}rā*(*h*) "(young (un)married) girl; maidservant"; *nʕr* (Ph., Amm.) "boy; servant".
naʕr "servant; soldier"	•CTX: **EB** *na-ʔa*$_5$*-rí, na-ʔa*$_5$*-la-ma* |naʕra(m?)=ma|; cf. UGULA *na-a-rum* → Fronzaroli SEL 12 53 fn. 8; Catagnoti QuSe 29 56, 212. •LL: **EB** Unc. cf. Á.TÚG = *na-a*-LUM → Conti QuSe 17 154; Fronzaroli SEL 52f. fn. 8. **EG** *n*(*a*)*-ʕa-ru*$_2$*-na, n-ʕ-ru*$_2$*-na, n-ʕ-ru*$_2$*-w-na*$_2$*, n-ʕ-ru*$_2$*-na/nu*$_4$ (pl. |naʕarūna|) → Hoch SWET 182f. no. 245.[254] •ONOM: **EB** Unc. *na*-LUM, *na-ru*$_{12}$ (GN ?) → Pagan ARES 3 226, 354.[255]
nʕr (A) "boy; servant"	•CTX: **UGA** Sg. abs. *nʕr*, suff. *nʕrh*; pl. abs. *nʕrm*; cstr. *nʕr*, suff. *nʕry*; du. *nʕrm* → DUL 607f.: *nʕr* (I). •ONOM: **UGA** *nʕr* → DUL 608: *nʕr* (III).
nʕrt "girl, maidservant"	•CTX: **UGA** Pl. *nʕrt* → DUL 608: *nʕrt.*

|n-ʕ-r| (2)	Sem.: *nʕr* (Hb.) "to shake off"; (JAram. D) id.
|**n-ʕ-r**| "to shake"	•CTX: **UGA** G/D prefc. *tnʕr*, suff. *ynʕrnh*; N prefc. *tnʕr* → DUL 607.

|n-ʕ-r| (3)	Sem. etym. unc.
nʕr (B) "a type of flour or grain"	•CTX: **UGA** → DUL 608: *nʕr* (II).

|n-b| (1)	Primary noun, Sem.: *nb*(*ʔ*) (JAram., Syr.) "nit, the egg of a louse"; *nābu*(*m*), *nēbu* (Akk.) "insect eggs; nit"; *nib*(*b*) (MSArab.) "nit"
nab "louse"	LL: **EB** *na-bù* → Sjöberg WO 27 18.

|n-b| (2)	Primary noun, Sem.: *npt* (*nopet*, Hb.) "virgin honey"; unc. *npt* (Pun.) "honey"; *nūbtu*(*m*) (Akk.) "honey-bee"; *nūb* (Arab.) "bees"; *nōbet, nūbōt, nibbɔt* (MSA) "bee"; *nəhb* (Eth.) id.
nubt "bee"	•ONOM: **EUPH** Cf. unc. *nu-ba-ta* , *nu-bu-ta*, *nu-ba-at-ta* → Gelb CAAA 168 (NUBAṬ); Durand MARI 8 618 fn. 265, 667.
nbt "honey"	•CTX: **UGA** Sg. *nbt*, suff. *nbtm* → DUL 610.
nūbiʔān "an insect (bee, caterpillar ?)"	•LL: **EB** Cf. NAM.NA.DU.DU = *nu-bí-a-núm* → Sjöberg Fs. Kienast 553; Fs. Oelsner 413; Militarev / Kogan SED 2 207f. no. 156; Bonechi QDLF 21 58.

254 Sivan / Cochavi-Rainey WSVES 82: *na-ʕa-rú-na* "warriors"; Helck Beziehungen no. 136.
255 Altern. \|nahr\| "river"; see \|n-h-r\| (1).

|n-b-ʔ|

Sem.: *nbyʔ* (*nābîʔ*, Hb.) “called, spoken to, prophet”, *nbʔ* (N, Hitp.) “to behave like a *nbyʔ*”, *nbyʔh* (*n*^{e}*bîʔāh*) “prophetess”, *nbwʔh* (*n*^{e}*bûʔāh*) “prophetic utterance”; *nby*(*ʔ*) (Aram., Syr.) “prophet, interpreter”, *naby* (JAram., Syr., D) “to predict, prophesy”, *nbwʔh, nbwʔtʔ, nbyw, nbywtʔ* “prophecy”; *nabû*(*m*), *nabāʔu*(*m*) (Akk.) “to name, nominate; invoke; decree”, *nabû*(*m*) “called, authorized person”, *munabbûm* “a lamentation priest”; *nabiyy* (Arab.) “prophet”, *nabbaʔa, ʔanbaʔa* “to inform, tell, advise, announce”, *tanabbaʔa* “to pass oneself off as a prophet, prophesy”, *nabaʔ* “news”, *mutanabbiʔ/n* “who passes oneself off as a prophet”; *nby* (*tnbʔ*, OSArab.) “to announce, promise”; *nebi, nəbī mbī* (MSArab.) “prophet”, *nəbō mbúh* “to inform”; *nabiyy* (Eth.) “prophet”, *nabiyyət, nabit* “prophetess”, *tanabbaya* “to act as a prophet”.
Non-Sem.: **nab*= (West Chadic) “to read, count”; **nab*= (Omotic) “name”.[256]

|n-b-ʔ| “to call (upon), proclaim, invoke, lament”

•CTX: **EB** D prefc. *ù-na-ba-ga-ma*, inf. *na-bù-u* |ʔunabbaʔ=ka=ma nabbuʔ=u(m)| → Catagnoti / Fronzaroli ARET 16 174, 256; Catagnoti QuSe 29 80, 114, 148, 152, 212.
EUPH Passim; cf. *i-na-ab-bu-ú* → Durand ARM 26/1 378 (A.450:6); Reculeau FM 16 376ff.
EM D juss. *lú-ú-na-ab-bi/bu* |lunabbi/u|; *tu-na-ab-bi, tù-na-bi, tu*$^{!}$*-nab-bi* |tunabbi|; cf. *lu-ú-tu*$_4$*-na-ab-bi* → Fleming JAOS 113 177f.; Pentiuc Vocabulary 111ff.; Ikeda BiOr 60 269, 271. See below: *nābiʔ, munabbiʔ.*
•LL: **EB** PÀ = *na-ba-um, na*<*-ba*>*-ù-um* → Krebernik RA 73 28.
•ONOM: **EB** Cf. *en-bí* |yinbiʔ|; |yibbiʔ=| (?) passim: cf. *i-bí-ù, i-bí-um, i-bí-u*$_4$, *ib-bí, ib-bí-um, i-bí-su/sù, i-bí-a-du, ib-bí-ì* |yibbiʔ=ʔi(l)|, and passim *i-bí*=DN; passim also aphaeretic *bí*= |(yi)bbiʔ=|: *bí-ḫa-lum*, etc.; unc. *i-da-bí*(*ù/um*) |yittabiʔ=| (?) → Pagan ARES 3 143f., 292, 305, 320f., 330.
U3 *ià-an-bi-ì-lum* → Buccellati Amorites 152; Gelb CAAA 26, 164: Golinets Onomastikon 2 26, 94, 322, 412.
EB *i-bí*-ZI.KIR[257] → Gelb LEbla 21f.; Krebernik PET 111.
EUPH *ia-ab-bi-um, ia-bi-*^{d}IM/^{d}*da-gan, ia-ab-ba-an-ni*-DINGIR, *ia-ab-bi-*^{d}IM, *ia-ab-bi-*^{d}*a-ba*$_4$, *ia-ab-bi-*^{d}*da-gan, ia-ba-an-ni*-DINGIR, *i-bi-*^{d}*da-gan, i-a-bi-na-im, i-bi-na-bu-ú*; cf. unc. *ia-na-bi-im, ia-na-bi-el, ia-na-*(*ab-*)*bi*-DINGIR → Huffmon APNMT 236; Gelb CAAA 26, 164; Golinets Onomastikon 2 87f., 98, 322, 412.
TU *a-ba-ni-il, i-ba-ni-il, ia-ba-an-ni-il* → Krebernik Tall Biʿa 208, 216, 218; Golinets Onomastikon 2 87f., 98, 322, 412.
EM *ia-ab-bi* → Pruzsinszky PTEm 165 [400].
UGA *nbʕm* (*nb*(*ʔ*)=*ʕm*) → Gröndahl PTU 17, 37, 39, 62, 109, 164; DUL 608f.
EG Cf. *n-ꜣ-b-w-y-ꜣ* → Schneider APÄQ 141 nos.299f.

nibʔ “nominal value”

•CTX: **EUPH** *ni-bu*(*-um*) → Michel MARI 6 194; Soubeyran ARM 23 381.

nabiʔ “called”

•ONOM: **EB** *na-bí* → Pagan ARES 3 143f., 353.

[256] Orel / Stolbova HSED 394 no. 1822: **nab*= “to speak, name”.
[257] Formerly read *i-bí-sí-piš* (Pettinato Culto 3, MEE 2 181).

nābiʔ "who names, calls, invokes"	•CTX: **EUPH** LÚ *na-bi-i* MEŠ → Fleming JAOS 113 179ff.; Durand ARM 22/1 378, 445f. (216:7). **EM** LÚ.MEŠ *na-bi-i* → Fleming JAOS 113 175ff.; Pentiuc Vocabulary 112. •ONOM: **EUPH** *na-bi-um, na-bi-ì-lí, na-bi-an-nu, na-bi-ka-ka, na-bi-*^{d}UTU, *an-nu-na-na-bi-iḫ* → Gelb CAAA 26, 162; Streck Onomastikon 1 329 § 5.24; Golinets Onomastikon 2 179, 412, 506, 510. **A7** *su-mu-un-na-bi, su-mu-na-a-bi, šu-mu-na-a-bi, su-mu-un-a-bi, a-ia-na-bi-i-la* |ʔaya=nābiʔ=ʔilā| → Wiseman AT 145; Arnaud AuOr 16 161f. **EM** *na-(a-)bi* → Pruzsinszky PTEm 174 [640].
nabāʔ "announce, new(s)" (?)	•ONOM: **EUPH** Unc. *na-ba-i-im, na-ba-yi-im* → Gelb CAAA 26, 162.[258]
munabbiʔ "he who invokes, laments"	•CTX: **EB** D act. ptc. fem. DAM *mu-na-bí-tum* → Paquali NABU 2018/38; 2019/3. **EM** D act. ptc. pl. fem. *mu*$_{x}$(A)*-na-bi-a-ti, mu*$_{x}$(A)*-nab-bi-a-ti*, MÍ.MEŠ *mu*$_{x}$(A)*-nab-bi-ia-ti*, MÍ.MEŠ *mu-na-bi-ia-ti* → Lion RA 94 22. 31f.; Fleming, JAOS 113, 175ff.; Pentiuc Vocabulary 112f.; Pasquali NABU 2019/3.

|n-b-ʕ|	Sem.: *nbʕ* (Hb.) "to gush forth", *mbwʕ* (*mabbûaʕ*) "spring, water source"; *nbʕ* (JAram., Syr.) "to gush forth", *nbʕ(ʔ), mbwʕ(ʔ), mbʕh, mbʕtʔ* "fountain"; *nabāʔu(m)* (Akk.) "to rise, well up" (?), *nambaʔu* "source, spring", *nābiḫum, nābiu(m)* "who rises"; *nabaʕa* (Arab.) "to well up, gush fort", *manbaʕ* "spring, well"; *nbʕn* (OSArab.) "who causes water to gush out"; *nabʕa, ʔanbəʕa* (Eth.) "to weep".
nibʕ "watered field" (?)	•CTX: **EUPH** *ni-ib-am, ni-ib-i-im* → Durand ARM 26/1 347; Zadok Fs. Hallo 327; Streck Onomastikon 1 108 § 1.95.
mabbaʕ "source, spring"	•LL: **EB** A.BAL = *ma-ba-ḫum*(LUM) → Pettinato MEE 4 (VE 640); Bonechi Proceedings 44 RAI 2 100

|n-b-b|	Sem.: *nabābu* (Akk.) "to play the flute", *ebbūbu(m), enbūbum, embūbu* "flute, pipe"; *nabba* (Arab.) "to bleat", *ʔunbūb* "tube, pipe, windpipe"; cf. further *nababa* (Eth.) "to murmur, utter a sound", *ʔanbaba* "to chant, recite".
|**n-b-b**| "to whistle, sound"	•LL: **EB** KA.GI.DI = *na-ba-bù-um*, var. gi.dé → Conti QuSe 17 99 *sub* (218); Sjöberg Fs. Kienast 550.
ʔumbūb "a kind of flute"	•CTX: **UGS** *um-bu-be* → CAD U/W 98.[259]
ʔanbūbt, ʔunbūbt "kind of tubular hairpin"	•CTX: **EB** *a/ù-na-bù-bi/bù-tum* → Fronzaroli SEL 12 60; Pasquali QuSe 23 104ff.

|n-b-x| Cf. **|x-b-t| (1)**	Sem.: Cf. *ḫabātu*(m) (Akk.) "to rob, plunder".
|**n-b-x**| "to rob, pillage" (?)	•CTX: **EB** Dtn prefc. cf. *nu-da-na-ba-ḫu* |nuttanabbax=u| → Catagnoti QuSe 29 137, 144, 213.

[258] Altern.: hypocoristica with the theophorous elem. (or PN?) *Nabû*; cf. ^{d}*na-bu-la-a-bu, na-bu-ia-tum,* ^{d}*na-bu-ú-ma-lik, iš-ḫi-na-bu-um, i-zi-na-bu-ú, i-bi-na-bu-ú*; see Durand REA 655, 687.
[259] Cf. diff. AHw 1413: *umbūbu*, Ug. for *šerʔān* "string".

|n-b-k|	Sem.: *nbk* (*nēbek*, pl. cstr. *nibkê*, Hb.,) "source, fountain", *mbk* (*mabbāk*, pl. cstr. *mabb^{e}kê*) "water-source". Cf. *nbg* (JAram.) "to break forth", (Syr.) "to gush out, emerge"; *nabağa* (Arab.) "to spout, spurt". See further: *nagbu*(m), *nagabbu* (Akk.) "underground water, source".
naBk "fountain, spring, well"	•CTX: **UGS** Pl. |nab(a)kūma|: *i-na* A.ŠÀ *: na-*AB-*ki-ma, i-na : na-*AB-*ki-ma, i-na* A.ŠÀ(.MEŠ) *:* NAB/*na-*AB-*ki-ma, i-na na-bá-ki-ma, i-na na-ba-ki-mi* → Sivan GAGl 252; Huehnergard UVST 151; vSoldt SAU 305 (96), 322 fn. 140; Tropper UG 137, 182, 295. •LL: **UGS** IDIM = *na*[*b-qu*(?)] = *tar-m*[*a*(?)-*n*]*i* = NAB-*ku* → Huehnergard UVST 97, 151, ^{2}UVST 390.[260] •ONOM: **EB** *nab-gu* → Pagan ARES 3 227, 354. **UGS** Cf. *na-*PA-*ak-ku* → Sivan GAGl 252; DUL 609: *nbk* (II).
nbk, npk "fountain, spring, well"	•CTX: **UGA** Sg. *nbk, npk* → Tropper UG 137; DUL 609: *nb*/*pk* (I) •ONOM: **UGA** Cf. unc. *gmnpk* → DUL 297; *nbk* → DUL 609: *nbk* (II).
mbk "fountain, spring, well"	•CTX: **UGA** Sg. *mbk*, pl. (?) *mbkm* → Tropper UG 137: |mabbak|; DUL 518.
|n-B-l| (1)	Culture word, Sem.: Cf. *nappillu, nabbillu, nappalu* (Akk.) "caterpillar".
nuppilān "caterpillar" (?)	•LL: **EB** Cf. NA.DU.DU =*nu-bí-a-núm* → Sjöberg Fs. Oelsner 413 fn. 11.
|n-b-l| (2)	Culture word, Sem.: *nablu*(*m*) (Akk.) "fire-arrow, flash of fire, flame"; *nabl* (Arab.) "arrow", denom. *nabala* "to shoot arrows", *nabbāl* "archer"; (Eth.) *nabal* "flame".
nabl "fire-arrow, flame"	•ONOM: **U3** Cf. *na-ab-la-núm*/*nu-um, lab-la-nu-um* → Buccellati Amorites 175; Gelb CAAA 27, 162; Owen JCS 33 257 (*na-ap-la-núm*); Zadok Fs. Hallo 327.[261]
nblů "fire-arrow, flame"	•CTX: **UGA** Sg./pl. suff. *nblůh*, pl. *nblåt* → Tropper UG 50; DUL 610.
nabbāl "the archer; DN"	•ONOM: **A7** Cf. *sa-am-su-*^{d}*na-ba-la* → Wiseman AT 145; Zadok OLA 28 96, 98 fn. 17.
|n-b-l| (3)	Sem.: *nabula* (Arab.) "to excel, surpass, show superiority", *nabl* "noble, exalted", *nubl* "nobility". See the antonym *nbl* (Hb.) "to be futile, foolish".
|**n-b-l**| "to excel, show superiority"	•ONOM: **U3** Cf. *ià-an-bu-li* → Buccellati Amorites 152f.; Gelb CAAA 27, 164; Golinets Onomastikon 2 26, 322, 412.
nablat "excellent, noble"	•ONOM: **EUPH** *na-ab-la-tum* → Golinets Onomastikon 2 154, 412
|n-b-r|	Sem.: *nbr* (JAram., Syr.) "to poke or dig up the ground", *nbr*(*?*) (Syr.) "claw"; cf. *nabara* (Arab.) "to raise, elevate".
|**n-b-r**| "to dig up / turn over (the ground)"	•ONOM: **EUPH** Cf. *na-bi-ru-um* → Zadock Fs. Hallo 327.[262]

[260] RS 94.2939 (trilingual Sumerian, Akkadian, and Hurrian LL) reads *nagbu* in the Akk. column.

[261] Zadok loc.cit. connects the PN *lab-la-nu-um* (< *nab-la-nu-um*) with the Hb. PN *Nbl* (*Nābāl*) "(ig)noble". Unlikely.

|n-B-S|	Culture word: Cf. *nabāsu(m)*, *nabassu*, *nabāšu*, *napāsu* (Akk.) "red(-dyed) wool".
nabāS "red(-dyed) wool"	•CTX: **EUPH** (SÍG) *na-ba-su* → Durand ARM 30 144.[263]
nps^{1} (B) "red(-dyed) wool"	•CTX: **UGA** → DUL 629: *npš* (II).
|n-b-ṯ|	Sem.: *nbṭ* (Hb. C) "to look"; *nabāṭu(m)* (Akk.) "to shine, be(come) bright"; see further: *nbṭ* (Aram.) "to grow, spew forth, spout"; *nabaṭa* (Arab.) "to well, issue forth"; *hnbṭ* (OSArab.) "to dig down to water"; *nebōṭ* (MSArab.) "to dig up, tale out". Cf. *nabaṭa* (Eth.) "to boil (over), grow".
|n-b-ṯ| "to shine, appear, look at"	•CTX: **UGA** G prefc. *tbṭ* → DUL 610f.: */n-b-ṭ/* •ONOM: **EB** Cf. *a-bí-du/dum* |yabbiṯ=| → Pagan ARES 3 144, 274. **U3** Cf. *e-bi-da-nu-um* → Buccellati Amorites 144; Gelb CAAA 27, 54 (?EB). **EB OBab.** *i-bi-iṭ-li-im* → Gelb CAAA 27, 164; Golinets Onomastikon 2 323, 413. **EUPH** *i-en-bi-iṭ-*^{d}TIŠPAK → Gelb CAAA 27, 164; Golinets Onomastikon 2 323, 413.
nabṯ "splendour"	•CTX: **EB** *na-ba-ti-iš* → Fronzaroli ARET 11 162; Catagnoti QuSe 29 113, 213.
nābiṯ "who shines, appears, looks at"	•ONOM: **EUPH** Cf. *an-nu-na-bi-ti*, *a-ta-na-bi-ti* → Gelb CAAA 27, 162.
nabuṯ "brillant, splendorous"	•ONOM: **EUPH** Cf. DINGIR-*na-bu-uṭ*, *na-bu-tum*, *na-bu-di-a* → Gelb CAAA 27, 162; Golinets Onomastikon 2 161, 413.
nubāṯ "the brillant, splendorous one"	•ONOM: **EUPH** Fem. cf. *nu-ba-ta* → Gelb CAAA 27, 168; Golinets Onomastikon 2 164, 413.
nubbūṯ "watched attentively, observed"	•ONOM: **EUPH** Fem. *nu-bu-ta*, nu-bu-ut-ta → Gelb CAAA 27, 168; Golinets Onomastikon 2 202, 413.
|n-d|	Akk. loanword: Cf. *nādu*, *nadû* (Akk. LL: *na(-ʔa-a)-du(-u/ú)*) "stela". Non-Sem.: Cf. NA$_4$ n a - d ù - a (Sum.) "stela".[264]
nad "stela"	•LL: **UGS** [N]A = *na-a-du* = *na-di* = *na-du* → Huehnergard UVST 49, 152; ^{2}UVST 382. Cf. NA$_4$ n a - d ù - a = *na-du* (RS Recension of Hh. XVI 243).[265]
|n-d-ʔ|	Sem.: Cf. *nadʔa* (Eth.) "drive away". See further: *nadaha* (Arab.) "to make walk".
|n-d-ʔ| "to eject, frighten away"	•CTX: **UGA** G suffc. *tdủ*, *ydủ*; impv. (?) *dỉ* → DUL 611: */n-d-ʔ/*.

262 Connection with the MN ITI *Nabrium*, *Nabrû(m)* (see Zadock loc.cit.) unc. See further: *ni-ip-ra-am*, *nu-pu-ri* (EUPH); *nu-bar*-LUGAL (A7); Gelb CAAA 166, 168.

263 For Mari-Akk. SÍG *na-ap-ša-tum* see Durand ARM 30 144f. ("étoffe cardée"), Akk. *napāšu(m)* "to pluck, pick (wool)".

264 Altern. rendering of n a - r ú - a. See under CAD N/1 68: *nadû* A; cf. AHw 705: *nadû* II.

265 Diff. vSoldt BiOr 47 732: "water skin"(?), from Hb. *noʔd* (see \|n-ʔ-d\| (1)). Unlikely Sivan GAGl 251: NÂDU "to care for"(?)).

|n-d-b| Cf. **|n-ṭ-p|**	Sem.: *ndb* (Hb. Hitp.) “to make a voluntary contribution”, *ndbh* (*nᵉdābāh*) “free motivation, voluntary offering”, *ndybh* (*nᵉdîbāh*) “dignity”; *ndb* (JAram. G) “to motivate to action”, (Dt) “to donate”, *ndbh*, *ndbtʔ* “free will offering”; *nadaba* (Arab.) “to appoint, assign”, *ʔintadaba* “to be willing, be prepared”, *naduba* “to be alert, agile”.
|n-d-b| “to be generous, give generously”	•ONOM: **EB** |yaddub=|: *a-du-bí, a-du-ba, a-du-bù, a-dub-da-mu*; |yiddub=|: *i-du-bù, i-dub-da-mu*, cf. *ì-du-bu*$_{17}$(KA);[266] |yindub=|: *en-du-bù*; |taddub=|: *da-dub, da-dub-si-nu, da-dub-da-mu* → Pagan ARES 3 144f., 277, 297, 306, 322, 328. **EUPH** *in-du-ub-ša-lim, ia-an-du-ub-li-im*; cf. *ia-ad-du-bi-im* → Gelb CAAA 27, 165; Zadok Fs. Hallo 327; Streck Onomastikon 1 327 § 5.21 fn. 2; Golinets Onomastikon 2 31, 159, 323, 413f. **UGA** *ndbd* → DUL 611; *ndbn* → DUL 611; *ydbỉl* → DUL 942; *ydbbʕl* → DUL 942; *ydbhd* → DUL 942.
nadab “willing, eager to give”	•ONOM: **EB** Fem. cf. *na-da/da*$_{5}$*-ba-du* → Pagan ARES 144f., 353. **U3** *na-da-ab-tum* → Zadok Fs. Hallo 327.
nadūb “generously given”	•ONOM: **U3** Cf. *na-du-be-lí* → Buccellati Amorites 175; Gelb CAAA 27, 162; Wilcke WO 5 29; Streck Onomastikon 1 327 § 5.21 fn. 2; Golinets Onomastikon 2 140, 413f. **EUPH** Cf. *na-du-bu-um*, fem. *na-du-ba*(?) → Gelb CAAA 27, 162; Streck Onomastikon 1 330 § 5.28; Golinets Onomastikon 2 139f., 413f.
mendib “generous gift”	•ONOM: **EUPH** *me-en-di-bu-um* → Gelb CAAA 27, 164; Streck Onomastikon 1 338 § 5.47.

|n-d-d| (1)	Sem.: *ndd* (Hb.) “to flee, escape”; (JAram., Syr.) “to move away from, give way”; *nadda* (Arab.) “to flee, run away”.[267] Non-Sem.: *nwd* (Eg.) “to move”; **nVyVd=* (Berb.) “to walk”; **nVd=* (West Chadic) “to go (away)”; **nad=* (Central Chadic) “to come”.[268]
|n-d-d| (A) “to move, escape, flee”	•CTX: **UGA** G prefc. *tdd*, suffc. *ndt* → Tropper UG 674, 676; cf. DUL 611f.: */n-d-d/* G 1, 2.
nādid “wandering labourer, vagrant”	•LL: **EB** SA.GÁZ = *na-ti-tum* → Conti QuSe 17 116f.; Bonechi QDLF 16 82.

|n-d-d| (2)	Sem.: Cf. *izuzzum, uzuzzu(m)* (Akk.) “to stand”;[269] further: *nādda* (Arab.) “to oppose, be opposed”.[270]
|n-d-d| (B) “to stand, step over to, step before”	•CTX: **UGA** G prefc. *ydd, tdd*, suffc. *ndd* → Tropper UG 101, 468, 534, 626, 674, 677: < **nðð*; cf. DUL 611f.: G. 3.

|n-d-ḥ|	Sem.: *ndḥ* (Hb.) “to wield (an axe)”, (N) “to be scattered”, (C) “to drive away, push away”; *ndḥ* (JAram.) “to mislead”; *nadaḥa* (Arab.) “to extend, expand”; *nadḥa* (Eth.) “to drive, push, throw down”.

---

266 Pagan ARES 3 328: *ì*?(NI)-*du-bu*$_{14}$?(KA).

267 Possibly loan in Akk.; see AHw *nadādu(m)*, “weichen” (?) (unc. mng according to CAD N/1 41).

268 Orel / Stolbova HSED 394f. no. 1826: **nad=*, **nid=* “to go, walk”.

269 Probl. < **nzz*. See Streck AfO 24/25 320ff.

270 See Tropper AoF 24 204ff.

|**n-d-ḫ**| "to swing (out)" (?)	•ONOM: **EG** Cf. *m-n:-ṯ-w₂-ḥ:-ty* → Schneider APÄQ 128 no. 273.
nidāḫ "kind of weapon"	•CTX: **EB** GIŠ *ni-da-ʔà* → Fronzaroli Fs. Limet 62 fn. 50; Pasquali QuSe 23 152f.

|n-d-n|
See |**n/w/y-D-n**|

|**n/w/y-D-n**| Cf. |**t-d-n**|	Sem. basis |=D-n| with augments in |n=|, |w/y=|. For |n-D-n| see *ntn* (Hb., Aram., Ammon., Edom., Nab., Palm.) "to give", *mtn* (*mattān*, Hb) "gift, present", *mtnh* (*matānāh*) id., *mtt* (*mattat*) id., *ntyn* (pl. *n*ᵉ*tînîm*) "temple slaves", *ndn* (cstr. *n*ᵉ*dānayk*) "present", *ʔtnh* (*ʔetnāh*), *ʔtnn* (*ʔetnan*) "gift"; *mtnʔ*, *mtnh*, *mtntʔ* (JAram., Syr.) "gift", *ntl* (*nettel*, Syr. < **ntn l*) "to give", *mtl*(*ʔ*) "gift"; *nadānu*(*m*) (Akk.) "to give", *nidnu*(*m*) "gift", *nādinum* "giver, donor", *mad*(*d*)*atu*(*m*), *mandattu* "payment, obligation" (> Aram., Syr. *mndh*, *mndtʔ*; Hb. *mdh*), *nidintu*(*m*), *nidittu*(*m*) "gift, dowry"; *nudunnû*(*m*) "marriage gift"; *ntn*, *natana* (Eth.) "to give" (< Hb.).[271] For |w/y-t-n| see *ytn* (Ph.) "to give", *mtt* (Ph.), *mtn*, *mtnt* (Pun.) "gift".
|**n-d-n**| "to give"	•CTX: **EB** G prefc. *i-ti* |yiddi(n)|, Gt prefc. *a-da-ti-in* |la=yittadin| → Fronzaroli ARET 13 19, 240; Catagnoti / Fronzaroli ARET 16 14, 242; Catagnoti QuSe 29 146f., 213.[272] **EA** Forms with occasional nasalization, see: *i-na-an-din-šu-nu-ti*, *a-na-an-din-šu-nu*, *a-na-an-din-šu-nu-ti*, *ta-na-an-di-in*, *i-na-an-din-ni*, *i-na-an-din-ni₇*; peculiar forms: *ia-di-in₄*, *ia-di-na*, *ia-di-nu*, *ya-di-in*, *ya-di-na*, *ya-di-nu*; *ti-na-din*; *ti-din*, *ti-di-in*, *ti-di-in₄*, *ti-id-di-in₄*; *na-ad-na*; *yu-da-na*, *yu-da-na₇*, *yu-da-nu*, *yu-da-na-ni* → Rainey CAT 2 21, 35, 37f., 57, 69; Izre'el Orient 38 83. **TA** *tu-da-nu-na* → Horowitz / Oshima CunCan 133. **UGS** Cf. *id-din*, *in-na-áš-šúm-ma*, *it-ta-din-me*, *it-ta-din-šu*, *id-dá-an-na*, *at-ta-na-ak-ku* → Arnaud AuOr 17/18 150; Huehnergard Syria 74 217; Lackenbacher / Malbran-Labat RSOu 23 22, 128, 131, 173. •ONOM: **EB** |din| (G imp.): *ti-in-da-mu*; |yaddi(n)| *i-ti*, *i-ti-um*, *i-ti-nu*, *i-ti-núm*, *i-ti-ne*, *i-ti-a*, *i-ti-u₉*; passim with DNN: cf. *i-ti-lum*, *i-ti-il*, *i-ti-ma-il*, *i-ti-da-mi-gu*, *i-ti*-DINGIR, *i-ti*-ᵈ*da-gan*, *i-ti*-ᵈEN.KI, *i-ti*-ᵈ*ga-me*/*mi-iš*, *i-ti*-ᵈ*ra-sa-ap*, *i-ti-ma-li*, etc.; |yiddin|: *i-ti-in*, *i-ti-nu*, *i-ti-in-ì-lam*, *i-ti-núm*, *i-ti-ne*; |yindi(n)|: *en-ti*, *in-ti*; |yaddi(n)|: *a-ti*, *a-ti*-DINGIR, *ʔa₅-ti*, *ʔa₅-ti-bí-du*; |taddi(n): *da-ti*, *da-te*-ᵈUTU, *da-ti*-ᵈ*gú-ša*, *da-ti-ga*, *da₅-ti*[273] → Pagan ARES 3 145, 272, 284, 299, 307, 325ff., 337, 370. **EUPH** |yiddin|: cf. *in-din-nu-um*, *id-di-nu*, *i-din-ia*, *i-din-ab-ba*, *i-din*-ᵈ*ad-mu*, *i-din*-ᵈIGI.KUR, *i-din-ak-ka*, *i-di-an-nu*, *i-din-ia-tum*, *id-di-ia-tim*, *i-din*-ᵈ*áš-ku-ur*, *i-din*-ᵈ*i-tur-me-er*, *i-din-bi-nu-um*, *i-din*-ᵈ*di-ri-tim*, *i-din*-ᵈ*da-gan*, *i-din-ka-ak-ka*, *i-din*-ᵈ*ka-ka*, *i-din*-ᵈ*la-ba*, *i-din*-ᵈ*me-er*, *i-din*-ᵈ*ma-ma*, *i-din*-ᵈ*ri-im*, *i-din*-ᵈ*ru-uš*/*úš-pa-an*, *i-din-ta-bu-bu* → Gelb CAAA 27, 164f.; Golinets Onomastikon 2 419ff., 504ff., 510. **A7** *id-di-na*, *id-di-na-ab-ba* → Wiseman AT 137; Gelb CAAA 27, 164; Golinets Onomastikon 2 506, 510.

[271] Note the dissimilated Phön. form *tntn* G prefc. |tantin| and Late Pun. N suffc. *nntn* |nantanū|; Amadassi Guzzo PPG 103. See also the EB and EUPH instances under |n-d-n| and |n-t-n|, below.
[272] For the imp. *i-ti* |yitti(n) < *|witin| see under |w/y-t-n|. Cf. also IN.NA.SUM |yinaddan|(?); Catagnoti QuSe 29 85 fn. 349.
[273] Altern. |dād=ī| "my beloved"; see |d-w/y-d|.

A4 *id-di-na-ba* → Wiseman AT 137; Gelb CAAA 27, 164; Golinets Onomastikon 2 506, 510.
EG Cf. *yw$_2$-d-y$_2$-n-ꜣ-y$_2$* ^{F} → Schneider APÄQ 50 no. 88.

|n-t-n| "to give" •CTX: **EA** G prefc. *an-ti-in$_4$-nu* (96:8) → Sivan GAGl 155, 255; Rainey CAT 2 398;
•ONOM: **U3** *in-ti-nu-um* → Buccellati Amorites 159; Wilcke WO 5 27; Golinets Onomastikon 2 31, 329, 419ff.
EUPH |yin/ttin|: *it-ti-in, i-ti-in-*^{d}IM, *ia-en-ti-nu-um, e-en-ti-nu-um*; |yan/ttin|: *ia-ti-nu, ia-at-ti-nu(-um), ia-an-ti-nu, ia-an-te/ti-nu-um, a-an- ti-nu-um, ia-ti-ia, ia-at-ti-ia, ia-an-te/ti-ia, ia-at-ti-in-a-ḫu, ia-an-ti-in-a-ḫu(-um), ia-an-ti-in-*^{d}IM, *ia-at-ti-in-*^{d}IM, *ia-ti-in-* ^{d}IM, *a-an-ti-in-*DINGIR, *ia-an-ti-na-du, ia-an/at-ti-in-*DINGIR, *ia-an-ti-ni-*DINGIR, *ia-an-ti-in-ḫa-mu, ia-an-ti-in-a-ra-aḫ, ia-an-ti-na-ra-aḫ, ia-an-ti-la/na-ra-aḫ, ia-an/at-ti-in-e-ra-aḫ, ia-an-ti-in-*^{d}*da-gan, ia-at-ti-in-*^{d}*da-gan, ia-ti-in-*^{d}*da-gan, ia-an-ti-in-ša-ma-aš* → Huffmon APNMT 244; Gelb CAAA 27, 167; Zadok Fs. Zadok 327; Golinets Onomastikon 2 31f., 35, 77, 328ff., 419ff., 478.
TU *ia-tin-*^{d}*ú-bi, ya-tin-*DINGIR → Krebernik Tall Biʿa 219, 221.
EG Cf. *y:-b-n-ty-t-y$_2$-n-ꜣ, y-ṯ-n-ꜣ* → Schneider APÄQ 18 no. 10, 63 no. 112.

|w/y-t-n| "to give" •CTX: **MBQ** G prefc. cf. *it-ti-nV, it-ti-in-ma, ti-it-ti-in, di-ti-in, it-tin:* 157 → Mayer Ekalte 38, 75, 140f., 157.
TA G prefc. *i-te-na* → Horowitz / Oshima CunCan 145.
EA G prefc. cf. *ia-ti-na* → Sivan GAGl 156, 255; Rainey CAT 2 57, 68.
UGA G prefc. *åtn* (*ỉtn* (?)), *ttn, ytn*, suff. *åtnk, ttnn, ytnk, ytn.hm, ytnn, ytnnn*, suffc. *ytt, ytnt, ytn*, imp. *tn*, inf. *tn, ttn*; N/Gpass. suffc. *ytn, ttn*, suff. *ytnm*, N ptc. *ntn*; C prefc. *ỉštn*; suffc. *štnt*, imp. *šnt* → DUL 974ff.
•ONOM: **EUPH** *ia-ta-nu-um*; cf. unc. *i-ti-li-im* → Zadok Fs. Hallo 332.
EA.[274]
UGS *ia-ta-nu* → Sivan GAGl 292.
UGA *bʕltn* → DUL 208, *bʕlytn* → DUL 209, *mlkytn* → DUL 551, *tnåbn* → DUL 860, *ytn* → DUL 977: *ytn* (II).
EG Cf. *y-ṯ-n-ꜣ* → Schneider APÄQ 63 no. 112.

nidn "gift" •ONOM: **EB** *ne-ti, ni-ti, ne-ti-i, ne-ti-la/ra-ì, ni-ti-bí-du* (probl. GN) → Pagan ARES 3 145, 355f.

nidint, niditt "gift, dowry" •CTX: **EUPH** *ni-di-in-ti/tam, ni-di-it-ti, ni-di-it-tim, ni-id-na-at, ni-id-na-tim* → Durand MARI 3 162; MARI 4 403; LAPO 18 396; Ziegler FM 4 41, 78.

nādin "giver, donor" •ONOM: **A7** *na-di-na* → Wiseman AT 142; Gelb CAAA 27, 162.

natūn "given" •ONOM: **EUPH** *na-tu-nu-um, ì-lí-na-tu-un* → Huffmon APNMT 244; Gelb CAAA 27, 164; Streck Onomastikon 1 200 § 2.95, 330f. § 5.28 fn. 5.

ntn "emission (of voice), lament" •CTX: **UGA** → DUL 642f.

mātan, mētan, mattan "gift" •ONOM: **EB** *ma-da-na/nu, mi-da-nu* → Pagan ARES 3 194, 347, 350; Catagnoti / Fronzaroli ARET 16 81.
EUPH *ma-ta-tum* → Streck Onomastikon 1 314 § 4.7, 335 § 5.43, 337 § 5.45 (Gelb CAAA 319: MʔT).
EG Cf. *ma$_4$-ta$_5$-n* (TN) → Hoch SWET 176 no. 235. Cf. Schneider APÄQ 136 no. 290 (PN *m-t:-y-n-t-ty*).

mandatt "tax, gift(s)" •CTX: **EG** *ma$_4$-n-da-ta* → Hoch SWET 131 no. 170.[275]

---

[274] Cf. PN *yatin*(SUM)- ^{d}IM, Tropper OLZ 91 55, against Sivan GAGl 255; Hess APN 165f., 209: *yantin* |n-t-n|.
[275] Sivan / Cochavi-Rainey WSVES 90: *ma-n-da-tá* "equipment"; Helck Beziehungen no. 93.

mantin, mattin "gift"	•ONOM: **EUPH** *ma-an-ti-nu-um* → Gelb CAAA 27, 167; Streck Onomastikon 1 338 § 5.57. **UGS** Cf. *ma-(at-)te-nu*, ^{d}U-*ma-te-ni*, ^{d}IM-*ma-tin*, *ma-an-ti-nu* → Gröndahl PTU 50, 147, 161f., 240, 284f.; Sivan GAGl 246; Huehnergard UVST 216.
mtn (B) "gift"	•CTX: **UGA** Sg. suff. *mtny*, *mtnh* → 592: *mtn* (II). •ONOM: **UGA** → 592: *mtn* (III); *mtnbʕl* → DUL 592; cf. unc. *mtnn* → DUL 592.
muttat "gift"	•ONOM: **EM** *mu-ta-at-te-e* → Pruzsinszky PTEm 174 [638]; Streck AfO 51 309.[276]
watin "given"	•ONOM: **EB** *wa-ti-nu* → Krebernik PET 42; Pagan ARES 3 194, 376.[277]
ỉtnn "present"	•CTX: **UGA** Sg. suff. *ỉtnny*, *ỉtnnk* → DUL 119; Richter BGH 519.[278]
yatin "given"	•ONOM: **UGS** *ia*-TE(*ti*$_7$)-*nu*, *ta*-TE(*ti*$_7$)-*nu* → Sivan GAGl 292.[279]
yatun "given"	•ONOM: **UGS** *ia-tu-nu* → Sivan GAGl 292.
ytn "a group or social class"	•CTX: **UGA** Pl. *ytnm* → DUL 977: *ytn* (I).
ytnt "gift, offering"	•CTX: **UGA** Sg. cstr. *ytnt* → DUL 977.

|n-d-p|	Sem.: *ndp* (Hb.) "to scatter"; (JAram.) "to blow, waft, spread (fragrance)"; *nadafa* (Arab.) "to tease, comb, card; to play (lute)", *mindaf* "carder, teasing bow"; *ndf* (MSArab.) "to expel (an outlaw)"; *nadafa* (Eth.) "to throw, strike, sting, card".
|n-d-p| "to throw"	•CTX: **UGA** C act. ptc. sg. fem. (altern.: Špass. ptc. sg. fem.) *mšdpt* → Tropper UG 599f., 606, 628; DUL 612: /*n-d-p*|.
mdpt "type of carder" (?)	•CTX: **UGA** → DUL 522.

|n-d-y| Cf. **|w-d-y|**	Sem.: *ndh* (Hb., D) "to push away, exclude"; *ndy* (JAram., Syr.) "to drop down, project out"; *nadû(m)* (Akk.) "to throw (down), lay down, emit; to apply, impose, load"; *ndy* (OSArab.) "to drive out". See further. *nadʔa* (Eth.) "to drive away", *nadya*, *nadaya* "to be poor".
|n-d-y| "to throw, remove, emit"	•CTX: **EB** C ptc. *mu-sa-ti-sa* |musaddiy=sa| → Fronzaroli QuSe 13 146; Catagnoti QuSe 29 140, 148, 166, 213. **EA** D suffc. *nu-di-ni* |nuddī=ni| → AHw 709; CAD N/II, p. 309; Rainey CAT 2 311, 3 59. **UGA** G suffc. *nd*; prefc. *td* → DUL 613: /*n-d(-y)*/.[280]
tanduy, taddiʔ "fabric with (golden) applications" (?)	•CTX: **EUPH** *ta-da-u*, GÚ.È.A / TÚG *ta-ad-di-ú*, TÚG *ta-ad-di-tim* / *ta-an-di-a-tum* / *ta-ad-di-a-tum* → Durand LAPO 16 271 fn. a; ARM 30 122f.

276 Pruzsinszky loc.cit.: "der Geber", but see Streck loc.cit.: "Gabe (des GN) [...]. *–te-e* ist wohl deminutives Suffix".

277 See also the spellings *ba-ti-nu*, *ba-ti-núm*, Pagan op.cit. 194, 291 (|b=| for *|w=| ?).

278 Hurr. *watann=* is probl. a Hurr.-Sem. hybrid form.

279 Cf. loc.cit. *at*-TE-*nu* (but Gröndahl PTU 221f.: Hurr. |att-| "Vater"); *ta*-TE-*nu* (but Gröndahl PTU 262: see Hurr. |tad-|).

280 Diff. Tropper UG 676, *nd:* G suffc. |n-d-d| (1) "fliehen"; 660, *td:* G prefc. |w-d-y| "niederlegen, ablegen".

tandiyat "(golden) application" (?)	•CTX: **EUPH** GÚ *ta-di-a-tum* / *ta-an-di-a-tum* / *ta-ad-di-a-tum*, GÚ.È.A *ta-ad-di-a-tum* → Durand ARM 30 71.
|n-ð-r| Cf. **|ʔ-d-r|**, **|d-r-r|**	Sem.: *ndr* (Hb.) "to perform a vow", *ndr* (*nē/eder*) "vow", *nzr* (N) "consecrate oneself to a deity", *nzr* (*nēzer*) "consecration, dedication", *nzyr* (*nāzîr*) "devoted, consecrated"; *ndr* (Ph., Pun., Amm., Palm.) "to vow", *ndr* (Ph., Pun.) "votive offering"; *nzr*, *ndr* (Aram., Syr.) "to vow", *ndr(ʔ)* "vow", *nzr* (JAram., Syr.) "to abstain", *nzyr* (JAram., Syr.) "Nazirite; abstinent, sacred"; *naḏara* (Arab.) "to dedicate, make a vow", *naḏr* "vow", *naḏīr* "consecrated", *manḏūr* "solemnly vowed"; *nḏr* (OSArab.) "to atone", tḏrm "penitential offering"; *nḏr* (MSArab.) "to make a vow", *néḏer* "vow, oath"; *nzr* (Eth.) *nāzara* "to be consecrated to God's service", *nəzur*, *nāzāri* „who is consecrated to God's service".[281]
|n-d-r| "to make a vow, promise"	•CTX: **UGA** G prefc. *ydr*; Gpass. prefc. *tdr* → Tropper UG 101; DUL 612f. •ONOM: **EUPH** Cf. *ia-an-du-rum*(?) → Gelb CAAA 27, 165. **A4** Cf. *na-dá*(TA)*-ru-ma* → Dietrich / Loretz UF 1 56 (23:34); Sivan GAGl 253.[282] **UGS** Cf. *id-da-ra(-na)* → Gröndahl PTU 164; Sivan GAGl 253.[283] **UGA** Cf. *ydrm* → DUL 944.
ndr "vow"	•CTX: **UGA** Sg. *ndr*; suff. *ndrh* → DUL 613.
mðr "vow"	•CTX: **UGA** → Tropper UG 116; DUL 523.
|n-g-ʕ| (1)	Sem.: *ngʕ* (Hb.) "to touch (violently), strike, reach, arrive"; (Aram.) "to touch, strike"; *nag*ʷ*ʕa* (Eth.) "to break". Non-Sem.: **nVg=* (Central Chadic) "to break".[284]
|n-g-ʕ| "to arrive, touch, smite"	•CTX: **EA** G prefc. *ig-gi-ú-šu* |yiggeʕū=| → Moran AmL 332 fn. 10 (on EAT 288:44); Rainey CAT 1 12, 2 25. **EG** Cf. *n-ga-ʕu* |nagaʕu| → Hoch SWET 195 no. 262.
|n-g-ʕ| (2)	Sem.: Cf. *nağaʕa* (Arab.) "to feed, take advantage of", *tanağğa*, *ʔintağa*, *ʔistanğa* "to forage"; *nuğʕa* "search for food", *nāğiʕ* "foraging, nourishing".
nigʕ "customary pastoral route"	•CTX: **EUPH** *ni-ig-ḫi*, *ni-ig-ḫu-um* (A.2730: 34, 37, 48; A.4182:42) → Kupper FM 6 195ff. (18); Durand Proceedings 46ᵉ RAI 119; Miglio Tribe and State 77; Lauinger STOBA 197f.
|n-g-b| (1)	No obvious Sem. connections.
|n-g-b| "to provide, supply (food)"	•CTX: **EB** G prefc. *na-gi-ba* → Fronzaroli ARET 11 162; Catagnoti QuSe 29 47, 126, 146, 213. **EUPH** G suffc. *na-gi-ib*, inf. (?) *na-gi-[bi-im* → Jean ARM 2 133f. (69.6'); Lackenbacher ARM 26/2 448 fn. a; Durand LAPO 16 538 fn. f.

[281] Note OBab. *lā a-du-ru*, AHw 1577: *nadārum* (kan. Fw.) "geloben"; Zadok Fs. Hallo 327. Vacat CAD; cf. CAD A/1 103ff.: *adāru* A.

[282] Unlikely altern. rdg in Sivan GAGl 255: *na-ta-ru-ma*, from \|n-t-r\| "to be free, loosen" (DUL 643: "to banish").

[283] Unlikely altern. rdg in Sivan GAGl 255: *it-tá-ra(-na)*, from \|n-t-r\| "to be free, loosen" (DUL 643: "to banish").

[284] Orel / Stolbova HSED 408f. no. 1899: **nVgVʕ=* "to break, strike".

nagb (A) "pile, heap, storage"	•LL: **B** Cf. Ì.DUB = *iš-pik-ki* = NAG-*bu* → Landsberger MSL 5 81 12a;[285] AHw 379: *išpikū*, 1578; CAD I 258: *išpikū*; Lafont Fs. Garelli 286 fn. g; Durand LAPO 16 537f. fn. f.
ngb "victualling"	•CTX: **UGA** → DUL 613f.
nagbat "(food) supply, stock"	•CTX: **EUPH** *na-ag-ba-tim* → Lafont Fs. Garelli 284, 286 fn. g.; Durand LAPO 16 537f. n. f.

|n-g-b| (2)	Sem.: *ngb* (*negeb*, Hb) "arid terrain; the South"; *ngb* (JAram.) "to dry up", *ngb(ʔ)* (JAram., Syr.) "dryness; the South"; *ngb* (MSArab.) "to be dry"; *nagaba* (Eth.) "to be dry, destroyed", *nageb* "the South".
nagb (B) "dryness, dry country"	•ONOM: **EG** In TN *n-g-bu/i*, *na-g-bu* → Hoch SWET 196 no. 263.

|n-G-d|	Sem.: Cf. *nkd* (*neked*, Hb.) "progeny"; *nagad* (Eth.) "tribe, clan".
niGdat "progeny, clan" (?)	•ONOM: **EUPH** Cf. unc. *ni*-KI-*da-tum* → Zadok Fs. Hallo 327.

|n-g-h| See **|g-y-ħ|**	Sem.: *ngh* (Hb.) "to gleam, shine", *ngh* (*nogah*) "gleam, bright light", *nghwt* (*n^egohôt*) "gleam of light"; *ngh* (Aram., Syr.) "to shine", *ngh(ʔ)*, *nwgh(ʔ)* (JAram., Syr.) "dawn"; *ngh* (OSArab.) "to become dawn"; *nagha*, *nagḫa* (Eth.) "to dawn, grow light". See further: *nagû(m)*, *negû* (Akk.) "to sing joyfully, carol", *nūgu* "jubilation", *nigûtu(m)* "joyful song"; *ghgh* (Syr. D) "to illuminate", *gwhghʔ* "morning time"; *gahəha* (Eth.) "to dawn, shine". Non-Sem: **nVgya=* (< **nVgVy=*, Central Chadic) "light".
|n-g-h| "to gleam, shine"	•ONOM: **EB** |yaggah|: cf. *a-ga*, *a-ga um*, *a-ga-iš*, *a-ga-li-im*, *a-ga-me/mi-nu*, *ag-ga ti*; |yiggah|: cf. *i-ga-iš-*ru_{12}, *i-ga-la-um*, *i-ga-li-im*; |yingah|: *en-ga-*u_4/u_9, *en-ga-um*, *en-ga-am*, *en-ga-šum*, *en-ga-da-ba-an*, *en-ga-da-mu*, *en-ga-li-im*, *en-ga-mu-ud*, *en-ga-mu-du*; |taggah|: *da-ga-da-mu*, *da-ga-du*; |yintagah|: cf. *en-da-ga* → Pagan ARES 3 146, 272, 277f., 286, 297, 305f., 322. **EM** Cf. *ia-gi*(?)-*^dda-gan* → Pruzsinszky PTEm 207 with fn. 550) [405].[286] **ASS** (late): *ia-an-gi* → Gelb CAAA 27, 165.
nigh "brightness, dawn" (?)	•ONOM: **EUPH** Fem. *ni-ig-ḫa-tum* → Gelb CAAA 27, 165; Streck Onomastikon 1 315 § 4.7.
nagah "brightness, dawn"	•ONOM: **EB** *na-ga-um* → Pagan ARES 3 146, 353.
nagih "shining"	•ONOM: **EB** Cf. *i-na-na-gi* → Pagan ARES 3 146, 324. **EUPH** *na-ki-ḫu-um*, *na-gi*$_4$*-a-nu-um*, fem. *na-gi-ia* → Gelb CAAA 27, 162; Streck Onomastikon 1 198, 200 § 2.95; Golinets Onomastikon 2 158, 414f., 494.

|n-g-ħ|	Sem.: *ngḥ* (Hb., JAram.) "to gore".
|n-g-ħ| "to butt each other"	•CTX: **UGA** N prefc. *ångḥ*, suff. *ynghn* → DUL 616: /*n-g-ḥ*/.

---

[285] LL ḪAR.gud I A; commentary on ḪAR.ra = *ḫubullu* II.

[286] Probl. \|*yaggih=dagān*\|. But the reading of the sign GI is uncertain; read perhaps with ZI: \|*yaxṣi=dagān*\|?

|n-G-p|

Culture word, Sem.: *nik/qiptu(m)* (Akk.) "spurge" (?; a shrub).

nikipt "an edible(?) plant and its oil"

•CTX: **EG Cf.** *n-k-*pi_2*-ta, n-k-fi-ta{-r}* → Hoch SWET 194f. nos. 260f.

|n-g-r|

Sem.: *nagāru(m)* (Akk. D) "to denounce", *nāgiru* "herald"; *nagara* (Eth.) "to say, recite, proclaim", *nagāri* "narrator".

nāgir "herald"

•ONOM: **UGS** Cf. *na-gi-r[a-na]* → Sivan GAGl 251: NĀGIRU.[287]
EG Cf. *n-ȝ-q-*y_2*-r* → Schneider APÄQ 146 no. 311.

ngr "herald"

•CTX: **UGA** Sg. *ngr* (fem. *ngrt* see below) → DUL 614f.

ngrt "herald"

•CTX: **UGA** → DUL 615.

|n-g-s¹|
Cf. |**n-g-θ**|

Sem.: Hb. *ngš* "to approach, step forward"; *nagāšu(m)* (Akk.) "to go to(wards)", *muttaggišu(m), muštaggišu* "bustling, restlessly busy".

|**n-g-s¹**| "to approach, go (towards); wander"

•CTX: **UGA** G suffc. *ngš*, suff. *ngšnn*, irregular spelling *ngṯhm*,[288] inf. *ngš* → DUL 615 */n-g-š/*.
•ONOM: **EB** Cf. *a-gú-šum, i-gú-uš* → Pagan ARES 3 147, 278, 322: *ngš* "to leave" (correct!).

nāgiS "approaching" (?)

•ONOM: **EB** Cf. *na-gi-sa/ša* → Pagan ARES 3 146f., 353.

muttaggiS "wandering" (?)

•ONOM: **EB** Cf. *mu-da*-KAS → Krebernik PET 97, cf. ibid. 271: nu-gal-mu-da-KASKAL (probl. sum. PN); see also Pagan ARES 3 147.

|n-g-s²|

Sem.: *ngŠ* (*ngś*, Hb.) "to force (to work), oppress", (*nogēś*) "tyrant"; *ngs²* (OSArab.) "to impose tribute upon, take control over"; *nagśa* (Eth.) "to become king", *nəgś* "reign, rule".

nagiS "ruler, chief"

•ONOM: **EUPH** Cf. *na-gi/*gi_4*-sa-nu-um* → Gelb CAAA 26, 162.

gan(i)s²a "violence, injustice" (?)

•CTX: **EG** Cf. *ga-ni-sa, ga-na-sa* (metath.) → Hoch SWET 349f. no. 512.[289]

|n-g-θ|
Cf. |**n-g-s¹**|

Sem.: *naǧaṯa* (Arab.) "to examine".

|**n-g-θ**| "to search, examine"

•CTX: **UGA** D prefc. suff. *tngṯh, tngṯnh* → DUL 615: */n-g-ṯ/*.[290]
•ONOM: **EB** Cf. *en-gi-su, en-gi-šum, en-gi-iš-ar, en-gi-iš*-KÁ |yingiθ=θaɣru| → Pagan ARES 3 146f., 306: *ngš* "to approach" (correct!).

|n-g-w/y|

Sem.: *naǧā* (Arab.) "to get away, escape, be quick".

|**n-g-w/y**| "to go away, depart"

•CTX: **UGA** G impv. *ng* → DUL 615f.: */n-g(-y)/*.

---

[287] Diff. Gröndahl PTU 165: NGR "Zimmermann", unlikely: this is always a *qattāl* pattern |naggār| in Akk., He., Arab.
[288] Tropper UG 109.
[289] Kilani VGW 135: |g'onsv|.
[290] For *ngṯhm* (correct DUL 615: */n-g-ṯ/* G suffc. suf.) cf. Tropper UG 109, and here |n-g-s¹|.

|n-g-z| Sem.: Cf. *nağaza* (Arab.) “to fulfil, carry out, execute”, *nağz*, *nağāz* “fulfillment, implementation”; *ngz* (OSArab., MSArab.) “put an end, finish”.

nagāz “fulfillment” (?) •ONOM: **EB** Cf. *na-ga-za* → Pagan ARES 3 147, 353.

|n-ɣ-ṣ́| Sem.: *naġaḍa* (Arab.) “to be in state of motion, agitation”.

|n-ɣ-ṣ| “to contract, shake; to buckle” •CTX: **UGA** G prefc. *tġṣ*; N. prefc. *tnġṣn*, “to buckle” → DUL 617: /*n-ġ-ṣ*/.

|n-H-B| Sem. etym. unc: Cf. *naʕfa* (Arab.) “strap”, *naʕafa* “thread, mane”, *naʕūf*, *nāʕifa* “hanging (ear)”; see also under |n-w-p|, below.[291]

nuHB “pendant (stone)” (?) •CTX: **EM** Cf. suff. NA$_4$ *nu-bi-šu-nu* → Pentiuc Vocabulary 134f.
•LL: **EM** [(NA4) MIN.NÍR.Á.ŠUBA = *a-š*]*u-ku-ut-tum* : *nu-ʔ-bu* → Seminara RSO 71 16f.; Pentiuc Vocabulary 134f.; Cohen Proceedings 53^{e} RAI 1 824f.
•ONOM: **EM** Cf. unc. *nu-bi*, *nu-bi-*^{d}*da-gan*/^{d}KUR → Pruzsinszky PTEm 175, 184 [654f.]. Altern. → Feliu Dagan 259 “DN is ten thousand”, from Hurr. *nube/i* “10000”.

naHuB(at) “pendant or necklace” (?) •CTX: **EB** Cf. *na-ù-ba-at*, *na-ù-bat* → Fronzaroli ARET 11 73, 163; Seminara RSO 71 16f.
•LL: **EB** Cf. IGI.KISAL = *na-ù-bu*$_{16}$, *na-ù-bù-um*, *na-ù-bu*$_{16}$*-um* → Conti QuSe 17 183 (unexplained).

|n-h-d| Sem.: *naʔādu*(*m*) (Akk.) “to be attentive; to pay attention”.

|n-h-d| “to be attentive; to pay attention” •CTX: **EB** D prefc. *nu-na-i-du* |nunahhid| → Catagnoti / Fronzaroli ARET 16 13, 260; Catagnoti QuSe 29 58, 213.

nahid “watchful, careful” •CTX: **EB** *na-da-ma* |nahidam=ma| → Fronzaroli ARET 13 14, 286; Catagnoti QuSe 29 48, 153, 213.

|n-h-ḳ| Sem.: *nhq* (Hb.) “to bray”; *nhq* (JAram.), “to bray, shout, cry out”; *nâqu*(*m*) (Akk.) “to cry, groan”, *tanūqātu*(*m*) “battle cry” (pl.t.); *nahaqa*, *nahiqa* (Arab.) “to bray”; *nəhēq* (MSArab.) id.; *nəhqa* (Eth.) id.

nhḳt “braying” •CTX: **UGA** Sg. / pl. *nhqt* → DUL 617f.

|n-h-l| (1) Sem.: *nhl* (Hb. D) “to escort with care (to a meadow, water); to provide with food”, *nhll* (pl. *nah*^{a}*lolîm*) “drinking place, watering place”; *naʔālu*(*m*) (Akk.) “to moisten”; *nahila* (Arab.) “to drink”, *ʔanhala* “to give to drink”, *nahla* “drink”, *manhal* “drinking place”.
Non-Sem.: **nVHul=* (Central Chadic) “to moisten”; **nyaHul=* (East Chadic) “rain”.[292]

[291] For Akk. *nību* (CAD N/2 206: *nību* B: “small piece”) see Sommerfeld Or 56 217, and Akk. *yābibu*.
[292] Orel / Stolbova HSED 400 no. 1851: **neʔul=* “to moisten”.

nih(i)l "a kind of sheep"	•CTX: **Q** UDU *ni-ḫi-lu* → Richter / Lange Idadda 117f., 191.[293]

|n-h-l| (2)	Sem.: *nâlu*(*m*), *niālu*(*m*) (Akk.) "to lie down (to sleep)", *mayyālu*(*m*) "bed, resting place", *mayyaltu*(*m*) "bed; stable"; *minhal* (Arab.) "grave", *manhūl* "emaciated (by disease)".
|**n-h-l**| "to lie down (to sleep)"	•LL: **EB** Ù.DI = *na-a-um* |nahālum|, AN.EN.EN = *na-u*$_9$*-lum* |nahhulum|, Ù.EN = *nu-u*$_9$*-lu-um* |nuhhulum|, Ù.DI.DI = *da-da-ì-lum* |tantahhilum| → Krebernik ZA 73 40; Conti QuSe 17 192; Catagnoti QuSe 29 17, 54, 58, 138, 148, 153, 213.
nahl "rest, sleep" (?)	•CTX: **EB** Cf. *na-am*$_6$ |naȟl=am| → Fronzaroli Fs. Kienast 102.
mahhal "resting place" (?)	•LL: **EB** AN.EN = *ma-ʔà-um* → Conti QuSe 17 38, 192; Pasquali QuSe 23 31; NABU 2002/33.

|n-h-r| (1)	Primary noun, Sem.: *nhr* (nāhār, Hb.) "river, stream", denom. *nhr* "to stream towards"; *nhr*(*ʔ*) (Aram., Syr.) id.; *nāru*(*m*) (Akk.) "river, watercourse, canal"; *nahr* (Arab.) "river, stream", denom. *nahara* "to flow copiously, stream forth"; *ʔnhr* (OSArab., pl.) "irrigation channels, conduits"; *nahār* (Eth.) "river", denom. *nahara* "to flow". Non-Sem.: Cf. **nyar=* (< **niHar=*, East Chadic) "to flow slowly".[294]
|**n-h-r**| "to flee, sail" (?)	•CTX: **EG** Cf. *na*$_2$*-h-ra*, *n-ha-r* |nahara| (verb, noun ?) → Hoch SWET 191 no. 254.[295]
nah(a)r (A) "river; DN"	•ONOM: **EB** Unc. *na*-LUM, *na-ru*$_{12}$ (probl. GN) → Pagan ARES 3 226, 354.[296] **EUPH** *na-ra-nu-um*, *um-mi-na-ru*, *bi-in-na-a-*[*ri*], *bi-in-na-rum*, *bi-na-ru-um*, *ḫa-na-na-ri-im*, *ki-in-na-ri-im*, *la-ri-im-na-ar*, *mu-ut-na-ri*(*-im*), *mu-tu-pi*$_4$*-na-ri*, *ia-šu-ub-na-ar* → Gelb CAAA 26, 161; Zadok Fs. Hallo 327; Streck Onomastikon 1 241 § 2.160, Suppl., 295 § 3.56.a.1.3. fn. 7; Durand REA 292.[297] **A7** Cf. *na-ri-im* → Wiseman AT 143; Gelb CAAA 26, 161. **TU** *šu-mu-na-ʔà-rí* → Krebernik Tall Bi`a 227; Streck Onomastikon 1 241 § 2.160, 326 § 5.17. **EM** Cf. DINGIR-*na-ru-*[→ Pruzsinszky PTEm 125 [481]. **EA** TN KUR KUR *na-aḫ-ri-ma/mi*(KI), *na-*<*aḫ-*>*ri-ma*, KUR *na-ah-*<*ri-*>*ma* → Belmonte RGTC 12/2 203f. **UGS** DUMU *na-ri*; *mi-il-ki-in-a-ri*; *ú-lu-na-a-ri* → Gröndahl PTU 165; Sivan GAGl 251.[298] **EG** TN; cf. *n-ha-r*, *n-ha-r-(n)nu-{t}*, *n-ha-r-ti*$_2$*-ya*, *n-h-ri-n*(*a*), *n-ha-rin-na*, *n-h-r-n*(*a*), *n-ha-ri*, *n-h-r-nu*, etc |nahara|, |nah(a)rêna| (Aram. pl.) → Hoch SWET 187ff. no. 253; cf. Schneider APÄQ 143 no. 306 (*n-h-r-y*$_2$*-n-ꜣ-y*$_2$).
nahar (B) "who runs away, fugitive"	•CTX: **EG** *n-ha-ru*$_2$*-ʔu* |naharû| (coll. "fugitives") → Hoch SWET 192 no. 255.[299]

[293] Probl. denoting a sheep that already goes to the watering place.
[294] Orel / Stolbova HSED 403 no. 1869: **nihar=* "to flow".
[295] Sivan / Cochavi-Rainey WSVES 82: *na-ha-ra* "to run"; Helck Beziehungen no. 140.
[296] Altern. \|naʕr\| "servant; soldier"; see \|n-ʕ-r\| (1).
[297] Some writings could point to Akk. *narû(m)* "stele", as e.g. in *ia-aḫ-wi-na-ri*, *mu-ut-na-ri*, etc.; see Durand SEL 8 90, REA 656.
[298] For the unrelated river name *naḫ*(*a*)*rā*(*yu*), UGA *nḫry*, see Belmonte RGTC 12/2 392; DUL 621; Huehnergard UVST 152; vSoldt SAU 331 fn. 160 bottom.
[299] Sivan / Cochavi-Rainey WSVES 82: *na-ha-rú-ʔu* "fugitive"; Helck Beziehungen no. 141.

nhr "river; DN"	•CTX: **UGA** Sg. *nhr*, pl./du. *nhrm*, suff. *nhrm* → DUL 618.[300] •ONOM: **UGA** *ủlnhr* → DUL 57.
|n-h-r| (2) Cf. **|n-w-r|**	Sem.: Hb. *nhr* "to shine, be radiant"; *nhr* (JAram., Syr.) "to shine, be clear", (JAram.) *nhr(?)* "light", *nhr* (Palm.) "illustrious"; *nahār* (Arab.) "daytime, day"; *nehōr* (MSArab.) "day".
nahīr "glorious, shining"	•CTX: **EG** *n-h-ri* (*i*-vowel after *r* displaced) → Hoch SWET 192 no. 256: title of a Syrian leader.[301]
|n-H-S| See **|n-ħ-S|**	Sem.: Cf. *nēšu(m)* (Akk.) "lion", *nēštu*, *nēltu* "lioness"; *nahūs*, *nahhas*, *minhas* (Arab.) "lion". Unlikely connection with *lyš* (*layiš*, Hb.) "lion"; *lyt(?)* (JAram.) "lion"; *layṯ*, *lāyiṯ* (Arab.) "lion".[302]
naHiS "lion" (?) **neHS** "lion" (?)	•LL: **EB** Cf. NIN.KI = *na-iš qàr-ga-rí-im* → Sjöberg WO 27 20f. •ONOM: **EB** Cf. *ne-šè/si*, *ne-šum*, *ne-ša-núm*, *ḫa-ra ne-iš*, *sa-da-ne-iš* → Pagan ARES 3 227, 317, 355, 360.[303]
|n-ħ-b|	Sem.: Cf. *naḥba*, *naḥḥab* (Arab.) "to vow, put himself under an obligation", *naḥḥab* "to strive, work with energy; to go at a quick pace". [304]
|n-ħ-b| "to vow, put himself under an obligation; to strive" (?)	•ONOM: **EUPH** Cf. *ia-ḫa-bu-um*, *ta-ḫa-ba-tum*, *ia-aḫ-ḫa-ab*-DINGIR, *ia-ḫa-ab-ḫa-mu*; *ia-ḫi-bu-um* → Gelb CAAA 27, 160.[305]
|n-ħ(-ħ)|	Cultural word, Sem.: Cf. *nāḫu(m)*, *nuḫḫu* (Akk.) "pig's fat, lard". Non-Sem.: Cf. *nḥḥ* (Eg.) "sesame oil, olive oil".
nħ "a type of oil / fat" (?)	•CTX: **UGA** → DUL 618: *nḥ*.
|n-ħ-l|	Sem.: *nḥl* (Hb., Ph., Nab.) "to maintain / take as a possession; to give, apportion as an inheritance", *nḥlh* (*naḥ*ᵃ*lāh*, Hb,) "inalienable, hereditary property", *nḥlh* (Nab.) "inheritance rights"; *naḥala* (Arab.) "to make a donation, a present; to ascribe, attribute", *niḥla* "present, gift, credit"; *nḥl* (OSArab.) "to give, to grant a lease", *nḥlt* "gift, lease, usufruct"; *naḥál*, *nəḥāl* (MSArab.) "to give the patrimony", *náḥəl*, *nēḥəl* "patrimony".

[300] See also the royal title *nahīr* "glorious, shining", |n-h-r| (2).
[301] According to Hoch, loc.cit., it is possible that *nhr*, the UGA epithet of the Sea God *Ym* (see above: *nhr*, |n-h-r (1)), is a title meaning "illustrious" rather than a by-name meaning "River".
[302] Cf. Militarev / Kogan SED 2 199f. no. 147; 210f. no. 159.
[303] Cf. |x-y-r|, |S-ʕ-d|. Altern., most instances could be read |neħ(i)S(=)| "alive; the living one"; see |n-ħ-S|.
[304] The Hb. PN *nḥby* (*naḥbî*) is probl. a *naqtīl* form of *ḥbʔ/y*; Zadok OLA 28 127.
[305] Read *me-en-ḫi-ma* instead of *me-en-ḫi-ba* (Gelb CAAA 27, 160); see Streck Onomastikon 1 338 § 5.47, 360 (Suppl.) and here *menʕim* "loveliness, delightfulness, grace" (|n-ʕ-m|).

|**n-ħ-l**| "to hand over property; to share an inheritance"	•CTX: **EUPH** G prefc. *i-na-aḫ-ḫi-il, in-ḫi-lu, in-ḫi-il, in-ḫi-lu-ni-in-ni, lu-uh-ḫi-il-ku-nu-ši-im*, inf. *na-ḫa-al, na-ḫa-li*; Gt *it-ta-aḫ-lu*; N suffc. *na-an-ḫu-lu* → AHw 712; CAD N/I 126; Durand, NABU 1989/20; Ziegler Proceedings 46^e RAI 96ff. (A.3297+:33); Durand ARM 26/1 178 (40:52); Streck Onomastikon 1 107f. § 1.95; Knudsen PIHANS 100 321. **Q** G prefc. *an-ḫa-lu*(KU) *: ḫa-la* → Richter / Lange Idadda 47ff. (TT 2:22). •ONOM: **EUPH** *mu-ut-na-ḫa-lim* → Zadok Fs. Hallo 327.[306]
nħl "feudatory, sharecropper"	•CTX: **UGA** Sg. suff. *nḥlh*, pl. cstr. *nḥlh, nḥlhm* → DUL 619: *nḥl*.
naħlat "inheritance, inalienable possession"	•CTX: **EM** Suff. *<<ta*[!]*->>na-aḫ-la-ti* → Pentiuc Vocabulary 177.[307]
naħilt "patrimonial estate"	•CTX: **A7** Pl. *na-ḫi-la-tim* → Lauinger STOBA 157ff. 158 (fn. 31), 269.
niħlat "property handed over"	•CTX: **EUPH** *ni-iḫ-la-at, ni-iḫ-la-tam, ni-iḫ-la-ti-šu* → CAD N/2 219; Streck Onomastikon 1 108 § 1.95. •ONOM: **EUPH** *ni-iḫ-la-tum* → Zadok Fs. Hallo 327.
nħlt "property; inheritance"	•CTX: **UGA** sg. suff. *nḥlty, nḥlth* → DUL 619: *nḥlt*.
|n-ħ-m| Cf. |**n-ʕ-m**|	Sem.: *nḥm* (Hb.) "to be compassionate, (D) to comfort, console"; *nḥm* (Aram., Syr.) "to comfort, console", *mnḥm(?)* (JAram.) "comforter". Cf. (onomatop.) *naḥama* (Arab.) "to groan, moan, wheeze", *naḥima, tanaḥḥama* "to expectorate".
|**n-ħ-m**| "to be compassionate; to comfort, console"	•ONOM: **A4** *ia-an-ḫa-mu*; cf. *mi-na-aḫ-mu* → Wiseman AT 136; Sivan GAGl 253; Golinets Onomastikon 2 36 fn. 135, 324, 415f. **EA** *ia-an-ḫa-mu/i/a/e(-mi), i-an-ḫa*(-am)*-mu, e-en-ḫa-mu*; *yi-í?*(AḪ)*-in*$_4$*-ḫa-mu* → Sivan GAGl 153, 253; Hess APN 82, 209; Moran AmL 385. **UGS** *mu-na-ḫi/ḫí-mu, ia-an-ḫa-(am-)mu/mi, [i]a?-na-ḫa-mu* → Sivan GAGl 153 178, 253; Huehnergard UVST 237, 240f.; vSoldt BiOr 46 650, SAU 22, 29f., 34, 325; Golinets Onomastikon 2 36 fn. 135, 324, 415f **UGA** *ỉlnḥm* → DUL 57; *mnḥm* → DUL 555; *ynḥm* → DUL 596. **EG** *ya-n-ḥam* → Hoch SWET 53f. no. 54; cf. Schneider APÄQ 56 no. 99 (*y-n:-ḥm*), 234 no. 499 (*t-w-n-ḥm-t-w*).
|n-ħ-r|	Sem.: *nḥr* (JAram.) "to stab, pierce, slaughter" (?); *nêru(m), nâru(m), neʔārum* (Akk.) "to strike, hit, kill, defeat", *nîrum, nêrum* "smiting, smiter"[308]; *naḥara* (Arab.) "to slaughter, butcher, kill".
|**n-ħ-r**| "to strike, overcome"	•CTX: **EB** G prefc. *en-àr-SÙ* → Fronzaroli ARET 13 178, 258; Catagnoti QuSe 29 25f., 38, 146, 155, 213. •ONOM: **EB** |yinħar=|: *en-àr-ì, en-àr-da-mu, en-àr-ga-ma-al*$_6$*, en-ar-ḫa-lam, en-ar/àr-li-im, en-àr-ar-mi.*KI; |yinħer=| (?): *en-ir-ma-lik*; |yintaħar=|: *en-da-ar* → Bonechi MARI 8 481, 483, 485; Pagan ARES 3 147, 305f.

[306] Cf. *mu-ut-na-ḫa* and see Durand SEL 8 93; Streck Onomastikon 1 Suppl. 361: read *mu-ut-na-ḫa-<lim?>*.
[307] Initial *ta*[!]- is a scribal plus: there is no theme *taqatlat* in Sem.
[308] Gelb MAD 3 191.

neħar "smiting, smiter; DN"	•ONOM: **EB** *ne-àr*, *ne-a-a*, *a-a-ne-àr*, *ne-àr-da-mu*, BE-*sù-ne*/*ni-àr*, *gi-ni-àr*, *i-bí-ni-àr*, *ib-ne-àr*[309], *i-ne-àr*, *iš-ne-àr*, *iš*/*iš*$_{11}$-*a-ne-àr*, *i-zi-ne-àr*, *šu-ne*/*ni-àr*, *zi-ne-àr*[310] → Bonechi MARI 8 481, 483, 485; Pagan ARES 3 147, 273, 292, 312, 320, 324, 327, 332, 340f., 355, 368, 387.

|n-ħ-S| See |**n-H-S**|	Sem.: *nêšu(m)*, *neʔāšum*, *naʔaśum* (Akk.) "to live, revive".
|**n-ħ-S**| "to live, be alive"	•CTX: **EB** Cf. G prefc. *i-na-ʔà-aš* |yin(aħ)ħaS|, inf. *na-ʔà-su* |naħāSu(m)| → Edzard ARET 5 19f., 54, 56. •ONOM: **EB** Cf. *i-du-na-sa* → Pagan ARES 3 148, 322.
naħiS "living, alive"	•LL: **EB** NÍG.KI = *na-iš g[àr-ga-rí-im]* → Civil BaE 91. •ONOM: **EB** *a-na-i-su*, LUGAL-*na-i-iš* → Pagan 3 148, 281, 347.
neħ(i)S "alive, the living one"	•ONOM: **EB** *ne-šè*/*si*, *ne-šum*, *ne-ša-núm*, *ne-iš-da-ar*, *ḫa-ra-ne-iš*, *sa-da-ne-iš* → Pagan ARES 3 148, 317, 355, 360.[311]
tanaħħiSt, **tinaħħiSt** "living, mankind"	•CTX: **EB** *ti-na-ì-si-du* → Conti QuSe 17 80f. •LL: **EB** NÌ.ZI.PA.ZI.PA (var. NÌ.PA.ZI.PA.ZI) = *da-na-i-si-du*/*tum* → Krebernik ZA 73 5, PIHANS 106 90f.; Civil BaE 84, 91; Conti QuSe 17 80f.; Sjöberg Fs. Oelsner 417.

|n-ħ-s¹| (1)	Culture word, Sem.: *nḥš* (*nāḥāš*, Hb.) "snake". Non-Sem.: Cf. **nyas=* (< **niHa*s=, West Chadic) "python".[312]
nħs¹ "serpent, snake"	•CTX: **UGA** Sg. *nḥš*, pl. *nḥšm* → DUL 619f.: *nḥš*.

|n-ħ-s¹| (2)	Culture word, Sem: *nḥšt*, *nḥwšh* (*nᵉḥošet*, *nᵉḥûšāh*, Hb.; Palm., Nab.) "copper, bronze"; *nḥš(ʔ)* (Aram., Syr.) id.; *nuḥās* (Arab.) "copper"; *nāḥs* (Eth.) "copper, brass".
naħs¹ "copper, bronze" (?)	•CTX: **EM** Cf. *na-a[ḫ-šu]*, *[na-a]ḫ-šu*, *na-aḫ-š[u*, *na-aḫ-šu* → Pentiuc Vocabulary 130: "bronze(-vessel)".
nuħus¹t "copper, bronze"	•CTX: **EA** U[RUDU?] : *nu-ḫu-uš-tu*$_4$ → CAD N/2 322.; Sivan GAGl 255; Gianto SEL 12 69.

|n-ħ-t|	Sem.: *nḥt* (Hb.) "to pull back"; (Aram.,[313] Syr., Nab., Palm.) "to descend"; cf. *naḥata* (Arab.) "to sculpt, carve; to exhaust".
|**n-ħ-t**| "to take down"	•CTX: **UGA** D prefc. *ynḥt*, suffc. *nḥt*, suff. *nḥtm*, prefc. *ynḥt* → DUL 620: /*n-ḥ-t*/.[314]

|n-ħ-w/y|	Sem.: *nḥh* (Hb.) "to lead"; *naʔû(m)*, *neʔû*(m) (Akk. D) "to set in motion"; *naḥā* (*naḥw*, Arab.) "to go towards, walk, move, turn".

[309] \|(yiʔ)hib=neħar\| "DN loved" (\|ʔ-h-b\|); altern. \|(yī)hib=neħar\| "DN gave" (\|w-h-b\|).
[310] \|ṣiʔ=neħar\| "come out, DN!" (\|w-ṣ-ʔ\|); altern. \|θi(l)=neħar\| "DN is protection"\| (\|θ-l-l\|).
[311] Cf. \|x-y-r\|, \|S-ʕ-d\|. Altern., most instances could be read \|neHS(=)\| "lion"; see \|n-H-S\|.
[312] Orel / Stolbova HSED 403 no. 1870: **niḥas=* "snake".
[313] Warka syll. C *aḫ-ḫi-te-e*.
[314] Diff. Hooker NABU 2014/23: from Eg. *nḥt* "to have an erection".

|**n-ħ-w/y**| "to proceed, turn, make for"	•CTX: **EB** G prefc. *in-i* |yinħī|, *i-ni-ʔa*$_5$*-a-am*$_6$ |yinħay=am|, D imp. *nu-u*$_9$*-nu* |naħħūnu| → Fronzaroli ARET 13 65f., 272; Catagnoti / Fronzaroli ARET 16 50, 241. **UGA** G prefc. *yḥ* → DUL 620: */n-ḥ(-y/w)/*. •ONOM: **EB** Cf. |yinħā| (?): *en-ʔà*, *en-ʔà-da-mu*; |yinħay| (?): *en-ʔà-u*$_4$*/um* → Pagan ARES 3 148, 305. **EUPH** Cf. *ia-a-ḫi*-DINGIR → Zadok Fs. Hallo 327; Streck Onomastikon 1 159 § 2.18 fn. 3. **A7 Cf.** *ia-aḫ-ḫi* → Wiseman AT 136; Streck Onomastikon 1 159 § 2.18 fn. 3. **A4** *ia-an-ḫu/ḫa* → Wiseman AT 136; Sivan GAGl 253. **UGS** *ia-an-ḫa-nu/a* → Gröndahl PTU 58, 165; Sivan GAGl 253. Cf. Gelb CAAA 27, 383: NḪ?N. **UGA** *ynḥn* → DUL 956f.
naħy "direction, way"	•CTX: **EB** *na-am*$_6$ → Fronzaroli ARET 13 21, 286; Catagnoti QuSe 29 109, 135, 214.
menħiy "direction, way" (?)	•ONOM: **EUPH** Cf. *me-en-ḫi-i-um* → Gelb CAAA 27, 160 (NḪ?J?).

|**n-x-l**|	Primary noun, Sem.: *nḥl* (*naḥal*, Hb.) "river valley, wadi, stream", also "date-palm"; *nḥl* (Aram., Syr.) "wadi, stream"; *naḫallu(m)*, *naḫlu(m)* (Akk.) "wadi, gorge"; *naḫl*, *naḫīl* (Arab.) "palm"; *nḫl* (OSArab.) "palmgrove"; *neḫelēt* / *néḫel* (MSArab.) "date-palm tree". Non-Sem.: *nḫr*(*n*) (*nḫl*) "river" (Eg.; Sem. loan, late).
nax(a)l "torrent, water course"	•CTX: **EM** *na-aḫ-li* → Pentiuc Vocabulary 129. **UGS** See A.ŠÀ.MEŠ *na-ḫa-li* → Huehnergard UVST 152; vSoldt SAU 305 (95); Tropper UG 169: altern. "Palmenhain". **EG** *n-ḫ-r*, *n-ḫ-r-ya-na*, *n-ḫ-ra* |naxla| → Hoch SWET 193 no. 258.[315] •ONOM: **EB** Cf. *na-ḫa-lu*[→ Pagan ARES 3 226, 353.[316]
nxl "torrent, water course"	•CTX: **UGA** Sg. *nḫl*, pl. *nḫlm* → DUL 621: *nḫl* (I). •ONOM: **UGA** Cf. TN (*gt*) *nḫl* → DUL 621: *nḫl* (II).

|**n-x-r**|	Sem.: *naḫāru*(*m*) (Akk.) "to snort"; *nāḫiru*(*m*) "snorter > dolphin, whale"; *naḫīru*(*m*) "nostril"; *naḫara* (Arab.) "to snort"; *nuḫra* "snout, nose"; *nāḫir* "pig"; *nḥr* (Hb., JAram., Syr.) "to snort", *nḥr* (*naḥar*, Hb.), *nḥrh* (*nah*^{a}*rāh*) "snorting"; *nəḫra* (Eth.) "to snort"; *nḥw/yr* (JAram.) "nostril"; *mnḥr* (Aram.) id.; **nḥyr*(*ym*) (du. Hb.) id.; **naḫrīr* (MSArab.) "nose". Non-Sem.: **nVḫur=* (Berber) "nose"; **nVwar=*, **nVɣwar=* (Chadic) „to snore".[317]
|**n-x-r**| "to snort, puff; to be angry"	•ONOM: **EUPH** *ia-an-ḫu-ru-um* → Gelb CAAA 27, 160.
naxar "snorting"	•ONOM: **EUPH** Fem. *na-ḫa-ra* → Gelb CAAA 27, 161.
ånxr "a marine animal ('dolphin')"	•CTX: **UGA** → DUL 76: *ảnḫr*.

315 Sivan / Cochavi-Rainey WSVES p. 82: *na-ḫa-l*, *na-ḫa-l-ya-na* "stream"; Helck Beziehungen no. 143.
316 The PN *na-ḫa-lu-du/ud* (Lahlouh / Catagnoti ARET 12 443) is probl. unrelated.
317 Orel / Stolbova HSED 397 no. 1839: **naḫür=* "nose", 409 no. 1901: **nVḫor=* "to snore".

|n-x-s|

Sem.: *naḫasu(m)* (Akk.) “to recede, return”; *nḫš* (Arab.) “to grow thin, slim”.

|n-x-s| “to move backwards, come back”

•CTX: **EB** G prefc. *ti-na-ḫu-zu* (< |tinaxxisū|) → Catagnoti / Fronzaroli ARET 16 82, 271; Catagnoti QuSe 29 53, 131, 147, 214.

|n-x-s^1|

Sem.: Cf. *naḫāšu(m)* (Akk.) “to be(come) luxuriant, prosper, be healthy”.

|n-x-s^1| “to be healthy; to prosper”

•ONOM: **UGS** Cf. *na-ḫi-ši-šal-mu* → PRU 5 141.[318]

|n-k-s^1| “to be healthy; to prosper”

•CTX: **EUPH** Cf. *a-lik-tum na-ak-ša-at* (with *k* for **x*) → Charpin / Durand MARI 8 388.

|n-k-h|

Sem.: *nakaha* (Arab.) “to blow, breathe (in someone’s face)”, *nukiha* “to have bad breath”.

|n-k-h| “to breathe in someone’s face”

•LL: **EB** KA.ḪAB = *na-ga-um* → Conti QuSe 17 93; Sjöberg Fs. Renger 523.

|n-k-l| (1)

DN; Sum. loan, < ^{d}nin.gal.

nik(k)al DN

•ONOM: **EUPH** Cf. *i-pí-iq-ni-ik-ka-al* (var. *i-pí-iq-*^{d}NIN.GAL) → Durand NABU 1987/14, REA 211.
UGS Cf. ÌR-*ni-kal/kál* → Gröndahl PTU 166; Huehnergard AkkUg 382, 386.

nkl DN

•ONOM: **UGA** DN → DUL 622. PNN: see *ʕbdnkl* → DUL 140; *bnnkl* → 226; *nklb* → DUL 622;[319] *nkly* → DUL 622.

|n-k-l| (2)

Sem.: *nakālu(m)* (Akk.) “to be(come) skilful, artful, clever”, *naklu* “skilful, elaborate, clever”, *takkalātu* (pl.) “clever, ingenious behaviour”; *nkl* (OSArab.) “to inlay”, *nkl* “skilled work of art”; see further: *nkl* (Hb., JAram., Syr.) “to act slickly, deceptively”; *nakala* (Arab.) “to recoil, shirk, draw back”; *nəkōl* (MSArab.) “to remove, overturn”.

nakl “artful, sophisticated”

•ONOM: **EUPH** Cf. *na-ak-lum*, fem. *na-ak-la-tum* → Gelb CAAA 26, 163.

takkalt “jewel, necklace”

•CTX: **EB** *da-ga-a-tum* → Fronzaroli Fs. Limet 52f., ARET 11 142; Pasquali QuSe 23 29.

|n-k-m|

Sem.: *nakāmu(m)* (Akk.) “to store, pile (up)”.

|n-k-m| “to store, pile (up)”

•CTX: **UGA** G prefc. *åkm* → DUL 622.[320]

---

318 Possibly Akk.; see Stamm ANG 160; diff. Sivan GAGl 253: *na-ḫí-ši-šal-mu* (NḪ/ḤŠ “practice divination”?

319 Add: 4.93 IV 20; 4.122:19; 4.260:94.708:4.; 4.432 (I) 11. Delete DUL 27: *bnnklb*.

320 Correct there the wrong statement “suffc. *åkm*” to “prefc. *åkm*”.

|n-k-p|	Sem.: *nakāpu(m)* (Akk.) "to push, thrust"; *nakafa* (Arab.) "to stop, disdain, reject"; *nəkūf* (MSArab.) "to drive out". See further: *nkp* (Syr.) "to be ashamed".
|**n-k-p**| "to push; gore, butt (each other)"	•LL: **EB** Á.DU$_7$ = *na-ga-bù(-um)* → Krebernik ZA 73 21; Conti QuSe 17 158; Á.DU$_7$.DU$_7$ = *da-da-ga-bù-um* (tGt / tGtn inf. |tattakipum / tattakkipum|) → Krebernik ZA 73 21, 47 [Nachtrag]; Rubio PIHANS 106 134; Catagnoti QuSe 29 48, 139, 144, 147, 214.

|n-k-r|	Sem.: *nkr* (Hb. N) "to be considered strange, behave as a stranger", *nkr* (*nēkār*) "foreigner, foreign country", (*nēker*) "unease, misfortune", *nkry* (*nokrî*) "foreign, strange"; *nkry* (Palm.) "stranger, foreigner"; *nkr* (Syr. D) "to repudiate, make foreign, distant", *nwkry* (Aram., Syr.) "alien, strange, unusual", *nwkry(?)*, *mnkryw(t?)* (Syr.) "alienation"; *nakāru(m)* (Akk.) "to be(come) different, strange, hostile", *nakru(m)* "strange, foreign, outsider", *nakaru(m)* "strange, unknown, enemy", *nukurtu(m)* "enmity"; *nakira* (Arab.) "not to know, have no knowledge, be ignorant", *nakir* "unknown", *nakīr* "denial", *nākir* "denying, unfriendly, hostile"; *nkr* (OSArab.) "ignorance", *nkrm* "anyone else, stranger, alien", *nkr(m)* "alteration, damage"; *šənkūr* (MSArab.) "to nag", *nəkərēt* "disliked", *mənkərāy* "rude"; *nakara* (Eth.) "to separate, make different, be strange, admirable", *nəkur* "uncommon, admirable", *nakir* "strange, foreign, stranger". See also: *nkr* (Hb. C) "to investigate, recognize, know"; *nkr* (JAram., Syr. C) "to recognize, acknowledge", *nkyr* (JAram.) "recognizable, obvious, known", *mkr(?)* (Aram.) "acquaintance"; *nīkər* (MSArab.) "to understand, catch on", *hənkūr* "to feel, realize, understand".
|**n-k-r**| "to look different, to be strange, stranger"	•ONOM: **EB** |yakkir|, cf. *ʔa$_5$-ki-rúm*, *a-gi-lu*; |yinkir|, cf. *en-kir!(ḫa)*, *en-gi-lum*, *en-ki-lu* → Krebernik PET 57; Pagan ARES 3 148, 272, 278, 306.
nakr, **nakar** "stranger, someone / something strange"	•ONOM: **EUPH** *na-ka-rum*/*ru-um*, *na-ak-ra-ḫu-um*, *a-bi-na-ka-ar*, *a-ḫi-na-ka-ar*, fem. *na-ka-ra*, *na-ka-ra-tum*, *na-ka-ar-tum* → Gelb CAAA 27, 162f.; Zadok Fs. Hallo 327; Golinets Onomastikon 2 150, 154, 416f.
nakir "stranger, someone / something strange"	•ONOM: **EM** *na-ki-ir*, *na-ki-rù* → Pruzsinszky PTEm 90 [644].
nikar "stranger, someone / something strange"	•CTX: **EM** (LÚ) *ni-ka-ri*/*rù* → Arnaud AuOrS 1 11, 20; Pentiuc Vocabulary 133f.; Ikeda BiOr 60 271; Westenholz Emar Tablets 13f., 16. •ONOM: **EUPH** Cf. *ni-ik-ru-um* → Gelb CAAA 27, 166
nukr, **nukar** "curiosity, something strange"	•CTX: **EUPH** *nu-uk-ra* → CAD N/2 328; Ziegler Fs. Hirsch 480 (185:16'); Durand Fs. Garelli 19. •ONOM: **U3** *nu-uk-ra-nu-um* → Buccellati Amorites 177; Gelb CAAA 27, 168. **EM** *nu-uk-ra*, *nu-ka$_4$-ri* → Pruzsinszky PTEm 91 [656f.].
nkr "stranger"	•CTX: **UGA** → DUL 622.
Sanakrat "recognised" (?)	•ONOM: **EUPH** Fem. *sa-na-ag*/*ak-ra-tum* → Gelb CAAA 31, 185 (ŚANAGR); Golinets Onomastikon 2 206f., 416f.

|n-k-S| (1)	Sem.: *nikkassu(m)* "account, property" (Sum. loan). Non-Sem.: n i g Š I D (Sum.) "account".

nks¹y "accounting, account(s)"	•CTX: **UGA** → DUL 622f.: *nkšy*.
|n-k-s| (2)	Sem.: *nks* (Pun., Aram., Syr.) "to slaughter"; *nakāsu(m)* (Akk.) "to fell, cut down"; *nakaša* (Arab.) "to stir up, rout up, break, rummage, ransack".
|n-k-s| "to interrupt, cut, stop"	•CTX: **EB** N suffc. *na-gú-zu-ma* |nakkusū=ma| → Catagnoti QuSe 29 54, 125, 148, 214.
|n-k-t|	Sem. etym. unc.: Cf. *nakata* (Arab.) "to beat, hit (the ground)".
|n-k-t| "to immolate"	•CTX: **UGA** G prefc. *nkt*, *tkt* → DUL 623.
mkt "immolation, offering" (?)	•CTX: **UGA** → DUL 539.
nkt "immolation, victim"	•CTX: **UGA** → DUL 623.
|n-k-θ| Cf. **|n-θ-k|**	Sem.: *nkt* (Aram., Syr.) "to bite"; *nkṯ* (Arab., OSArab.) "to break, violate"; *nakasa* (Eth., Amharism) "to bite".
|n-k-θ| "to bite"	•CTX: **EB** Gt prefc. *a-da-gú-šu* |lā yittakkaθū| → Catagnoti QuSe 29 46, 51, 105, 135, 144, 147, 214.
|n-k-y|	Sem.: *nkh* (Hb. N) "to be struck", (C) "to strike", *nkh* (*nākeh*, *nēkeh*) "crippled, broken"; *nky* (Aram., Syr.) "to beat, hit, injure", *nky* (JAram.) "injured"; *nakā* (Arab.) "to harm, hurt", *nikāya* "harm"; *nkyt* (OSArab.) "mischief"; MSArab.) *nkʔ* "to hit (with a knife")"; *nakaya* (Eth.) "to injure, hurt", *nəkuy* "damaged".
|n-k-y| "to smite"	•ONOM: **UGS** Cf. *en-ki-li* |ēnki=(ʔi)lī| (< |yanki-(ʔi)lī|) → Gröndahl PTU 21, 62, 166; Sivan GAGl 47, 254.
nky "beaten, distressed" (?)	•CTX: **UGA** Cf. fem. sg./pl. *nkyt* → DUL 623: *nkyt*.
|n-ḳ-b|	Sem.: *nqb* (Hb.) "to bore through", (N) "to be marked", *nqb* (*neqeb*) "subterranean passage, mine", *nqbh* (*nᵉqēbāh*) "woman, female", *mqbt* (*maqqebet*) "excavation, hammer"; *nqb* (Aram., Syr.) "to pierce", *nqb(ʔ)* (JAram., Syr.) "orifice, hole", *nqbh*, *nqbtʔ* "female; hole", *mqb(ʔ)* (Syr.) "awl", (JAram.) "mallet"; *nqb* (Nab.) "to mark"; *naqābu(m)* (Akk.) "to penetrate sexually, deflower"; *naqaba* (Arab.) "to bore, pierce", *naqqāb* "punch", *minqab* "punch, perforator, lancet"; *nqb* (OSArab.) "to cut channels (in the side of an aqueduct)"; *nīqəb* (MSArab.) "to be cracked", *nqɔb* "to break"; *naqaba* "(Eth.) "to disjoin, withdraw, perforate".
|n-ḳ-b| "to pierce; to mark"	•CTX: **UGA** G prefc. *yqb* → DUL 630.
maḳḳab "a tool (hammer, punch, pick ?)"	•CTX: **UGS** Pl. *ma-qa-b/pu-ma*.MEŠ |maqqabūma| → Sivan GAGl 244; Huehnergard UVST 153f.; vSoldt SAU 305 (86). •LL: **EB** DUB.NAGAR.URUDU = *ma-ga-bu₁₆* → Conti QuSe 17 188. •ONOM: **EG** Cf. *m-n:-g-ꜣ-b-w₂-ty* F.H3ST → Schneider APÄQ 127 no. 272.

maḳḳib "a tool (hammer, punch, pick ?)"	•CTX: **EA** *ma-qí-bu* → AHw 607; CAD M/1 252f.; Sivan GAGl 244.
mḳb, **mḳp** "a tool (hammer, punch, pick ?)"	•CTX: **UGA** Sg. *mqb*, *mqp*, du. *mqb/pm* → DUL 599: *mqb/p*; Del Olmo AuOr 37 290.
naḳḳab "a tool (hammer, punch, pick ?)"	•CTX: **EUPH** *na-qa-bu*, *na-aq-qa-bu/bi*, *na-aq-qa-bi-im* → Arkhipov ARM 32 139. **EM**: *na-qa-bu* → Pentiuc Vocabulary 131.

|n-ḳ-d|	Sem.: *nqd* (*noqēd*, Hb.) "shepherd, sheep-breeder"; *nqd(?)* (Syr.) "shepherd"; *nāqidu(m)* (Akk.) "stock-breeder, herdsman", *nāqidūtu* "position, task of a herdsman". Probl. unrelated: *naqādu(m)* (Akk.) "to be in danger"; *naqada* (Arab.) "to examine critically", *nāqid*, *naqqād* "critic". Non-Sem.: n a g a d a (Sum.) "herdsman" (Sem. loan).
nāḳid "stock-breeder, herdsman"	•LL: **EB** MU$_6$.SÙB = *na-gi-du-um* → FRonzaroli StEb 1 82; Krebernik ZA 73 35; Bonechi QDLF 16 83. •ONOM: **EG** Cf. *n-ꜣ-q-ꜣ-d-y$_2$-y* ^{F} → Schneider APÄQ 146f. no. 312.
nḳd "head shepherd, chief shepherd"	•CTX: **UGA** Sg. *nqd*, pl. *nqdm* → DUL 630f.
nḳṭ "head shepherd, chief shepherd" (?)	•ONOM: **UGA** Cf. *nqṭn* → Tropper UG 98; DUL 632.
maḳḳad "grazing tax"	•CTX: **UGS** UDU.MEŠ *ma-aq-qa-du* → Sivan GAGl 244, 249; Huehnergard UVST 154; vSoldt SAU 305 (87).
mḳd (A) "grazing tax"	•CTX: **UGA** Pg./pl. cstr. *mqd* → DUL 560: *mqd* (II).

|n-ḳ-ð|	Sem.: *naqaḏa* (Arab.) "to save, rescue".
|**n-ḳ-ð**| "to save, rescue"	•LL: **EB** KAR = *na-gi-sum* → Krebernik ZA 73 36f. (1025); Fronzaroli QuSe 13 147.

|n-ḳ-h|	Sem. etym. unc.: Cf. *naqiha* (Arab.) "to convalesce, recover", *naqha* (Eth.) "to wake up, convalesce, recuperate", *ʔanqəha* "rouse, stir up, revive".
|**n-ḳ-h**| "to gain strength, to stir up, revive" (?)	•CTX: **UGA** G suffc. *nqh* → DUL 631: */n-q-h/*, with a slightly diff. meaning: "to prepare, make ready".

|n-ḳ-ḳ|	Sem. etym. unc. Cf. *nqyq* (*nāqîq*, Hb.) "cleft, crack"; *nəqāq* (Eth.) "cleft, crevice", and see related *naqʕa* "to be split".
niḳāḳ "cleft (lip / palate)" (?)	•ONOM: **UGS** Cf. DUMU *ni-qa-qí* → Gröndahl PTU 168; Sivan GAGl 253.[321]
nḳḳ "cleft (lip / palate)" (?)	•ONOM: **UGA** Cf. *bn nqq* → DUL 632: *nqq*.[322]

[321] Altern. cf. *naqqa* (Arab.) "quaken", *naqqaqa* "frog".
[322] See previous fn.

|n-ḳ-l| Sem.: Cf. *nql* (Aram.) “to transport”; *naqala* (Arab.) “to carry, transport, deliver, pass on”.

niḳāl “supply, contribution” (?)
•CTX: **A7** In MN ITU *ni-qa-lim* → Wiseman AT 162 (rdg *niq/gaše*), AHw 792; Arnaud AuOr 16 166.
A4 In MN ITU *ni-qa*$_5$*-lì* → Wiseman AT 162 (rdg *niq/gaše*), AHw 792; Arnaud AuOr 16 166.
EM ITU *ni-qa-li* → Arnaud Emar 6/3 322 (364:2), 356 (373:185’), AuOr 16 166.
•ONOM: **UGS** PN *ni-qa-la-a* → Gröndahl PTU 168; vSoldt UF 21 370.

nḳl “supply, contribution” (?)
•CTX: **UGA** In MN → DUL 631: *yrḫ nql.*
•ONOM: **UGA** PN *nqly* → DUL 631.

|n-ḳ-m| Sem.: *nqm* (Hb.) “to take revenge”, (D) “to avenge”, *nqm* (*nāqām*) “revenge, vengeance”, *nqmh* (*n*^{e}*qāmāh*) “human revenge, divine retribution”; *nqm* (Aram., Syr.) “to avenge, take revenge”, *nqm* (Aram.) “(divine) avenger”, *nqm(?)*, *nqmh*, *nqmt?* (JAram.) “vengeance”; *naqa/ima* (Arab.) “to take vengeance, avenge”, *nāqim* “avenger”, *naqma*, *niqma*, *naqima* “revenge”; *nqm* (OSArab.) “to take vengeance”, *nqm* “penalty, payment of blood money”; *qym*, *taqayyama* (Eth.) “to take vengeance”, *qim* “revenge”.

|n-ḳ-m| “to avenge, save”
•CTX: **EA** G prefc. *yi-ki-im*, *li-ik-ki-im-mi*, suff. *yi-ki-im-ni-mi*, *yi-ik-ki-<mi>-ni* → CAD N/I 328f.
•ONOM: **EUPH** *ia-ki-ma*, *ia-ki-mu-um*, *ia-ki-ma-tum*, *ia-ki-im-*^{d}*da-gan*, *ia-ki-im-*DINGIR, *ia-ki-im-ḫa-mu*, *ia-ki-im-li-im*, *ia-ak-ki-im-li-im*, *ia-ak-ki-im-*^{d}IM, *ia-ak-ki-im-*^{d}IM, *a-an-ki-im-*DINGIR, *e-en-ki-im-*DINGIR, *ia-ak-ki-im-da-du*, *ia-an-ki-ma-nu*; *ia-an-ta-ki-im-*^{d}IM → Huffmon APNMT 241ff.; Gelb CAAA 27, 163, 166; Zadok Fs. Hallo 327; Streck Onomastikon 1 177 § 2.56, 180 § 2.63, 314 § 4.7, 346 § 5.64; Golinets Onomastikon 2 35, 39, 83, 188f., 324f., 417f., 487f.
U3 *en-gi-mu-um* → Huffmon APNMT 242; Buccellati Amorites 145f.; Gelb CAAA 27, 166; Bonechi SEL 13 12; Golinets Onomastikon 2 324, 417f.
UGS *na-qa-ma-du* → Sivan GAGl 254; Huehnergard UVST 248 fn.154.

niḳm “vengeance, salvation; DN”[323]
•CTX: **EUPH** *ni-iq-mi-šu*, *ni-iq-mi-im* → CAD N/2 251; Joannès ARM 26/2 337f. (435:26) fn. g; Zadok Fs. Hallo 327; Durand MARI 7 49; Streck Onomastikon 1 108f. § 1.95.
•ONOM: **EB** *dè-ni-g/ki-mu*, *i-da-ne/i-g/ki-mu*, *i-dè-ni-ki-mu*, *i-sa-ni-ki-mu*, *i-ša-ne-ig/ki-mu*, *i-ti-ne-ki-mu*, *ì:dè-ne/i-ki-mu*; cf. aphaeretic |(ni)ḳmu|: *i-da-ki-mu* → Pagan ARES 3 149, 301, 321f., 325f., 328; Bonechi SEL 13 12.
EUPH *ni-iq-ma-an*, *ni-iq-ma-nu-um*, *ni-iq-ma-a-nu-um*, *ni-iq-me-ia*, *ni-iq-ma/má-a/ad-du*, *ni-iq-mi-ia-ad-du*, *ni-iq-mi-e-pu-uḫ*, *ni-iq-mi-e-tar*, *ni-iq-mi-la-na-si* → Huffmon APNMT 241f.; Gelb CAAA 27, 166; Bonechi SEL 13 12; Streck Onomastikon 1 154 § 2.5, 156 § 2.11, 162 § 2.23 fn. 2, 200 § 2.95, 236 § 2.149, 242 § 2.165, 243 § 2.167, 344 § 5.59.
A7 *ni-iq-ma*, *ni-iq-mi-e-pu-uḫ*, *ni-iq-mi-ad-du*, *ni-iq-ma-a-bi*, *ni-iq-ma-a-du*, *ni-iq-me/i-pa*; *am-mu-ni-ik-ma* → Wiseman AT 127, 143; Gelb CAAA 27, 166; Arnaud AuOr 16 166, 173; Bonechi SEL 13 12; Streck Onomastikon 1 162 § 2.23 fn. 2, 253 § 2.179, 276 § 3.25, 323 § 5.11.
A4 *niq/ni-iq-me-pa*, *am-mu-ni-qí-ma* → Wiseman AT 127; Sivan GAGl 254.
EM *níq-me-*^{d}KUR → Pruzsinszky PTEm 184 [652]; Streck AfO 51 310.
EA *níq-ma-*^{d}IM → Sivan GAGl 254; Hess APN 119f.

---

[323] Also MN in OBab. (Mari, Chagar Bazar, Rimah, Diyala); AHw 792; CAD N/2 251; but see Streck Onomastikon 1 109 § 1.95.

	UGS *níq-ma-*^{d}IM, *níq-ma-an-du, níq-me-e-pa, ni-qi-ma/má-du, ni-iq-ma-du* → Huffmon APNMT 242; Gröndahl UPN 132, 144, 168; Huehnergard UVST 248 fn.154; Bonechi SEL 13 12.[324]
nāḳim "avenger, saviour"	•ONOM: **EUPH** *na-ki-mu(-um)* → AHw 721; Gelb CAAA 27, 163; Golinets Onomastikon 2 133f., 417.
nḳm "vengeance, salvation"	•ONOM: **UGA** Elem. in PNN: *nqmd* → DUL 631; *nqmpʕ* → DUL 632.
niḳitt "retaliation"	•CTX: **Late** *ni-qit-ti* → AHw 792: *niqittu* II; CAD N/2 251: *niqittu*.
menḳum "avenged, saved" (?)	•ONOM: **EUPH** Cf. unc. *me-en-gu-um* → Zadok Fs. Hallo 32 (Gelb-CAAA 323 under MNG).

|n-ḳ-p|	Sem.: *nqp* (Hb.) "to revolve, recur", *nqph* (*niqpāh*) "cord (around the body)", *tqwph* (*teqûpā*, < base **qwp*) "circuit, cycle"; *nqp* (JAram.) "to circle around", (Syr. C) "to complete a full cycle", *mqpn(ʔ)* (JAram.) "encircling wall", *tqwph* "cycle, turn" (< base **qwp*); *nāqaba* (Arab.) "to have a face-to-face encounter", *tanaqqaba, ʔintaqaba* "to put on a veil, veil one's face", *niqāb* "veil", *nuqba* "coat"; *nəqbat, nəqʷbat, ʔənqwəbat* (Eth.) "working garment, apron, loincloth".
nḳbn "animal harness, caparison" (?)	•CTX: **UGA** Pl. / du. *nqbnm*, suff. *nqbny* → DUL 630; Del Olmo AuOr 37 292.[325]
nḳpt, nḳpnt "turn, (yearly) cycle"	•CTX: **UGA** Pl. cstr. *nqpnt*, var. *nqpt* → DUL 632: *nqp(n)t*.
ʔanḳafḳaft "a wooden object carried on a chariot" (?)	•CTX: **EG** Cf. *ʔan-n-q-f-q-f-t* → Hoch SWET 26f. no. 15: etym. wholly unc.[326]

|n-ḳ-r|	Sem.: *nqr* (Hb.) "to dig out", (D) "to gouge out, pierce"; *nqr* (Aram., Syr.) "to excise", (Syr. D) "to cut out, perforate", *mqr(ʔ)* (Syr.) "chisel"; *naqāru(m)* (Akk.) "to demolish; to scratch", *maqqārum* "chisel"; *naqara* (Arab.) "to dig, pierce, bore", *minqār* "beak; pickax"; *nqər* (MSArab.) "to peck; to pick", *mengār, menqār, múnqur* "adze"; *naqʷara* (Eth.) "to peck, prick, pierce", *manqʷar* "beak, bill".
|n-ḳ-r| "to cut out; to scratch, engrave"	•CTX: **EB** *na-gu-lum, na-gu-um* |naḳḳur=, D | → Conti QDLF 4 104; Archi NABU 2005/40, PIHANS 106 108; Pasquali QuSe 23 183. •ONOM: **EB** Cf. unc. *a-gú-rúm, a-gur-il, a-gur-li-im* |yaḳḳur= | (?) → Pagan ARES 3 149, 278.[327] **EM** Unc. cf. *i-qir-x-x, iq-qir/qi-ir-da-ad-mu* → Pruzsinszky PTEm 135 with fn. 649 [500: "... die Wohnstätten"].
naḳir "engraved"	•CTX: **EB** *na-gi-lu* → Archi NABU 2005/40.

---

324 For attestations and var. see PRU 3 252; PRU 4 248; PRU 6 141; Ug 5 330.

325 For the *b/p* alternation see Tropper KWU 89: *nqbn**, with a diff. meaning: "Strick, Sattelriemen" (also Watson AuOr 29 159: "(saddle-)strap").

326 Sivan / Cochavi-Rainey WSVES 77: ʔ( )n-n-q-f-q-f-t "part of a chariot"; Helck Beziehungen no. 5.

327 Pagan loc.cit.: "he / DN demolished". Perhaps preferable: |yagūr=um| "he / DN sejourned"; see |g-w-r| (1).

maḳḳart “chisel”	•LL: **EB** ZÚ.UŠ = *ma-gàr-tum* → Conti QuSe 17 97.[328]

|n-ḳ-y| (1)	Sem.: *nqh* (Hb., N) “to be free, blameless”; *nqy* (Aram., D) “to remove a claim or obligation”; *naqiya* (Arab.) “to be pure, spotless”.
|**n-ḳ-y**| **(A)** “to be pure, free” (?)	•CTX: **UGA** G prefc. *åqy* → DUL 632f.: */n-q-y/*.
mnḳt “acquittal, exoneration” (?)	•CTX: **UGA** → DUL 557f.: *mnqt*.
taḳḳāt “an ornament or bead”	•CTX: **EUPH** *ta-qa-tim, ta-qa-at pappardilî* → CAD T 199: *taqqatu*; cf. Durand ARM 21 277 (249:6f.) “imitations”.

|n-ḳ-y| (2)	Sem.: *naqû(m)* (Akk.) “to pour a libation, to sacrifice”; hence *nqy* (Syr.) “to sacrifice”.
|**n-ḳ-y**| **(B)** “to pour a libation”	•CTX: **EB** G prefc. (perfect) |yittaqay| *i-da-ga-a* → Fronzaroli ARET 11 153; Catagnoti QuSe 29 132, 147, 165, 215. •ONOM: **EB** Cf. unc. |yinḳī| (?) *en-gi-da-du, en-gi-ma-lik* → Gelb MAD 3 204; Catagnoti QuSe 15 258; Pagan ARES 3 149f., 306.[329]

|n-m-ḳ|	Sem.: Cf. *nammaq* (Ar.): “to embellish, decorate”, *munammaq* “adorned”.
numaḳ “embellished” (?)	•ONOM: **UGS** Cf. *nu-ma-qi* → DUL 623: *nmq(n)*.
nmḳ “embellished” (?)	•ONOM: **UGA** Cf. *nmq(n)* → DUL 623 (unc.).

|n-m-l| (1)	Sem.: *nmlh* (*n^{e}mālāh*, Hb.) “ant”; *nml(?)* (Syr.) “ant hill”; *namālu(m), namlu* (Akk.) “ant”; *naml* (Arab.) “ant”; *nōmēl, nímhil, lōmē/ōl* (MSArab.) “ant”.
naml “ants, ant hill”	•CTX: **EA** *na-am-lu* (collective) → AHw 725; CAD N/1 208; Sivan GaGl 251; Rainey EAT 84, CAT 1 131; Izre’el Orient 38 85.
namal “ant”	•ONOM: **EUPH** *na-ma-lum, na-ma-la-tum* → Gelb CAAA 26, 163; CAD N/1 208: *namalu*; Golinets BuB 9 77.
lamn, lamatt[330] “ant”	•LL: **EB** KIŠI$_{6}$ = *la-ma-núm* → Civil BaE 91; Fronzaroli QuSe 13 144. Cf. la-ma-an → MEE 4 386 (0065); Sjöberg WO 27 24; Fs. Oelsner 414 fn. 16. **MŠ** *kul-ba-nu* = *la-ma-at-tu*$_{(4)}$ → AHw p. 533; CAD L, p. 67; Hrůša MŠ VI 61 255, 399.

|n-m-l| (2)	Sem.: *namala, namila* (Arab.) “to speak ill of”.
|**n-m-l**| “to speak ill of”	•LL: **EB** ÁŠ.DU$_{11}$ = *na-ma-lum, na-ma-lu-um, na-mar-tum* → Conti QuSe 17 103.

---

[328] For the var. ZÚ.UŠ = *ma-gàr-ru*$_{12}$ *si-nu(-me)*, GA.UŠ = *ma-a-šum* see Krebernik ZA 73 10; Conti QuSe 17 97f. fn. 158.

[329] See also the PN *ia-an-gi* under \|n-g-h\|.The forms \|yaqqī\|, \|yiqqī\|, \|tiqqī\| (cf. Pagan ARES 3 149f.: “to offer as a libation”) are most probably G prefc. of \|w-q-y\| (see Pagan ARES 3 190 and here \|w-q-y\|).

[330] Metath.; < *\|n-m-l\|. See further Fales QuSe 13 185 for VE 1189: ŠEG$_{9}$ = *la-ma-lum, la-ma-lum bar-su-um* “winged ant” and cf. Civil BaE 91 for KIŠI6.ḪU = *la-ma-núm bar-su-um*.

|n-m-r| (1)

Primary noun, Sem.: *nmr* (*nāmēr*, Hb.) "leopard, panther"; *nmr(?)* (Aram., Syr.) "leopard, panther"; *nimru(m)*, *namru*, *nammar* (Akk.) "leopard"; *nimr*, *namir* (Arab.) "leopard, tiger"; *nmr* (OSArab.) "panther, leopard"; *nemr* (MSArab.) "leopard"; *namr* (Eth.) "leopard".
Non-Sem.: Cf. **myar*= (Central Chadic) "serval, wild cat"; **mer* (Rift) "lion"; *mȝy* (Eg.) "lion", **muʔi*= (East Chadic) "lion"; **murum*= (West Chadic) "hyaena".[331]

namr (A) "leopard"

●LL: **EB** [PIRIG.TUR] = *na-me-ru*$_{12}$*-um*, *na-me-lum* → Civil BaE 93; Sjöberg Fs. Pettinato 279; Bonechi Fs. Fronzaroli 75ff.

|n-m-r| (2)
See |**n-w-r**|

|n-m-s¹| (1)

Culture word, Sem.: *nmš* (Hb.) "ichneumon, mongoose";[332] *nims* (Arab.) id.

namas¹, namis¹ "ichneumon, mongoose" (?)

●ONOM: **EUPH** *na-ma-šu*, *na-ma-ši*, *na-mi-šu* → Gelb CAAA 26, 163; Golinets BuB 9 80.

nms¹ "ichneumon, mongoose" (?)

●ONOM: **UGA** *nmš* → DUL 624.

|n-m-s¹| (2)

Sem.: Cf. *namāšu(m)* (Akk.) "to set in motion, start out", *nammaštû(m)*, *namaššû(m)*, *nammaštu* "moving (things, animals)".

tattam(m)iS "moving around a lot" (?)

●LL: **EB** Cf. NÌ.DI.DI = *da-da-mi-su* → Conti QuSe 17 82.

|n-m-y|

Sem.: Cf. *namā* (Arab.) "to increase, grow, become plentiful", *tanmiya* "increase".

tnmy "overflow" (?)

●CTX: **UGA** → DUL 860.

|n-m-z|
See |**n-z-m**|

|n-n-ʔ|

Culture word, Sem.: Cf. *nīnû(m)*, *nī/ēniu* (Akk.) "a medicinal plant".

nnủ "a medicinal plant"

●CTX: **UGA** Genit. *nnỉ* → DUL 624: *nnủ* (I).

|n-p-x|

Sem. |np=| with various H-extensions. See *npḥ* (Hb.) "to blow", *mpḥ* (*mappuᵃḥ*) "bellows"; *npḥ* (JAram., Syr.) "to blow", *mpwḥ(?)* "bellows"; *napāḫu(m)* (Akk.) "to blow", *munappiḫu(m)* "lighter of fires", *munappiḫtum* "bellows"(?); *nafaḥa* (Arab.) "to blow (wind), spread (fragrance)", *nafaḫa* "to blow, inflate", *minfaḫ*

---

[331] NOTE Orel / Stolbova HSED 382 no. 1760: **mer*= "beast of prey", 391 no. 1810: **müʔ*= "lion", 406 no. 1886: **numur*= "leopard, hyaena".
[332] Hebrew seal; Lemaire Semitica 37 47f.

"bellows"; *mnfḫthw* (OSArab.) "part of irrigation apparatus"; *hənfeġ* (MSArab.) "to blow"; *nafḫa, nafḥa, nafha* (Eth.) "to blow, inflate", *mənfāḫ* "bellows".

|**n-p-x**| "to blow"
●LL: **EB** KA.DIRI = *na-ba-ḫu(-um)* → Fronzaroli QuSe 13 147; Conti QuSe 17 102f.; Pasquali QuSe 23 69, Or 83 274.
●ONOM: **EUPH** *i-bi-ḫu, ib-bi-iḫ-li-di-ni* → Gelb CAAA 27 166.

mappax "bellows"
●LL: **EB** KA.DIRI = *ma-ba-ḫu-um* → Fronzaroli QuSe 13 147; Pasquali QuSe 23 69, Or 83 274; Catagnoti QuSe 29 59, 209.

mpx "(bellows of the) forge"
●CTX: **UGA** Du. *mpḫm* → DUL 559: *mpḫ*.

napx "shining, gleaming (stone)"
●CTX: **EB** *nab*$_x$*-ḫu*, NA *nab*$_x$(MUL)*-ḫu, na-ba-ḫu* → Pasquali NABU 2002/87; QuSe 23 67ff.: "cristallo di rocca".

|n-p-ḳ|
See |**p-w-ḳ**|, |**y-p-ḳ**|

Sem.: Cf. *npq* (Aram., Syr.) "to go out, come out; to turn into", (C) "to remove, produce, export".

|**n-p-ḳ**| "to come fort"
●ONOM: **U3** *i-bi-iq-ri-e-ú* → Buccellati Amorites 16, 154.

|n-p-l| (1)

Sem.: *npl* (Hb.) "to fall", *npl* (*nēpel*, Hb.) "miscarriage", *npylym* "giants"; *npl* (Aram., Nab., Palm., Syr.) "to fall", *npyl* (JAram.) "giant; premature birth"; *napālu(m)* (Akk.) "to dig out, tear down".

|**n-p-l**| **(A)** "to fall"
●CTX: **EA** G imp. *nu-pu-ul-mì* → AHw 734; CAD N/1 277; Sivan GAGl 254; Moran AmL 305; Rainey CAT 2 265, 3 40; Izre'el Orient 86.
UGA G suffc. *npl, nplt*, prefc. *tpl, tpln, ypl*; Gt prefc. *ttpl* → DUL 626.
●ONOM: Cf. npl → DUL 626.

|n-p-l| (2)

Sem.: *napālu(m)* (Akk.) "to pay balance"; *naffala, ʔanfala* (Arab.) "to cede the booty", *tanaffala, ʔintafal* "to do more than is required by duty or obligation".

|**n-p-l**| **(B)** "to supererogate"
●LL: **EB** É.NAM.AKA = *na-ba-um*, É.NAM.KI = *na-ba-u*$_9$ → Conti QuSe 17 119.

|n-p-p|

Sem.: *nwp* (Hb.) "to spray"; (Arab., Eth.) *nafnafa* "to drizzle".

|**n-p-p**| "to sprinkle"
●CTX: **EB** G prefc. *a-na-ba-ab* |la=yinappap|, inf. *na-ba-ba-šum* |napap=Sum|, cf. ptc. *na-ì-bù* |nāʔip|, *na-ì-bù-um* |nāʔip=|; Gt prefc. *lu-da-ba-ab* |la=yuttappap| → Fronzaroli NABU 1991/49, ARET 11 162; SEL 12 63; Catagnoti QuSe 29 45, 82, 140, 147f., 214.
UGA: Gt prefc. *ttpp* → DUL 626.

|n-p-r| (1)

Sem.: *npr* (Syr.) "to flee in fear"; *nafara* (Arab.) "to get frightened and fly", *nafūr, nāfir* "easily scared, shy"; *nafara* (Eth.) "to bubble".

|**n-p-r**| "to (start to) fly"
●CTX: **UGA** G prefc. *tpr*, suffc. *npr*, ptc. *npr* (see below: *npr*) → DUL 626.
●LL: **EB** DAL.DAL = *nu-bù-ru*$_{12}$*-um* → Sjöberg Fs. Pettinato 276; Catagnoti QuSe 29 138, 148, 214.

npr "flyer, bird"
●CTX: **UGA** Pl. *nprm* → DUL 626: *npr* (I).
●ONOM: Cf. *npr* → DUL 627: *npr* (2).

|n-p-r| (2)

Culture word, Sem.: *nupāru(m)*, *nubāru*, *nurpāru* (Akk.) "prison, workhouse".

nepar "workhouse, prison"

•CTX: **EUPH** Passim; cf. *ne-pa-ar*, *ne-pa-ra-am*, *ne-pa-ri*, *ne-pa-ri-im*, *né-pa-ri-im*, pl. *ne-pa-ra-ti*, *ne-pa-ra-tum/tim* → AHw 804: *nupāru(m)*; CADS N/2: *nupāru* A; Scouflaire Akkadica 53 25ff.; Lion Amurru 3 221; Charpin Fs. Veenhof 14.

|n-p-S|

Primary noun, Sem: *npš* (*nepeš*, Hb.) "throat, fauces";) *npš*(?) (JAram., Syr.) "throat"; *napaštum*, *napaltu*, *napištum*, *naʔištum*, *napuštu(m)*, *napultu*, *napšat(m)*, (Akk.) "throat, neck"; cf. *nafas* (Arab.) "swallow, gulp, draught". Denom. and further derivatives: *npš* (Hb. N) "to breathe freely", *npš* (*nepeš*) "breath, living being, life"; *nbš* (Ph., Aram., Syr.), *npš* (Ph., Pun., Nab., Palm. Hatra) *npš* "life, person"; *npš* (JAram., Syr.) "to breathe out", (Aram., Syr.) "soul, living person"; *napāšu(m)* (Akk.) "to breathe, be(come) wide"; *tanaffas* (Arab.) "to breathe, get his breath back", *nafs* "soul, spirit, life, a person", *nafas* "breath"; *hfsw* (OSArab.) "to cause to spread out", *nfs* "self, soul, life"; *néfoš* (MSArab.) "to breathe, live", *nefesét*, *nəfsét*, *nəfsēt* "soul, person, individual";*ʔanfasa* (Eth.) "to breathe", *nafsa* "to blow", *nafs* "soul, breath, self, a person", *nafās* "wind, air, spirit". See also: *nšb* (Hb., JAram., Syr.) "to blow"; *našāpu(m)* (Akk.) "to blow, winnow". Non-Sem.: *nf* (Eg.) "breath"; **naf*= (Saho-Afar, East Cushitic) "breath, soul";[333] *nfy* (Eg.) "to breathe"; **nif*= (Central Chadic) "breathe, smell";[334] **nVfas*= (Berber) "breath"; **nufas*= (West Chadic) "breath"; **na[f]us*= (Central Chadic) "soul"; **nafVs*= (Saho-Afar) "breathing";[335] **nufas*= (West Chadic) "breathe"; **nVfVs*= (Agaw) "blow".[336]

|n-p-S| "to breathe"

•ONOM: **EB** |yinpuS=|: *en-bù-uš-li-im* (also read ru_{12}*-bù-*), cf. *en-bù-uš*(!)*-ì*; |tappuS=|(?): *da-bù-šè* → Pagan ARES 3 149, 305.

nap(a)S, nap(i)S "throat; breath; life"

•ONOM: **EB** *nab-sa-su*, *na-bí-iš* → Pagan ARES 3 149, 353, 355.
U3 *na-ap-sa/ša-nu-um* → Buccellati Amorites 176; Gelb CAAA 26, 163; Wilcke WO 5 29; Owen JCS 33 257; Streck Onomastikon 1 223 § 2.122.
EUPH *na-pí-zu-um*, *na-ap-si-i-la*, *na-ap-si-in-ni*, *na-ap-si-ia-an-du*, *na-ap-zu-ba-al*, *na-ap-si-e-ra-aḫ*, *na-ap-si-*^{d}*da-gan*, *na-ap-si-bi-*DINGIR, *na-ap-su-na-i-la*, ^{d}*iš-ḫa-ra-na-ap-sí*, *la-ar-na-ap-su*, *na-ap-zum*, *na-ap-su-um*, *na-ap-ša/za-nu-um*, *na-ap-si-*^{d}IM, *na-ap-su-na-*^{d}IM, *na-ap-su-na-*^{d}*da-ra*, *ta-aḫ-wi-na-ap-su*, *a-bi-na-ap-si*, ^{d}*iš-ha-ra-na-ap-si* → Gelb CAAA 26, 163; Zadok Fs. Hallo 327; Streck Onomastikon 1 221 § 2.121, 223 § 2.122, 321 § 5.7.
A7 *na-ap-ši-a-du* → Wiseman AT 142; Gelb CAAA 26, 163; Arnaud AuOr 16 156; Streck Onomastikon 1 223 § 2.122.
Q *na-ap-ši-a-bi* → Richter / Lange Idadda 173, 175, 177.
EM *na-ap-ši*, *nap-ši* → Pruzsinszky PTEm 90 [648].
UGS Cf *nap-ša-na* → Sivan GAGl 252.

nip(i)S "throat" (?)

•CTX: **EM** Cf. *ni-pí*(?)*-šu* → Fleming Installation 269.

nupS "throat; breath; life"

•ONOM: **A7** *ka-ṣí-ra-nu-up-ši* → Wiseman AT 139; Arnaud AuOr 16 159.

nps[1] (A) "throat; breath; life"

•CTX: **UGA** Sg. *npš*, suff. *npšy*, *npšk*, *npšh*, *npškm*, *npskn*, *npšhm*, *npšm* → DUL 628f.: *npš* (I).

---

[333] Orel / Stolbova HSED 395 no. 1828: **naf*= "breath".
[334] Orel / Stolbova HSED 402 no. 1865: **nif*= "to smell, breathe".
[335] Orel / Stolbova HSED 395 no. 1830: **nafus*= "breath";
[336] Orel / Stolbova HSED 406 no. 1882: **nufas*= "blow, breathe".

nps^{1}n “place of / for ‘souls’” (?)	•CTX: **UGA** → DUL 629: *npšn.*
nbs^{1}t “living being(s), animal(s)”	•CTX: **UGA** Sg. / pl. *nbšt* → DUL 610: *nbšt.*
napiSat “throat; breath; life”	•ONOM: **EB** *na-bí-sa-dum* → Pagan ARES 3 149, 353.
nupuSt “throat; breath; life”	•LL: **EB** ZI = *nu-bù-uš-tum/du-um* → Krebernik ZA 73 37, PIHANS 106 91; Bonechi / Catagnoti Fs. Sommerfeld / Krebernik 190.

|n-p-ṣ| (1)	Sem. etym. unc. Cf. *npṣ* (Hb.) “to scatter, disperse”; *npṣ* (Aram., Syr.) “to shake, scatter; *napāṣu(m)* (Akk.) “to push away, abolish”.
nipṣ “clearance” (?)	•CTX: **R** *ni-pí-iṣ ni-ik-ka-si* → Dalley / Walker / Hawkins Tell Rimah 138 (176:2); CAD N/2 248: *nipṣu* 4; cf. Durand MARI 6 660: *nipiṣ nikkassī* “inventaire”.
npṣ “item, piece, single part of an equipment or outfit”	•CTX: **UGA** Pl. abs. *npṣm*; cstr. *npṣ*, suff. *npṣy/k/h* → DUL 627; Del Olmo AuOr 37 291.

|n-p-ṣ| (2)	Sem.: Cf. *nafaṣa* (Arab.) “to bring out fast”; *nfṣ* (OSArab.) “to go, march off”; *nafṣa* (Eth.) “to flee, escape”.
|n-p-ṣ| “to go, march off” (?)	•LL: **EB** Cf. SAG.SAR = *na-ba-zu*, *nab-zu* SAG, *ne-bí-zu-ù* → Conti QuSe 17 107. Diff. Sjöberg Fs. Wilcke 254: JAram. *nps/ṣ* “to hackle, comb (the hair)”

|n-p-y| (1)	Sem.: *nph* (cstr. *nāpat*, Hb.) “sieve”; *npy* (Aram.), “to winnow, sieve; to diminish”, *nph*, *npy* (JAram. D) “sieve”; *napû(m)* (Akk.) “to sieve, sift”, *nappû(m)*, *nappītu(m)* “sieve”; *nafaya* (Eth.) “to sift”, *manfe* “sieve”. See further: *nwp* (Hb.) “to move to and fro”; *nafā* (Arab.) “to drive away, expel, banish, dismiss, *nafy* “expulsion, banishment”.
|n-p-y| “to be driven away, expelled, banished”	•CTX: **EB** G prefc. *a-na-*[*ba*]*-m*[*a*] |lā yinappay=ma|, inf. suff. du. *na-ba-na-a* |napāy=i=nay(n)| → Fronzaroli ARET 13 14, 286; Catagnoti QuSe 29 45, 74, 105, 118, 147, 165, 215. **UGA** Gpass. / N. prefc. *tp* → DUL 629f.
nipīt “sieve, sifter”	•LL: **EB** Cf. KA.ZÌ = *ni-bí-tum* → Sjöberg Fs. Kienast 540; diff. Conti QuSe 19 46f.: KA.ŠÈ (eškiri) = NI-*bí-tum* “benda” (Akk. *nēbettu*).
npt “sieve, sifter”	•CTX: **UGA** → DUL 629.
npy “purification, expurgation”	•CTX: **UGA** → DUL 630.

|n-p-y| (2)	Culture word. Sem. cf. *nafya* (Arab.) “palm mat”. Non-Sem.: *mappa* (Latin) “tablecloth”.[337]
npyn “tunic”	•CTX: **UGA** Sg. suff. *npynh* → DUL 630.

[337] Loan: **mph* (Ph. / Pun.) “garment, cloth”.

|n-S-ʕ/x|	Sem.: *nsʕ* (Hb.) "to tear out; to journey further on", *msʕ* (*massaʕ*) "breaking (camp), departure", (*māssaʕ*) "(unhewn) stone"; *nsʕ* (Ph.) "to pull down"; *nazaʕa* (Arab.) "to pull out", *nazʕ* "removal"; *nazʕa*, *nazḫa* (Eth.) "to tear out, pull out". See also: *nsḥ* (Hb.)"to tear down / away"; *nsḥ* (Aram.) "to remove", *nzh*, *nzḥ* (JAram.) "to withdraw"; *nasāḫu*(*m*) (Akk.) "to tear out", *nisḫatu*(*m*) "a tax", *nisiḫtu* "desertion", *nusāḫu* "extract(ion)"; *nasaḫa* (Arab.) "to delete, withdraw", *nasaʕa* "to travel arround".
|**n-S-ʕ**| "to pull out, depart for a long journey; to pay"	•CTX: **EB** D prefc. *nu-na-zi* |nunaSSiʕ| → Catagnoti QuSe 29 148, 157, 215. Cf. SIKI *ni-za-ù* (inf. |nizāʕ=| ?) → Pasquali QuSe 19 258ff.: "lana dallo svellere". **EG** Cf. *na-ṯi*$_2$*-ʕa* |naSaʕa| (?) → Hoch SWET 196f. no. 265.[338] **UGA** G. prefc. *ysʕ*, *tśʕn*, *yśʕ*; act. ptc. sg./pl. cstr. suff. *nsʕk*; C suffc. *šsʕn* → DUL 634: /*n-s-ʕ*/ (I), 634f.: /*n-s:ś-ʕ*/ (II).
|**n-S-x**| "to pull out, withdraw"	•ONOM: **EB** Cf. *en-su-ḫu* → Pagan ARES 3 150, 307.
naSaʕt "removal"	•LL: **EB** KUR.KUR$_6$.NA.RÚ = *na-ša-du* → Conti QuSe 17 31, 33, 91. See also Fronzaroli ARET 13 87 for the gloss rdg.
nuSaʕt "tear, rip"	•CTX: **EB** SIKI *nu-za-a-tum* → Pasquali QuSe 19 258ff.
maSSaʕ "remoteness"	•CTX: **EB** *maš-za-im* → Fronzaroli ARET 11 160, 180; Catagnoti QuSe 29 31, 123, 210.

|n-S-G| Cf. |**n-s-k**|, |**n-θ-ḳ**|	Sem.: *nsk* (Hb.) "to entwine, plait, weave"; *nsg*, *nsk* (JAram.) "to weave", *nsyg* (Syr.) "weaving"; *nasağ* (Arab.) "to weave, intertwine", *nasīğ* "fabric".
|**n-S-G**| "to weave; to plot"	•CTX: **EUPH** Cf. G inf. *a-na na-sa*-KI-*im*, *a-wa-tam na-sa*-KI-*im* → Durand LAPO 16 273 fn. 41, 274f., LAPO 17 430 fn. 15;[339] Streck Onomastikon 1 107 § 1.95; Knudsen PIHANS 100 321 fn. 10.
naSiG "woven"	•CTX: **EUPH** *lu-ú na-sí*-IK → Streck Onomastikon 1 107 § 1.95.
niSG "a kind of hank" (?)	•CTX: **EUPH** Cf. *ni*-IS-KUM, *ni*-IS(*is*/*ìs*/*ís*?)-KU-*um*/*im* → Durand ARM 30 145.
ns^{1}g "cloth, fabric"	•CTX: **UGA** Gg. suff. *nšgh* → DUL 640: *nšg* "scabbard, sheath" (?).

\|n-S-x\|
See \|**n-S-ʕ/x**\|

|n-s-k| Cf. |**n-t-k**|, |**n-θ-ḳ**|	Sem.: *nsk* (Hb.) "to pour out", *nsk* (*nesek*) "drink offering, libation; statue of cast metal", *nsyk* (*nāsîk*) "libation, drink offering; cast statue, image; leader, chief of a tribe", *mskh* (*massēkāh*) "cast image; libation"; *nsk* (Ph., Pun.) "to pour out, found, privide", *nskt* (Pun.) "molten, cast metal"; *nsk* (Aram., Syr.) "to pour out, libate, cast metal", *nsk*(*ʔ*) (JAram.) "libation"; *nsyk*(*ʔ*) Syr. "cast image; flowing, fluid"; *nasāku*(*m*), *našaku* (Akk.) "to throw (down); to shoot"; see further: *nasaka* (Arab.) "to lead a devout life; to wash, clean", *na*/*i*/*usk* "piety"; *nāsik* "pious man, devotee".

[338] Altern. \|ðanaḫa\|, loc.cit. Cf. Sivan / Cochavi-Rainey WSVES 83: *na-śí-ʕá* "to depart"; Helck Beziehungen no. 146: "herausreisen".

[339] According to Durand ARM 30 145 the expression *awātam nasākum* means "ourdir une affaire"; cf. id. LAPO 17 430: "régler une affaire".

|**n-s-k**| "to throw (down); to pour (out)"	•CTX: **UGA** G/Gpass. prefc. *ảsk*, *ysk*; suff. *tskh*; suffc. suff. *nskh*; imp. *sk*; D prefc. *ynsk*; C imp. *šsk*. (?) → DUL 635: /*n-s-k*/. •LL: **EB** SÁ.SAG$_7$ =*na-za-gúm* → ContiQuSe 17 198; Catagnoti QuSe 29 21, 215.
nāsik "caster, metalsmith; chief"	•CTX: **EM** LÚ *na-sí-ku* → Pentiuc Vocabulary 132f.; Pruzsinszky PTEm 13 fn. 78.[340] **UGS** LÚ *na-s*[*í-ku*], *na-sí-ku* URUDU → Sivan GAGl 252; Huehnergard UVST 153, ^{2}UVST 394; vSoldt SAU 306. •ONOM: **UGS** *na-sí-ka-na* → Gröndahl PTU 426; Sivan GAGl 252; vSoldt SAU 40.
nasīk "cast metal object, ingot" (?)	•CTX: **EG** Cf. *n-ṯi$_2$-ku* (rdg unc.) → Hoch SWET 198f. no. 267.
nsk "caster, forger of metals"	•CTX: **UGA** Sg. *nsk*; pl. *nskm*; cstr. *nsk*; *nṣ*(!)*k* → DUL 635; Del Olmo AuOr 37 289. •ONOM: **UGA** Cf. *nskn* → DUL 636.
nskt "casting, cast metal or object; offering"	•CTX: **UGA** → DUL 636; Del Olmo AuOr 37 292.

|n-s-ḳ|	Sem.: Cf. *msq* (JAram.) "(sun)rise", *msq(ʔ)* (Syr.) "ascent, rising", *msqh*, *msqtʔ* (Syr.) "ascent"; see *slq* (Aram.) "to go up".[341]
nasḳ "ascent" (?)	•ONOM: **EUPH** *na-as-qa-tum* → Gelb CAAA 26, 164.

|n-s-s|	Sem.: *nss* (Hb.) "to stagger, dispair"; *nss* (JAram., Syr. D) "to trouble, make weak", *nsys* "vexed, frail, infirm"; *nasāsu*(*m*) (Akk.) "to lament, wail, moan", *nassu* "groaning"; *nss*, *nassa*, *nasasa* (Eth.) "to sway, move, shake". See further *nazāzu*(*m*) (Akk.) "to make swishing sound"; *nazza*·(Arab.)"to vibrate (string)", *nazz* "changeable, inconstant".
nass "wretched"	•ONOM: **EB** *na-sa*, *na-su-um* → Pagan ARES 3 150, 354.
nissat "weakness, indisposition"	•CTX: **EUPH** *i-na ni-is-sà-tim-ma* → CAD N/2 275; Durand LAPO 17 349 n. f.; Streck Onomastikon 1 109 § 1.95. **UGS** *i-na ni-is-sà-at* → Nougayrol PRU 3 56:24; CAD N/2 275; cf. Durand LAPO 17 349 n. f.

|n-s-y| (1)	Sem.: Cf. *nsh* (Hb. N) "to venture", (D) "to tempt, make an attempt"; *nsy* (JAram., Syr. D) "to tempt, attempt, try"; *nasawa* (Eth.) "to try, tempt".
|**n-s-y**| **(A)** "to venture; to try"	•CTX: **UGA** G/N prefc. *ysy* (?), Gt prefc. *ỉts* → DUL 636: /*n-s*(*-y*)/ (I).

|n-s-y| (2)	Sem.: Cf. *nesû*(*m*), *nasāʔum* "to be distant"; to withdraw". See further *nassa* (Arab.) "to push, drive".
|**n-s-y**| **(B)** "to remove"	•CTX: **UGA** G prefc. (?) *ysy*; suff. *ysynh* → DUL 636: /*n-s-y*/ (II).

340 For the shift "maître de forge" > "chef" ("le plus riche d'une communauté" see Abdallah / Durand BBVO 24 245ff. on a Tall Sakka text.

341 See further *nasāqu*(*m*) (Akk.) probl. "to ascend" (?) (CAD N/2 23: *nasāqu* B mng unc., C mng unkn.)

|n-ṣ-b| Cf **|w-ṣ-b|**	Sem.: *nṣb* (Hb. N) "to place oneself", (C) "to place, set up", *mṣb* (*maṣṣāb*) "place, (military) position", *mṣbh* (*maṣṣēbāh*), *mṣbt* (*maṣṣebet*) "memorial stone", *nṣyb* (*n^{e}ṣîb*) "overseer"; *nṣb* (Pun., Nab., Palm.) "to erect, to raise", *nṣb* (Ph.), *nṣyb* (Nab.) "raised stone, stele", *mṣb* (Nab., Palm.) "image in bas-relief", *mṣbh, mṣbt, mṣbtʔ* (Ph., Pun., Palm.) "stele"; *nṣb* (Aram., Syr.) "to plant, erect", *nṣb(ʔ)* (Aram.) "raised stone, stele", *nṣbh, nṣbtʔ* (Aram., Syr.) "plant, stele"; *naṣaba* (Arab.) "to set up", *naṣb* "setting up, signal, mark", *nuṣb* "statue, monument", *naṣība* "landmark, milestone", *manṣib* "origin, source; rank, quality", *ʔanṣāb* (pl.) "standard";[342] *nṣb* (OSArab.) "to erect", *nṣb* "funerary stela", *mnṣbt* (pl.) "pillars"; *nəṣáwb* (MSArab.) "to set up, erect", *neṣōb* "to begin, judge", *nəṣəbēt* "beam".
|n-ṣ-b| "to stay erect, take up a position, keep, wait for, expect; to erect, put, fix"	•CTX: **EB** G prefc. *a a-za-ab* |ʔay ʔaṣṣab|, *a-na-za-ab* |ʔanaṣṣab|, *da-na-za-ab* |tanaṣṣab|, *na-na-za-ab* |nanaṣṣab|, suffc. *na-zi-bu* |naṣib| → Fronzaroli ARET 11 162; ARET 13 25, 287; Catagnoti QuSe 29 10, 18, 46, 52, 105, 109, 125, 131, 134, 146, 216; Pasquali NABU 2018/39 fn. 6; 2018/94. **EA** Gt prefc. *it-ta-ṣa-ab*; suffc. *ni-ta-ṣ[a-ab]* → AHw 755; CAD N/2 33; Rainey EAT 84; Sivan GAGl 172, 182, 254; Rainey CAT 2 94f. **TA** G suffc. *n]a-ṣa-ab-ba* → Horowitz / Oshima CunCan 124, 150. **UGA** G ptc. *nṣb*; prefc. *yṣb* → DUL 637: /*n-ṣ-b*/. •ONOM: **EB** Cf. *en-zu-ub-bu*$_{16}$ → Krebernik PET 58; Pagan ARES 3 150, 308. **EUPH** *ia-an-zi-bu(-um), ia-an-zi-pa/ba-an, ia-an-zi-ib-*^{d}IM/DINGIR/^{d}*da-gan, ia az-zi-ib-*^{d}*da-gan, ia-an-ṣí-ib-ḫa-ad-nu* → Huffmon APNMT 241; Gelb CAAA 27, 166; Streck Onomastikon 1 207f. § 2.101 fn. 2, 229 § 2.138; Golinets Onomastikon 2 326f., 418. **UGS** Cf. *ia-ṣú-ba* → Gröndahl PTU 58, 169; Sivan GAGl 254: |yaṣṣub=|. **UGA** Cf. *yṣb* → DUL 971. **EG** *ya-n-di*$_{4}$*-bu* → Hoch SWET 54 no. 55; cf. Schneider APÄQ 57 no. 101 (*y-n:-dꜣ-b-w*).
mṣb (A) "beam, pointer"	•CTX: **UGA** → DUL 577: *mṣb* (I).
mṣb (B) "place in which something is put, deposit, reserve"	•CTX: **UGA** sg. *mṣb*; pl. (?) *mṣbm* → DUL 577: *mṣb* (II).
naṣb (A) "support"	•ONOM: **EUPH** *na-az-bu-um* → Gelb CAAA 27, 164.
naṣb (B) "reserve, setting apart" (?)	•CTX: **EUPH** Cf.A.ŠÀ *ù* É *na-aṣ-bu-um, na-aṣ-ba-am iṣ-ṣí-ib-[šu]* → CAD N/2 141: *nazbu*; Zadok Fs. Hallo 327; Streck Onomastikon 1 108 § 1.95.[343] •ONOM: **EM** Cf. *na-aṣ-bu* → Pruzsinszky PTEm 174 [649]: "Aufgerichteter, Schöpfung".
niṣb "support"	•ONOM: **EUPH** *ne-iz-bi-el/il* → Gelb CAAA 27, 166; Streck Onomastikon 1 323 § 5.11.
naṣab "erect, put / set upright"	•ONOM: **EUPH** *na-za-ba-nu-um* → Gelb CAAA 27, 164; Golinets Onomastikon 2 155, 418, 493.
nāṣib "keeper, one who is paying attention"	•LL: **EB** IGI.SI$_{11}$ = *na-zi-bù(-um)* → Fronzaroli QuSe 19 13; Bonechi QDLF 16 83. Bonechi MARI 8 491 n. 121; Sjöberg Fs. Renger 536; Catagnoti AAA 1 2019 25, 35f.; Pasquali NABU 2018/94.

[342] See Lackenbacher NABU 1991/12 fn. 2: "bétyle".

[343] Cf. Charpin AfO 34 40 fn. 26; Bonechi MARI 8 491 n. 121; Yamada Proceedings 54e RAI p. 593ff.

naṣub "erect, put / set upright"	•ONOM: **EB** Cf. *na-zu-bù* → Pagan ARES 3 150, 354.
nuṣab "erect, put / set upright"	•ONOM: **EUPH** *nu-za-ba-an*, *nu-za-bu*(*-um*), *nu-ṣa-ba-nu* → Gelb CAAA 27, 168; Zadok Fs. Hall 327; Streck Onomastikon 1 332 § 5.33; Golinets Onomastikon 2 164, 418, 494.
nṣbt "display, support" (?)	•CTX: **UGA** → DUL 637: *nṣbt*: "predilection" (etym. unc.).
taṣṣib "installation, camp"	•LL: **EB** KI.GÁ = *da-zi-bu-um* → Krebernik StEb 7 206; Bonechi MARI 8 491 fn. 121
|n-ṣ-ḥ (1)|	Sem.: *nṣḥ* (Ph.) "to excel, exert oneself"; *nṣḥ* (Aram., Syr.) "to be victorious", *nṣḥn*(*ʔ*) "victory".
nṣḥ "victory"	•CTX: **UGA** Sg. suff. *nṣḥy* → DUL 637f.: *nṣḥ*.
|n-ṣ-ḥ| (2)	Sem.: *naṣaḥa* (Arab.) "to be pure, sincere"; *naṣḥa* (Eth.) "to be pure, clean".
|**n-ṣ-ḥ**| "to be pure, clean" (?)	•LL: **UGS** Cf. [EL = *elēlu* = ... = *x*]-IZ-*ḫu* (read *ni*]-*iṣ*-*ḫu* ?) → Huehnergard ²UVST 383, 394.
|n-ṣ-ḳ| See |**y-ṣ-ḳ**|	Sem. by-form of |y-ṣ-ḳ| (?).
|n-ṣ-l|	Sem.: *nṣl* (Aram. C) "to free, save; take (away), retake, remove"; *naṣala* (Arab.) "to fall out, fade, get rid (of)", *ʔanṣala*, *tanaṣṣala* "to free, renounce, disavow, withdraw (from)"; *naṣala* (Eth.) "detach, separate".
|**n-ṣ-l**| "to retire, cease; to save"	•CTX: **UGA** N prefc. *ynṣl* → DUL 638. •ONOM: **EG** Cf. *h-ꜣ-ḏꜣ-r* (var. rdg) → Schneider APÄQ 162 no. 342 (altern. rdg: *h-ꜣ-b-w2-r*).[344]
|n-ṣ-p|	Primary noun: *nṣp* (Hb.) "certain weight"; *naṣf*, *niṣf*, *nuṣf* (Arab.) "half; middle; demi-", *niṣf* "medium, of medium size or quality", with several denom.: *naṣafa* "to reach the midst (day), *naṣṣafa* "to bisect", *nāṣafa* "to share", *ʔanṣafa* "to be just", *tanaṣṣafa* "to demand justice", *ʔintaṣṣafa* "to reach its midst".
nṣp "a weight (half a shekel / weak shekel)"	•CTX: **UGA** → DUL 638.
|n-ṣ-r|	Sem.: *nṣr* (Syr) "to whisper, murmur, grunt", *nṣr*(*ʔ*) "whisper".
|**n-ṣ-r**| "to sob" **mṣr** "sob"	•CTX: **UGA** G prefc. *tṣr*; act. ptc. fem. *nṣrt* → DUL 638. •CTX: **UGA** → DUL 580.
|n-ṣ-ṣ|	Primary noun, Sem.: *nṣ* (*nēṣ*), *nṣh* (*noṣāh*) (Hb.) "falcon"; *nṣ*(*ʔ*) (JAram., Syr.) "hawk, falcon"; *naṣnaṣu* (Akk. LL) "a bird"; *naṣṣa* (Arab.) "female sparrow".

[344] See also *m-ḏꜣ-r-y-ꜣ* (Schneider APÄQ 138 no. 294) under *maθθart* (\|n-θ-r\|).

|n-ṣ-ṣ| (A) "to take flight"	•CTX: **UGA** G prefc. *åṣṣ*; C ptc. cf. *mšṣṣ* (below) → DUL 638.
ms^{1}ṣṣ "one who drives out, scares off"	•CTX: **UGA** → DUL 587: *mšṣṣ*.
naṣṣ "a wild bird" (?)	•ONOM: **EB** Cf. *na-zu, na-zi, na-za, na-zú, na-zú-ù, na-zi-a, na-za-an* → Pagan ARES 3 227, 354. **A4** Cf. *na-aṣ-ṣú, na-(aṣ-)ṣí-ia* → Dietrich / Loretz WO 5 64 (8:15), 66 (9:53); Sivan GAGl 252. **UGS** Cf. *na-ṣi*; *na-ṣí-ya-a-nu* → Gröndahl PTU 169; Sivan GAGl 252.
nṣ "bird, wild bird"	•CTX: **UGA** → DUL 637: *nṣ* (I). •ONOM: **UGA** *nṣ* → Gröndahl PTU 28, 169; DUL 637: *nṣ* (II); unc. *nṣd* → DUL 637; *nṣdn* → DUL 637; *nṣṣn* → DUL 639; cf. Gröndahl PTU 170: Hb., Aram. "blühen, funkeln"; Arab. "bestimmen" (?).

|n-s^1-B| (1)	Sem.: *nšb, nšp* (Hb.) "to blow"; *nšb, nšp* (JAram., Syr.) "to blow", *nšb(?)* "blowing, wind storm"; *našāpu(m)* (Akk.) "to blow away", *našpu* "blown away (type of thin beer)", *nušaptum* "blown away" (brewing term)"; *nasafa* (Arab.) "to blow up, blast", *nasf* "blowing up, blasting".
|n-s^1-B| "to blow"	•ONOM: **A7** cf. *ia-ši-bi-il(-la)* → Wiseman AT 136; Arnaud AuOr 16 175. **EG** Cf. *yw-m-n-ꜣ-š-f-ty* → Schneider APÄQ 22 no. 21.
nas^{1}pat "blown, blowing" (?; fem.)	•ONOM: **EUPH** *na-aš-pa-tum* → Gelb CAAA 27, 164.
nus^1(s^1)up "blowing, blown" (?)	•ONOM: **EUPH** *nu-šu-bu-um* → Gelb CAAA 27, 168.

|n-s^1-b| (2)	Etym. unc. Sem. cf. *nšb?* (Syr.) "claw". Non-Sem. cf. *šbtyw* (Eg.) "two ribs (food)".
ns^{1}b "a piece of meat"	•CTX: **UGA** → 640: *nšb*.

|n-s^1-g|
See **|n-S-G|**

|n-s^1-ḳ| (1)	Sem.: *nšq* (Hb.) "to kiss", *nšq* (*nešeq*) "pleasant smells", *nšyqh* (*n^{e}šîqāh*) "kiss" *nšq* (Aram., Syr.) "to kiss", *nšyqh, nšyqt?* (JAram.) "kiss", *nwšqh, nwšqt?* (Syr.) "kiss"; *našaqu(m)* (Akk.) "to kiss". See further: *našiqa* (Arab.) "to smell, sniff".
|n-S-ḳ| "to kiss"	•CTX: **EB** G prefc.: *da-si-ig* |tassiḳ| → Fronzaroli ARET 13 21, 251; Catagnoti QuSe 29 26, 130, 146, 215. **UGA** G prefc. *yšq*, inf. *nšq*; D prefc. *ånšq* (?), *tnšq, ynšq* → DUL 640f.: /*n-š-q*/.
niSḳ "kissing"	•LL: **EB** NE.SUB$_5$ = *ne-sa-gu(-um)* → Krebernik ZA 73 33; Conti QuSe 17 203; Sjöberg Fs. Pettinato 269.
maSSaḳ "kissing, kiss"	•CTX: **EB** *mi-sa-ga- tim* |massaḳ ḳātim| → Fronzaroli / Catagnoti Fs. Pennachietti 222f.;[345] Catagnoti QuSe 29 28, 49, 115, 210.

[345] Fronzaroli / Catagnoti Fs. Pennachietti loc.cit.: *in* U$_4$ *mi-sa-ga- tim* EN "when the rite of the kiss of the hand of the king".

|n-s^1-ḳ| (2)

Sem.: *nšq* (Hb.) "to be armed"; *šutassuqu(m)* (Akk. *nasāqu(m)* Ct) "to put, keep in order"; *nasaqa* (Arab.) "to put in proper order"; *nasaqa* (Eth.) "to arrange in order, join closely".

|n-s^1-ḳ| "to put in proper array" — •CTX: **EG** Cf. *na₂-sa-k* → Hoch SWET 193 no. 259.[346]

|n-s^1-r| (1)

Primary noun, Sem.: *nšr* (*nešer*, Hb., Nab., Hatra) "eagle, vulture"; *nšr(?)* (Aram., Syr.) "vulture"; *našru* (Akk. LL) "eagle"; *nasr* (Arab.) "vulture, eagle", *nusārīyya* "eagle"; *nōher* (< *nšr*) (MSArab.) "big bird"; *nəsr* (Eth.) "eagle, vulture, hawk".

naSr "eagle, vulture" — •ONOM: **EB** Cf. *na-sa-ra-ì* → Pagan ARES 3 227, 354.

ns^1r "eagle, falcon" — •CTX: **UGA** Sg. *nšr*, pl. *nšrm*, suff. *nšrk* → DUL 641: *nšr*.

|n-s^1-r| (2)

Sem.: *našāru(m)* (Akk.) "to deduct, reduce, take something from something, reduce", *maššārtu(m)* "deduction, withdrawal"; *nasara* (Arab.) "to remove, take (away), tear".

|n-S-r| "to take away (the illness); to get better" — •CTX: **EB** D inf. *nu-su-rúm* |nuSSur=| → Fronzaroli Memoriae Diakonoff 92f.; Catagnoti QuSe 29 142, 148, 215.

taSSar "share, part set aside" — •CTX: **EB** Cf. *da-sa-lu-su* |taSSar=Su, taSSar=ū=Su| → Catagnoti / Fronzaroli ARET 16 90, 224.

|n-s^1-y| (1)

Primary noun, Sem.: *nšh* (*nāšeh*, Hb.) "sciatic nerve"; *gnšyʔ* (*gīd=našyāʔ*, Syr.) "ischial tendon", *ʔnšy* "sciatica"; *nasan* (Arab.) "tendon", *ʔansā* "lower leg muscle", *nasin* "suffering from sciatica", denom. *nasiya* "to feel pain in the sciatic nerve".
Non-Sem.: Cf. *ynst* (Eg.) "calf of leg, shank".

åns^1 "muscle, tendon" — •CTX: **UGA** Pl. cstr. *ånš* → DUL 80: *ånš*.

|n-s^1-y| (2)

Sem.: *nšh* (Hb.) "to forget"; *nšy* (Aram., Syr.) id.; *mašû(m)*, *mašāʔum*, *wašû* (Akk.) id.; *nasiya* (Arab.) id.; *ns^1y*(OSArab.) id.; *náyhi*, *nešə*, *anhō* (MSArab.) id.; *nasaya* (Eth.) "to be forgotten".

|n-s^1-y| "to forget" — •CTX: **UGA** N suffc. *nšt*; C prefc. *tššy* → DUL 641 */n-š-y/*: N "to be forgotten"; C "to cause, allow to forget".

|n-s^2-ʔ|

Sem: *nŠʔ* (*nśʔ*, Hb.) "to raise, lift up, carry", *nŠyʔ* (*nāśîʔ*), *nsy*, *nsyʔ* "ruler, chief", *mŠʔh* (*maśśāʔāh*) "exaltation"; *nšʔ* (Ph., Pun., Moab.) "to raise, lift up, carry", *nšʔ* "ruler, chief"; *nšʔ*, *nsy* (Aram.) "to lift up, take away"; *našû(m)* "to lift up, raise", *nāšû* "bearing, bearer, porter"; *našaʔa* (Arab.) "to rise, become elevated, appear", *naššaʔa* "to bring up, raise"; *nšʔ* (OSArab.) "to undertake a project"; *nəśū*, *nśe*

---

[346] Sivan / Cochavi-Rainey WSVES 82: *na-śá-ka* "to equip"; Helck Beziehungen no. 144 "vorbereiten".

(MSArab.) "to transhume"; *naśʔa* (Eth.) "to take (up), raise, lift".

|n-S-ʔ| "to raise, carry, accept"
•CTX: **EB** G prefc. *ʔa₅-si*, *ʔa₅-su* |ʔaSSi=|, *i-si* |yiSSiʔ|, *i-na-su* |yinaSSiʔ=ū|, *i-sa-ma* |yiSSiʔ=am-ma|, *i-ne-sa-nu* |yinaSSiʔ=am=nu|, *ne-na-sa-am₆*| ninaSSiʔ=am|, *ne-na-sa-nu* |ninaSSiʔ=am=nu|, *i-sa-ma* |yiSSiʔ=am=ma| → Fronzaroli ARET 13 189, 271; NABU 2016/88; Catagnoti / Fronzaroli ARET 16 114, 219; Catagnoti QuSe 29 79, 91, 136f., 146, 151, 215; Fronzaroli NABU 2016/88.
•LL: **EB** IGI.ÍL = *na-si-i a-na-a* → Fales QuSe 13 182: inf. "to raise, (said of) the eyes)"; diff.: Krebernik ZA 73 27f.: ptc. |nāśiʔ=|: "der die Augen erhebt" (see below: *nāSiʔ*).
•ONOM: **EB** *ʔa₅-si-li-gú*, *a-si*, *a-si-ar*, *a-si-ma-lik*, *da-si*, *da-si-a-ad*, *da-si-ḫu*, *da-si-ḫum*, *da-šè*, *da₅*-si-ga, *li-si* |liSSiʔ| → Pagan ARES 3 151, 272, 283, 299, 346.
U3 *ià-ši-li-im* → Buccellati Amorites 153; Gelb CAAA 27, 166; Streck Onomastikon 1 204f. § 2.96 fn. 5; Golinets Onomastikon 2 326, 417f.
EUPH *ia-áš-si-ia-an*, *i-si-*ᵈ*da-gan*, *i-si-iḫ-*ᵈ*da-gan*, *ia-si/ši*-DINGIR, *ia-si-*ᵈIM, *ia-si-li*, *ia-si-*ᵈUTU, *ia-si-(i-)lí*, *ia-si-lum*, *ia-si-ḫa-mu*, *ia-si-e/a-ra-aḫ*, *ia-si-ra-aḫ*, *ia-si-*ᵈ*da-gan*, *ia-si-su-uḫ*, *is-si-*ᵈ*da-gan*, *ia-si-iḫ-*ᵈ*da-gan*, *ia-áš-ši-*ᵈIM, *ia-áš-si-ia-an*, *ia-aš/áš-si-*ᵈ*da-gan* → Huffmon APNMT 239f.; Gelb CAAA 27, 166; Streck Onomastikon 1 204f. § 2.96 fn. 5, 187 § 2.79, 215 § 2.112, 221 § 2.121, 223 § 2.123, 236 § 2.149, 237 § 2.152, Suppl. 359; Golinets Onomastikon 2 325f., 417f.
A4 *ia-aš-ši*, *ia-ši*-DINGIR → Arnaud AuOr 16 175; vDassow SCCNH 17 496.
EM *la-na-ša* → Pruzsinszky PTEm 218 [590]; cf. unc. *ia-an-ša* → Arnaud SEL 8 41; Pruzsinszky PTEm 168 fn. 186 [419].
EG Cf. *y-n:-sꜣ* F, var. *y-n-y₂-sꜣ* F → Schneider APÄQ 56 no. 100.

|n-s¹-ʔ| "to raise, lift, carry"
•CTX: **EA** N Cf. *yi-na-aš-ši* : *na-aš-ša-a* → Rainey EAT 85; Rainey CAT 2 130, 308; Izre'el Orient 38 73.
UGA G prefc. *tšả*, suff.*tšản* (emph. *-n*), *tšủ*, *tšủn*, *yšủ*; suffc. *nšả*, *nšảt*, *nšủ*; imp. *šả*, *šủ*; inf. cstr. *nšỉ*; act. ptc. (?)*nšỉ*; Gt prefc. *ytšỉ*, *ytšủ*; N prefc. *tnšản* → DUL 639f.: */n-š-ʔ/*.

nāSiʔ "one who raises, accepts; chief, leader; ND"
•LL: **EB** IGI.ÍL = *na-si-i a-na-a* → Krebernik ZA 73 27f.: ptc. |nāśiʔ=|; diff.: Fales QuSe 13 182: inf. (see abowe: |n-S-ʔ|).
•ONOM: **EB** *na-si-um* → Pagan ARES 3 151, 354.
EUPH *ḫa-mu-la-na-sí*, *ia-aḫ-wi-na-si*, *ia-du-ur-na-si*, *ni-iq-mi-la-na-si*, *yi-it-mu/mi-na-si*, *zi-id-ku/kum-la-na-si*, *zi-ik-ru-la-na-si* → Huffmon APNMT 240; Gelb CAAA 27, 164; Streck Onomastikon 1 329 § 5.24, 236 § 2.149: Golinets Onomastikon 2 179f., 417f.
TU *ia-wi-ir-na-si* → Krebernik Tall Bi`a 219; Golinets Onomastikon 2 179, 417f.

naSūʔ "raised, accepted"
•ONOM: **EUPH** *la-na-su-ú*, *la-na-su-ú-um*, *la-na-su-wu-um*, *la-a-na-su-i-im*, *la-na-su-yi*, *la-ni-su-wu*, *la-na-su-ú(-um)*, *la-na-su-wu-um*, *mi-ia-na-su*, *la-na-su-ia*, cf. *la-ni-su*-PI → Huffmon APNMT 240; Gelb CAAA 27, 164; Streck Onomastikon 1 236 § 2.150, 330 § 5.28; Golinets Onomastikon 2 185f., 417f.
EG Cf. *n-ꜣ-sw-y* → Schneider APÄQ 144 no. 308.

miSSaʔ "predilection"
•ONOM: **A4** *mi-ša-ú* → Arnaud AuOr 16 170.

s¹uSSuʔ "handle, carrying device"
•CTX: **EUPH** *šu-uš-ši* → Guichard ARM 31 135; Durand LAPO 18 65 fn. b.

|n-s^2-r|	Sem.: Hb. *mŚwr* (*maśśôr*) "saw"; *nsr* (JAram. D, Syr. G) "to saw", *msr* (JAram.) "to saw", *msr*(*?*) "saw"; *našaru*(*m*) (Akk.) "to deduct, reduce", *maššartu*(*m*) "deduction", *šaššaru*(*m*), *šuššarum*, *šeššerum*, *šarsāru* "saw", probl. Aram.: *nasāru* "to saw", *massāru* "saw"; *našara* (Arab.) "to saw", *minšār* "saw"; see further: *wašara* (Arab.) "to saw", *mīšār* "saw", *mawšūr* "prism", *šaršara* "to split"; *mənšār*, *mənāšər* (MSArab.) "saw"; *waśara*, *waśśara*, *wasara* (Eth.) "to saw, split", *mośar*, *mośart*, *məśśar* "saw", *sarsara* "to bore a hole, saw".
SarSar "saw"[347]	•LL **EB** ŠUM.URUDU = *sar-sa-rum* → Conti QuSe 17 188; Catagnoti QuSe 29 31, 225.
|n-ṣ-m|	Sem.: Cf. *ḍmm* (Arab.) "to (com)press, tighten"; *ḍamama* (Eth.) "to bind, patch up, skin over".
niṣīm "thin layer, sheet, plate"	•CTX: **EB** Cf. *ne-zi-mu* → Waetzoldt LEbla 372f.; Fronzaroli Fs. Limet 63f.; Pasquali QuSe 23 87: < **naṣīm*.
|n-ṣ-ṣ|	Sem.: *nṣṣ* (G, Hb.) "to sparkle", (C) "to blossom", *nṣ* (*nēṣ*) "blossom", *nyṣwṣ* (*nîṣûṣ*) "spark", *nṣh* (*niṣṣāh*) "blossom, inflorescence"; (G, JAram.) "to blossom", (D, C) "to kindle", *nṣ*(*?*) "blossom"; *nāḍa* (*nawḍ*, Arab.) "to shine, sparkle".
|n-ṣ-ṣ| (B) "to sparkle, blossom"	•ONOM: **EUPH** Cf. *ni-ṣa-ta-nu-um*, *nu-ṣa-an* → Zadok Fs. Hallo 327.
|n-t-b| (1)	Sem.: *ntyb* (*nātîb*, Hb.) "pathway", *ntybh* (*nᵉtîbāh*) "path".
ntb "path"	•CTX: **UGA** → DUL 641f.
ntbt "path, (right of) way"	•CTX: **UGA** Sg. *ntbt*; suff. *ntbtk* → DUL 642.[348]
|n-t-b| (2)	Sem.: Cf. *nataba* (Arab.) "to swell, grow".
natib "swollen" (?)	•ONOM: **EUPH** *na-ti-ib-tim* → Zadok Fs. Hallo 327.
|n-t-k| See |s^1-t-k|, cf. |n-s-k|	Sem.: *ntk* (G / N, Hb.) "to gush forth, pour out", (C) "to pour out"; *ntk* (Aram.) "to melt, cast", *mtk* "cast metal"; *natāku*(*m*) (Akk.) "to drip", *nitku* "mineral or frit".
|**n-t-k**| "to spill, pour (out); to run, flow"	•CTX: **UGA** G prefc. *ytk*; N prefc. *tntkn* → DUL 642.[349]
nutk "a glass paste"	•CTX: **UGS** Cf. NA4 *ka-am-ma : nu-ut-ki* → Sanmartín NABU 1992/83; Huehnergard 2UVST 394.

[347] Akk. loan.
[348] For the writing *ntbtš* (KTU 4.288:6, *ntbt š*; DUL 642: *ntbt š* "cattle tracks" (?)) cf. Tropper UG 107: "Ug. ntbt "Weg + hurr. Abstraktendung –šše"; unlikely.
[349] For the forms *štk*, *išttk*, *ttkn*, considered by other scholars to be C and Gt of \|n-t-k\|, cf. \|s^1-t-k\|.

ntk "a glass paste"	•CTX: **UGA** → DUL 642.
mtk "libation"	•CTX: **UGA** → DUL 592.
|n-t-n| See **|n/w/y-D-n|**	
|n-t-r| See **|t-r-r|**, **|t-w-r|**	Sem.: Cf. *ntr* (Aram. C) "to release, take from someone's possession, unloosen", *natara* (Arab.) "to pull, draw vehemently". See further *natāru* (Late and SBab. Akk.) "to split open".
|n-t-r| "to take away by force, banish; to startle" (?)	•CTX: **UGA** G prefc. *ytr*; unc. C prefc. *tštr* → ²DUL 652; DUL 643.
|n-ṭ-ʕ|	Sem.: *nṭʕ* (Hb.) "to plant", *maṭṭāʕ* "planting"; *nṭʕ* (Ph.) "to plant", *nṭʕ* "plantation"; *nṭʕ* (OSArab.) "to plant", *nṭʕ* "ground".
|n-ṭ-ʕ| "to plant"	•ONOM: **EUPH** Cf. TN *ia-an-di-ḫa*-KI → Huffmon APNMT 239; Gelb CAAA 27, 167; Golinets Onomastikon 2 83f., 331, 419, 487.
mṭʕt "plantation"	•CTX: **UGA** Sg. / pl. *mṭʕt* → DUL 954.
|n-ṭ-l|	Sem.: *nṭl* (Hb.) "to impose, lay upon; to weigh", *nṭl* (*nēṭel*) "burden", *nṭyl* (*nāṭīl*) "weighing out"; *nṭl* (Aram.) "to lift up", *mṭl* (JAram., Syr.) "burden, weight"; *naṭālu*(*m*) (Akk.) "to look", *niṭlu*(*m*) "look, view", *nāṭilu* "seeing", *maṭṭaltu* "mirror image, reflection, counterpart".
|n-ṭ-l| "to lift, raise (eyes, voice)"	•CTX: **EB** G pref. *ti-na-da-ú* |tinaṭṭal=ū| → Fronzaroli QuSe 15 12, ARET 11 171; Archi PIHANS 106 104, Rubio PIHANS 106 121; Catagnoti QuSe 29 10, 18, 127, 131, 147, 216.
maṭṭal "inspection" (?)	•LL: **EB** Cf. IGI.GAR (GURUM$_7$) = *ma-da-u$_9$* → Conti QuSe 17 86f.; Sjöberg Fs. Kienast 537.
naṭl "lamentation"	•CTX: **EB** *na-da-a* → Fronzaroli ARET 11 162.
nāṭil "elegy singer"	•CTX: **EB** Pl. *na-ti-lu* |nāṭil=ū| → NABU 1991/49; Fronzaroli ARET 11 162; Bonechi QDLF 16 83, Catagnoti QuSe 29 111, 140, 147, 216. •LL: **EB** BALAG.DI = *na-ti-lu*(*-um*) → Conti QuSe 17 160; Bonechi QDLF 16 83.
|n-ṭ-p| Cf. **|n-d-b|**	Sem.: *nṭp* (Hb.) "to drip", *nṭp* (*nāṭāp*) "drops of stacte"; *nṭp* (Aram., Syr.) "to drip", *nwṭph*, *nwṭptʔ* (Syr.) "drop", *nṭwp* (JAram.) "stacte", *nṭph*, *nṭptʔ* (Syr.) "myrrh-oil", *nṭpyʔ* "dripping rain"; *naṭafa* (Arab.) "to dribble, trickle", *nuṭfa* "drop"; *hnṭf* (OSArab.) "to cause (blood) to flow"; *neṭefét*, *enṭefēt* (MSArab.) "drop"; *naṭba* (Eth.) "to drop, trickle", *naṭb*, *nəṭbat* "drop"; see further: *naṭafa* (Eth.) "to strain, filter".
naṭap "drop (of stacte)"	•ONOM: **UGS** Cf. unc. *na*-TAB-*pí* → Gröndahl PTU 14, 19, 29, 170: NTP;[350] Sivan GAGl 255: NṬP.[351]

[350] Unc. with reference to Arab. *natafa* "(Haare) ausrupfen, ausreissen"(?).
[351] Probl. not from |n-d-b|; for TAB see Huehnergard AkkUg 367.

nuṭ(ṭ)up "drop (of stacte)"	•ONOM: **EUPH** Cf. *nu-du-ub-tum*, *nu-du-pa-tum*, *nu-uṭ-tu-up-tum*; cf. unc. *nu-tu-ub-tum*, *nu-tu-pa-a-a* → Gelb CAAA 27, 168; Streck Onomastikon 202 § 2.95, 314 § 4.7, 333 § 5.37.
|n-ṭ-ṭ|	Sem.: *nṭṭ* (JAram.) (Gt) "to be frightened", (C) "to terrify"; *naṭṭa* (Arab.) "to spring, jump"; *neṭṭ* (MSArab.) "to shake"; *nṭṭ*, *naṭṭa*, *naṭaṭa* (Eth.) "to jump with joy"; see also: *nwṭ* (Hb.) "to tremble"; *nwṭ* (JAram. C) "to scare".
|**n-ṭ-ṭ**| "to shake"	•CTX: **UGA** G prefc. *tṭṭ*; suff. *tṭṭn*, pass. ptc. *nṭṭt* → DUL 643.
|n-ṭ-y|	Sem.: *nṭh* (Hb.) "to reach out, spread out", *mṭh* (*miṭṭāh*) "couch, bed"; *nṭy* (JAram.) "to incline towards"; *naṭā* (*naṭw*) "to be far (away); to stretch out, spread out"; *naṭû*(*m*), *natû*(*m*), *nadû*(*m*), *naṭāʔu* (Akk.) "to hit, beat", *miṭṭu*(*m*), *mī/ēṭu* "a divine weapon". See further: *nāṭa* (*nawṭ*, Arab.) "to hang, suspend".
maṭṭiy "sort of weapon"	•LL: **EB** GIŠ.GU.RU.(KAK.)URUDU = *ma-ti-um* → Conti QuSe 17 139.[352]
mṭt "bed"	•CTX: **UGA** Sg. suff. *mṭth* → DUL 595.
|n-θ-k| Cf. |**n-k-θ**|	Sem.: *nšk* (Hb.) "to bite", *nšk* (*nešek*) "deduction, interest"; *našāku*(*m*) (Akk.) "to bite", *nišku*(*m*) "bite"; *neṯōk*, *nəṯk* (MSArab.) "to bite"; *nasaka* (Eth.) "to bite".
|**n-θ-k**| "to bite"	•CTX: **EA** G prefc. *ta-an-šu-ku* → Rainey CAT 2 65; Izre'el Orient 38 85f. **UGA** G prefc. *yṯk*[, act. ptc. *nṯk* (see below *nṯk* (I)); N prefc. *ynṯkn* → DUL 643 */n-ṯ-k/*. •LL: **EB** KA.TAR = *na-ša-gúm/gú-um wa pur-ra-zu-um a-ba-a/lu* → Krebernik ZA 73 8; Fales QuSe 13 176.
naθk "bite"	•CTX: **UGS** ÚŠ.MEŠ *na-aš-ki-ša* → AHw 796; CAD N/2 281; Huehnergard AkkUg 120, ²UVST 394.
nθk (A) "biter"	•CTX: **UGA** → DUL 643f.: *nṯk* (I).
nθk (B) "bite; interest"	•CTX: **UGA** Sg. / pl. abs. *nṯk*, cstr. *nṯk*, suff. *nṯkh*. → DUL 644: *nṯk* (II).
|n-θ-ḳ| Cf. |**n-s-k**|	Sem. etym. unc. Cf. *nšq* (*nešeq*, Hb.) "equipment, weapons"; *nasāku*(*m*), *našāku* (Akk.) "to shoot (an arrow), hurl (weapons)", *nisku* "shot".
nθḳ "a missile (projectile, dart)" (?)	•CTX: **UGA** → DUL 644: *nṯq*; Watson Fs. Postgate 707; Del Olmo AuOr 37 291.

[352] For GIŠ.RU = *ma-du-um*, possibly related, cf. Fales WGE 207.

|n-θ̣-r| Sem.: *nṣr* (Hb., Pun., Old Aram.) "to keep watch, protect, preserve", *mṣwr* (conjectural rdg *maṣṣôr*, Hb.) "watchtower"; *nṭr* (Aram., Palm., Syr.) "to watch, guard, protect", *nṭr(?)* "guardian", *nṭrh, nṭrtʔ* "safekeeping, protection", *mṭrh, mṭrtʔ* "custody, care", *mnṭrn* (Syr.) "guard, guardian"; *naṣāru(m)* (Akk.) "to guard, protect", *niṣrum* "protection", *nāṣiru(m)* "guard, guardian", *maṣṣaru(m)*, *maṣṣuru* "guard, watchman", *maṣṣartu(m)* "observation, garrison"; *nẓr* (Arab.) "to perceive, see, eye", *naẓra* "look, glance", *naẓar* "protection, care", *nāẓir* "observer", *naẓẓār* "keen-eyed", *manẓar* "sight"; *nẓr* (OSArab.) "to observe, watch over", *nẓr* "protection, care"; *nḏ̣r* (*nəḏ̣awr*, MSArab.) "to see, find at"; (Eth.) *naṣṣara* "to look (at, on, towards), watch, examine", *nəṣṣāre* "view, glance", *naṣṣāri* "spectator, inspector".

|n-θ̣-r| "to protect, guard, watch"
•CTX: **EB** Cf. G prefc. *i-na-sar* → Edzard ARET 5 28; Krebernik QuSe 18 73, 112.[353]
•LL: **EB** EN.NUN.AK = *na-za-lum* (*na-za-lu-um, na-za-lu*) → Krebernik ZA 73 34, QuSe 18 112; Fronzaroli StEb 7 175f.; Bonechi QDLF 16 87;[354] Catagnoti AAA 1 22, 35f.; Pasquali NABU 2018/39.
•ONOM: **EB** *en-zu-ru*$_{12}$ |yinθ̣ur=| → Pagan ARES 3 150f., 308.
EUPH *ia-an-ṣur*-DINGIR, *ia-an-zu-ur-ìl*, *ia-an-zu-ur-*^{d}*da-gan*, *ia-aṣ-ṣu-ur-*^{d}IM, *ia-ṣur-*^{d}IM, *ia-zu-ur-*^{d}*da-gan*/^{d}IM/30, *i-zur-(a-)aš-du-um* → Gelb CAAA 27, 167; Zadok Fs. Hallo 327; Golinets Onomastikon 2 327, 418f.
R *ia-an-zu-ur*-DINGIR → Dalley / Walker / Hawkins Tell Rimah 175 (244 II 17); Golinets Onomastikon 2 327f., 418f.
UGA *nẓrỉl* → DUL 645.
EG Cf. *n-ꜣ-ḏꜣ-:r* ^{NSR} → Schneider APÄQ 148f. no. 315.

|n-ɣ-r| "to protect, guard, watch"
•CTX: **UGA** G prefc. *yġr* (?), *tġr*, suff. *tġrk*, *tġrkm*, *tġrn*; imp. *nġr*; act. ptc. *nġr* (see below); Gt prefc. *ttġr* → Tropper UG 94ff.; DUL 616.
•ONOM: **UGA** Unc. *nġry* → DUL 617.

naθ̣r, nuθ̣r "custody, protection"
•ONOM: **EUPH** *na-aṣ-ri-ia*; *be-lí-nu-uz-ri*, *ba-áš-ti-nu-uz-ri*, cf. *ba-aš-ti-nu-iz-ri* → Gelb CAAA 27, 164; CAAA 27, 168; Streck Onomastikon 1 325 § 5.15.

niɣr "custody, protection"
•LL: **UGS** [ŠEŠ = *naṣāru* = ...] = *ni-iḫ-rù* → Sivan GAGl 253; Huehnergard UVST 153; vSoldt SAU 306 (99).

nāθ̣ir "watchman, guard"
•ONOM: **EUPH** *ia-di-na-ṣir*, ^{d}*a-šar-na-ṣir*, ^{d}*da-gan-na-ṣir*, EŠ$_{4}$.DAR-*na-ṣí-ir-ti* → Gelb CAAA 27, 164; Zadok Fs. 327; Streck Onomastikon 1 265 § 3.12, 269 § 3.15, 281 § 3.40.

nāɣir "watchman, guard"
•CTX: **UGS** LÚ *na-ḫi-ru*[*-ma* → Sivan GAGl 251; Huehnergard UVST 153; vSoldt SAU 306 (98).

nɣr "watchman, guard"
•CTX: **UGA** → DUL 616f.: *nġr*.

nuθ̣ār "custody, protection" (?)
•ONOM: **EB** Cf. *nu-za-ar*, *nu-za-ru*$_{12}$ → Pagan ARES 3 150f., 357.

maθ̣θ̣ar "watchman, guard"
•CTX: **EB** *ma-za-lum* → Fronzaroli StEb 7 170f., QuSe 13 146; Archi ARET 1 294f.; Archi / Biga ARET 3 367f.; Biga / Milano ARET 4 312f.; Milano ARET 9 397; Conti Fs. Fronzaroli 126; Bonechi QDLF 16 87.[355]
•ONOM: **EB** *ma-za-lu*, *ma-za-ru*$_{12}$, *ma-za-lu*-DÙG (?) → Pagan ARES 3 150f., 349.
EG Cf. *m-ḏꜣ-r-y-ꜣ* → Schneider APÄQ 138 no. 294.

[353] ARET 5 6 III:1; // EN.NUN.AK in Abu Ṣalābīḫ IAS 326 (A2.6).
[354] Altern. rdg |naθ̣θ̣ārum| "guardian"; see Bonechi loc.cit. and below: *maθ̣θ̣ār*, *maθ̣θ̣ārt*.
[355] Altern. see *mazzāl* "courier, messenger", |m-z-l|.

maθ̣θ̣ur “watchman, guard”	•ONOM: **EB** *ma-zu-ra-ḫu* → Pagan ARES 3 150, 349.
maθ̣θ̣art “guard, watch, garrison”	•CTX: **EA** Cf. LÚ.MEŠ *: ma-ṣa-ar-ta*, cf. (BIL) *: ma-ṣa-ar-ta* → Moran AmL 217 fn. 3; Gianto SEL 12 71; Izre’el Orient 38 68 •LL: **EB** Cf. NÌ.ZÁḪ = *ma*-SUM(*zàr*?)-*tum* → Krebernik ZA 73 5.[356]
manṣart “guard, garrison”	•CTX: **EA** LÚ.MEŠ *ma-an-ṣa-ar-ta/ta*₅ (238:11, 244:35) → AHw 620; CAD M/1 335f.
mðrɣl “watchman, guard”	•CTX: **UGA** Sg. *mḏrġl*, pl. *mḏrġlm* → DUL 523f.: mḏrġl; Dietrich /Loretz WO 3/2 198f.; Márquez AfO 45 370; Richter BGH 532f.

|n-w-ʕ|	Sem.: Cf. *nwʕ* (Hb.) “to tremble, roam about, shake”; *nwʕ* (JAram.) “to move”; *nāʕa* (*nawʕ*, Arab.) “to sway, oscillate, shake”.
|n-w-ʕ| “to shake” (?)	•CTX: **UGA** Cf. Gt prefc. *ytʕn* → Tropper UG 522, 531, 628, 650: Gt “aneinander rütteln”. Altern.: related to Arab. *taʕtaʕa* “to compel, ill-treat, shake”; Krebernik Fs. Richter 264; DUL 843: */t-ʕ/* “to atack”.

|n-w/y-b| (1)	Sem.: Cf. *nwb* (Arab.) “to represent; to afflict, befall”, *niyāba* “representation, replacement”.
|n-w-b| (A) “to be coated (with)”	•CTX: **UGA** G/Gpass. suffc. / pass. ptc. fem. *nbt* → Tropper UG 517, 650, 675; DUL 609: */n-b/*.

|n-w/y-b| (2)	Sem.: Cf. *nwb* (Hb.) “to prosper”; unc. Pun. “to grow” (rdg ?); *nwb* (JAram.) “plant growth”; see further: *nayyaba*, *tanayyaba* (Arab.) “to take root”.
|n-w-b| (B) “to prosper, grow” (?)	•ONOM: **EUPH** Cf. unc. *in-na-ba-*(*a-*)*tum*, *in-ne-bu*, *in-ni-bi*, *in-ni-bu*(*-um*) → Gelb CAAA 27, 160. **EG** Cf. *n-ꜣ-b-w-y-ꜣ* → Schneider APÄQ 140f. nos. 299f.

|n-w-d|	Sem. *nwd* (Hb.) “to sway”; *nwd* (JAram., Syr.) “to shake rapidly, tremble”; *nāda* (*nawd*, Arab.), *tanawwada* “to sway”.
|n-w-d| “to shake (the head), nod, show mercy”	•ONOM: **EB** *a-nu-du*, *a-nu-ud-du*, *a-nu-ud-ḫa-lam*, *i-nu-du*, *i-nu-ud*, *i-nu-ud-da-mu*, *ti-nu-ud* → Bonechi QuSe 15 147f., MARI 8 481, 483; Pagan ARES 3 151, 282, 324, 370. **EUPH** *ia-nu-ud-li-im*, *ta-nu-da* → Huffmon 237; Gelb CAAA 27, 161; Zadok Fs. Hallo 327.
nūd “nodded, someone given the nod, granted mercy”	•ONOM: **U3** *nu-da-tum* → Buccellati Amorites 176; Gelb CAAA 27, 167.

|n-w-ħ|
Cf. **|(ʔ-)n-H|**

[356] For SUM = *zàr* see Borger AOAT 305 537 (292).

|n-w-x| Sem.: *nwḥ* (Hb.) "to settle down, rest, repose", *mnwḥ* (*manô*^{a}*ḥ*), *mnwḥh* (*manôḥāh*) "resting place, composure"; *nwḥ* (*ynḥ*, Ph.C) "to erect"; *nwḥ* (Aram., Syr.) "to rest, become quiet", *mnḥ* (JAram.) "rest, quiet, resting place", *nyḥ(?)* (JAram., Syr.) "quiet" "quiet"; *nâḫu*(*m*) (Akk.) "to be slow, take a rest", *neḫtu*(*m*) "calm, peace", *tanēḫtu*(*m*) "pacification, mollification"; *nawwaḫa* (Arab.) "to halt for a rest", *ʔanāḫa* "to stay, remain", *tanawwaḫa* "to kneel down", *nawḫa* "stop", *munāḫ* "halting place, abode"; cf. *nwḫ*, *noḫa* (Eth.) "to be high, tall, of long duration, distant, far off; to repose, linger", *noḫ* "tranquillity, quietness", *mənwāḫ* "resting place".

|**n-w-x**| "to rest" •CTX: **EB** G prefc. *da-nu-ḫu* → Catagnoti / Fronzaroli ARET 16 125, 224.
EA G suffc. *nu-uḫ-ti* → Sivan GAGl 144, 256; Rainey CAT 2 286; Izre'el Orient 38 74f.
UGA G prefc. *tnḫ*, suff. *ảnḫn*; suffc. *nḫt* → DUL 620f.: /*n-ḫ*/.
•ONOM: **EB** *a-nu-ḫu*, *i-nu-ḫi-li-im* → Pagan ARES 3 151, 282, 324.
EUPH *ia-ni-ḫa*, *a-ni-iḫ-li-ib-bi*, *e-ni-ḫu-um*; *ia-nu-ḫa-an*, *i-nu-uḫ-di-ta-an*, *i-nu-uḫ-li-bi*, *ia-nu-uḫ-li-im*, *i-nu-uḫ/ùḫ-sa-mar*, *ia-nu-uḫ-sa-mar/ma-ar*, *ta-nu-ḫa*, *ta-nu-uḫ-na-wu-um*, *ta-nu-uḫ-na-wu-ú*, *ta-nu-uḫ-ma-*DINGIR; cf. unc. *a-ḫi-ta-nu-a*, *ì-lí-ta-nu*, *ì-lí-ta-nu-uḫ*, ^{d}*a-mi-ta-nu-uḫ*, ^{d}*a-mi-ta-nu*, ^{d}*a-mi-ta-nu-a*, ^{d}*a-mu-ta-nu*, *a-mu-um-ta-nu-ú*, *sa-ka-aḫ-ta-nu-ú*; *in-na-ḫa-an* → Huffmon APNMT 237; Gelb CAAA 28, 160f.; Zadok Fs. Hallo 327; Durand REA 700; Golinets Onomastikon 2 38, 82, 151, 207, 283f., 293, 331ff., 421, 452, 480, 487f., 497, 500, 505, 511.
TU Cf. unc. *tá-nu-a*, *ta-nu-a-tum*, ^{d}*a-mu-ta-nu*, *a-mu-tá-nu-a* → Krebernik Tall Bi`a 210, 228; Golinets Onomastikon 2 497, 500.
R Cf. unc. *ḫa-at-nu-ta-nu-ḫa* → Dalley / Walker / Hawkins Tell Rimah 253 (12:1); Golinets Onomastikon 2 498.
A7 Cf. unc. *ḫa-li-ta-nu-a* → Wiseman AT 135; Gelb CAAA 28, 160; Golinets Onomastikon 2 498.

nāx "reassuring, calm granting, mercy showing; DN" •ONOM: **U3** *na-ḫa-nu-um* → Buccellati Amorites 176.
EUPH *na-ḫa-an*, *na-ḫa-ia*, *na-ḫa-ni-im*, *na-ḫi-*DINGIR, *na-ḫi-lum*, *na-ḫi-lu-um*, *na-ḫi-li-im*, ^{d}*na-ḫi-im-mi*, *na-ḫu-um-*^{d}*da-gan*, *mu-ut-na-ḫa* → Huffmon APNMT 237; Gelb CAAA 28, 162; Streck Onomastikon 1 127 § 1.103 fn. 2, 260 § 3.7, 329 § 5.25, 354 § 5.82; Golinets Onomastikon 2 303, 421, 489.
U3 *na-ḫa-nu-um* → Buccellati Amorites 114, 176; Golinets Onomastikon 2 303, 421.
UGS Cf. *na-ḫi*, *na-ḫu-ya* → Sivan GAGl 256.[357]

nīx, **nūx** "rest, calm" •ONOM: **EUPH** *ni-ḫa-tum*, *su-mu-ni-a*, *su-mu-ni-ḫu-um*, *gub-ba-ni-ḫi*; *nu-ḫi-*DINGIR, *ha-da-nu-ú-um* → Gelb CAAA 28 165, 167; Zadok Fs. Hallo 327.

nxt "divan" •CTX: **UGA** → DUL 621f.: *nḫt*.

manīx, **menīx**, **minīx** "calm, resting place" •ONOM: **EUPH** *ma-ni-ḫa*, *me-ni-ḫu-um*, *mi-ni-ḫu-um* *mi-ni-ḫu(-um)* → Gelb CAAA 28, 160; Streck Onomastikon 1 338 § 5.47.

mnx "calm, resting place" •CTX: **UGA** → DUL 556: *mnḫ*.

|n-w-ḳ| Sem.: *nâqu*(*m*) (Akk.) "to cry (out), wail", *tanūqātu*(*m*) "battle cry".

|**n-w-ḳ**| "to wail" •CTX: **EB** G prefc. *ti-na-ga* |du. tināḳay| → Fronzaroli ARET 13 109, 301; Catagnoti QuSe 29 127, 147, 161, 216.

[357] Diff. Gröndahl PTU: probl. from Hurr. / Anat. (?) *naḫ*= "Herz haben" (rather: *naḫ*(*ḫ*)= "to fear").

tnḳt (A) "scream" (?)	•CTX: **UGA** → DUL 861: *tnqt* (I).

|n-w-l|	Sem.: Cf. *nāla* (*nawl*, Arab.) "to give, donate, present", *nawāl*, *nāʔil* "gift".
nawil "affection, devotion"	•LL: **EB** Cf. KI.ÁGA = *na-ì-lum* → Sjöberg Fs. Pettinato 278.

|n-w-m|	Sem.: *nwm* (Hb.) "to fall asleep, slumber", *nwmh* (*nûmāh*) "drowsiness", *tnwmh* (*tenûmāh*) "slumber"; *nwm* (JAram., Syr.) "to sleep, slumber", *nwmh*, *nwmtʔ* (Syr.), "sleep"; *munattu* (pl. *munāmātu*, Akk.) "morning slumber"; *nāma* (Arab.) "sleep", *nawm*, *nīma*, *manām* "sleep"; *nwm*, *noma* (Eth.) "sleep, fall asleep", *nəwām* "sleep, death", *tanawwama* "slumber".[358]
|n-w-m| "to sleep"	•CTX: **EG** *nm-ʕ(u)*, *nm*, *nm-(m)a$_4$*, *nm-m-{t}* (|nâma|) → Hoch SWET 185f. no. 249.
nūma, nōma "sleep"	•CTX: **EG** *nm-ʕ* → Hoch SWET 186 no. 250:
nhmmt "drowsiness, fainting fit"	•CTX: **UGA** → DUL 617.

|n-w-p|	Sem.: *nāfa* (*nawf*, Arab.) "to be high, lofty, elevated", *nawf*, *munīf* "top, height, summit", *nayyāf* "long and high". Cf. *nwp* (*nôp*, Hb.) "height", *tnwph* (*t^{e}nûpāh*) "consecrated gift (raising of the object offered)". See further: *nwp* (Hb. C) "to move to and fro, brandish"; *nwp* (JAram., Syr. G) "to incline, to hang, to wave to and fro", (JAram.) *ʔnpw* "wave offering"; *nwf* (MSArab.) "to wave the hand".
|n-w-p| "to be high, lofty, exalted"	•CTX: **UGA** C prefc. *tšnpn* → DUL 625: /*n-p*/. •ONOM: **EB** *a-nu-bu$_{14}$*, *i-nu-ub-ì*, *i-nu-ub-il* → Pagan ARES 3 152, 282, 324. **EUPH** *ia-nu-bu-um* → Gelb CAAA 28, 161.
nāp "exalting" (?)	•ONOM: **EUPH** Cf. *na-ap-li-im-ma*, *na-ap-*^{d}UTU → Gelb CAAA 28, 162.
nūp, nūpat "rise, elevation" (?)	•ONOM: **EUPH** Cf. *nu-pa-nu-um*, *nu-pa-a-nu-um*, *nu-ba-ia*, *nu-bi-*DINGIR; *nu-ba-tum*, *nu-pa-tum*, *nu-pa-ti-ia* → Gelb CAAA 28, 168; Streck Onomastikon 154 1 § 2.5.
np "peak"	•CTX: **UGA** Sg. / pl. cstr. np → DUL 625.
nuwāp "elevated, exalted"	•ONOM: **EUPH** Cf. *nu-a-bu* → Gelb CAAA 28, 167.
s^{1}npt "the raising (a type of offering)"	•CTX: **UGA** → DUL 821: *šnpt*.

[358] For Akk. *nâmu* (AHw 726; CAD vacat) see *lamû*.

|n-w-r|	Sem.: *nhr* (Hb., Aram. loan) “to shine, be radiant”, *nr* (*nēr*), *nyr* (*nîr*) “light, lamp”, *mnwrh* (*m^{e}nôrāh*) “lampstand, light”; *nhr* (JAram., Syr.) “to shine, be clear”, *nhwr*(*?*) (Aram., Syr.) “light”, *nwhry* (JAram., Syr.) “shining”; *nawāru*(*m*), *namāru* (Akk.) “to be(come) bright, shine”, *nawru*(*m*), *namru*, *namiru* “bright, shining”, *nawir*(*a*)*tum*, *namir*(*a*)*tu* “brightness, light”, *nimru*(*m*), *niw*(*a*)*rum* “light”, *numūru* “torch”, *nūru*(*m*) “light”, *numru* “brightness”, *namurru*(*m*) “awe-inspiringly radiant”, *namrīrum*, *namrirru*, *namurratu*(*m*), *namruratu* “awe-inspiringly radiance”; *nār*, *nawr*, *niyar*, *nawwar*, *tanawwar*, *ʔistanar*, *ʔanār* (Arab.) “to shine”, *nūr* “light”, *nār* “fire”, *nayyir*, *nurāni* “luminous”, *manār* “lighthouse”, *manwar* “skylight”, cf. further: *nahār* “daytime”, *nahir* “light, pale”; *nwr* (OSArab.) “to make a burnt offering”, *mnrt* “altar”.
|n-w-r|, **|n-m-r|** “to shine; to burn; to brighten”	•CTX: **EB** G prefc. *a-nu-ra-am*$_6$ |ʔanūr=am| → Catagnoti / Fronzaroli ARET 16 105, 216: “io mi sono rallegrato”. **UGA** G suffc. *nr*, (L) pref. *tnrr* → DUL 633: /*n-r*/. •ONOM: **EB** *i-mi-ir-ì* |yimir=ʔi(l)| → Pagan ARES 3 152, 323. **EUPH** *ia-nu-ru-um*, *ia-wi-ru-um* → Gelb CAAA 28, 161; Golinets Onomastikon 2 274, 331, 422. **TU** *ia-wi-ir-na-si* → Krebernik Tall Bi`a 219; Golinets Onomastikon 2 179, 274, 331, 422.
nēr, **nīr**, **niwr** “light, fire, lamp; DN”	•CTX: **UGS** *ni-r*[*u* → Huehnergard UVST 152. •ONOM: **EB** (unc. due to the multiple rdgs of LUM, NE) cf. *ne-lum*, *ne-li*, *ne-rí*, *ù-ne-lum*, *a-dar-ne-lu*, *a-ša-ne-ra*, *da-bù-ne-li*, *du-ba-ne-lu*, *ne-il*-LU$_x$(C704), *šum-ra-ne-lu* → Pagan ARES 3 152, 277, 283, 296, 301, 355, 368. **EUPH** *ni-ir-ba-aḫ-li*, *a-ia-ni-ri*, *é-a-ne*/*i-ri*, *a-bi-ni-ri*, *a-bu-ni-ra*, ^{d}IM-*ni-ri*, $^{(d)}$*ad-mu-ne*/*i-ri*, *ì-lí-ne-ri*, *an-nu-ni-ri*, ^{d}*di-ri-tum-ni-ri*, ^{d}*iš-ḫa-ra-ni-ri*, EŠ$_4$.DAR-*ne-ri*, *ba-aḫ-li-ni-ri*, *be-lí-ne*/*i-ri*, ^{d}*da-gan-ne*/*i-ri*, *su-mu-ni-ri*, LUGAL-*ni-ri*, *la-aḫ-wi-ne-ri*, *ta-bu-bu-ni-ri* → Huffmon APNMT 243f.; Gelb CAAA 28, 165; Durand, NABU 1994/73; Zadok Fs. Hallo 327; Streck Onomastikon 1 278 § 3.32, 320 § 5.7, 324 § 5.13. **A7** *ni-e-ru*/*ra*, *ni-iw-ri-a-du*, *al-li-ni-ri*, *ia-mu-ut-ni-ri* → Wiseman AT 136, 143; Huffmon APNMT 243f.; Gelb CAAA 28, 165; Arnaud AuOr 16 154, 166. **EA** *am-mu-ni-ra*, *ḫa-mu-ni-ri* → Hess APN 32f., 208f.; Sivan GAGl 255; Moran AmL 380. **UGS** *ni*$_{(5)}$-*ra-nu* → Gröndahl PTU 165f.; Sivan GAGl 256; Watson AuOr 20 235.
nūr, **nuwr** “light, fire, lamp; DN”	•CTX: **EB** *nu-ru*$_{12}$-*um* → Krebernik QuSe 18 73, 144. •ONOM: **EB** *su-nu-rí* → Pagan ARES 3 152, 365. **U3** *nu-úr-*^{d}*da-gan* → Owen JCS 33 261. **EUPH** *nu-ra*, *nu-ru-a-ma-ar*, *nu-ur-me-er*, *nu-úr-a-qi-im*, *nu-úr-*^{d}*kap* → Gelb CAAA 28, 167f.; Streck Onomastikon 1 176 § 2.54 **Q** *nu-ri-ia*, *nu-ri-*^{d}IŠKUR → Richter / Lange Idadda 177. **EM** *nu-ru*, *nu-ri-ia*, *nu-ri-*^{d}*da-gan*, *nu-ra-li-mur* → Pruzsinszky PTEm 92 [658], 127 [283]. **A4** *nu-ur-i*, *nu-ri-i*, *nu-ri-ia*, *nu-ur-il-el-mu*, *ši-nu-ri* → Wiseman AT 143; Gelb CAAA 28, 168; Sivan GAGl 256. **UGS** *nu-ri-ia*(*-nu*/*a*), *nu-ra-nu*, *nu-ri-nu* → Gröndahl PTU 52, 166; Sivan GAGl 256; Huehnergard UVST 237; Watson AuOr 20 235. **EG** Cf. *nw-rw* → Schneider APÄQ 142f. no. 304.
nr “light, fire, lamp”	•CTX: **UGA** → DUL 633. •ONOM: **UGA** *ʕmnr* → DUL 161; *nrn* → DUL 633f.; *nryn* → 634.
namr (B) “shining”	•ONOM: **EB** *na-am*$_6$-*lu*-DINGIR → Pagan ARES 3 152, 353.
namār “dawn”	•ONOM: **EB** *na-mar* → Pagan ARES 3 152, 354.

nimīr "light, pale (oil)"	•CTX: **EB** *ne-mi-lum* (?) → Milano ARET 9 398; Catagnoti QuSe 29 30, 52, 62, 122, 217. Diff. Catagnoti Fs. Graziani 138: *šar*$_{x}$(NE)-*mi-núm*, "cypress".
namurr "shining"	•ONOM: **EB** *na-mu-ru*$_{12}$, *na-mu-lu*, *na-mu-lum* → Pagan ARES 3 152, 354.
namur(r)at "splendour; bright, shining (a stone)"	•CTX: **EB** → *na-mur-ra-tum* → Fronzaroli Fs. Kienast 102f.; Pasquali QuSe 23 71f.; Catagnoti QuSe 29 30, 62, 214.
nmrt "splendour"	•CTX: **UGA** Sg. suff. *nmrtk*, *nmrth* → DUL 624.
nrt (A) "light, lamp"	•CTX: **UGA** Sg. cstr. nrt → 634: *nrt* (I).
nūr(u)t "light, lamp"	•ONOM: **EB** *nu-lu-du*, *nu-lu-ud*, *nu-ru*$_{12}$-*ud* → Pagan ARES 4 152, 356. **EUPH** *nu-úr-tum* → Gelb CAAA 28, 168.
nyr "luminary"	•CTX: **UGA** → DUL 644f.
nawar "shining, light, lamp"	•ONOM: **EUPH** *na-wa-ar-*^{d}IM, *na-wa-ar-e-šar*, *ḫa-ab-du-na-wa-ar*, *ab-du-na-wa-ar*, *mu-ut-na-wa-ar*, *um-mi-na-wa-ar* → Huffmon APNMT 237; Gelb CAAA 28, 162; Streck Onomastikon 1 173 § 2.41 fn. 1; Golinets Onomastikon 2 244, 303f., 422. **TU** *na-wa-ar*-TU-UB-*qí* → Krebernik Tall Bi`a 224; Golinets Onomastikon 2 304, 422. **EM** ^{d}KUR-*na-wa-ri* → Pruzsinszky PTEm 121f. [281]
niwar, **nimar**, **nimer**, **niwer**, **niwir** "shining, light, lamp"	•CTX: **A7** Pl. genit. *ni-wa-re* → Arnaud AuOr 16 166. •ONOM: **EB** Cf. unc. NI-PI-*lum* |niwar=um| (?) → Pagan ARES 3 152, 356. **EUPH** *ni-wa-ar-me-er*, *ni-mar-*^{d}EN.ZU → CAAA 28, 165; Streck Onomastikon 1 173f §§ 2.41f., 2.44. **TU** *ni-me-er-*^{d}EN.ZU, *ni-wi-ir-*^{d}EN.ZU → Krebernik Tall Bi`a 224; Streck Onomastikon 1 174 §§ 2.44f. fn. 1. **EM** dKUR-*ni-wa-ru/ri* → Pruzsinszky PTEm [282]
nawrat, **namrat** "shining, light, lamp"	•ONOM: **EUPH** Cf. *na-am-ra-tum* → Gelb CAAA 26, 163.
menīr "candelabrum" (?)	•ONOM: **EUPH** *me-ni-ri-im* → Zadok Fs. Hallo 327.
mnrt "candelabrum"	•CTX: **UGA** → DUL 558.

|n-w-s|	Sem.: *nws* (Hb.) "to flee"; *nws* (Syr. G) "to tremble", (Aram. C) "to remove";. *nāsa* (*naws*, Arab.) "to dangle, swing back and forth"; see further: *nss* (Hb.) "to stagger"; *nussusu* (Akk.) "to shake (out hair), to wave (the tail)"; *nassa*, *nassasa* (Arab.) "to urge on", *nasnasa* "to fly swiftly"; *neśneś* (MSArab.) "to agitate"; *nsns*, *nasnasa* (Eth.) "to scatter, sprinkle, spread".
|n-w-s| "to move to and fro, flee, tremble"	•CTX: **UGA** G suffc. *ns*; prefc. *yns* → DUL 634: /*n-s*/. **EG** *na*$_{(2)}$-*wa-ṯi*$_{2}$, *nu-ṯi*$_{2}$ (|nawasa, nūsa|) → Hoch SWET 184f. no. 248.[359]

|n-w-ṣ|	Primary noun, Sem.: *nwṣh* (*nôṣāh*, Hb.) "plumage"; *nwṣṣ* (JAram.) id.; *nāṣu* (Akk.) id.; *nāṣiya* (Arab., pl. *nawāṣin*) "forelock".
nāṣ "plumage"	•LL: **MŠ** *na-a-ṣu* = MIN (: *naḫlaptu*) → Hrůša MŠ 131, 415 (VI 113).

[359] Sivan / Cochavi-Rainey WSVES 82: *na-wa-śí* "to tremble"; Helck Beziehungen no. 137.

|n-w-y|	Culture word, Sem.: *nwh* (*nāwāh*, *nāweh*, Hb.) "grazing place, stopping place, settlement"; *nwy*(*tʔ*) (Syr.) "pasture, fold"; *nawûm*, *namû*(*m*) (Akk.) "pasturage; steppe", denom. *nawûm*, *namû* "to turn into desert"; *nwy* (OSArab.) "watering place". See further: *nawā* (Arab.) "to aim to, go toward; to go away, move away", *ʔanwā* "to be far away", *nawān* "distance, absence", *niyya* "intend, destination".
nawiy, **namiy (A)** "pasturage; steppe, encampment; ND"[360]	•CTX: **EUPH**, **R** Cf. *na-wu-um*, *na-wu-ú-um*, *na-we-e-em*, *na-wa-a-am*, *na-wu-ú-ka*, *na-wu-šu*, *na-wa-ku-nu*, *na-wa-a-ku-nu*, etc. → AHw 771: *nawûm*, *namû*(*m*); CAD N/1 249f.: *namû* A, *nawû*; Rowton JESHO 17 18ff.; OrAn 15 17ff., 23; Anbar OBO 108 161ff. 710.; Durand ACF 1999-2000 **A7** *na-we-šu* → Wiseman JCS 12 125 (wrong rdg *x-na-wa* KI); Draffkorn-Kilmer JCS 13 94 fn. 3. •LL: **MŠ** *na-mu-ú* = MIN (*a-lum*) → Hrůša MŠ 45, 316. •ONOM: **EUPH**, **R** Cf. *bu-nu-na-wi-e*, *ta-gi-id-na-we-e*, *ta-nu-uḫ-na-wi-um*, *ta-nu-uḫ-na-wu-ú*, *ta-šu-ub-na-wu* → Huffmon APNMT 237; Gelb CAAA 26, 162; Dalley / Walker / Hawkins Tell Rimah 155 (208 I 20); Zadok Fs. Hallo 327; Durand REA 700.
namiy (B) "steppe-dweller"	•CTX: **A4** ERÍN.MEŠ *na-me*(*-e*) → Wiseman AT 162; Dietrich / Loretz WO 5 84, 87, 89f.; CCNH 17 105. **UGS** LÚ *na-mu-ú*, LÚ.ME *na-mu-ti* → Thureau-Dangin Syria 18 248, 253; Nougayrol PRU 3 116.

|n-y-l| Cf. **|t-y-l|**	Sem.: *nâlu*(*m*), *niālu*(*m*) (Akk.) "to lay down (to sleep)", *mayyālu*(*m*) "resting place".
|**n-y-l**| "to be, rest, settle"	•CTX: **EB** G prefc. *da-ne-a-al*$_6$ |tanīyal|; Gt prefc. *i-ti-ya* |yittīyal|, *i-ti-a-a* |yittīyalay| (du.), *a-ti-a* |la=ytīyal|, *a-ti-a-ù-ma* |la=ytīyalū=ma| → Fronzaroli ARET 11 142, ARET 13 53, 273; Catagnoti / Fronzaroli ARET 16 52f., 220; Catagnoti QuSe 29 130, 146, 162, 216. •LL: **EB** Ù.DI = *na-a-um* → Krebernik ZA 73 40; Fronzaroli StEb 7 176; QuSe 13 147.
mayyal "(resting) place, space; treasury"	•CTX: **EB** *ma-a-lum* → Fronzaroli ARET 13 67, 281. **EUPH** É *ma-*(*a-*)*ia-li* → Ziegler FM 4, p. 17; Durand Système palatial 39ff.; FM 8 86.
mas^{1}nāl "sleeping couch"	•CTX: **EM** *maš-na-lu* GAL → Westenholz Emar Tablets 52, 54.

|n-y-r|	Primary noun, Sem.: *nyr*(*ʔ*) (Aram., Syr.) "yoke", denom. *nwr* (JAram.) "to plow a field"; *nīru*(*m*) (Akk.) "yoke", denom. *mayyāru*(*m*) "breaking up (of the soil); *ʔanyār*, *nirān* (*nīr* pl. Arab.) "yoke"; cf. denom. *nyr* (Hb.) "to plow for the first time, make arable", *nyr* (*nîr*) "prepared virgin soil".
nrt (B) "ploughed land"	•CTX: **UGA** → DUL 634: *nrt* (II).
may(a)rīn "plow without seeder"	•LL: **EB** DÍM.SI.GA = *ma-rí-nu* → Civil AuOr(Suppl) 5 168; Sjöberg Fs. Kienast 557.

|n-z-ḳ|	Sem.: *nzq* (*nēzeq*, Hb.) "burden, damage"; *nzq* (Aram.) "to hurt"; *nazāqu*(*m*) (Akk.) "to worry, creak, be vexed"; *nazaqa* (Arab.) "to storm ahead, to be ruthless".

[360] Passim OBab., MBab., SBab.; see Edzard ZA 53 168ff.; AHw 771; CAD CAD N/1 249f.

|**n-z-ḳ**| "to get angry; to be injured, hurt"	•CTX: **Q** G prefc. *an-ziq* → Richter / Lange Idadda 185. **UGA** Gpass. suffc. *nzq* → DUL 645: /*n-z-q*/.
|n-z-l|	Sem.: *nzl* (Hb.) "to trickle, flow", *nzl* (*nozēl*) "rivulet"; *nzl* (Aram., Syr.) "to move down, shake", *nzl* (JAram.) "flowing"; *nazālu*(*m*) (Akk.) "to pour out", *mazzālu*(*m*) "(a pouring vessel) for water, oil"; *nazala* (Arab.) "to descend", *nazla* "catarrh"; *nazala* (Eth.) "to go down, flow, spill over".
|**n-z-l**| "to pour out, empty"	•LL: **EB** ZAL.A = *na-za-u*$_9$ → Conti QuSe 17 167. •ONOM: **EUPH** *an-za-la-tum* → Gelb CAAA 28, 168.
nizl "first quality oil"	•LL: **EB** SAG.Ì.GIŠ= *ni-zi*[!](GI)-*lu* → Conti QuSe 17 108.
nzl "kind of offering"	•CTX: **UGA** → DUL 645.
manzal, **mazzal** "pouring vessel"	•LL: **EB** NÌ.GÍD = *ma-ša-lu-um*, *ma-za-lu*, *zi-lum* (see below: *zil*) → Conti QuSe 17 75f. •ONOM: **EUPH** Cf. *ma-an-za-la-nu-um* → Gelb CAAA 28, 168.
zil "a vessel used as measure"	•CTX: **EB** *zi-lum* → Milano ARET 9 410. •LL: **EB** NÌ.GÍD = *zi-lum* → Conti QuSe 17 75f.
|n-z-m|	Sem.: *nazāmu*(*m*) (Akk.) "to moan, complain"; *nizmatu*(*m*) "desire", *tazzimtu*(*m*) "complaint".
|**n-z-m**| "to moan, complain"	•ONOM: **EB** *a-zu-ma-an*, *a-zu*/*zú-mu*, *e-zú-ma*, *en-zu*/*zú-ma*, *en-zu*/*zú-mu*, *en-zú:ma*; cf. unc. *na-zu*/*zú-mu* → Krebernik PTU 59; Pagan ARES 3 153, 285, 304, 308, 354.
|**n-m-z**| "to moan, complain"	•LL: **EB** Cf. metath. DIM.ZA = *na-ma-su-um*, DIM.DIM.ZA = *da-da-me-sum*$_6$ → Civil BaE 88; Sjöberg Fs. Kienast 553.
nizam, **nizim** "desire" (?)	•ONOM: **EB** Cf. *i-da-ne-za-mu*, *ne-zi-ma-ì*/*il*, *ne-zi-ma-a-ḫu*, *ne-zi-ma:a-ḫa* → Krebernik PET 103; Pagan ARES 3 153, 321, 356.

p

|p| (1) — Cf. |ʔ-p(-p)| (1)
|p| (2) — See |p(-w/y)|
|p-ʔ|
|p-ʔ-d|
|p-ʔ-l|
|p-ʔ-r|
|p-ʔ-S|
|p-ʕ-l|
|p-ʕ-m|
|p-ʕ-r| — Cf. |B-ɣ-r|
|p-d-d| — See |p-w/y-d| (2), |p-d-d|
|p-D-l
|p-d-m|
|p-d-n|
|p-D-r| (1)
|p-D-r| (2)
|p-d-y|
|p-ð-ð|
|p-g-ʔ|
|p-g-l|
|p-g-m|
|p-g-r|
|p-γ-(n-)d-r|
|p-γ-y|
|p-h-y|Cf. |y-p-y|
|p-ħ-l|
|p-ħ-m|
|p-x-d| (1)
|p-x-d| (2)
|p-x-r| (1)
|p-x-r| (2)
|p-k-r|
|p-k-y| — See |b-k-y|
|p-ḳ-d|
|p-ḳ-ħ|
|p-ḳ-r| — Cf. |b-ḳ-r| (2)
|p-l-d|
|p-l-g| — Cf. |p-l-x|
|p-l-G-G|
|p-l-x| — Cf. |p-l-g|
|p-l-l| (1)
|p-l-l/y| (2)
|p-l-s|
|p-l-ṭ|
|p-l-θ|
|p-l-y| — See |p-l-l/y| (2)
|p-n| — See |p-n-w/y|
|p-n-n|
|p-n-w/y| — See |p-n|
|p-n-y| — See |p-n-w/y|
|p-r|
|p-r-ʔ| (1)
|p-r-ʔ| (2)
|p-r-ʔ-r|
|p-r-ʕ| (1)
|p-r-ʕ| (2)
|p-r-d| (1)
|p-r-d| (2)
|p-r-γ-θ|
|p-r-x
|p-r-k|
|p-r-k-k|
|p-r-ḳ| (1)
|p-r-ḳ| (2)
|p-r(-l-n)|
|p-r-r| (1)
|p-r-r| (2)
|p-r-s| (1)
|p-r-s| (2)
|p-r-s| (3)
|p-r-s-ħ|
|p-r-s-y|
|p-r-ṣ|
|p-r-s^2|
|p-r-ṭ-l|
|p-r-θ|
|p-r(-w/y)| (1)
|p-r-y| (1) — See |p-r(-w/y)| (1)
|p-r-y| (2)
|p-r-z|
|p-s-ħ|
|p-s-x|
|p-s-l|
|p-s-m|
|p-s-s|
|p-ṣ-y|
|p-s^1-ʕ|
|p-s^1-ħ|
|p-s^1-ḳ|

|p-s¹-l| |p-w|
|p-s¹-ṭ| |p-w-d| (1)
|p-s²-ḳ| |p-w/y-d| (2),
|p-t-ḥ| |p-d-d|
|p-t-x| |p-w-ḳ| See |n-p-ḳ|,
|p-t-n| |y-p-ḳ|
|p-t-t| |p-w-l|
|p-t-y| |p-w(-t)|
|p-ṭ-r| |p-w-z|, |p-z-z|
|p-θ| |p(-y)| See| p(-w/y)| (1)
|p-θ(-θ)| |p-y-d| See |p-w/y-d| (2),
|p-θ̣-γ| |p-d-d|
|p-θ̣-l| |p-z-r|
|p(-w/y)| |p-z-z| See |p-w-z|, |p-z-z|

|p| (1)
Cf. |ʔ-p(-p)| (1)

Sem.: *p* (Aram., Nab., Palm.) "and moreover"; *fa* (Arab.) "and then, and so"; f (OSArab.) id. See also: *ʔ(w)p* (Aram.) "also, even".

p (A) "and; thus"   ●CTX: **UGA** → DUL 646f.: *p* (I).

---

p (2)
See |p(-w/y)|

|p-ʔ|

Primary noun, Sem.: *ʔpwtʔ* (JAram., Syr.) "forehead, front"; *pūtu, pâtum, pūtātu* (Akk.) "forehead, brow"; *fĭo* (MSArab.) "front". See further *pʔh* (*peʔāh*, Hb.) "side, edge"; *fe, lafe* (Eth.) "in the direction of, to this side, that way".

piʔat "edge, border, temple"
● CTX: **EUPH** *pí-a-e-<et>, pí-e-at, pí-a-tim, pí-a-at* → AHw 861: *piātum*; CAD P 358: *piātu*.
●LL: **EB** SAG.KI = *bí-a-tum* → Fronzaroli StEb 7 177, QuSe 13 138; Conti QuSe 17 108; Bonechi / Catagnoti Fs. Sommerfeld / Krebernik 177.

piʔt "edge, border, temple"
●LL: **UGS** [IB = *tubuqtu* = ...] = *pí-i(?)-[tu₄(?)]* → Sivan GAGl 258; Huehnergard UVST 73, 165.
●ONOM: **UGS** Cf. *pí-ʔ-TA-ya* → Gröndahl PTU 171; Sivan GAGl 258 (PIʔTU).[361]

pảt, pỉt "edge, border, temple"
●CTX: **UGA** Sg. *pỉt, pảt*; suff. *pỉth*; pl. *pảt* → DUL 649: *pỉt*.
●ONOM: **UGA** *pỉty* → DUL 649.

|p-ʔ-d|

Sem.: Cf. *fuʔād* (Arab.) "heart, entrails, spirit".
Non-Sem.: **pūd=* (West Chadic) "heart"; **pwad-pwad=* (East Chadic) "lungs".[362]

|p-ʔ-d| "to offer"
paʔ(a)d "offered"
●CTX: **EM** Cf. G prefc. *i-pa-a-du* → CAD P 1: *paʔādu*.
●CTX: **EM** Cf. Pl. fem. *pa-a-da-ti* → CAD P 6: **paʔdu*.

---

[361] Alternat. but less likely from PIʔDU, PʔD "mercy, kindness". Cf. Huehnergard JAOS 107 724. Note also in RS.- and Alalakh-Akk. *pāṭu, paṭṭu* (ZAG) "border (of a field)"; AHw 852: *pāṭu(m)*, 2; CAD P 307: *pāṭu*, 3.2'; Lauinger STOBA 19ff. and passim (436).
[362] Orel / Stolbova HSED 430f. no. 2016: **puwad=* "heart".

piʔd "mercy, kindness"	•ONOM: **EM** Cf. unc. *pí-da* → Pruzsinszky PTEm 175 [667]. **UGS** Cf. unc. *pí*-DI-*ya*, *pí*-ID-DA-*ya*, *pí*-ID-[DA(?)] → Gröndahl PTU 170f.; Sivan GAGl 258: PIʔDU, PIʔTU.[363]
pỉd "heart; goodness"	•CTX: **UGA** → DUL 648.
|p-ʔ-l|	Sem. etym. unc.; probl. by-form of |p-w/y-l|, |p-l-l| or several |p-l-C| bases with the general meaning "to split, break, crack".[364] Cf. *ply* (JAram.) "to split, cut open", *pyl(ʔ)* "split, crack"; *falla* (Arab.) "to nick, notch, dent, break, damage"; *fll* (OSArab.) "to cut chanels"; *falfala* (Eth.) "to break forth; to shell, pierce".[365]
paʔl, paʔal "a kind of flour"	•CTX: **EM** Cf. PA-*a-lu*, PA-*ʔa-a-lu* → Pentiuc Vocabulary 137; Watson LSU 98f.; NABU 2002/9.
pỉl "a kind of flour" (?)	•CTX: **UGA** → DUL 648.
pålt "cracked, fisured land"	•CTX: **UGA** Sg. *pålt*, suff. *pålth* → DUL 648.
|p-ʔ-r|	Primary noun, Sem.: *faʔr* (Arab.) "mouse, rat". See also: *pērūrūtu(m)* (Akk.) "mouse". Non-Sem.: * *ṗyar=* (emphatic |p|; West Chadic) "mouse, rat".[366]
paʔrat "mouse"	•LL: **EB** NIN.PÉŠ = *ba-ra-tum* → Krebernik ZA 73 33f. (873); Fronzaroli QuSe 13 138.
|p-ʔ-S|	Culture word, Sem.: *pustʔ* (Syr.) "axe"; *pāšu(m)* (Akk.) "axe, adze"; *faʔs*, *fās* (Arab.) "axe, adze". Non-Sem.: **paʔas=* (East Chadic) "axe"; **faʔas=* (East Cushitic) """axe"; *fat'so* (Dahalo) "axe".[367]
paʔS, pāS "axe"	•CTX: **EB** *ba-su* → Pasquali QuSe 23 171f., Or 83 274. •LL: **EB** TÙN.URUDU = *ba-šum* → Krebernik ZA 73 29.
pīs^{1}a "axe" (?)	•CTX: **EG** Cf. *bi-ša*, *b-šu*$_2$, *bi-ša-ʔu*, *bi*$_{2/4}$*-ša* → Hoch SWET 110f. no. 138.
|p-ʕ-l|	Sem.: *pʕl* (Hb., Ph., Pun.) "to make", *pʕl* (*poʕal*, Hb.) "deed, action"; *pwʕl* (Hb.) labourer"; *pʕl* (JAram., Syr.) "labour, work; worker, maker", *pʕlt* (Aram., Pun.) "work, act"; *faʕala* (Arab.) "to act, perform some activity", *fiʕl* "work, action", *fāʕil* "worker, labourer"; *fʕl* (OSArab.) "make, prepare", (C) "to work land", *fʕln* (pl.) "labourers". See further: *šupaʔʔulum*, *šupêlu(m)*, *šupellu(m)* (Akk.) "to exchange, overturn". Unrelated: *mabʕal/əl* (Eth.) "iron tool, axe". Non-Sem.: **pal=* (East Cushitic, Ometo) "to make"; *fal=* (Dahalo) "to do".[368]
|b-ʕ-l| (A) "to make, work"	•CTX: **UGA** G prefc. *ybʕl*, suff. *ybʕlnn*, *ybʕlhm*; act. ptc. *bʕl*; C(pass.?) prefc. *yšbʕl* → Tropper UG 137, 589; DUL 202f.

[363] In DUL 654 under *pdy* (II); probl. incorrect.
[364] See Renfroe AULS 159.
[365] See further Aram. *bʔlʔ* (*blʔ*) "rural area, open area"; Watson NABU 2018 77.
[366] Orel / Stolbova HSED 411 no. 1913: **paʔir=* "mouse, rat".
[367] Orel / Stolbova HSED 412 no. 1915: **paʔus=* "axe".
[368] Orel / Stolbova HSED 432 no. 2022: **pVʕal=* "to work, make".

|p-ʕ-l| "to make, work"	•CTX: **UGA** G suffc. *pʕl* → DUL 202: */b-ʕ-l/* G.1, 649: Ph. text. •ONOM: **A4** Cf. *pa-a-lu* → Dietrich / Loretz ZA 60 98 (12:37); Sivan GAGl 257. **UGA** Cf. *mnipʕl* → DUL 554.
puʕl "labour deed, work"	•ONOM: **A4** Cf. *pu-ú-la* → Wiseman AT 144; Sivan GAGl 259.
bʕl (A) "labourer, craftsman"	•CTX: **UGA** Sg. *bʕl*, pl. *bʕlm*, cstr. *bʕl*, du. *bʕlm* → DUL 203: *bʕl* (I).
pʕl "labour deed, work"	•CTX: **UGA** Sg. suff. *pʕlk* → 649f.

|p-ʕ-m|	Primary noun, Sem.: *pʕm* (*paʕam*, Hb.; Ph., Pun.) "foot, step, pace, time"; *pēmu*(*m*), *pēnu* (Akk.) "(upper) thigh"; *fawm*, *fām*, *faym*, *faʕm* (MSArab.) "foot, leg". Non-Sem. cf. **fān*= (Cushitic) "track (of an animal)", **paʕam*= (South Cushitic) "sole of foot"; **fun*= (West Chadic) "knee"; **pun*= (Central Chadic) "thigh".[369]
pʕn "foot"	•CTX: **UGA** Du. *pʕnm*, cstr. *pʕn*, suff. *pʕny*, *pʕnk*, *pʕnh*, *pʕnm*, pl. *pʕnt* → Tropper UG 154; DUL 650.
pȧmt "time"	•CTX: **UGA** Sg. *pȧm<t>*; pl. *pȧmt* → Tropper UG 153; DUL 648f.

|p-ʕ-r| Cf. **|B-ɣ-r|**	Sem.: *pʕr* (Hb.) "to open (the mouth)"; *pʕr* (Syr.) "to open the mouth wide". See further *phr* (Dt, Syr.) "to gape", *pwhr*(*?*) "gaping"; *faġara* (Arab.) "to open the mouth wide, gape".
|p-ʕ-r| "to open one's mouth; to shout, proclaim"	•CTX: **UGA** G suffc. *pʕrt*, *pʕr*; prefc. *tpʕr*, *ypʕr* → DUL **650:** ***/p-ʕ-r/***
paʕrit "scolding" (?)	•LL: **EB** INIM.ÉRIM = *ba-a-rí-tum* → Conti QuSe 17 31, 96.

|p-d-d| See **|p-w/y-d| (2)**, **|p-d-d|**	

|p-D-l|	Sem.: *ptl* (Hb. N) "to become entangled with one another; to wrestle", *ptyl* (*pātîl*) "cord", *ptltl* (*pᵉtaltol*) "tortuous"; *ptl* (Syr.) "to twist", *ptylh*, *ptylt?* (JAram.) "lamp-wick", *pwtl*(*?*) (Syr.) "twisting", *ptlwl*(*?*) "thin thread"; *patālu*(*m*), *petēlu*(*m*) (Akk.) "to twine, twist", *pitiltu*(*m*) "string, cord"; *fatala* (Arab.) "to twist together, wind, weave", *fatīl* "twisted" (pl.) *fatīlāt*, *fatāʔil* "wick"; *fatala* (Eth.) "to spin, twist".
patīl "bandages"	•CTX: **EG** *p-d-r* → Hoch SWET 124f. no. 158.[370]
prṯl "a kind of turban".	•CTX: **UGA** → Watson NABU 2018/105; NABU 2019/25; cf. diff. DUL 673: "a herb" (?).

|p-d-m|	Sem.: *fadama* (Arab.) "to seal (the mouth)", *fadm* "clumsy in speech".

---

369 For Afro-Asiatic etym. see Watson FO 52 338: *\|p-ʕ-m/n\|, and Orel / Stolbova HSED 187f. no. 828: **fuʕun*= "thigh, leg"; for the altern. bases **funuʕ*= and **paʕam*= see also Orel / Stolbova HSED 188.

370 Sivan / Cochavi-Rainey WSVES p. 80: *pa-ti-l* "cord"; Helck Beziehungen no. 82.

pādim "stutter(ing), stammer(ing)"	•LL: **EB** EME.LÁ = *ba-ti-mu, ba-ti-mu-um li-sa-nu, a-a-gú-um li-sa-nu, a-a-gú li-sa-nu* → Conti QuSe 17 94; Sjöberg Fs, Renger 524 fn. 20.[371]
|p-d-n|	Sem. etym. unc. Cf. *padānu(m)* (Akk.) "path, way"; see further *pdn(?)* (JAram., Syr.) "plow, yoke, plowed field"; *faddān* (Arab.) "yoke".
pad(d)an "road (through a plain)" (?)	•ONOM: **EB** Cf. unc. *ba-da-an, ba-da-nu* → Pagan ARES 3 228, 289.
pad(d)in "road (through a plain)" (?)	•LL: **EB** Cf. unc. KASKAL:ERIM = *ba-ti-na-tim, a-ti-mu ba-ti-na-tim* → Fales QuSe 13 183f.[372]
|p-D-r| (1)	Probl. loan. Cf. *patar(i)*= (Urartian) "hamlet, castle".[373]
pdr (A) "town, city"	•CTX: **UGA** Sg. *pdr*, suff. *pdrm* pl. *pdrm*, cstr. *pdr* → DUL 652: *pdr* (I).
|p-D-r| (2)	Probl. loan. Cf. *pe/idari* (*pit=ari, bit=ari*, Hurr.) "bull".[374]
pdr (B) "bull, DN"	•CTX: **EG** Cf. *p-w-tꜣ-rw* → Schneider AOAT 310 16. •ONOM: **UGA** → DUL 652f.: *pdr* (II), DN; *pdry* → DUL 653, fem. DN. Elem. in PNN: Cf. *ʕbdpdr* → DUL 140; *bnpdr* → DUL 227; *pdrn* → DUL 653.
ỉpdrð "a unit of measure (somehow connected with the keeping of oxen)"	•CTX: **UGA** → DUL 86: *ỉpdrḏ*; Tropper / Vita / Giorgieri UF 44 348ff.[375]
|p-d-y|	Sem.: *pdh* (Hb.) "to buy out, redeem", *pdwt* (*p^{e}dût*) "redemption"; *pdy* (Aram.) "to liberate"; *padû(m), pedû* (Akk.) "to spare, set free", *pādû* "forgiving", *pidītum* "pardon, indulgence"; *fadā* (Arab.) "to redeem, ransom", *fidya* "ransom, redemption"; *fdy* (OSArab.) "to repay, redeem"; *fede* (MSArab.) "ransom"; *fadaya* (Eth.) "to recompense, restore, pay a debt, avenge", *fadāy(i)* "avenger", *fəddā* "retribution", *fədyat* "paying".
|p-d-y| "to redeem, ransom"	•CTX: **UGA** G suffc. *pdy*, suff. *pdyhm* → DUL 653. •ONOM: **EUPH** Cf. *ia-ap-di/du-um* → Gelb CAAA 28, 170 (unpubl.); Zadok Fs. Hallo 327; Golinets Onomastikon 2 312, 423. **EM** *i-li-ia-ap-da* → Pruzsinszky PTEm 214 [475]; cf. unc. *Pada-šarri* (Hurr.?) 252 fn. 272 [CDISC *vacat*]. **EG** Cf. *pꜣ-t-w_2-y* → Schneider APÄQ 119 no. 254. **UGA** Cf. unc. *pdn* → DUL 652; *pdy* → DUL 653f.: *pdy* (II); *pdyn* → DUL 654.

[371] Diff. Fales QuSe 13 175: Sem |p-d-n| "pathway"; cf. *pdn(?)* (JAram., Syr.) "plow, yoke, plowed field"; *padānu(m)* (Akk.) "path, way". Unlikely.

[372] See here |p-d-m| for EME.LÁ = *ba-ti-mu, ba-ti-mu-um li-sa-nu, a-a-gú-um li-sa-nu, a-a-gú li-sa-nu*. Diff. Fales QuSe 13 175: from Sem. |p-d-n| "pathway". Unlikely.

[373] Sanmartín ALASP 7 133 fn. 4; Richter BGH 535.

[374] Laroche GLH 199; Richter BGH 319f.

[375] See CAD P 434: *pitaršu* "a building". For Hurr. *pidar(i)=ži* see Richter BGH 320.

pādiy "redeemer, ransomer"	•ONOM: **EB** *ba-ti*, *ba-ti-a* → Pagan ARES 3 153, 290.[376] **UGS** *pa-di/dì-ya* → Gröndahl PTU 71, 171; Sivan GAGl 256.
pidīt "ransom" (?)	•ONOM: **UGS** Cf. *pí-di-tu* → Sivan GAGl 24, 258 (< |padiyt| ?).
tapdēt "exchange"	•CTX: **UGS** Gt verbal noun / inf. (?) *ta-ap(/tap)-de*$_4$*-tu*$_4$ → Sivan GAGl 278; Huehnergard UVST 166; Tropper UG 280, 490.[377]
|p-ð-ð|	Culture word, Sem.: *pz* (p*az*, Hb.) "pure, refined gold"; *pz*, *pyzʔ* (JAram.) "gold", *pzwz* "gold plating".
pð "gold"	•CTX: **UGA** Sg. suff. *pḏh* → DUL 654: *pḏ*.
|p-g-ʔ|	Etym. unc.
pgủ "qualifying a garment"	•CTX: **UGA** Sg. *pgỉ*, du. *pgảm* → DUL 654, unexplained.
|p-g-l|	Sem.: Cf. *pgwl* (*piggûl*, Hb.) "meat for a sacrifice which has become unclean"; *pgl* (JAram. D) "to render unclean", *pgwl(ʔ)* "unclean, flawed"; see further: *faǧala* (Arab.) "to be flabby, plump, flaccid".
pglt "unclean offering"	•CTX: **UGA** Sg. / pl. *pglt* → DUL 654.
|p-g-m|	Sem.: *pgm* (JAram.) "to mutilate, cut", *pgm(h/tʔ)* "mutilation, defect".
pigm "section"	•CTX: **EM** *pí-ig-mi* → Pentiuc Vocabulary140.
pgm "harm" (?)	•CTX: **UGA** → DUL 654f.
|p-g-r|	Sem.: *pgr* (*peger*, Hb.) "corpse; offering for the dead (?)"; *pgr(ʔ)* (Aram., Palm., Syr.) "corpse, body"; *pagru(m)*, *paggar* (Akk.) "body, corpse". [378]
pagr "body, corpse (as a funerary offering)"	•CTX: **UGS** *pa-ag-ri-ma* (Pl. gen. |pagrīma|) as month name → vSoldt SAU 306; Huehnergard ^{2}UVST 396. **A7** ITI *pa-ag-ri* as month name → Cohen Calendars 294, 372ff.; CAD P 17: *pagru* B. •ONOM: **EM** *pa-ag-ri* → Pruzsinszky PTEm 92 [659]. **UGS** *pa-ag-ru-na* → Gröndahl PTU 172; Sivan GAGl 256.
pagraʔ "body, corpse (as a funerary offering)"	•CTX: **EUPH** Passim; written *pa-ag-re*, *pa-ag-ra-i*, *pa-ag-ra-yi*, *pa-ag-re-e*, *pa-ag-ri-im*, *pa-ag-ra-am*, *pa-ag-ri-a-im* → Sasson JCS 25 60 fn. 5; Durand ARM 21 160 fn. 20; 26/1 157 fn. h, 475 fn. i, REA 741, LAPO 18 114, 124, 297; Durand / Guichard FM 3 35; Birot ARM 27 122.
pugart "a funerary rite" (?)	•CTX: **EM** Cf. BU-GA-*ra-tu*$_4$ (pl. fem. |pugarāt| ?) → Pentiuc Vocabulary 141.
pgr "body, corpse (as a funerary offering)"	•CTX: **UGA** Sg. *pgr*, pl. *pgrm* as month name → DUL 655.

376 Altern. |baytī| "my household", |baitiya| "my household", Pagan ARES 3 105, 290; see GlOS 1 135: *bayt* (|b-y-t).

377 Diff. CAD T 179: *tapdētu* (mng unc.).

378 From OBab. on, also in Mari-Akk.; cf. Durand ARM 21 160 fn. 20, LAPO 18 82: "carcasse d'animal (pour les *pagrāʔu*)".

|p-γ-(n-)d-r|	Loanword. Cf. *p/waḫandar(r)i* (Hurr.) "kind of blanket or garment"; hence *paḫantarru, paḫattarru* (Akk.) "a blanket or garment".[379]
paγandarr, paγaddarr "a blanket or cloak"	•CTX: **Q** TÚG *: pá-ḫa-ad-da-ri* → Richter / Lange Idadda 88f. **EM**: TÚG *pa-ḫa-da-ra* → Pentiuc Vocabulary 137; Westenholz Emar Tablets 36, 38, 59f. **A4**: TÚG *pa-ḫa-an-t[a-ru* → AHw 810: *paḫantaru*; CAD P 20f.: *paḫantarru.* **UGS**: TÚG *pa-ḫa-dar*$_6$(TAR)*-ru* GADA → Huehnergard UVST 169, 317.
pγ(n)dr "a blanket or cloak"	•CTX: **UGA** Pl. / du. *pġndrm, pġdrm* → DUL 655: *pġ(n)dr*; Richter BGH 536.

|p-γ-y|	Sem. etym. unc.[380]
puγ(i)y "boy"	•ONOM: **UGS** Cf. unc. *pu-ḫi-ya-nu* → Virolleaud PRU 6 82 I 12; vSoldt SAU 361 fn. 235.
pγy "boy"	•CTX: **UGA** Sg. *pġy* (for the fem. *pγt* see below) → DUL 656: *pġy.* •ONOM: **UGA Cf.** unc. *pġyn* → DUL 656.
pγt "girl, princess"	•CTX: **UGA** Sg. *pġt*, du. *pġtm* → DUL 656: *pġt*, 1, 2. •ONOM: **UGA** *pġt* → DUL 656, 3.

|p-h-y| Cf. **|w-p-y|**	Sem. etym. unc.[381]
|p-h-y| "to see, look at; to know, recognise"	•CTX: **UGA** G prefc. *ỉph, tph, yph,* suff. *tphn, tphnh, tphhm, yphn, yphnh*; suffc. *pht, phy,* suff. *phnn*; imp. *ph*; N prefc. *ynphy* → Tropper UG 146, 427, 449, 500, 538, 655f., 662, 665, 668; DUL 656f.: */p-h-y/.*

|p-ḫ-l|	Sem.: *pḥl* (Syr.) "stallion", *pḥln, pḥltʔ* "testicles"; *puḫālu* (Akk.) "male animal"; *faḥl* (Arab.) "stallion"; *feḥl, faḥl, fēḥəl, fáḥəl* (MSArab.) "penis"; *faḥala* (Eth.) "to exult, be lascivious, sexually aroused".
puḫal "ram / stallion"	•CTX: **A4** (Image or likeness), SAG.DU *pu-ḫa-lu* → Wiseman AT 162 (390:6); Giacumakis AkkAl 95.[382]
pūḫil "ram / stallion"	•CTX: **EA** (Silver rhyton) 1 *bi-ib-ru* KÙ.BABBAR UDU.SIR$_4$ *: pu-u-ḫi-lu* (41:41, letter to the Hitt. court) → Moran AmL 115 fn. 12; Rainey EAC 1387.
pḫl "jackass; stallion of an equine species"	•CTX: **UGA** Sg. *pḥl*, (see below for fem. *pḥlt*) → DUL 657: *pḥl.*
pḫlt "mare"	•CTX: **UGA** → DUL 657: *pḥlt.*

|p-ḫ-m|	Primary noun, Sem.: *pḥm. (peḥḥām,* Hb.) "bright, reddish purple"; *pḥm* (JAram., Syr.) "coal"; *pēmtum, pēnt/du, pettu* (Akk.) "charcoal"; *faḥm* (Arab.) "charcoal"; *fḥam* (MSArab.) "charcoal"; *fəḥm* (Eth.) "coals, embers".
pḫm "ember; reddish, ruby (purple)"	•CTX: **UGA** Sg. *pḥm*, pl. *pḥmm* → DUL 657f.: *pḥm.*

[379] Laroche GLH 192: *paḫandari*; Richter BGH 287: *p/waḫandar(r)i.*
[380] For the hypothetical connection with the Hb. PN *pwʕh (pûʕāh)* see Zadok OLA 28 142.
[381] Probl. extended and lexicalised by-form of an deictic etymon *|p| with several Sem. isoglosses and their derivatives; see |p-w| (2), and cf. |w-p-y|.
[382] Probl. Akk.

|p-x-d| (1)	Sem.: *puḫādu*(*m*) (Akk.) "lamb".
pxd "yearling lamb"	•CTX: **UGA** → DUL 658f.: *pḫd*.

|p-x-d| (2)	Sem.: *pḥd* (Hb.) "to shiver, tremble", *pḥd* (*paḥad*) "trembling, dread"; *pḥd* (JAram.) "to fear", *pḥd*(*?*) "fear".[383]
|**p-x-d**| "to dread, fear"	•CTX: **UGS** *lip-ḫu-dú-ma* (Akkadianized Gt precative |lipHudū|) → AHw 810; Huehnergard UVST 166, 324.
paxd "fear, fright"	•CTX: **EB** *ba-ḫa-du* → Fronzaroli ARET 13 21, 249; Catagnoti QuSe 29 109, 218.

|p-x-r| (1)	Loanword, Sem.: *pḫr*(*?*) (JAram., Syr.) "clay; potter"; *pḫr* (Syr. D) "to turn into hard clay"; *paḫāru*(*m*) (Akk.) "potter"; *faḫḫār* (Arab.) "(fired) clay, pottery". Non-Sem.: b a ḫ a r (Sum.) "potter".[384]
paxxar "potter"	•ONOM: **EM** *pa-ḫa-ri* → Pruzsinszky PTEm 245 [660].[385]
pxr (A) "potter"	•CTX: **UGA** → DUL 659: *pḫr* (II).

|p-x-r| (2)	Sem.: *pḫr(?)*, *pwḫr?* (Palm., Hatra, Syr.) "assembly, banquet, crowds"; *paḫāru*(*m*) (Akk.) "to gather", *puḫru*(*m*) "assembly", *puḫḫuru*, *paḫḫuru* "assembled", *mupaḫḫirum* "who gathers, collector", *napḫaru*(*m*) "total, sum". Non-Sem.: **pVr=* (East Chadic) "to gather".[386]
|**p-x-r**| "to gather"	•LL: **EB** KA.KIN = *ba-ḫa-lum*^{um} → Conti QuSe 17 47, 100: |paxārum|; Fronzaroli SEL 12 57. Altern. rdg |paxr|; see below. •ONOM: **EB** *ib-ḫu-úr*, *ib-ḫur*^{úr}, *ib-ḫur-lu*, *ib-ḫur-ra/ru*$_{12}$, *ib-ḫur-ì*, *ib-ḫur-il/íl*, *ib-ḫur-*^{d}*ʔà-da*, *dab*$_{6}$*-ḫur-*^{d}*ʔà-da*, *ib-ḫur-*^{d}*ku-ra*, *ib-ḫur-li-im*; cf. unc. *ib-ur-da-mu* → Pagan ARES 3 153f., 332f. **EUPH** *ia-ap-ḫu-ru-um*, *ia-ap-ḫu-ra-nu*, *ia-ap-ḫu-ur-a-du*, *ia-ap-ḫu-ur-sin*, *ia-ap-ḫu-ur-li-im*; *pu-ùḫ-ra-na*, see below: *mupaxxir* → Huffmon APNMT 254; Gelb CAAA 28, 168, 172; Golinets Onomastikon 2 423f.
paxr "assembly" (?)	•LL: **EB** KA.KIN = *ba-ḫa-lum*^{um} → Conti QuSe 17 47, 100. Altern. rdg |paxārum|; see above |p-x-r|.
puxr "assembly, cluster, faction"	•LL: **UGS** ^{d}*pu-ḫur* DINGIR.MEŠ → Tropper UG 169, KWU 95: with vocalic /r/ (*ṛ*); Huehnergard UVST 166: bound form of Akk. *puḫru*.
paxūr "assembly / gathered" (?)	•ONOM: **A4** *pa-ḫu-ra* → Wiseman AT 144; Arnaud AuOr 16 164.
paxxur "reunited"	•ONOM: **EB** *ba-ḫu-rúm* → Pagan ARES 3 153f., 290.
puxxur "reunited"	•ONOM: **EUPH** *pu-ḫu-ur-*^{d}*nu-nu*, *pu-ḫu-ur-tum* → Golinets Onomastikon 2 201f.
pxr (B) "assembly, cluster, faction"	•CTX: **UGA** Sg. *pḫr*, suff. *pḫrk* NOTE For the writing *phr* (mistake ?) see Tropper UG 154. → DUL 659: *pḫr* (I).

---

[383] Neither Arab. nor UGA instances are available for this etymon and both |ħ| and |x| might be candidates for C_2. But the Eblaite evidence (with *ḫa*) speaks against |ħ| (normally written *ʔà*).
[384] Probl. a Sem. loan; see Rubio JCS 51 1ff.
[385] The PNN *pa-aʔ-ḫa-ri*, *pa-ḫu-ra/ru* (Pruzsinszky PTEm 245 [660f.], loc.cit.) are unrelated.
[386] Orel / Stolbova HSED 432 no. 2014: **pVḫVr=* "to gather".

pxyr "whole, totality"	•CTX: **UGA** Sg. *pẖyr*, suff. *pẖyrh* → DUL 659: *pẖyr*.
mupaxxir "who gathers"	•ONOM: **EUPH** Fem. *mu-pa-ḫi-ra* → Gelb CAAA 28, 169.
mpxrt "assembly, gathering"	•CTX: **UGA** → DUL 559: *mpẖrt*.

|p-k-r|	Sem.: *pkr* (JAram., Syr.) "to bind", *pwkr(?)* (Syr.) "connection, entangling"; *pakāru* (Akk.) "to tie up, tether". See further *fakara* (Arab.) "to reflect, ponder, think over".
|p-k-r| "to join"	•CTX: **EB** G prefc. *a-ba-ga-ra* | (du.) lā=yipakkarāy|, (pl.) *a-ba-ga-ru*$_{12}$ |lā=yipakkarū|; inf. *ba-ka-ru*$_{12}$ |pakāru| → Fronzaroli ARET 11 140; SEL 12 62; Catagnoti QuSe 29 45, 105, 129, 138, 218.

|p-k-y| See **|b-k-y|**	By-form of |b-k-y|.
|p-k-y| "to weep"	•CTX: **UGA** G prefc. *tpky* → Tropper UG 137; DUL 660.

|p-ḳ-d|	Sem.: *pqd* (Hb.) "to command, make a careful inspection, look at, see, instruct", *pqyd* (*pāqîd*) "overseer"; *pqd* (Ph.) "to command, survey"; *pqd* (Aram.) "to order, oversee", *pqyd* "officer, magistrate"; *pqd* (Syr.) "to care for, look for, visit"; *paqādu(m)* (Akk.) "to entrust, care for, hand over"; *piqdu*, *piqittu(m)* "allocation, mandate"; *tafaqqada*, *ʔiftaqada* (Arab.) "to seek, examine, inspect"; *faqada* (Eth.) "to wish, desire", *fāqəd* "inspector", *fəqd* "number, survey, surveillance". See further: *pqd* (Hb. N) "to be missed"; *faqada* (Arab.) "to fail to find, lose, miss", *faqd*, *fiqdān* "loss", *fāqid* "devoid"; *fqd* (OSArab.) "to lose", *fqdh* "loss".
|p-ḳ-d| "to command; provide, care for"	•CTX: **UGA** G prefc. *ypqd* → DUL 667: */p-q-d/*. •ONOM: **EB** *ib-gi-du!dum* → Pagan ARES 3 154, 331. **U3** *ap-ki-da* → Buccellati Amorites 102, Gelb CAAA 28, 171; Golinets Onomastikon 2 82, 84, 113, 428, 487. **EUPH** *ia-ap-ki-du-um* → Gelb CAAA 28, 171; Golinets Onomastikon 2 82, 113, 428. **R** *ia-ap-ki-id-* DINGIR, *ia-ap-ki-id-* ^{d}UTU → Dalley / Walker / Hawkins Tell Rimah 259; Zadok Fs. Hallo 327; Golinets Onomastikon 2 84, 113, 428. **EM** *ip-qí-de*$_{4}$, *ip-qí-di*, *ip-qí-dì*, *ip-qí-du* → Pruzsinszky PTEm 170: [498].
pāḳid "carer"	•ONOM: **EUPH** *pa-gi-du-um* → Gelb CAAA 28, 169.
piḳdāt "care, allocation"	•ONOM: **EUPH** *bi-ig-da-tum* → Gelb CAAA 28, 171; Zadok Fs. Hallo 327.
mapḳad "inspection, review"	•CTX: **EB** *ma-ba-ga-tum*, *ma-ba-ga-tim/ti*; *ma-ba-ga-dam*, *ma-ba-ag-da-mu* → Archi NABU 1997/147.

|p-ḳ-ħ|	Sem.: *pqḥ* (Hb., Aram.) "to open (eyes, ears)"; (Syr.) "to flourish"; *faqaḥa* (Arab.) "to open (eyes), to blossom"; *fqḥ* (OSArab.) "to open, release".
|p-ḳ-ħ| "to open"	•ONOM: **EB** *ib-ga-ì/il*, *ib-ga-a-gú*, *ib-ga-iš-lu/ru*$_{12}$ → Pagan ARES 3 154, 333. **EUPH** Cf. *ba-ga-a-tum*, *ba-ga-a-la-lum*; *pu-uq-ḫa-nu-um*; *pa-ta-aq-ḫi-im* → Gelb CAAA 28, 169; Zadok Fs. Hallo 327; Golinets Onomastikon 2 195, 428.

pataḳḫ "open"	•ONOM: **EUPH** *pa-ta-aq-ḫi-im* → Streck Onomastikon 1 340 § 5.50; Golinets Onomastikon 2 195, 428.
|p-ḳ-r| Cf. **|b-ḳ-r| (2)**	Sem.: Cf. *pqr* (JAram. C) "to abandon, declare free", *pqr* (JAram.) "lawless".
pḳr "manumited, enfranchised" (?)	•ONOM: **UGA** → Tropper / Vita UF 30 680f.; cf. DUL 667: *pqr*.
|p-l-d|	Sem. etym. unc. Cf. *palādu* (Akk.) "a garment" (?).
palid "a cloth or garment"	•CTX: **UGS** TÚG *pa-li-du*, TÚG *pa-li-du-ma* (pl. |pali/īdūma|) → Sivan GAGl 257; Huehnergard UVST 167f.; vSoldt SAU 306 (119).
pld "a cloth or garment"	•CTX: **UGA** Sg. *pld*; pl. and du. *pldm* →
|p-l-g| Cf. **|p-l-x|**	Sem.: *plg* (Hb.) "to be separated", (D) "to split", *plg* (*peleg*) "artificial water channel, canal"; *plg* (Aram., Syr.) "to divide" (Gt) "to be divided"; *plg(?)* (Aram., Nab., Palm.) "half", *plg?* (Aram.) "canal"; *palgu(m)* (Akk.) "irrigation ditch, canal"; falağa (Arab.) "to split, divide", *falğ* "crack, split, cleft, rift"; *mflq* (OSArab.) "exit channel, system of irrigation"; *felēg*, *félég* (MSArab.) *felēg*, *félég* "watercourse"; falaga (Eth.) "dig out, hollow out, to divide, split", *falag* "river, brook, valley". See also: *palāku(m)* (Akk.) "to divide off, demarcate", *palāk/qu(m)* "to slaughter, strike down"; *falaqa* (Arab.) "to split, cleave, tear asunder", *falq* "crack, split". Cf. further: *falaḥa* (Arab.) "to split, cleave, plow, till".
|p-l-g| "to be split"	•CTX: **UGA** N prefc. *tplg* → Tropper UG 538; DUL 660f.
plg "stream, brook	•CTX: **UGA** → DUL 661.
|p-l-G-G|	Culture word, Sem.: *plk* (*pelek*, Hb; Ph.) "spindle-whorf"; *plk(?)*, *plkh*, *plkt?* (JAram.) "spindle, distaff"; *pilakku(m)*, *pilaqqu(m)*, *pilaggu* (Akk.) "spindle"; *filka* (pl. *falak*, Arab.) "round point at the bottom of the spindle". Non-Sem.: b a l a k (Sum.) "spindle".
pilaḳḳ "spindle"	•LL: **EB** GIŠ.BAL = *bí-a-gu* → Krebernik ZA 73 16; Conti QuSe 17 133: |pilaḳḳu(m)=|[387]
pilakk "spindle"	•LL: **UGS** BAL = *pí-la-ak-ku* = *te-a-ri* = *pí-lak-ku* → Sivan GAGl 258; Huehnergard UVST 168; vSoldt SAU 306 (121).
palakk "spindle"	•LL: **EM** BAL = *pa-la-ak-ku* → Pentiuc Vocabulary 138.[388]
pilakkuγul "spinner"	•CTX: **A7** SAL.MEŠ *ṭe$_4$-mi-tum* (: ?) *pí-la-ku-ḫu-li* → Dietrich / Loretz WO 3 192f.; CAD P 373.
plk "spindle"	•CTX: **UGA** Sg. *plk*, suff. *plkh* → DUL 661.

[387] For \|ḳu\| written *gu* in the Ebl. "fonte D" see Conti QuSe 17 7.

[388] Arnaud Emar 6/4 68 reads: *pa-la-aq-qú*.

|p-l-x|
Cf. **|p-l-g|**

Sem.: *plḥ* (Aram., Syr.) "to serve, worship, adore", *p*(*w*)*lḥn*(*ʔ*) (JAram., Syr.) "worship"; *palāḫu*(*m*) (Akk.) "to fear, revere", *pulḫu* "fear". See also: *plḥ* (Hb. D) "to pierce through, cut to pieces, split (the womb)"; *plḥ* (Syr.) "to work, labour, plow". Cf. further: *falaḥa* (Arab.) "to split, cleave, plow, till".

|p-l-x| "to fear, worry about; to terrify"

•CTX: **EB** D suffc. *ba-lu-ḫu-du-nu* |palluxūtunu < palluxātunu| → Catagnoti / Fronzaroli ARET 16 90, 222; Catagnoti QuSe 29 51, 54, 126, 218.
•LL: **EB** Cf. IM(NÍ).TI = *ba-a-ḫu-um* → Krebernik Study ANE 237 fn. 6; Sjöberg Fs. Pettinato 276.
•ONOM: **EUPH** *ap-la-ḫa-an-da*/*du*, *ap-la-ḫa-da*, *ap-li-ḫa-an-da*, *ia-ap-la-ḫu*(*-um*), *ia-ap-la-aḫ*-DINGIR, *ia-ap-la-ḫi-il*, *ia-ap-la-aḫ-i-li-im*; cf. unc. *pu-la-ḫa-an* → Huffmon APNMT 255; Gelb CAAA 28, 171f.; Golinets Onomastikon 2 110f., 424f.

pilx "fear"

•ONOM: **EUPH** *bi-el-ḫu-*^{d}IM; cf. *bi-la-ḫu-um* → Gelb CAAA 28, 171; Streck Onomastikon 1 323 § 5.11.

|p-l-l| (1)

Sem.: *pll* (Syr.) "to break"; *falla* (Arab.) "to break, nick, dent", *ʔafalla* "to lose the flock, to be in an arid land", *fall*, *fill*, *ʔaflāl*, *filliya* "land in which is no herbage", *falla*, *falal* "dent, notch, nick"; *fll* (OSArab. C) "to cut".

|p-l-l| (A) "to be cracked, parched"

•CTX: **UGA** G suffc. *pl* → Tropper UG 676; DUL 661: */p-l*(*-l*)*/*.

|p-l-l/y| (2)

Sem.: Cf. *pll* (Hb. D) "to pronounce judgement; to be arbitrator, intercessor", (Hitp.) "to act as an intercessor, to pray"; *palālum* (Akk.) "to guard, watch over", *pālilu*(*m*) "guardian, watchman". See also: *plh* (Hb. N) "to be excellent", (C) "to treat excellently", *plʔ* (Hb. N) "to be unusual, wonderful"; *ply* (JAram.) "to split, cut open"; *falaya*, *falawa* (Eth.) "to separate, distinguish".

|p-l-l| (B), **|p-l-y| (A)** "to judge, distinguish, watch; to intercede, pray, invoke; to procure somebody's right"

•CTX: **EB** G prefc. *i-ba-la-al*$_6$ → Fronzaroli ARET 11 153; Rubio PIHANS 106 122; Catagnoti QuSe 29 40, 218.
A7 G suffc. cf. *pá-al-la-ti*;[389] D suffc. *pu-li-il-šu* → Tsevat HUCA 29 112: "to procure somebody's right" (G); Arnaud AuOr 16 179: "participer à" (G), 182: "attribuer (légalement)" (D).
UGA: G/D prefc. *tply* → DUL 663: */p-l-y/*.
•LL: **EB** GÙ.GÁ.II = *ba-a-lum*; GÙ.DI.II = *ba-a-lu-um*, *ba-la-lum* → Conti QuSe 17 95.[390]
•ONOM: **EB** Cf. *ib-lul*-NI → Catagnoti MARI 8 591.
EUPH *pa-la-*^{d}IM → Zadok Fs. Hallo 327.
UGS Cf. *ya-ap-lu*, *ya-ap-lu-nu*, *ia-ap-lu-na* → Gröndahl PTU 172; Sivan GAGl 258.
UGA Cf. unc. *pl* → DUL 660; *pll* → DUL 661; *pln* → DUL 672; *ply* → DUL 663; *ypln* → DUL 959.
EG Cf. *pꜣ-r-y*, *t-ꜣ-p-w*$_2$*-r-y* → Schneider APÄQ 109 no. 232g, 233 no. 495.

pall "invocation"[391]

•CTX: **EB** Cf. *ba-lu-um* → Fronzaroli NABU 1991/49, ARET 11 140.

---

[389] AT 7:5; cf. rdg *pá-al-la-*[*ku*] against *pá-al-la-t*[*i*] in AT 7:8.
[390] Cf. also IGI.GAR = *ba-la-um*; see Sjöberg Fs. Oelsner 414 fn. 13, Fs. Renger 522, Fs. Kienast 537: rdg *pá-la-um* "to inquire into, search for", and here GlOS 1 128: |*b-r-y*| (B) "to watch over, inspect, select, discern".
[391] Probl. abstract noun (theme PARS) denoting a "group of invoking men".

pālil (A) "guide, leader"	•LL: **EB** IGI.ŠÈ.DU = *ba-li-lum/lu-um*; PÁLIL = *ba-li-lu-um, ba-li-lum* → Fronzaroli StEb 7 176, QuSe 13 137; Conti QuSe 17 184 (720).
pālil (B) "kind of protective fabric, sac"	•CTX: **EUPH** *pa-li-lu* → Durand ARM 30 179.

|p-l-s|	Sem.: *pls* (Hb. D) "to observe"; *palāsu(m) (*Akk.) "to look (at)".[392]
|p-l-S| "to see, look (at); inquire"	•LL: **EB** IGI.BAR.DA = *ba-a-zu, ba-a-zu-um, ʔa$_5$-ša-um* → Conti QuSe 17 182.[393] •ONOM: **EB** *ib-lu$_5$-zú*[394] → Pagan ARES 3 154, 332. **EUPH**: *ia-ap-lu-sa-an, ia-ap-lu-zum, ia-ap-lu-si-su-ú-mi*; cf. *ip-pa-li-zu* → Huffmon APNMT 255; Gelb CAAA 28, 169, 171; Streck Onomastikon 1 227f. §§ 2.134, 2.136 fn. 3; Golinets Onomastikon 2 80, 112, 203, 425f. See also: *ú-pa-al-li-iš-ma, pu-ul-li-iš-ma, tu-pa-la-aš, nu-pa-al-li-iš, ú-pa-al-la-šu-ma* → Rouault Iraq 39 149 fn. 5; CAD P 61f. *pullušum* "to penetrate the meaning"; Durand LAPO 2 648 fn. g: "causer un souci"; Arkhipov NABU 2013/78: "to inquire". **EG** Cf. *pꜣ-:r-sꜣ, p-y$_2$-r- ṯꜣ-y* → Schneider APÄQ 110 no. 235, 112 no. 239. **UGS** Cf. *píl/píl-sú/sí, píl-si/sí-ya/ia, píl-sú-ya, pu-la-su* → Gröndahl PTU 172.[395] **UGA** *pls/ś* → DUL 661f.; *plsbʕl, plśbʕl* → DUL 662: *pls/śbʕl*; *plsy* → DUL 662.
palS "watched over, esteemed, cherished"	•ONOM: **EUPH** *pa-al-zu-um, pa-al-zi-ia* → Gelb CAAA 28, 169; Streck Onomastikon 1 203 § 2.95.
pilS, pulS "(merciful) look"	•ONOM: **EB** *bil-za-ì, bíl-za-ì, bil-za-il, bíl-za-il, bíl-za-ma-ni, bil-za-lum, bil-zi, bil-zi-ì, bíl-zi-ì, bil-zi-il, bíl-zi-il, bil-zi-lum, bíl-zi-da-ar, bíl-zi-ma-lik*; *a-da bil/bíl-zú* → Pagan ARES 3 154, 276, 292. **EUPH**: *bi-il-zi-*^{d}IM, *bil-za-nu-um*; *pu-ul-za-tum, pu-ul-za-an, pu-ul-zi-ia, pu-ul-zi-*^{d}IM, *pu-ul-zi-ra-aḫ, pu-u-si-e-ra-aḫ, pu-ul-zu-na-*^{d}IM → Huffmon APNMT 255; Gelb CAAA 28, 171f.; Streck Onomastikon 1 203 § 2.95, 227 § 2.134, 315 § 4.9, 323 § 5.11, 325 § 5.16,344 § 5.59. **EM**: *píl-sú, píl-sí-ia, píl-sú-*^{d}*da-gan* / ^{d}KUR; cf. *pí-sí-*^{d}*da-gan, pí-sú-*^{d}KUR → Pruzsinszky PTEm 175 [668-677]. **EG** f. *t-ꜣ-p-w2-r-sꜣ* → Schneider APÄQ 233no. 496.
palūS "watched over, esteemed, cherished"	•ONOM: **EB** *ba-lu-zú* → Pagan ARES 3 154, 290. **EUPH** *ba-lu-zum* → Gelb CAAA 28, 169; Streck Onomastikon 1 330 § 5.28; Golinets Onomastikon 2 139.
pilSūt "esteem"	•ONOM: **EB** *bíl-zú-du* → Pagan ARES 3 154, 292.
naplaSt "a kind of payment"	•CTX: **EUPH** *na-ap-la-ás-tam, na-ap-la-ás-ti, na-ap-la-ás-sa-at* → Kupper ARM 22 452 (286 rev. 5'); Soubeyran ARM 23 406f.

[392] Ph. in CTX and PNN: mng unc.; Hoftijzer / Jongeling DNWSI 916.
[393] Diff. Sjöberg Fs. Wilcke 258: rdg *pá-a-zu-um* ""to attain". See here: |p-w-z|, |p-z-z|.
[394] |yiplus=| "he looked over"; altern. |yiprus=| "he decided" (|p-r-s|); see Pagan ARES 3 155, 332.
[395] Cf. Gröndahl PTU 68 *pils* "Bahn"; PTU 172f.: PLS: "Bahn machen, ebnen", "schauen, beobachten". Altern. Sivan GAGl 258: PILSU "balance, scale"; 259 PLS "balance" (Hb. *pésel* "scales").

|p-l-ṭ|	Sem.:. *plṭ* (Hb. G) “to escape”, (D) “to bring out, save”; *plṭ* (G Aram., Syr.) “to escape, (D) “to free, rescue”; *balāṭu(m)* (Akk. G) “to live”, (D) “to revive, let live, cure, support”, *falata* (Arab.) “to escape, get away, be freed”, *ʔaflata* “to save, rescue”; *fēlet, fōlet, fult* (MSArab.) “to free oneself”, *flōt, flet* “to flee, escape”; *falaṭa* (Eth.) “to separate, put asunder, set apart”.
|**p-l-ṭ**| “to escape, slip away; to live; let live, save, cure”	•CTX: **UGA** N suffc. *npl̩ṭ*; D prefc. suff. *yplṭk* → DUL 662. •LL: **UGS** KAR = *šu-zu-bu* = *a-bu-uš-ku-me* = *pu-la-ṭu* |pullaṭu| → Sivan GAGl 259; Huehnergard UVST 168; vSoldt SAU 306 (120). •ONOM: **EUPH** *ia-ab-lu-te*$_9$*-el*; *a-ḫi-la-ap-la-aṭ*, *a-hu-la-ap-la-aṭ*, *a-ḫu-um-la-ap-la-aṭ*, *a-ḫi-li-ip-la-aṭ* → Golinets Onomastikon 2 113, 128, 426f. **EG** Cf. *pꜣ-r- ṯ-y-ꜣ* → Schneider APÄQ 112f. no. 240. **UGS** *ia-ap-lu-ṭu*$_4$, *ia-ap-lu-ṭá-nu/na* → DUL 959: *yplt/ṭ(n)*; Gröndahl PTU 173; Gelb CAAA 16, 119; Sivan GAGl 259; Huehnergard UVST 214, Golinets Onomastikon 2 79, 113, 426f., 491. **UGA** *plṭ* → DUL: 662; *yplṭ, ypltn, yplṭn* → DUL 959: *yplt/ṭ(n)*.
palaṭ “vivid, lasting, prevailing”	•ONOM: **EUPH** *pa-la-tum, pa-la-ta-an* → Gelb CAAA 16, 169; Golinets Onomastikon 2 151, 493.
pullaṭ “rescue, deliverance” (?)	•ONOM: **EUPH** Cf. *bu-la-tum, bu-la-da-tum* → Gelb CAAA 16, 120.

|p-l-θ|	Sem.: *plš* (Hb. Hitp.) “to roll about in mourning”.
plθt “humiliation”	•CTX: **UGA** → DUL 662: *pl̠tt*.

\|p-l-y\|
See \|**p-l-l/y**\| **(2)**

|p-n| See |**p-n-w/y**|	Primary noun, Sem.: *pnym* (*pānîm*, Hb. pl.) “front, face”; *pnm* (Ph. pl.), *pn* (Pun. pl. cstr.), *pny* (Moab. pl. cstr.) “front, face”; *panu(m)* (Akk.) “front”, (pl.) “face”; *fénɛ, fánə* (MSArab.) “face, front”. Denom. and derivatives: *pnh* (Hb. G) “to turn”; *pny* (Aram., Syr.) “to turn, face”; *panû(m), panāʔum, penû* (Akk.) “to face, be ahead, move forward”, *panû(m)* “first, earlier; front”; *fināʔ* (Arab.) “courtyard”; *fnw* (OSArab.) “front of building”, *fnwt* “in front of, in the direction of”.
|**p-n-w/y**| “to turn”	•CTX: **EB** G prefc. *ti-bí-na-ù, i-ba-na, i-ba-na-a* → Fronzaroli ARET 11 153, ARET 13 13, 301; Archi PIHANS 106 104; Rubio PIHANS 106 121; Catagnoti QuSe 29 127, 163, 218. •ONOM: **EUPH** Cf. *i-pa-an-ni-e-lum* → Gelb CAAA 28, 169; Golinets Onomastikon 2 87, 90, 94 fn. 439.
panw/y “front; (pl.) face”	•CTX: **EB** Pl. *ba-na-ù* |panwū|, suff. *ba-na-sa*, du. cstr. *ba-na-a* |panwā|, |panyiSa| → Fronzaroli ARET 11 20, 52, 140f.; Pasquali NABU 2010/60; Catagnoti QuSe 29 116, 218. **EA** Cf. *pa-ni-mu* |panīmū < paniy=humu| → Sivan GAGl 133, 257: “before them”; Rainey CAT 1 168, 175; 3 1, with question mark; diff. Moran AmL 241f. with fn. 3: “before him”; cf. Izre’el Orient 38 76ff. •LL: **EB** IGI.DUB(UM!) = *ba-nu ù* → Archi NABU 1988/77; Catagnoti QuSe 29 17, 61, 108, 218; Bonechi / Catagnoti Fs. Sommerfeld / Krebernik 170.

	•ONOM: **EUPH** *pa-ni-la*, *pa-(an-)ni-ia-tum* → Gelb CAAA 28, 169. **A7** *pa-ni-li* → Wiseman AT 144. **A4** *pa-ni-la* → Wiseman AT 144; Gelb CAAA 28, 169; Sivan GAGl 257. **UGS** *pa-ni-ya-nu* → Gröndahl PTU 173; Sivan GAGl 257.
pnm "face, countenance"	•CTX: **UGA** Pl.t. *pnm*, cstr. *pn*, suff. *pny*, *pnk*, *pnh*, *pnnh*, *pnwh*, *pnm* → DUL 664f.

|p-n-n|	Sem. etym. unc. Cf. *pnh* (*pinnāh*, Hb.) "corner".
pinn "button, stud (ornament)"	•CTX: **Q** *pí-in-nu*, suff. *pi-in-ni-šu-nu* → Bottéro RA 44 120; AHw 864: *pinnu*; CAD P 384: *pinnu*.
pnt "knuckle, joint, vertebra"	•CTX: **UGA** Pl. cstr. *pnt*, suff. *pnth* → DUL 665f.; Kogan Classification 302f.

|p-n-w/y| See **|p-n|**	Sem.: *pnh* (Hb. D) "to clear away, remove"; *faniya* (Arab.) "to pass by, dwindle away"; *fannawa* (Eth.) "to send".
|p-n-y| "to be removed" (?)	•CTX: **UGA** Cf. Dpass. prefc. *tpnn* → Tropper UG 568, 670 (cf. 579). Altern. cf. DUL 655: /*p-n-n*/ "to distort; to change". For a probl. frozen G imp. *pn* |pniy| see below: *pn*.[396]
pn "don't!; stop it!"	•CTX: **UGA** G imp. *pn* (frozen form) → Tropper UG 663, 790 fn., 913. Altern. cf. DUL 663: negative functor of intent "lest".

|p-n-y| See **|p-n-w/y|**	

|p-r|	Culture word, Sem.: *pyl(?)* (Aram., Syr.) "elephant"; *pīru(m)*, *pīlu*, *pēru* (Akk.) "elephant"; *fīl* (Arab.) "elephant"; *falfal* (Eth.) "water buffalo, elephant".
pīr "elephant"	•LL: **UGS** [GUL = *pīru* (?) = *pí-i-ri* = *pí-rù*; [UR] = *mit*[*ḫ*]*āri*[*š* = *piri* (?)] = *pí-ru* → Huehnergard ^{2}UVST 384, 397.

|p-r-ʔ| (1)	Primary noun, Sem.: *prʔ* (*pereʔ*, Hb.) "wild ass"; *parû(m)* (Akk.) "mule, hinny; *faraʔ*, *farāʔ* (Arab.) "wild ass, onager". Non-Sem.: **far*= (Omotic) "horse"; **farar*= (Saho-Afar) "horse"; **faraw*= (East Cushitic) "zebra".[397]
pār "an equid, wild ass"	•CTX: **EUPH** *pa-ar*, *pa-ra* → Talon ARM 24 6; George CUSAS 34 98f. •ONOM: **UGS** *pa-ri-ia-na* → Gröndahl PTU 174.
parʔ "an equid, wild ass"	•ONOM: **EB** *bar-i* → Pagan ARES 3 228, 291. **EM** *pa-ar-ú* → Pruzsinszky PTEm 92 [663]. **EG** Cf. *pꜣ-r-y* → Schneider APÄQ 108 no. 232.
parāʔ "an equid"	•ONOM: **EM** *pa-ra-i* → Pruzsinszky PTEm 92 [663].
prů "an equid, mule"	•ONOM: **UGA** *bn prỉ* → DUL 667: *prů*.

|p-r-ʔ| (2)	Sem.: *parāʔu(m)*, *parāḫu* (Akk.) "to cut off, slice through"; *farā* (Arab.) "to split lengthwise, cut lengthwise, chop".

[396] For the form *tpnn* in KTU 1.96:5,6 see Tropper UG 678: mng unc.

[397] Orel / Stolbova HSED 177 no. 780: **far*= "equid".

|**p-r-ʔ**| "to cut"	•CTX: **EB** D prefc. *du-ba-ra-ù* |tuparraʔū| → Fronzaroli QuSe 13 139.
|p-r-ʔ-r|	Etym. unc.; Sem. cf. *parû*, *parāʔum* (Akk.) "to speak basely"(?), *parû* "base, common", *parrû(m)* "base, common; homosexual lover".
paraʔur "(designation of an) homosexual"	•CTX: **A7** *pa-ra-ú-ra-am* → Lauinger STOBA 277 (rev. 5), 282ff.
|p-r-ʕ| (1)	Sem.: *farʕa* (Arab.) "to overtop, excel, surpass", *fāriʕ* "tall, lofty, towering", *farʕ*, *farʕa*, *fāriʕa* "top, summit"; *tftrʕ* (OSArab.)" summit"; see also *prʕ* (*peraʕ*, Hb.) "leader, prince" (?).
prʕ (A) "first fruit, early fruit"	•CTX: **UGA** Sg. / pl. cstr. *prʕ*, suff. *prʕm* → DUL 668: *prʕ* (I).
prʕ (B) "first"	•CTX: **UGA** → DUL 668: *prʕ* (II).
prʕt "height, peak"	•CTX: **UGA** Pl. fem. *prʕt* → DUL 668: *prʕt*.
|p-r-ʕ| (2)	Sem.: *prʕ* (Hb.) "to let free"; cf. *faraġa* (Arab.) "to finish, terminate", *farraġa*, *ʔafraġ* "to empty, void".
|**p-r-ʕ**| "to let free, to wash"	•CTX: **UGA** Gt prefc. *tptrʕ* → DUL 668: */p-r-ʕ/*.
|p-r-d| (1)	Primary noun, Sem.: *prd* (*pered*, Hb.) "mule", *prdh* (*pirdāh*) "female mule"; *prd(?)* (JAram.) "mule"; *perdum*, *pirdum*, *merdu* (Akk.) "an equid". Non-Sem.: **par(V)d=* (East Cushitic) "horse".[398]
perd "mount"	•ONOM: **EB** Cf. PI(*pi?*)-*ru₁₂-dum* → Pagan ARES 3 357: |biʔrutum|(?) "well".[399]
prd "mule"	•CTX: **UGA** → DUL 688. •ONOM: **UGA** Cf. unc. *prd* → DUL 668 *prd* (II); *prdy* → DUL 669; *prdny* → 669.
|p-r-d| (2)	Sem.: *prd* (Hb. N) "to be scattered, separated, (C) "to separate"; *prd* (JAram., Syr.) "to flee, go away", (D, C) "to put to flight, separate"; *farada* (Arab.) "to be single, sole", *ʔafrada* "to separate"; *frdm* (OSArab.) "sole, unique"; *farada* (Eth.) "to separate". See further: *parādu*(m) (Akk.) "to be fearful, disturbed".
|**p-r-d**| "to separate, decide; to detail (troops)"	•CTX: **EUPH** G imp. *pí-ir-dám* → Durand NABU 1988/68. **Late.**[400] •ONOM: **EUPH** *ip-ru-du* → Gelb CAAA 28, 171; Golinets Onomastikon 2 30, 113, 428f. **UGA** Cf. unc.*prd* → DUL 668: *prd* (II); *prdy* → DUL 669; *prdny* → DUL 669.

[398] Orel / Stolbova HSED 420 no. 1961: **parVd=* "equid".
[399] For a possible PN *Perdum* in OBab.-Ebla (written with PI= and WA=) see Kupper NABU 2001/82.
[400] For the form *ip-par-du-ma* (AHw 827: *parādu* II) see CAD P 144: *parādu* II and read probl. *ip-par-<ši->du-ma*; cf. *naparšudu(m)* "to escape, to flee", AHw 735; CAD N/1 283ff.

|b-r-d| “to divide, separate”	•CTX: **UGA** G / D prefc. *ybrd* → Tropper UG 137; DUL 233. •ONOM: **UGA** Cf. unc. *brdd* → DUL 233; *brdn* → DUL 234.
|p-r-γ-θ|	Culture word, Sem.: *prʕš* (*parʕoš*, Hb.) “flea”; *pwrtʕn(ʔ)*, *pwrṭʕnʔ* (Syr.) id.; *peršaʔum, perʔašum, pa/eršaʔu, puruʔzu* (Akk.) id; *burġūṯ* (Arab.) id. Non-Sem.: **burġuč=* (West Chadic) “mosquito”; *mV=bVrguč=* (Central Chadic) “louse”.[401]
puryaθ “flea”	•LL: **EB** *bur-ḫa-sum* → Catagnoti QuSe 29 28, 220 (Pettinato MEE 4 386 VE 0042: *bur-ḫa-šúm*).
puryuθ “flea”	•LL: **UGS** (?) Cf. [UH̬] =*pur-ḫu-šu* = *ta-me* (Sum.-Akk.-Hurr.) → André-Salvini / Salvini SCCNH 10 434; Golinets BuB 9 74. •ONOM: **EUPH** Cf. *pu-ur-ḫu-ša-nu* → Golinets BuB 9 74.
pryθ “flea”	•ONOM: **UGA** *prġṯ* → DUL 669.
|p-r-x|	Primary noun, Sem.: *prḥ* (*peraḥ*, Hb.) “bud, blossom”, *prḥ(ʔ)* (JAram.) “flower”; *perʔu(m), perḫu, parʔum, perwu* (Akk.) “bud, shoot”; *farḫ* (Arab.) “shoot, sprout”. Denom.: *prḥ* (Hb. C / G?) “to sprout, shoot; to cause to sprout, bring into bloom”; *parāʔu* (Akk.) “to sprout”, cf. *parāḫu* “to ferment”; *farraḫa, ʔafraḫa* (Arab.) “to germinate, sprout”; *farḫa* (Eth.) “to sprout, germinate”. Non-Sem.: for Eg. *prḫ* “flower”[402] see below.
|p-r-x | “to blossom, sprout, unfurl”	•CTX: **EG** *p-r-ḫu/i* |paraxa| (?) → Hoch SWET 118f. no. 151.[403]
pirx “blossom, sprout, shoot”	•CTX: **EG** *p-r-ḫ, p-r-ḫu* |pirḫa| → Hoch SWET 119f. no. 152. **EUPH** Cf. *pí-ir-ḫi-*ᵈEN.ZU → Dossin ARM 13 7.[404] **EA** Cf. UD(*pir?*)*-ḫi* → Kühne AOAT 19 17 fn. 84; Hess APN 123f.; Izre’el JAOS 116 271. **EG** *p-ḫi-r* (metath.) → Hoch SWET 120 no. 152.
prx “blossom, sprout, shoot”	•CTX: **UGA** → DUL 669: *prḫ* (I). •ONOM: **UGA** → DUL 669: *prḫ* (II); see also *prḫn* → DUL 669: PN?.
|p-r-k|	Sem.: *prk* (*perek*, Hb.) “violence, slavery”; *prk* (JAram.) “to crumble, crush, rub”, *prk(ʔ)* (JAram.) “refutation”, *prk* (Syr.) “cruel”; *parāku(m), parāḫu* (Akk.) “to lie across, obstruct”, *parku(m)* “transverse, lying across”; *faraka* (Arab.) “to rub”, *firk* “hate, hatred”.
|p-r-k| “to rub, crumble” (?)	•ONOM: **EUPH** Cf. unc. *ma-ab/p-ra-kam* → Zadok Fs. Hallo 328. **EG** Cf. unc. *pꜣ-rw-k-ꜣ* → Schneider APÄQ 110f. no. 236.
park “false(hood), wrong(fulness)”	•LL: **EB** NÌ.SA.RUM = *ba-ra-gúm, ba-la-gúm* → Conti QuSe 17 40, 78.

[401] Orel / Stolbova HSED 84 no. 345: **burġuč=* “insect”.
[402] Cf. Orel / Stolbova HSED 425 no. 1984: **piraḫ=* “sprout, flower”.
[403] Sivan / Cochavi-Rainey WSVES 79: *pa-r-ḫu* “flower”; Helck Beziehungen no. 75.
[404] For OBab. *pirḫum* in PNN see vSoldt JEOL 25 46; CAD P 418f.: *pirʔu* 2.d.

|p-r-k-k|	Culture word, Sem.: *prk(?)* (Syr.) "altar, shrine"; *parakku(m)* (Akk.) "cult dais, sanctuary". Non-Sem.: barag (Hellen. Sum.) "dais".
pirikk "a symbol or (movable ?) cultic installation"	•CTX: **EUPH** *pí-i-ik-ki, pí-ri-ik-ki-im, pí-ri-ik-ka-am* → CAD P 397: *pirikku* A: mng unkn.; vSoden Or 56, 103; Durand, MARI 6 298 fn. c; Feliu Dagan 133f; Streck AOAT 303 36 fn. 18.

|p-r-ḳ| (1)	Culture word, Sem. etym. unc.: Cf. *paraqqu* (Nuzi-Akk.) "a sack" (?).[405]
prḳt "a kind of cloth (container) or fabric"	•CTX: **UGA** Sg. / pl. *prqt* → DUL 670: *prqt*.

|p-r-ḳ| (2)	Sem: *prq* (Hb.) "to tear away, off, to drag away"; *prq* (Aram., Nab., Syr.) "to cut off, loosen, separate, redeem, rescue"; *parāqu* (Akk.; see below: |p-r-ḳ| Late); *faraqa* (Arab.) "to make a separation, split"; *frq* (OSArab.) "to save"; *faraqa* (Eth.) "to save, redeem, divide, separate". Non-Sem.: **park*= < **paVḳ* (West Chadic) "to rip and remove"; **parwak*= (East Chadic) "to tear, pluck feathers".[406]
|**p-r-ḳ**| "to release, slacken, unknit; to segregate"	•CTX: **UGA** G prefc. *yprq* → DUL 670: */p-r-q/*. **Late** G precative *lip-ra-aq* → CAD P 161: *parāqu*. •ONOM: **EUPH** *pa-ri-qì* → Zadok Fs. Hallo 328.
|p-r(-l-n)|	Loanword; **p/wur*= (Hurr.) "to look, see", *wurullini* "seer, diviner".[407]
purulin "seer, diviner"	•CTX: **EM** *pu-ru-li, pu-ru-li-na* (Hurr.) → Trémouille ChS I/8 322; Richter BGH 327. •LL: **UGS** [ḪAL = *ba-ru*]-*ú*(?) = *pu-ru-li-ni* = *pu-r*[*u-li-nu*] → vSoldt UF 21 365ff., BiOr 47 732; Huehnergard ^{2}UVST 397.
prln "seer, diviner"	•CTX: **UGA** → DUL 669f.; Richter BGH 536.

|p-r-r| (1)	Primary noun, Sem.: *pr* (*par*, Hb.) "bull, steer", *prh* (*pārāh*) "cow"; *prh, prt?* (JAram., Syr.) "ewe-lamb"; *parru* (Akk.) "(male) lamb", *parratu* "she lamb"; *farīr, farūr, furār* (Arab.) "lamb, young sheep"; see further *fʔr, fʕr* (MSArab. bases) "young bull". Non-Sem.: *pry* (Eg.) "bull-fight"; **par*= (Central Chadic) "cattle".[408]
pr (A) "young bull, bullock"	•CTX: **UGA** Sg. *pr*, du. *prm* → DUL 667: *pr* (II). •ONOM: **UGA** *prqdš* → DUL 670.
parr, part, parrat "weaned, weanling"	•CTX: **EB** Cf. *ì-la-bar, ba-ra, ìr-si/šè-bar-ru*$_{12}$, *ma-ba-ru*$_{12}$ → Pagan ARES 3 228, 290, 328, 339, 347. **EUPH** Cf. *pa*(?)-*ar-re*.ḪI.A, fem. *pa-ar-tum, pa-ra-tum*, pl. *pa-ar-ru-tu*, fem. *pa-ar-ra-tu* → Gelb CAAA 169 (PA?R); Durand NABU 1991/30; MARI 8 667; Charpin / Durand FM 2 36:8.

---

405 CAD P 153: *parakku* B.

406 Orel / Stolbova HSED 420 no. 1958: **paroḳ*= "to tear, rip".

407 See vSoldt UF 21 365ff.; Richter BGH 325f., 327.

408 Orel / Stolbova HSED 418 no. 1950: **par*= "cattle".

prt "heifer"	•CTX: **UGA** Sg. *prt*, pl. *prt* → DUL 673: *prt* (I). •ONOM: **UGA** Cf. unc. *prt* → DUL 673: *prt* (II).

|p-r-r| (2)	Sem.: *prr* (Hb. C) "to break, destroy"; *prr* (JAram. C) "to annul (a vow)"; *parāru(m)* (Akk.) "to be dissolved, broken up", (D) "to disperse, scatter, shatter"; *farra* (Arab.) "to flee", *ʔafarra* "to put to flight", *ʔiftarra* "to open up or part"; *frr, farra* (Eth.) "to shell, husk". Non-Sem.: **fVr=* (Berber) "to thresh, be threshed"; **par=* (West Chadic) "to smash; break into pieces".[409]
|p-r-r| "to be dissolved, confused; to break away, split"	•CTX: **EB** Gt prefc. *a-ba-da-ra-ar* |la=yiptarar|, *nab-da-ra-ar* |naptarar| → Fronzaroli ARET 13 110, 286; Catagnoti / Fronzaroli ARET 16 147, 210; Catagnoti QuSe 29 25, 31, 53, 129, 143, 218. **UGA** G prefc. *åpr* → Tropper UG 451, 674; DUL 670f.: */p-r(-r)/*. •ONOM: **EG** Cf. unc. *pꜣ-r-y* → Schneider APÄQ 108f. no. 232.

|p-r-s| (1)	Culture word, Sem. etym. unc.: Cf. *parīsu(m)* (Akk.) "picket, plank, pole, rib".
prs (A) "a part of a chariot"	•CTX: **UGA** → DUL 671: *prs* (I).

|p-r-s| (2)	Culture word, Sem.:[410] *prs* (Hb., Ph., Aram.) "half a measure"; *prys* (Aram.) "small dry measure"; *parīsu(m)* (Akk.) "a measure of capacity: half '*kurru*'".[411] Non-Sem.: *parissi* (*PA-RI-SI*, *PA-RI-IŠ-SI*, Hitt.); *parizzade* (Hurr.).[412]
parīs "a dry measure"	•CTX: **EB** *ba-rí-zu*, *ba-rí-zú* → Milano MARI 5 528f., ARET 9 379f.; Pomponio ARET 15/2 407. **EUPH**: *pa-ri-si* → Lafont ARM 26/2 537 (545:6, 9); CAD P 186: *parīsu* B 1.a. **A7** (GIŠ) *pa-ri-si* → Giacumakis AkkAl 94; CAD P 186: *parīsu* B 1.b.
prs (B), prS "a dry measure"	•CTX: **UGA** *prś*, *prs* → Tropper UG 47; DUL 671f.; *prś/s*.

|p-r-s| (3)	Sem.: *prs* (Hb.) "to break"; *prs* (Ph.) "portion"; *prs* (JAram., Syr.) "to divide, distribute", *prs(ʔ)* "allotment, salary"; *prs* (Ph.) "portion"; *parāsu(m)* (Akk.) "to cut (off), decide", *paras* "fraction", *purussû(m)*, *purussāʔum* "decision"; *farasa* (Arab.) "to kill, tear (a prey)"; *mfrs*^{3}*t* (OSArab.) "weir, boundary wall"; *ferōs* (MSArab.) "to eat carrion"; *farasa* (Eth.) "to be demolished, destroyed". See further: *prš* (Hb.) "to give a clear decision"; *prš* Aram., Syr., Nab. "to separate, specify, distinguish". Non-Sem.: **pirVs=* (East Chadic) "to crush (grain)"; **pVrVc=* (Central Chadic) "to grind"; **firis=* (Agaw) "to be destroyed"; **fVrVʒ*.[413]

[409] Orel / Stolbova HSED 418 no. 1951: **par=* "to break, thresh".

[410] Seemingly a PaRĪS theme derived from |p-r-s| (3); probl. lexicalization of Syrian origin.

[411] Durand MARI 6 43; Lafont Fs. Garelli 278f.; Westenholz Emar Tablets XIV.

[412] CAD P 186: *parīsu* B 1.d; Richter BGH 301.

[413] Orel / Stolbova HSED 425 no. 1986.: **piric=* "to break, grind"; 433 no. 2027: **pVriʒ=* "to cut, separate".

|p-r-s| "to separate, cut off, decide"	•CTX: **EB** G suffc. *ba-rí-zu* → Fronzaroli ARET 13 185f., 250; Catagnoti QuSe 29 22, 47, 125, 218. •LL: **EB** KA.TAR = *bù-ra-zu-um*; *na-ša-gúm/gú-um wa bur-ra-zu-um*; SAG.DÙ.BAD.BAD = *bur-zu-um* → Krebernik ZA 73 8 (195), 12 (258). •ONOM: **EB** *ib-lu$_5$-zú*,[414] *ib-da-ra-zu* → Pagan ARES 3 155, 330, 332.[415] **EUPH** *ia-ap-ru-us-a-bi* → Gelb CAAA 28, 171; Zadok Fs. Hallo 328 (*ia-ap-ru-uṣ-a-bi*); Golinets Onomastikon 2 113, 429. **EG** Cf. unc. *pꜣ-:r-sꜣ*, *t-ꜣ-p-w2-r-sꜣ* → Schneider APÄQ 110 no. 235, 233 no. 496. **UGA** Cf. unc. *prs* → DUL 671: *prs* (III), *prsn* → DUL 672.
pirs (A) "division, section (of troops, workers)"	•CTX: **EUPH** Passim KUD (KU$_5$); see *pí-ir-si-im*, *pí-ir-sà-am* → AHw 855: *pe/irsu*(*m*); CAD P 411: *pirsu* A; Soubeyran ARM 23 378 fn. b.
pirs (B) "a piece of fabric, cut"	•CTX: **EUPH** *pí-ir-su* → Durand ARM 30 85.
purs "weaning"	•CTX: **EUPH** *pu-ur-si-im* → Durand, MARI 7 52 fn. 47.
pirsēn "weaned animal"	•CTX: **EB** *bir$_5$-zi-núm* → Fronzaroli Lalies 26 11; Catagnoti QuSe 29 28, 123, 219.
paras "laceration" (?)	•CTX: **EG** Cf. unc. *pa$_2$-r-ṯi* → Hoch SWET 122f. no. 155.[416]
purrus "determined, decided"	•ONOM: **EUPH** Fem. *pu-ru-za-tum* → Gelb CAAA 28, 172; Zadok Fs. Hallo 328 (read *pu-ru-ṣa-tum*); Golinets Onomastikon 2 203, 429.
prz "decision, verdict" (?)	•CTX: **UGA** → DUL 674 (Hurr. ctx.).
purāsa "decision" (?)	•ONOM: **EB** Cf. unc. *bù-ra-za* → Pagan ARES 3 155, 294.
mapras "a cutting or splitting tool"	•LL: **EB** TÙN.BAR = *ma-ba-ra-zu-um*; UŠ.URUDU = *ma-ba-la-zu-um* → Krebernik ZA 73 29 (760); Conti QuSe 17 186f.

|p-r-s-ḫ|	Sem.: *napalsuḫu*(*m*), *naparsuḫu* (Akk.) "to fall to the ground"; see also *faršaḥ/ḫa* (Arab.) "to straddle".
|p-r-s-ḫ| "to collapse"	•CTX: **UGA** G prefc. *yprsḥ* → Tropper UG 539, 681; DUL 672: *prsḥ*.

|p-r-s-y|	Culture word, Sem.: *pursītu*(*m*), *pursû* (Akk.) "a bowl". Non-Sem.: burzi (Sum.) "a bowl".
prst "a bowl" (?)	•CTX: **UGA** Sg. / Pl. *prst* → DUL 672.

---

414 |yiplus=u| "he looked over"; altern. |yiprus=u| "he decided" (|p-r-s|); see Pagan ARES 3 155, 332.

415 |yiprus=| "he decided"; altern. |yiplus=| "he looked over"(|p-l-s|).

416 Sivan / Cochavi-Rainey WSVES 80: *pá-ra-śì* "to break(?)"; Helck Beziehungen no. 76.

|p-r-ṣ|	Sem.: *prṣ* (Hb.) "to break through", *prṣ* (*pereṣ*) "breach, gap"; *prṣ* (JAram.) "to make a breach", *prṣ(ʔ)* "hole, gap"; *parāṣu(m)* (Akk.) "to breach", *pe/irṣu(m)* "breach"; *faraṣa* (Arab.) "to cut, pierce", *furṣa* "opportunity, chance"; *faraṣa* (Eth.) "to break open, cut open, split". See also: *faraḍa* (Arab.) "to make an incision, to notch", *furḍa* "notch, nick", *prṭ* (Aram., Syr.) "to split, separate"; *farraṭa* (Arab.) "to abandon, desert, separate from". Non-Sem.: **pVrVç=* (Central Chadic) "to cut, break through".[417]
prṣ "breach, opening"	•CTX: **UGA** Sg. *prṣ*; pl. *prṣm* → DUL 672.

|p-r-s^2|	Sem.: *prŠ* (*prś* Hb.) "to spread out, stretch over"; *prs* (Palm.) "to extend (oneself)"; *faraša* (Arab.), "to spread"; *parāsu* (Akk. Dt) "to spread out"; *ferōś*, *fóróś* (MSArab.) "to spread". See further *rapāšu(m)* (Akk.) "to expand"; *naprušu(m)* "to fly".
|**p-r-s^1**| "to extend, apply a coat of a material, resurface"	•CTX: **UGA** G suffc. *pršả*, N prefc. *tprš* → DUL: 672f. */p-r-š/*.
parS "spreading (of the wings?)"	•LL: **EB** Cf. KIŠI$_6$ = *la-ma-núm bar-su-um*; cf. GÍR.MUŠEN = *šu-ga-ga-pù-um bar-su-um* → Fronzaroli QuSe 13 138, 144, 150; Krebernik ZA 73 39 (0205). Cf. Pettinato MEE 4 386 fn. r. I 8 for the rdg *x bar-su-um* (008).

|p-r-θ|	Sem.: *prt* (Syr. G) "to pierce", (D) "to tear apart". See also *prš* (Hb. C) "to sting"(?).[418]
|**p-r-θ**| "to split open, tear a portion" (?)	•CTX: **EG** Cf. *pa-r-ša, pa-r-šu, p-r-š-{t}* |paraθa| ? → Hoch SWET 120 no. 153. •ONOM: **UGA** Unc. *prṯ* → DUL 673.
prθt "a piece or portion (of meat)" (?)	•CTX: **UGA** → Diff. DUL 674: "secret" (?, Akk. *pirištu*).

|p-r(-w/y)| (1)	Sem.: *prh/ʔ* (Hb.) "to bear fruit", *pry* (*p^{e}rî*) "fruit"; *pr* (Ph.), *pry* (Pun.) "fruit"; *pry* (JAram., Syr.) "to be fruitful", *pyr(ʔ)* "fruit"; *farya, faraya* (Eth.) "to bear fruit", *fəre* "fruit". Non-Sem.: *prt* (Eg.) "fruit, crop, seed"; **fir=* (Agaw, Saho-Afar, East Cushitic) "fruit; corn, flowers".[419]
pr (B) "fruit"	•CTX: **UGA** → Tropper UG 192; DUL 667: *pr* (I).
purūwat "harvesting"	•CTX: **EB** *bù-lu-wa-da-sa-nu* → Fronzaroli ARET 13 108, 250; Catagnoti QuSe 29 78, 118 fn. 458, 220.

|p-r-y| (1)
See **|p-r(-w/y)| (1)**

---

[417] Orel / Stolbova HSED 420 no. 1959: **paruṣ=* "to cut, break through".
[418] See HALOT 976f.: *prš* hif. for Pr 23:32.
[419] Orel / Stolbova HSED 424 no. 1983: **pir=* "fruit, corn".

|p-r-y| (2)	Sem.: *parû, parāʔum* (Akk.) "to speak basely; to abuse"; *farā, ʔiftarā* (Arab.) "to invent lyingly, fabricate".
|p-r-y| "to be mendacious, base"	•CTX: **EB** D suffc. *ba-ru*$_{12}$*-a* |parruy=| → Fronzaroli ARET 13 199, 250; Catagnoti QuSe 29 124, 165, 219.

|p-r-z|	Sem.: Cf. *prz* (*pārāz / perez*, Hb.) "leader, warrior"; *faraza, ʔafraza* (Arab.) "to set apart, select, distinguish", *farz* "selection", *firz* (pl. *ʔafrāz, furūz*) "special portion or share".
pirz "champion, warrior"	•LL: **EB** Á.ZI.DA = *bir*$_5$*-zú* → Conti QuSe 17 152; Catagnoti QuSe 29 24, 219.

|p-s-ḫ|	Sem.: *psḥ* (Hb.) "to be lame, limp", *psḥ* (*pisseḥ*) "limping"; *pessû, passûm* (Akk.) "lame, limping".
psḫn "lame, limp"	•ONOM: **UGA** → DUL 674.

|p-s-x|	Sem.: Cf. *fasaḫa* (Arab.) "to straddle, dislocate, break up", *fasḫ* "dislocation", *fāsiḫ* "annulling, bringing to an end".
|p-s-x| "to break up, counteract" (?)	•CTX: **EUPH** Cf. *i*[*p-p*]*a-ás-si-ḫa-a*[*m*] → Birot ARM 14 103:21; AHW 838, 1582: *pasāḫu*(*m*) "vertreiben"?; CAD P 216: *pasāḫu*, mng unc.; cf. Durand LAPO 16 396 fn. 1.[420]
napsuxt "sudden attack, counteraction" (?)	•CTX: **EUPH** Cf. *na-ap-sú-uḫ-ti-ia* → Durand FM 8 150ff. (43:42).

|p-s-l|	Sem.: *psl* (Hb.) "to hew, cut straight", *psl* (*pesel*), *psyl* (*pāsîl*) "(divine) image"; *pslt* (Pun.) "hewn stone", *psl* (Aram., Syr.) "to cut, hew stone", *pslh* (Aram.) "hewn stone", *pswl*(*ʔ*) (Syr.) "stone-cutter"; *psl* (Nab., Palm.) "to sculpt", (Nab.) *pslʔ* "sculptor".
psl "engraver"	•CTX: **UGA** Sg. *psl*, pl. *pslm* → DUL 675; Del Olmo AuOr 37 289.
pasīlān "a peculiar pot shape"	•CTX: **UGS** Cf. DUG.SAG *pa-si*(?)*-la-nu* → Huehnergard UVST 168f.
pslt "sculpture"	•CTX: **UGA** → DUL 674f.: *pslt* (II).[421]

|p-s-m|	Loanword, Sem.: Cf. *pusmu, pussu* (Akk.) "a garment or a part thereof", *pasāmu*(*m*) "to cover", (D) "to veil", *pusummu, puṣunnu* "veil", *pusunnu* "veiled".
pusm "a garment (veil ?) or a part thereof (sleeve(s))" (?)	•LL: **MŠ** *pu-us-mu* (var. *pu-us-su*) = MIN (É *a-ḫi*) → Hrůša MŠ 132, 417.

[420] Wrong reference to Hb. *psʕ* (sic!) "marcher, s'avancer", and to the "Pass-over", "marche terrible de Dieu".

[421] For the unc. mng "braid, plait" (du. *psltm* ?) see DUL 674: *pslt* (I).

psm "a garment (veil ?) or a part thereof (sleeve(s))" (?)	•CTX: **UGA** Sg. (?) *psm* → DUL 675.
|p-s-s|	Sem: *pasāsu(m)* (Akk.) "to erase, delete"; *fašša* (Arab.) "to go down, subside".
|p-s-s| "to erase, delete"	•ONOM: **EG** Cf. *pꜣ-ṯ-w$_2$-ṯꜣ* SḎ.NḪT → Schneider APÄQ 123f. no. 264.
|p-ṣ-y|	Sem.: *pṣh* (Hb.) "to open (the mouth wide)"; *pṣy* (JAram., Syr. D, C) "to save"; *faṣā* (*faṣy*, Arab.) "to separate, take out", *fāšā* "to free oneself".
|p-ṣ-y| "to open, free"	•ONOM: **EG** Cf. *pꜣ-ḏꜣ-y-ꜣ* → Schneider APÄQ 124 no. 266.
|p-s^1-ʕ|	Sem.: *pšʕ* (Hb.) "to break with", *pšʕ* (*pešaʕ*) "crime, criminal action"; *pšʕ* (JAram., Syr.) "to act incorrectly; to be frightened"; *pšʕ(ʔ)* (JAram.) "sin".
ps^{1}ʕ "rebellion, transgression"	•CTX: **UGA** → DUL 675: *pšʕ*.
|p-s^1-ħ|	Sem.: *pšḥ* (Syr.) "to cease"; *pašāḫu(m)* (Akk.) "to be at rest, become tranquil", *tapšaḫu* "resting place"; *fasuḥa* (Arab.) "to be(come) wide, roomy". Probl. related: *fšḥ*, *tafaśśəḥa* (Eth.) "to rejoice, be glad".
paSaħ "tranquil" **tbθx** "bed"	•ONOM: **EB** *ba-sa-ḫu* → Pagan ARES 3 155, 290. •CTX: **UGA** (Akk. loan) → DUL 846: *tbṯḫ*; Del Olmo AuOr 37 290.
|p-s^1-ḳ|	Sem.:. *pšq* (Syr.) "to be easy", *pšyq* "easy"; *pašāqu(m)* (Akk.) "to be narrow, to be difficult", *pašqu* "narrow", *pušqu(m)* "narrowness".
|p-S-ḳ| "to be meagre, suffer difficulties"	•CTX: **EB** G prefc. *ib-da-su-gu* |yiptaSḳū|, *dib-ti-sa-ag* |tiptiSaḳ| (< |taptaSaḳ|) → Fronzaroli ARET 13 185, 267; Rubio PIHANS 106 122; Catagnoti QuSe 29 219.
puSḳ "hardship, need, necessity"	•CTX: **EB** *bù-su-gu*, *bù-su-ga* → Catagnoti / Fronzaroli ARET 16 46, 223; Catagnoti QuSe 29 115, 122, 220. •ONOM: **EB** Cf. *bù-su/si-gi*, *bù-uš-gi*, *a-bù-uš*!(*ìr*)-*gu*, *a-bù-su/uš-gú*, *a-a-bù-uš-gu/gú*, *du-bù-uš-bù-su-gú* → Pagan ARES 3 155, 273, 275, 294, 302.
|p-s^1-l|	Sem.: Cf. *pašālu(m)* (Akk.) "to crawl".
tps^{1}lt "oppression" (?)	•CTX: **UGA** Sg. cstr. *tpšlt* → DUL 862: *tpšlt*.
|p-s^1-ṭ|	Sem.: *pšṭ* (Hb.) "to spread out, take off clothes"; *pšṭ* (JAram., Syr.) "to extend, straighten";. *pašāṭu(m)* (Akk.) "to erase, cancel, revoke"; *basaṭa* (Arab.) "to spread out, extend", *bašṭ* "stretching, extension".

|p-S-ṭ| "to expand, widen, spread"	•LL: **EB** SAḪAR.GAR = *ba-sa-tum* → Pettinato MEE 4 314 (151); Sjöberg Fs. Kienast 538; diff. Conti QuSe 17 88; Catagnoti QuSe 29 19, 219: "cancellare".
pas^{1}ṭ "stretching, extension" (?)	•ONOM: **EUPH** Cf. *pa-aš-ṭi-ia* → Zadok Fs. Hallo 328.
pus^{1}s^{1}uṭ "discomfort" (?)	•LL: **EM** […] = *ni-is-sà-tum : pu-šu-uṭ-ṭú*(!) → Cohen Proceedings 53e RAI 1 825.

|p-s^2-ḳ|	Sem.: Cf. *pŠq* (*pśq*, Hb.) "to separate (lips), (C) "to open wide (legs)".
|p-s^2-ḳ| "open wide, cut, cleave"	•ONOM: **EUPH (OBab. Nippur)** Cf. *pa-zi-ga-ni-im* → Stone SAOC 44 273; Zadok Fs. Hallo 328.

|p-t-ħ|	Sem.: *ptḥ* (Hb.) "to open (up)", *ptḥ* (*petaḥ*) "opening, entrance"; *ptḥ* (Ph., Pun., Nab., Palm.) "to open", *ptḥ* (Ph., Pun.) "door, gateway"; *ptḥ* (Aram., Syr.) "to open", *ptḥ* (Aram., Syr.) "opening, gate", *mptḥ*(*ʔ*) (Aram.) "key"; *petûm*(*m*), *patû*, *patāʔum* (Akk.), *pītu*(*m*) "opening, aperture", *naptû* "key, opening device", *mupattītu* "opener (implement)"; *fataḥa* (Arab.) "to open", *fatḥ*, *futḥa* "opening", *miftāḥ* "key"; *fatḥa* (Eth.) "to open, loosen", *fətḥat* "opening", *maftəḥ* "key". Non-Sem.: **pVtVH*= (Central Chadic) "to open (eyes, anus)"; **pit*= (East Chadic) "to open".[422]
|p-t-ħ| "to open"	•CTX: **EB** N prefc. *i-ba-ti-ʔà-am₆* |yippatiħ=am|, D prefc. *du-ba-da-i* |tupattaħ=ī| → Fronzaroli ARET 9 163, ARET 13 15, 267 (with rdg *i-ba-ti-ʔà-an*); Catagnoti QuSe 29 135, 141, 157, 219. **UGA** G prefc. *tptḥ*, *yptḥ*, suffc. *ptḥ*, impv. *ptḥ*; Gpass. ptc. *ptḥ*; N prefc. *yptḥ* → DUL 675f.: /p-t-ḥ/. •LL: **EB** GIŠ.GÁL.TAKAx = *ba-da-um* → Pettinato MEE 331 (VE 1241'); Alberti BaE 65ff.; Krecher BaE 142. •ONOM: **EB** *ib-da-u₄/₉*, *ib-te-da-mu*, *dab₆-da-u₉* → Pagan ARES 3 155f., 300, 330, 332. **EUPH** *ia-ap-ta-ḫu*(*-um*), *ḫa-am-mu-pa-ta-a*; cf. unc. *me-ep-tu-um*, *me-ep-tu-ú*(*-um*), *mi-ip-ti-i*/*im* → Huffmon APNMT 255f.; Gelb CAAA 28, 169, 171; Golinets Onomastikon 2 58, 76, 113, 134, 147, 429f.[423] **A4** *ia-ap-ta-ḫu* → Gelb CAAA 28, 171; Sivan GAGl 259 (probl. not to PTʕ "surprise"); Arnaud AuOr 16 175. **EA** *ia-ab-ti-iḫ-*^{d}IM; *ia-ab-ti-ḫa-da* → Sivan GAGl 259;[424] Hess APN 86, 210; Rainey CAT 2 69; Golinets Onomastikon 2 67 fn. 263. **UGA** *yptḥ* → Bordreuil / Pardee RSOu 18 130 (KTU 4.868:6; DUL vacat); *yptḥd* → DUL 960.
pitH "spacer bead in a necklace"	•CTX: **EUPH** *pí-tu-šu*, *pí-tu-ša*, *pí-tu-šu-nu* → Dalley JSS 39 295; Arkhipov ARM 22 89f.: *pitûm*.

422 Orel / Stolbova HSED 425f. no. 1989: **pitaḥ*= "to open".

423 For *ip-ti-ia-mu-ta* (Gelb CAAA 171: \|yi=ptiħ=ya=mwut=a\|) see Golinets Onomastikon 2 282f. with fn. 883.

424 Both the altern. proposals by Sivan GAGl 212: BṬḤ "to trust" and 259: PTʕ "to surprise" are unlikely.

pitħ "opening"	•CTX: **EUPH** *pí-it-ḫa-t*[*um*] → Zadok Fs. Hallo 328. **EM** *pí-it-ḫa* → Zadok AION 51 118; Pentiuc Vocabulary 140f. •ONOM: **EUPH** *pi-it-ḫa-tim* → Yamada Proceedings 54e RAI 594 (Al-Rafidan TabT06-4:6). **UGS** Cf. BI-ID-*ḫa-na* → Sivan GAGl 212, 258f.: PITʕU "suddenness", PITḪU "entrance"; Gröndahl PTU vacat.
pātiħ "kind of chest with lock"	•CTX: **EUPH** KUŠ *pa-ti-ḫa-tum* → Durand ARM 30 179.
pitiħ "open"	•CTX: **EB** Fem. *bí*-[*ti-tum*] |pitiħt= | (< |patiħt=|) → Catagnoti QuSe 29 52, 121, 156, 219.
pātiħ "opener"	•ONOM: **EUPH** *pa-te-e-im*, *pa-te-ḫu-um*; fem. *pa-te-ḫa*, *pa-te/ti-ḫa-tum* → Gelb CAAA 28, 169; Zadok Fs. 328; Golinets Onomastikon 2 134, 136, 429f.
ptħ "entrance, door"	•CTX: **UGA** Sg. *ptḫ*, suff. *ptḫy*, du. *ptḫm* → DUL 676: *ptḫ*.
pitaħt "opening"	•CTX: **EB** *bí*(NE)-*da-ʔà-tum* → Pasquali NABU 2016/58
mupattiħ "opener"	•ONOM: **EUPH** *mu-pa-ti-yu-um*; cf. *mu-pa-*(*at-*)*ti-ia/tum* → Huffmon APNMT 255f.; Gelb CAAA 28, 169; Golinets Onomastikon 2 200, 429f., 506, 511.
mptħ "key"	•CTX: **UGA** → DUL 559: *mptḫ*.
|p-t-x|	Sem.: Cf. *patāḫu*(*m*) (Akk.) "to pierce, bore through", *pitḫu* "perforation".
tbtx "skewer, skewered meat" (?)	•CTX: **UGA** → DUL 846: *tbtḫ*.
|p-t-n|	Sem.: *ptnʔ* (Syr.) "tumult"; *patānu*(*m*) (Akk.) "to become strong, strengthen"; *fatana* (Arab.) "to tempt, charm, captivate, fascinate"; *fetōn*, *ftun* (MSArab.) "to cause trouble"; *fatana* (Eth.) "to try, test".
|p-t-n| "to prove to be strong / to strengthen" (?)	•ONOM: **EUPH** *ì-lí-ap-ta-an*, DINGIR-*ap-tan*, *ap-tu-na-nu-um*, *ia-ap-tu-na*, *ia-ap-tu-na-an*, *ia-ap-tu-na-*ᵈ*da-gan*, *ia-ap-tu-un*-DINGIR, *ip-ta-an* → Gelb CAAA 28, 171; Golinets Onomastikon 2 31f., 78, 81ff., 85, 113f., 430f., 491. **A7** *tap-ta-na-a-da*, *tap-tu-na-a-da* → Wiseman AT 149; Gelb CAAA 28, 171; Golinets Onomastikon 2 122f., 430f. **A4** *tap-da-na-ta* → Gelb CAAA 28, 171; Golinets Onomastikon 2 122f., 430f.
|p-t-t|	Sem.: *ptt* (Hb.) "to crumble"; *ptt* (JAram, Syr.) "to break off"; *pt*(*ʔ*), *pth*, *pttʔ* "piece of bread"; *fatta*, *fattata* (Arab.) "to crumble", *futāt* "piece, bit"; *ftt*, *fatta*, *fatata*, *fattata* (Eth.) "to break off a piece, fracture, crush", *fəttat* "piece, fragment".
patat "hunk, chunk (of bread)"	•LL: **EB** NINDA.TAR = *pá-tá-tum* → Sjöberg Fs. Renger 518.
|p-t-y|	Sem.: *pth* (Hb. D) "to persuade"; *pty* (JAram. D) "to entice", (Syr. C) "to expand, propagate"; *fatawa*, *fatwa* (Eth.) "to desire".
|p-t-y| "to seduce"	•CTX: **UGA** G prefc. *ypt* → DUL 676: /*p-t*(*-y*)/.

|p-ṭ-r|	Sem.: *pṭr* (Hb.) "to escape, to let go, let flow", *pṭr* (*peṭer*), *pṭrh* (*piṭrāh*) "first-born"; *pṭr* (Aram.) "to free, release, let go", *pṭyr* (JAram.) "pure, clear"; *pṭr* (Syr.) "to be separated, cease", *pṭr(?)* "fool"; *paṭāru(m)* (Akk.) "lo loosen, release", *paṭru* "released", *piṭru(m)* "release", *napṭaru(m)* "acquaintance, guest friend"; *faṭara* (Arab.) "to split, break apart, make, create", *faṭr* "crack, fisure", *fiṭr* "fast breaking", *faṭīr* "fresh, new"; *feṭōr* (MSArab.) "to break one's fast"; *faṭara* (Eth.) "to create, produce, make incisions on the flesh".
|p-ṭ-r| "to solve, redeem; to leave, desert (intrans. armies, etc.)"	•CTX: **EB** G prefc. *dib-da-ru*$_{12}$, *ni-i[b]-da-r[u*$_{12}$*]* → Fronzaroli ARET 13 108, 251; Archi PIHANS 106 104; Catagnoti QuSe 29 22, 129f., 219. **EUPH** Passim intrans. → CAD P 296: *paṭāru*, 9.a.1'; Durand LAPO 17 411ff. **EA** Passim intrans → CAD P 296: *paṭāru*, 9.a.1.a': also RS-Akk., Alalakh (OBab., MBab.). **UGS** N suffc. *na-ap-ṭa-ru* |napṭar=ū| → Huehnergard UVST 167, 397. See also: *napṭar*, below. •LL: **EB** NÍG.TUR.DU$_{11}$.GA = *ba-da-ru*$_{12}$, *ba-da-lum*, *ba-da-lu-um* → Conti QuSe 17 77; Catagnoti QuSe 29 20, 219. •ONOM: **EB** *dab*$_6$*-du-lu/lum*, *dab*$_6$*-dur-*^{d}UTU; see also DU$_8$?(GABA)-*da-mu*, DU$_8$?(GABA)-*li-im* → Pagan ARES 3 156, 300, 304. **EUPH** *ia-ap-tu-ur*, *ia-ap-tu-ri*, *ia-ap-tu-rum*, *ia-ap-tu-ru-um*, *ia-ap-tu-(ur-)ra-yi/yu*[425] → Gelb CAAA 28, 171; Golinets Onomastikon 2 114, 431, 494. **UGA** *pṭry* → DUL 677.
|p-θ-r| "to free, loosen"	•CTX: **UGA** G suffc. *pẓr*, inf. *pẓr* → DUL 679f.: */p-ẓ-r/*.
paṭr "release"	•ONOM: **EUPH** *ba-aṭ-ri-ia* → Streck Onomastikon 1 197 § 2.95.
piṭr "release"	•LL: **UGS** DU$_8$ = *pa-ṭá-[r]u* = *zu-lu-du-me* = *pí-iṭ-r[ù?]* → Sivan GAGl 259; Huehnergard UVST 95, 167; vSoldt SAU 306 (118); Tropper UG 485.
puṭr "release"	•ONOM: **EUPH** *an-nu-pu-uṭ-ri* → Streck Onomastikon 1 325 § 5.15.
paṭar "released"	•ONOM: **EUPH** *ba-da-ra-nu-um*, *pa-at-ta-rum* → Gelb CAAA 28, 170; Golinets Onomastikon 2 142,155, 493.
pāṭir "redeemer; deserter, off-duty soldier"	•CTX: **EUPH** Passim *pa-ṭe*$_4$*-ru*, var. spellings → vSoden Or 21 76; Sasson MilitEstabl 47; Durand LAPO 17 411ff.; Villard ARM 23 494f., 562; Charpin ARM 26/2 77 fn. i; CAD P 304: *pāṭiru*. •ONOM: **EUPH** *ba-di/ti-ru-um*, *pa-ti-rum* → Gelb CAAA 28, 170; Streck Onomastikon 1 197 § 2.95; Golinets Onomastikon 2 134, 431.
paṭur "redeemed" (?)	•ONOM: **EB** *ba-du-rí/rúm* → Pagan ARES 3 156, 289.
pṭr "breach, aperture"	•CTX: **UGA** → DUL 677.
bṭr "emancipated, free, deserted" (?)	•CTX: **UGA** → Tropper UG 139; DUL 249.
napṭar "exchange, ransom" (?)	•CTX: **UGS** *na-ap-ṭá-:ra* → Tropper UG 541; Huehnergard UVST 167.
napṭart "desertion"	•CTX: **EUPH** *na-ap-ṭà-ar-tum* → Kupper ARMT 6 50f. (60:32); Durand LAPO 17 183f. fn. i; cf. CAD P N/1 324: *napṭartu* B.[426]

[425] For the wrong rdg *ia-ap-di-rum* (Gelb CAAA 28, 171: PTIR) see now Golinets Onomastikon 2 54 fn. 199.

[426] Wrong text citation in CAD; see Kupper loc.cit.

|p-θ| Culture word, Sem.: *pšt* (*pēšet*, Hb.), “flax, linen”, *pšth* (*pištāh*) “flax, wick”; *pšt* (Ph., Pun.) “flax”.
Non-Sem.: *psšt* (Eg.) “mat”; **pič=* (West Chadic) “shroud”; **pVč* (East Chadic) “apron”.[427]

pθt (A) “flax; linen (fabric)” •CTX: **UGA** Sg. *p<u>t</u>t*, pl. *p<u>t</u>tm*, du. *p<u>t</u>tm* → DUL 677f.: *p<u>t</u>t* (I).

|p-θ-θ| Sem.: *pašāšu*(*m*) (Akk.) “to anoint”, *piššatu*(*m*) “ointment”.
Non-Sem.: **pwaĉi=* (West Chadic) “anoint, scatter”.[428]

|p-θ-θ| “to anoint” •CTX: **EM** D suffc. *pa-aš-šu-uš* → Westenholz Emar Tablets 13, 16.
•LL: **EB** ŠU.Ì = *ba-ša-šu-um*, *ba-ša-sum*; *bí-sum* (see below: *piθθ*) → Krebernik ZA 73 18; Conti QuSe 17 143f.; cf. Sjöberg ZA 88 250f. fn. 29.

piθθ “ointment” •LL: **EB** ŠU.Ì = *bí-sum* (verbal noun? See above |*p-θ-θ*|) → Krebernik ZA 73 18; Conti QuSe 17 143f.

piθθat “ointment spoon” •CTX: **EA** (Tušratta’s letter EA 25 II 43–51) *pí-iš-ša-tu*$_4$ → Adler AOAT 201 187, 313.

pθt (B) “ointment box” •CTX: **UGA** → DUL 678: *p<u>t</u>t* (II).

|p-θ̣-ɣ| Sem.: *pṣʕ* (Hb.) “to break into pieces”; (JAram.) “to split”. See further: *faḍaġa* (Arab.) “to break, crush”.

pθ̣γ “lacerator” •CTX: **UGA** Pl. *pẓġm* → Tropper UG 93; DUL 679: *pẓġ*.

|p-θ̣-l| Sem. etym. unc. Cf. *pṣl* (Hb.) “to skin, peel away”; (Syr. G) “to split”, (Gt) “to be separated”; *faṣala* (Arab.) “to separate”, *infaṣala* “to part, separate, break away”, *faḍala* (Arab.) “to exceed, surpass”.

|p-θ̣-l| “to overcome, break” (?) •CTX: **UGA** N suffc. *npẓ* → DUL 679: */p-ẓ-l/*.

|p(-w/y)| Primary noun, Sem.: *py*, *ph* (*peh*) Hb. “mouth; word”; *p* (suff. *py*, Ph., Pun.) id.; *pm*, *pwm*(*?*) (Aram., Syr.) id.; *pû*(*m*), *pāʔum*, *pīum* (Akk.) id.; *fa*/*i*/*um* (cstr. *fū*, Arab.), *fūha* id.; *f* (OSArab.) “mouth, voice, command”; *ʔaf* (Eth.) “mouth; word”.

pu(w), pū, pi(y), pī “mouth, word” •CTX: **EA** KA-*pí*, KA *: pí-i* → Gianto SEL 12 68; Rainey CAT 1 36.
•LL: **EB** Cf. SAGxIGI = *pù-wu* → Pettinato BaE 47 (for VE 267); Bonechi / Catagnoti Fs. Sommerfeld / Krebernik 170f., 178.
•ONOM: **EB** Passim; possible writings *bu*, *bù*, *bu*$_{14}$, *bu*$_{16}$, *pú* (LAGABxU, LAGABxÚŠ), *pi*, *bí*; cf. e.g.: *bu*, *bu*-^{d}EN.KI, *bu-gi-a*,; *bù-u*$_9$, *bù-ar*, *bù-da-mu*, *bù*-^{d}*da-gan*, *bù*-^{d}*ra-sa-ap*; *i-bù-bu*$_6$; *bu*$_{14}$*-ba-da*, *bu*$_{14}$*-gú-nu*, *bu*$_{14}$*-ma*, *bu*$_{14}$*-uš*-^{d}EŠ$_4$.DAR; *pú-šu*; *a-da-pi*, *ar*/*àr-pi*, *gú-nu-pi*, *din-pi-àr*, *din-pi-da-mu*, *i-ku-pi*-DINGIR, *pi-su-ga-du*; *ʔa*$_5$*-da-bí*, *gu*$_4$*-da-bí*, *i-bí-bí* → Pagan ARES 3 229, 272

---

[427] Orel / Stolbova HSED 423 no. 1975 **pič=* “cloth”.
[428] Orel / Stolbova HSED 426 no. 1992: **poĉ=* “to smear, scatter”.

276, 287f., 292ff., 295, 315, 323f., 320f., 357; Bonechi MARI 8 505.
U3 *da-dum-pi*$_5$-DINGIR, *i-da-bí*-DINGIR, *pi-a-núm*, *pi*$_5$*-a-nu-um*, *pu-me-il* → Buccellati Amorites 139, 177; Gelb CAAA 28 170.
EUPH Passim; possible writings *bu*, *pu*, *bi*, *pi*, *pí*, *ba*, *pa*; cf. e.g. *pu-ka-*^{d}*da-gan*, *pu-ú-*^{d}*da-gan*, *pu-ma-el*, *pu-um-e-el*, *ḫa-lam-bu-ú*, *a-lum-bu-mu*; *bi-ù*, *pi-i-la*, *bi-ka-ma-el*/DINGIR, *bi-na-aḫ-me-el*, *ia-ḫa-al-pi-lum*, *i-ḫi-il-bi*-DINGIR, *ḫa-a-iš-pí-ú*, *pí-ri-ip-i-im*, *i-ba-al-bi*/*pi-el*/DINGIR, *a-lum-bi-ú-mu*, *ha-lu-um*/*un-bi-ya-mu*, *ia-ḫu-un-pi-el*, *ḫu-un-bi-el*, *a-ru-uš-bi*-DINGIR, *aš-du-um-bi-ia-di-im*, *ia-su-ud-pi-el*, *ḫa-ta-an-bi*-DINGIR, *a-ku-pi-el*, *ḫa-ta-ak-pí-ìl*, *ia-ku-un-pi*, *ia*/*e-ku-bi*/*pi*, *ia-ku-(un-)bi-ia*, *i-ku-un-bi-i*, *ia-qú-ul-pí-*^{d}EN.ZU, *ia-ku-un-bi-*^{d}*ma-ma*, *a-mu-ut-bi-(i-)la*/DINGIR, *na-ap-si-bi*-DINGIR, *ta-aḫ-tu-bi*-DINGIR; *i-la-ba-i*, *pa-i-la*, *pa-(a-)ka-i-la*, *pa-ka*-DINGIR, *a-li*/*lí-pa*-DINGIR, *ḫa-a-li-pa*-DINGIR, *a-lí-pa-*^{d}UTU, *a*/*am-mu-ut-pa*-DINGIR, *mu-ut-pa-na-zi* → Huffmon APNMT 254; Gelb CAAA 28 168f., 170f.; Zadok Fs. Hallo 327; Streck Onomastikon 1 219f. § 2.118 fn. 1, 319 § 5.2, 357 Sup.
A4 *pi-i-la*; cf. DUMU *pu*-PI → Gelb CAAA 28 170; Dietrich / Loretz WO 5 65 9:28; Sivan GAGl 259.
TA *bi-*^{d}IM → Horowitz / Oshima CunCan 143.
EA *pu-ba-áʔ-la*, *pu-*^{d}IM → Sivan GAGl 259; Hess APN 126f., 210.[429]
UGS *pí-ṣí-id-qí*; cf. *il-pí-ya*, *i-li-pí-ya* → Gröndahl PTU 98 (ʔLP I), 170 (P); Sivan GAGl 199 (ʔILPU), 259 (PÛ).

p (B) "mouth, voice"
•CTX: **UGA** Sg. *p*, suff. *py*, *pk*, *ph*, *phm* → DUL 647f.: p (III).
•ONOM: **UGA** *pmlk* → DUL 663.

|p-w|

Sem.: *ph*, *pʔ*, *pw* (*poh*, *poʔ*, *pô*, Hb.) "here"; *PHO* (Pun.) id.

paw "here"
•CTX: **EB** *ba*, *ba-a*, *ba-wa* → Fronzaroli ARET 13 248; Catagnoti / Fronzaroli ARET 16 221; Catagnoti QuSe 29 61, 103f., 219

p (C) "here"
•CTX: **UGA** → DUL 647: *p* (II).

|p-w-d| (1)

Sem.: *fawd* (Arab.) "lock, hair (around the temples)"

pd "lock (of hair)"
•CTX: **UGA** Sg. *pd*; cstr. suff. du. / pl. *pdm* → DUL 651; Watson FO 52 325.

|p-w/y-d| (2), |p-d-d|

Sem.: Cf. *pyd* (*pîd*, Hb.) "disaster, misfortune"; *pwd* (Syr.) "to wander, fade", *pdd* "to vanish, slip away"; *pâdu(m)* (Akk.) "to confine, have someone bound", *pīdu*, *piddu* "imprisonment"; *fāda* (*fawd*, *fayd*, Arab.) "to die, fail", *fāwd* (Eth.) "tribulation. suffering".

|p-w/y-d| "to wear out, consume"
•CTX: **UGA** Dpass. prefc. *ypdd* → Tropper UG 583, 686: |yupādadu|; altern. cf. DUL 651: /*p-d-d*/ (G prefc.).

pdd "worn out" (?)
•CTX: **UGA** Pl. *pddm* → DUL 652.

taptayd, taptīd "putting away, making disappear"
•LL: **EB** NÌ.SIG = *dab-da-tum*, *dab*$_6$*-ti-du* (both |taptay(yi)dum|) → (both < |taptay(yi)dum| → Conti QuSe 17 35, 72; Catagnoti QuSe 29 28, 44, 162, 219.

---

[429] Delete the reading *pu*-AM(for AN?)-IM) in Hess APN 126f.

|p-w-ḳ| See|**n-p-ḳ**|, |**y-p-ḳ**|	Sem.: *pwq* (Hb. C) “to reach, obtain, find; to cause to reach, offer”; *pwq* (Ph. C) “to find, obtain, encounter”.
|**p-w-ḳ**| “to find, obtain, have something at one’s disposal”	•CTX: **UGA** G prefc. *ypq*, *tpq*, suffc. *pq*, inf. *pq*; Gt prefc. *tptq*; C suffc. *špq* → DUL 666f.: /*p-q*/. •ONOM: **UGA** *ypq* → DUL 960.
|p-w-l|	Primary noun, Sem.: *pwl* (*pûl*, Hb.) “bean”; *pwl(?)* (Aram., Syr.) id.; *fūl* (Arab.) id.; *fūl* (Eth.) id.
pūl “bean”	•CTX: **EG** *pu*$_2$*-r*, *pu*$_2$*-r-ya*, *pu*$_2$*-r-ʔa* (pl. |pūla|) → Hoch SWET 118 no. 150.[430]
|p-w(-t)|	Culture word, Sem.: *pwʔh*, *pwtʔ* (JAram., Syr.) “madder”; *fuwwah*, *fuwwa*, *fūwa* (Arab.) “madder”. Non-Sem.: Cf. *puwatti=* (Hitt.) “mark, colour”.[431]
puwwat “madder”	•CTX: **UGS** 1 *li-im* Ú : *pu-wa-ti*, 1 GUN *ḫu-re-tu*$_4$: *pu-wa-tu*$_4$ → Sivan GAGl 260; Huehnergard UVST 166, vSoldt SAU 306 (116), BiOr 47 734, UF 22 347f.[432]
pwt “madder”	•CTX: **UGA** → DUL 678.
|p-w-z|, **|p-z-z|**	Sem.: *fāza* (*fawz*) (Arab.)= “to be victorious”, *fāʔiz* “victorious, winner”, *fawz* “success, victory”. See also *pzz* (Hb.) “to be quickmoving”; *pzz* (Syr.) “to jump”, *pzyz* “rash, impetuous”.
|**p-w-z**| “to be victorious” (?)	•ONOM: **EG** Cf. *p-w*$_2$*-tȝ-y* ^{F}, *p-ṯ-b-ʕ-r*, *p-tȝ-b-ʕ-r* (altern. rdg *p-tȝ-b-r-ʕ*) → Schneider APÄQ 120f. nos. 257ff.
|p(-y)| See| **p(-w/y)**| **(1)**	
|p-y-d| See |**p-w/y-d**| **(2)**, |**p-d-d**|	
|p-z-r|	Sem.: *pazāru(m)* (Akk.) “to be hidden”, (D) “to hide, conceal”. See also *pzr* (Hb.) “to scatter, disperse”; *bdr* (Aram.D) “to disperse, scatter”; *baḏara* (Arab.) “to sow, disseminate”.
|**p-z-r**| “to shelter, hide”	•CTX: **A7** Cf. unc.(barley) *a-na* MUŠEN.ḪI.A *a-na pa-za-ri* → Wiseman JCS 13 26 (262:6).[433] •ONOM: **EG** Cf. *p-t-tȝ-r-y* → Schneider APÄQ 119f. no. 256. **UGA** Unc. *pzry* → Watson AuOr 8 1990 123; DUL 679.

[430] Sivan / Cochavi-Rainey WSVES 79: *pu-l*; Helck Beziehungen no. 74; Kilani VGW 119: |p'i/ur(yv)|.
[431] Lexicographically equated with Sum. ŠE.BE.DA and Akk. *ŠI-IN-DU* (*šimtu*) “mark”. For a discussion see Gzella BiOr 64 554; Kloekhorst EDHIL 685; Watson UF 42 837.
[432] Unrelated: *puati* or *puwati* (EA 14:74); see Moran AmL 35 fn. 20 (from Eg. *b/puati* “bracelet”).
[433] Cf. Sivan GAGl 260: G suffc. / noun?, PZR “scatter”.

pazr (A) "shelter, protection"	•ONOM: **EUPH** Cf. *pa-az-ri* → Gelb CAAA 28, 170.
pazr (B) "hub" (?)	•CTX: **EUPH** Cf. GIŠ *pa-az-ru*/ri, GIŠ *pa-az-ri-tim* → Durand LAPO 16 265f. fn. a, ARM 26/1 581; Arkhipov ARM 22 160f.[434]
puzr "shelter, protection"	•ONOM: **EB** Cf. passim logogr. PUZUR$_4$(pù-zur$_8$(ŠA))=; see e.g. PUZUR$_4^{ru12}$, PUZUR$_4$.RA, PUZUR$_4^{ru12}$-*um* PUZUR$_4$-*a-ḫu*, PUZUR$_4$.RA-*a-ḫu*, PUZUR$_4$-*ḫa-lu*/*al*$_6$, PUZUR$_4$.RA-*ḫa-al*$_6$, PUZUR$_4$-*il*, PUZUR$_4$.RA-*il*, PUZUR$_4$-^{d}EŠ$_4$.DAR, PUZUR^4.RA-^{d}EŠ$_4$.DAR, PUZUR$_4$.RA-*a-ba*$_4$, PUZUR$_4$-*ma-lik*, PUZUR$_4$.RA-*ma-lik* → Catagnoti QuSe 15 261; Pagan ARES 156f., 357f.[435] **EUPH** *bu-zu-ra-an*, PUZUR$_4$-*a-na* → Gelb CAAA 28, 172.
pazir "sheltered, placed under cover" (?)	•CTX: **A4** ANŠE.KUR.RA *pa-zi-ru* → AHw 852; diff. CAD P 313: mng unkn. •ONOM: **UGS** Cf. *pa-zi-ra*, BA-*zi-ra-na* → DUL 679: *pzry*.
puzar "sheltered, kept safe"	•ONOM: **EUPH** *bu-za-ru-um* → Gelb CAAA 28, 172.

|p-z-z|
See **|p-w-z|**, **|p-z-z|**

[434] AHw 836: *pasru*(*m*) "eine Stange"?, CAD P 224: *pasru* B "a wooden item".
[435] All probl. Akk. writings; cf. Gelb MAD 3 220f. (PÙ.ŠA=).

r

|r-ʔ-b|	See **|r-y-b|**
|r-ʔ-d|	
|r-ʔ-m| (1)	
|r-ʔ-m| (2)	
|r-ʔ-s^1|	
|r-ʔ-y|	
|r-ʕ|	
|r-ʕ-y| (1)	
|r-ʕ-y| (2)	See **|r-ʕ|**
|r-b-ʕ|	
|r-b-b| (1),	Cf. **|r-p-ʔ|**, **|r-y-b|**
|r-b-y|	
|r-b-b| (2)	
|r-b-d	
|r-b-k|	
|r-b-ḳ|	See **|r-p-ḳ|**
|r-b-ś|	
|r-b-θ|	
|r-b-y|	See **|r-b-b| (1)**
|r-D-B|	
|r-d-d|	
|r-d-m| (1)	
|r-d-m| (2)	
|r-d-y|	
|r-ð-l|	
|r-ð-y|	
|r-g-b|	
|r-g-l|	
|r-g-m|	
|r-γ-b|	
|r-γ-m|	Cf. **|r-m-m| (2)**
|r-γ-θ|	
|r-γ-w|	
|r-h-b|	See **|r-w-b| (2)**
|r-h-ṭ|	
|r-ħ|	
|r-ħ-b|	Cf. **|r-y-b|**
|r-ħ-ḳ|	
|r-ħ-l|	
|r-ħ-m|	
|r-ħ-ṣ|	Cf. **|r-w-θ̣|**
|r-ħ-s^1|	
|r-ħ-s^2|	Cf. **|r-s-ħ|**
|r-ħ-ś|	

|r-ħ-y|	
|r-x-l|	
|r-x-p|	
|r-x-ṣ|	
|r-x-θ|	See **|m-r-x-S|**
|r-x-w|	
|r-x-y|	
|r-k-b|	
|r-k-k|	
|r-k-n|	
|r-k-S|	
|r-k-s^1|	
|r-ḳ-d|	Cf. **|r-ḳ-ṣ|**
|r-ḳ-ħ|	
|r-ḳ-ḳ| (1)	
|r-ḳ-ḳ| (2)	
|r-ḳ-ṣ|	Cf. **|r-ḳ-d|**
|r-m-ħ|	
|r-m-k|	
|r-m-m| (1)	
|r-m-m| (2)	Cf. **|r-γ-m|**
|r-m-S|	See **|r-p-s|**
|r-m-ś|	
|r-m-θ|	
|r-m-y|	
|r-n-n|	
|r-p-ʔ|	
|r-p-d| (1)	
|r-p-d| (2)	
|r-p-ḳ|	See **|r-b-ḳ|**
|r-p-s|	See **|r-m-S|**
|r-p-s^1|	
|r-p-y|	
|r-s-ħ|	Cf. **|r-ħ-s^2|**, **|r-s-s|**
|r-S-p|	
|r-s-s|	Cf. **|r-s-ħ|**
|r-S-t|	
|r-S-y|	Cf. **|w-r-θ|**
|r-ṣ-ʕ|	
|r-s^1-ʕ|	
|r-s^1-p|	See **|r-S-p|**
|r-s^1-y|	
|r-ś-y|	
|r-t-ḳ|	

|r-ṭ-b|
|r-w-ʕ|
|r-w-b| (1)
|r-w-b| (2)
|r-w-ḥ|
|r-w/y-m|
|r-w/y-ṣ̌|
|r-w-θ|
|r-w-θ̣| Cf. |r-ḥ-ṣ|
|r-w-y|

|r-y-b| Cf. |r-b-b/y|, |r-ḥ-b|
|r-y-ḳ|
|r-y-m| See |r-w/y-m|
|r-y-ṣ̌| See |r-w/y-ṣ̌|
|r-y-ṭ|
|r-z-H|
|r-z-ḥ| See |m-r-z-ḥ|
|r-z-m|

|r-ʔ-b|

See |**r-y-b**|

|r-ʔ-d|

Etym. unc. Cf. *urīdum* (Mari-Akk.) "a vessel" and / or DN.[436]

rỉdn "a large cup / DN" (?) — •CTX: **UGA** → DUL 712: *rỉdn* (I, II).

|r-ʔ-m| (1)

Primary noun, Sem.: *rʔm*, *rym* (*r*^{e}*ʔēm*, *rêm* Hb.) "*bos primigenius*, wild bull"; *rym*, *rymʔ* (JAram.) "buffalo, aurochs", (Syr.) "unicorn"; *rīmu*(*m*), *rēmu* (Akk.) "wild bull", *rīmtu*(*m*) "wild cow"; *riʔm* (Arab.) "white antelope, addax"; *rəʔim*, *rəʔem* (Eth.) "wild bull, rhinoceros, unicorn".

riʔm (A) "wild bull, buffalo" — •LL: **MŠ** *ri-iʔ-mu* = *ri-i-mu* (V 49) → Hrůša MŠ 112, 399.[437]
•ONOM: **EB** Cf. *rí-ma*, *rí-ma-dum*,[438] ^{d}*da-gan-li-im*, *li-ma-*$^{(d)}$*da-gan* → Pagan ARES 3 231, 297, 346, 359.[439]

rủm "wild bull, buffalo" — •CTX: **UGA** Sg. *rủm*, pl. *rủmm* → DUL 712.[440]

rỉmt "bull-headed harp" — •CTX: **UGA** → Watson 2019/24; cf. DUL 712f.: "zither" (as the 'loved' object).

riʔnt (A) "wild cow" — •ONOM: **EB** Cf. *rí-in-du* → Pagan ARES 3 231, 359.[441]

---

[436] AHw 1429; CAD U/W 222. Cf. Guichard ARM 31 326ff., Semitica 59 36f. (M.9028:14; A.3325:6) "Uridu" (a protective genie); Arkhipov ARM 32 394.

[437] For Mari *riḫmum* see now Arkhipov ARM 32 91 ("un objet précieux"; diff. "a zoomorphic figurine" according to Zadok Fs. Hallo 328; and see Hrůša MŠ 254. Diff. Golinets BuB 9 66.

[438] Probl. hypocorism.

[439] Alternatively the instances could belong to the etymon |r-ʔ-m| (2), perhaps also to |l-ʔ-m| (1). Cf. Stamm ANG 259; Gelb MAD 231; Pagan ARES 3 161.

[440] For the wrong rdg *ru-ʔ*(?)*-mu* (Ug 5 97:6; Gröndahl PTU 178; Sivan GAGl 265) correct *šub-ʔa-mu* (see Huehnergard AkkUg 394).

[441] See the previous fn. to *riʔm* (A) (ONOM: EB) and below under |r-ʔ-m| (2).

|r-ʔ-m| (2)

Sem.: *râmu(m), raʔāmu(m), ramāmu* (Akk.) “to love”, *râmu(m), raʔāmu, rīmātum* “love”, *rîmtu(m), rîntum* (fem.) “beloved”, *raʔūmtu(m), ruʔūmtu, rûmtu, rûntu, rûmatu* (fem.) “beloved”, *rāʔimānu* “one who loves”; *raʔima* (Arab.) “to love tenderly”.

|r-ʔ-m| “to love” — •LL: **EB** MÍ.DU$_{15}$.GA = *ra-a-mu-um, la-a-mu-mu* → Krebernik ZA 73 11; Fronzaroli StEb 7 179, Fronzaroli QuSe 13 148; Conti QuSe 17 103f.; Catagnoti QuSe 29 20, 41, 221.
•ONOM: **EB** *dar-am$_{6}$-ma-lik, ìr-a-mu, íl-am$_{6}$-da-si-in, ìr-am$_{6}$-a-ḫir*(KEŠDA), *ìr-am$_{6}$-a-ḫu, ìr-am$_{6}$-na-gàr, ìr-am$_{6}$-sar*, and passim elem. *ìr-am$_{6}$*= with DNN → Krebernik PET 48; Catagnoti QuSe 15 261; Pagan ARES 3 161, 300, 337f.

rāʔim “lover” — •ONOM: **EB** *wa-da/ad-ra-im, wa-da-la-ì-mu* → Pagan ARES 3 161, 375.

riʔm (B) “love” — •ONOM: **EB** Cf. *rí-ma, rí-ma-dum,*[442] ^{d}*da-gan-li-im, li-ma-*$^{(d)}$*da-gan* → Pagan ARES 3 231, 297, 346, 359.[443]

riʔnt (B) “love” — •ONOM: **EB** *rí-in-du* → Pagan ARES 3 231, 359.[444]

|r-ʔ-s¹|

Primary noun, Sem.: *rʔš* (*roʔš*, Hb.) “head (summit, top (quality), chief, principal, individual, etc.)”, *rʔš(w)n* (*riʔšōn*) “first”, *rʔšyt* (*rēʔšît*) “beginning; the first and best”; *rʔš* (Ph., Pun., Moab., Nab.), *rš* (Palm.) “head”, etc., *rʔšt* (Ph.) “the choicest; first fruit”; *rʔš, ryš(ʔ)* (Aram., Syr.) “head” etc., *ryšw(tʔ), ryšy(tʔ)* (Syr.) “beginning”; *rēšu(m), rāšu(m)* (Akk.) “head”, etc., *rēštu(m)* “beginning, point, prime”, *rēštû(m)* “first, pre-eminent”; *raʔs* (Arab.) “head”, etc.; *rʔš* (OSArab.) “head”, etc.; *ḥə-rōh, ḥérih, réś, riy* (MSArab.) “head”, etc.; *rəʔ(ə)s* (Eth.) “head”, etc., denom. *rəsa, raʔasa* “to be(come) chief”.

|r-ʔ-s¹| “to toss the head” (?) — •CTX: **UGA** G prefc. *yrả̆š* → DUL 713 /*r-ʔ-š*/.

rāS, raʔs¹ “head, chief; detachment” — •CTX: **EUPH** *ra-si-im* → AHw 959: *rāsum*; Durand LAPO 17 466 fn. a; CAD R 183: mng unc.
•ONOM: **EUPH** Cf. *ma-a-ra-su-um* → Gelb CAAA 29, 175.
EM *ra-aḫ-ša* → Pruzsinszky PN PTEm 176 [691].[445]

rīS, riʔs¹ “head, chief” — •LL: **EB** SAG.KI.TÚM = *rí-še$_{6}$* KI.TÚM → Krebernik ZA 72 197f. (*še$_{6}$*), 73 46. See also Conti Problemi e metodi 6 fn. 21; Sjöberg Fs. Kienast 562 fn 52.
•ONOM: **EA** Cf. ÌR-*ri-ša* → Hess APN 16f., 211.

rōs¹ “head; summit” — •CTX: **EA** *ru-šu-nu* → CAD R 432: *rūšu* C; Sivan GAGl 30, 128, 265; Rainey CAT 1 85f., 92, 174.
EG metath. *ru$_{2}$-ša-ʔu* → Hoch SWET 209f. no. 285.[446]
•ONOM: **EG** *ru$_{2}$-sa; ru$_{2}$-ʔu$_{3}$-ša* → Hoch SWET 209f. no. 285.

ris̊¹ “head, chief, top, first(fruit)” — •CTX: **UGA** Sg. *ris̊*, suff. *ris̊k, ris̊h, ris̊hm*, pl. *ris̊t, rås̊t, rås̊m* → DUL 713f.: *ris̊*.
•ONOM: **UGA** *ris̊n* → DUL 715.[447]

rủs¹ “disease of the head” (?) — •CTX: **UGA** → DUL 715: *rủš*.

ris̊¹yt “beginning, primordial time” — •CTX: **UGA** → DUL 715: *ris̊yt*.

---

442 Probl. hypocorism.
443 Alternatively the instances could belong to the etymon |r-ʔ-m| (1), perhaps also to |l-ʔ-m| (1). Cf. Stamm ANG 259; Gelb MAD 231; Pagan ARES 3 231.
444 See the previous fn. to *riʔm* (B) (ONOM: EB) and above under |r-ʔ-m| (1).
445 For *ra-se-ia* (PTEm 176 fn. 271 [696]) see below: |r-s¹-y|.
446 Sivan / Chochavi-Rainey WSVES 83: *rú-ša-ʔu* “summit”; Helck Beziehungen no. 151.
447 Cf. the Ug. TN *raʔšu, riš*, and the GN SAG-*yu, rišy* (Belmonte RGTC 12/231f.; DUL 714: *riš* (II), 715: *rišy*. Note also the (EUPH) TN *ra-i-su*, Groneberg RGTC 3 194f.; Zadok WO 14 239.

|r-ʔ-y|	Sem.: *rʔh* (Hb.) “to see”, *mrʔh* (*marʔeh, marʔāh*) “seeing, appearance; vision”; *rʔy* (Pun., Moab.) “to see”; *rhy* (Syr.) “to observe”; *raʔā* (*raʔy*, Arab.) “to see”, *marʔiy* “seen, visible”, *mirʔāh, mirāya* “looking glass”; *rʔy* (OSArab.) “to see; to experience”; *rəʔya* (Eth.) “to see”, *mərʔāy* “sight”.
|**r-ʔ-y**| “to see”	•CTX: **UGA** Unc. G suffc. / imp. *rả* → Tropper UG 617; DUL 712: *rả* “?”. •ONOM: **EUPH** Cf. *ia-ar-i-i*[*l*(…) → Zadok Fs. Hallo 328. **UGA** Unc. *riʕbd* → DUL 712; *rảy* → DUL 715.
mirʔūt “seeing” (?)	•CTX: **EA** *a-na mi-ru-ti : ú-pu-ti* (EA 151:20) → AHw 658: *mirûtu*; CAD M/2 110: *mirûtu*; Sivan GAGl 248; Rainey EAC 1502 (discussion).

|r-ʕ|	Primary noun, Sem.: *rʕ* (*rēᵃʕ*, Hb.), extended by-form: *rʕy*, *rēʕeh*, Hb.) “friend, companion”, fem. *rʕh* (pl. cstr. *rēʕôt=, raʕyot=*) “companion, friend”, denom. *rʕh* (G) “to get involved, mixed up with”, (C) “to join oneself to”; *rʕ* (Aram.) “friend, companion”; *rūʔu(m), rûm, rūʔa* (Akk.; exceptionally: *rāʔum*) “friend, companion”, fem. *rūtum, ruttu(m), ruʔtu* “companion, associate”, denom. *râʔu* “to befriend”. Cf. *raʕawa* (Eth.) “to yoke, join”.
raʕ “friend, companion”	•LL: **EB** KU.LI = *la-ú-um* → Krebernik ZA 73 38. •ONOM: **EB** *ra-ù, la-ù, lá-ù-um, ra-ù-dum,*[448] *i-bí-la,*[449] *ì-lum-la, ì-la-la, kùn*(KUM)*-la, ne-ti-la/ra-ì, ʔa*$_5$*-za-ra-ù, ì-za-ra-ù, i-ga-la-um* → Krebernik PET 104; Pagan ARES 3 231, 272, 320, 322, 328f., 330, 344f., 355, 358.
reʕ “friend, companion”	•ONOM: **U3** *i-bi-iq-ri-e-ú, lú-ri-é-ú, lú-ri-ḫu* → Buccellati Amorites 16, 154, 166; Gelb CAAA 30, 178 (RIʕAJ).
rʕ “friend, companion”	•CTX: **UGA** Sg. suff. *rʕy, rʕh*, pl. (?) *rʕm*, suff. *rʕh* → DUL 715: *rʕ*. •ONOM: **UGA** Cf. unc. *rʕy* → DUL 716: *rʕy* (II).[450]

|r-ʕ-y| (1)	Sem.: *rʕh* (Hb.) “to feed; to (drive out to) pasture”, *rʕh* (*roʕeh*) “shepherd”, *mrʕh* (*mirʕeh*), *mrʕyt* (*marʕît*) “pasturage; *rʕm* (pl. Ph.) “shepherds”; *rʕy* (Aram., Syr., Palm.) “to feed, to graze”, *rʕy(ʔ)* “shepherd”, *mrʕy(tʔ), mrʕh, mrʕʔ* (JAram., Syr.) “pasture, meadow”; *reʔû(m)* (Akk.) “to pasture, shepherd, tend”, *rēʔītu(m)* “shepherd”, *mērītu(m)* “pasture”; *raʕā* (*raʕy*, Arab.) “to graze; to tend”, *rāʕin* “shepherd”, *marʕan* “grazing land, pasture”; *rʕy* (OSArab.) “to graze”, *rʕy* “shepherd”, *mrʕt* “pasture”; *rō(h), reʕe* (MSArab.) “to herd livestock”, *rēʕi, rewēʕi* “herdsman”; *rəʕya* (Eth.) “to graze; to herd, tend”, *raʕāyi* “shepherd”, *marʕet* “pasture”. Non-Sem. Cf. **ʔa=riʔ=* (Lowland East Cushitic) “to chase”.[451]
|r-ʕ-y| “to pasture, to graze”	•CTX: **EB** C prefc. u_9*-šar*$_x$(NE)*-ì* |yus¹arʕi| → Krebernik QuSe 18 75, 83, 144. •ONOM: **EUPH** Cf. *ya-ri-a-du, ia-ar-ḫi-*DINGIR → Gelb CAAA 29, 174, Zadok WO 14 236.
rāʕiy “shepherd”	•ONOM: **EUPH** Cf. *ra-ḫa-tum, ra-ḫa-an-nu-um,* DINGIR*-ra-ḫi-ia, i-la-ra-ḫi-a/e,* DINGIR*-ra-ḫi-e,* DINGIR*-ra-ḫa-a, ì-lí-ra-aḫ-e, ku-ul-pa-ra-ḫi-e* → Huffmon APNMT 260f.; Gelb CAAA 29, 174f. (RAWḤ); Zadok WO 14 236; Streck Onomastikon 1 352 § 5.79.
rʕy “shepherd”	•CTX: **UGA** Pl. abs. *rʕym*, du. cstr. *rʕy* → DUL 716: *rʕy* (I). •ONOM: **UGA** Cf. unc. *rʕy* → DUL 716: *rʕy* (II).[452]

---

[448] Probl. hypocorism.

[449] \|yibbiʔ=raʕ\| “the friend called”; altern. \|yibbiʔ=laʔ(ī)\| “the powerful one called”, Pagan ARES 3 136f.; see \|l-ʔ-w/y\| (1)\|.

[450] See also under \|r-ʕ-y\|, below.

[451] Orel / Stolbova HSED 449 no. 2115: **riʕ=* “to drive, chase”.

mrʕ "pasture land"	•CTX: **UGA** sg. / pl. suff. *mrʕh* → DUL 565. •ONOM: **UGA** *mrʕm* → DUL 565.
merʕuy "supervisor of the royal pasturage"	•CTX: **EUPH** Passim; e.g. LÚ.MEŠ *me-er-ḫu-ú* → AHw 646: *merḫum, merḫūtum*; CAD M/1 26: *merḫu, merḫūtu* "office of the *m.*"; see Marzal Sefarad 36 221ff.; JNES 30 194ff.; Finet Akkadica 26 6ff.; Safren Or 51 21ff.; Sasson JESHO 20 102 fn. 29; Durand Amurru 3 160ff.; ARM 26/1 225 fn. d (86:11); Streck Onomastikon 1 105f. •ONOM: **U3** Cf. *me-ra-aḫ-*[d]*šul-gi* → Gelb MAD 3 182. **EUPH** *me-er-ḫu-um* → Gelb CAAA 25, 155 (MRḪ); Zadok Fs. Hallo 328.
marʕayt "pasture land"	•LL: **EB** Ú.ŠIM(! ŠIMxNÌ) = *mar-a-tum* → Conti QuSe 17 113.

|r-ʕ-y| (2)

See |r-ʕ|

|r-b-ʕ|

Sem.: *ʔrbʕ* (*ʔarbaʕ*, Hb.) "four", fem. *ʔrbʕh* (*ʔarbāʕāh*) pl. *ʔrbʕym* (*ʔarbāʕîm*) "forty", *rbʕ* (*rebaʕ*, *robaʕ*) "fourth part, a quarter", *rbyʕy* "fourth", denom. *rbʕ* "to square"; *ʔrbʕ* (Ph., Pun., Nab., Palm.) "four", fem. *ʔrbʕʔ*, *ʔrbʕtʔ* (Palm.), pl. *ʔrbʕm* (Pun.), *ʔrbʕyn* (Nab., Palm.) "forty", *ʔrbʕy* (Pun.) "fourth", *rbʕ* (Ph., Pun., Palm., Nab.) "quarter"; *ʔrbʕ* (Aram., Syr.) "four", pl. *ʔrbʕyn* "forty", (Aram., Syr.) *rbʕ(ʔ* "quarter"; *arbaʔu(m)*, *erbe*, *arbe*, *rabbi* (Akk.) "four", *erbâ* "forty", *rebû(m)*, *rabû*, *rubû* "fourth"; *ʔarbaʕ* (Arab.) "four", pl. *ʔarbaʕūn* "forty", *rābiʕ* "fourth", *rubʕ*, *rabīʕ* "quarter", denom. *rabaʕa* "to take one-fourth", *mirbāʕ* "one-fourth of the booty", *rabbaʕa* "to quadruple"; *ʔrbʕ* (OSArab.) "four", *ʔrbʕy* "forty", *rbʕ* "one-fourth, quarter", *rbʕ* "fourth"; *árba*, *ōrbaʕ*, *ərbōt*, *órbəʕ*, *rəbōt* (MSArab.) "four", *rēbaʔ*, *rōbaʔ*, *rēʕ* "fourth", *rebáyt*, *riyʕét* "quarter"; *ʔarbāʕ* (Eth.) "four", *ʔarbəʕā* "forty", *rābəʕ* "fourth", *rubāʕe* "fourth part", denom. *rabbəʕa* "to make four".

|r-b-ʕ| "to quadruplicate"	•CTX: **UGA** C prefc. *åšrbʕ*, *yšrbʕ* → DUL 718. For Dpass. ptc. fem. *mrbʕt* see below.
ʔarbaʕt "square" (?)	•CTX: **EUPH** *ar-ba-aḫ-tim* → Kupper ARM 22 526 (328 rev. IV 11'); Zadok Fs. Hallo 328.
årbʕ "four"	•CTX: **UGA** Sg. m. *årbʕ*, fem. *årbʕt*, pl. *årbʕm* (see below: *årbʕm*) → DUL 92ff.
årbʕm "forty"	•CTX: **UGA** → DUL 94f.
årbʕtm "four times, fourfold"	•CTX: **UGA** → Tropper UG 347, 377, with reference to Hb. *ʔarbaʕtayim*; DUL *vacat.*
årbx "four year old (animal)" (?)	•CTX: **UGA** → DUL 95: *årbḫ*; Richter BGH 518.
mrbʕ "measure of capacity, quart"	•CTX: **UGA** → DUL 565.
mrbʕt "the fourth (wife)"	•CTX: **UGA** → Tropper UG 347, 370, 570: Dpass. ptc. fem. |murabbaʕ(a)t| "the one taken in fourth place"; DUL 565.
rbʕ "fourth"	•CTX: **UGA** → DUL 718.
rbʕt "a fourth, quarter"	•CTX: **UGA** Sg. *rbʕt*, pl. cstr. *rbʕt* → DUL 718f.

452 See also under |r-ʕ |, above.

|r-b-b| (1), |r-b-y| Cf. **|r-p-ʔ|**, **|r-y-b|**	Sem.: *rbb* / *rbh* (Hb.) "to be(come) numerous, large, great", *rb* (*rab*) "numerous, many; great", *r*(*w*)*b* (*rob*, *rôb*) "quantity, wealth", *rbbh* (*r*ᵉ*bābāh*), *rbw*(*ʔ*) (*ribbô*(*ʔ*)) "very great quantity, immense number", *rbybym* (*rebîbîm*) "(spring) shower, rain(s)", *trbyt* (*tarbît*) "profit, increase"; *rb* (Ph.) ""multitude", *rb* (Ph., Pun., Amm., Moab., Palm., Hatra) "numerous, big, important; head, chief, commander"; *rbb* (Syr.) "to be great", *rby* (Aram., Syr.) "to increase, grow", *rby*(*ʔ*) (JAram.) "young man", *rb*(*ʔ*) (Aram., Syr.) "large, great; chief, master", *rbw*(*tʔ*) "greatness; ten thousand", *rby*, *rbytʔ* (JAram.) "young girl", *rbbh* (Syr.) "tumult", *trby*(*tʔ*) (Syr.) "upbringing, growth, increase"; *rabû*(*m*), *rabāʔu*(*m*) "to be big, grow", *rabû*(*m*), *rabīu*(*m*) "big; grandee, chief", *rubāʔum*, *rubû*(*m*) "prince", *tarbītu*(*m*) "enlargement"; *rabba* (Arab.) "to be master, lord", *rabā* (*rabw*) "to increase"*rabb* "lord, master", *rabba* "mistress, lady", *rubba* "many", *ribwa* "myriad", *riban* "interest", *tarbiya* "upbringing"; *rbb* (OSArab.) "to be owner, possess; *rbw* "to cause to grow, cultivate", *rb* "lord".
|r-b-b/y| "to be big, great"	•CTX: **UGA** G suffc. *rbt* → DUL 719: /*r-b*(*-b:y*)/. •ONOM: **U3** *ra-ba-il* → Owen JCS 33 257. **EUPH** *i-ar-bi*-DINGIR, *ia-ar-bu*-DINGIR,*-ia-ar-bi- el*/DINGIR, *e-*[*er-*]*bu-ú-el*, *ta-ar-bi-an-nu-ni-tum*, *an-nu-tar-bi* → Huffmon APNMT 260; Gelb CAAA 30, 178; Golinets Onomastikon 2 25, 35, 312, 314, 436f. **EM** *ir-bi-ia*, *ir-bi*-^{d}KUR, *ir-bí-lu*/*li* → Pruzsinszky PTEm 84 [502f.].[453] **A4** Cf. unc. *ia-ar-ba-ú* → Wiseman AT 136; Sivan GAGl 264. **UGA Cf.** *yrbʕm* → DUL 962.
rabay "big"	•ONOM: **EUPH** Cf. *la-aḫ-ra-bu*, *še-la-ḫu-ra-bu-ú* → Zadok Fs. Hallo 328. **EM**: *ra-ba-a* → Pruzsinszky PTEm 175 [689]. **EG** Cf. *r-b-*y_2*-y-ꜣ* → Schneider APÄQ 150 no. 317.
rabb "great, large"	•CTX: **EM** ^{d}EN *ra-ab-ba*, fem. NINDA *ra-ba-*tu_4 (a large bread as dedication) → Pentiuc Vocabulary 151f. **UGS** GAL-*bu* |rabbu|, fem. *ra-ba-ti* |rabbatu| → Sivan GAGl 263; Huehnergard UVST 176; Tropper UG 185, 279. •ONOM: **EB** *ra-ba*, *ra-bù-šum*, *ra-ba-ì*, *ì-a-ra-bù*, *su ra-bù*, *wa-ad-ra-bù* → Pagan ARES 3 167, 328, 358, 375.[454] **EM** *ra-ab-ba-il*, *ra-ab-bi-il*, *ra-ab-bi-da-mi* → Pruzsinszky PTEm 175 [689]. **EA** GAL(*ràb*)*-ṣí-id-qí* → Sivan GAGl 269; Hess APN 131f.; Moran AmL 384.[455] **TA** *ra-ba-ia* → Horowitz / Oshima CunCan 173 (8:4'). **EG** *ra-*bi_3 |rabbi| → Hoch SWET 201f. no. 272.
rb (A), **rp** "great, large; chief, grandee"	•CTX: **UGA** Sg. *rb*, suff. *rbh*, *rbm*, f. *rbt* (see below: *rbt* (A)), pl. *rbm* → DUL 716f.: *rb* (I), 717f.: *rb* (II), 731: *rp*. •ONOM: **UGA** *ỉlrb* → DUL 61; *rbỉl* → DUL 718.
rb (B), **rbb** "type of dew, drizzle"	•CTX: **UGA** *rb*, *rbb* → DUL 719: *rb*(*b*).
ribab "ten thousand, myriad"	•CTX: **EB** *rí-bab* → Pettinato AfO 25 27; Catagnoti / Fronzaroli ARET 16 122, 261; Catagnoti QuSe 29 117, 223.

[453] Altern.: from |r-p-ʔ|; Pruzsinszky PTEm 84 fn. 143.

[454] Several writings *ra*/*la-b*= could belong to the etymon |r-y-b| "to compensate, replace; contest, plead". See Krebernik PET 49; Pagan ARES 3 162.

[455] Cf. GAL.DINGIR (170:36) and the ambiguous *ra*-BI-AN (333:24): possible rdgs *ra-bi-ilu*(DINGIR) "Great is Ilu / the god" (|r-b-b/y|; Sivan GAGl 263: RABBU; Gröndahl PTU 178f.: RB) respectively *ra-b(i)-ilu*(DINGIR) "Ilu / the god has pleaded" (|r-y-b|); or *ra-pí-ilu* (DINGIR) "my healer is Ilu / the god" (|r-p-ʔ|), see Moran AmL 383f.; Hess APN 130f., 211f.

rabīt (A) "great lady, queen"	•CTX: **UGS** (DUMU.SAL / DUMU.MEŠ / *bi-it-ti*) *ra-bi-ti* → vSoldt SAU 15; CAD R 26: *rabītu* A. **EG** Elem. in TN *ra-bi-tu*$_2$, *r-bi-tu*$_2$, *ru*$_2$*-bi-ta*$_{(5)}$ → Hoch SWET 204 no. 277.
rabīt (B) "capital city"	•CTX: **R** *ra-bi-ti-šu* → Dalley / Walker / Hawkins Tell Rimah 193 (277:6); CAD R 26: *rabītu* B.
rabbat "ten thousand, myriad"	•CTX: **EUPH** *ra-ab-ba-tim* → Guichard ARM 28 20f. (16:16); AHw 1585; CAD R 14: *rabbatu.*
rabbut "bigness, highness"	•ONOM: **EB** *ra-bù-du* → Pagan ARES 3 167, 358.[456]
ribbat "ten thousand, myriad"	•CTX: **EUPH** *rí-ba-at* → Durand MARI 3 278, MARI 5 605f. **A7** *ri-ib-ba-at* → AHw 980; CAD R 314; Giacumakis AkkAl 99; Arnaud AuOr 16 158; Zadok Fs. Hallo 328.
rbt (B), **rbbt** "myriad"	•CTX: **UGA** Sg. / pl. *rbt*, *rbbt*, du. *rbtm* → DUL 719: *rb*(*b*)*t*.
rubay "prince"	•LL: **MŠ** [*r*]*u-bu-u* = *ru-bu*[*-u* MAR.T]U (exp. I 35) → Hrůša MŠ 150, 280, 431, 544.[457]
tarbīy "promotion" (?)	•CTX: **EB** Cf. *tar*$_x$*-bí* → Fronzaroli NABU 2008/35.
tarbīyt "offspring"	•CTX: **EM** Fem. pl. *tar-bi-ia-ti* → Huehnergard RA 77 32; Pentiuc Vocabulary 179.
trbyt "profit, interest"	•CTX: **UGA** Sg. / pl. *trbyt* → DUL: 864.

|r-b-b| (2)	Sem.: *rabba* (Arab.) "to gather, increase, arrange, mend"; *rbb*, *rabba*, *rababa* (Eth.) "to stretch, extend", *marbabt*, *marbəbt* "net, fisherman's net".
rbt (C) "kind of fisherman's net; seine, trawl (?)"	•CTX: **UGA** → DUL 720f.; Watson 2018 75.

|r-b-d|	Sem.: *rbd* (Hb.) "to prepare a couch"; *rbd* (Pun.) "to pave"; *rabada* (Arab.) "to tie, bind", *mirbad* "berth; dryer of dates".
|r-b-d| "to prepare, get (a bed) ready; to cover"	•CTX: **Q** Cf. *ú-ra-ab-bá-du* → Fales Kaskal 1 104 fn. 106.[458] **UGA** G prefc. *trbd*, G inf.(?) *rbd* → DUL 720.
marbad "bedspread, counterpane"	•CTX: **EA** *ma-ar-*[*b*]*a-d*[*u*] (120:21) → Sivan GAGl 244; AHw 1573;[459] Rainey EAT 81; Moran AmL p. 199 fn. 11.
mrbd "bedspread, counterpane"	•CTX: **UGA** Sg. *mrbd*, pl. *mrbdt* → DUL 565f.: *mrbd* (I).

---

[456] The writing *ra-b=* could belong to the etymon \|r-y-b\| "to be big".

[457] A PaRaS theme \|rubay=u(=m)\| > *rubû*(*m*) Cf. vSoden GaG 14, 37, 61; Huehnergard Fs. Lambdin 185 fn. 24.

[458] Cf. Bottéro RA 43 36 fn. 3; AHw 954 *rapādu*(*m*) II, D.2; CAD R 412: *ruppudu* (mng unkn.); Richter / Lange Idadda 186: D ("?").

[459] Wrong rdgs AHw 617:-*ma-ar-zu*!?-*ú*!?; CAD M/1 290: *ma-a*[*r*]-[*ṣ*]*a*(?)-*ú*(?))

|r-b-k|	Sem.: *mrbkt* (Hb. *rbk* ptc. fem. Cpass. *murbāket*) "mixed"; *rbyk(?)* (JAram. *rbk* pass. ptc. fem.) "mixed", *rbyk(?)* "flour paste"; *rabāku(m)* (Akk.) "to boil down, decoct", *ribku(m)*, *rabīku* "concoction, infusion, decoction"; *rabaka* (Arab.) "to muddle, confuse", *rabik* "confused".
rabika "a fine bread or pastry"	•CTX: **EG** *–r-bi-ka* → Hoch SWET 204 no. 276.

|r-b-ḳ| See |r-p-ḳ|	Sem.: *rabaqa* (Arab.) "to lasso, to rope", *ribq*, *rabqa*, *ribqa* "lasso, lariat"; *mrbq* (*marbēq*, Hb.) "stall, tying-place"; cf. *rabāqum* (Akk.) mng unc., said of cattle.
|r-b-ḳ| "to act as a bond, to tie up" (?)	•ONOM: **EUPH** Cf. *ri-ib-qú*, *ra-bi-qa-nu* → Zadok Fs. Hallo 328.
rubḳ "rein, bridle"	•CTX: **EB** *lu-bù-gu/gù*, du. *lu-bù/ba-ga* → Waetzoldt NABU 1990/96; Conti / Bonechi NABU 1992/10; Conti QuSe 19 45.
marbiḳat, **marbaḳat**, **narbiḳat**, **narbaḳat** "a necklace" (?)	•CTX: **EUPH** Cf. *mar-bi-qa-at*, *mar/ma-ar-bi-qa-tum*, *mar-pa-qa-tum*; Akkadianized: *na-ar-bi-qa-tum*, *na-ar-pa-qat* → Limet MARI 3 194 fn. 18; Zadok Fs. Hallo 325; Streck Onomastikon 1 105 (to carry pendants, cylindrical seals, etc.); diff. Arkhipov ARM 32 86ff.: "monture de sceau" (see |r-p-ḳ|, below).

|r-b-ṣ́|	Sem.: *rbṣ* (Hb.) "to lie down, rest", *rbṣ* (*rēbeṣ*) "resting place, bed", *mrbṣ* (*marbēṣ*, *mirbāṣ*) "resting place"; *rbʕ* (Aram., Syr.) "to lie down", *mrbʕ(?)* (Syr.) "enclosure", *mrbwʕy(t?)* "place for lying down"; *trbṣ(?)* (Aram., Syr.) "courtyard"; *rabāṣu(m)* (Akk.) "to sit, be recumbent", *rābiṣu(m)* "'the lurker', an inspector", *rabṣu(m)* "recumbent", *narbāṣu* "lair", *tarba/āṣu(m)* "animal stall, courtyard"; *rabaḍa* (Arab.) "to lie down, sit, rest", *rabaḍ* "outskirts; place where animals lie down to rest", *marbiḍ* "sheep pen, fold"; *mrbḍn* (OSArab.) "sheep pen, fold"; *rebōź*, *rōź* (MSArab.) "to lie down, rest".
|r-b-ṣ| "to lie down, rest"	•CTX: **UGA** G imp. *rbṣ* → DUL 720.
rābiṣ "commissioner"	•CTX: **EA** LÚ MAŠKIN *:* LÚ *ra-bi-iṣ*, LÚ.MEŠ *ra-bi-ṣí : sú-ki-ni* → Gianto SEL 12 70.
rbṣ "'the lurker', an inspector"	•CTX: **UGA** → DUL 720.
ỉrbṣ "repose, resting place" (?)	•ONOM: **UGA** Elem. in TN *gt ỉrbṣ* → DUL 96.
marbiṣ́ "resting place, bed"	•LL: **EB** KI.NÁ = *mar-bí-zu* → Conti QuSe 17 200.
tarbaṣ "stable, yard"	•CTX: **UGS** É-*tu*$_4$ *: ta-ar-bá-ṣí* → Sivan GAGl 279; Huehnergard UVST 176; vSoldt SAU 307 (151).[460]
trbṣ(t) "yard, stable; reserve"	•CTX: **UGA** Sg. *trbṣ*, *trbṣt* → DUL 864: *trbṣ*.

|r-b-θ|	Sem.: *rabāšu(m)* (Akk.) "to substantiate a claim"; *rabaṯa* (Arab.) "to prevent, hinder".

[460] In Mari it seems to refer to a type of medaillon; Durand MARI 6 145f.; Guichard ARM 31 139; Arkhipov ARM 32 94.

|r-b-θ| "to substantiate a claim"	•CTX: **EB G** prefc. *ti-la-ba-šu* |tirabbaθ=ū|, suff. *i-ra-ba-ša-am*$_6$ |yirabbaθ=am|, *a-ra-ba-ša-ga* |ʔarabbaθ=am=ka|; *ìr-da-ba-ša-am*$_6$ |yirtabaθ=am|; inf. suff. *ra-ba-ša-ga* |rabāθ=ka| → Catagnoti / Fronzaroli ARET 16 91, 260; Catagnoti QuSe 29 25, 129, 131, 135, 221.
|r-b-y| See **|r-b-b| (1)**	
|r-D-B|	Sem.: Cf. *rdp* (Hb.) "to pursue"; *rdp* (Aram., Syr.) "to pursue, persecute"; *ratābu*(*m*), *raṭābu*(*m*) (Akk.) "to continue, begin, proceed (to do something)"; *radafa* (Arab.) "to come next, follow, succeed".
|r-t-b| "to hurry (to do something)"	•CTX: **EUPH** Passim; cf. G prefc. *ir-tu-up*, *ta-ar-tu-ba* → CAD R 217: *ratābu*; Kupper, NABU 1992/41; Durand ARM 26/1 91 fn. I; Joannès ARM 26/2 301, 307. **R** G prefc. *ta-ar-tu-bi*, cf. *ir-ta*(?)-*ub* → Dalley / Walker / Hawkins Tell Rimah 16:8, 115:15; CAD R 217: *ratābu*.[461]
|r-d-d|	Sem.: *rdd* (Hb.) "to subjugate, conquer"; *rdd* (JAram.) "to stamp, beat thin"; *radādu*(*m*) (Akk.) "to chase, pursue"; *radda* (Arab.) "to send back, to return, to repel".
|r-d-d| "to repel, chase, drive away" (?)	•ONOM: **EB** Cf. *tal-du-ud*, *tal-du-du* → Pagan ARES 3 163, 369.
|r-d-m| (1)	Sem. etym. unc. Cf. *nardamu* (Akk.) "pole", *nardamtu*, *nardamu* "track, footpath". [462]
mardimt "path" (?)	•LL: **UGS** GUD.DA.KALAM.MA = *mar-de*$_4$*-em-tu* → Huehnergard UVST 177; Tropper UG 172, 279.
mardam "a kind of walking stick" (?)	•ONOM: **U3** Cf. *mar-da-mu-um* → Buccellati Amorites 19, 170.
mardamān "a kind of walking stick" (?)	•CTX: **EB** *mar-da-ma-núm* → Pasquali QuSe 23 165f.
|r-d-m| (2)	Sem.: *rdm* (Hb. N) "to sleep deeply", *trdmh* (*tardēmāh*) "deep sleep"; *rdm* (JAram.) "to slumber".
|r-d-m| "to be sound asleep"	•LL: **EB** MA.MU = *ra-da-mu*, *la-da-mu-mu*, *la-da-mu-um* → Krebernik ZA 73 32; Conti QuSe 17 196f.
|r-d-y|	Sem.: *rdh* (Hb.) "to tread, rule", *rdy* (Aram., Syr.) "to plow, beat, chastise, train", (Syr.) "to flow; to follow, travel"; *redû*(*m*), *radāʔum* (Akk.) "to accompany, lead, drive, proceed", *rīdu*(*m*) "driving; succession, pursuit", *ridûtu*(*m*) "appropiation, (right of) succession, heritage"; *radiya*, *radan* (Arab.) "to perish, fall", *ʔardā* "to bring to the ground", *taraddā* "to fall".

[461] Cf. the unc. rdg *t/ša-ru-uB* in Tall Rimah 124:5; Eidem NABU 1991/87.
[462] For the dubious verbal forms of *radāmu* (mng unc.) see AHw 1585; CAD R 59.

|r-d-ʔ/y| “to lead”
•ONOM: **EB** *rí-dam-ma-lik, ìr-da-um, ìr-da-ar, ìr-da-ba, ìr-da-iš-lu/ru*$_{12}$, *ìr-da-lum, ìr-da-ma-lik, tal-da-nu, tal-da-gàr, tal-da-kam*$_4$, *tal-da-li-im* → Pagan ARES 3 162f., 338, 359, 369.
EG Cf. *r-t:*$_2$ ^{F} → Schneider APÄQ 160 no. 338.
UGA *rdn* → DUL 721: name of an ancestral king.

rīd, ridy “amount due”
•LL: **EB** KI.ZA = *rí-tum, rí-du-um* → Conti QuSe 17 201.

|r-ð-l|

Sem.: *radila* (Arab.) “to be low, base, vile”.

ʔarðāl “men of low condition”
•LL: **EB** AL$_6$.TAR.ŠÈ = *ar-ša-um*; AL.PAD(! GAR) = *ar-ša-lu* → Fronzaroli QuSe 13 136; Conti QuSe 17 36, 84.

|r-ð-y|

Sem.: *rzh* (Hb. N) “to dwindle, disappear”; *rzʔ* (Palm.) probl. mng “expense”; *rzy* (Syr.) “to grow weak”; *razaʔa* (Arab.) “to deprive”, *ruziʔa* “to suffer loss, lose”; *rzʔ* (OSArab.) “to spend, pay out”.

|r-ð-y| “to grow thin, weak”
•CTX: **UGS** N prefc. *ar-ra-zu* → vSoden UF 1 191; AHw 964: *razû*; CAD R 183: **rasû* (< 221: **razû*); Huehnergard UVST 177.

|r-g-b|

Sem.: *rağaba, rağiba* (Arab.) “to be afraid, awed, to get frightened”.

|r-g-b| “to be seized by fear; to terrify”
•CTX: **EA** G prefc. *tar-gu*$_5$*-ub* → De Moor UF 1 188; AHw p. 941; CAD R 62; Moran AmL 379 fn. 4; Izre’el Orient 38 74f.
•ONOM: **UGA** Royal ritual PNN *yrgbbʕl* → DUL 963; *yrgbhd* → DUL 963; *yrgblỉm* → DUL 963.

rgbt “respect, fear”
•CTX: **UGA** → DUL 721.

ʔargab “most frightening” (?)
•ONOM: **EUPH** Cf. *ar-ga-bu-um* → Zadok OLA 28 117, Fs. Hallo 328.

|r-g-l|

Primary noun, Sem.: *rgl* (*regel*, Hb.) “foot, leg”; *rgl(ʔ)* Aram., Syr. “foot, leg, march”; *riğl* (Arab.) “foot, leg”; *rgl* (OSArab.) “foot, leg”.[463]

rigl “foot, leg”
•LL: **UGS** [ÚR = *pēnu* = *ip...*] = *ri-ig-lu* → Sivan GAGl 264; Huehnergard UVST 176f.; vSoldt SAU 307 (131).
•ONOM: **UGS** Cf. *rgln* → DUL 721.

|r-g-m|

Sem.: *ragāmu* (Akk.) “to call (out), shout; prosecute, raise claim”, *rigmu*(m) “voice, sound, cry”, *rigimtum* “claim, request”; *trgmn(ʔ)* (JAram., Syr.) “interpreter”, *trgm* “to translate, preach”. Derivative mngs: *ragama* (Eth.) “to curse, insult”; *rağama* (Arab.) “to curse, damn, abuse, revile; to stone”; *rgm* (Hb., JAram., Syr.) to stone”.

|r-g-m| “to roar, speak”
•CTX: **UGA** G. prefc. *årgm, trgm*; *yrgm*, suff. *årgmk, årgmnk, årgmn*; suffc. *rgmt, rgmt, rgm*, imp. *rgm*; inf. *rgm*; Gpass. prefc. *yrgm* → DUL 721f.: /r-g-m/.
•LL: **UGS** [MU =] *za-ka*$_4$*-ru* = [...] = *ra-g[a?-mu?]* → Huehnergard UVST 50, 177; ²UVST 398; Tropper UG 481.
•ONOM: **EUPH** *ar-ga-ma-tum* → Gelb CAAA 30, 178.
A4 Cf. *ta-ar- ga*$_5$(QA)*-am-ma* → Wiseman AT 148; Arnaud AuOr 16 176.

---

[463] See further: *riglu* (Akk.) mng unc. (AHw 982: “ein Gegenstand”; CAD R 328 “a foodstuff”), *riğla* (Arab.) “common purslane”; *reglet, regēlet* (MSA) “tethering rope”.

rigm "yell, roar" (?)	•LL: **UGS.**[464] •ONOM: **EUPH** *ri-ig-ma-nu/num* → Gelb CAAA 30, 178.
rigatt "claim, request"	•LL: **EB** mu$_7$ (KA.LI) = *rí-ga-tum* → Conti QuSe 15 47 |rigamt=|; Bonechi / Catagnoti Fs. Sommerfeld / Krebernik 172.
|r-γ-b|	Sem.: *rʕb* (Hb.) "to be hungry", *rʕb* (*rāʕāb*), *rʕbwn* (*rᵉʕābôn*) "hunger"; *raġiba* (Arab.) "to desire, wish, crave", *raġba* "desire, wish, appetite"; *rəḫba* (Eth.) "to be hungry, desire", *raḫa/āb* "hunger, famine".
|**r-γ-b**| "to be hungry"	•CTX: **UGA** G suffc. *rġbt*, inf. *rġb* → DUL 724: */r-ġ-b/*.
rγbn "hunger"	•CTX: **UGA** → DUL 724: *rġbn*.
|r-γ-m| Cf. |**r-m-m**| **(2)**	Sem.: *rʕm* (Hb.) "to rage, roar", (C) "to cause to thunder", *rʕm* (*raʕam*) "uproar, thunder"; *rʕm* (JAram., Syr.) "to thunder, grieve", *rʕm(ʔ)*, *rʕym* "thunder, loud sound"; *raġama* (Arab.) "to loathe, detest", *raġima* "to be subjugated, humiliated", *ra/i/uġm* "coercion"; *rġm* (OSArab.) "coercion"; *raʕama*, *ʔarʕama* (Eth.) "to roar, thunder", *rāʕam* "roaring sound, noise", *raʕām* "shouting, thunder clap". See also *ramāmu*(m) (Akk.) "to roar, growl".
|**r-γ-m**| "to roar, thunder"	•ONOM: **UGA** Royal ritual PNN *yrġmbʕl* → DUL 963; *yrġmil* → DUL 963. **EG** Cf. *tu$_2$-r-m-gu* → Hoch SWET 358f. no. 530.
|r-γ-θ|	Sem.: *raġaṯa* (Arab.) "to suck (at the mother's teats)".
mrγθ "suckling, unweaned (lamb)"	•CTX: **UGA** Du *mrġṯm* → DUL 566f.: *mrġṯ* (Wrong morphol. analysis: sg. *mrġt*).
|r-γ-w|	Sem.: Cf. *raġā* (*raġw*, Arab.), *raġġā*, *ʔarġā* "to foam, froth; to fume with rage", *raġwa* "foam, lather, scum".
|**r-γ-w**| "to foam, be full of rage"	•CTX: **UGA** G prefc. *trġn* → DUL 723: */r-ġ/*.[465]
mrγt "scum, dross, dregs" (?)	•CTX: **UGA** → DUL 566: *mrġt* "corruption" (?).
|r-h-b| See |**r-w-b**| **(2)**	
|r-h-ṭ|	Culture word, Sem.: *rhṭ* (Hb.) "drinking trough"; *rhṭ(ʔ)* (JAram., Syr.) id.; *rāṭu(m)* (Akk.) "water-channel, pipe". Denom. cf. *rhṭ* (Syr.) "to irrigate"; *rahaṭa* (Arab.) "to gulp greedily".
rahṭ "a vessel"	•CTX: **EB** *la-a-tum* → Pasquali QuSe 23 156f. **EA** *ra-aḫ-ta* (14 i 46) → Moran AmL 28: *raḫda*; AHw 943: *raḫta* CAD R 76: *raḫta*. **EG** *r-h-d-{t}*, *r-h-da$_2$* → Hoch SWET 205 no. 279.

[464] For an altern. rdg of *rig(i)m* "word" (LL: UGS) as *talgim* "harness(ing)" ([DÍM (for DIM) = *riksu* = *x-x*[ ] = *tal-gi-mu*) see now Huehnergard NABU 2019/46, and here \|l-g-m\|.

[465] Diff. and unlikely Tropper UG 155: rdg *trġnw* (wrong) from *rġn* "verstört, verwirrt, bedrückt sein" (with Hb. *rʕm*).

|r-ħ|	Primary noun, Sem.: *rḥt* (*raḥat*, Hb.) "winnowing shovel"; *lḥt(?)* (Syr.) "central part of the hand or leg"; *rittu(m)* (Akk.) "hand, claw; handle";[466] *rāħa* (Arab.) "palm of hand"; *ərḥāt, rīḥet, rəḥāt, rḥót* (MSArab.) "palm of hand"; *ʔərāḥ* (Eth.) "palm of hand". Non-Sem.: **raH= / *riH=* (Central and West Chadic) "arm".[467]
rāħat "hand; kind of handle or grip"	•CTX: **EUPH** *ra-ʔà*(É)*-at, ra-ʔà*(É)*-te-šu-ni* → Limet ARM 19 148 (v. 10, 14) Westenholz BiOr 35 164ff.; CAD R 386: *rittu* A 4: "handle". •LL: **EB** ŠU.SAL = *ra-ʔà-tum, gi-bí-la-ti la-ʔà-tum, gi-bí-la-du ra-ʔà-tum*; ŠU.SÀ = *la-ʔà-tum* → Krebernik ZA 73 19; Conti QuSe 17 30, 145; QuSe 19 62; Pasquali NABU 2003/25; QuSe 23 74.[468]
rħt "palm of the hand"	•CTX: **UGA** Sg. suff. *rḥth*, du. *rḥtm* → DUL 727: *rḥt*.

|r-ħ-b| Cf. **|r-y-b|**	Sem.: *rḥb* (Hb.) "to open oneself wide", (C) "to make wide, extensive", *rḥb* (*rāḥāb*) "broad, wide", (*roḥab*) "breadth", *rḥb, rḥwb* (*r^eḥob, r^eḥôb*) "open plaza"; *rḥb* (Ph. C) "to enlarge, extend"; *rḥbh* (Aram.) "open land"; *raḥiba, raḥuba* (Arab.) "to be wide, spacious", *raḥb, raḥīb* "wide, spacious", *ruḥb, raḥab* "wideness", *raḥba, raḥaba* "public square"; *rḥb* (OSArab.) "width"; *reḥebét, rəḥbēt* (MSArab.) "place, land, town"; *rəḥba, rəḥba* (Eth.) "to be wide, large, broad", *rəḥb, rāḥb, raḥab, rəḥāb* "breadth, width", *rəḥib, rəḥub* "wide, broad".
|r-ħ-b| "to be wide, large, generous"	•ONOM: **EB** |yirħab| (?); cf. *ìr-a-ba*$_4$*/bu*$_{16}$(?) → Pagan ARES 3 163, 337. **EUPH** *ia-ar-ḫa-bu-um* → Gelb CAAA 30, 174; Golinets Onomastikon 2 57:207, 79, 114, 170, 172, 437.
ruħb "width"	•ONOM: **EUPH** *ru-uḫ-ba-tum, ru-ḫu-ba-tum* → Gelb CAAA 30, 179; Zadok Fs. Hallo 328.
raħāb "wide, broad, open space"	•ONOM: **EUPH** Cf. *a-na-ra-a-bu, ba-al-ku-úš-ra-ḫa-ab* → Gelb CAAA 30, 175. **EG** TN *ra-ḥ-bu, ra-ḥa-bu/a, ru*$_2$*-ḥa*$_2$*-bi-ʔa* → Hoch SWET 206f. no. 280. **UGS** River ÍD *ra-aḫ-ba/bá-na/ni* → Sivan GAGl 263; Huehnergard UVST 178f.: Tropper UgG 304.
raħīb "extended, expanded"	•ONOM: **EUPH** *ra-i-bu-um, ra-ḫi-ba* → Gelb CAAA 30, 175; Golinets Onomastikon 2 172.
rħb (A) "wide"	•CTX: **UGA** Sg. cstr. *rḥb*, fem. *rḥbt* → DUL 724: *rḥb* (I). •ONOM: **UGA** River *rḥbn* → DUL 725.
rħb (B) "width"	•CTX: **UGA** Sg. suff. *rḥbhm* → DUL 725: *rḥb* (II).
raħaba "a vessel"	•CTX: **EG** *ra-ḥa*$_2$*-ba, ra-ḥ-ba* → Hoch SWET 207 no. 281: *ra-ḥa*$_2$*-ba, ra-ḥ-ba*
riħbān "wide, spacious"	•LL: **EB** DÚR = *rí-ba-num* → Sjöberg Fs. Pettinato 276.
rħbt "amphora, jar"	•CTX: **UGA** Sg. / pl. *rḥbt* → DUL 725: *rḥbt*.

---

[466] For EA-Akk *rettu* "the lower part of the handle that fits into the hand"(?) see Moran AmL 58 fn. 9 on EAT 22 and passim.

[467] Orel / Stolbova HSED 444f. no. 2091: **raḥ=* "hand, arm".

[468] According to Pasquali (NABU 2003/25; QuSe 23 72ff.) *ra-ʔà-tum* (always CTX) was (also?) an aquatic animal whose shell could be used for decoration and as ornament.

|r-ħ-ḳ|	Sem.: *rḥq* (Hb. G) "to be far", (D, C) "to remove", *rḥ(w)q* (*raḥoq, rāḥôq*) "distant, remote", *mrḥq* (*merḥāq*) "distance, expanse"; *rḥq* (Aram.) "to be(come) distant", *rḥq* "distance; far(-away)", *rḥyq* "distant", *rwḥq(?)* (JAram., Syr.) "distance; *rḥq* (Palm.) "to leave, withdraw"; *rḥq* (Amm., Nab.) "far(-away); *rêqu(m), ruāqu(m)* (Akk.) "to be distant, go far off, depart", *rēqu(m), rēqû(m), rūqu(m)* "far, distant"; *rḥq* (OSArab.) "be distant, far", *rḥq(m)* "far"; *rəḥqa* (Eth.) "to be far off", *rəḥuq* "far, far away", *rəḥq(at)*, "distance"; see further *ruḥāq, raḥīq* (Arab.) "rich, full-bodied (: imported) wine".
|**r-ħ-ḳ**| "to be far, distant, to retreat, go away; to remove; to flee"	•CTX: **UGA** G imp. *rḥq*; D suffc. *rḥqt*; C suffc. *šrḥq* → DUL 726: */r-ḥ-q/*. **EG Cf.** *ma-ra-qi$_{(2)}$-ḫa-ta* (D ptc. fem. |maraħħiḳata|, metath. ?) → Hoch SWET 142f. no. 185;[469] *h-r-ti$_4$-qa-ḥa* (|hatraħħaḳa|) → Hoch SWET 216 no. 299.[470] •ONOM: **EB** *il-ʔà-ag-da-mu, ìr-ʔà-ag-da-mu, ìr-ag-da-mu, ìr*(!GUR)*-ag-da-mu*; cf. *zàr*(SUM)*-i-ig* → Sollberger ARET 8 12; Krebernik PET 48, 69; Pagan ARES 3 163f., 334, 337, 384. **EUPH**: *ir-ḫa-kum, ii-ir-ḫa-kum, e-er-ḫa-kum*; *ia-ar-ḫi-ku-um, ir-ḫi-ga* → Gelb CAAA 30, 174; Streck Onomastikon 1 181 § 2.64; Golinets Onomastikon 2 29f., 31, 35, 82, 115f., 438f.
raħḳ, reħḳ "distant"	•ONOM: **EB** *la-ga-a-gú*,[471] *ḫu-ba-rí-ga/gú, ḫu:ba-rí:ga, rí-ga-ì, rí-ga-gu* → Pagan ARES 3 163f., 319, 359.
ruħḳ "distant"	•ONOM: **EB** *ʔà-ma/mu-ru$_{12}$-gú, bù-lu/ru$_{12}$-gú, bù-ru$_{12}$-ù-gú, gi-lu-ù-gú* → Pagan ARES 3 163f., 270, 294, 312,
raħaḳ "distant"	•ONOM: **EM** *a-ḫi-ra-ḫa-aq* → Pruzsinszky PTEm 200 [99f.]
rħḳ "distant"	•CTX: **UGA** Sg. *rḥq*, pl. *rḥqm* → DUL 726: *rḥq*.
mrħḳ "distance"	•CTX: **UGA** Sg. suff. *mrḥqm* → DUL 567: *mrḥq*.
mrħḳt "distance, far away (place)"	•CTX: **UGA** Sg. suff. *mrḥqtm* → DUL 567: *mrḥqt*.

|r-ħ-l|	Sem.: *raḥala* (Arab.) "to wound (with a sword)".
|**r-ħ-l**| "to wound (with a sword?)"	•LL: **EB** ŠÀ.DAR = *ra-ʔa$_5$-lum, la-ʔa$_5$-lu-um, la-ʔa$_5$-lum* → Conti QuSe 17 30, 163; diff. Sjöberg Fs. Renger 534: *rʕl* "to tremble" (Hb., Aram., Syr.).

|r-ħ-m|	Primary noun, Sem.: *rḥm* (*reḥem*, Hb.) "womb"; *rḥm(?)* (Aram., Syr.) id.; *rēmu(m), rīmu* (Akk.) id.; *riḥm, raḥim* (Arab.) "uterus, womb"; *raḥm, mərḥam* (MSArab.) "womb". Denom. and derivatives: *rḥm* (Hb. D) "to meet someone with love, take pity", *rḥm* (*raḥam*) "slave girl", *rḥmym* (*raḥam*, pl. *raḥ^{a}mīm*) "feeling of love, mercy"; *rḥm* (Pun., Nab., Hatra G, C) "to love, care for", *rḥm* (Palm.) "affection, love", *rḥmn* (Palm.) "merciful", *rḥmnyt* (Palm.) "mercifulness", *rḥm* (Palm., Hatra) "friend", *rḥmt* (Moab.) "female slave", altern. "pregnant woman"; *rḥm* (Aram., Syr. G, D) "to love", *rḥmn* "merciful", *rḥmyn*

---

469 Diff. Sivan / Cochavi-Rainey WSVES 80: *ma-l-qa-ḥà-tá / ma-l-qi-ḥà-tá* "booty"; Helck Beziehungen no. 100.

470 "Fleeing, retreating"; diff. Sivan / Cochavi-Rainey WSVES *ha-r-ta$_2$-qa-ḥà* "entanglement"; Helck Beziehungen 163: "Verwirrung", from *rḥq* "mischen".

471 \|raħḳa=DN\| "DN is distant", altern. \|laʔka=DN\| "send, DN!"; see \|l-ʔ-k\|.

"mercy", *rḥm, rḥmh, rḥmtʔ* "affection, love; friend"; *rēmu(m), reʔāmu(m)* (Akk.) "to be merciful, have compassion", *rēmu(m), rīmu* "compassion, mercy", *rēmēnû(m), rēmānû, rēmēnānû* "compassionate, merciful"; *raḥima* (Arab.) "to have mercy", *raḥim, riḥm* "relationship, kinship", *raḥma* ""pity, compassion", *raḥīm* "merciful"; *rḥm* (OSArab.) "to have mercy", *rḥmt* "mercy", *rḥmn* "the merciful one"; *reḥām, rəḥām, rḥám* (MSArab.) "to pity"; metath. *maḥara, məḥra* (Eth.) "to have compassion, show mercy", *maḥāri* "merciful".
Non-Sem.: **riHim=* (Lowland East Cushitic) "pregnant".[472]

|**r-ħ-m**| "to have mercy, be compassionate"

•CTX: **UGA** G suffc. *rḥmt* → DUL 725: */r-ḥ-m/*.
•ONOM: **EUPH** *ia-ar-ḫa-mu, ia-ar-ḫa-ma-an, ia-ar-a-mu-um, ia-ar-ḫa-mi-*DINGIR, *ia-ar-ḫa-am-*DINGIR, *an-nu-ta-ar-am, an-nu-tar-(a-)am* → Huffmon APNMT 261; Gelb CAAA 30, 174; Streck Onomastikon 1 346 § 5.64; Golinets Onomastikon 2 76, 115 (fn. 484) 123, 437f., 491.
A7 *ir-ḫa-mi-*DINGIR, *ir-ḫa-mi-(il-)la* → Wiseman AT 138, JCS 8 20 (264:36; 274:26); Gelb CAAA 30, 174; Sivan GAGl 152, 264; Arnaud AuOr 16 176; Streck Onomastikon 1 239 § 2.156, 346 § 5.64; Golinets Onomastikon 2 30, 115,437f.
EG PN *yu$_2$-ra-ḥa-ma, yu$_2$-r-ḥ-m* (|yuroħam|(!) or D |yurúħħam|) → Hoch SWET 54 no. 56.

raħm "pity, mercy"

•ONOM: **EUPH** *ra-aḫ-ma-ia, ra-aḫ-mi-ì-lí, an-nu-ra-aḫ-mi,* EŠ$_4$.DAR*-ra-aḫ-mi, ra-aḫ-ma-^{d}da-gan* → Huffmon APNMT 261; Gelb CAAA 30, 175; Zadok Fs. Hallo 328; Streck Onomastikon 1 322 § 5.8, 354 § 5.82.

reħm, **riħm** "womb"

•LL: **EB** ÉxŠÀ = *rí-ʔe$_x$*(EN)*-mu, rí-mu-um* → Krebernik ZA 73 14; Conti QuSe 17 34, 119; Catagnoti QuSe 29 17.

raħim "merciful"

•ONOM: **EUPH** *ra-ḫi-ma, ra-i-mu-um* → Gelb CAAA 30, 175; Golinets Onomastikon 2 158, 160, 437f.

raħmān "the merciful one"

•ONOM: **EA** *ra-aḫ-ma-nu* → Huffmon APNMT 261; Sivan GAGl 263; Hess APN 211; Moran AmL 384.

rħm "womb; nubile girl, damsel"

•CTX: **UGA** Sg. *rḥm* → DUL 725f.: *rḥm.*
•ONOM: **UGA** DN *rḥmy* → DUL 726; see 725f.: *rḥm*

|r-ħ-ṣ|
Cf. |**r-w-θ̣**|

Sem.: Cf. *rêṣu(m)* (Akk.) "to help", *rēṣu(m)* "helper", *rēṣūtu(m)* "help, assistence".[473]

|**r-ħ-ṣ**| **(A)** "to help"

•LL: **EB** Cf. Á.E.GI$_4$.GI$_4$ = *da-la-za* (|taħrāṣā(n)|), *mar-a-za*; Á.E.DAḪ = *te-ra-za* (|teħrāṣā(n)|), *mar-a/ʔa$_5$-za* → Krebernik ZA 73 20f., StEb 7 209; Conti QuSe 17 29, 33, 155ff.; Fronzaroli SAOC 64 60f.; Catagnoti QuSe 29 33, 50, 221.
•ONOM: **EB** Cf. *ìr-a-zú*; passim with DNN, e.g. *i-az*(!ḪUŠ)*-ì, i-az*(!PÍŠ.ZA)*-ì, i-az*(!ḪUŠ.ZA$_x$)*-ma-lik, ìr-az*(!ḪUŠ)*-da-mu, ìr-az*(!ḪUŠ)*-zé, ìr-az*(!PIRIG)*-il, ìr-az-ì/il, ìr-az$_x$*(PÍŠ.ZA$_x$)*-ma-lik*; *ìr-da-az, ìr-da-az*(!ḪUŠ) → Bonechi MARI 8 505f.; Pagan ARES 3 166f. (*rwẓ*), 320, 337f.

raħ(a)ṣ, **riħṣ** "help"

•LL: **EB** Cf. Á.DAḪ = *ra-a-zu-um, rí-ì-zu-um, rí-zú* → Krebernik ZA 73 20f.; Conti QuSe 17 155ff.

---

[472] Orel / Stolbova HSED 449 no. 2118: **riḥim=* "uterus, pregnancy".

[473] This base should not be confounded with |r-w-θ̣| "to run" (cf. there) in spite of some inconsistent etymologies and lexical definitions: AHw 972: *rêṣu(m)* (*rʔ?ṣ*) "helfen"; CAD R 187f.: *râṣu* (*rêṣu, râṭu*) "to come; to come to help"; AHw 960: *râṣu(m)* "(zur Hilfe) laufen" (with reference to Hb. *rūṣ*, Eth. *rōṣa*, Aram. *rhṭ* "laufen"). Some semantic contamination between the bases can't be excluded. See Conti QuSe 17 155ff. for a detailed discussion.

•ONOM: **EB** *rí-za, rí-zú, ì r-kab-rí-zu/zú* → Pagan ARES 3 166f., 339, 359.
EG Cf. *sꜣ-rw-r-ṯꜣ* → Schneider APÄQ 189f. no. 399.

ruħṣ "help" — •ONOM: **EB** *ru$_{12}$-zu, ru$_{12}$-zi, ru$_{12}$-zi-gu-lu-ú, ru$_{12}$-zi-gú-lu/lum, ru$_{12}$-zi-a-aḫ/ḫu, ru$_{12}$-zi-da-du, ru$_{12}$-zi-du-du, ru$_{12}$-zu/zú*-GEŠTUG (|=xasīs| ?); passim with DNN, e.g. *ru$_{12}$-zu-ì/il, ru$_{12}$-zi-um* (|ruħṣī=(ʔil)um|), *ru$_{12}$-zi-lum, ru$_{12}$-zi-ì, ru$_{12}$-zi-ar, ru$_{12}$-zi-da-ar, ru$_{12}$-zi-da-mu, ru$_{12}$-zi-^{d}ku-ra, ru$_{12}$-zi-^{d}ì-lam, ru$_{12}$-zi-iš-lu, ru$_{12}$-zi-li-im, ru$_{12}$-zi-ma-lik, ru$_{12}$-zi-ma-rí, ru$_{12}$-zi-na-im, ru$_{12}$-zi-ša-ḫa-ru$_{12}$, ru$_{12}$-za-šum* → Bonechi MARI 8 505f.; Fronzaroli QuSe 19 12; Pagan ARES 3 166f., 359f.

rāħiṣ "helper" — •ONOM: **EB** *ra-i-zu/zú, ra-ì-zú* → Pagan ARES 3 166f., 358.

|r-ħ-s¹|

Sem.: Cf. *rḥš* (Hb.) "to be moved, aroused", *mrḥšt* (*marḥešet*) "baking pan".

raħas¹ "pan baked bread" (?) — •CTX: **EG** *ra-ḥa-su$_2$, ra-{ḫ}-ḥa-su$_2$, –r-ḥa-su$_2$*, metath. *ra-su$_2$-ḥa*, miswritings *ra-ḥa-su$_2$-ra, ra-su$_2$* → Hoch SWET 208f. no. 282.

|r-ħ-s²|

Cf. |r-s-ħ|

Sem.: Cf. *rḥś* (OSArab.) "to offer incense by sprinkling on a fire"; *rəḥsa* (Eth.) "to be moist", *ʔarḥasa* "to moisten", *rəḥus* "moistened". See further *rss* (Syr.) "to sprinkle"; *rašša* (Arab.) "to splash, spray, sprinkle".

ruħSat, ruħāSt "libation" — •LL: **EB** A.TAG = *ru$_{12}$-ʔa$_5$-ša-du, mu-sa-da-tum* → Conti QuSe 17 31, 169f.

|r-ħ-ṣ|

Sem.: *rḥṣ* (Hb.) "to wash, bathe, rinse", (*raḥaṣ*) "washing"; *rḥʕ, rʕʕ* (Aram.) "to wash"; *raḫāṣu(m)* (Akk.) "to flood, wash", *riḫṣu*(m) "flood(ing)"; *raḥada* (Arab.) "to rinse, wash"; *rḥḍ* (OSArab.) "to wash"; *reḥaź, raḥaź* (MSArab.) "to wash"; *rəḥḍa, raḥaḍa* (Eth.) "to sweat, perspire, wash, soak".

|r-ħ-ṣ| (B) "to wash (oneself); to clean, cleanse" — •CTX: **UGA** G prefc. *trḥṣ, yrḥṣ, trḥṣ*, suff. *trḥṣn, trḥṣnn*, imp. *rḥṣ*; ptc. *rḥṣ*; Gt prefc. *trtḥṣ, yrtḥṣ*; D act. ptc. pl. *mrḥṣm* → DUL 726f.

riħṣ "washing, flood(ing)" — •ONOM: **EUPH** *ì-lí-ri-iḫ-zi* → Gelb CAAA 30, 178.

raħaṣ "washed, overflowed" (?) — •ONOM: **EUPH** Cf. *ra-ḫa-zu* → Gelb CAAA 30, 175.

|r-ħ-y|

Primary noun, Sem.: *rḥym* (du. *rēḥayim*, Hb.) "hand-mill"; *rḥy(ʔ)* (Aram., Syr.) "millstone, mill"; *erû(m), irûm, erru* (Akk.) "grindstone"; *raḥan* (pl. *ʔarḥāʔ, ruḥiyy, ʔarḥiya*, du. *raḥawān*, Arab.) "hand mill", *raḥḥāy* "grinder".

rħ (A) "millstone" — •CTX: **UGA** Du. *rḥm* → DUL 724: *rḥ* (III).

|r-x-l|

Primary noun, Sem.: *rḥl* (*rāḥēl*, Hb.) "ewe"; *rḥl(ʔ)* (Aram.) "ewe"; *riḫl, raḫil, riḫla* (Arab.) "ewe"; *réḫloh* (MSArab.) "lamb"; metath. *laḫru(m)* (Akk.) "ewe, sheep".

laxr "ewe" (?) — •ONOM: **UGS** Cf. unc. *la-aḫ-ra* → Watson LSU 171 (Anatolian ?).

lħr "ewe" (?) — •ONOM: **UGA** Cf. unc. *lḫr* → KTU 4.69 III 20; DUL 493 (Akkadianism ?)[474]

---

474 Wrong rdg. *lḫr* in Watson LSU 171.

|r-x-p| — Sem.: *rḥp* (Hb. C) “to hover and tremble”; (Syr. D) “to brood, protect, hover over”.

|**r-x-p**| “to hover, fly about” — •CTX: **UGA** G ptc. f. *rḫpt*, D prefc. *årḫp*, *trḫp*, *trḫpn* → DUL 727f.: */r-ḫ-p/*.

|r-x-ṣ| — Sem.; etym. unc. Mng by the ctx.

|**r-x-ṣ**| “to hold a conference, to chat” (?) — •CTX: **EUPH** Passim; cf. G prefc. *ir-ḫa-ṣí*, *ir-ḫi-iṣ*, *i-ra-ḫi-ṣú*, *i-ra-aḫ-ḫi-ṣú* → CAD R *raḫaṣu* D; Durand ARM 26/1 178 fn. I, 181ff.

rixṣ “conference, chatting, endless talking” — •CTX: **EUPH** Passim; cf. *ri-iḫ-ṣí(-im)*, *ri-iḫ-ṣa-am* → CAD R 336f.: *riḫṣu* B; Durand ARM 26/1 181ff., 189f. (45); MARI 7 49; Amurru 3 189f.

|r-x-θ|
See |**m-r-x-S**|

|r-x-w| — Sem.: Cf. *riḫwa*, *raḫuwa*, *raḫawa* (Arab.) “to become relaxed, to relax”, *raḫw*, *riḫw*, *ruḫw* “soft, supple”, *raḫāʔ* “ease, happiness, welfare”.

rxnt “sweetness, tenderness” (?) — •CTX: **UGA** Cf. *rḫn{n}t* (sg. fem. ?; rdg unc.) → DUL 727: *rḫnt*.

|r-x-y| — Sem.: *reḫû(m)*, *raḫû* (Akk.) “to pour out; to have sexual intercourse”, *rāḫû(m)*, *rāḫium* “pourer, discharger”.

|**r-x-y**| “to procreate” — •ONOM: **EB** *a-rí-ḫi-il*, *i-rí-ḫi-ì*, *ìr-ḫi-ì* → Pagan ARES 3 164, 282, 324, 338.

rāxiy “inseminating” — •LL: **MŠ** *ra-a-ḫu-*[*ú* = MIN] → Hrůša MŠ 160, 436 (exp. I 170A).

|r-k-b| — Sem.: *rkb* (Hb.) “to ride, mount”, (C *hirkîb*) “to harness, yoke”, *rkb* (*rekeb*) “war chariot(s)”, *rkb* (*rakkāb*) “charioteer, driver”, *rkbh* (*rikbāh*) “riding”, *rkwb* (*rᵉkûb*) “vehicle, chariot”, *mrkbh* (*merkābāh*) “(war-)chariot”; *rkb* (Palm.) “to ride, mount”; *rkb* (Aram., Syr.) “to ride, mount”, *rkb(ʔ)* “rider, upper millstone”, *rkwb(ʔ)* “mount, chariot, vehicle, ship”, *mrkbh*, *mrkbtʔ* “chariot; ship”; *rakābu(m)* (Akk.) “to ride, mount”, *rakbû(m)* “mounted messenger”(?), *rikbu(m)* “crew”, *rākibu(m)* “rider”, *rakkābu(m)* “sailor, crew”, *rukūbu(m)* “chariot, boat”, *narkabu* “(upper) grindstone”, *narkabtu* “chariot”; *rakiba* (Arab.) “to ride, travel, go by boat; to overpower”, *rakb* “riders, caravan”, *rākib* “riding”, *rukūb* “riding”, *markab* “ship, vessel, boat”, *markūb* “riding animal, mount”, *markaba* “vehicle”; *rkb* (OSArab.) “to ride, mount”, *rkb* “rider, riding animals, saddle, trappings”; *rēkeb*, *rékeb*, *rekob* (MSArab.) “to ride, mount”, *márkeb*, *merkēb* “ship”. See further the secondary derivative *rakaba* (Eth.) “ride, go by boat”.[475]

---

[475] Leslau CDG 469: *rakaba* II. For Eth. *rakaba* “to find, get, reach, join” see Leslau GDG 469: *rakaba* I; Kogan Classification 457.

|r-k-b| "to mount, ride, load; to control, command, defeat"	•CTX: **EUPH** G prefc. *ni-ir-ka-ab-šu-nu-ti-ma*, *ir-ta-kab*, suffc. *ra-ki-ib*; C prefc. *nu-ša-ar-kib* → Birot ARM 27 219; Durand NABU 1993/113; Durand, ARM 26/1, 99; RA 82 107. **UGA** G suffc. *rkb*, imp. *rkb* → DUL 728. •ONOM: **EB** *ìr-ga-bù*, *ìr-kab-bù*, *ìr-kab-ar*, *ìr-kab-da-mu*, *ìr-kab-da-mu*, *ìr-kab-rí-zu/zú*, *dar-kab-bù*, *dar-kab-da-mu*, *dar-kab-du-lum* → Krebernik PET 51; Pagan ARES 3 164, 300, 338f. **EUPH** *ar-ga-bu-um*, *ar-ka-ba-tum*, *ia-ar-ka-ab-a-du*, *ia-ar-ka-ab-*^{d}IM, *ia-ar-ka-ab-li-im*, *ia-ar-ka-ba-*^{d}IM, *ia-ar-ki-ba-*^{d}IM, *ia-ar-ki-ib-a-du* → Huffmon APNMT 261; Gelb CAAA 30, 179; Zadok Fs. Hallo 328; Bonechi MARI 8 498; Golinets Onomastikon 2 69, 116, 439, 488. **A7** *ir-kab-tum* → Wiseman AT 138; Gelb CAAA 30, 179; Golinets Onomastikon 2 30, 116, 439. **R** *ia-ar-ki-ba-*^{d}IM → Dalley / Walker / Hawkins Tell Rimah 259 (136:3); Golinets Onomastikon 2 68, 81, 116, 439 (from |r-k-b| (1)). **A4** *ir-kab-du* → Wiseman AT 138; Gelb CAAA 30, 179; Golinets Onomastikon 2 30, 116, 439. **UGS** Cf. TN *Rakbā(yu)* → Belmonte RGTC 12/2 233. **UGA** Cf. TN *rkby* → DUL 729.
rakab "control, command, success"	•ONOM: **EB** *la-ga-ab* → Bonechi MARI 8 498. **EUPH** *ra-kab-tum* → Golinets Onomastikon 2 154, 439. Cf. TN *ra-ka-bat* → Groneberg RGTC 3 195.
rakub "successful"	•ONOM: **UGS** Cf. DINGIR-*ma-ra-kub*, *ra-kub-*^{d}U, *rak-bu-ya* → Sivan GAGl 265 diff.: RKB "ride"; cf. Gröndahl PTU 72, 179 "reitend, Reiter"?[476]
rikab "upper grindstone"	•LL: **EB** ḪAR.ŠU.2 = *rí-ga-bu*$_{16}$, *rí-kà-bu*$_{16}$ → Sjöberg Fs. Kienast 561.
rukab "successful"	•ONOM: **EUPH** *ru-ka-ba-tum* → Gelb CAAA 30, 179; Bonechi MARI 8 498; Golinets Onomastikon 2 164, 439.
rukub "a vehicle with wheels"	•CTX: **EB** (GIŠ) *ru*$_{12}$]-*gu-bù* → Fronzaroli ARET 11 150; Conti QuSe 19 25f. **EUPH** Cf. *qar-na-tim ša ru-ku-bi*, GIŠ *ru-[ku-b]i-im* → Kupper ARM 22/2 346f. (207 v. 8'), Durand ARM 21 158 (143:2), 159 fn. 19.
rākib "a type of levee"	•CTX: **EUPH, B** *ra-ki-bu-um*, *ra-ki-bi-im*, *ra-ki-ba-am* → AHw 947: *rakībum*; CAD R 107: *rākibu* A; Lafont FM 99; Durand, BAH 136, 126f.; ARM 26/1 206 fn. d.
rkb (A) "upper grindstone"	•CTX: **UGA** → Dietrich-Loretz ALAPS 1 190 fn. 150. Diff. DUL 728: *rkb* (III) "?".
rkb (B) "charioteer"	•CTX: **UGA** → DUL 728: *rkb* (I).[477]
rkb (C) "(an element of the) harness"	•CTX: **UGA** Cf. *rkb ả(!)tn* → Sanmartín UF 10 1978 353f.; cf. DUL 728f.: *rkb* (II) "?".[478]
rakabt "chariot"	•CTX: **EUPH** *ra-ka-a[b-tim]* → Guichard NABU 1994/31.
rakbūt "corps or rang of riders"	•CTX: **EUPH** LÚ.MEŠ *ra-ak-bu-ut* ANŠE.ḪI.A, LÚ *ták-lu-tim ra*(?)-*a*[*k*(?)-*bu-tim*] → Durand ARM 26/1 296f. (131:11), 26/2 171f. (368:6), LAPO 17 218ff., FM 8 110f. (32:23); Birot ARM 27 58f. (16:11).
mrkbt "(war-) chariot; chariot body"	•CTX: **UGA** Sg. *mrkbt*, pl. *mrkbt*, suff. *mrkbtk*, *mrkbthm*; du. *mrkbtm* → DUL 568f.; Del Olmo AuOr 37 290f.

[476] Altern. Sanmartín AuOr 9 168 fn. 10: "gatherer, joiner".
[477] Diff. Sanmartín AuOr 9 168 fn. 10: "gathering, gatherer". On the controversial meaning of the biblical *rkb b ʕrbwt* see Görg UF 6 57 fn. 15.
[478] Diff. Tropper KWU 107: *rkb*$_{2}$ "Wagen(ladung)" (?), Hb.

markabt "chariot; corps or rang of charioteer(s)"
•CTX: **UGS** Cf. (estate) *a-na mar-kab-te*[→ AHw 612; CAD M/1 282; Sivan GAGl 244; Huehnergard UVST 179; vSoldt SAU 305 (91); Tropper KWU 77, UG 279.
EG *ma–r-ka-ba-ta*, *ma*$_4$*-ra-k-b-ta*, *ma*$_3$*-ra-k-b-tu*$_2$, etc. (sg. |markabata| / pl. |markabāta| → Hoch SWET 147ff. no. 189.[479]

s¹akbarakba "upper and lower millstones"
•CTX: **EG** Compound word *š-ka-ba ra-ka-ba* (|s¹akba=rakba| ?) → Hoch SWET 289 no. 413 (Cf. |s¹-k-b|).

|r-k-k|

Sem.: Cf. *rkk* (Hb.) "to be tender, gentle"; *rkk* (JAram., Syr.) "to be tender, soft"; *rakka* (Arab.) "to be weak, feeble".

|r-k-k| "to be mild, delicate"
•ONOM: **EG**. *y:-:r-kȝ-k-kȝ*; cf. *ty-rw-k-ȝ-k* → Schneider APÄQ 39 no. 60, 238 no. 507.

|r-k-n|

Sem.: *rkn* (JAram., Syr.) "to incline", C "to lower, bend down"; *rakānu*(m) (Akk. LL) "to flatten with a maul"; *rakana*, *rakina* (Arab.) "to lean, rely on".

|r-k-n| "to rest on, lean against"
•CTX: **EB** G prefc. *ne-ra-ga-an* |nirakkan|, D suffc. *a-la-gú-nu* |rakkun|, D inf. *la-gu-ne-im* |rakkunim| → Fronzaroli ARET 11 163; SEL 12 63; Catagnoti QuSe 29 131, 138, 141f., 222.
•LL: **MŠ** *ra-ka-nu* = MIN (*da-a-ku*) → Hrůša MŠ (I 106) 36, 309.

|r-k-S|

Sem.: *rks* (Hb.) "to bind, tie"; *rkš* (Syr., Mand. also *rks*) "to bind, harness", *rkš(?)* (Mand.) "binding"; *rakāsu(m)* (Akk.) "to bind, tie", *raksu*, *raka/isu* "bound, tied", *riksu*(*m*) "binding, knot, bond"; *rakasa* (Arab.) "to hobble", *rikās* "hobble".

|r-k-S| "to bind, tie; to agree on"
•CTX: **EB** G ptrefc. *ìr-gú-zu* |yirkuS|, Gt prefc. *il-da-gú-su* |yirtakuSū| → Fronzaroli ARET 13 25, 273; Rubio PIHANS 106 122; Catagnoti QuSe 29 26, 38f., 51, 130, 143, 222.
Q *a-na ra-ka*$_4$*-ši-im* → Richter / Lange Idadda 78f. (TT 5:17).
EA G suffc. *ra-ak-ša-šu*, *ra-ak-šu*<*-šu*>*-nu* → Moran AmL 184 fn.7, 192 fn. 2; Rainey CAT 1 45.
UGA G prefc. *trks* → DUL 729: /*r-k-s*/.
•ONOM: **EB** *íl-gú-uš*, *íl-gú-ša*, *íl-*<*gú-*>*uš-su*, *íl-gú-uš-da-mu*, *íl-*<*gú-*>*uš-li-im*, *íl-gú-uš-ma-lik*, *íl-gú-uš-ti*, *íl-gú-uš-wa-bar*, *íl-da-kas/ga-áš* → Pagan ARES 3 164f., 335f.

rakS "knotting, closing / knotted, closed" (?)
•CTX: **EM** *aš-ša-aš-ḫu ra-ak-su* → Westenholz Emar Tablets 59.

rikS "bundle, knot; agreement"
•CTX: **EB** Sg. abs. *ìr-ki-iš* |?irkiS|, obl. GU.MU.TÚG *rí-ga-zi* |rikS=i|, cstr.GU.MU.TÚG *rí-ga-zú* |rikS=|, GU.MU.TÚG *rí-gi-za* |rikS=|, *rí-kas* |rikaS| → Edzard, QuSe 18 214; Pasquali QuSe 19 261f.; Fronzaroli ARET 13 25, 69, 273, 291; Catagnoti QuSe 29 29 39 223.
A7 *ri-ik-ši*, *ri-ik-ša-am* → Wiseman AT 31 (AT 3:1, 4).[480]

rks "belt"
•CTX: **UGA** *r*<*k*>*s* → DUL 729.

---

[479] Sivan / Cochavi-Rainey WSVES 81: *ma-r-ka-bu-tá* / *mà-r-ka-ba-tu* / *mà-r-ka-b-tu* "chariot(s)"; Helck Beziehungen no. 102; Kilani VGW 120, 131: |mvrk'a/obtv|,

[480] The same writing with *š* in texts from Carchemish according to the Hitt. treaty terminology. For further bibliographical references see Rainey CAT 1 45.

|r-k-s[1]|	Sem.: Hb. *rkwš* (*rᵉkûš*) "possession, goods, equipment", denom. *rkš* "to acquire".
rakūs[1]u "equipment, gear"	•CTX: **EG** *r-k-su*$_2$ → Hoch SWET 210f. no. 286.[481]

|r-ḳ-d| Cf. |**r-ḳ-ṣ**|	Sem.: *rqd* (Hb.) "to spring, leap", (D) "to dance"; *rqd* (JAram., Syr.) "to dance", *rqd(?)*, *rqdn* "dancer"; *raqādu*(*m*) (Akk.) "to dance, skip", *raqqidu*(*m*) "(cultic) dancer".
|**r-ḳ-d**| "to spring, leap, dance"	•ONOM: **UGA** Cf. *rqdn* → DUL 734.[482]
mrḳd "an instrument for accompanying the dance (castanet ?)"	•CTX: **UGA** Pl. / du. *mrqdm* → DUL 569: *mrqd.*

|r-ḳ-ḫ|	Sem.: *rqḥ* (Hb.) "to prepare, mix spiced ointment", *rqḥ* (*reqaḥ, roqaḥ*) "spice mixture", (*raqqāḥ*) "ointment-mixer", (*riqquᵃḥ*) "ointment"; *rqḥ* (Aram., Ph., Pun.) "to prepare perfumes", *rqḥ* (Aram.) "perfume", *mrqḥ* (Aram.) "ointment (?), perfume (?)"; *rīqu(m), riqqu* (Akk.) "aromatic substance", *ruqqû, raqqû* "to process oil", *raqqû* "oil-perfumer", *raqqûtu* "spice(s)".
rāḳiḫ "oil-perfumer"	•LL: **EB** Ì.RÁ.RA = *ra-gi-um* → Fronzaroli QuSe 13 148; Catagnoti QuSe 29 40, 140, 156, 222.
rḳḫ (A) "perfume, ointment"	•CTX: **UGA** Cf. *r*[*qḥ* (sg. ?) → DUL 735: *rqḥ* (II).
rḳḫ (B) "perfumer, druggist"	•CTX: **UGA** → DUL 734f.: *rqḥ* (I).
riḳaḫt "spiced, oily ointment"	•LL: **EB** GIŠ.NAGA = *rí-ga-tum* → Conti QuSe 17 31, 33, 126. See also Catagnoti Fs. Scandone Matthiae 141.

|r-ḳ-ḳ| (1)	Sem.: *rq* (raq, Hb.) "thin, gaunt", *rāqîq* "flat cakes, thin bread", *rqh* (*raqqāh*) "temple"; *rqq* (Syr. C) "to beat thin with a hammer"; *raqāqu*(*m*) (Akk.) "to be(come) thin, fine", *raqqu*(*m*) "thin, fine", *ruqqu*(*m*), "cauldron"; *raqqa* (Arab.) "to be(come) thin, delicate, fine", *raqq, riqq* "parchment", *riqqa* "thinness", *raqīq* "thin, slender", *ruqāq* "flat loaf of bread"; *reḳéḳ, reḳáyk* (MSArab.) "transparent, fine"; *rqq, raqqa, raqaqa* (Eth.) "to be subtle, soft, thin, slight", *raqiq* "soft, thin, slight".
|**r-ḳ-ḳ**| "to be(come) thin, fine"	•ONOM: **UGS** Cf. unc. *ra*-GA-*na* → DUL 735: *rqn.* **UGA** Cf. unc. *rqn* → DUL 735.
raḳḳ "thin, fine"	•LL: **EB** NÍG.SAL = *ra-gu* → Krebernik ZA 73 4; Conti QuSe 17 39, 74; Catagnoti QuSe 29 23, 36, 222.

---

481 For Akk. *ra-ki-su* and *raksu* (Hoch op.cit.) see rather \|r-k-S\|.

482 No convincing etym. are given for the Ug. TN *rqd / Raqdu* (Belmonte RGTC 12/2 233f., DUL 734; see DUL 734: GN *rqdy* (I), PN *rqdy* (II)). Cf. Arab. *raqada* "to rest, lie", *raqda* "manner of lying".

ruḳḳ "sheet of metal"	•CTX: **EUPH** *ru-qí, ru-qú-ú, ru-uq-qú/qí, ru-qí-im, ru-uq-qí-im* → Durand MARI 2 134; Guichard ARM 31 289ff.; Arkhipov ARM 32 18f.
rḳ (A) "fine, thin"	•CTX: **UGA** → DUL 733: *rq* (II).
rḳ (B) "sheet"	•CTX: **UGA** Pl. *rqm* → DUL 733: *rq* (I).
raḳaḳ "thin cake, waffle"	•LL: **EB** NÍG.ŠU.DU.DU = *ra-ga-gu* → Sjöberg Fs. Kienast 529.
ruḳḳān "thin cake, waffle"	•CTX: **EM** NINDA *ru-qa-nu* → Pentiuc Vocabulary 153.
raḳḳat (A) "a type of bread"	•CTX: **EM** NINDA *ra-qa-tum* → CAD R 171: *raqqatu* D.
raḳḳat (B) "a fine textile"	•CTX: **ASS**, **EUPH** Passim GÚ / TÚG *ra-qa-tum*; cf. [GÚ / TÚG *r*]*a-aq-qa-tum* → CAD R 168ff.: *raqqatu* A; Durand ARM 30 87ff., 429f.[483]
raḳḳat (C) "a part of the head" (?)	•CTX: **B** Cf. *ra-aq-qa-at šumēlišu* ("his left *r.*") → CAD R 170f.: *raqqatu* C.
rḳt "temple"	•CTX: **UGA** Sg. / pl. suff. *rqth* → DUL 735: *rqt*; Watson FO 52 326.
trḳ "a container" (?)	•CTX: **UGA** Unc. → Du. *trqm* → DUL 867: *trq*.

|r-ḳ-ḳ| (2)	Primary noun, Sem.: *rqq*(?) (Aram., Nab., Syr.) "swamp, ford"; *raqqatu* (Akk.) "river-flats"; *raqqa* (Arab.) "riverside", cf. *riqq*, *ruqq* "area of level ground"; *reḳ* (MSArab.) "shallow". Cf. further *raqaʔa* (Arab.) "to cease to flow".
raḳḳat (D) "meadow, swamp, marsh"	•CTX: **B** A.GÀR *ra-aq-qa-tim* → Kraus AbB 4 95:5; Fiette ARCHIBAB 3 167, 190 (n. 679). **EUPH** *ra-qa-tum* → Villard ARM 23 556f. (590:6); CAD R 170: *raqqatu* B. **EM** A.ŠÀ [...] *i-na ra-qa-ti*, (orchard) *ša ra-qa-ti* → Arnaud Emar 6 146:1, 169:4; CAD R 170: *raqqatu* B; Westenholz Emar Tablets 19. **MBQ** *ra-qa-ti* → Mayer Ekalte 38, 166. •LL: **MŠ** *raq-qa-tu*$_4$ = *ú-šal-la* (II 44) → Hrůša MŠ 54, 332.

|r-ḳ-ṣ| Cf. **|r-ḳ-d|**	Sem.: *raqaṣa* (Arab.) "to dance"; *reḳōṣ*, *reḳáwṣ* (MSArab.) "to dance".
|r-ḳ-ṣ| "to jump, leap"	•CTX: **UGA** Gt prefc. *trtqṣ*, *yrtqṣ* → DUL 735: */r-q-ṣ/*.[484]

|r-m-ħ|	Primary noun, Sem.: *rmḥ* (*romaḥ*, Hb.) "lance, spear"; *rwmḥ*(?) (JAram., Syr.) id.; (Arab.) *rumḥ* id.; *rmḥ* (OSArab.) id.; *rəmḥat* (MSArab.) id.; *ramḥ*, *rəmḥ* (Eth.) id.
murħ "lance, spear"	•CTX: **EG** (metath.) *ma-r-ḥa*, *ma-ra-ḥa* → Hoch SWET 138f. no. 179.[485]
mrħ "lance, spear"	•CTX: **UGA** (metath.) Sg. *mrḥ*, suff. *mrḥh*, du. *mrḥm*, pl. cstr. *mrḥy* → Tropper UG 166, KWU 77; DUL 567: *mrḥ*; Del Olmo AuPr 37 291.

|r-m-k|	Sem.: Cf. *ramāku*(*m*) (Akk.) "to bathe, wash (in)", *ramku*(*m*) "bathed".

---

483 See also Ziegler FM 4 158ff. (9 I 28'): *ra-aq-qa*]*-tum*.

484 Read *brltk* for wrong *m*]*rqṣtk* in KTU[(3)] 1.16 I 42.

485 Sivan / Cochavi-Rainey WSVES 80: *ma-r-ḥà* / *mi-r-ḥa* "lance"; Helck Beziehungen no. 98; Kilani VGW 119: \|m'i/urḥv\|.

|r-m-k| "to soak, bathe; to purify, prune; to macerate"	•CTX: **EUPH** D prefc. *ú-ra-mi-ik*, inf. *a-na ru-mu-ki-šu* → Lion FM 108; Chambon FM 11 186 (187); Durand LAPO 16 359f. fn. a (225); .Joannès MARI 7 259f. (A.4446).
ramik "bathed, washed"	•ONOM: **EUPH** Cf. *ra-mi-ga-nu-um* → Gelb CAAA 30, 176.[486]
tarmikt "purification, pruning" (?)	•CTX: **EUPH** *ta-ar-mi-ik-ti, ta-ar-mi-ik-tum, ta-ar-mi-ik-tim* → CAD T 238: *tarmiktu*; Lion FM 108; Durand LAPO 16 359f. fn. a (225).
|r-m-m| (1)	Primary noun, Sem.: *rmh* (*rimmāh*, Hb.) "maggot"; *rmh, rmtʔ* (Aram., Syr.) "maggot"; *rimmā* (Arab.) "wood-fretter", also "cadaver". See *rmm* (Hb.) "to decay"; *ramma, rimma, ramim, ʔaramm* (Arab.) "to decay, rot".
|r-m-m| (A) "to decay"	•CTX: **EB** G prefc. *a-la-mi-im* |lā=yirammim| → Fronzaroli ARET 13 26, 242; Catagnoti QuSe 29 45, 105, 222.
rimmat "a bead (shaped as a maggot ?)"	•CTX: **EUPH** *ri-im-ma-tim* → Durand ARM 21 235; Durand Fs. Perrot 160ff.; Anbar EI 24 159f.; Lion / Michel MARI 8 722f.
|r-m-m| (2) Cf. **|r-γ-m|**	Sem.: *ramāmu(m)* (Akk.) "to roar, growl", *ramīmu*(m) "roar (of Adad)", *rimmu(m)* "roaring".
|r-m-m| (B) "to roar, thunder"	•ONOM: **EUPH** *ra-ma-ma-nu-um, bu-ra-ma-nim*; cf. *ra-ma-ma*-AN → Greenfield IEJ 26 196ff.; Gelb CAAA 29, 176; Zadok Fs. Hallo 328.
|r-m-S| See **|r-p-s|**	Sem. lexicalized variants: Cf. *rms* (Hb.) "to trample with one's feet, crush to pieces", *mrms* (*mirmās*) "trampling, overtrodden land", *rmŠ* (*rmś*) "to slink, crawl", *rmŠ* (*remeś*) "creature(s)"; *rms* (JAram.) "to creep, crawl, to trample", *rms(ʔ)* "creeping thing"; *namāšu(m)* (Akk.) "to set oneself in motion, start out", *nammaštû(m)* "moving things, animals".
|r-m-S| "to set oneself in motion in a particular manner" (?)	•ONOM: **EB** Cf. *il-maš-il, dar-ma-áš, tar*$_x$(BAN)*-maš-da-mu* → Krebernik PET 52; Pagan ARES 3 165, 300, 334, 369.
rimS "moving, setting in motion in a particular manner" (?)	•ONOM: **EUPH** Cf. *ri-im-ši*-DINGIR, *ri-im-ši-ì-lí, ri-im-ši-ì-lí, ka-ak-ka-ri-im-ši* → Gelb CAAA 30, 178.
ramaS, ramiS "being on the move in a particular manner" (?)	•ONOM: **EB Cf.** *ra-maš* → Pagan ARES 3 135, 358. **EUPH** Cf. *ra-ma(-a)-ši, ra-mi-šum* → Gelb CAAA 30, 176.
|r-m-ṣ́|	Sem.: Cf. *ramaḍa, ramiḍa* (Arab.) "to burn, be hot, burning", *ramḍāʔ* "hot, sun-baked ground"; *rmḥ* (JAram. < *rmʕ* "to cook in ash") "hot ash"; *ramaḍa, ramaṣa* (Eth.) "to scorch, burn", *ramaḍ* "hot ashes, heat of ashes".

486 Cf. Gelb MAD 3 235: RMK (*ir-mu-uk-ìr-ra*, Ur III). For the probl. Non-Sem. PNN *i-ne/ni-ir-mu-uk* (Gelb CAAA 30, 179), and *i-ni-ik-mu-uq/uk-pa/tab-li* see Golinets Onomastikon 2 203f.

rmṣ "embers, hot stones"	•CTX: **UGA** Pl.t. *rmṣt* → DUL 730. Diff. Tropper KWU 107: "Röstopfer".
|r-m-θ|	Culture word, Sem. etym. unc.: Cf. *armašītu*, *arbašītu* (Akk.) "a pottery vessel", "a type of pot".
rmθt "a vessel" (?)	•CTX: **UGA** → DUL 730: *rmṯt*.
|r-m-y|	Sem.: *rmh* (Hb.) "to cast, to throw, shoot"; *rmy* (Aram., Syr.) "to throw, put down, shoot"; *ramû(m)* (Akk.) "to throw, cast down, cast over someone"; *ramā*, *rimāya* (Arab.) "to throw, fling, hurl, shoot"; *ramaya* (Eth.) "to throw, strike, shoot".
|r-m-y| "to throw, cast, shoot"	•CTX: **UGA** G prefc. *yrmy* → DUL 730. •ONOM: **EB** *íl-mi*, *íl-mi-lum*, *íl-mi-ì*, *ir-mi-*^{d}*ša-ma-gan*, cf. *ìr(uš)-mi-ì*, *dar-mi-a*, *dar-mi-lu* → Pagan ARES 3 165, 300, 336f., 339.
|r-n-n|	Sem.: *rnn* (Hb.) "to call loudly, shrilly, to shout"; *rnn* (Palm.) "to announce, to sing" (?); *rnn* (JAram.) "to murmur", D "to praise aloud joyfully"; *ranna* (Arab.) "to cry, wail, lament".
|r-n-n| "to shout, raise one's voice"	•CTX: **UGA** G prefc. *årnn* → Tropper KWU 107, UG 955; DUL 731: /*r-n*(-*n*)/. •ONOM: **UGA** Cf. unc. *rny* → DUL 731. **EG** Cf. *y:-r-n:-n-ꜣ* → Schneider APÄQ 36 no. 53.
|r-p-ʔ|	Sem.:. *rpʔ* (Hb.) "to heal", *rpʔym* (pl. t. *rāpāʔîm*, *r*^{e}*pāʔîm*) "dead spirits; legendary peoples", *rpwʔh* (pl. *r*^{e}*puʔôt*) "healing, medication"; *rpʔ* (Aram., Ph., Pun.) "to heal", *rpʔh* (Aram.) "healing", *rpʔm* (Ph., Pun.) "dead spirits"; *rpy* (Syr.) "to make firm", (Aram. D) "to heal"; *rafaʔa* (Arab.) "to sew, mend, repair"; *rfʔ* (OSArab.) "to, protect"; *rafʔa* (Eth.) "to sew, mend, heal".
|r-p-ʔ| "to heal"	•CTX: **UGA** G prefc. *trpå* → DUL 731: /*r-p-ʔ*/. •ONOM: **EUPH** *ia-ar-pa-*^{d}IM → Huffmon APNMT 263f.; Gelb CAAA 30, 179; Golinets Onomastikon 2 178. **A7** *ir-pa-a-bi*, *ir-pa-da*, *ir-pa-a-da*, *ir-pa-*^{d}IM → Wiseman AT 138; Huffmon APNMT 263f.; Gelb CAAA 30, 179; Arnaud AuOr 16 176, 180; Streck ArOr 67 655ff.; Golinets Onomastikon 2 30, 175, 178f., 439f. **EM** *ia-ra-pi-iʔ* → Pruzsinszky PTEm 210 fn. 573 [421]. **EG** *r-pꜣ-y*; cf. unc. *r-f-y*$_2$, *r-y*$_2$*-f-y*$_2$, *rw-f-y*$_2$, *tꜣ-r-f-y*$_2$ → Schneider APÄQ 151f. no. 319. **UGA** *yrpủ* → DUL 966.
rapʔ "purification" (?)	•LL: **UGS** [SIKIL ? = *tēliltu* ? / *ebbu* ??] = *x-x-x-ni-ḫi* = *rap-u*(?) → Huehnergard UVST 58, 179.
riʔp "healing, salvation"	•ONOM: **EUPH** *pí-ri-ip-i-im*, *ri-ip-a-*DINGIR, *ri-ip-a-ma-lik*, *ri-ip-i/e-*dIM, *ri-ip-*(*i-*)^{d}*da-gan*, *ri-i-pi-*^{d}*da-gan*, *ri-ip-i-li-im*, *ri-ip-i-sa-ma-ás* → Huffmon APNMT 264; Gelb CAAA 30, 179; Zadok Fs. Hallo 328, Streck ArOr 67 664,

Onomastikon 1 199 § 2.95, 201 § 2.95, 233f. § 2.145f., 238 § 2.154, 323 § 5.11, Suppl. 361.
TU *ri-ip-ḫi-*^{d}*da-gan* → Krebernik Tall Bi`a 226; Streck Onomastikon 1 232 § 2.144.
A4 *šu-me/i-ri-pa* → Gelb CAAA 30, 177; Streck Onomastikon 1 224 § 2.127, 253 § 2.179.
EM *ri-ib-i* → Pruzsinszky PTEm 176 [704].

rāpiʔ "healer (ancestral hero; DN)"
•ONOM: **U3** LÚ-*ra-bí* → Buccellati Amorites 111; Gelb CAAA 30, 177; Streck ArOr 67 661; Onomastikon 1 267 § 3.14; Golinets Onomastikon 2 180,439f.
EUPH Written *ra-pi=*, e.g. *a-bi-ra-pi, al-la-ra-pi, am-mu-ra-pi, am-mi-ra-pi, ḫa-am-mu-um-ra-pi, ḫa-at-nu-ra-pi*; written *=ra-pi=*, e.g. *ḫa-am-mu-um-ra-pi-li-wi-ir*; written *ra-pa=* (< |rāpiʔ=a=|) *ra-pa-nu-um*; written *ra-bi=*, e.g. *ra-bi-um, ra-bi-i-im, ra-bi-ú-um, ra-bi-mi-il, ra-bi-mi-lum*; (fem.) *ra-bi-a, ra-bi-ia, ra-bi-a-tum, ra-bi-tum*; written *=ra-bi*, e.g. ^{d}*a-*[*ba*$_4$*-*]*ra-bi, a-bi-ra-bi, a-mi-ra-bi, ab-nu-ra-bi, a-pa-aḫ-ra-bi, áš-du-ra-bi, be-lí-ra-bi, da-du-ra-bi*, DINGIR-*ra-bi, é-a-ra-bi*, ^{d}EN.ZU-*ra-bi*, $^{(d)}$*ḫa-am-mu-ra-bi, ḫa-am-mu-ú-ra-bi, ḫa-am-mu-um-ra-bi, ḫa-ad-nu-ra-bi*, (cf. *ḫa-at-nu-ra-bi*), *ḫa-am-na-ra-bi, ḫa-am-ru-ra-bi, ḫa-*(*a-*)*yu-um-ra-bi, ḫa-lu-ra-bi, ḫa-mu-ra-bi, ḫa-mu-ú-ra-bi, ḫa-mu-um-ra-bi, ḫa-mu-úr-ra-bi, ì-lí-ra-bi*, ^{d}IM-*ra-bi*, ^{d}ID-*ra-bi, iz-kur-ra-bi*, [*mu-u*]*l-ki-ra-bi, mu-ut-*[*r*]*a-bi, ša-am-*[*si-*]*ra-bi*, ^{d}UTU-ra-bi, *su-ma-ra-bi, sú-mu-ra-bi, ya-ku-un-ra-bi*; written *=ra-bi=*, e.g. *a-mu-ra-bi-ì-*[*lí*], *ḫa-am-mu-ra-bi-*DINGIR, *ḫa-am-mu-ra-bi-ba-ni, ḫa-am-mu-ra-bi-lu-da-ri*; written *=ra-bi-i*, e.g. *ia-ku-un-ra-bi-i, zi-me-er-ra-bi-i, ḫa-lu-ra-bi-i*; written *ra-bi-iḫ=*, e.g. *a-bi-ra-bi-iḫ, am-mi-ra-bi-ih, ḫa-am-mu-ra-bi-iḫ, ḫa-lu-ra-bi-iḫ* → Huffmon APNMT 263f.; Gelb CAAA 30, 176f.; Streck ArOr 67 659ff., Onomastikon 1 158 § 2.15, 200 § 2.95, 265 § 3.12, 267 § 3.14, 268 § 3.15, 277 § 3.30, 281 § 3.40, 329 § 5.24; Golinets Onomastikon 2 174, 180ff., 439ff.
TU *a-mu-ra-bi-i, ḫa-lu-ra-bi-i* → Krebernik Tall Bi`a 209 (*=ra-pí*); Golinets Onomastikon 2 181f., 439ff.
A7 Written *=ra-pa*: *su-mi-ra-pa*; written *=ra-bi*: *am-mu-ra-bi, ḫa-am-mu-ra-bi, ia-šu-ub-ra-bi, ši-nu-ra-bi*; written *=ra-bi-i*: *am-mu-ra-bi-i* → Wiseman AT 135, 138, 145f.; Huffmon APNMT 264; Gelb CAAA 30, 176f.; Sivan GAGl 264; Arnaud AuOr 16 162f.; Streck ArOr 67 659ff., Onomastikon 1 158 § 2.15, 191 § 2.88, 224 § 2.127, 235 § 2.148, 265 § 3.12, 267 § 3.14; Golinets Onomastikon 2 180ff., 439ff.
A4 Cf. *a-bi-ra-a-bi* → Wiseman AT 126; Dietrich / Loretz ZA 60 92 (4:5); Sivan GAGl 264.
EM *ra-pí-ú*, A.A-*x x x-ra-pí-i?*, $^{\langle d\rangle}$KUR-*ra-pí-iḫ*, dÉ.A-*ra-pí-iḫ* → Pruzsinszky PTEm 191 [112], 176 [690], 195 [284], [304].
TA DINGIR-*ra-bi-i* → Horowitz / Oshima CunCan 133 (2:21); Golinets Onomastikon 2 182, 439ff.
EG *r-pꜣ-y*; cf. unc. *r-f-y*$_2$, *r-y*$_2$*-f-y*$_2$, *rw-f-y*$_2$, *tꜣ-r-f-y*$_2$ → Schneider APÄQ 151f. no. 319.
UGS |rāpiʔ=ān|: *rap-a-na, ra-ap-a-na*; |rāpiʔ=|: *am/a-mu-ra-bi*, ÌR-*rap-i*, DUMU.SAL *ra-ap-i, šu-mu-ra-bi*; cf. *a-bir*$_x$*-pí-i* → Gröndahl PTU 180; Sivan GAGl 264.

rōpiʔ "healer (ancestral hero; DN)"
•ONOM: **EM** *ru-pí-*^{d}*da-gan* → Pruzsinszky PTEm 197 fn. 470, 219 [704]; Streck AfO 52 311.

rapūʔ "healed"
•ONOM: **EUPH** *ra-pu-ú-um*, (fem.) *ra-pu-a-tum* → Gelb CAAA 30, 177; Streck ArOr 67 664, Onomastikon 1 198 § 2.95, 233f § 2.145f., 315 § 4.9, 330 § 5.28; Golinets Onomastikon 2 185f., 439ff.

rpủ “healer (ancestral hero; DN)”	•CTX: **UGA** sg. abs. / cstr. *rpủ*, *rpỉ*, pl. abs. *rpủm*, *rpỉm*, cstr. *rpỉ* → DUL 731f. •ONOM: **UGA** *ảbrpủ* → DUL 13; *ỉlrpỉ* → DUL 62; *ʕbdrpủ* → DUL 140; *ʕmrpỉ* (var. *ʕmrbỉ*) → DUL 162f.; *mlkrpỉ* → DUL 549; *rpỉl* → DUL 732; *rpản* → DUL 732; *rpỉy* → DUL 732; *rpỉyn* → DUL 732
ripʔūt “care, medication”	•CTX: **EA** *ri-pu-ú-ti* → Huffmon APNMT 264; AHw 987; CAD R 367; Sivan GAGl 265.

|r-p-d| (1)	Sem.: *rpd* (Hb. G, D) “to spread out, extend”; *rpd* (Syr.) “to creep”; *rapādu(m)* (Akk.) “to roam, wander”, *murtappidu(m)* “wandering, roving”; *rafada*, *ʔarfada* (Arab.) “to put a saddle-pad on a beast”, *rifāda* “saddle-pad”; *rafada* (Eth.) “to spread out a mat”.
|r-p-d| “to roam, wander”	•LL: **EB** EDEN.DU.DU = *ra-ba-tum* → Krebernik ZA 73 43.
rāpid “raider”	•CTX: **EB** *ra-[bu_{16}-]du-nu-ma*, *a-la-bu_{16}-[d]u-nu-ma* (< |(la=)rāpidūnu=ma|) → Catagnoti / Fronzaroli ARET 16 121, 261; Catagnoti QuSe 29 53, 75, 107, 222.
tartappid “trek” (?)	•LL: **EB** EDEN.DU.DU = *dar-da-bí-tum* → Krebernik ZA 73 43; Rubio PIHANS 106 135: tGtn nomen actionis (< |tartanpid|); Catagnoti QuSe 29 123, 139, 144, 222.

|r-p-d| (2)	Sem.: *rpd* (Hb. D) “to support”; *rafada* (Arab.) “to support”, *rāfida* “main beam, support”; *rfd* (OSArab.) “to support, help”, *rfdt* “revetment(s), base of a column”.
ripād “support, pedestal”	•LL: **EB** DAG = *ri-b[a-du]* → Waetzoldt MEE 12 52 (EV 051); Pasquali QuSe 23 118.
tarpīd “support, pedestal” (?)	•CTX: **EB** *da-bí-tum* → Pasquali QuSe 23 117f.

|r-p-ḳ| See **|r-b-ḳ|**	Sem.: *mtrpqt* (*mitrēpeqet* Hb., ptc. fem. Hitp.) “who leans oneself against, support oneself”; *mrqp(ʔ)* (JAram.) “elbow (as support)”; *rāfaqa* (Arab.) “to be companion, to accompany, escort”, *mirfaq*, *marfiq* “elbow; cushion; implement”, *murtafaq* “support”, *ʔarfaqa* “to attach, enclose, append”, *ʔirtafaqa* “to lean one’s elbows, rest one’s arms”; *rəfiq* (MSArab.) “one another”; *rafaqa* (Eth.) “to recline, lie down, sit”, *marfāq*, *mərfāq*, *marfaq* “place where one reclines or sits”.
|r-p-ḳ| “to prop, support”	•LL: **EB** SA[G.GUB] = *ra-ba-gu(-um)* → Conti QuSe 17 107.
rapaḳt “support”	•LL: **EB** SAG.E_{11} = *ra-ba-ga-tum* → Conti QuSe 17 108.
ripiḳt “support”	•LL: **EB** SAG.KI.GUB = *rí-bí-ki-tum* → Krebernik PIHANS 106 91.
marpiḳt “support, tray”	•CTX: **EB** *mar-pi-ga-tum* → Pasquali QuSe 23 168ff.; Or 83 272f.
tartappiḳ “supporting”	•LL: **EB** SAG.E_{11} = *dar-da-bí-gu-um* → Conti QuSe 17 108; Catagnoti QuSE 29 28, 123, 139, 144, 222.

|r-p-s| See **|r-m-S|**	Sem.: *rps*, *rpŠ* (*rpś*) “to disturb (water), make muddy”; *rps* (Aram., Syr.) “to trample”; rapāsu(m) (Akk.) “to beat, thrash”; *rafasa* (Arab.) “to kick”.
|r-p-s| “to trample on”	•CTX: **UGA** G prefc. *yrps* → DUL 732.

|r-p-s^1|	Sem.: *rapāšu(m)* (Akk.) "to be(come) broad, expand", (D) "to widen, extend", *rapšu*(m) "wide, extended", *rupšu(m)* "width, breadth", *narpašû* "broadening, extension", *tarpašû(m)* "open space".
|r-p-s^1| "to widen, extend; to be generous"	•ONOM: **EB** Cf. *íl-ba-šum, ìr-ba-su,*[487] *ìr-píš-da-mu, ìr-píš-zé, la*/*ra-píš-dum, ra-bù-šum,*[488] *li-ba-su,*[489] *rí-píš, ru$_{12}$-bù-uš-li-im* → Krebernik PET 50; Bonechi MARI 8 498; Pagan ARES 3 165.
raps^1 "wide, extended" (?)	•ONOM: **UGS** Cf. TN URU *ḫal-bi rap-ši* → Belmonte RGTC 12/2 112. Cf. *rps*^{1} below.[490]
rips^1 "wide, extended"	•CTX: **EB** *rí-péš* abs. |ripiS| → Catagnoti QuSe 29 27, 117, 223: "largamente".
rapis^1 "wide, extended, generous"	•ONOM: **EB** *la*/*ra-píš-dum* → Bonechi MARI 8 498; Pagan ARES 3 165, 345, 358.
rps^1 "wide, extended, generous; open country"	•CTX: **UGA** Pl. cstr. *rpš* → DUL 732f.: *rpš* (I). •ONOM: **UGA** Cf. *rpš* → DUL 733: *rpš* (II).[491]

|r-p-y|	Sem. Cf. *rph* (Hb.) "to grow slack, release, wither, collapse"; *rpy* (Aram., Syr.) "to be(come) lax, weaken"; see also *ramû(m), remû, ramāʔu(m)* (Akk.) "to slacken, become loose".
|r-p-y| "to slacken, loosen"	•CTX: **UGA** Dt prefc. *ttrp* → DUL 733.[492]

|r-s-ḫ| Cf. **|r-ḫ-s^2|**, **|r-s-s|**	Sem.: *rasḥa* (Eth.) "to be unclean, filthy, defiled"; see also *rəḥsa*, metath. *rasḥa* (Eth.) "to be moist".
|r-s-ḫ| "to dissolve, sully" (?)	•LL: **EB** Cf. NÌ.GÚG.GÚG = *ra-sa-um* → Conti QuSe 17 12, 36, 82.[493]

|r-S-p|	Sem.: *ršp* (*rešep*, Hb.) "flame, glow, blaze"; *ršp* (Aram., Palm.) "a demon"(?). Cf. *ršpm* (Ph.) "manes, shades" (?; cf. *ʔrṣ ršpm*).
|r-S-p| "to flame, blaze"	•ONOM: **EUPH** *ia-ar-sa-ap-la-*DINGIR, *ia-ar-sa-ap-la-il, ia-ar-sa-ap-la-i-la, ia-ar-sà-ap-la-*DINGIR, *ia-ar-sa-ab-ba, ta-ar-sa-ba* → Gelb CAAA 30, 179; Zadok Fs. Hallo 328f.; Streck Onomastikon 1 211 § 2.121, 223 § 2.124; Golinets Onomastikon 2 83,116, 117, 123, 441f., 478, 487.

---

487 Diff. Pagan ARES 335: |yilbā=šum| "DN encircled" (see |l-w-y|), |ʕirba=s^{1}u| "his gift".

488 Diff. Pagan ARES 3 |rabbu=Sum| "great is DN" (see here |r-b-b| (1), |r-b-y|), altern. |raybu=Sum| "compensation is DN" (see here |r-y-b|).

489 Diff. Pagan ARES 3 346 |rība=s^{1}u| "his compensation" (see here |r-y-b|).

490 See the following fn.

491 For the TN UGS URU *ḫal-bi rap-ši* / UGA *ḫlb rpš* see Dietrich / Loretz UF 10 430; DUL 386: *ḫlb rpš*, and cf. Hb. rpš (repeš) "mud".

492 Altern. Tropper KWU 129: |t-r-p| "schändlich behandeln, verachten, verderben" (with JAram. *trp*, C).

493 Cf. NÌ.Ì.GÚG = var. A rdg [*í*]*l*(?)-*za-um* |ʔirsāḫum| (?) for [S]AG(?)-*za-um*; Conti QuSe 17 53. Critically Sjöberg Fs. Pettinato 258: *il* representing |ʔir| seems unlikely.

raSap "flame, blaze; DN"	•LL: **EB** ^{d}GÌR.UNU(^{d}nergal$_{x}^{irigal}$$_{x}$) = *ra-sa-ab* → Krebernik ZA 73 31; Conti QuSe 17 194. •ONOM: **EB** *bù-^{d}ra-sa-ap*, *en-na-$^{(d)}$ra-sa-ap*, *i-ti-^{d}ra-sa-ap*, *ib-du-^{d}ra-sa-ap* → Krebernik PET 104, 277; Pagan ARES 3 165f., 294, 307, 327, 331. **EUPH** *a-bi-ra-sa-ap*, *ia-aḫ-ba-^{d}ra-sa-ap*, *ì-lí-^{d}ra-sa-ap*, *ia-aḫ-zu-^{d}ra-sa-ap*, *i-ṣí-ra-sa-ap* → Huffmon APNMT 263; Gelb CAAA 30, 177; Zadok Fs. Hallo 328f.;[494] Zadok Fs. Hallo 328f.; Durand REA 660. **EM** *ra-ša-ap*-TI, *ra-ša-ap*-DINGIR, *ra-ša/ša$_{10}$-ì-lí*, *ra-šap*-DINGIR-*lì*, *ra-ša$_{10}$-ap-ka-bar*, *ra-ša-ap-la-i*, *ra-šap-pa*-DINGIR-*lì*; cf. *zu-ra* → Pruzsinszky PTEm 128 [692ff.], 187 [857], 201 [695f.].
riSp, ruSp, raSip, rSap "flame, blaze; DN"	•ONOM: **EUPH**: Elem. |ruSp=| in the DN *RuSpān*: *i-din-ru-uš/úš-pa-an* → Huffmon APNMT 263; Streck 203 § 2.95; Durand REA 660; Golinets Onomastikon 2 441. **EA** Hurr.-Sem. elem. |(i)rSap|: *ir-ša-ap-pa* → vSoldt BiOr 46 647; Hess APN 91.[495] **UGS** Allomorphic elems |riSp=|, |raSip|: *ri-iš-pa-ia*, ÌR-*ra-ši-ip*, *nu-ma-re-ša-ip*; Hurr.-Sem. elem. |(i)rSap|: ÌR-*ir-šap(-pa)* → Gröndahl PTU 163, 181, 225f.; vSoldt BiOr 46 647.
rs^{1}p "flame, blaze; DN"	•LL: **UGA** *ršp* → DUL 736: *ršp*, b.[496] •ONOM: **UGA** DN *ršp*, pl. / du. *rpšm* → DUL 736: *rpš*, a, c.[497] Elem. in PNN: *ảbršp* → DUL 14; *ả/iḫršp*, *ảḫrṯp* → DUL 39: *ả/iḫršp*; *ỉlršp* → DUL 62; *ʕbdršp* → DUL 140; *ʕdršp* → DUL 147; *bnršp* → DUL 227; *ḫḏpršp* → DUL 383; *mlkršp* → DUL 549; *mršp* → DUL 571; *ngršp* → DUL 615; *ršpảb* → DUL 737; *ršpn* → DUL 737; *ršpy* → DUL 737; *tgrš* → DUL 849; *tgršp* → DUL 849; *ytršp* → DUL 978.

|r-s-s| Cf. **|r-s-ħ|** **|r-s-s|** "to sprinkle, spray"	Sem.: *rss* (Hb.) "to splash, spray"; *rss* (Syr.) "to sprinkle, drip"; *rašša* (Arab.) "to spatter, splash, spray, sprinkle"; see also *russû(m)* (Akk.) "to dissolve, sully" (?). •ONOM: **EG** Cf. *r-sꜣ-sꜣ* $^{SY.SḎ.MḎ3T}$ → Schneider APÄQ 155f. nos. 331f.

|r-S-t|	Culture word, Sem. etym. unc. Cf. *ruštu* (NBab. Akk.) "an ornament".
ruSt "an ornament"	•CTX: **EM** *ru-uš-tù*, *ru-uš-tì* → CAD R 430: *ruštu*; Westenholz Emar Tablets 71, 75.

|r-S-y| Cf. |**w-r-θ**|	Sem.: *ršy* (JAram., Syr.) "to obligate, bring suit; to have authority", (C) "to empower, permit"; *rašû(m)* (Akk.) "to get, acquire", *rāšû(m)* "rich, well-off"; *rašā* (*rašw*) (Arab.) "to bribe, obtain a favour by gifts"; *rs^{2}w/y* (OSArab.) "to offer, dedicate, make a grant" (?), *rs^{2}y* "gift"; *reśō* (MSArab.) "to bribe". See also *ršt* (*rešet*, Hb.) "net".
|**r-S-y**| **(A)** "to acquire, get"	•ONOM: **EB** *ar-šè*, *a-ḫa-ar-šè*, *ar-šè-a-ḫa/ḫu*, *ar-si-aḫ*, *ar-šè-ti-lu*, *ar-si-a-ḫa/ḫu/ḫum*, *ar-si-da-mu*, cf. *ìr-si/šè-bar-ru$_{12}$* → Krebernik PET 52f.; Pagan ARES 3 166, 278, 288, 339.

494 For the doubtful DN *Rušpān* of Tuttul cf. now Krebernik Tall Bi`a 203 and the rdg *ru*-X-*Ba-an* (KTT 35 (I) 4, 46 (I) 6).
495 Diff.: Sivan GAGl 265: from a verbal root RŠP.
496 Cf. the writing ^{d}GÌR.UNU.GAL(nergal), Ug 5 18:26.
497 Cf. the writings ^{d}MAŠ.MAŠ, ^{d}KAL, ^{d}GÌR.UNU.GAL; Huehnergard AkkUg 69, 360, 382, 399.

	U3 *a-ḫa-am-ar-ši, ar-si*(!?)*-a-núm* → Buccellati Amorites 134f.; Gelb CAAA 30, 179; Golinets Onomastikon 2 313, 442, 491. **EUPH** *a-ar-ši*-DINGIR, *ar-ši-a-da*(*-a*), *ar-ši-a-ḫu-um, ar-ši-e-da-ku, ia-ar-ši-a-ša-ri, ia-ar-ši*-DINGIR(*-um*), *ia-ar-ši-ḫa-*(*am-*)*mu, la-ar-ši-ù-um*; cf. unc. *ra-si-a*[498] → Huffmon APNMT 265 (RŠY **rṯw/y* "lament, feel pity"); Gelb CAAA 30, 177, 179; Golinets Onomastikon 2 313 (with fn. 935), 442. **EM** Cf. unc. *ra-se-ia* → Pruzsinszky PTEm 176 fn. 271 [696].
|**r-s**^{1}**-y**| "to receive, have"	•CTX: **UGA** G suffc. *yrš* → DUL 737: */r-š-y/*.
|**r-θ-y**| "to receive, possess"	•CTX: **EB** G prefc. suff. *a-a-la-ša-su-nu* |la=ʔarθay=Sunu| → Catagnoti / Fronzaroli ARET 16 169, 211; Catagnoti QuSe 29 81, 164, 222. **UGA** G prefc. *yrṯy* → DUL 738: */r-ṯ-y/*.
rθt "net"	•CTX: **UGA** → DUL 738.[499]
tartaθtiy "owed amount"	•CTX: **EB** *tar*$_x$*-da-šu* Catagnoti / Fronzaroli ARET 16 169, 271; Catagnoti QuSe 29 139, 144, 165, 222.
|**r-ṣ-ʕ**|	Sem.: *rṣʕ* (Hb.) "to pierce through", *mrṣʕ* (*marṣēᵃʕ*) "awl"; *rṣʕ* (JAram. C) "to bore through", *mrṣʕ(ʔ)* "awl"; *marṣāʔu* (Akk. LL) "a tool (awl ?)"; *raṣaʕa, ʔarṣaʕa* (Arab.) "to nail, hammer", *ʔarṣaʕ* "sharp"; *réṣaʕ* (MSArab.) "to stitch, mend delicately".
riṣaʕ "point, tip"	•CTX: **EB** Sg. genit. *ri-za-im* → Fronzaroli QuSe 15 24f., ARET 11 25, 165.
|**r-s**^{1}**-ʕ**|	Sem.: *ršʕ* (Hb.) "to be(come) guilty, to err", (C) "to make oneself guilty; to declare guilty", *ršʕ* (*rāšāʕ*) "guilty, wicked person", (*rešaʕ*) "wrong, offence", *ršʕh* (*rišʕāh*) "offence"; *ršʕ* (JAram., Syr.) "to be wicked", (C) "to commit evil, to be godless", (Aram., Syr.) *ršyʕ* "wicked", *ršʕ(ʔ)* (JAram., Syr.) "evil"; *ruššû*(*m*) (Akk. D) "to harass, treat ruthlessly, act in contempt or disrespect of others", *rešûm* "reckless"; *rasaʕa* (Arab.) "to be slack, to lack vigor"; *rasʕa* (Eth.) "to neglect, be negligent, be(come) godless, wicked", *rāsəʕ, rəsuʕ, rasiʕ* "negligent, impious".
|**r-s**^{1}**-ʕ**| "to harm, injure, harass" (?)	•CTX: **UGA** G / D (?) prefc. *tršʕ* → Tropper UG 456; DUL 736: */r-š-ʕ/*.
rs^1**ʕ** "bad person"	•CTX: **UGA** → DUL 736: *ršʕ*.
|**r-s**^{1}**-p**| See |**r-S-p**|	
|**r-s**^{1}**-y**|	Sem.: *rasā* (*rasw*, Arab.), *ʔarsā* "to be firm, stable; to anchor, cast anchor"; *resō, hersō* (MSArab.) "to stand firm, be firm", *arsō* "to anchor"; *rsy, ʔarsaya* (Eth.) "to drop anchor, bring to rest".
|**r-S-y**| **(B)** "to fix, (drop) anchor"	•LL: **EB** DA.KEŠDA = *ra-sa-um* → Conti QuSe 17 159.
|**r-ṣ́-y**|	Sem. *rṣh* (Hb.) "to be favourable to, well disposed, pay, redeem", (C) "to bring for payment"; *rṣy* (JAram.) "to consent", *rʕy* (Aram., Syr.) "to desire", (JAram. C) "to satisfy (the obligations)", *rqy* (Aram.) "to look favourable to"; *raḍiya*

[498] Cf. the TNN *ra-sa-ia, ra-sé-e-em, ra-sú-ú*; Groneberg RGTC 3 194f.; Zadok WO 14 239.
[499] Altern.: culture word. Cf. *ršt*, Hb.

(Arab.) "to be satisfied, content"; *rḍy* (OSArab.) "to be willing, consent", *rḍy(m)* "negotiable currency, current coin".

|r-ṣ-y| "to be content, satisfied; to give in payment"
•CTX: **B** Cf. unc. [*š*]*u-ur-ṣi-am* (C) → AHw 960: *raṣûm* "in Zahlung geben"?; Walters YNER 4 86f. (65:14). Cf. CAD R 187: **raṣû* (mng unkn.).
•ONOM: **EB** *al*$_{6}$*-za-li-im*, *ìr-za-il* (cf. *ìr-za*$_{x}$(LAK384)*-ì*), *tal-za-gú-bí* (cf. *tal*!(*rí*)*-zi*, *tar*$_{x}$(BAN)*-zi-na-u*$_{9}$) → Pagan ARES 3 163, 286, 339, 369.
EUPH *ra-za-*^{d}*da-gan* → Huffmon APNMT 265; Gelb CAAA 30, 177; Golinets Onomastikon 2 147.
•ONOM: **B** *ra-zu-um* → Gelb CAAA 175 (from R?Z).

raṣiy "content, satisfied"
•ONOM: **EB** *lá-zi* → Pagan ARES 3 163, 345.

marṣiy "love, choice"
•CTX: **A7** *mar-ṣí* → Arnaud AuOr 16 170.

tarṣiyat "pleasure"
•CTX: **B** Sg. suff. *ta-ar-ṣi-à-ta-ki* → AHw 1331; CAD T 241.

|r-t-ḳ|
Sem.: *rtq* (Hb. Dpass.) "to be fettered", *rt(w/y)qh* (*r*^{e}*tu*/*û*/*îqāh*) "something bound together; chains" (?); *rtq(ʔ)* (JAram.) "impediment, parapet"; *rataqa* (Arab.) "to mend, repair", *raqt* "patching, mending, repair".[500]

|r-t-ḳ| "to tie up, close"
•CTX: **UGA** G suffc. *rtqt*; pass. ptc.(?) *rtq* → DUL 737: /*r-t-q*/.

rutuḳt "binding, clamping, holding together"
•CTX: **EB** *ru*$_{12}$*-du-ga-tum* → Pettinato, Or 53 325 fn. 37; Waetzoldt OrAn 29 11; Pasquali QuSe 19 241f., QuSe 23 88f.

|r-ṭ-b|
Sem.: *rṭb* "to be(come) wet", *rṭb* (*rāṭob*) "to be in sap"; *rṭb* (JAram., Syr.) "to be moist", *rṭyb* "moist", *rṭb(ʔ)*, *rwṭb(ʔ)* "juice, moisture"; *raṭābu*(m) (Akk.) "to be damp, fresh", *raṭbu*(m) "damp, fresh"; *raṭiba*, *raṭuba* (Arab.) "to be moist, damp, humid, wet", *raṭb*, *rāṭib*, *raṭīb* "moist, damp, humid"; *raṭba* (Eth.) "to be moist, damp, humid, wet, juicy", *rəṭb* "sap", *rəṭub* "damp, wet, sappy, juicy".

|r-ṭ-b| "to be wet, juicy"
•ONOM: **EG** Cf. *r*(?)*-t-ꜣ-bꜣ* → Schneider APÄQ 160 no. 339.

riṭb "(sprouting) precious stone trim"
•LL: **EM** [NA$_{4}$.NUNUZ.TU]R = *ṣi-ip-ru* = : *ri-i*[*ṭ-bu*] → Cohen Proceedings 53^{e} RAI 1 826.

raṭibt "fresh, juicy"
•CTX: **EUPH** *ra-ṭì-ib-tum* → Birot ARM 27 130f. (66:18); CAD R 218: *raṭbu*.

|r-w-ʕ|
Sem.: *rwʕ* (Hb. C) "to cry, shout", *rʕ* (*rē*^{a}*ʕ*) "thundering voice"; *rāʕa* (*rawʕ*, Arab.) "to frighten, scare, alarm", *rawʕa* "fright, alarm".

rʕt "terrific shouting"
•CTX: **UGA** Sg. / pl. *rʕt* → DUL 716.

---

500 Cf. Akk. *rapāqu(m)* "to rivet, fasten, put together", and the LL entries DA.GUL = *ra-pa-qu*, DA.GUL.LA = *ra-ta-qu*; see CAD R 218: *ratāqu* "to join together" (?); vacat AHw.

|r-w-b| (1)

Sem.: *rāba* (*rawb*, Arab.) "to be troubled, become uneasy, perplexed", *rawwaba* "to get tired", *rawbān* "dull, blunt"; cf. *rawaba* (Eth.) "to become muddy" (?).

|r-w-b| (A) "to languish, grow drowsy"

•LL: **EB** ME.GAR = *ra-wa-bù, me/i-a-tum* → Conti QuSe 17 84.

|r-w-b| (2)

Sem.: *rwb* (Aram., Syr.) "to quarrel, make a loud noise"; *râbu*(*m*) (Akk.) "to quake". See also: rhb (Hb.) "to storm, assault", (C) "to harry, confuse"; *rhb* (Syr.) "to be quick, agitated"; *raʔābu*(*m*), *raḫābu* (Akk.) "to shake, tremble"; *rahiba* (Arab.) "to be frightened", *rahhaba* "to frighten".

|r-w-b| (B) "to tremble, quake"

•LL: **EB** SAG.SÌG = *ra-wa-bù, la-bù-um* → Krebernik ZA 73 11; Conti QuSe 17 105.

|r-w-ħ|

Primary noun, Sem: *rwḥ* (*rū^{a}ḥ*, Hb.) "wind, breath, spirit", *ryḥ* (*rêḥ*) "odour, fragrance", denom. *rwḥ* (C) "to smell"; *rḥ* (Pun.), *rwḥʔ* (Nab.) "wind, breath, spirit"; *rwḥ*(*ʔ*) (Aram., Syr.) "wind, breath, spirit; odour", *ryḥ*(*ʔ*) "smell";· *rūḥ* (pl. *ʔarwāḥ*, Arab.) "breath, soul, spirit", *rawḥ* "breeze", *riḥ* (pl. *riyāḥ, ʔarw/yāḥ*) "wind, smell, odour", *rīḥa* "smell, odour", denom. *rīḥa* "to be windy", *rawwaḥa* "to fan, air", *rayḥa* "to sniff", *rayyiḥ* "windy"; *rəḫe* (Eth.) "perfume, flavor", denom. *rwḥ, roḥa* "to fan, make a breeze by fanning", *rəḥya, rəhya, rəḫya* "emit an odour, be fragrant".
Non-Sem.: *roḥ= (Saho-Afar) "breath, soul"; *ruḥ= (Lowland East Cushitic) "breath, soul".[501]

|r-w-ħ| "to blow, smell" (?) — •ONOM: **EUPH** Cf. *ka-na-ak-ra-ḫu*(*-um*) → Gelb CAAA 30, 176.

riwħ "odour, fragrance" — •ONOM: **EUPH** Cf. *ri-ḫa-an, ri-ḫa-tum* → Gelb CAAA 30, 178.

ruwħ "wind" — •ONOM: **EUPH** Cf. *ka-ni-ik-ru-um, ka-ni-ik-rum* → Gelb CAAA 30, 179.

rħ (B), rx "wind" — •CTX: **UGA** Sg. *rḥ*, suff. *rḥk*, var. suff. *rḫh* → DUL 724: *rḥ* (I).

rħ (C) "aroma, perfume" — •CTX: **UGA** → DUL 724: *rḥ* (II).

|r-w/y-m|

Sem.: *rwm* (Hb.) "to be high above, reach high, be exalted, rise, go up" (by-form *rmm* (N) "to exalt oneself, lift oneself out of"), *r*(*w*)*m* (*rûm*) "height", *rwmm* (*rômam*) "exaltation, praise", *mrwm* (*mārôm*) "elevated site", *trwmh* (*t^{e}rûmāh*) "contribution"; *rm* (Edom. C) "to elevate"; *rm* (Ph.) "high, elevated", *mrm* (Pun.) "height"; *rwm* (Aram., Syr.) "to be high", (C) "to elevate, put up", *rmh, rmtʔ* (Aram., Syr.) "mountain, hill", *rm* (Aram., Syr.) "heigh", *rwm*(*ʔ*), *mrwm*(*ʔ*) (Aram., Syr.) "height", *rym*(*ʔ*) (Syr.) "raising up", *mrym* (Syr.) "high"; *rāma* (*raym*, Arab.) "to go away, move", *rayyama* "to exceed", *raym* "excess"; *rym* (OSArab.) "to raise", *rym* "exalted", *rymm* "height", *mrym* "top, roof"; *rihm* (MSArab.) "tall, long"; *rayama* (Eth.) "to be high, raised", *rāmā* "elevated place", *rəyyum, rayyām* "elevated", *ʔaryām* "heights, the highest".

|r-y-m| "to go up, get up, to show off; to erect, raise"

•CTX: **UGA** G prefc. *trm*, suffc. *rm*, L prefc. *trmm, trmmn, yrmm*, suff. *yrmmh*, imp. *rmm* → Tropper UG 498, 578, 580, 646, 648, 650f.; DUL 729: */r-m/*.
•ONOM: **EB** Cf. *ʔa$_5$-rí-mu* → Pagan ARES 3 167, 272.
EUPH Passim: *ia-ri-im*=DN; passim: *la-ri-im*=DN; see *i-ri-im-^{d}da-gan, ia-ri-im-*

---

[501] Orel / Solbova HSED 451f. no. 2132: *ruḥ= "breath, soul".

su-mu-a-bi, passim: *ia-ri-im*=DN, *áš-du-ni-a/e-ri-im*, *su-um-mu-na-a-ri-im*, *su-mu-un-a-bi-ia-ri-im*, *su-mu-na-bi-ia-ri-im*, *ta-ra-am-nu*, *ta-ra-am-*^{d}IM, *ta-ra-am-*EŠ$_4$.DAR, *ta-ri-im-*EŠ$_4$.DAR, *ta-ra-am-ša-ki-im*, *ta-ri-im-ša-ki-im*, *ta-ri-im-*DINGIR-*ma*(?), *ḫa-ab-du-ta*(!)*-ri-im*, *la-ri-im*, *la-ri-mu-um*, l*a-ri-im-ḫa-zi-ir*, *ḫa-mu-la-ri-im*, *ka-bi-la-ri-im*, *ṣú-ri-la-ri-im*; cf. *ru-ma-an*, *ru-ma-tum*, *ad-mu-ru-ma* → Huffmon APNMT 261f.; Gelb CAAA 30, 175, 178f.; Zadok Fs. Hallo 239; Golinets Onomastikon 2 127, 129, 285f., 293f., 298, 300f., 443f.
A7 *ia-ri-im-li-im* → Wiseman AT 136.[502]
TU *a-rí-im-la-*^{d}IM, *a-ri-ni-ḫi-im*, *lá-rí-im-a-ʔà-ad*, *kà-pí-lá-rí-im* → Krebernik Tall Bi`a 210, 221f.; Golinets Onomastikon 2 240, 285, 300, 443f., 478.
EM *ia-ri-im-*EN, *ia-ri-im-1*+EN → Pruzsinszky PTEm 211 [423f.].
A4 *ia-ri-im-mu*, *i-ri-im/mi-il-la*, *i-ri-mil-la* → Wiseman AT 136, 138; Gelb CAAA 30, 174; Sivan GAGl 266; Golinets Onomastikon 2 286.[503]
UGS *ia-ri-mu*, *ia-ri-im-mu*, *ia-ri-ma-nu*, *ia-ri-im-ma-nu*, *ia-ri-im-*^{d}IM, *ia-ri-*LUGAL, DUMU-*ia-ri-mì*, DUMU-*ia-ri-ma-na* → Gröndahl PTU 182; Sivan GAGl 266.
UGA *yrm* → DUL 965f.; *yrmʕl* → DUL 966; *yrmbʕl* → DUL 966; *yrmhd* → DUL 966; *yrmn* → DUL 966.

rām "high, sublime, exalted; a kind of monument, DN"
•LL: **UGS** Cf. [IDIM = *kabtu*(?) = … = [*r*]*a-m*[*u*] → Huehnergard ²UVST 390, 398.
•ONOM: **EB** *la-ma*, *ʔa₅-za ra-mu*; cf. *la-mi*, *ab ra-am₆*(?)(AN) → Pagan ARES 3 167f., 272, 345.
U3 *a-du-ra-mu* → Buccellati Amorites 131; Gelb CAAA 30, 176.
EUPH *ra-am*, *ra-ma-tum*, *ra-ma-nu-um*, *ra-ma-ia-tum*, *ḫa-mu-ra-ma*, *ra-ma-é-a*, *ra-ma-ì-lí*, *ra-ma-*^{d}IM, *mu-ut/tu-ra-ma*, *mu-ut-ra-me-im*, *mu-ut-ra-mi-e*, *a-bi-ra-am*, *a-bi-ra-ma-a*, cf. *ra-ma-ma* → Huffmon APN 261f.; Gelb CAAA 30, 176; Zadok Fs. Hallo 239; Streck Onomastikon 1 276 § 3.25; Golinets Onomastikon 2 304, 443f.[504]
TU *a-mu-ra-am* → Krebernik Tall Bi`a 209; Golinets Onomastikon 2 304, 443f.
EM *id-di-iḫ-ra-mi*, *id-di-ra-mu* → Pruzsinszky PTEm 213 [446].
A4 *qa-zi-ra-ma*, *šu-ra-mu/ma*, *si-i-ra-ma* → Wiseman AT 145, 147; Gelb CAAA 30, 176.
TA *e-lu-ra-ma* → Horowitz / Oshima CunCan 143 (7 rev.3).
EA ÌR-*i-ra-ma* → Sivan GAGl 263; Hess APN 15, 211, 239; Moran AmL 379.[505]
EG Elements =*ra-ma*$_{(3/4)}$, =*ru₂-mu₆*, =*ru₂-ma₄*; cf. *y:-d-y₂-r-m*, *r-m*, *rw-mꜣ*, *b-ʕ-r-y₂-rw-m-w* → Schneider APÄQ 51f. no. 89, 87 no. 166, 152f. nos. 320ff.; Hoch SWET 204f. no. 278.
UGS *a-bi-ra-mì*, *a-ḫi-ra-mu*, DINGIR-*ra-mu*, *šu-mu-ra*[*-ma*] → Gröndahl PTU 182; Sivan GAGl 263, 266.

rīm "high, sublime, exalted; DN"
•ONOM: **U3** *ri-ma-nu-um* → Buccellati Amorites 178; Gelb CAAA 30, 178
ASS *ri-im-i-la* → Gelb CAAA 30, 178.
EUPH *ri-im/mu-*^{d}IM, *ri-im-*^{d}*da-gan*, *i-din-*^{d}*ri-im* → Gelb CAAA 30, 178.
UGS Cf. *re-mi-ia*, *ri-mi-ya*, unc. DUMU *ri-im*(?)*-mu-na* → Gröndahl PTU 182; Sivan GAGl 264.[506]

---

[502] Diff. Arnaud AuOr 16 176: "offrir".
[503] See the previous fn.
[504] Durand REA 659: "monument commémoratif dans le rite du *kispum*".
[505] "Servant of Ramu", DN; Moran op.cit. 387: DN Ramu, WSem. "the exalted one".
[506] For DUMU *ri-im*(?)*-mu-na* cf. diff. Sivan GAGl 264: RIMMŌNU "pomegranate", but see here |l-r-m-n|.

rm (A) "high, sublime, exalted"	•CTX: **UGA** Sg. *rm*, pl. *rmm*, fem. *rmt* → DUL 730: *rm* (I). •ONOM: **UGA** *ảbrm* → DUL 13; *ảḫrm* → DUL 39; *ỉlrm* → DUL 61f.; *bʕlrm* → DUL 207; *rmib* → DUL 730; *šmrm* → DUL 818, *ymrm* → DUL 954; cf. *rmy* → DUL 731; *rmyy* → DUL 731.
rm (B) "rising, height" (?)	•CTX: **UGA** Sg. cstr. *rm* → DUL 730: *rm* (II).
marōma/ēma "height(s)"	•ONOM: **EG** Elem. in TN *ma*$_{2/3/4}$*-ra-ma*$_{3/4}$; perhaps pl. in *ma*$_{3/4}$*-ra-mi*$_{3/4}$*-im*(?), *m-ra-mi*$_{3}$*-im*(?) → Hoch SWET 137f. no. 177.
mrm, mrym "height"	•CTX: **UGA** Sg. *mrm*, mrym, pl. *mrmt* → Tropper UG 191; DUL 569: *mrm*, 572: *mrym*.
trmt "offering"	•CTX: **UGA** → DUL 866.

|r-w/y-ṣ̂|	Sem.: Cf. *rāḍa* (*rawḍ*) "to tame, domesticate, train, coach", *rāʔiḍ*, *rayyāḍi* "trainer".
rayyāṣ̂ "trainer, tamer" (?)	•CTX: **EM** Cf. KASKAL.GAL *ša* LÚ.MEŠ *ra-ya-ṣí* → Pentiuc Vocabulary 152; Ikeda BiOr 60 275.

|r-w-θ|	Primary noun, Sem.: *rawṯ* (Arab.) "dung, droppings", denom. *rāṯa* "to drop dung", *marāṯ* "anus"; *rūšu*(*m*), *ruššu* (Akkad.) "dirt", denom. (*w*)*arāšum*, *marāšu* "to be(come) dirty", (D) "to defile", (*w*)*aršu*(*m*), *maršu*, *arašu* "dirty".
rθ(n) "dirt"	•CTX: **UGA** → DUL 738: *rṯ*, *rṯn*.

|r-w-θ̣| Cf. **|r-ḥ-ṣ|**	Sem.: *rwṣ* (Hb.) "to run"; *rwṣ* (Aram.) "to run"; *rhṭ* (Aram., Syr.) "to run"; *râṣu*(*m*) (Akk.) "to rush (to help)"; *rwṣ*, *roṣa* (Eth.) "to run, run about". See further *ʔaraḍḍa* "to hurry (up)".
|**r-w-θ̣**| "to run, compete" (?)	•CTX: **UGA** G prefc. *yrẓ*[507] → DUL 738f.: /*r-ẓ*/. •ONOM: **EA.**[508] **EG** Cf. *pꜣ-r-wꜣ- ṯꜣ* → Schneider APÄQ 109 no. 234. **UGS** Cf. unc. *ri-ZA-na*, *ya-ri-ZA-na* → Gröndahl PTU 179: RY/WṢ; Sivan GAGl 265f.: RĪṢU, RYṢ. **UGA** Cf. unc. *rṣn* → DUL 735.
rāwiθ̣ "runner"	•ONOM: **EG** Elem. in PN *Pꜣ ra-wi*$_{2}$*-ṯi* → Hoch SWET 201 no. 271.[509]
trθ̣θ̣ "light march, speed" (?)	•CTX: **UGA** Sg. suff. *trẓẓh* → DUL 867f.: *trẓẓ*.[510]

|r-w-y|	Sem.: *rwh* (Hb.) "to drink one's fill, be refreshed", (C, D) "to give drink abundantly, water thoroughly"; *rwy* (Aram., Syr.) "to be sated with drink", (D) "to make drunk, provide with moisture", (C) "to offer drink"; *rawiya* (Arab.) "to give to drink, to water"; *rwy* (OSArab.) "to provide with irrigation"; *rēʔ*, *ráywi*, *rəwō*

507 Rdg unc.; cf. KTU 1.16 I 50: *yr*q.

508 In EA 226:3 read probl. PN *ši-ip-ṭú-ri*[...ÌR-*ka*] (Rainey EAC: "Shipturi[... your servant]") against *ši-ip-ṭú-ri-ṣ*[*a*] (Hess APN 144, 212; Moran AmL 384, 388: WS? "Šipṭu, come to the rescue"[?]).

509 Sivan / Cochavi-Rainey WSVES 83: *ra-wa-ṣí* "to run"; Helck Beziehungen no. 149.

510 See further the unc. rdg *ti-tar-ri-*ZA (Ug 5 3 r. 10'), for which cf. Huehnergard ²UVST 390: possibly "D *yaqtula* of a root *trZ* \|tirarriZa\|; [...] denominative form from the noun *trẓẓ*, itself a derivative of the verb *rwẓ* 'to run'? Or read altern. *ti-tar-ḫu-*ZA, mng unexplained. Very dubious.

(MSArab.) "to drink to repletion"; *rawaya*, *rawya* (Eth.) "to drink one's fill, be watered".

|**r-w-y**| "to be well watered; to be brimming with water"

•ONOM: **EUPH** Cf. *ia-ar-wi-um*, *a-ar-wi-*DINGIR → Gelb CAAA 30, 175.
EG Cf. Elem. in TN *Šbrt Ngbry*, perhaps *n-g-bi=ru*$_2$*-ya* |rôya / rūya| (?)
UGA Cf. *rwy* → Gröndahl PTU 312,409; DUL 738.

|r-y-b|
Cf. |**r-b-b/y**|, |**r-ḥ-b**|

Sem.: *ryb* (Hb.) "to quarrel, contest a lawsuit, complain to", *rb*, *ryb* (*ri/îb*), *rybh* (pl. *ribôt*) "dispute, quarrel"; *rw/yb* (Aram., Syr.) "to quarrel"; *rbb* (Syr.) "to make a disturbance", *rwyb* (Syr.) "tumult"; *riābu*(*m*), *râbu* (Akk.), *raʔābum* (OAkk.)[511] "to replace; to requite", *rību*, *ruʔubbāʔum* "replacement, compensation", *tarību*(*m*), *tarībtu*(*m*) "replacement"; *rāba* (*rayb*, Arab.) "to disquiet, doubt, question, suspect", *rayb*, *rība* "doubt". See further Arab. *raʔaba* "to mend, rectify, set right".

|**r-ʔ/y-b**| "to compensate, replace; contest, plead"

•ONOM: **EB** |yirīb=|: *i-rí-bù*, *i-rí-íb-a-ḫu*, *i-rí-íb-il*; |yirʔib=|: *ìr-ì-ba/bù*, *ir-íb-a-ḫu*, *ìr-ì-ba-hu*, *ìr-ib-da-mu*, *ìr-ib-ga-ar*, *ìr-ib-i-sar*, *ìr-íb-ì*, *ìr-íb-ga-ma-al*$_6$; |tarʔib=|: *dar-ib/íb-da-mu* → Krebernik PTU 47, 49; Pagan ARES 3 167, 300, 324f., 338.
•**U3** |yirīb=|:*ìr-ib*, *i-ri-ib* → Streck Onomastikon 1 346 § 5.64 fn. 1. Cf. Buccellati Amorites 160: possibly also from |r-ʔ-p| "to be compassionate" (cf. Pagan ARES 3 161); diff. Gelb CAAA 30, 174: RḤAB, RḤIB (|r-ḥ-b| "to be wide, to be broad").
EUPH |yarʔib=|: *ia-ar-ḫi-bi*(?)*-im*, *ia-ar-i-ib-*^{d}*ab-ba*, =^{d}IM/DINGIR, =*ak-ka*, *ia-ar-ib-*^{d}*ab-ba*, =DINGIR, ^{d}*da-gan*, ^{d}*é-a*, =*èr/ìr-ra*, ^{d}IM, =^{d}*nin-si*$_4$*-an-na*, *ia-ar-i-ba-an*, *ia-ar-i-bu*, *ia-ar-i-bu-um*; |ya/irīb=|: *ia-ri-i-bu-um*, *ia-ri-ba-a-tum*, *a-ri-ib-*^{d}*ab-ba*, =DINGIR, ^{d}IM → Huffmon APNMT 260; Gelb CAAA 30, 174 (RḪIB); Zadok Fs. Hallo 328f.; Streck Onomastikon 1 346 § 5.64 fn. 1; Golinets Onomastikon 2 57 fn. 207, 170f., 263, 287, 435f., 444f., 491, 505, 512.
EA Cf. *ri-ib-*(*ḫa-*)*ad-di*, =^{d}IM$^{(di)}$, =*ad-da*, =*id-di* → Sivan GAGl 264, 266; Moran AmL 384; Hess APN 132ff., 211.
UGA Cf. *mrbd* → DUL 566: *mrbd* (II); *yrbʕm* → DUL 962.

rayb "compensation; plea"

•ONOM: **EB** *ra-ba*, *ra-bù-šum*, *ra-ba-ì*, *ì-a-ra-bù*, *la-bu*$_{17}$*-bù-lu*, *su ra-bù*, *wa-ad-ra-bù* → Pagan ARES 3 167, 328, 345, 358, 375.[512]
EUPH *ra-ba-*(*a-*)*nu-um*, *ra-ba-zi-it-ru-ú* → Gelb CAAA 30, 176.[513]
EA Cf. *ri-ib-*(*ḫa-*)*ad-di*, =^{d}IM$^{(di)}$, =*ad-da*, =*id-di* → Sivan GAGl 264, 266; Moran AmL 384; Hess APN 132ff., 211.

riyb "compensation; plea"

•ONOM: **EB** *rí-íb*, *rí-bí*, *rí-bu*$_{17}$, *rí-íb-a-ḫu*, *rí-ba-il*, *ʔà-da-rí-ba*, *li-ba-su* → Pagan ARES 3 167, 269, 346, 359.
U3 *ri-i-bu-um* → Gelb CAAA 30, 178; Golinets Onomastikon 2 512; cf.

---

[511] According to Krebernik PET 47 C$_2$:ʔ |r-ʔ-b| is an old allomorphism of the base C$_2$:y |r-y-b|. Slightly diff. Gelb MAD 2 186: "[In OAkk.] verbs secundae ʔ$_3$ frequently behave like verbs secundae ʔ$_7$. See also Gelb MAD 3 229f. and CAD R 53ff.: *râbu* A (*riābu*).
[512] Several writings *ra/la-b=* could belong to the etymon |r-b-b/y| "to be big". See Krebernik PET 49; Pagan ARES 3 162.
[513] Cf. the previous fn.

	Buccellati Amorites 160: possibly also from |r-ʔ-p| "to be compassionate". **EUPH** *ri-ba-tum,*[514] *ri-bu-ú, ri-bu-*^{d}*da-gan* → Gelb CAAA 30, 178; Golinets Onomastikon 2 512. **A7** *ri-ba-am-mu, su-mi-ri-ba, ti-im-ri-pa* → Gelb CAAA 30, 178 **A4** *šu-me/mi-ri-ba/pa* → Wiseman AT 147; Gelb CAAA 30, 178. **EA** Cf. *ri-ib-(ḫa-)ad-di,* =^{d}IM$^{(di)}$, *=ad-da, =id-di* → Sivan GAGl 264, 266; Moran AmL 384; Hess APN 132ff., 211.
rīb "compensation; plea"	•CTX: **UGA** *rīb ksp* → Tropper KWU 103;[515] diff. DUL 712: *rīb* "a metal container" (? Akk. *raʔabum* (?), *rību*(*m*) "a vessel").
riybān "strife, plea"	•LL: **EB** AN.AK = *rí-ba-nu, za-du-um* |ṣaltum| → Conti QuSe 17 194.
raybat "compensation; plea"	•ONOM: **EUPH** *ra-ba-tum* → Gelb CAAA 30, 176.[516]
raybūt "compensation; plea"	•ONOM: **EB** *ra-bù-du* → Pagan ARES 3 167, 358.[517]
riybat "compensation; plea"	•ONOM: **EB** *li-ba-ad, rí-bad, rí-ba-du* → Pagan ARES 3 167, 358. **EUPH** *ri-ba-tum* → Gelb CAAA 30, 178; Zadok Fs. Hallo 32: R-W/Y-B^2, possibly connected with JAram. *rybʔ* [sic!] "maiden" (see JAram. *rby*(*tʔ*) "young girl").
taryib "compensation"	•ONOM: **EUPH** *ta-ri-bu-um* → Gelb CAAA 30, 175; Golinets Onomastikon 2 512.

|r-y-ḳ|	Sem.: *ryq* (Hb. C) "to empty, pour out", *ryq* (*rîq, rēyq, rēq*) "void, empty"; *ryq* (JAram. C) "to pour out, empty", *ryq* (*rîq*) "void, empty"; *riāqu*(*m*), *râqu* (Akk.) "to be empty; to be unemployed", *rīqu*(*m*) "empty", *rīqūtu*(m) "emptiness"; *rāq* (*rayq*, Arab.) "to flow out, pour forth", *ʔarāqa* "to pour out, shed, spill", *rayq* "useless, empty, dry".
|r-y-ḳ| "to be void"	•CTX: **EB** G suffc. *ra-aq* |rāḳ| → Catagnoti QuSe 29 125, 222.
riḳāta "compartments or hollow spaces"	•CTX: **EG** *ra-ga-ta-{t}* → Hoch SWET 211f. no. 287.
marwaḳat "a (small) pot" (?)	•CTX: **EB** Cf. *mar-wa-ga-tum* → Waetzoldt MEE 12 243ff; Archi NABU 20105 39.[518]

|r-y-m|
See **|r-w/y-m|**

|r-y-ṣ|
See **|r-w/y-ṣ|**

[514] See Zadok Fs. Hallo 329 R-W/Y-B^2: cf. Aram. *rybʔ* "maiden, young woman".
[515] Only one instance; probl. loan.
[516] For Ebl. cf. Pagan ARES 3 345: *la-ba*$_{x}$?(ḪUŠ)*-dum* "compensation".
[517] The writing *ra-b=* could belong to the etymon \|r-b-b/y\| "to be big".
[518] With reference to a var. *mar-wa-zàr-tum* (*G* > [ḍ] ?). See Catagnoti QuSe 29 209: rdg *mar-pi-ga-tum* "sostegno, piedistallo".

|r-y-ṭ|	Culture word. Sem. cf. *rayṭa* (Arab., pl. *rayṭ*, *riyāṭ*) "(seamless) tunic, veil".
rṭ "(seamless) tunic, veil"	•CTX: **UGA** Sg. *rṭ*, pl. *rṭm* → DUL 738.

|r-z-H|	Sem.: *rzh* (Hb., N) "to dwindle, disappear", *rzh* (*rāzeh*) "thin, gaunt", *rzwn* (*rāzôn*) "emaciation"; *rzʔ* (Palm.) "(business) expense"; *rzy* (Syr.) "to grow weak"; *razaʔa* (Arab.) "to deprive", *ruziʔa* "to suffer loss", *ruzʔ*, *razīʔa* "heavy loss, calamity"; *rzʔ* (OSArab.) "to spend", *rzʔn* "cost, harm", *trzʔ* "loss".
tarzuHm "hunger, starvation" (?)	•LL: **EB** ŠÀ.ŠUR = *tár-zu-um* → Sjöberg Fs. Kienast 539f.

|r-z-ħ|
See |**m-r-z-ħ**|

|r-z-m|	Sem.: Cf. *ʔarzam* (Arab.) "to howl, roar, groan", *razama* "wail, howl".
rāzimt, **rāzitt** "wailing woman"	•CTX: **EB** Sg. *ra-zi-tum*, pl. *ra-zi-ma-tum* → Pasquali / Mangiarotti NABU 1999/7; Paquali NABU 2018/28; 2019/3.

s (s^3)
and
S
(for undetermined sibilants / interdentals)

|S-ʔ|	
|s-ʔ-n| (1)	
|S-ʔ-n| (2)	
|s-ʔ-p|	
|S-ʔ-r|	
|S-ʕ-ḳ|	
|s-ʕ-y|	
|S-b-b| (1)	
|s-b-b| (2)	
|S-b-b-y-n|	
|s-b-k|	Cf. |s^2-p-ḳ|
|S-b-l	Cf. |w/y-b-l|
|S-b-S|	
|S-B-S-G|	
|S-b-t|	
|s-b-y|	
|S-d/ð|	
|S-d-d|	
|S-d-n| (1)	
|S-D-n| (2)	
|s-d-r|	
|S-ð|	See |S-d/ð|
|S-ð-b|	
|S-G-b|	
|s-g-d|	
|S-g-g|	Cf. |s^2-g-y|
|S-g-g-ʔ|	
|s-G-l|	
|s-g-n| (1)	
|s-g-n| (2)	
|s-G-r|	
|S-G-S|	
|s-H-d|	
|S-H-r|	
|S-H-ṭ|	
|s-ħ-b|	Cf. |s^1-ʔ-b|
|S-ħ-n|	
|s-ħ-r|	
|s-ħ-y|	
|s-x-l|	
|S-x-p|	
|s-x-r|	
|S-x-r-r|	
|s-k-k| (1)	
|s-k-k| (2)	
|S-k-l|	
|s-k-n| (1)	
|s-k-n| (2)	See |s^1-k-n|
|S-ḳ-b|	
|S-ḳ-ḳ|	
|S-ḳ-n	See |ð-ḳ-n|
|S-ḳ-r|	Cf. |ð-k-r| (2), |s^2-k-r| (2)
|s-l-ʕ|	
|S-l-B|	
|S-l-x|	
|s-l-l|	
|s-l-m| (1)	Cf. |s^1-l-m|
|s-l-m| (2)	
|S-l-m-x|	
|s-l-t|	
|S-L(-y)|	
|s-m-d| (1)	
|s-m-d| (2)	

|s-m-x|	
|s-m-k|	
|s-m-m|	
|S-m-r| (1)	
|S-m-r| (2)	See **|ð-m-r| (1)**
|S-m-r| (3)	
|S-m-S|	
|S-m-s^1|	
|s-m-w/y|	
|s-m-y|	See **|s-m-w/y|**
|s-n-ḳ|	
|s-n-n|	
|S-n-r|, |S-r-n| (1)	
|s-n-s-n|	
|S-n-s^1|	
|s-p-ʔ|	
|s-p-d|	
|S-p-ħ|	
|s-p-x|	
|s-p-l|	
|s-p-p| (1)	
|s-p-p| (2)	
|S-p-p-r|	
|S-p-r| (1)	
|s-p-r| (2)	
|S-p-S-k|	
|s-p-y|	
|s-r-d| (1)	
|s-r-d| (2)	
|s-r-d-n-n|	
|S-r-m|	
|S-r-m-n|	
|S-r-n| (1)	See **|S-n-r|, |S-r-n| (1)**
|S-r-n| (2)	
|S-r-p|	
|s-r-r| (1)	Cf. **|s^2-r-r|**
|s-r-r| (2)	
|s-r-r| (3)|	
|S-r(-r)| (4)	
|s-r-θ|	Cf. **|(w/y)-r-θ|**
|S-r-(y-)n|	
|s-s|	
|S-S-B-n|	
|S-s-s|	
|S-S-S-k|	
|s-t-r| (1)	
|S-t-r| (2)	
|s-w-d|	
|s-w-p|	
|S-(w-)r|	
|s-w-s-w|	
|S-y-ʕ|	
|S-y-d|	See **|S-d/ð|**
|S-y-m|	
|s-y-n|	
|S-y-p|	
|S-y-r|	

|S-ʔ|	Culture word, Sem.: *sʔh* (*s^{e}ʔāh*, Hb.) "a grain measure"; *sʔh, sʔtʔ* (Aram., Nab., Syr.) "a grain measure"; *sūtu*(*m*) (Akk.) "a measuring vessel of standard capacity". Non-Sem.: *ŠA-A-DU, ŠU-Ú-TUM* (Akkadogram in Hitt.).[519]
Sūt "measure of capacity"	•LL: **EB** Cf. BÁN = *šu-tum* → Krebernik ZA 73 29.
s^{1}aʔīt "a liquid measure"	•CTX: **UGS** Cf. *ša-i-tum* → AHw 1134; CAD Š/1 112.
s^{1}t (B) "measure of capacity"	•CTX: **UGA** → DUL 838: *št* (II).
xamiSSāt "five *S*.-measures"	•CTX: **EUPH** *ḫa-mi-sà-tum* (sandhi) → Charpin AfO 40/41 23.

|s-ʔ-n| (1)	Culture word, Sem.: *sʔwn* (*s^{e}ʔôn*, Hb.) "hem, trim(ming)", denom. *sʔn* "to whirl";[520] *sūnu* (Akk.) "hem, trim(ming)".[521]

[519] CAD S 420: *sūtu*,1; see CHD Š/2 314: GIŠ *šādu*.
[520] Dietrich / Loretz OLZ 62 544: *sʔwn* "Schleife"; *sʔn* "wirbeln".
[521] Moran RA 77 93f.

suʔn "hem, trimming"	•CTX: **EUPH** TÚG *su-nu-ú*, *ša* (*la*) *su*/*sú-ni* / *sú-nim*, *sú-nu-šu* → Durand LAPO 16 94f.; ARM 30 93ff. **EA** TÚG LÚGUD!(PÚ).DA *ša sú-nu-šu* GÙN.A → Moran AmL 60 fn. 60 (for EA 22 IV 14). **UGS** *su-na-te-šu-nu*; cf TÚG.TÙN(!?) *:* !?*su-nu* → Huehnergard UVST 155; Lackenbacher / Malbran-Labat RSOu 23 82.
sỉn "hem, trimming"	•CTX: **UGA** → Moran RA 77 93f.; DUL 740.
|S-ʔ-n| (2)	Culture word, Sem.:[522] *šʔn*, *sʔwn*(*ʔ*) (Aram., Syr.) "shoe, sandal", denom. *sʔn* "to put on a shoe", *msn*(*ʔ*) "shoe", *syn*(*ʔ*) (JAram.) "shoe"; *šēnu*(*m*) (Akk.) "sandal",[523] *mašʔanum*, *mašʔenum*, *mešēnu* "a type of shoe"; *śāʔn* (Eth.) "shoe, sandal", *taśəʔna*, *taśaʔana*, *tasaʔana* "to put on sandals".
Saʔn "sandal"	•LL: **EB** E.LAK-173 = *sa-na* → Fronzaroli StEb 7 180; QuSeS 13 149.
s^{1}ỉn "sandal(s); rim"(?)	•CTX: **UGA** Du. *šỉnm*, pl. *šảnt* → DUL 785f.: *šỉn*.
mỏnt "sandal" (?)	•CTX: **UGA** Sg. / pl. *mỏnt* → DUL 523: *mḏnt*.
|s-ʔ-p|	Sem.: Cf. *saʔāb*/*pu* (Akk.) "to chew, bite, grind" (?).
sỉp "who chews, grinds" (?)	•ONOM: **UGA** Cf. *bʕlsỉp* → DUL 207.[524]
|S-ʔ-r|	Culture word, Sem.: Cf. *Šʔr* (*śeʔor*, Hb.) "sour (leavened) dough", *mŠʔrt* (*mišʔeret*) "kneading trough".
mas^{1}ʔirt "kneading trough" (?)	•CTX: **EM** *ma-aš-ir-ta* → Pentiuc Vocabulary 117.
|S-ʕ-ḳ|	Sem, with allomorphs. C$_1$:*ṣ*, *ṣʕq* (Hb.) "to shout, call out", *ṣʕq* (*ṣaʕaq*) "scream"; *ṣʕq* (Aram.) "to cry out", *ṣʕqh* "shout"; *ṣaʕaqa* (Arab.) "to strike someone down with lightning, hit, slay (of lightning)", *ṣaʕq* "thunder", *ṣaʕiqa* "bolt of lightning"; C$_1$:*z*, *zʕq* (Hb.) "to call for help", *zʕqh* (*zeʕāqāh*) "cry for help"; *zʕq* (Aram., Syr.) "to shout, sound out", *zʕq*(*ʔ*), *zʕqh*, *zʕqtʔ* (JAram., Syr.) "outcry"; *zaʕaqa* "to cry, yell, shriek, scream", *zaʕq*, *zaʕqa*, *zaʕīq* "clamor, shouting".
|S-ʕ-ḳ| "to cry, call"	•CTX: **EA** N suffc. *in$_4$-né-ri-ru : na-az-a-qú* (366:24) → Sivan GAGl 293; Moran AmL 364 (fn. 3); Rainey EAT 35; CAT 2 128f., 308. **EG** *ḏa-ʕu-q* (inf.?) → Hoch SWET 381 no. 570.[525]

522 For Hb. *sʔwn* (*s^{e}ʔôn*) see above: \|s-ʔ-n\| (1).
523 Nuzi-Akk.: *šīnu*; Guichard NABU 1994/31: Hurr.; see Richter BGH 349: *šanni*.
524 Other suggested cognates (cf. Gröndahl PTU 37, 40, 116, 184) seem rather unlikely: Hb. *swp* "to come to an end"(?), Aram. *swp* "to be fulfilled" (D / C) "to destroy"; Arab. *sawwafa* ""to postpone, delay".
525 Sivan / Cochavi-Rainey WSVES 87: *s̱á-ʕu-q* "to cry out"; Helck Beziehungen no. 302.

Saʕaḳāta, **Saʕaḳōta** "cries, calls"	•CTX: **EG** *d̲a-ʕa-qa-ta*, altern. *d̲a-ʕa-qu$_4$-ta* → Hoch SWET 381 no. 571.
Suʕḳ "cry, outcry"	•ONOM: **A4** Cf. ZU-*ú-qa* → Wiseman AT 153; Sivan GAGl 270.
|s-ʕ-y|	Sem.: *sʕh* (Hb.) "to sweep away, winnow"; *sʕy* (Syr.) "to attempt, attack (sexually)"; *seʔû* (Akk.) "to press down, suppress, oppress"; *saʕā* (*saʕy*, Arab.) "to move quickly, attempt".
|**s-ʕ-y**| "to assault, remove"	•CTX: **UGA** G pass. ptc. *sʕt* → DUL 740: /*s-ʕ*/.
|S-b-b| (1)	Sem.: *šbyb* (*šābîb*, Hb.) "spark"; *šbyb(ʔ)* (Aram., Syr.) "spark"; *šabābu(m)* (Akk.) "to glow, to be parched"; *šabba* (Arab.) "to burn, blaze". Cf. *səhbo* (Eth.) "slow fire".
Sabbab "brightness, dawn"	•LL: **EB** DÁG.DAG = *sa-ba-ba-bú(-um)* → Conti QuSe 17 188f.; Sjöberg Fs. Wilcke 260f.
Sababt "brightness, dawn"	•LL: **EB** [DADAG.DAG.DAG] = *sa-ba-ba-tum* → Civil BaE 84: Conti QuSe 17 188.
s^{1}bb "spark, flame; DN" (?)	•ONOM: **UGA** Mythical female being defeated by Anat; miswritten *d̲bb* (?) → vSoldt UF 21 373; DUL 282: *d̲bb*.
|s-b-b| (2)	Sem.: *sbb* (Hb.) "to turn oneself around, to go around"; *sbb* (Ph., C) "to turn over"; *sbb* (Aram.) "to encircle, surround"; *sbb, sabba, sababa* (Eth.) "to go around, circle". See also *šibbu(m), šippu(m)* (Akk.) "belt, girdle"; *sibb* (Arab.) "turban", *sabab* "rope", *sabīb* "strand of hair"; *səbēt, səbtēt, sebtét, səbat, səbṭəh* (MSArab.) "belt"; *śabśaba* (Eth.) "to intertwine".
|**s-b-b**| "to turn (round, towards, into); to be changed into"	•CTX: **UGA** G prefc. *ysb*, suffc. *sb*, suff. *sbny*, imp. *sb*; N suffc. *nsb* → DUL 740f.: /*s:ś-b-b*/.[526] •ONOM: **B** Cf. *sa-bi-bu-um* → Hinson NABU 2013/25 ("he who guards", |sābib|)
|S-b-b-y-n|	Culture word, Sem.: *šbbwn(ʔ)* (Syr.) "black cumin"; *zibibiānum, zizibiānum, zi/abibânu, šibibānu, s/šib/pib/piānu, sabubânu, zibibiannu* (Akk.) "black cummin" (apocopated (?) *zību, zibû, zēbu, zīpu*; see also *zibītum, zibibītum* "a kind of spice / seed").
sbbyn "black cumin"	•CTX: **UGA** Sg. *sbbyn, sbbym* → DUL 741.
|s-b-k| Cf. |**s^{2}-p-ḳ**|	Sem.: Cf. *sbk* (Hb.) "to entangle, entwine"; *sbk* (Syr.) "to adhere, be interwoven with"; *šabaka* (Arab.) "to interjoin, intertwine".

[526] For the problematic writing *šśb* (DUL 741: C suffc.; in bkn ctx.) see Tropper UG 49, 601.

|s-b-k| "to interweave; to contamine" (?)	•CTX: **EUPH** Cf. G prefc. *i-sa-ab-bi-ik* → AHw 999: *sabāku*(*m*); CAD S 2: *sabāku*; Charpin AfO 40/41 1; Streck Onomastikon 1 112 § 1.95; cf. Golinets Onomastikon 2 452f. (ŚPQ).

|S-b-l| Cf. **|w/y-b-l|**	Sem.; merger of several etyma: Cf. *zbl* (Hb.) "to raise", *zbl* (*z*^{e}*bul*) "lofty residence", *sbl* "to carry, support", *sbl* (*sēbel*, *sobel*) "burden"; *zbl* (Ph.) "prince"; *sbl* (JAram., Syr.) "to carry, bear", *sbl*(*?*) (Syr.) "porter", "burden"; *zabālu*(*m*), *s*/*ṣabālu*(*m*), *zebēlu* (Akk.) "to carry, deliver", *zabbilu*(*m*), *zābilum*, *zanbilum* "bearer"; *zabīl*, *zibbil*, *zinbil* (Arab.) "basket, pannier".
|ð-b-l| "to carry, deliver"	•LL: **EB** ŠU.GÍD = *iš*$_{(11)}$*-ba-lum*; SAG.SUM = [*za*]*-ba-lu-um* → Conti QuSe 17 148ff.; Sjöberg Fs. Renger 526; Catagnoti QuSe 29 49, 66, 195.
Sabl "work team"	•CTX: **EUPH** *sa-bi-il*, *sa-ab-la-am* → AHw 999; CAD S 4; Held JAOS 88, 94; Streck Onomastikon 1 112 § 1.95.[527]
Sibl "principality, highness" (?)	•ONOM: **EUPH** *zi-ib-la-nu-um* → Huffmon APNMT 186; Gelb CAAA 35, 203 (ZBL); cf. *si-bi-lu-um* → Gelb 31, 187 (ŚBL). **TA** *zi-bi-lu* → Glock BASOR 204 27; Horowitz / Oshima CunCan 150 (TT 950:4). **UGS** *pi-zi-ib*/*bi-li* → Gröndahl PTU 19, 31, 55, 170, 183.
ðābil "bearer, porter"	•LL: **EB** SAG.SUM =*za-bí-lu-um*; cf. SAG.GÍD.GÍD = *za-bí-lum* SAG → Conti QuSe 17 109; Bonechi QDLF 16 82; cf. Castellino BaE 368; Fales QuSe 13 185; Vattioni EDA 215ff.
Sabil, **Sabul** "princely"	•ONOM: **EUPH** *za-bi-lim*, *za-bu-lum*, fem. *za-bi-la-tum* → Gelb CAAA 35, 202.
Subāl "exalted, prince"	•ONOM: **EUPH** *zu-ba-li-im*, *zu-ba la-an*, fem. *zu*(?)*-ba-la-tum* → Huffmon APNMT 186; Gelb CAAA 35 203; Streck Onomastikon 1 331 § 5.32. **UGS** *zu-ba-li* → Huehnergard Syria 74 214.
Subīl "(little) prince"	•ONOM: **A7** *zu-bi-lu* |Subayl| → Arnaud AuOu 16 169.
sbl, **Sbl** "prince" (?)	•ONOM: **UGA** Cf. unc. *sbl*, *śbl* → DUL 741: *śbl*.
zbl (A) "prince"	•CTX: **UGA** Sg. *zbl*; pl. cstr. (?) *zbl* → DUL 982: *zbl* (I).
zbl (B) "principality"	•CTX: **UGA** Sg. suff. *zblkm*, *zblhm* → DUL 982: *zbl* (II). •ONOM: **UGA** Cf. Elem. in TN *qrzbl* → Belmonte RGTC 12/2 353; DUL 982: *zbl* (IV).
zbl (C) "one carried, an invalid person"	•CTX: **UGA** → DUL 982: *zbl* (III).
zbln "sickness, illness"	•CTX: **UGA** Sg. *zbln*, suff. *zblnm* → DUL 982.
Sub(b)ul "excellency"	•CTX: **EUPH** *su-bu-lu-um* → Gelb CAAA 31, 189 (ŚBL); fem. *zu-bu-ul-tim* → AHw 1536; Streck Onomastikon 1 122 § 1.95.
muðtabbil "servant" (?)	•LL: **EB** ŠU.GÍD.GÍD = *mu-da-bíl-du* (fem.) → Conti QuSe 17 14, 150; Catagnoti QuSe 29 27, 66, 140, 144, 195.

|S-b-S|	Sem. with several lexicalized allophones: Cf. *šbš* (JAram., Syr. D) "to flatter", *šwbš*(*?*) "friendship"; *šabāšu*(*m*), *šabāsu*, *šapāšu* (Akk.) "to gather"; *šabiṯa*, *tašabbaṯa* (Arab.) "to hold fast, cling, adhere".

[527] Diff. Durand ARM 26/1 15f. fn. 42; ARM 26/2 226f. (393 rev. 5') fn. d; Kupper ARM 28 13f. (13:5) fn. a: "population".

|s^1-b-s^1| "to attract, collect" (?)	•CTX: **UGA** D suffc. *šbšt* → DUL 794f.: /*š-b-š*/.
|S-B-S-G|	Culture word, Sem.: Cf. *zabzabgû* (Akk.) "a glaze". Non-Sem: *zapzagai=*, *zapzaki=*, *zapziki=* (Hitt.) "glass; glaze".
sbsg, spsg, SpSg "a glaze"	•CTX: **UGA** Sg. *sbsg*, *spsg*, *śpśg*, pl. *spsgm* → DUL 758: *ś:sp/bś:sg.*
|S-b-t|	Culture word, Sem.: Cf. *sabītu*(*m*) "(a kind of) lyre". Non-Sem.: sabitum (BALAG.TUR, Sum.) "an instrument".
Sebit "(a kind of) lyre, harp"	•CTX: **EUPH** Cf. *še*$_{20}$*-bi-tam*, *še-bi-tu-ia* → vSoden NABU 1988/59; OLZ 89 537; Ziegler FM 9 180ff. (n°38:22).
|s-b-y|	Culture word, loan: *sabû* (Akk.) "to brew beer", *sābû*(*m*), *sābium*, *sêbû*, *sā/ēbiʔu* "brewer, innkeeper", *sābītu*(*m*) "female brewer, alehouse keeper", *sabûtu*, *sibûtu*(*m*) "innkeeper's trade"; cf. *sbʔ* (Hb.) "to tipple", *sbʔ* (*sobeʔ*) "drink, tipple".
sabayt "brewing (supplies)" **sābiyt** "female brewer, alehouse keeper"	•LL: **EB** MUNU$_4$.GÚG = *sa-ba-tum*/*tù-um* → Civil OrAn 21 14; Sjöberg Fs. Oelsner 411 (fn. 8); Fs. Pettinato 280. •LL: **EB** GÉME.KAR.AG / GÉME.GAR.A = *za-bí-tum* → Krebernik ZA 73 45, PIHANS 106 90; Bonechi QDLF 16 84.
|S-d/ð|	Primary noun; Sem. with several allomorphs: Basis |θ-d(-y)|: *šd* (*šad*, *šōd*, Hb.) "breast"; *td*(*?*) (Aram., Syr.) "breast"; *ṯady*, *ṯadan* (Arab.) "female breast, udder"; *ṯōdi*, *tɔdɛ*, *tódi* (MSArab.) "breast, bosom". Basis |z-ð|: *zyz* (*zîz*, Hb.) "breast"; *zīzu* (Akk.) "teat". Non-Sem.: *čid=* (East Chadic) "breast".[528] Sem. loanword: *zeze*, *zizzi* (Hurr.) "breast".[529]
ðd (A) "breast, bosom" **θd** "breast, bosom, chest, teat, udder" **zd** "breast, chest"	•CTX: **UGA** → DUL 282: *ḏd* (I).[530] •CTX: **UGA** Sg. *ṯd*, suff. *ṯdh*, pl. cstr. *ṯd*, suff. *ṯdn* → DUL 886: *ṯd*.[531] •CTX: **UGA** → DUL 983.[532]
|S-d-d|	Sem. with allomorphs. Basis |s^3-d-d|: *sadādum* (Akk.) "to make a raid" (see below: |S-d-d|); basis |s^1-d-d|: *šdd* (Hb.) "to devastate, despoil", *šd* (*šod*, suff. *sodd=*) "violent action, devastation"; *šadādu*(*m*), *śadādum* (Akk.) "to drag, draw (down, up, away, off)"; *sadda* (Arab.) "to obstruct, block"; *sadada* (Eth.) "to chase away, drive out, pursue"; basis |s^2-d-d|: *šādda* (Arab.) "to assault, attack".

[528] Orel / Stolbova HSED 109 no. 462: **čad=* / **čid=* "breast".
[529] Laroche GLH 303: *ze-(e)-zi*, 306: *zizzi* "seins"; Richter BGH 397f.: "breast".
[530] Basis |θ-d(-y)|.
[531] Basis |θ-d(-y)|.
[532] Basis |z-ð|.

|S-d-d| "to make a raid, to pursue"	•CTX: **EUPH** G prefc. *ìs-du-ud-ma, ìs-du-dam-ma, ni-ìs-du-ud-ma, i-sa-ad-da-ad, ta-sa-ad-da-ma*, inf. *sa-da-di-im* → CAD S 10: *sadādu* A; Zadok Fs. Hallo 329f.; Charpin AfO 40/41 2; Streck Onomastikon 1 113 § 1.95.
|s^1-d-d| (A) "to be drawn (off)"	•CTX: **UGA** N suffc. *nšdd* → DUL 798: */š-d-d/* (I).
|s^1-d-d| (B) "to assail, beset; to devastate"	•CTX: **UGA:** G prefc. *yšdd* → DUL 799: */š-d-d/* (II). **EG** *ša-da* → Hoch SWET 290 no. 418.
Sadd "raid"	•CTX: **EUPH** *sa-di-im, sa-ad-da-am, sa-ad-di-im* → CAD S 17: *saddu*; Charpin AfO 40/41 2; Streck Onomastikon 1 113 § 1.95.
Sādid "raiding party"	•CTX: **EUPH** *sa-di-du, sa-di-id-ka, sa-di-di-ka, sa-di-dam* → CAD S 18: *sādidu*; Charpin AfO 40/41 2. •LL: **MŠ** *sa-di-du* = MIN (*maḫru*, III 74) → Hrůša MŠ 78f., 231, 364.
Saddat "raid, expedition"	•CTX: **EB** *sa-da-tum* → Fronzaroli ARET 13 185, 292; Catagnoti QuSe 29 122, 224.
maSadd "(pulling) pole"	•CTX: **EB** Du. *ma-sa-da* |maSadd=ayn| → Fronzaroli ARET 11 160; Archi PIHANS 106 106.

|S-d-n| (1)	Culture word, Sem. etym. unc. Cf. Hb. *sdyn* (*sādîn*, Hb.) "vest" (?); *sdyn(?)* (JAram., Syr.) "linen sheet"; *s/šaddinnu* (Akk.) "a tunic" (?); *sadan* (Arab.) "warp (of a fabric)". See further *šty(?)* (Aram., Syr.) "warp", denom. *šty* (JAram., Syr., C) "to weave"; *šatû(m)* (Akk.) "to knot together, weave".
Sad(d)in(n) "a shirt or chemise"	•CTX: **EA** *sa-dì-in-nu* (22 I 44; also Nuzi-Akk.) → AHw 1001f.: *s/šaddinu*; CAD S 17: *saddinnu*; Waetzoldt RlA 6 22; Moran AmL 315. **EM** Cf. TÚG *ša-ti-na* → Westenholz Emar Tablets 52, 54.
sdn "a horse-cloth"	•CTX: **UGA** Pl. *sdnt* → DUL 742.

|S-D-n| (2)	Culture word, Sem.: *šut(t)innu(m)*, *sut(t)innu* (Akk.) "bat (also a part of a chariot or plough)". Non-Sem.: sudin (Sum.) "bat (a part of a chariot)".
Sudan, Sudun(n)iyat "collar"	•CTX: **EB** *su-da-nu, su-du-ni-a-tum* → Waetzoldt NABU 1997/95.

|s-d-r|	Culture word, Sem.: Cf. *sidr* (Arab.) "a kind of lotus", cf. *sadīr* "grass".
sid(a)r "a plant"	•LL: **EB** Cf. GÀR.SAR = *si-da-*ru_{12} → Sjöberg Fs. Kienast 553.

|S-ð|
See **|S-d/ð|**

|S-ð-b|	Culture word, Sem.: *šizbu*(m), *ši/ezibbu* (Akk.) "milk", *šizbānu* "a plant with milky sap".
Saðb, Siðb "a milkweed"	•LL: **EB** Ú.ŠIM.GA = *sa-ša-bù, si-ša-bù, si-sa-ša-bù* → Civil Or 56 238; Krebernik ZA 73 22 fn. 75; Conti QuSe 17 113; Catagnoti QuSe 29 20, 64, 224.

|S-G-b|	Sem. etym. unc. Cf. *Šgb* (*śgb*, Hb.) "to be too high, strong"; *Šgb* (*śgb*, Aram.) "to lift high, raise up", *Šgb* (*śgb*, Aram., rdg unc.) "supporter (?), nobleman (?)".
SaGb(iy) "a special troop (patrol ?)"	•CTX: **EUPH** *sa-ag-bu, sa-ag-bi, sa-ag-bi-im, sa-ag-bu-ia, sa-ag-bi-šu-nu* → AHw 1002: *sag/kbu(m), sagbû(m)*; CAD S 22f.: *sagbû*; vKoppen MARI 8 421; Charpin AfO 40/41 2f. "patrouille(s), patrouilleur(s)"; Streck Onomastikon 1 113f. § 1.95.
|s-g-d|	Sem.: *sgd* (Hb.) "to bow down in adoration"; *sgd* (Aram., Syr.) "to bow down in respect", *sgd(ʔ)* (JAram.) "worship"; *sağada* (Arab.) "to bow down, bow in worship", *sağda, suğūd* "prostration"; *sagada* (Eth.) "to bow, prostrate", *sagid* "adoration".
sigad "adoration"	•ONOM: **A4** *sí-ga-du*, nasalised var. *sí-en-ga-du* → Wiseman AT 152; Arnaud AuOr 16 166.
|S-g-g| Cf. |s^2-g-y|	Culture word; Sem. with several by-forms: Cf. *Šgg* (*śgg*, Hb. C) "to cause to grow", (Ct) "to grow upwards", see *Šgʔ* (*śgʔ*, G) "to grow", *Šgh* (*śgh*, G) "to increase"; *sgy* (Aram., Syr., G) "to become many, to grow", D/C "to make numerous".
Sugāg "the big one, sheikh"	•CTX: **EUPH** Passim; cf. *su-ga-gu, su-ga-gu-um, su-ga-gu-šu-nu*, LÚ *su-ga-gu*, LÚ *su-ga-gu-um*, LÚ *su-ga-ag-šu*, LÚ *su-ga-gi-ni*, LÚ *su-ga-gi-šu-nu*, LÚ.MEŠ *su-ga-gu-šu-nu*, LÚ *su-ga-gi*(.MEŠ), LÚ.MEŠ *su-ga-gu* → AHw 1053: *sugāgum*; CAD S 343f.: *sugāgu*; Durand Amurru 3 173; LAPO 16 206ff.; LAPO 17 494ff.; Charpin AfO 40/41 21; Streck BaM 33 179ff.; AOAT 271/1 53f.; Onomastikon 1 116 § 1.95. **R** *su-ga-gi* → Dalley / Walker / Hawkins Tell Rimah 84 (100:16); CAD S 343f.: *sugāgu* c. •ONOM: **U3** Cf. *zu/su-ga-kum* → Gelb MAD 3 240. **EUPH** *su-ga-gi, sú-ga-gu-um*; cf. *zu-ga-ga, zu/su-ga-kum* → Gelb MAD 3 240: SQQ?; CAAA 33, 189; Zadok Fs. Hallo 329; Streck Onomastikon 1 331f. fn. 2.
Sugāgūt "post as sheikh"	•CTX: **EUPH** *su-ga-gu-ut, su-ga-gu-tim, su-ga-gu-ti-šu, su-ga-gu-ti-šu-nu* → AHw 1053: *sugāgūtum*; CAD S 344: *sugāgūtu*; Charpin AfO 40/41 21f.; Streck Onomastikon 1 116 § 1.95.
|S-g-g-ʔ|	Culture word, loan: *sāgu, sagû* (Akk.) "sanctuary, cella". Non-Sem.: zaggula, zagŋara (Sum.) "shrine".
Saggaʔ "sanctuary"	•CTX: **EB** *za$_x$-ga-ù* → Fronzaroli ARET 13 174, 311; Catagnoti QuSe 29 19, 224 (*saggaʔum*), 229 (*ˈsaggaʔum*).
|s-G-l|	Sem.: *sglh* (*s^{e}gullāh*, Hb.) "property"; *sgl* (JAram., D) "to acquire"; *sakālu(m)* (Akk.) "to acquire, hoard", *sikiltu(m)* "acquisition(s), (hoarded) property", *sugullu(m), sukullu(m)* "herd, cattle". See also *šikāl* (Arab.) "fetter, hobble", *šakala* "to hobble".
SiG(i)l, SiGilt "acquisition, treasure, private property"	•CTX: **EB** *zi-ga-lum* → Fronzaroli ARET 13 105, 311. •ONOM: **EUPH** Cf. *ṣi-ki-lum, zi-ik-lum, zi-ki-li-im, zi-ki-li-ia, zi-gi-il-da-nu-um* → Gelb CAAA 30 (SKL), 179f. **A7** Cf. *zi-gi-il-te, zi-ki-il-da* → Wiseman AT 153; Gelb CAAA 30, 179. **A4** *zi-ki-il/el-ta* → Wiseman AT 153; Gelb CAAA 30, 179.

SaGul(a)t “acquisition, treasure, private property”	•LL: **EB** SAG.NÍG.DU = *sá-gú-la-tum* → Sjöberg Fs. Pettinato 275.
sglt “acquisition, treasure, private property”	•CTX: **UGA** Sg. suff. *sglth* → DUL 742f.
|s-g-n| (1)	Sem.: *saǧǧana* (Arab.) “to crack, split, dig”.
masgin “pick, pickaxe”	•LL: **EB** GIŠ.NÌ.GUL = *ma-za-gi-núm*, *ma-zi-gi-num*, *mar-gi-nu* → Conti QuSe 17 142.
|s-g-n| (2)	Culture word, etym. unc.
sugun “an ornament (handle?)”	•CTX: **EUPH** Cf. *su-gu-ni*, *sú-gu-nim*, *su-gu-nu-šu* → Talon ARMT 24 52; Guichard ARM 31 133f.; Charpin, AfO 40/41 22.
|s-G-r|	Sem.: *sgr* (Hb.) “to shut”, *sgwr* (*s*^{e}*gûr*) “lock”, *msgrt* (*misgeret*) “prison”, *swgr* (*sûgar*) “collar”; *skr*, *sgr* (Aram., Syr.) “to stop up, to shut (up)”, *swkr(?)* (JAram., Syr.) “bolt; stable”, *swgr(?)* (Syr.) “chain for the neck”, *msgr* (Aram.) “prison, enclosure”, *mskr(?)* (Syr.) “barrier”; *sekēru(m)*, *sakāru(m)* (Akk.) “to shut off, block up”, *sikru(m)* “dam, barrage”, *sikkūru(m)* “bar, bolt”, *meskertum* “barrage, dam”; *sāǧur* (Arab.) “clamp, collar”. See further: *śagara* (Eth.) “to catch in a net, snare, bar a gate”; *šigaru*(m), *sigaru* (Akk.) “clamp”. Non-Sem.: Cf. siŋar (Sum.) “bolt, clamp”, gišukur “enclosure”.
|S-G-r| “to close, shut”	•CTX: **EB** G suffc. *za-gi-ir* |SaGir|; N prefc. *na-zi-ga-la-am*$_6$ |naSSiGar=am| → Catagnoti / Fronzaroli ARET 16 175, 282; Catagnoti QuSe 29 9, 53, 125f., 136, 142, 229. **UGA** G prefc. *ysgr*, suffc. *sgrt*; imp. *sgr*; pass. ptc. *sgr* → DUL 743: */s-g-r/*. •ONOM: **UGA** Cf. unc. *sgr* → DUL 743: *sgr* (III); *s/śgryn* → DUL 744.
SiGr “sluice”	•LL: **EB** A.UŠx(LAK 672).KI = *zi-gi-lum* → Conti QuSe 17 169; Bonechi Proceedings 44^{e} RAI 101; Sjöberg Fs. Kienast 550.
SaGar, **SiGar** “ritual closing (of doors)”	•CTX: **EB** *za-ga-ri-iš*, *zi-ga-ri-iš* → Pasquali NABU 2020/39.
SaGir “sluice”	•LL: **EB** A.UŠ$_x$(LAK 672).KI = *za-gi-rí* A (*māwī*) → Conti QuSe 17 169; Bonechi Proceedings 44e RAI 101; Sjöberg Fs. Kienast 550.
SāGir “who closes, controls”	•CTX: **EB** *za-gi-lum* → Catagnoti QuSe 29 140, 229.
sigar “fort; magazine” (?)	•CTX: **EG** Cf. *s-ga-r* → Hoch SWET 270f. no. 385.[533]
sikar “tower gate” (?)	•CTX: **EG** Cf. *ṯi*$_2$*-ka-r* → Hoch SWET 371 no. 555.[534]
sikkur “clasp”	•CTX: **EUPH** *sí-ik-ku-ur*, *sí-ku-ru*, *sí-ik-ku-ru*, *sí-ik-ku-ur-ša*. *sí-ik-ku-ru-ša* → Arkhipov ARM 32 92.

533 A connection with *θayr* “gate” (see \|θ-γ-r\|; Hoch loc.cit.) is less likely. Cf. Sivan / Cochavi-Rainey WSVES 84: *śa-ga-r* “fortress”; Helck Beziehungen no. 209.

534 Sivan / Cochavi-Rainey WSVES 87: *śi-ka-r* “door with bolt”; Helck Beziehungen no. 297.

suGir "bolt"	•CTX: **UGS** GIŠ *sú-qi-ri* → vSoldt SAU 306 (102): *sú-qi-ri* |su(k)kiri|; Or 60 119; cf. Sivan GAGl 267 (SUGIRU / SŌGIRU), 268 (SUKIRU / SŌKIRU); Huehnergard UVST 155f.: GIŠ *sú*-KU!(QI)-*ri* |sug/kuru|. •ONOM: **UGS** Cf. unc. ZU-*ug-ri-ia-nu* → Gröndahl PTU 255f.: Hurr.; Sivan GAGl 267f. (SUGRĪYĀNU / SUKRĪYĀNU < SGR / SKR).
suGur "bolt"	•LL: **UGS** GIŠ.SAG.GÚL = *si-ik-ku-ru* = *sú*-KU-*ru*, GÚL.LA.LA = *sik-kur šá-qí-li* = ŠU-KU-*ru sà*-GI-*ru*, GIŠ.ÉŠ.SAG.GÚL = *e-bi-il si-ku-ri* =*eb-lu sú*-KU-*ri*, GIŠ.MUD.SAG.GÚL = *šul-bu-ú* = *up-pu sú*-KU-*ri* → Huehnergard UVST 155f.
sgr (A) "enclosure, closed courtyard" (?)	•CTX: **UGA** Pl. *sgrm* → DUL 743: *sgr* (I).
sgr (B) "(a dress or fabric) sewn or decorated in a certain way"	•CTX: **UGA** → DUL 743: *sgr* (II).
skr "bolt"	•CTX: **UGA** → DUL 749.
SaGirat "sluice"	•LL: **EB** NÍG.NIGIN = *za-gi-ra-tum* (VE 38) → Conti QuSe 17 65; Fronzaroli QuSe 19 51f.; Bonechi Proceedings 44e RAI 101.
sgrt "room, chamber"	•CTX: **UGA** → DUL 743.
SiGirrat, **SiGurrit** "a fastening, hook, buckle" (?)	•CTX: **EB** 1 *zi-kir-ra-tum*, 4 *zi-kir-ra-tum* → Conti QuSe 19 51f. **EUPH**: Cf. *zi-gu-ri-tum* → Durand MARI 6 146ff.; ARM 30 139.
msgr "closed building"	•CTX: **UGA** → DUL 574f.

|S-G-S|	Sem. Cf. *šgš* (Syr.) "to disturb", *šgwš* "disturber", *šgyš* "disturbed"; *šagāšu*(*m*), *šakāšu*(*m*) (Akk.) "to kill (in battle), slaughter", *šagšu* "slain, ruined, afflicted", *šaggāšu*(*m*), *šāgišu*, *šaggišu*, "murderer", *mašgašu*(*m*), *maškašu*(*m*) "a battle mace" (?).
|S-G-S| "to slay, slaughter"	•ONOM: **EB** *iš-gú-uš-da-mu* → Bonechi MARI 8 481; Pagan ARES 3 173, 340.[535]
Sā/ēGiS "killer"	•ONOM: **EB** *sa-gi-iš*, *sa-gi-su*, *en-sa-kis*$_x$(KAS), *en-sa-gi*, *en-sa-gi-iš*, *en-sa-gi-su*, *en-sa-ki-iš*; *ma-sa-gi-ba-um*, *ma-sa-gi-iš-ba-um*, *ma-gi:si-ba-u*$_4$, *ma-si-gi-sa-<ba>-um*, *ma-si-gi-si-ba*, *ma-an-sa:gi:si-ba-um*[536] → Pagan ARES 3 173, 307, 347f., 349, 361.
SaGiS "dead"	•ONOM: **EUPH** *ḫa-am-mi-ša-gi-iš*, *am-mi-ša-gi-iš*, *ḫa-mu-ša-ki-iš*, *bu-nu-um-ša-gi-iš* → Huffmon APNMT 266f.; Gelb CAAA 33, 194.
SaGuS "afflicted" (?)	•ONOM: **EB** *sá-gu*/*gú-si*, *sá-gu*/*gú-šum* → Pagan ARES 3 173, 362.
maSGaSat "battle mace" (?)	•ONOM: **EB** Cf. *maš-ga-sa-du*, *maš-ga-ša-du* → Pagan ARES 3 173, 350.

[535] Further study is required in order to ascertain the occurrence of \|s²\| (*ś*) in the basis **šg/qš* (Bonechi SEL 18 33).

[536] In all instances \|man=Sā/ēGiS=baʕl=\| "who is the killer, Baʕlu?"; cf. diff. Bonechi SEL 18 32f.: *Mašgiš=Baʕlu* (unlikely).

|s-H-d|	Sem.: Cf. *sʕd* (Hb.) "support, sustain"; *sʕd* (Aram.) "to help, aid", *sʕd(?)* (JAram.) "helper, supporter"; *sēdu* (Akk.) "to support, assist", *sāʔidum* "helper";[537] *sāʕda, ʔasʕada* (Arab.) "to help, support", *sʕd* (OSArab.) "to favour someone with, grant".
|**s-ʔ-d**| "to support, comfort"	•CTX: **UGA** G prefc. *ysảd*, imp. *sảd* → DUL 740.
|**s-ʕ-d**| "to support, protect"	•ONOM: **EUPH** Cf. *sa-a-di-ia, ia-ás-ta-aḫ-di-el* → Huffmon APNMT 245; Gelb CAAA 180 (ŚʔD); Zadok Fs. Hallo 329.
sỉd "chief butler"	•CTX: **UGA** (as tittle of a DN) → DUL 740.

|S-H-r|	Sem.: Cf. *šaʔāru*(m) (Akk.) "to win, conquer"; *ṯaġara* (Arab.) "to nick, damage, break"; *saʕara, səʕra* (Eth.) "to remove, destroy".
|**S-H-r**| "to defeat, beat" (?)	•CTX: **EUPH** Cf. G prefc. *ta-aš-ḫa-ru, a-ša-i-ra-kum*, D prefc. [*u*]*š-ta-aʔ*$_4$*-ir-šu* → Durand Fs. De Meyer 15ff., LAPO 17 171 (556:21) fn. c.; Charpin MARI 6 263ff.; Durand LAPO 18 257f. (1084):12 fn. b.; Eidem PIHANS 117 134f. (64:22); Streck Onomastikon 1 117 § 1.95.
maSHart "a priestess"	•CTX: **EM** Passim: *maš-ar-ti, ma-aš-ar-tu*$_4$, *ma-aš-ar-ti* → Fleming Installation 98f., 322f.: *mašʔartu*.

|S-H-ṭ|	Culture word, etym. unkn.
maSHaṭ "a cloth item"	•CTX: **UGS** Pl. TÚG.MEŠ GIŠ.MÁ.MEŠ *ma*-ÁŠ-ḪA-*ṭu-ma* → Huehnergard UVAS 186, ²UVST 399.

|s-ḥ-b| Cf. |**s¹-ʔ-b**|	Sem.: *sḥb* (Hb., Moab.) "to drag (away)"; *saḥaba* (Arab.) "to drag, pull"; *sḥab, sḥob, səḥab* (MSArab.) "to drag"; *saḥaba* (Eth.) "to draw, pull". See also *sāba* (*sayb* < ? **sḥb*, Arab.) "to flow, run".
|**s-ḥ-b**| "to drag away"	•LL: **EB** NÌ.KAR = *sa-ʔà-bu* → Conti QuSe 17 73; É.PAP = [*s*]*a-u*$_9$-[*b*]*ù-um, sa-ʔà-bu* → Conti QuSe 17 117; Fronzaroli QuSe 19 17 fn. 43; NÌ.KAR.KAR = *dal-da-i-bù* |taStaḥ(ḥ)īb| → Kienast BaE 243; Krebernik ZA 72 191 (I, *i*); Conti QuSe 17 74; Catagnoti QuSe 29 65, 224; Kogan Classification 97f.

|S-ḥ-n|	Sem.: Cf. *šaḥana* (Arab.) "to load, freight".
|**S-ḥ-n**| "to load, freight"	•LL: **EB** MÁ.GAR = *ša-a-nu-um* → Conti QuSe 17 85f.

|s-ḥ-r|	Sem.: Cf. *saḥara, saḥḥara* (Arab.) "to bewitch, put a spell on", *sāḥir*, "magician".
sāḥirat "witch"	•ONOM: **EUPH** *sà-ḫi-ra-tim* → Sasson BiOr 43 129; Zadok Fs. Hallo 329.

|s-ḥ-y|	Sem.: *sḥh* (Hb. C) "to sweep away"; *sḥy* (Aram., Syr.) "to bathe", (C) "to wash"; *saḥā* (*saḥy*) (Arab.) "to scrape off, unstick"; *sḥy, saḥaya, səḥya* (Eth.) "to rub, scrub".
|**s-ḥ-y**| "to sweep away"	•LL: **EB** [Á.A].TAG = *za-ʔà-um* → Conti QuSe 17 30, 36, 158; Bonechi / Catagnoti Fs. Sommerfeld / Krebernik 161.

[537] Thus with AHw 1010; diff. CAD S 67f.: "inn, road-station" (?).

|s-x-l|	Sem.: *saḫālu(m)*, *seḫēlu* (Akk.) "to prick, pierce"; *səḥāl* (MSArab.) "to scratch, grind".
sāxil "who pierces"	•LL: **EB** SAG.DU$_7$ = *za-ḫi-lu* → Conti QuSe 17 109 (257); Sjöberg Fs. Renger 526; Bonechi / Catagnoti Fs. Sommerfeld / Krebernik 176f.: "headache"(?).
sxl "grinder, polisher, engraver" (?)	•CTX: **UGA** Pl. *sḫlm* → Watson JSS 47 206 fn. 27; DUL 744: *sḫl*.

|S-x-p|	Loanword, Sem.: *šuḫuppatu*, *suḫuppatu*, *šuḫuptu*, *šaḫuppatu* (Akk.) "boot" (?). Non-Sem.: suḫub (Sum.) "boot".
Saxuppat, **Suxuppat** "a complement for foot-wear (gaiter ?)"	•CTX: **EUPH** Written *me-še-en* ŠUḪÚB; cf. *maš-a-nu šu-ḫu-pá-tum*, 2 KUŠ *ša-ḫu-pá-tin* → Durand ARM 30 167f., 171. **EA** ŠU KUŠ *šu-ḫu-up-pát-tum* → CAD Š/3 211: *šuḫuppatu*, c.[538]

|s-x-r|	Sem.: Cf. *sḥr* (Hb.) "to pass through", *swḥr* (*sôḥēr*) "trader, dealer"; *sḥr* (Ph., Pun.) "peddler, merchant"; *sḥr* (JAram.) "to go about, turn around", *sḥwr(?)* (JAram., Syr.) "merchant, beggar"; *saḫāru(m)* (Akk.) "to go around, search (for)" *saḫḫiru(m)* "peripatetic, peddler".[539]
|s-x-r| "to turn around, search for" (?)	•ONOM: **UGA** *sḫr* → DUL 745; *sḫrn* → DUL 745.[540]
Suxar "gang leader, recruiter"	•LL: **EB** zilulu$_x$(PA.URU) =*zu-ḫa-lum*/*lu-um* → Bonechi QDLF 16 85.
saxūr "requested, sought" (?)	•ONOM: **UGS** Cf. *sa-ḫu-ra-nu/na* → Huehnergard UVST 226; AkkUg 363f.; vSoldt SAU 313 fn. 118.
sāxirt "female peddler; DN"	•CTX: **EUPH** Cf. *sa/sà-ḫi-ir-tim* → Durand Fs. Kupper 162 fn. 14; Charpin AfO 40/41 4f.
masxarūt "putting / pushing aside"	•CTX: **EUPH** *ma-as-ḫa-ru-tim* → Durand, MARI 6 293 fn. a.

|S-x-r-r|	Culture word, Sem.: *šaḫarru*, *šuḫarru*, *šuḫarrû* (Akk.) "porous" (?). For Mari-Akk. see below: *Suxurr*. Non-Sem.: sahar (Sum.) "a vessel".
Suxurr, **Suxarr** "(qualifying a) clay vessel"	•CTX: **EUPH** Pl. masc. *šu-ḫu-ur-ri*, fem. *šu-ḫu(-úr)-ra-tum* → AHw 1262: *šuḫurru*(m); CAD Š/1 80: *šaḫarru*. **UGS** *šu-ḫar-ri-tu*$_4$ → AHw 1262: *šuḫurru*(m); CAD Š/1 80: *šaḫarru*; Huehnergard AkkUg 395.
Saxurrat "clay vessel"	•CTX: **EB** Pl. *sa-ḫu-ra-ti* → Fronzaroli ARET 11 167; Catagnoti QuSe 29 100, 224.

---

538 Also in Nuzi.

539 Steinkeller JCS 35 245; Gelb / Steinkeller / Whiting Ancient Kudurrus 99.

540 For *saḫāru* in MBab. PNN (Ugarit and other places) see vSoldt Or 60 117.

|s-k-k| (1)

Sem.: *skk* (Hb.) “to shut off (as protection)”, *sk* (*sok*), *skh* (*sukkāh*) “hut, refuge”, *skk* (*sokēk*) “mantelet”; *sakāku*(*m*) (Akk.) “to block; to be hard of hearing”, *sukkuku*(*m*) “deaf; mentally handicapped”; *sakka* (Arab.) “to lock, bolt”, *sakaka* “to be(come) deaf”, *ʔistakka* “to have a hearing problem”; *sukk* “tight coat of mail”.

sakk “ a kind of close, dense fabric” — •CTX: **EUPH** (GÚ) *sa-kum*, GÚ *sa-ak-kum*, TÚG *sa-kum*, TÚG *sa-ku-um*, TÚG *sa-ak-kum*, TÚG *sa-ak-ku*(*-um*) → Durand ARM 30 90ff.

sikk “secret affaire” — •CTX: **EUPH** (official) *ša sí-ki*, *ša sí-ik-ki-šu* → Charpin AfO 40/41 17.[541]

sukk “coverlet, cloak” — •CTX: **UGS** Cf. TÚG ZU/SU(?)-*ku*(?)-*ma* MEŠ → Huehnergard UVST 156.

sk (A) “coverlet, cloak; lid (?)” — •CTX: **UGA** Sg. *sk*, du. *skm*; pl. *skm* → DUL 745: *sk* (I).

sk (B) “den, cove” — •CTX: **UGA** Sg. suff. *skh*, pl. (?)*skt* → DUL 745: *sk* (II).

sakkakk “private, secretary’s office” — •CTX: **EUPH** *sà-ka-ki-im*, *sà-kà-ak-ki-im*, *sà-ka-ki-ia*, *sà-ka-ki-ka* → Charpin AfO 40/41 6.

sukkuk “deaf” — •CTX: **EUPH** *sú-qú-*{KU}*-qú ša an-dùl-li* → Durand ARM 30 469 fn. a.

|s-k-k| (2)

Culture word, Sem. etym. unc. For a probabl. general mng “to stick in” (Syr.) see *skh*, *sktʔ* (JAram., Syr.) “peg, nail, spike”; *sikkatu*(*m*), *s/ziqqatu* (Akk.) “nail, peg; cone; pyramid, pinnacle”;[542] *sikka* (Arab.) “die, shapping tool”, *sakkiyy* “nail”, etc.[543]
Non-Sem.: NA.ZA.KIN (*huwasi=*, Hitt.) “stela, pillar”.

sikkan, sigann “(inscribed?) stela, standing stone”[544] — •CTX: **EUPH** *sí-ik-ka-nu-um*, *sí-ka-nim*, *sí-ik-ka-nam*, pl. *sí-ik-ka-na-tim* → Durand Fs. Birot 81ff., FM 8 32ff., OBO 287 15ff.; Charpin NABU 87/77; Dietrich / Loretz / Mayer UF 21 133ff.; Lackenbacher, NABU 1991/12; Ziegler WZKM 86 482 fn. 1; Durand RA 24ff.; Charpin AfO 40/41 16f.; Guichard NABU 2017/65.
TU *si-ga-nu-um ša* ^{d}*da-gan* → Krebernik Tall Bi`a 99 (157:4), 241.
EM NA$_4$ *si-ka-ni*, NA$_4$ *si-kà-na*$_7$, NA$_4$ *sí-ka-na*, NA$_4$ *sí-ka-ni*, NA$_4$ *sí-kà-na*; pl. NA$_4$ *si-ik-ka-na-ti*, NA$_4$ *si-ka-na-ti*, NA$_4$ *si-ka*<*-ne-e-*>*ti*, NA$_4$ *sí-ka-na-ti*, NA$_4$ *sí-ka-na-tì* → Fleming Installation 75ff.; Pentiuc Vocabulary 156ff.; Ikeda BiOr 60 271; Dietrich / Loretz / Mayer UF 21 133ff.; Westenholz Emar Tablets 76f.; Durand MARI 7 49; LAPO 18 141ff.; FM 8 1ff., 35ff.
TMB NA$_4$ *sí-kà-na*, NA$_4$ *sí-kan-nu-mi* → Dietrich / Loretz / Mayer UF 21 136; Mayer Ekalte 35:25ff., 36:14ff., 69:25ff., 78:8ff.; Marti NABU 2006/58.
UGS Pl |sikānūma| genit. É AN.ZA.GÀR *sí-kà/ka*$_4$*-ni-ma* → Huehnergard UVST 157, ^{2}UVST 395; Dietrich / Loretz / Mayer UF 21 133ff.

---

541 Durand ARM 21 510f.: *siqqum* “bourse”, from SQQ “boucher”.
542 For Ugarit LL see RS 17.98 (Hh. V-VII):9 GIŠ.KAK.MUD = *sí-ka-at up-pí*; vSoldt Or 60 119.
543 See further Huehnergard Fs.Leslau 1991 703, for OSArab. and Eth. (Gur. “drive a peg […] into the ground”), Amh. *skk* “thread through, drive through”.
544 Abode of a deity. Probably a *qitlān* form of |s-k-k|; Huehnergard ^{2}UVST 395.

	•LL: **EB** KUR.PAD.NA.RÚ = *ma-da-ù zi-ga-na-tim*; *ma-da-*u_9 $NA_4.NA_4$ → Durand NABU 1988/8; Conti QuSe 17 91; Catagnoti QuSe 29 112, 115, 229. •ONOM: **EUPH** Cf. ÌR-*sí-ka-ni*, *wa-ra-ad-sí-ka-ni* → Charpin NABU 87/77, AfO 40/41 17.
skn (B) "stela"	•CTX: **UGA** Sg. *skn*, pl. *sknm* → DUL 747f.: *skn* (II).
|S-k-l|	Culture word, Non-Sem.: tukul (Sum.) "weapon".
Sukull "a weapon" (?)	•LL: **EB** GIŠ.TUKUL = *zu-gul-lum*, *zu-gú-lum* → Krebernik ZA 73 17. Altern. Conti QuSe 17 142: |ṣukūr=| "big hammer" (cf. Arab. *ṣaqāra* "to hit with a stick", *ṣaqūr* "big hammer").[545]
|s-k-n| (1)	Sem.: *skn* (JAram.) "to be in danger", *sknh*, *skntʔ*, *sknw* "danger".
skn (A) "dangerous moment"	•CTX: **UGA** → 748: *skn* (III).
|s-k-n| (2) See **|s^1-k-n|**	
|S-ḳ-b|	Culture word, Sem.: Cf. *šiqaba* (Arab.) "fissure", hence (?) *šiqb*, *šaqab* "a species of tree with lotus-like flowers". Non-Sem.: Cf. *śqb* (Eg.) "sandalwood / ash" (?).[546]
ʕθḳb, θḳb "a species of tree, ash tree" (?)	•CTX: **UGA** pl. *ʕṯqbm*, *ṯqbm* → DUL 190: *ʕṯqb*, 913: *ṯqb*. •ONOM: **UGA** Cf. *ṯqbn* → DUL 913f.; *ṯqby* → DUL 914.
θaḳabān "the little ash tree" (?)	•ONOM: **UGS** Cf. *šá-qa-ba-ni* → Huehnergard UVST 231; AkkUg 414.
|S-ḳ-ḳ|	Culture word, Sem.:. *Šq* (*śaq*, Hb) "sack"; *šq* (Aram.) "sack"; *sq(ʔ)* (JAram., Syr.) "sack(-cloth)"; *saqqu(m)* (Akk.) "sack(-cloth)", *saqqāya*, *šaqqāya* "sack maker"; *śeqah* (MSArab.) "coat"; *śaqq* (Eth.) "sack(-cloth)".
Saḳḳa "a cloth or fabric, sack"	•CTX: **EG** *sa-ga* → Hoch SWET 269 no. 383.
θḳ "a cloth or fabric, sack"	•CTX: **UGA** Sg. *ṯq*, pl. *ṯqt* → DUL 913: *ṯq*.
|S-ḳ-n| See **|ð-ḳ-n|**	
|S-ḳ-r| Cf. **|ð-k-r| (2)**, **|s^2-k-r| (2)**	Sem.: *zaqāru(m)*, *saqāru* (Akk.) "to project, stick up", *zaqru* "high, tall", cf. *ziqqurratu(m)*, *siqqurrutu* "temple tower", *zuqqurtu* "elevation". See also *sqr* (JAram., Syr.) "to look at, stare, envy".

[545] See Sjöberg Fs. Wilcke 255f. + fn. 10.

[546] Noegel UF 32 385ff.

ʔaSḳur "the very high one; DN"	•ONOM: **EUPH** Cf. *aš-ku-ra-an*, *aš-kur-*^{d}IM, *aš*/*áš -ku-ur-*^{d}IM, *aš-kur-li-im*, *bu-nu-áš-ku-ur*, *mu-ut-*$^{(d)}$*aš-kur*, *i-din-dáš-ku-ur*, *šu-mu-áš-ku-ra* → Gelb CAAA 32, 188; Durand SEL 8 88, REA 672.[547] **A7** *aš-kur-e-da* → Wiseman AT 54:25; Durand SEL 8 88, REA 672; Streck Onomastikon 1 200 § 2.95, 243 § 2.166; 295 § 3.56.[548]
|s-l-ʕ|	Primary noun, Sem.: *slʕ* (*selaʕ*, Hb.) "rock, cliffs"; *salʕ*, *silʕ* (Arab.) "cleft, crack".[549]
silʕ "cliff, rock" (?)	•CTX: **UGS** A.SÀ (:) *sí-il-a* → Sivan GAGl 267; Huehnergard UVST 157.[550] •ONOM: **UGS** Cf. *sí-il-a-*[*na*], *si-il-ʔa-nu* → Gröndahl PTU 185; Sivan GAGl 267.
slʕ "cliff, rock" (?)	•ONOM: **UGA** Cf. *slʕn* → DUL 749; *slʕy* → DUL 749.
|S-l-B|	Sem.: Bases C_1:*s*^{1}-C_2:*l*- C_3:*p*, cf. *šlp* (Hb.) "to pull out, pull off, take out"; *šlp* (JAram., Syr.) "to pull, draw out, remove"; *šalāpu*(*m*) (Akk.) "to pull out, draw, tear out; to wipe". Bases C_1:*s*^{3}-C_2:*l*-C_3:*b*, cf. *salaba* (Arab.) "to take away, deprive"; OSArab. *s*^{3}*lb* "to draw water improperly"; *salaba* (Eth.) "to take off, strip off, deprive".
|**s**^{1}**-l-p**| "to be dishevelled" (?)	•CTX: **EG** Cf. *ša-n-ra-fi*, *ša-n-r-fi* → Hoch SWET 283 no. 404.[551]
|S-l-x|	Sem.: Cf. *zlḥ* (JAram.) "to sprinkle"; *salāḫu*(*m*) (Akk.) "to sprinkle", (D) "lustrate", *maslaḫu*(*m*) "a libation tube", *maslaḫtu*(*m*), *musalliḫtu* "a libation vessel". See also: *slḥ* (Hb., JAram.) "to forgive".[552]
slx "a certain material for sacrifice" (?)	•CTX: **UGA** → DUL 749f.: *slḫ* (I).
Salaxxiy, Suluxxiy "ritually sprinkled animal; garment made from this wool"	•CTX: **EUPH** *su-lu-ḫi*, TÚG *sà-la-ḫi* → Durand ARM 30 148
maSxalt "a vessel with lip or spout"	•CTX: **EB** *maš-ḫa-tum*, *ma-sa-ḫa-tum* → Fronzaroli ARET 11 48, 160.
mðlɣ "watering can" (?)	•CTX: **UGA** Cf. unc. *mḏlġ* → DUL *mḏlġ*: 523.

547 Diff. Golinets Onomastikon 2 117f.: prefc. ŚKR.
548 See the previous fn.
549 Unrelated: Arab. *ṣaliʕa* "to be bald", with *ṣullaʕ*, *ṣullāʕ* "rock", and Eth. *ṣolāʕ*, *solʕat* "rock".
550 Cf. TN *Silʕu*, Belmonte RGTC 12/2 399, 403.
551 Sivan / Cochavi-Rainey WSVES 95: *šá-la*$_2$*-fi* "to bristle, to be disheveled(?)"; Helck Beziehungen no. 222.
552 Unrelated: *zuluḥ* (Arab.) "wide vessels", *mezelaḥ* "vessel for drawing water"; *zalḥa*, *zalləḥa* (Eth.) "to drain out, empty all the liquid, squeeze".

|s-l-l|

Sem.: Cf. *sll* (Hb.) "pile up", *mstwll* (*mistôlēl*, ptc. Hitpol.) "to behave high-handedly, insolently", *sllh* (*sol^{e}lāh*) "assault ramp", *mslh* (*m^{e}sillāh*) "a track firmed with stones"; *swlm(?)* (JAram.) "ladder". Cf. *musallil* (Akk.) "torturer" (?).[553]

|s-l-l| "to be in distress, sleepless" (?)

●CTX: **EUPH** G prefc. *i-sa-al-lu(-la)*, suffc. *sà-al-la-at*; cf. unc. *sa-li-il* → Heimpel NABU 1995/93; Charpin MARI 7 202 (ln.47, 52); AfO 40/41 7 (no etym. explanation).
●ONOM: **EG** Cf. *sꜣ-n:-r* → Schneider APÄQ 185 no. 390 (a).

sol^{e}lā "siege-mound"

●CTX: **EG** *ṯ-r-r-ya*, *ṯ-r-r-t* → Hoch SWET 368f. no. 548.

|s-l-m| (1)
Cf.-|**s^1-l-m**|

Sem.:[554] *šlwm* (*šālôm*, Hb.) "peace, friendliness", *šlm* (G) "to keep peace" (?), (C) "to make peace" (?); *šlm* (Ph., Palm.) "peace, good relations"; *šlm(?)* (Aram., Syr.) "peace"; *salāmu(m)*, *selēmu* (Akk.)[555] "to be(come) at peace", (D) "conciliate, propitiate, bring peace to", *salīmu(m)* "peace, amity", *salmu*, *sālimu* "peaceful, friendly"; *silm*, *salām* (Arab.) "peace", *sallama* "greet, salute", *sālama* "to keep the peace", *tasālama* "to make peace with one another", *musālim* "peaceable"; *slm* (OSArab.) "peace", *hslm* "to make peace, sue for peace"; *səlōm* (MSArab.) "peace", *séləm* "to greet"; *salām* (Eth.) "peace, salutation, safety", *salama* "to greet", *tasālama* "to salute, make peace with one another".

|**S-l-m**| **(A)** "to be friendly, show friendliness, greet, seek peace, surrender"

●CTX: **EUPH** Passim; see *is$_7$-la-am-ma*, *l*[*a-is$_7$*]*-li-ma*, *is-sa-lim* → Charpin AfO 40/41 7f.: "se rendre".
A7 Cf. *ís*(IŠ)*-li-mu* → Lauinger STOBA 330 (AT 58 u.e. 1), 332.
EG *ša-r-ma*, *ša-ra-ma*$_{(2/4)}$ |šalama| (?), |šallema| (?), miswritten: *ša-ma* → Hoch SWET 283f. no. 406: "to greet, do homage"; *ša-ra-ma*$_{(2)}$, *ša-r-m* (|šalama| (?), |šallema| (?)) → Hoch SWET 285 no. 407: "to lay down (arms), seek peace".[556]
●ONOM: **EUPH**, **B** *e-es-li-mu-um*, *ia-áš-la-mu-um*, *iš-la-ma-na*, *ia-áš-li-ma-an*, *ia-ás-li-im-ia-*[*an-d*]*u*, *ia-áš-lam*-DINGIR; cf. *ti-is-li-mu* → Huffmon APNMT 246f.; Gelb CAAA 32 188; Zadok Fs. Hallo 330; Golinets Onomastikon 2 32, 57 fn. 206, 57, 60f., 82, 118f., 142, 447f., 491f.
TU *iš-la-am-*^{d}IM → Krebernik Tall Bi`a 221; Golinets Onomastikon 2 32, 118, 447f.
UGS *iš-la-ma-na*, *ia-aš-li-ma-na* → Gröndahl PTU 193; Sivan GAGl 274; Golinets Onomastikon 2 63 fn. 248, 74 fn. 290.

Salm (A) "peace"

●CTX: **EA** *šal-ma* (136:13) → AHw 1149: *šalmu* II; CAD S/1 100: *salīmu*; Moran AmL 217 fn. 1.

Salam "friendly; DN"

●ONOM: **EUPH** *sa-la-ma-an*, *ša-la-mu-um*, *i-lu-um-ša-al-ma*, fem.: *sa-la-ma-tum* → Huffmon APNMT 246f.; Gelb CAAA 32, 181f.; Golinets Onomastikon 2 142, 151, 154, 447f., 493.

---

[553] Grayson / Sollberger RA 70 111 (M 8): *mu-sa-li-il-šu-nu*; Charpin MARI 7 202: "tourmenteur". Unrelated (see Hb. *šll* ""to stalk, sheaf") are: Arab. *salla*, *ʔistalla* "to pull out, withdraw", *tasallala* "to infiltrate, advance singly or in small groups"; Eth. *sassala* "to withdraw".

[554] Due to their semantic and phonetic neighbourhood, the bases |s-l-m| (1) "to be friendly" and |s^1-l-m| "to be complete, well" may intersect or merge in some languages. For each language see also under |s^1-l-m|.

[555] AHw 1013: 'Sekundärwurzel zu *šlm*' (also Golinets Onomastikon 2 447f.). For a discussion of this opinion see Streck Onomastikon 1 115f. § 1.95.

[556] Sivan / Cochavi-Rainey WSVES 85: *šá-la-ma* "to greet, to sue for peace"; Helck Beziehungen no. 225: "Frieden erbitten".

Salām (A) "peace, greetings"	•CTX: **EUPH** *sa-la-am, a-sa-la-am* (*ana salām*) → Charpin AfO 40/41 7. **EG** *ša-ra-ma$_4$, ša-r-ma$_4$* |Salāma| → Hoch SWET 285f. no. 408.
Salim (A) "friendly; DN Dusk"	•LL: **UGS** ^{d}*sa-li-mu* (// *šlm*, KTU 1.47:34; 1.118:33) → Huehnergard UVST 181 (diff.: "whole, sound", from |s^1-l-m|). •ONOM: **EB** Cf. *ku-un-sá-lim* → Catagnoti Mari 8 591. **EUPH, B** *sa-li-ma-an, sa-li-ma-nu(-um), ša-lim-a-nu-um, ša-lim-a-šar, i-la-sa-lim, mu-ut-sa-lim, i-ṣi-sa-lim, i-dur-sa-lim, i-uš-sa-lim, ia-ku-un-sa-lim, ia/ya-tar-sa-lim, in-du-ub-ša-lim, ša-al-mu-ṭà-ba*; fem.: *sa-li-ma, sa-li-ma-tum* → Huffmon APNMT 247; Gelb CAAA 32 181f.; Lafont Amurru 2 255ff.; Zadok Fs. Hallo 330; Streck Onomastikon 1 265 § 3.12 + fn.3, 267 § 3.14, 278 § 3.33, 326 § 5.20; Golinets Onomastikon 2 129, 159f., 305, 447f., 506, 512. **R** *ia-ku-un-di-ri/rum, ia-ku-un-*^{d}IM, *ia-ku-un-*^{d}*lim, ia-ku-un-sa-lim* → Dalley / Walker / Hawkins Tell Rimah 259; Golinets Onomastikon 2 159, 447f. **TU** *sá-li-ma-an* → Krebernik Tall Bi`a 226; Golinets Onomastikon 2 159, 447f. **UGS** DINGIR-*ša-lim*, DINGIR-*ša-li-ma*, DINGIR-*šal-ma, na-ḫi-ši-šal-mu*; cf. DINGIR-*ša-al-mi* → Gröndahl PTU 193; Sivan GAGl 272, 274.
Salim (B) "capitulation, surrender"	•CTX: **EUPH** *sa-li-im, sa-l[i-im]-šu*, pl. *sa-li-ma-tim* → Charpin AfO 40/41 9f.
Silām "friendly"	•ONOM: **EB** Cf. *si-la-mu-du, si-la-mu-da, si-la-mu-*UTU/*ud* (?) → Colonna d'Istria NABU 2013/74.[557] **EUPH** *še-la-mu* → Millet AlbàbTopoi Suppl 2 487 fn. 21; Colonna d'Istria NABU 2013/74.
Sulām "friendly"	•ONOM: **B** *su-la-mu-um* → Gelb CAAA 32, 189; Golinets Onomastikon 2 164, 447f. **UGS** *šu-la-mu*, ^{d}IM-*šu-la-mu*, EN-*šu-la-mu* → Gröndahl PTU 193; Sivan GAGl 274.
Sulīm "(little) friend" (?)	•ONOM: **EM** *sú-li-mu* → Pruzsinszky PTEm 176 [709]; Streck AfO 51 309.
Sullum "reconciled"	•ONOM: **EB** Cf. *zu-lum, zu-lu-mu* → Pagan ARES 3 169, 389. **A4** *šu-lu-ma* → Sivan GAGl 275.
s^1lm (A) "friendly; DN Dusk"	•CTX: **UGA** *šlm, šḥr w šlm* → DUL 809: *šlm* (IV). •LL: **UGA** *šlm* → DUL 809: *šlm* (IV). •ONOM: **UGA** *ỉlšlm* → DUL 62; *bʕlšlm* → DUL 208; *šlmym* → DUL 810; cf. *šlmn* → DUL 809.
Sulmān (A) "(little) friend"	•ONOM: **U3** *šu-ul-ma-nu-um* → Buccellati Amorites 29, 182; Gelb CAAA 32, 189.
s^1lmn "(little) friend"	•ONOM: **UGA** Cf. *šlmn* → DUL 809.
meSlim "friendliness"	•ONOM: **EUPH** *me-iš-li-mu-um* → Gelb CAAA 32, 188; Streck Onomastikon 1 199 § 2.95, 338 § 5.47.
miSlam "shown friendly, reconciled" (?)	•ONOM: **UGS** Cf. ^{d}IM-*mi-iš-lam* → Sivan GAGl 274. **UGS** Cf. *bʕlmšlm* → DUL 207.
muSallim "conciliator"	•ONOM: **EUPH** *mu-sa-li-mu(-um)*, fem.: *mu-sa-li-ma-tim* → Gelb CAAA 32 181f.; Golinets Onomastikon 2 199, 506, 512.

[557] Cf. Sum. silim-$^{(d)}$UTU; Steinkeller Fs. Hallo 239.

|s-l-m| (2)	Sem. etym. unc.: Cf. *slm* (*sullām*, Hb.) "stepped ramp, flight of steps"; *swlm(ʔ)* (JAram.) "ladder", metath. *sblh, sbltʔ* (Syr.) "ladder"; *sullam* (Arab.) "ladder". Further: *sll (*Hb.) "to pile up, exalt".
slm "staircase" (?)	•CTX: **UGA** → DUL 750.
mslmt "ascent, slope" (?)	•CTX: **UGA** → DUL 575.
|S-l-m-x|	Culture word, Sem.: *sulumḫû(m), zulumḫû, s/zuluḫḫû* (Akk.) "a kind of long-fleeced sheep; a garment". Non –Sem.: zulumḫi (Sum.) "a sheep".
Salāx, Sulūx "a long-fleeced garment"	•CTX: **EUPH** TÚG *sà-la-ḫi, su-lu-ḫi* → Durand ARM 21 220 (221:4); ARM 30 148f.; Charpin AfO 40/41 22.
|s-l-t|	Primary noun, Sem.: *slt* (*solet*, Hb.) "wheat porridge"; *swlt(ʔ)* (JAram.) "fine floor"; *siltu* (Akk.) "a kind of groats"; *sult* (Arab.) "rye".
Salt, sulta "finely ground wheat flour"	•CTX: **EB** Cf. *za-la-tum* → Milano ARET 9 409. **EG** *t̠u-ru*$_2$*-ta, t̠u*$_2$*-ru*$_2$*-ta, t̠i*$_2$*-r-ta* |sulta|, misspellings: *t̠i*$_2$*-ru*$_2$*-ʔa, t̠i*$_2$*-r-ya* → Hoch SWET 369f. no. 550.[558]
|S-L(-y)|	Sem. etym. unc. Cf. *slh* (Hb.) "to treat as worthless", (D) "to throw away"; *sly* (Syr., C) "to reject"; *salāʔu* (Akk., C) "disdain, neglect".
SaLu(y) "a lower status or menial occupation (in the textile craft)" (?)	•LL: **EB** Cf. NE.RA = *sa-ru*$_{12}$*-um, sá-lum* → Conti QuSe 17 204; Sjöberg Fs. Wilcke 261f.
|s-m-d| (1)	Sem.: *smd(ʔ)* (JAram., Syr.) "barley bread; pottage", *smyd(ʔ)* "fine flour" *samādu(m), semēdu* (Akk.) "to grind (finely)", *samīdu(m)* "a fine flour", *sumidātu, summiddītu* "a kind of flour".
simmidat "a kind of flour"	CTX: **EM** 17 GIŠ *pa* ZÌ *si-im-mi-da-ti* → Pentiuc Vocabulary 156.
|s-m-d| (2)	Loanword. Non-Sem.: *smdt* (Eg.) "pearls, string of pearls".
smd "bead, pearl (necklace)"	•CTX: **UGA** Sg. / pl. cstr. *smd lbnn* → DUL 751.
|s-m-x|	Sem.: *samāḫu(m)* (Akk.) "to mix", *summuḫu, sammuḫu* "mixed, miscellaneous".

[558] Sivan / Cochavi-Rainey WSVES 86: *śu-lú-tá* "meal, flour"; Helck Beziehungen no. 294.

samīx "unskilled agricultural labourer" — •CTX: **EUPH** LÚ *sa-mi-iḫ*, LÚ(.MEŠ) *sa-mi-hi*, LÚ *sa-mi-hi-ša* → vKoppen FM 6 35; Durand FM 7 88f.; LAPO 17 351, 651, 654, 657; ARM 33 473ff. (227:9f.) fn.9; Lauinger STOBA 128f.
R *sa-mi-ḫi-ša* → Dalley / Walker / Hawkins Tell Rimah 146ff. (145:14).

|s-m-k|

Sem.: *smk* (Hb.) "to support, sustain, help", *Šmykh* (*ś^{e}mîkāh*) "cover, covering" (cf. Akk.); *smk* (Palm.) "pillar / banquet-room" (?); *smk* (Aram., Syr.) "to prop up, support", *smk(?)* (JAram., Syr.) "base, support", *smwk* (Syr.) "support", *swmk(?)* (Syr.) "prop, support"; *samaka* (Arab.) "to lift, erect, raise", *samk* "height; roof, ceiling", *masmūkāt*, *musmakāt* "the heavens"; *s^3mk* (OSArab.) "to go up, ascend, raise"; *samaka* (Eth.) "to lean on, take refuge". See also *samāku(m)* (Akk.) "to cover up" (?).[559]

|S-m-k| "to support" — •ONOM: **EUPH** Cf. *su-mu-uk-li-im* → Gelb CAAA 30, 32, 193 (ŚUMUK).

Sumk "support" — •ONOM: **EUPH** *zum-ga-nu-um* → Gelb CAAA 30, 32, 192 (ŚUMK).

Sam(a)k "support" — •ONOM: **EUPH** Cf. *a-bi-sa-ma-ku*, *sa-ma-gu-um*, *sa-am-ka-ia*, *za-am(?)-ga-nu-um* → Gelb CAAA 30, 32, 183 (ŚAMAK, ŚAMK).
R *sa-am-ka-nu/ni/nim* → Dalley / Walker / Hawkins Tell Rimah 262; Zadok Fs. Hallo 329.

Samūk "supporting" (?) — •ONOM: **EUPH** Cf. *sa-mu-ki-el*, *sa-mu-kum*, *sa-mu-uk*, *sa-mu-ki-im*, *sa-mu-ka-nu-um* → Gelb CAAA 30, 32, 185 (ŚAMUK).

smkt "height, ceiling" — •CTX: **UGA** Sg. / pl. *smkt* → DUL 751.

|s-m-m|

Primary noun, Sem: *sm* (Hb., pl. *sammîm*) "spices, fragrant perfumes", *smm* (C) "to paint the face, colour"; *sm(?)* (JAram., Syr.) "medicine, poison, pigment", (D, C) "to poison"; *samm* "poison, toxin" (Arab., pl. *sumūm*, *simām*), *samma* "to poison".

sm "perfume" — •CTX: **UGA** Sg. suff. *smm* → DUL 751: *smm*.

|S-m-r| (1)

Culture word, Sem. etym. unc.: Cf. *msmr* (*masmēr*, Hb.) "nail, peg"; *msmr(?)* (Aram.) id.; *mismār* (Arab.) id.

Samrat, Samrūt "a kind of spear" — •CTX: **EUPH** Cf. *za-am-ra-at*, (GIŠ) *za-am-ra-tum*, (GIŠ) *za-am-ru-tum*, *za-am-re-tim*, *zi-im-ra-ti-im* → Durand ARM 21 346; Charpin AfO 40/41 10f. (rdg *sà*=); Arkhipov ARM 32 129f.

|S-m-r| (2)

See **|ð-m-r| (1)**

|S-m-r| (3)

Culture word, Sem.: Cf. *šmr(?)* (JAram., Syr.) "fennel"; *šimru*, *šibru*, *šimrānu*, *simru* (Akk.) id.; *šamar*, *šamār*, *šamra*, *šumra* (Arab.) "fennel"; see also *šamru* (Akk. LL) "a plant".

θmr (A) "fennel" (?) — •CTX: **UGA** Cf. *ṯmr{g}* → DUL 904: *ṯmr*.

---

[559] AHw 1017: "überdecken"; CAD S 109: 1. "to dam a canal", 2. "to reject(?), to remove (?)".

|S-m-S|	Sem. etym. unc. Cf. Hb. *mw/yš* "to withdraw from a place", (C) "to remove"; *mašāšu(m)* (Akk.) "to wipe out, clean"; see also *mšš* (Hb.) "to touch"; *mš* (Syr.) "to feel, touch", *mšmš* (JAram., Syr.) "to feel, touch"; *massa* (Arab.) "to feel, touch"; *marsasa* (Eth.) "to search (for something)".
|S-m-S| "to hide"	•CTX: **EUPH** D prefc. *ú-sa-am-mi-iš$_7$, ú-sa-mi-šu, ú-sà-am-mi-šu, ú-sà-am-ma-šu-šu-nu-ti, ú-sa-am-ma-šu-šu-nu-ti, ú-sà-mi-šu-ši-na-ti*; suffc. *sú-um-mu-šu* → Charpin AfO 40/41 10.
SummuS "hidden, secret"	•CTX: **EUPH** Fem. pl. *sú-mu-ša-tum* → Charpin AfO 40/41 22.
SimmiSt "secret"	•CTX: **EUPH** *sí-mì-iš-tim* → Charpin AfO 40/41 18f.
|S-m-s^1|	Primary noun, Sem. C_1:*$š^1$/s^2*-C_2:*m*-C_3: *s^1*: *šmš* (*šemeš*, Hb.) "sun"; *šmš* (Ph. Pun.) "sun"; *šmš* (Aram., Syr.) "sun", *šmš* (Syr. D) "to be sunny"; *šamšu*(m), *śamśu(m)* (Akk.) "sun, sun-god", *šamsātu(m)* "(sun-)disc"; *šams* (Arab.) "sun", *šamasa, šamisa* "to be sunny"; *s^2ms^1* (OSArab.) "sun".
$Sams^1$ "the Sun, DN"	•ONOM: **U3** *ša-ma-aš-ki-ti* → Owen JCS 258. **EUPH, B** Passim; cf. among other variant writings *ša-am-si-*^{d}IM, *sa-am-si-ma-lik, sa-am-šu-*^{d}IM, *sa-am-ši-*^{d}IM, *za-am-si-*^{d}UTU, *sa-am-si-e-ra-aḫ; ia-ku-un-sa-am-si; ša-ma-ši, a-bi-sa-ma-aš, ḫa-ad-ni-sa-ma-áš, ḫi-im-di-sa-ma-ás, ri-ip-i-sa-ma-ás, zi-im-ri-sa-maš/ma-áš*; cf. *sa-am-sa-tum* → Huffmon APNMT 250f.; Gelb CAAA 32, 183ff. (ŚAMAŚ, ŚAMŚ); Zadok Fs. Hallo 330; Streck Onomastikon 1 200 § 2.95; 226 § 2.132, 321 § 5.7, 323 § 5.11, 345 § 5.62f.; Durand REA 663.[560] **A7** *sa-am-šu-*^{d}IM (on seal), *sa-am-si-*dIM, *sa-am-si-e-da, sa-am-su-na-ba-la, zi-im-ri-sa-maš* → Wiseman AT 36, 145, 153; Arnaud AuOr 16 156;
s^1ams^1a "the Sun, DN"	•ONOM: **EG** Elem. in TN *ša-m-ša, ša-ma$_3$-ša, š-m-šu$_3$, š-m-š* Hoch SWET 280 no. 402.
$Saps^1$ "the Sun, DN"	•ONOM: **A7** *ša-ap-ši, sa-ap-si-ia, ša-ap-ši-a-bi, sa-ap-si-a-du, sa-ap-si-e-da* → Huffmon APNMT 250f.; Gelb CAAA 185 (ŚAPŚ); Arnaud AuOr 16 156; Streck Onomastikon 1 223 § 2.125, 225 § 2.130f.
s^1aps^1 "the Sun; DN"	•LL: **UGS** [UTU = *šamšu* / *Šamaš* = ...] = *ša-ap-šu*; ^{d}[UT]U = *ši-mi-gi* = *ša-ap-šu*; [^{d}...] = *ši-mi-gi* = *ša-ap-šu* → Sivan GAGl 273; Huehnergard UVST 183f.; vSoldt SAU 307 (143); Tropper KWU 122.[561] •ONOM: **A4** *ša-ap-ša, ka$_4$-mil-ša-pa-ši* → Hess UF 24 114.
s^1ps^1 "sun; the Sun (DN and royal title)"	•CTX: **UGA** Sg. *špš*, suff. *špšm, špšn* → DUL 824: *špš*; Tropper UG 139, 286.[562] •ONOM: **UGA** *ỉlšpš* → DUL 63; *blšpš* → DUL 220; *špšm* → DUL 825; *špšmlk* → DUL 825; *špšn* → DUL 825f.; *špšy* → DUL 826; *špšyn* → DUL 826.
|s-m-w/y|	Sem.: *smy* (JAram., Syr.) "to be blind" (Syr. C) "to be lame"; *samû, samāʔu(m)* (Akk.) "to vacillate, be undecided".
|S-m-w| "to hesitate"	•CTX: **EB** G prefc. *iz-mu* |yiSmū| → Catagnoti / Fronzaroli ARET 16 175, 243; Catagnoti QuSe 29 26, 39, 163, 229.

[560] For EB OBab. *i-bí*-ZI.KIR, read formerly *i-bí-sí-piš* (Pettinato Or 44 366 fn. 34; Culto 3; MEE 2 181), see GlOS 1 162: *ðikr* "remembrance, name" (\|ð/S-k-r\| (2)).

[561] \|s^1aps^1u\| < *\|s^1amps^1u\| < *\|$Sams^1u$\|; Tropper loc.cit.

[562] Note the unexplained *ṯpš* (DUL 912: "a kind of bird"(?)), a variant reading for *špš* (?; Del Olmo CR 68f. fn. 11).

|s-m-y| See **|s-m-w/y|**	
|s-n-ḳ|	Sem.: *sanāqu*(*m*) (Akk.) "to check, approach".[563]
|**S-n-ḳ**| "to approach"	•CTX: **UGS** G pref. *iš-ni-qu*, *iš-ni-qu-ú-ma*, *na-aš-ša-ni-iq-mi* → AHw 1021b: *sanāqu*(*m*) G.B.3; CAD S 137b: *sanāqu* A 2. •ONOM: **EUPH** Cf. *ia-as-ni-ka-an*, *ia-as*/*áš-ni-iq*-DINGIR, *zi-na-gi*, *si-nu-ga* → Gelb CAAA 30f. (SNQ), 180.
Saniḳ "approached" (?)	•ONOM: **EUPH** *za-ni-kum* → Gelb CAAA 31 (SNQ), 179.
Simḳat "action, performance" (?)	•CTX: **Q** Cf. *ši-im*-KA-*ti-šu-nu* → Richter / Lange Idadda 71 (TT 5 r. 24).
|s-n-n|	Culture word, Sem.: *snwny*(*tʔ*) (JAram., Syr.) "swallow"; *sinuntu*, *ṣinundu*, *sinundu* (Akk.) "swallow"; *sunūnū*, *sunūniya* (Arab.) "swallow". Cf. *sw*/*ys* (*sûs*, *sîs*, Hb.) "swift"; *ss ʕgr* (Aram.) "a kind of swift".[564]
snnt "swallow"	•CTX: **UGA** Pl. *snnt* → DUL 752.
sas(u)gaL "a kind of swift" (?)	•LL: **EB** Cf. NAM.DAR.MUŠEN = *sa-su-ga-lum* → Rendsburg Eblaitica 3 151f.; Müller SEL 12 137; Sjöberg Fs. Pettinato 271; Kogan SED 2 259.[565]
|S-n-r|, **|S-r-n| (1)**	Culture word, Sem.: *šwnrh*, *šwnrtʔ*, *šwnr*(*ʔ*), *šwrn*(*ʔ*) (JAram., Syr.) "cat"; *šurānu*(*m*) (Akk.) "cat"; *sinnawr* (Arab.) "cat"; *sənnáwrət*, *sínórt* (MSArab.) "cat".
Sinar "cat" (?)	•ONOM: **UGS** Cf. unc. ZI/ṢI-*na-ru*/*a*/*i*, ZI-*na-ra-na* → Gröndahl PTU 189.[566]
snr, **Snr** "cat" (?)	•ONOM: **UGA** Cf. unc. *snr* → DUL 753:*snr* (II*)*, *Snrn* → DUL 753: *s*/*śnrn*.
Surān "cat"	•ONOM: **EUPH** *šu-ra-na-tum* → Gelb CAAA 196.
|s-n-s-n|	Culture word, Sem.: *snsnh* (*sansinnāh*, Hb.) "panicle of the date"; *snsn* (JAram.) "fruit stalk (of the palm)"; *sysn*(*ʔ*) (JAram., Syr.) "date-palm spadix"; *sissinnu*(*m*), *šissinnu*, *sissintu*, *šissintu* (?) "date-palm spadix"; *sinsin* (Arab.) "uppermost part of the hump", *sinsina* "apophysis of the dorsal vertebra".
ssn "date-palm branch"	•CTX: **UGA** Sg. suff. *ssnm* → DUL 760: *ssn* (I). •ONOM: **UGA** Cf. unc. *ssn* → 760: *ssn* (II).
|S-n-s^1|	Sem.: *sanāšu*, *šanāšu* (Akk.) "to stick in", *sunnušu* "pierced, perforated".
SannuS "kind of filling"	•CTX: **EB** D verbal adj. pl. obl. *sa-nu-si* → Catagnoti / Fronzaroli ARET 16 96, 261; Catagnoti QuSe 29 71f., 225.
|s-p-ʔ|	Sem.: *mspwʔ* (*mispôʔ*, Hb.) "fodder"; *spy* (JAram., G) "to feed".

---

[563] Including Gelb CAAA 30f.: SNQ.

[564] For Hb. and Aram. *sVs* "swift" (< *sVns*=, < *sVnsVn*=, < **sVn*=) see Kogan SED 2 259.

[565] For the lexical entry SIM.MAḪ.MUŠEN = *si-nu-un-tum* :*ša-?-ba* in Emar see Cohen Proceedings 53ᵉ RAI 1 828 (38).

[566] Diff.: Sivan GAGl 269: ṢINNĀRU "waterfall, pipe". See also there: URU ZI-*na-ru*/*i* (TN).

|s-p-ʔ| "to devour, consume"	•CTX: **UGA** G prefc. *ìspå, tspì, yspů, yspì*, ptc. *spů*; inf. *spů*, suff. *spůy*; N prefc.(?) *ìspì* → Tropper UG 445, 538, 621ff.; DUL 754.
|s-p-d|	Sem.: *spd* (Hb.) "to mourn, bewail"; *spd* (JAram.) "to lament", (Syr.) "to tremble", (JAram. C) "to mourn, to lament", (JAram.) *mspd(?)* "mourning"; *sapādu(m)* (Akk.) "to mourn", (C) "to cause to mourn".
ms^{1}spdt "wailing woman, hired mourner"	•CTX: **UGA** Pl. *mšspdt* → DUL 587: *mšspdt*.
|S-p-ħ|	Sem.: *mšpḥh* (*mišpāḥāh*, Hb.) "extended family, clan"; *špḥ* (Ph., Pun.) id. Probl. related: *sapāḫu(m), šapāḫu* (Akk.) "to scatter, disperse; to sprinkle", *sapḫu(m)* "scattered material", *sipḫu*(m) "scatterings"; *safaḥa* (Arab.) "to pour out, spill, shed"; *safḥa* (Eth.) "to extend, spread out", *səfuḥ* "flat, large, generous".
Saph "scion, heir"	•ONOM: **EUPH** *sa-ap-ḫu-um-li-ip-ḫu-ur* → Zadok Fs. Hallo 330.
s^{1}aph "scion, heir"	•LL: **UGS** [GIBIL = *perʔu*(?) = *ḫ*]*í*(?)-*iš-ši* = *šap-ḫu* → Sivan GAGl 273; Huehnergard UVST 183; vSoldt SAU 307 (142); BiOr 47 732.
supāħ "scattered bread (?, as offering)"	•CTX: **EM** NINDA *su-pa-ḫu* → Pentiuc Vocabulary 159.
s^{1}pħ, s^{1}bħ, θpħ "family, stock"	•CTX: **UGA** Sg. *šbḥ, špḥ, ṯpḥ* → DUL 793: *šbḥ*; DUL 823: *špḥ*; DUL 911: *ṯpḥ*.
|s-p-x|	Sem.: Cf. *spḥ* (Hb.) "to associate", *spyḥ* (*sāpîḥ*) "second growth".
|s-p-x| "to associate" (?)	•ONOM: **UGA** Cf. unc. *spḫy* → DUL 754.
sipx "new alluvial land" (?)	•CTX: **EM** *sí-ip-ḫu/ḫi*, metah. *pí-is-ḫi* → Zadok AION 51 119.[567]
|s-p-l|	Culture word, Sem.: *spl* (*sēpel*, Hb.) "a bowl"; *spl, swplʔ* (JAram.) "a bowl"; *saplu* (Akk.) "a bowl". See further: *safala* (Eth.) "to hit, work with a hammer". Non-Sem.: *zabl=* (Hurr.) "platter, tray".[568]
sapl "platter, bowl, cauldron"	•CTX: **Q** *sà-ap-lu* ZABAR → Richter / Lange Idadda 83ff., 186. **EA** *sà-ap-lu* ZABAR (22 IV 21, Tušratta) → AHw 1027; CAD S 165; Sivan GAGl 266. **A4** *sà-ap-lu* (...) ZABAR, *sà-pa/pá-lum* ZABAR / URUDU, *sà-pá-al-la*[569] → AHw 1027; CAD S 165; Giacumakis AkkAl 99. **UGS** *sà-ap-lu* URUDU GAL / ZABAR (MEŠ), *sa-ap-lu*; cf. *sà*!(A)-*a*[*p-l*]*u* → AHw 1027; CAD S 165; Sivan GAGl 266; Huehnergard UVST 157f.

[567] Altern. Pentiuc Vocabulary 163f.; Ikeda BiOr 60 272, 275: "broad, flat (surface); platform"; see |ṣ-p-ħ|. Cf. diff. Reculeau 53e RAI 513f., according to Durand RA 97 147 fn. 32: Akk. *sipḫum (SPḪ) "disperser, éparpiller".

[568] Richter BGH 353: *zabl=* I

[569] < Hurr. *|sabli=na|; Wilhelm SCCNH 8 355f.

sipl "large drinking bowl, crater"	•CTX: **EG** *ṯi₂-pa-ra*; *ṯi₂-ra-ba*, *ṯi₂-r-ba* (metath. ?) → Hoch SWET 364 no. 541, 367 no. 547:
spl "platter, tray"	•CTX: **UGA** Sg. *spl*, du. / pl. *splm* → DUL 754f.

|s-p-p| (1)	Culture word, Sem.: *sp* (*sap*, Hb.; Ph. Pun.) "bowl"; *sappu*(*m*), *šappu*(*m*) (Akk.) "bowl", *šappatu*, *šabbatu*, *sappatu*, *šapputu* "a pottery vessel". Non-Sem.: *zuppa*= (Hit.) "a silver vessel";[570] cf. *su-pu* (Minoan) "a vessel".[571]
sapp (A) "a type of bowl"	•CTX: **EUPH** Cf. *sà-ap-pu*, *sà-pu-um*, *sà-ap-pu-um*, GAL *sà-pu-ú/um* → Durand ARM 21 358; Guichard ARM 31 292ff.; cf. GAL *sà-ap-pu* ZABAR → Arkhipov ARM 32 172, 463 (M.8132 III 18').
supp "a type of glass"	•CTX: **EB** Cf. *zu-bù*, *zú-bù* → Waetzoldt MEE 12 385; Pasquali QuSe 23 185f.
Sapt "bowl" (?)	•CTX: **A7** Cf. DUG *ša-ap-tum* → AHw 1175: *šappatu*, 4; CAD Š/1 478: *šappatu*, d; Giacumakis AkkAl 103: *šaptu*.
sp "bowl"	•CTX: **UGA** Sg. *sp*, du. *spm* pl. abs. *spm*; cstr. *sp* → DUL 753f.

|s-p-p| (2)	Culture word, Sem. etim. unc. Non-Sem.: LL equivalence *sap-pu* = šaʾuša (Sum.) "lance".[572]
sapp (B) "lance (as emblem ?)"	•CTX: **EUPH** GÍŠ.TUKUL *sà-ap-pí*, GÍŠ.TUKUL *sà-ap-pí*, ᵈ*sà-ap-pí-im*, *ka-ak sà-pí*; cf. *ka-ak-sà- pu* → Catagnoti NABU 1992/61; FM 26f.; Charpin AfO 40/41 13; Arkhipov ARM 32 112f.: *kaksappum*, 172, 263 (A.3140: 5).
sapp (C) "rod"	•CTX: **EUPH** *sà-ap-pi* → Durand Fs. Kupper 166; Charpin AfO 40/41 13.

|S-p-p-r|	Culture word, Sem.: *sappāru*(*m*), *šappāru*(*m*) (Akk) "a wild animal (wild ram ?)". Non-Sem.: Cf. šeŋbar (Sum.) "an animal".
Sip(p)arr "a wild animal"	LL: **EB** *ši₄-bar-ru₁₂* → Sjöberg WO 27 10.

|S-p-r| (1)	Sem., with allomorphs C₁:*s*¹/*s*³. Basis |s¹-p-r|: *šapāru*(*m*), *śapārum* (Akk.) "to send (a message), write (to)", *šapru*(m) "envoy, messenger", *šipru*(m) "sending, mission, work", *šāpiru*(*m*) "ruler, overseer", *šipāru*(*m*) "regulations, instructions", *šipirtu*(*m*) "message, letter, instruction", *našparu*(*m*) "messenger", *našpartu*(*m*) "message, commission"; *s¹frt* (OSArab.) "extent, measure". Basis |s³-p-r|: *spr* (Hb.) "to count, write", (D) "to count (out, up), announce, tell", *spr* (*sōper*) "scribe, secretary", *spr* (*sēper*) "inscription, letter, scroll", *sprh* (*siprāh*) "book", *spr* (*sᵉpār*) "calculation", *mspr* (mispār) "number, quantity, narrative"; *spr* (Ph., Pun., Amm., Moab., Hatra) "scribe", *spr* (Ph., Palm.) "writing, inscription, letter, document", *mspr* (Ph., Pun.) "number"; *spr* (JAram.) "to count", (Syr.) "to narrate, tell", *spr(ʔ)* (Aram., Syr.) "scribe", *spr(ʔ)* (Aram., Syr.) "document, book, letter", *spyr* (Syr.) "learned"; *sepēru* (Akk.) "to write (in Aramaic script)", *sipru* "document", *sepīru*, *sepirru* "interpreter-scribe"; *sifr* (Arab.) "book (of the Scriptures)", *safara* (*safr*) "to write"; *sufra* (MSArab.) "board"; *safara* (Eth.) "to

570 Tischler EGH 784: *zuppa*=.

571 Gordon Or 32 293; Stieglitz Kadmos 10 110.

572 See RS 21.09 (Hh XI-XII) ZA.RÍ.ŠA MIN = *sà-ap-pu*; vSoldt Or 60 119.

	measure (out)", *səfr* "size, measure", *masfar*(*t*), *məsfār* "measure, means of measuring".
|S-p-r| (A) "to write, send"	•CTX: **EB** G prefc. *ne-sa-bar* |nisappar|, *a*^{nu}-*s*[*a*]-*ba-r*[*a*]-*am*$_6$ |la= ʔaSappar=am| → Fronzaroli ARET 13 141, 288; Catagnoti / Fronzaroli ARET 16 44, 216; Catagnoti QuSe 29 45, 105, 131, 135, 225. •ONOM: **A4** Cf. unc. ZA-*pa-ar-ma* → Wiseman AT 152; Arnaud AuOr 16 180: |sapar=ma(lik)|(?).
|s-p-r| (B) "to count, number, recite; to write"	•CTX: **UGA** N prefc. *tspr*; G/D prefc. *yspr*, *tspr*; suffc. *spr*, suff. *sprhm*; inf. *spr*; act. ptc. *mspr* (see below: *mspr*), C prefc. suff. *åšsprk* → Tropper UG 539, 591, 869; DUL 755: /*s-p-r*/.
sōpir "scribe"	•CTX: **EG** *ṯu-pi*$_3$-*r* → Hoch SWET 364 no. 540.[573] •ONOM: **EG** In TN: *ṯu-pi*$_3$-*ra* → Hoch SWET 364 no. 540.
Sapur "sent"	•ONOM: **B** *sa-pu-ru-um* → Gelb CAAA 32, 185; Streck Onomastikon 1 330 § 5.28.[574]
Sipar "regulation(s), instruction(s)" (?)	•LL: **EB** Cf. Ú.U$_4$.MA.ŠÈ = *šè-ba-lu* → Sjöberg Fs. Kienast 556f.
spr (A) "scribe"	•CTX: **UGA** Sg. *spr*, pl. *sprm* → DUL 755f. *spr* (I).
spr (B) "tablet, writing, letter"	•CTX: **UGA** Sg. *spr*, *sprn* → DUL 756f.: *spr* (II).
spr (C) "number, inventory"	•CTX: **UGA** Sg. *spr*, suff. *sprhn* → DUL 757: *spr* (III).
Sipirt "allocation, forfeit"	•CTX: **EUPH** *ši-pi-ir-tim* → Charpin NABU 2009/59. •LL: **EB** ŠU.GAR = *si-bíl-tum* → Conti QuSe 17 88; Krebernik ZA 73 6; PIHANS 106 91; Catagnoti QuSe 29 22, 226.
sprt "instruction, prescription"	•CTX: **UGA** Sg. / pl. *sprt* → DUL 758.
maSpar, maSpir "sending" (?)	•ONOM: **EB** Cf. *maš-bar* → Pagan ARES 3 176, 350. **B** *maš-pa-ru-um*, *ma-áš-pa-ru-um*, *maš-pi-ru-um* → Gelb CAAA 32, 188; Streck Onomastikon 1 335 § 5.43, 337f. §§ 5.45, 5.47.
mspr (A) "reciter"	•CTX: **UGA** → DUL 755. /*s-p-r*/ (D act. ptc.).
mspr (B) "recitation, story, tale"	•CTX: **UGA** → DUL 575f.: *mspr*.

|s-p-r| (2)	Culture word, Sem.: Cf. *siparru*(*m*) (Akk.) "bronze (items)".[575] Non-Sem.: zabar (Sum.) "bronze (items)".
saparr, siparr "bronze covered chariot" (?)	•CTX: **EG** Cf. *ṯu-pi-ra-ta*$_5$, *ṯ-pa-r* → Hoch SWET 365 no. 542.
spr (D) "bronze"	•CTX: **UGA** Sg. *spr*, suff. *sprn* → DUL 757f.: *spr* (IV).
sbrdn "lancer, spear-bearer / maker" (?)	•CTX: **UGA** Pl. *sbrdnm* → Richter BGH 537; Vidal Gladius 27 10; Watson NABU 2013/30; Fs. Postgate 711; cf. DUL 741f.: "bronze-smith"; Del Olmo AuOr 37 289.

573 Sivan / Cochavi-Rainey WSVES 86: *śu-pí-r*, *śu-pu-r* "scribe"; Helck Beziehungen no. 283; Kilani VGW 68: \|ṯUpAr\|.

574 Altern. Golinets Onomastikon 2 162: "schön" (\|s¹-p-r\| (1)).

575 For Ugarit LL see RS 22.401 (Diri I) ii 22' *za-bar* UD.KA.BAR = *sí-pí-*[*ir-ru*]; vSoldt Or 60 119.

|S-p-S-k|	Loan. *šupšikkum*, *tupšikku*(*m*), *dupšikku* (Akk.) "hod, earth basket". Non-Sem.: d u p s i k (Sum) "basket".
tupSikkān "earth-moving troops"	•CTX: **EUPH** *ṣa-ab tu-ši-ik-ka-nim* → CAD T 476: *tupšikkānu*; Charpin ARM 26/2 164f. (362:6, 19) + fn. a.

|s-p-y|	Sem.: *suppû* (Akk.) "to pray, supplicate", *supû*, *suppû* "prayer", *sīpu* "(act of) prayer".
|s-p-y| "to pray"	•LL: **EB** [...] = *za-bù-um* → Sjöberg Fs. Kienast 550: |sappûm|, altern. rdg: |sapʔum| (*sāpum*) "prayer".

|s-r-d| (1)	Culture word, Sem.: *se/irdu*(m) (Akk.) "olive tree".
se/ird "olive orchard"	•CTX: **A4** GIŠ *zi-ir-te* → Wiseman AT 53f. (84:4; 87:15: "olive(s)" ?); AHw 1037: *serdu*(*m*) 2; CAD S 311f.: *sirdu* A b. **EA** GIŠ *se*$_{20}$*-er-du* → Rainey EAT 15 (359 rev.25). **UGS** GIŠ *sé-er-di*-MEŠ-*šu*, GIŠ *zé-er-ti-šu*, GIŠ *zi-ir-te* → AHw 1037: *serdu*(*m*); CAD S 311f.: *sirdu* A. •ONOM: **UGS** Cf. *sí-ir-da-ya* → PRU 6 38 (RS 17.356):3; DUL 758: *srd*.
srd "olive orchard" (?)	•ONOM: **UGA** Cf. *srd* → Watson AuOr 22 116; DUL 758.

|s-r-d| (2)	Sem.: *sarādu*(*m*) (Akk.) "to tie up; to pack", *sardum* "packed, loaded".
sard "load"	•CTX: **UGS** *sà-ar-du-šu-nu* → Lackenbacher / Malbran-Labat RSOu 23 97.

|s-r-d-n-n|	Culture word; etym. unknown.
srdnn "type of projectile or missile"	•CTX: **UGA** Pl. *srdnnm* → DUL 759; Watson Fs. Postgate 708.

|S-r-m|	Sem., with several partly lexicalized allomorphs: Cf. *šrm* (Syr.) "to break; *sarāmu*(*m*) (Akk.) "to cut open", *sirendu*, *sarindu* (**sirimtu*) "a cutting tool", *šarāmu*(m), *šerēmu* "to trim, peel off", *šarmu* "lopped, trimmed", *šerimtum*, *širimtu*, *širindu* "cutting, weeding"; *sarrama* (Arab.) "to cut up (into pieces)", *šarama* "to split, slit, slash", *ṯarama*, *ʔaṯrama* "to nick, chip", *ṯarima*, *ʔinṯarama* "to get a dent chipped".
|θ-r-m| "to carve, cut up (into pieces), feed (meat)"	•CTX: **UGA** G prefc. *iṯrm*, *yṯrm*, inf. *ṯrm*, D prefc. *tṯrm* → DUL 917f.: /*ṯ-r-m*/.
Sarm, Sarim "cut off, portion" (?)	•ONOM: **EB** Cf. unc. *sar-ma*, *sar-mu*, *ša-rí-mu* → Pagan ARES 3 184, 362, 367.
Sirm, Serm "cut, cutting off" (?)	•CTX: **EUPH** Passim desig. a cup: *širim qarni* → AHw 1248: *ši/ermu*(*m*), 1, "Kappen von Hörnern"; CAD Š/3 112: *širmu*, 2, "a cut-off horn" (?); Bry AuOrS 20 205ff.; Guichard ARM 31 306ff.

θurme(h), **θurum** "cut off, portion" (?)	•CTX: **EM** Cf. UZU *šu-ur-me* → Arnaud Emar 6/3 405 (410:9'); Pentiuc Vocabulary 174; Watson NABU 2002/16. •ONOM: **A4** *šu-ru-ma* → Arnaud AuOr 16 168.
Sarrām "cutter, carver" (?)	•ONOM: **EB** Cf. *ša-ra-mu* → Pagan ARES 3 184, 366.
θrmt "meat, victuals"	•CTX: **UGA** → DUL 919: *ṯrmt*.
|S-r-m-n|	Culture word, Sem.: *šrwyn(ʔ)* (JAram., Syr.) "a type of cypress", *twrny(tʔ)* "cypress or acacia"; *šurmē/īnu(m)*, *šurmānu*, *šurʔīnu* (Akk.) "cypress"; *sarw* (Arab.) "cypress".
Sarmīn, **Sirmīn** "cypress"	•CTX: **EB** GIŠ.ŠU.ME = *ša-mi-nu*, *še-rí-mi-nu* → Krebernik ZA 73 14; Conti QuSe 17 125.
θrmn (B) "cypress" (?)	•ONOM: **UGA** Cf. unc. TN *gt ṯrmn* → DUL 918f.: *ṯrmn* (II).[576]
|S-r-n| (1) See **|S-n-r|**, **|S-r-n| (1)**	
|S-r-n| (2)	Sem.: Cf. *srnym* (Hb. pl. *s^{e}rānîm*) "(title of the Philistine) governors".
srn "prince" (?)	•CTX: **UGA** Pl. *srnm* → DUL 759.
|S-r-p|	Loan. Non-Sem.: *Sarpa=* (Hitt.) "an object on which one can sit", *SarpaSSi=* "a drape, chair-cover".
s^1arpas^1s^1 "a drape, chair-cover" (?)	•CTX: **EM** Cf. *šar-pá-aš-ši* → Huehnergard RA 77 34; Pentiuc Vocabulary 171.
|s-r-p-D|	Culture word, Sem.: Cf. *srpd* (*sirpād*, Hb.) "stinging nettle". Non-Sem.: *sꜣpt* (Eg.) "lotus".
sarpat "lotus"	CTX: **EG** Cf. *srpt* |sArpAt| → Kilani VGW 113.
|s-r-r| (1) Cf. **|s^2-r-r|**	Sem.: *srr* (Hb.) "to be stubborn, obstinate", *sr* (*sar*) "ill-humoured", *srh* (*sarāh*) "obstinacy, falsehood"; *sarāru(m)*, *ṣarāru* (Akk.) "to be false", *sarru* "false, criminal",[577] *sarrārum* "criminal". Cf *šarra* (Arab., sibilant irreg.) "to be bad", *šarr* "ill, evil".

[576] Altern. see *θrmn* "royal" (\|s^2-r-r-\|).

[577] For Ugarit LL see RS 25.434+ (Diri I) v 13' [*li-lí*]*b* ŠI.ŠI = *sa-ar-rum*, RS 22.229 (Lu I) vii 16' AMA.LUL.A = MIN (= *ummi*?) *sà-a-ri*; vSoldt Or 60 119.

sarr "stubborn; malicious"	•LL: **UGS** Cf. [ḪUL = *sarru* = ...]-*ri* = *sar-rù* → Sivan GAGl 266; Huehnergard UVST 88, 158; vSoldt SAU 306 (103). Altern. rdg: [MAḪ = *rubû* = *ewe*]*ri* = *šar-rù* → Huehnergard ^{2}UVST 388, 395: "prince" (see |s^2-r-r|).[578]
	•ONOM: **EB** Cf. *zàr*(SUM)-*rí*, *zàr*(SUM)-*rúm* → Pagan ARES 3 169, 383f.
sarrān "stubborn; malicious"	•ONOM: **EB** *za-ra-an* → Pagan ARES 3 169, 383. **UGS** Cf. unc. *sa-ar-ʔa-nu* → Sivan GAGl 266.
sarrār "stubborn; malicious; out of control"	•CTX: **EUPH** Passim; *sà-ar-ra-ru*(-um), *sà-ar-ra-ri* → AHw 1030; CAD S 178f.; Durand MARI 5 198; Fs. Garelli 64; Charpin AfO 40/41 14.
	•ONOM: **EB** *za-la-li*, *za-la-rúm* → Pagan ARES 3 169, 383.
sarrat "ignominy"	•ONOM: **UGS** Cf. DUMU *sà-ra-ti* → Sivan GAGl 266.

|s-r-r| (2)	Sem.: *swr* (Hb., JAram.) "to turn aside, go off, retreat"; *swr* (Ph., Pun. C) "to remove"; *sārra*, *ʔasarra* (Arab.) "confide a secret", *sirr*, *sirrī*, *sirrīya* "secret", *surra* "middle", *mustasarr* "place of concealment"; *sawwara*, *śawwara* (Eth.) "to hide, conceal", *məsəwwār* "hiding place".
|**s-r-r**| **(B)** "to set, hide"	•CTX: **UGA** G inf. cst. *srr* → DUL 759.
srr "sunset" (?)	•ONOM: **UGA** Elem. in DN *ngh w srr* → DUL 759.
msrr "entrails, viscera" (?)	•CTX: **UGA** → DUL 576; Watson FO 52 336.

|s-r-r| (3)|	Sem.: Cf. *sarra* (Arab.) "to cheer up, gladden, delight", *surra* "to rejoice, be glad"; *sarara*, *śarara* (Eth.) "to fly, leap in the air".
|**s-r(-r)**| "to exult inwardly" (?)	•CTX: **UGA** Gt prefc. *ystrn* → DUL 758: /*s-r*/.

|S-r(-r)| (4)	Culture word, Sem.: *sarru*(*m*), *zarru*(m), *sāru*, *zāru* (Akk.) "grain heap". Non-Sem.: Cf. šezar (Sum.) "grain heap".
Sarr (A) "grain heap"	•LL: **EB** Cf. ŠE.DUB = *za-lu-um* → Conti QuSe 17 176.

|s-r-θ| Cf. |**(w/y)-r-θ**|	Culture word, Sem.: *sīrāšu*, *sērāšu*, *sīrīšu*, *šīrīsu*, *širāš* (Akk.) "beer", *sīrāšû*(*m*) "brewer", *sīrāšītum* "female brewer", *širāšûtu*(*m*) "brewing". Non-Sem.: siraš (Sum.) "beer".
Sāriθt "female brewer"	•LL: **EB** MUNUS.LUNGA(ŠIM) = *za-rí-iš*$_{11}$*-tum* → Sjöberg Fs. Kienast 563; Bonechi QDLF 16 84.
Surθ "a metal vessel"	•CTX: **EUPH** Cf. unc. ZU-*ur-šu*/*šum*, GAL ZU-*ur-šum*/*šu-um* (GAL / TUR) → Guichard ARM 31 133, 298ff.: *ṣuršu*; cf. AHw 115: *ṣuršu*(*m*), 2 (*z*/*suršum*?).

|S-r-(y-)n|	Culture word, Sem.: *srywn*, *šrywn* (*siryôn*, *širyôn*, Hb.) "coat of mail"; *sryn* (JAram.) "coat of mail"; *sari*(*y*)*am*, *siri*(*y*)*am*, *siri*, *še*/*iryam* (Akk.) "(coat of) armour". Non-Sem: *šariyanni*= (Hit. / Hurr.) "a coat of scale armour".[579]

[578] For the PN UGS DUMU ZA-*ra-ti* see Sivan GAGl 266: SARRATU "ignomity" [sic!], unlikely.

ʔaSaryān "coat of armour"	CTX: **EB** *a-sar-a-nu/núm* → Conti-Bonechi NABU 1992/10; Conti QuSe 19 62f.; TIE A 1/1 41.
Siryān "coat of armour"	•CTX: **EG** *ṯi$_2$-ra-ya-na, ṯi$_2$-r-ya-na, ṯi$_2$-ru$_2$-yu-na, ṯu-r-na* → Hoch SWET 366f. no. 546.[580]
Sirenn "protective padding"	•CTX: **EUPH** Cf. GAD *ḫi-rum* ZI-*ri-ni* → Durand ARM 30 157f. (fn. g).
θryn "(suit of) armour, protective padding"	•CTX: **UGA** Sg. *ṯryn*, pl. cstr. *ṯryn* → DUL 921: *ṯryn* (I). •ONOM: **UGA** Cf. *ṯryn* → DUL 921: *ṯryn* (II).
|s-s|	Primary word, Sem.: *ss* (sās, Hb.) "clothes moth"; *ss(?)* (Aram., Syr.) "moth, maggot"; *sāsu(m)* (Akk.) "moth"; *sūs* (Arab.) "woodworm, moth". Non-Sem.: Cf. **čači=* (Central Chadic) "louse".[581]
sās "moth"	•LL: **EB** = *sà-sú-um* (0040 monoling. vocab. MEE 4 116) → Sjöberg WO 27 18. •ONOM: **EB** Cf. *za-zu/zi, za-zu/zú-um* → Pagan ARES 3 231, 384.
|S-S-B-n|	Culture word, Sem.:*ššbyn* (Palm.) "groomsman"; *šwšbyn(?)* (Aram., Syr.) id., *šwšbynw(t?)* "office of a groomsman"; *susapinnu* (Akk.) "best man, accompanying bridegroom".
susapinnūt "function of best man"	•CTX: **UGS** *sú-sà-pí-in-nu-ti* → AHw 1063; CAD S 416.
|S-s-s|	Culture word, Sem.: Cf. *sassu(m)* (Akk.) "base, floor(-boards of chariot)".[582]
sass "base (of the mace)" (?)	•CTX: **EUPH** Cf. *sà-as-sú ša* GIŠ.TUKUL → Charpin AfO 40/41 14; Arkhipov ARM 32 122.
Sst "baseboard, floor (of a chariot)"	•CTX: **UGA** Du. (?) *śstm* → DUL 760: *śst*.
|S-S-S-k|	Culture word, Sem.: *sissiktu*(m), *šiššiktu*, *zizziktu* (Akk.) "hem, fringe".
SiSSikt "a thin cord"	•CTX: **EUPH** Cf. *sí-sí-ik-tum/tim/tam, sí-sí-ik-ti* → Durand ARM 26/1 40 fn. 179; ARM 30 51, 147f.; Lafont Amurru 2 258; Charpin AfO 40/41 21.
|s-t-r| (1)	Sem.: *str* (Hb. N) to hide oneself", (C) "to hide"; *str* (JAram. G) "to hide (oneself)", Syr. (D) "to hide"; Palm (D) "to hide"; *satara* (Arab.) "to cover, conceal, protect"; *stər, sətūr* (MSArab.) "to cover, veil"; *satara* (Eth.) "to hide, conceal".

[579] The alleged Hurr. origin is unlikely; see Wilhelm AdS 2, 132 for *s/zariam* (no. 34 § 9); Richter BGH 357f.
[580] Sivan / Cochavi-Rainey WSVES 86: *śí-r-ya-na* "armour"; Helck Beziehungen no. 288.
[581] Orel / Stolbova HSED 233 no. 1034: **ʕačuč=* "insect"
[582] For Ugarit LL see RS 22.416+ (Hh. XI-XII) ii 5' KUŠ.KI.KAL.NÍG.NA$_4$ = *sà-a[s-sú* MIN (= *kīsu*)]; vSoldt Or 60 119.

|s-t-r| "to hide, provide cover, protect"

●CTX: **EG** Cf. *ha-r-ṯi$_2$-ṯi$_2$* |ha<t>stattira| → Hoch SWET 217f. no. 300.[583]
●ONOM: **UGA** Cf. *strn* → DUL 762; *stry* → DUL 762.
EG Cf. *sw-tr-y-r-y*, *ṯ ꜣ-ty-:r-y* → Schneider APÄQ 195 no. 413, 258 no. 556.

sitr "shelter, cover"

●ONOM: **EUPH** *sí-it-ra-an*, *zi-it-ru-ú*, *sí-it-ra-tum*, *zi-it-ri-ia/ya*, *zi-it-ra-a-du*, *zi-it-ri-e-ba-al*, *zi-it-ri-e-*^{d}IM, *zi-it-ri-e-lum*, *zi-it-ri-*DINGIR, *si/zi-it-ri-*^{d}IM, *li-ia-zi-it-ru-ú*, *ra-ba-zi-it-ru-ú* → Huffmon APNMT 253f.; Gelb CAAA 30, 180; Zadok Fs. Hallo 329; Streck Onomastikon 1 227f. § 2.134f., § 2.167, 203 § 2.95, 243 § 2.166, 323 § 5.11, 351 § 5.75.

satūr "covered, protected"

●ONOM: **EUPH** *za-tu-ru-um* → Gelb CAAA 30, 179; Golinets Onomastikon 2 139, 445.
R Cf. *sà-tu-ri* → Dalley / Walker / Hawkins Tell Rimah 263 (*za-tu-ri*); Zadok Fs. Hallo 329.
A4 *sà-tu-ú-ri* → Wiseman AT 152; Arnaud AuOr 16 164.

|S-t-r| (2)

Culture word, Non-Sem.: Cf. *sittar(i)=* (Hitt.) "sun-disk, sun-emblem".

ztr "cippus, votive stela"

●CTX: **UGA** → DUL 985.

|s-w-d|

Sem.: Cf. *swd* (Hb.) "to chatter", *swd* (*sôd*) "circle of confidents"; *swd(?)* (Syr.) "conversing"; *sāwada* (Arab.) "to confide a secret"; *mswdn* (OSArab.) "council, assembly of clan-heads; counselor". See further *ysd* (N, Hb.) "to get together, conspire".

sd "council" (?)

●CTX: **UGA** → DUL 742.

|s-w-p|

Sem.: Cf. *swp* (Hb., Aram., Syr.) "to come to an end", *swp* (Hb., Aram., Syr.) "end", *swpt* (*sôpet*, Hb.) "late fruit".

sawpuy "late barley" (?)

●LL: **EB** Cf. ŠE.ŠU.TAG / ŠE.BAD = *za-a-bù-um* → Sjöberg Fs. Pettinato 267.

|S-(w-)r|

Culture word, loan. Cf. *šauri*, *šawuri* (Hurr.) "a weapon" (?).[584]

s^{1}ůrt "a weapon" (?)

●CTX: **UGA** Sg./pl. *šůrt*, du. *šůrtm* → DUL 786f.: *šůrt*; Richter BGH 538f.

|s-w-s-w|

Culture word, Sem.: *sws* (*sûs*, Hb.) "horse", *swsh* (*sûsāh*) "mare"; *ss* (Ph.) "horse"; *swsy(?)* (Nab., Palm., Demotic Eg.) "horse"; *swsy(?)* (Aram., Syr.) "horse", *swsh*, *swst?* "mare"; *sīsû(m)*, *sīsum*, *sisium* (Akk.) "horse"; *sīsī* (Arab.) "pony".
Non-Sem.: For *áśva=ḥ* (Old Indian), *aspa=* (Avestic), *asa=* (Old Persian), etc. see Indo European **ek̯u̯o=s* "horse".[585]

sīs(w) "horse" (?)

●CTX: **UGS** Cf. unc. elem. in ZI-ZA-*ḫal-li-ma* (pl.) → Márquez AOAT 335 239 n. 95; Huehnergard ^{2}UVST 400.[586]

---

583 According to the author HtD [hatpaʕʕil] "to do stealthily", with *r*-meth. and assimilation of C$_2$:*t* > *s*.
584 Laroche GLH 219; Richter BGH 340f.
585 Pokorny IEW 301f.
586 Cf. Sivan GAGl 267 (SISAḪALLU / ZIZAḪALLU); Huehnergard UVST 193: loanword (?).

sūs(w) "horse"	•CTX: **EA** Pl. ANŠE.KUR.<RA.>MEŠ : *sú-ú-[sí-ma]* → AHw 1051: *sīsû(m)*; CAD S 418: *sīsû*; Rainey EAT 89; Sivan GAGl 268; Rainey EAC 1567 (263:25). •LL: **EB** SU.SÚM = *su-su-um* → Sjöberg Fs. Oelsner 409. •ONOM: **A4** Unc. cf. *su-su-*PI(*wa/ya*), *su-*ZI*-a-e* → Sivan GAGl 268; Wiseman / Hess UF 26 506 (AT 457:40).[587] **UGS** Unc. cf. *su-su*, ZU-ZI*-na* → Sivan 268.[588]
ssw, SSw "horse"	•CTX: **UGA** Sg. *śśw*; fem. *śśwt* (see below: *śśwt*); cstr. *śśw*, pl. *sswm*, *śśwm*; cstr. *śśw*; du. (?) *śśwm* → DUL 760f.: *s:śs/św*. •ONOM: **UGA** Cf. in bkn ctx. *śśw* → DUL 761.
sswt "mare" (?)	•CTX: **UGA** Pl. *sswt* → DUL 761f.; cf. Tropper UG 195: "Pferdezucht" (?).
SiSaxal(l) "horseman, courier" (?)	•CTX: **UGS** Pl. cf. ZI-ZA*-ḫal-li-ma* → Márquez AOAT 335 239 n. 95; Huehnergard ^{2}UVST 400; Richter BGH 397.

|S-y-ʕ|	Sem.: Cf. *šayyaʕa* (Arab.) "to burn, consume by burning".
Sayʕat "roasted barley" (?)	•LL: **EB** ŠE.SA = *sa-a-tum* → Conti QuSe 17 30, 35, 178.

|S-y-d|
See **|S-d/ð|**

|S-y-m|	Sem.: *siāmum*, *sâmu* (Akk.) "to be red, brown"; *sāmu(m)*, *saʔmu* "red, brown", *sāmtu(m)* "redness; carnelian", *sūmu(m)*, *suʔmu*, *simūtu* "redness".
Sām "red, carnelian"	•LL: **EM** Cf. GADA ŠAG$_4$.GA.DÚ SA$_5$ = *né-be-ḫu sa*$_{19}$(ŠÀ)*-mu* → Gantzert ELT 1 192 (13058c), 2 110 (13058c). **UGS** Cf. NA$_4$.NUNUZ.SA$_5$ = *ša-mu* → MSL 10 43 (A 154); vSoden OLZ 82 458; Huehnergard AkkUg 113, 387; vSoldt UF 22 343 fn. 157. •ONOM: **EB** *za-a-mi*, *za-i-mu*, *za-mu-du*, *za-ma-ʔà-ru*$_{12}$, *za-ma-sum*, *a-bu*$_{16}$*/bí-za-mu*, cf. *a-na-za-mu*[589] → Pagan ARES 3 169 (*sʔm*), 274f., 382f.
Sīm "red wine"	•CTX: **EUPH** Passim; cf. *sà-a-mi(-im)*, GEŠTIM *ša sí-mi*, GEŠTIM *sí-mi-im* → AHw 1020: *sāmu(m)* 6; CAD S/1 129: *sāmu* a.7'; Durand ARM 26/1 210 (70:5), FM 7 19:13, MARI 6 629f.; Chambon FM 11 8:1 (etc.); Charpin AfO 40/41 11f.[590]
Sāmt "red(ness); sunset"	•CTX: **EB** *sa-ma-ti* → Fronzaroli ARET 13 186, 292. •LL: **EB** É.SI$_4$.AN = *sa-ma-du sa-rí-im/mu* → Civil BaE 89; Sjöberg Fs. Kienast 546.
Sīmt "carnelian"	•LL: **UGS** Cf. NA$_4$.GUG = *ši-im-tu* → MSL 10 41 (A 90); Huehnergard AkkUg 113, 120, 387; vSoldt UF 22 343 fn. 157.
s^{1}mt (B) "reddish shade"	•CTX: **UGA** → DUL 818f.: *šmt* (II).
s^{1}amutt, s^{1}umutt "reddish shade"	•CTX: **EM** *ša-mut-tu*$_4$ ^{d}KUR, *ša-mut-ta* ^{d}*iš*$_8$*-tár*, *šu-mut-tu*$_4$ → Pentiuc Vocabulary 169.

---

[587] But cf. Gröndahl PTU 291 for the Anatolian elem. |zuz=|. For the alleged Amorite |sūs| "horse" see Golinets BuB 9 68.
[588] See the previous fn.
[589] Probably |ʔāna=Sām=| "the red one is strong", or altern. |ħanna=Sām=| "the red one is gracious"; Pagan loc.cit.
[590] Diff. Mayer Or 60 112: Wine from Sâmum/Samûm?

|s-y-n|	Sem.: *Suʔē/īn*, *Sîn*, *Sê/îʔ*, *sînu* (Akk.) “the moon(-god)”.[591]
Suyīn “the moon(-god)” **Sīn(iy)** “a crescent- shaped jewel”	•LL: **EB** ^{d}EN.[ZI] = *zu-i-nu* |suyīn| (=) → Conti QuSe 17 191f. •ONOM: **EB** *du-bí-zu-i-nu* → Pagan ARES 3 232, 302. •CTX: **EUPH** Cf. *sí-nu*, *sí-ni*, *sí-nu-ú*, *sí-nu-um*, *sí-ni-im*, *sí-na-am* → Arkhipov ARM 32 92f., 432f. (VIII T. 8’): *sînûm*. **Q** *ṣí-nu* ZA.GÌN, *ṣí-nu ug-gur*, *ṣí-nu* KÙ.SIG$_{17}$, *ṣí-nu* AN.GUG.ME → Richter / Lange Idadda 170f., 186: *ṣ/zīnu*.
sn “the moon (-god)	•CTX: **UGA** Cf. *aḏmr sn* (Akk. in cuneiform script) → KTU 1.70 4.

|S-y-p|	Sem.: *šēpu(m)*, *šīpu(m)* (Akk.) “foot”; *śab* (MSArab.) “foot”, *śaf*, *śēf*, *śɛf* “trace, track(s)”.
Sayp “foot”	•CTX: **EB** Du. nom. *si-ba* |Sēp=ā(n)| → Fronzaroli ARET 13 21f., 292; Catagnoti QuSe 29 88 fn. 360, 110, 223: *saʔpum*. •ONOM: **EB** *si-íb*, *si-bí-su*, *si-íb-da-mu*, *si-íb-i-sar* → Pagan ARES 3 235, 363.

|S-y-r| (1)	Culture word, Sem.: *syr* (*sîr*, Hb.) “cooking-pot”; *zīr* (Arab.) “a large jar for storing water”.[592]
Sīr (A) “cooking pot, cauldron”	•CTX: **EB** *zi-ru*$_{12}$ → Pasquali QuSe 23 181ff. **Q** *zi-ru* → Richter / Lange Idadda 94 (TT 17:4). **EA** *ki-ma ri-qí* URUDU *: sí-ri* → CAD Z 134; Rainey EAT 89; Sivan GAGl 267; Rainey CAT 2 335f.; Moran AmL 339 fn. 1; Liverani NABU 1997/130.

591 The alleged connection with OSArab. *Syn* “the Sun-god” of Hadhramawt is unlikely (see Ryckmans RHR 206 165).

592 Unrelated: *swr*, *zwr*, *swy* (Eg.) “to drink”, *swrw* (*zwrw*) “bowl; drink”.

Ṣ

|ṣ-ʕ-l|
|ṣ-ʕ-r|
|ṣ-ʕ-ṣ|
|ṣ-b-γ|
|ṣ-b-r| (1)
|ṣ-b-r| (2)
|ṣ-b-y| Cf. |ṣ́-b-ʔ|
|ṣ-d-ḳ|
|ṣ-γ-d|
|ṣ-γ-r| Cf. |z-ʕ-r|
|ṣ-γ-w|
Cf. |ṣ-w-γ
|ṣ-h-l|
|ṣ-ħ-r| Cf. |θ̣-h-r|
|ṣ-ḳ-l|
|ṣ-l-ħ|,
|ṣ-ħ-l|
|ṣ-l-ḳ| Cf. |s^{1}-l-ḳ|
|ṣ-l-l| (1) Cf. |θ̣-l-l|
|ṣ-l-l| (2) Cf. |ṣ-r-ṣ-r|
|ṣ-l-m| Cf. |θ̣-l-m|
|ṣ-l-p|
|ṣ-l-w/y|
|ṣ-l-y| See |ṣ-l-w/y|
|ṣ-m-ħ|
|ṣ-m-ḳ|
|ṣ-m-l|
|ṣ-m-r|
|ṣ-m-t| (1)
|ṣ-m-t| (2) See |ṣ́-m-d|
|ṣ-n-ʕ|
|ṣ-n-n| (1),
|ṣ-w-n|
|ṣ-n-n-| (2)
|ṣ-n-p|
|ṣ-n-r|
|ṣ-p-d|
|ṣ-p-ħ|
|ṣ-p-n| (1) Cf. |ṣ-p-y| (2)
|ṣ-p-n| (2)
|ṣ-p-p|
|ṣ-p-r| Cf. |θ̣-p-r|
|ṣ-p-ṣ-p|
|ṣ-p-y| (1)
|ṣ-p-y| (2)
|ṣ-r-ʕ|
|ṣ-r-d|
|ṣ-r-H|
|ṣ-r-ħ| (1)
|ṣ-r-ħ| (2)
|ṣ-r-x|
|ṣ-r-m|
|ṣ-r-p|
|ṣ-r-r| (1),
|ṣ-w-r|
|ṣ-r-r| (2),
|ṣ-y-r|
|ṣ-r-r| (3)
|ṣ-r-r| (4)
|ṣ-r-ṣ-r| Cf. |ṣ-l-l| (2)
|ṣ-w-ʕ|
|ṣ-w/y-d|
|ṣ-w-γ| Cf. |ṣ-γ-w|
|ṣ-w/y-ħ|
|ṣ-w-l| (1)
|ṣ-w-l| (2) Cf. |ṣ-l-l| (2)
|ṣ-w-m|
|ṣ-w-n| See |ṣ-n-n| (1),
|ṣ-w-n|
|ṣ-w-r| See |ṣ-r-r| (1),
|ṣ-w-r|
|ṣ-y-ħ| See |ṣ-w/y-ħ|

|ṣ-ʕ-l| Sem.: *ṣâlu(m)*, *ṣêlu(m)* (Akk.) "to fight, quarrel", *ṣāltu(m)*, *ṣē/īltum* "discord, strife, quarrel"; *ṣaʕala* (Eth.) "to reproach", *ṣəʕl* "spite", *ṣəʕlat* "reproach". See further: *ṣʕl* (Syr.) "unclean".

ṣiʕl "reproach" •CTX: **EM** *ṣí-iʔ-li* → Pentiuc Vocabulary163; Ikeda BiOr 60 275.

|ṣ-ʕ-r| Sem.: *ṣʕr* (JAram., Syr.) "to suffer, be in pain, be disgraced"; *ṣəʕra* (Eth.) "to be in pain, suffer". See also: *zêru(m)*, *zeʔārum* (Akk.) "to dislike, hate".

|ṣ-ʕ-r| "to be in pain, suffer" •CTX: **EM** Cf. rdg *i-ze-ru-ni-ni* (for *um-ḫir-ru-ni-ni*) → Durand NABU 2013/07.
•LL: **EB** ŠÀ.ḪUL = *za-a-rúm*, *ʔà-la-lum*, *ʔà-a-lum* → Conti QuSe 17 165.

|ṣ-ʕ-ṣ| Sem.: Cf. *ṣaʕṣaʕa* "to shake, scatter; to fear".

ṣʕṣ "terror, agitation" (?) •CTX: **UGA** → DUL 765.

|ṣ-b-γ| Sem.: *ṣbʕ* (*ṣobēᵃʕ* ?, Hb.) "dyer", (*ṣebaʕ*) "coloured cloth"; *ṣbʕ* (Aram., Syr.) "to moisten, dip, dye", *ṣbʕ(ʔ)* (JAram.) "dyer", *ṣwbʕ(ʔ)* (JAram., Syr.) "colour, dyed garment", *ṣwbʕnyn*, *ṣwbʕnʔ* "colours, dye"; *ṣapû(m)*, *ṣabû* (Akk.) "to soak, dench", *šapû(m)* "soaked, dyed", *ṣābû* "dyer", *ṣīpu* "submersion, soaking, drenching", *ṣubītu* "dyed wool", *muṣappiu* "dyer"; *ṣabaġa* (Arab.) "to dye, stain", *ṣibġ*, *ṣibġa*, *ṣibāġ* "colour, dye(stuff), *ṣabbaġ* "dyer", *maṣbaġa* "dyehouse"; see further: *ṣabḫa* (Eth.) "to dip".

ṣibīγ "soaked cloth, poultice" •CTX: **EB** *zi-bí-um* → Catagnoti QuSe 29 52, 122, 230.

ṣabaγbaγa "dunking, soaking" •CTX: **EG** *ḏa-b-q-b-q*, *ḏa-ba$_2$-ga-ya*, *ḏa-b-ga-ba$_3$-qa* → Hoch SWET 383f. no. 575.[593]

ṣ-b-r| (1) Sem.: Cf. *ṣbr* (Syr.) "to chatter, be confused, delirious", *ṣbr(ʔ)* "chattering, garrulous", *ṣbwr* "foolish"; *ṣabāru(m)* (Akk.) "to twinkle, blink, mutter", *ṣabru(m)* "blinker, winker"; see further: *ṣapāru(m)* (Akk.) "to press down; to wink".

ṣabr "squinting, muttering" •ONOM: **B** *za-ab-rum*, *za-ab-ri-ia* → Gelb CAAA 34, 186.

ṣabur "squinting, muttering" •ONOM: **EB** *za-bur-rúm*; cf. *za-bur-X* → Pagan ARES 3 170, 382f. (*ṣbr* "to squint").[594]

ṣabrān "the squinting / muttering one" •ONOM: **U3** *za-ab-ra-nu-um* → Buccellati Amorites 28, 179; Gelb CAAA 34, 186.

|ṣ-b-r| (2) Culture word, Sem.: Cf. *ṣbr(ʔ)* (JAram., Syr.) "alone"; *ṣibaru*, *ṣiburu* (Akk.) "aloe"; see further: *ṣapru*, *ṣaparu*, *ṣap(a)ratu* (Akk.) "a spice".

---

593 Patern QaTalTal; cf. Sivan / Cochavi-Rainey WSVES 87: *ṣá-b-ga-ba-qa* "to tumble head over heel"; Helck Beziehungen no. 306: "kopfüber eintauchen".

594 Altern. Pagan loc.cit.: Arab. *ṣabara* "to be patient, enduring".

ṣabar, **ṣibar** "aloe" (?)	•ONOM: **EB** Cf. *za-ba-ra*, *za-ba-rúm*, *za-ba-ru*$_{12}$, *za-ba-lum* → Pagan ARES 3 232f., 382. **B** Cf. *zi-ba-ru-um*, *ṣi-ba-ra-tum* → Gelb CAAA 34, 197.

|ṣ-b-y| Cf. **|ṣ-b-ʔ|**	Sem.: *ṣby* (*ṣebî*, Hb.) "splendour"; *ṣbʔ* (Palm.) "to want, long for", *ṣbw* (cstr. *ṣbwt*) "desire, longing for"; *ṣby* (Aram.) "to desire", (Syr.) "to prefer, be pleased with", *ṣbw(ʔ)*, *ṣbwtʔ* (Aram., Syr.) "desire; matter, thing", *ṣbt* (Aram.) "valuable"; *ṣabû(m)*, *ṣebû* (Akk.) "to wish, want", *ṣabûm* "wished for, expected", *šibûtu(m)*, *ṣabûtu(m)*, *ṣabiātum* "wishes, designs", *ṣubûtu* "wish, desire, plan"; *ṣabā* (*ṣabw*, Arab.) "to bend, incline (to), feel desire", *ṣabwa* "(youthful) passion, (sensual) desire".
ṣaby "beauty, desire"	•ONOM: **EB** *a-lu-za*-NE (*bí?*) → Pagan ARES 3 170, 279. **U3** *za-bí* → Buccellati Amorites 46, 179; Gelb CAAA 34, 196.[595]
ṣiby "beauty, desire"	•ONOM: **EUPH**, **B** *zi-bu*, *zé-bi-li-lum*, *zi-bi-li-im*, *zi-bi-ni-ḫi-im* → Gelb CAAA 34, 197.
ṣuby "beauty, desire"	•ONOM: **EB** Cf. *zu-bù*, *zu*-NE (*bí?*), *zu-bu*$_{16}$ → Pagan ARES 3 170, 388. **EUPH** *la-ka-zu-bu-um* → Gelb CAAA 34, 198.
ṣabay "desired"	•ONOM: **EUPH**, **B** *za-ba-ad-du*, *za-ba-ia-tum*, fem. *za-ba-te-el* → Gelb CAAA 34. **EG** Cf. unc. *t-ꜣ-ḏꜣ-b-w* → Schneider APÄQ 247 no. 528 (b).
ṣubyān "the gorgeous, desired one"	•ONOM: **EB** *zu-ba-an* → Pagan ARES 3 170, 388.

|ṣ-d-ḳ|	Sem.: *ṣdq* (Hb.) "to be right", *ṣdq* (*ṣedeq*) "accuracy, equity", *ṣdyq* (*ṣadîq*) "just", *ṣdqh* (*ṣᵉdāqāh*) "honesty, justice"; *ṣdq* (Ph., Pun.) "correct, legitimate"; *zdq* (Palm.) "just"; *ṣqd* (Aram.) "to be just, guiltless, prevail in court", *ṣdq* "correct, justifiable conduct", *ṣdq* "correct, legitimate", *ṣdqh*, *ṣdqtʔ* "merit, righteousness"; *zdq* (Syr. D) "to justify", *zdk(ʔ)* "that which is right", *zdyq* "just, honest"; *ṣadaqa* (Arab.) "to speak the truth, prove to be true", *ṣidq* "truth, veracity", *ṣādiq* "true, truthful", *ṣadūq* "truthful"; *ṣdq* (OSArab.) "to fulfil an obligation, to grant", *ṣdq* "due, right; proper"; *ṣadq* (MSArab.) "truth", *sədūq*, *sədəq*, *ṣadōq* "to tell the truth"; *ṣadqa* (Eth.) "to be just, righteous, faithful", *ṣədq* "justice, truth", *ṣəduq* "true", *ṣādeq* "just, true".
|ṣ-d-ḳ| "to be / show oneself just"	•ONOM: **EUPH**, **B** *ia-áš-du-qa-an*, *ia-aš-du-kum*, *ia-aš/áš-du-uq*-DINGIR, *ia-áš-du-qí*-DINGIR → Huffmon APNMT 256f.; Gelb CAAA 34, 196; Streck Onomastikon 1 229f. §§ 2.133f.; Golinets Onomastikon 2 122, 459f.
ṣidḳ "justice, legitimacy; DN"	•ONOM: **EUPH**, **B** *zi-id-kum*, *zi-id-qa-an*, *ṣi-id-ga-nu-um*, *zi-id-ki-ia*, *zi-id-qa*-ᵈIM, *zi-id-qé-e-tar*, *zi-id-qé-e-pa*, *zi-id-qé-e-pu-uḫ*, *zi-id-ku-la-na-si*, *zi-id-kum-ma-zi*, *ṣí-id-qí-li-im*, *ṣí-id-qú-li*-DINGIR, *ṣí-id-qum-e-mu-qí*; *ì-lí-zi-id-ki/kum*, *su-mu-zi-id-kum*, *su-mu-zi-id-kum-di-ta-na* → Huffmon APNMT 256f.; Gelb CAAA 34, 197; Durand REA 662; Streck Onomastikon 1 201 § 2.95, 206 § 2.99, 324 § 5.13, 344 § 5.59, 351 § 5.75. **EA** GAL-*ṣí-id-qí* → Sivan GAGl 269; Moran AmL 384, 388; Hess APN 131f., 240. **UGS** SAL.DUMU.SAL-*ṣí-id-qí*, *pí-ṣí-id-qí*, *ṣi-id-qa-nu/na* → Gröndahl PTU 187; Sivan GAGl 269.
ṣadaḳ "just, right"	•ONOM: **U3** *za-da-ga* → Buccellati Amorites 59, 179; Gelb CAAA 34, 196.

[595] Diff.: Knudsen PIHANS 100 322 fn. 12 "a type of gazelle"; see |θ̣-b-y|.

ṣaduḳ "just, right, just case; DN"

•CTX: **EA** *ṣa-du-uq* (287:32) → AHw 1074; CAD Ṣ 59; Moran AmL 329 fn. 8; Izre'el Orient 38 79, 81.
•ONOM: **EUPH, B** *za-du-kum, ṣa-du-qa-nu-um, a-bi-ṣa-du-uq, a-ḫi-za-du-uq, am-ma/mi-za-du-ga, a-mi-za-du-ga-i-lu-ni, ba-aḫ-li-ṣa-du-uq, ḫa-(am-)mi-za-du-uq, ì-lí-za-du-uq, ṣa-du-qí-il, ṣa-du-qí*-DINGIR, *ṣa-tu-qí*-DINGIR → Huffmon APNMT 256f.; Gelb CAAA 34, 196; Durand REA 662; Zadok Fs. Hallo 329; Golinets Onomastikon 2 163, 459f.
R *ṣa-du-uq-qí, ṣa-du-uq-*^{d}*a-šár*(?) → Dalley / Walker / Hawkins Tell Rimah 212, 13, 215:1, 3; Golinets Onomastikon 2 162f., 459f.
A7 *la-ḫi-ṣa-du-uq* → Wiseman AT 141; Gelb CAAA 34, 196; Arnaud AuOr 16 164.
EM *a-du-ni-ṣa-du-qi* → Pruzsinszky PTEm 200 [75].
UGS *ṣa-du-qu* → Gröndahl PTU 187; Sivan GAGl 268.

ṣdḳ (A) "justice, legitimacy; DN"

•CTX: **UGA** Sg. suff. *ṣdqh* → DUL 768, cf. *ṣdq* (I), *ṣdq* (II).
•ONOM: **UGA** *ṣdqỉl* → DUL 768; *ṣdqn, ṣdkn, ṣtkn* → DUL 768: *ṣdqn*; *ṣdqšlm, štqšlm* → 768: *ṣdqšlm*; cf. *ṣdqm* → DUL 768; *ṣdqy* → DUL 768.

ṣdḳ (B) "lawful, righteous; DN"

•CTX: **UGA** Sg. *ṣdq* → DUL 768, cf. *ṣdq* (I).
•ONOM: **UGA** Cf. *ảbṣdq* → DUL 14; *ảdnṣdq* → DUL 21; *ỉlṣdq* → DUL 62; *bʕlṣdq* → DUL 207; *yḥṣdq* → DUL 947; cf. *ṣdqm* → DUL 768; *ṣdqy* → DUL 768.

|ṣ-ɣ-d|

Sem.: *ṣʕd* (Hb.) "to stride solemnly, walk along". See further *ṣaʕida* (Arab.) "to rise, go up".

|ṣ-ɣ-d| "to go, make for"

•CTX: **UGA** G prefc. *yṣġd* → DUL 769: /*ṣ-ġ-d*/.

|ṣ-ɣ-r|
Cf. |**z-ʕ-r**|

Sem.: *ṣʕr* (Hb.) "to become lowly", *ṣʕyr* (*ṣāʕîr*) "the smaller one, younger one, little", *ṣʕyrh* (*ṣeʕîrāh*) "smallness, youth", *zʕyr* (*zeʕîr*) "little", *mṣʕr* (*miṣʕār*) "small amount, few", *mzʕr* (*mizʕār*) "trifling"; *zʕr* (Aram., Syr.) "to be small, be lacking", *ṣʕr* (JAram., Syr. D) "to afflict, reproach", *ṣʕr(ʔ)* "pain, insult", *zʕyr* (Aram.) "small", *zʕwr* (JAram., Syr.) "small"; *ṣeḫēru(m), ṣaḫāru(m)* (Akk.) "to be(come) small, young, little", *ṣeḫru(m)* "small, young", *ṣuḫru(m)* "youth(s)", *ṣaḫartu(m), ṣeḫertu(m), ṣaḫḫartu, ṣeḫḫertu(m)* "(little) girl", *ṣuḫāru(m)* "boy, male child, servant", *ṣuḫartu(m)* "girl, young woman", *ṣeḫrūtu, ṣuḫrētu* "(time of) youth", *meṣḫerūtu, meṣḫarūtu* "childhood, youth", and cf. *ṣaḫḫaru(m), ṣaḫarru* "a kind of crop", *ṣeḫḫertu(m)* "minor crops"; *ṣaġura, ṣaġira* (Arab.) "to be(come) small, little, scanty", *ṣaġīr* "small, little", *ṣaġara* "littleness", *muṣaġġar* "diminished"; *ṣġr* (OSArab.) "small, unimportant".

ṣaɣ(i)r "small"

•ONOM: **EB** *za-ḫa-li/lí-a, za-ḫi-lu, ʔà-za-za-ḫir* → Pagan ARES 3 170f., 271, 383.

ṣaɣur "servant, (shepherd-)boy"

•LL: **EB** SA.ḪUR = *sa-ḫu-ru$_{12}$-um* → Sjöberg Fs. Renger 545.

ṣiɣ(i)ru "child"

•ONOM: **EB** *zi-iḫ-lu, zi-hi-lu* → Pagan ARES 3 170f., 385f.

ṣuɣar "junior servant, employee"

•CTX:[596] **Shechem** Pl. *ṣú-ḫa-ru-ú* → Horowitz / Oshima CunCan 122 (Shechem 1:10).
•LL: **EB** Cf. UGULA.URU = *zu-ḫa-lum, zu-ḫa-lu-um* → Sjöberg Fs. Wilcke 262.

---

596 For Mari *ṣuḫārum, ṣuḫrum* see Macdonald JAOS 96, 57ff.; Michel Ktema 22, 94f.

ṣuɣur "youth"	•ONOM: **EB** *zu-hu-rí* → Pagan ARES 3 170f., 388.
sɣr, **Sɣr** "servant, (shepherd-)boy"	•CTX: **UGA** Sg. *śġr*, cstr. *sġr*; suff. *sġrh*, *śġrh*, pl. *śġrm* → DUL 744: *s*/*śġr*; Tropper UG 46, 103, 125.
ṣɣr "small, of tender years, young"	•CTX: **UGA** Sg. *ṣġr*, fem. *ṣġrt*, suff. *ṣġrthn* (see below: *ṣġrt* (A)); pl. *ṣġrm* → DUL 769: *ṣġr* (I). •ONOM: **UGA** *ṣġr* → DUL 769.
ṣiɣara "youthfulness" (?)	•ONOM: **EB** *zi-ḫa-ra-ni* → Pagan ARES 3 170f., 385.
ṣɣrt (A) "girl, youngest, small, of tender years"	•CTX: **UGA** Sg. *ṣġrt*; suff. *ṣġrthn* → DUL 769f.: *ṣġrt* (I).
ṣɣrt (B) "babyhood, tender years, infancy" (?)	•CTX: **UGA** Sg. suff. *ṣġrth* → DUL 770: *ṣġrt* (II).
ṣaɣirt "a kind of crop" (?)	•CTX: **EUPH** Cf. *ṣa-ḫir-tum* → CAD S 59: *saḫirtu* (rdg *sà-ḫir-tum*); Streck Onomastikon 1 114 § 1.95.
maṣɣarat "youth, childhood"	•LL: **EM** (ŠÀ.TAM) MIN.NAM.DUMU.A.NI = MIN (=ŠÀ.TAM) *ma-ru-ut-ti-šu : zu ma-aṣ-ḫa-ra-ta-šu* → Pentiuc Vocabulary 116; Ikeda BiOr 60 268; Cohen Proceedings 53e RAI 1 831f.

|ṣ-ɣ-w| Cf. **|ṣ-w-ɣ**	Sem.: Cf. *ṣʕh* (Hb.) "to lie down"; *ṣʕy* (Aram.) "to fall"; *ṣaġā* (*ṣaġw*, Arab.) "to incline, bend, lean".
ṣuɣwat "pendent"	•CTX: **EB** Cf. *zú-ḫu-a-tum*, *zu-ḫu-wa-ti* → Pasquali QuSe 23 184f.

|ṣ-h-l|	Sem.: *ṣhl* (Hb. C) "to gleam, shine".
|ṣ-h-l| "to (make) shine, gleam"	•CTX: **UGA** G prefc. *yṣhl* → DUL 770.

|ṣ-ħ-l| See **|ṣ-l-ħ|**	

|ṣ-ħ-r| Cf. **|θ̣-h-r|**	Sem.: *ṣḥr* (Syr.) "to redden, blush"; *ṣēru*(*m*) "steppe, open country";[597] *ṣaḥara* (Arab.) "to boil; to cause a sunstroke", *ʔiṣḥārra* "to become whitish-reddish"; *ṣəḥār*, *ṣaḥár*, *ṣóʕər* (MSArab.) "to brand".
|ṣ-ħ-r(-r)| "to roast, burn"	•CTX: **UGA** L suffc. *ṣḥrrt*, suff. (?) *ṣḥrrm* → Whiting Or 50 17; DUL 771f. /*ṣ-ḥ-r-r*/. •ONOM: **UGA** Cf. *ṣḥrn* → DUL 771.
ṣaħr, **ṣiħr** "steppe, open country"	•CTX: **EB** Cf. *zi-ru*$_{12}$ → Butz EDA 347; Bonechi WO 30 33f. •LL: **EB** Cf. EDEN = *za-lum* → Krebernik ZA 73 47 (for VE 1247).

|ṣ-ḳ-l|	Sem.: Cf. *ṣaqala* (Arab.) "to smooth, polish", *ṣaqqāl* "polisher, smoother".
ṣaḳḳāl "polisher"	•ONOM: **A4** Cf. *ṣa-qa-la* → Wiseman AT 152; Arnaud AuOr 16 161.

[597] For the distinction of two different lexemes in Akk. (*ṣēru* "back" < \|θ̣-h-r\|, and *ṣēru* "steppe, open country" < \|ṣ-ħ-r\|) see Whiting Or 50 17 fn. 71.

|ṣ-l-ħ|, **|ṣ-ħ-l|**	Culture word, dimorphism by metath.: *ṣlḥt* (*ṣallaḥat*, Hb.) "bowl", *ṣlḥyt* (*ṣeloḥît*) "jar"; *ṣlwḥy(t?)* (JAram., Syr.) "jar, vial"; *ṣaḥn* (Arab.) "bowl, dish"; *ṣāḥl* (Eth.) "bowl, dish".
ṣallaħt, ṣillaħt "jar; bowl"	•CTX: **EA** (gold / stone bowls) *ṣí-il-la-aḫ-tá* (*šum-šu*) (14 II 1, 54, III 70) → Lambdin Or 22 69; Sivan GAGl 269; Moran AmL 29f., 33: *zillaḫta*, untranslated. **EG** *ḏa-ḥa-r-ta*, metath. *ra-ḥa-ḏa-ta* → Hoch SWET 394 no. 593.[598]
|ṣ-l-ḳ| Cf. |s^1-l-ḳ|	Sem.: *ṣlq* (JAram.) "to split", *ṣlq(?)* "fissure".
ṣalaḳ "fissured" (?)	•ONOM: **B** *ṣa-la-qù* → Zadok Fs. Hallo 329.
|ṣ-l-l| (1) Cf. |θ̣-l-l|	Sem.: Cf. *ṣll* (JAram., Syr.) "to cleanse, strain", *ṣlyl* "pure"; *ṣalla* (Arab.) "to strain, filter; to cleanse the grain"; *ṣll*, *ṣalala* (Eth.) "to percolate, filter, winnow".
ṣalil "pure" (?)	•ONOM: **B** *za-li-lum/li* → Gelb CAAA 34, 196; Zadok Fs. Hallo 329.
|ṣ-l-l| (2) Cf. |ṣ-r-ṣ-r|	Sem.: *ṣll* (Hb.) "to resonate, ring", *ṣlṣl* (*ṣ^{e}lāṣal*, Hb.) "kind of insect"; *mṣlh* (*m^{e}ṣillāh*) "little bell", *mṣltym* (*m^{e}ṣiltayim*) "cymbals"; *ṣll* (JAram., Syr.) "to tingle", *ṣll(?)* (Syr.) "ringing", *ṣllh*, *ṣllt?* (JAram., Syr.) "clattering"; *ṣalla* (Arab.) "to ring, clink, rattle", *ṣalīl* "rattler, clatter". See allomorph C_1-C_1-C_2: *ṣṣl(?)* (Syr.) "cymbal"; allomorphs C_1-C_2-C_1-C_2: *ṣlṣlym* (*ṣelṣ^{e}lîm*, Hb.) "clanging pans, cymbals"; *ṣlṣl(?/h)* (JAram.) "cymbal"; *ṣalṣala* (Arab.) "to clink, jingle", *ṣalṣala* "sound, tinkle"; *ṣanṣalat*, *ṣanṣal* (Eth.) "cymbal, sistrum".
ṣulṣul "an insect"	•LL: **EB** *zu-lu-lu* → Sjöberg WO 27 19.
maṣill "cymbalist"	•CTX: **UGS** LÚ *ma-ṣi-lu* → Sivan GAGl 245; Huehnergard UVST 171; vSoldt SAU 305 (85).
mṣl "cymbalist"	•CTX: **UGA** Sg. *mṣl*, pl. *mṣlm* → DUL 579.
mṣlt (A) "cymbal(s)"	•CTX: **UGA** Du. *mṣltm* → DUL 579: *mṣlt* (I).
mṣlt (B) "clang"	•CTX: **UGA** → DUL 579: *mṣlt* (II).
|ṣ-l-m| Cf. |θ̣-l-m|	Primary noun, Sem.: *ṣlm* (*ṣelem*, Hb.) "statue, image"; *ṣlm* (Ph., Nab., Palm., Hatra) "statue"; *ṣlm(?)* (Aram., Syr.) "image, idol"; *ṣalmu(m)* (Akk.) "effigy, image, statue"; further: *ṣanam* (Arab.) "image, idol"; *ṣlm*, *ẓlm* (OSArab.) "statue".
ṣlm "image, statue" (?)	•CTX: **UGA** Sg. *ṣlm*, pl. *ṣlmm* (unc. ctx.) → DUL 772.[599]
|ṣ-l-p|	Sem.: Cf. *ṣlp* (Syr.) "to split, wound"; *ṣalāpu(m)*, *ṣelēpu* (Akk.) "to cut (at an angle), cross out".
|ṣ-l-p| "to be slant, deform" (?)	•ONOM: **UGA** Cf. unc. *ṣlpn* → DUL 772.

[598] For Coptic *dʒəl'aḥtəs* "deep pit, vessel" see Kilani VGW 130.
[599] Altern. from *ṣalm* (Arab.) "courageous man (as DN ?)"; Arnaud SEL 8 33: "brave, bravoure".

|ṣ-l-w/y|	Sem.: *ṣly* (Aram., Syr. D) “to pray”, *ṣlw*, *ṣlwtʔ* “prayer”, *tṣlwt* (Aram.) “prayer”; *ṣullû*, *ṣallû* (Akk.) “to beseech, pray to”, *ṣulû*, *ṣullû* “supplication, prayer”, *sullû(m)* “to appeal, pray to”, *sulû* “prayer”, *teslītu*(m), *taslītum* “appeal, prayer”; *ṣallā*, *ṣallāha* (Arab.) “to pray”, *ṣalāh* “prayer”; *ṣlt* (OSArab.) “prayer(s)”; *ṣallaya* (Eth.) “to pray, make a vow”, *ṣalot* “prayer, vow”.
|**ṣ-l-y**| “to pray, cast a spell”	•CTX: **UGA** D prefc. *yṣly* → DUL 772. See also *ṣly*, below. •ONOM: **EUPH** Cf. unc. *ia*-AŠ-*li-ba-al*, *ia*-AZ-*li-ìl* → Gelb CAAA 188 (ŚLIJ); Zadok Fs. Hallo 329 (Ś-L-Y / Š-L-Y ?).
ṣily “curse, spell”	•LL: **UGS** [EN = *a-r*]*a-ru* = *ši-da-ar-ni* = *ṣi-il*-PI(*yV*) → Sivan GAGl 269; Huehnergard UVST 57, 170; vSoldt SAU 307 (123); BiOr 648.
ṣly “prayer, spell” (?)	•CTX: **UGA** Cf. unc. sg. suff. *ṣlyh* (rdg *ʕlyh* ?) → Tropper KWU 113; vacat DUL (cf. DUL 773: /*ṣ-l-y*/).
ṣlt “prayer”	•CTX: **UGA** Sg. suff. *ṣltkm* → DUL 772.

|ṣ-l-y| See |**ṣ-l-w/y**|	

|ṣ-m-ḫ|	Sem.: Cf. *ṣmḥ* (Hb.) “to sprout, grow”, *ṣmḥ* (*ṣemaḥ*) “sprouting, shoot”; *ṣmḥ* (Ph., Pun.) “scion, offspring”; *ṣmḥ* (JAram., Syr.) “to sprout, shine”, *ṣmḥ(ʔ)* “splendour, growth”.
|**ṣ-m-ḫ**| “to grow, cultivate” (?)	•CTX: **EG** Cf. *ma$_4$-ḏa-ʕa* (metath. |ṣamḫa, ṣamaxa| ?) → Hoch SWET 178 no. 240.
ṣamḫa, ṣamaxa “produce, croops” (?)	•CTX: **EG** Cf. *ma-ḏa-ʕa* (metath.) → Hoch SWET 177f. no. 239.

|ṣ-m-ḳ|	Culture word, Sem.: *ṣm(w)qym* (*ṣimmūqîm*, Hb.) “cake of dried grapes”, *ṣmq* “to shrink, dry up” (only ptc. pl. *ṣomᵉqîm*); *ṣymwqyn* (JAram.) “raisins”; *muzīqu*, *munziqu* (Akk.) “raisin”.
ṣammūḳ “raisin”	•ONOM: **B** *ṣa-am-mu-uq-qu* → Zadok Fs. Hallo 329. **EG** Elem. in TN *ḏa-ma$_3$-qa* → Hoch SWET 388 no. 583.
ṣmḳ “raisin”	•CTX: **UGA** Pl. *ṣmqm* → DUL 775.

|ṣ-m-l|	Sem. etym. unc.: Cf. *ṣamala* (Arab.) “to be firm, hard, dry; to last, hold out”, *ṣamīl*, *ṣāmil* “dry”.
ṣml “dried out (barley) draff” (?)	•CTX: **UGA** → DUL 774f.: *ṣml* (I).[600]

|ṣ-m-r|	Sem. etym. unc. Cf. *ṣamāru(m)* (Akk. G, D) “to wish, strive, aim for, make effort”, *ṣimru* “wealth”, *ṣumru* “desire, purpose”, *ṣummirātu(m)*, *ṣummu*/*erātu(m)*, *ṣumrātu* “desires, aims”; *ṣamara*, *ṣammara*, *ʔaṣmara* (Arab.) “to be miserly, mean”. Altern. cf. *ṣmrt* (*ṣammeret*, Hb.) “top”; *ṣemēru(m)*, *ṣamāru* “to swell up, be swollen, bloated”, *ṣimertu(m)*, *ṣimru* “swollen state, bloatedness”. See further: *ṣamra*, *ṣamira*, *ṣamara*, *ʔaṣmara* (Arab.) “to turn sour”, *ṣamra*, *ṣāmūra* “very sour milk”, *ṣumr* “edge”.

[600] The DN *ṣml* lacks still for a plausible explanation; see DUL 775: *ṣml* (II).

ṣimirt (A) "top, wealth; the highest utmost good" (?)	•ONOM: **EM** Cf. ^{d}*da-gan* ZI(*ṣí*)*-me-er-ti*, ^{d}KUR-SI(*ṣì*)*-me-er-ti* → Pruzsinszky PTEm 195 [285].
ṣimirt (B) "morbid boldness" (?)	•CTX: **EUPH** *ṣí-im-ra-at* → Durand LAPO 17 162 fn. m; MARI 7 199ff. (A.319:34) fn. ad 34.
ṣmrt "top, wealth; the highest, utmost good" (?)	•ONOM: **UGA** Cf. *ṣmrt* → DUL 775.

|ṣ-m-t| (1)	Sem.: *ṣmt* (Hb.) "to destroy, silence" (?), (N) "to disappear, vanish", (D, C) "to destroy, silence"; *ṣmt* (JAram.) "to contract, inhibit", (Syr. D) "put to silence", *ṣmtʔ* (Syr.) "cuffs"; *ṣamata, ṣāmata* (Eth.) "to be destroyed, disappear, perish", *ʔaṣmata* "to destroy, root out", *ṣamatā* "booty".
|**ṣ-m-t**| "to silence, destroy"	•CTX: **UGA** D prefc. *tṣmt*, suffc. *ṣmt*, *ṣmt*, inf. *ṣmt* (cf. *ṣmt*, below) → DUL 775.[601]
ṣmt "disappearance, destruction"	•CTX: **UGA** Cstr. *ṣmt* → DUL 775f.

|ṣ-m-t| (2) See |**ṣ́-m-d**|	

|ṣ-n-ʕ|	Sem.: *ṣnʕ* (Nab.) "to make, construct"; *ṣnʕh, ṣnʕtʔ* (Syr.) "craft"; *ṣnʕ* (OSArab.) "to fortify"; *ṣanʕa, ṣanʔa* (Eth.) "to be strong, powerful".
ṣanīʕ "strength, strong"	•LL: **EB** ŠU.TA.KAL = *za-ni-um* → Conti QuSe 17 144. •ONOM: **EB** Cf. *za-ne-ma-rí*.KI, *za-ne/ni-ḫi-ma-rí*(.KI) → Pagan ARES 3 171, 383.
tuṣtanniʕ "exerting, enduring"	•LL: **EB** ŠU.TA.KAL = *du-uš-da-ne-um*, *du-uš-da-ne-ḫum*, *du-uš-da-ne-*LU(*um*?) → Conti QuSe 17 144; Catagnoti QuSe 29 27, 230.

|ṣ-n-n| (1), |ṣ-w-n|	Sem.:. *ṣnh* (*ṣinnāh*, Hb) "(large) shield"; also: *ṣāna* (*ṣawn*, Arab.) "to preserve, safeguard, keep", *ṣawn* "guarding, care", *ṣāʔin* "keeper"; *ta=ṣawwana* (MSArab.) "to take shelter"; *ṣawwana, ḍawwana* (Eth.) "to protect, defend, shelter", *ṣawan* "refuge, shelter".
ṣinnat "(large) shield"	•CTX: **EUPH** (GI) *ṣí-na-tum*, *ṣí-in-na-tum*, *ṣí-in-na-a-tim*, *ṣí-in-na-as-sú* → Abrahami JAOS 119 132f., NABU 1991/26; Charpin AfO 40/41 20 (rdg *sí=*); Durand LAPO 17 391; Stol BiOr 57 626; Schrakamp RlA 12 177; Arkhipov ARM 32 122f.[602]
ṣn "protection, shelter" (?)	•ONOM: **UGA** Cf. *åbṣn* → DUL 14; *bʕlṣn* → DUL 208.

|ṣ-n-n-| (2)	Sem.: *ṣnynym* (pl. *ṣenînîm*, Hb.) "pricks"; *ṣnn* (JAram.) "thorn".

[601] The Syll.Ug. section belongs under |ṣ́-m-d|.

[602] Cf. Akk. dictionaries under *sinnatum* (AHw 1047), *sinnatum* (CSD S 285f.), both "a lance ?".

ṣanna "bristling of hair"	•CTX: **EG** *d̲a-n-na, d̲-n* → Hoch SWET 388 no. 584.
|ṣ-n-p|	Primary noun, Sem.: *ṣnyp* (*ṣānîp*, Hb.) "headband", denom. *ṣnp* "to wind around"; *ṣnyp, ṣnph, ṣnptʔ* "border, fringe, edge", denom. *ṣnp* (JAram.) "to wrap oneself"; *ṣinf, ṣinfa, ṣanifa* (Arab.) "border, fringe"; *ṣənf, ṣanf, ṣanafi, ṣannāfe* "border, fringe", denom. *ṣanfa* "to be(come) a border".
ṣanipt "border, fringe"	•CTX: **EB** Sg. cstr. *zi-na-ba-ti, zi-ne-íb-ti* |(ṣinapt|) → Catagnoti QuSe 29 52, 116, 230.
|ṣ-n-r|	Sem. etym. unc. Cf. *ṣnwr* (*ṣinnōr*, Hb.) "waterfall, stream, flood" (?).
ṣin(n)ar "fast-flowing stream" (?)	•ONON: **UGS** Cf. unc. *ṣi-na-ru, ṣí-na-ra/ri, ṣí-na-ra-na* → Sivan GAGl 269; Huehnergard 228.[603]
ṣnr "fast-flowing stream" (?)	•ONON: **UGA** Cf. unc. *ṣnr* → DUL 776; *ṣnrn* → DUL 776.[604]
|ṣ-p-d|	Sem.: *ṣpd* (Hb.) "to contract, shrink"; *ṣpd* (JAram.) "to weave"; *ṣafada* (Arab.) "to bind, fetter".
ṣapputt, ṣupputt, ṣuppatt "a kind of bread"	•CTX: **EM** NINDA *ṣa-ap-pu-ta*, NINDA *ṣa-ap-pu-ut-tù*, NINDA *ṣa-pu-ta/tu*$_4$; NINDA *ṣu-pu*(BU)*-tu*$_4$, NINDA *ṣu-pu*(BU)*-ut-tu*$_4$; cf. NINDA *ṣú*(ZU)*-pa-*[→ Pentiuc Vocabulary 160.
|ṣ-p-ḥ|	Sem.: *ṣpḥt* (*ṣapaḥat*, Hb.) "pitcher, broad (jug)", *ṣpyḥt* (*ṣapîḥit*) "flat (pastry)"; *ṣpḥ(ʔ)* (Aram., Syr.) "plate, dish"; *ṣafaḥa* (Arab.) "to broaden, widen", *ṣafḥa* "plane, leaf, sheet", *ṣafīḥ* "broad side, sheet iron, tinplate", *ṣafīḥa* "plate, sheet, leaf, slab"; *ʔṣfḥt* (OSArab.) "platform"; *ṣəfḥ, d̲əfḥ* "breadth", *ṣəfuḥ* "broad".
ṣipḥ "flat field"	•CTX: **EM** A.ŠÀ(.ḪI.A) *ṣí-ip-ḫu*; cf. A.ŠÀ.MEŠ (...) *i-di ṣì-pa-ḫi* → Pentiuc Vocabulary 163f.
ṣapaḥa "plank, panel"	•CTX: **EG** *d̲a-pa*$_2$*-ḥa* → Hoch SWET 384f. no. 578.[605]
ṣ-p-n| (1) Cf. **|ṣ-p-y| (2)**	Culture word (?), Sem.: Cf. *ṣpwn* (Hb.) "the north".
ṣapān "northwind"	•CTX: **EA** *i-na ṣa-pa-ni-šu* (147:10) → Grave Or 51 161ff.; UF 12 221ff; OrAn 19 205ff.; Rainey EAC 743.[606] •ONOM: **EUPH** Cf. *ṣa-pa-an, ṣa-pa-nu-iš-tár* → Zadok Fs. Hallo 329.
ṣapōn "North (TN / DN)"	•ONOM: **EA** TN URU *ṣa-pu-*MA(*na*!) → Belmonte RGTC 12/2 246. **EG** DN *d̲a-pu*$_2$*-na, d̲a-pu*$_3$*-n* |ṣapōna| → Hoch SWET 384 no. 576.

[603] Probl. unrelated: URU *Sinā ru* (TN), Belmonte RGTC 12/2 239.

[604] Probl. unrelated: TN *snr* (*miḫd*), Belmonte RGTC 12/2 239, DUL 752f.: *snr* (I); GN *snry*, DUL 753: *snry* (I); PNN *snr*, DUL 753: *snr* (II); *snry*, DUL 753: *snry* (II), *s/śnrn*, DUL 753.

[605] Cf. Sivan / Cochavi-Rainey WSVES 87: *s̲á-pá-ḥa* "broad board"; Helck Beziehungen no. 307a.

[606] Diff. and unlikely: AHw 1082: "bergen"; CAD Ṣ 96 "to hide"; Sivan GAGl 270: ṢPN "hide".

ṣpn "the mountain dwelling of BaʕI; DN"	•ONOM: **UGA** TN / DN *ṣpn*, *ṣpʕn*, *ẓpn*, suff. *ṣpnhm* → DUL 777; Belmonte RGTC 12/2 246f.
|ṣ-p-n| (2)	Sem.: Cf. *ṣufn* (Arab.) "a small drinking-vessel (of skin or leather); bag", *taṣafana* "to divide or share the water", *muṣāfana* "dividing of water"; *ṣfn*, *ṣafana* (Eth.) "to draw water", *ṣafan*, *ṣəfn* "pitcher", *maṣāfən* "satchel".
maṣtapin "watering hole"	•LL: **EB** ŠU.A = *maš-da-bí-num/nú-um* → Conti QuSe 17 146; Bonechi Proceedings 44e RAI 2 100.
|ṣ-p-p|	Culture word, Sem.: *ṣuppu(m)*, *ṣuʔbu* (Akk.) "white sheep".
ṣp (C) "white ewe"	CTX: **UGA** Sg. cstr. *ṣp* → DUL 776f.: *ṣp* (III).
|ṣ-p-r| **Cf. |θ̣-p-r|**	Primary noun, Sem.: *ṣpwr* (*ṣipôr*) "bird"; *ṣpr(ʔ)*, *ṣnpr* (Aram., Syr.) "bird"; *ṣafara* (Arab.) "to whistle, chirp", *ṣafīr* "whistle", *ṣāfir* "who whistles"; *ṣəfər*, *həṣfōr* (MSArab.) "to whistle, pipe", *əṣféroh* "bird".
ṣip(p)ār, **ṣip(p)ōra** "bird" (?)	•ONOM: **EG** Cf. *ḏi_4-pa-r*, *ḏi_4-pu_2-r* (?) → Hoch SWET 384 no. 577.
|ṣ-p-ṣ-p|	Culture word, Sem.: Cf. *ṣpṣph* (*ṣapṣapāh*) "willow"; *ṣafṣāfa* (Arab.) "willow".
ṣapṣap "willow"	•ONOM: **B** *ṣa-ap-ṣa-pu-um* → Zadok Fs. Hallo 329.[607]
|ṣ-p-y| (1)	Sem.: *ṣph* (Hb. D) "to overlay", *ṣpwy* (*ṣipûy*) "platting"; *ṣph* (Pun.) "broad purple stripe / tunic with the same" (?); *ṣuppu*, *ṣaʔʔupu* (Akk.) "to decorate, inlay (?), overlay (?)", *ṣuppu* "decorated, overlaid, covered, clad"; *ṣaffa* (Arab.) "to put in a row, arrange, set, compose", *ṣaff* "row, line"; *ṣf* (OSArab.) "stone facing of a building" (?); *ṣəf*, *ṣeff* (MSArab.) "to align, stitch roughly"; *ṣfṣf*, *ṣafṣafa*, *ḍafḍafa* (Eth.) "pave a road, coat a wall".
|ṣ-p-y| (A) "to plate, cover, embroider"	•CTX: **UGA** G inf. *ṣpy*, pass. ptc. pl. *ṣpym*, fem. *ṣpyt* → DUL 778.
ṣipy "platting"	•CTX: **EB** *zi-bù* → Pasquali QuSe 23 93f.; QuSe 25 288.
ṣp (A) "embroidered garment"	•CTX: **UGA** Pl. *ṣpm* → DUL 776: *ṣp* (II).
ṣipayt "platting"	•CTX: **EB** *zi-ba-du/tum* → Pasquali QuSe 23 90ff.; Or 83 272.
ṣuṣṣup(a)t "a metallic sheet or plate"	•CTX: **EB** Pl. *zu-zu-ba-tum*, *zú-zú-ba-tum* |ṣupṣupāt=| → Fronzaroli QuSe 13 127, 153; Conti QuSe 19 52f.; Catagnoti QuSe 29 24, 37, 112, 230.

[607] Referring also to Late/ NBab. *ṣap-ṣap*.

|ṣ-p-y| (2)	Sem.: *ṣph* (Hb.) "to keep watch, look, spy", *mṣph* (miṣpeh) "watch-tower"; *ṣpy* (JAram.) "to look out, observe", *ṣpy, ṣpytʔ* "watch-tower"; *ṣubbû(m), ṣabbû(m)* (Akk.) "to observe (from a distance", *ṣāpītu, ṣābītu* "watch-tower".
|ṣ-p-y| (B) "to spy, observe"	•ONOM: **EUPH** *la-ṣa-pa-tim* → Zadok Fs. Hallo 329.
|γ-p-y| "to spy, observe"	•CTX: **UGA** G prefc. *tġpy* → DUL 319: /*ġ-p-y*/; Tropper UG 95: *γ* for etym. *ṣ*.
ṣp (B) "look, glance"	•CTX: **UGA** → DUL 776: *ṣp* (I).
mṣpt "crow's nest"	•CTX: **UGA** → DUL 580.

|ṣ-r-ʕ|	Sem.: *ṣaraʕa* (Arab.) "to throw down, fell".
|ṣ-r-ʕ| "to lay low; to overthrow"	•CTX: **EG** *ḏa-ra-ʕa* (|ṣaraʕa|) → Hoch SWET 392f. no. 590.[608]

|ṣ-r-d|	Sem. etym. unc. Cf. *ṣard* (Arab.) "numerous", *ṣarad* "large army".
ṣrdt "a large group (of servants)" (?)	•CTX: **UGA** Suff. *ṣrdth* → DUL 779: "?".

|ṣ-r-H|	Culture word, Sem.: *ṣērru(m), ṣēru(m)* (Akk.) "snake".
ṣarH "snake"	•LL: **MŠ** *ṣa-ar-ú* = *ṣe-[ru]* → AHw p. 1086; CAD Ṣ 115; Hrůša MŠ 112, 254, 399 (V 53).
ṣirH "snake"	•CTX: **EB** *zi-lu-um* → Fronzaroli ARET 13 13, 311: the constellation 'Snake'. •LL: **UGS** Cf. (MU.UŠ) MUŠ = *ṣi-i-ru* → Nougayrol Ugaritica 5 239:15.
ṣāriH "snake charmer"	•LL: **EB** MUŠ.LAḪ$_4$= *za-rí-um* → Mander Or 48 337 fn. 27; Krebernik ZA 73 28+ fn. 91.
ṣert "female snake"	•LL: **EB** *ṣé-er-tum* → Sjöberg WO 27, 17.

|ṣ-r-ḥ| (1)	Primary noun, Sem.: *ṣryḥ* (*ṣ*^{e}*rî*^{a}*ḥ*, Hb.) "vault"; *ṣryḥ(?)* (Nab., JAram.) "room, chamber"; *ṣarḥ* (Arab.) "castle, lofty edifice"; *ṣrḥn* (OSArab.) "upper chamber, upper storey"; *ṣərḥ* (Eth.) "(upper) chamber, fortress, palace".
ṣarḥ "tower, lofty building, upper chamber"	•CTX: **EB** *za-ra ba-tum* → Bonechi WO 30 32f. •LL: **EB** ÙR = [*za-r*]*a ba-tum, za-ra ba-tim* → Bonechi WO 30 32f.; Catagnoti QuSe 29 115, 230.

|ṣ-r-ḥ| (2)	Sem.: Cf. *ṣrḥ* (Syr.) "to be inflamed", *ṣarāḫu* "to heat up, flare up", (D) "to keep warm (horse)"; *ṣaruḥa* (Arab.) "to be clear", *ṣarraḥa* "to be clear", *ṣāraḥa* "to clarify, enlighten".
taṣrāḥ "warmer (of the horses)"	•CTX: **EA** LÚ *ta-a*[*ṣ-r*]*a-ḫi* ANŠE.KUR.RA.ḪI.A (143:27) → AHw 1337; CAD T 284; Moran AmL 229f. fn. 5.

[608] Cf. Sivan / Cochavi-Rainey WSVES 87: *ṣá-ra-ʕá* "to throw down"; Helck Beziehungen no. 314.

|ṣ-r-x|

Sem.: *ṣrḥ* (Hb.) "to shout, scream shrilly", *ṣrḥ* (cj. *ṣeraḥ*) "war-cry"; *ṣrḥ* (JAram., Syr.) "to cry out"; *ṣarāḫu(m)* (Akk.) "to cry out, wail, complain", *ṣerḫu(m)* "shout, lamentation"; *ṣaraḫa* (Arab.) "to cry, yell, scream", *ṣarḫa* "cry, outcry, yell, scream"; *ṣrḫ* (OSArab.) "to call for help, summon"; *ṣarḫa, ṣarḥa* (Eth.) "to cry, shout", *ṣərāḫ* "outcry, shout".

ṣir(a)x "lamentation" — •CTX: **EM** DUB *an-nu-ú ša ṣi-ra-ḫi* → Pentiuc Vocabulary 163.

|ṣ-r-m|

Sem.: *ṣrm* (Syr.) "to dare", *ṣrymw(t?)* "audacity; *ṣarāmu(m)* (Akk.) "to make an effort, strive"; *ṣaruma* (Arab.) "to be sharp, incisive, determined", *ṣarm* "severance", *ṣarāma* "sharpness, harshness"; *ṣátrəm, ṣɔtrəm* (MSArab.) "to scowl".

ṣirm "effort, zeal" — •CTX: **EUPH** *ṣé-er-mi-im-ma, ṣí-ir-ma-am, ṣí-ri-*WA(*im*$_x$)*-šu-nu* → AHw 1092: *ṣermum*; CAD Ṣ 208: *ṣirmu*; Charpin ARM 26/2 205 + fn. b (386:4'f.).

ṣirimt "effort, zeal" — •CTX: **EUPH** ZI-*ri-im-tam* → Joannès ARM 26/2 307 + fn. e (419:10').

|ṣ-r-p|

Sem.: *ṣrp* (Hb.) "to smelt (metal), to refine", *ṣrpy* (*ṣorᵉpî*) "metal smelters, refiners"; *ṣrp* (Moab.) "goldsmith"; *ṣrp* (JAram., Syr.) "to refine", *ṣrp(?)* (Syr.) "alum", *ṣryp* (Aram.) "refined", *ṣrwp(?)* (Syr.) "refiner", *ṣrpwn(?)* "scarlet dye"; *ṣarāpu(m)* (Akk.) "to burn, fire, bake; to smelt, refine; to dye (with red); make something glow", *ṣarpu(m)*, *ṣarriptu* "burnt, reddened, refined", *ṣirpu(m)* "red (wool), bright colour", *ṣurpu(m)* "burning of heart", *ṣāripu* "dyer", *ṣarīpu* "dyed (red) sheep"; *ṣarafa* (Arab.) "to avert, turn away, keep away", *ṣarrafa* "to cause to flow off, draw off, drain", *ṣirf* "pure, unmixed", *ṣarīf* "refined silver"; *ṣrf* (OSArab.) "silver". Late lexicalized dimorphism C$_3$:*b*: *ṣrb* (Hb. N) "to be scorched", *ṣrb* (*ṣārāb*) "scorching"; *ṣrb* (JAram.) "to be scorched"; *ṣarābu* (NBab. Akk.), see *ṣarāpu(m)*, above.

|ṣ-r-p| "to dye reddish" — •ONOM: **EM** Cf. unc. *ṣa-ri-ip-tu*$_4$ (fem. |ṣāript| "dyeing" / |ṣaript| "dyed" ?) Pruzsinszky PTEm 95 [710].
UGA Cf. unc. *ṣrpt* → DUL 780.

ṣirp (A) "bright dye, brilliant fabric" — •CTX: **EUPH** GÚ *ṣi-ri-ip* DUḪ.ŠÚ.A; cf. GÚ.É.A ṣi-ri-ip (ARM 18:11), ṣi-ir-pu-um (A.1285:44) → Durand ARM 30 96; Arkhipov ARM 32 11.

ṣirp (B) "a glazed earthenware" (?) — •CTX: **EUPH** *ṣí-ri-ip tu-uk-ri-ši-im, ṣí-ir-pu, ṣí-ir-pí, ṣí-ir-pu-um,* (NA$_4$) *ṣí-ir-pí-im* → Guichard ARM 31 127f.; Arkhipov ARM 32 37.

ṣurp (A) "refined silver" — •CTX: **EB** *sùr-bù-um, sùr-bí-im, sùr-ba-am*$_6$ → Pasquali QuSe 23 76f.; QuSe 25 286; NABU 2003/108; Catagnoti QuSe 29 31, 109, 122, 230.
Q *ṣur-pu* → Richter / Lange Idadda 171 (62:40f.), 186.
A4 *ṣur-pu* → Giacumakis AkkAl 100.
UGS *ṣur-pu* (PRU 3 169:14) → AHw 1114: *ṣurpu*(m), 3 (*ṣorpu*; vSoden UF 11 750).[609]

ṣurp (B) "reddish glowing" (?) — •ONOM: **A4** Cf. *zur-ba* → Sivan GAGl 270: from ṢRB "burn, scorch".

ṣrp "reddish dye" — •CTX: **UGA** → DUL 779f.

---

609 For the altern. rdg *ṣár-pu* see Huehnergard AkkUg 279, 398 (437 ZUR); vSoldt SAU 413.

ṣurpān "refined silver"	•CTX: **EB** *sùr-ba-núm* → Pasquali QuSe 23 76f.; Or. 83 270f.
|ṣ-r-r| (1), |ṣ-w-r|	Sem. dimorphism: Bases C_1-C_2-C_2:. *ṣrr* (Hb.) "to wrap (up), tie up, lock up", *ṣrwr* (*ṣerôr*) "bag, little pack"; *ṣrr* (Aram., Syr.) "to wrap up, bind together, tie up"; *ṣarra* (Arab.) "to lace, tie up, bind", *ṣurra* "bundle, parcel"; *ṣarārum* (Akk.) "to pack up", *ṣerretu(m)*, *ṣerratum* "nose-rope, leading rope". Bases C_1-C_2, *ṣwr* (Hb.) "to tie up, encircle, lay siege to", *mṣwr* (*māṣôr*) "distress, siege"; *ṣwr* (JAram.) "to hold tightly, shut in", *ṣyr(?)* "siege".
|ṣ-w-r| "to besiege, lay siege to, confine"	•CTX: **EA** G suffc *la ma-ṣa-kú : ṣí-ir-ti* (127:34) → Moran AmL 208 fn. 9; Rainey CAT 2 286, 353; EAC 1472. **UGA** G prefc. *tṣr* → DUL 779: */ṣ-r(-r)/*.[610]
mṣrrt "bundle, parcel" (?)	•CTX: **UGA** Sg. / pl. *mṣrrt* → DUL 581: *mṣrr(t)*: "a piece of fabric or a garment"
|ṣ-r-r| (2), |ṣ-y-r|	Sem., probl. dimorphic. Cf. *ṣurrum* (Akk.) "to exalt", *ṣīru(m)* "exalted, supreme, splendid", *ṣīrūtu(m)* "supremacy, exaltedness".
ṣrrt "height(s)"	•CTX: **UGA** Sg. / pl. *ṣrrt* → DUL 780.
ṣrry "height(s)"	•CTX: **UGA** → DUL 780.
|ṣ-r-r| (3)	Sem.: Cf. *ṣarāru(m)*, *ṣerēru* (Akk.) "to flash", *ṣarru* "flashing".
ṣarr "flash(ing)"	•ONOM: **B** Cf. *za-ar-rum*, *la-za-ra-a* → Gelb CAAA 34, 196 (unexplained).
ṣirr "flash(ing)"	•ONOM: **EUPH** Cf. *zi-ir-ri* → Gelb CAAA 34, 197 (unexplained). **A7** Cf. *zi-ir-ri* → Wiseman AT 153; Gelb CAAA 34, 197 (unexplained).
ṣurr "flash(ing)"	•ONOM: **EUPH** Cf. *zu-ur-ri* → Gelb CAAA 34, 198 (unexplained).
ṣārir "the flashing one; DN"	•ONOM: **B** Cf. *za-ri-ru-um*, *i-zi-za-ri-ru-um* → Gelb CAAA 34, 196 (unexplained).
|ṣ-r-r| (4)	Sem. etym. unc.: Cf. *ʔaṣarr* (Arab.) "to get a husk (ear of corn)", *ṣarar* "ear with its husk".
ṣrr "corn (ear with its husk ?)"	•CTX: **UGA** → DUL 780.
|ṣ-r-ṣ-r| Cf. **|ṣ-l-l| (2)**	Primary noun, Sem.: *ṣṣr(?)*, *ṣṣwr(?)* (Syr.) "cricket"; *ṣarṣaru*, *ṣāṣiru(m)* (Akk.) "cricket"; *ṣarṣar*, *ṣurṣur*, *ṣurṣūr* (Arab.) "cricket".
ṣarṣar, ṣaṣṣar, ṣanṣar "cricket"	•CTX: **EUPH** *ṣa-ar-ṣa-ar*, *ṣa-aṣ-ṣa-ar*, BURU$_5$ *ṣa-an-ṣa-ar* → Lion / Michel MARI 8 707ff.; Zadok Fs. Hallo 329 (Ṣ-R-R). •LL: **EB** *za-za-ru*$_{12}$*-um* → Sjöberg WO 27 22. •ONOM: **EB** *za-za-lum* → Pagan ARES 3 233, 384.
ṣirrōra, ṣinnōra "cricket" (?)	•ONOM: **EG** Cf. elem. in TN *ḏi*$_2$*-nu*$_2$*-ra*, *ḏi*$_4$*-nu*$_2$*-ru*$_2$ → Hoch SWET 391f. no. 587.

[610] See above for the correct etym. justification.

|ṣ-w-ʕ|	Culture word, Sem.: Cf. *ṣʕ(ʔ)* (JAram., Syr.) "plate"; *ṣāʕ* (Arab.) "a cubic measure", *ṣuwāʕ* "cup"; *ṣəwwāʕ* (Eth.) "cup, goblet". Non-Sem.: Cf. (GIŠ) *zau=* (Hitt.) "a type of plate".[611]
ṣāʕ "plate, bassin"	•CTX: **UGS** *ṣa-(a-)i*, pl. *ṣa-ʔa-tu* → AHw p. 1087; CAD Ṣ 65; Sivan GAGl 268; Huehnergard UVST 170; vSoldt SAU 307 (124).
ṣʕ "plate, bassin"	•CTX: **UGA** → DUL 764f.
ṣāʕy "a type of plate"	•CTX: **EUPH** Cf. *za-a-yu(-um)* → Durand MARI 7 377 fn. 3; Guichard ARM 31 218. 295ff.; Guichard RA 98 23.
ṣāʕt "a vessel"	•CTX: **EM** (DUG.ḪA) *ṣa-tù/tu₄* → Fleming Installation 146 fn. 248 (*za-du*); Pentiuc Vocabulary 162.

|ṣ-w/y-d|	Sem.: *ṣwd* (Hb.) "to hunt", *ṣyd* (*ṣayid*) "game, venison", *ṣyd* (*ṣayyād*) "hunter"; *ṣd* (Pun.) "hunt (offering), game" (?); *ṣwd* (Aram., Syr.) "to take game, catch; to grasp, hold fast", *ṣyd(ʔ)* (Aram., Syr.) "hunter", *ṣyd(ʔ)* (Aram., Syr.) "game, provisions", *ṣwd* (Syr.) "provisions"; *ṣâdu(m)* (Akk.) "to prowl, roam (around); turn", *ṣayyādu* "vagrant, hunter", *ṣāʔidu(m)*, *ṣayyidu* "roaming, restless"; *ṣāda* (*ṣayd*, Arab.) "to catch, trap, hunt", *ṣayd* "game, venison", *ṣāʔid*, *ṣayyād* "hunter"; *ṣyd* (OSArab.) "game; (ritual) hunt"; *əṣtəyūd*, *əṣtəd* (MSArab.) "to fish".
|ṣ-w/y-d| "to hunt; to scour, comb"	•CTX: **UGA** G prefc. *åṣd*, *tṣd*, *tṣdn*, *yṣd*, inf. *ṣd*, (?) act. ptc. fem. *ṣwdt* → DUL 767: /*ṣ-d*/. •ONOM: **U3** Cf. unc. *e-zi-da-nu-um* (rdg ?) → Gelb CAAA 34, 196 (ṢJID, 1649 I).[612]
ṣaw/yd "round(s) (?)	•CTX: **EM** Cf. *ṣa-du* → Fleming Installation 269.
ṣāyid "hunter, vagrant"	•ONOM: **B** Cf. *za-i-di-im*, fem. *za-i-da-tum* → Gelb CAAA 34, 196.
ṣayyād "hunter"	•ONOM: **EB** *za-a-ti* → Pagan ARES 3 171, 382. B *za-ia-du-um*, *za-a-da-an* → Gelb CAAA 34, 196.
ṣd (A) "hunt, game"	•CTX: **UGA** Sg. *ṣd*, suff. *ṣdk* → DUL 767: *ṣd* (I).
ṣd (B) "roamer, vagrant" (?)	•CTX: **UGA** → DUL 767: *ṣd* (II).
ṣdt "roaming, hunting party" (?)	•CTX: **UGA** Cf. suff. *b ṣdtk* → DUL 768: "?"
mṣd (B) "(feast of) game"	•CTX: **UGA** Sg. *mṣd*, suff. *mṣdy*?, *mṣdk*, *mṣdh* → DUL 578 *mṣd* (I).

|ṣ-w-γ| Cf. **|ṣ-γ-w|**	Sem.: Cf. *ṣʕṣʕym* (*ṣaʕᵃṣuʕîm*, Hb.) "casting, cast"; *ṣāġā* (*ṣawġ*, Arab.) "to form, shape, mold".
ṣiγṣiγt "cast figurine (jewel)"	•CTX: **EB** *zi-zi-ḫi-tum* → Pasquali QuSe 23 183f.

[611] Tischler HethEtymGl 679f.: (GIŠ) *zau=* "eine Art Teller oder Platte".

[612] Vacat. Buccellati Amorites; cf. op.cit. 84, 144 rdg *e-bi-da-nu-um*, and Gelb CAAA 54 (1595 U).

|ṣ-w/y-ḥ|	Sem.: *ṣwḥ* (Hb.) "to shout loudly", *ṣwḥh* (*ṣ^ewāḥāh*) "cry of lament"; *ṣwḥ* (JAram., Syr.) "to cry out", *ṣwḥh*, *ṣwḥtʔ* "shout"; *ṣāḥa* (*ṣayḥ*, Arab.) "to cry, yell, shout", *ṣayḥ*, *ṣayḥa*, *ṣiyāḥ* "cry, crying, outcry", *ṣayyāḥ* "crier, crying". See further *ṣawwəʕa*, *ṣawwəʔa* (Eth.) "to call (upon, out), shout, cry out".[613]
|ṣ-w/y-ḥ| "to exclaim, shout, call, claim" **ṣayaḥ** "outcry, loud cry" **ṣiyḥ** "shouting, crying"	•CTX: **UGA** G prefc. *åṣḥ*, *tṣḥ*, *htṣḥn*, *yṣḥ*, *tṣḥny*, suff. *åṣḥkm*, *yṣḥn*; suffc. *ṣḥ*, *ṣḥt*, *ṣḥ*, suff. *ṣḥtkm*, imp. *ṣḥ*, suff. *ṣḥn* → DUL 770 f.: */ṣ-ḥ/*. •ONOM: **UGA** *yṣḥn* → DUL 971.[614] •LL: **EB** ŠÀ.NE.DU(ŠA$_4$) = *za-a-ḫu-um* → Conti QuSe 17 165; Sjöberg Fs. Kienast 550. •ONOM: **EUPH**, **B** Unc. *zi-ḫa-tum*, *zi-ḫa-da*, cf. *ma-na-zi-a-tum* → Gelb CAAA 34 (ṢJḪ "to rejoice"), 196f. (ṢIJḪ).

|ṣ-w-l| (1)	Sem.: Cf. *ṣwlh* (*ṣûlāh*, Hb.) "abyss, depths", *mṣwlh* (*m^eṣûlāh*) "the deep, the depths"; *mṣlh*, *mṣwlh*, *mṣwltʔ* (Aram.) "depth, abyss".
ṣuwl "depth, abyss; DN ?"	•ONOM: Cf. **B** *zu-la-nu-um* → Gelb CAAA 203 (ZULAN); Zadok Fs. Hallo 329 (Ṣ-W/Y-L).

|ṣ-w-l| (2)
Cf. **|ṣ-l-l| (2)**

|ṣ-w-m|	Sem.: *ṣwm* (Hb.) "to fast", *ṣwm* (*ṣôm*) "fast"; *ṣwm* (Aram., Syr.) "to fast", *ṣwm(ʔ)* "fast"; *ṣām*, *ṣiyāma* (*ṣawn*, Arab.) "to abstain, fast", *ṣawm* "fast", *ṣāʔim* "fastener"; *ṣawm*, *ṣum*, *ṣíəm* (MSArab.) "to fast", *ṣawm*, *ṣuhm* "fasting"; *ṣwm*, *ṣoma* (Eth.) "to fast", *ṣom* "fast, fasting", *ṣəwwəm* "who fasts".
θ̣ēmēn "the little fastener" (?) **θ̣m** "fasting" **θ̣mn** "the little fastener" (?)	•ONOM: **UGS** Cf. unc. ZI-*me-ni*, ZÍ-*me-nu* (|θ̣āymān| ?) → Nougayrol PRU 6 147:2; Malbran-Labat RSOu 7 2 r. 2'; Huehnergard UVST 226. •CTX: **UGA** → DUL 987: *ẓm*. •ONOM: **UGA** Cf. unc. *ẓmn* → Huehnergard UVST 226; DUL 987.

|ṣ-w-n|
See **|ṣ-n-n| (1)**, **|ṣ-w-n|**

|ṣ-w-r|
See **|ṣ-r-r| (1)**, **|ṣ-w-r|**

|ṣ-y-ḥ|
See **|ṣ-w/y-ḥ|**

[613] For Akk. *ṣiāḫu(m)*, *ṣâḫu* "to laugh" see Militarev / Kogan SED 1 325.
[614] Add KTU 4.853:6.

s^1 (š)

|s^1|
|s^1-ʔ-b| Cf. |s-ħ-b|
|s^1-ʔ-l|
|s^1-ʔ-m|
|s^1-ʔ-n|
|s^1-ʔ-r| (1)
|s^1-ʔ-r| (2) Cf. |θ-ʔ-r|
|s^1-ʔ-r| (3)
|s^1-ʔ-y|
|s^1-ʕ-d| Cf. |s^2-d-w|
|s^1-ʕ-r|
|s^1-b-ʕ|
|s^1-b-ħ| Cf. |l-b-x|
|s^1-B-x-t|
|s^1-b-l|
|s^1-b-r| (1)
|s^1-b-r| (2)
|s^1-b-t|
|s^1-b-ṭ|
|s^1-b-y| (1)
|s^1-b-y| (2)
|s^1-d-d|
|s^1-D-G|, |s^1-G-D|
|s^1-d-l|
|s^1-d-m|
|s^1-d-n|
|s^1-d-p|
|s^1-d-θ|
|s^1-d-y|
|s^1-G-D| See |s^1-D-G|
|s^1-G-m|
|s^1-G-r| (1)
|s^1-g-r| (2)
|s^1-g-s^1|
|s^1-g-y|
|s^1-H-d|
|s^1-ħ-ḳ|
|s^1-ħ-l| (1)
|s^1-ħ-l| (2), |s^1-l-ħ|
|s^1-ħ-r| (1)
|s^1-ħ-r| (2)
|s^1-ħ-t|, |s^1-w/y-ħ|
|s^1-ħ-y|
|s^1-x-d|
|s^1-x-l|
|s^1-x-n|
|s^1-x-p|
|s^1-x-r|
|s^1-x-ṭ|
|s^1-x-w|
|s^1-x-w/y|
|s^1-k-b|
|s^1-k-H-n| Cf. |k-n-ʕ|
|s^1-k-ħ|
|s^1-k-k| (1)
|s^1-k-k| (2)
|s^1-k-n|
|s^1-k-r| (1)
|s^1-k-r| (2)
|s^1-ḳ-d| (1)
|s^1-ḳ-d| (2)
|s^1-ḳ-l|
|s^1-ḳ-p|
|s^1-ḳ-r|
|s^1-ḳ-y|
|s^1-l-ħ| (1)
|s^1-l-ħ| (2) See |s^1-ħ-l| (2), |s^1-l-ħ|
|s^1-l-ħ-p-w/y|
|s^1-l-ḳ|
|s^1-l-m| Cf. |s-l-m| (1)
|s^1-l-m-m|
|s^1-l-n|
|s^1-l-ṭ|
|s^1-l-w|
|s^1-m| (1)
|s^1-m| (2) Cf. |h-m|
|s^1-m-ʕ|
|s^1-m-x| (1)
|s^1-m-x| (2)
|s^1-m-l-l|
|s^1-m-m|
|s^1-m-(m-)n|
|s^1-m-n|
|s^1-m-r|
|s^1-m-S-k-l|

|s^{1}-m-s^{1}-m| (1)	
s^{1}-m-s^{1}-m (2)	
|s^{1}-m-w/y|	
|s^{1}-m-y|	See **|s^{1}-m-w/y|**
|s^{1}-n| (1)	
|s^{1}-n| (2)	
|s^{1}-n-m|	
|s^{1}-n-n|	
|s^{1}-n-S|	
|s^{1}-n-w/y|	
|š^{1}-n-y| (1)	
|s^{1}-n-y| (2)	See **|s^{1}-n-w/y|**
|s^{1}-p-ʔ|	
|s^{1}-p-H-l|	
|s^{1}-p-k|	
|s^{1}-p-l|	
|s^{1}-p(-p)-r|	
|s^{1}-p-r|	
|s^{1}-p-y|	
|s^{1}-r-ʕ|	See **|s^{2}-ʕ-r| (2)**
|s^{1}-r-b|	
|s^{1}-r-D|	
|s^{1}-r-d-n|	Cf. **|θ-r-t-n-n|**
|s^{1}-r-g|	
|s^{1}-r-γ|	
|s^{1}-r-H|	
|s^{1}-r-x-l|	
|s^{1}-r-r| (1)	
|s^{1}-r-r| (2)	
|s^{1}-r-r| (3)	
|s^{1}-r-r| (4)	
|s^{1}-r(-r)| (5)	
|s^{1}-r-s^{1}-r| (1)	
|s^{1}-r-s^{1}-r| (2)	
|s^{1}-r-t|	
|s^{1}-r-w/y|	
|s^{1}-r-w-n-s^{1}|	
|s^{1}-r-y|	See **|s^{1}-r-w/y|**
|s^{1}-s-y| (1)	
|s^{1}-s-y| (2)	
|s^{1}-s^{1}|	
|s^{1}-s^{1}-m-t(-t)|	
|s^{1}-s^{1}-n-n|	
|s^{1}-t|	Cf. **|ʔ/y-S-D|**
|s^{1}-t-G(-G)|	
|s^{1}-t-l|	
|s^{1}-t-m|	
|s^{1}-t-p|	
|s^{1}-t-y| (1)	
|s^{1}-t-y| (2)	
|s^{1}-ṭ-p|	
|s^{1}-ṭ-r|	
|s^{1}-w/y-ħ|	See **|s^{1}-ħ-t|**, **|s^{1}-w/y-ħ|**
|s^{1}-w-ḳ| (1)	
|s^{1}-w-ḳ| (2)	
|s^{1}-w-l|	
|s^{1}-w/y-p|	
|s^{1}-w-r| (1)	
|s^{1}-w-r| (2)	
|s^{1}-w-s^{1}|	
|s^{1}-w-ṭ|	
|s^{1}-w/y-ṭ|	
|s^{1}-w-y| (1)	
|s^{1}-w-y| (2)	
|s^{1}-y-B|	See **|s^{1}-w/y-p|**
|s^{1}-y-d|	
|s^{1}-y-ħ|	See **|s^{1}-w/y-ħ|**
|s^{1}-y-p|	See **|s^{1}-w/y-p|**
|s^{1}-y-r| (1)	
|s^{1}-y-r| (2)	See **|s^{1}-w/y-r|**
|s^{1}-y-t|	
|s^{1}-y-ṭ|	See **|s^{1}-w/y-ṭ|**

|s^{1}| — Sem.; Akk. loan: *šu*.[615]

s^{1}= "he of" — •ONOM: **UGA** *šbʕl* → DUL 792.[616]

|s^{1}-ʔ-b|
Cf. **|s-ħ-b|**

Sem.: *šʔb* (Hb.) "to draw water", *mšʔb* (*mašʔāb*) "trough, drinking pipe"; *šʔbh*, *šʔwbtʔ* (JAram.) "drawing water"; *s^{1}tʔb* (OSArab.) "to draw water"; *saʔaba* (Eth.) "to drag, pull"; cf. *sâbu*(*m*), *sâpu* (Akk., sibilant irregularity) "to draw water".

|s^{1}-ʔ-b| "to draw, carry water" — •CTX: **UGA** G prefc. *yšảbn, tšảbn*, inf. *šỉb*; act. ptc. m. *šỉb* (see below: *šỉb)*; act. ptc. fem. pl. *šỉbt* (see below: *šỉbt*) → DUL **783**f.: /*š-ʔ-b*/.

---

[615] Often denoting dependence and not family relation, as in Alalaḫ PN$_{1}$ *šu* PN$_{2}$ (against PN$_{1}$ *mār* PN$_{2}$); see Liverani AfO 48/49 181.

[616] Cf. RS-Akk. *šu*-^{d}IM, PRU 3 34 (RS 8.207) rev. 7; see Sivan GAGl 275, and GlOS 1 158: *ðū/ī/a* (|ð|).

s^{1}ōʔibt "vessel for water"	•CTX: **EA** *šu-i-ib-tá* → Rainey EAT 95; EAC 1346 (14 III 61); Sivan GAGl 274.
s^{1}åb, s^{1}ỉb, s^{1}ỉbt "water bearer, water carrier"	•CTX: **UGA** Pl. cstr. *šỉb*, *šåb*, fem. pl. abs. / cstr. *šỉbt* → DUL 784: *šå:ỉb*, *šỉbt*.
mas^{1}ʔab "watering place"	•ONOM: **EG** Elem. in TN *ma-ša-ʔaba$_{(3)}$(-ya)* → Hoch SWET 156 no. 205.[617]

|s^1-ʔ-l|	Sem.: *šʔl* (Hb.) "to ask, consult, claim", *šʔlh* (*š^{e}ʔēlāh*) "request", *mšʔlh* (*mišʔālāh*) "desire"; *šʔl* (Pun.,[618] Nab., Palm.) "to ask, interrogate; *šʔl* (Aram., Syr.) "to ask", *šʔlh* "what one asks for, request", *šʔwl(ʔ)* "questioner, one who requests", *šwʔl(ʔ)* (Syr.) "inquiring", *mšʔln* (Syr.) "interrogator", *mšʔlh, mšʔltʔ* "interrogation"; *šâlu(m), šaʔālu(m)* (Akk.) "to ask; to call to reckoning, punish", *šaltum* "interrogation", *šāʔilu* "asker; dream interpreter", *mašʔaltu* "questioning, interrogation", *muštālu(m)* "who considers, deliberate", *muštālūtum* "consideration, deliberation"; *saʔala* (Arab.) "to ask, inquire", *suʔl(a)* "demand, request, wish", *sāʔil* "questioner, beggar", *masʔala* "question", *musāʔla, tasāʔul* "questioning"; *s^{1}ʔl* (OSArab.) "to ask, request, claim", *sʔl(m)* "request, claim", *msʔl(m)* "oracle"; *sōl* (MSArab.) "to ask for payment of a debt"; *saʔala* (Eth.) "to ask, enquire, make a petition, beseech, beg", *səlat* "request, petition", *masʔəl* "who asks, petitioner, beggar, sorcerer, soothsayer", *məsʔāl* "petition, place of entreaty", *tasəlo(t)* "question, dialogue".
|S-ʔ-l| "to ask, inquire, beg"	•CTX:[619] **EB** G prefc. *iš-al-su* |yiSʔal=|, inf. *sa-al-li-iš, sa-a-li<-iš>-ki* |Saʔāl=| → Fronzaroli ARET 13 19, 26, 292; Catagnoti QuSe 29 60, 80, 113, 138, 150, 223. •LL: **EB** AD.GAR = *sa-da-um* |Sataʔlum / Satālum | "to discuss, converse" → Conti QuSe 17 87f.; cf. IGI.TÙR = *da-aš-da-ì*(? NI)*-lum* |taStaʔʔil=| → Krebernik QuSe 18 121; further Ù.EN = *tíš-tá-i-lum* → Kienast BaE 247f. •ONOM: **EB** |yiSʔal| *iš-al$_6$-li, iš-al$_6$-da-mu, iš-al$_6$-ma-lik*; |yiStaʔ(a)l| *iš-da-al$_6$, iš-da-lá* → Krebernik PET 61; Pagan ARES 3 171f., 339. **A7** Cf. unc. *ta-ša-al- qú-ni* → Wiseman AT 149; Arnaud AuOr 16 176.[620]
|s^1-ʔ-l| "to ask, request; to order a cultic reply, to require a cultic reply"	•CTX: **UGA** G prefc. *yšål*, *[y]šỉl* (?), *yšůl*, *tšål*; suffc. *šỉlt*, suff. *šỉln*; inf. *šål* (see below: *s^{1}ål*); Gt prefc. *yštål*, cf. *tštỉl* (?) → DUL 784f. */š-ʔ-l/*.
Saʔl "claim, request, demand"	•ONOM: **EUPH** *sa-li-ia, ša-la-nu-um, sa-li*-DINGIR, *sa-lu-ma-dar*, fem. *sa-la-tum* → Gelb CAAA 31, 181.
Saʔal "asked for, requested, desired, begged"	•ONOM: **EUPH** *sa-a-la* → Gelb CAAA 31, 180.
Sāʔil "diviner"	•ONOM: **EUPH**: Fem. *sa-i-la-tum, ša-il-tum* → Gelb CAAA 31, 180.
Saʔul "asked for, requested, desired, begged"	•ONOM: **EB** *sa/sá-ù-lum* → Krebernik PET 28; Pagan ARES 3 171f., 361f.

[617] Sivan / Cochavi-Rainey WSVES 81: *ma-ša-ʔab-u, ma-š^ə-ʔab* "scoop"; Helck Beziehungen no. 117.

[618] Writings *YSLYM* and *YSTHYALM* (with several vars) in Poenulus.

[619] For Mari *šaʔālum* mng·"faire exécuter" see Joannès ARM 26/2 245 fn. h.

[620] Arnaud loc.cit.: \|tašʔal=qūnī(?)\| "(La déesse) demande ma création".

Suʔʔul "carefully requested, desired, begged"	•ONOM: **EUPH** *su-ú-lu-um* → Gelb CAAA 31, 189.
s^1ål "claim, demand"	•CTX: **UGA** Pl. *šålm* → DUL 785: *šål*.
s^1ỉl "interrogator, cultic questioner, diviner"	•CTX: **UGA** → DUL 785: *šỉl* (I). •ONOM: **UGA** *šỉl* → DUL 785: *šỉl* (II).
Sāʔilt "diviner" (fem.)	•LL: **EB** Fem. EN.LI = *sa-il-tum* → Krebernik ZA 73 34, PIHANS 106 90; Bonechi QDLF 16 83; Catagnoti QuSe 29 38, 151, 223.
Saʔʔult "carefully requested, desired, begged" (fem.)	•LL: **EB** Fem. AL.ÈN.TAR = *sa-ul-tum*, *sá-ul-du-um* → Krebernik ZA 73 36, PIHANS 106 90 (VE 987!); Catagnoti QuSe 29 20, 27, 33, 151, 223.
muSaʔʔilt "who asks carefully, desires, begs" (fem.)	•CTX: **EB** *mu-sa-il-da* → Fronzaroli ARET 13 19, 292; Catagnoti QuSe 29 38, 115, 140, 151, 223.
maSʔal "oracle"(?)	•CTX: **UGS** Cf. A.ŠÀ.MEŠ *ma-aš-a-li* → Sivan GAGl 245; Huehnergard ^{1}UVST 180, ^{2}UVST 398.

|s^1-ʔ-m|	Sem.: *šâmu(m)*, *š/šaʔāmum* (Akk.) "to buy, purchase", *šāʔimum* "buyer", *šāmu(m)*, *šīmu* "purchased", *šīmu(m)* "purchase (price)". Cf. *sāma* (*sawm*) (Arab.) "to offer for sale".
Siʔm "price"	•CTX: **EB** Pl. obl. *si-mi* → Fronzaroli QuSe 13 149, ARET 13 91, 294; Catagnoti / Fronzaroli ARET 16 26 fn. 21, 32, 264; Catagnoti QuSe 29 108, 116, 226.
Saʔūm "bought" (?)	•ONOM: **EB** Cf. *sa-ù-mu*, *sá-ù-um*, *sá-ù-mu*, *ša-ù-um* → Pettinato AuOr 13 85; Pagan ARES 3 172, 361f., 367.

|s^1-ʔ-n|	Sem.: *šʔn* (Hb. D *šaʔᵃnan*) "to be quiet"; *šyn*, *šyn(ʔ)* (Aram., Syr.) "peace", *šyn* (Syr. D) "to make peace". See also *šanānu(m)* (Akk.) "to equal, rival"; *sənʔ* (Eth.) "peace", *snʔw*, *tasanāʔawa*, *tasanāʕawa* "to be at peace with".
|**S-ʔ-n**| "to be quiet, in agreement"	•CTX: **EB** G prefc. *ʔa₅-si-in* |ʔaSʔin|, *da-si-in* |taSʔin|, *ne-si-im* |niSʔin|; Gt prefc. [*da*]-*sa-da-an* |taStaʔin|, *ne-si-da-an* |niStaʔin| → Fronzaroli ARET 13 200, 288; Catagnoti / Fronzaroli ARET 16 33, 50, 219; Catagnoti QuSe 29 110, 143, 150f., 223.[621]

|s^1-ʔ-r| (1)	Sem.: *šʔr* (Hb.) "to be remaining, (N) "to remain over", (C) "to leave over"; *šʔr* (Aram.) "to remain", (JAram., Syr. Gt/ Dt) "to remain"; *saʔira* (Arab.) "to remain, be left"; *s^1ʔr* (OSArab.) "remainder".
|**s^1-ʔ-r**| "to remain (to be paid)"	•CTX: **UGA** Gt suffc. *ištỉr*, imp. (?) *ištỉr* → DUL 786: /*š-ʔ-r*/.

|s^1-ʔ-r| (2) Cf. |θ-ʔ-r|	Primary noun, Sem.: *šʔr* (*šᵉʔēr*, Hb.) "body, flesh, meat"; *šʔr* (Pun.) "meat, flesh"; *šīru(m)*, *šēru*, *tīru* (Akk.) "flesh, body, entrails".

[621] Obsolete: Fronzaroli SEb 5 108 n. 33; QuSe 13 137: **wašānum* "to know" (?).

Siʔr "flesh, entrails"	•CTX: **EB** *si-rí* |Siʔri|, |Siʔrī| → Catagnoti / Fronzaroli ARET 16 173, 264; Catagnoti QuSe 29 73(fn. 274), 226. •LL: **EB** É.DUR = *si-ru₁₂-um*, *ga-ba-ru₁₂* → Conti QuSe 17 118; Catagnoti QuSe 29 226.[622]
s^1iʔr "flesh, entrails"	•LL: **UGS** [Z]U = *ši-i-ru* = *ú-zi* = *ši-i-ru* → Huehnergard UVST 180; vSoldt SAU 307 (133), BiOr 47 731; cf. Sivan GAGl 281: ṮIʔRU.
s^1ỉr (A) "flesh"	•CTX: **UGA** Sg. *šỉr*, suff. *šỉrh* → DUL 786: *šỉr* (I).
|s^1-ʔ-r| (3)	Culture word, Sem. etym. unc. Non-Sem. Cf. šar (Sum.) "a unit of area".[623]
s^1ỉr (B) "unit of area measure"	•CTX: **UGA** Sg. *šỉr*, du. *šỉrm* → DUL 786: *šỉr* (II).
|s^1-ʔ-y|	Metath. of CSem. |s^1-w-ʔ|: Cf. *šwʔ* (Hb. C) "to treat badly" (?), *šāw(ʔ)* "worthless; destruction, magic"; *sāʔa*, *sawāʔa* (Arab.) "to be evil, wicked", *sayiʔ*, *sayyiʔ* "bad, evil"; *s^1wʔ* (OSArab.) "evil, ill, adverse"; *sayʔa* (Eth.) "to commit a depraved act", *sayəʔ*, *śayəʔ* "depraved act". See further *šhy* (Syr.) "to grow faint, be extinguished"; *saʔā* (*saʔw*, Arab.) "to tear by tugging; to cause a rift".
|**S-ʔ-y**| "to lay desolate" (?)	•LL: **EB** Cf. ŠÀ.GAR = *ša-u₉* → Sjöberg Fs. Kienast 538f.
s^1ỉy "murderer"	•CTX: **UGA** → Renfroe AULS 143f.; DUL 787: *šỉy* (I).
|s^1-ʕ-d| Cf. |**s^2-d-w**|	Sem.: *šd* (*šēd*, Hb. loanword) "demon"; *šēdu(m)* (Akk.) "protective deity, luck";[624] *saʕada* "to be favourable", *saʕida*, *suʕida* "to be happy, lucky" (Arab.), *saʕd* "good luck", *saʕīd* "happy, lucky".
Saʕd "protective deity, luck; DN"	•ONOM: **EB** Cf. *sa-du*, *sa-du-um*, *sá-du-um*, *a-sa-sa-du*, *sa-da*-NE-*iš*, NI-*sa-du*, NI-*a-sa-du* → Krebernik PET 105, 279; Pagan ARES 3 233f., 283, 328f., 360.[625]
s^1d (C) "demon; DN"	•CTX: **UGA** (Akkadism) → DUL 798: *šd* (III).
|s^1-ʕ-r|	Primary noun, Sem. *šʕr* (*šaʕar*, Hb.) "weight (of grain)", *šʕr* (*šaʕar*) "to calculate"; *šʕr(ʔ)* (Aram.) "estimate, fixed measure, market price", *šʕr* (JAram. D) "to estimate, calculate"; *siʕr* (Arab.) "price, rate", *saʕʕar* "to value, rate".
s^1aʕar "market price"	•CTX: **EG** *ša-ʕa-r* → Hoch SWET no. 389.

[622] See also *Sēr*, *Sīr* "song" (\|s^1-y-r\|) for alleged onom. material from Ebla (Pagan ARES 3 236).
[623] Powell RlA 7 479.
[624] For Mari see Durand REA 303. Cf. 1 ALAN *še-di-im*, Arkhipov ARM 32 407 (M.10463: 4).
[625] Note that *ša*, *sa* and *za* are spellings rendering different phonemes; see Catagnoti QuSe 29 20f. In some instances these PNN could be read \|Sadaw=\| "mountain; DN" (cf. \|s^2-d-w\|).

|s^1-b-ʕ|	Primary noun, Sem.: *šbʕ* (*šebaʕ*, Hb.) “seven”, *šbyʕy* (*šᵉbîʕî*) “seventh”, pl. *šbʕym* (*šibᵉʕîm*) “seventy”; *šbʕ* (Ph., Pun., Moab., Nab., Palm.) “seven”, *šbʕm* (Pun., Palm.) “seventy”; *šbʕ* (Aram., Syr.) “seven”, *šbyʕy* “seventh”, pl. *šbʕyn* “seventy”; *sebe, seba, šabe* (Akk.)[626] “seven”, *sebû(m), šibû, šabû, sabāʔiu* “seventh”, *sebettu* “group of seven”, *sebūtum* “seventh day”, *sebîšu, šabîšu, šibîšu* “seven times”; *sabʕa* (Arab.) “seven”, *sabbaʕa* “to make sevenfold, to divide into seven parts”, *sābiʕ* “seventh”, pl. *sabʕūn* “seventy”, *s^1bʕ* (OSArab.) “seven”; *hōba, sōʕ, yhóbəʕ* (MSArab.) “seven”, *hōbaʔ, šīʕ, hēbaʔ* “seventh”, pl. *səbʕay, səbʕīn* “seventy”;. *sabʕ, səbʕ, sabʕu* (Eth.) “seven”, *sbʕ, sabbəʕa* “to make seven”, *sābəʕāwi* “seventh”, pl. *sabʕā* “seventy”.
|**s^1-b-ʕ**| **(A)** “to repeat for the seventh time”	•CTX: **UGA** D prefc. *yšbʕ* → DUL 790: */š-b-ʕ/* (I).
Sabaʕ “seven”	•ONOM: **EB** Cf. *sá-ba* → Pagan ARES 3 234, 361.
s^1bʕ (A) “seven”	•CTX: **UGA** Sg. *šbʕ*, fem. *šbʕt*; pl. *šbʕm* → DUL 790ff.: *šbʕ* (I); 792f.: *šbʕm* (pl., see below: *s^1bʕm*).
s^1bʕ (B) “seventh”	•CTX: **UGA** Sg. *šbʕ*, fem. *šbʕt* → DUL 792: *šbʕ* (II).
s^1bʕm “seventy”	•CTX: **UGA** → DUL 792f.: *šbʕm*.
Sebuʕt “the seventh day of the month”	•CTX: **EUPH** Cf. *se-bu / se-bu-ut se-bi-im* → Charpin NABU 1989/93; AfO 40/41 15f.[627]
Sabaʕt “septenary”(?)	•CTX: **EB** Sg. *sa-ba-tum*, pl. obl. *sa-ba-a-ti-im* |Sabaʕāt=|, suff. *sa-ba-a-ti-su-ma* |Sabʕātī=|, du. suff. *sa-ba-da-su-ma* |Sabaʕtay=| → Stieglitz Eblaitica 4 212f.; Fronzaroli QuSe 15 19; ARET 11 166; Catagnoti QuSe 29 78, 86, 112, 119, 224. See also Catagnoti Studia Eblaitica 5 15ff.
s^1ebʕi “seven”	•CTX: **A4** *še-eb-i* (Idrimi 29, 45) → AHw 1033: *sebe*; Giacumakis AkkAl 104 § 3.10.
s^1bʕ(ī)d “seven times”	•CTX: **UGA** *šbʕd, šbʕid*, suff. *šbʕdm* → DUL 792: *šbʕ(i)d.*
s^1ibʕitān “seven times”	•CTX: **EA** *ši-bi-ta-a-an, ši-ib-e/i-ta-an* (EA 211:4; 215:6; 196:4) → Rainey CAT 1 46, 186, 194.
ms^{1}bʕ “the seventh, taken in seventh place”	•CTX: **UGA** Fem. sg. suff. *mšbʕthn* → DUL 582: *mšbʕt.*

|s^1-b-ḥ| Cf. |**l-b-x**|	Sem.: *šbḥ* (Hb. D) “to sing praises, laud”; *šbḥ* (Hatra, Palm., D) “to praise”; *šbḥ* (Aram., Syr. D) “to praise”,[628] *šbḥ, šwbḥʔ* “praise”, *šbyḥ* (Syr.) “praised, praiseworthy”; *sabbaḥa* (Arab.) “to praise, extol”; *sabbəḥa* (Eth.) “to praise, extol”, *səbbuḥ* “praised”, *səbḥat, sabbəḥo* “glory, praise”.
|**S-b-ḥ**| “to praise”	•LL: **EB** Cf. ŠÀ.KALAG = *dal-da-bí-ḫum* |taStab(b)iḥum| → Krebernik StEb 7 195; Conti QuSe 17 166.[629]
|**s^1-b-ḥ**| “to praise”	•ONOM: **EG** *ya-sa-ba-ḥa* |yas^{1}baḥa| → Hoch SWET 55 no. 59.

---

[626] Note the irregular consonantal correspondence; see vSoden GAG 30 § 30.d; Faber JCS 37 106 fn. 34: the change *\|s^1\| > \|s^3\| may have been catalized by the labial \|b\|.
[627] Charpin loc.cit.: “septième jour (*sebûtum*) du septième (mois) (*sebûm*)”.
[628] Akk. *šubbuḫu* “to praise God”.
[629] Sjöberg Fs. Pettinato 265 reads À.KAL = *tal-ta-bi-ḫum*, from \|l-b-x\| “to be fleshy, corpulent, fat” (see there).

Sabiḥ "praiseworthy"	•ONOM: **EUPH** *sa-bi-ḫu-um* → Zadok Fs. Hallo 329.
Subāħ, Subūħ "praise"	•LL: **EB** IGI.ÁR = *su-ba-um, su*(!)*-bu$_x$-um* → Conti QuSe 17 12, 185; Bonechi / Catagnoti Fs. Sommerfeld / Krebernik 169f.
ås^{1}bħ "most praiseworthy"	•ONOM: **UGA** *åšbḥ* → Gröndahl PTU 75; DUL 112 (*åšbú*, wrong).
|s^1-B-x-t|	Culture word, etym. unc.
s^{1}uBxat "a golden ornament"	•CTX: **Q** *šu*-UB-*ḫa-tu*$_4$, *šu*-UB-*ḫa-tù* → Bottéro RA 44 120; AHw 1280: *šupḫatu*; CAD Š/3 172: *šubḫatu*.
|s^1-b-l|	Primary noun, Sem.: *šblt* (*šibbolet*, Hb.) "ear of grain"; *šblh, šblt?* (JAram., Syr.) "ear of grain", *šbl* (Syr. D) "to make a stem"; *šubultu*(*m*), *šubiltu* (Akk.) "ear"; *sabal, sunbul* (Arab.) "ears", *sanbala, ʔasbala* "to form ears"; *s^{1}blt* (OSArab.) "ears"; *səbəlēt, sebólet* (MSArab.) "ear (of rice)"; *sabl* "ear of corn" (Eth.), *sabla* "to grow, ripen".
s^{1}abal, s^{1}ubl "spikes (of fruit trees), shoots"	•CTX: **EG** *sa-ba*$_{2/4}$*-r* → Hoch SWET 258f. no. 365.[630] •ONOM: **EUPH** Cf. *sa-ba-la* → Collon CWAS 3 258; cf. Zadok Fs. Hallo 329.[631]
Sabalt "ear"	•LL: **EB** SÙ.PA.SIKIL = *sa-ba-tum* → Fronzaroli QuSe 15 20, 33; Sjöberg Fs. Oelsner 411 (fn. 8).
s^{1}blt "ear, spike (of corn)"	•CTX: **UGA** Sg. / pl. *šblt* → DUL 793: *šblt*.
|s^1-b-r| (1)	Culture word, Sem.: *šibirru*(*m*), *šipirru* (Akk.) "shepherd's staff, sceptre". Non-Sem.: šibir (Sum.) "staff".[632]
s^{1}br "stick, staff"	•CTX: **UGA** Sg. suff. *šbrh*, (?) pl. *šbrm* → DUL 794: *šbr*; Watson Fs. Postgate 709; UF 50 425.t
|s^1-b-r| (2)	Etym. unc.[633]
Subar "handle (of a tool)"	•CTX: **EUPH** *šu-ba-ar ḫa-ṣi-ni, šu-ba-ru pa-ši* → Arkhipov ARM 32 143f., 482 (I 8, 9).
|s^1-b-t|	Sem.: Cf. *šbt* (Hb. G) "to cease, stop" (C) "to put to an end, remove"; *šbt* (Pun. C) "to destroy". Lexical Hebraisms: *šbt* (JAram., Syr.) "to cease from doing something, observe the Sabbath"; *sabata* (Arab.) "to rest, keep the Sabbath", *sanbata* (Eth.) "to take a rest", *ʔasanbata* "to keep the Sabbath".
|s^1-b-t| "to stop, detain, suspend" (?)	•CTX: **UGA** D suffc. suff. *šbtm* → DUL 795: */š-b-t/*.

630 Sivan / Cochavi-Rainey 84: *šá-bi-r* "branch"; Helck Beziehungen no. 191.
631 Diff. explanation: Hb. *šbyl*, Aram. *šbyl?*, Arab. *sabīl* "way".
632 Cf. the logogr. writing GIŠ.(GÚ.)ŠUBUR, CAD S/2 170: *šubaru*.
633 Cf. GIŠ.(GÚ.)ŠUBUR, CAD S/2 170: *šubaru*.

|s^1-b-ṭ| Primary noun, Sem.: *šbṭ* (*šēbeṭ*) "stick, rod, tribe", *šbṭ(ʔ)* "stick, rod, tribe"; *šibṭu* (Akk.) "blow, epidemic", *šabbitu* "staff, sceptre"; *s^{1}bṭm* (OSArab. pl.) "strokes, blows"; *səbṭ* (Eth.) "pointed rod". Secondary derivatives: *šbṭ* (JAram., Syr. D) "to engrave, straighten, beat"; *šabāṭu(m)* (Akk.) "to beat, sweep (away)"; *səbūṭ*, *səṭ* "to beat, hit", *zabaṭa* (Eth.) "to strike, beat".

s^{1}ibṭ "staff; rod" •CTX: **EG** *ši$_2$-b-da$_2$*, *ši$_2$-b-d*, *ši$_2$-ba-d*, *ši$_2$-b-di*, *ši$_2$-b-di-ya*, etc.; metath.: *ši$_2$-d-b*, *ši$_2$-ta-ba* → Hoch SWET 276ff. no. 397.[634]

s^{1}abbuṭ "staff" •LL: **EM** (GI) MIN.IZI.LÁ = *gi-zi-lu-u* :*šab-bu-ṭu* → Pentiuc Vocabulary 170; Cohen Proceedings 53^e RAI 1 828.

|s^1-b-y| (1) Culture word, Sem.: *šbw* (*š^{e}bû*, Hb.) "agate"; *šubû(m)*, *šabû* (Akk.) "a semiprecious stone".[635]

s^{1}ubay "a precious stone, agate (?)" •CTX: **EG** Cf. Pl. (?) *šu$_5$-ba-ya* → Hoch SWET 275f. no. 395.

|s^1-b-y| (2) Sem.: Cf. *šbh* (Hb.) "to deport", *šbyh* (*šibyāh*) "captivity, captive", *šbyt* (*š^{e}bît*) "captivity"; *šby* (Aram., Syr.) "to take captive", *šby* (Syr.) "captive", *šby*, *šbyʔ*, *šbytʔ* (JAram., Syr.) "captivity", *šbwy*, *šbwʔh* (JAram.) "captor"; *sabā* (*saby*, Arab.) "to take prisoner", *sabīy* "captive", *saby* "capture, captivity"; *s^{1}by* (OSArab.) "to take captive", *s^{1}by* "captive".

|S-b-y| "to take captive" •ONOM: **EUPH**, **B** Cf. *ia-aš-bi*-DINGIR, *ia-aš-bi-i-la*, *iš-bi-*$^{(d)}$*ìr-ra* → Gelb CAAA 31 (ŠBJ), 186.

|s^1-b-y| "to take captive" •ONOM: **EG** Cf. *yw-m-n-ꜣ-š-f-ty* ^{F} → Schneider APÄQ 22 no. 21 (b).

s^{1}by "captive •CTX: **UGA** Sg. suff. *šbyn* → DUL 795: *šby*; Watson Fs. Postgate 712.

|s^1-d-d| Culture word, Sem.: *šiddu(m)* (Akk.) "(longer) side (of a piece of immovable property)".

s^{1}idd "a measure of area" •CTX: **A4** *ši-dum* → Giacumakis AkkAl 104; CAD Š/2 407: *šiddu* B, 3.b; Westenholz Emar Tablets XIV.
EM *ši-id-du*/*dum* → CAD Š/2 407: *šiddu* B, 3.b; Westenholz Emar Tablets XIV.

s^{1}d (B) "a measure of area" •CTX: **UGA** → DUL 797f.: *šd* (II).

|s^1-D-G|, |s^1-G-D| Sem. with several lexicalized allomorphisms:[636] Cf. *štq* (Hb.) "to grow silent", and *šqṭ* "to be at rest, quiet", *šqṭ* (*šeqeṭ*) "peacefulness"; *štq* (Aram., Syr.) "to be quiet", (D) "to silence", and *šqṭ* (JAram.) "to rest from activity, dwell in calm", *šqṭ(ʔ)* (Syr.) "quiescence"; *sakata* (Arab.) "to be silent, become quiet". See further: *šaqāṭu(m)* (Akk.) "to make fall, trip up"(?), and *sakātu(m)* (Akk.) "to be

[634] Sivan / Cochavi-Rainey WSVES 85: *šá-b-d* / *šá-ba-da* "staff"; Helck Beziehungen no. 220; Kilani VGW 113:|švb'adyv|, |švb'a:dv|, 125: |švb'ad|, |švb'o:dv|, pl. |švb'o:dv|, |švb'adyv|.
[635] Note NA$_4$.SUBA(ZA + MÙŠ)$^{(ša-bi)}$ = *ša-bu*, MSL 10 42 126 (Ras Shamra recension of ḪAR-ra XVI).
[636] Tropper UG 97.

silent";[637] *saqaṭa* (Arab.) "to fall, drop (dawn), tumble", *saqṭa* "fall, tumble"; *səḳáwṭ* (MSArab.) "to be a worthless fellow", *sɔḳɔṭ* "to fall, fail".

|S-ḳ-ṭ| "to cease, be quiet; to cede"
●ONOM: **EUPH, B** *ye-eš-ki-it-an*, *ia-aš-ki-iṭ*-DINGIR → Huffmon APNMT 253; Gelb CAAA 33, 188; Zadok Fs. Hallo 330; Golinets Onomastikon 2 36, 121, 454, 492.

Saḳṭ "calm, stillness" (?)
●ONOM: **B** Cf. *ša-aq-ti* → Gelb CAAA 33, 185.

|s^1-t-k| "to cease, be quiet; to cede"
●CTX: **UGA** G inf. *štk*; Gt suffc. / inf. *ištk* → DUL 838f.: /*š-t-k*/.[638]

|s^1-d-l|
Sem.: *sadala* (Arab.) "to let down, drop", *sidl* "veil, curtain".

Sidilt "pendant"
CTX: **EB** *si-ti-tum*, pl. *si-ti-a-tum* → Pasquali QuSe 23 175f.

|s^1-d-m|
Sem.: *šdmh* (*šᵉdēmāh*, Hb.) "terrace".

s^1dmt "terrace"
●CTX: **UGA** Sg. / pl. *šdmt*, suff. *šdmth* → DUL 799: *šdmt*.

|s^1-d-n|
Culture word, Sem.: *šdnʔ* (Syr.) "hematite"; *šadānu*(*m*), *šaduānum* (Akk.) id.

s^1adan "hematite" (?)
●LL: **EM** ZA.KI.I[N] NA₄ ZA.GÌN = *uq-nu :ša-a-da-*[*nu*?] → Pentiuc Vocabulary 165 (with reservations); Cohen Proceedings 53ᵉ RAI 1 828 (non local).[639]

|s^1-d-p|
Sem.: Cf. *šdp* (Hb.) "to dry out", *šdph* (*šᵉdēpāh*) "scorching heat"; *ʔasdafa* (Arab.) "to become shaded, be dark", *sidāfa* "a veil or covering". Cf. *šzb* (Hb.) "to turn brown, scorch".

Sidipt "a veil or covering" (?)
●LL: **EB** TÚG.MU / MU.TUG = *si-díb-tum* → Sjöberg Fs. Pettinato 273. See also Pasquali NABU 1996/128.

ʔus¹dupp "plaque"
●CTX: **EM** NA₄ *uš-dup-pu* → CAD U/W 326: *uštuppu*.
●LL: **EM** [... *d*]*u-up-pu* = *uš-du-pu* → Pentiuc Vocabulary 191 (rdg *uš*-DU-TE); CAD U/W 326: *uštuppu*.

niSdupp "plaque"
●CTX: **EUPH** *ni-iš-ta-ap*, *ni-iš-du-up*; also written GIŠ.DUB(*-pu*/*pí*) → Arkhipov ARM 32 51f.

|s^1-d-θ|
Primary noun, Sem.: *šš* (*šēš*, Hb.), *ššh* (*šiššāh*) "six", *ššy* (*šiššî*) "sixth; sixth part", *ššym* (*šiššîm*) "sixty"; *šš* (Pun.), *št* (Nab., Palm.) "six", *ššm* (Pun., Nab., Palm.) "sixty"; *št*, *ʔštʔ* (Aram., Syr.) "six", *ʔšty*, *štyty* "sixth", *štyn*, *ʔštyn* "sixty"; *sediš*, *še*/*iššet* (Akk.) "six", *šeššu*(*m*), *šiššu*(*m*), *šedištum* (fem. OAkk.), *šadāšium* "sixth; one-sixth", *šūši*, *šūš*, *šūša*, *šuššu* "sixty"; *sitta* (Arab.) "six", *sādis* "sixth", *suds*, *sudus* "one-sixth", *sadasa* "to be the sixth", *saddasa* "to make six (times)", *sittūn* "sixty"; *s^1t*, *s^1ṯ* (OSArab.) "six", *s^1dṯ* "sixth", *s^1ty*, *s^1ṯy*, *s^1dṯy* "sixty"; *hət*, *yətēt*, *šīdət* (MSArab.) "six", *šədṯēt* "sixth", *stayn*, *stīn* "sixty"; *səds*, *səssu*, *səddəstu* (Eth.) "six", *sādes*, *sādəsāwi* "sixth", *səssā* "sixty", *saddasa* "to make six (times)".

---

[637] For Akk. *šaqātu* see CAD Š/1 14 (mng unc.), and cf. AHw 1179: "zu Fall bringen".
[638] See also |n-t-k|.
[639] Note the odd *ša-a=* spelling.

|θ-d-θ| "to repeat for the sixth time"	•CTX: **UGA** D prefc. *yṯdṯ*, pass. ptc. *mṯdṯt* (see below: *mθdθ*) → DUL 887: */ṯ-d-ṯ/*.
θθ "six	•CTX: **UGA** Sg. *ṯṯ*, *šš*. fem. *ṯṯt*, du. *ṯṯtm*; pl. *ṯṯm* "sixty" (see below: *θθm*) → DUL 922ff.: *ṯṯ*; Tropper UG 347.
θdθ "sixth"	•CTX: **UGA** → DUL 887: *ṯdṯ*.[640]
θaθθa "sixth" (?)	•ONOM: **EB** Cf. *ša-ša-su* → Pagan ARES 3 239, 367.
θθm "sixty"	•CTX: **UGA** → DUL 924: *ṯṯm*.
mθdθ "the sixth"	•CTX: **UGA** Fem. *mṯdṯt* → DUL 596: *mṯdṯt*.

|s¹-d-y|	Sem.: *šdy* (Palm. Gt) "to be cast out, expelled"; *šdy* (Aram., Syr. G) "to throw".
|s¹-d-y| "to pour"	•CTX: **UGA** G impv. *šd*; (?) Gt prefc. *yštd* → DUL 799: */š-d-y/*.

\|s¹-G-D\|
See \|**s¹-D-G**\|

|s¹-G-m|	Sem.: Cf. *šgm* (Syr.) "to impact", *šgm(?)* "hard force, very heavy rains"; *šagāmu(m)* (Akk.) "to roar", *šāgimu* "braying (donkey)", *šagīmu* "roaring, clamor"; *sağama* (Arab.) "to flow, stream".
|s¹-g-m| "to rage, roar" (?)	•CTX: **EG** Cf. *h-s-mi₃-q(u₂)* |has¹gimu| (?C) → Hoch SWET 218f. no. 301.[641]
s¹agm "uproar, thunder"	•CTX: **EM** EN *šag-ma* → Pentiuc Vocabulary 170f.
s¹km "one who brays"	•CTX: **UGA** → DUL 803: *škm*.

|s¹-G-r| (1)	Culture word, Sem.: Cf. *šakarûm*, *šagarû*, *šag/krû* (Akk.) "a metal object", *šekarû*, *šakaraḫḫu* (Nuzi-Akk.) "a metal object". Non-Sem. Cf. **šagare* (*šgr*, loan in Hurr., origin unknown) "a cultic vessel of metal".[642]
SaGariy "a metal object (container ?)"	•CTX: **EUPH** Cf. *ša-ka-ri-im*, *ša-ka-ru-ú* → Arkhipov ARM 32 123. **A4** *ša-ga-ru-we-e* → Wiseman AT 79 (229:3); CAD Š/1 66: *šagaru*.
s¹kr "a kind of container"	•CTX: **UGA** Du. / pl. *škrm* → DUL 804f.: *škr*.

|s¹-g-r| (2)	Sem.: *šgr* (*šeger*, Hb.) "what is dropped, thrown"; *šgr* (Syr.) "to flow", (JAram., Syr., D) "to cast off, throw away", cf. *tgrʔ* (JAram.) "ditch", DN *šgr* ("offspring", Deir ʕAllā I 14); *saǧǧara* (Arab.) "to cause to overflow". Non-Sem.: Cf. Hurr. PN *Šaḫari*.[643]

---

[640] Read |θādiθu|. For an additional rdg |θadūθu| see Tropper UG 384f. "Sechszahl", collective.
[641] The writing could be related also to bases such as |g-s¹-m|, |g-ʕ-s¹|, |s¹-g-ʕ|.
[642] For Hurr.-Alph. *šgr* (KTU 1.131:13) see Dietrich Mayer UF 26 101: "metallenes Opfergefäss".
[643] Wilhelm AdS 4 110 (*šá-ḫa-ri*, 251:101); KlBHurr 389.

s^1agara "a body of water; ditch, dyke" (?)	•CTX: **EG** *ša-ga-r* → Hoch SWET 290 no. 415
s^1aggar "offspring; DN"	•CTX: **EM** *šag-gàr*, *ša-ag-ga-ru/ri*; ^{d}*ša-ag-ga-ar* → Pentiuc Vocabulary 165ff.[644]
s^1gr "offspring of cattle; DN"	•CTX: **UGA** → DUL 800: *šgr* (I), *šgr* (II).

|s^1-g-s^1|	Culture word, Sem.: *šigūšu*, *šēgūšu*, *šegušš u* (Akk.) "a type of barley".
SiguS(S) "a type of barley"	•LL: **EB** ŠE.MÙŠ =*zi-gú-sum* → CAD Š/2 262: *šeguššu*, end; Sjöberg Fs. Pettinato 267 (rdg *sí-*).

|s^1-g-y|	Sem.: Cf. *šgh* (Hb.) "to stray", *šgyʔh* (*š^{e}gîʔāh*) "oversight, transgression"; *šgʔ*, *šgy* (Aram., Syr.) "to err, be missing", (D, C) "to lead astray", *šgy(ʔ)* (Syr.), *šgw(tʔ)* (JAram.) "error"; *sak^{w}aya*, *sāk^{w}aya* (Eth.) "to go astray, wander about", *səykat* "going astray, wandering". See further: *sgy* (JAram.) "to go, walk".
|S-g-y| (A) "to go astray, roam; to swerve"	•CTX: **EUPH** G prefc. *i-sa-ag-gu-ú*, inf. *sa-gi-im* → CAD S 28: *sagû*; Kupper ARM 28 79:13, 15 (110ff.), 144:11 (203f.), 155:16 (225f.); Charpin AfO 40/41 3 (A.1307:69, Syria Suppl. 2/1 407f.); Streck Onomastikon 1 114 § 1.95. **EG**: Cf. *ha-s-t-ka-ta* (|haStaggata|) → Hoch SWET 220 no. 302: infixed doubled stem.[645]
Sagīt "roaming people"	•CTX: **EUPH** *sa-gi$_5$-tum* → Streck Onomastikon 1 114 § 1.95; diff. Kupper ARM 28 175f. (117:10): "gens razziés".[646]

|s^1-H-d|	Sem.: *šḥd* (Hb.) "to give a present"; *šḥd* (Aram., Syr.) "to bribe". For Akk. *šaḫādum* see below: |s^1-x-d|.
|s^1-H-d| "to give, present"	•CTX: **B** G prefc. *ta-aš-ta*-AḪ-*da* → AHw 1128: *šaḫādum*; CAD Š/1 75: *šaḫādu* "to bestow"; Zadok Fs. Hallo 330.

|s^1-ħ-ḳ|	Sem.: *šḥq* (Hb.) "to crumble, crush together", *šaħaḳ* "(layer of / clouds of) dust";*šḥq* (Aram., Syr.) "to grind"; *šêqu(m)* (Akk.) "to level off", *šīqu(m)* "levelling off"; *saḥaqa* (Arab.) "to crush", *saḥq* ""crushing, pulverization".
s^1aħaḳ "dust cloud; pulverized grain (a type of bread)"	•CTX: **EG** *ša-ḥa-qa*, *ša-ḥa-{ḥ}-q*, *ša-ḥa-qa-{-r}* → Hoch SWET 287f. no. 411.[647]

|s^1-ħ-l| (1)	Sem.: Cf. *sāḥil* (Arab.) "seashore".

[644] Probl. a Moon-God; see Theuer OBO 173 32, 115.
[645] Sivan / Cochavi-Rainey WSVES 83: *ha-ś-ta-ka-tá* "to tatter, stagger"; Helck Beziehungen no. 162: "hin und her schwanken", Hb. *škh*.
[646] Cf. CAD S 28: *sagû*; Kupper ARM 28 79:13, 15 (110ff.), 144:11 (203f.), 155:16 (225f.); Charpin AfO 40/41 3 (A.1307:69, Syria Suppl. 2/1 407f.).
[647] Kilani VGW 114: \|švḥ'i:/u:qv\|, 126: \|švḥ'i:/u:qv\|.

s^1ħlmmt "Mortality Shore" (?)	•ONOM: **UGA** → DUL 800: *šḥlmmt*; TN; mythical place of the divine dead, antechamber to the underworld (see |m-w-t|).

|s^1-ħ-l| (2), |s^1-l-ħ|	Sem.: *šêlu(m)* (Akk.) "to sharpen, whet", *šēltu, šessu* "sharp blade, point", *šēlūtu* "pointed blade", *mešēltu* "whetstone"; *saḥala* (Arab.) "to shave off, peel, scrape off", *misḥal* "file, brush, jack plane"; *səḥāl* (MSArab.) "to scratch; to grind a knife"; *saḥala* (Eth.) "to sharpen", *masḥal* "whetstone". Metath. derivatives of a basis |s^1-l-ħ|: *šlḥ* (Hb.) "to forge", *šlḥ* (*šelaḥ*) "a weapon, missile"; *silāḥ* (Arab.) "weapon".
|s^1-ħ-l| "to sharpen"	•LL: **EB** Ù.SAR.AK = = *sa-ʔà-lum, sa-ʔà-a-um* → Civil BaE 87; Sjöberg Fs. Pettinato 272f. Unlikely altern. Krebernik ZA 73 40: "new moon, month" (|s^2-h-r|).
ms^{1}lt (B) "a (sharp / sharpening) tool"	•CTX: **UGA** → DUL 584f.: *mšlt* (II); basis |s^1-ħ-l|.
|s^1-l-ħ| (B) "to laminate, forge"	•CTX: **UGA** G prefc. *yšlḥ* → DUL 805: */š-l-ḥ/* (II).
Silaħ "sword; DN" (?)	•ONOM: **EUPH** Cf. *še-la-ḫu-ra-bu-ú* → Zadok Fs. Hallo 330.
s^1lħ "sword; DN" (?)	•ONOM: **UGA** DN *šlḥ* → DUL 805; Watson Fs. Postgate 709.

|s^1-ħ-r| (1)	Primary noun, Sem.: *šḥr* (*šaḥar*, Hb.) "dawn"; *šḥrt* (Moab.) "dawn"; *šḥr(ʔ)* (JAram.) "early morning"; *šēru(m), šīru, ši(ʔ)ārum, šiyāru, šeāru, šērtu(m), šīrtu(m)* (Akk.) "morning"; *saḥar* (Arab.) "time before daybreak, dawn".
Saħ(a)r, Seħ(e)r "dawn"	•LL: **EB** UD.TE =*šè-er a-me-mu, ša-ar* UD → Fales QuSe 73 182; Krebernik ZA 72 216f.; ZA 73 29; PIHANS 106 87; UD(DÁG).DAG = *si-ʔe$_x$*(EN)*-lum* → Krebernik ZA 72 216f.; ZA 73 29; Conti QuSe 17 188f.; Sjöberg Fs. Wilcke 260f. **MŠ**: [*še*]*-e-ri* = *še-ḫe-ri* (VI 211, right and left columns reversed) → Hrůša MŠ 271.
s^1aħr, s^1iħr "dawn; DN"	•CTX: **EM** ^{d}*ša-aḫ-ri* → Pentiuc Vocabulary 167. •ONOM: **EM** *a-ia-ši-iḫ-ra* → Pruzsinszky PTEm 191 (fn. 415) [112].
s^1ħr "dawn; DN"	•CTX: **UGA** → DUL 801: *šḥr*. •ONOM: **UGA** *ilšḥr* → DUL 62.[648]

|s^1-ħ-r| (2)	Sem.: *šḥr* (Hb.) "to become black", *šḥr* (*šāḥor*) "coal-black", *šḥwr* (*š^{e}ḥôr*) "blackness" (?), *šḥrḥr* (*š^{e}ḥarḥor*) "darkish colour"; *šḥr* (Syr.) "to be black", (JAram., Syr. C) "blacken", *šwḥr(ʔ)* "black", *šḥyr* (JAram.) "black", *šyḥwr(ʔ)* (JAram.) "soot"; *šaḫḫara* (Arab.) "to soot, blacken with soot";[649] see also *mazḫart* (Eth.) "ebony".
Saħir "black, scorched (barley)"	•LL: **EB** ŠE.ZÌ.SA = *sa-i-lum, sa-ì-lu-um*; ŠE.ZÌ.ZÌ = *sa-ì-lu-um* → Conti QuSe 17 179; Catagnoti QuSe 29 17, 58, 120, 224.
ʔis^{1}ħar "black"	•ONOM: **EG** Cf. *yw$_2$-šꜣ-ḥ:-r-w$_2$* → Schneider APÄQ 44 no. 72.

[648] Note the PNN *ảbšḫr*, DUL 14, and *ʕbdšḫr*, DUL 140f.

[649] Eastern dialects; note the irregular consonantal correspondence; probl. < Aram.

|s^1-ħ-t|, **|s^1-w/y-ħ|**	Culture word, Sem.: *šḥt* (*šaḥat*, Hb.) "pit, trap", *šwḥh* (*šûḥāh*) "trapper's pit", *mšḥyt* (*mašḥît*) "snare for birds";[650] *ʔšwḥ* (Moab.), *ʔšḥt* (Amm.) "water reservoir, cistern"; *šwḥh* (JAram.) "pit"; *šuttatu*(*m*), *šuttu* (Akk.) "(hunter's) pitfall"; see also metath.: *ḫaštu*, *ḫaltu* (Akk.) "hole, pit".
Saħat "pitfall, trap"	•CTX: **EUPH** *sa-ḫa-tam*, *sa-ḫa-tim* → AHw 1008; CAD S 54; Limet ARM 25 282; Charpin AfO 40/41 4; Durand LAPO 16 350 fn. c; Zadok Fs. Hallo 330;[651] Streck Onomastikon 1 114 § 1.95.
s^1uttat "well, cistern" (?)	•CTX: **EM** Cf. A.ŠÀ [*q*]*í-i-ra* :*šu-ut-ta-ti*; TÚL :*šu-ut-te-ti* → Pentiuc Vocabulary 174f.
mas^1ħīta "trap, snare"	•CTX: **EG** *ma$_4$-sa-ta-ḥa* (metath.) → Hoch SWET 155f. no. 203.
|s^1-ħ-y|	Sem. etym. unc. Cf. *šḥh* (Hb.) "to stoop down" (C) "to subdue, oppress".[652]
|**s^1-ħ-y**| "to bend down" (?)	•CTX: **UGA** Ct prefc. *tštšḥ* → DUL 800: /*š-ḥ-y*/.
|s^1-x-d|	Sem.: *šḥd* (Hb.) "to give a present"; *šḥd* (Aram., Syr.) "to bribe"; Akk.: WSem. loanword, see below |s^1-x-d|.
|**s^1-x-d**| "to give, present"	•CTX: **EB** G inf. suff. *sa-ḫa-da-šum* → Fronzaroli ARET 11 34, 167; Catagnoti QuSe 29 82, 224. **B** G prefc. *ta-aš-ta-aḫ-da* → AHw 1128: *šaḫādum*; CAD Š/1 75: *šaḫādu*; Streck Onomastikon 1 117 § 1.95.
|s^1-x-l|	Sem.: *šḫl* (Syr.) "to drip", *šḫlh*, *šḫlt?* (Aram., Syr.) "strainer"; *šaḫālu*(*m*) (Akk.) "to sieve, filter", *šāḫilu* "strainer".
Sāxil "strainer"	•CTX: **EUPH** *ša-ḫi-li* → Arkhipov ARM 32 173f.
|s^1-x-n|	Sem.: *šḫyn* (*šeḫîn*, Hb.) "inflamed spot, boil"; *šḫn* (JAram., Syr.) id.; *šaḫānu*(*m*) (Akk.) id.; *saḫuna*, *saḫana*, *saḫina* (Arab.) "to be(come) warm, hot"; *səḫna*, *saḫana* (Eth.) id.
|**s^1-x-n**| "to be hot, to warm (oneself)"	•CTX: **UGA** G prefc. *yšḫn*, imp. *išḫn* → DUL 801f.: /*š-ḫ-n*/.
|s^1-x-p|	Sem. etym. unc. Cf. *šḫp* (JAram.) "to move slowly, crawl"; *saḫufa*, *saḫāfa* (Arab.) "to be weak, feeble, thin", *saḫfa*, *suḫfa* "weakness, thinness"; altern. *šḫp*(*ʔ*) (Syr.) "colostrum".
s^1xp "weakness, thinness / colostrum" (?)	•CTX: **UGA** (Bkn ctx.) Sg. *šḫp*, cstr. *šḫp*, suff. *šḫph* → DUL 802: *šḫp* "colostrum".

[650] The alleged connection with a verbal basis *šḥt* "to go to ruin, be(come) destroyed" is open to question.
[651] For the TNN *a-su-ḫi*, *a-ši-ḫi-im*, *a-šu-uḫ* see Zadok WO 14 237 fn. 3; Fs. Hallo 330.
[652] Arab. *saḥā* "to scrape off, unstick" is probl. unrelated, as well as Hb. *sḥh* (C) "to sweep away", and Eth. *sḥy*, *saḥaya*, *səḥya* "to rub, scrub".

|s^1-x-r|	Sem. etym. unc.
s^{1}ixr "(leather) brace, strap"	•CTX: **EUPH** *ši-iḫ-ru ša* GIŠ.GU.ZA → Durand ARM 30 170.
|s^1-x-ṭ|	Sem.: Cf. *šḥṭ* (Hb.) "to slaughter"; *šḥṭ* (Syr., D) "to damage, wound"; *šaḫāṭu*(m) (Akk.) "to tear away, off, down", *zaḫaṭû* (*m*) "battle-axe".[653] See also: *saḥaṭa* (Arab.) "to slaughter", *masḥaṭ* "gullet, throttle"; *saḥaṭa, səḥṭa* (Eth.) "to wound". Non-Sem. Cf. zaḫada (since OBab. Sum.) "axe".
s^{1}xṭ "butcher, slaughterer"	•CTX: **UGA** → DUL 802: *šḫṭ*.
maSxaṭ "butchers knife"	•CTX: **EB** Cf. *m*[*a*]-*sa*-[*ḫa-tum*] → Fronzaroli QuSe 15 20f.
mas^{1}xaṭ "a kind of (axe-shaped?) sail"	•CTX: **UGS** 7 TÚG.MEŠ GIŠ.MÁ.MEŠ *ma-áš-ḫa-ṭu-ma* → Sivan GAGl 245 (diff.: MAŠḪ/ḪAṬU "type of garment"); Huehnergard UVST 186, ^{2}UVST 399 (*maθḫatu* ?, pl. *maθḫatūma* ? "a cloth item"); vSoldt SAU 305 (92): "?"; Sanmartín UF 21 342.
ms^{1}xṭ "a kind of axe or cleaver"	•CTX: **UGA** → DUL 583: *mšḫṭ*.
|s^1-x-w|	Sem.: *šaḫāḫu*(*m*) (Akk.) "to be(come) loose, fall out"; see further *šwḥ* "to sink, collapse" (Hb.), *šḥh* "to stoop down", *šḥḥ* "to bow down, bent over"; *sāḫa* (Arab. *sawḫ*) "to be(come) slippery, sink (in the ground), be(come) faint, swoon".[654]
Saxwat "pendant"	•CTX: **EB** *sa-ḫa-wa* (vars *sa, sa-ḫa*) → Pasquali QuSe 23 173. •LL: **EB** GIŠ.GEŠTU.LÁ.KA = *sa-ḫa-wa-tum* → Fronzaroli MAARAV 5/6 118 fn. 27; Pasquali QuSe 23 35 fn. 165, 173; Sjöberg Fs. Kienast 547.
|s^1-x-w/y|	Primary noun, Sem.: *šḥy, šḥyt*(*?*) (JAram., Syr.) "armpit"; *šaḫātu*(*m*) (Akk.) "armpit"; *xōt, šxɔt / šɔt, šḥoh, məšxáwt* (MSArab.) "armpit".
Saxat, ?iSxat "armpit"	•LL: **EB** DA = *sa-ḫa-tum, iš-ḫa-tum* → Krebernik ZA 72 216; ZA 73 21; Conti QuSe 17 159; Catagnoti QuSe 29 20, 26, 39, 49, 59, 224.
|s^1-k-b|	Sem.: *škb* (Hb.) "to lie (down, with)", *mškb* (*miškāb*) "lodging place, bed", *škbh* (*šikbāh*) "what is laid down, layer"; *škb* (Ph., Pun.) "to repose, lie down", *mškb*(*?*) (Ph., Nab.) "lying. resting"; *škb* (Aram., Syr.) "to lie (down, with)", *mškb*(*?*) "bed", *škb*(*?*) "lying down"; *sakaba, sakba* (Eth.) "to lie (down, with)", *məskāb* "resting place, couch, bed", *səkub, səkbat* "(act of) lying down". Phonologically irregular: *sakāpu*(m) "to rest, lie down", *sakpu* "resting", *sākipu* "resting".
|S-k-b| "to lie down (for the night)"	•LL: **EB** Cf. Ù.SÁ.SÁ = *si-ga-bù-um* → Krebernik ZA 73 40; Catagnoti QuSe 29 48, 224. •ONOM: **EUPH** Cf. unc. ^{d}*iš-ḫa-ra-ta-aš-ku-ub* → Gelb CAAA 32 (ŚKB), 188.
|s^1-k-b| "to lie (down, with)"	•CTX: **UGA** G prefc. *yškb*, suffc. *škb* → DUL 802: */š-k-b/*.

[653] Hence Sum. zaḫada, see below: Non-Sem.

[654] Unrelated: *šwḥ, šḥy, šḥḥ* (JAram., Syr.) "to melt"; *šāḥa* (*sayḥ*, Arab.) "to run, flow; to melt"; *sayḥa* (Eth.) "to melt".

Sakb "resting" (?)	•ONOM: **EUPH** Cf. unc. *sa-ak-bi-ia*, *sa-ak-bi-*^{d}IM → Gelb CAAA 32, 181.
maSkabt "shelter for the night"	•CTX: **EUPH** Pl. *ma-áš-ka-ba-ti-šu-nu* → AHw 626: *maškabum*; Durand LAPO 17 426f. fn. d; Streck Onomastikon 1 105 § 1.95.[655]
ms¹kb(t) "place of rest, bed"	•CTX: **UGA** Sg. *mškb*, *mškbt* → DUL 583: *mškb*(*t*).
s¹akbarakba "upper and lower millstones"	•CTX: **EG** Cf. *š-ka-ba ra-ka-ba* (|šakba=rakba| ?) → Hoch SWET 289 no. 413.

|s¹-k-H-n| Cf. **|k-n-ʕ|**	Culture word, Sem.: *muškēnu*(*m*), *maškēnu* "a social designation; dependant, private individual"; prob. denom. *šukênu*(*m*), *šukaʔʔunu*(*m*), *šukennu* (Akk.) "to prostrate oneself, bow before someone; to submit to".
|s¹-x-x-n| "to get low, bow before someone"	•CTX: **EM** Prefc. *tu-uš-ḫé-ḫa-an*, *uš-ḫé-ḫa-nu* → CAD Š/3 218: *šukênu*, 2.b.2';[656] Pentiuc Vocabulary 185f. **EA** Prefc. *uš-ḫé-ḫi-in*, *uš-ḫe-ḫi-in*$_4$, *uš-ḫé-ḫi-in*$_4$, *aš-ḫi-ḫi-en*, cf. *ḫé-ḫi-in*$_4$ (defective ?); *t*-infix (?) prefc. *iš-ti-ḫi-ḫi-in*, *iš-ta-ḫa-ḫi-in*, *iš-ti-ḫa-ḫi-in*, *iš-tu-ḫa-ḫi-in* → AHw 1263: *šukênu*(*m*); CAD Š/3 218: *šukênu*, 2.b.2'; Rainey CAT 2 43, 109f., 185, 3 193. **UGS** Prefc. *uš-ḫé-ḫi-in* → Nougayrol Ugaritica 5 135 fn. 1; AHw 1263: *šukênu*(*m*); CAD Š/3 218: *šukênu*, 2.b.2'.
mas¹kēn "a social designation"	•CTX: **A4** *maš-ki-en* → Wiseman AT 162.

|s¹-k-ḥ|	Sem.: *škḥ* (Aram., Syr.) "to find".
|s¹-k-ḥ| "to find, meet"	•CTX: **UGA** G prefc. *tškḥ*; N prefc./ptc. *nškḥ* → DUL 803: /*š-k-ḥ*/.
Sakuḥ "found, met"	•ONOM: **EUPH** *sà-ku-ḫu-um* → Zadok Fs. Hallo 330.
Sukaḥ "found, met"	•ONOM: **EUPH** Cf. *sú-ka-ḫi-ia* → Zadok Fs. Hallo 330.
miSkiḥ "find, finding"	•ONOM: **EUPH** Cf. *mi-is-ki-ḫi* → Zadok Fs. Hallo 330

|s¹-k-k| (1)	Sem.: *škk* (Hb.) "to subside, lessen, quieten". See further: *tasaksaka* (Arab.) "to behave slavishly", *sakkwasa* (Eth.) "to come to an end, cease, recede".
Sakk "calm, quietness"	•ONOM: **EUPH** *sa-ak-ki-im* → Zadok Fs. Hallo 330.

|s¹-k-k| (2)	Sem.: *šakāku*(*m*) (Akk.) "to put in a line or row, thread (on string); to harrow", *šakku*(*m*) "harrowed", *šikkatu*(*m*) "harrowed (land)", *šakikātu* "strung row", *šikkūtu* "string of beads".
Sikkat "string of beads"	•CTX: **EUPH** *ši-ka-at*, *ši-ik-ka-at*, *ši-ka-tum/tim*, *ši-ik-ka-tum/tim*, *ši-ka-sú-nu* → Arkhipov ARM 32 99,

---

655 Cf. CAD 370a under *maškanu* 1.a.1': "threshing floor, empty lot" rdg *ma-áš-ka-na*(text *-ba*)*-ti-šu-nu*.

656 See op.cit., loc.cit. for references to Bogh. *ul-te-ḫé-ḫi-in*, *ul-tu*$_4$*-ḫé-ḫi-in*.

SiGGat "trimmings, a kind of lace"	•CTX: **EUPH** SÍG *ši-ka/qa-tum* BABAR → Durand ARM 30 152.
|s^1-k-n|	Sem.: *škn* (Hb.) "to settle, reside, dwell", *škn* (*šākēn*) "resident", *mškn* (*miškān*) "abode"; *škn* (Ph.) "to dwell, to reside"; *škn* (Aram., Syr.) "to inhabit, dwell", *škn* "dwelling-place", *sgn* (Aram.) "prefect, governor, chief", *mškn*(*?*) "tent"; *šakānu*(*m*) (Akk.) "to put, place; be placed, present, settled; provide, supply with", *šaknu*(m) "placed, governor", *šiknu*(m) "act of putting", *šākinu*(m) "that places", *šikittu*(*m*) "form, shape", *šukuttu*(*m*) "adornment, jewellery", *iškinū* (pl.t.) "supplementary payment"; *maškānum* "deposit", *maškānu*(*m*) "place of putting, threshing floor, tent, chain, shackles; pledge", *maškattu*(*m*) "depot, account"; *sakana* (Arab.) "to be tranquil, to repose; to live, dwell", *sukna, sakan, sakina, maskan, maskin* "dwelling"; *səkūn, skun* (MSArab.) "to settle, dwell". Akk. loans: *mškn* (Nab., JAram., Syr.) "to give as a pledge", *mškn* (Nab., Palm., Syr.) "pledge". Non-Sem.: **sikun=* (West Chadic) "to sit; to rest"; **sukunun=* (Rift) "to squat".[657]
|**S-k-n**| "to be placed, settle, stay; to establish oneself; to assign, establish"	•CTX: **EUPH** G suffc. *sa-ak-na, sa-ak-na-at, sa-ak-nu-ma, sa-ka-ni-ša*(!), imp. *su-uk-na*; D prefc. *ú-ša-ak-ki-in* → AHw 1011: *sakānu* see *šakānu*; CAD S 117b: *šakānu*; Zadok Fs. Hallo 329 (*sukkunum*, SKN); Charpin AfO 49/41 5f.; Streck Onomastikon 1 114f. § 1.95. **EA** G precat. *li-is-kí-in, li-is-kín* (285:26, 286:38, 287:13, 17; 290:29) → AHw 1011: *sakānu*; CAD S 69f.: *sakānu*; Sivan GAGl 267; Rainey EAT 88, CAT 2 212; Moran AmL 330 fn. 22. **UGA** G prefc. cf. *tskn*; C imp. *šskn* → DUL 745f.: */s-k-n/*. •ONOM: **EB** *iš*$_{11}$*-gú-nu* |yiSkun|, cf. *íl-gú-nu* |yilkun| → Pagan ARES 3 173f., 335, 342. **U3** *a-bí-iš-ki-in* → Golinets Onomastikon 2 117, 445f.; cf. diff. Buccellati Amorites 101, 128; Gelb CAAA 137 (?AB=IŠ=KIWN); Wilcke WO 5 26. **EUPH** *áš-ki-na-nu-um, ia-áš-ki-in-*^{d}[→ Huffmon APNMT 245; Gelb CAAA 32, 187; Golinets Onomastikon 2 117, 445f. **UGA** Cf. *bʕlskn* → DUL 207; *bʕlyskn* → DUL 209; *skn* → DUL 748: *skn* (IV); *šknt* → DUL 749.
|**s^1-k-n**| "to be placed, settle, stay; to establish oneself; to assign, establish"	•CTX: **EA** *ia-aš-ku-un, ti-ìš-ku-nu, ti-ša-kàn* → CAD S 117b: *šakānu*; Rainey CAT 2 35, 59. **UGA** G prefc. *tškn*, suffc. *šknt*, ptc. ?) *šknm*; Gt prefc. *yštkn*; D *åškn, tšknn* [*tšknnnn*], *yškn*; imp. *škn* → DUL 803f.: */š-k-n/*. •ONOM: **UGS** Cf. *šu-ku-nu/na* → DUL 804: *škn* (II). **UGA** Cf. *škn* → DUL 804; *šknn* → DUL 804: *škny* → DUL 804.
Sakn (A) "appointed, established"	•ONOM: **EUPH** *sa-ak-nu(-um), ša-ak-nu*, fem. *sa-ak-na-tum* → Gelb CAAA 32, 181.[658]
Sakn (B) "camp"	•CTX: **EUPH** *sa-ak-na-am, sa-ak-nim, sa-ak-nam-ma* → Charpin AfO 40/41 6f.
Sik(i)n (A) "appointed, established"	•CTX: **EB** *si-gi-ma, si-gi-su-ma* → Fronzaroli ARET 13 82, 293; Tonietti PrepEb 30; QuSe 25 322; Fronzaroli / Catagnoti Fs. Pennachietti 279; Fronzaroli / Catagnoti ARET 16 18, 262; Catagnoti QuSe 29 77, 226.[659]
Sik(i)n (B) "food allocation"	•LL: **EB** SÁ.DU$_{11}$.GA = *zi-gi-nu* → Conti QuSe 17 103:

[657] Orel / Stolbova HSED 473 no. 2240: **sikun=* "to dwell, sit".
[658] See Durand ARM 26/1 529 fn. d.
[659] Cf. *si-gi-iš*, mng unc. (Catagnoti QuSe 29 113 with fn. 437, 226: "punta").

Sakan "appointed, established"	•ONOM: **EUPH** *sa-ka-nu-um* → Gelb CAAA 32, 181; Golinets Onomastikon 2 155, 445f.
Sakin "appointed, established"	•ONOM: **EB** *sa-gi-na* → Pagan ARES 3 173f., 361.
Sakun "appointed, established"	•ONOM: **EUPH** *sa-ku-nu-um* → Gelb CAAA 32, 181; Golinets Onomastikon 2 139, 445f.
Sākin "provisor; prefect, governor"[660]	•CTX: **A7** LÚ *sà-ki-ni* → Wiseman passim JCS 8 1ff., 13 19ff.; Giacumakis AkkAl 98; Arnaud AuOr 163; Zeeb AOAT 282 408ff. **EM** LÚ *sà-kìn* → Pentiuc Vocabulary 155f. **UGS** LÚ *sà-ki-ni, sà-ak-ki-ni, sà-ki-in-ni, sà-ki-ni, sà-ki-in* → Sivan GAGl 267; Huehnergard UVST 157, 203, 210; vSoldt SAU 306 (101); UF 33 579ff.; UF 34 805ff.; UF 38 675ff.; Tropper UG 167, 472. •ONOM: **UGS** Cf. *sà-ki-ni* → Gröndahl PTU 185; Sivan GAGl 267: *sà-ki-ni*; diff.: Huehnergard UVST 157, 203: "prefect", noun.
Sōkin "provisor; prefect, governor"	•CTX: **EA** LÚ.MEŠ *ra-bi-ṣí : sú-ki-ni*, LÚ.MAŠKÍM *sú-ki-na* → AHw 1011; CAD 354; Rainey EAT 88; Sivan GAGl 267; Rainey CAT 1 20; Moran AmL xxvi fn. 70; Gianto SEL 12 70; vSoldt Or 60 117.
skn (C), Skn "provisor; prefect, governor"	•CTX: **UGA** Sg. *skn, śkn, s̱kn, škn*, pl. *sknm* → DUL 746f.: *s:śkn* (I); DUL 804: *škn*.
sknt "form"	•CTX: **UGA** → DUL 748.
ʔiSkin "addition, additional payment"	•ONOM: **EB** Cf. *iš₁₁-gi-nu-šu-bar-zú* → Krebernik PET 93; Pagan ARES 3 173f., 341.
maSkan (A) "shackle, rein; addition"[661]	•CTX: **EUPH** URUDU *ma-aš-ka-nu, ma-aš-ka-ni, ma-aš-ka-nim, ma-aš-ka-nam/na-am, ma-aš-ka-an-šu* → Durand ARM 26/1 282 fn. a; Arkhipov ARM 32 169f. •LL: **EB** NÍG.ANŠE.AKA = *maš-ga-nu*, var. *ma-ša-ga-nu*; NÍG.KI.GAR = *maš-ga-nu* → Krebernik ZA 73 5 (110a/b, 125); Fronzaroli StEb 7 171f., QuSe 13 146f.; Conti QuSe 17 82, 19 45f.
maSkan (B) "dwelling place"	•CTX: **EUPH** *ma-às-ka-an-šu-nu* → Lafont ARM 26/2 492f. fn. d (519:16); Zadok Fs. Hallo 329.
maSkan (C) "dweller"	•CTX: **EUPH** LÚ *ma-ás-ka-nu-ú*, LÚ *ma-ás-ka-ni-i* → Durand FM 7 78, 99ff. (26:6); 125ff. (35:3'); 128ff. (36:13, 42); 137ff. (39:32, 42).
meSkin "firmness" (?)	•ONOM: **EUPH** *me-èš-ki-nu-um, me-èš-ki-nim* → Gelb CAAA 32, 197; Streck Onomastikon 1 196 § 2.95.
mas¹katt, mas¹kant, "dwelling place, (store)house"	•CTX: **EA** KISLAḪ *: ma-aš-ka-na-*[*ti*]*-ka* (306:31) → Moran AmL 344 fn. 6. •ONOM: **EM** Cf. *maš-kat* → Pruzsinszky PTEm 89 [612]. **EG** Elem. in TN *ma₄-ša-ka-ta* → Hoch SWET 163f. no. 210.
ms¹knt "residence, mansion"	•CTX: **UGA** Sg. suff. *mšknth, mšknthm* → DUL 583f.: *mšknt*.
tiSkan "established" (?)	•ONOM: **EB** *ti-iš-ga-nu/núm, tíš*(UR)*-ga-na-ḫu*[662] → Pagan ARES 3 173f., 370f.

[660] AHw p. 1012, *sakinnu, sakkinu*; CAD S 76 *sākinu, sakkinu, sak(k)innu*.
[661] Actually "imposition, depot", meaning an additional payment. See OAkk. *maškattum, maskanāt* "depot"; Hasselbach SargAkk 276.
[662] Read *taš*(UR)*-ga-na-ḫu* by Pettinato MEE 2 283, and *daš-ga-na-ḫu* by Catagnoti QuSe 15 213, 264.

θkt "adornment, jewellery" (?) — •CTX: **UGA** → Tropper KWU 133, loan < Akk. *šukuttu(m)*, *šakuttu*; unc.; see Tropper loc.cit., and DUL 891f.: *ṯkt* ("type of boat") for other opinions.

|s^1-k-r| (1) — Culture word, Sem.: *šukurru(m)* (Akk.) "lance". Non-Sem.: šukur (Sum.) "lance".

Sakurr "lance" — •CTX: **EUPH** *ša-ku-ur-ri* → Durand ARM 26/2 205 (386) fn. c; Charpin Cahiers de NABU 1 120 (ln. 34) fn. f; Arkhipov ARM 32 124ff.

|s^1-k-r| (2) — Sem.: *škr* (Hb.) "to be drunk", *škr* (*šēkār*) "intoxicating drink, beer", *škrwn* (*šikkārôn*) "drunkenness, intoxication"; *škr* (JAram., Syr.) "to be drunk", *škr(ʔ)* (Aram., Syr.) "intoxicating drink"; *šakāru* (Akk.) "to be inebriated, drunk", *šikaru(m)*, *šikru* "beer, alcoholic drink", *maškuru*, *maškiru* "(inflatable) animal skin"; *sakira* (Arab.) "to be drunk", *sukr*, *sakra* "inebriety", *sakar* "intoxicating, wine", *muskir* "alcoholic beverage"; *sīkər*, *sékər* (MSArab.) "to be drunk"; *sakra* (Eth.) "to be drunk, intoxicated", *səkār*, *səkrat* "drunkenness, intoxication".

|s^1-**k-r| (B)** "to be(come) drunk" — •CTX: **UGA** G inf. *škr* → DUL 804: /*š-k-r*/ (II).[663]

Sakār "a kind of beer" (?) — •LL: **EB** Cf. (rdg unc.) ŠE+TIN = *sa/ʔà*(?)-*x-lum* → Fronzaroli ARET 11 170: *sa*(?)-[*g*]*a*(?)-*lum*; Conti QuSe 17 174.

s^1ikrinn "beer vat" (?) — •CTX: **EM** *ši-ik-ri-nu* → Pentiuc Vocabulary 172; Westenholz Emar Tablets 60.

s^1krn "intoxication" — •CTX: **UGA** → DUL 805: *škrn.*

maSkirt "a drink vessel" — •CTX: **EUPH** Pl. *ma-aš-ki-ra-tum* → Birot ARM 12 254; AHw 627; CAD M/1 376:

ms^1krt (A) "skin" (?). — •CTX: **UGA** Sg./pl. (?) *mškrt* → DUL 584: *mškrt* (I).

|s^1-ḳ-d| (2) — Sem.: Cf. *šqd* (Hb.) "to watch, be wakeful"; *šqd* (Pun.) "to pay attention to"; *šqd* (JAram.) "to lie awake".

|S-ḳ-d| "to watch, be wakeful" (?) — •LL: **EB** DU.MA = *ša-ga-dum*/*du-um* → Sjöberg Fs. Wilcke 263.
•ONOM: **EUPH** Cf. *šu-ku-du-um* → Gelb 196 (ŠUKUD); Zadok Fs. Hallo 331 (Ṯ-Q-D).

|s^1-ḳ-l| — Sem.: Cf. *šql* (JAram., Syr.) "to lift, take away", *šql(ʔ)* (Syr.) "lifting up, taking, portion; burden, tribute"; *šql* (Palm.) "to take"; *saqālu*, *šaqālu* (Akk.) "to take away".[664]

Siḳl "taking, portion" (?) — •ONOM: **B** Cf. *ši-iq-li-im*, *ši-iq-la-nu*, *si-iq-la-nim*, *si/ši-iq-la-nu-um* → Gelb CAAA 33, 195 (ŠQL "to weigh"); Streck Onomastikon 1 214f. § 2.111f.: "tragen".

Sataḳl "the carried one" — •ONOM: **EUPH** Cf. *ša-ta-aq-lum*, *ša-ta-ka-lim*, ^{d}UTU-*ša-ta-ka-lim* → Gelb CAAA 33, 194 (ŠQL "to weigh"); Streck Onomastikon 1 340 § 5.50; Golinets Onomastikon 2 195, 454.

---

[663] The recourse to |s^1-k-r| "to become drunk" regarding the PN read IŠ-*ku-ru* (Hess APN 91f. 212) is probably wrong. See instead under *milk* (B) "ruler; (the) king; DN" (|m-l-k|).

[664] For the var. *šaqālu* (seldom; SBab.) see AHw 1178: *šaqālu(m)*, G.5: "wegführen".

|s^1-ḳ-p|	Sem.: *šqp* (Hb. N, C) "to look down from above".
|s^1-ḳ-p| "to notice, realise" (?)	•CTX: **UGA** G prefc. *yšqp* → DUL 827: /*š-q-p*/.

|s^1-ḳ-r|	Sem.: Cf. *šaqāru* (Akk.) "to pierce"; *śuqahar* (MSArab.) "morning"; *saq^w ara* (Eth.) "to perforate, pierce". See further *dqr* (Hb.) "to pierce through".
|S-ḳ-r| "to pierce"	•LL: **EB** KA.GÍR = *sa-ga-ru₁₂-um, si-ga-lum* → Conti QuSe 17 100.
Suḳr "a tool"	•CTX: **EUPH** *šu-uq-ru*/*rum* → Arkhipov ARM 32 143f.
Siḳr "piercing time, dawn"	•CTX: **EB** *si-gi-lum* → Fronzaroli QuSe16 15; ARET 13 186, 293. •LL: **EB** GI₆.SÁ = *si-gi-lu-um, si-gi-lum, ù-ru mu-si-im* → Fronzaroli QuSe16 15; Conti QuSe 17 196.
Sāḳir "a craftsman who drills, perforates, pierces" (?)	•LL: **EB** Cf. GIŠ.TI.SÁR(?) = *sa-gi-lum* → Bonechi QDLF 16 82.
maSḳart "an agricultural implement"	CTX: **EUPH**, **B** Cf. GIŠ *ma-aš-qa-ra-tim*; *ma-aš-qa-ra-tum, ma-aš-ka*(!)*-ra-tim* → CAD M/1 382: *mašqartu* (*maškartu*); Charpin FM 32 fn. d.

|s^1-ḳ-y|	Sem.: *šqh* (Hb., C) "to provide drink for, irrigate", *mšqh* (*mašqeh*) "cupbearer", *šqwy* (*šiqqûy*) "drink", *šqt* (*šoqet*) "watering channel"; *šqy* (Palm.) "to irrigate, water", "irrigator, waterer"; *šqy* (Aram. C) "to offer to drink, irrigate", *šqy(?)* (Aram., Syr.) "cupbearer", *mšqy(?)* "drinking", *mšqyn* (Syr.) "irrigator, cupbearer"; *šaqû*(*m*) (Akk.) "to give to drink, irrigate, water animals", *šāqû*(*m*), *šāqiu*(*m*) "steward, cupbearer", *šāqītu*(*m*) "female cupbearer",[665] *mašqû*(*m*) "watering place; watering can, drinking vessel"; *saqā* (*saqy*, Arab.) "to give to drink", *saqy* "watering", sāqiya "irrigation channel", *siqāya, suqāya* "watering place, vessel", *misqān* "irrigation canal"; *s^1qy* (OSArab.) "to irrigate", *ms^1qy* "irrigated land; canals"; *həḳū, šeḳé, eššōḳi* (MSArab.) "to give a drink; to irrigate"; *saqaya* (Eth.) "to irrigate, water", *səqyat* "irrigation", *masqe*(*t*) "jug, vessel (for oil)", *məsqāy* "water reservoir". Non-Sem.: **syaḳu*= (West Chadic) "to pour into vessel; give water"; **syaχwa*= (Central Chadic) "to drink".[666]
|S-ḳ-y| "to give to drink"	•ONOM: **EB** Cf. *si-gi, si-gi-da-mu* → Pagan ARES 3 177, 363.[667]
|s^1-ḳ-y| "to offer (something to) drink; to give drink"	•CTX: **UGA** G prefc. *tšqy, yšqy*, suff. *tšqyn, yšqyn*, suffc. *šqy*; C prefc. *tššqy, yššq*, suffc. *ššqy* → DUL 827: /*š-q-y*/.
s^1aḳōn "watering place" (?)	•CTX: **EG** *ša-ku-na* → Hoch SWET 289f. no. 414.[668]
Sāḳiy "waterer, irrigator; an official" (?)	•CTX: **A7** Cf. *ša-qum* → Lauinger STOBA 97 fn. 53, 102f., 331, 349. •ONOM: **EUPH** *ša-gi-ia-an* → Gelb CAAA 181 (ŚAʔQ); Zadok Fs. Hallo 330. **UGS** Cf. *ša-qí-ia-nu* → Sivan GAGl 274.

665 See also *s^1āḳīt*, below EUPH (CTX).

666 Orel / Stolbova HSED 468 no. 2220: **seḳ*= "to drink, give a drink".

667 For the glosse [ŠE+TIN.KUR] = *ša-gúm, ša-gú-um* see Conti QuSe 17 174f., and here ADDITIONS and CORRECTIONS to Vol. 1 p. XXX: |ð-ʔ-g|.

668 Unless read |šakuna|, from Hitt. *šak(k)uni*= "spring, well", Kloekhorst EDHIL 702f.

s¹ḳy "cupbearer, wine waiter" (?)	•CTX: **UGA** Du. / pl. *šqym* → 828: *šqy*.
Saḳat "libation"	•CTX: **EB** Sg. suff. *za-ga-ti-ig* → Krebernik Beschwörungen 137; Catagnoti QuSe 29 76, 119, 225.
s¹āḳīt "female cupbearer"	•CTX: **EA**: MUNUS.DÉ : *ša-qí-tu₄* → Rainey EAT 40ff. (369:8; cf. 14f.: MUNUS.DÉ.MEŠ), EAC 369ff.; Moran RA 69 151 fn. 2, AmSt 280 fn. 17.
Sāḳit "irrigation channel"	•CTX: **EUPH** *ša-qí-ti-šu* → AHw 1179: *šaqītum*; CAD Š/2 15: *šaqītu*; Reculeau FM 16 352ff. (A.477:13); Durand LAPO 17 608ff. (no.804) fn. g.
Siḳūt "drinking trough"	•CTX: **EB** *si-gu-dam* → Catagnoti / Fronzaroli ARET 16 22, 262; Catagnoti QuSe 29 28, 110, 227.
mas¹ḳ "office of cupbearer"	•LL: **UGS** [SIG = *šāqûtu* = *t*]*ap- ša-ḫal-še* = *ma-aš-q*[*u-ú*(?)] → Huehnergard ²UVST 398f.; cf. UVST 80 for the rdg KUM (*qu*).
mis¹ḳ "cup" (?)	•CTX: **UGS** *miš-qú* → AHw 661: *mišqu*; CAD M/2 129: *mišqu*; Sivan GAGl 248.
ms¹ḳ "cup"	•CTX: **UGA** → DUL 585: *mšq*.
muSaḳḳiy "(man) that waters (the field)"	•CTX: **EUPH** *mu-ša-qú-ú* → CAD M/2 260: *mušaqqû*; vKoppen JESHO 44 469.

|s¹-l-ḫ| (1)	Sem.: *šlḥ* (Hb.) "to stretch out, let free, send, despatch", *šlwḥym* (*šillûḥîm*) "dismissal, gift, dowry", *šlḥwt* (*šᵉluḥôt*) "tendril, *mšlḥ* (*mišlāḥ*) "undertaking, pastureland", (*mišlōᵃḥ*) "contribution", *mšlḥt* (*mišlaḥat*) "release, troop"; *šlḥ* (Ph., Pun.) "to send; send word (command)", *šlḥ* (Ph.) "deputy"; *šlḥ* (Aram., Syr.) "to send", *šlyḥ* (Aram., Syr.) "messenger", *šlwḥ* (JAram.) "messenger", *mšlḥh* (JAram.) "mission, emissary"; *šalû(m)*, *salû*, *šalāʔu*, *šelû* (Akk.) "to fling, cast away", *šilūtum* "thrown-up material", *šilūtu*(*m*) "shot".[669]
|S-l-ḫ| "to send, grant"	•ONOM: **EUPH** *ia-áš-la-aḫ-*ᵈIM → Gelb CAAA 32, 188 (ŚLAḤ); Golinets Onomastikon 2 118, 447.
|s¹-l-ḫ| (A) "to throw, send, grant"	•CTX: **UGA** G prefc. *išlḥ*, *tšlḥ*, *nšlḥ*, suff. *åšlḥk*, *yšlḥn*, suffc. *šlḫt* → DUL 805: /*š-l-ḥ*/ (I).
Sāliḫ "who grants, sends"	•ONOM: **EUPH** *sa-li-ḫu(-um)*, fem. *sa-li-ḫa* → Gelb CAAA 32 181 (ŚALIḤ); Golinets Onomastikon 2 134, 136, 447.
Saluḫ "sent, granted"	•ONOM: **B** *sa-al-lu-ḫi* → Gelb CAAA 32, 182 (ŚALUḤ); Golinets Onomastikon 2 139, 447.
Sulāḫ "sent, granted"	•ONOM: **EUPH** *su-la-ḫa-nu* → Gelb CAAA 32, 189 (ŚULAḤ); Golinets Onomastikon 2 164 (fn. 602), 447, 494.
Sulluḫ "sent, messenger"	•ONOM: **U3** *su-lu-ḫu* → Gelb CAAA 32 189 (ŚULUḤ); Golinets Onomastikon 2 202, 447. **EUPH** *su-lu-ḫu-um* → Gelb CAAA 32 189 (ŚULUḤ); Golinets Onomastikon 2 202, 447.
Suluḫt "sending, shipment"	•CTX: **EA** *šu-lu-uḫ-ta* (265:8) → Sivan GAGl 275; Rainey CAT 3 54; Moran AmL 314; Izre'el Orient 38 88.
s¹aluḫata "stalk, bunches" (?)	•CTX: **EG** *s-r-ḥut-ta* → SWET 263 no. 373:
ms¹lḫ "battering-ram" (?)	•CTX: **UGA** → DUL 584: *mšlḥ*.

669 For OAss. *šalāḫum* see Kogan PIHANS 106 185, 211.

|s^1-l-ḫ| (2) See **|s^1-ḫ-l| (2)**, **|s^1-l-ḫ|**	
|s^1-l-ḫ-p-w/y|	Culture word, Sem.: *slwpy(t?)* (Syr.) "turtle"; *šeleppû(m)*, *šilippû*, *šelappû* (Akk.) "turtle"; *silaḥfāh*, *sulaḥfā(?)*, *sulaḥfiya* (Arab.) "turtle".
Salaḫpuy "turtle"	•LL: **EB** NÌ.BÀD.NA = *ša-la-bù-um* → Conti QuSe 17 31, 33, 36, 67.
|s^1-l-ḳ|	Sem.: Cf. *šalāqu(m)* (Akk.) "to cut open", *šilqum* "split piece". See further: *salaqa* (Arab.) "to lacerate the skin, hurt"; *śalaqa* (Eth.) "to peel, husk, crush".
Silḳ "decision"	•CTX: **EB** *si-ki*, *si-ki-ma* → Fronzaroli ARET 13 22, 294, 317:
|s^1-l-m| Cf. **|s-l-m| (1)**	Sem.:[670] *šlm* (Hb.) "to be complete, remain healthy" (D) "to make intact, make restitution, reward", (C) "to finish, carry out", *šlm* (*šālēm*) "well, intact, whole", *šlwm* (*šālôm*) "well-being, salvation", *šlm* (*šelem*), *šlmym* (pl.t. *šᵉlāmîm*); *šlm* (Ph. Pun. D) "to requite, accomplish, fulfil, pay", *šlm*, *šlwm* (Ph., Pun., Edom., Nab., Palm.) "welfare, well-being, health", *šlm* (Pun.) "a certain type of sacrifice"; *šlm* (Aram., Syr.) "to be whole, complete, finished" (D) "to finish", (C) "to complete", *šlm* (Aram., Syr.) "whole, fitting", *šlm(?)* "well-being, safety", *šlwm* (JAram., Syr.) "payment, ending, completion"; *šalāmu(m)*, *śalāmum* (Akk.)[671] "to be(come) healthy, intact", *šalāmu* "well-being", *šalmu(m)* "intact, healthy, sound", *šulmu(m)* "completeness, well-being, health", *šalimtu(m)*, *šalmūtu(m)* "well-being, health", *šulmānu* "(greeting) gift, fee", *mušallimu*(m) "that delivers safely, escort", *našlamtu* "completed payment", *tašlimtu(m)* "payment of balance due"; *salima*, *salāma* (Arab.) "to be safe and sound, intact, secure", *sallama* "to preserve, protect from harm; surrender, resign", *tasallama* "to receive, take possession of", *salam* "forward buying", *salīm*, *sālim* "safe", *salām* "soundness, well-being, security", *salāma* "blameless", *musallam* "intact", *taslim* "handling over"; *slm* (OSArab.) "to be well, healthy", *slm* "soundness, health"; *sīləm* (MSArab.) "to be safe, saved", *sōləm* "to rescue, save"; *tasallama* (Eth.) "to receive, take possession of".
|S-l-m| (B) "to be well, complete; re-establish, pay, deliver"	•CTX: **EB** G prefc. *i-si-a-ma-ma* |lā yiSlam=ma|, D prefc. *a-sa-a-ma* |la=yaSullam=ma| → Fronzaroli ARET 13 16, 273; Catagnoti QuSe 29 45, 129, 141, 225. **UGS** D suffc. (*la*) *šal/ša-li-ma* → Sivan GAGl 274; Huehnergard UVST 182; Tropper UG 464. •LL: **EB** IGI.DU_8 = *sa-lu-mu* → Fronzaroli QuSe 15 18; Conti QuSe 17 183; Catagnoti QuSe 29 138, 142, 225.
|s^1-l-m| "to be well; to re-establish, restore health"	•CTX: **UGA** G prefc. *yšlm*;, suffc. *šlm* (?), D prefc. *yšlm*], *tšlm*, *tš{š}lmn*, suff. *tšlmk*, *tšlmkm*., suffc. *šlm*, *šlmt* (?) → DUL 806f.: /*š-l-m*/.

[670] Due to their semantic and phonetic neighbourhood, the bases-|s^1-l-m| "to be well" and |s-l-m| (1) "to be friendly" may intersect or merge in several languages. For each language see also under |s-l-m| (1).

[671] For the alleged relationship between Akk. *šalāmu(m)* and *salāmu(m)* see Streck Onomastikon 1 115f. § 1.95; Golinets Onomastikon 2 447ff.

Salm (B) "well-being, health"	•LL: **EB** SILIM NA.E = *sa-ma*, É(*sa*!)-*ma* → Civil Or 56 241; Conti QuSe 17 198. •ONOM.[672]
Salām (B) "well-being, health"	•ONOM: **EM** *na-aḫ-mi-ša-la-mu* → Pruzsinszky PTEm 197 [646].
Salim (C) "whole, sound"	•ONOM: **EB** *sá-li-mu* → Bonechi QuSe 15 150f.; Pagan ARES 3 174, 362.[673]
Sulum "well-being, health"	•ONOM: **EB** *su-lum* → Pagan ARES 3 174, 365.
s¹lm (B) "well-being, health"	•CTX: **UGA** Sg. *šlm*, suff. *šlmy*, *šlmk* → DUL 807f.: *šlm* (I).
s¹lm (C) "a type of sacrifice"	•CTX: **UGA** Sg. suff. *šlmm*, pl. *šlmm* → DUL 808: *šlm* (II).
s¹lm (D) "pure"	•CTX: **UGA** → DUL 808: *šlm* (III).
Sulmān (B) "well-being, health"	•CTX: **EA** *šu-ul-ma-na*, *šu-ul-ma-ni*, *šul-ma-an-šu* → CAD Š/3 244f.: *šulmānu* 1. **UGS** *šul-ma-nu*, *šul-ma-ni* → CAD Š/3 244f.: *šulmānu* 1.
Sulmān (C) "present, gift"	•CTX: **A4** *šul-ma-ni* → Wiseman JCS 8 9 (117:5, copy); CAD Š/3 245: *šulmānu* 2. **EA** *šu-ul-ma-an*, *šu-ul-ma-nu*, *šul-ma-ni*, *šul-ma-na*, *šu-ul-ma-na*, *šu-ul-ma-an-šu* → CAD Š/3 245: *šulmānu* 2. **UGS** *šul-ma-ni*, *šul-ma-ni-šu*, *šul-ma-na-ti* (MEŠ), *šul-ma-na-tum* MEŠ → CAD Š/3 245: *šulmānu* 2; Lackenbacher / Malbran-Labat RSOu 23 79.
Salmata "supplies"	•CTX: **EG** *ša-r-ma*$_{(2)}$*-ta* |s¹almata| → Hoch SWET 286f. no. 409.[674]
s¹lmt (A) "well-being, health"	•CTX: **UGA** Sg. suff. *šlmtn* → DUL 809: *šlmt* (I).
s¹lmt (B) "compensation"	•CTX: **UGA** Sg. suff. *šlmth* → DUL 809: *šlmt* (II).
Sulumm "a kind of scabbard" (?)	•CTX: **EUPH** KUŠ *su-lum-mu*, *šu-lum-mu* (*ša* KUŠ) → Durand ARM 30 171.
Silimmiy "fulfilling, observance"	•CTX: **EUPH** *si-li-im-me-e-em* → Charpin AfO 40/41 18.
ns¹lm "guarantee, pledge" (?)	•CTX: **UGA** → DUL 640: *nšlm*; Kogan Classification 375.
s¹s¹lmt "supplementary delivery or ration"	•CTX: **UGA** → DUL 834: *ššlmt*; Kogan Classification 368.
ts¹lm "due, final payment"	•CTX: **UGA** → DUL 869: *tšlm*.

|s¹-l-m-m|	Sem.: Cf. *šalummu* "radiant" (Akk.), *šalummatu(m)* "radiance".

[672] Cf. the TN *Šalmā*, *Šalmiya*, *Šalmā=Yammi*; Belmonte RGTC 12/2 260f.; alph. *šlmy* (DUL 809f.: *šlmy* (I)), with the GN URU *šal-mi/mì-yu*; alph. *šlmy* (DUL 810: *šlmy* (II)) and the PN *ša-al-mi-ya*, alph. *šlmy* (DUL 810 (III)).

[673] For UGS ᵈ*sa-li-mu* (Huehnergard UVST 181: "whole, sound"), see *Salim* "friendly; DN Dusk" (\|s-l-m\|).

[674] Sivan / Cochavi-Rainey WSVES 85: *šá-l-ma-tá* / *ši-l-ma-ta* "provisions"; Helck Beziehungen no. 226.

s^{1}alummat "a type of metal jewellery"	•CTX: **Q** *ša-lum-ma-tum*, *ša-lum-ma-tù* → Bottéro RA 44 120; AHw 1152f.: *šalummatu*(*m*), 6 ('Goldschmuck'); CAD Š/1 285: *šalummatu* B (mng unkn.).
|s^{1}-l-n|	Culture word, etym. unc. Non-Sem.: Cf. unc. *šillē=na* (*š.* with Hurr. pl. *=na*).[675]
s^{1}ilina "an ornament"	•CTX: **Q** 1 *ši-li-na*, 2 *ši-li-na* → Bottéro RA 44 120; AHw 1236: *šilina*; CAD Š/2 444: *šilina*.
|s^{1}-l-ṭ|	Sem.: *šlṭ* (Hb.) "to have power", *šlyṭ* (*šallîṭ*) "ruler", *šlṭwn* (*šilṭûn*) "mighty"; *šlṭ* (Nab., Palm.) "to exercise power", *šlṭnʔ* (Palm.) "power, control"; *šlṭ* (Aram., Syr.) "to have power", *šlyṭ* "ruling, ruler", *šlṭn*, *šwlṭn* "power, rule", *šlṭwn* (Aram.) "governor"; *šalāṭu*(*m*) (Akk.) "to rule, be in authority", *šalṭu*(*m*) "authoritative", *šulluṭu* "triumphant"; *saliṭa* (Arab.) "to be authoritative", *saluṭa* "to gain power", *sallaṭa* "to give power", *sulṭa* "power, authority", *salṭ*, *salīṭ* "strong, domineering"; *śallaṭa* (Eth.) "to gain dominion", *śəlluṭ* "who has power", cf. *salaṭa* "to be whole, perfect".
|**s^{1}-l-ṭ**| "to rule, dominate"	•ONOM: **EM** Cf. *ša-la-ṭi* → Pruzsinszky PTEm 176 [732]; Streck AfO 51 309.
Salṭ "triumphant"	•ONOM: **EB** *sal-ti*; cf. *sal*(?)-*da*-NI(?) → Pagan ARES 3 174, 362 (.
s^{1}lyṭ "tyrant, "powerful"	•CTX: **UGA** → DUL 810: *šlyṭ*.
θlṭ "tyrant, "powerful"	•ONOM: **UGA** Cf. *ṯlṭ* → DUL 894.
|s^{1}-l-w|	Sem.: *šlh* (Hb.) "to have rest, be at ease", *šlw*, *šlyw* (*šᵉlē*(*y*)*w*) "quiet, at ease"; *šly* (JAram., Syr.) "to cease, be silent, calm", *šlw*, *šlwtʔ* "error", *šlw*(*ʔ*) (Syr.) "cessation"; *šelû* (Akk.) "to be neglectful, neglect"; *salā* (*salw*), *saliya* (Arab.) "to get rid of the memory, forget", *salwa*, *sulwa* "solace, comfort, oblivion"; *śāhlawa* (Eth.) "to keep quiet".
|**s^{1}-l-w**| "to rest" (?)	•CTX: **UGA** G prefc. *åšlw* → DUL 810: /*š-l-w*/.[676]
|s^{1}-m| (1)	Primary noun, Sem.: *šm* (*šēm*, Hb.) "name, reputation, fame"; *šm* (Ph., Pun., Nab., Palm., Hatra) name, fame"; *šm*(*ʔ*) (Aram., Syr.) "name, reputation, fame"; *šumu*(*m*) (Akk.)"name, son, posterity"; *ʔism* / *ʔusm*, *sam*, *sim*, *sum* (Arab.) "name, noun"; *s^{1}m* (OSArab.) "name"; *ham*, *šum*, *šem* (MSArab.) "name"; *səm* (Eth.) "name", *samaya* "to call, name".
Sam "name, posterity, community; DN"	•ONOM: **EB** *sa-ma*, *sá-ma*, *sá-mu*, *sa-mu-um*, *sá-mu-um*, *sa-mu-ù* → Catagnoti QuSe 15 188 n. 14, 239ff.; Pagan ARES 3 236f. 361f.[677]

[675] According to Wilhelm SCCNH 10 418f (for ln. 20), *š.* "Schmuckelement"; cf. Richter BGH 377: *šilina* ("Hurrizität ungewiss bzw. nicht allgemein anerkannt").

[676] Altern. Tropper UG 590, 671: C of |l-w-y| (?) "umwinden, umhüllen".

[677] Several instances cited by Pagan could be also assigned to the basis |s^{2}-y-m|. For *ša-ma-ni* see also |ṯ-m-n-y|. Note that *ša*, *sa* and *za* are spellings rendering different phonemes; see Catagnoti QuSe 29 20f.

U3 *ša-ma-bu-um, ša-ma-núm, sa-ma-mu-um, ša-ma-mu-um* → Buccellati Amorites 180f.; Wilcke WO 5 29; Gelb CAAA 182f. (ŚAM, ŚAMAM); Zadok Fs. Hallo 330; Streck Onomastikon 1 166 § 2.31.[678]
EUPH Passim; cf. *sa-mu-mu-ú*,[679] *sa-mu-a-bi-im, sa-mu-la*-DINGIR, *sa-me-e-ra-aḫ, ša/sa-ma-me-el, sa-mu-ìl, sa-mu-*^{d}DUR.ÙL → Huffmon APNMT 247ff.; Gelb CAAA 182 (ŚAM), 185 (ŚAMUM); Zadok Fs. Hallo 330; Streck Onomastikon 1 171 § 2.29, 224 § 2.127, 291f. § 3.53.[680]
EA *ša-mu-*^{d}IM → Hess APN 140f.; Tropper OLZ 91 56.

Sim "name, posterity, community; DN"
•ONOM: **U3** Cf. *si-mu* → Owen JCS 33 258.
EUPH Cf. *si-im-me-a-tar* → Gelb CAAA 187 (ŚIMM); Streck Onomastikon 1 171 § 2.39.

Sum "name, posterity, community; DN"
•CTX: **A4** DUMU *mu-ta šu-ma*; DUMU *šu-ma šu-ma* → Dietrich / Loretz WO 5 62 (5:38), 77 (31:46).[681]
•LL: **EB** MU.NÍ.ZA = *su-mu-um* → Krebernik ZA 73 40; Catagnoti QuSe 29 122, 228.
•ONOM: **EB** *zu-um, šu-ma, su-ma-nu, su-mi-a, su-mi, šu-mi-a, su-mi-a-ù, sum-ù* → Catagnoti QuSe 15 188 n. 14, 239ff.; Pagan ARES 3 236f., 365f., 389.
U3 *šu-mi-in-ni* → Buccellati Amorites 182; Gelb CAAA 33, 189.
EUPH Passim; cf. e.g. *su-ma-an, su-mu-mu, su-mu/mi-ia-ma-am, su-mu-a-bu-um, su-mu-a-la-ab, su-mu-la*-DINGIR, *su-mu-ra-aḫ, i-la-su-mu-ú, su-mu-*^{d}DUR.ÙL, *su-um-na-*^{d}IM, *su-mu-bi-na-šu, su-mu-ḫa-zí-ir, su-mu-i-ba-al, su-mu/mi-ia-ma-am*; *i-gu-ur*$_{x}$*-su-um*; cf. *su-ú-mi(-im), ḫa-ià-su-ú-mu(-ú)* → Huffmon APNMT 247ff.; Gelb CAAA 33, 189ff. (ŚUM); Zadok Fs. Hallo 330; Streck Onomastikon 1 171 § 2.39,221f. § 2.121, 224 § 2.127 (with fn. 1), 225 § 2.130, 278 § 3.33,291f. § 3.53 fn.4, 342 § 5.55; Durand REA 695.[682]
R *su-mu-še-rum* → Dalley / Walker / Hawkins Tell Rimah 166 (231:8); Zadok Fs. Hallo 330.
A7 *su-ma-a-bi, šu-ma-a-du, su-me-a-bu-um, su-mi-a-du, su-mi-ri-ba, su-mi-ra-pa su-mu-na-(a-)bi, su-mi-lam-mu, su-mu-un-na-(a-)bi, ia-pa-aḫ-su-mu-a-bi* → Wiseman AT 145, 147, Gelb CAAA 33, 189ff. (ŚUM); Arnaud AuOr 16 152f.; Streck Onomastikon 1 224 § 2.127.
A4 *šu-um-i-la, šu-ma-ú, šu-mat-ti, šu-ma-at-ti* (and *=ad-di*), *šu-mi-ia, šu-mi-*GAL, *šu-me/mi-ri-pa, šu-mi-ta-ru*; cf. unc. *šu-me-pa, šu-ma-ri* → Wiseman AT 147; Gelb CAAA 33, 189ff. (ŚUM); Dietrich / Loretz WO 5 69 (15:8), 99 (198:20), UF 1 42 (215:10); Sivan GAGl 276; Arnaud AuOr 16 152f.; Streck Onomastikon 1 224 § 2.127.
EM Cf. *šu-mi-ia-an-ni, šu-mi-*^{d}*da-gan* → Pruzsinszky PTEm 177 (fn. 285) [754].
EA *šu-mu-ḫa-di, šu-um/šum-ad-da*; cf. *šu-mi-it-ti* → Hess APN 145ff.; cf. Tropper OLZ 91 56.
TU *šu-mu-na-ʔà-rí* Krebernik Tall Bi`a 227; cf. Streck Onomastikon 1 224 § 2.127.
UGS *šùm-a-dì, šùm-a-da-ti*$_{7}$, *šu-um-*^{d}IM, *šu-um-a-na-ti, šu-me-ya-na, šu-mi-[ia-n]a, šu-mu-a-bi, šu-mu-a-sa, šu-mu-ra[-ma*(?)], *šu-mu-ra-pí*; cf. *šu-mi-i[t-ti]* → Gröndahl PTU 193f.; Sivan GAGl 276; see vSoldt BiOr 46 648.
EG *šu*$_{5}$*-ma* (sg. cstr. |s^{1}uma|) → Hoch SWET 279 no. 399.[683]

---

678 Altern. see *Samam* (|s^{1}-m-m|).
679 Altern. see *Samum* (|s^{1}-m-m|).
680 For *a-bi-sa-ma-ta* (Gelb CAAA 183: ŚAMAT) see Golinets Onomastikon 2 148.
681 Scribal note for an unknown name; diff. Sivan GAGl 276: PN.
682 Cf. also Durand loc.cit. for the spelling *šu-ḫu-um, la-na-su-ú-um*, etc. (|Suʔ(u)m| ?).
683 See also *šꜣ -m-y*, Schneider APÄQ 196f. no. 417.

s^1m "name, posterity, community, DN"

●CTX: **UGA** sg. *šm*, suff. *šmy*, *šmk*, pl. *šmt*, suff. *šmthm* → DUL 810f.: *šm* (I).
●ONOM: **UGA** *šm* → DUL 811: *šm* (II); *šmʕnt* → DUL 813;[684] *šmbʕl* → DUL 813; *šmlbů* → DUL 814; *šmmlk* → DUL 815; *šmrm* → DUL 818; *šmyn* → DUL 819. Cf. unc. *šmym* → DUL 819 (II).

|s^1-m| (2)

Cf. |**h-m**|

Sem. *|s^1im(-ma)|: *šumma* (Akk.) "if".[685]

Summa "if"

●CTX: **EB** *su-ma* → Fronzaroli ARET 13 295f.; Catagnoti / Fronzaroli ARET 16 265; Catagnoti QuSe 29 85, 87, 102, 111, 228.

|s^1-m-ʕ|

Sem.: *šmʕ* (Hb.) "to hear, listen (to), obey, understand", *mšmʕt* (*mišmaʕat*) "bodyguard"; *šmʕ* (Ph., Pun., Palm., Hatra) "to hear, become acquainted with", *mšmʕt* (Moab.) "subjects"; *šmʕ* (Aram., Syr.) "to hear, listen (to)", *šmʕ(ʔ)* (JAram.) "servant", *šmʕ(ʔ)*, *mšmʕ(ʔ)*, *mšmʕh*, *mšmʕtʔ* (JAram., Syr.) "hearing, fame, obedience", *šmwʔ(ʔ)* (JAram., Syr.) "auditor"; *šemûm(m)*, *šamû* (Akk.) "to hear, listen (to), obey, understand", *šēmû(m)* "hearer; that hears", *šāmeʔānu* "hearsay witness", *nešmû(m)* "hearing"; *samiʕa* (Arab.) "to hear, give ear, listen (to), learn", *samʕ*, *samāʕ* "hearing", *sāmiʔ* "hearer, listener, witness", *nasmaʕ* "hearing"; *s^1mʕ* OSArab. "to hear", *s^1mʕ* "witness"; *hīma*, *hūma*, *hyəma* (MSArab.) "to hear"; *samʕa* (Eth.) "to hear, listen (to), be obedient, understand", *səmʕ* "rumor, testimony", *samiʕ* "obedience", *səmuʕ* "notable", *samāʕi* "auditor, listening to", *məsmāʕ* "hearing".
Non-Sem.: **ŝim=* (Central Chadic) "ear"; **sim=* / **sum=* (East Chadic) id.[686]

|**S-m-ʕ**| "to hear, listen (to), notice"

●CTX: **EB** G prefc. *iš-má-ma* |yiSmaʕ=ma|, *áš-da-ma* |ʔaStamaʕ| → Catagnoti / Fronzaroli ARES 16 171, 242; Catagnoti QuSe 29 26, 32, 39, 57, 157, 225.
●LL: **EB** GIŠ.BA.TUKU$_x$ = *sa-ma-um* → Krebernik ZA 73 15; Conti QuSe 17 126; Sjöberg Fs. Renger 529.
EUPH, B: Passim *ia-áš-ma-aḫ*=DN, *iš-ma/má(-aḫ)*=DN, *iš-me(-eḫ)*=DN; see also: *si-im-ḫe-e-ra-aḫ*, *si-ma-aḫ-ni-i-la*, *ši-ma-aḫ-ni*-DINGIR, *si-ma-aḫ-la-a-ni* (with vars: *si-ma=*, *su-ma-aḫ=*, *su-ma-ḫa=*), *ia-áš-ma-ḫu*, *ia-áš-ma-ḫu-um*, *ia-aš-ma-ḫi-im*, *ia-áš-mi-iḫ*-^{d}IM, *iš-mi-il-la*, *iz-me*-DINGIR, *ta-às-ma-aḫ*-^{d}*ma-ma*, *sa-am-si-ia-ás-ma-aḫ*-^{d}IM, *i-zi-iš-ma-aḫ*, *an-nu-taš/ta-aš-ma-aḫ* → Huffmon APNMT 249f.; Gelb CAAA 32, 187f.; Streck Onomastikon 1 169 § 2.26; 221f. § 2.121, 223f. § 2.126, 225 § 2.130f.; Golinets Onomastikon 2 15f., 30, 119f., 121, 123ff., 449f., 506, 514.
R *iš-me-e-ra-aḫ* → Dalley / Walker / Hawkins Tell Rimah 220 (305:5); Zadok Fs. Hallo 330; Golinets Onomastikon 2 15, 449f.
TU Cf. *ì-lí-sa-ma-aḫ* → Krebernik Tall Bi`a 217; Golinets Onomastikon 2 146, 157, 449f.[687]
A7 *iš-ma-a-da*, *iš-mi-il-la*; cf. *am-mu-sa-ma*[688] → Wiseman AT 139; Gelb CAAA 32, 188; Arnaud AuOr 16 176, 180; Golinets Onomastikon 2 120, 449f.

---

684 For *šmʕn* see |s^1-m-ʕ|.
685 Unrelated: Arab. *ṯumma*, *ṯummat* "then, thereupon, later (on), afterwards" (diff. AHw 1272: *šumma* (Arab. *ṯumma* "dann").
686 Orel / Stolbova HSED 474 no. 2245: **sim=* / **simaʕ=* "to hear; ear".
687 Golinets loc.cit. |ʔilī=Samaʕ| "Mein Gott erhört" (?).
688 Gelb CAAA 183 (ŚAM).

|s^1**-m-ʕ**| "to hear, listen (to), notice"	•CTX: **EA** G prefc. *yi-iš-ma* (82:23), suffc. *ša-mi-ti$_7$* (362:5) → Sivan GAGl 141, 151, 274; Rainey CAT 2 36, 286, 302; Moran Or 29 4 fn. 4; AmL 152. **UGA** G prefc. *išmʕ*, *tšmʕ*, *yšmʕ*, suff. *yšmʕk*; *tšmʕm*, suffc. *šmʕt*; imp. *šmʕ*; inf. *šmʕ*; Gt impv. *ištmʕ* → DUL 811f.: /*š-m-ʕ*/. •ONOM: **EM** *iš-ma-aḫ-^{d}da-gan*, *iš-ma*(*-aʔ*)-^{d}KUR, *iš-me-*[^{d}*da-gan*], *iš-me-*^{d}KUR, *ši-im-i*, *ši-mi-da-ru*/*ri*, *ši-mi-na-ni* → Pruzsinszky PTEm 129, 177, 215 [524, 752]. **A4** *iš-mi-il-a-du*; cf. *ša-ma*-AN → Wiseman AT 139, 145; Arnaud AuOr 16 176, 180. **EA** Cf. *be-e*[*l*]*-ša-a*[*m*]*-ma* (37:26) → Hess APN 56, 212.[689] **UGS** *ša-am-ú-na*, *ìš-ma-ʔa-nu*, *ia-aš-me-*[, *ia-aš-mu-u*, *ia-aš-mu-nu*, *aš-ta-me-šar-ri* → Gröndahl PTU 194; Berger WO 5 274; Sivan GAGl 272 (ŠAMʕŌNU), 274 (ŠMʕ); Huehnergard UVST 251f.; vSoldt SAU 24, 331f. fn. 160.[690] **UGA** *šmʕn* → DUL 812; *šmʕy* → DUL 813; *yšmʕ* → DUL 972.[691] **EG** *ša-m-ʕ* |s^{1}amaʕa| → Hoch SWET 279 no. 400.[692]
Samʕ "hearing, testimony" (?)	•ONOM: **B** Cf. *sa-am-ḫa-nu-um*, *ša-am-ḫa-nu-um* → Gelb CAAA 32, 183.[693]
Samaʕ "who has been heard"	•ONOM: **EUPH**, **B** *ša-ma-ḫa-tim*, *ša-ma-*(*a-*)*ia-tum* → Gelb CAAA 32, 183; Golinets Onomastikon 2 156, 449f.
Sāmiʕ "who hears; listener"	•ONOM: **EB** *sa-mi-um*, *sá-me-um* → Pagan ARES 3 174f., 361f. **U3** *lu-ḫa-a-a-sa-mu*/*mi-um* → Gelb CAAA 32, 183; Golinets Onomastikon 2 135f., 449f. **EUPH**, **B**: *sa-me-ḫu-um*, *sa-mi-um*, *sa-mu*(*-ú*)*-um*, fem. *sa-me-ḫa* → Gelb CAAA 32, 183; Streck Onomastikon 1 152f. § 2.2, 223f. § 2.126, 253 § 2.180; Golinets Onomastikon 2 135f., 449f. **EG** Cf. *su$_2$-ma$_2$-ʕi*(?)*-n* (|s^{1}imʕōn|, probl. with vowel displacement) → Hoch SWET 260 n0. 368.
s^{1}mʕ "auditor"	•CTX: **UGA** Sg. cstr. *šmʕ*; suff. *šmʕh* → DUL 812 *šmʕ*.
maSmiʕ "hearing"	•ONOM: **EUPH** *ma-aš-mi-a-na-am* → Gelb CAAA 32, 188; Streck Onomastikon 1 208 § 2.103, 338 § 5.47(fn. 10), 347 § 5.68.
ms^{1}mʕt "(body)guard"	•CTX: **UGA** → DUL 585: *mšmʕt*.
taSmaʕ "attention, acceptance"	•CTX: **EUPH** *taš-ma-un* → Durand MARI 4 152 fn. 30 (nunation).

|s^1-m-x| (1)	Sem.: *Šmḥ* (*śmḥ*, Hb.) "to be glad, rejoice", *Šmḥ* (*śāmēᵃḥ*) "happy", *Šmḥh* (*śimḥāh*) "joy"; *šmḥ* (Amm.) "to be glad, rejoice".
|S-m-x| **(A)** "to be glad, rejoice; to light up"	•ONOM: **EB** Cf. *dùl*(SÚR)*-da-ma-ḫa*/*ḫu*, *íl-da-ma-ḫu* → Krebernik PET 64; Pagan ARES 3 175f., 304., 335.
|s^1**-m-x**| "to be glad, rejoice; to light up"	•CTX: **UGA** G prefc. *yšmḫ*, *tšmḫ*, *nšmḫ*; suffc. *šmḫ*, *šmḥ*; inf. *šmḫ*; D prefc. *tšmḫ*; C suffc. *ššmḫt* → DUL 813: /*š-m-ḫ*/.[694] •ONOM: **UGA** Cf. unc. *ilšmḥ* → DUL 62.[695]

[689] The doubling of the consonant poses a problem. See the diff. rdg [*b*]*e-*[*e*]*l-x-y-x* in Moran AmL 111 fn. 10.
[690] Cf. the TN URU DINGIR-*iš-tam-i* \|*ʔilis^{1}tamʕ=*\|, Belmonte RGTC 12/2 141.
[691] Cf. the TN *ilštmʕ*, GN *ilštmʕy*; DUL 63.
[692] See also *my-ṯ-r-šȝ-m-ʕ*, Schneider APÄQ 137 no. 292; *sw-mȝ- ʕ-n-y$_2$*, Schneider APÄQ 182 no. 387; *šȝ-m-y*, Schneider APÄQ 196f. no. 417; [*///*]*m-šȝ-m-ʕȝ*, Schneider APÄQ 272 no. 606.
[693] Cf. Golinets Onomastikon 2 156: "Erhört".

s^1mxt "joy"	•CTX: **UGA** → DUG 814: *šmḫt*.[696]

|s^1-m-x| (2)	Sem.:[697] *šamāḫu(m)* (Akk.) "to grow, flourish", *šamḫu(m)* "luxuriant", *šamḫatum* "voluptuous"; *samaḫa* (Arab.) "to germinate", *simḫa* "growth, development".[698]
|S-m-x| **(B)** "to prosper, flourish"	•ONOM: **EB** Cf. *íl-da-ma-ḫu*, *daš*(UR)*-da-ma-ḫu*, *tal-da-ma-ḫu*, *dùl*(SÚR)*-da-ma-ḫa/ḫu* → Krebernik PET 64; Pagan ARES 3 175f. (*šmḫ* "to rejoice"), 301, 304, 335, 369 ("he / she rejoiced").
Simx "splendour, radiance"	•ONOM: **EUPH** *ši-im-ḫa-a-ia*, *si-im-ḫi-ᵈda-gan*, *é-a-ši-im-ḫi*, *⁽ᵈ⁾ad-mu-ši-im-ḫi*, *ì-lí-ši-im-ḫi*, *ì-lí-ši-im-ḫa-ia*, *an-nu-ši-im-ḫi*, ES4.DAR*-ši-im-ḫi*, *ta-bu-bu-ši-im-ḫi* → Gelb CAAA 32 (*śimḫum* "joy"), 187 (ŚIMḪ); Streck Onomastikon 1 324 § 5.13.
Sumx "splendour, radiance"	•ONOM: **EUPH, B** *su-um-ḫu-ba-al*, *su-um-ḫu-ra-bi* → Gelb CAAA 32 (*śumḫum* "joy", 192 (ŚUMḪ).
Samux "stately, luxuriant"	•ONOM: **EUPH** *sa-mu-ḫi-el*, *sa-mu-ḫi-il*, *da-mi-sa-mu-uḫ*, *da-di-sa-mu-uḫ*, *ḫa-lu-sa-mu-uḫ*, *ì-lí-sa-mu-uḫ*, [ᵈEN.ZU]*-ša-mu-uḫ* → Huffmon APNMT 250 (from **šmʕ*); Gelb CAAA 32, 185 (ŚAMUʕ); Streck Onomastikon 1 327 § 5.21; Golinets Onomastikon 2 162, 451f.
Sumāx "stately, luxuriant"	•ONOM: **EUPH** Fem. *šu-ma-ḫa-tum* → Golinets Onomastikon 2 165 (fn. 603).
Summux "most stately, luxuriant"	•ONOM: **EUPH, B** *su-mu-ḫu-um*, *zu-mu-ḫu-um*, *su-mu-uḫ-ba-la*, fem. *šu-mu-uḫ-tum* → Gelb CAAA 32 (*śum(m)uḫum* "very joyful", 192 (ŚUMUḪ); Streck Onomastikon 1 333 § 5.36; Golinets Onomastikon 2 202f., 451f.
s^1mħ "stately, luxuriant" (?)	•ONOM: **UGA** Cf. unc. *ỉlšmḥ* → DUL 62.[699]
Samakt "prostitute"	•LL: **EB** GÉME.KAR.AG = *ša-ma-ag-tum* → Krebernik ZA 73 45 (1412a).[700]

|s^1-m-l-l|	Culture word, Sem.: Cf. *šamallû(m)*, *šamallāʔum*, *šamlû* (Akk.) "purse-bearer, merchant's assistant". Non-Sem.: šaŋanla (Sum.) "trader".
s^1ml " agent, assistant" (?)	•CTX: **UGA** Sg. cstr. *šml* → DUL 814: *šml* (I). •ONOM: **UGA** Cf. *sml* → DUL 815: *šml* (II).

|s^1-m-m|	Sem.: Cf. *šmm* (Hb.) "to be deserted, desolate", *šmm* (*šāmēm*) "desolated"; *šmm* (JAram.) "to be desolate", *šmm(h)* "desolation"; *šamāmu* (Akk.) "to injure".
Samm, Simm "damage"	•ONOM: **EUPH** *sam-am-mi-a-ta-ar*, *sa-am-me-tar*, *sa-am-me-e-tar*, *sa-mi-a-ta-ar*, *sa-am-mi-e-tar*, *sa-am-mi-tar*; *si-im-mi-a-tar* → Gelb CAAA 32 (ŚMM), 183, 187.

694 The alleged EA-Akk. writing *iš-mu-ḫu₅* (109:50; Rainey EAT 92: *šamāḫu* "to rejoice") is controversial. See altern. rdgs and interpretations in Moran AmL 184 fn. 13; Rainey CAT 3 185f.; EAC 590.

695 See also *s^1mħ* (|s^2-m-x| (2)).

696 For *Simx*, *Sumx* (Gelb CAAA 32: *śimḫum* "joy", *śumḫum* "joy") see |s^2-m-x| (2).

697 Some entries in this etymon may belong to |s^2-m-x| (1).

698 Unrelated: Arab. *samuḥa* "to be kind, magnanimous".

699 See also |*s^1-m-x*| (|s^1-m-x| (1)).

700 See *sābiyt* (|s-b-y|).

Samam, Samim, Samum “damaged”	•ONOM: **U3** Cf. *sa-ma-mu-um, ša-ma-mu-um* → Gelb CAAA 32 (ŚMM), 183.[701] **EUPH, B** *sa-mi-mu(-um), sa-mu-mu-ú,*[702] *sa-mu-ma-nim* → Gelb CAAA 32 (ŚMM), 183, 185. Altern. see *Sam* “name” (see |s¹-m|).

|s¹-m-(m-)n|	Culture word, Sem.: *šummannu(m), šimmannum* (Akk.) “halter, tether”. Non-Sem.: saman (Sum.) “rope”.
Sum(m)att, Sum(m)utt “halter, tether”	•CTX: **EB** Pl. *su-ma-du, su-[m]a-ti* → Fronzaroli ARET 11 169; Catagnoti QuSe 29 116, 227. •LL: **EB** GIŠ.ÉŠ.NU.EŠ = *su-ma-tum*; NÍG.ÉŠ.NU.ÉŠ = *su-mu-tum* → Krebernik ZA 73 2 (40a, 483); Conti QuSe 17 38, 66; QuSe 19 55; Sjöberg Fs. Kienast 529f.

|s¹-m-n|	Primary noun, Sem.: *šmn* (*šemen*, Hb.) “olive) oil, fat”; *šmn* (Pun., Edom., Palm) “oil”; *šmn, šwmn(?)* (Aram., Syr.) “fat”, *šmn* “to grow fat / mature”, *šmyn* (JAram., Syr.) “fat; fatty”; *šamnu(m)* (Akk.) “oil, fat, cream”, *šummunu* (Dt) “to be oiled”; *samn* (Arab.) “clarified butter, ghee”, *samina* “to be(come) fat”, *samīn* “fat, corpulent”; *šəmnún* (MSArab.) “fat”, *šūn* “to become fat”. Non-Sem.: **sinam=* (West Chadic) “oil”; **sVmVn=* (Central Chadic) “thick, fat”, *siwan=* (East Chaic) “oil”.[703]
Samn “oil”	•LL: **EB** Ì.DU$_{10}$ = *sa-ma-nu da-bù* → Krebernik ZA 73 34; Fales QuSe 13 183; Fronzaroli QuSe 13 149, StEb 7 181 (rdg *sa-ma-nu-um da-pù-um*).
Samīn “fat, fatty” (?)	•ONOM: **EUPH** Cf. *sa-mi-nu-ú, sà-mi-núm/nu-um* → Gelb CAAA 183 (ŚAMIN), 202 (ZAMIN); Zadok Fs. Hallo 330.
s¹amān “fatty” (?)	•ONOM: **EM** *ša-ma-nu, ša-ma-ni* → Pruzsinszky PTEm 177 (fn. 281) [733].
Sammun “fat, fatty”	•ONOM: **EB** *sa-mu-nu* → Pagan ARES 3 234f., 361.
s¹amun “an oily dish”	•CTX: **EM** GIŠ *ša-mu-nu, ša-mu-ú-[n]a*(?) → Zadok AION 51 119.
s¹mn (A) “oil, fat, butter”	•CTX: **UGA** Sg. *šmn, šmn* → DUL 815ff.: *šmn* (I). •ONOM: **UGA** Cf. *šmn* → DUL 817: *šmn* (III) DN?, *šmn* (IV); *šmny* → DUL 818.
s¹mn (B) “fat, fatling”	•CTX: **UGA** → DUL 817: *šmn* (II).
s¹amna “oil” (?)	•ONOM: **EG** Cf. elem. *su₃-mi3-n* in TN → Hoch SWET 260f. no. 369.[704]
Summun “the fat one”	•ONOM: **EB** *zu-mu-na, zu-mu-na-nu* → Pagan ARES 3 234f., 389.
Sammanūt, Sammunūt “fat”	•ONOM: **EB** *sa-ma-nu-du, sa-mu-nu-du, ša-mu-nu-du,* Ì.GIŠ-*nu-du* → Pagan ARES 3 234f., 328, 361, 366.
s¹mt (A) “fat, grease”	•CTX: **UGA** → DUL 818: *šmt* (I).[705]

|s¹-m-r|	Sem.: *šamāru(m)* (Akk.) “to rage, be furious”, *šamru(m)* “furious, impetuous”.

---

[701] Altern. see *Sam* “name” (s¹-m|).
[702] Altern. see *Sam* “name” (s¹-m|).
[703] Orel / Stolbova HSED 474f. no. 2247: **siman=* “oil, fat”.
[704] See also *šumēlu* (|s²-m-ʔ-l|).
[705] Probl. |s¹ama/itt| < |s¹ama/int|; Tropper KWU 121; Kogan Classification 248 fn. 714.

Samar "the boisterous, furious one; DN"	•ONOM: **U3** *i-la-ša-ma-ar* → Buccellati Amorites 17, 108, 157f.; Gelb CAAA 183; Golinets Onomastikon 2 152, 452. Cf. Huffmon APNMT 252 (SMR^1 "to guard, watch"); Gelb CAAA 32 (ŚMR "to guard, to protect"); Wilcke WO 5 27. **EUPH**, **B** *sa-ma-ra-an, sa-ma-ra-nu, a-bi-sa-mar, ba-aḫ-li-sa-mar, ḫa(-am)-mu-sa-mar, i-nu-uḫ/ùḫ-sa-mar/ma-ar, ia-nu-uḫ-sa-mar* → Gelb CAAA 183; Golinets Onomastikon 2 151f., 452; Durand REA 688. Cf. Huffmon APNMT 252 (SMR^1 "to guard, watch"); Gelb CAAA 32 (ŚMR "to guard, to protect"). **TU** *sa-ma-ra-an* → Krebernik Tall Bi`a 226; Golinets Onomastikon 2 152, 452. **A7** *ša-am-ma-ra-a-du, sa-ma-ri-*DINGIR → Wiseman JCS 368:8; AT 455:46; Gelb CAAA 183; Streck Onomastikon 1 172 § 2.40 fn. 3 (cf. 163f. § 2.26 fn. 4); Golinets Onomastikon 2 152 (fn. 584), 452. Cf. Gelb CAAA 32 (ŚMR "to guard, to protect").
|s^1-m-S-k-l|	Culture word, Sem.: *šamaškil(l)u(m), šamaškillānu, šusikilu* "a type of onion". Non-Sem.: šumsikil (Sum.) "an alliaceous vegetable, onion".
s^{1}amaSkil "a type of onion"	•LL: **EB** ŠÚM.SAR.SIKIL = *ša-maš-gi-lu* → Sjöberg Fs. Renger 543.
s^{1}umatkil "a type of onion"	•CTX: **EUPH** *šu-ma-at-ki-lu* → Durand ARM 21 122 fn. 2 (103:5); CAD Š/1 300: *šamaškillu*, b,1'.
|s^1-m-s^1-m| (1)	Primary noun, Sem: *šwšmn(?)* (JAram., Syr.) "ant"; *sumsum* (Arab.) "red ant". Non-Sem.: **sam=sam=* (East Chadic) "flea".[706]
SaSSamān "ant"	•ONOM: **EB** *sa-sa-ma-nu* → Pagan ARES 3 235, 361.
|s^1-m-s^1-m| (2)	Culture word, Sem.: *šmšm* (Hb.) conventionally "sesame"; *ššmn* (Ph.) id.; *šwmšm* (Aram.) id., *šwšm(?)* (JAram., Syr.) id.; *šamaššamū* (pl. Akk.),[707] *šamsāmū* "sesame (?) / (altern.) "flax and its seed" (?); *simsim* (Arab.) "sesame". Non-Sem.: *sapsama=* (*ša-ap-ša-ma=*, *ŠA-AM-ŠA-AM-MI*, Hitt.) "an oil producing plant and / or its seeds";[708] *šum(m)išum(m)i* (Hurr.) "sesame / linseed" (?);[709] *sēsamon* (Gk.) "sesame". See šeŋeši (Sum.) "sesame (plant, seed)".
s^{1}s^{1}mn "sesame / linseed(s)"	•CTX: **UGA** 834: *ššmn*.
|s^1-m-w/y|	Primary noun, Sem. (mostly pl. / du.): *šmym* (*šāmayim*, Hb.) "heavens, sky"; *šmm* (Ph. Pun., Nab., Palm.) id.; *šmyn, šmyʔ* (Aram., Syr.) id.; *šamû, šamāʔū, šamāmū* (pl.) (Akk.) id.; *samāʔ* (Arab., pl. *samawāt*) "heavens, sky"; *samā* (*smw*) "to be high"; *s^{1}myn* (OSArab.) "heavens, sky"; *samāy* (Eth.) id. See further: *háytəm, hətəm, šétəm, sútum* (MSArab.) "heaven, sky". Non-Sem.: Cf. **sam=* (West Chadic) "sky" (probl. Arab. loan).[710]

706 Orel / Stolbova HSED 461 no. 2187: **sam-sam* "insect".
707 Probl. a popular etym., from Akk. **šaman=šammī* "oil-plant" (ŠE.GIŠ.Ì).
708 CHD Š/1 207. Unrelated: *ša(m)ma(m)ma=* "a tree or its fruit (a kind of nut?)".
709 Richter BGH 412.
710 Orel / Stolbova HSED 461 no. 2188: **samaʔ=* "sky".

Samay, s^{1}amayūma (pl.) "heavens, sky"	•CTX: **EA** AN.ḪI.A : *ša-mu-ma* (211:17); *ša-mì-ma* (264:16); cf. *ša-me*, AN *sa-mi*, AN *ša-me*, *ša-mé-ú*, *ša-me-e*, AN *sa-mì-i*, AN *sa-me-e*, AN.MEŠ *sa-me*, AN.MEŠ *: ša-me-ma* → Sivan GAGl 272; Rainey CAT 1 26, 145. •LL: **UGA** [AN = *šamû* = *ḫa-b*]*ur-ni* = [*š*]*a*(!?)-[*m*]*u*(?)-*ma*(?); [IDIM = *šamû* = *ḫa-bur*]-*ni* = *ša-mu-ma*; [AN = *a-n*]*i* = *ša-mu-ma* → Sivan GAGl 272; Huehnergard UVST 182; vSoldt SAU 307 (136); BiOr 47 731; Tropper UG 198, 301; KWU 120. •ONOM: **EUPH** Cf. *sa-mi-ma-ia-si-im*, *zu-sa-mi-ma* → Zadok Fs. Hallo 330. **A4** *ša-ma*, *ša-ma-ia*, *ša-ma-an* → Wiseman AT 145; vSoldt BiOr 46 648; diff. Sivan p. 276: ŠUMU "name" var. **UGS** *ša-mu-*^{d}U (cf. AN.^{d}U), *ša-mu-nu*, *ša-mu-ma-nu*/*na* → Gröndahl PTU 195; vSoldt BiOr 46 648.
s^{1}mm "heavens, sky"	•CTX: **UGA** Pl.t. *šmm*, *šmym*, suff. *šmmh* → DUL: 814f. *šmm* (I). loc.). •ONOM: **UGA** *šmm* → DUL 815 *šmm* (II); *šmmn* → DUL 815.

|s^{1}-m-y| See |**s^{1}-m-w/y**|	

|s^{1}-n| (1)	Sem.: *s^{1}n*, *s^{1}nn*, *s^{1}wn* (OSArab.)"to, toward", see also *ʕd s^{2}nn*, *ʕd s^{3}nn* "to, up to, against".
Sin (A) "to, toward, for, through, by"	•CTX: **EB** Passim *si-in*, suff. *si-ma* |Sin=ma| → Fronzaroli StEb 1 13; Pennachietti LdE 302; Hecker EdA 242 fn. 91; Archi Eblaitica 4 8ff., PIHANS 106 100, 105; Rubio PIHANS 106 135; Fronzaroli ARET 13 26 (64), 293f.; Tonietti QuSe 25, 329; PrepEb 90ff.; Catagnoti QuSe 29 26, 98, 116, 226. **TB** *ši-in* → Ismail, etc. Tell Beydar 77 I 2.

|s^{1}-n| (2)	Primary noun, Sem.: *šnh* (*šānāh*, Hb.) "year"; *št* (pl. *šnt*, Ph., Pun., Moab., Amm.) id., *šnʔ* (Palm.) id.; *šnh*, *štʔ* (Aram., Syr.) id.; *šattu*(*m*), *šantu*(*m*) (pl. *šanātu*, Akk.) id.; *sana* (Arab.) id.
s^{1}an(a)t "year"	•CTX: **EA** Sg. MU *: ša-ni-ta* → Rainey EAC 1236 (362:66). •LL: **UGS** [...] = *ša-an-tu$_{4}$* → vSoldt SAU 307, 336 fn. 169; BiOr 47 731; Huehnergard ^{2}UVST 383; Tropper UG 146, 185.
s^{1}nt (A) "year"	•CTX: **UGA** Sg. *šnt*, suff. *šntm*, du. *šntm*, pl. *šnt*,*šnm*, suff. *šntk* → DUL 821f.: *šnt* (I).

|s^{1}-n-m|	Etym. unc.
s^{1}nm "DN"	•ONOM: **UGA** Cf. *ṯkmn w šnm* → DUL 820: *šnm*.

|s^{1}-n-n|	Primary noun, Sem.: *šn* (*šēn*, Hb.) "tooth"; *šn*(*ʔ*) (Aram., Syr.) "tooth", *šnn* (JAram. D, Syr. D) "to sharpen; to test, assay"; *šinnu*(*m*) (Akk.) "tooth; elephant tusk, ivory"; *sinn* (Arab.) "tooth", *sanna* "to sharpen, whet"; *šnin* (MSArab.) "tooth"; *sənn* (Eth.) "tooth". Non-Sem.: *šinni* (Loan in Hurr.) "tooth";[711] **sin*= (Berber, West Chadic) "tooth"; **ŝin*= (Central Chadic) "tooth"; **siHan*= (East Chadic) "tooth", **sihin*= (Rift) "tooth".[712]

[711] Richter BGH 386.

|s^1-n-n| "to grind teeth"	•CTX: **UGA** G / D prefc. *tšnn, yšnn* → DUL 821: */š-n-n/*.
Sinn, Sinnat "tooth, point"	•LL: **EB** ZÚ.URUDU = *si-nu-um, si-na-tum*; ZÚ.^{d}ÍD = *si-nu a-ḫa-mu*; ZÚ.UR$_5$ = *si-na-tum ʔà-la-um, si-na-ti ʔà-la-mu*; ZÚ.UŠ = *ma-gàr-ru*$_{12}$ *si-nu(-me)*; ^{d}NAMMU = *si-nu ḫa-mi-um* → Krebernik ZA 73 6f. (174), 8f. (202b, 1344), 9 (209), 10 (227); Conti QuSe 17 93 (174); cf. Fales QuSe 13 176 (202b, 1344, esp. 209); Bonechi / Catagnoti Fs. Sommerfeld / Krebernik 190.
s^1n "tooth; ivory"	•CTX: **UGA** Sg. *sn*, pl. suff. *šntk, šnth* → DUL 819f.: *šn*.
|s^1-n-S|	Sem.: *šns* (Hb. D) "to gird", *šnṣ* (JAram.) "to tighten", *šnṣ(?)* "strap, lace".
|**s^1-n-s**| "to gird (oneself)"	•CTX: **UGA** G suffc. *šnst* → DUL 821: */š-n-s/*.
|s^1-n-w/y|	Sem.: *šnh* (Hb.) "to change"; *šny* (JAram., Syr.) "to be different, go away"; *šanû(m)* (Akk.) "to be changed, become different", (?) "to run, trot".
|**s^1-n-w**| "to change, leave for, depart" (?)	•CTX: **UGA** G suffc. *šn, šnt*; (?) act. ptc. *šnwt* → DUL 822: */š-n-w/*; Tropper UG 597f.
|s^1-n-y| (1)	Culture word, Sem.: Cf. *šanā/âtu* (Akk.) "an oil-bearing aromatic plant".
Sanayt "an oil-bearing aromatic plant"	•LL: **EB** Ú.GUDU = *sa-na-tum, sa-na-du-um* → Conti QuSe 17 113f.; see Catagnoti Fs. Scandone Matthiae 1234ff.: "acacia".
|s^1-n-y| (2) See |**s^1-n-w/y**|	
|s^1-p-ʔ|	Culture word, etym. unc.
s^1upi(ʔ) "an ornament"	•CTX: **Q** Cf. *šu-pí-ú* → Bottéro ZA 44 120; AHw 1280: *šupiu*; CAD Š/3 323: *šupiu*.
|s^1-p-H-l|	Sem.: *šupêlu(m)* (Akk.) "to exchange", *šupêltu(m)* "exchange".
tes^{1}pēl "exchange"	•CTX: **EM** Suff. *téš-pe-li-šu* → CAD T 374f.
|s^1-p-k|	Sem.: *špk* (Hb.) "to shed, pour"; *špk* (JAram.) id.;. *šapāku(m)* (Akk.) "to heap up, pour on"; *safaka* (Arab.) "to shed, pour"; see also *sabaka* (Arab.) "to found, cast (metal)"; *sabaka, sabbaka* (Eth.) "to smelt, melt down".
|**s^1-p-k**| "to spill, shed"	•CTX: **UGA** G prefc. suff. *tšpkm*, imp. *špk* → DUL 823: */š-p-k/*.
Sipk (A) "a general term for cereal(s)"	•CTX: **EUPH** Passim *ši-ip-ku* → CAD Š/3 71: *šipku* B.

[712] Orel / Stolbova HSED 475f. no. 2250: **sin*= "tooth".

Sipk (B) “a kind of holdall”	•CTX: **EUPH** KUŠ *ši-ip-ku-um* → Durand ARM 30 170f.
Sipk (C) “in loose quantity, in bulk”	•CTX: **EUPH** SÍG *ši-ip-ku* → Durand ARM 30 163.

|s^1-p-l|	Sem.: *špl* (Hb.) “to be, become low, to fall”, *špl* (*šāpāl*) “”low (lying, in height)”, (*šēpel*) “lowliness”; *špl* (Aram., Syr.) “to be low”, *špl(?)* “plain, lower part”, *špwl(?)* “base, foot (of a mountain)”; *šapālu*(*m*) (Akk.) “to become low, deep”, *šaplu*(*m*) “underside, bottom”, *šaplû*(*m*) “lower(-lying)”, *šuplu*(*m*); “depth, deepness”, *šapiltu*(*m*) “lower part”; *safala* (Arab.) “to be(come) low, to be below, turn downward”, *sufl* “bottom”, *sifla* “lowly people”; *s^{1}fl* (OSArab.) “lowland, bottom, lower part”.
|S-p-l| “to be low, descend” (?)	•ONOM: **EB** Cf. *iš-ba-al$_6$-ma-lik* → Krebernik PET 61; Pagan ARES 3 176, 339.
|s^1-p-l| “to stoop, plunge (oneself); to knock down”	•CTX: **UGA** G *tšpl*; imp. *špl*; D prefc. *tšpl*, imp. *špl* → DUL 823: /*š-p-l*/.
Sapl “low (place); (lowly) people”	•CTX: **EUPH** *sa-ap-lim*, *sa-ap-la-am*; cf. *sa-bi-il*, *sa-ab-la-am*, *sa-bi-il-ku-nu* → Durand ARM 26/1 15f. fn. 42; ARM 26/2 226f. fn. d; LAPO 17 198f. (n°575) fn. c; Kupper ARM 28 13f. (13:5) fn. a; Zadok Fs. Hallo 330; Charpin AfO 40/41 1; Streck Onomastikon 1 112 § 1.95. **UGS** Cf. É IM X DI/KI *šap-li-mi* → vSoldt BiOr 47 733; Huehnergard ^{2}UVST 391, 398.
Sipl “lower part, lowliness”	•LL: **EB** AN.KI = *si-bí-lum* → Krebernik ZA 73 30 (781, fn. 96); Conti QuSe 17 189.
Sapilt “lowly people”	•CTX: **EUPH** Cf. *sa-bi-la-tum* → Durand ARM 26/1 16 fn. 42.

|s^1-p(-p)-r|	Culture word, Sem.: *š(w)pr* (*šōpār*, Hb.) “horn”; *šypwr(?)* (JAram., Syr.) “trumpet”; *sappāru*(*m*), *šappāru*(*m*) (Akk.) “wild ram”, *sappartu*, *šappartu* “point, tip (of horn?)”; *s^{1}frt* (OSArab.) “goats, small cattle”; *sappira* (Eth.) “rhinoceros”.
Sibbār “a larger (horned?) animal”	•LL: **EB** Cf. *ši$_4$-bar-ru$_{12}$* → Sjöberg WO 27 10.
s^{1}pr “horn(ed animal)” (?)	•CTX: **UGA** → DUL 824: *špr*.

|s^1-p-r|	Sem.: *špr* (Hb.) “to please”; *špr* (Palm.) “to please, do good”, *špr* (Palm., Hatra) “beautiful”; *špr* (Aram., Syr.) “to be beautiful, pleasing”, *špr*, *šwpr?* “beauty, best part”, *špyr* (Aram., Syr.) “beautiful, good”, *šwprn(?)* (Syr.) “grace”; *sibr* (Arab.) “beauty”, *masbūr* “beautiful”; see also *śamra* (Eth.) “to delight in, be pleased”.
Sapr “fairness, beauty”	•ONOM: **EUPH** *ša-ap-ra-kum* → Gelb CAAA 32, 185. **A7** *sa-ap-ra-ia*, *sa-ap-ra-a-du*; cf. ZA(*sà*)-*ap-ra*-AN → Wiseman AT 145; Gelb CAAA 32, 185; Arnaud AuOr 16 157.
Sipr “fairness, beauty”	•ONOM: **U3** *še-ep-ra-nu-um*, *ši-ip*(?)-*ra*(?)-*nu-um* → Buccellati Amorites 29, 182; Gelb CAAA 32, 187. **EUPH** *še-ip-ra-tu* → Gelb CAAA 32, 187.
s^{1}ipr, **s^{1}upr** “fairness, beauty”	•ONOM: **A4** *še-ap-ra*, *ši-ip-ra-an*, *ši-ip-ri-an*-TA(*dá*), *šu-up-ra* → Wiseman AT 146f.; Gelb CAAA 32, 187; Arnaud AuOr 26 158f.

Sapar "beautiful, pleasing"	•ONOM: **U3** *ša-ba-ar-kum* → Buccellati Amorites 68, 179f. **EUPH**, **B** *sa-pa-ra-an*, *a-bi-sa-pár/pa-ar*, *ba-aḫ-li-sa- pár/pa-ar*, *be-lí-sa-par/pár*, *i-zu-sa-pár/pa-ar* → Huffmon APNMT 252; Gelb CAAA 32, 185; Golinets Onomastikon 2 152f., 453.
Sapir "beautiful, pleasing"	•ONOM: **EB** Cf. *bu*$_{14}$*-sa-*^{bí}*bir*$_5$, *ša-bir*$_5$*-gi-nu*, *ša-pi-a/ra* → Pagan ARES 3 176, 295, 366. **U3** *ša-bi-ru-um* → Buccellati Amorites 117, 181; Gelb CAAA 32, 185; Golinets Onomastikon 2 159, 453. **EUPH**, **B** *sa-bi-ru(-um)*, *a-bi-ša-pí-ir*; fem. *sa-bi-ra-a-ia*, *sa-bi/pi-ra-tum* → Huffmon APNMT 252; Gelb CAAA 32, 185; Zadok Fs. Hallo 330 (see under Ś-B-R); Golinets Onomastikon 2 159f., 453. **TU** Cf. *sá-pí-ru-um* → Krebernik Tall Bi`a 226; Golinets Onomastikon 2 159, 453.
Suppur "very pleasing"	•ONOM: **B** *su-pu-ur-tum* → Gelb CAAA 32, 193 (ŚUPUR).

|s^1-p-y|	Sem.: Cf. *šph* (Hb. N) "to be swept down flat (by de wind)", *špy* (*š*^{e}*pî*) "plain on a higher level of land"; *špy* (JAram., Syr.) "to smooth", *špy*(*?*) "flat, plain"; *safā* (*safy*, Arab.) "to raise and scatter (said of the wind)", *sāfiyāʔ* "dust", *masfan* "something whirled up".
s^{1}p "tableland, dune" (?)	•CTX: **UGA** Pl. *špm* → DUL 822: *šp*.
ms^{1}p, ms^{1}py "elevated (place)" (?)	•CTX: **UGA** → DUL 585: *mšpy*. •ONOM: **UGA** Cf. unc. *mšp* → KTU 4.868:8 (vacat DUL).

|s^1-r-ʕ| See **|s^2-ʕ-r| (2)**	

|s^1-r-b|	Sem.: Cf. *šarbu* (Akk.) "rainy season"; *sariba* (Arab.) "to flow, leak, drizzle", *masrab* "course, river bed"; *saraba* (Eth.) "to flood".
|S-r-b| "to drip, drizzle, rain" (?)	•LL: **EB** Cf. ŠÀ.TAR.SUR = *dal-da-li-bù* |taStar(r)ib=| → Conti QuSe 17 164f.; altern. rdg |dalt=ay libb=u| → Krebernik ZA 73 22.

|s^1-r-D|	Sem.: *šrt* (Hb. D) "to serve, attend to the service of God"; *šrt* (Pun. D) "to serve".
|s^1-r-d| "to serve"	•CTX: **UGA** D suffc. *šrd*, imp. *šrd* → DUL 830f.: */š-r-d/*.

|s^1-r-d-n| Cf. **|θ-r-t-n-n|**	Loan. Non-Sem.: Cf. *Šrdn* (Eg.) "Sardinian (??; *sherden*)".
s^{1}erdan "appellative / GN"	•CTX: **EA** LÚ *ši-ir-da-nu*, LÚ *še-er-da-ni* (81:16; 122:35; 123:15) → AHw 1216; CAD Š/2 313. **UGS** LÚ *še-er-da-na* → Nougayrol PRU 4 234:6; AHw 1216; CAD Š/2 313. •ONOM: **UGS** Cf. unc. *sè-er-da-na* → Thureau-Dangin Syria 18 250 (RS 8.145):27 (Nougayrol PRU 3 257); AHw 1216; CAD Š/2 313.

|s^1-r-g|	Sem.: *saraǧa*, *sariǧa* (Arab.) "to lie"; see also *šaraǧa* "to lie, mix".

|s^1-r-g| "to lie, deceive"	•CTX: **UGA** G prefc. suff. *tšrgn*, inf. / verbal noun. suff. *šrgk* → Renfroe AULS 149f.; cf. DUL 831: /*š-r-g*/: "to twist, tangle up".
|s^1-r-γ|	Sem.: Cf. *šrʕ*, *šrg*, *šrq* (JAram.) "to slip, slide"; *šerû* (Akk.) "to take refuge".
Sarrāḳ "refugee, asylum seeker" (?)	•CTX: **A7** Cf. pl. *šar-ra-aq-qí* → Hess UF 24 465f.
|s^1-r-H|	Culture word, Sem.: *šerʔu*(*m*), *širʔu*(*m*), *še*/*irḫu*(*m*) (Akk.) "furrow".
s^{1}erHat "furrow"	•LL: **EM** (GIŠ).APIN/ÀBSIN = [*e-pu-u*]*n-nu* : *ši-ir-ḫa-tù* → Civil AuOr 7 12 (125'); Pentiuc Vocabulary 172; Cohen Proceedings 53^e RAI 1 828f.
SurHat "plough"	•LL: **EB** GIŠ.APIN = *su-ḫa-tum* → Sjöberg Fs. Kienast 547f.
|s^1-r-x-l|	Etym. unc., Sem.: Cf. *šerḫullum*, *šurḫullu* (Akk.) "a gold or silver bead; a necklace".
Sarxull (A) "a piece of jewellery"	•CTX: **EUPH** *šar-ḫu-lu*, *ša-ar-ḫu-lu* → Arkhipov ARM 32 96 (1).
Sarxull (B) "a bronze item"	•CTX: **EUPH** *ša-ar-ḫu-ul-lu*, *ša-ar-ḫu-ul-li* → Arkhipov ARM 32 96 (2, 3).
|s^1-r-r| (1)	Primary noun, Sem.: *šr* (*šor*, Hb.) "navel, navel cord"; *šwr*(*?*), *šrh*, *šrt*(*?*) (JAram., Syr.) "navel, navel cord"; *surr*, *surra*, *surur* (Arab.) "umbilical cord"; *šīrɛ*, *šírɔ*, *šərā* (MSArab.) "navel".
s^{1}r (A) "navel"	•CTX: **UGA** Sg. *šr*, suff. *šrh* → DUL 829f.: *šr* (IV).
|s^1-r-r| (2)	Sem.: *šrr* (Aram., Syr.) "to be firm, tight, true", (C) "to stablish", *šrr*(*?*) "firmness, truth", *šryr* (Aram., Syr.) "firm, true", *mšrr* (Syr.) "firm, stable", *mšrn* "constant, trustworthy", *mšrrn*(*?*) "affirmer"; *śarr* (MSArab.) "to attach"; *śārara*, *sārara* "to lay a foundation, establish". Cf. *šryr* (*šārîr*, Hb.) "sinew, muscle" (?); *ša*/*urumma* (Nuzi-Akk.) "indeed, certainly, forthwith" (?; see below: *s^{1}arrumma*, *s^{1}urrumma*). See further: *šarāru*(m) (Akk.) "to go ahead" (?).[713]
|s^1-r-r| "to be firm"	•CTX: **EG** *ma-ša-ra-ra* (|mas^{1}arrira| D ptc. ['attached, said of a pole'] → Hoch SWET 159f. no. 208.[714]
s^{1}irar "the firm one"	•ONOM: **EM** *še-ra-ru* → Pruzsinszky PTEm 177 [753].
s^{1}arrumma, s^{1}urrumma "indeed, certainly, forthwith" (?)	•CTX: **EA** Cf. *ša-ar-ru-um-ma*, *šar-ru-um-ma*, *šu-ur-ru-um-ma* → AHw 1190: *šarrumma*, 1286: *šurrumma*; CAD Š/3 361f.: *šurrumma*. **UGS** *šur-ru-um-ma* → AHw 1190: *šarrumma*, 1286: *šurrumma*; CAD Š/3 361f.: *šurrumma*.
ms^{1}rr "pointer (of the balance), pivot" (?)	•CTX: **UGA** Sg. suff. *mšrrm* → DUL 586f.: *mšrr*.

[713] Unc. Ebl. LL Á.GÍR.TAG = *sa-la-lum*, *sa-ra-ra-du*; Conti QuSe 17 153 (543).

[714] Sivan / Cochavi-Rainey WSVES 81: *ma-ša-ra-ra* "polished"; Helck Beziehungen no. 119.

|s^1-r-r| (3)

Sem.: *šarāru*(m) (Akk.) “to go ahead”, (D) “encourage” (?), *šarūr*(*m*) “brilliance, ray”.

|S-r-r| (A) “to lean out of, lean toward, bend; shine”

•CTX: **EUPH** Gtn prefc. Cf. *a-na ra-ma-ni-šu iš-ta-na-ar-*[*ra*]*-ar*, *a-na ra-ma-ni-ka la ta-áš*/*-ta-na-ar-ra-a*[*r*] → Durand ARM 26/1 424 (197:26f.) fn. e; LAPO 18 404 fn. e (“briller”).
•LL: **EB** Á.GÍR.TAG = *sa-la-lum* → Conti QuSe 17 153.

Sari/ur “leaned, bent”

•CTX: **EUPH** G suffc. *ša*-RU-*ir* (!) → Durand ARM 26/1 (155:13), 322 fn. e.

Sarart “lean, tilt, inclination”

•LL: **EB** Á.GÍR.TAG = *sa-ra-ra-dum* → Conti QuSe 17 153.

|s^1-r-r| (4)

Sem.: *šry* (Aram., Syr., D) “to begin”; *šurrû*(*m*), *šarrû*(*m*) (Akk.) “to begin, start, inaugurate”.

tas^1rit “beginning, inauguration”

•LL: **EM** [NA$_4$.BA]LA = NA$_4$ *ta-aš-ri-*[*ti*] → Arnaud EMAR 6/4 127; Kleber NABU 2016/89.[715]

|s^1-r(-r)| (5)

Etym. unc.

Sur(r) “a piece of jewellery”

•CTX: **EUPH** *šu-ru*/*rum* → Arkhipov ARM 32 100.

s^1ur(r) “a valuable object”

•CTX: **A4** *šu-u-ur-ra*, *šu-u-ri* → Wiseman AT 112 (440: 9f.); CAD S/3 370: *šūru* E.

|s^1-r-s^1-r| (1)

Culture word, Sem.: *šršrt* (*šaršeret*, Hb.) “chain”; *šlšlh*, *šlšlt?* JAram. “chain”, *šlšl* “to let down by chain”; *šeršer*(*r*)*u*(*m*) “link (in a chain)” (Akk.), *šeršerratu*(*m*), *šeršerretu*, *šaršarratu*(m) “chain, set of rings”; *silsila* (Arab.) “chain”, *salsala* “to link together, concatenate”; *s^1s^1lt* (OSArab.) “chain”; *senselet*, *silsileh* (MSArab.) “chain”; *sansal* (Eth.) “chain”, *sansala* “to chain, link”.

s^1as^1s^1ar “chain”

•ONOM: **EUPH** *ša-ša-ra-nu*(*-um*) → Gelb CAAA 33 (ŠARŠAR), 194.[716]

s^1s^1rt “chain”

•CTX: **UGA** → Tropper UG 301; DUL 835: *ššrt*.

s^1us^1ara(h) “chain” (?)

•CTX: **EM** Cf. *šu-ša-ra* → Pentiuc Vocabulary 174.

|s^1-r-s^1-r| (2)

Culture word, Sem.: Cf. *ššr* (*šāšar*, *šāšēr*, Hb.) “vermillon”; *šaršerru*, *šaršarru*, *šeršerru*, *šaššēru* (Akk.) “red paste”.

s^1s^1r “reddish colouring agent, (?) minium”

•CTX: UGA → DUL 834f.: *ššr*.

|s^1-r-t|

Culture word, Sem. etym. unc. Cf. *ešertu(m)*, *išertum*, *aširtu*, *iširtu* (Akk.) “chapel, shrine”; see also *šrt* (Hb., D) “to serve, to attend to the service of God”, *šrt* (*šārēt*) “ritual service”; *šrt* (Pun., D) “to serve”, *mšrt* (Ph.) “service”.

---

715 Read NA$_4$.BALA = *ab-nu ta-ši-ri-tu*$_4$ in Hh. XVI 189.

716 See also Arkhipov ARM 32 174: *šaršarr*(*at*)*um* (?).

Sirat "chapel, shrine"	•LL: **EB** É.SAG = *si-la-tum* → Conti QuSe 17 120; Catagnoti QuSe 29 20, 227; Sjöberg Fs. Wilcke 254.
|s^1-r-w/y|	Sem.: *šrh* (Hb.) "to let loose", (D) "to release" (?), *šryh* (*širyāh*) "small arrow"; *šry* (Aram., Syr.) "to loosen, untie", *šry(?)* "releasing, release", *šry* "free, unrestrained"; *sarā* (*sarw*), *sarrā*, *ʔasrā* "to rid someone of worries, remove, pull off (clothes)", *sarwa*, *sirwa*, *surwa* "dart"; *saraya* (Eth.) "to absolve, pardon".
|S-r-y| **(A)** "to release" (?)	•CTX: **EB** G imp. *si-rí* → Fronzaroli MARI 5 269; Bonechi MARI 6 235.
|s^1-r-y/w| "to release"	•CTX: **UGA** G inf. suff. *šrh* → DUL 833: */š-r-y/w/*.
Sīr (B) "sending"·	•CTX: **EB** Sg. suff. *si-la-ga*, *si-ra-ga*, *si-la-na*, *si-la-su-ma* → Catagnoti / Fronzaroli ARET 16 36, 264; Catagnoti QuSe 29 76, 72, 227.
s^{1}rt "dart-throver squad" (?)	•CTX: **UGA** Sg. *šrt*, du. *šrtm* → DUL 833: *šrt* (II).
|s^1-r-w-n-s^1|	Loanword. Non-Sem.: *še/irwanaše* (Hurr.) mng unc.[717]
s^{1}e/irwanas^{1}e "a variety of gold" (?)	•CTX: **Q** *še-er-wa-na-še*, *ši-ir-wa-na-še* → Bottéro RA 43 17 fn. 5; 44 120; AHw 1220: *še/irwanaše*; CAD Š/2 336: *šerwanaše*, *širwanaše*; Richter BGH 395.
|s^1-r-y| See **|s^1-r-w/y|**	
|s^1-s-y| (1)	Sem.: *šasû(m)*, *šasāʔum* (Akk.) "to shout, call (out); read (out)".
|S-s-y| "to shout"	•CTX: **EB** Gt prefc. *il-da-zu* |yiStasay=ū| → Catagnoti / Fronzaroli ARET 16 81, 238; Catagnoti QuSe 29 28, 65, 165, 225. •ONOM: **EB** *daš*?(UR)-*zi*, *íl-zi*, *il*$_x$(NE)-*zi*, *iš*$_{12}$(LAM)-*zi*, *íl-zi-du*, *íl-zi-dum*, *íl-zi-ma-lik*, *íl-zi*-BE, *íl-zi-da-mu*, *iš*$_{12}$(LAM)-*zi-da-mu*; cf. unc. rdgs NE-*zi-ma*-NI, NE-*zi-ma-a-ḫu*, NE-*zi-ma-lik* → Pagan ARES 3 177f., 301, 336, 342.
Sasay "calling"	•ONOM: **EB** *sa-sa-ì*, *sa-za-ì*, *sa:za-ì*, *ša-za-ì*, *sa-za-iš*, *sa-za-iš-lu*, *ša-za-iš* → Krebernik PET 107, Pagan ARES 3 177f., 361f., 367.
|s^1-s-y| (2)	Sem. *šsh*, *šss* (Hb.) "to spoil, plunder". Non-Sem. Cf. *šꜣsw* (Eg.) "Shasu-bedouin".
s^{1}ōsiy "despoiler"	•CTX: **EA** Pl. cstr. *šu-sú-mì* (|šōsû=mi)| *a-bi-ia* → Rainey EAT 95, CAT 3 236; Sivan GAGl 274; Moran AmL 306 fn. 6; Izre'el Orient 38 82.
|s^1-s^1|	Culture word, Sem.: *šwš* (JAram., Syr.) "liquorice"; *šūšu(m)* (Akk.) id.; *sūs* (Arab.) id.
SuS "liquorice"	•CTX: **EB** GIŠ.ŠUŠ$_x$(ŠÉ+NÁM) = *su-šum* → Conti QuSe 17 138f.; Catagnoti QuSe 29 24. 228.

[717] Richter BGH 395.

|s^1-s^1-m-t(-t)| Culture word, etym. unc.

s^{1}es^{1}mit(t) "a stone" •CTX: **Q** *še-eš-mi-tù*, *še-eš-mi-it-tu*$_4$, *še-eš-mi-it-tù* → Bottéro RA 44 120; AHw 1220; *šešmittu*; CAD Š/2 337: *šešmittu*.

|s^1-s^1-n-n| Culture word, etym. unc.

s^{1}as^{1}s^{1}inn "a gem" •CTX: **Q** *ša-aš-ši-in-nu* → Bottéro RA 44 120; AHw 1198: *šaššinnu* ('eine Gemme' ?); CAD Š/2 176: *šaššinnu* ('an ornament').

|s^1-t| Cf. **|ʔ/y-S-D|**, **|w-s-d|** Primary noun, Sem.: *št* (*sēt*) "base, foundation, buttocks"; *ʔšt*(*h*?) "(Ph.) "pillar" (?); *ʔ ist*, *satah* (Arab.) "podex, buttocks"; *šīt*, *šét*, *šéh* (MSArab.) "backside, buttocks; privates".[718]

s^{1}t (A) "base, foot" •CTX: **UGA** → DUL 837f.: *št* (I); Watson FO 52 338.

|s^1-t-G(-G)| Culture word, Sem.: *šutukku*(*m*) (Akad.) "reed-hut, reed shelter". Non-Sem.: šutug (Sum.) "reed hut".

Sutuḳḳ "a chapel" •LL: **EB** AGRUN = *šu-du-gu*; É.SAG.KÉŠ = *šu-du-gu gal-la-tum* → Conti QuSe 17 39, 118ff.[719]

|s^1-t-l| Sem.: *štl* (Hb.) "to plant", *štyl* (*šatîl*) "offshoot"; *štl* (JAram., Syr.) "to plant", *štl*(*ʔ*) "plant, offspring", *štyl*(*ʔ*) (JAram.) "plant, planting"; *satālu* (Akk.) "to plant", *šitlu*(*m*) "sprout, seedling"; *šatala* (Arab., sibilant irregularity?) "to plant", *šatla* "seedling".

Satil "bud, shoot" •LL: **EB** GIŠ.KUL = *sa-ti-um* → Conti QuSe 17 36, 134.

|s^1-t-m| Culture word, Sem.: *šatammu*(*m*), *šattammu*(*m*) (Akk.) "administrator, government auditor". Non-Sem: šatam (Sum.) "an administrative official (government auditor)".

θutum(m) "an administrative official" •CTX: **EB** Sg. cstr. *šu-du-mu* → Fronzaroli ARET 13 127, 300; Catagnoti QuSe 29 234.

|s^1-t-p| Sem.: Cf. *šatāpu* (Akk.) "to cut out", *ši/etiptu*(*m*) "excision" (?), *naštiptum* "bandage".

Sata/ipt, Sitipt "allocation of garment(s)" (?) •CTX: **EB** Cf. *sa-ti-bù*, *sa-díp-tum*, *sa-da-bí-iš*, *ša-dab-tíš* → Fronzaroli ARET 11 27f., 160; Pasquali QuSe 19 248ff., 251ff.
•LL: **EB** Cf. MU.TÚG (^{mu}mu$_4$)= *si-díb-tum* (MEE 4 1142, 0213) → Krebernik PIHANS 106 91; Pasquali QuSe 19 251.

---

[718] In part the mngs may merge with the the (probl. related) basis |ʔ/y-S-D| (GlOS 1 45). See Militarev / Kogan SED 1 226 (no. 255).

[719] For *gal-la-tum* see Krebernik ZA 73 14: read |qallātim| "Sklavinnen".

maStap "(ceremonial) bandage, *pallium*" (?)	•CTX: **EB** *maš-da-bù*; cf. *maš-da-ù, ma-sa-da-ù* → Archi NABU 2005/42; NABU 2019/40; Fronzaroli ARET 11 160, 180; Pasquali QuSe 19 248ff.; NABU 2011/3; 2012/04.

|s^1-t-y| (1)	Sem.: *šth* (Hb.) "to drink", *mšth* (*mišteh*) "drinking, banquet"; *šty* (Aram., Syr.) "to drink", *mšty(?)* "drinking"; *šatû*(m) (Akk.) "to drink", *maštû(m)* "drinking vessel, drink", *maštītu*(m) "drinking vessel, drink"; *ms¹ty* (OSArab.) "drink, libation"; *satya* (Eth.) "to drink", *maste* "drinking vessel, drink.
|S-t-y| "to drink"	•ONOM: **EB** *šè-ti, si-ti, si-ti-gi-lu*, passim with DNN: *si-ti-àr-ru*$_{12}$, *si-ti-da-mu, si-ti-gú-nu, si-ti-ì-lum, si-ti-li-im, si-ti-ma-lik*; *tíš-da-um, tíš-da*-AD.MU, *ti-iš-da-mu, ti-iš-te-da-mu,*[720] *tíš-da-ma-lik* → Krebernik PET 62, 106; Müller BaE 179f., 184; Fronzaroli ARES 1 23; Pagan ARES 3 178, 364, 367, 370f.
|s^1-t-y| "to drink"	•CTX: **UGA** G prefc. *tšty, tšt, yšt, nšt, tštyn*, suff. *ištn, ištynh*, suffc. *šty*; imp. *št, šty*, suff. *štym, štm*; inf. *šty*; act. ptc. *štyt* → DUL 840: */š-t-y/*.
s^1itiy, s^1utiy "drinking"	•CTX: **EA** *ši-ti, ši-it-yi, ši-te-šu, šu-ta-ia* → Rainey CAT 2 376, 379, 403; CAD Š/3 142f.: *šitû* A, (*šutû*).
muStayt "drink, libation"	•LL: **EB** A.TAG = *mu-sa-da-tum* → Conti QuSe 17 169f.
ms^1t "banquet" (?)	•CTX: **UGA** → Tropper KWU 81; cf. DUL 587: *mšt* (I) "?".
ms^1tt "drink, libation"	•CTX: **UGA** → DUL 588: *mštt*.
tas^1it "goblet"	•CTX: **EM** *ta-ši-ti*, pl. *ta-ši-ia-ti* → Fleming Installation 122, 144f.

|s^1-t-y| (2)	Sem.: *šty* (*šᵉtî*, Hb.) "warp", base *šth* (conjecture G ptc.**šātôy* "weaver"), *šty(?)* (Aram., Syr.) "warp", *šty* (JAram., Syr.) "to weave (together)"; *šatû(m)* (Akk.) "to knot together, weave", *šatû(m)* "weaved, knotted", *šītu* "textile", *šutû(m), sutû* "woven material, warp".
s^1ut(t)uy "type of cloth"	•CTX: **EUPH** TÚG *šu-ti* (Tall Leilān 97:1); TÚG *šu-tu-um, šu-tu*-WA(*ya*)-*tin*, cf. TÚG.BAR.SI *šu-ti-im* → Ismail WTL 102; Durand ARM 30 119f. **EM** Cf. TÚG *zu-du la-be-ru* → Westenholz Emar Tablets 42, 44 (15:13).
s^1etayt "a garment"	•CTX: **UGS** Cf. TÚG *še-ta-ti* → AHw 1253: *šitûtu*; CAD Š/2 339: *šetâtu*.
s^1tt "spun, woven (wool)"	•CTX: **UGA** Fem. *štt* → DUL 839: *štt*.

|s^1-ṭ-p|	Sem.: Cf. *šaṭāpu(m), śatāpum* (Akk.) "to preserve life, rescue", *šaṭpu, śaṭpum* "rescued".
|S-ṭ-p| "to rescue, save"	•ONOM: **EB** *iš-dub-ì, iš-dub-il, iš-dub*-^{d}UTU, *iš-dub-sar* → Krebernik ET 62; 92; Pagan ARES 3 178, 339.
Saṭp, Saṭip "rescued, saved"	•ONOM: **EB** *sa-ti-bù* → Pagan ARES 3 178, 361. Diff. Pasquali NABU 1996/128: not a PN. **EUPH** Fem. *ša-aṭ-ba* → Gelb CAAA 33, 194.
Saṭūp "rescued, saved"	•ONOM: **EUPH** *ša-ṭu-bi*-DINGIR, *ša-ṭu-bi-el*[721] → Gelb CAAA 33, 194.

[720] See Bonechi QuSe 15 151ff.

[721] |šaṭūb=ʔil| "(he is been) rescued, oh DN".

|s¹-ṭ-r|	Sem.: *š(w)ṭr* (*šōṭēr*, Hb.) "civil servant, office holder", *mšṭr* (*mišṭār*) "writing (in heavens)"; *šṭr* (Pun.) "to inscribe, write", *mšṭr* "officer", *mšṭrt* "administration", *šṭr* (Nab., Palm.) "document"; *šṭr(?)* (Aram., Syr) "document"; *šaṭāru(m)*, *śaṭārum*, *saṭāru* (Akk.) "to write (down)", *šaṭāru* "writing", *šaṭṭiru* "eager to write", *mašṭaru* "inscription"; *saṭara*, *saṭṭara* (Arab.) "to write, record, draw lines", *saṭr* "writing"; *s¹ṭr* (OSArab.) "to write, inscribe".
Sāṭir "registrar" (?)	•ONOM: **EB** Cf. unc. ŠA-*ti-ir*, ŠA-*ti-lu* → Pagan ARES 3 178f., 367. For the writings with ŠA see Catagnoti QuSe 29 20: |ṯa|.
Saṭṭār "scribe" (?)	•ONOM: **EB** Cf. unc. ŠA-*da-lum* → Pagan ARES 178f., 366. See above.
mas¹ṭir "office, chancellery"	•CTX: **EG** *mas-ti₃-ra* / *mas-ta-ya-r* → Hoch SWET 134f. no. 202.[722]
|s¹-w/y-ḫ| See |**s¹-ḫ-t**|, |**s¹-w/y-ḫ**|	
|s¹-w-ḳ| (1)	Primary noun, Sem.: *šwq* (*šôq*, Hb.) "thigh, fibula, shank"; *šq(?)* (Aram., Syr.) "thigh, leg"; *sāqu(m)*, *sīqu* (Akk.) "thigh"; *sāq* (Arab.) "thigh". Non-Sem.: **saḳu=* (West Chadic) "leg"; **sak=* (Central Chadic) "leg".[723]
s¹ḳ "thigh, leg"	•CTX: **UGA** → DUL 826: *šq*.
|s¹-w-ḳ| (2)	Sem.: Cf. *tšwqh* (*tᵉšûqāh*) "desire, longing"; *šwq(?)* (JAram.) "desire"; *sāqa* (*sawq*, Arab.) "to drive, urge on"; *tasaqqʷa* (Eth.) "to covet".
|**s¹-w-ḳ**| "to be impelled, urged"	•CTX: **EG** Cf. *ša-qa* → Hoch SWET 288f. no. 412.
|s¹-w-l|	Culture word, Sem.: *šwl* (*šûl*, Hb.) "seam".
s¹awala "trapper (the horse's skirt)"	•CTX: **EG** *s-wa-r* → Hoch SWET 257 no. 361.
|s¹-w/y-p|	Sem.: Cf. *šwp* (Hb.) "to grip, strike someone hard"; *šwp* (JAram., Syr.) "to grind down, rub down".[724] Cf. *su(p)pannum* (OAss.) "a container"
Sawp "fine flour"	•LL: **EB** ŠE.ZÌ.[GU] = *sa-bù-um* → Fronzaroli QuSe 13 149; ARET 9 406; Conti QuSe 17 179.
Sawpān "a wide vessel (for flour ?)"	•CTX: **EB** *sá-ba-núm* → Fronzaroli ARET 11 25, 166, 181.

[722] Sivan / Cochavi-Rainey WSVES 81: *máś-tá-r* "office"; Helck Beziehungen no. 113.
[723] Orel / Stolbova HSED 460 no. 2179: **saḳ=* "leg".
[724] Unrelated: *šāfa*, *šawwafa* (*šawf*, Arab.) "to polish, adorn".

yaSīB "battering ram"	•CTX: **EUPH**, **B** GIŠ *ia-si-bu*, GIŠ *ia-si-bi-im*, GIŠ *ia-ši-bi*, and other writings: *ia/ya-ši-ba-am*, *ia-šu-ba*, *ia-šu-bu-ú*, *a-ši-bi*, *šu-pi-i* → AHw 412, 1565: *jāšibum*, *wāšibum* (?); CAD A/2 428: *ašibu*; Zadok Fs. Hallo 330; Durand ARM 21 346ff. **R** → GIŠ *ya-si-bi-*[*im* → Dalley / Walker / Hawkins Tell Rimah 21 (9:8').

|s^1-w-r| (1)	Sem.: Cf. *š*(*w*)*rr* (*šōrēr*, Hb.) "enemy"; *šwr* (JAram., Syr.) "to jump over, attack"; *šurru*(*m*) (Akk.) "to bend forwards"; *sāra* (*sawr*, Arab.), *sāwara* "to leap, attack, assault", *sawra* "violence, vehemence"; *sarara* (Eth.) "to leap upon; assault".[725]
|s^1-w-r| "to threaten, trap, besiege"	•CTX: **EA** Cf. unc. *ša-a-i-ru* (act. ptc.?) → AHw 1134: *šāʔiru*; Moran AmL 237: "traitor"; Rainey CAT 1 16, 46. **UGA** G suffc. suff. *šrn*, imp. suff. *šrnn* → DUL 828: /*š-r*/ (II).[726]
s^1rr "enemy"	•CTX: **UGA** → DUL 832: *šrr*; Watson Fs. Postgate 712.
s^1ār (A) "hostile, inimical; enemy"	•CTX: **EA** Sg. *ša-ru*, *ša-ra*, pl. *ša-*(*a-*)*ru-tu*, *ša-ru-te*, *ša-ru-ta*$_{(5)}$; sg. LÚ *ša-ru*, LÚ *ša-ra*, cstr. LÚ *ša-ri*, pl. LÚ *ša-ri* MEŠ, LÚ.MEŠ *ša-ru-tu*$_{(4)}$, LÚ.MEŠ *ša-ru-ta*, LÚ *ša-ru-ta* MEŠ → AHw 1193: *šāru* III; CAD Š/2 132f.: *šāru*; Rainey CAT 1 46. **UGS** Cf. unc. *ša-r*[*u*(?)] → PRU 4 215 (RS 17.288) 12; CAD Š/2 132f.: *šāru*.
s^1r (E) "violence, vehemence" (?)	•CTX: **UGA** Sg. *šr* → Tropper KWU 123: *šr*$_5$ (ctx.?); diff. cf. DUL 830: *šr* (V) "disgrace" (?).

|s^1-w-r| (2)	Primary noun, Sem.: *šwr* (*šûr*, Hb.) "wall"; *šwr*(*ʔ*) (Aram., Hatra, Syr.) "wall; *sūr* (Arab.) "wall", *sawwar* "to enclose, fence in".
s^1ār (B) "wall; a kind of building (caravansery ?)"	•CTX: **EM** Cf. É-*tu*$_4$ *ša-ra* → Pentiuc Vocabulary 169f.[727] •ONOM: **EUPH**, **B** Cf. *sa-ri*, *sa-ru-um*, *sa-ri-ia*, *sa-ra-nu-um* → Gelb CAAA 181 (ŚAʔR); Zadok Fs. Hallo 330.
s^1ūr "wall"	•ONOM: **EG** *šw-r-y* → Schneider APÄQ 198 no. 420.

|s^1-w-s^1|	Sem.: Cf. *sāsa* (Arab.) "to dominate, govern", *siyāsa* "administration"; *šyš* (Syr. D) "to placate".
s^1awas^1ata "governing" (?)	•CTX: **EG** *ša-wa-ša-ta* → Hoch SWET 275 no. 394.

|s^1-w-ṭ|	Sem.: *šwṭ* (Hb.) "to rove about, roam, row across water", *šyṭ* (*šayiṭ*) "oar", *mšwṭ* (*māšôṭ*) "rudder"; *šwṭ* / *šṭṭ* (Aram.) "to roam", *šwṭ* (JAram., Syr.) "to swim, float; to sail", *šyṭ*(*ʔ*) (Aram.) "swimmer; sailor", *mšwṭ* (JAram.) "rudder or oar"; *šâṭu* (Akk.) "to pull, tow". See also *sāṭa* (*sawṭ*, Arab.) "to whip, lash", *sawṭ* "whip", *miswaṭ* "stick used for stirring"; *swṭ*, *soṭa* (Eth.) "to mix", *masoṭ* "mixing-vessel".
mas^{1}ōṭa "small galley propelled by oars"	•CTX: **EG** *mas-ta*, *mas-ta-ʔu*$_3$*-t* (< |mas^{1}awṭ=|) → Hoch SWET 153f. no. 201.
mθṭ "oar" (?)	•CTX: **UGA** Pl. *mṯṭm* → DUL 598: *mṯṭ*; Huehnergard ²UVST 399.[728]

[725] Arab. *ṯāra* (*ṯawr*) "to stir, revolt, rage" is a denominative of *ṯawr* "bull, steer".

[726] Gt prefc. there is probably wrong; see \|n-t-r\| Š, and Tropper KWU 92: *ntr*.

[727] Probl. a kind of caravansery built near the city wall; see Pentiuc loc.cit. with reference to Hatra *šwrʔ* "wall". For EM É-*tu*$_4$ *ša-ra ù É ḫa-ab-lu* cf. Hatra *šwrʔ w ʔbwlʔ* "the wall and the gateway".

[728] Probl. a direct loan. See Tropper UG 109f. for the occasional Ug. *θ* instead of the expected Sem. *s^1*.

|s^1-w/y-ṭ|

Sem.: *šwṭ* (*šôṭ*, Hb.) "outburst, sudden spate of water"; *sawṭ* (Arab.) "pond, pool"; *ʔs^1yṭ* (pl. OSArab.) "ponds, rainwater cisterns"; *swṭ*, *soṭa* (Eth.) "to pour, spill".

Sawṭ, Siyṭ "cisterne, pond"

•LL: **EB** ŠÀ.A.UŠ$_x$(LAK 672) = *sa-a-tum*, *si-a-tum* → Conti QuSe 17 162f.; Sjöberg Fs. Pettinato 265; Bonechi Proceedings 44 RAI 2 101.

|s^1-w-y| (1)

Culture word, Sem. etym. unc. Cf. *šwh* (*šāweh*, Hb.) "plain", elem. in TN *šwh qrytym*, probl. from a basis meaning "to be equal" (*šwh* Hb., *šwy* Aram.; Arab. *sawwā* "to make equal, to level, make even"; *sōwi* [MSArab.] "to level"). Unlikely: *šwʔh* (*šôʔāh*, Hb.) "storm, trouble, ruin", probl. from *šwʔ* (cf. Arab., OSArab., Eth.) "to be bad, wicked".

Sawuy "barren plain, flat wasteland"

•CTX: **EUPH**, **B** *sa-we-e* → AHw 1033: *sawûm*; CAD S 202f.: *sawû*; Zadok Fs. Hallo 330; Streck Onomastikon 1 115 § 1.95.

|s^1-w-y| (2)

Sem.: Cf. *šʔh* (Hb.) "to roar, foam", with a by-form *šwʔ*; cf. *tšwʔh* (*t^{e}šûʔāh*) "noise(s), crash", *šʔwn* (*šāʔôn*) "noise, roar".

ts^1yt "roar, shouting" (?)

•CTX: **UGA** → DUL 869: *tšyt*.[729]

|s^1-y-B|
See **|s^1-w/y-p|**

|s^1-y-d|

Sem.: Cf. *sāda*, *siyāda* (Arab.) "to be(come) master", *sayyid*, *sāʔid* "master, chef, prince", *sayyida*, *sitt* (modern and colloquial) "lady"; *sāydā* (Eth.) "lady".

s^1t (C) "dame, lady"

•CTX: **UGA** → DUL 838: *št* (IV).[730]

|s^1-y-H|
See **|s^1-w/y-H|**

|s^1-y-p|
See **|s^1-w/y-p|**

|s^1-y-r| (1)

Primary noun, Sem.: *šyr* (*šîr*, Hb.) "song", *šyrh* (*šîrāh*) "song", *šyr* "to sing", *šr* (*šār*), *mšrr* (*m^{e}šorēr*) "singer"; *šr* (Ph.) "singer", *šyr*(*?*) (JAram.) "song", *šyr* (JAram., Syr.) "to sing", *šry* (JAram.) "to sing", *šyrh*, *šyrtʔ* "song".[731]
Non-Sem: **sir=* (East Chadic) "to sing", **sur=* (Omotic) id.[732] Cf. šir (Sum.) "to sing; song";[733] *šaḫri* (Hurr.) "musical interval".[734]

---

[729] "Triumph, success", although the connection with Hb. *twšyh* (*tûšiyyāh*, mng and etym. unc.) is highly problematic.
[730] The passages listed in DUL 838 under *št* (III) ("tearing apart, separation, desolation" (?)) belong probl. to this entry; see Tropper KWU 124: *št₂*.
[731] For Akk. *šēru*(*m*) "song, chant" see below: *Sēr*.
[732] Orel / Stolbova HSED 477 no. [2258]: **sir=* / **sur=* "to sing".
[733] Since Lagash II (Gudea, seldom); mostly OBab.

|s^1-y-r| "to sing"	•CTX: **UGA** G prefc. *åšr, tšr, yšr*, imp. *šr* → DUL 828: */š-r/* (I).
s^1ār (C) "singer"	•CTX: **EM** Pl. LÚ.MEŠ *šàr-ru* → Zadok AION 51 119.
Sēr, **Sīr (C)** "song"	•CTX: **EUPH** *še-ra-am* → AHw 1219: *šēru*(m) III; CAD Š/2 335: *šēru* B; Durand LAPO 16 547 fn. c.[735] •ONOM: **EB** Cf. *si-lu*(DIB), *si-rí, sì*(SUM)*-ìr, sì*(SUM)*-rí,*[736] *sì*(SUM)*-rúm, šè*(KU)*-ir-ma-lik, si-ir-ma-lik, si-la-mu-ud, si-li-mu-du* → Pagan ARES 3 180, 363f., 367.[737]
s^1īr "song"	•LL: **UGS** EZEN = *za-am-ma-ru* = *ḫal-mi* = *ši-i-ru* → Sivan GAGl 277; Huehnergard UVST 181; vSoldt SAU 307.
s^1r (C) "song"	•CTX: **UGA** Sg. cstr. *šr* → DUL 828: *šr* (I).
s^1r (D) "musician, singer"	•CTX: **UGA** Sg. *šr*, pl. *šrm* → DUL 828f.: *šr* (II).
ms^1r (A) "song"	•CTX: **UGA** → DUL 586: *mšr* (II).

|s^1-y-r| (2)
See **|s^1-w/y-r|**

|s^1-y-t|	Sem.: *šyt* (Hb.) "to set, place, establish", *št* (Ph., Pun.) "to place, put, establish", *šêtu(m), sêtu(m), šiātu, šâtu* (Akk.) "to leave remaining".
|S-y-t| "to place, put, establish"	•LL: **EB** Cf. IGI.KAL-KAL = *šè-a-du bu$_y$-ti(-í)*; [IGI.KÙ.DUB.IGI.GAR] = *šè-a-du ma-ḫa-rí a-na-a* → Fales QuSe 13 181 (705a, 728b); Conti QuSe 17 185 (728b).[738] •ONOM: **EUPH, B** *ia-si-tum, ia-si-ta-am, ia-si-ta-an, i-si-it-na, ia-si-it-na, ia-si-it-a-bi(-im), ia-si-it-a-bu-(um), ia-si-it-*A.GI.E, *ia-si-it-na-a- bi, ia-si-it-na-a-bu(-m), ia-si-it-na-a-ḫu-um, ia-si-it-na-*DINGIR, *ia-si-it-na-el*; *a-ḫi-si-it, su-mu-ia-si-it* → Huffmon APNMT 253; Gelb CAAA 32, 180; Golinets Onomastikon 2 290, 456.[739] **R** *ia-si-it-na-a-bu-um* → Dalley / Walker / Hawkins Tell Rimah 122 (150:2); Golinets Onomastikon 2 290, 456. **TU** *a-si-it-a-ḫa, i-si-it-na-a-na* → Krebernik Tall Bi`a 210, 217; Golinets Onomastikon 2 289f., 456.
|s^1-y-t| "to place, put, establish"	•CTX: **UGS** G prefc. *åšt, tšt, yšt*, suff. *åštk, åštm, åštn, tštk, tštn, tštnn, yštk*; suffc. *št, štt*; imp. *št*, suff. *štn*; Gpass. prefc. *yšt*; suffc. *št, štt* → DUL 835ff.: */š-t/*. •LL: **UGS** [MAL / GÁN] = *ša*(?)-[*ka-nu*(?)] = *ke-um-mi* = *ši-tu* → Sivan GAGl 277; UVST 55, 181; SAU 307 (145); Tropper UG 189, 485. •ONOM: **EM** *ia-ši-it-a-bu* → Pruzsinszky PTEm 211 [426]; Streck AfO 51 311. **UGS** Cf. unc. *ša-ti-ya* → Gröndahl PTU 196; *ša-ta-na* → Gröndahl PTU 196. **UGA** Cf. unc. *štn* → DUL 839; *šty* → DUL 840.
Siyt (A) "established"	•ONOM: **EB** Cf. *si-da* → Pagan ARES 3 180, 363. **EUPH** Fem. *si-ta-tum* → Gelb CAAA 32, 187 (ŚIJT); Golinets Onomastikon 2 302, 456 (act. ptc.?).

---

734 Richter BGH 342: *šaḫri* I.
735 For the alleged rdg *a-na ša-ru-te* (Taanakh 1:29; Albright BASOR 94 20 fn. 40; AHw 1194: *šarûtu*; CAD Š/2 144: *šarūtu*) see Horowitz / Oshima CunCan 131: *a-na* KÙ:BABBAR *ip-ṭe-ri*.
736 See Bonechi MARI 6 235, and here: |S-r-y| "to release" (?) (|s^1-r-w/y|).
737 Unlikely altern.: from |s^1-ʔ-r| (2) (Pagan ARES 3 236: šiʔr "flesh").
738 Cf. Krebernik ZA 73 28 (728b), unexplained.
739 According to Zadok, Fs. Hallo 330, the DN *Šut* DN (Hb. Seth; > GN 'Sutean') is related to the basis |S-y-t| (Š-W/Y-T); the author adduces as support the PNN (EUPH, B) *su-tu-i-lum*, ÌR-*sú-tim*; *i-ša-ab/p-su-tim*. See Wilhelm RlA 13 365ff., 369 (§ 6).

Siyt (B) "remnant"	•LL: **EB** GÍN.IR = *si-tum* → Conti QuSe 17 187 (761)
maSyit "halt, support"	•ONOM: **U3** *ma-si-id-a-nu-um* → Gelb CAAA 32, 180; Streck Onomastikon 1 338 § 5.47.
ts¹t "wish; proposal" (?)	•CTX: **UGA** Sg. suff. *tštk* → DUL 869: *tšt*.

|s¹-y-ṭ|
See |**s¹-w/y-ṭ**|

s^{2} (ś)

|s^{2}-ʕ-l|	
|s^{2}-ʕ-r| (1)	
|s^{2}-ʕ-r| (2)	
|s^{2}-ʕ-r| (3)	
|s^{2}-b-ʕ|	
|s^{2}-b-m|	
|s^{2}-d-w|	Cf. **|s^{1}-ʕ-d|**
|s^{2}-g-b|	
|s^{2}-g-y|	Cf. **|S-g-g|**
|s^{2}-h-r|	
|s^{2}-ħ-t|	
|s^{2}-k-r| (2)	Cf. **|ð-k-r| (2)**, **|S-ḳ-r|**
|s^{2}-k-y|	
|s^{2}-ḳ-ḳ|	
|s^{2}-l-ħ|	
|s^{2}-l-θ|	
|s^{2}-m-ʔ-l|	
|s^{2}-n-ʔ|	
|s^{2}-p|	
|s^{2}-p-ḳ|	Cf. **|s-b-k|**
|s^{2}-r-ʕ|	See **|s^{2}-ʕ-r| (3)**
|s^{2}-r-x|	
|s^{2}-r-k| (1)	
|s^{2}-r-k| (2)	
|s^{2}-r-p|	
|s^{2}-r-r-|	Cf. **|s-r-r| (1)**
|s^{2}-r-s^{1}|	
|s^{2}-r-ṭ|	
|s^{2}-r-y|	
|s^{2}-t-m|	
|s^{2}-t-t|	
|s^{2}-ṭ-ḳ|	
|s^{2}-ṭ-y|	
|s^{2}-w|	Cf. **|θ-ʔ|**
|s^{2}-w/y-s^{2}|	
|s^{2}-y-ʔ|	
|s^{2}-y-b|	
|s^{2}-y-ḳ|	
|s^{2}-y-m|	Cf. **|s^{1}-m| (1)**
|s^{2}-y-s^{2}|	See **|s^{2}-w/y-s^{2}|**

|s^{2}-ʕ-l|

Sem.: *šaʕala, šaʕʕala, ašʕala* (Arab.) "lo light, kindle, ignite", *suʕla* "fire, blaze".

Saʕl "fire, blaze" — LL: **EB** NE.DAG = *ša-lu-um, ša-lum* → Conti QuSe 17 203 (unexplained); Anderson NABU 2013/58.

|s^{2}-ʕ-r| (1)

Primary noun, Sem: *Šʕr* (*śēʕār*, Hb.) "hairiness, body hair", *Šʕrh* (*śaʕᵃrāh*) "an individual hair"; *sʕr(ʔ), sʕrh, sʕrtʔ* (Aram., Syr.) "hair"; *šārtu(m)*,[740] *šaḫratu* (Akk.) "hair, pelt"; *šaʕr, šaʕar* (Arab.) "hair, fur, pelt", cf. *šaʕira* "to be hairy"; *śaʕər, śōr* (MSArab.) " hair, wool"; *śəʕərt, səʕərt* (Eth.) "hair of body or head".

s^{1}ʕr "hair, pelisse" — •CTX: **UGA** Sg. *šʕr*, cstr. *šʕr* → DUL 787: *šʕr*.

Seʕrt "hair" — •CTX: **EA** *še-er-tá* → Moran AmL 31(with fn. 36).

---

740 < |s^{2}aʕart|, vSoden 58 § 55b. See below *Seʕrt* (EA) for the 'regular' shift |ā|> |ē: in context of |ʕ|.

SaʕratSeʕrat, **Seʕrat** "hair, pelt"	•LL: **EB** LAK-175 = *sa-ra-tum*, *šè(?)-ra-du-um*; IGI.LAK-672(munsub, $uš_x$) = *si-rí-a-du* → Fronzaroli QuSe 13 149; StEb 7 180f.; Krebernik ZA 73 35; Fronzaroli SEL 12 58;[741] Conti QuSe 17 185; Sjöberg Fs. Wilcke 259; Fs. Kienast 544. •ONOM: **B** *sa-e-ra-tum*/*tim* → Gelb CAAA 180f. (ŚAʔIR); Zadok Fs. Hallo 330.
s^2aʕrata "wool"	•CTX: **EG** Pl. *sa-ʕa-ra-ta* |s^2aʕ(^{ə})rata| → Hoch SWET 256 no. 359.[742]
Saʕart "wool"	•CTX: **UGS** TÚG *šá-ḫar-tu* → Sivan GAGl 271; Huehnergard UVST 183; vSoldt SAU 307 (139); Tropper UG 168, 279.
s^1ʕrt "wool, woollen textile"	•CTX: **UGA** Sg. / pl. *šʕrt* → DUL 788f.: *šʕrt* (I). •ONOM: In TN *šʕrt* → Belmonte RGTC 12/2 257: **Šaʕartu* (URU SÍG); DUL 789 *šʕrt* (II).
Saʕirāy "hairy (mouse / rat)"	•LL: **EB** *ší-ḫi-ra-um*; NIN.PÉŠ(LAK-244).ḪUL = *si-ḫi-ra-um* → Civil BaE 92; Sjöberg WeOr 27 14.

|s^2-ʕ-r| (2)	Primary noun, Sem.: *Šʕrh*, *Šʕrym* (*ś^{e}ʕorāh*, Hb.; pl. *ś^{e}ʕorîm*) "barley corn, kernels", (pl.) "barley"; *sʕrh*, *sʕrtʔ*, pl. *sʕryn*, *šʕrn*, *šʕryn* (Aram. pl., Syr.) "barley"; *šaʕīr* (Arab.) "barley", *šaʕār* "undergrowth, vegetation, trees"; *s^2ʕr* (OSArab.) "barley"; *šəʕīr*, *šʕír*, *šiʕir* (MSArab.) "barley". See also: *šaʕār* (Arab.) "undergrowth, vegetation, trees"; *śɛr* (MSArab.) "straw"; *śəʕra* (Eth.) "to grow green", *śāʕr* "herb, grass", cf. *śərnāy* (<? **śəʕərnāy*) "wheat".
s^1iʕr "barley" (?)	•LL: **UGS** Cf. [ŠE(?) = *šeʔu*(?) = ... *š*]*i*(?)-*i-ru* → Huehnergard UVST 100, 183.
s^2aʕarū, **s^2aʕara** "barley (field) / scrub country" (?)	•CTX: **EG** *sa-ʕa-ru₂*, *sa-ʕa-r* → Hoch SWET 255f. no. 358.[743]
s^1ʕrm "barley"	•CTX: **UGA** Pl.t. *šʕrm* → DUL 787f.: *šʕrm*.

|s^2-ʕ-r| (3)	Sem.:*Šʕr* (*śʕr*, Hb.) "to blow away", *sʕr* "to be stormy", *sʕr* (*saʕar*) "heavy gale"; *sʕr* (JAram.) "to be upset"; *šāru*(*m*), *šeʔēru* (Akk.) "to whirl around" (?),[744] *sāru* "wind, breath".
|S-ʕ-r| "to blow away, whirl around"	•CTX: **EUPH** G prefc. suff. *a-ša-i-ra-kum*, cf. D precf. suff.? *uš-ta-aʔ₄-ir-šu* → Durand Fs. De Meyer 15ff. (A.6:21); LAPO 17 170f. fn. c.; Charpin MARI 6 263ff.-265 (M.11009+:12); Durand LAPO 18 257f fn. b ("venir à bout de").
Saʕr "wind, breath"	•CTX: **UGS** *ša-a-ru* (RSOu 7 35:15) → Huehnergard Syria 74 219. •ONOM: **EB** Cf. *sá-a-ra*, *sa-ra-an* → Pagan ARES 3 234, 361.
s^1rʕ "storm, gale" (?)	•CTX: **UGA** Metath. *šrʕ* → Renfroe AULS 146f.; cf. DUL 830: *šrʕ* "flow".

|s^2-b-ʕ|	Sem.: *Šbʕ* (*śbʕ*, Hb.) "to eat one's fill, be(come) sated, satisfy oneself", *Sbʕ* (*śābē^{a}ʕ*) "satiated"; *šbʕ* (Ph., Palm.) "to be full, to be(come) sated"; *Šbʕ*, *sbʕ* (Aram., Syr.) "to be(come) sated", *sbʕ*, *sbyʕ* (Syr.) "satiated"; *šebû*(*m*), *šabû*(*m*) (Akk.) "to be full, to become sated", *šebû*(*m*) "satisfied, sated";[745] *s^2bʕ* (OSArab.) (C) "to give in abundance"; *šabiʕa* (Arab.) "to satisfy one's appetite", *šubʕa*

[741] Fronzaroli loc.cit.: "'capelli' […] la rete dei vasi sanguigni".

[742] Kilani VGW 113: \|svʕ'artv\|.

[743] Sivan / Cochavi-Rainey WSVES 84: *śá-ʕá-rú* "hair", "thicket"; Helck Beziehungen no. 187.

[744] See Lambert JNES 33, 294; Hasselbach SargAkk 85 fn. 173.

[745] For Mari-Akk. *šabīʔum* see below: *Sabiʕ*.

"fill"; *śība, śōba, śēʕ* (MSArab.) "to be satisfied". See also *ṣagba* (Eth.) "to be satiated, filled".

|**S-b-ʕ**| "to be sated"

•ONOM: **EB** *iš*$_{11}$*-ba um, áš-ba-ì, iš-ba-ì, iš-ba-il* → Pagan ARES 3 172, 288, 339, 341.
EM *ia-aš-bi, iš-bi-ia, iš-bi*-^{d}EN/^{d}1+EN, *iš-bi*-^{d}*da-gan*/^{d}KUR, *iš-bi*-EN, *iš-ta-bu* → Pruzsinszky PTEm 168 [426], 172 [517, 526], 215 [518ff.]; Streck AfO 51 311.

|**s^1-b-ʕ**| **(B)** "to be sated; to sate, satiate"

•CTX: **UGA** G prefc. *tšbʕ, tšbʕn*, suffc. *šbʕ, šbʕt*, inf. *šbʕ*; D prefc. *yšbʕ* → DUL 790: */š-b-ʕ/* (II).

Sabiʕ "satisfied" (?)

•CTX: **EUPH** *ša-bi*-ḪU-*um* → AHw 1120: *šabīʔum*; CAD Š/1 11: *šabīʔu*; Durand LAPO 16 443f. (fn. c); Zadok Fs. Hallo 330.
•ONOM: **EB** Cf. *sa-bi* (NE) → Pagan ARES 3 172, 360.

|s^2-b-m|

Sem. Cf. *šibbam, šibām* (Arab.) "a kind of muzzle or gag (for weaned kids); cords for affixing the veil to the face", *šabama, šabbama* "to put the *š*. (in the mouth of a kid)".[746]

|**s^1-b-m**| "to muzzle" (?)

•CTX: **UGA** Gt prefc. *ištbm* → DUL 793: */š-b-m/*.

s^1bm "muzzle" (?)

•CTX: **UGA** → DUL 793f.: *šbm*.

|s^2-d-w|
Cf. |**s^1-ʕ-d**|

Primary noun, Sem.: *Śdh, Śdy* (*śādeh, śāday*, Hb.) "pasture(s), open field(s), arable land"; *šd* (Ph., Pun.) "field, plain";[747] *šadû(m), šaddû* (Akk.)[748] "mountain(s), open country, desert"; cf. *s^2dw* (OSArab.) "pasture(s), cultivated land" (?).

Sadaw/y "open field, field, steppe, mountain; DN"

•CTX: **EB** Suff. *ša-da-ga* |Sadā=ka| → Fronzaroli ARET 13 162, 297; Krebernik PIHANS 106 87.
UGS Cf. unc. *ša*-TI-I |šadî| (?) → Huehnergard UVST 180.
EA *ú-ga-ri* : *ša-de*$_4$*-e* (287:56) → Sivan GAGl 277; Rainey CAT 1 10, 16; Izre'el Orient 38 79, 81f.
•LL: **EB** Cf. ŠÀ.DAḪ.TÚG = *gi-bí-la-ti sa-dim* (VE 1416) → Fales QuSe 13 186; Civil EDA 146.[749]
UGS [MAL / GÁN = *e*]*q*(?)-[*lu*](?) = *a-wa-ar-re* = : *ša-d*[*u-ú*(?)]; [MAḪ = *ṣēru* = *a-wa-a*]*r-re* = : *ša-du-u* → Sivan GAGl 271; Huehnergard UVST 55, 180; SAU 307 (134); Tropper UG 198. Cf. [...] / GA.AB.ḪUL / [IM.KUR.RA] / [...]= *šad*(KUR)*-du-ú*, MSL 17 44 (RS 25.425) 4', 8', 12', 16' → Huehnergard AkkUg 388.
•ONOM: **EB** Cf. *sa-du, sa-du-um, sá-du-um, a-sa-sa-du, ì-sa-du, ì-a-sa-du* → Krebernik PET 105; Pagan ARES 3 234, 283, 328f., 360, 362.[750]
EUPH Cf. *ša-di*-^{d}IM, *sa-di*-DINGIR, *ša-di-ma*-DINGIR, *ša-du-i-la, ša-du-(um-)la-ba, ša-du-um-la-bi, ša-du-um-la-bu-a, ša-du*-LUGAL, *ša-du-šar-ri, ša-*

---

[746] The PNN *iš-bi-mu, sa-bi-mu(-um), sa-bi-ma-tim*, Gelb CAAA 31 (ŚB?M), 181, 186 remain unexplained.
[747] Gr.-Pun. *sadoi, sade*; Lat.-Pun. *SADE*.
[748] Hasselbach SargAkk. 284: ŚDW.
[749] For *za-du-um* (= AN.AK) see Conti QuSe 17 194 fn. 202.
[750] Note that in several instances these PNN could be read |Saʕd=| "protective deity" (cf. |s^1-ʕ-d|).

du-ša-ar-ri, ša-du-um-šar-ri; ḫa-li-sa-da, a-bi-sa-da-a, ^{d}IM-*ša-da* → Huffmon APNMT 267; Gelb CAAA 33, 193f. (ŠADW); Streck Onomastikon 1 215 § 2.111f.[751]
A4 Cf. *ša-di-ma-ra* → Dietrich / Loretz ZA 60 99 (13:9); Sivan GAGl 271.
EM Cf. *šad-da, šad-de*$_4$, *sa-dá-a, ša-dì-ia, šad-di*$_{12}$*-ia, ša*$_{10}$*-di*$_{12}$*-ia, ša*$_{10}$*-a-dì, ša-a-da, ša*$_{10}$*-ad-da, ša-da-aʔ-e, ša-dì-i, šad-ni, ša-du-ú-na, na-aʔ-mi-ša-da,* SIG$_5$*-ša-da, ša*$_{10}$*-dì-da(-gan)*; cf. *ša-du-mi-e* → Wiseman / Hess UF 26 506; Pruzsinszky PTEm 96 [714f., 718], 128 [645],197 [645].
Kāmid el-Loz Cf. *ša-a-te* → Edzard ZA 66 64:9, 65f.
EA Unc. ŠA-TI-*ya* → Hess APN 139f., 212: "field, floor" (rdg *ša-di*$_9$*-ya*).[752]
UGS *ša-du-ya, ša-de*$_4$*-ya, ša-dì-ia; ša-de*$_4$*-ia-nu,* [*ša*]*-di-ia-a-nu, ša-di-nu*; cf. A.ŠÀ-*ia-nu*, KUR-*du*(?)[-*ya*], *ša*-TA*(dá)-ya*; *ša-da-ia-nu* → Gröndahl PTU 191f.; Sivan GAGl 271; Huehnergard AkkUg 388; DUL 799: *šdy* (II), 799f. *šdyn*.
EG Cf. *sȝ-d-y*$_2$*-ʕ-m-y*$_2$*-y* → Schneider APÄQ 196 no. 414f. (altern. rdg: *sȝ-d-y*$_2$*-m-y*$_2$*-y*).

s^{1}d (A) "open field, field, steppe, mountain; DN"
•CTX: **UGA** sg. *šd*, cstr. *šd*, suff. *šdk, šdh*, pl. *šdm* → DUL 795ff.: *šd* (I).
•ONOM: **UGA** Cf. *šdy* → DUL 799 *šdy* (II); *šdyn* → DUL 799f.

s^{1}dy "land labourer, mountain-dweller" (?)
•CTX: **UGA** Pl. *šdym* → DUL 799: *šdy* (I).

|s^2-g-b|
Sem.: *Šgb* (*śgb*, Hb.) "to be too high, to strong"; *Šgb* (*śgb*, Aram.) "to lift high, save".

|s^2-g-b| "to be exalted, saved"
•ONOM: **EG** Elem. in PN and TN: *sa-qa-ba, sa-qa-bi, sa-q-ba* → Hoch SWET 268 no. 380; see Schneider APÄQ 192 no. 406: *sȝ-q- ȝ-b-w*$_2$.

|s^2-g-y|
Cf. **|S-g-g|**
Sem.: Cf. *Šgh* (*śgh*, Hb.) "to increase, become large"; by-forms: *Šgg* (*śgg*, Hb. C) "to cause to grow", (Ct) "to grow upwards", *ŠgȜ* (*śgʔ*, G) "to grow", *sgy* (Aram., Syr., G) "to become many, to grow", D/C "to make numerous".

|S-g-y| (B) "to grow, increase"
•ONOM: **B** Cf. *sa-ga-a-nu-um, sa-gu-ú*; cf. *ḫa-am-mi-zu-gu-ú* → Gelb CAAA 181 (ŚAʔQ), 203 (ZUʔG); Zadok Fs. Hallo 330.

|s^2-h-r|
Sem.: *Šhrnym* (*śah^{a}ronîm*, pl. Hb.) "little moons (amulets, jewellery)"; *šhr* (Aram.) "Moon god", *shr(ʔ)* (Aram., Syr.) "moon"; *šahr* (Arab.) "new moon, month"; *s^{2}hr* (OSArab.) "new moon"; *śeher* (MSArab.) "moon"; *śāhr* (Eth.) "moon, first day of the month".

s^{1}ihar "a crescent shaped sickle" (?)
•CTX: **UGS** Cf. *ši-a-ru*(?)[→ Sivan GAGl 273; Huehnergard UVST 180.

|s^2-ħ-t|
Primary noun, Sem.: *Šyḥ* (*śîḥ*, Hb.) "shrub, bush"; *šḥ* (Pun.) "shrub"; *sḥʔ* (Syr.) "plant name"; *šīḥ* (Arab.) "wormwood".

---

[751] Durand (REA 290) reads *Šaddûm* "le Montagnard". For KUR = *šadûm* (not: *eqlum*) in Mari-Akk. (*sakanakku*) see Cavigneaux / Colonna d'Istria, Studia Orontica 6 56.
[752] The rdg *di*$_9$ (TI) is questionable; see Moran AmL 384: language unc. Cf. Ug. PN *šty* (DUL 840: *šty* (I).

s^{1}ḫt "shrub, bush"	•CTX: **UGA** Sg. / pl. *šḫt* → DUL 801: *šḫt*.

|s^2-k-r| (2) Cf. **|ð-k-r| (2)**, **|S-ḳ-r|**	Sem: *Škr* (*śkr*, Hb) "to hire", *mŠkrt* (*maśkoret*) "wage"; *škr* (Ph., Palm.) "to hire; to reward", *škr* (Palm.) "rewarding"; *śakara* (Eth.) "to hire", *śəkur* "hired, hireling".
|S-k-r| "to hire, favour, reward"	•ONOM: **EUPH, B** *aš-ku-ra-an*, *ia-aš/áš-ku-rum*, *ia-áš-ku-rum*, *ia-uš ku-ru-um*, *aš/áš-ku-ur-*^{d}IM, *aš-kur-li-im*, *ia-áš-kur*-DINGIR, *ia-aš/áš-ku-ur*-DINGIR, *ia-áš-ku-úr*-DINGIR, *ia-àš-kur-*^{d}IM, *ia-aš/áš-kur/ku-ur-*^{d}*da-gan*, *iš-kur-e-li* → Huffmon APNMT 245f.; Streck Onomastikon 1 156 § 2.9 fn. 2, 211 § 2.105 fn. 1, 337 § 5.45; Golinets Onomastikon 2 32, 35, 117f., 446f., 491f.[753] **TU** *iš-ku-ra-an* → Krebernik Tall Bi`a 221; Golinets Onomastikon 2 32, 118, 446f., 492. **A7** *aš-kur-e-da* → Wiseman AT 54:25; Golinets Onomastikon 2 117, 446.
|s^1-k-r| **(A)** "to hire out"	•CTX: **UGA** G prefc. *tškr*, inf. *škr* → DUL 804 */š-k-r/* (I). •ONOM: **EA** *iš-kur*, *iš-ku-ru*, *iš-ku-ra* → Golinets Onomastikon 2 447. **UGS** *ia-aš-ku-ra-na* → Gröndahl PTU 193; Golinets Onomastikon 2 446.[754]
Sikr "wage(s), pay"	•ONOM: **EUPH** *si-ik-ri-ḫa-da* → Gelb CAAA 32, 187; Streck Onomastikon 1 323 § 5.11.
Sakir "favoured, rewarded"	•ONOM: **EUPH** *sa-ki-rum*, fem. *sa-ki-ra* → Huffmon APNMT 245f.; Gelb CAAA 32, 181; Golinets Onomastikon 2 158.
Sakūr "favoured, rewarded"	•ONOM: **EUPH** *sa-ku-ra-an*, *sa-ku-ra-nu(-um)* → Huffmon APNMT 245f.; Gelb CAAA 32, 181; Streck Onomastikon 1 330 § 5.28; Golinets Onomastikon 2 139, 494.
Sakkār "one who favours, rewards" (?)	•ONOM: **EUPH** Cf. *sa-ka-rum/ru-um*, *i-la-sa-qar*, *i-la-sa-ka-ar* → Gelb CAAA 32, 181; Streck Onomastikon 1 333 § 5.38, 358.[755]
Sukkur "very much favoured, rewarded" (?)	•ONOM: **EUPH** Fem. cf. *šu-ku-ra-tum* → Gelb CAAA 32, 189.
maSkar, miSkir "wage(s), pay"	•ONOM: **EUPH** *maš-ga-ru-um*, *me/mi-iš-ki-rum* → Gelb CAAA 32, 187f.; Streck Onomastikon 1 330f. § 5.28 fn. 7, 335 § 5.43, 337 § 5.45.
ms^{1}krt (B) "wage(s)"	•CTX: **UGS** → DUL 584: *mškrt* (II).

|s^2-k-y|	Sem.: Cf. *mŠkyt* (*maśkît*, Hb.) "image, imagination"; *sky* (JAram., Syr.) "to expect, watch for", *skwy(ʔ)* (JAram.) "watchman".
|S-k-y| "to watch"	•ONOM: **EB** Cf. *iš*$_{11}$*-gi*-UTU → Bonechi NABU 2016/1 (2, TM.75.G.2014 = MEE 3 59 obv. I 4).
s^{2}āki? "scout, guard" (?)	•CTX: **EG** Cf. *sa-ka-ʔu*, *sa-ku*$_3$, *sa-ka-ʔu* → Hoch SWET 268f. no. 381. •ONOM: **EG** Cf. *sa-ku*$_3$, *sa-ka-ʔa* → Hoch SWET 268f. no. 381.

|s^2-ḳ-ḳ|	Sem.: Cf. *šaqqa* (Arab.) "to split, break (up), cross, travel".
|s^2-ḳ-ḳ| "to open the way, break the trail" (?)	•CTX: **EG** *sa-ga* → Hoch SWET 269 no. 382.[756]

---

[753] Diff. Gelb CAAA 32: ŚKR "to remember".

[754] See also UGS |ð-k-r| (|ð/S-k-r| (2)), GlOS 1 161.

[755] "Gott ist der Belohner"; diff. Golinets Onomastikon 2 156f.: śakar "Belohnt; der Gott belohnt (?)".

|s^2-l-ħ|	Sem. etym. unc.: Cf. *šalaḥa* (Arab.) "to take off (clothes), shed the cloth", *mašlaḥ* "long, flowing cloack".
maSlaħ "a garment"	•CTX: **UGS** Cf. *ma-aš-la-ḫa-ma* → Huehnergard UVST 181; Tropper UG 289.

|s^2-l-θ|	Primary noun, Sem.:[757] *Šlš*, *Šlwš* (*šālōš*, Hb.) "three", *šl(y)šy* (*šᵉlišī*) "third", *šlyš* (*šālîš*) "third man, adjutant, fighting charioteer", *šlšym* (*šᵉlošîm*) "thirty"; *šlš* (Ph., Pun.) "three", *šlšy* (Ph.) "third", *šlšm* (Ph., Pun.) "thirty"; *tlt* (Nab., Palm., Hatra) "three", *tlt*, *twlt?* (Nab.) "one third", *tltyn* (Nab., Palm.) "thirty"; *tlt* (Aram., Syr.) "three", *tlyty* "third", *tlty*, *tltyt?*, *tlytyh*, *tlytyt?* (Aram., Syr.) "third part", *šlšn*, *tltyn* "thirty"; *šalāš*, *šalassu* (Akk.) "drei", *šalšu(m)*, *šaššu(m)*, *šalāšiu* "third, one-third", *tašlīšu*, *taššalīšu* "third man (of a chariot crew)", *šalāšā*, *šelāšā* "thirty", *šullušu(m)* "trebled, tripled, threefold", *šalāšu(m)* "to do for a third time, do three times"; *ṯalāṯa* (Arab.) "three", *ṯāliṯ* "third", *ṯulṯ* "one-third" *ṯalāṯūn*, "thirty", *ṯulāṯa* "thrice", *muṯallaṯ* "tripled, threefold", *ṯallaṯa* "to triple, do three times"; *s^2lṯ*, *ṯlṯ* (OSArab.) "three", *s^2lṯn*, *ṯlṯ* "one third", *s^2lṯy*, *ṯlṯy* "thirty"; *śhəlēṯ*, *śhəlīṯ*, *śāṯáyt* (MSArab.) "three", *śōleṯ*, *śəwṯīt* "third", *śəlāṯáyn*, *śāṯáyn* "thirty";*śalās* (Eth.) "three", *śāləs* "third", *śalāsā*, "thirty", *maśləst* "triple, threefold, third rank" *śallasa* "to triple, do three times, for the third time". Non-Sem.: Cf. LÚ *šalašḫa/i=* (Hitt.) "an official whose duties involve equids and carriages".[758]
|**θ-l-θ**| "to repeat for the third time; to ridge, plough alternate strips"	•CTX: **UGA** D prefc. *ṯlṯ*, *yṯlṯ*; pass. ptc. fem. *mṯlṯt* (see below: *mθlθ* (B)) → DUL 894: /*ṯ-l-ṯ*/.
θlθ (A) "three; set of three"	•CTX: **UGA** Sg. *ṯlṯ*, *šlš*; fem. *ṯlṯt*, *šlšt*, suff. *ṯlṯtm*, du. *ṯlṯtm*, pl. *ṯlṯm* (see below: *θlθm*) → DUL 894ff.: *ṯlṯ* (I).[759]
θlθ (B) "third"	•CTX: **UGA** Sg. *ṯlṯ*, fem. *ṯlṯt* → DUL 897: *ṯlṯ* (II).[760]
θlθ (C) "third man"	•CTX: **UGA** Pl. cstr. *ṯlṯ* → DUL 897: *ṯlṯ* (III).
θlθ (D) "triple, three times"	•CTX: **UGA** Sg. suff. *ṯlṯh*, (?) fem. suff. *ṯlṯth* → DUL 897: *ṯlṯ* (IV).
θlθid "three times"	•CTX: **UGA** → DUL 898: *ṯlṯid*.
θlθm "thirty"	•CTX: **UGA** → DUL 899: *ṯlṯm*.
SulluS "plated three times" (?)	•CTX: **EUPH** Cf. *šu-lu-úš*, *šu-ul-lu-úš* → CAD S/3 244: *šullušu* B; mng unc.; Arkhipov ARM 32 68f.
mθlθ (A) "a third"	•CTX: **UGA** Sg. *mṯlṯ*, (?) du. *mṯlṯm* → DUL 597: *mṯlṯ*.
mθlθ (B) "the third (one)"	•CTX: **UGA** Fem. sg. *mṯlṯt* → DUL 597: *mṯlṯt*.

756 Sivan / Cochavi-Rainey WSVES 84: *śá-ga* "to step forth"; Helck Beziehungen no. 207: "weichen", cf. Hb. *swg*.

757 For the original base C_1:*s^2* see Tropper UG 142; 346f.

758 Note CHD Š/1 89f.: Not to be equated with the LU KUŠ₇ "chariot fighter" or the *KARTAPPU* "chariot / carriage driver".

759 Cf. further Tropper KWU 133: *ṯlṯ*₁ |ṯalāṯu|; *ṯlṯ*₃ |ṯalūṯu| "Dreizahl, Triade"; *ṯlṯt*₁ "Drittelschekel"; *ṯlṯt*₂ |ṯāliṯta?| ""am dritten Tag, übermorgen"; *ṯlṯt*₃ ""das Dreifache"; *ṯlṯt*₄ |ṯalāṯatu| "Dreiergruppe".

760 Cf. Tropper KWU 133: *ṯlṯ*₂ |ṯāliṯu|].

|s^2-m-ʔ-l|	Primary noun, Sem.: *Šmʔ(w)l* (*śemōʔl*, Hb.) "left side", *Šmʔly* (*śemāʔlî*) "on the left"; *šml* (Palm.) "left", *šmly* "northern; north"; *smʔl(ʔ)* (Aram., Syr.) "left hand, side", *smly* "left"; *šumēlu(m)*, *šumilu(m)* (Akk.) "the left", *šumēlû(m)* "left-hand"; *šamāl*, *šimāl* (Arab.) "north (wind); left (hand, side)", *šamālī*, *šimālī* "northern, on the left"; *śáymǝl*, *śǝmōwǝl*, *śīl*, *śímhel*, *śǝmǝl* (MSArab.) "left (hand, direction)".
Samʔāl, **Samʔīl**, **Simʔāl** "the north, left side"	•ONOM: **EUPH** TN as DN *sa-am-a-al*, *sa-am-a-la*-DINGIR, *sa-am-ḫi-li*-DINGIR; as tribe name: *si-ma-al*, *si-im-a-al*, *si-im-a-lu-um*, *si-im-ḫa-al* → Gelb CAAA 31, 183, 187; Stol BiOr 35 221.
s^2umēlu "north, left" (?)	•ONOM: **EG** Cf. elem. in TN *su3-mi3-n* → Hoch SWET 260f. no. 369.[761]
s^1mål "left (hand, side)"	•CTX. **UGA** Sg. *šmål*, suff. *šmålh* → DUL 811: *šmål*.
|s^2-n-ʔ|	Sem.: *Šnʔ* (*śnʔ*, Hb.) "to hate, loathe, detest", *Ś(w)nʔ* (G act. ptc. *śōnēʔ*, *šônēʔ*) "enemy"; *sny* (Aram., Syr.) "to hate, loathe, detest", *snʔ(ʔ)* "enemy"; *šanaʔa*, *šaniʔa* (Arab.) "to hate, loathe, detest", *šāniʔ* "enemy"; *s^2ny* (OSArab.) "enemy".[762]
|s^1-n-ʔ| "to hate, loathe"	•CTX: **UGA** G suffc. *šnå* → 820: /*š-n-ʔ*/.
s^1nů "enemy"	•CTX: **UGA** Pl. cstr. *šnů* → DUL 820: *šnů*.
Sannāʔ "one who hates"	•CTX **B** [*ša*]-*na-i-šu* AHw 1164; CAD Š/1 388.; Zadok Fs. Hallo 331; Streck Onomastikon 1 117 § 1.95.
maSnuʔ "enemy" (?)	•LL: **UGS** Cf. [ḪUL? = *zīru*? = TA]R(?)-*du-bar-ri* = *ma-aš-nu-ú*(?) → Huehnergard UVST 90f., 182f.[763]
|s^2-p|	Primary noun, Sem.: *Šph* (*śāpāh*, Hb.) "lip, margin, edge"; *sph*, *sptʔ* (Aram., Syr.) "lip, margin, edge"; *šaptu(m)*, *śaptum*, *šabdu* (Akk.) "lip, margin, edge"; *šafa* (Arab.) "lip, margin, edge"; *s^2ft* (OSArab.) "promise; to promise; *śábǝh*, *śǝbht* (MSArab.) "lip". Non-Sem.: *spt* (Eg.) "lip"; **ŝuf*= (Rift) "lip".[764]
Sap(a)t "lip, rim" (?)	•CTX: **EB** *sa-ba-du-na-a* |Sapātū=nayn| → Catagnoti QuSe 29 74, 119, 225; •LL: **EB** SAG.DAR = *sa-ba-tum*, *sa-íb-tum*; cf. SAG.DIMxNI = *sa-bí-tù* SAG → Krebernik ZA 73 11; Sjöberg Fs. Pettinato 279; Bonechi / Catagnoti Fs. Sommerfeld / Krebernik 176f. •ONOM: **EM** Cf. unc. *šap-ta* → Streck AfO 51 309.[765]
s^1pt "lip"	•CTX: **UGA** Sg. / pl *špt*, suff. *špty*, *šptk*, *špth*, *špthm* → DUL 826: *špt*.
|s^2-p-ḳ| Cf. |s-b-k|	Sem.: *Špq* (*śpq*, Hb.) "to be sufficient", *spq* "to vomit", *Špq* (*śepeq*) "surfeit, excess", *spq* (*sepeq*) "abundance"; *spq* (Aram., Syr.) "to be sufficient", (Syr. D) "to vomit", *špq* (Aram.) "abundance", *spq* (Aram., Syr.) "able, sufficient"; *sapāqu* (Akk.) "to be sufficient", *sapqu* "able, competent"; *s^2pq* (OSArab. C) "to satiate", *s^2pqm* "abundance".

[761] See also *s^1amna* (\|s^1-m-n\|).
[762] Unrelated: Eth. *tasannana* "to quarrel" (see *sanana* "to grow teeth").
[763] Diff. and unlikely: Sivan GAGl 246: MAṮNÛ "answer, response".
[764] Orel / Stolbova HSED 132 no. 572: *ĉup*= "lip".
[765] Pruzsinszky PTEm 176 [737f.]: *Šapṭa/u* "Richter", unlikely.

|S-p-ḳ| "to give abundantly"	•ONOM: **EUPH**, **B** *ia-áš-pu-kum*, *ia-ás-pu-uk-*DINGIR, *ia-ás-pu-ki-*DINGIR, *ì-lí-iš-bi-ik* → Huffmon APNMT 252 (SPK **špk* "to pour out"); Gelb CAAA 32 (ŚPQ), 188; Golinets Onomastikon 2 121, 452f.
Sipḳ "abundance"	•ONOM: **EUPH** *si-ip-ku-na-da*, *si-ip-ku-na-*^{d}IM → Gelb CAAA 32, 187.
Sapaḳ "who is given abundantly"	•ONOM: **B** *sa-ba-kum* → Gelb CAAA 32, 185; Golinets Onomastikon 2 156, 452f.
Sāpiḳ "who gives abundantly" (?)	•ONOM: **B** *sa-bi-kum* → Gelb CAAA 32, 185; Streck Onomastikon 1 112 § 1.95; Golinets Onomastikon 2 135.

|s^2-r-ʕ| See **|s^2-ʕ-r| (3)**	

|s^2-r-x|	Sem.: *šrḫ* (Syr. Gt) "to exult", (C) "to become refreshed", *ʔšrḫw* "wantonness"; *šarāḫu(m)* (Akk.) "to take pride in, make splendid", *šarḫu(m)* "proud, splendid"; *šaraḫa* (Arab.) "to become a youth", *šarḫ* "prime of youth", *šarīḫ* "young man"; *śār(ə)ḫa*, (also *śār(ə)ḥa*, *sarḫa*, Eth.) "to light up, shine, glitter", *śəruḫ* "brilliant, splendid".
Sarx "proud" (?)	•ONOM: **EB** Rdg unc. *sar-ḫé*(?)*-a-a* → Pagan ARES 3 177, 362. Diff. rdg Pomponio ARET 15 no. 6 r. 11,8: *sar-gan-a-a*.

|s^2-r-k| (1)	Sem.: *srk* (JAram.) "to adhere", (Syr. D) "to affix", *sryk* "adhering"; *šarāku(m)* (Akk.) "to present, give", *šerku(m)*, *širku(m)*, *širaku* "gift; temple oblate"; *širka*, *šarika*, *šārak* (Arab.) "to share, participate", *šarīk* "partner, companion"; *s^2rk* (OSArab.) "to share out, make an agreement".
|S-r-k| "to present (ex voto)"	•ONOM: **EUPH** *ia-áš-ku-ka-an*, *ia-áš-ru-ki-el*, *ia-ás-ru-uk-*^{d}IM → Gelb CAAA 33, 188; Golinets Onomastikon 2 121, 455.
|s^1-r-k| "to team up with, to join"	•CTX: **UGA** G suffc. / act. ptc. *šrk* → DUL 831: */š-r-k/*.
Sarik "donated, given ex voto" (?)	•ONOM: **B** Cf. *sa-ri-kum* → Gelb CAAA 33, 186.
muSarrik "most open-handed"	•ONOM: **EUPH** Fem. *mu-sa-ar-ri-ka* → Gelb CAAA 33, 186; Golinets Onomastikon 2 200, 455.

|s^2-r-k| (2)	Sem.: Cf. *širka*, *šarika*, *šāraka* (Arab.) "to share, participate, be(come) partner", *šarika* "partnership", *šarīk* "partner, sharer".
Surk "profit sharing" (?)	CTX: **A7** Cf. KÙ.BABBAR *ša šu-ur-ki-im* → Arnaud AuOr 16 185.
Sarrāk "pedlar, transporter" (?)	CTX: **A7** LÚ.MEŠ *šar-ra-ki* → CAD Š/2 68: *šarraku*; Arnaud AuOr 16 184f.; Lauinger STOBA 96 fn. 52.

|s^2-r-p|	Sem.: *Šrp* (*śrp*, Hb.) "to burn", *Šrph* (*śᵉrēpāh*) "fire, incineration"; *srp*, *šrp* (Aram.) "to burn"; *šarāpu(m)* (Akk.) "to burn", *šarpu*, *šurpu(m)* "burning, incineration", *šuruptu(m)* "burning, cremation".
|s^1-r-p| "to burn"	•CTX: **UGA** G prefc. suff. *tšrpnn*, inf. / verbal noun *šrp* → DUL 831: */š-r-p/*.
Sarpat "burnt sacrifice"	•CTX: **EB** Cf. *sà-ra-pá-tum* → Pettinato Culto 42, 93. See also Bonechi WO 30 32f.
s^1rp "burnt sacrifice"	•CTX: **UGA** Sg. *šrp*, suff. *šrpm* → DUL 831: *šrp*.

|s^2-r-r| Cf. **|s-r-r| (1)**	Primary noun, Sem.: *Šr* (*śar*, Hb.) "high functionary, head, chief, prince", denom. *Šrr* (*śrr*, G; or *swr* ?) "to rule, reign" (open to question); *šr* (Ph., Palm., Aram.) "prince, high functionary, chief, master"; *šarru(m)* (Akk.) "king, prince". Non-Sem.: *šarri* (Hurr.) "king".
Sarr (B), s^{1}arr "king, prince; DN"	•CTX: **EM** LÚ.MEŠ *šar/šàr-ru* (pl. |Sarrū|) → Pentiuc Vocabulary 171. •LL: **EB** Cf. GAL.GAL = *sa-la-lum, sa-ra-ru*$_{12}$*-um* |Sarrum| → Krebernik ZA 73 45.[766] **UGS** Cf. [MAḪ = *rubû* =] = *šar-rù* → Huehnergard ^{2}UVST 388, 395. Altern. rdg: [ḪUL = *sarru* = ...]-*ri* = *sar-rù* → Sivan GAGl 266; Huehnergard UVST 88, 158; vSoldt SAU 306 (103) (see |s-r-r| (1). •ONOM: **EB** *sar-ma, sar-rí, sal-li, sa-li-ì-lum, sar-a-ba*$_4$, *sar*-BÀD, *sar-da-mu, sar-du-du, sar-ì-lum-ma, sar-ì-sa, sar*-KU-*da, sar-ma-ì, sar-ma-ì-lum, sar-mi-lu*;[767] *bù-da-sar, en-na-sar, i-nu-sar, ìr-am*$_6$*-sar, iš-dub-sar, la-a-sar* → Pagan ARES 3 235, 293, 307, 324, 337, 339, 354, 362f., 361; Bonechi NABU 2016/1. **EM** *šar-ra, li-im/mì-šar-ra* → Pruzsinszky PTEm 177 [740], 184 [595]. **UGS** Cf. unc. *šá-ra-na, šar-ra-nu* → Nougayrol PRU 6 73:20; PRU 6 80:1; Huehnergard UVST 414; AkkUg 414.
s^{1}r (B) "prince, sovereign; DN"	•CTX: **UGA** Sg. *šr* → DUL 829: *šr* (III). •ONOM: **UGA** Cf. *åbšr* → DUL 9: *åbḏ/šr*; *å/ỉnšr(m)* → DUL 81; *yḥšr* → DUL 947; *ymtšr* → DUL 954: *ymtḏ/šr*. Unc. *šr* → DUL 830: *šr* (VII), *šrm* → Gröndahl PTU 196 (vacat DUL), *šrn, šrny*[768] → Gröndahl PTU 196 (vacat DUL). Unc. DN *ʕd w šr, mt w šr* → DUL 830: *šr* (VI); *šrġzz* → DUL 831.
ðr, θr (A) "prince, sovereign; DN"	•ONOM: **UGA** Passim elem. in Hurr.-Ug. PNN; cf. *åbḏr* → DUL 9: *åbḏ/šr*; *ib/wrḏr* → DUL 12; *ågb/pṯr* → DUL 25; *åġlḏrm* → DUL 29; *ỉllḏr(m)* → DUL 54; *ỉlṯr* → DUL 65; *ånnḏr* → DUL 78; *å/ỉrpṯr* → DUL 101; *ġlpṯr* → DUL 317; *ḥbgḏr* → DUL 352; *ḫbdṯr* → DUL 379; *ḫdpṯr* → DUL 382; *ḫdmḏr* → DUL 383; *nwrḏr* → DUL 644; *pbṯr* → DUL 651; *ymtḏr* → DUL 954: *ymtḏ/šr*; *ḏrdn* → DUL 285; *ṯrdn* → DUL 917; *ṯrdnt* → DUL 917. Unc. *ṯrn* → DUL 919: *ṯrn* (II); *ṯryl* → DUL 920; unc. *ṯryn* → DUL 921: *ṯryn* (II). See further the Hurr.-Anat. hybrids *ʕbdṯrm* → DUL 141; *ḏ/ṯrm* DUL 285, *ḏrn* → Gröndahl PTU 197 (vacat DUL), and the elem. *šarruma*, Gröndahl PTU 250.[769]
θrmn (A) "royal"	•CTX: **UGA** Sg. *ṯrmn*; pl. *ṯrmnm* → DUL 918: *ṯrmn* (I), *ṯrmn* (II).
Sarrat "queen"	•ONOM: **EB** *ḫu-pi-sa-ra-du* → Pagan ARES 3 235, 319.
Sarrūt "sovereignty, power" (?)	•ONOM: **EB** Cf. *sa-lu-ud* → Pagan ARES 3 235, 361.
Sarratūtt, s^{1}arratūtt "dignity of a queen"	•CTX: **EUPH** *šar-ra-tu-tam* → Durand MARI 6 277f. **UGS** Cf. SAL.LUGAL-*ut-ti* → Nougayrol PRU 3 176 (RS 17.159):36; Durand MARI 6 277f.; CAD Š/2 75f.: *šarratuttu*.
θrry (A), θrrt "powerful" (?)	•CTX: **UGA** Sg. / pl. cstr.(?) *ṯrry*; sg. fem. *ṯrrt* → DUL 919f.; 920: *ṯrry* (I). •ONOM: **UGA** Cf. unc. *ṯrry* → DUL 920: *ṯrry* (II).[770]

[766] See Krebernik ZA 72 226: writing C$_1$v-C$_2$v-C$_2$v for C$_1$-C$_2$C$_2$v. Unlikely altern. rdg: inf. |Sarārum| (?, questionable: GAL.ME.DI =*du-da-rí-lum* |tus^{2}tarrir=|; Krebernik ZA 73 45). For the alleged fem. |śarratum| (*sa-ra-du-um*, VE 260) cf. Conti QuSe 17 110 (260; see |s^2-r-ṭ).

[767] For *šar-mi-lu* see also Bonechi Fs. Buccellati 70 fn. 8.

[768] See vSoldt Fs. Groneberg 313; unrelated: *šu-ru-na*-PI (RS 25.132 i 8').

[769] For the queen's name *ṯryl* / *Ṯaryelli* (*šar-e-li, šar-el-li*) and its onomastic interpretation see among others vSoldt JEOL 29 71; SAU 15ff. (especially fn. 142); DUL 920: *ṯryl*.

[770] Altern. see |θ-r-r|; Gröndahl PTU 200.

|s^2-r-s^1|	Primary noun, Sem.:. *šrš* (*šoreš*, Hb.) "root", *šrš* (D) "to uproot, to take root"; *šrš* (Ph.) "root"; *šrš*(*?*) (Aram., Syr.) "root", *šrš* (JAram., Syr. C; D) "to uproot", "to take root"; *šuršu*(*m*), *śurśum* (Akk.) "root; base, foundation". For variant consonantal structures and their lexicalisations see aslo: *sirr* (Arab.) "source, origin", *širs* "small thorny trees"; *s^2rs^1* (OSArab.) "beginning, foundation", (C) "to eradicate"; *śəríḥo*, *śírɔx* (MSArab.) "root"; *śərw* (Eth.) "sinew, root, stock", *śarwe* "beam of wood".[771]
SirS "root, foundation"	•LL: **EB** GIŠ.ŠUŠx(ŠÉ+NÁM) = *si-su* → Krebernik ZA 72 236; Conti QuSe 17 138f.; Catagnoti QuSe 29 24, 228. Cf. AN.KI = *si-li-sa-a*, *si-li-sa*(!) → Fronzaroli QuSe 13 149; Krebernik ZA 73 30.
SurS "root, foundation"	•ONOM: **EB** Cf. *sùr*(HIxMAŠ)-*si*, *sùr*(HIxMAŠ)-*sa-ar* → Pagan ARES 3 237, 366.
s^1urs^1 "root, offspring"	•ONOM: **EM** *šur-ši*, *šur-ši-ia*, *šur-ši-ia*-É-^{d}*aš-tár*, *šur-ši-da*/^{d}KUR → Pruzsinszky PTEm 97, 106, 131 [755ff., [758]. **UGS** Elem. in the PN *šur-ša-am-mi* → Sivan GAGl 276.
s^1rs^1 "root, offspring"	•CTX: **UGA** Sg. *šrš*, suff. *šršk* → DUL 832: *šrš* (I). •ONOM: **UGA** *šršʕm* → DUL 833; *šršn* → DUL 833. See the TN *Šurašu*, Belmonte RGTC 12/2 278f., and the GN *šršy* → DUL 833; Belmonte RGTC 12/2 279.

|s^2-r-ṭ|	Sem.: *Šrṭ* (*śrṭ*, Hb.) "to make gashes in oneself, injure oneself badly"; *srṭ*, *šrṭ* (JAram., Syr.) "to scratch, draw"; *šarāṭu*(*m*) (Akk.) "to tear, shred"; *šaraṭa* (Arab.) "to tear, make incisions". See also: *šaṭara* (Arab.) "to divide in two", *šaṣara* "to pierce"; *śaṣṣara*, *śaṣara*, *śaḍara* (Eth.) "to split, cut up, tear".
|S-r-ṭ| "to tear"	•LL: **EB** SAGxTAG$_4$ = *sa-ra-du-um* → Conti QuSe 17 110; Sjöberg Fs. Kienast 543f. Diff. Bonechi / Catagnoti Fs. Sommerfeld / Krebernik 170: *šaʕrātum* "hair". •ONOM: **EM** Cf. EN-*ša-ri-iṭ* → Pruzsinszky PTEm 120 [233]

|s^2-r-y|	Sem.: *s^2ry* (OSArab.) "to save, protect"; *śaraya*, *śarraya* (Eth.) "to heal, cure, give medicine". See also: *sry* (JAram., Syr.) "to stink"; *šary* "colocynth"; *s*(*w*)*ry* (rdg *sôriyyāh*) "stinking".
|S-r-y| **(B)** "to protect, cure"	•ONOM: **EB** Cf. *áš-ra*, *iš-la-nu*, *iš-la-ab*, *iš-la-a-ba*$_4$, *iš-la-da-du*; passim: *iš-la*=, *iš-ra*= |yiSrā=| with DNN: *iš-la-ku*(*-tu*), *iš-la-ì*, *iš-la*-BE, *iš-la-ma-lik*, *iš-ra-ì*/*il* → Pagan ARES 3 177 (diff., *šry* "to struggle / contend with"), 289, 340; Golinets Onomastikon 2 455.[772] **EUPH** *ia-as-ra*(!), *ia-ás-ra*-^{d}*da-gan* → Golinets Onomastikon 2 313, 455. **UGA** Cf. *yšrỉl* → Kogan BuB 3 240; DUL 973.
Saray "saved, protected"	•ONOM: **B** *ša-ra-zi-id-kum*, *ša-ra-ṣur-ru-um* → Gelb CAAA 33 (ŚRJ "to contend with"), 185.
Sarayt "salvation"	•ONOM: **B** *ša-ra-te*/*ti-el* → Gelb CAAA 33 (ŚRJ "to contend with"), 185.

|s^2-t-m|	Sem.: *Štm* (*śtm*, Hb.) "to shut off (ears), close the way, silence", *stm* "to stop up, shut off, keep secret"; *stm* (JAram.) "to close up".

[771] All etyma probl. originated from biconsonantal bases. See Leslau CDG 535; Kogan Classification 42.
[772] With reference to Kogan BuB 3 240f.

|s^1-t-m| "to close (the mouth), to silence" (?)	•CTX: **UGA** G prefc. *ištm* (rdg?) → DUL 839: */š-t-m/*.
|s^2-t-t|	Sem.: Cf. *šatta* (Arab.) "to be(come) broken, dissolved,", *šattata* "to break, dissolve".
|s^1-t-t| "to devastate, break" (?)	•CTX: **UGA** G prefc. *yšt* (bkn) → DUL 839: */š-t(-t)/*.
|s^2-ṭ-ḳ|	Sem.: *sdq* (Aram., Syr.) "to split apart, cleave"; *šatāqu(m)* (Akk.) "to split, crack (off)"; *śaṭaqa* (Eth.) "to cleave, split, break through".
|S-t-ḳ| "to squash, crush" (?)	•CTX: **EUPH** G prefc. cf. *li-iš-tu-uq*, *ta-ša-at-ta-aq*, suffc. *ša-at-qa*; N inf. cf. *na-áš-tu-qí-im* → AHw 1200; CAD Š/2 193f.; vSoden NABU 1989/76; Groneberg NABU 1989/77; Charpin MARI 8 350 fn. 26 (A.2976+:26); cf. Durand RA 82 107: "remettre, confier"; LAPO 17 52f. (475:4'); LAPO 17 273 fn. g.
|s^2-ṭ-y|	Sem.: Cf. *Šṭh* (*śṭh*, Hb.), *Šwṭ* (*śwṭ*) "to deviate, turn aside", *st* (*sēṭ*) "deviation, transgression"; *sṭy* (JAram., Syr.) "to turn aside, deviate", *swṭ* (JAram. C) "to move"; *śaṭaya* (Eth.) "to be drunk", *taśaṭya* "to deviate from the right path, be bent". See *šaṭṭa* (Arab.) "to go to extremes, too far; to exceed proper bounds; to deviate, stray".
Saṭiy "bent, curved" (?)	•ONOM: **EUPH** Fem. cf. *za-di-ia-tum* → Gelb CAAA 31, 179 (ŚAṬI?); Zadok Fs. Hallo 331 (*sà-ṭi-ia-tum*).
|s^2-w| Cf. |θ-ʔ|	Primary noun, Sem.: *Šh* (*śeh*, Hb.) "small livestock beast, sheep or goat"; *š* (Ph.) "sheep"; *syh*, *sytʔ* (JAram.) "ewe"; *šāh* (Arab., pl. *šāʔ*, *šiyāh*) "ewe; woman"; *s^{2}h* (OSArab.) "sheep".
Say "small livestock beast" (?)	•ONOM: **EB** Cf. *sá-u$_4$* → Pagan ARES 3 235f.
s^{1}iy "ram; sheep" (?)	•ONOM: **UGS** Cf. unc. *šu-ia*, *šu-ya-a*, *šu-ia-a*, *šu-ia-nu*, *šu-*^{d}IM → Sivan GAGl 275: ŠŪ (< **šiyu*).[773] **A4** *šu-ya* → Wiseman AT 147; Sivan GAGl 275: ŠŪ (< **šiyu*).[774]
s^1 "ram; sheep"	•CTX: **UGA** Sg. *š*, suff. *šy*, *šh*, du. *šm* → DUL 783: *š*.
|s^2-w/y-s^2|	Sem.: *Św/yŠ* (*św/yś*, Hb.) "to rejoice", *ŚŚwn* (*śāśôn*) "joy, jubilation", *mŚwŚ* (*māśôś*) "joy".
|s^2-w/y-s^2| "to be pleased" (?)	•ONOM: **EG** Cf. *t-ȝ-y:-:r-sȝ-sw* ^{F} → Schneider APÄQ 228 no. 481. **UGA** Cf. unc. *ss* → DUL 760; *šš* → DUL 834; *ššy* → DUL 835.
|s^2-y-ʔ|	Sem.: Cf. *šāʔa* (Arab.) "to want, wish".

[773] Altern.: Hurr, see Gröndahl PTU 255: *šuya*, *zuya*, *ŠY*.
[774] Altern.: Hurr, see Gröndahl PTU 255: *šuya*, *zuya*, *ŠY*.

|**s^2-y-ʔ**| "to want, wish" (?)	•ONOM: **EG** Cf. *sȝ-w-y$_2$-ty* → Schneider APÄQ 180 no. 381.
|s^2-y-b|	Sem.: *Šyb* (śyb, Hb.) "to be grey headed, old", *Šyb* (*śēb*) "grey-headness, old age", *Šybh* (*śêbāh*) "grey hair, advanced age"; *sʔb*, *syb* (JAram., Syr.) "to be(come) old", *šb*, *sb(ʔ)* "elders, old man", *sybh*, *sybtʔ* "old age"; *šiābu(m)*, *šêbu* (Akk.) "to be(come) old", *šibu* "old, elder, witness", *šībtu(m)* "greyness, grey hair; old woman", *šībūtu(m)*, *šēbūtu*, *ši/ebuttu(m)* "old age, function as witness, testimony"; *šāba* (Arab.) "to become white-haired", *šayba* "greyness of the hair, old age", *šāʔib* "white, grey (hair)"; *śyīb*, *eśśeb* (MSArab.) "to go white (in the hair)", *śayb* "white hair"; *śyb*, *śeba* (Eth.) "to turn grey (hair), *śibat* "grey hair".
Siyb, **Siybt**, **Siybat** "old age / man / woman"	•LL: **EB** NÌ.UL = *si-bù-um* → Conti QuSe 17 79; Sjöberg Fs. Renger 518. **EM** [BUR].ŠÚM.MA = *pu-ur-šum-tum* = MUNUS *ši-ib-tu* → Cohen Proceedings 53^{e} RAI 1 828. •ONOM: **EB** *si-bù*, *si-bu$_{14}$*(KA), fem.: *sì*(SUM)-*bad*, *si-ba-dum*, *sì*(SUM)-*ba$_x$*(HUŠ)-*du*, cf. NAM-*bíʔ*(NE)-*na-du* → Pagan ARES 3 179, 355, 363f. **EUPH** *ši-bu-na-a-ta-am*, *si-ba-ta-nu*, fem. *ši-ib-tu*, *ši-ib-tum/tu-um*, *ši-ba-tum*, *si-ba-ti-ia* → Gelb CAAA 31, 186f.
Saybat "grey or white fabric"	•CTX: **EUPH** *ša-ba-tum* (SAG, ÚS) → Durand ARM 30 114.
s^{1}b "old man, elderly man"	•CTX: **UGA** Pl. *šbm* → DUL 789: *šb*.
s^{1}bt "greyness, old age"	•CTX: **UGA** Sg. cstr. *šbt*, suff. *šbtk*, *šbth* → DUL 795: *šbt*.
|s^2-y-m| Cf. |**s^1-m**| **(1)**	Sem.: *Św/ym* (*św/ym*, Hb.) "to lay / set down, arrange, fix", *tŚwmh* (*teśûmet*) "deposited property"; *š(y)m* (Ph., Pun.) "to place, set up, put"; sw/*ym* (Aram., Syr.) "to place, put, install", *sym(ʔ)* (Syr.) "placing", *symh*, *symtʔ* "treasure"; *šiāmu(m)*, *šâmu* (Akk.) "to fix, decree", *šīmtu(m)* "what is fixed, will, destiny"; *šayma* (Arab.) "to sheathe; to enter", *šīma* "nature, constitution, character"; *s^2(y)m* (OSArab.) "to set up, erect; to secure, protect", *ms^{2}ym* "cultivated area"; *śym*, *śema* (Eth.) "to set (in order), put, place, appoint", *śimat* "placement", *maśyam*, *maśyəm*, *məśyām* "container; location where something is placed".
|**S-y-m**| "to place, fix, establish"	•CTX: **EB** G suffc. *si-mi*, D prefc. *u$_9$-si-ma-am$_6$*, suffc. *su-mu* → Mander MEE 10 35; Fronzaroli QuSe 19 16; Catagnoti / Fronzaroli ARET 16 153, 265; Catagnoti QuSe 29 125, 136, 162, 225f. •ONOM: **EB** *i-šè-mu*; cf. DAŠ(*talʔ*)-*ti-mu* → Pagan ARES 3 179, 325, 369. **EUPH, B** *ia-si-ma-tum*, *la(-a)-ia-si-im*, *la-ia-si-i-im*, *ia-si-im-su-mu(-ú)*, *ia-si-im-zu-mu-ú*, *ia-si-im-ad-da-šu-nu*; passim with DNN and epith.: *ia-si/ši-im*-DINGIR, *ia-si/ši-im-^{d}da-gan*, *i-ši-im-*^{d}IM, *ia-si/ši-im-*^{d}IM, *ia-si-im-ba-li*, *i-ši-im-é-a*, *ia-ši-im-*$^{(d)}$*é-a*, *ia-ši-im-ìr-ra*, *e-si-im-ḫa-mu-ú*, *ia-si-im-ḫa-mu(-ú)*, *ia-si-im-ḫa-am-mu (-ú)*, *ia-si-im-ki-*DINGIR, *ia-si-im-li-im*, *ia-si-im-ma-ḫar/ḫa-ar*; *ḫa-am-mi-e-si-im*, *sa-mi-ma-ia-si-im*, *su-mu-ia-si-im* → Gelb CAAA 32, 180; Zadok Fs. Hallo 331; Streck 221 § 2.121, 224 § 2.128; Golinets Onomastikon 2 287f., 301, 455f., 478.[775] **TU** *ia-si-mu-um* → Krebernik Tall Biʿa 219; Golinets Onomastikon 2 289, 455f. **R** *ia-si-im-ka-nu* → Dalley / Walker / Hawkins Tell Rimah 176 (244 III 20); Zadok Fs. Hallo 331; Golinets Onomastikon 2 288, 455f.

775 Cf. Huffmon APNMT 211: YSM (**wsm*) "be pretty, ornamental".

Saym “destiny”	•ONOM: **EB Cf.** *sa-ma, sá-ma, sa-mu, sá-mu, sa-mu-um, sá-mu-um, sa-mu-ù* → Krebernik PET 105; Pagan ARES 3 179, 361f.[776]
Siym, **Siym(a)t** “destiny”	•ONOM: **EB** *si-mi-dum* → Pagan ARES 3 179, 364. **EUPH**: *si-mu-da-ra, la-si-ma, ši-ma-tum, ši-ma-at-*^{d}*da-gan, ši-ma-at-*EŠ$_4$.DAR → Gelb CAAA 32, 187. **A7** *ta-ab-si-im-tum* → Wiseman AT 147; Gelb CAAA 32, 187.
maSiym “granary, storage place”	•CTX: **EM** *na-aš-ka-pu : ma-ši-mu* → Pentiuc Vocabulary 123.

|s^2-y-ḳ|	Sem.: Cf. *šīq, šīqa* (Arab.) “summit, top”.
Siyḳ “summit, top”	•ONOM: **EB** Cf. *si-ig-da-mu* → Pagan ARES 3 236, 363.

|s^2-y-s^2|
See **|s^2-w/y-s^2|**

[776] Several instances could be also assigned to the basis |s^1-m| (1).

Ṣ́

|ş-ʔ-n|
|ş-b-ʕ|
|ş-b-r|
|ş-b-ṭ|
|ş-ħ-ḳ|
|ş-l-ʕ|
|ş-m-d|
|ş-m-r|
|ş-p-r|
|ş-r-ʕ|
|ş-r-b|
|ş-r-k|
|ş-r-r|
|ş-r-s^1|
|ş-r-ṭ|
|ş-r-w|
|ş-w/y-ḳ|
|ş-y-ḳ See |ş-w/y-ḳ

|ş-ʔ-n|	Primary noun, Sem.: *ṣʔn* (*ṣoʔn*, Hb.) "flocks, small cattle, sheep (collective)"; *ṣʔn* (Ph., Amm., Moab.) id.; *qn(ʔ)*, *ʕn*, *ʕʔn*, *ʕnʔ* (Aram., Syr., Palm.) id., *ġn* (Aram. in Demotic script) id.; *ṣēnu(m)*, *ṣānum* (Akk.) id.; *ḍaʔn* (Arab.) id.; *ḍāʔin* "sheep" *ḍʔn* (OSArab.) "sheep".
şaʔn, **şān** "small cattle, sheep" **şōn** "small cattle, sheep" **şỉn** "small cattle, sheep"	•LL: **MŠ** *ṣa-a-nu*, [*-a*]*ʔ-nu* = *ṣe-e-nu* → AHw 1081: *ṣānu*; CAD Ṣ 96: *ṣānu*; Hrůša MŠ 111, 398 (only in MŠ).[777] •CTX: **EA** UDU.UDU.MEŠ *: ṣú-ú-nu* (263:12) → Sivan GAGl 270; Rainey CAT 1 20. •CTX: **UGA** Sg. *ṣỉn*, suff. *ṣỉnk*, (?)*ṣỉnh* → DUL 764: *ṣỉn* (I). •ONOM: **UGA** *ṣỉn* → DUL 764: *ṣỉn* (II).
|ş-b-ʔ| Cf. |ṣ-b-y|	Sem.: *ḍabaʔa* (Arab.) "to lurk, lie in ambush, in wait for"; see further: *ṣbʔ* (Hb.) "to fight against; to be on duty", *ṣbʔ* (*ṣābāʔ*) "troops, military service"; *ṣabāʔum*, *ṣabûm* (Akk.) "to take the field, put army into the field", *ṣābu(m)*, *ṣabbu* "troops, people"; *ṣbʔ*, *ḍbʔ* (OSArab.) "to wage war, fight", *ḍbʔ* "battle"; *ṣabʔa*, *ḍabʕa*, *ḍabʔa* (Eth.) "to make war, fight, attack", *ṣabʔ* "warfare", *ṣabāʔ* "fighting", *ṣabāʔit* "army, troops".
şābiʔ, **şābiy** "warrior(s), troop(s), army"	•CTX: **EUPH** *ṣa-bu-ú-um*, *ṣa-ba-a-am*, *ṣa-bi-i-im*, *ṣa-bi-e-em* → AHw 1072; CAD Ṣ 49: *ṣābu*, d,2', 54; Lafont Fs. Birot 161ff. **EG** *ḏa-bi-ʔi*, *ḏa-bi*$_2$*-ʔu*$_3$ (|ṣābiʔu|) → Hoch SWET 382 no. 573.[778]

[777] For the MN *Za-ʔà-na(-at)*, *Za-ʔà-tum* in pre-Sarg. Ebla and Mari see Gelb MariRe 137f., 142.

[778] Cf. Sivan / Cochavi-Rainey WSVES 87: *ṣ́á-bì-ʔu* "army"; Helck Beziehungen no. 305.

	•ONOM: **EB** *za*-NE(*bí*?), *za*-NE(*bí*?)-*ù* → Pagan ARES 3 232, 382. **EUPH** *za-bi-um*, *za-bu-ú-um* → Knudsen JCS 34 15; Streck Onomastikon 1 156 § 2.12 fn. 1.Diff. Gelb CAAA 196 (34: ṢB? "to desire"). **EG** Cf. *ḏa*-bi_2 → Hoch SWET 382 no. 573.
ṣ́bů (A) "troops, army"	•CTX: **UGA** Sg. *ṣbů*, *ṣbỉ*, suff. *ṣbůk*, pl. *ṣbỉm*, cstr. *ṣbỉ* → DUL 765f.: *ṣbů* (I).
ṣ́bů (B) "ducking, setting"	•CTX: **UGA** *ṣbů*, *ṣbỉ*, *ṣbả*, *ṣb{ỉ}ả* → DUL 766: *ṣbů* (II).
maṣ́biʔt "troops, army"	•CTX: **EB** *maš-bí-tum* → Fronzaroli ARET 13 139, 282. •LL: **EB** ÉREN.KI.GAR = *maš-bí-tum* → Conti QuSe 17 84f.

|ṣ́-b-ʕ|	Culture word, Sem.: *ṣbwʕ* (*ṣābûᵃʕ*, Hb.) "hyena"; *ḍab*(*u*)*ʕ* (Arab.) "hyena"; *ḍəbʕ* (Eth.) "hyena". See further: *būṣu*(*m*) (Akk.) "hyena"; *ṣəʕb* (Eth.) "rapacious animal, hyena".
ṣ́abaʕ "a rapacious animal"	•LL: **EM** AZ = *a-su* :*za-ba-ú* → Pentiuc Vocabulary 160f.; Cohen Proceedings 53ᵉ RAI 1 831.[779]

|ṣ́-b-r|	Sem.: *ṣbr* (Hb.) "to pour into a heap", *ṣbr* (*ṣibbur*) "heap"; *ṣbr* (Aram.) "to heap up", *ṣybwr*(*?*) "congregation", cf. *ʕbwr* (Aram., Syr.) "grain; crops"; *ḍabara* (Arab.) "to collect, gather, assemble", *ḍibāra*, *ḍubāra*, *ʔiḍbāra* "dossier, file".See further *ṣubrum* (Akk.) "(group of domestic) servants, labourers"; *ḍamara*, *ḍammara* (Eth.) "to unite, connect, fasten together".
ṣ́ibar "clan, community"	•ONOM: **B** Cf. unc. *zi-ba-ru-um*, *zi-ba-ra-tum* → Gelb CAAA 34, 197 (ṢIBAR).
θ̣br "clan, community" (?)	•ONOM: **UGA** → DUL 986: *ẓbr*; Tropper UG 93.
ṣ́brt "clan, community"	•CTX: **UGA** → DUL 766.[780]

|ṣ́-b-ṭ|	Sem.: *ṣbṭ* (Hb.) "to pick up"; *ʕbṭ* (Man. D) "to fetter", (JAram. Dt) to be seized"; *ṣabātu*(*m*) (Akk.) "to seize, take, hold", *ṣabtu*(*m*) "captured, taken", *ṣibittu*(*m*) "seizure", *muṣabbit*(*t*)*u* "part of a loom; an implement"; *ḍabaṭa* (Arab.) "to seize, capture", *ḍabṭ* "capture"; *źāṭ*, *źébaṭ*, *źáybɛṭ* (MSArab.) "to take"; *ḍabaṭa*, *ṣabaṭa* (Eth.) "to grasp, take hold of", *ḍəbuṭ* "grasped, seized".
|ṣ́-b-t| "to seize, take, hold"	•CTX: **EB** G prefc. *ni-za-ba-ad* |niṣ́bat|, *ne-il-da-ba-ad* |niṣ́tabat|, suff. *i-zi-ba-dè-ga* |yiṣ́batay=ka|; N verbal adj. suff. *ne-zi*-bu_{14}-*ud-kum* |naṣ́but=kum| → Edzard ARET 5 229; Fronzaroli Fs. Kienast 100f.; ARET 13 139, 141, 290; Catagnoti QuSe 29 21, 27, 29, 48, 68, 80, 82, 130, 132, 143, 229.
|ṣ-b-ṭ| "to seize, take, hold"	•CTX: **UGS** Cf. G prefc. *i-ṣa-ba-ṭu-na* → Nougayrol PRU 4 110:21.[781]
ṣ́abṭ "captured, taken" (?)	•ONOM: **B** Cf. *a-mi-za-ab-ti* → Gelb CAAA 34, 196 (ṢABṬ).

[779] For Sum. / Akk. AZ = asu "bear" see the Akk- dictionaries (CAD A/1 344: *asu* B; AHw 76: *asu*(*m*) II), lexical sections.
[780] For the alleged *ṣbr* / *ṣibbir* (DUL 766 "type of field (?) or special farming system, communal plot"; Sivan GAGl 269; Huehnergard UVST 169; vSoldt SAU 306) see Belmonte Fs. Sanmartín 43, and here \|z-b-r\|.
[781] Nougayrol loc.cit.: *i-ṣa-ba*-tu_x-*na*; cf. Huehnergard AkkUg 413 no. 595 for ṬU/GÍN and the spelling *ṣa-bi*-ṬU (for *ṣābitu*) in Ug. LL.

ṣibiṭt "seizure" (?)	•ONOM: **EUPH** Cf. *zi-bi-it-ta* → Gelb CAAA 34, 197 (ṢIBIṬ).
mṣbṭ "a tool or part of one (handle ?)"	•CTX: **UGA** Du. *mṣbṭm* → DUL 577f.
|ṣ-ḥ-ḳ|	Sem.:[782] *ṣḥq*, *śḥq* (Hb.) "to laugh", *ṣḥq* (*ṣ^{e}ḥoq*), *śḥwq* (*ś^{e}ḥôq*) "laughter"; *šḥq* (Hatra) "to laugh"; *ḥwk* (JAram.) "to laugh", *ʔḥk* (JAram.) "to laugh", *gḥk* (JAram., Syr.) "to laugh", *gḥwk(ʔ)* "laughter", *dḥk* (Aram.) "to laugh", *dḥwk(ʔ)* (JAram.) "laughter", *mḥk* (JAram.) "to laugh"; *ḍaḥika* (Arab.) "to laugh", *ḍaḥk*, *ḍiḥk*, *ḍaḥik* "laughter"; *źḥak*, *źəḥāk*, *źaḥák*, *źáḥak* (MSArab.) "to laugh", *źəḥāk* "laughter"; *śaḥaqa*, *śəḥqa*, *saḥaqa* (Eth.) "to laugh", *śāḥq*, *śaḥaq*, *śəḥāq* "laughter".[783]
|ṣ-ḥ-k| "to laugh"	•LL: **EB** ZÚ.NE.NE (su$_{11}$.li$_9$.li$_9$ = *za-ʔà-gú-um* → Conti QuSe 30, 40, 99; Sjöberg Fs. Renger 524, Fs. Kienast 550; Bonechi / Catagnoti Fs. Sommerfeld / Krebernik 186. •ONOM: **EUPH** Cf. *ia-az-ḫa-ki*(?)*-im* (rdg ?) → Gelb CAAA 34, 196 (ṢḤAQ); Golinets Onomastikon 2 122, 460.
|ṣ-ḥ-ḳ| "to laugh"	•CTX: **UGA** G prefc. *tṣḥq*, *yṣḥq*, suffc. *ṣḥq*, inf. *ṣḥq*, C prefc. *tšṣḥq* → DUL 771: /*ṣ-ḥ-q*/.
|θ̣-ḥ-ḳ| "to laugh"	•CTX: **UGA** G prefc. *yẓḥq* → DUL 986: /*ẓ-ḥ-q*/; Tropper UG 93.
ṣiḥḳ "laughter"	•ONOM: **B** Cf. *zi-ḫa-ka-a-a* → Gelb CAAA 34, 196 (ṢIḤAQ);
ṣḥḳ "laughter"	•CTX: **UGA** → DUL 771: *ṣḥq*.
|ṣ-l-ʕ|	Primary noun, Sem.: *ṣlʕ* (*ṣēlāʕ*, Hb.) "rib; side, (fir) plank"; *ʕlʕ(ʔ)* (Aram., Syr.) "rib; side", *ʕlʕh*, *ʕlʕth* (JAram.) id.; *ṣēlu(m)*, *ṣīlu(m)*, *ṣellu(m)*, *ṣillu(m)* (Akk.) "rib; side, flank"; *ḍilʕ* "rib", *ḍilʕa* (Arab.) "side"; *źālaʔ*, *źalʕ*, *źélaʕ* (MSArab.) "rib". Non-Sem.: *selis* (Gr.) "crossbeam".
ṣilaʕat "plank"	•CTX: **EG** *ḏi$_4$-ra-ʕ-tu*, *ḏi$_4$-r-ʕu-*(?) → Hoch SWET 394 no. 592.
ṣlʕ "rib, chops"	•CTX: **UGA** Pl. cstr. *ṣlʕ* → DUL 772.
|ṣ-m-d|	Primary noun, Sem.: *ṣmd* (*ṣemed*, Hb.) "(yoke-)team", *ṣmd* (C) "to tighten, harness"; *ṣimdu(m)*, *ṣindu*, *šimittu(m)*, *šimmitu* (Akk.) "binding, (yoke-)team; pair; 'yoke' (area measure)", *ṣamādu(m)* "to tie up, bind up, yoke", *naṣmattu(m)* "bandage"; *ḍamada* (Arab.) "to bind, bandage", *ḍimād* "bandage"; *ḍəmd* (Eth.) "yoke, pair", *ḍamada*, *ṣamada* "to bind", *maḍmad* "rope, thong"; with irregular consonantism: *ṣmd* (JAram., Syr.) "to bind (together)", *ṣmd* (Syr.) "yoke", *mṣmdw*, *mṣmdwtʔ* "fastening".
|ṣ-m-d|, "to tie up, bind"	•CTX: **EB** G prefc. *a-za-me-du* |ʔaṣmid|; N ptc. *mu-za-da* |muṣṣamd| → Rubio PIHANS 106 122; Catagnoti QuSe 29 125, 140, 143, 230.
|ṣ-m-d| "to harness, yoke; to tie, bind"	•CTX: **UGS** Cf. G suffc. *:ṣa-ma-ta*, *:ṣa-ma-tu*, D suffc. *ṣú-um-mu-ta* → vSoldt SAU 244 + fn. 9, 442 +fn. 112; Márquez AOAT 335 227f.[784] **UGA** G prefc. *tṣmd*, suff. *yṣmdnn*, suffc. *ṣmd*, impv. *ṣmd*, act. ptc. pl. *ṣmdm* →

[782] For the probl. dissimilation C3:*ḳ > C3:*k* see Militarev / Kogan SED 1 326f., and cf. Kogan Classification 98.

[783] For Akk. *ṣiāḫu*(m), *ṣâḫu* "to laugh" see Militarev / Kogan SED 1 325.

[784] Altern. Huehnergard UVST 171f.; ²UVST 397f.: \|ṣ-m-t\| "to transfer", with scanty etym. basis (Hb. *ṣ^{e}mimut* etym. and mng unc.). See also AHw 1081: *ṣamātu* (ug. Fw.) "definitiv übergeben";

	DUL 773: /ṣ-m-d/.
	•ONOM: **UGS** Cf. *ṣa-ma-da-na* → Nougayrol PRU 6 83 I 15'.
ṣamad, ṣamid "bound"	•CTX: **UGS** *ṣa-ma-at, ṣa-mì-it* → vSoldt SAU 437 + fn. 95, 484, 500. Nougayrol PRU 6 154 fn. 2; Márquez AOAT 335 227f.
ṣmd "pair, team; 'yoke' (area measure); a weapon"	•CTX: **UGA** Sg. *ṣmd*, pl. *ṣmdm*, du. *ṣmdm* → DUL 773f.
mṣmt "treaty, agreement"	•CTX: **UGA** → DUL 579; Tropper KWU 80.

|ṣ-m-r|	Primary noun, Sem.: *ṣmr* (*ṣemer*, Hb) "wool"; *ʕmr(ʔ)*, *qmr* (Aram., Syr.) "wool"; *ḍamr* (Eth.) "wool, fleece, woollen garment".
ṣamr "wool; a variety of sheep(?)"	•CTX: **EUPH** Sg. *za-mu-ra-tum*, pl. *za-ma-ra-tum/tim, za-mu-ra-tum/im* → Talon ARM 24/1 249: *zamartum, zamurtum*; Streck Onomastikon 1 111, 116f. § 1.95; Krebernik Tall Bi'a 45; Knudsen PIHANS 100 325 fn. 24.[785] **TU** Sg. *za-am-ru-um, za-am-ra-am, zu-am-ra-am*, fem. *za-am-ra-tum, zu-am-ra-tum, zu-am-ra-ta-am*, pl. *za-ma-ra-tum*, du. *za-am-ra-tá-an, zu-am-ra-ta-in* → Krebernik Fs. Fronzaroli 306ff.; Tall Bi'a 245 (notice the transcription *Zamrum* with *Z*). •ONOM: **EUPH** Cf. *za-am-ra* → Kupper ARM 22/2 494 (321:4, "laine"); Zadok Fs. Hallo 322: "wool".

|ṣ-p-r|	Sem.: Cf. *ḍafara* (Arab.) "to plait, braid; to case with stones (without mortar), ḍāfara "to aid"; *ḍfr* (OSArab.) "to case with stones (without mortar)"; see further: *źəfūr* (MSArab.) "to plait the hair", *źəfīr* "plait of hair", *ḍafreh* "braid"; *ḍafara, ḍaffara, ṣafara* (Eth.) "to braid, entangle, drape, twist", *maḍfart, maṣfart* "interwoven work"; *ṣpyrh* (*ṣepîrāh*, Hb.) "thread, wreath"; *ṣipirtu* (Akk.) "a clothing"(?).
ṣippar "plaited wool"	•CTX: **EUPH** Cf. GÚ(.È.A) / TÚG *ḫa-li/al ṣí-pa-ri / ṣí-pa-li / ṣí-ip-pa-ri / ṣí-pa-ri-im* → Durand ARM 30 38f.
mṣpr "who arranges, reinforces" (?)	•CTX: **UGA** G act. ptc. fem. sg. *mṣprt* → DUL 579: *mṣprt*.

|ṣ-r-ʕ|	Primary noun, Sem.: *ṣrʕh* (*ṣirʕāh*, Hb.) "wasp, hornet"; *ʕrʕy, ʕrʕtʔ, ʔwrʕytʔ* (JAram.) id.
ṣirʕu "hornets"	•ONOM: **EG** Elem. in TN *ḏi*$_4$*-r-ʕw* → Hoch SWET 393 no. 591.

|ṣ-r-b|	Culture word, Sem.: *ʕrbh* (*ʕᵃrābāh*, Hb.) "willow, poplar" (?); *ʕrbh, ʕrbtʔ* (JAram., Syr.) "willow, poplar" (?); *ṣarbatu(m), ṣerba/etu(m)* "poplar"; see further: *ġarab* (Arab.) "a species of tree".

CAD Ṣ 93: *ṣamātu* (or *ṣamādu*) "to transfer (real estate)"; Sivan GAGl 269: ṢMT 1. "destroy", 2. "transfer property" ?

[785] Add perhaps *za-am-ra*; Kupper ARM 22/2 494 (321:4, "laine"); Zadok Fs. Hallo 322: "wool".

ṣarbat "a species of tree (poplar / willow?)"

•LL: **EB** GIŠ.ASAL$_x$ = *zàr-ba-tum*; ASAL$_x$ = *gú-a-lu za-la-ba-tim*; *gú-ʔà-lu zàr-ba-tum* → Krebernik ZA 73 15, 26; PIHANS 106 91; Conti QuSe 17 127, 177; Archi NABU 2005/39; Catagnoti QuSe 29 32, 109, 230.
•ONOM: **EB** Cf. *zàr*-BAD(*bad*?), *zàr*- HUŠ(*ba$_x$*?)-*du* → Pagan ARES 3 233, 384.

|ṣ-r-k|

Sem.: *ṣrk* (Hb.) "to fail, be missing"; *ḍaraka* (Arab.) "to be decrepit, poor"; with irregular consonantism: *ṣrk* (JAram., Syr.) "to be in want, to need".

|ṣ-r-k| "to weaken, fail, be missing"

•CTX: **UGA** G prefc. *yṣrk* → DUL 779.

|ṣ-r-r|

Sem.: *ṣwr*, *ṣrr* (He.) "to show hostility, attack", *ṣr* (*ṣar*) "enemy", *ṣrh* (*ṣārāh*) "second, rival wife, concubine", *ṣrr* "to be a concubine"; *ʕrr* (Aram.) "to protest", *ʕrʕr* "to contest", *ʕr*(*?*) "enemy"; *ṣerru* (Akk.) "enmity, enemy, rival", *ṣerretu*(*m*) "concubine, subsidiary wife", *ḍarra* (Arab.) "to harm, damage", *ḍirr* "polygamy, bygamy", *ḍarra* "wife other than the first one"; *ḍrr* (OSArab.) "to wage war, launch an attack"; *źər*, *źer* (MSArab.) "to harm, beat"; *ḍarara* (Eth.) "to become an enemy, be hostile", *ḍərur*, *ḍarāri* "enemy, hostile".

ṣarrār "rival; spouse (man / wife ?) other than the first one" (?)

•CTX: **EM** Cf. unc LÚ ZA(*ṣa*?)-*ra-ri*, LÚ [ZA(*ṣa*?)]-*ar-ra-ri* → Pentiuc Vocabulary 161f. (Huehnergard); altern. Ikeda BiOr 60 272 reading LÚ *sà*(SAR)-*ra-ri* (see Tsukimoto ASJ 16, 1n. 19-20) "false, unfaithful".[786]

ṣrt "enmity, enemy"

•CTX: **UGA** Sg. *ṣrt*, suff. *ṣrtk* → DUL 780f.[787]

|ṣ-r-s^1|

Primary noun, Sem.: *ʕrš*(*?*) (Syr.) "molar tooth"; *ṣeršu* (Akk.) "offshoot, growth, point (moon's horns)"; *ḍirs* (Arab.) "molar tooth", *ḍarasa* "to bit firmly", *ḍarisa* "to be dull (teeth)"; *ʔḍrs*^{1} (OSArab.)"molar tooth"; *máźrəh*, *məẓréšto*, *məźrāḥ* (MSArab.) "(molar) tooth"; *ḍərs*, *ṭərs* (Eth.) "molar tooth", *ḍarsa*, *ṭarsa* "to be set on edge (teeth)".

ṣaras^1, **ṣaras^{1}t**, **ṣaris^{1}t** "point, moon's horn(s); splintering; chipping of a tooth"

•LL: **EB** ZÚ.GUL = *za-la-šum*, *za-ra-sa-tum^{um}*, *za-rí-iš-tum* (var.: *ḫa-zi-lum si-nu*); GIŠ.GUL = *za-rí-iš-tum*; Ù.SAKAR = *za-la-sa* → Krebernik ZA 73 10; Conti QuSe 17 101f.; Sjöberg Fs. Pettinato 272.

|ṣ-r-ṭ|

Sem.: *ʕrṭ* (Syr.) "to break wind"; *ṣarātu*(*m*), *ṣarādu* (Akk.) "to fart", *ṣāritu* "farter"; *ḍaraṭa* (Arab.) "to fart", *ḍart* "fart"; *źərūṭ*, *źérəṭ* (MSArab.) "to fart, break wind".

ṣāriṭān "little farter"

•ONOM: **UGS** Cf. *ṣa-ri-ṭá-na* → Malbran-Labat RSOu 7 3 r. 6'; Huehnergard UVST 214; AkkUg 368 (139).

ṣrṭn "little farter"

•ONOM: **UGA** Cf. *ṣrṭn* → DUL 781.

---

[786] Cf. Akk. *sarrāru* I < *sarāru* "robber, criminal"; AHw 1030; CAD S 178f., and here |s-r-r| (1).

[787] The Ug. PNN DUMU ZA-*ra-ti* and ZA-*ri-ri* remain unexplained; Gröndahl PTU 307; Sivan GAGl 270: ṢRR "tie up, be hostile towards". For DUMU ZA-*ra-ti* see Sivan GAGl 266: SARRATU "ignomity" [sic!].

|ṣ́-r-w|	Culture word, Sem.: Cf. *ṣry* (Hb.) "(a kind of) balsam / resin" (?); *ṣrw(ʔ)* (Syr.) "fragrant cedar product"; *ḍarw* (Arab.) "mastic"; (OSArab.) *ḍrw* "an aromatic".
ṣ́urw "(aromatic) resin, balsam"	•CTX: **EA** DUG *riq-qú*: *zu-ur-wu* → CAD Ṣ 261; Sivan GAGl 270; Huehnergard UVST 131f., ^{2}UVST 392; vSoldt SAU 304 (52); Moran AmL 120 fn. 2.
θ̣rw "(aromatic) resin, balsam"	•CTX: **UGA** → DUL 988: *ẓrw*; Tropper UG 93, 192.

|ṣ́-w/y-ḳ|	Sem.: *ṣwq* (Hb., C *hṣyq*) "to harass, press hard", *mṣwq* (*māṣûq*), *mṣwqh* (*m*^{e}*ṣûqāh*) "distress, hardship"; *ʕwq* (JAram., Syr.) "to be in trouble", *ʕyq* "distressed person", *ʕyyq* "narrow, distressed", see also *ṣwq* (JAram.) "to be distressed", *ṣwqh*, *ṣwqtʔ* "distress"; *ḍāqa* (*ḍayq*, Arab.) "to be(come) narrow", *ḍayyaqa* "oppress, constrain"; *ḍīq* " narrowness, lack of space", *ḍayyiq* "narrow"; *ṭwq*, *ṭoqa* (Eth.) "to be in dire straits, oppressed, constrain", *ṭəwwuq* "afflicted, oppressed". See also *siāqu(m)*, *sâqu* (Akk.) "to be(come) narrow", *sīqu* "narrow, tight".
|ṣ-y-ḳ| "to grasp; to push, put pressure on"	•CTX: **UGA** C prefc. suff. *tšṣqnh*, suffc. *šṣq* → DUL 778: /*ṣ-q*/.[788] •ONOM: **UGA** Cf. unc *ṣqm* → DUL. 779; *ṣqn* → DUL 779.
ṣḳ "distressed" (?)	•CTX: **UGA** → DUL 778.
ṣ́iyḳ "the narrow one (said of a small barge?)"	•CTX: **EB** Cf. *zi-kam*$_4$ → Fronzaroli ARET 13 67, 311.[789]
mṣḳt "difficult situation, trouble"	•CTX: **UGA** → DUL 580.

|ṣ́-y-ḳ
See |ṣ́-w/y-ḳ

[788] Read *ta-za-qa-pu* in EA 287:41 against Moran AmL 330 fn. 11: *ta-ṣa-qa*.
[789] For the alleged advb. / prep. *si-gi*(=) "together (with)" (Fronzaroli Amurru 1 130; Archi Eblaitica 4 20) see Tonietti PrepEb 30.

t

|t-ʔ-l| Cf. **|t-w-l|**
|t-ʔ-m|
|t-ʔ-n|
|t-ʔ-r|
|t-ʔ-s¹-r| See **|ʔ-s¹-r| (2)**
|t-ʕ-ʕ| See **|n-w-ʕ|**
|t-ʕ-b|
|t-b-ʔ| See **|ṭ-w-b|**
|t-b-ʕ|
|t-b-k| (1)
|t-b-k| (2)
|t-b-l|
|t-b-n|
|t-b-r-r|
|t-d-n| Cf. **|n/w/y-D-n|**
|t-γ-p-θ| Cf. **|ħ-b-S|**
|t-h-m| Cf. **|d-h-m| (2)**
|t-h-w|
|t-H-y|
|t-ħ-m| See **|D-H-m| (1)**
|t-ħ-t|
|t-k-k| (1)
|t-k-k| (2)
|t-k-l| (1)
|t-k-l| (2)
|t-k/ḳ-n| Cf. **|ḳ-n-w/y|**
|t-ḳ-ʕ|
|t-ḳ-n| See **t-k/ḳ-n|**
|t-ḳ-p| See **|θ-ḳ-p|**
|t-l-ʕ|
|t-l-ħ
|t-l-l| (1)
|t-l-l| (2)
|t-l-l| (3)
|t-l-l/y|
|t-l-m| (1)
|t-l-m| (2)
|t-l-y| See **|t-l-l/y|**
|t-m-ʔ|
|t-m-g|
|t-m-h|
|t-m-k|
|t-m-l|
|t-m-m|
|t-m-n|
|t-m-r| (1)
|t-m-r| (2) Cf. **|ṭ-m-r|**
|t-n-d-H|
|t-n-n-n|
|t-n-r|
|t-p-ħ|
|t-p-p|
|t-p-r|
|t-r-ʔ|
|t-r-ʕ|
|t-r-D-n|
|t-r-ħ|
|t-r-x| (1)
|t-r-x| (2)
|t-r-m|
|t-r-n| (1)
|t-r-n| (2)
|t-r-n| (3)
|t-r-r| (1)
|t-r-r| (2)
|t-r(-r)| (3)
|t-r-S|
|t-r-S-m|
|t-r-ṣ|
|t-r-t-r|
|t-r-w| Cf. **|w-r-w/y|**
|t-S|
|t-S-n|
|t-s¹-ʕ|
|t-t-p|
|t-w-k|
|t-w-l| Cf. **|t-ʔ-l|**
|t-w-l-ʕ|
|t-w-r|
|t-y-l| Cf. **|n-y-l|**
|t-y-s¹|
|t-y-t|

|t-ʔ-l|
Cf. **|t-w-l|**

Sem.: Probl. by-form of |t-w-l|. Cf. *tʔl* (Safaitic elem. in PNN) "to practice magic".

|**t-ʔ-l**| "to practice magic" (?)

•ONOM: **R** Cf. *ta-aḫ-li*-DINGIR → Dalley / Walker / Hawkins Tell Rimah 175 (244 II 46).
EM Cf. *ta-aḫ-li*[→ Pruzsinszky PTEm 177 [762]: "?"
EG Cf. *t-ꜣ-y:-:r* → Schneider APÄQ 227 no. 477.

|t-ʔ-m|

Primary noun, Sem.: *twʔmm* (pl. *tôʔᵃmim*, Hb.) "twins"; *tywm(ʔ)*, *twm* (JAram.) "twin", *tywmh*, *tywmtʔ* (fem.) "twin"; *tʔm(ʔ)* (Syr.) "twin"; *tū(ʔ)amu(m)*, *tuʔīmum*, *tūmamu*, *tuʔû* (Akk.) "twin", *tū(ʔ)amtu(m)*, *tūʔimtum*, *tūmamtu*, *tūʔintu* "twin, twinned (item)"; *tawʔam* (Arab.) "twin", *tawʔama* (fem.) "twin", *tiʔm* "double".[790]

taʔm, tuʔam "twin"
tuʔimt "twin vessel"

•ONOM: **EUPH** *ta-mi*, *tu-ma-nu-um*, fem. *tu-a-ma-tum* → Gelb CAAA 34, 198 (TAʔM); Zadok Fs. Hallo 331.
•CTX: **EUPH** *tu-im-tum* → Guichard ARM 31 315; Charpin MARI 3 48f.

|t-ʔ-n|

Primary noun, Sem.: *tʔnh* (*tᵉʔēnāh*, Hb.) "fig (tree)"; *tyn* (Pun.) "fig"; *tʔnh*, *tʔntʔ* (Aram., Syr.) "fig (tree)"; *tittu(m)*, *tiʔ(it)tu* (Akk.) "fig (tree)"; *tīn*, *tīna* (Arab.) "fig". Non-Sem.: Cf. **tiyin=* (Central Chadic) "mahogany".[791]

tiʔn, ti/eʔ "fig"

•CTX: **Q** Cf. *ti-ú* → CAD T 438f.: *tiʔu* A.[792]
•LL: **MŠ** *ti-ʔu-u/ú* = *ti-it-tú/ti* (II 127), [*ti-i*]-*nu* = *ti-it-tú* (MŠ exp. III 208), *ti-ʔu-u/ú* = *ti-ta* (exp. III 209) → Hrůša MŠ 60f., 182f., 341, 452.

tiʔnat "fig"

•LL: **UGS** [PÈŠ = *tittu* = ... = *ti-*[*n*]*a-tu*$_4$ → Huehnergard UVST 184, ^{2}UVST 383.[793]

tiʔitt "fig (tree)"

•LL: **EB** GIŠ.PÈŠ = *ti-ì-tum*, *ti-ì-du* → Krebernik ZA 73 14; Conti QuSe 17 124; PIHANS 106 91.

|t-ʔ-r|

Sem.: Cf. *tʔr* (*toʔar*) "appearance; beautiful in form", cf. *tʔr* (D) "to make an outline"; *tʔr* (Ph., Pun.) "plan (?); renown, imposing presence; dignity (?)"; *tʔr* (Syr.) "to notice", *twʔry*, *twʔytʔ* (JAram.) "appearance"; *ʔatʔara*, *ʔitʔāra* (Arab.) "to look at fixedly, to continue to look at".

tår "glory, splendour" (?)

•CTX: **UGA** → DUL 842.

|t-ʔ-s¹-r|
See **|ʔ-s¹-r| (2)**

|t-ʕ-ʕ|
See **|n-w-ʕ|**

|t-ʕ-b|

Sem.: Cf. *taʕiba* (Arab.) "to be(come) tired, weary".

---

[790] Probl. unrelated: Eth. *mantā* "twins, both", *mantawā* "to be twinborn".
[791] Orel / Stolbova HSED 502 no. 2392: **tiʔin=* "tree".
[792] Cf. AHw 1363: *tittu(m)* ['Q. nicht', see *ḫiddu* 4].
[793] Altern. rdg: vSoldt SAU 307 (154); BiOr 47 731; KWU 129: *ti-*[*i*]*t-tu*$_4$ |titt|.

|t-ʕ-b| "to be exhausted, weary" (?)	•CTX: **UGA** D suffc. suff. *t[ʕ]bthn* → DUL 843.[794]
|t-b-ʔ| See |ṭ-w-b|	For writings *tab-a-an*, *tab-ú-tum* listed in CAD T 33 as *tabʔu* adj.; (mng unkn.); Mari. Limet ARM 19 101 and passim: "excellentes"; AHw *vacat.*
|t-b-ʕ|	Sem.: *tbʕ* (JAram., Syr.) "to seek, follow"; *tebû(m)* (Akk.) "to get up, arise, set out"; *tabiʕa* (Arab.) "to follow, succeed"; *tabʕa*, *tabbəʕa* (Eth.) "to be brave, courageous".
|t-b-ʕ| "to raise, get up, stand up, go, leave, depart"	•CTX: **EB G** prefc. *i-da-ba-am*$_6$ |yitbaʕ=am|, *i-da-ba-ma* |yitabbaʕ=ma|, *a-da-ba-gú-ma-a* |la=yitabbaʕ=kum=ay(n)| → Fronzaroli ARET 13 72, 268; Catagnoti / Fronzaroli ARET 16 158, 212; Catagnoti QuSe 29 45, 82, 129f., 131, 135, 157, 231f. **UGS** G suffc. *ta-ba-ʔa* → Rainey IOS 3 40; Huehnergard UVST 184; vSoldt BiOr 46 647; SAU 307 (147); Tropper UG 464. **UGA** G prefc. *ttbʕ*, *ytbʕ*, suffc. *tbʕ*, *tbʕt*, inf. *tbʕ* → DUL 844f. •ONOM: **UGA** Cf. *tbʕ* → DUL 845.
tibʕ "rising, lifting"	•CTX: **EB** *ti-ib-ù-ma*, *dib-ù* → Fronzaroli ARET 11 41, 171; ARET 13 106, 251.
|t-b-k| (1)	Sem.: *tabāku(m)* (Akk.) "to pour (out)".[795]
|t-b-k| "to pour out"	•CTX: **EB** G prefc. *ti-da-ba-gu-ne* |titabbakū=nē(n)| → Catagnoti QuSe 29 22, 36, 79, 127, 131, 231: "essi versano a noi (d.)".
|t-b-k| (2)	Culture word, Sem.: Cf. *tubku* (Nuzi-Akk.) "a kind of leather".
tbk "a kind of leather"	•CTX: **UGA** → DUL 845.
|t-b-l|	Loanword. Non-Sem.: *tab/w=* (Hurr.) "to cast", *tabli=* "blacksmith, smelter (of metal)".[796]
tbl "blacksmith, smelter (of metal)"	•CTX: **UGA** Pl. *tblm* → DUL 845; Del Olmo AuOr 37 289.
|t-b-n|	Primary noun, Sem.: *tbn* (*teben*, Hb.) "straw, chaff"; *tbn(ʔ)* (Aram., Syr.)id.; *tibnu(m)* (Akk.) id.; *tibn* (Arab.) id.
tibn "straw"	•LL: **UGS** [IN = *ti-i*]*b-nu* = *ti-ib-ni* = *ti-ib-nu* → Sivan GAGl 279; Huehnergard UVST 57f., 184; vSoldt SAU 307 (146).
|t-b-r-r|	Loan, Hurr. Cf. *tab/warri/w/ba*, *tabarriani* (Nuzi-Akk.) "red wool".[797]

794 D-stem: "to exhaust, use up". See DUL loc.cit. for altern. solutions.

795 Heavily polysemic; see dictionaries. For the transferred mng "weaken" see Kouwenberg ZA 95 100.

796 Richter BGH 438ff.

tabarr, **tubarr** "a red dye; reddish dyed fabric"	•CTX: **EUPH** GÚ / TÚG *ta-ba-ru*, GÚ (*ša*) *da-ba-ri*, GÚ.È.A *da-ba-ri*, TÚG *tu-ba-ru* / *tu-ba-ra-tum* → Durand ARM 30 120f. (|tobarr=|). **A4** *ta-wa-ar-ri-na* → Wiseman AT 111 (434:3), 163. **UGS** Cf. SÍG.SA$_5$ *:ta-ba*(!)*-ri* → Huehnergard UVST 206; vSoldt UF 22 343f.
|t-d-n| Cf. **|n/w/y-D-n|**	Ass. by-form of |n/w/y-D-n|: *tadānu*(*m*) (Ass.) "to give", *tidintu*, *tidittu* (NAss.) "gift".
taditt "gift"	•CTX: **EM** Pl. *ta-ad-na-ti* → Pentiuc Vocabulary 176.
|t-γ-p-θ| Cf. **|ḫ-b-S|**	Culture word, Sem.: *taḫapšu* "felt, (felt-)rug" (Akk.).[798]
tγpθ "a type of (felt-)rug"	•CTX: **UGA** Sg. *tġpṯ*, pl. *tġpṯm* → DUL 850: *tġpṯ*.
taγapθ "a type of (felt-)rug"	•CTX: **A4** Pl. *ta-ḫa-ap-še-na* → Wiseman AT 163 (433:6); AHw 1301; CAD T 40f. **EM** LÚ *e-piš ta-ḫap-ši* → Pruzsinszky PTEm 8.
taγapθuγul "weaver of *t.*-rugs"	•CTX: **A4** LÚ *ta-ḫa-ap-šu-ḫu-li* → Wiseman AT 159 (301:8, 10); AHw 1301; CAD T 41f.
|t-h-m| Cf. **|d-h-m| (2)**	Primary noun, Sem.: *thwm* (*tᵉhôm*, Hb.) "primeval ocean"; *thwm*(*ʔ*) (JAram., Syr.) "abyss; subterranean waters, flood"; *tiamtu*(*m*), *tāmtu*(*m*), *tâm*/*ndu*, *tâw*/*matu* (Akk.) "sea, lake";[799] *thmy* (OSArab., du.) "low-laying fields", *thmt* "Coastal Plain" (TN); see also Arab. TN *tihāma* (Tihāma, Mekka).
tēmt "stretch of water, sea, lake"	•CTX: **EUPH** Passim; cf. *er-bi te-em-ti* ('shrimps'), *i-na te-em-tim*, *it-ti te-em-tim*, *li-it te-em-tim*, BURU$_5$ *te-em-tim* → Lion / Michel Topoi Suppl 2 103 (A.2661:9); Charpin ARM 26/2 135 (358:4); FM 7 38 (A.1968:3); Charpin RA 92 84ff (M.5423:12'); Arkhipov ARM 32 397 (M.15238:1').[800] **R** *er-bi te-em-ti* ('shrimps') → Dalley / Walker / Hawkins Tell Rimah 150f. (204:7).
thm "primordial ocean, abyss, DN"	•CTX: **UGA** → DUL 851.
tahāmat "primordial ocean, abyss"	•LL: **UGS** [AN-*tu*$_4$] = [*a*]*š*-[*t*]e-*a-ni-wi* = *ta-a-ma-tu*$_4$ → Huehnergard UVST 184f.; vSoldt SAU 307 (148); Tropper UG 174.
tihām(a)t "sea"	•CTX: **EB** *ti-ʔà-ma-du*, *ti-ʔà-ma-tum*, *ti-ʔà-ma-dím* → Edzard ARES 5 30, 58, 61; Bonechi QuSe 15 132f.; Proceedings 44ᵉ RAI 2 100; Catagnoti QuSe 29 93, 110, 231. •LL: **EB** AB.A = *ti-ʔà-ma-tum* → Krebernik ZA 73 43; PIHANS 106 91; Fronzaroli StEb 7 183; Fronzaroli QuSe 13 151; Bonechi QuSe 15 132f.; Proceedings 44ᵉ RAI 2 100.
thmt "primordial ocean, abyss"	•CTX: **UGA** du. *thmtm*, sg. (?) / pl. *thmt* → DUL 851.

797 Cf. Richter BGH 440: *tabarru*. See AHw 1298 and CAD T 21 for EA (Egypt, Tušratta), MAss., SBab., NBab.

798 Hurr. loan; Richter BGH 425f.: *taḫapšu*, *taḫapšuḫuli*.

799 DN *Tiāmat*; AHw 1354: *tiamtu*(*m*), *tâmtu*(*m*), 7; CAD T 156: *tâmtu*, 4. See *tēmt*, below.

800 For the DN *Têmtum* in Mari see Durand REA 213 (missing in the onomastics from Mari).

tēmāy "overseas" (?)	•CTX: **EUPH** Cf. URUDU LUḪ.ḪA *te-ma-yu/yi* → Arkhipov ARM 32 15f. + fn. 40.
|t-h-w|	Culture word, Sem.: Cf. *thw* (*tohû*, Hb.) "wilderness, wasteland". See further, *tayha*, *tayahāna* (Arab.) "to wander about, be lost, get lost", *tayyaha* "to lose, mislay", *tīh* "desert, wasteland".
thw "steppe, desert"	•CTX: **UGA** → DUL 851.
|t-H-y|	Sem.: *taʔû(m)* (Akk.) "to eat, graze", *tīʔu*, *tû*, *tîtu(m)*, *tiʔûtu*, *teʔûtu* "nourishment, sustenance"; *tw* (OSArab.) "nourishment"; *təwū*, *təwō*, *té* (MSArab.) "to eat", *táywi*, *təwi*, *tē*, *tɛh* "meat".
taHāy "food"	CTX: **EB** *da-ʔà*, *da<-ʔà>* → Lahlouh / Catagnoti ARET 12 520; suff. *da-a-su* |tahāy=i=Su| → Catagnoti / Fronzaroli ARET 16 29, 223.
taHyūt "food"	CTX: **EB** Cstr. *da-ʔà-ut* |taHy=ūt| → Fronzaroli StEb 7 9 +fn. 13; ARET 13 86, 250.
|t-ħ-m| See **|D-H-m| (1)**	
|t-ħ-t|	Sem.: *tḥt* (*taḥat*, Hb.) "what is located underneath, below, instead of", *tḥty* (*taḥtîy*), *tḥtn*, *tḥtwn* (*taḥtûn*) "lower, lowest"; *tḥt* (Ph., Pun., Nab., Palm.) "what is lower, below; under, instead of"; *tḥt* (Aram., Syr.) "that which is below, which follows, nether region", *tḥt*, *tḥwt*, *tḥyt* "under, instead of", *tḥth*, *tḥty*, *tḥtyh*, *tḥtyy*, *tḥtn* "below, under; lower one", cf. *ti-ḫu-ú-tú* (Warka-Aram.); *taḥt* (Arab.) "lower part, bottom", *taḥta*, *taḥtu* "under, below", *taḥtiyy*, *taḥtānī* "lower"; *tḥt* (OSArab.) "under", *tḥtyn* "lower, lowest"; *tāḥt* (Eth.) "lower part", *tāḥ(ə)ta* "below, under", *tāḥtu* "below, under", *tāḥtit* "lower part", *tāḥtay*, *tāḥtāwi* "lower, inferior", *təḥta*, *taḥata* "to be humble, stoop".
taħt "underneath, below; instead of"	•CTX: **EA** *ta-aḫ-ta-mu* (252:26, |taħtamô| < |taħt=a=himu| ?) → AHw 1302: *taḫta*; Sivan GAGl 128, 278; Rainey CAT 1 92, 168, 174; 3 1; EAC 1025; Moran AmL 305; Izre'el Orient 38 78.[801] •ONOM: **EUPH**, **B** Cf. *ta-aḫ-tu-bi*-DINGIR, *bu-un/nu-taḫ-tu-un-i-la*, *ta-aḫ-ti$_4$-li-im*, *ta-aḫ-ti-in-ìl* → Gelb CAAA 34 198f.; Zadok Fs. Hallo 331.
tħt "under, beneath; underneath"	•CTX: **UGA** Suff. *tḥth*, *tḥtn* (?), *tḥtm* → DUL 852f.: *tḥt* (I), 853: *tḥt* (II).
tħtn "lower"	•CTX: **UGA** → DUL 853: *tḥtn*.
tħty "lower	•CTX: **UGA** Fem. *tḥ<t>yt* → DUL 853: *tḥtyt*.
|t-k-k| (1)	Culture word, Sem.: Cf. *tikku(m)* (Akk.) "neck".
tikkat "neck-line"	•CTX: **EUPH** *ti-ka-ti-ia* → Dossin ARM 4 35ff. (20:16): "mes laisses"; Oppenheim JNES 13 142; cf. CAD T 400: *tikātu* (sic!); Charpin MARI 7 173; Durand LAPO 16 632 (no. 436) fn. b.

[801] Altern. Durand QuSe 16 39f.; CAD T 299: *taʔtamu*, b, EA: "assembly" (?).

tkyγ "a type of harness or trappings"	•CTX: **UGA** → DUL 855: *tkyġ*.
|t-k-k| (2)	Sem.: *tkk* (Syr.) "to oppress, subdue", *twk(ʔ)* "oppression"; *takāku(m)* (Akk.) "to(op)press", *tukku* "oppression"; *takka* (Arab.) "to trample down".
tukk "labour camp, workshop"	•CTX: **EUPH** (LÚ) NAGAR *ša tu-uk-ki-im* → Bardet / Joannès ARM 23 55f. (66:8), 145f.; Durand NABU 1989/111. **EM** É *tu*-UG-GI → Durand NABU 1989/111; Pentiuc Vocabulary 185.
|t-k-l| (1)	Sem.: *tkl* (JAram., Syr.) "to trust"; *takālu(m)* (Akk.) id.; *tukultu(m)* "trust".[802]
|t-k-l| "to trust"	•ONOM: **EA** (d)*da-ga-an-ta-ka-la* → Moran AmL 381; Hess APN 64f., 212. **EG** Cf. *t-ꜣ-k-ꜣ-r-n-ꜣ-y* → Schneider APÄQ 241f. no. 517.
tukl "safe repository, storehouse" (?)	•CTX: **EUPH** Cf. É *tu-[u]k-la* → CAD T 459: *tuklu* (*bīt tukli*); Dossin ARM 14 (13 1 XIV 59). **EM** Cf. É *tùk-li*, É *tu-uk-li* → CAD T 459: *tuklu* (*bīt tukli*); Dietrich UF 21 81 + fn. 72; Fleming Installation 114f.; Pentiuc Vocabulary 185.
|t-k-l| (2)	Culture word, Sem.: *tklt* (*tᵉkēlet*, Hb.) "blueish (/ violet coloured) purple wool"; *tklh, tkltʔ* (JAram., Syr.) "purple thread, purple dye"; *takiltu* (Akk.) "purple (wool)".[803]
takilt, tikilt "purple (wool)"	•CTX: **EM** SÍG *ti-kíl-ti* → Westenholz Emar Tablets 61. **UGS** Cf. SÍG.ZA.GIN *ta-kíl-tu*$_4$, SÍG *ta-kíl-ta* → vSoldt UF 22 329ff., 335f., 341.
|t-k/ḳ-n| Cf. **|ḳ-n-w/y|**	Sem. dimorphic base. C_2:*k*: *tkn* (Hb.) "to allocate, examine, check". C_2:*ḳ*: *tqn* (Hb.) "to be(come) straight"; *tqn* (Aram., Syr.) "to be firmly positioned", (D) "to establish properly, correct", *tqn* "proper", *tqyn* "firm, stable"; *taqānu(m)*, *taqāmu*, *tagānu* (Akk.) "to be in good order", *taqnu* "in order, good", *tiqnu(m)*, *teqnu* "ornament", *tuqnu(m)*, *tuq/gunu* "good order", *tuqqunu* "laid out in order"; *ʔatqana* (Arab.) "to perfect", *tiqn* "skilful".
|t-ḳ-n| "to be in good order"	•CTX: **EB** G prefc. *[lu-d]a-gú-nu* |(lu=yitḳun|), *lu-d[u]gú-nu* (|lu=yitḳunū|) → Fronzaroli ARET 13 92, 280; Catagnoti / Fronzaroli ARET 16 23, 250; Catagnoti QuSe 29 46, 134, 231.
taḳn "good order"	•ONOM: **A4** *ta-qa-an* → Wiseman AT 149. **UGS** Cf. *il-taq-nu* → Gröndahl PTU 201; Sivan GAGl 279. **EG** Cf. *t:*$_2$*-q-ꜣ-y*$_2$*-n-ꜣ* → Schneider APÄQ 241 no. 516.
tiḳin "a kind of necklace"	•CTX: **EB** *ti-gi-na, ti-ki-na, ti-ki-núm* → Pasquali QuSe 23 20ff.
taḳḳan "perfect, straight"	•ONOM: **UGS** *táq-qa-na* → Nougayrol PRU 3 32 (RS 16.129):2; vSoldt SAU 40.
tkn "inspector, measurer" (?)	•CTX: **UGA** Pl. *tknm* → DUL 854.
tḳn "perfect, straight"	•ONOM: **UGA** → DUL 862.

[802] Also in Ebl. LL: Krebernik ZA 73 17, 45; Catagnoti QuSe 29 232.

[803] See AHw 1306 and CAD T 70ff. for Nuzi, EA (Tušratta) etc.: from MBab. on. Cf. OAkk. SIG da.gál.túm and vars (AHw 1306: *takiltu*, 6; CAD T 73).

|t-ḳ-ʕ|	Sem.: Cf. *tqʕ* (Hb.) “to strike the hands together, to blow the trumpet”, *tqʕ* (*tēqaʕ*) “a blast of the horn”, *twqyʕ* (ptc. pl. *tôqeʕîm*) “who strikes (the hand)”; *tqʕ* (JAram.) “to sound a horn”, *tqwʕ* “one who blows the trumpet”; *ṭaqʕa*, *ṭaqʔa* (Eth.) “to sound, blow a trumpet”. Non-Sem.: Cf. **taq*= (West Chadic) “to strike”; **tuḳ*= (East Cushitic) “to strike”[804]
tḳʕt “she who applauds; DN” (?)	•ONOM: **UGA** → DUL 862: *tqʕt*.
t-ḳ-n| See **t-k/ḳ-n|**	
|t-ḳ-p| See **|θ-ḳ-p|**	WSem. by-form.
|t-l-ʕ|	Primary noun, Sem.: Cf. *tulû(m)*, *telû*, *tilû* (Akk.) “breast, teat”; *təlōt* (OSArab.) “nipple”; *tallāʕ*, *tallāʔ* (Eth.) “breast”.
tulʕuy “breast-shaped” **tlʕ** “nipple, pectoral(s)”	•CTX: **EUPH** *tu-lu-ú*, GAL *tu-lu-ú* → Durand Fs. Veenhof 125 fn. i; (vessel) Guichard ARM 31 140, 324. •CTX: **UGA** Sg. suff. *tlʕm* → DUL 856.
|t-l-ħ|	Sem.: Cf. *tlḥ* (Syr.) “to split, tear”.
|t-l-ħ| “to split, tear”	•ONOM: **B** *ta-la-ḫu-um* → Gelb CAAA 199 (TL?); Zadok Fs. Hallo 331.
|t-l-l| (1)	Sem.: Cf. *talālu*(*m*) (Akk.) “to stretch”; *tillatu*(*m*) “help”, *tillūtu*(*m*) “assistance”. See further: *talla* (Arab.) “to take down, get down”.
|t-l-l| “to assist, help; to achieve an alliance (?)” **tālil** “auxiliary”	•CTX: **EUPH** G suffc. *ta-al-lu*, *ta-al-la-nu-ma*, inf. suff. [*ta-la-l*]*i-šu-nu* (A.4515: 28’. 32’), D cf. *ú-ta-la-al* → Charpin MARI 8 365; Ziegler AfO 46/47 332; Lackenbacher ARM 26/2 393; Lafont ARM 26/2 484. •CTX: **EUPH** *ta-li-lu* → Birot ARM 13 60 (35:27); Durand LAPO 18 21f. +fn. e.[805]
|t-l-l| (2)	Loan. Non-Sem.: Cf. elem. *tilla* (Hurr.) “bull”.[806]
till (A) “bull; DN” (?)	•LL: **EB** Cf. ^{d}BAD.KALAM.TIM = BAD (*til*?)-*lu ma-tim*, ^{d}<BAD.>KALAM.TIM = *ti-lu ma-tim* → Krebernik ZA 73 31; cf. Lambert MARI 4 529 fn. 4 (read: BAD-*lu ma-tim* “king / lord of the land”).

[804] Relation controversial; cf. Orel / Stolbova HSED 498 no. 2370: **taq*= / **tiq*= “to strike”; 503 no. 2399: **tuḳ*= “to strike”.
[805] Cf. AHw 1310, I (cf. *talālu* G) “Bogenschütze”; CAD T 94, A: “boat-tower(?)”.
[806] GN and elem. in PNN; Deller Or 45 44; Gröndahl PTU 265; Haas SCCNH 1 183ff.; Richter BGH 459.

|t-l-l| (3)

Primary noun, Sem.: *tl* (suff. *till=*, Hb.) “rubbish heap”; *tl(ʔ)* (Aram., Syr.) “tell, mound, hill”; *tīlu(m)*, *tillu*, *tēlu* (Akk.) “(ruin) mound, heap”;[807] with irregular vocalism: *tall* (Arab.) “hill, elevation” (cf. *talʕa* “hill, hillside”).
Non-Sem.: **tul=* (West Chadic, Cushitic) “hill, hill-top”.[808]

till (B) “mound, heap”
●CTX: **EG** *ti$_2$-ra*, *ta-n-ra-{t}* (pl. |tilla|) → Hoch SWET 356f. no. 527; cf. Kilani VGW 128: *t'i/u^{n}r(rv).

tl (B) “hill”
●CTX: **UGA** Sg. *tl*, pl. *tlm* → DUL 855.

|t-l-l/y|

Sem. dimorphic base. C$_3$:*w/y*: *tlh* “to hang up”, *tly* (*t^{e}lî*) “quiver-belt”; *tly* (Aram., Syr.) “to suspend, hang”, *tly(ʔ)* “suspension; a weapon”, *tlyh*, *tlytʔ* (Syr.) “handle”; *talā*, *tuluwwa*, *tallā* (Arab.) “to follow, continue”, *tilw* “rear(ing)”; *tlw* (OSArab.) “to follow, continue to do”; *talawa* (Eth.) “to follow, cling to, accompany”, *taliw* “adherence”. C$_2$=C$_3$: *tullû* (Akk.) “to accoutre”, *tillu*, *tillû(m)* “appendage, trappings”.

tily, **tillay** “a kind of appendage, strap” (?)
●CTX: **EB** *dè-li*, *dé-lu*, *dè-lum* → Pasquali QuSe 23 121ff.
EUPH *til-le-e*, *ti-il-le-e* → Arkhipov ARM 32 100; Pasquali Or 83 273.

tl (A) “holder, strap; weapon”
●CTX: **UGA** Sg. *tl*, pl. *tlm* → DUL 855f.

|t-l-m| (1)

Primary noun, Sem.: *tlm* (*telem*, Hb.) “furrow”; *tlm* (JAram). id.; *talam* (Arab.) “furrow”, and cf. *tilm* “servant”; *təlm* (Eth.) “furrow”.

talama “furrow”
●CTX: **EG** *d-nm* → Hoch SWET 378 no. 564.

tlm (A) “furrow” (?)
●CTX: **UGA** Cf. *tlm* (bkn ctx.) → DUL 857.

|t-l-m| (2)

Sem.: *tlym(ʔ)* (JAram.) “(twin) brother”; *talīmu(m)* (Akk.) “favourite brother”.

talīm “nice, lovable (brother); own” (?)
●LL: **EB** NÌ.Ú.RUM =*da-li-mu* → Krebernik ZA 73 4; Conti QuSe 17 78.
●ONOM: **EB** Cf. *du*-NE(*bí*?)-*da-li-im* → Krebernik PET 80; Pagan ARES 3 237, 302.

tlm (B) “nice, lovable (brother); own” (?)
●ONOM: **UGA** Cf. *tlmn* → DUL 857.

|t-l-y|
See |**t-l-l/y**|

|t-m-ʔ|

Sem.: *tamû(m)*, *tamāʔu(m)*, *taʔû*, *temû* (Akk.) “to swear”, *tamītu* “oath”, *tam(m)āmû* “one who swears oaths”, *tumāmītu(m)* “oath(-taking)”; see also *ymy* (Aram., Syr.) “to swear”; *wamāʔum* (Akk.) “to swear”.

|t-m-ʔ| “to exorcise, charm”
●CTX: **EB** Cf. G prefc. *ad-da-ma-ʔa$_5$-ki* (|ʔattamaʔ=am=ki|) → Krebernik Beschwörungen 157; Catagnoti QuSe 29 60, 80, 83, 152, 231.

tamāmiyt “asseveration”
CTX: **EUPH** *ta-ma-mi-tum* → AHw 1316: *tammāmītu*; CAD T 111: *tamāmītu*; Dossin ARM 10 202f. (141:17).

---

[807] For a poss. var. |dul| (cf. Sum. du$_6$) as basis for |du(l)dul=| (TN *Tuttul*) see Archi NABU 2019 86.

[808] Orel / Stolbova HSED 509 no. 2429: **tül=* “hill”.

|t-m-g|	Culture word, etym. unkn. Sem: *tumāgu* (Akk. LL) “a kind of flour”.
tumag “a kind of flour” (?)	•CTX: **EM** *tu-ma-gu* → Pentiuc Vocabulary 182.
|t-m-h|	Sem.: Cf.: *tmh* (Hb.) “to be astonished, amazed”, *tmhwn* (*timmāhôn*) “confusion, bewilderment”; *tmh* (Aram., Syr.) “to wonder at, be amazed”, *mtmh* (JAram.) “surprising”.
metmiħ “surprise” (?)	•ONOM: **EUPH** *me-it-mi-yu*, *me-it-mu-um*, *me-it-me-ú-um* → Gelb CAAA 34, 200.
|t-m-k|	Sem.: Cf. *tmk* (Hb.) “to hold, take hold of”; *tmk* (Ph., Pun.) “to take, seize”; *tamāku* (SBab., once) “to grasp”, Akk. otherwise *tamaḫu(m)*.
tamk “fixed abode, residence” (?)	•CTX: **UGS** Cf. É KISLAḪ *:ta-am-*GI → Sivan GAGl 278; Huehnergard UVST 185: “?”.
|t-m-l|	Primary noun, Sem.: *ʔtmwl* (*ʔē/e/itmôl/ûl*, Hb.) “yesterday”; *ʔtml(y)*, *tmly* (Aram., Syr.) id.; *timāli*, *timālu* (Akk.) id.;[809] *təmāləm* (Eth.) id.
tumāl “the previous day, yesterday”	•CTX: **EA** *tu-ma-al* (362:14f.) → Rainey CAT 1 179, 3 10, 127f.
ỉtml “the previous day, yesterday”	•CTX: **UGA** *ỉtml* (rdg ?) → DUL 119: *ủ/ỉtml*.
|t-m-m|	Sem.: *tmm* (Hb.) “to be(come) completed, finished”, *tm* (*tām*, pl. *tammìm*) “complete, perfect”, *tm* (*tom*, pl. *tummîm*) “perfection”, *tmym* (*tāmîm*) “complete, intact”; *tmh* (*tummāh*) “completeness”; *tmm* (Ph., Pun.) “to be completed, decided”, *tm* (Ph., Pun.) “totality, completion”, *tm* (Pun.) “perfect, undamaged”, *tmh* (Pun.) “perfection”; *tmm* (JAram.) “to come to an end”, (Syr., D) “to make perfect”, *twm* (JAram.) “innocence, completion”, *tmym* (Aram., Syr.) “perfect, honest”, *tamma* (Arab.) “to be(come) complete”, *tamām*, *tāmm* “complete”; *tymm* (OSArab.) “perpetuity”; *təm*, *tem*, *tim*, *timm*, *tumm* (MSArab.) “to finish, be finished”; *tamām* (Eth.) “complete”.
|t-m-m| “to be completed; to complete”	•ONOM: **EG** Cf. *pȝ-y-t-ȝ-m-y*, *ṯ-mȝ-m-*w_2 → Schneider APÄQ 107 no. 226, 250 no. 534.
tamm “complete, full”	•ONOM: **UGA** Unc. *ta-mì-ia*, *ta-mu-mu*, *ta-me-nu* → Gröndahl PTU 201; Sivan GAGl 278; Malbran-Labat RSOu 7 16 (2:5).[810]
tm “complete, full”	• CTX: **UGA** Sg. (?) *tm*, pl. f. *tmt* → DUL 858. •ONOM: **UGA** *ỉltm* → DUL 64; cf. unc. *tmn* → DUL 858: *tmn* (II); *tmnn* → DUL 858; *tmy* → DUL 860; *tmyn* → DUL 860.
|t-m-n|	Etym. unkn.

[809] For NAss. *i/it-ti-ma-li* see vSoden GAG 95 §72 b.

[810] Cf. Hurr.-Ug. *ta-me* “flea” (LL; = Akk. *pur-ḫu-šu*); Richter BGH 435.

tuman "a beam" (?)	•LL: **EB** GIŠ.ÙR = *tù-ma-nu*/*núm* → Sjöberg Fs. Pettinato 262. **MŠ** *tu-ma-a-nu* = *gu-šu-ri* / GIŠ.ÙR (II 139B, exp. III 250) → Hrůša MŠ 62, 185, 217, 342, 454.
|t-m-r| (1)	Primary noun, Sem.: *tmr* (*tāmār*, Hb.) "date palm"; *tmr* (Pun., Nab.) id.; *twmrh*, *t*(*w*)*mrtʔ* (Aram., Syr.) "date, date palm"; *tamr* (Arab.) "dates", *tamra* "date"; *tmrm* (OSArab.) "dates"; *tōmər* (MSArab.) "dates", *təmərēt* "date", *təmrəh* "date palm"; *tamr*, *tamart* (Eth.) "date, date palm".
tamar "date palm; DN"	•LL: **UGS** Cf. [GIŠIMMAR = *gišimmaru* ? = ... = *ta*-[*ma*?-*ru*?] → Sivan GAGl 278; Huehnergard UVST 185; vSoldt SAU 307 (149). •ONOM: **EUPH** *qí-iš-ti-*ᵈ*ta-ma-ru* → Dossin RA 64 44 fn. 2; Zadok Fs. Hallo 331.
tmr "date palm"	•CTX: **UGA** Cf. *tmrym* (pl. GN) → DUL 859: *tmry*; Belmonte RGTC 12/2 285. •ONOM: **UGA** Cf. *tmr* (PN) → DUL 859; *tmrm* (TN) → DUL 859.
|t-m-r| (2) Cf. **|ṭ-m-r|**	Sem.: *temēru*(*m*), *tamāru* (Akk.) "to cover (in earth), bury, conceal", *timru* "buried", *tumru*(*m*) "charcoal ashes".
temr "a ritual or cultic meal" (?)	•CTX: **EUPH** Ì.GIŠ *a-na te-em-ri-im ša* ᵈDUMU.ZI → Dossin RA 69 27 (4:4: "enterrement"; Jacquet FM 12 139 (A.4540:4); AHw 1346: *temrum*, *timru*: "ein Kultmahl"(?); CAD T 419: *timru* (*temru*), 1: "embers(?)".
timert "buried deposit"	•CTX: **EUPH** *ti-me-er-tam*, *ti-mi-ir-tam* → AHw 1360: *time*/*irtum*; CAD T 418: *timirtu*; Durand MARI 3 138 fn. 67; LAPO 18 285 fn. f.
|t-n-d-H|	Culture word, etym. unkn. Sem.: Cf. *tindû* (Akk. LL) "a lyre" (?).
tinduH "lyre" (?)	•LL: **EM** ZA.AN.MÙŠ MIN (: À. ZA.AN.MÙŠ) = *ti-in-du-u* → Pentiuc Vocabulary 182.
|t-n-n-n|	Culture word, Sem.: *tnyn* (*tannîn*, Hb.) "sea-monster, -dragon; serpent"; *tnyn*(*ʔ*) (Aram., Demotic script, Syr.) id.; *tinnīn* (Arab.) id.; with modified consonantism: *tamān* (Eth.) "snake, dragon".[811]
tunnan "dragon, snake; DN"	•LL: **UGS** [MUŠ = *ṣīru* = *apši*...] = *tu-un-na-nu* → Sivan GAGl 280; Huehnergard UVST 185f.; vSoldt SAU 307 (150).[812] •ONOM: **EUPH** *tu-na-nu*(*-um*) → Zadok Fs. Hallo 331.
tnn "dragon, snake; DN"	•CTX: **UGA** → DUL 860: *tnn* (I). •ONOM: **UGA** *bntnn* → DUL 860: *tnn* (II).
|t-n-r|	Culture word, Sem.: *tnwr* (tannûr, Hb.) "oven"; *tnwr*(*ʔ*), *tnwrh*, *tnwrtʔ* (JAram., Syr.) id.; *tinūru*(*m*), *tenūru* (Akk.) id.; *tannūr* (Arab.) id.
tannūra "oven"	•CTX: **EG** *ta-ru*$_2$*-ru*$_2$, *ta*$_3$*-ru*$_2$*-ru*$_2$, miswritten *ta-ha-ru*$_2$ → Hoch SWET 359 no. 531; Kilani VGW 129: *tvr´i:/u:r(v).[813]

[811] Cf. *tan= (West Chadic) "earth worm", according to Orel / Stolbova HSED 498 no. 2367: *tan= "snake, worm"; questionable.

[812] See further the PN *tu-ni-in-na*, Nougayrol PRU 6 51 (RS 17.426) rev. 11, and the TN URU *tu-na-a-na*, Nougayrol Ug 5 95 (RS 20.01):20; probl. unrelated.

[813] Cf. Sivan / Cochavi-Rainey WSVES 86: *tá-rú-rú* "oven, kiln"; Helck Beziehungen no. 277.

|t-p-ħ| — Culture word, Sem.: *tpwḥ* (*tapû*^{a}*ḥ*, Hb.) “apple, apple-tree”; *twpḥ* (Aram. Pehlevi ideograms, JAram.) id.; *tuffāḥ* (Arab.) “apple”; *təffuḥ, təffāḥ, taffaḥ, taffuḥ, tuffāḥ* (Eth.) “apple, apple-tree”.
Non-Sem.: Cf. **tVfaḥ*= (Berb.) “apple”.[814]

tappuħ “apple” — •CTX: **EG** *d-p-ḫu, d-p-ḫ-{t}, ḏ-p-{t}-ḥ* → Hoch SWET 377 no. 563.
•ONOM: **EG** *ḏ-p-ḥu* → Hoch SWET 377 no. 563.

tuppuħ “apple” — •LL: **EB** GIŠ ḪAŠḪUR (!?) = *du-bù-*u_9 → Conti QuSe 17 123; Catagnoti QDFL 18 181..

tpħ “apple” — •CTX: **UGA** → DUL 861f.: *tpḥ* (I).
•ONOM: **UGA** TN *tpḥ* → DUL 862: *tpḥ* (II).

|t-p-p| — Sem. onomatopoeia: *tpp* (part. pl. fem. G *tôpēpôt*, D *m*^{e}*top*^{e}*pôt*, Hb.) “to beat the timbrel”, *tp* (*top*) “hand-drum, tambourine”; *tpp* (part. sg. m. D *mtpp*, Ph.) “to strike”; *tpp* (Aram.) “to play the timbrel”, *twp(ʔ)* (JAram.) “drum”; *duff, daff* (Arab.) “tambourine”. See further *dabdaba* (Arab.) “to treat, tap”, *dabdāb* “drum”; *dəbb(a) ʕanbasā* (Eth.) “kettledrum”.

tp (A) “drum, tambourine” — •CTX: **UGA** Sg. *tp*, suff. *tpk* (rdg ?) → DUL 861: *tp* (I).

|t-p-r| — Sem.: Cf. *tpr* (Hb.) “to stitch together, tack”; *tpr* (JAram.) “to sew”.

tuppur “a bronze (sewing ?) tool” — •CTX: **EM** *tù-up-pu-ru* ZABAR → Pentiuc Vocabulary 186.

|t-r-ʔ| — Sem.: *trʔ(ʔ)* (Syr.) “guide, educator”, *trʔʔ/y* “to educate”; *tarû(m)* (Akk.) “to lift up”, *tāriu* “(child) minder”, *tāritu(m)* “nurse”.

|t-r-ʔ| “to lift up” — •LL: **EB** Cf. ME.DA.GÍR = *da-rí-ì šu-ga-ga-bí* (G inf. ?) → Fales QuSe 13 186 (for EV 0205).

tāriʔ “female keeper, attendant” — •CTX: **EM** LÚ.MEŠ *ta-ri-i* → Fleming Installation 18, 102f
•ONOM: **A4** *ta-ar-i* → Wiseman AT 147; Arnaud AuOr 16 157; AuOrS 1 79.

tāriʔt “keeper, attendant” — •LL: **EM** Fem. EME.DA = *ta-ri-tu* = *ta-ri-ʔ-*tu_4 → Arnaud AuOr 16 157; Pentiuc Vocabulary 178; Cohen Proceedings 53^e RAI 1 829f.

|t-r-ʕ| — Sem.: Cf. *trʕ* (JAram., Syr.) “to break through (flooding)”, (D) “to destroy, break down (hemorrhage)”; *tariʕa* (Arab.) “to be full”, *ʔatraʕ* “to fill”.

|t-r-ʕ| “to be overwhelmed by flooding” (?) — •CTX: **UGA** Gpass. suffc. suff. *trʕn*, inf. *trʕ* → DUL 864: /*t-r-ʕ*/ “to be cracked” (?)

|t-r-D-n| — Culture word, Sem.: *tartānu, tartannu, turtānu, turtannu* (Akk.) “deputy, second in command”; see also *trtn* (*tartān*, Hb.) “commander in chief”; *trtn* (Aram.) id.; *tardennu, tartennu, terd/tennu* (Akk.) “second, secondary, successor”, *tardennūtu, ta/erd/tennūtu* “position of *t*.”
Non-Sem.: *tartānu, tartannu* (Hurr.-Akk.) “deputy, second (in command)”.[815]

---

[814] From Arab. See Orel / Stolbova HSED 508 no. 2422: **tupaḥ*= “apple”.
[815] Richter BGH 448: *tartānu, tartannu* (u. ä).

tarDan(n), tarDenn, terDenn, tur(a)Dan(n) "second in rank; younger brother, son"	•CTX: **EM** *tar-ta-an-ni*, (LÚ) *tar-ta-ni* → Pentiuc Vocabulary 181: "a high official". **UGS** LÚ *tar-te-ni*, LÚ *tar-te-en-ni*, LÚ *tar-te-in-nu* → AHw 1329: *ta/erd/tennu*; CAD T 228: *tardennu*, 2; Wilhelm UF 2 277: "Kronprinz"; Dietrich / Loretz WO 3 239. •LL: **EM** UGULA.É.DUB.BA.A = [*šatam é*] *du-bi :tu-ra-ta-nu* → Pentiuc Vocabulary 181; Cohen SSCE 57 fn. 199; Proceedings 53e RAI 1 830: "supervisor". **MŠ** *te-er-de-en-nu* = MIN (*ma-a-ru*) → Hrůša MŠ 162, 285, 438 (exp. I 200): "son". •ONOM: **UGS** *ta-ar-da-a*(?)-*nu* → Nougayrol PRU 6 75 rev. 5'.
tarDennūt "position of *t.*"	•CTX: **EM** Cf. *a-na tar*(!)-*te-nu-ti* → Arnaud AuOrS 1 76 (40:19: "en échange".[816] **UGS** [LÚ *ta*]*r-te-in-nu-ut-ti* → AHw 1329; CAD T 228; Wilhelm UF 2 277.
trdn, trtn "second in rank; younger brother, son"	•ONOM: **UGA** *trdn*, *trtn* → DUL 865: *trd/tn*.
|t-r-ħ|	Culture word, Sem.: Cf. *tarīḫu* (Akk.) "a valuable vessel".
trħ "flask"	•CTX: **UGA** sg. cstr. *trḥ* → DUL 865: *trḥ*.
|t-r-x| (1)	Sem.: *terḫatu*(*m*), *tirḫatu*(*m*), *tarḫātu* (Akk.) "bride payment".[817]
|**t-r-x**| "to marry, get married"	•CTX: **UGA** Denom. G prefc. *ỉtrḫ*, *ttrḫ*, *ytrḫ*, suffc. *trḫ*, impv. *trḫ*, act. ptc. *trḫ* (see *trḫ* below); G pass. ptc. *mtrḫt* (see *mtrḫt* below) → DUL 865: /*t-r-ḫ*/; Tropper UG 449, 477, 570.
tarx (A) "dowry, bride price"	•CTX: **EB** *da-ḫa-ma* (|tarx=am=ma|) → Catagnoti / Fronzaroli ARET 16 31, 223.
trx "newlywed, groom"	•CTX: **UGA** → DUL 866: *trḫ*.
trxt "dowry, bride price"	•CTX: **UGA** → DUL 866: *trḫt*.
mtrxt "consort, wife"	•CTX: **UGA** → 593: *mtrḫt*; see alsoTropper UG 477, 570.
|t-r-x| (2)	Sem. etym. unc. Cf. *terḫu*(*m*) (Akk.) "beer mug".
tarx (B) "beer mug"	•CTX: **EUPH** *ta-ar-ḫu* → CAD T 230; Charpin / Durand FM 6 486 (73:3); Guichard ARM 31 315.
|t-r-m|	Culture word, Sem.: Cf. *terinnu*, *tirinnu*, *tarinnum*? (Akk.) "cone (of conifer)".[818]
tarimt, taritt "cone (of conifer)"	•LL: **EB** ŠE.Ù.SUḪ$_5$ = *da-rí-tum*, *da-rí-ma-tum*, → Conti QuSe 17 27, 37, 180f.; Sjöberg Fs. Oelsner 258.

[816] Cf. Durand NABU 2012/70: read *a-na* {TE}*te-nu-ti* ("pour replacement").
[817] Note also Milano Or 56 85f. for [*t*]*ir*$_5$(BAN)-*ḫa-tum* in OAkk. Tell Asmar.
[818] See for Mari Charpin NABU 2015/68.

|t-r-n| (1)	Culture word, Sem.: *trn* (*toren*, Hb.) "post, mast"; *twrn(?)* (JAram.) "mast".
tarn "mast (of a ship)"	•CTX: **UGS** GIŠ *ta-ar-ni* GAL → CAD T 239; vSoldt BiOr 47 734; SAU 307; Huehnergard ²UVST 399.
trn "mast (of a ship)"	•CTX: **UGA** → DUL 866: *trn* (I).
|t-r-n| (2)	Loanword. Non-Sem.: Cf. *tarna=* (Hitt.) "a small capacity measure".
tarna, **tarnann** "a small capacity measure"	•CTX: **EM** Cf. *tar-na-nu*, *tar-na-an-ni*, *tar-na-aš* → CAT T 239: *tarnannu*;[819] Pentiuc Vocabulary 179f.
|t-r-n| (3)	Loan. Non-Sem.: Cf. *turi=* (Hurr.) "low, lower", *turuni* (|tur(i)=o=ni|) "a setting for jewellery".[820]
turunn "a setting for jewellery"	•CTX: **Q** (Stone) *ina tu-ru-ni ḫurāṣi* → CAD T 493: *turunnu*; Gichard ARM 31 140 fn. 86; Durand MARI 6 155f.[821]
|t-r-r| (1)	Sem. etym. unc.: Cf. *tarāru(m)* (Akk.) "to tremble, shake"; *tartara*, *tatartara* (Arab.) "to shake, stir"; *tantana* (Eth.) "to shake".
|t-r-r| "to shake, tremble"	•CTX: **UGA** G/D prefc. (?) *y*]*trr* → DUL 867.
|t-r-r| (2)	Etym. unkn.
tārir "a profession or social class"	•CTX: **UGS** LÚ *ta-ri-ru-ma* → AHw 1330; CAD T 231; Rainey IOS 3 44; Sivan GAGl 279; Huehnergard UVST 186; vSoldt SAU 307 (153).
trr "a profession or social class"	•CTX: **UGA** Pl. *trrm* → DUL 867.
|t-r(-r)| (3)	Culture word, Sem.: *t(w)r* (*tor*, *tôr*, Hb.) "turtle dove"; *tr* (JAram.) "turtle dove"; *tarru* (Akk.) "a bird". Non-Sem.: Cf. dar (Sum.) "bird".[822]
tr (B) "turtle dove"	•CTX: **UGA** → 863: *tr* (II).
|t-r-S|	Loan. Sem.: *turāšu(m)*, *turēzu*, *turazzu* (Akk.) "harvest". Non-Sem.: *turezzi* (Hurr.) "harvest (time)".[823]
turis¹ "harvest"	•CTX: **EM** ᵈINANNA *tu/tù-ri-ši* → vSoden NABU 1987/46; Pentiuc Vocabulary 183.

819 Obsolete CAD T 239: *tarnaš*.
820 Richter BGH 477f.: *turi* II; *turuni*.
821 For Mari *tarnum* see Guichard ARM 31 138f.
822 See further *tr* (Syr.) "water bird", probl.< Iranian.
823 Richter BGH 478: *turezzi*.

|t-r-S-m|	Loan; etym. unc. Non-Sem.: Cf. sumun (Sum.) "vessel, beer mash".
turSumm "a type of wine (must, wine-dregs, plonk?)"	•CTX: **EUPH** Cf. (DUG.GEŠTIN) *tu-ur-šu-um-mu/mi* → CAD T 489: *turšummu* B; Chambon FM 11 68 (26:5), 110ff. (71:12), 139f. (114:4), 167 (158:17), 168 (161:19)
|t-r-ṣ|	Sem.: Cf. *trṣ* (Aram., Syr.) "to set right", *twrṣ(?)* "correction", *tryṣ* "erect, straight, upright"; *tarāṣu*(m) (Akk.) "to stretch out, over", *tarṣu* "stretched out", *terṣu(m)* "stretching out, extension".
tarṣ "stretched out, over"	•ONOM: **EB** Cf. *da-ar-zu* → Pagan ARES 3 180, 296.
turṣ "alteration, remodelling, enlargement" (?)	•LL: **EB** Cf. DUB.LÁ = *dur-zu-um* → Sjöberg Fs. Wilcke 264: "an architectural term" ?; Catagnoti QuSe 29 29, 232.
|t-r-t-r|	Culture word, Sem.: Cf. *tuttur(r)u(m)* (Akk.) "an elem. in jewellery (leaf?)".
tuttur "an elem. in jewellery"	•CTX: **EB** Cf. Pl. GIŠ *d[u-du]-lu* |tutturū| → Fronzaroli ARET 11 32, 149. **EUPH** Cf. (gold) *ša tu-tu-ri, tu-ut-tu-ru/ri* → Durand NABU 1992/34 (from **wtr*); Arkhipov ARM 32 69f. (pl.t.?, "une technique particulière de finissage"). **Q** Passim (gold) *ša tu-(ut-)tu-ri / tù-ud-tù-ri* → Bottéro RA 44 121 ("à soudure"); Fales Kaskal 1 98 fn.74 ("a granitura"). **EA** Passim (gold) *ša tù-ud-tù-ri* (letters from Babylon and Mitanni) → AHw 1375; CAD T 499; Adler AOAT 201 ad.loc.: mng unkn; Rainey EAC 147 ad loc., 1301 ("gold leaf").
|t-r-w| Cf. **|w-r-w/y|**	Sem.: *tarû(m), tarāʔum* (Akk.) "to lead away".
|t-r-w| "to lead away" **tarw** "(foreign) horde" (?)	•LL: **EB** Cf. GÁ.DU = *da-la-wu* → Pettinato MEE 4 336 (VE 1339); Milano ARET 9 274 fn. 2. •CTX: **EM** Cf. unc. ERIM.MEŠ *tar*-PI(*wu*?) → Arnaud AuOsS 1 58 (25:2), 83 (44.2); Pruzsinszky PTEm 26f. fn. 29; altern.: Pentiuc Vocabulary 180: unlikely connexion with Hurr. *tarwišša.*[824]
|t-S|	Loanword. Non-Sem.: Cf. *taš=* "to give", *taše/i=* (Hurr.) "gift", *tašuḫḫe/i=* "a sacrificial term (offering table?)".[825]
tzγ "offering (table)"	•CTX: **UGA** Sg. *tzġ*, suff. *tzġm*, pl. *tzġm* → DUL 871: *tzġ*.
|t-S-n|	Loanword. Non-Sem.: Cf. *tiššan=* (Hurr.) "very (much)".[826]

[824] See Richter BGH 446f.: TAR-PI, and *tarwišša, tarwiššu* (Nuzi-Akk.)
[825] Richter BGH 449f.
[826] Cf. Richter BGH 463: *tiššan*.

tiSn "a container"	•CTX: **A7** *ti-iš-nu*, GAL.ḪI.A *ti-iš-nu*, GAL KÙ.BABBAR *ti-iš-nu*, URUDU *ti-iš-nu*, *ti-iš-ni* UD.KA.BAR → CAD T 433; Wiseman AT 162; Giacumakis AkkAl 108.
tθnt "a container"	•CTX: **UGA** → DUL 871: *ṯṯnt*.

|t-s^1-ʕ|	Primary noun, Sem. *tšʕ* (*tēšaʕ*, Hb.) "nine", *tšʕym* (*tišʕîm*) "ninety"; *tšʕ* (Pun., Nab., Palm.) "nine", *tšʕm* (Ph.) "ninety"; *tšʕ* (Aram., Syr.) "nine", *tšʕyn* "ninety", *tšwʕ* (JAram.) "one ninth"; *tiše* (Akk.) "nine", *tešê* "ninety", *tišāt*, *tišû*(*m*) "one ninth"; *tisʕa* (Arab.) "nine", *tisʕūn* "ninety", *tusʕ* "one tinth"; *tšʕ* (OSArab.) "nine", *tšʕy* "ninety"; *tīsa*, *tesʕ*, *sē* (MSArab.) "nine", *təsʕayn*, *təsʕín*, *tisáyn* "ninety"; *təsʕ* (Eth.) "nine", *tasʕā*, *təsʕā* "ninety" .
tis^{1}ʕ "nine"	•ONOM: **UGS** *ti$_7$-iš-ʔu* → Sivan GAGl 130, 279.
ts^{1}ʕ "nine"	•CTX: **UGA** *tšʕ*, fem. *tšʕt*, pl. *tšʕm* (see *tšʕm* below) → DUL 868: *tšʕ*.
tuSuʔ "ennead"	•ONOM: **B** Elem. in DN ^{d}*i-lu-um-tu-su-ú* → Gelb CAAA 34, 201.
ts^{1}ʕm "ninety"	•CTX: **UGA** → DUL 868f.: *tšʕm*.
tas^{1}iʕt, tas^{1}iʕat "a ninth"	•CTX: **EM** Sg. *ta-ši-ti*, var. *ta-ši-ia-ta*, *ta-ši-a*<*-ta*>, pl. *ta-ši-a-ti*, *ta*-ŠE(*ši$_x$*)*-ia-ti* → Pentiuc Vocabulary 178f.[827]

|t-t-p|	Culture word, Sem.: *titapū* (Akk. pl.t.) "beer mash". Non-Sem.: titab (Sum.) "an ingredient in beer-making; beer mash".
tatāp, tutāp "beer mash"	•LL: **EB** ŠE.TITAB = *du-da-bù(-um)*, *da-da*-NI(*bu$_{16}$*) → Pettinato MEE 4 275 (EV 668); Milano ARET 9 406.

|t-w-k|	Sem.: *twk* (*tāwek*, cstr. *tôk*, Hb.) "midst, middle", *tyk*(*w*)*n* (*tikōn*) "middle"; *btkt*, *bmtkt* (Ph.) "in the middle of".[828]
tk "centre, middle"	•CTX: **UGA** Cstr. *tk* → DUL 853f.
tōkiy "inner"	•ONOM: **UGS** Elem. (< |tawkiy=|) in TN URU *ga-li-li tu-ki-yi* → Sivan GAGl 279; Huehnergard UVST 185; vSoldt SAU 377 fn. 177; Tropper UG 197; Belmonte RGTC 12/2 77.
tky "inner"	•ONOM: **UGA** Elem. in TN *glltky*, *gll.tky* → DUL 295: *glltky*.

|t-w-l| Cf. **|t-ʔ-l|**	Sem.: Probl. by-form of |t-ʔ-l|. Cf. *tiwala*, *tuwala* (Arab.) "spell, charm", *tāla* (*tawl*) "to cast a spell".
taw(i)l "spell, charm" (?)	•LL: **EB** UD.DU$_{11}$.GA = *da*-WA-*um*/*u$_9$* → Conti QuSe 17 21, 104f.[829]

|t-w-l-ʕ|	Primary noun, Sem.: *twlʕ* (*tôlāʕ*) "(crimson-)worm, crimson"; *twlʕ*(*ʔ*), *twlʕh*, *twlʕtʔ* (JAram., Syr.) "worm, scarlet"; *tûltu*(*m*), *tuʔiltu*, *tuʔissu* (Akk.) "worm"; *təwālot*, *təbʕáləṭ*, metath. *taʕáləh* (MSArab.) "worm".
tawlaʕt "worm"	•LL: **EB** NIN.LÚ.UḪ = *du-lá-tum* → Sjöberg Fs. Kienast 561f.; Catagnoti QuSe 29 19, 231.

827 Obsolete CAD T 289: *tašiu* "a container for liquids".

828 Unlikely altern. *mtkt* "oppression", cf. Syr. *tkk* "to oppress".

829 Diff. Mander Or 48 337: from *tamû*(*m*), *tamāʔum* "to swear". Cf. further Akk. *awātu*(*m*) "word", and Conti loc.cit. + fn. 184 for other altern. solutions.

tolaʕa "dressed in crimson; worm"	•ONOM: **EG** *tu-ra-ʕa* → Hoch SWET 358 no. 529.
|t-w-r|	Sem.: Cf. *twr* (Hb.) "to spy out, reconnoitre; to follow, seek out, discover"; *târu(m)*, *tūaru(m)* (Akk.) "to turn, return", *tūru(m)* "return, retreat", *tūrtu(m)* "turning, reversion", *tayyāru(m)* "relenting, merciful"; *tāra* (*tawr*, Arab.) "to run, flow, turn", *tawr* "turn".
|**t-w-r**| **(A)** "to come back, return"	•CTX: **EB** G prefc. *a-da-a-ra-am*$_6$ |ʔatwar=am|; cf. unc. *lu-ti-ir* |lū yutīr|(?) → Fronzaroli QuSe 13 145; Catagnoti / Fronzaroli ARET 16 82, 212; Catagnoti QuSe 29 16, 61, 135, 161, 231. **EM** D imp. *te-er-ra* → Yamada NABU 2014/90: "pay back (money)!". **UGS** G prefc. *ia-tu-ru, i-tu-ru, <i->túr-ru, i-tù-ur-ni, ti-tu-ru-na, e-te-e-ru* → Huehnergard AkkUg 160; vSoldt SAU 441; Tropper UG 447. •LL: **EB** A.NÍGIN = *du-lum* |turr=um|, *da-wu-lum* |tawwur=um| → Conti QuSe 17 173. •ONOM: **EB** Passim |yatūr, tatūr|, cf. *a-du-ur, a-du-ul, a-du-lu, a-du-lum, a-du-ru*$_{12}$, *a-du-ul-li-im, da-du-úr, da-du-lu, da*$_5$*-du-lu, da*$_5$*-du-lum, da*$_5$*-dur-*^{d}UTU; |yitūr|, cf. EN(*ʔe*$_x$)*-du-lu*; |tur|, cf. *dur-ì, du-ur-ì, dur-ì-lum, dur-du:lum, dur-*BE, *dur-da-ar, dur-du-lum, dur-lim, dur-ma-lik*; *i-dúr-*UTU → Krebernik PET 40; Pagan ARES 3 180f., 272, 277, 297, 299, 303f.; Bonechi NABU 2016/1. **U3** *i-túr-*AN, *tu-ra-nu-um* → Owen JCS 33 248; Zadok Fs. Hallo 331. **EUPH**, **B** Passim; |yitūr|, cf. *i-tu-ra-an, i-túr-li-ib-bi, i-tar-ad-an*; |tatūr|, cf. *ta-tu-ur-*EŠ$_4$-DAR, *ta-dur-ḫa-tum, ta-dur-ma-tum, ta-tu-ur-ma-tum*; |tūr|, cf. *tu-ur-ma-tum* → Gelb CAAA 34, 198: |TWUR|; Zadok Fs. Hallo 331. Elem. |yatūr=|, |yitūr=| in the DN *Yitûr-/ Yatūr-Mêr* (*Wēr, Mēr*, the city god of Mari, and in several PNN: see |yatūr| ^{d}*ia-tu-ur-me-ir*; |yitūr| ^{d}*i-dur-me-ir, ḫa-an-na-*^{d}*i-dur-me-er, ip-ku-*^{d}*i-dur-me-er, i-din-*^{d}*i-dur-me-er* → Gelb CAAA 34 155 |MEʔR|, 198; Durand REA 189f., 245, 647. **EM** *ia-tu-ur-a-ḫu, ia-túr-*EN, *ia-túr-*^{d}*da-gan* → Pruzsinszky PTEm 212 [429].[830] **EG** Cf. *ty-:r, ty-r-y, t-r-w-r-ʕ* → Schneider APÄQ 235 nos. 500f., 237f. no. 506.
|**t-w-r**| **(B)** "to scour, travel through"	•CTX: **UGA** G prefc. *ytr*, inf. *tr*, C prefc. *tštr* → DUL 862f. */t-r/*; Tropper UG 484.[831]
tawr, tuwr "return"	•LL: **EB** ŠU MU.NÍGIN = *da-lum*; A.NÍGIN = *du-lum* → Conti QuSe 17 144, 173; Sjöberg Fs. Pettinato 263f.
tawir, tāʔir, tār "relenting, merciful" (?)	•ONOM: **B** Cf. *ta-e-ru/rum, ma-na-ta-ri* → Gelb CAAA 34, 199.
tiwr, tīr "returned" (?)	•ONOM: **EUPH**, **B** *ti-ir-*É.A, *ti-ir-*EŠ$_4$.DAR, *ti-ir-ma-na, an-nu-ti-ri*, ^{d}EN.ZU*-ti-ri(-im)*, ^{d}*da-gan-ti-ri, ma-ti-ti-rum*, fem. *ti-ra-tum* → Gelb CAAA 34, 199. **A7** ^{d}EŠ$_4$.DAR*-te-ir-ra* → Wiseman AT 139; CAAA 34, 199.
tr (A) "steering pole (chariot); log" (?)	•CTX: **UGA** Pl. *trm*, suff. *trh*, [*t*]*rhm, trhn* → DUL 863: *tr* (I).[832]

[830] WSem. variant of Akk. *Itūr*-PNN? Cf. Pruzsinszky PTEm 216*: Itūr-baʕlu, /-Dagān, /-ʔilu, /-libbu* [530ff.]; Tropper BiOr 62 67.

[831] For a base *yry* (II) "aller, marcher" (?) see also Del Olmo NABU 2013/31.

[832] Note UGA *mtrt*, mng unc.; cf. DUL 594 "chariot with reinforced wheels"; diff. Tropper UG 203, 584, 651: Lp ptc. from denom. *twr* "mit Deichsel versehen werden" (< *tr)* "Deichsel"; see GlOS *tr* (A), (\|t-w-r\|); Vita Ejército 52ff.: "cajas de carro provistas de timón", **twr*; also Watson LSU 96f.

tūrt "circuit" (?)	•CTX: **EM** Cf. *tù-ur-tu*, *ina tu-ur-ti*, suff. *ina tu-ur-ti-[šu-nu]* → CAD T 491: *tūrtu* B.
|t-y-l| Cf. **|n-y-l|**	Sem.: Lexicalized by-form of |n-y-l|. Cf. *itūlu(m)*, *utūlu*(m) (Akk.) "to lie down, sleep".[833]
|t-y-l| "to lie down to sleep, rest"	•CTX: **EB** G prefc. *i-ti-a* |yittīyal|, *i-ti-a-a* |yittīyal=ay|, a-ti-a |la=yittīyal|, *a-ti-a-ú-ma* |la=yittīyal=ū=| → Fronzaroli ARET 13 110, 273, 313; Catagnoti / Fronzaroli ARET 16 16 52f., 63, 174, 220f. **EUPH** Prefc. *it-te-el* |yittīyal| → vSoden GAG 18 § 16 k, 155 § 107 j (i-m), 46* (36); AHw 407: *i/utūlu(m)* G, 1564; CAD U 344: *utūlu*, a.
|t-y-s¹|	Primary noun, Sem.: *tyš* (*tayiš*, Hb.) "billy goat"; *tyš(?)* (JAram., Syr.) "he-goat"; *daššu(m)*, *taššu* (Akk.) "buck, ram";[834] *tays* (Arab.) "billy goat"; *tys¹* (OSArab.) "billy goat"; *tuš*, *tɛš*, *táyh*, *tāyəh* (MSArab.) "goat, black goat, billy goat"; see also: *tästay* (Tigre) "young bull accustomed to yoke".
tīSān "a caprid (moufflon?)"	•CTX: **EB** *ti-sa-na*, *ti-sa-na-a*, *ti-ša-nu* → Conti / Bonechi NABU 1992/11. **EUPH** UDU.ḪI.A *ti-ša-ne* → Durand NABU 1988/15; ARM 26/1 108f. (11:24); Lion NABU 1991/60.
|t-y-t|	Culture word, Sem.: *tiyatu*, *tiat* (Akk.) "a medicinal plant".
tiyat "a plant or vegetable substance"	•CTX: **UGS** Ú.LUḪ.ḪA *:ti-ia-tu₄* → vSoldt UF 22 348f., 350
tyt "a plant or vegetable substance"	•CTX: **UGA** → DUL 871.

833 Several prefc. forms with prothetic *n=*. See the discussion in CAD U 345 on *i/utūlu*.

834 See for Tuttul Krebernik Tall Bi`a 234: *daššum* "Bock".

ṭ

|ṭ-ʕ-n|		**|ṭ-n-p|**	
|ṭ-b-x|	See **|ð-b-ħ|**	**|ṭ-p-ħ|**	
|ṭ-b-ḳ|	Cf. **|d-b-ḳ|**	**|ṭ-p-l|**	
|ṭ-B-l|		**|ṭ-p-r|**	
|ṭ-h-r|		**|ṭ-r-d|**	
|ṭ-ħ-l|		**|ṭ-r-ḳ|**	
|ṭ-ħ-n|		**|ṭ-r-y| (1)**	
|ṭ-x-d|		**|ṭ-r-y| (2)**	
|ṭ-x-w|		**|ṭ-w/y-b|**	
|ṭ-l-l|		**|ṭ-w-x|**	
|ṭ-m-r|	Cf. **|t-m-r|**	**|ṭ-y-b|**	See **|ṭ-w/y-b|**
|ṭ-m-θ|		**|ṭ-y-n|**	
|ṭ-n-ʔ|			

|ṭ-ʕ-n|	Sem.: *ṭʕn* (Hb. Dpass.) "to be pierced"; *ṭʕn* (JAram. D) "to pierce"; *ṭaʕana* (Arab.) "to thrust, pierce"; see further *naṭû(m)*, *naṭāʔum* (Akk.) "to hit, beat".
|ṭ-ʕ-n| "to run through, stab to death; to hurt" **ṭaʕn** "injured, hurt"(?)	•CTX: **EUPH** D precf. *ú-ṭá-ḫi-nu* → Durand LAPO 17 229 fn. d; Streck Onomastikon 1 119 § 1.95. **UGA** G prefc. suff. *iṭʕnk*, *nṭʕn*, inf. *ṭʕn* → DUL 873: "to smite, destroy" (?). •CTX: **EUPH** Cf. *ta-aḫ-nu* → Durand LAPO 17 228f. fn. d; Streck Onomastikon 1 119 § 1.95.
|ṭ-b-x| See |ð-b-ħ|	Sem.: *ṭbḥ* (Hb.) "to slaughter, kill", *ṭbḥ* (*ṭabbāḥ*) "butcher, cook", *ṭbḥ* (*ṭebaḥ*) "slaughtering, butchery"; *ṭbḥ* (Pun., Palm.) "butcher, cook"; *ṭbḥ* (JAram., Syr.) "to slaughter", *ṭbḥ(ʔ)* (Aram.) "butcher, cook", *ṭbḥʔ* (JAram.) "meat"; *ṭabāḫu(m)* (Akk.) "to slaughter", *ṭābiḫu(m)* "slaughterer, butcher", *ṭabbiḫu* "butcher"; *ṭabaḫa* (Arab.) "to cook (meat)", *ṭabbāḫ* "cook"; *ṭbḫ* (OSArab.) "animals for butchering, meat"; *ṭəbōḫ*, *ṭabōḫ* (MSArab.) "to cook, boil"; *ṭabḥa* "to slaughter, cut up, sacrifice", *ṭabāḥi* "slaughterer".
|ṭ-b-x| "to slaughter"	•CTX: **EB** G prefc. *a-da-ba-aḫ* |la=yiṭabbax|, Gt prefc. *a-a-da-ba-aḫ* |ʔay=yiṭṭabax| → Fronzaroli ARET 13 80f., 240; Catagnoti QuSe 29 25, 45f., 105f., 134, 143, 232.[835] **UGA** G prefc. *yṭbḫ*, *tṭbḫ*, suffc. *ṭbḫ*, imp. *ṭbḫ* → DUL 873f. /*ṭ-b-ḫ*/.

[835] For *da-ba-um* (LL 531a: Fales QuSe 13 179 (531a: *ṭbḫ*) see here \|ṭ-p-ħ\|.

ṭābix "slaughterer, butcher"	•ONOM: **B** Cf. fem. *ta-bi-ḫa-tum* → Gelb CAAA 35, 201. **EM** EN-*ṭa-bi*, EN-*ṭa*/*ṭá-bi-i?*, EN-*ṭá-bi-iḫ* → Pruzsinszky PTEm 123 [320f.].
ṭabīx "an ornamental dagger" (?)	•CTX: **EUPH** *ṭa-bi-ḫu*, *ṭa-bi-ḫi*, *ṭa-bi-ḫi-im*, *ṭa-bi-ḫa-am* → CAD Ṭ 6; Streck Onomastikon 1 119 § 1.95; Arkhipov ARM 32 108f., 128f.
ṭubix, ṭubux "slaughtering, sacrifice"	•CTX: **EB** *du-bù-ḫi* |ṭubx=ī| → Fronzaroli QuSe 13 139; Catagnoti / Fronzaroli ARET 16 185, 226. •ONOM: **EB** *du-bù-ḫu-ù*, *du-bí-ḫu-ma-lik*, *du-bu-hu-da-mu*, *du-bù-ḫi*/*ḫu-ma-lik*, *du-bù-ḫu-ì*, *du-bu*/*bù-ḫu-*^{d}*ʔà-da*, *du-bù-ḫu-i-sar*; shortened forms: *du-bù-da-mu*, *du-bù-*^{d}*ʔà-da*, *du-bù-i-sar*, *du-bù-ma-lik* → Krebernik PET 81f.; Pagan ARES 3 181, 302. **EA** Elem. in TN URU *ṭú-bi-ḫi* (179:15, and passim) → Belmonte RGTC 12/2: 298. **EG** Elem. in TN *d-b-ḫu*$_3$, *du-bi-ḫi* → Hoch SWET 376f. no. 562.
ṭbx "sacrificer"	•CTX: **UGA** Sg. *ṭbḫ* → DUL 874: *ṭbḫ*.
ṭabixūt "slaughter, butchering"	•CTX: **Q** É.ḪI.A *ṭá-bi-ḫu-te* MEŠ → Richter / Lange Idadda 130f.

|ṭ-b-ḳ| Cf. **|d-b-ḳ|**	Sem.: *ṭabbaqa* (Arab.) "to cover up", *ʔaṭbaqa* "to close, shut, cover (up)".[836]
|ṭ-b-ḳ| "to shut, close"	•CTX: **UGA** G act. ptc. *ṭbq* → DUL 874: /*ṭ-b-q*/.
ṭubḳ "covering, shielding"	•ONOM: **EUPH**, **B** Cf. *tu-ub-ki*, *tu-ub-ga-tum*, *tu-bu-ga* → Gelb CAAA 35, 201 (unexplained).

|ṭ-B-l|	Culture word. Cf. *ṭbwlym* (pl.t. *ṭᵉbûlîm*, Hb.) "turban"; *ṭbl*(*?*) (Syr.) "women's ornament"; *ṭablala* (Eth.) "to fold up, wrap up". Non-Sem.: *adupli=* (Hitt.) "a formal dress, cloak".[837]
ʔuṭupl "a serge"	•CTX: **EUPH** Passim; cf. (GÚ / GÚ.E.A / TÚG) *ú-ṭub-lu*, *ú-ṭú-ub-lu* → AHw 1446: *utuplu*(*m*) "ein langer Schal?", CAD U/W *utuplu* "a fabric or weaving"; Durand ARM 21 404; ARM 30 131ff. LL: **MŠ** *ú-ṭúp-lu*$_4$ = *na-aḫ-lu*$_4$ / *sa-an-qu* (VI 96) → Hrůša MŠ 128, 266, 414.

|ṭ-h-r|	Sem.: *ṭhr* (Hb.) "to be clean", *ṭhr* (*ṭohar*) "purity", *ṭh*(*w*)*r* (*ṭāhōr*) "clean, pure"; *ṭr*, *ṭʔr* (Pun.) "pure"; *ṭhr* (JAram. rare) "to be clean (ritually)"; *ṭahara*, *ṭahura* (Arab.) "to be clean, pure", *ṭuhr* "cleanness, purity", *ṭāhir* "clean, pure"; *ṭahara*, *ṭaḫara* (Eth.) "to be pure", *ṭəhr* "purity", *ṭəhur* "pure"; *ṭhr* (OSArab.) "cleanness (ritual)"; *ṭəhēr*, *ṭɛhɛ́r* (MSArab.) "to be pure (ritually)", *ṭəháyr*, *ṭhír*, *ṭəhər* "(ritually) clean".
ṭuhur "pure"	•LL: **UGS** [SIKIL = *ellu*] = *ši-ḫa-la-e* = *ṭu-ú-ru*; [KÚ = *ellu*? = *ši-ḫ*]*a-la-e* = *ṭu-ú-ru* → Sivan GAGl 280; Huehnergard UVST 26, 38, 58, 76, 131; vSoldt SAU 304 (51); Tropper UG 176.
ṭhr, θ̣hr "pure, sparkling"	•CTX: **UGA** Pl. *ṭhrm*, *ẓhrm* → DUL 875: *ṭhr*; 986: *ẓhr*.

---

836 Eth. *ṭabaqa* is probl. a by-form of \|d-b-ḳ\| (CGD 586). The PNN *tu-ub-ki*, *tu-ub-ga-tum*, *tu-bu-ga* in Gelb CAAA 35 (ṬBQ), 201 remain unexplained.

837 A loan from Hurr.?; Richter BGH 69.

|ṭ-ħ-l|	Primary noun, Sem.: *ṭḥl(?)* (JAram., Syr.) "spleen"; *ṭulīmu(m), tulīmu* (Akk.) id.; *ṭiḥāl* (Arab.) id.; *ṭəlḥáym, ṭɛlḥím* (MSArab.) id. Non-Sem.: **tyaHal=* (East Chadic) "liver".[838]
ṭħl "spleen"	•CTX: **UGA** → DUL 875: *ṭḥl.*
|ṭ-ħ-n|	Sem.: *ṭḥn* (Hb.) "to grind", *ṭḥnh (ṭaḥᵃnāh)* "mill", *ṭḥwn (ṭᵉḥôn)* "hand-mill"; *ṭḥn* (Aram., Syr.) "to grind", *dwḥn(?), ṭwḥnh, ṭwḥnt?* "mill"; *ṭênu(m), ṭeānu* (Akk.) "to grind", *meṭēnu(m)* "floor bin"; *ṭaḥana* (Arab.) "to grind, mill", *ṭāḥūn(a)* "mill, grinder", *maṭḥana, miṭḥana,* "mill"; *ṭḥnm* (OSArab.) "flour"; *ṭḥan, ṭəḥān, ṭáḥan* (MSArab.) "to grind", *məṭḥənēt, məṭḫénút, muṭḫénút* "grind-stone"; *ṭaḥana, təḥna* (Eth.) "to grind flour, grind fine", *ṭāḥn* "grind-stone". Non-Sem.: **ṭaHan=* (West Chadic) "to press down, forge".[839]
|**ṭ-ħ-n**| "to grind"	•CTX: **EB** G prefc. *a-da-i-in* |lā yiṭaħħan| → Fronzaroli ARET 13 15, 240, 317; Catagnoti QuSe 29 50, 60, 155, 232. **UGA** G prefc. suff. *tṭḥnn*; inf. *ṭḥn* → DUL 875: */ṭ-ḥ-n/.* •LL: **EB** ŠE.ÀR.ÀR = *da-ʔà-núm/nu-um* → Fronzaroli StEb 7 184; QuSe 13 138; Krebernik ZA 73 25.
maṭħatta "mortar, quern"	•CTX: **EG** Cf. *ma-d̠a-ḥa-t, ma-d̠i₃-ḥ-ta-t, ma-d̠i-ḥa-ta* → Hoch SWET 179 no. 242.
|ṭ-x-d|	Sem.: Cf. *ṭaḫādu(m)* "to prosper, flourish", *ṭaḫdu(m)* "luxuriant", *ṭuḫdu* "plenty, abundance".
ṭaxd "abundance" (?)	•ONOM: **EUPH** Cf. *ta-aḫ-di-li-im* → Gelb CAAA 35, 201 (unexplained).
|ṭ-x-w|	Sem.: *teḫû(m), taḫû, taḫāʔu(m)* (Akk.) "to be(come) near to, approach; (D) "to bring close, present (offerings)".
|**ṭ-x-w**| "to come near; to bring near, claim; to annex"	•CTX: **EB** G prefc. *i-da-ḫa-ú* |yiṭaxxawū|, suff. *a-da-ḫa-gú-ma-a* |lā=yiṭaxxaw=kum=ay(n)| → Catagnoti / Fronzaroli ARET 16 158, 212; Catagnoti QuSe 29 232.[840] **A7** D suffc. *ú-ul ṭu-uḫ-ḫu* → Lauinger STOBA 331 (AT 58 low.e. 4).
mṭx "present, gift, offering"	•CTX: **UGA** → DUL 594: *mṭḫ.*
ṭēxiyt "delegation, embassy"	•CTX: **EUPH** *ṭe₄-ḫi-tum* → AHw 1383: *ṭēḫītum*; CAD Ṭ 71: *ṭēḫītu.*

[838] Orel / Stolbova HSED 501 no. 2387: **teḥal=* "spleen, liver".
[839] Orel / Stolbova HSED 515 no. 2455: **ṭaḥan=* "to grind, forge".
[840] Probl. an etymon C₃:*w* (against Catagnoti / Fronzaroli: C₃:ʕ) in view of the absence of the guttural in UGA (see below: *mṭx*).

|ṭ-l-l|	Primary noun, Sem.: *ṭl* (*ṭal*, suff. *ṭall=*, Hb.) "dew"; *ṭl(ʔ)* (Aram., Syr.) "dew", *ṭll* (Syr. C) "to make drip down like dew"; *ṭall* (Arab.) "dew, fine rain", *ṭalla* "to bespray, be dew"; *ṭal, ṭəl, ṭɛhl* (MSArab.) "dew", *šəṭlel* "to be covered with dew"; *ṭall* (Eth.) "dew, moisture", *ṭll, ṭalla, ṭalala* (Eth.) "to be moist, wet, covered with dew", *ʔanṭalṭala* "to drip".
|ṭ-l-l| "to drop dew"	•CTX: **UGA** D prefc. *yṭll* → 876 /*ṭ-l-l*/.
ṭall, ṭill "dripping, filtering; dew, (light) rain"	•LL: **EB** A.SUR = *ti-lum* (BAPPIR) → Conti QuSe 17 89. •ONOM: **U3** *i-la-ab-ti-il* → Buccellati Amorites 75, 157; Gelb CAAA 35, 201. **EUPH**, **B** Cf. *ta-li-ib-ni, i-la-ap-ta-lu-ú, ḫa-(am-)mi-ta/te/ti-lu-ú, ṣi-ḫar-ti-lu-uk* → Gelb CAAA 35, 201. **UGS** Cf. TA-*la-ia* → Gröndahl PTU 202; Sivan GAGl 280; Huehnergard UVST 214.[841]
ṭl "dew, (light) rain"	•CTX: **UGA** → DUL 876. •ONOM: **UGA** Cf. *ṭly* (DN) → DUL 876.[842]
|ṭ-m-r| Cf. |**t-m-r**|	Sem.: *ṭmr* (Aram., Syr.) "to bury", *ṭmr(ʔ)* (Syr.) "burying"; *ṭamra, ṭammara* (Arab.) "to bury"; see further: *ṭmn* (Hb.) "to hide".
ṭamr "tumulus; earth hole, crack" (?)	•CTX: **EB** *da-ma-rúm*, cf. adverbial *da-ma-rí-iš* → Bonechi MARI 8 526f.
|ṭ-m-θ|	Sem.: *ṭmš* (JAram., Syr.) "to immerse, soak", *ṭmš(ʔ)* "immersion"; *ṭamaṯa* (Arab.) "to menstruate", *ṭamṯ* "menstruation".
ṭmθ "(menstrual) blood"	•CTX: **UGA** → DUL 876: *ṭmṯ*.
|ṭ-n-ʔ|	Sem.: *ṭnʔ* (Ph., Pun.) "to erect, install", *mṭnʔ* (Ph.) "(votive) offering"; see also *ṭny* (OSArab.) "to erect".
maṭniʔ "provision(s), supplies"	•CTX: **EA** IGI.KÁR.MEŠ (GAL.MEŠ) <:> *ma-aṭ-ni-a* (337:9, 21) → Moran AmL 358 fn. 1; Rainey EAC 1625 ad loc.
|ṭ-n-p|	Sem.: *ṭnp* (Hb. D) "to soil"; *ṭnp* (JAram., Syr., D) "to pollute", *ṭnwp(ʔ)* (JAram.) "filth"; *ṭanāpu* (Akk.) "to be(come) dirty"; *ṭanafa* (Arab.) "to be evil, wicked".
ṭannāp "dirty"	•LL: **EM** PI.IN.ZI.IR = *li-pí-iš-si*$_{20}$*-tum* ("vulva") *:ṭá-an-na-pu* → Pentiuc Vocabulary 186f.; Cohen Proceedings 53e RAI 1 830f.
|ṭ-p-ħ|	Sem.: *ṭpḥ* (Hb., D) "to spread out (by striking ?)", *ṭpḥ* (*ṭepaḥ, ṭopaḥ*) "hand-breadth"; *ṭpḥ* (Syr.) "to spread out", (JAram.) "to strike, clap the hands", *ṭpḥ(ʔ)* (JAram., Syr.) "hand-breadth, expanse"; *ṭepû(m), ṭapû, ṭapāʔum* (Akk.) "to extend, apply, add"; *ṭafḥa* (Eth.) "to clap (the hands); to make flat by patting with

841 Only if TA = *ṭá*. For unmarked consonant doublings see Huehnergard UVST 208f.

842 Zadok Fs. Hallo 331 (ṬLY) proposes a connection of this DN with Aram. *ṭlyṯʔ* "girl"; unlikely in view of the secondary semantic character of this Aram. mng See Militarev / Kogan SED 2 297ff.: **ṭalay=* "lamb, kid", and the above mentioned PN TA-*la-ia*.

	the hands"; metath. *faṭaḥa, faṭṭaḥa* (Arab.) "to spread out, flatten".
|ṭ-p-ḥ| "to clap the hands"	•LL: **EB** ŠU.ŠU.RA = *da-ba-um / ma-ḫa-zi i-da* → Krebernik ZA 73 20; Conti QuSe 17 36, 151; Sjöberg Fs. Pettinato 264.
|ṭ-p-l|	Sem.: *ṭpl* (Hb.) "to smear"; *ṭpl* (JAram., Syr.) "to stain, smear", *ṭpl(?)* (Syr.) "dirt"; *ṭapālu(m)* (Akk.) "to slander, insult", *ṭiplu, ṭapiltu, ṭapultu(m)* "slander"; *ṭafāl* (Arab.) "clay, mud".
|ṭ-p-l| "to abuse; to humiliate"	•CTX: **EA** D prefc. *tu-ṭe$_4$-pí-il$_5$-šu-nu* (EA 1:91) → Moran Or 53 302, AmL 5 fn. 36. •LL: **EB** LÚxKÁR = *ṭá-pá-lum* → Sjöberg Fs. Kienast 557; see also Catagnoti RA 106 49 fn 29 " prisoner" (with previous bibliography).
ṭupl "slander(ing)"	•CTX: **UGS** Cstr. *ṭu-púl* → AHw 1394:*ṭuplu*; CAD Ṭ 126: *ṭuplu*.
ṭupult "abuse"	•CTX: **EUPH** *ṭú-pu-ul-ta$_8$*(ḪI), suff. *ṭú-pu-<ul->ta-šu* → CAD Ṭ 163f.; Charpin ARM 26/2 57f. (303:25', 30') fn. 1.
|ṭ-p-r|	Sem.: Cf. *ṭafara* (Eth.) "to cover a house, to roof over", *ṭafar* "vault, roof".
ṭapar "wooden board"	•LL: **EM** DUR.GIŠ.DÚR = *ki-iš-kàr-rum* = *:*TA-*pa-rum* → Pentiuc Vocabulary 187; Cohen Proceedings 53e RAI 1 817.
|ṭ-r-d|	Sem.: *ṭrd* (Hb.) "to drip continually"; *ṭrd* (Aram., Syr.) "to shut up, confine; to drive out"; *ṭarādu(m)* (Akk.) "to send off / away, despatch", *ṭardu(m)* "driven off", *ṭarīdum* "fugitive"; *ṭarada* (Arab.) "to drive away / out", *ṭarida* "to hunt", *ṭard* "expulsion, chase", *ṭārid* "he who expels", *ṭarīd* "outcast, fugitive"; *ṭrd* (OSArab.) "to hunt, chase"; *ṭərūd, ṭérəd, ṭérəd* (MSArab.) "to follow (flocks / a theft), to drive away; to hunt".
|ṭ-r-d| "to send, drive out, expel"	•CTX: **EB** G imp. *du-ru$_{12}$-da-A* |ṭurday=|, N prefc. *id$_x$-da-ra-da-A* |yiṭṭarad=| → Fronzaroli ARET 13 16f., 255, 317; Catagnoti QuSe 29 25, 48, 73f., 133, 143, 232f. **UGA** G act. ptc. *ṭrd* → DUL 876f.: */ṭ-r-d/*. •ONOM: **UGA** Cf. *ṭrd* → DUL 877.
ṭard "sending, present"	•ONOM: **EB** Cf. *dar-du* → Pagan ARES 3 181, 300.
ṭerd "deportation, persecution; DN"	•ONOM: **EA** DN *^{d}ṭe-ri-id* → AHw 1388: *ṭe/irdu*, 2; CAD Ṭ 102: **ṭerdu* B (357:69 lit.; Nergal and Ereškigal).
ṭārid "he who sends"	•ONOM: **EUPH, B** *da-ri-du-um, ta-ri-du-um, ta-ri-da-ad-mu* → Gelb CAAA 35, 201; Golinets Onomastikon 2 129, 135,460.
ṭarūd "sent"	•ONOM: **B** *da-ru-du-um* → Gelb CAAA 35, 201; Golinets Onomastikon 2 140, 460.
|ṭ-r-ḳ|	Sem.: Cf. *ṭaraqa* (Arab.) "to knock, beat, slam, hammer"; *ṭaraqa* (Eth.) "to crush".
|ṭ-r-ḳ| "to beat"	•ONOM: **A4** Cf. *ia-aṭ-ru-qa* → Wiseman AT 136; Sivan GAGl 280.
|ṭ-r-y| (1)	Sem.: Cf. *ṭerû, ṭarāʔum* (Akk.) "to penetrate, rub into, rub in".

maṭray "kind of (tanned) strap, girth or welt"	•CTX: **EB** Cf. *ma-da-lum*, du. *ma-da-ra* |*maṭray=ay*(*n*)|, advb. *ma*<*-da*>*-rí-iš*, *ma-da-rí-ša* → Conti QuSe 19 29ff.; Catagnoti QuSe 29 113, 210: "cinghia". **EM** ÉŠ *ma-at-ru-ú* → Durand RA 84 81; ARM 30 184: "lanière". **EA** Cf. *ma-aṭ-ru-ú-šu* (22 II 18, of a dagger; Tušratta's letter) → AHw 635: "Griff?"; CAD M/1 428: "a pole or stick"; Adler AOAT 201 302: "Gehenk".
maṭarayt "a container made from goatskin"	•CTX: **EUPH** Cf. *ma-ṭà-ra-at*, *ma-ṭà-ra-tum* → Durand ARM 30 512 (M.6056+:24'f.)
|ṭ-r-y| (2)	Sem.: *ṭry* (*ṭārî*, Hb.) "fresh"; *ṭrwn* (Syr.) "fresh"; *ṭaruwa*, *ṭariya*, *ṭarawa* (Arab.) "to be(come) fresh, tender, succulent", *ṭarīy* "fresh, succulent, tender"; *ṭáyri*, *ṭéri* (MSArab.) "to get wet, damp", *ṭɛráy*, *ṭériʔ*, *ṭərīʔ* "wet, damp, fresh"; *ṭərāy* (Eth.) "raw, crude".
ṭry "fresh, tender"	•CTX: **UGA** → DUL 877: *ṭry* (I). •ONOM: **UGA** Cf. unc. *ṭry* → DUL 877: *ṭry* (II).
|ṭ-w/y-b|	Sem.: *ṭwb* (Hb.) "to be good", *ṭwb* (*ṭôb*) "merry, pleasant", (*ṭûb*) "goodness, happiness", *ṭb*, *ṭwbh* (*ṭôbāh*) id.; *ṭb* (Nab., Palm., Hatra) "good", *ṭbtʔ* (Hatra) "goodness, benevolence"; *ṭwb* (JAram.) "to be(come) good", *yṭb* "to be good, go well", *ṭʔb* (Aram., Syr.) "to be good, be pleased with", *ṭb*, *ṭwb*, *ṭbh*, *ṭbtʔ*, *ṭbwt*, (Aram.) "good; goodness, well-being"; *ṭiabu*(*m*), *ṭâbu* (Akk.) "to be(come) good", *ṭābu*(*m*) "good", *ṭābtu*(*m*), *ṭābtātu* "goodness", *ṭābtu*(*m*) "salt",[843] *ṭābūtu*, *ṭabuttu* "friendship", *ṭūbu*, *ṭubbu* "goodness", *ṭūbtu* "peace", *ṭābtānu* "doer of good"; *ṭāba*, *ṭība*, *taṭyāb* (Arab.) "to be good, pleasant, delicious, sweet", *ṭāb* "good, pleasant", *ṭayyib* id.; *ṭyb* (OSArab.) "to be well disposed (towards someone)", *ṭyb* "good, precious"; *ṭəyūb*, *ṭɔb*, *ṭɛ:b* (MSArab.) "to enjoy, to have had enough", *ṭəyōb* "goodness".
|**ṭ-w/y-b**| "to be good, pleasing"	•ONOM: **EB** Cf. *i-ti-ib*, *i-ti*-NE(*bí*?), *i-ti-ba-li:im* → Pagan ARES 3 181f., 326. **EUPH** *ia-ṭà-bu-um*, *ta-da-ab-e-šar* → Gelb CAAA 199 (TADAB); Zadok Fs. Hallo 331; Golinets Onomastikon 2 226 fn. 764, 295, 461. **EM** *ia-ṭa-ab-*^{d}*da-gan* → Pruzsinszky PTEm 212 + fn. 591 [429].
ṭawb, ṭayb "good, friendly"	•CTX: **EB** Pl. m. *la da-bù-du* |lā ṭābūtu| → Fronzaroli ARET 13 127, 251, 317; Catagnoti QuSe 29 105, 120 + fn.463, 232. •LL: **EB** NÌ.DU$_{10}$.DU$_{10}$ = *da-bù*; NÌ.KI.LUḪ = GIŠ *da-bù*; Ì.DU$_{10}$ = *sa-ma-nu-um da-bù* → Fronzaroli QuSe 13 139; StEb 7 184; Krebernik ZA 73 3, 34; Conti QuSe 17 69, 81; Catagnoti QuSe 29 23, 232. **UGS** [DÙG = *ṭa-a-bu* = … =] *ṭa-bu* → Sivan GAGl 280; Huehnergard UVST 28, 60, 131; vSoldt SAU 304 (50); Tropper UG 200. •ONOM: **EB** Passim; cf. e.g. *dab-ar-ru*$_{12}$, *dab*$_{6}$*-da-ar*, *tab-li-im*, *zi-ru*$_{12}$*-dab*$_{6}$, *da-a-bù*, *da-a-bu*$_{14}$, *a-da-bù*, NI (*ʔa*$_{5}$?)*-da-da-bu*$_{16}$, *da-bù*-NE(*ne*?)*-li*, *da-bù-ma-lik*, *da-bu*$_{16}$*-zi-ma-lik*, *dab*$_{6}$*-bù-ma-lik*, DINGIR-*da-bu*$_{16}$, EN-*da-bù*, *da-ba*$_{4}$, *da-ba*$_{(4)}$*-a-du*, *da-ba-ga*, *dab*$_{6}$*-ba-*^{d}*ku-ra*, EN-*da-ba*; cf. fem.(?) *da-bù-du*[844] → Krebernik PET 41; Pagan ARES 3 181f., 272, 276, 296f., 299ff., 301, 305, 368, 388.

[843] A peculiar Akk. development from the fem. *ṭābt*= "good, tasty"; Fronzaroli Studi 1971 621. See further RS-Akk. *ṭābūtu*; CAD Ṭ 42: "brine" (?).

[844] \|ṭawbut\|, allomorph of fem. \|ṭawbat\|?; see Hecker LEbla 174 fn. 79.

U3 *la-da-bu-um*, fem. *da-ba-tum* → Buccellati Amorites 61, 68, 163f., 182; Gelb CAAA 35, 201; Streck Onomastikon 1 198 § 2.95.
EUPH, B Passim; cf. e.g. *ta-a-ba, ṭà-ab-su-mu-ú, ṭà-ab-ṣi-lu-ú, a-mi-ṭa-bi, sa-mar-ṭa-bu, su-mu-da-bi, ša-al-mu-ṭà-ba*; fem. |ṭābat / ṭābt / ṭāba|: *da-ba-tum, la-ṭà-ab-tum, bi-in-du-ṭà-ba, um-mi-ṭà-ba*, cf. *ṭà-bi-a* → Huffmon APNMT 207; Gelb CAAA 35, 201; Streck Onomastikon 1 201f. § 2.95, 351 § 5.76 fn. 1; Golinets Onomastikon 2 305, 461.
TU *ba-aḫ-li-ṭà-ab* → Krebernik Tall Bi`a 212 (279:11); Golinets Onomastikon 2 305, 461.
A7 *ta-pa-aš-šu-ra, ṭa-ba*-DINGIR, *ta-ab-si-im-tum, a-bi-ṭa-ba, ì-lí-da-ba, am-mi-ṭa-ba, su*(?)*-mi-da-ba* → Wiseman AT 125, 148f.; Gelb CAAA 35, 201; Arnaud AuOr 16 180; Streck Onomastikon 1 275 §3.25.
A4 *ṭá-bi-ia, a-ḫu-ṭá-bi*; cf. TN URU *ṭá-ba-ya* → Wiseman AT 148, 156; Dietrich / Loretz UF 1 42 (4:4); Sivan GAGl 280; Arnaud AuOr 16 180.
EM Cf. *ṭà-ab-da-ad-mu*; cf. *ṭá-ab-x-x*[→ Pruzsinszky PTEm 130 [794f.].
EA Cf. ŠEŠ-*ṭa-a-bu* (a Babylonian messenger) → Sivan GAGl 66; Huehnergard JAOS 107 719; Hess APN 23; Moran AmL 380.
UGS DINGIR-*ṭa-ab-i*; *ṭa-bíl* → Sivan GAGl 280.
EG *t-ꜣ-bꜣ-y*; cf. *r*(?)*-t-ꜣ-bꜣ* → Schneider 231 no. 491; cf. 160 no. 339.

ṭōb "merry, pleasant" (?)
•ONOM: **A4** Cf. *ṭú-bi-ia* → Sivan GAGl 280.
EA Cf. TN URU *ṭù-bu* → Belmonte RGTC 12/12 298; Sivan GAGl 66, 280.
EG Elem. in TN *tu*$_2$*-b-ya*, *tu*$_2$*-ʔu*$_3$*-b* → Hoch SWET 356 no. 525.

ṭuwb "goodness, well-being"
•ONOM: **EB** *dub-bí, dub-da-ar, ar-du-pi, du-bí* (passim: *du-bí*=DN), *du-bù-uš, du-bù-uš-bù-su-gú, du-bù/bí-uš-da-mu, du-bù-uš-li-im, du-ba-ne-lu* → Krebernik PET 81; Pagan ARES 3 181f., 287, 301f., 304.
EM Cf. *ṭú/ṭù-ba-a* → Pruzsinszky PTEm [795].

ṭb "good, sweet, pleasant"
•CTX: **UGA** Sg. *ṭb*, pl. (?) *ṭbm*[845] → DUL 873.

ṭbn "sweetness"
•CTX: **UGA** Cstr. *ṭbn* → DUL 874.

ṭuwbāt, ṭuwbūt, ṭuwbuwat "goodness"
•LL: **EB** NÌ.DU$_{10}$ = *du-bù-du, du-bù-a-tum* → Krebernik ZA 73 3; Conti QuSe 17 69.
•ONOM: **EB** *du-ba-du* → Pagan ARES 3 181f., 301.

ṭbt "well-being"
•CTX: **UGA** → DUL 875.

|ṭ-w-x|
Sem.: *ṭwḥ* (Hb.) "to plaster"; *ṭwḥ* (JAram.) "to smear", *ṭḥy* "to glaze, plaster"; *ṭāḫa* (*ṭayḫ*, Arab.) "to get dirty". See further: *ṭāʔa* (Arab.) "mud"; *ṭyʕ, ṭeʕa, ṭeʔa* "to plaster with mud".

|**ṭ-w-x**| "to plaster"
•CTX: **UGA** G act. ptc. *ṭḫ* → DUL 875f.: /*ṭ-ḫ*/.

|ṭ-y-b|
See |**ṭ-w/y-b**|

|ṭ-y-n|
Primary noun; Sem.: *ṭyṭ* (*ṭîṭ*, Hb.) "wet loam, mud, potter's clay"; *ṭyn*(*?*) (Aram., Syr.) "clay, mud", *ṭyn* (D) "to smear with mud"; *ṭīdu, ṭīṭu, ṭidd/ttu*(*m*) (Akk.) "clay, mud";[846] *ṭīn* (Arab.) "clay", *ṭāna, ṭayyana* "to daub or coat with clay", *maṭīn* "plastered, coated with clay".

[845] For this rdg see Tropper UG 114; probl. incorrect KTU ad loc. and DUL 906: *ẓbm* (I).
[846] For RS-Akk. *ṭiddu* "earwax" see Nougayrol Ug 5 38.

ṭiṭṭ "a sort of malt"	•LL: **EB** ŠE.ŠILIG.TITAB = *ti-du-um*, *ti-du*, *ti-tum* → Conti QuSe 17 38, 175.
ṭt "mud"	•CTX: **UGA** Sl. / pl. suff. *ṭtm* → DUL 877.
mṭnt "clay container" (?)	•CTX: **UGA** → DUL 595.

θ (ṯ)

|θ-ʔ|	Cf. **|s²-w|**	**|θ-l-l-r|**	
|θ-ʔ-g|		**|θ-l-t-x|**	
|θ-ʔ-r|		**|θ-l-θ|**	
|θ-ʔ-ṭ|		**|θ-m-d|**	
|θ-ʕ-d| (1)		**|θ-m-m| (1)**	
|θ-ʕ-D| (2)		**|θ-m-m| (2)**	
|θ-ʕ-l(-b)|		**|θ-m-n-y|**	
|θ-ʕ-r|		**|θ-m-r|**	Cf. **|ð-m-r|**, **|S-m-r|**
|θ-ʕ-y|			
|θ-b-r|		**|θ-n|**	
|θ-d-l|		**|θ-n-n|**	Cf. **|θ-n|**
|θ-d-r|		**|θ-n-ṭ|**	
|θ-d(-y)|	See **|S-d/ð|**	**|θ-n-y|**	
|θ-γ-r| (1)		**|θ-p-d|**	
|θ-γ-r| (2)		**|θ-p-r|**	
|θ-h|		**|θ-p-ṭ|**	
|θ-ħ-l|		**|θ-r| (1)**	
|θ-x|		**|θ-r| (2)**	
|θ-x-ṭ|	See **|S-H-ṭ|**	**|θ-r-k|**	
|θ-k-ħ|		**|θ-r-m-l|**	
|θ-k-l|		**|θ-r-n**	
|θ-k-m|		**|θ-r-p|**	See **|θ-p-r|**
|θ-k-p|		**|θ-r-r|**	
|θ-k-r|		**|θ-r-t-n-n|**	Cf. **|s¹-r-d-n|**
|θ-ḳ-b|	See **|S-ḳ-b|**	**|θ-r-y| (1)**	
|θ-ḳ-D| (1)		**|θ-r-y| (2)**	
|θ-ḳ-d| (2)		**|θ-t-ʕ|**	
|θ-ḳ-l|		**|θ-t-ḳ|**	Cf. **|s²-ḳ-ḳ|**
|θ-ḳ-p|		**|θ-θ-y|**	
|θ-ḳ-y|		**|θ-w-ʕ|**	
|θ-l-b|		**|θ-w-b|**	
|θ-l-g|		**|θ-w-r|**	
|θ-l-ħ-n|		**|θ-w-y|**	
|θ-l-l|		**|θ-y-n|**	

|θ-ʔ|
Cf. |**s²-w**|

Primary noun, Sem.: *šʔh, šʔt, tʔh, tʔtʔ* (Aram.) "ewe, sheep"; *šûm, šuʔu* (Akk.) "sheep (for sacrifice)", *šuʔātu, šâtu* "ewe"; *ṯāwa, ṯāya* (Arab.) "sheepfold"; *ṯīwīt, ṯēt, tīt, séʔah* (MSArab.) "sheep".

θaʔ "ewe"

●LL: **MŠ** Cf. [*šá*]-*a*-*u*₅ = MIN (: *im-me-ru*) (V 31) → Hrůša MŠ 111, 251, 397, 545.

θāt "ewe"	•CTX: **TU** UDU *ša-ta-am* → Krebernik Tall Bi`a 243.
θiʔat "ewe"	•CTX: **EM** Pl. cf. MÍ.MEŠ *ši-a-ti* → Pentiuc Vocabulary 171f.
θåt "ewe"	•CTX: **UGA** Sg. *ṯåt*, pl. *ṯåt*, *ṯủt* → DUL 879: *ṯåt*.
|θ-ʔ-g|	Sem.: Cf. *šʔg* (Hb.) "to roar", *šʔgh* (*šᵉʔāgāh*) "roaring, screaming"; *ṯaʔaġa* (Arab.) "to bleat", *ṯuʔaġ* "bleat".
|S-ʔ-g| "to roar" (?)	•LL: **EB** Cf. KA.NI (gù.zal) = *sa-ù-gú*, *su-ù-gúm* → Conti QuSe 17 39, 92f.; Bonechi / Catagnoti Fs. Sommerfeld / Krebernik 166.
θāʔig "screaming"	•ONOM: **EUPH** *ša-i-gu-um* → Zadok Fs. Hallo 331; cf. Gelb CAAA 180: ŚAʔIQ.
θỉgt "neighing"	•CTX: **UGA** → DUL 879: *ṯỉgt*.
|θ-ʔ-r|	Sem.: *ṯaʔara* "to avenge the blood, take blood revenge", *ṯaʔr* "(blood) revenge, retaliation".
|**θ-ʔ-r**| "to protect"	•CTX: **UGA** G/D prefc. *yṯỉr* → DUL 878: /*ṯ-ʔ-r*/.
θår "protection" (?)	•CTX: **UGA** Sg. *ṯår*, pl. suff. (?) *ṯỉrk* → DUL 878f.: *ṯår*
|θ-ʔ-ṭ|	Sem.: *ṯaʔiṭa*, *ṯaʔaṭa* (Arab.) "to stink", *ṯaʔṭ*(*a*) "mud".
θỉṭ "mud"	•CTX: **UGA** Sg. / pl. *ṯỉṭ* → DUL 879: *ṯỉṭ*
|θ-ʕ-d| (1)	Sem.: Cf. *ṯʕd* (OSArab.) "to own, have".
|**θ-ʕ-d**| "to own, have"	•ONOM: **UGS** Cf. *ia-aš-ad-dì*/*du* → Müller WO 10 27; Golinets Onomastikon 2 472; diff. and unlikely Gröndahl PTU 147; Sivan GaGl 292 (altern. 266: *ia-rum-ad-dì*, RWM). **UGA** Cf. *yṯʕd* → DUL 978.
|θ-ʕ-D| (2)	Culture word, etym. unc.
θaʕitt "a container and measure of capacity"	•CTX: **UGS** Cf. *1 ša-i-tu*$_4$ *a-na* LÚ.MEŠ.ḪUN.GÁ → Huehnergard UVST 188.
θʕt "a container and measure of capacity"	•CTX: **UGA** Sg. *ṯʕt*, pl. *ṯʕdt* → DUL 880f.: *ṯʕt*.
|θ-ʕ-l(-b)|	Culture word, Sem.: *šwʕl* (*šūʕāl*, Hb.) "jackal, fox"; *šʕl*, *tʕl*(*?*) (Aram., Syr.) "jackal, fox"; *šelebu*(*m*), *šellebu*, *šēlubu*, *tālabum* (Akk.) "fox"; *ṯuʕāla*, *ṯaʕlab* (Arab.) "fox"; *iṯʕēl*, *yəṯáyl*, *hīṯáyl* (MSArab.) "fox". Non-Sem.: **či=čVlVb=* (Central Chadic) "jackal", *čulib=* (East Chadic) "wolf".[847]
θaʕal "fox"	•ONOM: **EB** *ša-al*$_6$, *ša-la* → Pagan ARES 3 238, 366. **UGS** *ša-a-la-na* → Gröndahl PTU 198; Sivan GAGl 281.

[847] Orel / Stolbova HSED 109f. no. 464: **čaʕlib=* / *čuʕlib=* "fox, jackal".

θuʕal "fox"	•ONOM: **EUPH** *šu-ḫa-la-nu/an* → Gelb CAAA 33, 195; Kogan AuOr 21 253; Knudsen PIHANS 100 322; Golinets BuB 9 72.
θʕl "fox"	•ONOM: **UGA** *ṯʕl* → DUL 880; *ṯʕln* → DUL 880; *ṯʕly* → DUL 880.
θuʕalt "vixen; DN 'The Vixen'"	•ONOM: **EG** *šu$_5$-ʕa-ru$_2$-ta* → Hoch SWET 274f. no. 391.
θaʕlab "fox"	•ONOM: **EB** *ša-a-ab, ša-la-ab* → Pagan ARES 3 238, 366. **EUPH** *sà-aḫ-la-ba-nu/an* → Zadok Fs. Hallo 331; Dirbas NABU 2017/12. **EM** *ša-la-bi/bu* → Pruzsinszky PTEm 97 (fn. 291) [731].
θeʕlib "fox"	•ONOM: **EB** *šè-lí-bù* → Pagan ARES 3 238, 367.
θʕlb "fox"	•ONOM: **UGA** *ṯʕlb* → DUL 880.

|θ-ʕ-r|	Sem.: Cf. *šʕr* (He.) "to calculate, reckon", *šʕr* (*šaʕar*) "weight"; *šʕr* (JAram. D) "to estimate, calculate", *šʕr(ʔ)* (Aram.) "fixed measure", *šyʕwr(ʔ)* (JAram.) "size"; see further: *šaraʕa* (Arab.) "to establish, lift, raise, prescribe"; *s^{2}rʕ* (OSArab.) "to erect"; *śarʕa* (Eth.) "to establish (order), prepare, arrange".
|**θ-ʕ-r**| "to arrange (the table)"	•CTX: **UGA** G prefc. *ṯṯʕr*, *yṯʕr*; inf.(?) *ṯʕr* → Tropper UG 110; DUL 880: /*ṯ-ʕ-r*/.
θaʕara "calculation; scheme"	•CTX: **EG** *ša-ʕ-ra, ša-ʕa-r, ša-ʕa-r* → Hoch SWET 272f. no. 387.
maθʕart "a priestess (kind of waitress?)"	•CTX: **EM** MÍ *ma-aš-ar-tu/ti*, (MÍ) *maš-ar-tu$_4$/ti* → Pentiuc Vocabulary 116f.

|θ-ʕ-y|	Sem.: Cf. *šʕh* (Hb.) "to gaze, look at"; *šeʔû(m), šeʔāʔu(m), šêʔu* (Akk.) "to seek (out); to probe, scrutinize".[848]
|**θ-ʕ-y**| "search, scrutinize; examine (the exta)"	•CTX: **EB** G imp. *ša-a* → Fronzaroli ARET 13 140, 297; Catagnoti QuSe 29 133, 156, 165, 233. **UGA** G prefc. *nṯʕy*; act. ptc. *ṯʕy* (cf. *ṯʕy* (I)) → DUL 881: /*ṯ-ʕ-y*/ ("to offer, sacrifice"). •ONOM: **EB** *šè-a*; *iš$_{11}$-a, iš$_x$*(LAM)*-a*; *iš$_{11}$-a-il, iš$_{11}$-a-da-mu, iš/iš$_{11}$-a-ne-àr, iš$_x$*(LAM)*-a-ma-lik, iš$_{11}$-a ma-lik* → Pagan ARES 3 182f., 339, 341f. **EM** Cf. *še-a, še-(-i)-ia, še-i-ba-aḫ-li/*^{d}U, *še-i-*^{d}*da-gan/*^{d}KUR, *še-i-*EN; cf. *še-um-ka/*GAL → Pruzsinszky PTEm 97 [741, 743ff.], 129 [750].
θāʕiy "supervisor, examiner of the exta" (?)	•ONOM: **UGS** Cf. *ša-i-ya* → Gröndahl PTU 71, 197; Berger WO 5 280; Huehnergard UVST 238f.; Sivan GAGl 281.
θʕy "an official; supervisor, examiner of the exta" (?)	•CTX: **UGA** → DUL 881: *ṯʕy* (I). •ONOM: **UGA** Cf. *ṯiy* → DUL 879 (unc.); *ṯʕy* → DUL 881: *ṯʕy* (II).
θʕ (A) "search, supervision, examination of the exta" (?)	•CTX: **UGA** → DUL 879: *ṯʕ* (I) ("offering").

[848] The isoglosses alleged in support of a mng "to offer" are lexically and phonologically questionable: OSArab. *mṯʕy* "incense (offering)" (DOSA 548: ṮʕY; vacat SB); *šayyaʕa* (Arab.) "to consume, burn (up)"; *śwʕ, śawʕa* (Eth.) "to sacrifice".

|θ-b-r|	Sem.: *šbr* (Hb.) "to shatter, smash, break", *šbr* (*šeber*) "breaking, break",*šbrwn* (*šibbarôn*) "destruction"; *šbr* (Ph.) "to break"; *šbr*, *tbr* (Aram., Syr.) "to break", *tbr*(?) (JAram., Syr.) "breaking"; *šebēru*(*m*), *śabārum*, *šabāru*(*m*) (Akk.) "to break", *šebru*(*m*) "broken", *šabburum* "broken"; *tabara*, *ṯabara* (Arab.) "to destroy, ruin", *tibr* "gold dust", *tabār*, *ṯubūr* "ruin"; *ṯbr* (OSArab.) "to damage, destroy"; *tiber* (MSArab.) "to be broken"; *sabara* (Eth.) "to break (off)", *səbr* "fragment", *səbbār* "fragment", *sēbrat* "breaking".
|θ-b-r| "to break, shatter; to grind, powder"	•CTX: **UGA** G prefc. *yṯbr*, suffc. *ṯbr*; N prefc. *ṯṯbr*, *yṯbr* → DUL 884f.: /*ṯ-b-r*/. •LL: **EB** Cf. ZÌ = *ì-ša-ba-lum*/*lu-um* |ʔiθbār=| (VE 1175); ZÚ.ÀR.ŠA₄ = *dal-da-bí-lum*/*lu-um* |taθab(b)ir=| → Fronzaroli Fs. Leslau 467; Conti QuSe 15 39; Catagnoti QuSe 29 23, 49, 64, 66; 233. •ONOM: **UGS** Cf. *ša-ba-ra-na* → Gröndahl PTU 198; Sivan GAGl 281. **UGA** Cf. *ṯbrn* → DUL 885: *ṯbrn* (II); *ṯbry* → DUL 885.
θbr "opening"	•CTX: **UGA** Sg. / pl. cstr. *ṯbr* → DUL 885: *ṯbr*.
θbrn "opening"	•CTX: **UGA** Sg. cstr. *ṯbrn* → DUL 885: *ṯbrn* (I).
ʔiθbīr "a fine flour"	•CTX: **EB** *iš-bí-na* |ʔiθbīr=nay(n)| → Catagnoti / Fronzaroli ARET 16 82, 242; Catagnoti QuSe 29 26, 39, 74, 118, 189. •LL: **EB** NÌ.SAL.SAL = *iš-bí-lu* → Civil BaE 84; Conti QuSe 17 75; Catagnoti QuSe 29 49, 64, 189.

|θ-d-l|	Sem.: Cf. *šadālu*(*m*) (Akk.) "to be(come) wide", *šadlu* "broad, spacious", *šuddulum*, *šum*/*ndulu* "very wide".
θmdl "gapping" (?)	•CTX: **UGA** → Watson UF 39 685; altern. DUL 900: *ṯmdl* "exhaustion, destruction" (?).

|θ-d-r|	Loan. Non-Sem.: *šiduri* (Hurr.) "girl".[849]
θiduri "girl"	•LL: **MŠ** *ši-du-ri* = MIN (*ar-da-tu₄*, exp. MŠ I 78) → Hrůša MŠ 152f., 282, 432, 547.
θdr "waitress, girl"	•CTX: **UGA** → DUL 886: *ṯdr*.

\|θ-d(-y)\|
See \|**S-d/ð**\|

|θ-γ-r| (1)	Primary noun, Sem.: *šʕr* (*šaʕar*, Hb.) "gate"; *šʕr* (Ph., Moab.) "gate", *šʕr* (Hb., Ph.) "porter"; *trʕ* (Aram., Syr., Nab., Palm., Hatra) "gate", *trʕ* (Hatra) "gatekeeper"; *taraḫu* "gate" (*ta-ra-ḫa*/*ḫi*, Warka-Akk., Aram. loan); *ṯaġr* (Arab.) "mouth, port, inlet".

[849] Richter BGH 400f.

θaγr "gate; DN"	•CTX: **EA** KÁ *a-bu-ul-lí* : *ša-aḫ-ri* (244:16) → CAD Š/1 100; Sivan GAGl 43, 281; Izre'el Orient 38 91. **UGS** Cf. unc. Pl. GIŠ *ša-[ḫ]a*(!?)*-ru-ma* |θaγarūma| (?) → Huehnergard UVST 188. **EG** *ša-ʕa-ra*, metath. *ša-r-ʕa* → Hoch SWET 273f. no. 390. •ONOM: **EB** *gi-a-ša-ḫa-ru*$_{12}$, *gi-a-sa-ru*$_{12}$, NAM(sim?)-*ša-ḫa-lu*/*ru*$_{12}$, *ru*$_{12}$-*gi*(!?)-*iš-ša-ru*$_{12}$, ru$_{12}$-*zi-ša-ḫa-ru*$_{12}$ → Krebernik PET 93; Pagan ARES 3 238, 311, 360, 365; Bonechi MARI 8 504.
θaγγār "porter, gatekeeper"	•LL: **EB** KÍD.SAG = *ša-ḫa-lum* → Fronzaroli QuSe 13 150; Milano ARET 9 393; Conti QuSe 17:110; Bonechi MARI 8 504 fn. 216; QDLF 16 86; Catagnoti QuSe 29 20, 59, 64, 80, 122, 233.
θγr (A) "gate, door"	•CTX: **UGA** Sg. *ṯġr*, pl. cst. *ṯġrt*, suff. *ṯġrh*, *ṯġrny*, *ṯġrkm* → DUL 888: *ṯġr* (I); Tropper UG 287, 299.
θγr (B) "gatekeeper"	•CTX: **UGA** Sg. *ṯġr*, suff. *ṯġrh*; pl. *ṯġrm* → DUL 888f.: *ṯġr* (II). •ONOM: **UGA** Cf. unc. *ṯġr* → DUL 889: *ṯġr* (III).

|θ-γ-r| (2)	Sem.: *šoʕār* (Hb.) "rotten, burst open (figs)" (?); *trʕ* (JAram., Syr.) "to break through"; *šaʔāru(m)* (Akk.) "to win, conquer"; *ṯaġara* (Arab.) "to break, breach", *ṯuġra* "breach"; *(y)hoʔor* (MSArab.) "to split"; *saʕara*, *səʕra* (Eth.) "to remove, withdraw, violate, break (oath)".
|θ-γ-r| "to break, win, defeat"	•CTX: **EB** D precf. suff. *lu-sa-ir-su* |lā=yuθaγγir=| → Fronzaroli ARET 13 115, 280; Catagnoti QuSe 59, 64, 106, 156, 233. •ONOM: **EB** *iš*$_{11}$*-ar*, *iš*$_{11}$*-a-rúm*, *iš*$_{11}$*-ar-ì*, *iš*$_{11}$*-ar-da-mu* → Krebernik PET 61; Pagan ARES 3 182 (*ṯʕr*), 341.
θuγr "victory" (?)	•ONOM: **EB** Cf. elem. (=)*šu-ra(=)*, KU-*ra(=)* → Bonechi MARI 8 500.[850]

|θ-h|	Sem.: Cf. *šēʔu*, *šīʔu* (Akk.) "neighbour", fem. *šiʔītum*, *šeʔītu*, *šīttu*(m) / *šittu*, *šettu*.
θh "neighbour, vicinity" (?)	•CTX: **UGA** → DUL 889: *ṯh*.

|θ-ħ-l|	Culture word, Sem.: Cf. *šḥlt* (*šᵉḥēlet*, Hb.) mng unc. ("garden cress?"); *tḥl* (Syr.) "cress", *šḥly*, *tḥlyʔ/n* (Aram.) "weeds, cress"; seee also *saḫlium*, *saḫlû(m)*, *saḫlânu* (Akk.) "cress plant / seed", *saḫlûtu* "cress seed". Non-Sem.: Cf. *zaḫḫeli=* (Hitt., mistaken for *ḫaḫḫeli=* ?) "weed, undergrowth"; *sélinon* (Gr.) "celery".
θaħlat, θeħlat "a vegetable (cress?)"	•CTX:[851] **EUPH** Cf. *ša-aḫ-la-tum*, *še-eḫ-la-tim* → AHw 1209: *šeḫlātum*; CAD Š/2 264: *šeḫlātu*; Zadok Fs. Hallo 331 (ṮḪL); Joannès ARM 23 132 (123:3); Durand FM 2 49:27; Streck Onomastikon 1 118 § 2.95.[852]
s¹ħlt "cress seeds" (?)	•CTX: **UGA** Sg. / pl. *šḥlt* → DUL 800f.: *šḥlt*.

|θ-x|	Culture word, Sem.: *šēḫtu* (Akk.) "incense burner".

---

[850] For an altern. rdg of the elems *šu*/KU-*ra* as \|θuwr=\| "bull; DN" see Pagan ARES 3 238, and here \|θ-w-r\|.

[851] For an Ebl. *si-ʔà-tum* "Onyx marinus" related to Hb. *šḥlt* "a smelling shell" (?) see Pasquali NABU 2009/61.

[852] Diff. Jacquet NABU 2003/44: "farine tamisée", Akk. *šaḫālu(m)* "to sieve, filter".

ủθxt "incense burner; DN"	•CTX: **UGA** → DUL 122: *ủṯḫt.*
|θ-x-ṭ| See **|S-H-ṭ|**	
|θ-k-ħ|	Sem.: Cf. *škḥ* (Hb.) "to forget", (N) "to be careless, thoughtless".
|θ-k-ħ| "to forget oneself" (?)	•CTX: **UGA** N (?) prefc. *tṯkḥ, yṯkḥ* → DUL 889f.: */ṭ-k-ḥ/* "to burn, inflame"; "to be inflamed (sexual meaning), get excited".
|θ-k-l|	Sem.: *škl* (Hb.) "to become childless", *škwl* (*š^{e}kôl*) "childlessness", (*šākûl*) "bereaved of children"; *tkl* (JAram.) "to be childless", *tkl(?)* (JAram., Syr.) "bereavement", (JAram.) "childless person"; *ṯakila* (Arab.) "to lose a child / a loved person", *ṯakal, ṯukal* "state of one who has lost a loved one", *ṯākil, ṯaklān* "bereaved of a child".
|θ-k-l| "to be deprived of children"	•CTX: **UGA** G / Dpass. prefc. *tṯkl* → DUL 890: */ṯ-k-l/.*
θkl "sterility, loss of children"	•CTX: **UGA** → DUL 890: *ṯkl.*
|θ-k-m|	Primary noun, Sem.: *škm* (*š^{e}kem*, Hb.) "shoulder", *škm* (C *hiškîm*) "to load on the backs in the early morning, to do early"; *tkmh* (Aram., Demotic script) "back"; *sakm* (Eth.) "load", *sakama* "to carry on the shoulders". Non-Sem.: **sagam=* (Lowland East Cushitic) "nape".[853]
θākim "he who carries on the shoulders; DN"	•ONOM: **EUPH**, **B** *ša-ki-mu-um, ša-ki-ma-num, a-ḫi-ša-ki-im, bi-ni-ša-ki-im, i-la-ša-ki-im, ìl-lí-ša-ki-im, mu-ut-ša-ki-im, sa*(!)*-mu-ša-ki-im,*[854] *ta-ri-im-ša-ki-im* → Gelb CAAA 33, 194; Zadok Fs. Hallo 331; Durand REA 678.[855]
θakūm "carried on the shoulders"	•ONOM: **EB** Cf. *ša-gú-um, ša-gú-mu* → Pagan ARES 3 183, 366. **EUPH**, **B** *sa-ku-mu-um*, cf. *sa-ku-mi*-DINGIR |θakūm=ʔil| "carried on the shoulders by DN" ? → Gelb CAAA 33, 194.
θkm "shoulder, top"	•CTX: **UGA** Sg. *ṯkm*, cstr. *ṯkm*, du. cstr. suff. *ṯkmm* → DUL 890: *ṯkm.*
θkmt "she who carries on her shoulders, who shoulders"	•CTX: **UGA** → DUL 890f.: *ṯkmt.*
ʔiθkimt "shoulder"	•LL: **EB** Á.KU$_5$ = [*iš*]-*gim*-[*t*]*um*, var. *iš$_{11}$-gi-du-núm* → Conti QuSe 17 37, 159; Catagnoti QuSe 29 29, 49, 64, 67, 189.
ʔiθkittān "the one with misshapen shoulder"	•LL: **EB** Á.KU$_5$ = *iš-gi-da-nu* → Conti QuSe 17 12, 38, 153; Catagnoti QuSe 29 29, 49, 189; Bonechi / Catagnoti Fs. Sommerfeld / Krebernik 160.

[853] Orel / Stolbova HSED 110 no. 468: **čakam=* "shoulders, nape".
[854] For this rdg see Durand REA 663 fn. 66.
[855] With a diff. mng: "rendre libre", hence *Šakim* "libérateur" (with no etym. support).

|θ-k-p|

Sem. etym. unc. Cf. *tkp* (JAram. D) "to place next to each other", cf. advb. *b tkyp* (JAram.) "suddenly".

|**θ-k-p**| "to press, urge" (?)

•CTX: **UGA** Cf. N suffc. (?) *nṯkp* → De Moor AuOr 27 290 (mng); Tropper UG 535 (form); DUL 891: /*ṯ-k-p*/ "?".

|θ-k-r|

Loan, Sem.: Cf. *ʔškr* (*ʔeškār*, Hb.) "tribute", *iškāru*(*m*), *eškāru*(*m*) "work assignment".
Non-Sem.: e š g a r (Sum.) "assignment".

|**θ-k-r**| "to deliver (in payment or tribute)" (?)

•CTX: **UGA** C prefc suff.?, cf. *tṯtkrn* → DUL 891: /*ṯ-k-r*/; Tropper UG 142, 594.

|θ-ḳ-b|
See |**S-ḳ-b**|

|θ-ḳ-D| (1)

Sem. etym. unc. Cf. *kašāṭu*(*m*) (Akk.) "to cut off"; *qašaṭa* (Arab.) "to pay, take off"; *qs*^{1}*ṭ* (OSArab.) "to pay"(?); *qaśaṭa* (Eth.) "to steal, carry off".

|**θ-ḳ-D**| "to contribute, pay, carry" (?)

• CTX: **EB** Gtn prefc. *iš*$_{11}$*-da-ga-*SU |yiθtaḳḳaD=|, D prefc. *nu-ša-ga-ad* |nuθaḳḳaD|, *a du-ša-ga-du* |la tuθaḳḳadū|, *uš-da-ki-du* |yuθtaḳḳidū| → Edzard ARET 5 18, 20; Krebernik Beschwörungen 323f.; Fronzaroli VO 8 18f.; ARET 16 30, 80, 260, 289; Catagnoti QuSe 29 21, 27, 142, 144, 233.
•LL: **EB** Cf. TÚM.MA = *ša-ga-dum*/*du-um* (VE 988) → Pettinato MEE 4 309; Fronzaroli ARET 16 80 (4).

|θ-ḳ-d| (2)

Culture word, Sem.: *šqd* (*šāqēd*, Hb.) "almond (tree)"; *šgdh, šgdtʔ, šqdh, šgrʔ* (JAram., Syr.) "almond"; *šiqdu*(*m*), *šuqdu, siqdu* (Akk.) "almond (tree)", *šiqdīum* "of almond wood"(?); *səgd* (Eth.) "almond tree, nut tree".

θuḳd "almond"

•CTX: **UGS** GIŠ *šu-uq-du-ma* → Sivan GAGl 282; Huehnergard UVST 188f.; vSoldt SAU 307 (156).

θḳd "almond"

•CTX: **UGA** → DUL 914: *ṯqd*.
•ONOM: **UGA** *ṯqdy* → DUL 914.

|θ-ḳ-l|

Sem.: *šql* (Hb.) "to weigh (out)", *šql* (*šeqel*) "shekel, weight", *mšqwl* (*mišqôl*), *mšql* (*mišqāl*) "weight", *mšqlt* (*mišqelet, mišqolet*) "mason's level"; *šql* (Pun.) "to weigh out", *šql* (Pun.) "shekel, weight"; *tql* (Aram., Syr.) "to hang, weigh", *šql, tql* "shekel", *mtql*(*ʔ*) "weight, scale", *mtqlh, mtqltʔ* (Aram.) "weight"; *šaqālu*(*m*) (Akk.) "to weigh, pay, balance, suspend", *šiql*(*m*) "shekel", *šuqlum* "load", *šāqilu*(*m*) "a wooden lock or bolt, beam", *šuqultu*(*m*) "(stone) weight", *mašqaltum* "payment"; *ṯaqula, ṯaqāla* (Arab.) "to be heavy, weigh heavily", *ṯaqala* "to weigh out", *ṯiql* "weight, burden", *ṯiqal* "heaviness", *miṯqāl* "weight"; *saqala* (Eth.) "to suspend, hang (up)".
Non-Sem: *šiklade* (Hurr.) "shekel";[856] *síglos* (Gr.) id.

|**θ-ḳ-l**| "to hang (up), weigh (out)"

•CTX: **EB** G prefc. *daš*(TUKU$_x$)*-gul* |taθḳul| → Catagnoti QuSe 29 28, 130, 233. Cf. Fronzaroli ARET 13 176, 302: TUKU$_x$:GUL.
•LL: **EB** Cf. GIŠ.GI.DA.LA = *ša-ga-lum* → Conti QuSe 17 131; LÁ.LÁ = *ti-iš-da-gi-lum* → Krebernik ZA 73 42; Hecker BaE 218; Kienast BaE 247.

856 Richter BGH 373.

θāḳil "beam"	•LL: **EB** GIŠ.MÁḪ = *ša-gi-lum* → Fronzaroli QuSe 13 149; Krebernik ZA 73 16; Conti QuSe 17 130; Bonechi QDLF 16 82: "pesatore".
θaḳul "weighed, measured"	•LL: **EB** NÌ.ÁGA = *ša-gú-um* → Conti QuSe 17 65.
θuḳult "weight"	•ONOM: **EUPH** *šu-gul-tum* → Gelb CAAA 33, 196.
ʔaθḳaliy "very heavy" (?)	•ONOM: **A4** Cf. *a-aš-qa-li-ia* → Wiseman AT 125; Dietrich / Loretz WO 5 67 (139:17); Arnaud AuOr 16 170f.
maθḳal "weight"	•CTX: **EA** Cf. 50 MEŠ NI LAL *: maš-qa-al*[*-šu-nu* (?)] (235+327:20) → AHw 628; CAD M/1 382; Sivan GAGl 246.
miθḳul "weighed out" (?)	•CTX: **UGS** Cf. rdg *mi-iš-qú*(!)*-la-t*[*i* (pl., of tears) → vSoden UF 1 194f.
θḳl "shekel"	•CTX: **UGA** Sg. *ṯql*, *šql*, du. / pl. *ṯqlm* → DUL 914ff.: *ṯql*. •ONOM: **UGA** Cf. unc. *šqln* → DUL 827.

|θ-ḳ-p|	Sem.: *tqp* (Hb.)[857] "to overpower", *tqp* (*toqep*) "might, power", *tqyp* (*taqqîf*) "mighty"; *tqp* (Aram., Syr.) "to be strong, prevail, overpower", *tqwp*(*?*) "strength, vigor", *tqyp* "strong"; *ṯaqafa* "to defeat, beat in intelligence", *ṯaqifa*, *ṯaqufa* "to be skilful, smart", *ṯaqf*, *ṯaqīf* "smart, very clever"; *hṯqf* (OSArab. C) "to make known".
|**t-ḳ-p**| "to prevail over" (?)	•ONOM: **A4** Cf. unc. *ta*-KA(*qà*)*-pu* → Wiseman AT 148; Sivan GaGl 279.
tuḳ(ḳ)up "prevailing" (?)	•ONOM: **B** Cf. unc. DU(*tù*)-GU(*qù*)*-pu-um* → Zadok Fs. Hallo 331.

|θ-ḳ-y|	Sem.: Cf. *šaqû*(*m*) (Akk.) "to be(come) high, elevated", (D) "to rise up".
|**θ-ḳ-y**| "to be(come) high, elevated; to elevate, take up"	•CTX: **UGA** D prefc. *yṯq* → DUL 916: /*ṯ-q-y*/. •LL: **EB** IL.IL = *du-uš-da-gi-um* |tuθtaḳḳiy=| → Kienast BaE 250; Krebernik StEb 7 200; Fronzaroli ARET 11 78, 154: "to rise up again and again".

|θ-l-b|	Culture word, Sem.: Cf. *šulpu*(*m*) (Akk.) "stalk, straw". Non-Sem.: *šnp* (Eg.) "a kind of grass; reed, reed matting".
s¹ulb "trumpet, tube" (?)	•CTX: **EG** Cf. *šu*$_5$*-n-b-ʔu*, *šu*$_5$*-n-b-i̓*, *šu*$_5$*-n-b-ʔu*, *šn-b-ʔu*, *šu*$_5$*-n-b-t* → Hoch SWET 281f. no. 403.
θlb "flute"	•CTX: **UGA** Sg. *ṯlb*, pl. *ṯlbm* → DUL 892: *ṯlb*.

|θ-l-g|	Primary noun, Sem.: *šlg* (*šeleg*, Hb.) "snow", *šlg* (C) "to snow"; *tlg*(*?*) (Aram., Syr.) "snow", *tlg* (Syr. C) "to become white"; *šalgu*(*m*) (Akk.) "snow, sleet" (for the denom. Mari-Akk *šalāgum* see below: |θ-l-g|); *ṯalǧ* (Arab.) "snow, ice", *ṯalağa* "it snowed"; *ṯalǧ*, *falg* (MSArab.) "ice, snow".
|**θ-l-g**| "to snow"	•CTX: **EUPH** G prefc. *i-ša-al-la-gu* → CAD Š/1 193: *šalāgu*.
θalg "snow(-white ?)"	•CTX: **EG** *sa-ra-qu*$_2$, *s-r-qu*, *sa-ra-qa/qu*$_4$, defective writings: *sa-qu*, *sa-r* → Hoch SWET 264f. no. 375.[858] •ONOM: **EUPH** *ša-al-ga-an* → Gelb CAAA 33, 194.
θalk "snow"	•CTX: **EUPH** *sa-al-ku* → Kupper ARM 28 185 (123:9).

---

857 Aram. loan.

858 Sivan / Cochavi-Rainey WSVES 84: *šá-l-qu* "snow"; Helck Beziehungen no. 199.

|θ-l-ħ-n|	Culture word, Sem.: *šlḥn* (*šulḥān*, Hb.) "table".
θulħān "table"	•ONOM: **UGS** Cf. TN URU *šul-ḫa-na/nu* → vSoldt SAU 338 n. 177; UF 28 690; Sivan GAGl 267; Huehnergard UVST 230 n. 86, 244 n. 130; AkkUg 365; Belmonte RGTC 12/2 302.
θlħn "table"	•CTX: **UGA** Sg. *ṯlḥn*, cstr. *ṯlḥn*, suff. *ṯlḥny*, pl. *ṯlḥnm*, *ṯlḥnt* → DUL 892f.: *ṯlḥn*. •ONOM: **UGA** Cf. PN *ṯlḥny* → DUL 893: *ṯlḥny* (III); TN *ṯlḥn*, *ṯlḥny* → DUL 893: *ṯlḥn*(*y*) (I); GN *ṯlḥny* → DUL 893: *ṯlḥny* (II).

|θ-l-l|	Sem.: *šll* (Hb.) "to plunder, capture", *šll* (*šālāl*) "booty, spoil", *šwll* (*šôlāl*) "stripped off"; *šll* (JAram.) "to despoil", *šll*, *šwll*(?) "spoil"; *šalālu*(*m*) (Akk.) "to carry off, plunder", *šallu* "plundered, captive", *šallatu*(*m*), *šillatu* "booty, plundered thing(s)"; *ṯalla* (Arab.) "to destroy, break something apart"; *ṯll* (OSArab.) "to plunder, take as booty".
|**θ-l-l**| "to take (away), take booty" (?)	•CTX: **EUPH** Cf. *ša ša-la-lim* → Lafont FM 98 fn. 5. •ONOM: **Tall Brak** Cf. *iš-lul*-ᵈEN.ZU → Catagnoti Mari 8 590f. **EUPH, B** Cf. *da-aš-la-lum/lu-um*, *uš-ta-li-li* → Gelb CAAA 32, 181, 188f.
|**s¹-l-l**| "to plunder, rob"	•CTX: **UGA** G suffc. *šl* → Tropper UG 676; 806: /*š-l*(*-l*)/.[859]
Salal, Salil, Sullal, Sullul "captive" (?)	•ONOM: **EUPH, B** *ša-la-lum*, *sa-li-lum*, *su-ul-la-li*, *su-ul-lu-lum* → Gelb CAAA 32, 188f.
θālil "plunderer"	•ONOM: **EB** *ša-li-lu* → Pagan ARES 3 183, 366.
θall "captive"	•CTX: **EG** *s-r-ta* (|θallatu|, fem.) → Hoch SWET 265f. no. 376.[860]
θlln "captive" (?)	•ONOM: **UGA** Cf. unc. *ṯlln* → DUL 893.
θallat "booty"	•LL: **EB** NAM.RA.AG = *ša-la-tum* → Fronzaroli StEb 7 183; QuSe 13 150; Krebernik ZA 73 38f.
θllt "booty" (?)	•CTX: **UGA** Unc. *ṯllt khn*[→ DUL 893: *ṯllt* "?".
maθall "conduit, pipe, tube"	•CTX: **EUPH** *ma-ša-al-lim*, *ma-ša-al-lam* → Lafont FM 98 fn. 5.

|θ-l-l-r|	Culture word, Sem: *šallūru*(*m*), *šannūru* "plum"(?).[861] Non-Sem.: *salor* (Armenian) "plum";[862] šennur (Sum.) "plum".
θallur "plum" (?)	•LL: **EB** Cf. ŠENNUR ZA.GÌN = *ša-lu-ra* KUR → Civil EDA 143 ((iv 1), 149f. fn. 24.

|θ-l-t-x|	Culture word, Sem.: Cf. *šiltāḫu*(*m*), *šiltaḫḫu*, (?)*lištāḫu* (Akk.) "arrow(head); Syrius".
θltx "arrow(head)"	•ONOM: **UGA** Cf. *ṯltḫ* → DUL 894.

[859] For the UGA PN *ṯlln* and the fem. (?) noun *ṯllt* cf. DUL 893 (both unc.).
[860] Sivan / Cochavi-Rainey WSVES 84: <*ʔa*>*-śa-r-tá* / <*ʔa*>*-śi-r-tá* "female prisoner"; Helck Beziehungen 200: from Akk. *esirtu* "Gefangene" (\|ʔ-s-r\|), as EG *ʔaśīr* (but see Hoch SWET 45f. no. 40: *ʔa₂-ṯi₂-ra*, and GlOS 1 46: \|ʔ-s-r\| (1)).
[861] "Apricot" in Ass. according to Postgate BSA 3 115ff.
[862] Greppin JNES 50 203 fn. 4f.

|θ-l-θ|	Culture word; etym. unc.
θalθ "copper, bronze" (?)	•CTX: **UGS** Cf. 1 *ša-al-šu-ma* → Sivan GAGl 281; Huehnergard UVST 186f.; vSoldt SAU 307 (155).
θlθ (E) "copper, bronze(-bolt)"	•CTX: **UGA** Sg. *ṯlṯ* → DUL 897f.: *ṯlṯ* (V); Del Olmo AuOr 37 287f., 290.
|θ-m-d|	Sem.: Cf. *ṯamada* (Arab.) "to retain, collect (water)", *ṯamd*, *ṯamad* "pond, pool".
|**θ-m-d**| "to be, or to grow, fat"	•ONOM: **EG** Cf. *s-m-d-t-ty* [F] → Schneider APÄQ 184 no. 389. **UGA** Cf. *ṯṯmd* → DUL 871.
|θ-m-m| (1)	Sem.: *šm*, *šmh* (Hb.) "there"; *šm*, *tm* (Aram.) "there", *tmh*, *tmn* (Aram., Syr.) "there"; *ṯamma* (Arab.) "there", *ṯumma* "then, furthermore", *ṯammata* "there"; *šumma* (Akk.) "when; now".
θm "there; then"	•CTX: **UGA** *ṯm*, suff. *ṯmm*, *ṯmn*, *ṯmny*, *ṯmt* → DUL 900: *ṯm*.
|θ-m-m| (2)	Sem. etym. unc. Cf. *ṯamma* (Arab.) "to fix, arrange"; see further *šmm* (Hb.) "to shudder, be appalled".
|**θ-m-m**| "to fix, resolve to do, be about to do" (?)	•CTX: **UGA** Cf. G impv. (?) *ṯmm* → Tropper UG 58: "ordnen"; cf. DUL 901: /*ṯ-m-m*/ "to be appalled" (?).
|θ-m-n-y|	Primary noun, Sem.: *šm(w)nh* (*šᵉmōneh*, Hb.) "eight", *šmyny* (*šᵉmînî*) "eighth", *šm(w)nym* (*šᵉmōnîm*) "eighty"; *šmn* (Ph., Pun.) "eight", *šmnm* (Pun.) "eighty": *tm(w)nʔ* (Nab., Palm.) "eight"; *tmnyh*, *tmny* (Aram.) "eight", *tmyny* "eighth", *tmnyn* "eighty"; *samāne*, *šamāne* (Akk.) "eight", *samanû* "eighth, one-eighth"; *ṯamāniya* (Arab.) "eight", *ṯamin* "eighth", *ṯumn* "one-eighth", *ṯamānūn* "eighty"; *ṯmny* (OSArab.) "eight", *ṯmnyy* "eighty", *ṯmn* "one-eighth"; *ṯəmōni*, *ṯōni*, *ṯəmən* (MSArab.) "eight", *ṯōmən*, "eighth", *ṯəmənáyn* "eighty"; *səmn*, *samāni* (Eth.) "eight", *sāmən* "eighth", *samānəyā* "eighty", *sammana* "to make eight (times)".
|**θ-m-n**| "to make eight (times)"	•CTX: **UGA** D prefc. (?) suff. *ṯṯ{t}mnm* (rdg?) → DUL 901: /*ṯ-m-n*/; Tropper UG 348. •ONOM: **UGA** Cf. *ṯṯmnt* → DUL 921f.; Tropper UG 530.
θmn (A) "eight"	•CTX: **UGA** → Masc. *ṯmn*, fem. *ṯmnt*, *šmnt*, pl. *ṯmnym* (see below: *ṯmnym*) → Huehnergard UVST 292 fn. 115; DUL 901f.: *ṯmn*(*y*) (I).
θmn (B) "eighth"	•CTX: **UGA** → DUL 903 *ṯmn* (II).
θamānay "eight" (?)	•ONOM: **EB** Cf. *ša-ma-ni* → Pagan ARES 3 238, 366.[863] **UGS** Cf. [*ša*]-*ma-né-e* → Sivan GAGl 130, 281.
θmnỉd "eight times"	•CTX: **UGA** → DUL 903: *ṯmnỉd*.
θmnym "eighty"	•CTX: **UGA** → DUL 903f.: *ṯmnym*.

863 Rdg |θamāne|; altern. rdgs |s^{1}am=a=ni| "our name" (see |s^1-m| (1)), |s^{2}aym=a=ni| "our destiny" (|s^2-y-m|), Pagan ARES 3 368.

|θ-m-r| Cf. **|ð-m-r|**, **|S-m-r|**	Sem.: Cf. *ṯamara* (Arab.) "to bear fruit", *ṯamara*, *ṯamar* "fruit(s), yield"; *ṯmr* (OSArab.) "to cause to bear fruit", *ṯmr* "crop(s)"; *samra*, *śamra* (Eth.) "to be fruitful, flourish", *samr*, *samar* "produce, productiveness".
|θ-m-r| "to be fruitful"	•ONOM: **EG** Cf. *sm-:r-m-yw*$_2$ → Schneider APÄQ 183 no. 387.
θamr "crop(s), fruit(s)"	•CTX: **EB** Cstr. *ša-ma-la* → Fronzaroli ARET 13 207, 297. •ONOM: **UGS** Cf. PN *ša-am-ra-na* → Nougayrol PRU 3 202 (RS 16.257+) III 49; vSoldt SAU 34; Gröndahl PTU 199; Sivan GAGl 281.[864] Cf. unc. TN *Ṯamrā* (URU *šam*(Ú)*-ra-a*, URU *šàm-ra-a*, URU *šá-am-ra-a*) → vSoldt Topography 47, 187; Belmonte RGTC 12/2 300; Fs. Watson 114.
θmr (B) "crop(s), fruit(s)"	•ONOM: **UGA** Cf. PN *ṯmrn* → DUL 904;[865] TN *ṯmr*, *ṯmry* → DUL 904f.; GN *ṯmry* → DUL 905.

|θ-n|	Primary noun, Sem.: *šnym* (*š*^{e}*nayim*, Hb. du.) "two", *šny* (*šēnî*) "following, second", *šnh* "to repeat", *mšnh* (*mišneh*) "in second position, copy"; *šnm*, *ʔšnm* (Ph., Pun.) "two, second", *šny* (Ph.) "second", *šny* (Nab. D) "to change"; *tryn* (Aram., Syr.) "two", *tnyn*(*y*) (Aram. Syr.) "second", *šny* (Aram. D) "to change", *tny* (JAram., Syr.) "to repeat";[866] *šina*, *šena* (Akk.) "two", *šanû*(*m*), *šanāʔu*(*m*) "to do twice, repeat", *šanû*(*m*), *šanium*(*m*) "second, next; (an)other, different", *šanā* "two by two", *šanāʔum*, *šanûti*=, *šanuttē*=, *šaniānu*, *šaniyānu* "for a second time", *šinīšu* "twice"; *ʔiṯnāni* (Arab.) "two", *ṯanī* "second"; *ṯanā* (*ṯany*) "to double, fold", *ṯannā*, *taṯniya* "to double, repeat", *ṯāniyan* "secondly", *ṯunāʔ*, *maṯnāy* "two at a time"; *ṯny* (OSArab.) "two; second", *hṯny* "to double", *mṯny* "doubled, two"; *ṯərō*, *ṯroh*, *trɔ* (MSArab.) "two"; see *sānəy* (Eth.) "the next day". Non-Sem.: *šin*=, *šina*= (Hurr.) "two";[867] see further **sin*= (East Chadic) (elder) brother", **šan*= (Agaw) "brothers".[868]
|θ-n-y| "to repeat, reiterate"	•CTX: **UGA** G prefc. *yṯny*, suff. *aṯnyk*, csuff. *ṯnt*, *ṯn*, imp. *ṯn*, *ṯny*, suff. *ṯnm*; inf.(?) *ṯn*, *ṯny*; Gt (?) prefc. *tṯtnyn* → DUL 910f.: /*ṯ-n-y*/. •ONOM: **EB** Cf. UR(*daš*?)*-ne*/*ni*, UR(*daš*?)*-ni-ga* → Krebernik PET 298; Pagan ARES 3 183f., 301. **EUPH, B** *iš-ta-aš-ni*-DINGIR, *iš-ta-aš-ni-el*/*il*, *ša-ta-aš-ni-il*; cf. *uš-taš*/*ta-aš-ni*-DINGIR, *uš-ta-an-ni* → Gelb CAAA 33, 195; Golinets Onomastikon 2 30ff., 319f., 456f. **A7** *iš-ni*-^{d}IM; cf. *uš-ta-an-ni*, *uš-ta-ni-i-la* → Wiseman AT 139, 151; Gelb CAAA 33, 194f.; Golinets Onomastikon 2 305, 319f., 456f., 506, 514.
θn (A) "two"	•CTX: **UGA** Masc. *ṯn*, suff. *ṯnh*, *ṯnm*, fem. *ṯt*, suff. *ṯth*, (?) *ṯtm* → DUL 905ff.: *ṯn* (I).
θn (B) "second, vice-"	•CTX: **UGA** Sg. masc. *ṯn*, suff. *ṯnn*, fem. (rdg ?) *ṯnt* → DUL 907f.: *ṯn* (II).[869] •ONOM: **UGA** Cf. unc. *ṯny* → DUL 911; *ṯnyn* → DUL 911.
θaniy "second"	•CTX: **EB** *sa-ne* → Fronzaroli ARET 13 108, 292; Catagnoti QuSe 29 64, 120, 233. •ONOM: **EB** *ša-ni* → Krebernik PET 298f.; Pagan ARES 3 183f., 366. **EUPH, B** *sa-ni-i*, *sa-ni-ú-um* → Gelb CAAA 33, 194.

[864] Cf. also Krebernik PET 64f.: S-M-L, and GlOS 1 164f.: |ð-m-r|.

[865] Cf. PN *ḏmrn*, GlOS 1 164: |ð-m-r| (A), ONOM: UGA.

[866] Allomorph *tryn* "two" (Aram., Syr.); see MSArab. *ṯərō*, *ṯroh*, *trɔ*, and Kogan Classification 404, 581.

[867] Richter BGH 380: *šin*= I, *šina* I, *šine*/*i*.

[868] Orel / Stolbova HSED 462f.: **san*= / **sin*= "brother".

[869] For *θn* in alph. Hurr. ctx. see Richter BGH 542: *ṯn* I (šn), *ṯny*.

θnỉd "twice"	•CTX: **UGA** *ṯnỉd*, suff. *ṯnỉdy*, *ṯnỉdm* → DUL 908: *ṯnỉd*.
θinaγili "of secondary quality"	•CTX: **EM** NINDA.MEŠ ZI *: ši-na-ḫi-li* → Pentiuc Vocabulary 172; Westenholz Emar Tablets 76, 78.
θnγly "deputy, second"	•CTX: **UGA** → DUL 908f.: *ṯnġly*; Richter BGH 542f.; fem. sg. suff. *ṯnġlyt* → DUL 909: *ṯnġlyt*.
mθn "repetition"	•CTX: **UGA** Sg. cstr. *mṯn*, suff. (?) *mṯnn* → DUL 597: *mṯn*.
maθnay "secondly" (?)	•CTX: **UGS** Cf. *ma-aš-na* (altern. *ma-aš-na-<a>* (?) |maθna/ā| (?)) → Sivan GAGl 246; Huehnergard UVST 187, 290; Tropper UG 200, 312, 346.

|θ-n-n| Cf. **|θ-n|**	Culture word, etym. unc.
θanānu "chariot soldier; archer"	•CTX: **EG** *s-n-ni*, *s-n-n-ni*, *sa-ni-ni* → Hoch SWET 261ff. no. 371.[870]
θannan "a class-designation (archer?)"	•CTX: **A4** *ša-na-nu*, ERÍN.MEŠ *ša-na-an-nu*, LÚ:MEŠ *ša-na-a-an-ni* → AHw 1161: *šanannu* "Streitwagen-Bogenschütze"; CAD Š/1 166: *šanannu* "archer"(?); Wiseman AT 163: "a class-designation"; Giacumakis AkkAl 102: "archer, bowman"; Rainey IOS 18 446f.; vDassow UF 34 883f.; SCCNH 17 558: *šannanu* "archer (using composite bow)".[871] **UGS** LÚ *ša-na-ni*, pl. LÚ *ša-na-nu-ma* → Sivan GAGl 281; Huehnergard UVST 187; vSoldt SAU 307(137).
θnn "a class-designation (archer?)"	•CTX: **UGA** Sg. *ṯnn*, pl. *ṯnnm* → DUL 909: *ṯnn* (I).[872]
θanan(n)uγ(γ) "a class-designation (archer?)"	•CTX: **A4** Pl. LÚ.MEŠ *sa-na-nu-ḫé* → Wiseman AT 350:9; Laroche GLH 214; Richter BGH 349.
θanannūt "function of the *θ.*-class"	•CTX: **Q** *a-na ša₁₀-na-an-nu-ti* → Richter / Lange Idadda 76.

|θ-n-ṭ|	Loan; Sem. cf. *šnṭ?* (Aram.) "a garment". Non-Sem.: Cf. *šnḏwt* (Eg.) "apron".[873]
θṭ "a piece of cloth or a garment"	•CTX: **UGA** → DUL 922: *ṯṭ*

|θ-n-y|	Culture word, Sem.: *šny* (*šānî*, Hb.) "crimson".
θn (C) "crimson, scarlet"	•CTX: **UGA** → DUL 908: *ṯn* (III).[874] •ONOM: **UGA** Cf. unc. *ṯny* → DUL 911; *ṯnyn* → DUL 911.

---

870 Cf. Sivan / Cochavi-Rainey WSVES 84: *śa-na-na* "chariot warrior"; Helck Beziehungen no. 195.

871 For the Alalaḫ class *ašannu* and its (unlikely) relation to *šanannu* see Dietrich / Loretz ZA 60 117; vDassow SCCNH 17 554.

872 There is also a PN *ṯnn*; cf. DUL 909f.: ṭnn (II): etym. unc.

873 Hannig WbÄgD 899; cf. Muchiki Egyptian 173.

874 For an unkn. commodity *ṯnt* see DUL 910 *ṯnt* (I); phonol. unrelated to Akk. *šanû* "to sluice, apply water", *šinītu*(*m*) "dyed textile".

|θ-p-d|	Sem.: Cf. *špt* (Hb.) "to set on", *mšptym* (*mišpᵉtayim*, du.) "the two saddle-baskets of a packmule"; *ṯaffada* (Arab.) "to line, pad (a cuirass)", *miṯfad* "fold".
|θ-p-d| "to place, rest (the feet)"	•CTX: **UGA** G prefc. *yṯpd* → DUL 911: /*ṯ-p-d*/. •ONOM: **UGS Cf.** *ša/šá-pí*-DA-*na* → Sivan GAGl 282 (ṮPṬ); Huehnergard UVST 230f.
mθpd "layer, stratum"	•CTX: **UGA** Du. *mṯpdm* → DUL 597: *mṯpd.*
|θ-p-r|	Primary noun, Sem.: Cf. *šapru*(*m*) (Akk.) "thigh"; *ṯafr*, *ṯufr* (Arab.) "vagina (of an animal)", derivatives: *ṯafar*, *ʔaṯfar* "crupper", *ṯaffara*, *ʔaṯfara* "to harness", *ʔistaṯfara* "to put the waist-wrapper between the thighs twisted together".
|θ-r-p| "to spur on" (?)	•CTX: **UGA** (Metath.) D prefc. *tṯrp*; inf. *ṯrp* → DUL 919: /*ṯ-r-p*/.
θprt "a woman's intimate garment"	•CTX: **UGA** Sg. *ṯprt*, du. *ṯprtm* → Watson NABU 2003/64; DUL 912: *ṯprt* "garment".
|θ-p-ṭ|	Sem.: *špṭ* (Hb.) "to pass judgement, to rule", *špṭ* (*šepeṭ*) "penalty", *š*(*w*)*pṭ* (*sōpeṭ*) "judge, ruler", *špwṭ* (*šᵉpôṭ*) "judgement", *mšpṭ* (*mišpāṭ*) "decision, judgement"; *špṭ* (Pun.) "to pass judgement, to rule", *špṭ* (Ph., Pun.) "magistrate", *mšpṭ* (Ph.) "rule, dominion"; *špṭ* (Aram.) "to begin a process, to litigate", *špṭ* (JAram.) "rule", *špṭ*(*ʔ*) (JAram.) "judge"; *šapāṭu*(*m*), *šapātu*(*m*), *šabātu* (Akk.) "to give judgement, exercise authority", semantic splitting with different vocalization: *šapāṭum* "to inform strictly, reprimand",[875].*šipṭu*(*m*) "judgement, verdict", *šāpiṭu*(m) "district governor"; *ṯfṭ* (OSArab.) "to decide, direct", *ṯfṭ* "judgement, legal decision".
|θ-p-ṭ| **(A)** "to pass judgement, exercise authority"	•CTX: **EUPH** G prefc. *a-ša-pí-iṭ*, *ni-iš-pí-iṭ*, *iš-pí-iṭ-ma*, *li-ša-pí-iṭ*, suff. *ta-ša-ap-pi-ṭam*, *iš-pí-ṭam*, imp. *šu-pí-iṭ*, inf. cstr. *ša-pa-aṭ*, Gt prefc. suff. *li-iš-t*[*a*]*-ap-ṭe*$_4$*-ši* → AHw 1172: *šapāṭu*(m); CAD Š/1 450f.: *šapāṭu* A; Dossin ARM 10 32:16'; Kupper ARM 13 103:11; Birot ARM 14 88ff. (49:11, 19); Durand ARM 26/1 163f. (31:5); ARM 26/2 26f. (298:29); Arkhipov ARM 33 280f. (118:25); Charpin / Durand / Birot FM 2 100ff. (60:7'); Charpin / Durand FM 6 390ff. (50:30f.); Ziegler RA 118ff. (A.1246:2'); Streck Onomastikon 1 117f. § 2.95. **UGA** G prefc. *tṯpṭ*, *yṯpṭ*, act. ptc. *ṯpṭ*, *ṯpẓ* (see below: *θpṭ* (B)) → DUL 912: /*ṯ-p-ṭ*/. •ONOM: **EB** *iš*$_{11}$-NE(*bí*)-*du* → Krebernik PTU 61; Pagan ARES 3 184, 341. **UGS** *ia-aš-pu-ṭù*/*ṭì* → Gröndahl PTU 199f.; Sivan GAGl 282; DUL 980: *yṯpṭ*. **UGA** Cf. *ṯbṭ* → Tropper UG 139; DUL 886. **EG** *ša-pa-ta*, *š-f-ta*, *sa-pa-ta*, (?) *ša-f-ta* |θapaṭa| → Hoch SWET 278 no. 398; Schneider APÄQ 115f. no 247: *pꜣ -sꜣ-p-w*$_2$*-ty*.
|θ-p-ṭ| **(B)** "threaten, raise a warning"	•CTX: **EUPH** G prefc. *iš-pa-aṭ-ma*, suff. *aš-pu-uṭ-šu-nu-ti*, Dt prefc. *uš-ta-pa-aṭ-ma* → CAD Š/1 451; Durand ARM 26/2 90ff. (323:12); Küpper ARM 28 100f. (70:10); Durand LAPO 17 425 fn. a. •ONOM: **EB** Cf. *iš-bù-du* → Pagan ARES 3 184, 339.
θipṭ "justice, judgement, verdict; warning"	•CTX: **EUPH** Passim; cf. *ši-ip-ṭám*, *ši-ip-ṭà*/*ṭá-am*, *ši-ip-ṭì*/*ṭim*, *ši-ip-ṭi*$_4$*-im*, suff. *ši-ip-ṭà-ṭi-šu-nu* → AHw 1247; CAD Š/3 91ff.; Durand ARM 26/1 163f. (31:17), 196:3', 13'; ARM 26/2 15ff. (285.19'), 85f. (320:5, 9); Durand LAPO 17 343 fn. a; Zadok Fs. Hallo 331 ("threat(ening)"); Streck Onomastikon 1 118 § 2.95. •ONOM: **B** *ši-ip-ta-a-ḫu-um*, *ši-ip-ti-a-ḫa-ar* → Gelb CAAA 33, 195. **A7** Cf. *ši*-BAD(*pít*)-*ra-bi* → Wiseman AT 147; Arnaud AuOr 16 159. **A4** *ši-ip-ti*-ᵈIM, *ši-ip-ti-an-ta*, *ši-ip-ti-ia-an-ta* → Wiseman AT 146; Huffmon

[875] CAD Š/1 451: *šapātu* B "to inform"(?); vacat AHw.

	APNMT 268; Gelb CAAA 33, 195; Arnaud AuOr 16 159; Streck Onomastikon 1 323 § 5.11. **EA** *ši-ip-ṭì/ti₄-*^{d}IM, *ši-ip-ṭú-ri-ṣa* → Sivan GAGl 281; Hess APN 143f. **UGS** *ši-ip-ṭí-ia*; *ši-paṭ-*^{d}IM, *ši-pì-iṭ-*^{d}IM, *ši-ip-ṭì-*^{d}IM, cfr. *ši-* BAD(*píṭ*)-^{d}IM → Gröndahl PTU 199f.; Sivan GAGl 281. **EG** *spd=bʕl* → vSoldt SAU 13 fn. 115; Vita / Galán UF 29 709f. fn. 8.
θapaṭ "judged, passed, proved"	•ONOM: **EUPH** *ša-pa-ta-an* → Huffmon APNMT 268; Gelb CAAA 33, 194; Golinets Onomastikon 2 156, 457, 493, DUL 912f.
θāpiṭ "judge, ruler"	•CTX: **EUPH**, **B** Passim; cf. *ša-pí-ṭú/ṭum*, *ša-pí-ṭa/ ṭám/ṭà-am*, *ša-pí-ṭí/ṭim*, *ša-pí-ṭú-ú/um*, *ša-pí-ṭe₄-em*, *ša-pí-ṭì-im*, *ša-pí-ṭì-ia* → AHw 1173; CAD Š/1 459; Durand ARM 26/1 51:8, 28; ARM 26/2 329:56', 398:18, 435:4; ARM 27 100:29, 151:2; ARM 28 151:27; Lion Amurru 2 142ff., 203ff.; Zadok Fs. Hallo 331. **R** *ša-pí-ṭim*, *ša-pí-ṭum-ma* → AHw 1173; CAD Š/1 459; Dalley / Walker / Hawkins Tell Rimah 296:4, 303:3, 304:3; Streck Onomastikon 1 118 § 2.95. •ONOM: **UGS** *ša-pí-ṭa-na* → Sivan GAGl 282.
θapuṭ "process"	•CTX: **A4** / **B** Cf. *ṭup-pí-ni la ša -pu-ṭí* → Arnaud AuOr 16 164.[876]
θpṭ (A) "lawsuit, judgement"	•CTX: **UGA** → DUL 912f.: *ṯpṭ* (I). •ONOM: **UGA** *ṯpṭbʕl* → DUL 913; *ṯpṭy[* → DUL 913 (bkn?).
θpṭ (B), **θpθ̣** "judge, ruler"	•CTX: **UGA** Sg. *ṯpṭ*, *ṯpẓ*, suff. *ṯpṭn* → DUL 913: *ṯpṭ* (II.
θāpiṭūt "governorship"	•CTX: **EUPH** *ša-pí-ṭú-ut*, *ša-pí-ṭú-ti/tim/tam*, *s*uff. *ša-pí-ṭú-us-sú* → FM 2:76f. (40:15'); FM 8 21:14; Durand ARM 26/1 178ff. (41:12'); Arkhipov ARM 33 429f. (203:10'); Streck Onomastikon 1 118 § 2.95.
mθpṭ, **mθpθ̣** "command, oracle"	•CTX: **UGA**. *mṯpṭk*, sg. cstr. *mṯpẓ* → DUL 597f.: *mṯpṭ/ẓ*. •ONOM: **UGA** *bʕlmṯpṭ* → DUL 207; *mṯpṭ* → DUL 598.

|θ-r| (1)	Etym. unc.; Cf. *šēru*(*m*) (Akk.) "a kind of mat".
θr (C) "a plant or vegetable product" (?)	•CTX: **UGA** → Watson LSU 113: "a mat"; DUL 917: *ṯr* (III) "a plant"(?).

|θ-r| (2)	Etym. unc.
θr (D) "a bird" (?)	•CTX: **UGA** → DUL 917: *ṯr* (IV); mng from ctx.

|θ-r-k|	Sem.: Cf. *šarāku*(*m*) "to present, give", *šerku*(*m*), *širku*(*m*) "gift".
|θ-r-k| "to present"	•ONOM: **UGA** Cf. unc. *ṯrk* → DUL: 917; *ṯrkn* → DUL 917.
θarrāk "openhanded"	•ONOM: **UGS** *šar-ra-ka-nu* → Gröndahl PTU 200.
θirk "a taxe"	•CTX: **UGS** Sg. suff. *ši-ir-ki-ša* → Nougayrol PRU 3 70 (16.276): 10; CAD Š/3 111: *širku* B, 2.

|θ-r-m-l|	Culture word.

[876] Arnaud loc.cit.: "notre tablette est de non-procès"; the text is a mix of Babylonian and a local dialect.

θarmil "a noble material"	•ONOM: **EB** Cf. *sar-mi-lu* → Pagan ARES 3 238, 363: "alabaster". **A7** Cf. *šar-ru-me-(el-)la* → Wiseman AT 146. **UGS** Cf. *šar-mi-la* → Gröndahl PTU 354 (Hurr.?).
θrml "a noble material"	•CTX: **UGA** → DUL 918: *ṯrml*; Bonechi Fs. Buccellati 70f.
|θ-r-n|	Etym. unc. Cf. *šarānu(m)* (Akk.) "a wood; a medicinal plant"; *šurnû* "a medicinal plant".
θrn "a vegetable product" (?)	•CTX: **UGA** → DUL 919: *ṯrn* (I).
|θ-r-p| See **|θ-p-r|**	
|θ-r-r|	Sem.: Cf. *šerru(m)*, *šarrum* (Akk.) "baby, infant".
θerr "baby, infant"	•ONOM: **EB** Cf. *mi-ti-šè-lu* → Pagan ARES 3 239, 351.
θrry (B) "baby, infant"	•ONOM: **UGA** Cf. unc. *ṯrry* → Gröndahl PTU 200; DUL 920: *ṯrry* (II).[877]
|θ-r-t-n-n| Cf. **|s¹-r-d-n|**	Loan. Cf. LÚ *še/irtennu*, *sartennu*, *sartinnu* (Hurr.-Akk.) "chief judge".
θertann "a kind of bailiff / sheriff" (?)	•ONOM: **UGS** Cf. unc. *še-er-da/ta-an-ni* → Nougayrol PRU 3 124:13; 131:5, 257; PRU 4 234:6, 263. Altern. Dietrich / Loretz UF 42 109ff.: "Šerdana".
θrtn "a kind of bailiff / sheriff" (?)	•CTX: **UGA** Pl. *ṯrtnm* → Sanmartín UF 21 345ff.; Richter BGH 543. Altern.: DUL 920: *ṯrtn* "Šerdana".[878]
|θ-r-y| (1)	Sem.: *šarû(m)* (Akk.) "to be(come) rich", *šarû(m)*, *šarium* "rich"; *ṯariya*, *ʔaṯrā* (Arab.) "to become wealthy", *ṯariyy* "wealthy", *ṯarwa*, *ṯarāʔ* "wealth"
θariy "wealthy"	•ONOM: **EB** *ša-rí* → Pagan ARES 184, 367.[879]
θrt "abundance"	•CTX: **UGA** → DUL 920: *ṯrt*.
ʔiθrūt "abundance" (?)	•ONOM: **EB** Cf. *iš*$_{11}$*-ru*$_{13}$*-ud-da-mu*, *iš*$_{11}$*-ru*$_{13}$*-ud-ḫa- lab*$_{x}$ → Fronzaroli ARET 1 8; Bonechi MARI 8 483.
|θ-r-y| (2)	Sem.: Cf. *mšrh* (*mišrāh*, Hb.) "liquid, juice"; *try* (JAram., Syr.) "to soak, to dissolve", *mtrw(tʔ)* (JAram.) "liquid", *trywn(ʔ)*, *myrywnʔ* (Syr.) "piece of bread soaked in water"; *ṯariya*, *ʔaṯrā* (Arab.) "to get damp, wet"; *ṯaran*, *ʔaṯraʔ* "moist earth".
mes¹aru "wetland" (?)	•ONOM: **EG** Cf. elem. *ma-š-r-ru*$_{2}$, *ma-š-r-ʔu-ru*$_{2}$ in / as TN → Hoch SWET 158f. no. 207.[880]

[877] Altern. see |s²-r-r-|.

[878] Altern. cf. Hurr.-Akk. LÚ *sartennu*, *še/irtennu*; Sanmartín UF 21 345ff.; Richter BGH 337f. "chief judge, magistrate".

[879] For the PN *iš*$_{11}$*-ru*$_{12}$*-ud*-DN (Fronzaroli ARES 1 8: |ʔiṯrut=DN| "richesse de DN"; Bonechi MARI 8 483) read rather |yis¹rut=DN|; see here |y-s1-r|.

|θ-t-ʕ|

Sem.: *štʕ* (Hb.) “to be afraid”; *štʕ* (Ph.) “to dread, fear”.

|θ-t-ʕ| “to be frightened, scared”

•CTX: **UGA** G csuff. *ṯtʕ*, suff. *ṯtʕnn* → DUL 921: */ṯ-t-ʕ/*.

|θ-t-ḳ|
Cf. |s^2-ḳ-ḳ|

Sem. etym. unc.[881]

θtḳt “she who splits” (?)

•ONOM: **UGA** *ṯtqt* → DUL 922.

|θ-θ-y|

Culture word, Sem.: Cf. *ššy* (JAram., pl. *ʔšyšyn*) “a type of cake”; *ʔšyšh* (*ʔᵃšîšāh*, Hb.) “raisin cake”.

ʔaθaθu(wā)t “a type of pancake”

•LL: **EB** Cf. SAG.GUR$_8$ = *a-ša-šu-tum*, pl. *a-ša-šu-wa-tum* → Sjöberg Fs. Wilcke 253.

|θ-w-ʕ|

Sem.: *šwʕ* (*šûᵃʕ*, Hb.) “noble, eminent”; *šuwāʔum*, *šuʔu*/*û* (Akk.) “master, lord”.

θuwʕ “hero, noble; DN”
θʕ (B) “hero, noble (as title); DN”

•ONOM: **EUPH** *šu-ḫu-um*, *šu-uḫ-ma-ba-il*, *al-la-šu-ḫu*, fem. *šu-ḫa-tum* → Gelb CAAA 195 (ŠUʔḪ); Zadok Fs. Hallo 331.
•CTX: **UGA** Sg. *ṯʕ*, suff. *ṯʕh*, pl. *ṯʕm* → DUL 879f.: *ṯʕ* (II).

|θ-w-b|

Sem.: *šwb* (Hb.) “to turn back, return”, (D) “to requite, restore”, (C) “to reverse, answer”; *šb* (Moab.) id.; *twb* (Aram., Syr., Nab.) id., (Aram., Syr. C) “to restore, answer”, *twb* “turning back, reply”, *šybh* (Aram.) “restoration”; *šâbu*(*m*) (Akk.) “to tremble, quake”, (D) “to make vacillate”; *ṯāba* (*ṯawb*, Arab.) “to return”, *ṯawwaba* “to reward, repay”; *ṯwb* (OSArab.) “to return, render; to succeed, torn over”.

|θ-w-b| “to return, turn round, attend to, pardon; to vacillate”

•CTX: **EB** G prefc. *iš-šu-bù* |yiθūb| → Catagnoti QuSe 29 161, 233.[882]
UGA G prefc. *ṯtb*, *ṯtbn*, *yṯb*, *yṯbn*, *nṯb* (?), suffc. *ṯb*, imp. *ṯb*; inf. suff. (?) *ṯby*, *ṯbh*; D prefc. *ṯṯbb*; C prefc. *tṯṯb*, *yṯṯb*, *tṯṯbn*, imp. *ṯṯb* inf. *ṯṯb* → DUL 882f.: */ṯ-b/*.
EG Cf. *sa-wa-bi-bi* |θawbib| → Hoch SWET 256f. no. 360.[883]
•ONOM: **EB** *a-šu-bu*$_{16}$(NI), *a-šu-bù* → Pagan ARES 3 179, 283.
U3 *šu-bi-ga-ra-ad* → Gelb CAAA 33 (ŠWB), 195 (vacat Buccellati Amorites).
EUPH, B *ia-šu-ba*, *ta-šu-ba*, *ia-šu-bu-um*, *ia-su-bi-im*, *ta-šu-ba-tum*, *ia-šu-ba-an*, *ia-šu-ub-a-du*, *ia-šu-ub-a-šar*, *e-šu-ub*-DINGIR, *ie-e-šu-bi*-DINGIR, *ia-šu-ub*-DINGIR, *ia-šu-ub-*^{d}*da-gan*, *ia-šu-ub-*^{d}IM, *ia-šu-ub-*^{d}*i-pi-uḫ*, *ia-šu-ub-*^{d}*ma-lik*, *ia-šu-ub-ia-ḫa-ad*, *i-šu-ub-ya-ʔà-ad*, *i-*<*šu-*>*ub-*^{d}*nu-nu*, ia-*šu-ub-ḫa-al*, *ia-šu-ub-li-im*, *ia-šu-ub-na-ar*, *ta-šu-ub-na-wu*, *a-šu-ub-la*, *a-šu-ub-la-nim*, *a-šu-ub-la-*

---

880 Altern. “plain”, from |y-s^1-r / w-ṯ-r| “to be level”, Hoch loc.cit.

881 Phonol. unrelated to Aram. *sd*/*tq*, Eth. *śaṭaqa* “to split”, Arab. *šaqqa*“to split”. Folk etymological echoing of these bases should not be excluded.

882 Formerly read *iš-da-bù* |yiṯṯab| by Fronzaroli ARET 13 174, 273; see also Rubio PIHANS 106 122 fn. 38.

883 Sivan / Cochavi-Rainey WSVES 84: *śá-wa-bí-bi* “to turn”; Helck Beziehungen no. 189: “Umweg machen”.

DINGIR, *a-šu-ub-la-el*, *a-šu-ub-li-el*, *šu-ub-*^{d}*i-la*, *šu-ba*-DINGIR.DINGIR, *šu-ub-ni*-DINGIR, *šu-ba-ni*-DINGIR, *šu-bi-*^{d}IM, *šu-ub-na*-DINGIR, *šu-ub-na-il*, *šu-ub-ba-ḫi-lu*, *šu-ub-na-lu-ú*, *šu-bu-ra-bu* → Huffmon APNMT 266; Gelb CAAA 33, 193, 195; Zadok Fs. Hallo 331; Streck Onomastikon 1 214f. § 2.111f., 306 § 3.72; Golinets Onomastikon 2 291f., 295, 297, 458.
A7 *ia-ši-bi-il*, *ia-ši-ib*-DINGIR, *a-ši-bi-i-la*, *ia-šu-ub-ra-bi*, *su-ub-ḫa-li*, *šu-ba-ḫa-li*, *su-ba/pa-ḫa-li*, *šu-ba-am-mi* → Wiseman AT 136f., 145; Gelb CAAA 33, 195; Sivan GAGl 157, 178, 282; Arnaud AuOr 16 177; Streck Onomastikon 1 207 § 2.101f. fn. 3; Golinets Onomastikon 2 290ff., 297, 458.
TU *ta-šu-ub-ša-ki-ni* → Krebernik Tall Bi`a 228; Golinets Onomastikon 2 294, 484.
A4 *a-šu-ub-i-la*, *šu-bi*$_4$*-ia*, *šu-bi-la* → Wiseman AT 147; Gelb CAAA 33, 193; Sivan GAGl 282; Arnaud AuOr 16 177, 181; Golinets Onomastikon 2 291, 485.
EA *šu-ba-an-du/di* → Sivan GAGl 204, 222, 282; Moran AmL 384; Hess APN 144f., 213; Golinets Onomastikon 2 458.
EG Elem. in PN, TN, DN: *s-bi*$_4$, *s-b*, *sa-bi*$_3$, *s-ba*, *sa-b*, *s-bi*$_4$ |θāba, θuba| → Hoch SWET 258 no. 364; *sꜣ-b-y*$_2$*-y-ꜣ* → Schneider APÄQ 181 no. 382. Unc. *ya-ši*$_2$*-p*, *ya-ši*$_2$*-pi* → Hoch SWET 56 no. 60 (|yaθib| / |yaθub| ?. Altern. see |w-θ-b|).
UGS *ia-šu-ub*-DINGIR, *šu-bu-ia*, *šub-am-mu*, *šu-ub-am-mu*, *šu-ba-ʔa-mu*, *šu-ba-an-tu* → Gelb CAAA 33 (ŠWB), 195; Gröndahl PTU 200, 299; Sivan GAGl 282; Golinets Onomastikon 2 297, 458.
UGA: *ṯbil* → DUL 883: *ṯbil* (I);[884] *ṯbʕm* → DUL 884; *ṯbʕnq* → DUL 884; *ṯbln* → DUL 884; *ṯby* → DUL 886.

θuwb "return"
•CTX: **EM** Cf. *šu-bi* → Zadok AION 51 119; Pentiuc Vocabulary 173: *šu*-BI "?".

θawb "attending to, devoted towards"
•ONOM: **EUPH**, **B** *ša-bi*-DINGIR, *sa-ba-a-ú-um*, *ša-a-bi*-É, *ša-bi-pí*-DINGIR → Gelb CAAA 33, 193; Streck Onomastikon 1 329 § 5.25; Golinets Onomastikon 2 302, 458.
A4 *ša-bi*$_4$*-lu*, *ša-bi-i-la* → Wiseman AT 145; Sivan GAGl 282; AuOr 16 178, 181.
EA Cf. *ša-bi*-DINGIR → Sivan GAGl 282; Moran AmL 384; Hess APN 138f., 213.
UGS *ša-bi*-DINGIR, *ša-bi*-DINGIR-lì, *šá-bi*$_4$*-ya*, *ša-ba-i-ni-qi* → Gröndahl PTU 200f.; Rainey UF 3 164.; Sivan GAGl 157, 82.

θb "repetition, intercalary month"
•CTX: **UGA** → DUL 883: *ṯb*.

|θ-w-r|

Primary noun, Sem.: *šwr* (*šôr*, Hb.) "bovid (one single beast)"; *twrʔ* (Palm.) "bull, ox"; *swr*, *šwr*, *twr*(*ʔ*) (Aram.; Syr.) "bull, ox"; *šūru*(*m*) (Akk.) "bull"; *ṯawr* (Arab.) "bull, steer, ox"; *ṯr*, *ṯwr* (OSArab.) "bull, steer"; *ṯawr*, *ṯawer* (MSArab.) "bull"; *sor* (Eth.) "ox, bull".
Non-Sem.: *šsr* (Eg.) "bull (for slaughtering)"; **tawVr=* ·(West Chadic) "bull"; (East Chadic) "cow, antelope".[885]

Suwr, θuwr "bull; DN"
•LL: **EB** GU$_4$.TUR =*šu-lum* → Krebernik ZA 73 23f. fn. 78: |θō/ūr=|.
•ONOM: **EB** *šu-ra*, *su-rí-a*, *šu-ru*$_{12}$, AD-*su-ra*, *šu-ra-da-mu*, KU(*dúr*?)*-ra-da-mu*, *šu-ra-ga-mu*, *šu-ra-ma-lik*, HIxMAŠ(*sur*$_x$)*-kam*$_4$, *šu-ra-gàr-ru*$_{12}$, KU(*dúr*?)*-ra-gàr-ru*$_{12}$ → Pagan ARES 3 238f., 286, 304, 365, 368.[886]

---

[884] Cf. the TN *ṯbil* (*Ṯabaʔil*), Belmonte RGTC 12/2 299; DUL 883: *ṯbil* (II).
[885] Orel / Stolbova HSED 112: **čawVr=* / **čVr=* "bull".

	EUPH, **B** *šu-ra-nu*, *ab-du-šu-ri-im* → Zadok Fs. Hallo 331. **R** *ab-du-šu-ri* → Dalley / Walker / Hawkins Tell Rimah 257; Gelb CAAA 33, 195. **EM** *šu-ri* → Pruzsinszky PTEm 177 [758].
θr (B) "bull; DN"	•CTX: **UGA** Sg. *ṯr*, pl. *ṯrm*, cstr. *ṯr*, suff. *ṯry*, *ṯrh* → DUL 916: *ṯr* (I). •ONOM: **UGA** Cf. unc. *ỉlṯr* → DUL 65; *ṯr* → DUL 917: *ṯr* (II), *ṯr* (V). Cf. unc. *šr* → DUL 830: *šr* (VII).[887]

|θ-w-y|	Sem.: *ṯawā* (*ṯwy*, Arab.) "to stay, live, settle down".
|θ-w-y| "come to a halt, live, to stay"	•CTX: **EB** G prefc. *i-ša* |yiθawway|, Gt prefc. *iš*$_{11}$*-da-wa* |yiθtawwayay| → Milano ARET 9 17 r. IV 10; Fronzaroli ARET 11 90, 155; Catagnoti QuSe 29 39, 143, 161, 164f., 234. **UGA** D prefc. *ṯṯwy* → DUL 925: /*ṯ-w-y*/. •ONOM: **EG** Cf. *sꜣ-w-y*$_2$*-ty* → Schneider APÄQ 180 no. 381.

|θ-y-n|	Sem.:[888] *šyn* (ptc *maštîn*, Hb. Gt / C *štn*?) "to pass water, urinate", *šyn* (*šayin*) "urine"; *twn* (Syr.) "to urinate", *štn* (JAram. C) "to urinate", *twn*(*ʔ*) (JAram., Syr.) "urine", *tyn*(*ʔ*) (Syr.) "urine", *tʔnh*, *tʔntʔ* (Syr.) "urine"; *šânu* (Akk). "to urinate", *šatānu* (*šiānum* Gt) id., *šīnātu*(m) "urine", *muštin*(*n*)*u*(*m*) "urethra"; *śyn*, *śena* (Eth.)[889] "to urinate", *śənt* "urine"; see also: *maṯāna* (Arab.) "bladder". Non-Sem.: **kV=ʒin=H=* (West Chadic) "urine".[890]
|θ-y-n| "to urinate"	•CTX: **UGA** Gt prefc. (|θ-y-n|) / altern. G prefc. (|θ-t-n|) *yṯtn* → DUL 905: /*ṯ-n*/; Tropper UG 526, 650.
θnt "urine"	•CTX: **UGA** → DUL 910: *ṯnt* (II).[891]

---

[886] See also Pasquali NABU 2018/39 fn. 7. For an altern. rdg of the elems *šu*/KU-*ra* as |θuγra| (DN: "victoire, arme victorieuse") see Bonechi MARI 8 500, and here |θ-γ-r| (2).

[887] All PNN entries perhaps from Hurr.-Akk. *šarr(i)* (Gröndahl PTU 249); see here *ðr*, *θr* (A) (|s²-r-r|). See further |θ-r| (3).

[888] Hb., Akk. and some JAram. vb. themes only Gt (respect. reflexive infix =t=). For Ug. see *yṯtn* (|θ-y-n / |θ-t-n|, CTX: UGA).

[889] Irregular consonantism; read probl. **syn*.

[890] Orel / Stolbova HSED 546 no. 2627: **ʒinaʔ=* "urine".

[891] For an unkn. commodity *ṯnt* see DUL 910 *ṯnt* (I).

θ̣ (ẓ)

|θ̣-b-y|	
|θ̣-h-r|	Cf. **|ṣ-ħ-r|**
|θ̣-l-l-|	
|θ̣-l-m|	See **|γ-l-m| (2)**; cf. **|ṣ-l-m|**
|θ̣-m-ʔ|	
|θ̣-p-n|	Cf. **|ṣ-p-n| (1)**
|θ̣-p-r|	Cf. **|ṣ-p-r|**
|θ̣-r-r|	See **|θ̣-w-r|**
|θ̣-w-r|	See **|θ̣-r-r|**
|θ̣-y|	

|θ̣-b-y|

Primary noun, Sem.: *ṣby* (*ṣ*^e^*bî̂y*, Hb.) "gazelle", *ṣbyh* (*ṣ*^e^*bîyyāh*) "female gazelle"; *ṣby*, *ṭby*(*?*) (Aram., Syr.) "gazelle, deer"; *ṣabītu*(*m*) (Akk.) "gazelle"; *ẓaby* (Arab.) "gazelle", *ẓabya* "female gazelle"; *ṣby* (OSArab.) "gazelles", cf. *ẓby* "kind of she-camel > 'gazelle-aged'".

θ̣abayt "gazelle" — •LL: **EB** *za-ba-a-tum* → Krebernik ZA 73 42; PIHANS 106 92; Sjöberg Fs. Pettinato 275.

θ̣abiy, θ̣abiyat "gazelle" — •ONOM: **EUPH** Cf. *za-bu-um*, *za-bu-ú-um*, *za-bi-ia-tum* → Gelb CAAA 196 (ṢABU?); Knudsen PIHANS 100 322 fn. 12.[892]

θ̣by "gazelle" — •CTX: **UGA** Pl. *ẓbm* (?), suff. *ẓbyy*, *ẓbyh* → DUL 986: *ẓby*; for *ẓbm* seeTropper UG 114, 198, 295.

|θ̣-h-r|
Cf. |ṣ-ħ-r|

Primary noun, Sem.: *ṣhr* (*ṣōhar*, Hb.) "roof"; *ṣēru*(*m*) (Akk.) "back, upperside";[893] *ẓahr* (Arab.) "back".

---

[892] For U3 *za-bí* see Buccellati Amorites 179, and here |ṣ-b-y|.

[893] For the distinction of two different lexemes in Akk. (*ṣēru* "back" < |θ̣-h-r|, and *ṣēru* "steppe, open country" < |ṣ-ħ-r|) see Whiting Or 50 17 fn. 71.

θ̣ahr "back"	•LL: **EB** MURGU = *za-lum* → Krebernik ZA 73 47. •ONOM: **EB** Cf. *za-lum, za-ʔà-la, za-a-rí-im, za-a-rúm* → Pagan ARES 3 241f., 382f.
θ̣uhr "back"	CTX: **EA** *ṣe-ru-ma :ṣú-uḫ-ru-ma* (64:7; 65:5; 232:11), *ṣú-ri-ia* (147:39), *ṣ[ú]-ru-ma* (281:7) → AHw 1115: *ṣuʔru, ṣūru*; CAD Ṣ 261: *ṣūru*; Sivan GAGl 131, 270; Izre'el Orient 38 68, 76; Rainey CAT 1 20; 3 232.[894]
θ̣r "back"	•CTX: **UGA** Sg. cstr. *ẓr*, suff. *ẓrh* → DUL 988: *ẓr* (I). •ONOM: **UGA** Cf. unc. *ẓrm* → DUL 988.
|θ̣-l-l|	Primary noun, Sem.: *ṣl* (*ṣēl*) "shadow, protection", *ṣll* (C) "to give shade"; *ṭwl(?)*, *ṭll(?)* (Aram.) "shadow, shade; protection", *ṭll* (Aram., Syr., D, C) "to cast shade on, roof over"; *ṣillu(m)* (Akk.) "shadow, shade; protection", *ṣallulu* (D), *ṣullulu(m)* "to roof over, cover"; *ẓill* (Arab.) "shadow", *ẓallala* "to shade, overshadow", *ẓalīl* "shady"; *ẓll* (OSArab.) "shelter, covered structure"; *aẓlēl* (MSArab.) "to make shade"; *ṣəlālot* (Eth.) "shade", *ṣll, ṣallala, ṣalala* "to (make) shade, to be shady, to darken, cover".
θ̣ill "shade, protection; DN"	•ONOM: **EB** Passim *zi-la*=DN; cf. *zi-la, zi-lu, zi-la-ì, zi-la-il, zi-lu-su*-DÙG, *a-mi-zi-lí, zé-ìl-da-mu, zi-il*-DÙG, *zi-la*-NE(*še*$_{6}$)-*gi*; passim abbrev. =*zé*, =*zi*,[895] cf. e.g. *a-bù-zi, gú-ra-zi, gul-zé, i-rí-ig-zé, i-sar-zé, in-zé, ìr-ʔa*$_{5}$*-zé, kùn-zé, šè-íb-zé* → Krebernik PET 110f.; Pagan ARES 3 200, 275, 280, 314f., 325, 337, 344, 367, 384, 386f. **EUPH**, **B** Cf. *zi-la-an, zi-il-la-an, ṣíl-lí-ak-ka, ṣíl-lí-i-da, ṣíl-lí-ba-aḫ-li, ṣíl-lí-*^{d}*ḫa-na-at, ṣíl-lí-an-nu, ka-ma-zi-lum, ku-mu-zi-li, ṭà-ab-ṣi-lu-ú* → Huffmon APNMT 257; Gelb CAAA 34, 197 (ṢILL); Streck Onomastikon 1 182 § 2.66, 201 § 2.95. **A7** *zi-il-la-ad-du*, GA(*kà*)-*bar-zi-li* (first element surely dialectal) → Gelb CAAA 34, 197 (ṢILL); Arnaud AuOr 16 159; Streck Onomastikon 1 203 § 2.95. **A4** *zi-il-lu, zi-il-e, zi-li-ia, zi-il-la-nu* → Wiseman AT 153; Dietrich / Loretz ZA 60 90 1:7; WO 5 64 8:30; Sivan GAGl 295; Arnaud AuOr 16 159. **EM** *ṣil-la, ṣíl-la-*^{d}*ba-aḫ-la-ka, ṣíl-la-da, ṣíl-la-ḫa-li, ṣíl-la-*^{d}*u*$_{4}$*-ḫa, ṣi-li-*^{d}EN, *ṣíl-lu-ud-da, ṣíl-lu-*^{d}*da-gan*; cf. ŠAMÁN-*la*, ŠAMÁN-*la*-^{d}IŠKUR, ŠAMÁN-^{d}UTU, ŠAMÁN-*lu*-^{d}*da-gan* → Pruzsinszky PTEm 95, 711f.; Fleming JAOS 124 598ñ **EG** Cf. *ty-:r, ty-r-y* → Schneider APÄQ 235 no. 500-501.
θ̣alil "shady, umbrageous" (?)	•ONOM: **B** Cf. *za-li-lum/li* → Gelb CAAA 34, 196 (ṢALIL).
θ̣l "shade, reflection sheen, spirit"	•CTX: **UGA** Sg. *ẓl*, pl. *ẓlm*, allomorph sg. / pl. cstr. *zl* → DUL 986f.: *ẓl* (I). •ONOM: **UGA** Cf. unc. *ẓl* → DUL 987: *ẓl* (II); *ẓll* → DUL 987: *ẓll*.
|θ̣-l-m| See |**γ-l-m**| **(2)**; cf. |**ṣ-l-m**|	Sem.: Cf. *ṣlmwt* (*ṣalmāwet* < **ṣalmût*, Hb.) "gloom"; *ṣalāmu(m)* (Akk.) "to be black, dark", *ṣalmu(m)* "black, dark", *ṣulmu(m)* "blackness, black spot"; *ẓalima* (Arab.) "to be dark, gloomy", *ẓulma* "gloom", *ʔaẓlam* "darker", *ʔiẓlām* "gloom", *muẓlim* "gloomy"; *ṣalma, ṣalama* (Eth.) "to be black, grow dark", *ṣəlum* "dark, obscured, blinded", *ṣallim* "black, dark, gloomy", *ṣəlmat* "darkness".[896]

---

894 Cf. *i-na* KUR.ḪÁ *ṣu-uh-ri* (145:22), Moran AmL 231 n. 5: "in the hinterlands" / "back-lands" / provinces?; diff. Rainey CAT 3 319: "in the lands of Ṣuḫri".

895 Altern. see *zé*=, *zi*=, |w-θ̣-ʔ|.

896 Unrelated: *ṭlm* (JAram., Syr.) "to oppress"; *ẓalama* (Arab.) "to wrong".

θ̣alm "black, dark, gloomy"	•ONOM:[897] **U3** *ṣa-al-ma-nu-um* → Owen JCS 33 257; Zadok Fs. Hallo 332. **EM** Cf. *ṣa-al-mu/mi* → Arnaud AuOrS (1) 189; Pruzsinszky PTEm 95 (*Ẓ/Ṣalmu*) [709: "Schwarzer", Akk.][898] **A4** Cf. *zal-ma* → Dietrich / Loretz UF 1 40 (207:77); Sivan GAGl 268 (ṢALMU "image"). **UGS** Cf. dIM-*ṣa-al-mì* → Gröndahl PTU 188 (ṢLM I "Bild"); Sivan GAGl 268 (ṢALMU "image").
θ̣lmt "darkness"	•CTX: **UGA** → DUL 987: *ẓlmt*.

|θ̣-m-ʔ|	Sem.: *ṣmʔ* (Hb.) "to thirst, be thirsty", *ṣmʔ* (*ṣāmāʔ*) "thirst", (*ṣāmēʔ*) "thirsty"; *ṣamû(m)*, *ṣamāʔu* (Akk.) "to be(come) thirsty, to thirst for", *ṣamû(m)* "thirsty"; *ẓamiʔa* (Arab.) "to be(come) thirsty"; *ẓmʔ* (OSArab.) "to be(come) thirsty"; *ẓáyma*, *ṭáyme* (MSArab.) "to be(come) thirsty", *ẓawma* "thirst"; *ṣamʔa* (Eth.) "to be(come) thirsty", *məṣmāʔ* "parched place".
|**θ̣-m-ʔ**| "to be thirsty, parched"	•CTX: **EG** *ḏa-ma-{ʕ}ʕu* (|tamiʔa|) → Hoch SWET 386 no. 581. •ONOM: **B** Cf. *za-ma-a-a-tum* (ZAMAʔ) → Gelb CAAA 202; Zadok Fs. Hallo 332 (Ẓ-M-Y).[899]
|**γ-m-ʔ**| "to be thirsty"	•CTX: **UGA** G suffc. *ġmỉt*; inf. *ġmủ* → DUL 318; Tropper UG 94.
θ̣amiʔ "thirsty"	•CTX: **EG** Adj. fem. *ḏa-ma-t* (θ̣amêtu|) → Hoch SWET 386 no. 581. •ONOM: **EB** *za-mi-ù*[*-X*] → Pagan ARES 3 171, 383.
mθ̣mủ "thirsty"	•CTX: **UGA** Sg. accus. *mẓmả* → DUL 600.

|θ̣-p-n| Cf. **|ṣ-p-n| (1)**	Sem.: *ṣpn* (Hb.) "to hide, keep, store"; *ṣpn* (Aram. C) "to hide".
|**θ̣-p-n**| "to hide, shelter"	•CTX: **UGA** G prefc. *tẓpn* → DUL 988: */ẓ-p-n/*.

|θ̣-p-r| Cf. **|ṣ-p-r|**	Primary noun, Sem.: *ṣprn* (*ṣipporen*, Hb.) "(finger- / toe)nail"; *ṭpr* (Aram., Syr.) "(finger- / toe)nail, hoof"; *ṣupru(m)*, *ṣupuru* (Akk.) "(finger- / toe)nail, claw, hoof"; *ẓufur*, *ẓufr*, *ẓifr* (Arab.) "(finger- / toe)nail, claw"; *ẓfēr*, *ẓífər*, *ṭayfēr* (MSArab.) "(finger- / toe)nail, claw"; *ṣəfr* (Eth.) "fingernail, claw".
θ̣upr "nail, claw, hoof"	•CTX: **EM** Cf. unc. pl. |θ̣uparāt| d*iš8-tár ṣu-pa-r*[*a-ti*], dINANNA *ṣu-pá-ra-ti*, cf. ḪUR.SAG *ṣu-pa-r*[*a-ti*] → Diff.: Arnaud EMAR 6/3 375 (379:6), Arnaud Emar 6/3 268 (274:8), Arnaud Emar 6/3 431 (452:29'):TN *Ṣuparatu*; Fleming Installation 272, 298: id.; Pentiuc Vocabulary 164f.: "goats". •ONOM: **EUPH**, **B** Cf. *zu-up-rum*, *zu-up-ra-an*, *zu-up-ri-e-ra-aḫ* → Huffmon APNMT 258; Gelb CAAA 34, 198. **UGS** Cf. ZUM(*ṣu*)*-pa-ri*, ZUM(*ṣu*)*-pa-ra-nu* → Gröndahl PTU 73, 190; Sivan GAGl 270: ṢŪPARU "siren, hooter".
θ̣pr "(sharp) claw(ed)"	•CTX: **UGA** Cf. unc. *klb ṣpr* → Diff.: DUL 777f. "bird". •ONOM: **UGA** *ṣpr* → DUL 778: *ṣpr* (II), *ṣprn* → DUL 778.

---

[897] Many if not all PNN instances could be just Akk. *ṣalmu(m)* "black, dark" (as *ṣa-al-mV* in EA 7:73, 80; see Hess APN 137; Moran AmL 384) or derivatives (*ṣalm* "image, likeness") from the basis \|ṣ-l-m\|.

[898] Altern. cf. Arnaud SEL 8 33: "brave, bravoure", as in *ṣālim* (Arab.) "fearless, courageous man". See also Stark PNPI 47, 109: Palm. PN *ṣlmʔ/y* "strong man".

[899] Cf. Gelb CAAA 203: **B** *iz-me*-DINGIR (ZMEʔ).

|θ̣-r-r| See **|θ̣-w-r|**	Culture word, Sem.:*ṣr* (*ṣor*, pl. *ṣ^{e}rôrôt*, Hb.) "flint"; *ṭynr(ʔ)* (JAram.) "flint, rock", *ṭrn(ʔ)* (Syr.) "rock, flint"; *ṣurru(m)* (Akk.) "obsidian, flint"; *ẓirr* (Arab.) "sharp-edged stone, flint".
θ̣arir "sharp blade"	•LL: **EB** Cf. "GIŠGAL" = *da-ri-du-um* |θ̣arirt=| (fem.) → Fronzaroli Fs. Cohen 228f. + fn. 34; Catagnoti QuSe 29 121, 233.
θ̣urrān "flint"	•LL: **EB** KA.GÍR:GAL = *zu-ra-nu-um* → Conti QuSe 17 99.

|θ̣-w-r| See **|θ̣-r-r|**	Sem.:[900] *ṣ(w)r* (*ṣūr*, Hb.) "rock, hill, mountain"; *ṭwr(ʔ)* (JAram., Syr.) "mountain"; *ṣūru(m)* (Akk.) "cliff, rock"; *ẓrn* (*ẓwr*, OSArab) "rock".
θ̣uwr "rock, mountain"	•ONOM: **EUPH**, **B** Passim; cf. *zu-ra-a, zu-ri-ia, zu-ra-ta-an, zu-ra-ta-nu, zu-ra-ḫa-am-mu, zu-ri-ḫa-am-mu(-ú), zu-ri-^{d}da-gan, zu-ri-*^{d}IM, *zu-ri-*DINGIR, *zu-ri-la-ri-im, zu-ri-e-ra-aḫ, a-be-zu-ra, a-bi-ṣu-ra, a-bi-zu-ri, am-mi-zu-ra, ḫa-am-mi/mu-zu-ri, ḫa-a-ià-zu-ru, i-la-zu-ur, ^{d}iš-ḫa-ra-zu-ri,* ^{d}ÍD-*zu-ri, ša-ra-ṣur-ru-um, ka-zu-ri-ḫa-la, ka-zu-ra-*DINGIR → Huffmon APNMT 258; Gelb CAAA 34, 197f. (ṢUWR); Zadok Fs. Hallo 332; Streck Onomastikon 1 117 § 1.95; 204 §2.96 fn. 1, 229 § 2.138, 258 § 3.4 fn. 1, 270 § 3.18, 281 § 3.40, 324 § 5.14; Gray NABU 2019/62. **A7** *il-ab-zu-ra* → Arnaud AuOr 16 154. **EA** *ṣú-ra-šar* → Hess APN 138, 210, 325; Moran AmL 384, 387; Zadok JSOAS 59 131.
γuwr "rock, mountain"	•ONOM: **EB** Cf. unc. *ḫu-ra-na-dum* → Pagan ARES 3 214, 319.[901]
γr (A) "mountain; DN"	•CTX: **UGA** Sg. *ġr*, suff. *ġry, ġrk, ġrh*, pl. *ġrm* → DUL 319f.: *ġr* (I). •ONOM: **UGA** Elem. in TN *ġr* → DUL 321: *ġr* (VI); elem. in PN *ġrn* → DUL 322.
γr (D) "an installation for the funerary cult"	•CTX: **UGA** → 320: *ġr* (II); etym. connection unc.
γrt "rock" (?)	•CTX: **UGA** Sg. / pl. *ġrt* → DUL 322: *ġrt* (I). •ONOM: **UGA** Cf. PN *ġrt* → DUL 322: *ġrt* (II).

|θ̣-y|	Primary noun, Sem.: Hb. *ṣʔh* (*ṣoʔāh, ṣēʔāh*, Hb.) "dung, excrement"; *zû(m)* (Akk.) "excrement", *ezûm, teṣû(m), tezû(m)* "to defecate", *nezû* "to void (urine, excrement)"; see *ẓiya* (Arab.) "putrefying body"; *ẓyw* (OSArab.) "to putrefy" (?), *ṣyy* (*ystṣyn*) "to stink"; *ḏ̣áwya, ḏ̣éʔ, ṭéʔa* MSArab. "to smell, scent"; *ṣyʔ, ṣeʔa, ḍeʔa* (Eth.) "to rot, putrefy, stink", *ṣiʔ* "bad smell", *ṣiʔat* "rot, filth, excrement".
θ̣ủ "secretion, excrement"	•CTX: **UGA** Sg. suff. *ẓủh* → DUL 986: *ẓủ*.

[900] Probl. a secondary lexicalization of \|θ̣-r-r\|; see Fronzaroli Studi 271, 287, 298; Kogan Classification 203.

[901] Normalized ibid. \|γūra=naʔdum\| "exalted is the mountain". But for Ebla the phonetic neighbourhood of interdentals and laterals (as it is the case in Ugaritic; Tropper UG 94f.) remains unproved.

W

|w|	
|w-ʔ-r|	
|w-ʕ-b|	
|w-ʕ-d|	Cf. |ʕ-w-d| (1)
|w-ʕ-l| (1)	
|w-ʕ-l| (2)	
|w-ʕ-r| (1)	
|w-ʕ-r| (2)	
|w-ʕ-y|	
|w-b-ʔ|	Cf. |b-h-m| (2)
|w-b-l| (1)	
|w-b-l| (2)	
|w-b-m|	
|w-b-r|	Cf. |H-b-r| (2)
|w-d-ʕ|	
|w-d-d|	
|w/y-D-n|	See |n/w/y-D-n|
|w-d-y| (1)	Cf. |n-d-y|
|w-d-y| (2)	
|w-d-y| (3)	
|w-ð-ʕ|	
|w-ð-y|	
|w-g-ʕ|	
|w-g-r|	
|w-γ-l|	
|w-h-b|	
|w-ħ-l|	
|w-h-y|	
|w-ħ-d|	
|w-ħ-m|	Cf. |ħ-m-m|
|w-ħ-y|	
|w-x-m|	
|w-x-z|	
|w-k-l|	
|w-k-y|	
|w-ḳ-h|	
|w-ḳ-r|	
|w-ḳ-y|	
|w-l-d|	
|w-l-θ|	
|w-l-y|	
|w-m-ʔ|	
|w-n-y|	
|w-p-d|	
|w-p-θ|	
|w-p-y|	Cf. |p-h-y|, |w-h-b|, |y-p-ʕ|
|w-r-ʔ|	
|w-r-d| (1)	
|w-r-d| (2)	
|w-r-x|	
|w-r-k|	
|w-r-ḳ|	
|w-r-r|	
|w-r-s| (1)	
|w-r-S| (2)	
|w-r-θ| (1)	Cf. |r-S-y|
|w-r-θ| (2)	
|(w/y)-r-θ|	Cf. |s-r-θ|
|w-r-w/y|	Cf. |t-r-w|
|w-r-y| (1)	
|w-r-y| (2)	
|w-r-y| (3)	See |w-r-w/y|
|w-s-d|	See |ʔ/y-S-D|, |s^1-t|
|w-s-m|	
|w-s-n|	
|w-s-r|	
|w-ṣ-b|	Cf. |n-ṣ-b|
|w-ṣ-r|	
|w-ṣ-y|	
|w-s^1-m|	See |ʔ/w-s^1-m|
w-s^1-n|	
|w-s^1-p|	
|w-s^1-r|	
|w-s^1-ṭ|	
|w-ṣ́-ʔ|	Cf. |w-ṣ́-ʕ|
|w-ṣ́-ʕ|	Cf. |w-ṣ́-ʔ|
|w-ṣ́-ħ|	
|w-t-H|	

|w-t-n| See **|n/w/y-D-n|**
|w-t-r| (1)
|w-t-r| (2)
|w-θ-b|
|w-θ-ḳ|
|w-θ-r|
|w-y-n|
|w-z-n|
|w-z-r|

|w|

Sem.: *w* (West Sem. languages) "and"; see *w* (*w^e^*, *wa*, *wā*, Hb.; Aram., Syr.); *U*, *Y*, *UY* (Pun.); *wʔ* (Samalian); *ú-ma-ʔ* (Warka-Aram.). Other Sem. areas: *u* (Akk.; occasionally OAss. *wa*) "and, but, also, then"; *wa* (Arab.) id.;. *w* (OSArab.) id.; *w*, *əw*, *wə* (MSArab.) id.; *wa* (Eth.) id.

wa "and (also); namely, or (else)"
●CTX: **EB** *wa*, *wa-a* (rdg *wa^a^*), Ù, suff. *ù-ma* → Hecker EdA 240 fn. 81; Fronzaroli QuSe 15 5ff.; Krebernik ZA 72 221; ARET 11 173, 175ff., 181; 179; 13 305, 310, 314, 317; Catagnoti Fronzaroli ARET 16 273f., 276ff., 285, 289; Catagnoti QuSe 29 87, 99f., 106f., 111, 116, 234.
UGS Cf. PI(*wa*?) → Huehnergard UVST 122.

w "and (also); namely, or (else)"
●CTX: **UGA** *w*, *wn* → DUL 926ff.

|w-ʔ-r|

Sem.: (*w*)*âru*(*m*), (*m*)*aʔāru*, *mâru* (Akk.) "to go (up to)", (*w*)*uʔʔurtu*(*m*), (*w*)*ûrtu*(*m*), *mûrtu* "commission, command".

|w-ʔ-r| "to go, approach; to send"
●CTX: **EUPH** (*wêrum*?); cf. e.g. G inf. *we-e-ra-am* → Birot ARM 14 22f. (2:31).[902]
A7 Cf. D prefc. *ú-wa-ru-šu* → Lauinger STOBA 324 (55 obv. 14).

waʔr "way(s), instruction(s); journey"
●CTX: **EB** Suff. *a-lu-na-a* |waʔr=nay(n)| → Fronzaroli ARET 13 22, 243; Catagnoti QuSe 29 73, 234.
●LL: **EB** DI.DI = *a-lu-um* → Conti QuSe 17 198.

|w-ʕ-b|

Sem.: Cf. *waʕaba* (Arab.) "to take the whole", *waʕib* "ample, wide".

yaʕ(a)b "ample, wide"
●ONOM: **Tall Hadidi** Elem. in TN URU *ia-aḫ-bi* → Belmonte RGTC 12/2 337: **yaʕbā*(*yu*).

yʕb "ample, wide"
●ONOM: **UGA** Elem. in DN *yʕbdr* → DUL 932. Cf. PN *yʕbd* → DUL 932; TN *yʕby* → DUL 933.

|w-ʕ-d|
Cf. **|ʕ-w-d| (1)**

Sem.: Cf. *ʕdh* (*ʕēdāh*, Hb.) "assembly", *mwʕd* (*môʕēd*) "assembly point", *tʕwdh* (*t^e^ʕûdāh*) "confirmation, corroboration, attestation"; *yʕd* (JAram. D) "to be appointed", *wʕd*(*ʔ*) "appointed time or place", *ʕdh*, *ʕdtʔ* "community, assembly; (?)time", *mwʕd*(*ʔ*) "holiday"; *adānum*, *ḫadānum*, *adannu*, *adiānu*, *edānu*(*m*), *idānu* (Akk.) "fixed date, time limit"; *waʕada* (Arab.) "to promise", *waʕd*, *mīʕād*, *mawʕid* "promise"; *wʕd* (OSArab.) "to promise", (C) "to make an appointment", *mʕd* "limit, deadline; feast-day", *mʕwd* "promise", *mʕdtn* "pledge, commitment"; *šəwēd*, *šəʕēd* (MSArab.) "to make a rendez-vous, arrange a meeting; to vow to do something", *wɛd*, *wɛdīn*, *wɛdūtən* "place appointed for a meeting; promise", *mʕūd*, *muʕūd*, *mīʕēd* "appointment". See further *waʕala*, *wəla* (Eth.) "to stay, remain".

---

902 For the OBab. forms *uwaʔʔer=* (D prefc., also Mari-Akk.) see vSoden GAG 132 § q, 150 § f.

|**w-ʕ-d**| "to determine, promise"	•CTX: **EB** D prefc. suff. *ù-wa-ì-da-am*$_6$ |ʔuwaʕʕid=am|, *ù-wa-ì-da-ga* |ʔuwaʕʕid=am=ka| → Fronzaroli QuSe 13 152; Catagnoti / Fronzaroli ARET 16 89, 276; Catagnoti QuSe 29 80, 83, 85, 136, 156, 159, 234.
ʕidān "fixed date, time limit"	•CTX: **EUPH** *ḫi-da-an*, *ḫi-da-nim*, *ḫi-da-na-am* → AHw 184: (*ʕ*)*edānu*(*m*); CAD A/1 97ff.: *adannu*; Kupper ARM 28 95:15; Durand ARM 33 80:8, 118:24, 151:14.
ʕdt (A) "assembly; confluence; overflowing, flooding"	•CTX: **UGA** Sg. *ʕdt*, suff. *ʕdtm* → DUL 148 *ʕdt* (I).
mōʕid "assembly"	•CTX: **EG** *mu*$_3$-*ʕid* → Hoch SWET 126 no. 161.[903]
mʕd "convention, assembly"	•CTX: **UGA** → DUL 514.
tʕdt "embassy, accreditation"	•CTX: **UGA** Sg. cstr. *tʕdt* → DUL 843.

|w-ʕ-l| (1)	Primary noun, Sem.: *yʕl* (*yāʕēl*, Hb.) "mountain goat"; *yʕl*(*ʔ*) (JAram., Syr.) id.; *waʕl*, *waʕil* (Arab.) id.; *wʕl* (OSArab.) id.; *wɛl*, *wāl* (MSArab.) id.; *wəʕəlā*, *waʕālā*, *wāʔəlā* (Eth.) id. Non-Sem.: **wul=* (West Chadic) "antelope"; **wayil* (East Chadic) id.; **ʔaw*(*V*)*l=* (East Cushitic) "gazelle".[904]
waʕil "mountain goat"	LL: **EB** IGI.DÀRA = *wa-ʔa*$_5$(NI)-*lum* → Bonechi / Conti NABU 1992/11; Militarev / Kogan SED 2 312 no. 244: rdg *wa-ì-lum*.
yaʕ(i)l "mountain goat"	•ONOM: **EUPH** *ia-aḫ-la-tan*, *ya-i-la-nim*, *ya-i-la-an*, fem. *ya-ḫi-la*, *ya-ḫi-la-tum* → Gelb CAAA 21 102 (JAʕIL); Zadok Fs. Hallo 331; Streck Onomastikon 1 349 § 5.71 fn.2.[905]
yʕl "mountain goat"	•CTX: **UGA** Pl. *yʕlm* → DUL 933f. •ONOM: **UGA** Cf. *yʕl* → DUL 934: *yʕl* (II).

|w-ʕ-l| (2)	Sem.: Cf. *yʕl* (Hb., JAram., C) "to profit; to effect, accomplish"; *waʕl* (Arab.) "eminent, noble"; *wʕl* (OSArab.) "to tower above, rule over"(?).
|**y-ʕ-l**| "to accomplish, effect"	•ONOM: **EUPH, B** Cf. *ia-ḫi-il-li-im*, *i-ḫi-il-bi*-DINGIR; *ia-ḫu-ul-*^{d}*da-gan*; *ia-ḫa-la*, *ia-ḫa-al-pi-lum* → Gelb CAAA 21 101 (JʕIL, JʕUL), 102 (JAʕAL).

|w-ʕ-r| (1)	Sem.: *waʕara* (Eth.) "to be amazed, overawed"; metath. *yrʕ* (Hb.) "to be apprehensive"; *waraʕa*, *waruʕa*, *warāʕa* (Arab.) "to weak, coward, lazy"; *wrʕ* (OSArab.) "intimidate, frighten, overawe".
|**y-ʕ-r**| "to be frightened"	•CTX: **UGA** G suffc. *yʕr* → DUL 934.

[903] Sivan / Cochavi-Rainey WSVES 80: *mú-ʕ( )d-(t)* "council"; Helck Beziehungen no. 90.
[904] Orel / Stolbova HSED 523 no. 2505: **waʕül=* "antelope".
[905] For the tribe name *Yaʕil(ān)* see Durand REA 689: *Ya'ila*.

|w-ʕ-r| (2)	Primary noun, Sem.: *yʕr* (*yaʕar*, Hb.) "thicket, wood"; *yr*, *JAR* (Pun.) "wood, forest"; *yʕr* (Moab.) id.; *yʕr(ʔ)* (JAram., Syr.) id., *yʕr* (JAram., C) "to be in difficulty"; *waʕr* (Arab.) "wild, rough", *waʕīr* id., *waʕra* (Yemeni-Arab.) "thicket", *waʕara* "to be rough, difficult"; *waʕara* (Eth.) "to be rough, coarse".
waʕr "rugged, coarse"	•ONOM: **EB** Cf. *wa-a-rúm*, PI(*wa*?)-*ra-an*/*nu*, *a-da*-PI(*wa*?)-*ar* → Pagan ARES 3 185, 276, 376.
yuʕr "difficult, rugged (place)"	•LL: **EB** GIŠ.LAGABxA = *u*$_9$-*ru*$_{12}$-*um* → Sjöberg Fs. Kienast 548.
yʕr (B) "wood, thicket; rugged, coarse"[906]	•CTX: **UGA** Pl. *yʕrm* → DUL 934 *yʕr* (II). •ONOM: **UGA** *yʕr* → DUL 934: *yʕr* (III); *yʕrn* → DUL 934.
yaʕart "roughness, coarseness"	•ONOM: **A4** Cf. *ia-ar-tu-na* → Dietrich / Loretz WO 5 61 5:2; Sivan GAGl 285. **UGS** Cf. *ia-ar-ta-na* → Gröndahl PTU 142; Sivan GAGl 285; cf. TN *Yaʕartu*, Belmonte RGTC 12/2 337.
yʕrt "wood, thicket"	•ONOM: **UGA** Cf. TN *yʕrt* → DUL 934f.; GN *yʕrty* (pl. / du. *yʕrtym*) → DUL 935.
|w-ʕ-y|	Sem.: Cf. *waʕā* (*waʕy*, Arab.) "to retain in one's memory, know by heart, pay attention", *waʕy* "awareness, wakefulness".
waʕy "remembrance, awareness" (?)	•ONOM: **EM** Cf. *wa-a-we*, *wa-a-e* → Arnaud SEL 8 44: |wāʕi| (act. ptc.); Pruzsinszky PTEm 178 fn. 178 [813] (untranslated).
|w-b-ʔ| Cf. **|b-h-m| (2)**	Sem.: Cf. *wabiʔa* (Arab.) "to be plague-stricken, infected", *mawbūʔ* "poisoned, infested", (*w*)*abāʔu*(*m*) (Akk.) "to weed", *wabûtum* "weeding"; *wabā* (Eth.) "plague, pestilence".
|w-b-ʔ| "to be plague-stricken" **mawbaʔt** "back"	•LL: **EB** Cf. SA.NÁ = *wa-ba-um*, *wa-ba-ù-um* → Conti QuSe 17 117; Sjöberg Fs. Pettinato 261. •LL: **EB** Cf. SA.SAL = *ma-ba-tum*, *mu-ba-tum* → Conti QuSe 17 116; Bonechi / Catagnoti Fs. Sommerfeld / Krebernik 174f.
|w-b-l| (1)	Sem.: *ybl* (Hb., C) "to bring", *ybwl* (*y*^{e}*bûl*) "yield of soil", *ʔbl* (*ʔubāl*), *ybl* (*yābāl*), *ywbl* (*yûbal*) "water-course, canal", *mbwl* (*mabbûl*) "the celestial sea; the Deluge"; *ybl* (Aram.) "to bear, bring, to convey", (Syr., D) "to lead", *blw* "tribute", *ybl(ʔ)* (JAram., Syr.) "stream", *mwbl* (Aram., Syr.) "shipment, load"; *wabālu*(*m*), *abālu*, *ubālu*, *babālu*(*m*), *tabālu*(*m*) "to carry, bring", *biltu*(*m*), *bissu*, *bīsu* "load; yield, rent", *babbilu*(*m*), *wābilum* "bearer, carrier", *biblu*(*m*) "bringing; (said of) high water", *bibbulu*(*m*) "spate, flood"; *wabala* (Arab.) "to shed heavy rain", *wabl*, *wābil* "(heavy) downpour", *wābila* "the extremity of the scapula"; *wbl* (OSArab.) "pay tribute, prescribe taxes", *wblm*, *hwbltm* "tribute". See further *tanbala* (Eth.) "to be ambassador", *tanbal* "envoy".
|w-b-l| (A) "to carry, bring, take, supply"	•CTX: **EB** G prefc. *du-ba* |tubbal|, Gtn precf. *ad-da-ba-al*$_6$-*ma* |ʔattabbal=|, D prefc. suff. *nu-da-bí-am*$_6$ |nūtabbil=am|, C prefc. *nu-su-bí-a-am*$_6$ |nuSūbil=am| → Rubio PIHANS 106 122; Fronzaroli ARET 13 115, 291; Catagnoti / Fronzaroli ARET 16 39, 43, 45f., 226; Catagnoti QuSe 29 25, 107, 136, 144, 158f., 235.[907]

[906] For *yʕr* (A) "razor" see GlOS 1 86: \|ʕ-r\| (?).

[907] See *tuwtabbil*(*t*), below.

•LL: **EB** ŠU.GÍD.GÍG = *mu-da-bíl-du* |muttabbil=| → Krebernik ZA 73 20; Fronzaroli QuSe 13 146.
•ONOM: **EB** Cf. *bíl-ma-lik*, GIBIL(*bíl*?)-*mu-su*, *da-bil-da-mu*, *du-bíl-da-mu*, *du-bíl-ma-lik* → Conti QuSe 15 60f.; Krebernik PET 38f., 67f., 78; Pagan ARES 3 185, 292, 296, 302.

|y-b-l| "to carry, bring, take, supply"
•CTX: **EM** G prefc. *i-ba-la* |yibbala|(?) → Pentiuc Vocabulary 80.
UGS G prefc. *i-bi-la* |yabila|(?), C prefc. *i*]*a(-)šu-bi-lu* < |yVs^{1}awbilu|, altern. G imp. *šu-bi-lu* |s^{1}awbilū| → Huehnergard UVST 132f.
UGA G prefc. *ybl*, *ybln*, *tbl*, *nbl*, *nbln*, suff. *yblnh*, *yblnn*, *yblk*, *tblk*, suffc. *ảbl*, (?)*ybl*, *yblt*, imp. *bl*; Gpass. prefc. *ybl* → DUL 935f.; Tropper UG 963 (*wbl*), 964 (*ybl*).
•ONOM: **U3** Cf. *yi-ba-la-tum* → Buccellati Amorites 47, 156, 184; Gelb CAAA 21 107; Golinets Onomastikon 2 222, 461f.
EUPH, **B** Passim; cf. *i-ba-la-an*, *i-ba-lim*, *i-ba-lu*/*lum*/*lu-um*, *ia-ba-al-*^{d}IM, *e-ba-al-e-ra-aḫ*, *i-bal-*^{d}*da-gan*, *i-ba-al-*^{d}*da-gan*, *i-ba-al-*DINGIR, *i-ba-al-da-mu-um*, *i-ba-al-e-ra-aḫ*, *i-ba-al-*EŠ$_{4}$.DAR, *i-ba-al-*^{d}ḪAR, *i-ba-al-*^{d}IM, *i-ba-al-*^{d}*iš-ḫa-ra*, *i-ba-al-*KA-DINGIR, *i-ba-al-bi-*DINGIR/*el*, *i-ba-al-pi-el*, *i-ba-al-pi*$_{4}$*-il*, *i-ba-al-pi*4-^{d}EN.ZU, *i-ba-al-la-*DINGIR, *i-ba-al-na-ap-zu*, *i-ba-al-sa-am-si*; *a-bi-a-ba-al*, *mu-ti-a-ba-al*, *su-mu-mu-ti-a-ba-la*, *a-ḫi-e-ba-al*, *da-mi-e-ba-al*, *ás-di-e-ba-al*, *da-di-e-ba-al*, ^{d}EN.ZU-*e-ba-al*, *ḫa-na-ti-e-ba-al*, ^{d}*ḫa-mi-e-ba-al*, *ḫa-mi-i-ba-al*, *ḫa-am-mu-e-ba-al*, *iš-ḫi-e-ba-al*, *nu-uḫ-me-e-ba-al*, *zi-it-ri-e-ba-al*, *da-mi-i-ba-al*, ^{d}GÌR-*i-ba-al*, ^{d}ḪAR-*i-ba-al*, *ḫa-na-ti-i-ba-al*, *i-ia-ti-i-ba-al*, *ì-lí-ma-i-ba-al*, *ia-i-ti-i-ba-al*, *iš*(!)-*ḫi-i-ba-al*, *su-mu-i-ba-al*, *su-mu-ti-ba-al* → Huffmon APNMT 154f. (?BL); Gelb CAAA 21, 102 (JABAL), 107f. (JBAL); Zadok Fs. Hallo 331; Golinets Onomastikon 2 221ff., 461f.
R i-*ba-al-a-pí-iḫ* → Dalley / Walker / Hawkins Tell Rimah 174 (244 I 42).
TU *i-ba-lum*, *i-ba-a-lum*, *i-ba-lu-um*, *i-ba-la-ḫu-um* → Krebernik Tall Bi`a 215f.

wābil "holder, support"
•CTX: **EB** *a-bí-lum* → Pasquali QuSe 23 97.

yābil "porter, bearer"
•ONOM: **U3** *ya-bí-ìl* → Zadok Fs. Hallo 331.
B *ia-bi-il-wi-ir-ra* → Gelb CAAA 21 108 (JBIL); Golinets Onomastikon 2 238f., 461f.

yōbil "porter, bearer"
•CTX: **EA** Cf. *ú-bi-il* GUN (288:12), LÚ.MEŠ *ú-bi-li-mi* KASKAL.ḪÁ (287:55) → Sivan GAGl 159f., 256; Moran AmL 328, 331; Rainey CAT 1 49; 3 236, 256; Izre'el Orient 38 79, 81, 95.

wabbāl "porter, runner"
•LL: **EB** KAS$_{4}$ = *wa-ba-lu*, AL.KÉŠ = *gi-zi-lum a-ti wa-ba-lu-um*, ŠE+TIN = *gi-za-lu a-ti wa-ba-um* → Bonechi QDLF 16 87. Diff.: Krebernik ZA 73 35f.; Fronzaroli StEb 7 185; Fronzaroli QuSe 13 152; Catagnoti QuSe 29 235: |wabāl=)| "to carry, bring".

ybl (A) "produce"
•CTX: **UGA** → DUL 936: *ybl* (I).

ybl (B) "rod"
•CTX: **UGA** Pl. suff. *yblhm* → DUL 936: *ybl* (II).

yābilt "irrigation ditch"
•CTX: **EUPH** *ia-bi-il-tum*/*tim* → Birot ARM 14 40ff. (14:5, 10, 26, 31f.), 220; Durand LAPO 17 607 fn. a; Reculeau Proceedings 53^{e} RAI 511; Zadok Fs. Hallo 331.

yubila, ʔubalaya "stream"
•ONOM: **EG** Elem. in TN *yu-bi-r*, *yu-bi-ru*$_{2}$, *yu-ba-ra*; cf. *ʔu-ba-ra-ya* → Hoch SWET 50f. no. 49.

yblt "flowing current, stream"
•CTX: **UGA** Sg. suff. *ybltm* → DUL 936f.

(ỉ)blbl "messenger, bearer" (?)
•CTX: **UGA** Pl. *blblm*, suff. *ỉblblhm* → DUL 9, 219; Tropper UG 275.

bibilt "(improper) conduct or tendency"	•CTX: **EUPH** *bi-bi-il-tum/tim-ma*, pl. *bi-ib-la-tim, bi-ib-la-tim-ma* → Kupper MARI 6 337ff. (A.1025:22, 66); Durand ARM 26/1 102 fn. 43: "prétexte mensonger".
mawbal (A) "flood"	•LL: **EB** Cf. A.KUL = *ma-ba-lum* → Fales QuSe 13 181 (640b).
mawbal (B) "produce, load" (?)	•CTX: **UGS** *mu-ba-li* |mōbal|(?) → Sivan GAGl 248; Huehnergard UVST 132; Tropper UG 188.
mawbil, mawbal (C) "neck (-sinew)"	•LL: **EB** SA.GÚ = *ma-bíl-tum, ma-bal-tum, ma-ba-al*$_6$*-tum* → Krebernik ZA 73 13; Sjöberg Fs. Pettinato 261; Bonechi / Catagnoti Fs. Sommerfeld / Krebernik 174.
muwabbil "(standard) bearer (a priest class?)"	•CTX: **EUPH** pl. LÚ.MEŠ *mu-ba-bi-li*, LÚ.MEŠ *mu-ba-ab-bi-lu*, LÚ(.MEŠ) *mu-ba-bi-lu-tum* → Birot ARM 14 144f. (82:17); Villard FM (1) 147ff.; Arkhipov ARM 32 381 (M.6206:7'); Durand LAPO 17 202ff., 204 fn. g.; LAPO 18 195f. fn. c. •ONOM: **EB** Cf. *mu-a-bí-lum* → Pagan ARES 3 185, 351.
tuwtabbil(t) "supply, sustenance, maintenance"	•CTX: **EB** Suff. *du-da-bí-na* |tūtabbil=nay(n)|, *du-da-bí-nu* |tūtabbil=nu|, *du-da-bí-du*-SÙ |tūtabbilt=a=Sunu| → Catagnoti / Fronzaroli ARET 16 13, 226; Catagnoti QuSe 29 74, 139, 145, 160, 235.

|w-b-l| (2)	Sem.: *wabala* (Arab.) "to run vehemently; give chase to, pursue".
|w-b-l| (B) "to run, pursue"	•LL: **EB** KAŠ$_4$ = *wa-ba-lum* → Sjöberg Fs. Wilcke 262f.

|w-b-m|	Sem.: *ybm* (*yābām*) "husband's brother", *ybmh* / *ybmt* (*y*^{e}*bāmāh* / *yābemet*) "brother's widow", *ybm* (D) "consummate a marriage with a brother-in-law"; *ybm(ʔ)* (JAram., Syr.) "brother-in-law", *ybmh, ybmtʔ* "sister-in-law", *ybm* (D)"to marry a brother's widow".
|y-b-m| "to consummate the marriage with a brother-in-law" (?)	•CTX: **UGS** Cf. *štbm* (Št prefc.?; rdg?) → Tropper UG 608f.; altern. rdg DUL 937 /y-b-m/: *t*(!)*štbm* (Št prefc.) "to proclaim oneself a nubile widow" (?).
yabam "brother-in-law"	•CTX: **R** Suff. *ia-ba-mi-ša* → Dalley / Walker / Hawkins Tell Rimah 117 (143:10); AHw 1565; Zadok Fs. Hallo 331. •ONOM: **U3** Cf. unc. *ià-ma-am-ú* → Moran Or 26 340; Huffmon APNMT 211; diff. Buccellati Amorites 151f. (II); Gelb CAAA 103, 607 (3628: JAMAM=HU).[908]
ybm "brother-in-law"	•CTX: **UGA** Sg. *ybm*, suff.(?) *ybmh* → DUL 937.
ybmt "widow sister-in-law, nubile widow"	•CTX: **UGA** Sg. cstr. *ybmt*; *ymmt* → DUL 937.

[908] For EUPH *ia-ma-(a-)ma* see further Durand REA 669 "Yamam", Zadok Fs. Hallo 332 Y-M-M², Streck Onomastikon 1 328 § 5.22 with fn. A, referring to Arab. *yamāma* "rock dove". See \|y-w-n\|.

|w-b-r|
Cf. **|H-b-r| (2)**

Sem.: Var. of |H-b-r|; cf. *wabrum*, *ubru*(*m*) "a type of foreigner".[909]

wabar "guest-friend"

•ONOM: **EB** Cf. *wa-ba-lum*, *wa-ba-rúm*, *wa-ba-rí-a*, *íl-gú-uš-wa-bar*, *su*/*zu-wa-ma-wa-ba-ar* → Krebernik PET 104; Pagan ARES 3 240, 336, 365, 375, 389.

|w-d-ʕ|

Sem.: *ydʕ* (Hb.) "to notice, know", *dʕh* (*daʕāh*) "wisdom", *dʕt* (*daʕat*) "knowledge", *mdwʕ* (*maddûaʕ*) "why?", *mdʕ* (*modāʕ*), *mdʕt* (*modaʕat*) "relative"; *ydʕ* (Ph., Pun.) "to know, be informed"; *ydʕ* (Palm.) id.; *ydʕ* (Aram., Syr.) "to know", *dʕt*(*ʔ*), *dyʕh*, *dʕtʔ* (JAram.) "knowledge", *ydʕ*(*ʔ*), *ydʕh*, *ydʕtʔ*, *ʔydʕtʔ* (Syr.) "information, knowledge"; *edû*(*m*), *idû*(*m*), *idāʔum*, *wadûm*, *udāʔu* (Akk.) "to know", *diʔ*(*a*)*tum*, *daʔtum* "information, knowledge", *mūdû*(*m*), *mūdaʔum*, *mūdiʔum*, *muddû* "knowing, wise, experienced", *minde* "perhaps"; *hydʕ* (OSArab., C) "to cause to know", *mydʕ* "information"; *wīda*, *édaʕ*, *ədaʕ*, *yōda* (MSArab.) "to know"; *ydʕ*, *ʔaydəʕa* (Eth.) "to make know, inform".

|w-d-ʕ| "to know, to recognise, distinguish"

•CTX: **EB** G inf. *wa-da-iš* |wadāʕ=iS|, D precf. *du-da-ù* |tuddaʕu|, *du-ti-ù* |tuddiʕū|, *nu-ti-ì* |nuddiʕ|, C prefc. *ù-sa-ti-am*$_6$ |ʔuSadiʕ=am|, *lu-sa-ti-am*$_6$ |lā=yuSādiʕ=am| → Fronzaroli NABU 1991/49; ARET 11 45, 52, 143f.; ARET 13 197, 306; Catagnoti QuSe 29 45, 60, 113, 121, 125, 136f., 157ff., 160, 235.
•ONOM: **EB** Cf. *a-da*-AD.MU, PI(*ya*$_8$?)-*da-ù-um*; *i-da-ù*, passim. elem. *i-da*=DNN (also *i-da-a-ba*$_4$, *i-da-am*), see *ì-da*-DINGIR, *ì-da*-NE(*il*$_x$?), *i-dè-ni-ki-mu* (vars *ì:dè*=, *dè*=); *ti-da*, *ti-da-na-ù* → Krebernik PET 40, 71, 118; Conti QuSe 15 64f.; Catagnoti QuSe 15 266; Pagan ARES 3 185f., 276, 301, 321f., 328, 369, 382.

|y-d-ʕ| (A) "to know, to recognise, distinguish"

•CTX: **UGA** G prefc. *idʕ*, *tdʕ*, *tdʕ*, suff. *ydʕnn*; suffc. *ydʕt*, *ydʕ*, imp. *dʕ*, inf. *ydʕ*, suff. *ydʕm*, act. ptc. *ydʕ*; pass. ptc. *ydʕt* → DUL 941 /*y-d-ʕ*/ (I); Tropper UG 963 (*wdʕ*), 964 (*ydʕ*).
•ONOM: **U3** *e-ti-um* → Buccellati Amorites 105, 146f.; Gelb CAAA 21, 108; Golinets Onomastikon 2 228, 463.
EUPH, B Passim; elem.|yadaʕ=|, writings *a-da*= (*a-da*-DINGIR),[910] *a-da-aḫ*= (*a-da-aḫ*-[*bi*?]-*el*), ia-*da*= (*ia-da-am-mu*), *ia-da-aḫ*= (*ia-da-aḫ*-DINGIR), *ia-daḫ*= (*ia-daḫ*-DINGIR), *ia-da*=*ḫ*= (*ia-da-aḫ-ḫa-lum*), *ia-ṭà-aḫ*= (*ia-ṭà-aḫ*-^{d}IM), =*ia-da-ḫ*= (*ḫa-ma-ma-ia-da-ḫa*), =*e-da-aḫ* (*ka-bi-e-da-aḫ*), *i-da*= (*i-da-lim-ma*), *i-daḫ*= (*i-daḫ-ra-am*); elem. |yadiʕ=|, writings *ia-di*= (*ia-di-ḫa*-(*tum*)), *ia-di-ḫ*= (*ia-di-ḫa-el*) → Huffmon APNMT 209; Gelb CAAA 21 108f. (JDAʕ, JDIʕ); Zadok Fs. Hallo 332; Streck Onomastikon 1 155 § 2.8 fn. 2, 160 § 2.20; Golinets Onomastikon 2 225ff., 463f.[911]
EM *ia-da-il*$_5$*-ti*, *ia-dì*, *ia-di*/*dì*-^{d}*da-gan*/^{d}KUR, *i-da*, *id-da*, *i-da-aḫ-a*, *i-da-da*, *id-di*, *id-di-id-da-ḫi*, *id-dì*-EN, *id-di*-1+EN, *id-di-id-da*, *id-di*-^{d}*da-gan*, *id-di*/*dì-e*, *id-dì-iʔ-e*, *id-di-il-li*, *id-di-li-mu*, *id-di-im-ma* → Pruzsinszky PTEm 166, 169f., 183f., 207, 212 [401f., 440ff.]; Streck AfO 51 308f.
UGS ^{d}IM-*i-da-ʔa* → Sivan GAGl 140, 291; Huehnergard UVST 246.
UGA *ảdʕ*(*y*) → DUL 17; *bʕldʕ* → DUL 207; *ydʕ* → DUL 942; *ydʕn* → DUL 942.
EG *t*$_2$*-ʕ-b-ʕ-r-y* → Schneider 229 no. 486.

---

909 For LL: EB NÌ.ŠUBUR = *ù-ba-ra-tum*, *u*$_9$*-ba-ra-du-um* see also GlOS 1 211: *Hubārat* "companionship" (|H-b-r| (2)). Untranslated in Conti QuSe 17 77; Bonechi QuSe 19 140f. + fn. 11.
910 Only selected instances.
911 No clear instances of PāRiS forms available (Gelb CAAA 21: *yādiʕ* "knowing").

wadiʕ "available, present, complete"	•CTX: **EB** *wa-ti-a* |wadiʕay|, pl. *wa-ti-a-ti* |wadiʕāti(m)| → Catagnoti QuSe 29 107, 121, 125, 157f., 235. •LL: **EB** ZÀ.ME = *wa-ti-um* → Fronzaroli ARET 11 177; Catagnoti QuSe 29 122, 157, 159, 235.
daʕ, daʕat, diʕat "knowledge, friendship"	•LL: **EB** Cf. UMUN(?) = *ba-lu da-a-tim* → Krebernik ZA 73 42. •ONOM: **EB** Cf. *da-ḫu, da-ḫu-um, da-ḫu-šum, a-da-ad, a-da-a-ad, a-da-a-du, la-da-ad, la-da-ù, la-da-gi-nu, kùn-a-da-ù, la-ti-ad, la-ti-a-ad* → Pagan ARES 185f., 276, 297, 344f. **EUPH**, **B** ^{d}UTU-*da-ḫi-i, i-la-da-ḫa-at*, DINGIR-*da-ḫa-at, sa-mi-da-ḫu-um* → Gelb CAAA 21, 122; Streck Onomastikon 1 319 § 5.4. **EM** *da-i, da-a-i, da-aḫ-a, a-bi-da-i, ia-ša-ar-da-i, ia-ša-ru-dá-i*, DUMU-*da-i*, dUTU-*da-i* → Pruzsinszky PTEm 159, 189, 195,197f. [35, 296f., 425, 610, 734]; Streck AfO 51 310.
daʕūt "knowledge, friendship"	•ONOM: **EB** *da-ḫu-du, da-ù-du* → Pagan ARES 3 185f., 297, 299.
dʕt (A) "knowledge, friendship"	•CTX: **UGA** Sg. suff. *dʕtk, dʕtkm, dʕthm*, pl. suff. *dʕtm* → DUL 257f.: *dʕt* (I).
yaydāʕ, yaydāʕt "knowledge, friendship; DN"	•ONOM: **EUPH**, **B** *ia-da-aḫ-ta*-DINGIR, *sa-ma-a-da-ḫu(-um), su-mu-a-da-ḫu-um* → Gelb CAAA 21, 103; Streck Onomastikon 1 163f. § 2.26 fn. 1, 303 § 3.67, 328 § 5.23.
yadūʕ "known, familiar"	•ONOM: **B** Cf. *ia-du-a-bu-um* → Gelb CAAA 21, 108 (JDIʕ); Golinets Onomastikon 2 227, 463 (|yayduʕ|?); see **EM** below. **EM** *ia-du*-EN → Pruzsinszky PTEm 184 [404]; Streck AfO 51 309. **EG** *y-t-w*$_2$*-ʕ-w*$_2$*-b-ʕ-r*^{STH}, *y-t-w-ʕ-w-bʕl-y* → Schneider APÄQ 63 no. 111.
yōdiʕa "skilled, learned"	•CTX: **EG** *ya-di-ʕa* → Hoch SWET 58 no. 64: act. ptc. |y-d-ʕ|.[912] •ONOM: **EG** Cf. *ya-tu*$_2$*-ʕu, ya-tu*$_2$*-ʕu*$_2$ → Hoch SWET 58 no. 64: act. ptc. |y-d-ʕ|.
mēdiʕ "knowledge"	•ONOM: **U3** *me-te-um* → Buccellati Amorites 32, 172; Gelb CAAA 21, 109.
muwdaʕ "knowing, wise, experienced"	•ONOM: **EB** *mu-da-ar, mu-da-bí, a-ḫu-mu-da-a*, cf. *mu-da*-ḪUM(*ḫum*?), *mu-da*-LUM (*ḫum*?) → Krebernik PET 97, 252; Pagan ARES 3 185f., 278, 352.
muwdiy[913] "class or corporation (knowing, wise, experienced)"	•CTX: **UGS** (LÚ) *mu-du* LUGAL, pl. LÚ *mu-du-ú* LUGAL, *mu-de*$_4$ MÍ.LUGAL, LÚ.MEŠ *mu-de*$_4$ LUGAL, LÚ *mu-du-ma* → Sivan GAGl 249; Huehnergard UVST 144; vSoldt SAU 421, 427f., 428 fn. 53. •LL: **UGS** NU.NU = *mu-du-ú* → Huehnergard UVST 144.
md (B) "class or corporation (knowing, wise, experienced)"	•CTX: **UGA** Pl. *mdm*, cstr. *md* → DUL 518 *md* (II).
mdʕ (A) "why?"[914]	•CTX: **UGA** → DUL 519: *mdʕ* (I).
mdʕ (B) "(royal) family"	•CTX: **UGA** → DUL 519: *mdʕ* (II).
mndʕ "perhaps"[915]	•CTX: **UGA** → DUL 554f.

[912] Sivan / Cochavi-Rainey WSVES 78: *y(u)-di-ʕá*; Helck Beziehungen p. 530: *ya-di-ʕá*.

[913] *\|muwda/iʕ=\| > *mūdû*; Akk. loan in Ugarit.

[914] Elems *m(h)*=\|w-d-ʕ\|; cf. Hb. *mdwʕ*.

[915] Probl. *mn* (A)=\|w-d-ʕ\|.

|w-d-d|

Sem.: *yd* (*yād*, Hb.), *ydydwt* (*y^e dîdôt*) "love", *ydyd* (*yādîd*) "beloved"; *ydd* (Syr. Dt) "to be beloved", *ydyd* (JAram., Syr.) "beloved", *ydydw*(*t?*) (Syr.) "love", *mwdd*(*?*), *mwddw* (Aram.) "friend, ally; love(?)"; *namaddu* (Akk.) "darling"; *wadda, wādda* (Arab.) "to love", *tawaddada* "to try to gain favour", *wadd, widd, wudd* "love; loving", *wadīd, wadūd, waddiyy, widdiyy, wuddiyy* "friendly", *mawadda* "love"; *s^1twdd* (OSArab.) "to love", *wdh* "offering (to win favour)", *mwd* "friend, ally", *wdm* "friendship"; *wdd, wadda* "to join together, put into", *ʔastawādada* "to join, make agree", *dəd* "joint", *wədud* "joined, suitable".

dawd "beloved" •LL: **EB** ŠÀ.KI.ÁG = *du-du, du-du-du* → Conti QuSe 17 164.
•ONOM: **EG** Cf. *d-y_2-d-y_2* → Schneider APÄQ 261 no. 561ff.

yd (B) "love" •CTX: **UGA** Sg. cstr. *yd*, suff. *ydh* → DUL 941: *yd* (II).[916]

yadīd "beloved" •ONOM: **EUPH**, **B** *a-di-du*(*-um*), *a-di-dum, ia-ad-du-um, ia-di-du, ia-di-dum*/*du-um*; fem. *ia-di-da, ia-di-da-tum*, cf. *wa-di-it-tum* → Huffmon APNMT 209; Gelb CAAA 21, 103; Zadok WO 14 236; Fs. Hallo 331; Streck Onomastikon 1 330 § 5.27; Golinets Onomastikon 2 338f., 464f.
R *ia-ad-da-tim* → Dalley / Walker / Hawkins Tell Rimah 136 (171:7).
EM *ia-di-du_4* → Pruzsinszky PTEm 166 [404].

yadūd "beloved" •ONOM: **UGS** Cf. *ia-du-da-na* → Gröndahl PTU 143.[917]

yudād "darling" •ONOM: **U3** *ú-da-du-um* → Zadok WO 14 236; Streck Onomastikon 1 183 § 2.70; Golinets Onomastikon 2 346, 464f.

ydd "the loved one" •CTX: **UGA** → DUL 943 *ydd* (I).
•ONOM: **UGA** *ydd* → 943 *ydd* (II); *yddn* → DUL 943; fem. *yddt* → DUL 943.

mawdad "beloved" •ONOM: **U3** *mu-da-du-um* → Buccellati Amorites 23, 173; Gelb CAAA 21, 100.
B *mu-da-du* → Gelb CAAA 21, 100; AHw 665: *mūdādum*, CAD M/2 160 *mudādu*.
EG Cf. *my* ^{SJ}*-d-ȝ-d-ȝ-m*^{F} → Schneider APÄQ 137f. no. 293.

mdd "beloved, friend" •CTX: **UGA** → DUL 520: *mdd* (I).
•ONOM: **UGA** *mdd* → DUL 520: *mdd* (II); *mddbʕl* → DUL 520.

mddt (A) "beloved" •CTX: **UGA** Sg. suff. *mddth* → DUL 520f.: *mddt* (I).

|w/y-D-n|

See |n/w/y-D-n|

|w-d-y| (1)

Cf. |n-d-y|

Sem.: *ydh* (Hb.) "to cast, shoot"; *ʔawdā* (Arab.) "to perish, die; to snatch away"; *wadaya* (Eth.) "to put, set, throw, cast".

|y-d-y| (A) "to throw, expel" •CTX: **UGA** G prefc. *tdy, yd, ydy*; imp. *ydy*; inf. *ydy* act. ptc. m. *ydy* (see below *ydy* (A)); fem. *ydt* (see below *ydt*) → DUL 944: */y-d-y/* (I)

ydy (A) "one who casts out, expels" •CTX: **UGA** → DUL 945: *ydy* (I).

ydy (B) "banishment" •CTX: **UGA** → DUL 945 *ydy* (II).

ydt "she who casts out, expels" •CTX: **UGA** → DUL 944.

ydyt "untilled, barren" •CTX: **UGA** Sg. / pl. *ydyt* → DUL 945

---

916 For the argued *tdd* "Liebe" (Tropper UG 270) see DUL 611: /n-d-d/ G, 3,"to prepare, hurry, rush, launch oneself", "to arise", inchoative mng

917 Unlikely altern. Sivan GAGl 285: from |y-d|. For the spellings *ia/ya-dV(=)*, all probl. from |y-d|, see here *yad* (|y-d|). Altern. Gröndahl PTU 142: |y-d|.

|w-d-y| (2)	Sem.: *ydh* (Hb. C) "to praise", *htydh* (*hityaddāh*) "to confess"; *ydy* (Palm. C) "to return thanks"; *ydy* (JAram., Syr.) "to give thanks, praise; to confess"; *ʔistawdā* (Arab.) "to be grateful for something". See further: *wadûm* (Akk.) "to know", (D) "to recognize".
|**w-d-y**| "to praise, thank"	•ONOM: **U3** *a-ù-da-il, a-aw-te-il, ú-da-ma* → Buccellati Amorites 18, 67, 135f.; Gelb CAAA 35, 100 (WDAJ).
|**y-d-y**| **(B)** "to praise, thank"	•ONOM: **EA** Cf. unc. *yi-id-ia, i-dì-ya* → Tropper OLZ 91 56; Fleming BASOR 303 98; altern. Sivan GAGl 285: *yad* "hand" (see |y-d|); Hess APN 167f.: Akk. *nadû* "to throw, plant".
wadiy "praised, celebrated" (?)	•LL: **EB** Cf. ZÀ.ME = *wa-ti-um* → Krebernik ZA 73 41.

|w-d-y| (3)	Sem.: Cf. *diya* (Arab.) "blood money, indemnity", *wadā* "to pay blood money".
duyt "blood money, indemnity"	•CTX: **EB** *du-tum* → Fronzaroli ARET 13 60, 255; Catagnoti QuSe 29 23, 44, 122, 195.

|w-ð-ʕ|	Sem.: *zʕh* (*zēʕāh*, Hb.), *yzʕ* (*yezaʕ*) "sweat"; *dwʕ* (JAram., C), *dʕt* (Syr.) "to sweat", *dyʕh, dyʕth* (JAram.), *dwʕh, dwʕth* (Syr.) "sweat"; *zūtu*(*m*), *zuʔtu, izūtu* (Akk.) "sweat, exudation"; *wadaʕa* (Arab.) "to run, flow".
|**y-d-ʕ**| **(B)** "to sweat"	•CTX: **UGA** G prefc. *tdʕ* → DUL 942 */y-d-ʕ/* (II).
ðuʕt "sweat"	•LL: **EB** IR = *šu-du-um* → Krebernik ZA 73 37.
dʕt (B) "sweat"	•CTX: **UGA** → DUL 258: *dʕt* (II).

|w-ð-y|	Sem.: *wadā* (*wady*, Arab.) "scratch, rip (out)".
|**y-d-y**| **(C)** "scratch, rip (out)"	•CTX: **UGA** G prefc. *td, ydy* → DUL 944: */y-d-y/* (II); Tropper UG 101, 633, 660 (*wdy*₂).

|w-g-ʕ|	Sem.: *ygʕ* (Hb.) "to grow weary", *ygʕ* (*yāgāʕ*) "product of labour", (*yāgēᵃʕ*) "weary", *ygyʕ*(*h*) (*yᵉgîᵃʕ, yᵉgîʕāh*)) "labour", (*yāgîᵃʕ*) "exhausted"; *egû*(*m*) (Akk.) "to be(come) lazy, be negligent";[918] *wağiʕa, wağaʕa* (Arab.) "to hurt, suffer", *wağaʕ* "pain, suffering", *wağiʕ* "sorrowful, patient".
w/yagāʕ "negligence"	•CTX: **EB** *a-ga-a* (vb. noun, cstr.) → Fronzaroli ARET 13 21, 241.
yagāʕt "sorrow(s)"	•CTX: **EUPH** *ia-ga-(a-)tum* → AHw 411: *jagâtum*; CAD I/J 321: *jagâtu*; Jean ARM 2 198f. (118 12, 15); Durand LAPO 17 200f. fn. c; Zadok Fs. Hallo 331; Streck Onomastikon 1 121 § 1.95.

|w-g-r|	Sem.: Cf. *ygr* (*yᵉgar*, Hb.) "stone monument"; *ygr*(*?*) (JAram.) "heap of stones"; *wgr* (OSArab.) "to construct a superstructure".

[918] For AHw 1456: *wagûm* "sich kümmern um"(?) see CAD U/W 400.

tuggur "a kind of auxiliar structure or building"	•CTX: **EM** Cf. É *tu-gu-ru*, E *tu-gu$_5$-rù*, É *tu-ku-rù*, É *tu-ug-gu-ri*, É *tu-ug-gu$_{(8)}$-rù*, É *tu-gu-ra-tu* MEŠ → CAD T 450f. *tugguru*; Arnaud AuOrS 1 12, 14; Westenholz Emar Tablets 19, 57f.
|w-γ-l|	Sem.: Cf. *waġil* (Arab.) "undernourished", cf. *waġla* "to be a sponger, cadger, parasite".
yγl "poor, barren land"	•CTX: **UGA** Pl. / sg. suff *yġlm* → DUL 945: *yġl*.
|w-h-b|	Sem.: *hb* (*hab*, Hb. imp.) "give!, come!"; *yhb* (JAram., Syr.) "to give"; *mwhbh*, *mwhbtʔ* (Nab., JAram., Syr.) "deed of gift"; *wahaba* (Arab.) "to give", *hiba* "gift", *wahba* "tip", *mawhiba* "gift, talent"; *whb* (OSArab.) "yo give", *hbtn* "gift", *mwhbt* "donations"; *hábə* (MSArab.) "give!"; *wahaba* (Eth.) "to give", *hab*(*i*), *habu*, *habā* "let (me, us)!".
|**w-h-b**| "to give"	•ONOM: **EB** Cf. *a*-DUM(*íb*?), *a*-DUM(*íb*?)=DNN,[919] *i-i-bù*, *i-ì-bu*, *i-i-bu$_{14}$*, *i-i-bu$_{16}$*, *i-i-ì-bù*, *i-ib-ma-lik*, *i-ib-na-im*,[920] *ti-i-bù*,[921] abbreviated: *ib*, *ib*=DNN,[922] → Krebernik PET 35; Conti QuSe 15 69; Pagan ARES 3 187, 277, 322f., 330, 370.
|**y-h-b**| "to give"	**EUPH** Cf. *ia-a-ab-el* → Zadok Fs. Hallo 331.
wahb "gift"	•ONOM: **EB** Unc. cf. *wa-bu* → Pagan ARES 3 187, 375.[923]
mawhaba "gift"	•ONOM: **EB** Cf. *mu-ʔà-ba-ù* → Pagan ARES 3 187, 351.
|w-h-y|	Sem.: *wahā* (*wahy*, Arab.) "to be weak, feeble".
|**y-h-y**| "to wane"	•CTX: **UGA** G prefc. *yh* → DUL 946 /*y-h(-y)*/.
|w-ḥ-d|	Primary noun, Sem.: *ʔḥd* (*ʔeḥād*, Hb.) "one", *yḥyd* (*yāḥîd*) "only", *yḥd* (*yaḥad*) "together", *yḥd* "to be united"; *ʔḥd* (Ph., Pun.) "one", *ʔḥdy* (Pun.) "together"; (*ʔ*)*ḥd* (Palm., Hatra) "one"; *ḥwd* (Nab.) "alone, only"; *ḥd* (Aram. Syr.) "one", *ʔḥyd* "singled out", *yḥyd* "lone, unique", *yḥd* (D, C) "to unite", *hwḥd* (Aram. C) "to gather", *ḥwd* (Syr. D) "to join, unite"; (*w*)*ēdu*(*m*) (Akk.) "single, sole, alone", *ēdēnu*, *ēdānu*, *ēdennu*, *īdīnu* "alone", *ēdumānu* "single", *ēdāniš*, *ēdiš* "alone"; *ʔaḥad* (Arab.) "one", *ʔaḥāda* "one by one", *waḥad*, *waḥid*, *waḥīd*, *wāḥid* "only", *waḥada* "to be alone, unique, singular", *waḥḥada* "to unite" *tawaḥḥada* "to be one, alone", *ittaḥada* "to form a unity"; *ʔḥd* (OSArab.) "one", *kwḥd* "together"; *wəḥáyd*, *aḥdí* (MSArab.) "alone"; *ʔaḥadu* (Eth.) "one", *ʔaḥād* "unit, unique", *ʔəḥud* "first", *ʔawāḥada* "to unite one thing with another", *wāḥəd* "only, one".
ʔaḥad "one"	•LL: **UGS** [AŠ = *it-te-tù* = … = *a-ḫ*]*a-du* → Huehnergard UVST 67, 105; vSoldt SAU 302 (4).
åḥd (A) "one, oneself; together with"	•CTX: **UGA** Sg. *åḥd*; suff. *åḥdy*, *åḥdh*; fem. *åḥt* → Tropper UG 162; DUL 31f.: *åḥd* (I).
åḥd (B) "solitary, single"	•CTX: **UGA** Sg. *åḥd*, du. *åḥdm* → Tropper UG 162; DUL 32f.: *åḥd* (II).

919 |yāhib|; altern. |yaʔhib| "he loved", see GlOS 1 13: |ʔ-h-b|.
920 |yīhib=|; altern. |yiʔhib=u| "he loved", see GlOS 1 13: |ʔ-h-b|.
921 |tīhib=u|; altern. |tiʔhib=u| "she loved", see GlOS 1 13: |ʔ-h-b|.
922 |(yī)hib|, altern. |(yiʔ)hib| "he loved", see GlOS 1 13: |ʔ-h-b|.
923 |wahbu|(?); altern. |wapiy| "beautiful", see |w-p-y|.

waħ(a)d "single (person); unique; individually; big landowner"	•CTX: **EB** *wa-tum, wa-ʔà-tum* → Fronzaroli ARET 13 65, 310; Catagnoti QuSe 29 58, 122, 236. Adverbialised *wa-ad, wa-ad-ma, wa-da-ma, wa-ʔa₅-da, wa-a-da-ma* → Fronzaroli ARET 13 185, 310; Catagnoti / Fronzaroli ARET 16 74, 281f.; Catagnoti QuSe 29 9, 16, 25, 59, 91, 117, 235f. **A7** LÚ *we-du-tum* → Durand FM 7 78; Lauinger STOBA 121f., 126, 128 fn. 28, 131f. •ONOM: **EB** *ù-a-ad, ù-wa-da, wa-ad*-BE, *wa-ad-ra-bú, wa-ad-ra-im, wa-ad-zi-kir, wa-da-ʔà, wa-da-a-i-bù, wa-da-bí-zú, wa-da-ra-im, wa-da-la-ì-mu, wa-da-za-ir, mu-lu-wa-du* → Conti QuSe 15 71 fn. 201 (partly from |w-d-ʕ|?); Krebernik PET 103; Pagan ARES 3 240, 352, 371, 373, 375.
yaħad, **yaħid**, **yiħad** "unique, being the only of its kind"	•ONOM: **EUPH**, **B** By-form |yaħad|, cf. *ia-ḫa-ad, ia-ḫa-du, ia-ḫa-dum/du-um, ia-aḫ-da-nu-um, ia-ḫa-ad-a-bu-um, ia-ḫa-ad*-DINGIR, *ia-ḫa-ad-ḫa(-am)-mu, ia-ḫa-ad-e-ra-aḫ, ia-ḫa-ad-e-lum, ia-ḫa-ad-ḫa-mu-ú, ia-ḫa-ad-ḫa-ri-ru-ú, ia-ḫa-ad-li-im, ia-ḫa-ad-ma-aṣ, ia-ḫa-ad-ú-ṣu-ur*; *a-ḫu-ia-ḫa-ad, ḫa-at-ri-e-ḫa-ad, ia-šu-ub-ia-ḫa-ad*; by-form |yaħid|, cf. *ia-ḫi-da-ar-ru, ia-ḫi-id-ar-ru*; by-form |yiħad|, cf. *ad-ri-ḫa-ad, ad-ri-e-ḫa-ad, ḫa-ad-ri e-ḫa-ad* → Huffmon APNMT 210; Gelb CAAA 21, 102; Zadok Fs. Hallo 318; Streck Onomastikon 1 152 § 2.2, 265 § 3.12, 268 § 3.15, 326 § 5.18; Golinets Onomastikon 2 239ff. (|yaħad|), 241 (|yiħad|), 253 (|yaħid|), 465. **TU** *a-ḫu-a/ia-ḫa-ad, ḫa-mu-ḫa-ad*(?), *lá-rí-im-a-ʔà-ad*(!) → Krebernik Tall Bi`a 209, 215, 222.
yħd "solitary, single"	•CTX: **UGA** → DUL 946: *yḥd.*
yaħatt "uniqueness, singularity"	•ONOM: **B** *ia-ḫa-ti-el, ia-ḫa-ti-lum, ia-ḫa-ti*-DINGIR, *ia-ḫa-at-ti*-DINGIR, *ia-ḫa-at-ti-*ᵈUTU → Gelb CAAA 223 (ḪATI?); Streck Onomastikon 1 152f. § 2.2 fn. 5, 326 § 5.18
åħdh, **yħdh** "together"	•CTX: **UGA** → Tropper UG 344; DUL 31f.: *åḥd*, 2; 946: *yḥdh.*
yaħdōn "alone"	•CTX: **EA** Cf. *a-na-ku-ma : ya-ḫu-du-un-ni* → Sivan GAGl 286; Moran AmL 363; Rainey EAT 73; CAT 1 52, 72; 3 1, 149; Izre'el Orient 38 90; altern. CAD I/J 321: "together with".
yaħudiy "simple (-minded?)"	•CTX: **B** *i-a-ḫu-di-a-ku, ia-ḫu-di-a-am* → AHw 1565: *jaḫudû(m)*; Frankena Fs. Beek 43; Zadok Fs. Hallo 318.

|w-ħ-l|	Sem.: Cf. *yḥl* (Hb. D, C) "to wait"; *yḥl* (Syr. C) "to despair, weaken"; *waḥila* (Arab.) "to get stuck in the mud", *ʔawḥala* "to put somebody in a predicament"; *wḥl* (OSArab.) "to wait, allow time".
|w-ħ-l| "to be worried, despair, lose hope"	•CTX: **UGA** Dpass. prefc. *twḥln* → DUL 946: */y/w-ḥ-l/.*

|w-ħ-m| Cf. **|ħ-m-m|**	Sem.: Cf. *waḥimat, waḥama, tawaḥḥamat* (Arab.) "to have cravings".
ħaħħam "craving"	•ONOM: **EB** Cf. *ḫa-ḫa-ma-núm* → Pagan ARES 3 188, 316.

|w-ħ-y|	Sem.: *yḥy* (JAram. C) "to hurry"; *waḥā, tawaḥḥā* (Arab.) "to hasten", *waḥḥā* "to urge (on)", *waḥiyy* "hasty, quick"; *wḥy* (OSArab. C) "to accelerate"; *waḥaya* (Eth.) "to visit, inspect, watch for".

|**w-ħ-y**| "to hurry, hasten, inspect"	•CTX: **UGA** Gt prefc. *twtḥ* → DUL 929: */w-ḥ-y/*. •LL: **EB** Cf. ŠU.RA = *wa-ʔà-um* → Sjöberg Fs. Pettinato 263; Milano ARET 9 407; •ONOM: **B** Cf. *ia-ú-ḫi*-DINGIR → Gelb CAAA 35, 100.
|w-x-m|	Sem.: Cf. *waḫuma, waḫāma* (Arab.) "to be unhealthy", *waḫam* "unhealthy, dirty", *waḫīm* "unhealthy, bad, evil".
waxim "unhealthy"	•ONOM: **EB** Cf. PI(*wa*?)-*ḫi-mu* → Pagan ARES 3 188, 375.
watxam, watax(xa)m "dirty, rotten (liar?)"	•LL: **EB** Cf. NÌ.LUL.AKA = *a-da-ḫi-mu-um, a-da-ḫa-mu* → Conti QuSe 17 78.
|w-x-z|	Sem.: Cf. *waḫaza* (Arab.) "to sting, prick", *wāḫiz* "stinging, pricking, sharp".
wāxiz "stinging, pricking"	•ONOM: **EB** Cf. *wa-hi-zu/zú/zu-um* → Pagan ARES 3 188, 375.
|w-k-l|	Sem: *wakālum* (Akk. D) "to appoint as overseer", (*w*)*aklu*(*m*), *uklu* "overseer, inspector", see passim *takālu*(*m*) "to trust", with several derivatives; *wakala* (Arab.) "to entrust, assign, charge", *wakkala* "to delegate", *tawakkala* "to be appointed as agent, rely", *wakīl* "authorized representative, manager", *tawkīl* "delegation, authorization", *tawakkul* "trust"; *wkl* (OSArab.) "to entrust"; *awōkəl, úkəl, ōkəl* (MSArab.) "to entrust with", *əwtəkūl, əbt*(*ə*)*kél* "to rely", *wəkáyl* "agent"; *wkl, tawakkala* (Eth.) "to confide, trust", *wəkkul* "dependent, confident", *təwkəlt* "confidence".
|**w-k-l**| "to have authority (over)" **wakil** "person in charge, overseer"	•CTX: **EB** D prefc. suff. *ù-wa-gi-a*-SÙ-*ma* |ʔuwakkilam=Sumay(n)| → Catagnoti QuSe 29 81, 83, 159, 236. •CTX: **EB** Pl. suff. *wa-gi-lu-na, wa-ki-lu-na* |wakilū=nay(n)| → Fronzaroli QuSe 13 152; Catagnoti / Fronzaroli ARET 16 45, 55, 285; Catagnoti QuSe 29 34, 74, 111, 119, 159, 236. •ONOM: **EB** *la-wa-gi-a, ma*-PI(*wa*)-*gi, ma-wa-gi-a, la-wa-gi/ki-lu, ma-wa-gi-lu* → Krebernik PET 104; Pagan ARES 3 240, 345, 349.
|w-k-y|	Sem.: Cf. *ekû*(*m*) (Akk.) "to deprive", *ekûtu* (Nuzi) "orphanhood", *mēkûtu* "shortage".
wakāyt "orphanhood"	•LL: **EB** KI.GUL = *wa-ga-du* → Conti QuSe 17 199f.
|w-ḳ-h|	Sem.: *yqhh* (y^e*qāhāh* / *yiqhāh*, Hb.) "obedience"; *waqiha* (Arab.) "to obey"; *wqh* (OSArab.) "to obey".
|**w-ḳ-h**| "to obey"	•ONOM: **EB** *ù-ga, ù-ga-ù, da-a-ga-ù, da-a-ga-a-ba, da-a-ga-ba-*al_6*/lu, da-a-ga-*ba_4*-lu*; cf. NI-*a-ga-ba-*al_6 → Pagan ARES 3 190, 296, 371, 382. **U3** *ù-ga* → Buccellati Amorites 20, 79, 183. **B** Cf. *ù-ga-a, ú-qa/ga*-^{d}IM, *ú-qa/ga*-DINGIR, *ú-qa-il, ú-qa-i-la, ú-qa*-DINGIR-*lum, ú-qa-ki-el, ú-ga-*(*a-*)^{d}UTU, *ú-qí-el* → Gelb CAAA 22, 100f. (WQAH, WQIH).

|y-ḳ-h| "to obey"	•ONOM: **B** Cf. *i-ka-aḫ*-DINGIR → Gelb CAAA 22, 110 (JQAH). **A7** Cf. *ia-qa-am-mu* → Wiseman AT 136; Gelb CAAA 22, 110 (JQAH).

|w-ḳ-r|	Sem.:[924] *yqr* (Hb.): "to be difficult, carry weight, be esteemed", *yqr* (*yāqār*) "scarce, precious", (*yᵉqār*) "preciousness, honour", *yqyr* (*yaqqîr*) "scarce, precious, dear"; *yqr* (Palm. C) "to make heavy", *yqr* (Palm., Hatra) "honour"; *yqr* (Aram., Syr.) "to be heavy", *yqr*(*?*) "honour", *yqyr* "heavy, precious, dear", *ywqr*(*?*) "weight, heaviness"; *(w)aqāru(m)* (Akk.): "to become rare, precious", (*w*)*aqru*(*m*), *uqru*, fem. (*w*)*aqartu*(*m*), *baqartum*, *maqartu* "rare, valuable", (*w*)*aqqaru* "very precious"; *waqura*, *qira* (Arab.) "to be dignified, grave", *wuqūra* "to sit with dignity", *waqqar* "to honor, revere", *waqār* "dignity", *waqūr* "grave, dignified".
|y-ḳ-r| "to be heavy, precious, esteemed"	•ONOM: **EUPH** *ia-ki-ra-nu*, *ia-ki-ra-a-bu-um*, *ia-ki-ra-a-ḫi*, *ia-ki-ra-ḫu-um* → Gelb CAAA 22, 110; Zadok Fs. Hallo 331; Streck Onomastikon 1 200 § 2.95, 346 § 5.64; Golinets Onomastikon 2 229f., 468.[925]
yaḳr "dear, precious, esteemed"	•ONOM: **B** ia-aq-ra-an, *ia-aq-ri*-DINGIR, *ia-aq-rum*-DINGIR, LUGAL-*ya-aq-ra*, vocalic assimil. |yiqar=|: *a-bi-e-qar*, *ba-aḫ-li-e-qar*, cf. *a-ḫu-um i-qar*; fem. *a-ḫa-ta-ya-aq-ra*, *um-mi-ia-aq-ra*, vocalic assimil. |yiqrah/t=|: *a-ḫa-ti-iq-ra*, *a-ḫa-at-iq-ra*, *a-ḫa-ti-iq-ra-at*, nisbe fem.? |yaqrīt=|: *ia-aq-ri-tum* → Gelb CAAA 22, 104 (JAQR), 109 (JIQR); Streck Onomastikon 1 161 § 2.21, 165 § 2.29, 275 § 3.34, 312 § 4.3, 316 § 4.10, 344 § 5.60; Golinets Onomastikon 2 242, 251f., 468. **R** *ì-lí-aq-ra* → Dalley / Walker / Hawkins Tell Rimah 27 (16:3); Page Iraq 30 90; Golinets Onomastikon 2 252, 468. **EM** *ia-aq-ri* → Pruzsinszky PTEm 168 [420].
yaḳar "dear, precious, esteemed"	•ONOM: **EUPH**, **B** *ia-qar*(-DINGIR), *ia-qa-ru*, *ia-ga/qa-rum*, *ia-ga-ru-um*, *ḫa-mu-ia-qar*, *a-bi-e-qar*, *a-bu-qar*, fem. |yaqarah|, |yaqart=|: *ia-qar-tum*, *um-mi-ya-qar-ra* → Huffmon APNMT 214; Gelb CAAA 22, 104; Streck 1 205 § 2.97; Golinets Onomastikon 2 251f., 468. **A4** *ia-qa-ru/i* → Wiseman AT 136; Dietrich / Loretz ZA 60 102 (197:37); Arnaud AuOr 16 177; Sivan GAGl 288; vDassow SCCNH 17 496. **UGS** *ia-qa-ru*, *ia-qa-rum*, *ia-qar-mi* → Gröndahl PTU 145; Sivan GAGl 288.
yaḳir, **yaḳḳir** "(most) dear, precious, esteemed"	•ONOM: **EUPH** *à-ki-rí-im* → Golinets Onomastikon 2 254, 468.: |yaḳir=| **TU** *ya-qí-ru-um* → Krebernik Tall Bi`a 221: |*yaḳḳir*|; Golinets Onomastikon 2 254, 468: |yaḳir=|.
yaḳur, **yaḳḳur** "(most) dear, precious, esteemed"	•ONOM: **U3** Cf. *ia*-GU-*ra* → Zadok Fs. Hallo 323.[926] **EUPH**, **B** *ia-ku-ra-an*, *i-ku-ur-ba-li*, *ia-ku-ur-ᵈda-gan*, *ia-ku-ri*(?)-*im*(?) → Huffmon APNMT 214: |*yaqur*=|; Gelb CAAA 72 (?KUR!); Streck Onomastikon 1 333 § 5.36 fn. 2: |*yaqqur*|, 359 (3313, rdg?); Golinets Onomastikon 2 262, 468. **UGS** *ia-qú-ru* → Gröndahl PTU 145; Sivan GAGl 288. **R** *ia-qú-ra* → Dalley / Walker / Hawkins Tell Rimah 175 (244 II 26'); Zadok Fs. Hallo 331.
yḳr "(most) dear, precious, esteemed"	•ONOM: **UGA** → DUL 961: *yqr*.
wuḳḳur "dear, precious, esteemed"	•ONOM: **EB** Cf. *ù-gú-ra* → Pagan ARES 3 190, 372 (|ʔuqqur=|).

---

924 Unrelated to \|n/w/y-q-r\| "pierce, incise, excavate".

925 Altern. Huffmon APNMT 145, 214: qatil / qatīl / qattīl\| "valuable"(Hb. *yaqqīr*).

926 Altern. see \|g-w-r\| "to lodge, dwell", GlOS 1 193 (\|g-w-r\| (1)).

yaḳrān "dear, precious, esteemed"	•ONOM: See above *yaḳr*.
yaḳarah, yaḳart "dear, precious, esteemed"	•ONOM: See above *yaḳar*.
yaḳrīt "dear, precious, esteemed"	•ONOM: See above *yaḳr*.
mayḳarat "dear, precious, esteemed"	•ONOM: **EB** *ma-ga-ra-du, ma-ga-ra-dum, má-ga-ra-du*, cfr. *ma-ga-du, ma-ga-da, ma-ga-dum, ma-ga-a-du* → Krebernik PET 245; Pagan ARES 3 190, 347f., 350.
mawḳir "dearness"	•ONOM: **U3** *mu-gi-ra-nu-um* → Buccellati Amorites 62, 174; Gelb CAAA 22, 101 (WQIR); Streck Onomastikon 1 176 § 2.52.

|w-ḳ-y|	Sem.: *ʔwqy, ʔqytʔ* (Syr.) "hair band"; *waqā* (*waqy*, Arab.) "to guard, preserve, safeguard", *waqqāya* "protective covering"; *wəqyat* (Eth.) "wraparound".
|**y-ḳ-y**| "to protect"	•CTX: **UGA** G prefc. suff. *tqh, tqyn, tqynh* → DUL 961: /*y-q-y*/. •ONOM: **B** *ú-qe-e-ra-aḫ* → Zadok Fs. Hallo 331.
mawḳuwuy "kind of band or collar for yokes"	•LL: **EB** Cf. NÍG.LÁ.GU.SAG.KEŠDA = *ma-wa-gu-wu* → Conti QuSe 17 63f.

|w-l-d|	Sem.: *yld* (Hb.) "to bear, give birth", *wld* (*wālād*) "child", *yld* (*yeled*) "boy, male child", *yldh* (*yaldāh*) "girl", *ylyd* (*yālîd*) "son", *ylwd* (*yillod*) "born", *yldwt* (*yaldût*) "youth", *ldh* (*lēdāh*) "giving birth", *mwldt* (*môledet*) "descendants, relatives", *twldwt* (*tôlēdôt*) "descendants, successors"; *yld* (Ph.) "to bear, give birth"; *yld, wld(?)* (Nab., Palm.) "children"; *yld* (Hatra) "birth"; *yld* (Aram., Syr.) "to bear, give birth", *yld* (JAram.) "children", *yldʔ* (Aram., Syr.) "birth", *yld* (Aram.) "born", *yldh, yldtʔ* (JAram., Syr.) "one giving birth", *yldn, yldtʔ* (Syr.) "descendants"; *(w)alādu(m), ulādu* (Akk.) "to give birth", *līdu(m)* "child, offspring", *waldum, (m)aldu* "born", *(w)ildu(m)* "young, offspring", *wālidu(m)* "progenitor", *(w)ālittu(m)* "one giving birth", *tālittu(m), tamlittu* "offspring of animals"; *walada, wilāda* (Arab.) "to bear, give birth", *wālid* "father", *wālida* "mother", *walad, walīd* "child, son", *walīda* "girl", *walda, lida, wilāda, mīlad, mawlūd* "birth", *walūd* "prolific", *muwallid* "progenitor", *tawlīd* "procreation"; *wld* (OSArab.) "to bear, give birth", *wld* "son, child", *mwld, tldm* "birth"; *wəlēd, éléd* (MSArab.) "children"; *walada* (Eth.) "to bear, give birth", *lədat* "birth", *wald* "son, child", *walatt* "daughter, girl", *wəlud* "born", *mulād, mulādāt* "birth, origin, genealogy", *tuladd, ta/əwlədd* "offspring, family".
|**w-l-d**| "to bear, sire"	•ONOM: **EB** Cf. unc. *u*$_9$*-li*-NI(*ni*?) → Krebernik PET 53; Pagan ARES 3 188, 373: |yūli(d)=ni|.
|**y-l-d**| "to bear, sire"	•CTX: **UGA** G prefc. *tld*. suffc. *ylt*, imp. *ld*, inf. abs. (*y*)*ld*; N suffc. *yld*; C prefc. *åšld* → DUL 948f. /*y-l-d*/; Tropper UG 963f. (*wld, yld*). •ONOM: **EUPH** Cf. *ia-li-id*-^{d}IM → Zadok Fs. Hallo 331.
lād "child"	•ONOM: **EM** *la-di*$_{12}$*-ia, la-ad/dá*-^{d}KUR → Pruzsinszky PTEm 173 [584]: 184 fn. 349 [583f.].[927]
yald "child"	•LL: **UGS** Cf. [TUR = *šerru*(?) = [*z*]*u*(?)-[*k*]*i*(?) = P[I(?)-*al*/*la*(?)-*d*]*u*(?) → Huehnergard UVST 77, 133 (rdg ?).

[927] For *Luʔād-Dagan* see Feliu Dagan p. 258.

yld "son; young (animal)"	•CTX: **UGA** Sg. *yld*, pl. cstr. *yld*, du. suff. *yldy* → DUL 949.
wallādt "midwife"	•LL: **EB** ŠÀ.ZU = *wa-a-tum* → Fronzaroli QuSe 13 152; StEb 7 185; Bonechi QDLF 16 89.
mld "newly born"	•ONOM: **UGA** → DUL 541: *mld* (II).
mald(iy) "newly born (stock)"	•CTX: **EUPH** *ma-al-du* → vSoden Or 56 100 (< *waldû*); Durand ARMT 21 30 fn. 36; Charpin / Durand MARI 2 92.
muwallidt "midwife"	•CTX: **EB** *mu-wa-li-tum* → Archi ARET 1 296; Bonechi QDLF 16 84; Catagnoti QuSe 29 140, 160, 236 •LL: **EB** ŠÀ.ZU = *mu-li-tum/du* → Fronzaroli QuSe 13 146; StEb 7 174; Krebernik ZA 73 22f. (581, 609); Conti QuSe 17 163; Bonechi QDLF 16 84; Catagnoti QuSe 29 22, 140, 160, 236: |mullittum|.
tawladt "first offspring of animals"	•CTX: **EB** Pl. *du-la-ti* |tūlattī|, suff. *du-la-ti*-SÙ, *du-la-ti-su-ma* |tūlattī=Sumay(n)| → Fronzaroli ARET 11 81, 143; Catagnoti QuSe 29 19, 78, 232.

|w-l-θ|

Sem.: *walaṯa* (Arab.) "to beat, crush".

|**w-l-θ**| "to crush"	•LL: **EB** ḪI = *wa-la-sum* → Fronzaroli StEb 1 77; QuSe 13 152.

|w-l-y|

Sem.: *waliya* (Arab.) "to be near, be close, lie next", *waliyy* "near, neighbouring, close".

yly "comrade, companion"	•CTX: **UGA** Pl. suff. *ylyh* → DUL 949 *yly* (I). •ONOM: **UGA** *yly* → DUL 949: *yly* (II).

|w-m-ʔ|

Sem.: *ymy* (Aram., Syr.) "to swear"; *wamāʔum*, with allomorphs *tamû*, *tamāʔum*, *taʔû*, *temû* (Akk.) "to swear".

|**w-m-ʔ**| "to swear"	•LL: **EB.**[928] •ONOM: **EB** u_9*-ma-li-im* → Krebernik PET 53; Pagan ARES 3 189, 373. **U3** *ù-ma-il* → Buccellati Amorites 51, 183, Gelb CAAA 35, 100 (WMA?). **EUPH**, **B** Cf. *ú-ma-*ᵈDINGIR, *ya-ma-a-ḫu-um*, *ya/ia-ma-ḫa-nu-um* → Gelb CAAA 35, 100 (WMA?).

|w-n-y|

Sem.: Cf. *ynh* (Hb. C) "to oppress"; *yny* (Aram. C) "to vex, oppress"; *wanāʔum* (Akk.) "to put under pressure"; *wanā* (*wany*, Arab.) "to be(come) weak", *ʔawnā* "to weaken".

|**y-n-y**| "to be lowered in value, reduced"	•CTX: **UGA** N prefc. *nyn* → DUL 957.

|w-p-d|

Sem.: *wafada* (Arab.) "to come, travel (as an envoy)", *wafd* "delegation", *wāfid* "envoy".

wappād "envoy"	•LL: **EB** IGI.ME.DA = *wa-ba-tum*, [*wa-ba*]-*du*; IGI.KI.DA = *wa-ba-tum*, *wa-ba-tù-um* → Conti QuSe 17 182; Sjöberg Fs. Wilcke 258f.; Bonechi QDLF 16 87.

---

[928] For PAP.A = *wa-mu*, *wa-mu-um* (Krebernik ZA 73 24: from *wamāʔum* "(be)schwören", unlikely) see *yamm* "(primeval) stream, watercourse" (|y-m-m|).

|w-p-θ|	Sem.: *wapāšu(m)* (Akk.) "to insult".
|**w-p-θ**| "to scold, grumble"	•CTX: **UGA** D prefc. *ywpṯ*; inf. suff. *wpṯm* → DUL 929f.: /*w-p-ṯ*/ ("to spit"). •LL: **EB** Cf. Ì.I = *wa-ba-sum* → Fronzaroli QuSe 13 152. •ONOM: **EB** Cf. unc. *wa-bí-sum*, *wa-bí-šu-um*, *wa-ba-sum* → Pagan ARES 3 189, 375: "spitter"(?).

|w-p-y| Cf. |**p-h-y**|, |**w-h-b**|, |**y-p-ʕ**|	Sem.: *yph* (Hb.) "to become beautiful, clean", *yph* (*yāpeh*) "beautiful", *ypy* (*yopî*) "beauty"; *pʔy* (Syr.) "to be beautiful", *pʔy* "beautiful". See further: (*w*)*apû*(*m*) (Akk.) "to appear, be(come) visible"; *wafā* (Arab.) "to be perfect, complete"; *wfy* (OSArab.) "to be safe"; *wfy*, *ʔawaffaya* (Eth.) "receive, grant, transmit".
|**w-p-y**| "to be beautiful"	•ONOM: **EB** Cf. *a-pi*, *a-pi-i-sar* (var. *a-pi-i+sar*), EN(*ʔe*$_x$)*-pi-i-sar*; *u*$_9$*-pi-i-sar*, *a-pi-s*/*šum*; unc. cf. *šu*-NE(*bí*?), *su-ba*$_4$*-a-bù* → Krebernik PET 59; Pagan ARES 3 189f. 282, 365, 367, 374. **EG** Cf. *y-w-pꜣ*, *y-p-w*, *y-pꜣ*, *y-w*$_2$*-pꜣ*, *y-w-p-w* → Schneider APÄQ 53f. no. 91ff. (Zus. 1ff.).
wapiy "beautiful"	•LL: **EB** Cf. AN.EDIN = *wa-bí-um* → Conti QuSe 17 194; Catagnoti QuSe 29 21, 61, 236. •ONOM: **EB** Cf. *wa-bu* → Pagan ARES 3 189f., 375.[929]
wappuy "made beautiful"	•LL: **EB** Cf. AN.EDIN = *a-bu*$_{16}$*-um*, *wu-bù-um* → Conti QuSe 17 194; Catagnoti QuSe 29 36, 61, 236.
yapiy "beautiful; nice thing, beauty"	•CTX: **EA** *ia-pu* :*ḫa-mu-du* (138:126) → AHw 412: *japu*; CAD I/J 325: *japu*. •ONOM: **A4** *ia-pi* → Wiseman AT 136; Sivan GAGl 288.
yp "beauty, dignity"	•CTX: **UGA** Sg. *yp*, suff. *ypkm*, *ypkn* → DUL 958: *yp*. •ONOM: **UGA** Cf. *ypy* → DUL 960.
tp (B) "beauty; countenance"	•CTX: **UGA** → Tropper UG 199, 269; DUL 861: *tp* (II).

|w-r-ʔ|	•Sem.: *yrʔ* (Hb.) "to fear"; metath. *waʔara*, *ʔawʔar* (Arab.) "to frighten"; see *morāʔ*, *morəʔ*, *morāʕ*, *morʕā* (Eth.) "waistband, apron".
|**y-r-ʔ**| "to fear"	•CTX: **UGA** G prefc. *yrảun*, suffc. *yrả*(!), *yrỉtn* → DUL 962. •ONOM: **EUPH, B** *ia-ra-a-nu*; cf. *ya-ri-ni-im*, *ia-ri-en*[930] → Zadok Fs. Hallo 331f. **A4** Cf. *ia-ri-la*, *ya-ra-a-ni*[931] → Wiseman AT 136; Sivan GAGl 292; Zadok Fs. Hallo 331 (?).
wariʔt "fear"	•CTX: **EB** Suff. *wa-rí-a-da-ag* |wariʔt=a=ka| → Fronzaroli ARET 13 115, 310; Catagnoti QuSe 29 76, 118f. (fn. 459), 237.
mawraʔ (A) "fright, fear" (?)	•CTX: **EG** Cf. *ma*$_2$*-ru*$_2$*-ʔa* |môraʔa| → Hoch SWET 134f. no. 174.
mawraʔ (B) "a garment (apron?)"	•CTX: **UGS** Cf. Pl. TÚG.MEŠ *mu-ru-ú-ma* |mōruʔ=ūma| → Sivan GAGl 250; Huehnergard UVST 134.

|w-r-d| (1)	Akk. loan: (*w*)*ardu*(*m*),[932] *urdu*(*m*), *aradu* "slave, servant", (*w*)*ardatu*(*m*) "girl, woman", (*w*)*ardūtu*(*m*), *warduttum*, *urduttu* "slavery".

[929] Altern. \| wahbu\| "gift", see \|w-h-b\|.
[930] Gelb CAAA 276: JRN.
[931] Gelb CAAA 276: JRN.
[932] Lex. isoglosses not known; see denom. base \|ʔ-r-d\|, GlOS 1 38.

---

ward "servant"
•ONOM: **EB** Cf. *ar-da-ša* → Pagan ARES 3 191, 287.

wardat "girl"
•LL: **EB** Cf. SIKIL = *àr<-da?>-tum* → Krebernik ZA 73 41.
•CTX: **EB** Pl. *àr-da-du* |wardāt=| (// SIKIL). → Catagnoti QuSe 29 62, 237.

wurdūt "vassalage, (political) servitude"
•CTX: **EUPH** *wu-ur-du-tam* → Jean ARM 2 104f. (49:8, 10); Charpin ARM 26/2 156 fn. 100; Durand LAPO 16 488f. (309) fn. a.

|w-r-d| (2)

Sem.: *yrd* (Hb.) "to go down, descend"; *yrd* (Ph., Pun., Moab.) id.; *yrd(?)* (Syr.) "stream"; *(w)arādu(m)* (Akk.) "to go down, descend"; *(w)ārittu(m)* "descending"; *warada* (Arab.) "to come to the watering place, to arrive, come closer", *wird* "watering place", *ʔīrād* "adduction, supply"; *wrd* (OSArab.) "to descend, go down"; *wərūd*, *ərəd* (MSArab.) "to go down to the water"; *warada* (Eth.) "to descend, go down", *rədat* "descent", *wərud* "descending".

|**w-r-d**| "to go down, descend"
•CTX: **EB** G prefc. suff. *u*$_{9}$*-li-da-am*$_{6}$ |yūrid=am| → Catagnoti QuSe 29 158, 236. See further *u*$_{9}$*-ru*$_{12}$*-du* |yurdu/ū| → Krebernik QuSe 18 79 (C13:4), 85 fn. 8, 144.

|**y-r-d**| "to go down, descend"
•CTX: **UGA** G prefc. *ảrd*, *trd*, *yrd*, *nrd*, suff. *yrdnn*, suffc. *yrd*, *yrt*, imp. *rd*; act. ptc. pl. *yrdm*, fem. *yrdt* → DUL 962f.
•ONOM: **EUPH**, **B** Cf. *ia-ri-du-um*, *i-ri-da-nu-um*, *ma-ri-du-nu-um* → Gelb CAAA 22, 110 (JRID); *ia-a-er/ir-du-ú* → Zadok Fs. Hallo 332.
A4 *ya-ra-du* → Wiseman AT 151; Sivan GAGl 292.
EG Cf. *y-r-ty* → Schneider 57 no. 102.

yardān "watercourse; DN"
•CTX: **EM** Sg. m. ID-*dá-an*, *ia-ar-da/dá-ni*, pl. *ia-ra-dá-a-ni* (|yaradān=|, fem. ^{d}*ya-ar-da-na*-TI (|yardanāt=| "the river goddesses" → Arnaud AuOrS 1 12; Pentiuc Vocabulary 86f.; Ikeda BiOr 60 270; Reculeau Proceedings 53e RAI 511f.: "le(s) Dévalante(s)"; Westenholz Emar Tablets 32; Sigrist Kutscher Memorial 172 (4:1).

yrdt "step, stair"
•CTX: **UGA** → Pl. *yrdt* → DUL: 963.

|w-r-x|

Primary noun, Sem.: *yrḥ* (*yārēᵃḥ*, Hb.) "moon", (*yerēḥ*) "month"; *yrḥ* (Ph.) "moon", (Ph., Pun., Nab., Palm., Hatra) "month"; *yrḥ(?)* (Aram., Syr.) "month", (JAram.) "moon"; *(w)arḫu(m)*, *urḫu(m)*, *barḫum* (Akk.) "the moon; month"; *wrḫ* (OSArab.) "month"; *warḫ*, *ɔrḫ*, *wōrəḫ*, *wārəḫ* (MSArab.) "month"; *warḫ* (Eth.) "moon, month".

yar(i)x, yarax "(new) moon, DN"
•ONOM: **EB** Cf. *a-ra-ḫé-iš*, *a-ra-ḫé-su*, *a-ra-ḫé-zu*, *a-ra-ḫi-su* → Pagan ARES 3 240, 282.
U3(?) Cf. *ia-ar-ḫa* → Gomi MVN 12 237f.; Zadok Fs. Hallo 332.
EUPH, **B** *ia-ra-aḫ-tum/tim*; passim DN in second position =*yaraḫ*, written =*ia-ra-aḫ*, =*a-ra-aḫ*, =*Ca-ra-aḫ*, =*e-ra-aḫ*, =*Ce-ra-aḫ*, =*ra-aḫ*; see also *a-di-e-ra-aḫ*, *ḫa-ià-e-ra-aḫ*, *is-me-e-ra-aḫ*, *ki-ib-sí/ṣí-e-ra-aḫ*, *ú-qe-e-ra-aḫ* → Gelb CAAA 21, 104f. (JARAḪ) 104f.); Durand REA 214, 670; Zadok Fs. Hallo 332; Streck Onomastikon 1 184f. § 2.76, 269 § 3.17.
TU *ia-ra-aḫ*-^{d}EN.ZU → Krebernik Tall Bi`a 219; Streck Onomastikon 1 262 § 3.10.
A7 *a-bi-ra-aḫ* → Wiseman AT 126; Gelb CAAA 21, 104; Streck Onomastikon 1 185 § 2.76.
A4 Cf. PI(*wa/ya*)*-ar-ḫi*; *a-ar-ḫu-um-ma* → Dietrich / Loretz ZA 60 101 (16:24); WO 5 72 (21:4); Sivan GAGl 56, 289.
UGS *ia-ri-ḫi-ma-nu* → Gröndahl PTU 145; Sivan GAGl 289.

yrx "(new) moon, DN; month"
•CTX: **UGA** Sg. cstr. *yrḫ*, du. / pl. *yrḫm* → 963ff.: *yrḫ*.
•ONOM: **UGA** *ʕbdyrġ*, *ʕbdyrḫ* → DUL 141; *yrḫm* → DUL 965.

|w-r-k|	Primary noun, Sem: *yrk* (*yārēk*, Hb.) "upper thigh, side", *yrkh* (*y*^{e}*rēkāh*) "rear, far part"; *yrk(?)* (JAram.) "thigh, buttocks"; (*w*)*arkû*(*m*), *warkīum*, *urkīu*(*m*) "rear, later", (*w*)*arkatu*(*m*), *urkatu*(*m*) (Akk.) "rear, backside; buttocks", (*w*)*arkītu*(*m*), *urkītum*, *urkittu* "posterity; remainder"; *wark*, *wirk*, *warik* (Arab.) "hip, haunch; thigh"; *wrk* (OSArab.) "hip, thigh"; *wərkīt* (MSArab.) "hip, hip-bone and flesh".
warik "side, hip"	•LL: **EB** ÍB.ÁŠ = *wa-rí-gúm*, *wa-rí-gú-um*, *wa-rí*<*-gú*>*-um* → Krebernik ZA 73, 1983, 33; PIHANS 106 88; Conti QuSe 17 204; Catagnoti QuSe 29 23, 29, 237.
yrk "body back part, flank; side"	•CTX: **UGA** → DUL 965.
yrkt "support, thigh" (?)	•CTX: **UGA** → DUL 965.
|w-r-ḳ|	Sem.: *yrq* (*yārāq*, *yereq*, Hb.), *yrwq* (*yārôq*) "greens, greenery", *yrqwn* (*y*^{e}*rāqôn*) "yellowness, paleness"; *yrq* (Syr.) "to be pale, be green", *yrq(?)* (Aram., Syr.) "vegetation, vegetables", *yrq* (JAram.) "green", *yrqh*, *yrqt?* "a gem", *yrqwn* (JAram., Syr.) "a herb"; (*w*)*arāqu*(*m*) (Akk.) "to be(come) green-yellow, pale", (*w*)*arqu*(*m*) "yellow, green; greenery", *arqūtu* "greenness, freshness", (*w*)*urqu*(*m*), *murqu* "yellow-green colour", *yarqānu* "a garden plant"; *waraqa*, *warraqa*, *ʔawraqa* (Arab.) "to leaf out", *waraq* "foliage, leaves", *wariq* "leafy, green", *warq*, *wirq*, *wurq* "coins"; *wrq* (OSArab.) "gold, greenstuff, vegetables"; *warq* (Eth.) "gold (coin)".
|w-r-ḳ| "to be green, make green, plant"	LL: **EB** A.MÚ = *su-da-ra-gu*[933] → Krebernik ZA 73 24; Bonechi WO 30 28.
werḳ "pale; garden, orchard"	•CTX: **EB** WA(*wi*)*-rí-gu*, WA(*wi*)*-rí-gúm* → Milano ARET 9 409; Bonechi WO 30 27ff.; Catagnoti / Fronzaroli ARET 16 180, 282; Catagnoti QuSe 29 51, 62, 237. •LL: **EB** ŠE.SU:SU.SAR = *da-da-ma-du* WA(*wi*)*-rí-gi* → Krebernik ZA 73 24; Bonechi WO 30 28 (+ fn. 34). •ONOM: **EB** WA(*wi*)*-ra-gúm*, WA(*wi*)*-rí-gi*, WA(*wi*)*-rí-gu* → Bonechi WO 30 28; Pagan ARES 3 191, 376.
waraḳ, **waruḳ**, **wurḳ** "verdant, greenish (a gem)"	•CTX: **EB** Cf. *wa-ru*$_{12}$*/ra-ga-tum*, *wa-ru*$_{12}$*-ga-na-tum* → Bonechi WO 30 28; Pasquali QuSe 23 77ff.; Or 83 273f. •LL: **EB** *ù-ra-gú* (= Ebla Sum. version: ŠÈ.li za) → Civil EdA 143 (EB vi 4), 152: Pasquali NABU 2002/86; QuSe23 78. •ONOM: **EB** *wa-ru*$_{12}$*-ga-nu*; cf. *a-ru*$_{12}$*-gú*, *ar-ru*$_{12}$-LUM(*gúm*?) → Pagan ARES 3 191, 283, 287.
yarḳ "garden, orchard"	•ONOM: **EUPH** *ia-ar-qa-an* → Huffmon APNMT 215; Gelb CAAA 105 (JARQ).
yariḳ "green, verdant"	•ONOM: **B** *mu-tum-ya-ri-iq* → Gelb CAAA 105. **A4** *ia-ar-qa-an* → AuOr 16 177.[934]
yrḳ "greenish yellow (gold)"	•CTX: **UGA** Sg. cstr. *yrq* → DUL 966f.: *yrq*.

[933] C-stem |s^{1}utawraḳ=| "to make green, to plant".

[934] Arnaud loc.cit.: Sab. *wrq* "to order, decree"; unfounded.

yarḳān "garden, orchard"	•CTX: **UGS** *ia-ar-qa-ni* → Sivan GAGl 289; Huehnergard UVST 134; vSoldt SAU 304 (58); Belmonte RGTC RGTC 12/2 403. •ONOM: **A4** TN i_{15}*-ia-ar-qà-[ni]* → Belmonte RGTC 12/2 343: **Yarqānu*. **UGS** TN *ia-ar-qa-ni, i-ia-ar-qa-ni* → Belmonte RGTC 12/2 343: **Yarqānu*.
yrḳn "garden, orchard"	•ONOM: **UGA** Elem. in TN *yrḳn* → Belmonte RGTC 12/2 343; DUL 967: *yrqn*.
werḳān "garden, orchard"	•ONOM: **EB** Cf. WA(*wi*)*-rí-ga-nu* → Bonechi WO 30 28.
|w-r-r|	Sem.: Cf. (*w*)*erru*(*m*) (Akk.) "mighty".
(w)irrat "a weight (strong weight?)"	•CTX: **EB** *ìr-ra-tum*-SÙ, suff. *ìr-ra-ti-ga* → Fronzaroli ARET 13 177, 273; Catagnoti QuSe 29 110, 119, 201.
|w-r-s| (1)	Sem.: Cf. *warasa* (Arab.) "to be(come) covered with verdigris", *warrasa* "to dye with *wars* ('kamala')", *ʔawrasa* "to be(come) yellowish", *waris, wāris* "reddish".
wirs "a greenish-yellow dye or plant"	•CTX: **EB** GIŠ *ir-zú* → Pasquali QuSe 19 238ff.; QuSe 23 79; Pomponio ARET 15/2 423.
|w-r-S| (2)	Loanword. Non-Sem.: *wrs* (Eg.) "head-rest".[935]
(w)uruSS "head-rest"	•CTX: **EA** *ú-r[u-u]š-ša* (5:22; cf. 14 II 20) → CAD U/W 272: *uruššu* A (also Bog.-Akk.).
|w-r-θ| (1) Cf. **|r-S-y|**	Sem.: *yrš* (Hb.) "to take possession", *yršh* (*y*^{e}*rēšāh, y*^{e}*ruššāh*) "possession", *mwrš*(*h*) (*môrāš, môrāšāḫ*) "inheritance, property"; *YRYSOTH* (Pun.) "heritage"; *yrš* (Moab., Palm.) "to inherit"; *wršt?* (Palm.) "heiress"; *yrt* (Nab.) "heir"; *yrt* (Aram., Syr.) "to inherit", *yrt*(*?*), *yrwt*(*?*) "heir", *yrtw, yrtwt?, myryt?* "inheritance"; *yāritūtu* (Akk.) "inheritance"; *wariṯa* (Arab.) "to inherit", *ʔirṯ, wirṯ, wirāṯa, turāṯ, mīrāṯ* "inheritance", *warīṯ, wāriṯ* "heir"; *wrṯ* (OSArab.) "to inherit"; *wērəṯ, wīrəṯ, ərt* (MSArab.) "to inherit"; *warasa* (Eth.) "to inherit", *rəst, wərsat* "inheritance", *warāsi* "heir".
|y-r-θ| "to inherit, possess; to take possession" **yarθ** "inheritance, possession" **yāriθ** "heir"	•CTX: **EM** G prefc. *tu-ri-iš, lu-ri-iš*, suff. *tù-ur-ša-šu-nu* → Pentiuc Vocabulary 183, 204; CAD W/U 404: *warāšu*. **UGA** G prefc. suff. *ảrṯm*; act. ptc. *yrṯ* (see below: *yrθ*); Gt *ỉtrṯ* → DUL 967: */y-r-ṯ/* •ONOM: **A4** Cf. *ya-ar-ši-i[a]* → Dietrich / Loretz ZA 60 101 188:12; Sivan GAGl 289. •ONOM: **A4** DUMU *ya-ri-ša* → Dietrich / Loretz WO 5 73 (23:5); Sivan GAGl 292. **UGS** DUMU *ya-ri-ši*; cf. *ya-ri-šu-nu* (Syria 18 252 / RS 8.213bis:26) → Gröndahl PTU 145; Sivan GAGl 162, 292.
warrāθ / yarrāθ "heir"	•CTX: **EM** LÚ Cf. PI(*ya*?)*-ra-šu/ša*, cf. {A} PI(*ya*?)*-ra-ša* → Huehnergard RA 77 31; Pentiuc Vocabulary 139f., 235; Ikeda BiOr 60 271, 274; CAD U/W 405: *warrāšu*. **MBQ** Cf. PI(*ya*?)*-ra-ša* → Mayer Ekalte 38, 170 (43:20); CAD U/W 405: *warrāšu*.

935 Cochavi-Rainey UF 29 102: Eg. *wrś*, Late Eg. *wrśw*, Demotic *wrs*.

yrθ "heir"	•CTX: **UGA** Sg. *yrṯ*; suff.(?) *yrṯy* → DUL 967f.: *yrṯ* (I). •ONOM: **UGA** *yrṯ* → 968: *yrṯ* (II).
ʔurāθ "house, estate"	•LL: **MŠ** *ú-ra-šu/šú* = MIN (: *bītu*, I 257); *ú-ra-šu/šú* = *ki-ru-u/ú* (II 117) → Hrůša MŠ 48f., 60f., 210, 340.
mrθ (B) "estate" (?)	•CTX: **UGA** → DUL 572: *mrṯ* (II). •ONOM: **UGA** Cf. *mrṯd* → DUL 572.
|w-r-θ| (2)	Sem.: *warāšum*, *arāšu*, *marāšu* (Akk.) "to be(come) dirty", (*w*)*aršu*(*m*), *maršu*, *arašu* "dirty"; cf. *warraṯ*, *ʔawraṯ* (Arab.) "to stoke (fire)".
waruθ "unclean"	•LL: **EB** Ú.SAL.ZÚ = *wa-ru*$_{12}$*-šu/šúm* (1.)DAM, *wa-ra-šúm* 1.DAM → Krebernik PIHANS 106 88f. (VE 1214).
|(w/y)-r-θ| Cf. **|s-r-θ|**	Culture word-cluster, Sem.: Cf. *mryt*, *mrytʔ* (JAram., Syr.) "juice, must", *tyrwš* (*tîrôš*, Hb.) "sweet wine, must", *tyrwš* (*tîrôš*, G prefc. Hb.) "to tread, press"; *trš* (Ph.) "must, new wine".[936] Non-Sem.: *tuwarsa=* (Luwian) "wine".
wirS, **wurS** "flow, gush, spurt"	•LL: **EB** Cf. ZAL.A.ENGUR = *wa-ru*$_{12}$*-sum*, *wa-rí-šu* → Conti QuSe 17 167f.; Bonechi Proceedings 44e RAI 2 100.[937]
tiriS "must"	•CTX: **EB** Cf. unc. *ti-ri-su* → Fronzaroli ZA 88 231.
trθ "new wine; DN"	•CTX: **UGA** → DUL 867: *trṯ*; Zamora Vid 242ff.
|w-r-w/y| Cf. **|t-r-w|**	Sem.: *yrh* (Hb.) "to throw, cast, shoot"; *warû*(*m*), *warāʔum*, *urāʔu*, *arû* (Akk.) "to lead, conduct", (C) "to direct, conduct"; *wrw* (OSArab.) "to fight, attack"; *warawa* (Eth.) "to throw (away)".
|w-r-w| "to send, deliver"	•LL: **EB** ḪI.MU.TÚM = *su-lu-wu-um* → Catagnoti QuSe 29 139, 160, 164, 236; GIŠ.RU = *wa-ru*$_{12}$*-um* → Sjöberg Fs. Wilcke 255.
|y-r-y| "to throw, fire, shoot arrows"	•CTX: **EA** Gpass. prefc. *tu-ra* (245:8) → Sivan GAGl GaGl 170, 292; Rainey CAT 2 38, 76, 78; Moran AmL 299. **UGA** G prefc. *yr* → DUL 968. •ONOM: **EB** Cf. *i-rí-da-mu*, *i-rí-il* → Pagan ARES 3 191, 324f.
tiyriy "throwing" (?)	•LL: **EB** Cf. Ì.GAR = *ti-ri-um*, *ti-rí-u*$_{9}$*-um* → Bonechi QuSe 15 172; Conti QuSe 17 90.
|w-r-y| (1)	Sem.: *ywrh* (*yôreh*, Hb.) "early rain", *mwrh* (*môrēh*) "rain", *yrh* (C) "to water".[938]
waray "cloud heavy with rain"	•LL: **EB** IM.UD = *wa-la-um* → Sjöberg Fs. Kienast 558.
yr "early rain"	•CTX: **UGA** → DUL 961f.
|w-r-y| (2)	Loanword. Non-Sem.: Cf. *wrt* (Eg.) "a type of boat" (?).

[936] WSem. derivatives through C$_1$:*s* > *t* dissimilation of \|s-r-θ\|.
[937] Secondary base \|w-r-θ\| "to flow, gush, spurt" like Hb. vb. *yrš* "to tread, press".
[938] For other questionable isoglosses see Watson LSU 27.

wry "a type of boat"	•CTX: **UGA** Cf. unc. *wry* (bkn ctx.) → DUL 930. Altern.: (Hurr.) PN.
|w-r-y| (3) See **|w-r-w/y|**	
|w-s-d| See **|ʔ/y-S-D|**, **|s^1-t|**	Sem.: *ysd* (Hb.) "to found, establish", *mwsd* (*môsād*) "foundation", (*mûsād*) "founding", *yswd* (*yᵉsôd*) "base"; *ysd* (JAram. D) "to found, establish", *ʔsd*(*?*) (JAram., Syr.) "pillow"; *wassada* (Arab.) "to rest, lay", *wasād, wisād, wusād, wisāda* "pillow, cushion"; *ms*^{3}*d* (OSArab.) "base".
mūsdōt "foundations"	•ONOM: **EG** Cf. *m-ṯꜣ-*^{HWY}*d-w*$_2$*-ty-w*$_2$ → Schneider APÄQ 139 no. 296.
msdt "foundation(s)"	•CTX: **UGA** Pl. *msdt* → DUL 574.
ysd, ySd "base"	•ONOM: **UGA** Cf. *ysd, yśd* → DUL 968: *ys/śd*.
|w-s-m|	Sem.: *wasāmu*(*m*), *usāmu* (Akk.) "to be(come) fitting, suitable, appropriate; seasonable", *wasmu*(*m*) "fitting, suitable", *wassumum, wussumum* "especially suitable", (*w*)*usmu*(*m*) "appropriateness; worthy", *simtu*(*m*) "appropriate symbol, proper sign", *simānu*(m) "right occasion, season";[939] *wasuma* "to be beautiful", *wasīm* "beautiful", *wasāma* "beauty, elegance, charm". Non-Sem.: *žamāna* (Old Persian < Aram.) "time"
wussum "especially suitable, worthy, nice"	•ONOM: **EB** Cf. PI(*wa*?)*-sum/su-um* → Pagan ARES 3 191, 376.
ysm (A) "handsome, pleasant"	•CTX: **UGA** Pl. *ysmm* → DUL 968: *ysm* (I).
ysm (B) "elegance" (?)	•CTX: **UGA** Cf. unc. Sg. suff. / pl. *ysmm* → DUL 968: *ysm* (II); Gsella BiOr 64 564: *ysm* (A).
ysmsm "most handsome"	•CTX: **UGA** → DUL 968.
ysmsmt "exceptional handsomeness"	•CTX: **UGA** Sg. cstr. *ysmsmt* → DUL 969.
ysmt "handsomeness, beauty"	•CTX: **UGA** *ysmt* → DUL 969.
simin "right time, fitting time; DN"	•ONOM: **EB** Cf. *zi-mi-nu, zi-mi-sa, zi-mi-su, zi-mi-zu, zi-mi-ga, zi-mi-ne, zi-mi-na-nu, zi-mi-*BABBAR.KÙ, *zi-mi-ni-*BABBAR.KÙ, *zi-mi-na-ì, zi-mi-a-ḫu, zi-mi-na-ḫu, zi-mi-na-a-ḫu, zi-mi-na-ar, zi-mi-na-*BE, *zi-mi-na-da-mu, zi-min-na-da-mu, zi-mi-na-ma-lik; gi-ba-zi-mi-nu* → Krebernik PET 111; Pagan ARES 3 231, 387; Fronzaroli ProsEbl G 31.

---

939 Probl. semant. developments herefrom (C_1:\|s\| > \|z\| because of C_2:\|m\|): *zmn* (*zᵉmān*, Hb., late) "appointed time"; *zmn*(*?*) (Aram.) "set time", *zbn*(?) (Aram., Syr.) "time"; *zaman, zamana, zamanīya* (Arab.) "given time, period; *zəbōn, zəmōn, zɛm* (MSArab.) "time";. zaman (Eth.) "time, period".

sitt "exquisite ornament, decoration"	•CTX: **EB** *zi-du/da* < |simt| → Pasquali QuSe 23 93f.: |simt|.[940]
ʔus(a)m "exquisite ornament, decoration"	•CTX: **EB** *u₉-za-mu*, *u₉*-SU(*zu*!)-*mu gu-zi-tum*, *u₉*-SU(*zu*!)-*mu ʔà-da-um*-TUG → Pasquali QuSe 19 266f.
tawsam "exquisite ornament, decoration"	•CTX: **EB** *du-za-mu* → Fronzaroli ARET 11 34f., 144; Pasquali QuSe 19 231f.; Textile terminologies 175; Pomponio ARET 15/2 411.
tsm "beauty"	•CTX: **UGA** Sg. *tsm*, suff. *tsmh* → DUL 868.

|w-s-n|	Sem.: Cf. *wasina* (Arab.) "to feel sick because of the smell of a well".
|**w-s-n**| "to feel sick" (?)	•LL: **EB** EME.IR = *wa-si-nu-um* → Sjöberg Fs. Wilcke 252; cf. Krebernik ZA 73 7; Conti QuSe 13 170; Bonechi / Catagnoti Fs. Sommerfeld / Krebernik 164.

|w-s-r|	Sem.: *ysr* (Hb.) "to teach, instruct", *ysr* (*yāsor*) "supervisor", *yswr* (*yissôr*) "reprover"; *ysr* (JAram. D) "to try, chastise"; *esēru*(*m*), *esāru*(*m*) (Akk.) "to exact payment", *isru* "exacter payment", *isirtu*(*m*), *esirtu* "(debt-)collection", *usertu*, *usištu* "exaction". See also: *šawwara*, *ʔašāra* (*šawr*, Arab.) "to make a sign, to advise, command".
|**w-s-r**| **(A)** "to put pressure; teach, instruct"	•CTX: **EB** G prefc. suff. *ù-zu-ra-am₆*(!ḪAL) |ʔūsir=| → Fronzaroli ARET 16 60f., 276; Catagnoti QuSe 29 48, 158, 238: *waʕsārum*. **UGA** G prefc. suff. *tsrk*, D prefc. with suff. *ywsrnn* → Tropper UG 195; DUL 930.
ʔasar "obliged to pay a tax"	•CTX: **EUPH** *a-sa-rum* → Durand MARI 6 60f.
sīr "a tax revenue"	•CTX: **EUPH** Cf. *si-ir*, *si-ri-im*, *si-ra-am*, *si-ir-šu* → Durand MARI 6 58ff.; FM 8 113ff (33:22); ARM 26/1 444 fn. g; QuSe 16 33 fn. 20; Zadok Fs. Hallo 332; Charpin AfO 40/41 20f.; Streck Onomastikon 1 115 § 1.95.

|w-ṣ-b| Cf. |**n-ṣ-b**|	Sem.: *yṣb* (*hityaṣṣēb*, Hb.) "to take ones'stand (firmly)"; *yṣb* (Aram. D) "to validate", (JAram. Dt) "to be steadfast"; *waṣaba* (Arab.) "to last".
|**y-ṣ-b**| "to put, set; to load (a bow)"	•CTX: **UGA** G suffc. *yṣbt*, N prefc. *tṣb* → DUL 971. •ONOM: **UGS** Cf. *i*[*a*?]-*ṣa*-[*bu*] → Sivan GAGl 292: YṢB. **UGA** Cf. *yṣb* → DUL 971.
yaṣib "firm, steadfast"	•ONOM: **U3** *ya-ṣí-b/pu-um* → Zadok Fs. Hallo 332.
yaṣūb "firmly set, made firm"	•ONOM: **UGS Cf.** *ia-ṣú-ba* → GaGl 292; altern. Gröndahl PTU 58, 169; Sivan GAGl 254, 292: |yaṣṣub| (|n-ṣ-b|).

|w-ṣ-m|	Sem.: *waṣama* (Arab.) "to disgrace, blemish".
|**y-ṣ-m**| "to curse"	•CTX: **UGA** G prefc. *yṣm* → DUL 971f.

940 For the alleged Mari-Akk. *sīmu*(*m*) (Pasquali QuSe 19 232 fn. 73f.: 'elemento decorativo') see *zīmu*(*m*) "face, appearance" (AHw 1528f.).

|w-ṣ-r|	Sem.: *yṣr* (Hb.) "to form, fashion", *yṣr* (*yōṣēr*) "potter, caster"; *yṣr* (Pun.) "potter"; *eṣēru(m)* (Akk.) "to draw, design", *ēṣiru* "(stone) carver"; *wiṣr* (Arab.) "drawn agreement (entered in an official register)".
wāṣir "potter"	•LL: **EB** BÁḪAR= *wa-zi-lu-um* → Fronzaroli QuSe 13 152f.; Krebernik ZA 73 36; Bonechi QDLF 16 83; Catagnoti QuSe 29 140, 159, 238. •ONOM: **EB** *wa-zi-ra* → Pagan ARES 3 192, 376.[941]
yāṣir "potter"	•CTX: **UGS** Pl. *ia-ṣi-ru-ma*; cf. LÚ *ia-ṣí-[ru* → AHw 412; CAD I/J 326; Huehnergard UVST 134. Altern. reading LÚ *ia-ṣí-[ḫu-ma*(??), vSoldt SAU 304 (54); see *yāṣiḥ* "bleacher" (|w-ṣ-ħ|).
yṣr "potter"	•CTX: **UGA** Sg. *yṣr*, du. *yṣrm*, pl. *yṣrm* → DUL 972: *yṣr* (I). •ONOM: **UGA** *yṣr* → DUL 972: *yṣr* (II).

|w-ṣ-y|	Sem.: *ṣwy* (Hb.) "to give an order, command"; *waṣṣā*, *ʔawṣā* (Arab.) "to entrust, commend, commit; to order, will"; *awōṣi*, *úṣi* (MSArab.) "to give (o's) dying instructions".
|w-ṣ-y| "to be joined (together), destine; to entrust"	•CTX: **EB** G inf. [*w*]*a-za-u_9* |waṣāy=|; D prefc. suff. *u_9-za-u_9*-SÙ |yuṣṣayū=| → Fronzaroli ARET 16 14, 193, 276; Catagnoti QuSe 29 159, 165, 238.

|w-s^1-m| See |**ʔ/w-s^1-m**|	Sem.: *šimtu(m)*, *simtu(m)*, *sind/tu* (Akk.) "mark, colour, paint", denom. *šamātu* "to mark, brand"; *wasama* (Arab.) "to brand, stamp, mark", *sima* "sign, mark", *wasm* "brand".
Sitt (A) "dye-stuff; stamp; paint, colour"	•LL: **EB** ŠE.GÍN = *si-tum* (< |simt=|) → Fronzaroli StEb 7 181f.; Fronzaroli QuSe 13 149; Krebernik ZA 73 38 fn.136; PIHANS 106 88 (VE 693, !761);[942] Conti QuSe 17 181.

|w-s^1-n| Cf. |**y-θ-n**|	Sem.: *yšn* (Hb.) "to fall asleep", *yšn* (*yāšēn*) "asleep", *šnh* (*šēnāh*) "sleep"; *šnh*, *šntʔ* (Aram., Syr.) "sleep"; *šittu(m)*, *šiṭṭu* (Akk.) "sleep",*šuttu(m)*, *šunatu(m)* "dream"; *wasina* (Arab.) "to sleep deeply, slumber", *wasan*, *sina* "slumber, doze", *wasin* "sleepy"; *s^1nt* (OSArab.) "sleep"; *šənēt*, *šonút* (MSArab.) "sleep".
|**w-s^1-n**| "to sleep"	•CTX: **UGA** Cf. G prefc. *yšn* → Tropper UG 632; 634; DUL 973: */y-š-n/*. •ONOM: **EB** Cf. *si-na-du*,[943] *si-na-ha-um*, *si-na-ḫu*, *si-na-ma-lik*, *si-na-mu-du* → Pagan ARES 3 192f., 364. **UGS** Cf. *ia-ši-nu* → Gröndahl PTU 146; Sivan 292: YŠN. **UGA** Cf. *yšn* → DUL 973.
Sin (B) "oracle"	•CTX: **EB** Sg. cstr. *si-ni*, suff. *si-ni* |Sin=ī| → Fronzaroli ARET 13 15, 295.
Sinat "sleep"	•ONOM: **EB** Cf. *si-na-du* → Pagan ARES 3 192f., 364.
s^1nt (B) "sleep"	•CTX: **UGA** Sg. *šnt*, suff. *šnth* → DUL 822: *šnt* (II).
Sitt (B) "sleep"	•CTX: **EB** Sg. *si-dè* → Fronzaroli StEb 7 186; ARET 13 15, 292; Catagnoti QuSe 29 65, 79, 115, 122, 227. •LL: **EB** Ù.SÁ = *si-tum* → Fronzaroli StEb 7 182; QuSe 13 149; Krebernik ZA 73 40; PIHANS 106 88; Conti QuSe 17 192f.; Catagnoti QuSe 29 121, 227.

---

941 For the writings *ù-zi-ra*, *u_9-zi-ra* see op.cit. 192, 373f.: \|ʔūṣir=\| "potter"; questionable.

942 For GÍN.IR = *si-tum* (VE761 see *Siyt* (B) "remnant" (\|s^1-y-t\|).

943 \|Sina=(ʔa)du\| "sleep, father!"; altern. see below: *Sinat* "sleep", and (unlikely) *Sinnāt* "tooth" (\|s^1-n-n\|).

|w-s^{1}-p|	Sem.: (*w*)*ašāpu*(*m*) (Akk.) "to exorcise", *šiptu*(*m*) "incantation, spell".
Sipt "incantation, spell"	•CTX: **EB** *si-ba-du-ne-a* |Sipātū=neyn| → Krebernik Beschwörungen 114f., Catagnoti QuSe 29 74, 119, 227.

|w-s^{1}-r|	Sem.: *yšr* (Aram. C) "to send, transmit, release"; (*w*)*ašāru*(*m*) (Akk.) "to sink down, be submissive", *wuššurum*, *muššuru*, (*w*)*uššuru*, *uššuru* "release, let go".
|w-S-r| **(B)** "to release, dismiss"	•CTX: **EB** D prefc. suff. *nu-wa-sa-ra-si* |nuwaSSar=am=Si| → Fronzaroli ARET 11 40, 165; Catagnoti QuSe 29 80, 83, 159, 237. **EUPH**, **R**, **A7** Passim D *waššurum* → AHw 1484: *wašārum*, *ašāru*, D.[944] •LL: **EB** Cf. BAR.AN.DAG = *wa-sa*-NI(*lí*)-*um* (vars. *wa-sa*-NI<-*um*>, or *wa-sa-bu*$_{x}$-*um* → Sjöberg Fs. Pettinato 275 (discussion). •ONOM: **EUPH** Cf. *mu-ša-ra-an*, *tu-ša-ru-um* → Gelb CAAA 158, 201 (MUŠAR, TUŠAR); Zadok Fs. Hallo 332.
(w)aSr, **waSir** "submissive"	•ONOM: **EB** Cf. *aš-ra-gal-lu*, *ù-aš-ra-sá-mu*, *uš-ra-sá-mu*, *uš-la-sá-mu*; PI(*wa*?)-*si-lí*/*lu*/*ru*$_{12}$ → Pagan ARES 3 193, 288, 371, 374f., 376.
maSSur, **waSSur** "set free"	•ONOM: **EB** *ma-šu-lu*, *wa-su-lum* → Pagan ARES 3 193, 349, 376.
mawSar "release, dismissal"	•LL: **EB** Cf. AMA.GI$_{4}$ = *ma-sa-lu-um* → Krebernik ZA 73 37f.[945] •ONOM: **A4** Cf. *mu-ša-ri* → Wiseman AT 142; Sivan GAGl 13, 249 (diff.: MŌŠARU < **mawšaru* "evenness, uprightness", unlikely).[946]

|w-s^{1}-ṭ|	Primary noun, Sem.: *išti*, *ište*, *ašte*/*i*, *išta*=, *ištu* (Akk.) "with; from", *ištu*(*m*), *ultu*, *e*/*uštu*, *iltu*/*a*/*i*, *issu*, *ildu* "from, out of; since, after", *ištūma* "if indeed"; *wasaṭa* "to be in the middle" (Arab.), *wassaṭa* "to be, place, put in the middle", *wasṭ*, *wasaṭ*, *ʔausaṭ* "middle, centre", *wasīṭ* "middle, medial"; *ws*^{1}*ṭ*, *mws*^{1}*ṭ*, *ys*^{1}*ṭ* (OSArab.) "middle, interior; during"; *wašṭ* (MSArab.) "in, inside"; *wəsṭ* (Eth.) "interior, middle", *wəsta* "in, into, inside, on, to, among".
waSt "at; from; after"	•CTX: **EB** *áš-du*, *áš-tum*, *áš-du-ma*, suff. *áš-du-nu* |waSt=um=nu|, *áš-du-na*, *áš-du-ne* |waSt=um-nayn| → Archi Ebla 71ff.; PIHANS 106 100; Rubio PIHANS 106 135; Fronzaroli ARET 13 19 247; ARET 16 220; Tonietti PrepEb 62ff., 65; Catagnoti QuSe 29 94, 101, 111, 237.
waStay "at, with; from, since"	•CTX: **EB** *áš-da*, *áš-da-ma*, *áš-ti*, suff. *áš-ti* |waStī|, *ás-da-a* |waStay=ya| *áš ti-ga* |waStay=ka|, *áš-da-su* |waStay=Su|, *áš-da-sa* |waStay=Sa|, *áš-da-g*[*ú-n*]*u* |waStay=kunu| → Archi Ebla 68ff., 70f.; PIHANS 106 100; Rubio PIHANS 106 135; Fronzaroli ARET 13 86, 246f.; ARET 16 219f.; Tonietti PrepEb 57ff., 65ff.; Pomponio ARET 15/2 406; Catagnoti QuSe 29 62, 73, 94, 237. •ONOM: **EB** *aš*/*áš-da-ì*, *áš-da-il*, *áš-da-ma-ì*, *áš-da*-^{d}*ku-ra*, *áš-da-ma*-^{d}*ku-ra* → Krebernik PET 76; Pagan ARES 3 257f., 288f.[947]
waStayma "if indeed"	•CTX: **EB** *áš-ti-ma* |waStay=ma| → Fronzaroli ARET 13 108, 247; Catagnoti QuSe 29 101, 237.
waStumma "if indeed"	•CTX: **EB** *áš-du-ma* | waSt=um=ma| → Fronzaroli ARET 13 108, 247; Catagnoti QuSe 29 101, 238.

---

[944] For A7 *wuššurum* cf. Lauinger STOBA 79 fn. 22, 368, 397. For R see also Dalley / Walker / Hawkins Tell Rimah 49 (34:14f.).

[945] Altern. see *maySar* "justice" (y-s^{1}-r\|).

[946] Cf. *mays*^{1}*ar* "justice" (y-s^{1}-r\|). Altern. cf. Arnaud AuOr 16 170: Hurr. \|muš=ari/adal\|.

[947] Altern. cf. *ʔaS*(*a*)*d* "warrior" (\|ʔ-S-d\|), see GlOS 1 44. Forms with base *ʔiSt*=, *ʔuSt*= (Pagan ARES 3 257f., if related to *waStay*) are probl. Akkadisms.

|w-ṣ̂-ʔ| Cf. |w-ṣ̂-ʕ|	Sem.: *yṣʔ* (Hb.) "to come out, go out", *yṣyʔ* (*yāṣîʔ*) "produced", *mwṣʔ* (*môṣāʔ*) "place of departure"; *yṣʔ* (Ph., Pun.) "to go out, leave"; *yʕy* (JAram., Syr.) "to sprout", *yʕyh*, *yʕytʔ*, *mwʕy*(*tʔ*) (Syr.) "sprout"; (*w*)*aṣû*(*m*), *waṣaʔum*, *uṣāʔum*, *uṣû* (Akk.) "to go out", (*w*)*āṣû*(*m*) "going out", (*w*)*āṣītu*(*m*) "that what goes out; a garment (with sleeves ?)", *ṣītu*(*m*) "exit; a kind of waistcoat (with neck opening)", *mûṣû*(*m*), *mūṣāʔu*, *muṣṣû* "exit; outflow, outlet"; *mušēṣû* "one who leases; an official"; *wḍʔ* (OSArab.) "to go out", *mwḍʔ* "tribute"(?); *waḍʔa*, *waṣʔa* (Eth.) "to go out", *ḍaʔat* "exit", *wəḍuʔ* "departing", *mawḍəʔi* "instrument serving to take things out".
|w-ṣ̂-ʔ| "to go out, appear"	•CTX: **EB** G prefc. *da-za-a* |taṣ̂ṣ̂aʔā| → Fronzaroli QuSE 13 139. For G inf. *zé* see *ṣ̂iʔ*, below. **EA** G prefc. *li-sà-ḫir :yu-ṣa* (151:70) → Rainey EAT 88; C prefc. suff. *yi-ki-im-ni :ia-ṣí-ni* |yāṣiʔ=nī| (282:14) → Rainey EAT 69; Huehnergard JAOS 107 721: read *ia<-aw>-ṣí-ni*; Moran AmL 323; Rainey CAT 2 192. Izre'el Orient 38 82f.: "may he [...] take me out". Cf. unc. G / C *ú-ṣa-ka* (82:29) → Moran Or 29 18: volitive yaqtula |ʔawṣ̂iʔ=|; Sivan GAGl 175, 292: C prefc. suff. |ʔōṣ̂ā=(k=)ka|; Huehnergard BASOR 310 70: C prefc. suff. |ʔawṣ̂iʔa=ka|; Rainey CAT 2 192f.: Cpass. suffc. suff. |huwṣ̂aʔka| > |(h)ûṣaʔka|; cf. Moran AmL 152: "*can get out* to you"; Izre'el Orient 38 83f.: "I will send you". •LL: **EB** Cf. MA.RA.DAG = *sa-zu-wa-tum*, *sa-zu-tum*, *sa-zu-du-um* → Krebernik ZA 73 18f. fn. 65; Conti QuSe 17 197 fn. 616.[948] •ONOM: **EB** *ù-zi*, *zé*, *zé-i-sar*, *zé-ma-lik*, passim *zi*=DNN,[949] *da-zi*, *da-zi-ma-ad*, =*ma-du*, =*ma-ad-um*, *da₅-zi-ma-lik*, *du-zi-i-sar*, *a-zi*, *a-zi-um*, *a-zi-ga-ù*, *i-zi-ma*, *i-zi-lum*, *i-zi-ne-àr*, *du-za*, *i-za-iš-lu*, *ì-za-ra-ù*, *du-za-ma-lik* → Krebernik PET 59f.; Pagan ARES 3 186f., 285, 299, 303, 327, 330. **EUPH, B** *ú-zi*, *ú-zi-a-la-šum*, *i-ia-ú-zi*, *ia-ú-zi*-DINGIR, *ia-aw-zi*-DINGIR, *ia-aw-zi*-ᵈIM, *ia-ú-zi-lum*, *ia-aw-zi-el*(?) → Gelb CAAA 22, 101 (WṢIʔ); Streck Onomastikon 1 176 § 2.52; Golinets Onomastikon 2 230f., 474.
|y-ṣ̂-ʔ| "to go out, appear"	•ONOM: **EUPH, B** *i-zi-ia*, *i-zi-ia-tum*, *a-zu-um*, *i-a-zu-um*, *ia-zu-um*, *i-ṣi-a-šar*, *i-ṣi-da-ri-e*, *i-za-ar-ri-e*, *i-zi-da-ri*, *i-zi-da-ri-e*, *i-zi-za-ri-e*, *ia-zi-e*, *ia-zu*-ᵈ*da-gan*, *ia-zi*-ᵈ*da-gan*, *ia-zi-lum*, *ia-ṣi*-DINGIR, *ia-zi*-DINGIR, *ia-zi-a-ḫu*, *ia-zi-e-ra-aḫ*, *ia*(!)-*zi-é-a*, *ia-zu-ìr-ra*, *ia-zu-ra-aḫ*, *ia*(!)-*zu-e-ra*-[*aḫ*], *i-zi-ga-dar*, =*ga-ta-ar*, =*ga-tar*, =*ga-dar-i*, *i-ṣi-ga-tar*/*ta-ar*, *ia-ṣi-qa-tar*, *ia-zi-ša-ki-im*; *a-bi-ia-zi*, *i-zi-ia-zi*-[*iḫ*], *i-ṣi-ma-ri-e*, *i-ṣi-sa-lim*, *ia-zu*-ᵈIM, *ia-zu-ba-al*; passim *i-zi*=DNN (and deceased family members, etc.), *ta-a-zi-an-nu*, *tu-ṣa-a*/*ia*, *ia-tum-zi-a* → Huffmon APNMT 184; Gelb CAAA 22, 111f. (JṢIʔ); Zadok Fs. Hallo 331; Streck Onomastikon 1 192 § 2.91; Golinets Onomastikon 2 218, 230ff., 238, 474. **TU** *i-ṣí-e-ḫu-um*, *i-ṣí-qa-ta-ar*, *i-ṣí-ra-a*/*ha-a*, *i-ṣí-za-re-e*, *i-ṣí-ki-in*-ᵈ*da-gan*, *i-ṣí-na-bu-ú*, *ia-ṣí-li-im*, *ia-ṣí-ú*, *ia-ṣí-lu*, *ia-si-it-na-a-na*, → Krebernik Tall Bi`a 217, 219; Golinets Onomastikon 2 232f., 474. **A7** *a-bi-a-zi* → Wiseman AT 53 v. 10; Gelb CAAA 54 (ʔAZJ); Golinets Onomastikon 2 232, 474. **A4** *ia-ṣí* → Wiseman AT 137; Arnaud AuOr 16 177.
|w/y-ṣ-ʔ|-"to go out, appear"	•CTX: **UGS** G suffc. *i-ṣa-ʔa*; cf. *i-ṣa-ma* → Huehnergard UVST 133; ²UVST 392; vSoldt SAU 304 (57); Tropper UG 464, 636; cf. BiOr 46 650. **UGA** G prefc. *tṣỉ*, *tṣủ*, *yṣủ*, *yṣỉ*, *yṣỉn*, *yṣản*[; suffc. *yṣả*, *yṣảt*; imp. *ẓỉ*, inf. *ṣảt* (see below: *ṣảt*); C prefc. *ảšṣỉ*, *yšṣỉ*; suffc. *šṣả*, *šṣảt* (?); act. ptc. *mšṣủ* (see below: *mšṣủ*) → DUL 969f.; Tropper UG 964 (*wṣʔ*; *yṣʔ*).

---

948 See also\|w-ṣ̂-ʕ\|, LL: EB.

949 Altern. *zé*=, *zi*=, *θill* "shade, protection; DN", \|θ-l-l-\|.

	•ONOM: **UGS** Cf. *ta-a-zi*, *ia-ʔa-za-na* → diff. Gröndahl PTU 112; Sivan GAGl 208: |ʕ-z-y| (See GlOS 1 99: |ʕ-z-z|, fn. 692, and |y-ṣ̂-ʔ| ONOM: EUPH above). **UGA** *yṣủ* → DUL 971: *yṣủ* (II).
yṣủ "exit, departure"	•CTX: **UGA** Sg. *yṣủ*, *yṣỉ*, suff. *yṣỉhm* → DUL 970: *yṣủ* (I).
ṣt "a garment" (?)	•CTX: **UGA** Sg. suff. *ṣth* → DUL 781f.[950]
ṣ̂iʔ (A) "exit, issue, statement"	•CTX: **EB** *zé*, *zé* KA, suff. *zé-ga*, *zé-sù*, *zé-gú-nu* → Conti QuSe 15 73 fn. 221; Fronzaroli QuSe 13 153, StEb 7 180; ARET 13 22, 311; Catagnoti / Fronzaroli ARET 16 91, 283; Catagnoti QuSe 29 22, 122, 238.
ṣ̂iʔ (B) "offspring"	•ONOM: **EB** *zi-du*, *zi-ti*, *zi-da*, *zi-da-su*, *zi-du-ḫa-ru*$_{12}$ → Pagan ARES 3 186f., 385, 388.
ṣảt "issue"	•CTX: **UGA** Cstr. *ṣảt* → DUL 764.
mawṣ̂iʔ "appearance"	•ONOM: **EUPH** *mu-zi-ia* → Gelb CAAA 22, Streck Onomastikon 2 176 § 2.52.
mawṣ̂aʔ "export, produce"	•CTX: **EA** *mu-ú-*[*ṣ*]*a* (85:35) → Sivan GAGl 248.
ms¹ṣủ "one who leads out"	•CTX: **UGA** → DUL 587: *mšṣủ*.
tuwṣ̂at "offspring"	•ONOM: **EUPH** Cf. *tu-ṣa-ta-an* → Gelb CAAA 200 (TUʔZ); Durand MARI 5 622; Zadok Fs. Hallo 331.
|w-ṣ̂-ʕ| Cf. **|w-ṣ̂-ʔ|**	Sem.: Cf. *yṣʕ* (Hb., C) "to make one's bed", *yṣwʕ* (*yāṣûᵃʕ*) "couch", *mṣʕ* (*maṣṣāʕ*) "couch"; *yṣʕ* (JAram., D, C) "to install a resting area on a flat surface"; *waḍaʕa* (Arab.) "to lay (on, down), set down"; *wḍʕ* (OSArab.) "to lay low".
|**w-ṣ̂-ʕ**| "to spread, put down"	•LL: **EB** NI.BA.BÀRA = *wa-za-ù*; ŠU.GUB = *wa-za-um*, *wa-za-ù-um*, *wu-zu-um* → Fronzaroli StEb 7 186; QuSe 13 152; Conti QuSe 17 83, 144; Catagnoti QuSe 29 18, 21, 56, 60, 157f., 160, 238. Altern. see |w-θ̣-ʔ|; Krebernik ZA 73 18; QuSe 18 139; Conti QuSe 13 164.
waṣ̂aʕ "lowliness" (?)	•ONOM: **EB** Cf. PI(*wa*?)-*za-ù* → Pagan ARES 3 187, 376.
wiṣ̂ṣ̂aʕ "couch" (?)	•CTX: **A4** Cf. Hurr.-Akk. GIŠ.NÚ/NÁ *ša wi-iṣ-ṣa-e-na* → Giacumakis AkkAl 112; Arnaud AuOr 16 168f.; Richter BGH 317: *wizz/ssaʔena*.
|w-ṣ̂-ħ|	Sem.: Cf. *waḍaḥa* (Arab.) "to be clear, plain, patent", *waḍaḥ* "light, brightness", *wāḍiḥ* "clear, lucid".
yāṣ̂iḥ "bleacher"	•CTX: **UGS** Cf. LÚ *ia-ṣí-*[*ḫu-ma*(??) → vSoldt SAU 304 (54). Altern. reading LÚ *ia-ṣí-*[*ru*, Huehnergard UVST 134: "potter"; see *yāṣir* "potter" (|w-ṣ-r|).
yṣħ "bleacher"	•CTX: **UGA** Pl. *yṣḥm* → DUL 971: *yṣḥ*.
|w-t-H|	Sem.: *watû*(*m*), *watāʔum* (Akk.) "to find, discover", *itûtu*(*m*) "selection, choice".
|**w-t-ʔ**| "to search, find"	•ONOM: **EB** *ù-da-sa*, *ù-da-aḫ*, *ù-da-a-ḫu*, *ù-da-bù*, cf. unc. *u*$_4$-*da-da-bir*$_5$ → Krebernik PET 40; Pagan ARES 3 194, 371, 373. **EUPH** *ú-ta-tum*, *ú-ta-a-ḫi* → Gelb CAAA 35, 101 (WTAʔ).
|w-t-n| See **|n/w/y-D-n|**	

[950] Akk. loan (*ṣītu*). Etym. unrelated: Hb. *swt* "garment", *mswh* "covering", Ph. *swt* "garment", cf. Pun. *swyh*.

|w-t-r| (1)	Primary noun, Sem.: *ytr* (*yeter*, Hb.) "tendon, cord", *mytr* (*mîtār*) "bow-string"; *ytr*(*ʔ*) (JAram., Syr.) "rope, cord, tendon", *mytr* (Syr. pass. ptc. D) "strung"; *watar* (Arab.) "tendon, string", *wattara* "to draw a bow", *watara* "frenum, membrane, cartilage; *watr* (Eth.) "sinew, cord, string", *watara* "to bend, stretch tight", *wətur* "bent (bow)".
mētara "cordage"	•CTX: **EG** Cf. *mt-r-t* → Hoch SWET 174f. no. 232.

|w-t-r| (2)	Sem.: *ytr* (Hb. N) " to be left over", (C) "to leave over, have left over", *ytr* (*yeter*) "rest, remainder", *ywtr* (*yôtēr*) "the rest, what is too much", *ytrwy* (*yitrôy*) "result", *mwtr* (*môtār*) "advantage, profit"; *ytr* (Aram., Syr.) "to be left over, remain", (C) "to leave a remainder, make to excel", *ytyr* "excessive; more", *ywtrn*(*ʔ*) "excess, increase", *ytyrw*, *ytyrwtʔ* (Syr.) excess, advantage, *mytr* "excellent, more", *mwtrn*(*ʔ*) "useful", *twtr*(*ʔ*) "remainder", *mwtr*(*ʔ*) (JAram.) "surplus, remainder"; (*w*)*atāru*(*m*), *utāru*, *matāru* (Akk.) "to be(come) outsize, surplus", (*w*)*atru*(*m*), *utru*(*m*), *matru* "huge, excellent, additional, surplus, too much", (*w*)*attaru*(*m*) "substitute, replacement", (*w*)*atartu*(*m*) "surplus, extra piece", *tertum* "surplus"; *tawatāra* (Arab.) "to follow one another, take turns regularly", *tawātur* "succession, sequence, series, frequency"; *watr* (Eth.) "continuous, uninterrupted time".
|w-t-r| "to be / show oneself excellent" **|y-t-r|** "to be / show oneself excellent"	•CTX: **EB** G suffc. *a*-BAN(*tar*$_x$)-*ma* |watar=|; D prefc. *lu-ti-ir* |lu=yuttir| → Fronzaroli ARET 13 70f., 177, 247; Rubio PIHANS 106 123; Catagnoti QuSe 29 46, 61, 124, 134, 148, 159, 238. •ONOM: **EUPH** *a-bi-li-tar*; passim elems *ya-te-ir*=, *ya-ti-ir*= → Golinets Onomastikon 2 237. **A7** *ia-te-ra*, *ia-te-ri-da*, *ia-te-ir-e-da* → Wiseman AT 137; Gelb CAAA 22, 112; Arnaud AuOr 16 177; Streck Onomastikon 1 152f. § 2.2 fn. 3; Golinets Onomastikon 2 237f., 474f. **A4** *ia-ti-ra-mu* → Wiseman AT 137; Gelb CAAA 22, 112; Arnaud AuOr 16 177; Streck Onomastikon 1 152f. § 2.2 fn. 3; Golinets Onomastikon 2 237, 474f. **EG** Cf. *my-ṯ-r-šꜣ-m-ʕ* → Schneider APÄQ 137 no. 292.
watar "excellent, outstanding; too much"	•CTX: **A7** *at-rù* → Lauinger STOBA 367 (368 obv. 4). •ONOM: **EB** *a-bù-wa-dar* → Pagan ARES 3 194f., 375. **EG** Cf. *b-ʕ-:r-w-t-:r-m-g-w* → Schneider APÄQ 85 no. 159.[951]
yatar "excellent, outstanding"	•ONOM: **U3** *ya-at-ra-il*, *ya-ta-ar-ḫu-um*, *a-bí-wa-dar* → Buccellati Amorites 25, 32f., 77, 128, 153f., 184; Gelb CAAA 22 107; Streck Onomastikon 1 281 § 3.39 (*yatru*); Golinets Onomastikon 2 246, 474f. **EUPH**, **B** *ia-ta-ru*/*rum*/*ru-um*, *ia-ta-ri*(*-im*), *ia-at-ta-ar*, *ia-at-ri-im*; fem. *ia-ta-ra*, *ia-ta-ra-tum*, *ia-at-ra-tum*, *ia-tar-a-ia*, *ia-ta-ar-a-ia*, *ia-ta-ra-*(*a-*)*ia*; passim elems *ia-tar*=, *ya-tar*=, *ia-ta-ar*=; =*ia-tar*, =*ia-ta-ar*, =(*C*)*a-ta-ar*, =(*C*)*a-tar*, =(*C*)*a-dar*/*dár*, =(*C*)*i-tar*, =*tar*, =*ta-ar* → Huffmon APNMT 217f. (*qatala*); Gelb CAAA 22 106f.; Zadok Fs. Hallo 332; Streck Onomastikon 1 268 § 3.15, 326 § 5.18; Golinets Onomastikon 2 244ff., 252f., 474f. **A7** *ia-tar-ma-lik* → Wiseman AT 137; Gelb CAAA 22, 107, Arnaud AuOr 16 177; Golinets Onomastikon 2 246. **UGS** *ia-ta-ri*, *ia-tar-mu*/*mi*, *ia-tar*-^{d}NERGAL → Gröndahl PTU 148; Sivan GAGl 292.
watār "abundance"	•CTX: **EB** *a*-BAN(*tar*$_x$) → Catagnoti / Fronzaroli ARET 16 171, 220; Catagnoti QuSe 29 16, 28, 61, 160f., 238.

[951] See also \|m-g-g\| "to fight, battle".

yitar "excellent, outstanding"	•ONOM: **EUPH**, **B** *i-ta-ru-um*, *i-tar-ad-an*, *i-tar-i-li*, *i-tar-mu-luk*; *sa-am-me*/*mi-*(*e-*)*tar*; passim elems =(*C*)*e-tar*, =*e-ta-ar* → Gelb CAAA 22 107 (JATAR); Zadok Fs. Hallo 332; Golinets Onomastikon 2 249f., 474f. **TU** *i-ta-ar-li-im*, *i-tár-ba-al*, *bu-nu-i-ta-ar* → Streck Onomastikon 1 266 § 3.14 (*yitar*); Krebernik Tall Bi`a 213, 217 (*yatar*); Golinets Onomastikon 2 250 (*ʔitar*), 474f. **R** *ki-ib-sí-e-tar* → Dalley / Walker / Hawkins Tell Rimah 260. **A4** *e-tar-ma-lik*, *i-ta-ar-mu* → Wiseman AT 133; Dietrich / Loretz UF 1 45 (7:59); Arnaud AuOr 16 177f.; Sivan GAGl 292.
watir "excellent, outstanding"	•ONOM: **EB** *wa-ti-lu* → Pagan ARES 3 194f., 376.
yatir "excellent, outstanding"	•ONOM: **A4** *ia-at-i-ra* → Wiseman AT 137; Dietrich / Loretz WO 5 63 (136:10); Arnaud AuOr 16 177f.; Sivan GAGl 292. **UGS** *ia-ti-r*[*i*(?)] → Gröndahl PTU 58, 148; Sivan GAGl 292.
ytr "excellent, outstanding"	•ONOM: **UGA** *ytr* → DUL 977;[952] *ytrt* → DUL 978; *ytrʕm* → DUL 977; *ytrhd* → DUL 977; *ytrm* → DUL 978; *ytršp* → DUL 978.
wattār "substitute"	•CTX: **EB** Suff. *wa*^{a}*-ad*-BAN(*tar*$_{x}$)*-su-nu* |wattar=Sunu| → Catagnoti / Fronzaroli ARET 16 170, 281; Catagnoti QuSe 29 62, 78, 118, 122, 238. **EUPH** *wa-at-ta-ar* AGA.ÚS; *ṣa-ba-am wa-at-ta-ar-tam*, cf. LÚ *wa-t*[*a-ri*], L]Ú *w*[*a*(?)*-ta-ru*] → Birot RA 62 19ff. (2:27', 3"); Guichard Semitica 58 49 (5:7); Guichard JA 307 35ff. (2:17', 21').[953]
wattur "superior"	•ONOM: **EB** Cf. PI(*wa*?)*-du-lum* → Pagan ARES 3 194f., 375.
maytir "excellence"	•ONOM: **B** *me-te-ra-nu-um* → Gelb CAAA 22, 112; Streck Onomastikon 1 338 § 5.47.
mtr "besides, in addition"	•CTX: **UGA** → DUL 593.
mtrn "surplus, supplementary"	•CTX: **UGA** → DUL 593.[954]
tirt "excess, increase, abundance"	•CTX: **EB** *ti-ra-du-um*, *ti-la-du-um* → Fronzaroli ARET 11 44, 79 (!*ti-la-tum*), 171; Catagnoti QuSe 29 41, 110, 232. •LL: **EB** LAMxKUR.DÙ = *ti-ra-tum* → Fronzaroli ARET 11 44, 79.
tawtar "wealth"	•CTX: **EB** Pl. *da-da-ri* |tawtar=ī| → Fronzaroli ARET 13 159, 251.
tuwtir, tuwtur "abundance, surplus"	•LL: **EB** A.DIRI = *du-ti-lum*, *du-ti-lu-um*, *du-du-lum* → Krebernik ZA 73 23; Conti QuSe 17 168.
ti/uwtattir "excess, increase, abundance"	•CTX: **EB** Suff. *ti-da-ti-lu-su* |tī/tūtattir=Su| → Fronzaroli ARET 13 157, 301; Catagnoti QuSe 29 77, 238.

|w-θ-b| Sem.: *yšb* (Hb.) "to sit (down), to dwell", *mwšb* (*môšāb*) "seat, dwelling place", cf. *šbt* (*šebet*) mng unc.; *yšb* (Ph., Pun., Moab.) "to sit down, to reside, dwell", *mšb* (Pun.) "seat"; *ytb* (Palm.) *ytb* "to sit down, to reside, dwell", *mytb* "seat, throne", *mwtbh* (Nab.) id.; *yšb*, *ytb* (Aram., Syr.) "to sit (down), dwell, stay", *mytb*(*?*), *mwtb*(*?*) (Aram.) "seat, setting", *ytb*(*?*) (Syr.) "seat, dwelling", (JAram.)

---

[952] Cf. unc. GN pl. UGS LÚ.MEŠ KUR PI-*at-ri* / UGA *wtrym*, DUL 930.

[953] For the LÚ.DIRI.GA.MEŠ (*wattarū*) "fermier" in A7 (as opposed to the *maskānū* "exploitant direct") see Durand FM 7 79; Lauinger STOBA 121, 128 fn. 28, 132.

[954] Note UGA *mtrt*, mng unc.; cf. DUL 594 "chariot with reinforced wheels"; diff. Tropper UG 203, 584, 651: Lp ptc. from denom. *twr* "mit Deichsel versehen werden" (< *tr)* "Deichsel"; see GlOS *tr* (A) (\|t-w-r\|); Vita Ejército 52ff.: "cajas de carro provistas de timón", **twr*; also Watson LSU 96f.

"inhabitant", *twtb(?)* (Aram., Syr.) "resident, sojourner"; *wašābu(m)*, *ušabu(m)* (Akk.) "to sit (down), dwell", *(w)āšibu(m)* "sitting, dwelling, inhabitant", *(w)ašbu(m)*, *ušbum* "inhabited; present"; *mūšabu(m)* "dwelling; seat", *šubtu (m)* "seat, residence, dwelling"; *waṯṯaba* (Arab.) "to offer a cushion, to seat / place on a cushion"; *wṯb* (OSArab.) "to sit, reside", *ṯbt*, *mwṯb* "seat"; *ʔawsaba* (Eth.) "to marry".

|w-θ-b| "to sit (down), stay"
•ONOM: **EB** *a-šè-bù*, *a-šè-bu*$_{14}$ → Pagan ARES 195, 283.
EUPH *ia-aw-ši-bu* → Huffmon APNMT 185; Gelb CAAA 22, 101 (WŠIB); Golinets Onomastikon 2 230, 473f.

|y-θ-b| "to sit (down), stay"
•CTX: **EA** Cf. unc. *a-ša-bu* (138:62) → Rainey EAT 65; CAT 2 292, 382, AfO 36/37 63. (G suffc.); altern. Moran AmL 224 fn. 15: *aššābu* "residents" (of inferior status). See also LÚ.MEŠ *ša aš-bu-ni*$_7$ *i-na* E.GAL-*ši* (62:25).[955]
UGS G prefc. 1cs.(?) *la-a a-ši-ib* |lā ʔaθib| → Huehnergard UVST 135; vSoldt SAU 437.
UGA G prefc. *åṯb*, *ṯṯb*, *yṯb*; suff. *åṯbn*, suffc. *yṯb*, *yṯbt*, impv. *ṯb*; act. ptc. *yṯb* (see below: *yšb*, *yṯb*); C prefc. *yṯṯb*; suff. *yṯṯbn* → DUL 978ff. */y-ṯ-b/*.
EG Cf. *ya-ši*$_2$*-p*, *ya-ši*$_2$*-pi* → Hoch SWET 56 no. 60 (|yaθib| / |yaθub| ?. Altern. see |θ-w-b|).
•ONOM: **UGS** Cf. *ú-ši-b[u]* → Sivan GAGl 292.

waθab "dweller" (?)
•CTX: **EB** Cf. unc. *a-sa-bu*$_{16}$*-um* → Pomponio ARET 15/2 405.

yaθab "dweller"
•ONOM: **EUPH** *ia-ša-ba-an* → Gelb CAAA 22, 106 (JAŠAB); Golinets 244, 473f.

yθb "assistant"
•CTX: **UGA** Sg. *yšb*, cstr. *yṯb* → DUL 972: *yšb*, 980: *yṯb*.

yθbt "residence, dwelling"
•CTX: **UGA** Sg. suff. *yšbtn* → DUL 980: *yṯbt*.

wuSbub "temporary guest"
•CTX: **EB** *wu-su-bu*$_{14}$*-bu*$_{14}$ → Fronzaroli ARET 13 72, 310.[956]

mōθab (A) "residence; seat"
•LL: **UGS** [BARAG = *mūšabu* = …] = *mu-ša-bu* → Sivan GAGl 249; Huehnergard UVST 102, 135; vSoldt SAU 305, 337 n. 175.

mōθab (B), **mūθub** "cushion"
•CTX: **Q** TÚG *mu-ša*(!)*-bu*(!), suff. *mu-ša-bi-šu*, TÚG *mu-šu-bi-šu* → Richter / Lange Idadda 86, 185.

mθb (A) "seat, throne"
•CTX: **UGA** Pl. cstr. *mṯbt*, suff. *mṯbtkm* → DUL 596: *mṯb*, 2.

mθb (B) "residence, shelter"
•CTX: **UGA** Sg. *mṯb*, suff. *mṯbk*; *mṯbh*, pl. suff. *mṯbth* → DUL 596: *mṯb*, 1, 3.

nūθab "cushion"
•CTX: **EM** Cf. TÚG *nu-ša-bu* → Arnaud Emar 6/3 290 (303:4'. Passim Nuzi-Akk.; CAD N/2 354).

ʔaθba (A) "chair, throne"
•CTX: **EG** *ʔ-s-b-t*, *ʔ-s-p-t*, *ʔas-ba-t*, *ʔ-s-bu-t*, *ʔ-s-ba*, *ʔ-s-b*, *i-s-b*, *i-s-b-y*, miswritten *ʔas-ba-pa*, *s-b-ʔu* → Hoch SWET 36ff. no. 30.

ʔaθba (B) "shelter, hut, residence"
•CTX: **EG** *ʔas-ba*, *ʔ-s-b-t*, miswritten *s-b-ya-ni* → Hoch SWET 39f. no. 31.

θub(a)t, **Sub(a)t** "(family) seat, residence"
•LL: **EB** GAR.DÚR = *šu-ba-tum/du* → Krebernik ZA 73 4; Conti QuSe 17 76.
•ONOM: **EB** Cf. *su-ba-ti* → Pagan ARES 3 195, 365.[957]

---

[955] No reference is made here to the forms of *ašabu* in *Šar tamḫari*-epic EA 359 (passim), for which see Rainey EAT 65 (*ašābu*), Izre'el CunMon 9 66f., Westenholz Legends 102ff.
[956] Note the somewhat problematical writing *su*= instead of normal *šu*=.
[957] See the previous note.

θbt "(family) seat, sitting (down)"
•CTX: **UGA** Sg. cstr. *ṯbt*, suff. *ṯbtk*, *ṯbth* → DUL 885f.: *ṯbt*.

|w-θ-ḳ|
Sem.: *waṯiqa* (Arab.) "to place one's confidence, put faith, rely", *ṯiqa* "trust, confidence", *waṯīq* "firm, strong", *wātiq* "trusting"; *wṯq* (OSArab.) "to entrust, have faith", *ʔwṯq* "hostage", *tqt* "guarantee"; *wīṯəq* (MSArab.) "to be fixed", *wēṯəq* "firm, secure".

(w)aθ(i)ḳ "firm, secured" (?)
•ONOM: **EB** Cf. *uš-ga*, *uš-ga-ti*, *uš-kùn-nu-nu*, *iš-kùn-nu-nu*, *ba-ba-uš-gú*, *i-na-uš-gú* → Pagan ARES 3 195, 289, 324, 340, 374.

θaḳ "reliability"
•LL: **EB** IGI.ḪI-DU$_8$ = *ša-gúm*/*gu-um* → Fronzaroli QuSe 15 18; Conti QuSe 17 185f.

θiḳ "trust" (?)
•ONOM: **EB** Cf. *su-šè-gú*, *ʔà-lu-šè-gi*, *ʔà-la-áš*-NE(*še*$_6$?)-*gi*, NE(*še*$_6$?)-*gi-sa*, *ù*-NE(*še*$_6$?)-*gi* → Pagan ARES 3 195, 270, 365, 367, 373.

mūθaḳ "reliability"
•LL: **EB** IGI.ḪI-DU$_8$ = *mu-ša-gu-um* → Fronzaroli QuSe 15 18; Conti QuSe 17 185f.

|w-θ-r|
Sem.: Cf. *ašaru*(m) (Akk.) "to muster, review, check".

|w-θ-r| "to organize, instruct"
•LL: **EB** Cf. NA.DE$_5$ = *wa-ša-lu-um*, *wa*-LI (*ša*!)-*lu-um* → Fronzaroli ARET 13 136 ((1) for VE 901).

wuθr "(unresolved) question(s)"
•CTX: **EB** Cf. DUB *ù-su-rí*, DUB *ù-šu-rí* → Fronzaroli ARET 13 136, 307; Sallaberger Kaskal 5 95f.; Catagnoti / Fronzaroli ARET 16 133, 276.

|w-y-n|
Culture word, Sem.: *yyn* (*yayin*, Hb.) "wine"; *yn* (Ph., Amm.) id.; *yyn*(?) (Aram.) id.; *īnu* (Akk.) "wine"; *wayn* (Arab.) "black grapes"; *wyn*, *yyn* (OSArab.) "grapes, vineyard"; *wayn* (Eth.) "vine, wine, grapes".
Non-Sem.: *wiyan=* (Hitt.) "wine"; *wo-no* (Myc.) id.; *ya-ne* (Min.) id.; *oĩnos* (Gk.) id.; *vinum* (Lat.) id.ι

wayn "wine" (?)
•ONOM: **EB** Cf. unc. *wa-na* → Pagan ARES → Pagan ARES 241, 375.[958]

yēn "wine; vineyard"
•CTX: **EA** Cf. DUG.]SAR *ye-ni* (84:44) → Moran AmL 156 fn. 15; Rainey EAC 1428.
•LL: **APHEK** GEŠTI]N.MEŠ = *ka-ra-nu* = *ye-nu* (Aphek 2:2') → Horowitz / Oshima CunCan 32.
•ONOM: **UGS** Elem. in TN URU *ye-na*, URU GEŠTIN-*na*, URU *ye-na-a*; cf. URU <*ye-na*> *ša-pí-il* → Huehnergard AkkUg 375; Belmonte RGTC 12/2 345f.

yn "wine"
•CTX: **UGA** Sg. *yn*, suff. *ynh*, *ynm* → DUL 945ff.
•ONOM: **UGA** Elem. in TN *yny* → DUL 957f. (I), hence GN *yny* → DUL 958: *yny* (II); PN *yny* → DUL 958: *yny* (III).

|w-z-n|
Sem.: *mʔznym* (*moʔz*^{e}*naym*, Hb.) "balances"; *mwznʔ*, *mzynʔ*, *mwznyn*, *mʔznyʔ*, *mwdn*(?) (Aram.) "(pair) of scales"; *wazana* (Arab.) "to weigh", *wazn*(*a*) "weight", *wāzin* "weighing",*mīzan* "balance, scales", *wāzin* "weighing"; *mizān* (Eth.) "scales, balance", *mazzana* "to weigh, measure".

|w-z-n| "to weigh"
•CTX: **EB** G prefc. *u*$_9$-*za-an* |yuzzan|, *du-za-an* |tuzzan|, *ni-da-za-an* |nittazan|, imp. *zi-in* |zin|, suffc. *wa-zi-in* |wazin| → Fronzaroli ARET 13 112, 176, 310; Catagnoti QuSe 29 132f., 158f, 239 (*wa*^{d}*zānum*).

---

958 A more plausible altern. rdg is |wawn=a| "dove" (see |y-w-n|).

|y-z-n| "to weigh, pay out" (?)	•CTX: **UGA** Cf. G prefc. / suffc. *yzn* → Tropper UG 634; DUL 981, unexplained.
wazzān "weigher"	•LL: **EB** GIŠ.DILMUN = *wa-za-núm*, *wa-za-nu-um* → Fronzaroli QuSe 13 152; Bonechi QDLF 16 87 (cf. 82f.); diff.: Krebernik ZA 73 16: |waz(a)n=| "Gewicht".
mzn "weight, scales"	•CTX: **UGA** Sg. *mzn*, suff. *mznh*, du. *mznm* → DUL 599f.

|w-z-r|	Sem.: *wazra* (Arab.) "to plug, block, fill up", *wazara* "moulding"; *wazara* (Eth.) "to plaster, overlay, decorate".
wazār "decorating"	•CTX: **EB** *wa-za-ru*$_{12}$, var. advb. *wa-za-rí-iš* → Pasquali QuSe 23 89f.; QuSe 25 287.

y

|y| (1)
|y| (2)
|y| (3)
|y-ʔ-y|
|y-b-b|
|y-b-l|
|y-b-s¹|
|y-d|
|y-G-B|
|y-ħ-m-r|
|y-k-l|
|y-ḳ-s¹|
|y-ḳ-θ̣|
|y-m-m|
|y-m-n|
|y-n-ḳ|
|y-p-ʕ| Cf. |ʕ-b-ʔ|, |w-p-y|
|y-p-ħ|
|y-p-ḳ| See |n-p-ḳ|, |p-w-ḳ|
|y-p-n|
|y-r-b-ʕ|
|(y)-r-θ| See |(w/y)-r-θ|
|y-r-y|
|y-S-B(-y)|
|y-ṣ-ḳ|
|y-s¹-r|
|y-t-m|
|y-θ| See |ʔ/y-θ|
|y-θ-ʕ|
|y-θ-n| Cf. |w-s¹-n|
|y-w-m|
|y-w-n|

|y| (1)

Sem. formative elem. in first person pronouns. Sg. c. genit. Hb. *=ī*; Syr. *=ī*, *=ay*; Akk. *=ī*, *=ya*; Arab. *=ī*, *=ya*; MSArab. *=i*; Eth. *=ya*. Indep. forms: Akk. *yāti* (genit. / accus.), *yāši*(*m*) (dat.), attrib. possessor m. sg. *yaʔum*, *yû*(*m*), fem. sg. *yattum*, m. pl. *yûtun*, *yāʔūt*(*t*)*um*, fem. pl. *yâttun*, *yāt*(*t*)*um*; Arab. *ʔiyyāya* (accus.); Eth. *kiyaya* (accus.).

=ī, =ya "my, mine, (...) me"

•CTX: **EB** Passim; suff. |ī| cf. e.g. *áš-ti*, *ba-li*, *si-ri*; suff. |=ya| cf. eg. *áš-da-a*, *du-ru₁₂-da*-A, *me-li-ga*-A, *za-ti-a*-A, *ba-li*-A, *si-la*-A, DUMU.NITA-A → Fronzaroli StEb 596; Fronzaroli ARET 13 16f., 238; Catagnoti / Fronzaroli ARET 16 82, 90, 111, 211; Catagnoti QuSe 29 72f., 239.
EA Suff. |=ya| *ḫe-na-ia*, LÚ *a-bu-ti-ia* → Sivan GAGl 127.
UGS Suff. |=ya| cf. *la-ša-na-ia*[959] → Huehnergard UVST 132, 293.

[959] "My tongue" (Huehnergard loc.cit.), if Ug 5 153 is Ugaritic. For RS-Akk. texts (legal and letters, including EA 45, 46, 47, 49, and Aphek 7 [Horowitz / Oshima CunCan 35ff.]) see Huehnergard AkkUg 126.

	•ONOM: **U3**, **EUPH**, **B**, **A7** Passim; suff. |=ī|, e.g. *a-ḫi-da-nu-um*, *a-ḫi-ì-lí*, *a-ia-a-ḫa-ti*, *a-ḫi-iš-du-ka*, *a-bi-a-sa-ad*; suff. =ya, e.g. *la-a-a*, *ì-lí-aš-ra-ia*, *a-bu-la-ia*; suff. =ye, e.g. *i-zi-da-ri-e*, *zi-im-ri-e-*^{d}IM, *ka-ba-az-zi-e* → Gelb Lingua 151f.; CAAA 438ff. (I), 526ff. (JA, JE). **EA** *bá-a-lu*/ ^{d}IM-*lu-ia* → Sivan GAGl 127, 208; Hess APN 48f., 201f., 236. **UGS** Suff. |=ī|(?) cf. *a-ḫi*-LUGAL → Sivan GAGl 127;
=y (A) "my, mine, (...) me"	•CTX: **UGA** → DUL 931.
ya(?) "(is) mine"	•ONOM: **EB** *su-mi-a-ù* → Pagan ARES 3 255, 365. **U3** *i-a-um*, *ià-a-um* → Buccellati Amorites 84, 86, 150; Gelb CAAA 21, 101. **B** Passim, e.g. *ia-a-um*, *ia-ú-a-lí*, *ia-ú-i-lí*, *ia-ú*/*wu-um*-DINGIR, *ì-lí-ia-um*, *ì-lí-i-ú-um*, *ia-a-a-tum*, → Gelb CAAA 21 101.
|y| (2)	Sem. enclitic intensifying / reinforcing the mng of the affected lexeme / syntagm. Etym. unc.; irrespective of its historical origins it seems semantically and functionally unrelated to the *nisba* endings.[960]
=āy, **=īy** "(is really, indeed!)" **=īya** "(is really, indeed!)"	•CTX: **UGS** *uḫ-ra-a-yi*, URU *ga-li-li tu-ki-ii*, *uš-r*[*i-ia*]*-ni* |ʔuθr=īy=ānu| → Huehnergard UVST 106, 112, 185, 315f. •LL: **UGS** *al-li-ni-ya* → Huehnergard UVST 121; Tropper UG 833. •ONOM: **EB** Passim (also |=īy(ān=)| → Pagan ARES 3 259. **EUPH**, **B**, **A7**, **etc.** Passim (also |=īy(ān)| → Gelb CAAA 464ff. (IJA, IJAN); Streck Onomastikon 1 349ff. §§5.73-78. **A4** (also |=īy(ān)|, **EA**, **UGS** Passim → Gelb CAAA 466; Sivan GAGl 99f. (8.5.2); Gröndahl PTU 50f. (§ 83 b), 52f. (§ 85); Hess APN 202 (see Tropper OLZ 91 57).
=y (B) "(is really, indeed!)"	•CTX: **UGA** → DUL 931f.; Tropper UG 833ff. •ONOM: **UGA** (also *=yn*) → Gröndahl PTU 50f. (§ 83 d, e), 52f. (§ 85).
|y| (3)	Sem. exclamative morphem void of decomposable lexical content ('interjection'). Several (extended) allomorphs; cf. *yh*, *ʔwy*, *ʔwyh* (*ʔôy*, *ʔôyaḥ*, Hb.); *yh*, *yʔ* (Aram.), *wy*, *wyʔ* (Syr.); *ūʔa*, *ūʔi*, *ūya*, *wā*(*ya*) (Akk.); *yā*, *wā*, *way* (Arab.); *ʔā*, *ʔō* (*ʔō*), *yā*, *ʔɛ́* (MSArab.); *ye* (*ye*), *yo* (*yo*) (Eth.) (all: "oh, ah!, what!, woe!", etc.).
y "oh!, woe!"	•CTX: **UGA** → DUL 932.
|y-ʔ-y|	Sem.: *yʔh* (Hb.) "to be proper, fitting"; *yʔ* (Pun.) "beautiful"; *yʔy* (JAram, Syr.) "beautiful, suited, fitting", *yʔyw*(*tʔ*) "beauty"; *yaʔyaʔa* (Arab.) "to flatter"; *yawwəha*, *yawha*, *yawḥa* "to be gentle, to charm, flatter".
|y-ʔ-y| "to be right, fitting"	•ONOM: **U3** Cf. *i-a-um*, *ià-a-um* → Buccellati Amorites 150; Gelb CAAA 21 101 (JA?); Zadok Fs. Hallo 331. **B** Cf. *ia-a-um*, *ia-a-a-tum*, *ia-a-a-nu-um* → Gelb CAAA 21 101 (JA?); Zadok Fs. Hallo 331.
|y-b-b|	Sem.: *ybb* (Hb. D) "to lament"; *ybb* (JAram., Syr. D) "to sound a trumpet, shout for joy"; *yab*(*b*)*aba* (Eth.) "jubilate, shout with joy, triumph"; see also *ʔabbaba* (Arab.) "to shout".

[960] Cohen Semitica 14 73ff.; Moscati Grammar 83 § 12.23; Aartun AOAT 21/1; Tropper UF 26 481; UG 481.

|y-b-b| "to shout, whinge"	ONOM: **B** Cf. *e-bi-bu-um* → Zadok OLA 28 25, 105.[961] **EM** Cf. *e/i-bi-bu* → Pruzsinszky PTEm 169 fn. 195 [432].
|y-b-l|	Primary noun, Sem.: *y(w)bl* (*yōbēl*) "ram"; *ybl* (Ph.) id.; *ybl* (Aram.) "ram", *ʔybl* (Aram. Demotic writing) id. Non-Sem.: *ybꜣw* (Eg.) "a kind of sheep (Ammotragus lervia)"; **bVl=* (Central Chadic) "kind of ram"; **bilVy=* (East Chadic) "buffalo".[962]
yabil "ram"	•LL: **NAss**. UDU.NITÁ.MEŠ = *ia-bi-le* → AHw 411; CAD I/J 321.
|y-b-s^{1}|	Sem.: *ybš* (Hb.) "to dry up, become dry", *ybš* (*yābēš*) "dried, dry", *ybšh* (*yabbašāh*), *ybšt* (*yabbešet*) "dry land, mainland"; *ybšʔ* (Palm.) "dry ground, land"; *ybš* (JAram., Syr.) "to dry up", *ybš(ʔ)* "dry ground, land", *ybyš* (Aram., Syr.) "dry", *ybšh*, *ybštʔ* "dry land, earth", *ʔbštʔ* (Syr.) "dried berries or grapes"; *yabisa* (Arab.) "to be(come) dry, to dry", *yabis*, *yābis* "dried (out), arid, land"; *ybs^{1}* (OSArab.) "to dry up", *ybs^{1}m* "dry land"; *yabsa* (Eth.) "to be dry, arid", *yabs* "dry land, earth", *yəbus* "dry, arid".
yabaS "dry; Dry Land (TN)"	•ONOM: **EUPH B** Fem. *ia-ba-sa*, *ia-ab-za*(?)-*tum*; elem. in TN *ya-ba-si-im*-KI, and GNN *ya-ba-su-ú*, *ya-ba-si*(-*i-im*) → Golinets Onomastikon 2 239, 251, 462f.
yabiS, **yabis^{1}** "dry"	•CTX: **EUPH** *700* ÙZ *ya-bi-sa-tum* → Streck Onomastikon 1 121 § 1.95: "(milchlose) Ziegen". **EM** Pentiuc NINDA.ḪÁD.DU *ša ya-biš-ti* (fem. |yabis^{1}t=|) → Zadok AION 51 117; Pentiuc Vocabulary 87 " biscuits with dry (fruit?)". •LL: **EB** Fem. |yabiSt=| in ESIR$_x$.ḪÁD = *ì-da-um a-bí-iš-tum* → Krebernik ZA 73 42; Conti QuSe 17 13; Bonechi Proceedings 44e RAI 2 101. •ONOM: **EUPH**, **B** *ia-bi-šu/šum*, *ia-bi-su-um*; cf. *i-bi-šu* → Zadok Fs. Hallo 332; Golinets Onomastikon 2 253, 462f.[963]
yabuS "dry"	•ONOM: **EUPH**, **B** *ia-bu-uš*, *ia-bu-šum*, *ia-bu-sú-um*; fem. *ia-bu-za-tum*, cf. *i-bu-za-tum* → Golinets Onomastikon 2 255, 260, 462f.
ʔābis^{1}tu, **ʔābes^{1}tu**, **yābis^{1}ta** "hardtack, biscuit" (?)	•CTX: **EG** *ʔa$_2$-bi-š-tu/tu$_2$*, *ʔa^2-bi-ša-*(*ta*), *ʔi-bi-ša-ta*, *ya-bi-ša-*(*ta*), *ya-bi-š-ta* → Hoch SWET 19f. no. 5.
mēbiS "dryness, drought" (?)	•ONOM: **EUPH** Cf. *me-bi-sa*, *me-bi-šum* → Gelb CAAA 108; Streck Onomastikon 1 202 § 2.95.
|y-d|	Primary noun, Sem.: *yd* (*yād*, Hb.) "hand, arm, power"; *yd* (Ph.) id., *IADEM* (Pun., du.), id.; *yd* (Nab., Palm.) id.; *yd(ʔ)*, *ʔyd(ʔ)* (Aram., Syr.) id.; *idu(m)* (Akk.) "hand, arm, power, wage(s), rental"; *yad* (Arab.) "hand, arm, power"; *yd* (OSArab.) id.; *ḥayd*, *éd*, *ə́ʔəd*, *ḥēd* (MSArab.) "hand, arm"; *ʔəd* (Eth.) "hand, arm, power".
yad "hand, power, portion"	•ONOM: **EB** Cf. *a-du-na* → Pagan ARES 3 241, 277. **B** *ia-di-im*, *ia-da-nu-um*, *ia-di-na-ṣir*, *aš-du-um-bi-ia-di-im* → Gelb CAAA 21, 102. **UGS** Cf. *ia-du*, *ya-a-du-na*, *ia-dì-ia-na*, *ia-du-ya*, *ia-du*-^{d}IM, *ia-du*-LUGAL, *ya-du-mì-nu*;[964] unc. *ia-ad-li-nu*, *ia-ad-la-na*[965] → Sivan GAGl 285.

[961] Diff. Gelb CAAA 15, 99: ʕBB "to be pure", *ʕebibum* "pure".
[962] Orel / Stolbova HSED 535 no. 2570: **yabil=* "bull, ram".
[963] For the elem. *i-bi/bí-iš=* (Buccellati Amorites 154; Gelb CAAA 108: JBIŠ) see Golinets Onomastikon 2 462.
[964] Altern. see Gröndahl PTU 142: *yd* "Liebe".

yid, **yidat** "hand, arm, power; rental"	•CTX: **EB** Sg. accus. *i-da* (|yid=am), *i-da-da* (|yid=at=am) → Catagnoti / Fronzaroli ARET 16 68f., 237. •LL: **EB** ŠU.TAR = *ba-da-gi* / *bí-da-gi i-tim*; ŠU.ŠU.RA = *ma-ḫa-zi i-da*; Á.ḪUM = *ga-ba-zi i-da*; A.ŠU.LUḪ = *ma-wu i-da-a*, *ma-u*$_9$ *i-da* → Krecher BaE 159, 165; Fronzaroli QuSe 13 144, 172; Fales QuSe 13 179; Krebernik ZA 73 19ff., 24; Conti QuSe 17 172; Catagnoti QuSe 29 48, 62, 108, 121, 239. •ONOM: **EB** *i-du-na*, *ì-du-na*, *i-du-a*, *i-du-ì-a*, *i-du-ì-la*, *i-du-na-ì*, *i-du-ì:a*, *i-du-na-sa*, *i-du-nu-na*, *i-du-ù-na*, *i-du-nu-ù-na* → Krebernik PET 200; Pagan ARES 3 241, 322, 328. **U3** Cf. *i-da-nu-um* → Buccellati Amorites 24, 156; Gelb CAAA 21, 109. **EUPH**, **B** *i-di*, *i-di-ia*, *i-di-ia-tum*, *i-du-ú*, *i-di*-DINGIR, *i-di-ya-an* → Gelb CAAA 21, 109. **Q** *id-a-da*, *id-a-an-da*, *id-a an-ta* → Richter / Lange Idadda 118, 176. **EA** Cf. unc. *yi-id-ia*, *i-dì-ya* → Sivan GAGl 285; altern. see Hess APN 167f.: Akk. *nadû* "to throw, plant"; Tropper OLZ 91 56; Fleming BASOR 303 98: *ydy* (see |w-d-y| (2)).
yōd "hand (stele)" (?)	•ONOM: **EG** Elem. in TN *yu*$_2$*-d* → Hoch SWET 57f. no. 63.
yd (A) "hand, power, portion"	•CTX: **UGA** Sg. *yd*, cstr. *yd*, du. *ydm*, suff. *ydy*, *ydk*, *ydh*, pl. *ydt*, suff. *ydty* → DUL 938ff.: *yd* (I). •ONOM: **UGA** Cf. *ydbʕl* → DUL 942; *ydn* → DUL 943f.; *ydnm* → DUL 944; *ydy* → DUL 945: *ydy* (III);[966] unc. *ydln* → DUL 943.
ʔid "hand"	•ONOM: **A4** Cf. *id-a-ad*[*-dV* → Wiseman AT 137; Arnaud AuOr 16 154.[967]
bad "through (into / from) the hands of"[968]	•CTX: **EA** Suff. ŠU-*ti-šu* :*ba-di-ú* |b(i=y)adi=hu| (245:35) → Sivan GAGl 56, 133, 209, 285; Rainey CAT 1 76, 92; 3 23, 31, 54, 56; Izre'el Orient 38 91, 93. •ONOM: **TA**[969] **UGS** Unc. *ba-du-ni*[970] → DUL 215: *bdn*; unc. *ba-di/dí-da-nu*[971] → DUL 214: *bddn*.
bd (A) "through (into / from) the hands of"[972]	•CTX: **UGA** *bd*; suff. *bdy*, *bdk*, *bdh*, *bdhm*; with encl. *bdm* → DUL 211f.: *bd* (IV) •ONOM: **UGA** *bdìl* → DUL 213. Unc. *bdn*[973] → DUL 215; unc. *bdy*(*n*) → DUL 215; unc. *bddn*[974] → DUL 214.

|y-G-B|	Etym. unc. Cf. *akabbu* / *akappu* / *agabb*/*ppu* (*a*-KAB-*pu*, Nuzi-Akk.) "a kind of tree".
ygb "a commodity"	•CTX: **UGA** → DUL 945.

|y-ħ-m-r|
See **|ħ-m-r|**

---

965 Altern. Sivan GAGL 214: |d-l-y|.
966 Altern. see Gröndahl PTU 142: *yd* "Liebe".
967 The ending =(*i*)*d* "(x) time(s)" (GLOS 1 11: |ʔ-ð|) is probl. related to this morpheme.
968 See *bad* under |b|, GlOS 1 103, and below *bd*.
969 The PN *ba-du-na* (Taanakh, cit. Zadok OLA 28 97f. with fn. 56), doesn't exist; see Horowitz / Oshima / Sanders CunCan 138 for TA 14 obv. 13'.
970 Altern. *s*ee |b-d-n|.
971 Altern. see |b-d-d|, |d-y-n|.
972 See *bd* under |b|, GlOS 1 103, and above *bad*.
973 Cf. |b-d-n|; diff. Zadok OLA 28 97: Arab. *badan* "mountain goat".
974 Altern. see |b-d-d|, |d-y-n|.

|y-k-l|

Sem.: *ykl* (Hb., Aram., Syr.) "to endure, be able to". Related to: *khl* (Aram.) "to be able"; *kahala, kahula* (Arab.) "to reach maturity", *kahl* "man of mature age"; *khl* (OSArab.) "to be able, succeed in", *khltm* "power"; *kəhēl, khɛl, kɔl, həhēl* (MSArab.) "to be able"; *kəhla* (Eth.) "to be able, prevail".

|**y-k-l**| "to endure"

•ONOM: **EUPH** Cf. LÚ.MEŠ *ga-yi i-ka-li-it* (hypocoristic fem. |yiykal=it| ?) → Kupper ARM 22/1 109 (22 40 II' 15'); Zadok Fs. Hallo 331.

|y-ḳ-s^1|

Sem.: *yqš* (Hb., with by-forms *nqš, qwš*) "to catch a bird with a snare", *yqwš* (*yāqôš, yāqûs*) "fowler", *mwqš* (*môqēš*) "wooden snare for catching birds". The connection with *nāqaša* (Arab.) "to argue, dispute"; *waqaśa* (Eth.) "reprimand, strive, quarrel" is problematic for phonological and semantic reasons

|**y-ḳ-s^1**| "to catch birds"

•ONOM: **EG** Cf. *ya-k-sa-mu$_2$* |yaḳs^{1}amu|(?) → Hoch SWET 56 no. 61.

yāḳis^1 "fowler, bird catcher"

•CTX: **UGS** LÚ *ia-qí-š[u-* → Sivan GAGl 288; Huehnergard UVST 134; vSoldt SAU 304 (56); Tropper UG 471.

yḳs^1 (A) "fowler, bird-catcher"

•CTX: **UGA** Pl. *yqšm* → DUL 961: *yqš* (I).
•ONOM: **UGA** *yqš* → DUL 961: *yqš* (III).

yḳs^1 (B) "game" (?)

•CTX: **UGA** → DUL 961 *yqš* (II).

|y-ḳ-θ̣|

Sem.: *yqṣ* (Hb.) "to awake"; *yaqiẓa* (Arab.) "to wake"; *awōqeθ̣, ōquθ̣, óqeṭ, awqáwθ̣θ̣*(MSArab.) "to waken".

|**y-ḳ-ɣ**| "to be alert, pay attention"

•CTX: **UGA** C prefc. *tqġ* → DUL 960f.: */y-q-ġ/*.

|y-m-m|

Primary noun, Sem.: *ym* (*yām*, Hb.) "sea"; *ym* (Ph.) id.; *ym(ʔ)* (Aram., Syr.) id.; *yamm* (Arab.) "(open) sea".

yamm "(primeval) stream, watercourse; sea, lake; DN"

•CTX: **EB** Cf. LÚ ŠÀ PI(*ya*?)-*mu-mu* (ARET 5 4 V [v.II] 6f.) → Fronzaroli NABU 1998/89: "he of the middle of the stream (*wammum*)".[975]
EG *ya-ma, ya-mu$_{2/3/4}$, ya-n-ma$_4$, yu-ma* → Hoch SWET 52f. no. 52.[976]
•LL: **EB** Cf. PAP.A = PI-*mu-um*, PI-*mu* → Krebernik ZA 73 24 (from *wamāʔum* "(be)schwören", unlikely); Conti QuSe 17 171f. (untranslated); Sjöberg Fs. Pettinato 266 (indecisive); Fronzaroli NABU 1998/89: (*wammum* "watercourse, stream").[977]
B late Ú *ku-sa*-A.AB.BA / *ia*(-*a*)-*mì* ("sea-covering; algae ?", in plant list) → AHw 411, 514; CAD I/J 322.
•ONOM: **EB** Cf. *ma-na-a-a-mu* → Pagan ARES 3 241, 348.
EUPH, B *a-bi-ia-ma, ma-di-ia-ma, ia-mi-i-la, ia-am-ma-a*(-*ia*), *ia-am-ma*-DINGIR, *im-ma*-DINGIR, *ia-am-mu-ú, ia-am-mu*(?)-*qa-du-um*, DUMU-^{d}*a-am-ma-a, ia-ku-un-ia-mu, ḫa-lu-pi$_4$-a*[-*mu*], *ḫa-lu-pí-ia-mu, su-mu*/*mi-ia-ma-am, su-mu-mu*(-*ú*) → CAAA 21, 103; Zadok Fs. Hallo 332; Streck Onomastikon 1 167 §

---

[975] Diff. Fronzaroli loc.cit.: Ebl. *wammum* is the etymon of the NWSem. **yamm-* (with the characteristic development of *w*>*y* in initial position). See also Kogan Classification 239 fn. 701.
[976] Sivan / Cochavi-Rainey WSVES 78: *ya-m*; Helck Beziehungen no. 25.
[977] Fronzaroli NABU 1998/89.

2.33, 266 § 3.14, 272 § 3.19, 274 § 3.22, 301 § 3.60.[978]
TU *a-ab-du-e-mi(-im)*, *im-ma*-DINGIR → Krebernik Tall Bi`a 208, 220 (rdg *im-ma-an* (?)); Streck Onomastikon 1 270 § 3.18.
EM DN ^d^*ia-a-mi* → Pentiuc Vocabulary 86.
A4 *ia-am-mu/ma*, *ia-ma*-DINGIR → Wiseman AT 136; Dietrich / Loretz UF 1 39 (1:39); Sivan GAGl 287; Arnaud AuOr 16 157.
UGS *ia/ya-mu-na* → Gröndahl PTU 144; Sivan GAGl 287.

yomm "sea, lake" — •ONOM: **EG** Elem. in TN *pa-yu-mu*$_3$ → Hoch SWET 52f. no. 52.

ym (A) "(primeval) sea; DN" — •CTX: **UGA** Sg. *ym*, suff. *ymm* → DUL 951f.: *ym* (II).
•ONOM: **UGA** *ilym* → DUL 66; *ảym* → DUL 131; *ʕbdym* → DUL 141;[979] *šmym* (2) → DUL 819: *šmym* (II); *ymỉl* → DUL 952; *ymn* → DUL 953: *ymn* (II); *ymrm* → DUL 954; *ymy* → DUL 954. Cf. unc. *mlkym* → DUL 550; cf. *šlmym* PN DUL 810.

yw "Sea (?), DN" — •ONOM: **UGA** → DUL 980: altern. / ancient name; miswritten?

|y-m-n|

Primary noun, Sem.: *ymyn* (*yāmîn*, Hb.) "right side / hand", denom. *ymn* (C) "to keep to the right", *ymny* (*yemānî*) "right"; *ymyn(ʔ)* (Nab., Palm.) "right side", *ymny* (Palm.) "right"; *ymyn(ʔ)* (Aram., Syr.) "right, right hand", denom. *ymn* (Syr. D) "to greet with the right hand", *ymyny* (JArasm., Syr.) "pertaining to the right"; *imnu(m)* (Akk.) "right (side, hand)", *imnû(m)* "(lying) on the right", *imittu* (*m*), *emittu(m)* "right side, the right"; *yamīn* (Arab.) "right side, right hand", *yamīnī* "pertaining to the right (side, hand)", *maymana* "right side"; *ymn* (OSArab.) "right hand"; *yamān* (Eth.) "right, right side, right hand", *yəmn* id., *yamāni* "right, one who uses only his right hand".
Non-Sem.: *ymn* (Eg.) "right side", *ymnt* id.; **(yV)mVn=* (Berb.) "direct".[980]

|y-m-n-n| "to take with the right" — •CTX: **UGA** G suffc. *ymnn*; act. ptc. suff. *mmnnm* |muyamnin=ma|[981] → DUL 953f.

yamin, ya/imitt "right (side, arm); the South" — •LL: **EB** Á.ZI = *a-me-núm*, *a-me-tum*, *i-me-tum* → Fronzaroli StEb 7 186; QuSe 13 135; Krecher BaE 158; Krebernik ZA 73 20; PIHANS 106 88 (VE 534); Conti QuSe 17 152; Catagnoti QuSe 29 22, 47, 62, 120f., 239.
•ONOM: **EUPH** *ia-mi-na* → Gelb CAAA 21 103; passim tribe name *Yamīn*, Anbar OBO 108; Streck Onomastikon 1 51 § 1.45, 329 § 5.26.[982]

yimnay "pertaining to the right, southerner" — •ONOM: **EM** Cf. *im-na-a* → Pruzsinszky PTEm 84 [486].

ymn "right (side, hand)" — •CTX: **UGA** Sg. *ymn*, suff. *ymny*, *ymnh* → DUL 952f.: *ymn* (I).

|y-n-ḳ|

Sem.: *ynq* (Hb.) "to suck", (C) "to suckle, nurse", *ywnq* (*yônēq*) "suckling, child", *mynqt* (*mêneqet*) "(wet) nurse"; *ynq* (Aram., Syr.) "to suck", (C) "to give suck, nurse", *ynwq(ʔ)* (JAram., Syr.) "one who gives suck, youngster", *mynqh*, *mynqtʔ* "wet nurse", *mynwq(ʔ)* (JAram.) "child", *tynwq(ʔ)* "infant"; *enēqu(m)* (Akk.) "to suck", (C) "to suckle, give suck to", *ēniqu* "suckling", *museniqtu(m)* "wet nurse", *šūnuqu* "milk-giving", *tēnīqu*(m) "(act of) suckling"; metath. *naqā* (*naqw*, *naqy*,

---

[978] For the DN *Yamma/um* see Durand REA 293.
[979] Cf. (DUMU) ÌR.A.AB.BA; Gröndahl 144, 316.
[980] Orel / Stolbova HSED 537 no. 2578: **yamin=* "right (side)".
[981] For a discussion of this form see also Tropper UG 581, 678, unlikely.
[982] For the general mng "the South" in Mari see also Stol BiOr 35 221.

	Arab.), *ʔintaqā* "to get out the bone marrow"; *qənū*, *qéní* (MSArab.) "to rear, to suckle".
|**y-n-ḳ**| "to suck; to suckle, nurse"	•CTX: **EB** C prefc. *uš-a-na-ga* |yuSyannaḳ=ā| → Fronzaroli ARET 13 157, 307; Huehnergard PIHANS 106 5; Catagnoti QuSe 29 142, 160, 239. **UGA** See below *ynq*, *mšnqt*.
ynḳ "who sucks, suckling"	•CTX: **UGA** Sg. *ynq*, pl. *ynqm* → DUL 957: /y-n-q/ (|y-n-ḳ| G act. ptc.).
yunnuḳ "suckled"	•CTX: **EB** NU (*lā*) *u*$_9$*-nu-gú* → Catagnoti / Fronzaroli ARET 16 32, 274; Catagnoti QuSe 29 160, 239
mus^{1}**ēniḳtāt** "wet nurses"	•CTX: **A7** Pl. MUNUS(.MEŠ) *mu-še-ni-iq-ta-ti* → Wiseman AT 158; AHw 682: *mušēniqtu*(*m*); CAD M/2 266: *mušēniqtu*.
ms^{1}**nḳt** "she who breast-feeds"	•CTX: **UGA** → DUL 585: *mšnqt* (|y-n-ḳ| C ptc. fem.).
tnḳt (B) "lactation, nursing" (?)	•CTX: **UGA** → DUL 861: *tnqt* (II).
|y-p-ʕ| Cf. |**ʕ-b-ʔ**|, |**w-p-y**|	Sem.: *ypʕ* (Hb. C) "to cause to shine", *ypʕh* (*yipʕāh*) "beaming splendour"; *yafaʕa* (Arab.) "to reach adolescence", *tayyafaʕa* "to climb", *yafʕ* "puberty", *yafaʕ* "hill, highland", *yāfiʕ* "grown-up, high", *wafʕ* "adolescent; lofty building; high cloud(s)"; *yfʕ* (OSArab.) "to rise, go up", "to announce".
|**y-p-ʕ**| "to go up, arise; to grow; to shine"	•CTX: **UGA** G / N prefc. *ypʕ*, *tpʕ*, suffc. *ypʕt*, N prefc. *ynpʕ* → DUL 958: */y-p-ʕ/*. •ONOM: **EB** Cf. *i-pi zi-nu* |yibēʕ=|(?) → Pagan ARES 3 196, 324.[983] **U3** *ià-pá-um* → Zadok Fs. Hallo 331. **EUPH**, **B** *ia-a-pa-aḫ*, *ia-pa-ḫu-um*, *ti-pa-ḫu*, *te-pa-ḫu*(*-um*), *te-pa-ḫi-im*, *te-a-pa-ḫu*, *ia-pa-*DINGIR, *a-ba-aḫ-na-nu-um*, *a-pa-aḫ-a-bi*, *a-pa-aḫ-ra-bi*, *ia-pa-aḫ-*DINGIR, *ia-pa-aḫ-*^{d}*da-gan*, *ia-pa-aḫ-*^{d}IM, *ia-pa-ḫa-*^{d}IM, *ia-a-pa-aḫ-*^{d}IM, *ia-a-pa-aḫ-li-im*; *a-bi-ia-pa-aḫ*, *i-zi-a-pa-aḫ* → Huffmon APNMT 212; Gelb CAAA 22, 109f. (JPAʕ); Durand REA 670 (***Yâpah*, *ºYâpah*); Streck Onomastikon 1 158 § 2.14 A 2, 250f. §§ 2.173f.; Golinets Onomastikon 2 216, 228f., 238, 465ff. **A7** *ia-pa*, *ia-pa-aḫ-su-mu-a-bi*, *i*[*a-pa*]*-aḫ-*^{d}IM → Wiseman AT 147, and 7 seal a obv, 56:47; Gelb CAAA 22, 109f.; AuOr 16 177; Golinets Onomastikon 2 229, 465ff. **EM** *ia-pa-e* → Pruzsinszky PTEm 168 [420]; Streck AfO 61 308. **EA** *ia-pa-ḫi*, *ia-pa-*^{d}IM, *a-pa-aḫ-*^{d}IM, *ia-ap-pa-aḫ-*^{d}IM → Moran AmL 385; Sivan GAGl 208, 291; Hess APN 84ff., 206, 236; Tropper OLZ 91 56. **A4** *ia-pa-na* → Dietrich / Loretz WO 5 70 (129:4); Sivan GAGl 291; Arnaud AuOr 16 177. **UGS** *ya-pa-ú*, *ia-pa-i*, *ia-pa-a*, *ya-a-pa-ʔu*, *ia-pa-*LUGAL, *níq-ma/me/mu-pa(-a)*, *níq-me-e-pa* → Gröndahl PTU 155f.; Sivan GAGl 291. **UGA** *nqmpʕ* → DUL 632; *ybʕ* → DUL 935; *ypʕ* → DUL 958: *ypʕ* (I);[984] *ypʕbʕl* → DUL 959; *ypʕmlk* → DUL 959; *ypʕn* → DUL 959. **EG** *y-w-pꜣ-ʕ:*^{F}, *y- w*$_2$*-pꜣ-ʕ:*^{F}, *y-p-ʕ* → Schneider APÄQ 53 no. 93f.
yipʕ "splendour"	•ONOM: **EB** Cf. *i-bù-mu-du* → Pagan ARES 3 196, 321.[985]

983 PNN spellings *da-ba-ù*, *da-ba*$_4$*-a*, *i-ba=*, *i-ba*$_4$*=*, *ti-ba=* derive prob. from \|b-w-ʔ\| "to come, enter" (see GlOS 1 133), not from \|y-p-ʕ\| (Pagan ARES 3 196).

984 For the TN *ypʕ* see DUL 958f.: *ypʕ* (II).

985 Altern. \|ʕibʔ\| "burden", Pagan ARES 3 93, 321.

yapaʕ "radiant"	•ONOM: **EUPH**, B Fem. |yapʕa / yapaʕa|, yapʕat| / yapaʕat|, cf. *ia-ap-ha, ia-ap-ḫa-tum, a-nu-ia-ap-ḫa, a-nu-ip-ḫa*, EŠ$_4$.DAR-*ip-ḫa*, EŠ$_4$.DAR-*ia-ap-ḫa-tum*, ^{d}*iš-ḫa*<*-ra*>*-ia-ap-ḫa* → Huffmon APNMT 213; Durand REA 689 (*Yâpah*); Streck Onomastikon 1 281 § 3.40; Golinets Onomastikon 2 251, 465ff.
yapiʕ "radiant"	•ONOM: **EUPH** *mu-tu-ab-bi-iḫ, ia-bi-iḫ*-^{d}IM → Gelb CAAA 22, 110 (JBIʕ); Golinets Onomastikon 2 254, 265ff. **R** *i-ba-al-a-pí-iḫ* → Dalley / Walker / Hawkins Tell Rimah 174 (244 I 42); Zadok Fs. Hallo 331; Golinets Onomastikon 2 254, 465ff. **EM** Cf. ^{d}IM-PI-*pí-iʔ*, ^{d}U-PI-*pí-iʔ*,]-PI-*pí-iḫ* → Pruzsinszky PTEm 196: DN-*Wāpiʕ* [335f.].
yapuʕ "radiant"	•ONOM: **EUPH, B** *ia-pu-ḫu(-um), mu-ta-a-pu-uḫ, a-bi-ia-pu-uḫ*, ^{d}*da-gan-a-pu-uḫ, ba-li-a-pu-uḫ*, fem. *ia-pu-ḫa-ia, ia-pu-ḫa-tum*, ^{d}UTU-*ia-pu-ḫa-at*, cf. *ia-pu-ḫu*-IS → Huffmon APNMT 212f.; Gelb CAAA 22, 110 (JPUʕ); Durand REA 670 (***Yapuh*, °*Yapuh*), 690 (*Yapuhum*); Streck Onomastikon 1 160 § 2.20, 268 § 3.15, 327 § 5.21; Golinets Onomastikon 2 255ff., 260, 465ff.
yipaʕ "radiant"	•ONOM: **TU** *e-pa-aḫ-šu*(?)-AN-*a-bi* → Krebernik Tall Bi`a 214; Golinets Onomastikon 2 241, 465ff. **Q** *zi-id-ki-e-pa* → Bottéro RA43 37; Golinets Onomastikon 2 241, 465ff. **A7** *ba-li-e-pa, ì-lí-e-pa, ia-al-e-pa-aḫ*(!), *níq-me-pa, ni-iq-me/mi-pa* → Wiseman AT 143; Arnaud AuOr 16 177, Golinets Onomastikon 2 241, 465ff. **A4** Cf. *šu-me-pa* → Wiseman AT 147; Sivan GAGl 291.
yipuʕ "radiant; DN"	•ONOM: **EUPH, B** *a-bi-e-pu-uḫ*, ^{d}*a-mi-e-pu-uḫ, ba-li-pu-uḫ*, ^{d}*da-gan-e-pu-uḫ, ḫa-mu-e-pu-uḫ, ḫa(-am)-mi-e-pu-uḫ, ì-lí-e-pu-uḫ, ka-bi-e-pu-uḫ, ni-iq-mi-e-pu-uḫ, nu-uḫ-mi-e-pu-uḫ, sa/su-mi-e-pu-uḫ, su-mu-e-pu-uḫ, zi-id-ki-e-pu-uḫ, zi-im-ri-e-pu-uḫ, ia-šu-ub*-^{d}*i-pu-uḫ* → Huffmon APNMT 212f.; Gelb CAAA 22, 110 (JPUʕ); Zadok Fs. Hallo 331; Golinets Onomastikon 2 256, 465ff. **A7** *ni-iq-mi-e-pu-uḫ* → Wiseman AT 143; Golinets Onomastikon 2 256, 465ff.[986]
yipʕūt "splendour"	•ONOM: **EB** *i-bù-du* → Pagan ARES 3 196, 321.[987]
yatapʕ "shiny"	•ONOM: **EUPH** *ia-ta-ap-ḫu(-um)*, fem. *ia-tap-ḫa-tum* → Golinets Onomastikon 2 262, 465ff.
mēpiʕ "splendour"	•ONOM: **U3** *me-pi-um* → Buccellati Amorites 28, 172; Gelb CAAA 22, 110; Streck Onomastikon 1 192 § 2.89, 249 § 2.172, 338 § 5.47, 340 § 5.50 fn. 3. **EUPH** *me-bi-ḫu-um* → Huffmon APNMT 148, 212; Gelb CAAA 22, 110; Streck Onomastikon 1 192 § 2.89, 193 § 2.93, 200 § 2.95, 249 § 2.172.

|y-p-ḥ|	Culture word, Sem.: *ypḥ* (*yāpēᵃḥ*, Hb.) "witness".[988]
ypḥ "witness"	•CTX: **UGA** Sg. *ypḥ*; allograph *ypḫ*, pl. *ypḥm* → DUL 959: *ypḥ*.

|y-p-ḳ| See **|n-p-ḳ|**, **|p-w-ḳ|**	Sem., with by-forms |n-p-ḳ|, |p-w-ḳ| (see there for lexical isoglosses).
|y-p-ḳ| "to issue, send on" (?)	•CTX: **EA** G suffc. *ia-pa-aq-ti* (64:23) → Hoftijzer / Jongeling DNWSI 464f.; Sivan GAGl 138, 291; Loretz / Mayer UF 6 493f.; Moran AmL 135f. fn. 2; Rainey CAT 2 286, 296; Izre'el Orient 38 83; Mazzini UF 50 241ff. **UGA**.[989]

986 See Durand REA 690 for the DN *Yapuhum* (sic).

987 Altern. \|ʕibʔut\| "burden", Pagan ARES 3 93, 321.

988 For its problematical connection with a CSem. etymon **bwḥ* "to reveal a secret" (Arab., Eth.) see Watson SEL 34-36 83ff.

|y-p-n|	Culture word, Sem.: *yafan* (Arab.) "four-year-old bullock", fem. *yafana* "cow with calf". See further *tayfan, tafen, tefan* (Eth.) "young bullock".[990]
ypt "cow, yearling calf"	●CTX: **UGA** → DUL 960: *ypt* (I). ●ONOM: **UGA** Cf. *ypt* → DUL 960: *ypt* (II).
|y-r-b-ʕ| **yarbuʕ** "a rodent"	Primary noun, Sem.: *yrbwʕ(ʔ)* Syr.) "jerboa"; *arrabu(m), arrapu* (Akk.) "dormouse"; *yarbūʕ, yurbūʕ* (Arab.) "jerboa". ●LL: **EB** NI.PÉŠ = *a-ra-bù(-um)* → Krebernik ZA 73 33f.; Fronzaroli QuSe 13 136; Conti QuSe 17 205; Sjöberg WO 27 14.
|(y)-r-θ| See **|(w/y)-r-θ|**	
|y-r-y┼| **yryt** "coral" (?)	Culture word, etym. and mng unc. Cf. *ayyartu(m), yartu* (Akk.) "white coral" (?) altern. "cowrie" (?).[991] ●CTX: **UGA** Pl.? *yryt* → DUL 698.
|y-S-B(-y)| **yaSuB(uy)** "a stone (jasper ?)"	Culture word, Sem.: *yšph* (*yāšᵉpēh*, Hb.) "jasper"; *yšph* (JAram., Syr.) "jasper", *ʔyspwn* (Syr.) id.; *yašpû, ašpû* (Akk.) "jasper"; *yašb, yašf* (Arab.) id. Non-Sem.: *iaspis* (Gr.) "jasper"; hence Eth. *yāsbis, ʔiyyāspid* id. ●CTX: **EM** NA₄ *i-ia-šu-BU* → Pentiuc Vocabulary 82.
|y-ṣ-ḳ| **|y-ṣ-ḳ|** "to pour (out); to smelt, cast" **māṣiḳta, manṣiḳta** "a (large) vessel"	Sem.: *yṣq* (Hb.) "to pour out"; *yṣq* (Ph.) "cast statue" (?). ●CTX: **UGA** G suffc. *yṣq*, prefc. *yṣq*, suff. *yṣqm* → DUL 972: /y-ṣ-q/. ●CTX: **EA** Cf. *ma-ṣí-iq-tá* (14 III 40) → CAD M/1 438: *maziqda* (*maṣiqta*) "an alabastron"; Moran AmL 33 (untranslated); Sivan GAGl 245: "ladle". **EG** *ma-ḏ-q-ta, ma-ḏ-q* |māṣiḳta|, miswritten *ma-ḏi₃-ta, ma-ḏ-b-ta* → Hoch SWET 180 no. 243; with initial *n=: ma-n-ḏ-q-ta* |manṣiqta| → Hoch SWET 131f. no. 171.[992]
|y-s¹-r|	Sem.: *yšr* (Hb.) "to be straight, right", (D) "to smooth", (C) "to level", *yšr* (*yāšār*) "straight, level, smooth", (*yošer*) "straightness, honesty", *myšwr* (*mîšôr*) "level ground, plain", *myšrym* (*mêšārîm*) "order, integrity"; *myšr* (Pun. ptc. D) "regent"(?), *mšrt* "justice"; *yšyr* (JAram., Syr.) "upright, firm", *yšyrw, yšyrwtʔ* "uprightness", *myšr, mšrʔ* "plain"; *ešēru(m), i/ešāru(m)* (Akk.) "to be / go well, be straight; to direct (towards)", *išaru(m)* "straight, normal", *mīšaru(m)* "justice"; *yasara* (Arab.) "to be(come) easy", *yassara* "to level, smoothen, ease", *yusr,*

---

[989] The form *ypq* (KTU 1.14 I 12) is probl. to be read as G prefc. of \|p-w-ḳ\|; see Tropper UG 645: *ypq* \|yapûḳ\|; Gzella BiOr 64 563; diff. DUL 959f.: /y-p-q/, G suffc.

[990] For other proposals see Watson NABU 2019/71.

[991] For other questionable proposals see Tropper KWU 141: "Zeltdecke"(?), Hb. *yryʕh*; Watson SEL 6 46, LSU 114: Akk. *yarītu* (TÚG *ia-ri-a-te*) "a textile".

[992] Sivan / Cochavi-Rainey WSVES 80: *ma-n-ṣa-q-tá* "flask"; by-form in WSVES 82, Helck Beziehungen 135: *ma-ṣa-q-tá / ma-n-ṣa-q-tá*.

yusur, *yasār* "ease, facility", *yasar*, *yasīr*, *maysūr* "easy", *maysara* "ease, facility"; *ys*^{1}*r* (OSArab. D) "to cause to go straight", *mys*^{1}*rm* "plain".

|**y-S-r**| "to be just, straight"

●CTX: **EB** Ct *uš-da-si-ir* |yus^{1}taySir| → Fronzaroli QuSe 13 151: "he has prepared".
●ONOM: **EB** Cf. *ti-sar*, *ti-sa-lum*, *ti-ša-lum*, *i-si-lum*, *i-si-rúm*, *ti-si-lum* → Krebernik PET 63; Pagan ARES 3 196ff., 325, 370f.
EUPH, **B** *ia-si-rum*/*ru-um*, *ia-šir-ti-im* → Huffmon APNMT 212 (YSR), 216 (YŠR); Gelb CAAA 22, 110 (JŚIR); Streck Onomastikon 1 152 § 2.2 fn. 4; Golinets Onomastikon 2 230, 469.
A7 *ia-še-re-da* → Gelb CAAA 22, 110 (JŚIR); Streck Onomastikon 1 152 § 2.2; Golinets Onomastikon 2 230 fn. 774, 469.

yiSr "just, straight; DN"

●ONOM: **EB** Passim DN *YiSr* written =*iš-lu*, =*iš-ru*$_{12}$, =iš, *iš-lu*=, *iš*$_{11}$-*lu*= → Krebernik PET 92; Pagan ARES 3 196ff.

yaSar, **yaSarah** "just, straight upright"

●ONOM: **EB** *a-sa-ar*, *a-sa-ra*, *a-sar-a-nu*, *a-ša*-LUM(*lum*?), *a-sar-a*-LUM(*ḫum*? / lum? / núm), *a-sar-gi-nu*, cf. *a:sar*(?) → Krebernik PET 73; Pagan ARES 3 196ff., 283.
EUPH, **B** *a-ša-ru-um*, *ia-sa-rum*, *ia-ša-ru-um*, *ia-sa-ru-um*, *ia-sa-ra*, *bu-nu-ma-šar*, *bu-nu-um-ma-a-šar*, *ḫa-mu-ya-šar*, *ḫa-am-mu-sa-ar* → Gelb CAAA 22, 106 (JAŚAR); Golinets Onomastikon 2 243, 252, 469.[993]
TU *ia-ša-ri-il* → Krebernik Tall Bi`a 219; Golinets Onomastikon 2 243, 469.
A7 *ia-aš-ri-e-da* → Wiseman AT 136; Gelb CAAA 22, 110 (JŚIR); Streck Onomastikon 1 224 § 2.129; Golinets Onomastikon 2 243, 469.
UGS *ia-aš-ra-n*[*u*] → Sivan GAGl 290.

yiSar, **yiSart** "just; DN; favourable (prayer)"

●CTX: **EB** *i-sa-rí*, *i-sa-i* → Catagnoti QuSe 29 41, 240.
●LL: **EB** SI.SÁ = *i-sa-lum* → Fronzaroli QuSe 13 143; StEb 7 187; QuSe 18 103; Krebernik ZA 73 39; PIHANS 106 88; Catagnoti QuSe 29 10, 62, 240.
●ONOM: **EB** *i-sar*, *i-sa-rúm*, <*i*?>-*sar-dum*, *i-sar-dum*, *i-sar-il*, *i-sar-ma-lik*, *ì-sar-ma-lik*, *i-sar-zé*; *bù-i-sar*, *du-bù-i-sar*; passim DN *YiSar* written =*i-sar* → Krebernik PET 63,107, 202; Pagan ARES 3 196ff., 294, 302, 325.
EUPH, **B** *i-ša-rum*, *a-bi-e-sa-ar*, *áš-di-e-sa-ar*, *da-di-e-sa-ar*, *ha-am-mi-e-sa-ar*, *la-aḫ-wi-e-sa-ar*, *na-wa-ar-e-šar*, *ya-da-ab-e-šar*; *i-šar-li-im* → Gelb CAAA 22, 110 (JŚAR); Streck Onomastikon 1 326 § 5.18; Golinets Onomastikon 2 243f., 469.
TU *ba-aḫ-li-e-sa-ar*, *ḫa-li-e-sa-ar* → Krebernik Tall Bi`a 212, 215; Golinets Onomastikon 2 244, 469.
A7 *i-ša-ri* → Wiseman AT 139; Gelb CAAA 22, 110 (JŚAR); Golinets Onomastikon 2 244, 469.
EM Cf. *i-ša-ra*/*ri*, *i-šar*-DINGIR-*lì*, ^{d}*i-ša-ru-ma-x*, fem. *i-šar-te*, *i-ša-ar-te* → Pruzsinszky PTEm 84 [516], 171 [515], 196 [516].[994]

yaSur "just, upright"

●ONOM: **EUPH** Cf. *ia-šu-ur-ak-ka*, *ia-šu-ur-*^{d}*da-gan*, *ia-šu-ur-é-a* → Zadok Fs. Hallo 332

ys^{1}r "justice, uprightness"

●CTX: **UGA** Sg. suff. *yšrh* → DUL 973: *yšr* (I).
●ONOM: **UGA** *yšr* → DUL 973: *yšr* (II).

yaSart "justice, uprightness"

●ONOM: **EUPH** *ia-sa-ar-ti*-DINGIR → Gelb CAAA 22, 106; Streck Onomastikon 1 326 § 5.19 fn. 1.

yiSrut "just"

●ONOM: **EB** *iš-ru*$_{12}$-*ud*, *iš*$_{11}$-*ru*$_{12}$-*ud*, *iš-lu-du*, *iš-ru*$_{12}$-*ud-da-mu*, *iš*$_{11}$-*ru*$_{12}$-*ud-da-mu*, *iš*$_{11}$-*ru*$_{12}$-*ud-ḫa-lam* → Pagan ARES 3 196ff., 340, 342.

---

993 for the DNN *yaSarum* (var. *Yašarum* ?) see Durand REA 690.
994 For the PNN *iašur*=, *išur*= see Streck AfO 51 311.

yataSr "justly treated"	•ONOM: **EUPH** *ia-ta-áš-rum* → Streck Onomastikon 1 224 § 2.129; Golinets Onomastikon 2 262. **TU** *ia-ta-áš-ri-im* → Krebernik Tall Bi`a 219; Streck Onomastikon 1 224 § 2.129; Golinets Onomastikon 2 262, 469.
maySar "justice"	•LL: **EB** Cf. AMA.GI_4 = *ma-sa-lu-um* → Krebernik ZA 73 37f.; Fronzaroli QuSe 13 145; Fronzaroli StEb 7 172f.[995] •ONOM: **EB** *mi-sa-lu* → Pagan ARES 3 196ff., 351. **A7** Cf. *mi-ša-re* (month name) → Wiseman AT 162; Arnaud AuOr 16 166.
mays^{1}ar "justice"	•ONOM: **UGS** *me-sa-ra-nu*/*ni*, cf. *mè-ša-r*[*a-nu*?] → Sivan GAGl 14, 247.[996]
mays^{1}ur "justice"	•ONOM: **A4** *mi-šu-ri* → Wiseman AT 142; Arnaud AuOr 16 170.
ms^{1}r (B) "justice"	•CTX: **UGA** → DUL 586: *mšr* (I). •ONOM: **UGA** *mšrn* → DUL 586.

|y-t-m|	Primary noun, Sem.: *ytwm* (*yātôm*, Hb.) "orphan, fatherless"; *ytm* (Ph.) id.; *ytm*(*ʔ*) (JAram., Syr.), fem. *ytmh*, *ytmtʔ* (JAram.) "orphan", denom. *ytm* (Syr. D) "to orphan"; *yatīm*, fem. *yatīma* (Arab.) "orphan", *yatam* "orphanage, helplessness", *yatama* "to be(come) fatherless", *maytama* "calamity that causes orphanage".
yatām, **yatūm**, **yitūm** "orphan"	•ONOM: **B** *ia-ta-mu-um*, *ia-tam-ma*-DINGIR, *ia-tu-mu*(*-um*); cf. *i-tu-ma-nim* → Gelb CAAA 21, 106f., 109; Streck Onomastikon 1 168 § 2.35, 328 § 5.22 fn. 3.[997] **A4** *ia-ta-mu* → CAAA 21, 106.
ytm "orphan"	•CTX: **UGA** → DUL 973f.
ytmt "orphan girl"	•CTX: **UGA** → DUL 974.
maytmiy "orphaned"	•ONOM: **EUPH** Cf. *me-et-mi-iu-um* → Zadok Fs. Hallo 332.

|y-t-n|
See |**n/w/y-D-n**|

|y-θ|
See |**ʔ/y-θ**|

|y-θ-ʕ|	Sem.: *yšʕ* (Hb.N) "to receive help", (C) "to help, save", *yšʕ* (*yēšaʕ*, *yošaʕ*), *yšwʕh* (*yᵉšûʕāh*), *mwšʕh* (*môšāʕāh*) "help, salvation", *mwšyʕ* (*môšīᵃʕ*) "deliverer"; *yšʕ* (Moab. C) "to save, deliver".[998]

[995] Altern. see *mawSar* "release, dismissal" (|w-s^1-r|).

[996] Cf. *mawSar* "release, dismissal" (|w-s^1-r|).

[997] For PI(*wa*?)-*at-mu-um* see Streck Onomastikon 1 328 § 5.22 fn. 3: Akk. (*w*)*atmu*(*m*) "hatchling".

[998] Passim. in Moab. and Ammon PNN; for a detailed inventory cf. Golinets Onomastikon 2 472.

|y-θ-ʕ| "to help, save"	•ONOM: **EB** Cf. *a-sa-ì, a-sa-ì-um, a-sa-sa-du, a-ša-lum, a-ša-ne-ra, a-ša-rí-gú, ʔa$_5$-ša-gá, da-ša*; *i-ša, i-sa-ni-ki-mu, i-ša-ne-ig-mu, i-ša-ne-ki-mu, ì-sa-ga-u$_9$, ì-sa-il, sar-ì-sa, ti-sa, ti-ša-nu, ti-ša-li-im, ti-ša-mi-nu, ti-šè-li-im*; *ù-ša, ù-ša-il, ù-ša-lu, u$_9$-si-ma*-DINGIR, *du-si, du-si-li-im* → Krebernik PET 59f.; Pagan ARES 3 192, 272, 283, 299, 303, 325, 329, 362, 370f., 373f. **U3** *la-šu-il* → Buccellati Amorites 165. **EUPH** *ia-a-ši-ḫu* → Zadok Fs. Hallo 332; Streck Onomastikon 1 161 § 2.20 fn. 4; Golinets Onomastikon 2 213, 230, 254, 469ff. **EM** *iš-a, i-ša-aḫ-a, i-ša-^{d}da-gan, la-ti-iʔ-ša* → Pruzsinszky PTEm 171 [514], 215 [515], 218 [591].[999]
yaθʕ, yaθʕat, yiθʕ, yiθʕah, yiθʕat "help, salvation"	•ONOM: **EUPH**, **B** *bu-nu-ia-aš-ḫa*, ^{d}UTU-*ia-aš-ḫa*, EŠ$_4$.DAR-*ia-aš-ḫa*; *iš-ḫa, iš-a-ti, iš-i-ra-aḫ*, passim elem. (=)*iš-ḫa*/*ḫi*(=) with DNN / deceased relatives, cf. *iš-ḫi-^{d}da-gan, iš-ḫi-e-ra-aḫ, iš-ḫi-ìl-a-ba$_4$, iš-ḫi-la-ba-an, iš-ha-at-a-bu-um, iš-ḫa-ba-al, iš-ḫa-ga-al, $^{(d)}$ad-mu-iš-ḫa, an-nu-(-un)-iš-ḫa*, EŠ$_4$.DAR-*iš-ḫa, ka-ka-iš-ḫa* → Gelb CAAA 22, 106 (JAŠʕ), 109 (JIŠʕ); Zadok Fs. Hallo 332; Streck Onomastikon 1 249 § 2.172, 268 § 3.15, 281 § 3.40; Golinets Onomastikon 2 261, 469ff.
yaθiʕ, yaθiʕah, yiθiʕ "helpful, saviour"	•ONOM: **EUPH**, **B** *ia-še-ia, e-še-eḫ-ba-la*(?), *ia-ši-iḫ-ìl, ḫa-ab-di-e-si-iḫ* → Golinets Onomastikon 2 254f., 469ff. **A7** *zu-ia-še-ia* → Wiseman AT 153; Gelb CAAA 22, 106; Zadok Fs. Hallo 332; Golinets Onomastikon 2 255, 469ff.
yaθuʕ, yaθuʕah, yaθuʕat, yiθuʕ "helpful, saviour"	•ONOM: **EUPH**, **B** *ia-šu-ḫu-um, ia-šu-ḫa, ia-šu-ḫa-tum, ia-su/sú*-^{d}IM, *ia-su-ra-aḫ, ia-šu*-DINGIR, *mu-ta-ia-šu-uḫ, ia-si-su-uḫ, a-bi-ia-šu-ḫa, a-ḫi-ia-šu, a-ḫi-ia-šu-uḫ*; *a-a-e-šu-uḫ, mu-tu-e-šu-uḫ, mu-ta-šu-uḫ, ia-si-su-uḫ*, passim: DNN / ancestors =*e-šu-uḫ* → Huffmon 215f.; Gelb CAAA 22 109ff. (JIŠʕ, JŠUʕ); Zadok Fs. Hallo 332; Streck Onomastikon 1 160 § 2.20 fn. 4, 215 § 2.112, 250 § 2.173, 265 § 3.12, 267 § 3.14, 327 § 5.21f. fn. 5; Golinets Onomastikon 2 257ff., 469ff. **TU** *i-šu-ḫa-am-mu, i-šu-ma-da-ri, ia-su/sú-um, ia-su*-DINGIR, *ia-su-^{d}da-gan, ^{d}a-mi-(e-)šu-uḫ, ka-bi-e-šu-uḫ* → Krebernik Tall Bi`a 209, 217, 219, 221; Golinets Onomastikon 2 257f., 260, 469ff. **EA** Cf. *ya-šu-ia* → Moran AmL 385; Hess APN 166f., 207; Tropper OLZ 91 56.
yataθʕ "helped"	•ONOM: **EUPH** Fem. |yataθʕah, yataθʕat| *ia-taš-ḫa, ia-ta-aš-ḫa, ia-taš-ḫa-tum* → Gelb CAAA 22, 106 (T JAŠʕ); Zadok Fs. Hallo 332; Streck Onomastikon 1 328 § 5.21 fn.5, 340 § 5.50; Golinets Onomastikon 2 262, 469ff.
mēθiʕ "help"	•ONOM: B *me-si-um* → Gelb CAAA 22, 110; Streck Onomastikon 1 338 § 5.47, 340 § 5.50 fn. 4

|y-θ-n| Cf. **|w-s^1-n|**	Sem.: *yšn* (Hb. N) "to grow old", *yšn* (*yāšān*) "old".
|**y-θ-n**| "to be(come) old"	•CTX: **UGA** G suffc. *yṯn* → DUL 980: */y-ṯ-n/*.
yaθan "old"	•ONOM: **EB** *ya-sa-na*, fem. *a-sa-du* |yaθattu|, *a-sa-na-du* |yaθanatu| → Krebernik PET 186; Pagan ARES 3 196, 283, 382.
yaθun "old"	•ONOM: **U3** *e-šu-nu-um* → Buccellati Amorites 62, 146; Gelb CAAA 21, 106. **A7** *ia-šu-na* → Wiseman AT 137; Gelb CAAA 21, 106.
yθn "old, rancid"	•CTX: **UGA** Pl. *yṯnm*, fem. *yṯnt* → DUL 980: *yṯn*.

[999] Cf. op.cit. 172 fn. 224: *Išeia* [523: "Mann"(?), or *yšʕ* ?].

|y-w-m|	Primary noun, Sem.: *ywm* (*yôm*, Hb.) "day"; *ym* (Ph., Pun.) id.; *ywm* (Ammon., Nab., Palm., Hatra) id.; *ywm(ʔ)* (Aram., Syr.) id.; *ūmu(m)* (Akk.) id.; *yawm* (Arab.) id.; *ywm*, *ym* (OSArab.) id.; *ḥə=yūm*, *yum*, *yhɔm* (MSArab.) "day";[1000] *yom* (Eth.) "today".
yawm "day; DN"	•CTX: **EB** Sg. abs. / cstr. u_9-*mu* → Catagnoti / Fronzaroli ARET 16 80f., 274; Catagnoti QuSe 29 44, 62, 102, 117, 239. •LL: **EB** UD.TE = *šè-er a-me-mu* → Krebernik ZA 73 29; Fales QuSe 3 182; UD.GÁN = *a-wa-mu ʔà-mu-tum*, *a-mu ʔà-mu-tum* → Krebernik ZA 73 30; Fronzaroli QuSe 13 137; Catagnoti QuSe 29 16, 24, 44, 61, 107, 239. •ONOM: **EUPH** Cf. *ú-mu-ša-ki-in*, *yu-mi-i-la*, *ḫa-lu-bi-ia-mu*, *a-lum-bi-ú-mu*, *a-lum-bu-mu*, *ḫa-lu-um/un-bi-yu-mu*, *ia-al-ú-mu*, *ia-al-wi-mu*, *ia-al-ú-mu*, *ra-ba-aḫ-du-yu-mu*, *ra-ba-aḫ-du-ú-mu* → Zadok Fs. Hallo 332; Streck Onomastikon 1 166 § 2.30 fn. 1, 176 § 2.52, 219 § 2.118.
yōm "day; DN"	•CTX: **UGS** Cf. *im-mi* < |in(a=yō)mi| (?; RS 94.2389:2') → Lackenbacher / Malbran-Labat RSOu 23 70, 210. •LL: **UGS** [UD = *ūmu* = … = *yu-mu*; ^{d}[U]D = *tu-en-ni* = *yu-mu* → Sivan GAGl 291; Huehnergard UVST 67, 133; SAU 304 (53); Tropper UG 188.
ym (B) "day"	•CTX: **UGA** Sg. *ym*, cstr. *ym*, du.(?) *ymm*, pl. *ymm*, *ymt*, cstr. *ymy* → DUL 950f: *ym*(I).
|y-w-n|	Primary noun, Sem.: *ywnh* (*yônāh*) "dove"; *ywn(ʔ)*, *ywnh*, *ywntʔ* (Aram., Syr.) id.; cf. *yamāma* (Arab.)[1001] "(rock-)dove".
wawn, **wawnat** "dove" (?)	•CTX: **EUPH** (Sakanakku) Cf. WA-*an-tum*, pl. WA-*na-tum*, du. WA-*an-tá-an* → Cavigneaux / Colonna d'Istria *Studia Orontica* 6 56. •ONOM: **EB** Cf. unc. *wa-na* → Pagan ARES 241, 375.[1002]
w/yatt "dove"	•LL: **EM** Cf. MIN / TU <MUŠEN> = *su-um-ma-*tu_4 = PI-*at-*tu_4 → Pentiuc Vocabulary 139; Cohen Proceedings 53e RAI 1 831.
ynt "dove"	•CTX. **UGA** Sg. abs. / cstr. *ynt* → DUL 957.
yamāmah "(a kind of) dove"	•ONOM: **EUPH** Cf. *ia-ma(-a)-ma* → Gelb CAAA 103 (JAMAM); Durand REA 669: "Yamam", Zadok Fs. Hallo 332: Y-M-M^2, Streck Onomastikon 1 313 § 4.5, 328 § 5.22 with fn. 2.

[1000] See also *ḥə=yawm*, *yum* "sun; heat of the sun".
[1001] Secondary form through shift |wawn=| > |wām=| > |yām=| and reduplication |yamā=m=|. See below *yamāmah*.
[1002] An altern. rdg is |wayn=a| "wine" (questionable; see |w-y-n|).

Z

|z-ʔ-B|	
|z-ʕ-r|	Cf. **|ṣ-γ-r|**
|z-b-b|	
|z-b-b-r|	
|z-b-g|	
|z-b-l|	See **|S-b-l|**
|z-b-n|	
|z-b/m-r|	
|z-ð|	See **|S-d/ð|**
|z-G-g|	
|z-γ-w|	
|z-h-w|	
|z-k-k|	Cf. **|ð-k-y|**
|z-ḳ-ḳ|	
|z-ḳ-t|	
|z-l-g|	See **|g-z-r**
|z-l-l|	
|z-m-b-r|	Cf. **|d-b-r| (4)**
|z-m-r| (1)	
|z-m-r| (2)	See **|z-b/m-r|**
|z-n-ḳ|	
|z-n-n|	
|z-n-y|	
|z-r-ḳ|	
|z-r-z|	
|z-w-n|	
|z-w-r|	
|z-w-z|	
|z-y-d|	
|z-y-ḳ|	
|z-y-m|	
|z-y-n|	
|z-y-t|	

|z-ʔ-B|

Culture word, Sem.: Cf. *zyb(ʔ)* (Syr.) "case, sheath"; *ziʔpu*, *zīpu* (Akk.) "mould; impression".

zaʔaBt "incision, engraving (on a jewel)"

•CTX: **EB** Cf. *za-a-ba-tum* → Pasquali QuSe 23 180f.

|z-ʕ-r|
Cf. |ṣ-γ-r|

Sem.: *zʕyr* (*z*ᵉ*ʕêr*, Hb.) "a litle"; *zʕr(ʔ)* (Nab., Palm.) "small"; *zʕyr* (Aram.) "small", *zʕr* (Aram., Syr.) "to be(come) small"; *zaʕir* (Arab.) "thin haired", *zaʕira* "to be thin, sparse".

ủzʕr "the smallest, youngest"

•CTX: **UGA** Sg. fem. *ủzʕrt* → DUL 132f.: *ủzʕrt*.

|z-b-b|

Culture word, Sem.: *zabāba* (Arab.) "rat".

zabab "a rat"

•LL: **EB** NIN.NA.NI = *za-ba-bù-um* → Sjöberg Fs. Oelsner 410 fn. 6; Fs. Renger 546.

|z-b-b-r|	Culture word, Sem.: Cf. *zbwr(ʔ)* (Syr., JAram.) "thyme" (several JAram. and Syr. variants, e.g. *ʔbrh*, *ʔbrtʔ*, *zrbwz(ʔ)*); *zambūru* (Akk.) "thyme".
zibbīr "thyme"	•ONOM: **UGS** Elem. in TN A.ŠA(.ḪI.A / MEŠ) *zi-ib-bi-ri* → Belmonte RGTC 12/2 400; Fs. Sanmartín 43. Altern. reading *ṣí-bi-ri* |ṣibbi/īrV|: Sivan GAGl 269 "collective fields"; Huehnergard UVST 169 "collective land"; vSoldt SAU 306 (122): "a type of field".
ṣbr "field rich in thyme"	•CTX: **UGA** Sg. *ṣbr*, pl. *ṣbrm* → Belmonte Fs. Sanmartín 43; cf. DUL 766.

|z-b-g|	Sem.: Cf. *zbwg(ʔ)* (JAram.) "lizard".
zabug "lizard" (?)	•ONOM Cf. *za-bu-ug* → Zadok Fs. Hallo 332.

|z-b-l|
See **|S-b-l|**

|z-b-n|	Sem.: Cf. *zbn* (Aram., Syr., Palm., Hatra) "to buy", (D) "to sell".
zabin "bought" (?)	•ONOM: **EUPH**, **B** *za-bi-nim*, *za-bi-in-nu-ú-a*, fem. *za-bi-na* → Zadok Fs. Hallo 332.

|z-b/m-r|	Sem.: *zmr* (Hb.) "to prune", *zmwrh* (*z*^{e}*môrāh*) "shoot"; *zmr* (JAram.) "to prune"; with alternance of labials: *zabara* (Arab.) "to cut, prune (the vine)"; *zabara* (Eth.) "to break".
|z-b-r| "to prune"	•CTX: **UGA** G prefc. suff. *yzbrnn*, act. ptc. pl. *zbrm* → DUL 983. •ONOM: **EG** Cf. *ṯꜣ(?)-m*^{MḎꜣT}*?-b-w-r-y*$^{\text{RNPY.Rʕ}}$ → Schneider APÄQ 249f. no. 533.
åzmr "foliage, branches"	•CTX: **UGA** → DUL 133f.

|z-ð|
See **|S-d/ð|**

|z-G-g|	Loan. Non-Sem.: ZÚ(?).GIG.GA (Sum.);[1003] cf. zu "tooth", gig "sick".[1004]
zakigay "toothache"	•CTX: **UGS** *za-ki-ga-a* → Nougayrol Ug 5 17 (RS 17.155 and dupl.): 36; Dietrich SEL 5 84.

|z-γ-w|	Sem.: Cf. *zʕh* (only ptc. pilpel **m*^{e}*zaʕzeʕ*, Hb.) "to bark"; *zaġā* (Arab.) "to weep, cry (baby)", *zaġzaġa* "to banter".
|z-γ-w| "to low, bellow"	•CTX: **UGA** G prefc. *tzġ* → DUL 983: /*z-ġ(-y)*/.
zγt "howl, bark"	•CTX: **UGA** Cstr. *zġt* → DUL 983: *zġt*.

[1003] Nougayrol Ug 5 30; "Sumérien macaronique".
[1004] Nougayrol op.cit. 34 "mal […] de dent"; AHw 1505: *zakigû* "Zahnschmerz"; cf. diff. Krecher UF 1 154: Sum. ZÀ(?).GIG.GA "Seiten(?)-Krankheit".

|z-h-w|	Sem.: Cf. *zahā* (*zahw*, Arab.) "to blossom, flower", *zahw* "bloom, beauty, splendour".
zahw "splendour"	•ONOM: **EB** Cf. *za-ù-nu*, *za-ù-su* → Pagan ARES 3 199, 384.
|z-k-k| Cf. **|ð-k-y|**	Sem.: Cf. *zkk* (Hb.) "to be bright", *zk* (*zak*, fem. *zakkāh*) "clear", *zkwkyt* (*zekûkît*) "glass"; *zkyk* (JAram.) "clear", *zgzg* (Syr.) "to shine", *zgwgy*(*tʔ*) (JAram., Syr.) "glass"; zağağ (Arab.) "glass"; *zuğāğiyy* "vitreous, crystal-clear"; *zakakātu*, *zakukūtu* (Akk.) "glass, glaze".
zakukiyt "glaze, glass"	•CTX: **EUPH** NA_4 *za-zu-ki-tim* → Kupper Fs. De Meyer 268ff. (A.2178:5); Groneberg MARI 6 180.
zakzakiy "crystal-clear"	•ONOM: **B** Cf. *za-ak-za-ku-um* → Zadok Fs. Hallo 332.
|z-ḳ-ḳ|	Culture word, Sem.: Cf. *zyq*(*ʔ*) (Aram., Syr.) "(water) skin, bag".
ziḳḳ "a skin (for wine)"	•CTX: **R** KUŠ *zi-qú* → Dalley / Walker / Hawkins Tell Rimah 183f. (251:10). •LL: **MŠ** *ziq-qu* = [*t*]*a-kal-tú ik-*[(III 67) → Hrůša MŠ 78, 364.
|z-ḳ-t|	Sem.: Cf. *zqt* (Syr.) "to goad", *zqt*(*ʔ*), *zqwt*(*ʔ*) (Syr.) "goad", *zqt*(*ʔ*) (Syr.) "spasm"; *zaqātu*(*m*) "to sting", *ziqtu*(*m*) "sting (mark)".
zaḳt "stung" (?)	•ONOM: **EB** Cf. *za-ga-du* → Pagan ARES 3 199, 383.
|z-l-g| See **|g-z-r|**	
|z-l-l|	Sem.: Cf. *zll*(Hb., N) "to quake", *zlzl* (*zalzal*) "vine shoot"; *zll* (JAram., Syr.) "to be light, of little value", *zlylw*(*ʔt*) "lightness"; *zalzala* (Arab.) "to shake", *zalzala* "earthquake"; *zalala* (Eth.) "to move, be shaken".
zalzala "switch; stick; branch" (?)	•CTX: **EG** Cf. *ḏa-n-ḏa-n-r-*{*t*}, *ḏa-na-ḏa-na*, *ḏa-n-ḏa-r-*{*t*}, *ḏa-n-ḏa-r*, *ḏa-n-ra-ḏa-n-r*, *ḏa-r-ḏa-r*, *ḏa-n-ḏa-w-t*, *ḏa-n-ḏa-t*, *ḏa-ḏa-n-r*, *ḏa-ḏa-n-ra*, *ḏa-ḏa-r*, *ḏa-n-ra*, *ḏa-n-r* → Hoch SWET 389 no. 586.
|z-m-b-r| Cf. **|d-b-r| (4)**	Primary noun, Sem.: Cf. *zunbūr* (Arab.) "hornet"; *zbwr*(*ʔ*), *zbwrh*, *zbwrtʔ* (JAram., Mandean) "hornet".
zumbar "hornet"	•LL: **EB** GIŠ.BALAG = *zu-mu-ba-*ru_{12} → Conti QuSe 17 37, 123.
|z-m-m|	Sem.: *nzm* (*nezem*, Hb.) "(nose- / ear-)ring"; *zmm* (JAram.) "to muzzle", *zmm*(*ʔ*) "muzzle-ring", *zmywn* "plan"; *zamma* "to tie up, fasten", *zimām* (Arab.) nose-rope".
|z-m-m| "to muzzle, fasten"	•ONOM: **EUPH**, **B** Cf. *zi-im-mi-da-di*, *za-am-ma-*(*a-*)*nu-um* → Gelb CAAA 202f.; Zadok OLA 28 151 fn. 7; Fs. Hallo 332.

|z-m-r| (1)	Sem.: *zmr* (Hb.) "to sing, play an instrument"; *zmr* (Aram., Syr.) "to sing", *zmr(?)* "singer, psalmist"; *zamāru(m)* (Akk.) "to sing (of)", *zammāru, zammeru* "singer, musician", *zammertu* "female singer"; *zamara* (Arab.) "to blow, play (a wind instrument)", *zammār* "player (on a wind instrument)"; *zammara* (Eth.) "to sing, play a musical instrument", *zammāri* "who plays a musical instrument".
zammār "singer"	•CTX: **EM** LÚ *za-ma-ru*, pl. LÚ.MEŠ *za-ma-ru*, fem. *za-mi-ra-ta*, pl. MÍ.MEŠ *za-mi-ra-tu* → Fleming Installation 92f.
zammirt "female singer"	•CTX: **EM** Sg. *za-mi-ra-ta*, pl. MÍ.MEŠ *za-mi-ra-tu* → Fleming Installation 93.

|z-m-r| (2)
See **|z-b/m-r|**

|z-n-ḳ|	Sem.: Cf. *znq* (Hb.) "to leap forth"; *znq* (Syr.) "to throw"; metath. nazaqa (Arab.) "to storm ahead, rush forward".
|**z-n-ḳ**| "to leap"	•ONOM: **TA** Cf. unc. *za-na-na-qum*, DUMU-*za-nu-qí-ma* → Zadok Fs. Hallo 329 (Ṣ-N-Q "to shut up"); Sivan GAGl 293; Horowitz / Oshima CunCan 138.

|z-n-n|	Sem.: *zanānu(m)* (Akk.) "to rain"; *zinnu(m), zīnu* (NAss.), *zinnānu, zunnu(m)* "rain"; see *zanma* (Eth.) "to rain", *zənām* "rain".
zīn "rain"	•CTX: **UGS** Cf. *zi-i-nu i-za-an-ni-nu* → Nougayrol Ug 5 71 (20): 7 fn. 8.

|z-n-y|	Sem.: *znh* (Hb.) "to commit fornication", *znh (zonāh)* "prostitute, harlot", *znwt (zᵉnût)* "fornication"; *znyt?* (Palm.) "prostitute"; *zny* (JAram., Syr.) "to commit fornication, adultery", *znyh, znyt?* "prostitute"; *zanā* (Arab.) "to commit adultery", *zāniya* "whore, harlot", *zinan, zinā?* "adultery, fornication"; *t̠d̠nt* (OSArab.) "fornication"; *zənū, zíni, zíní* (MSArab.) "to commit adultery, fornicate"; *zanaya* (Eth.) "to fornicate", *zənet, zənyat* "fornication".
dnt (B) "lechery, fornication"[1005]	•CTX: **UGA** → DUL 274: *dnt* (I).
zāniy(a)t "prostitute"	•CTX: **EB** DUMU.MÍ *za-ni-tum* → Pasquali NABU 2015/60 (for Pomponio ARET 15/1 38 (40-47)). •LL: **EB** Cf. GÉME.KAR.AK = *za*-NE-*tum*, VE 1412 → Viganò *apud* Civil Biling. 89 fn. 18; Glassner NABU 2003/55. •ONOM: **B** *za-ni-ia-tum* → Gelb CAAA 35, 202.
mazniyat "fornication"	•ONOM: **B** *ma-az-ni-a-tum* → Gelb CAAA 35, 203.

|z-r-ḳ|	Sem.: *zrq* (Hb.) "to toss, sprinkle"; *zrq* (Aram., Syr.) "to throw, sprinkle, disperse", *drq* (JAram.) "to toss"; *zarāqu(m)* (Akk.) "to sprinkle, strew", *zirīqu(m)* "an irrigation device ('shaduf?)"; *zaraqa* (also *d̠araqa*, Arab.) "to drop excrement (birds)".
zirḳ "sprinkling (of a sacrificial sheep)"	•CTX: **EUPH** UDU *zi-ir-qí* → Charpin NABU 2005/98.

[1005] For *dnt* (A) see *dnt* (|d-n-n|), GlOS 1 149.

ziriḳ "a kind of (wooden?) bucket, scoop, watering can"	•ONOM: **EB** Cf. *zi-rí-ig/gú* → Pagan ARES 3 199, 388.
mazraḳ, mazriḳ "a long wooden device (for hoisting water?)"	•LL: **EB** Cf. GIŠ.GÍD = *ma-za-rí-gú, ma-zi-rí-gúm* → Conti QuSe 17 40, 129; 4 62; Sjöberg Fs. Wilcke 255. •ONOM: **EUPH** Cf. *ma-az-ra-qa-tum* → Gelb CAAA 35, 203 (ZRAQ).

|z-r-z|	Culture word, Sem.: *zrz(?)* (JAram.) "girding; belt-saddle".
zurz "(double) packsack"	•CTX: **ASS** (OAss.) *zu-ur-zu-um, zu-ur-ze* → AHw 1539; CAD Z 167; Kogan PIHANS 106 212, 214 fn. 214. Also Nuzi-Akk. and NAss.

|z-w-n|	Sem.: *zwn* (Hb.) "to feed", *mzwn* (*māzôn*) "food, provisions"; *zwn* (JAram., Syr.) "to provide food", *mzwn(?)* "food", *zyn(?)*, *zywn(?)* (Syr.) "nourisher"; *zanānu(m)* (Akk.) "to provision, provide", *zāninu(m)* "provisioner", *zinnātu(m)* "support, sustenance".
|z-w-n| "to nourish"	•ONOM: **EUPH** Cf. *a-zu-na-an* → Gelb CAAA 51 (ʔASUN); Zadok Fs. Hallo 332. **EG** Cf. *ṯꜣ-n:-n-y_2, ṯꜣ-n:-n-ꜣ* → Schneider APÄQ 251 no. 536.
zn "provider, supplies official"	•CTX: **UGA** Pl. *znm* → DUL 984.
znt "sustenance, provision(s)"	•CTX: **UGA** Sg. suff. *zntn* → DUL 984.
tznt "provisions"	•CTX: **UGA** → DUL 872.

|z-w-r|	Sem.: *zwr* (Hb.) "to turn aside", *zr* (*zār*) "strange"; *zwr* (JAram.) "to turn aside"; *zâru* (Akk.) "to turn (round), twist", *zīru* "twisted (garlic)"; *zāra* (Arab.) "to visit, call on", *zawwara* "to incline toward (a visitor)", *izwa/ārra* "to turn aside"; *zwr, zora* (Eth.) "to go / turn around", *zawr* "circle".
|z-w-r| "to divert, go"	•CTX: **UGA** G suffc. suff. *zrm* → DUL 984: */z-r/*.
ziwr (A) "braid; ball, plait of wool"	•CTX: **EB** *zi-rí* SIKI → Bonechi QuSe 16 143; Pasquali QuSe 19 267f. 9); Textile terminologies 174.
ziwr (B) "a close-woven textile"	•CTX: **EUPH** Cf. (TÚG) *zi-rum, zi-ru-um*, pl. (TÚG) *zi-ra-tum*, pl. cstr. (TÚG) *zi-ra-at* → Durand ARM 21 15f. n. 91; ARM 30 140f., 560. **R** Pl. GÚ.ḪA *zi-ra-ti* → Durand ARM 21 416 fn. 91; ARM 30 140.[1006]
ziwr (C) "fork, junction"	CTX: **EB** *zi-il* TN → Fronzaroli ARET 11 37, 178; Bonechi WO 30 33.
ziwrt "a woollen fabric; a turban (?)"	•CTX: **Q** Cf. *zi-ir-ri-tu_4* → Bottéro RA 43 13. **EM:** SÍK *zi-ir-tu_4*, TÚG *zi-ir-ta* → Fleming Installation 26, 148 n. 57; Dietrich UF 21 95; Pentiuc Vocabulary 195.
zāwir "who turns on / against somebody"	•CTX: **MBQ** Cf. *za-a-wi*(PI)*-ri* → Mayer Ekalte 38, 170.
zayyār "stranger"	•CTX: **EM** Cf. LÚ *za-ia-ri* → Huehnergard RA 77 30; Zadok AION 51 119.

[1006] Corrected rdg; diff. Dalley / Walker / Hawkins Tell Rimah 59 (57:5): *nam-ra-ti*.

mazwur "wound" (?)	•ONOM: **EUPH** Cf. unc. *ma-zu-ra-tum* → Zadok Fs. Hallo 332.
|z-w-z|	Sem.: Cf. *zwz* (JAram., Syr.) "to move", (C) "to move something".
|z-w-z| "to move"	•ONOM: **EB** Cf. *za-zi, za-zu, za-zú, za-zu-um, za-zú-um* → Pagan ARES 3 199, 384.[1007] **A4** Cf. *za-za, za-zi-ia* → Wiseman AT 152; Sivan GAGl 294. **EG** Cf. *ṯ-w*$_2$*-ṯ-w*$_2$, *ṯꜣ- ṯꜣ-w*$_2$*-y*$_2$ → Schneider APÄQ 259f. no. 557f.
|z-y-d|	Sem.: *zyd* (Hb.) "to behave insolently", (C) "to become hot"; *zyd(ʔ)* (Mandaean) "rage"; *zāda* (*zayd*, Arab.) "to become greater, increase", *zayd* "excess", *zāʔid* "excessive, immoderate".
|z-y-d| "to boil, become inflamed, yearn for"	•CTX: **UGA** G prefc. *tzd*, suff. *tzdn* → DUL 983: /z-d/. •ONOM: **EG** Cf. *ṯ-w-t-n-y-ꜣ* → Schneider APÄQ 258 no. 555.
|z-y-ḳ|	Sem.: *zyq(ʔ)* (Aram., Syr.) "flash of fire, strong wind, storm"; *ziāqu(m), zâqu* (Akk.) "to blow, waft, gust", *zīqu(m), sīqu, ziqqu* "draught, breeze".
ziyḳ "waft, breath"	•CTX: **EUPH** *zi-iq a-wa-ti-šu* → Jean ARM 2 56 (23:9'); Durand LAPO 17 233 (590): "le ton de ses dires". •ONOM: **EB** Cf. *zi-gi, zi-gi-iš, zi-ki-ar* → Pagan ARES 3 200, 385f. **R** *zi-iq-*^{d}EŠ$_4$.DAR → Dalley / Walker / Hawkins Tell Rimah 241 (323:7).
|z-y-m|	Primary noun, Sem.: *zīmu(m)* (Akk.) "face, appearance"; see also *zyw(ʔ)* (Aram., Syr.) "(splendours) appearance"; *ziyy* (Arab.) "dress, apparel, attire", *zayyā* "to dress, costume".
ziym "bearing, appearance; DN"	•ONOM: **EB** Cf. *zi-mu, zi-me-ḫa-du, dar-zi-mu, i-bí-zi-mu* → Pagan ARES 3 242, 300, 321, 387.
|z-y-n|	Sem.: Cf. *zaʔānu(m), zânu* (Akk.) "to be adorned", *zuʔʔunu(m)* "decorated"; *zāna, zayyana* (*zayn*, Arab.) "to decorate, adorn, grace", *zayn* "beauty, ornament", *zayān* "beautiful"; *zyn, zena* (Eth.) "to decorate".
zayn "attired" (?) **zaynūt** "attire, ornament" (?)	•ONOM: **EB** Cf. *za-na, za-na-ma, za-a-na, za-a-nu*, cf. *za-ni, za-a-ni* → Pagan ARES 3 199f., 382f.[1008] •ONOM: **EB** Cf. *za-nu-du* → Pagan ARES 3 199f., 383.
|z-y-t|	Primary noun, Sem.: *zyt* (*zayit*, Hb.) "olive, olive tree"; *zt* (Ph.) id. (?); *zyt(ʔ)* (Aram., Syr.) "olive, olive tree, olive oil";[1009] *zayt* (Arab.) "(olive) oil", *zaytūn* "olive tree"; *zét, zayt* (MSArab.) "oil", *zaytún, zétún* "olive tree"; *zayt* (Eth.) "olive, olive tree, olive oil", *zayton* "olive tree".

[1007] Altern. "moth" (Pagan loc.cit.) unlikely in view of Proto-Sem. *zīz=; Militarev / Kogan SED 2 324f. no. 255.
[1008] For ***zīnu(m)* (Mari, Qatna, AHw 1529: *zīnu(m)* "eine Gemme") see *Sīn(iy)* "a crescent-shaped jewel" (|s-y-n|).
[1009] See Late Bab. *za-(a)-aʔ-it, za-ʔi-tu*$_4$; Finkel Fs. Lambert 151 fn. 11.

zētu "olive, olive tree, olive oil"	•CTX: **EG** *ḏi*$_3$*-tu*, *ḏ-t*, cf. *ḏ-du* → Hoch SWET 395 no. 594.[1010]
zt "olive, olive tree(s)"	•CTX: **UGA** Sg. *zt*, pl. *ztm*, cstr. *zt* → DUL 984f.

[1010] Sivan / Cochavi-Rainey WSVES 87: *s̠i-t* / *s̠e-t* "olive oil"; Helck Beziehungen no. 316.

Indexes

A. Verbal roots

		Etymon	CTX	LL	ONOM	page
ʔ - ḳ						
|b-ʕ-l| (A)	to make, work	**|p-ʕ-l|**	CTX			120
|b-r-d|	to divide, separate	**|p-r-d| (2)**	CTX		ONOM	133
|ð-b-l|	to carry, deliver	**|S-b-l**		LL		185
|γ-m-ʔ|	to be thirsty	**|θ̣-m-ʔ|**	CTX			334
|γ-p-y|	to spy, observe	**|ṣ-p-y| (2)**	CTX			222
l						
|l-ʔ-k|	to send	**|l-ʔ-k|**	CTX		ONOM	4
|l-ʔ-w/y| (A)	to be able, (to show oneself) to be powerful	**|l-ʔ-w/y| (1)**	CTX		ONOM	6
|l-ʔ-w/y| (B)	to be drained, weaken	**|l-ʔ-w/y| (2)**	CTX		ONOM	7
|l-b-x|	to be fleshy, corpulent, fat	**|l-b-x|**		LL		9
|l-b-n|	to make bricks	**|l-b-n| (2)**	CTX			10
|l-b-s^1|	to clothe oneself, wear	**|l-b-s^1|**	CTX			10
|l-ħ-ħ|	to moisten	**|l-ħ-ħ|**	CTX		ONOM	11
|l-ħ-k|	to lick	**|l-ħ-k|**	CTX			12
|l-ħ-m| (A)	to eat	**|l-ħ-m| (1)**	CTX			12
|l-ħ-m| (B)	to fight	**|l-ħ-m| (2)**	CTX			12
|l-ħ-n|	to be intelligent	**|l-ħ-n|**			ONOM	12
|l-ħ-y|	to revile, verbally abuse	**|l-ħ-y| (2)**	CTX		ONOM	13
|l-ḳ-ħ|	to take; to receive	**|l-ḳ-ħ|**	CTX		ONOM	13
|l-ḳ-ḳ|	to lick up, lap	**|l-ḳ-ḳ|**			ONOM	13
|l-ḳ-ṭ|	to gather out, pick out	**|l-ḳ-ṭ|**		LL	ONOM	14
|l-ḳ-θ̣|	to gather out, pick out (?)	**|l-ḳ-ṭ|**	CTX			14
|l-m-d|	to learn	**|l-m-d|**	CTX			15
|l-p-ḳ|	to join and sew together (?)	**|l-p-ḳ|**		LL		15
|l-p-t|	to play, strike	**|l-p-t|**	CTX			15
|l-s-m|	to run	**|l-s-m|**	CTX			16
|l-s^1-n|	to slander	**|l-s^1-n|**	CTX			17
|l-ṭ-s^1|	to sharpen	**|l-ṭ-s^1|**	CTX			17
|l-w-s^1|	to knead	**|l-w-S|**	CTX			18
|l-w-ṭ|	to cover (?)	**|l-w-ṭ|**		LL	ONOM	18
|l-w-y|	to surround	**|l-w-y|**	CTX		ONOM	19

m

|l-y-n|	to sleep, stay the night	|l-y-l(-y)|	CTX			20
|l-y-ṣ|	to speak loudly (?)	|l-y-θ|			ONOM	20
|m-ʔ-d|	to be numerous	|m-ʔ-d|	CTX		ONOM	28
|m-ʔ-S|	to forgive (?)	|m-ʔ-S|			ONOM	28
|m-d-d|	to measure	|m-d-d| (1)			ONOM	29
|m-d-l|	to bridle (?)	|m-d-l(-l)|	CTX			30
|m-g-g|	to fight	|m-g-g|	CTX		ONOM	31
|m-g-n|	to regale	|m-g-n|	CTX			31
|m-ɣ-y|	to come, arrive	|m-θ-ʔ/y|	CTX		ONOM	61
|m-ḥ-y|	to clean, wipe	|m-ḥ-w/y|	CTX			33
|m-x-r|	to approach; to receive; to fight	|m-x-r|	CTX	LL	ONOM	33
|m-x-ṣ|	to hit, beat	|m-x-ṣ́|	CTX			34
|m-x-s¹|	to hit, beat	|m-x-ṣ́|	CTX			34
|m-x-ṣ́|	to hit, beat	|m-x-ṣ́|	CTX	LL		34
|m-x-w/y|	to be frenzied	|m-x-w|	CTX			35
|m-k(-k)|	to fall, be cast down	|m-k(-k)|	CTX			35
|m-k-r|	to trade, sell	|m-k-r|	CTX			36
|m-k-s|	to put a tax	|m-k-s|	CTX			36
|m-ḳ-ḳ|	to melt, dissolve (?)	|m-ḳ-ḳ|		LL		36
|m-ḳ-s¹|	to emboss, hammer (?)	|m-ḳ-s¹|	CTX			36
|m-ḳ-ṭ|	to fall, go down	|m-ḳ-ṭ|	CTX		ONOM	37
|m-l-ʔ|	to be full	|m-l-ʔ|	CTX		ONOM	37
|m-l-ḥ|	to pull out, draw	|m-l-x| (1)	CTX			38
|m-l-x|	to tear out	|m-l-x| (1)	CTX	LL		38
|m-l-k|	to rule, give advice	|m-l-k|	CTX		ONOM	39
|m-l-ḳ|	to uproot	|m-l-ḳ|		LL		42
|m-l-l|	to rub with the fingers, caress (?)	|m-l-l|	CTX		ONOM	43
|m-l-ṭ|	to save, rescue	|m-l-ṭ|			ONOM	44
|m-n-ḥ|	to deliver	|m-n-ḥ|	CTX			44
|m-n-w/y| (A)	to count; to deliver	|m-n-w/y| (1)	CTX		ONOM	44
|m-n-w/y| (B)	to love	|m-n-w/y| (2)			ONOM	45
|m-r-ʔ|	to fatten	|m-r-ʔ| (2)	CTX			46
|m-r-x|	to be coated	|m-r-x|	CTX			47
|m-r(-r)| (A)	to go away; to travel through	|m-r(-r)| (1)	CTX			48
|m-r(-r)| (B)	to strengthen	|m-r(-r)| (2)	CTX		ONOM	49

|m-r-ṣ|	to fall ill	**|m-r-ṣ́|**	CTX			51
|m-r-ṣ́|	to be worried	**|m-r-ṣ́|**			ONOM	51
|m-r-ṭ|	to be plucked out, be bald (?)	**|m-r-ṭ|**			ONOM	51
|m-S-ħ|	to rub, anoint	**|m-s¹-ħ|**	CTX		ONOM	55
|m-s-k|	to mix, combine	**|m-s-k|**	CTX			53
|m-s-r|	to deliver up	**|m-s-r| (2)**			ONOM	53
|m-s-S|	to liquefy, dissolve	**|m-S-S/w/y| (1)**	CTX			53
|m-S-y|	to become evening, get dark	**|m-s¹-y|**		LL		56
|m-s¹-k|	to adhere, give support (?)	**|m-s¹-k| (2)**	CTX			56
|m-s¹-l|	to rule, reign	**|m-s¹-l| (1)**			ONOM	56
|m-s¹-r|	to set a vehicle in motion, to drive it (?)	**|m-s¹-r|**	CTX			56
|m-s²-w/y|	to wash, purify	**|m-s²-w/y|**	CTX		ONOM	57
|m-t-ʕ|	to take away; to help	**|m-t-ʕ|**	CTX		ONOM	58
|m-t-ħ|	to erect	**|m-t-ħ|**		LL		58
|m-t-n|	to wait (?)	**|m-t-n| (2)**	CTX			59
|m-ṭ-r|	to rain	**|m-ṭ–r|**	CTX		ONOM	59
|m-ṭ-y|	to be scarce, lacking	**|m-ṭ-y|**	CTX			60
|m-θ-k|	to carry, take	**|m-s¹-k| (2)**	CTX			56
|m-θ̣-ʔ|	to meet, find; to be successful	**|m-θ̣-ʔ/y|**	CTX		ONOM	61
|m-w-s¹|	to feel, look over (?)	**|m-w-s¹|**			ONOM	62
|m-w-t|	to die	**|m-w-t|**	CTX	LL	ONOM	62
|m-y-ʕ|	to soak in water	**|m-y-ʕ|**	CTX			63
|m-z-ʕ|	to tear to pieces	**|m-z-ʕ|**	CTX			63
|m-z-g|	to mix drinks	**|m-z-g|**			ONOM	63
|m-z-l|	to go, run	**|m-z-l|**	CTX	LL		63
|m-z-y/z|	to be weak; to suck (?)	**|m-z-y/z|**			ONOM	64

n

|n-ʔ-m|	to advance	**|n-ʔ-m|**	CTX			69
|n-ʔ-ṣ|	to despise, insult	**|n-ʔ-ṣ|**	CTX			69
|n-ʕ-m|	to be large, rich	**|n-ʕ-m|**	CTX		ONOM	69
|n-ʕ-r|	to shake	**|n-ʕ-r| (2)**	CTX			71
|n-b-ʔ|	to call (upon)	**|n-b-ʔ|**	CTX	LL	ONOM	72
|n-b-b|	to whistle, sound	**|n-b-b|**		LL		73
|n-b-x|	to rob (?)	**|n-b-x|**	CTX			73
|n-b-l|	to excel	**|n-b-l| (3)**			ONOM	74
|n-b-r|	to dig up / turn	**|n-b-r|**			ONOM	74

	over (the ground)					
|n-b-ṭ|	to shine, look at	**|n-b-ṭ|**	CTX		ONOM	75
|n-d-ʔ|	to eject, frighten away	**|n-d-ʔ|**	CTX			75
|n-d-b|	to be generous	**|n-d-b|**			ONOM	76
|n-d-d| (A)	to move, escape	**|n-d-d| (1)**	CTX			76
|n-d-d| (B)	to stand, step over to, step before	**|n-d-d| (2)**	CTX			76
|n-d-ħ|	to swing (out) (?)	**|n-d-ħ|**			ONOM	77
|n-d-n|	to give	**|n/w/y-D-n|**	CTX		ONOM	77
|n-d-p|	to throw	**|n-d-p|**	CTX			79
|n-d-r|	to make a vow, promise	**|n-ð-r|**	CTX		ONOM	80
|n-d-y|	to throw, emit	**|n-d-y|**	CTX			79
|n-g-ʕ|	to arrive, touch, smite	**|n-g-ʕ| (1)**	CTX			80
|n-g-b|	to provide, supply (food)	**|n-g-b| (1)**	CTX			80
|n-g-h|	to gleam, shine	**|n-g-h|**			ONOM	81
|n-g-ħ|	to butt each other	**|n-g-ħ|**	CTX			81
|n-g-s¹|	to approach; to wander	**|n-g-s¹|**	CTX		ONOM	82
|n-g-θ|	to search, examine	**|n-g-θ|**	CTX		ONOM	83
|n-g-w/y|	to go away	**|n-g-w/y|**	CTX			82
|n-ɣ-r|	to protect, guard, watch	**|n-θ̣-r|**	CTX			110
|n-ɣ-ṣ|	to contract, shake; to buckle	**|n-ɣ-ṣ́|**	CTX			83
|n-h-d|	to be attentive; to pay attention	**|n-h-d|**	CTX			83
|n-h-l|	to lie down (to sleep)	**|n-h-l| (2)**		LL		84
|n-h-r|	to flee, sail (?)	**|n-h-r| (1)**	CTX			84
|n-ħ-b|	to vow; to strive (?)	**|n-ħ-b|**			ONOM	85
|n-ħ-l|	to hand over property; to share an inheritance	**|n-ħ-l|**	CTX		ONOM	85
|n-ħ-m|	to be compassionate	**|n-ħ-m|**			ONOM	86
|n-ħ-r|	to strike, overcome	**|n-ħ-r|**	CTX		ONOM	86
|n-ħ-S|	to live, be alive	**|n-ħ-S|**	CTX		ONOM	87
|n-ħ-t|	to take down	**|n-ħ-t|**	CTX			87
|n-ħ-w/y|	to proceed, turn, make for	**|n-ħ-w/y|**	CTX		ONOM	88
|n-x-r|	to snort, puff; to be angry	**|n-x-r|**			ONOM	88
|n-x-s|	to move backwards	**|n-x-s|**	CTX			89
|n-x-s¹|	to be healthy; to	**|n-x-s¹|**			ONOM	89

<table>
<tr><td></td><td>prosper</td><td></td><td></td><td></td><td></td><td></td></tr>
<tr><td>|n-k-h|</td><td>to breathe in someone's face</td><td>|n-k-h|</td><td></td><td>LL</td><td></td><td>89</td></tr>
<tr><td>|n-k-m|</td><td>to store, pile (up)</td><td>|n-k-m|</td><td>CTX</td><td></td><td></td><td>89</td></tr>
<tr><td>|n-k-p|</td><td>to push; gore, butt (each other)</td><td>|n-k-p|</td><td></td><td>LL</td><td></td><td>90</td></tr>
<tr><td>|n-k-r|</td><td>to look different, to be strange, stranger</td><td>|n-k-r|</td><td></td><td></td><td>ONOM</td><td>90</td></tr>
<tr><td>|n-k-s|</td><td>to interrupt</td><td>|n-k-s| (2)</td><td>CTX</td><td></td><td></td><td>91</td></tr>
<tr><td>|n-k-s^{1}|</td><td>to be healthy; to prosper</td><td>|n-x-s^{1}|</td><td>CTX</td><td></td><td></td><td>89</td></tr>
<tr><td>|n-k-t|</td><td>to immolate</td><td>|n-k-t|</td><td>CTX</td><td></td><td></td><td>91</td></tr>
<tr><td>|n-k-θ|</td><td>to bite</td><td>|n-k-θ|</td><td>CTX</td><td></td><td></td><td>91</td></tr>
<tr><td>|n-k-y|</td><td>to smite</td><td>|n-k-y|</td><td></td><td></td><td>ONOM</td><td>91</td></tr>
<tr><td>|n-ḳ-b|</td><td>to pierce; to mark</td><td>|n-ḳ-b|</td><td>CTX</td><td></td><td></td><td>91</td></tr>
<tr><td>|n-ḳ-ð |</td><td>to save, rescue</td><td>|n-ḳ-ð|</td><td></td><td>LL</td><td></td><td>92</td></tr>
<tr><td>|n-ḳ-h|</td><td>to gain strength, to stir up, revive (?)</td><td>|n-ḳ-h|</td><td>CTX</td><td></td><td></td><td>92</td></tr>
<tr><td>|n-ḳ-m|</td><td>to avenge, save</td><td>|n-ḳ-m|</td><td>CTX</td><td></td><td>ONOM</td><td>93</td></tr>
<tr><td>|n-ḳ-r|</td><td>to cut out; engrave</td><td>|n-ḳ-r|</td><td>CTX</td><td></td><td></td><td>94</td></tr>
<tr><td>|n-ḳ-y| (A)</td><td>to be pure, free (?)</td><td>|n-ḳ-y| (1)</td><td>CTX</td><td></td><td></td><td>95</td></tr>
<tr><td>|n-ḳ-y| (B)</td><td>to pour a libation</td><td>|n-ḳ-y| (2)</td><td>CTX</td><td></td><td>ONOM</td><td>95</td></tr>
<tr><td>|n-m-l|</td><td>to speak ill of</td><td>|n-m-l| (2)</td><td></td><td>LL</td><td></td><td>95</td></tr>
<tr><td>|n-m-r|
See |n-w-r|, |n-m-r|</td><td></td><td></td><td></td><td></td><td></td><td></td></tr>
<tr><td>|n-m-z|</td><td>to moan, complain</td><td>|n-z-m|</td><td></td><td>LL</td><td></td><td>117</td></tr>
<tr><td>|n-p-x|</td><td>to blow</td><td>|n-p-x|</td><td></td><td>LL</td><td>ONOM</td><td>97</td></tr>
<tr><td>|n-p-ḳ|</td><td>to come fort</td><td>|n-p-ḳ|</td><td></td><td></td><td>ONOM</td><td>97</td></tr>
<tr><td>|n-p-l| (A)</td><td>to fall</td><td>|n-p-l| (1)</td><td>CTX</td><td></td><td>ONOM</td><td>97</td></tr>
<tr><td>|n-p-l| (B)</td><td>to supererogate</td><td>|n-p-l| (2)</td><td></td><td>LL</td><td></td><td>97</td></tr>
<tr><td>|n-p-p|</td><td>to sprinkle</td><td>|n-p-p|</td><td>CTX</td><td></td><td></td><td>97</td></tr>
<tr><td>|n-p-r|</td><td>to (start to) fly</td><td>|n-p-r| (1)</td><td>CTX</td><td>LL</td><td></td><td>97</td></tr>
<tr><td>|n-p-S|</td><td>to breathe</td><td>|n-p-S|</td><td></td><td></td><td>ONOM</td><td>98</td></tr>
<tr><td>|n-p-ṣ|</td><td>to go, march off (?)</td><td>|n-p-ṣ| (2)</td><td></td><td>LL</td><td></td><td>99</td></tr>
<tr><td>|n-p-y|</td><td>to be driven away</td><td>|n-p-y| (1)</td><td>CTX</td><td></td><td></td><td>99</td></tr>
<tr><td>|n-S-ʔ|</td><td>to raise, carry, accept</td><td>|n-s^{2}-ʔ|</td><td>CTX</td><td>LL</td><td>ONOM</td><td>106</td></tr>
<tr><td>|n-S-ʕ|</td><td>to pull out, depart for a long journey; to pay</td><td>|n-S-ʕ/x|</td><td>CTX</td><td></td><td></td><td>100</td></tr>
<tr><td>|n-S-G|</td><td>to weave; to plot</td><td>|n-S-G|</td><td>CTX</td><td></td><td></td><td>101</td></tr>
<tr><td>|n-S-x|</td><td>to pull out, withdraw</td><td>|n-S-ʕ/x|</td><td></td><td></td><td>ONOM</td><td>100</td></tr>
<tr><td>|n-s-k|</td><td>to throw (down); to pour (out)</td><td>|n-s-k|</td><td>CTX</td><td>LL</td><td></td><td>101</td></tr>
</table>

<table>
<tr><td>|n-S-ḳ|</td><td>to kiss</td><td>|n-s^1-ḳ| (1)</td><td>CTX</td><td></td><td></td><td>104</td></tr>
<tr><td>|n-S-r|</td><td>to take away (the illness); to get better</td><td>|n-s^1-r| (2)</td><td>CTX</td><td></td><td></td><td>105</td></tr>
<tr><td>|n-s-y| (A)</td><td>to venture; to try</td><td>|n-s-y| (1)</td><td>CTX</td><td></td><td></td><td>101</td></tr>
<tr><td>|n-s-y| (B)</td><td>to remove</td><td>|n-s-y| (2)</td><td>CTX</td><td></td><td></td><td>101</td></tr>
<tr><td>|n-ṣ-b|</td><td>to stay erect; to put, fix,</td><td>|n-ṣ-b|</td><td>CTX</td><td></td><td>ONOM</td><td>102</td></tr>
<tr><td>|n-ṣ-ħ|</td><td>to be pure, clean (?)</td><td>|n-ṣ-ħ| (2)</td><td></td><td>LL</td><td></td><td>103</td></tr>
<tr><td>|n-ṣ-l|</td><td>to retire, cease; to save</td><td>|n-ṣ-l|</td><td>CTX</td><td></td><td>ONOM</td><td>103</td></tr>
<tr><td>|n-ṣ-r|</td><td>to sob</td><td>|n-ṣ-r|</td><td>CTX</td><td></td><td></td><td>103</td></tr>
<tr><td>|n-ṣ-ṣ| (A)</td><td>to take flight</td><td>|n-ṣ-ṣ|</td><td>CTX</td><td></td><td></td><td>104</td></tr>
<tr><td>|n-ṣ-ṣ| (B)</td><td>to sparkle, blossom</td><td>|n-ṣ́-ṣ́|</td><td></td><td></td><td>ONOM</td><td>107</td></tr>
<tr><td>|n-s^1-ʔ|</td><td>to raise, lift, carry</td><td>|n-s^2-ʔ|</td><td>CTX</td><td></td><td></td><td>106</td></tr>
<tr><td>|n-s^1-B|</td><td>to blow</td><td>|n-s^1-B| (1)</td><td></td><td></td><td>ONOM</td><td>104</td></tr>
<tr><td>|n-s^1-ḳ|</td><td>to put in proper array</td><td>|n-s^1-ḳ| (2)</td><td>CTX</td><td></td><td></td><td>105</td></tr>
<tr><td>|n-s^1-y|</td><td>to forget</td><td>|n-s^1-y| (2)</td><td>CTX</td><td></td><td></td><td>105</td></tr>
<tr><td>|n-t-k|</td><td>to spill, pour (out); to run, flow</td><td>|n-t-k|</td><td>CTX</td><td></td><td></td><td>107</td></tr>
<tr><td>|n-t-n|</td><td>to give</td><td>|n/w/y-D-n|</td><td>CTX</td><td></td><td>ONOM</td><td>78</td></tr>
<tr><td>|n-t-r|</td><td>to take away by force, banish; to startle (?)</td><td>|n-t-r|</td><td>CTX</td><td></td><td></td><td>108</td></tr>
<tr><td>|n-ṭ-ʕ|</td><td>to plant</td><td>|n-ṭ-ʕ|</td><td></td><td></td><td>ONOM</td><td>108</td></tr>
<tr><td>|n-ṭ-l|</td><td>to lift, raise (eyes, voice)</td><td>|n-ṭ-l|</td><td>CTX</td><td></td><td></td><td>108</td></tr>
<tr><td>|n-ṭ-ṭ|</td><td>to shake</td><td>|n-ṭ-ṭ|</td><td>CTX</td><td></td><td></td><td>109</td></tr>
<tr><td>|n-θ-k|</td><td>to bite</td><td>|n-θ-k|</td><td>CTX</td><td>LL</td><td></td><td>109</td></tr>
<tr><td>|n-θ̣-r|</td><td>to protect, guard, watch</td><td>|n-θ̣-r|</td><td>CTX</td><td>LL</td><td>ONOM</td><td>110</td></tr>
<tr><td>|n-w-ʕ|</td><td>to shake (?)</td><td>|n-w-ʕ|</td><td>CTX</td><td></td><td></td><td>111</td></tr>
<tr><td>|n-w-b| (A)</td><td>to be coated (with)</td><td>|n-w/y-b| (1)</td><td>CTX</td><td></td><td></td><td>111</td></tr>
<tr><td>|n-w-b| (B)</td><td>to prosper, grow (?)</td><td>|n-w/y-b| (2)</td><td></td><td></td><td>ONOM</td><td>111</td></tr>
<tr><td>|n-w-d|</td><td>to shake (the head), nod, show mercy</td><td>|n-w-d|</td><td></td><td></td><td>ONOM</td><td>111</td></tr>
<tr><td>|n-w-x|</td><td>to rest</td><td>|n-w-x|</td><td>CTX</td><td></td><td></td><td>111</td></tr>
<tr><td>|n-w-ḳ|</td><td>to wail</td><td>|n-w-ḳ|</td><td>CTX</td><td></td><td></td><td>112</td></tr>
<tr><td>|n-w-m|</td><td>to sleep</td><td>|n-w-m|</td><td>CTX</td><td></td><td></td><td>113</td></tr>
<tr><td>|n-w-p|</td><td>to be high, lofty, exalted</td><td>|n-w-p|</td><td>CTX</td><td></td><td>ONOM</td><td>113</td></tr>
<tr><td>|n-w-r|, |n-m-r|</td><td>to shine; to burn; to brighten</td><td>|n-w-r|</td><td>CTX</td><td></td><td>ONOM</td><td>113</td></tr>
<tr><td>|n-w-s|</td><td>to move to and fro, flee, tremble</td><td>|n-w-s|</td><td>CTX</td><td></td><td></td><td>115</td></tr>
</table>

|n-y-l|	to be, rest, settle	**|n-y-l|**	CTX	LL		116
|n-z-ḳ|	to get angry; to be injured, hurt	**|n-z-ḳ|**	CTX			116
|n-z-l|	to pour out, empty	**|n-z-l|**		LL	ONOM	116
|n-z-m|	to moan, complain	**|n-z-m|**			ONOM	117

p

|p-ʔ-d|	to offer	**|p-ʔ-d|**	CTX			119
|p-ʕ-l|	to make, work	**|p-ʕ-l|**	CTX		ONOM	121
|p-ʕ-r|	to open one's mouth; to shout	**|p-ʕ-r|**	CTX			121
|p-d-y|	to redeem, ransom	**|p-d-y|**	CTX		ONOM	122
|p-h-y|	to see, look at; to know, recognise	**|p-h-y|**	CTX			124
|p-x-d|	to dread, fear	**|p-x-d| (2)**	CTX			125
|p-x-r|	to gather	**|p-x-r| (2)**		LL	ONOM	125
|p-k-r|	to join	**|p-k-r|**	CTX			126
|p-k-y|	to weep	**|p-k-y|**	CTX			126
|p-ḳ-d|	to command; provide	**|p-ḳ-d|**	CTX		ONOM	126
|p-ḳ-ħ|	to open	**|p-ḳ-ħ|**			ONOM	126
|p-l-g|	to be split	**|p-l-g|**	CTX			127
|p-l-x|	to fear; to terrify	**|p-l-x|**	CTX	LL	ONOM	128
|p-l-l| (A)	to be cracked, parched	**|p-l-l| (1)**	CTX			128
|p-l-l| (B), |p-l-y| (A)	to judge; to pray, invoke; to procure somebody's right	**|p-l-l/y| (2)**	CTX	LL	ONOM	128
|p-l-S|	to see, look (at); inquire	**|p-l-s|**		LL	ONOM	129
|p-l-ṭ|	to escape; to live; to save	**|p-l-ṭ|**	CTX	LL	ONOM	130
|p-l-y| (A) See *|p-l-l|* (B), *|p-l-y|* (A)						
|p-n-w/y|	to turn	**|p-n|**	CTX		ONOM	130
|p-n-y|	to be removed (?)	**|p-n-w/y|**	CTX			131
|p-r-ʔ|	to cut	**|p-r-ʔ| (2)**	CTX			132
|p-r-ʕ|	to let free, to wash	**|p-r-ʕ| (2)**	CTX			132
|p-r-d|	to separate; to detail (troops)	**|p-r-d| (2)**	CTX		ONOM	132
|p-r-x |	to blossom, sprout, unfurl	**|p-r-x|**	CTX			133
|p-r-k|	to rub, crumble (?)	**|p-r-k|**			ONOM	133
|p-r-ḳ|	to release, slacken, unknit; to	**|p-r-ḳ| (2)**	CTX		ONOM	134

	segregate					
|p-r-r|	to be dissolved; to split	**|p-r-r| (2)**	CTX		ONOM	135
|p-r-s|	to separate, cut off, decide	**|p-r-s| (3)**	CTX	LL	ONOM	136
|p-r-s-ħ|	to collapse	**|p-r-s-ħ|**	CTX			136
|p-r-s^1|	to extend, resurface	**|p-r-s^2|**	CTX			137
|p-r-θ|	to split open (?)	**|p-r-θ|**	CTX		ONOM	137
|p-r-y|	to be mendacious	**|p-r-y| (2)**	CTX			138
|p-s-x|	to break up, counteract (?)	**|p-s-x|**	CTX			138
|p-s-s|	to erase, delete	**|p-s-s|**			ONOM	139
|p-S-ḳ|	to be meagre, suffer difficulties	**|p-s^1-ḳ|**	CTX			139
|p-S-ṭ|	to expand, widen, spread	**|p-s^1-ṭ|**		LL		140
|p-s^2-ḳ|	open wide, cut	**|p-s^2-ḳ|**			ONOM	140
|p-t-ħ|	to open	**|p-t-ħ|**	CTX	LL	ONOM	140
|p-t-n|	to prove to be strong / to strengthen (?)	**|p-t-n|**			ONOM	141
|p-t-y|	to seduce	**|p-t-y|**	CTX			141
|p-ṭ-r|	to solve, redeem; to leave, desert	**|p-ṭ-r|**	CTX	LL	ONOM	142
|p-θ-θ|	to anoint	**|p-θ-θ|**	CTX	LL		143
|p-θ̣-l|	to overcome, break (?)	**|p-θ̣-l|**	CTX			143
|p-θ̣-r|	to free, loosen	**|p-ṭ-r|**	CTX			142
|p-w/y-d|	to wear out, consume	**|p-w/y-d| (2), |p-d-d|**	CTX			144
|p-w-ḳ|	to find, obtain	**|p-w-ḳ|**	CTX		ONOM	145
|p-w-z|	to be victorious(?)	**|p-w-z|, |p-z-z|**			ONOM	145
|p-z-r|	to shelter, hide	**|p-z-r|**	CTX		ONOM	145

r

|r-ʔ/y-b|	to compensate; contest, plead	**|r-y-b|**			ONOM	179
|r-ʔ-m|	to love	**|r-ʔ-m| (2)**		LL	ONOM	149
|r-ʔ-s^1|	to toss the head(?)	**|r-ʔ-s^1|**	CTX			149
|r-ʔ-y|	to see	**|r-ʔ-y|**	CTX		ONOM	150
|r-ʕ-y|	to pasture, to graze	**|r-ʕ-y| (1)**	CTX		ONOM	150
|r-b-ʕ|	to quadruplicate	**|r-b-ʕ|**	CTX			151
|r-b-b/y|	to be big, great	**|r-b-b| (1), |r-b-y|**	CTX		ONOM	152
|r-b-d|	to prepare, get (a bed) ready; to cover	**|r-b-d|**	CTX			153
|r-b-ḳ|	to act as a bond,	**|r-b-ḳ|**			ONOM	154

	to tie up (?)					
|r-b-ṣ|	to lie down, rest	**|r-b-ṣ̂|**	CTX			154
|r-b-θ|	to substantiate a claim	**|r-b-θ|**	CTX			155
|r-b-y| See |*r-b-b/y*|						
|r-d-ʔ/y|	to lead	**|r-d-y| (1)**			ONOM	156
|r-d-d|	to repel, chase, drive away (?)	**|r-d-d|**			ONOM	155
|r-d-m|	to be sound asleep	**|r-d-m| (2)**		LL		155
|r-d-y| See |*r-d-ʔ/y*|						
|r-ð-y|	to grow thin, weak	**|r-ð-y|**	CTX			156
|r-g-b|	to be seized by fear; to terrify	**|r-g-b|**	CTX		ONOM	156
|r-g-m|	to roar, speak	**|r-g-m|**	CTX	LL	ONOM	156
|r-γ-b|	to be hungry	**|r-γ-b|**	CTX			157
|r-γ-m|	to roar, thunder	**|r-γ-m|**			ONOM	157
|r-γ-w|	to foam, be full of rage	**|r-γ-w|**	CTX			157
|r-ħ-b|	to be wide, large, generous	**|r-ħ-b|**			ONOM	158
|r-ħ-ḳ|	to be far, go away; to flee	**|r-ħ-ḳ|**	CTX		ONOM	159
|r-ħ-l|	to wound (with a sword?)	**|r-ħ-l|**		LL		159
|r-ħ-m|	to have mercy	**|r-ħ-m|**	CTX		ONOM	160
|r-ħ-ṣ| (A)	to help	**|r-ħ-ṣ|**		LL	ONOM	160
|r-ħ-ṣ| (B)	to wash (oneself); to clean, cleanse	**|r-ħ-ṣ̂|**	CTX			161
|r-x-p|	to hover	**|r-x-p|**	CTX			162
|r-x-ṣ|	to hold a conference (?)	**|r-x-ṣ|**	CTX			162
|r-x-y|	to procreate	**|r-x-y|**			ONOM	162
|r-k-b|	to mount; to control, defeat	**|r-k-b|**	CTX		ONOM	163
|r-k-k|	to be mild, delicate	**|r-k-k|**			ONOM	164
|r-k-n|	to rest on, lean against	**|r-k-n|**	CTX	LL		164
|r-k-S|	to bind, tie; to agree on	**|r-k-S|**	CTX		ONOM	164
|r-ḳ-d|	to spring, leap, dance	**|r-ḳ-d|**	CTX			165
|r-ḳ-ḳ|	to be(come) thin, fine	**|r-ḳ-ḳ| (1)**			ONOM	165
|r-ḳ-ṣ|	to jump, leap	**|r-ḳ-ṣ|**	CTX			166
|r-m-k|	to soak; to macerate	**|r-m-k|**	CTX			167

|r-m-m| (A)	to decay	**|r-m-m| (1)**	CTX			167
|r-m-m| (B)	to roar, thunder	**|r-m-m| (2)**			ONOM	167
|r-m-S|	to set oneself in motion (?)	**|r-m-S|**			ONOM	167
|r-m-y|	to throw, cast, shoot	**|r-m-y|**	CTX		ONOM	168
|r-n-n|	to shout, raise one's voice	**|r-n-n|**	CTX		ONOM	168
|r-p-ʔ|	to heal	**|r-p-ʔ|**	CTX		ONOM	168
|r-p-d|	to roam, wander	**|r-p-d| (1)**		LL		170
|r-p-ḳ|	to prop, support	**|r-p-ḳ|**		LL		171
|r-p-s|	to trample on	**|r-p-s|**	CTX			170
|r-p-s^1|	to widen, extend; to be generous	**|r-p-s^1|**			ONOM	171
|r-p-y|	to slacken, loosen	**|r-p-y|**	CTX			171
|r-s-ħ|	to dissolve, sully (?)	**|r-s-ħ|**		LL		171
|r-S-p|	to flame, blaze	**|r-S-p|**			ONOM	171
|r-s-s|	to sprinkle, spray	**|r-s-s|**			ONOM	172
|r-S-y| (A)	to acquire, get	**|r-S-y|**			ONOM	172
|r-S-y| (B)	to fix, (drop) anchor	**|r-s^1-y|**		LL		173
|r-s^1-ʕ|	to harm, injure (?)	**|r-s^1-ʕ|**	CTX			173
|r-s^1-y|	to receive, have	**|r-S-y|**			CTX	173
|r-ṣ-y|	to be content; to give in payment	**|r-ṣ-y|**	CTX			174
|r-t-ḳ|	to tie up, close	**|r-t-ḳ|**	CTX			174
|r-t-b|	to hurry (to do something)	**|r-D-B|**	CTX			155
|r-ṭ-b|	to be wet, juicy	**|r-ṭ-b|**			ONOM	174
|r-θ-y|	to receive, possess	**|r-S-y|**	CTX			173
|r-w-b| (A)	to languish, grow drowsy	**|r-w-b| (1)**		LL		175
|r-w-b| (B)	to tremble, quake	**|r-w-b| (2)**		LL		175
|r-w-ħ|	to blow, smell (?)	**|r-w-ħ|**			ONOM	175
|r-y-m|	to go up; to erect, raise	**|r-w/y-m|**	CTX		ONOM	175
|r-w-θ̣|	to run, compete	**|r-w-θ̣|**	CTX		ONOM	177
|r-w-y|	to be well watered	**|r-w-y|**			ONOM	178
|r-y-b| See *|r-ʔ/y-b|*						
|r-y-ḳ|	to be void	**|r-y-ḳ|**	CTX			179

s (s^3, and S)

|s-ʔ-d|	to support, comfort	**|s-H-d|**	CTX		ONOM	191
|S-ʔ-g|	to roar (?)	**|θ-ʔ-g|**		LL		315
|S-ʔ-n|	to be quiet, in	**|s^1-ʔ-n|**	CTX			232

	agreement					
|S-ʔ-y|	to lay desolate (?)	**|s^1-ʔ-y|**		LL		231
|s-ʕ-d|	to support, protect	**|s-H-d|**			ONOM	191
|S-ʕ-ḳ|	to cry, call	**|S-ʕ-ḳ|**	CTX			183
|S-ʕ-r|	to blow away, whirl around	**|s^2-ʕ-r| (3)**	CTX			271
|s-ʕ-y|	to assault, remove	**|s-ʕ-y|**	CTX			184
|S-ʔ-y|	to lay desolate (?)	**|s^1-ʔ-y|**		LL		231
|S-b-ʕ|	to be sated	**|s^2-b-ʕ|**			ONOM	272
|s-b-b|	to turn; to be changed into	**|s-b-b| (2)**	CTX		ONOM	184
|S-b-ħ|	to praise	**|s^1-b-ħ|**		LL		232
|s-b-k|	to interweave; to contamine (?)	**|s-b-k|**	CTX			185
|S-b-y|	to take captive	**|s^1-b-y| (2)**			ONOM	234
|S-d-d|	to make a raid, to pursue	**|S-d-d|**	CTX			187
|S-G-r|	to close, shut	**|s-G-r|**	CTX		ONOM	189
|S-G-S|	to slay, slaughter	**|S-G-S|**			ONOM	190
|S-g-y| (A)	to go astray, roam; to swerve	**|s^1-g-y|**	CTX			237
|S-g-y| (B)	to grow, increase	**|s^2-g-y|**			ONOM	273
|S-H-r|	to defeat, beat (?)	**|S-H-r|**	CTX			191
|S-ħ-b|	to drag away	**|s-ħ-b|**		LL		191
|S-ħ-n|	to load, freight	**|S-ħ-n|**		LL		191
|s-ħ-y|	to sweep away	**|s-ħ-y|**		LL		191
|s-x-r|	to turn around, search for (?)	**|s-x-r|**			ONOM	192
|S-k-b|	to lie down (for the night)	**|s^1-k-b|**		LL	ONOM	240
|S-k-n|	to be placed, to settle; to establish	**|s^1-k-n|**	CTX		ONOM	242
|S-k-r|	to hire, favour, reward	**|s^2-k-r| (2)**			ONOM	274
|S-k-y|	to watch	**|s^2-k-y|**			ONOM	274
|S-ḳ-d|	to watch, be wakeful (?)	**|s^1-ḳ-d| (2)**		LL	ONOM	244
|S-ḳ-r|	to pierce	**|s^1-ḳ-r|**		LL		245
|S-ḳ-ṯ|	to cease, be quiet; to cede	**|s^1-D-G|**, **|s^1-G-D|**			ONOM	235
|S-ḳ-y|	to give to drink	**|s^1-ḳ-y|**			ONOM	245
|S-l-ħ|	to send, grant	**|s^1-l-ħ| (1)**			ONOM	246
|s-l-l|	to be in distress, sleepless (?)	**|s-l-l|**	CTX		ONOM	196
|S-l-m| (A)	to be friendly, seek peace, surrender	**|s-l-m| (1)**	CTX		ONOM	196
|S-l-m| (B)	to be complete; to pay, deliver	**|s^1-l-m|**	CTX	LL		247
|S-m-ʕ|	to hear, listen (to), notice	**|s^1-m-ʕ|**	CTX	LL	ONOM	251

|S-m-x| (A)	to be glad, rejoice; to light up	**|s¹-m-x| (1)**			ONOM	252
|S-m-x| (B)	to prosper, flourish	**|s¹-m-x| (2)**			ONOM	253
|S-m-k|	to support	**|s-m-k|**			ONOM	199
|S-m-S|	to hide	**|S-m-S|**	CTX			200
|S-m-w|	to hesitate	**|s-m-w/y|**	CTX			200
|S-n-ḳ|	to approach	**|s-n-ḳ|**	CTX		ONOM	201
|s-p-ʔ|	to devour	**|s-p-ʔ|**	CTX			202
|s-p-x|	to associate (?)	**|s-p-x|**			ONOM	202
|S-p-ḳ|	to give abundantly	**|s²-p-ḳ|**			ONOM	277
|S-p-l|	to be low, descend (?)	**|s¹-p-l|**			ONOM	258
|S-p-r| (A)	to write, send	**|S-p-r| (1)**	CTX		ONOM	204
|s-p-r| (B)	to count, recite; to write	**|S-p-r| (1)**	CTX			204
|s-p-y	to pray	**|s-p-y|**		LL		205
|S-r-b|	to drip, drizzle, rain (?)	**|s¹-r-b|**				259
|S-r-k|	to present (ex-voto)	**|s²-r-k| (1)**			ONOM	277
|S-r-r| (A)	to lean out of, lean toward, bend; shine	**|s¹-r-r| (3)**	CTX	LL		261
|s-r-r| (B)	to set, hide	**|s-r-r| (2)**	CTX			207
|s-r(-r)|	to exult inwardly (?)	**|s-r-r| (3)|**	CTX			207
|S-r-ṭ|	to tear	**|s²-r-ṭ|**		LL	ONOM	279
|S-r-y| (A)	to release (?)	**|s¹-r-w/y|**	CTX			262
|S-r-y| (B)	to protect, cure	**|s²-r-y|**			ONOM	279
|S-s-y|	to shout	**|s¹-s-y| (1)**	CTX		ONOM	262
|S-t-ḳ|	to squash, crush (?)	**|s²-ṭ-ḳ|**	CTX			280
|s-t-r|	to hide, provide cover, protect	**|s-t-r| (1)**	CTX		ONOM	209
|S-t-y|	to drink	**|s¹-t-y| (1)**			ONOM	264
|S-ṭ-p|	to rescue, save	**|s¹-ṭ-p|**			ONOM	264
|S-y-m|	to place, fix, establish	**|s²-y-m|**	CTX		ONOM	281
|S-y-t|	to place, put, establish	**|s¹-y-t|**		LL	ONOM	268

Ṣ

|ṣ-ʕ-r|	to be in pain, suffer	**|ṣ-ʕ-r|**	CTX	LL		213
|ṣ-b-ṭ|	to seize, take, hold	**|ṣ̂-b-ṭ|**	CTX			284
|ṣ-d-ḳ|	to be / show oneself just	**|ṣ-d-ḳ|**			ONOM	214
|ṣ-γ-d|	to go, make for	**|ṣ-γ-d|**	CTX			215

|ṣ-h-l|	to (make) shine, gleam	**|ṣ-h-l|**	CTX		216
|ṣ-ħ-ḳ|	to laugh	**|ṣ́-ħ-ḳ|**	CTX		285
|ṣ-ħ-r(-r)|	to roast, burn	**|ṣ-ħ-r|**	CTX		216
|ṣ-l-p|	to be slant, deform (?)	**|ṣ-l-p|**	CTX		217
|ṣ-l-y|	to pray, cast a spell	**|ṣ-l-w/y|**	CTX	ONOM	218
|ṣ-m-d|	to harness, yoke; to tie, bind	**|ṣ́-m-d|**	CTX	ONOM	285
|ṣ-m-ħ|	to grow, cultivate (?)	**|ṣ-m-ħ|**	CTX		218
|ṣ-m-t|	to silence, destroy	**|ṣ-m-t| (1)**	CTX		219
|ṣ-p-y| (A)	to plate, cover, embroider	**|ṣ-p-y| (1)**	CTX		221
|ṣ-p-y| (B)	to spy, observe	**|ṣ-p-y| (2)**		ONOM	222
|ṣ-r-ʕ|	to lay low; to overthrow	**|ṣ-r-ʕ|**	CTX		222
|ṣ-r-k|	to weaken, fail, be missing	**|ṣ́-r-k|**	CTX		287
|ṣ-r-p|	to dye reddish	**|ṣ-r-p|**		ONOM	223
|ṣ-w-r|	to besiege, lay siege to, confine	**|ṣ-r-r| (1), |ṣ-w-r|**	CTX		224
|ṣ-w/y-d|	to hunt; to scour	**|ṣ-w/y-d|**	CTX	ONOM	225
|ṣ-w/y-ħ|	to exclaim, shout, call, claim	**|ṣ-w/y-ħ|**	CTX		226
|ṣ-y-ḳ|	to grasp; to push, put pressure on	**|ṣ́-w/y-ḳ|**	CTX	ONOM	288

s^1 (š)

|s¹-ʔ-b|	to draw, carry water	**|s¹-ʔ-b|**	CTX			228
|S-ʔ-l|	to ask, inquire, beg	**|s¹-ʔ-l|**	CTX	LL	ONOM	229
|s¹-ʔ-l|	to ask, inquire; to require a cultic reply	**|s¹-ʔ-l|**	CTX			229
|s¹-ʔ-r|	to remain (to be paid)	**|s¹-ʔ-r| (1)**	CTX			230
|s¹-b-ʕ| (A)	to repeat for the seventh time	**|s¹-b-ʕ|**	CTX			232
|s¹-b-ʕ| (B)	to be sated; to sate, satiate	**|s²-b-ʕ|**	CTX			272
|s¹-b-ħ|	to praise	**|s¹-b-ħ|**			ONOM	232
|s¹-b-s¹|	to attract, collect (?)	**|S-b-S|**	CTX			186
|s¹-b-m|	to muzzle (?)	**|s²-b-m|**	CTX			272
|s¹-b-t|	to stop, detain, suspend (?)	**|s¹-b-t|**	CTX			233
|s¹-b-y|	to take captive	**|s¹-b-y| (2)**			ONOM	236

<table>
<tr><td>|s^1-d-d| (A)</td><td>to be drawn (off)</td><td>|S-d-d|</td><td>CTX</td><td></td><td></td><td>187</td></tr>
<tr><td>|s^1-d-d| (B)</td><td>to assail, beset; to devastate</td><td>|S-d-d|</td><td>CTX</td><td></td><td></td><td>187</td></tr>
<tr><td>|s^1-d-y|</td><td>to pour</td><td>|s^1-d-y|</td><td>CTX</td><td></td><td></td><td>236</td></tr>
<tr><td>|s^1-g-m|</td><td>to rage, roar (?)</td><td>|s^1-G-m|</td><td>CTX</td><td></td><td></td><td>236</td></tr>
<tr><td>|s^1-H-d|</td><td>to give, present</td><td>|s^1-H-d|</td><td>CTX</td><td></td><td></td><td>237</td></tr>
<tr><td>|s^1-ħ-l|</td><td>to sharpen</td><td>|s^1-ħ-l| (2),
|s^1-l-ħ|</td><td></td><td>LL</td><td></td><td>238</td></tr>
<tr><td>|s^1-ħ-y|</td><td>to bend down (?)</td><td>|s^1-ħ-y|</td><td>CTX</td><td></td><td></td><td>239</td></tr>
<tr><td>|s^1-x-d|</td><td>to give, present</td><td>|s^1-x-d|</td><td>CTX</td><td></td><td></td><td>239</td></tr>
<tr><td>|s^1-x-x-n|</td><td>to get low, bow before someone</td><td>|s^1-k-H-n|</td><td></td><td></td><td></td><td>241</td></tr>
<tr><td>|s^1-x-n|</td><td>to be hot, to warm (oneself)</td><td>|s^1-x-n|</td><td>CTX</td><td></td><td></td><td>239</td></tr>
<tr><td>|s^1-k-b|</td><td>to lie (down, with)</td><td>|s^1-k-b|</td><td>CTX</td><td></td><td></td><td>240</td></tr>
<tr><td>|s^1-k-ħ|</td><td>to find, meet</td><td>|s^1-k-ħ|</td><td>CTX</td><td></td><td></td><td>241</td></tr>
<tr><td>|s^1-k-n|</td><td>to be placed, settle; to establish</td><td>|s^1-k-n|</td><td>CTX</td><td></td><td>ONOM</td><td>242</td></tr>
<tr><td>|s^1-k-r| (A)</td><td>to hire out</td><td>|s^2-k-r| (2)</td><td>CTX</td><td></td><td>ONOM</td><td>274</td></tr>
<tr><td>|s^1-k-r| (B)</td><td>to be(come) drunk</td><td>|s^1-k-r| (2)</td><td>CTX</td><td></td><td></td><td>244</td></tr>
<tr><td>|s^1-ḳ-p|</td><td>to notice (?)</td><td>|s^1-ḳ-p|</td><td>CTX</td><td></td><td></td><td>245</td></tr>
<tr><td>|s^1-ḳ-y|</td><td>to give drink</td><td>|s^1-ḳ-y|</td><td>CTX</td><td></td><td></td><td>245</td></tr>
<tr><td>|s^1-l-ħ| (A)</td><td>to throw, send, grant</td><td>|s^1-l-ħ| (1)</td><td>CTX</td><td></td><td></td><td>246</td></tr>
<tr><td>|s^1-l-ħ| (B)</td><td>to laminate, forge</td><td>|s^1-ħ-l| (2),
|s^1-l-ħ|</td><td>CTX</td><td></td><td></td><td>238</td></tr>
<tr><td>|s^1-l-l|</td><td>to plunder, rob</td><td>|θ-l-l|</td><td>CTX</td><td></td><td></td><td>322</td></tr>
<tr><td>|s^1-l-m|</td><td>to be well; to re-establish, restore health</td><td>|s^1-l-m|</td><td>CTX</td><td></td><td></td><td>248</td></tr>
<tr><td>|s^1-l-p|</td><td>to be dishevelled (?)</td><td>|S-l-B|</td><td>CTX</td><td></td><td></td><td>195</td></tr>
<tr><td>|s^1-l-ṭ|</td><td>to rule, dominate</td><td>|s^1-l-ṭ|</td><td></td><td></td><td>ONOM</td><td>249</td></tr>
<tr><td>|s^1-l-w|</td><td>to rest (?)</td><td>|s^1-l-w|</td><td>CTX</td><td></td><td></td><td>249</td></tr>
<tr><td>|s^1-m-ʕ|</td><td>to hear, listen (to), notice</td><td>|s^1-m-ʕ|</td><td>CTX</td><td></td><td>ONOM</td><td>252</td></tr>
<tr><td>|s^1-m-x|</td><td>to be glad, rejoice; to light up</td><td>|s^1-m-x| (1)</td><td>CTX</td><td></td><td>ONOM</td><td>255</td></tr>
<tr><td>|s^1-n-ʔ|</td><td>to hate, loathe</td><td>|s^2-n-ʔ|</td><td>CTX</td><td></td><td></td><td>276</td></tr>
<tr><td>|s^1-n-n|</td><td>to grind teeth</td><td>|s^1-n-n|</td><td>CTX</td><td></td><td></td><td>257</td></tr>
<tr><td>|s^1-n-s|</td><td>to gird (oneself)</td><td>|s^1-n-S|</td><td>CTX</td><td></td><td></td><td>257</td></tr>
<tr><td>|s^1-n-w|</td><td>to change, leave for, depart (?)</td><td>|s^1-n-w/y|</td><td>CTX</td><td></td><td></td><td>257</td></tr>
<tr><td>|s^1-p-k|</td><td>to spill, shed</td><td>|s^1-p-k|</td><td>CTX</td><td></td><td></td><td>257</td></tr>
<tr><td>|s^1-p-l|</td><td>to stoop, plunge (oneself); to knock down</td><td>|s^1-p-l|</td><td>CTX</td><td></td><td></td><td>258</td></tr>
<tr><td>|s^1-r-d|</td><td>to serve</td><td>|s^1-r-D|</td><td>CTX</td><td></td><td></td><td>259</td></tr>
<tr><td>|s^1-r-g|</td><td>to lie, deceive</td><td>|s^1-r-g|</td><td>CTX</td><td></td><td></td><td>260</td></tr>
<tr><td>|s^1-r-k|</td><td>to team up with, to join</td><td>|s^2-r-k| (1)</td><td>CTX</td><td></td><td></td><td>277</td></tr>
<tr><td>|s^1-r-p|</td><td>to burn</td><td>|s^2-r-p|</td><td>CTX</td><td></td><td></td><td>277</td></tr>
</table>

<table>
<tr><td>|s^1-r-r|</td><td>to be firm</td><td>|s^1-r-r| (2)</td><td>CTX</td><td></td><td></td><td>263</td></tr>
<tr><td>|s^1-r-y/w|</td><td>to release</td><td>|s^1-r-w/y|</td><td>CTX</td><td></td><td></td><td>262</td></tr>
<tr><td>|s^1-t-k|</td><td>to cease, be quiet; to cede</td><td>|s^1-D-G|, |s^1-G-D|</td><td>CTX</td><td></td><td></td><td>235</td></tr>
<tr><td>|s^1-t-m|</td><td>to close (the mouth), to silence (?)</td><td>|s^2-t-m|</td><td>CTX</td><td></td><td></td><td>280</td></tr>
<tr><td>|s^1-t-t|</td><td>to devastate, break (?)</td><td>|s^2-t-t|</td><td>CTX</td><td></td><td></td><td>280</td></tr>
<tr><td>|s^1-t-y|</td><td>to drink</td><td>|s^1-t-y| (1)</td><td>CTX</td><td></td><td></td><td>264</td></tr>
<tr><td>|s^1-w-ḳ|</td><td>to be impelled, urged (?)</td><td>|s^1-w-ḳ| (2)</td><td>CTX</td><td></td><td></td><td>265</td></tr>
<tr><td>|s^1-w-r|</td><td>to threaten, trap, besiege</td><td>|s^1-w-r| (1)</td><td>CTX</td><td></td><td></td><td>266</td></tr>
<tr><td>|s^1-y-r|</td><td>to sing</td><td>|s^1-y-r| (1)</td><td>CTX</td><td></td><td></td><td>268</td></tr>
<tr><td>|s^1-y-t|</td><td>to place, put, establish</td><td>|s^1-y-t|</td><td>CTX</td><td></td><td>ONOM</td><td>268</td></tr>
<tr><td colspan="7">s^2 (ś)</td></tr>
<tr><td>|s^2-g-b|</td><td>to be exalted, saved</td><td>|s^2-g-b|</td><td></td><td></td><td>ONOM</td><td>273</td></tr>
<tr><td>|s^2-ḳ-ḳ|</td><td>to open the way, break the trail (?)</td><td>|s^2-ḳ-ḳ|</td><td>CTX</td><td></td><td></td><td>274</td></tr>
<tr><td>|s^2-w/y-s^2|</td><td>to be pleased (?)</td><td>|s^2-w/y-s^2|</td><td></td><td></td><td>ONOM</td><td>280</td></tr>
<tr><td>|s^2-y-ʔ|</td><td>to want, wish (?)</td><td>|s^2-y-ʔ|</td><td></td><td></td><td>ONOM</td><td>281</td></tr>
<tr><td colspan="7">ṣ́</td></tr>
<tr><td>|ṣ́-b-t|</td><td>to seize, take, hold</td><td>|ṣ́-b-ṭ|</td><td>CTX</td><td></td><td></td><td>284</td></tr>
<tr><td>|ṣ́-ħ-k|</td><td>to laugh</td><td>|ṣ́-ħ-ḳ|</td><td></td><td>LL</td><td>ONOM</td><td>285</td></tr>
<tr><td>|ṣ́-m-d|</td><td>to tie up, bind</td><td>|ṣ́-m-d|</td><td>CTX</td><td></td><td></td><td>285</td></tr>
<tr><td colspan="7">t</td></tr>
<tr><td>|t-ʔ-l|</td><td>to practice magic (?)</td><td>|t-ʔ-l|</td><td></td><td></td><td>ONOM</td><td>290</td></tr>
<tr><td>|t-ʕ-b|</td><td>to be exhausted, weary (?)</td><td>|t-ʕ-b|</td><td>CTX</td><td></td><td></td><td>291</td></tr>
<tr><td>|t-b-ʕ|</td><td>to raise, get up, stand up, go, leave, depart</td><td>|t-b-ʕ|</td><td>CTX</td><td></td><td>ONOM</td><td>291</td></tr>
<tr><td>|t-b-k|</td><td>to pour out</td><td>|t-b-k| (1)</td><td>CTX</td><td></td><td></td><td>291</td></tr>
<tr><td>|t-k-l|</td><td>to trust</td><td>|t-k-l| (1)</td><td></td><td></td><td>ONOM</td><td>294</td></tr>
<tr><td>|t-ḳ-n|</td><td>to be in good order</td><td>t-k/ḳ-n|</td><td>CTX</td><td></td><td></td><td>294</td></tr>
<tr><td>|t-l-ħ|</td><td>to split, tear</td><td>|t-l-ħ|</td><td></td><td></td><td>ONOM</td><td>295</td></tr>
<tr><td>|t-l-l|</td><td>to assist; to achieve an alliance (?)</td><td>|t-l-l| (1)</td><td>CTX</td><td></td><td></td><td>295</td></tr>
<tr><td>|t-m-ʔ|</td><td>to exorcise, charm</td><td>|t-m-ʔ|</td><td>CTX</td><td></td><td></td><td>296</td></tr>
</table>

<table>
<tr><td>|t-m-m|</td><td>to be completed; to complete</td><td>|t-m-m|</td><td></td><td></td><td>ONOM</td><td>297</td></tr>
<tr><td>|t-r-ʔ|</td><td>to lift up</td><td>|t-r-ʔ|</td><td></td><td>LL</td><td></td><td>299</td></tr>
<tr><td>|t-r-ʕ|</td><td>to be overwhelmed by flooding (?)</td><td>|t-r-ʕ|</td><td>CTX</td><td></td><td></td><td>299</td></tr>
<tr><td>|t-r-x|</td><td>to marry, get married</td><td>|t-r-x| (1)</td><td>CTX</td><td></td><td></td><td>300</td></tr>
<tr><td>|t-r-r|</td><td>to shake, tremble</td><td>|t-r-r| (1)</td><td>CTX</td><td></td><td></td><td>301</td></tr>
<tr><td>|t-r-w|</td><td>to lead away</td><td>|t-r-w|</td><td></td><td>LL</td><td></td><td>302</td></tr>
<tr><td>|t-w-r| (A)</td><td>to come back, return</td><td>|t-w-r|</td><td>CTX</td><td>LL</td><td>ONOM</td><td>304</td></tr>
<tr><td>|t-w-r| (B)</td><td>to scour, travel through</td><td>|t-w-r|</td><td>CTX</td><td></td><td></td><td>304</td></tr>
<tr><td>|t-y-l|</td><td>to lie down to sleep, rest</td><td>|t-y-l|</td><td>CTX</td><td></td><td></td><td>305</td></tr>
</table>

ṭ

<table>
<tr><td>|ṭ-ʕ-n|</td><td>to run through, stab to death; to hurt</td><td>|ṭ-ʕ-n|</td><td>CTX</td><td></td><td></td><td>306</td></tr>
<tr><td>|ṭ-b-x|</td><td>to slaughter</td><td>|ṭ-b-x|</td><td>CTX</td><td></td><td></td><td>306</td></tr>
<tr><td>|ṭ-b-ḳ|</td><td>to shut, close</td><td>|ṭ-b-ḳ|</td><td>CTX</td><td></td><td></td><td>307</td></tr>
<tr><td>|ṭ-ħ-n|</td><td>to grind</td><td>|ṭ-ħ-n|</td><td>CTX</td><td>LL</td><td></td><td>308</td></tr>
<tr><td>|ṭ-x-w|</td><td>to come near; to bring near, claim; to annex</td><td>|ṭ-x-w|</td><td>CTX</td><td></td><td></td><td>308</td></tr>
<tr><td>|ṭ-l-l|</td><td>to drop dew</td><td>|ṭ-l-l|</td><td>CTX</td><td></td><td></td><td>309</td></tr>
<tr><td>|ṭ-p-ħ|</td><td>to clap the hands</td><td>|ṭ-p-ħ|</td><td></td><td>LL</td><td></td><td>310</td></tr>
<tr><td>|ṭ-p-l|</td><td>to abuse; to humiliate</td><td>|ṭ-p-l|</td><td>CTX</td><td>LL</td><td></td><td>310</td></tr>
<tr><td>|ṭ-r-d|</td><td>to send, drive out, expel</td><td>|ṭ-r-d|</td><td>CTX</td><td></td><td>ONOM</td><td>310</td></tr>
<tr><td>|ṭ-r-ḳ|</td><td>to beat</td><td>|ṭ-r-ḳ|</td><td></td><td></td><td>ONOM</td><td>310</td></tr>
<tr><td>|ṭ-w/y-b|</td><td>to be good, pleasing</td><td>|ṭ-w/y-b|</td><td></td><td></td><td>ONOM</td><td>311</td></tr>
<tr><td>|ṭ-w-x|</td><td>to plaster</td><td>|ṭ-w-x|</td><td>CTX</td><td></td><td></td><td>312</td></tr>
</table>

θ (ṯ)

<table>
<tr><td>|θ-ʔ-r|</td><td>to protect</td><td>|θ-ʔ-r|</td><td>CTX</td><td></td><td></td><td>315</td></tr>
<tr><td>|θ-ʕ-d|</td><td>to own, have</td><td>|θ-ʕ-d| (1)</td><td></td><td></td><td>ONOM</td><td>315</td></tr>
<tr><td>|θ-ʕ-r|</td><td>to arrange (the table)</td><td>|θ-ʕ-r|</td><td>CTX</td><td></td><td></td><td>316</td></tr>
<tr><td>|θ-ʕ-y|</td><td>search, scrutrinize; examine (the exta)</td><td>|θ-ʕ-y|</td><td>CTX</td><td></td><td>ONOM</td><td>316</td></tr>
<tr><td>|θ-b-r|</td><td>to break, shatter; to grind, powder</td><td>|θ-b-r|</td><td>CTX</td><td>LL</td><td>ONOM</td><td>317</td></tr>
<tr><td>|θ-d-θ|</td><td>to repeat for the</td><td>|s^1-d-θ|</td><td>CTX</td><td></td><td></td><td>236</td></tr>
</table>

	sixth time					
|θ-γ-r|	to break, win, defeat	**|θ-γ-r| (2)**	CTX		ONOM	318
|θ-k-ħ|	to forget oneself (?)	**|θ-k-ħ|**	CTX			319
|θ-k-l|	to be deprived of children	**|θ-k-l|**	CTX			319
|θ-k-p|	to press, urge (?)	**|θ-k-p|**	CTX			320
|θ-k-r|	to deliver (in payment or tribute) (?)	**|θ-k-r|**	CTX			320
|θ-ḳ-D|	to contribute, pay, carry (?)	**|θ-ḳ-D| (1)**	CTX	LL		320
|θ-ḳ-l|	to hang (up), weigh (out)	**|θ-ḳ-l|**	CTX	LL		320
|t-ḳ-p|	to prevail over (?)	**|θ-ḳ-p|**			ONOM	321
|θ-ḳ-y|	to be(come) high; to elevate, take up	**|θ-ḳ-y|**	CTX	LL		321
|θ-l-g|	to snow	**|θ-l-g|**	CTX			32°
|θ-l-l|	to take (away), take booty (?)	**|θ-l-l|**	CTX		ONOM	322
|θ-m-d|	to be, or to grow, fat	**|θ-m-d|**			ONOM	323
|θ-l-θ|	to repeat for the third time; to ridge, plough alternate strips	**|s^2-l-θ|**	CTX			275
|θ-m-m|	to fix, resolve to do (?)	**|θ-m-m| (2)**	CTX			323
|θ-m-r|	to be fruitful	**|θ-m-r|**			ONOM	324
|θ-n-y|	to repeat, reiterate	**|θ-n|**	CTX		ONOM	324
|θ-p-d|	to place, rest (the feet)	**|θ-p-d|**	CTX		ONOM	326
|θ-p-ṭ| (A)	to pass judgement	**|θ-p-ṭ|**	CTX		ONOM	326
|θ-p-ṭ| (B)	threaten, raise a warning	**|θ-p-ṭ|**	CTX		ONOM	326
|θ-r-k|	to present	**|θ-r-k|**			ONOM	327
|θ-r-m|	to carve, cut up (into pieces), feed (meat)	**|S-r-m|**	CTX			205
|θ-r-p|	to spur on (?)	**|θ-p-r|**	CTX			326
|θ-t-ʕ|	to be frightened, scared	**|θ-t-ʕ|**	CTX			329
|θ-t-n| See *|θ-y-n|*, *|θ-t-n|*						
|θ-w-b|	to return, pardon; to vacillate	**|θ-w-b|**	CTX		ONOM	329
|θ-w-y|	come to a halt, live, to stay	**|θ-w-y|**	CTX		ONOM	331
|θ-y-n|	to urinate	**|θ-y-n|**	CTX			331

θ̣(ẓ)

|θ̣-m-ʔ|	to be thirsty, parched	**|θ̣-m-ʔ|**	CTX		ONOM	334
|θ̣-p-n|	to hide, shelter	**|θ̣-p-n|**	CTX			334

w

|w-ʔ-r|	to go, approach; to send	**|w-ʔ-r|**	CTX			337
|w-ʕ-d|	to determine, promise	**|w-ʕ-d|**	CTX			338
|w-b-ʔ|	to be plague-stricken	**|w-b-ʔ|**		LL		339
|w-b-l| (A)	to carry, bring, take, supply	**|w-b-l| (1)**	CTX	LL	ONOM	339
|w-b-l| (B)	to run, pursue	**|w-b-l| (2)**		LL		341
|w-d-ʕ|	to know, to recognise, distinguish	**|w-d-ʕ|**	CTX		ONOM	342
|w-d-y|	to praise, thank	**|w-d-y| (2)**			ONOM	345
|w-h-b|	to give	**|w-h-b|**			ONOM	346
|w-ħ-l|	to be worried, despair, lose hope	**|w-ħ-l|**	CTX			347
|w-ħ-y|	to hurry, hasten, inspect	**|w-ħ-y|**	CTX			348
|w-k-l|	to have authority (over)	**|w-k-l|**	CTX			348
|w-ḳ-h|	to obey	**|w-ḳ-h|**			ONOM	348
|w-l-d|	to bear, sire	**|w-l-d|**			ONOM	350
|w-l-θ|	to crush	**|w-l-θ|**		LL		351
|w-m-ʔ|	to swear	**|w-m-ʔ|**		LL	ONOM	352
|w-p-θ|	to scold, grumble	**|w-p-θ|**	CTX	LL	ONOM	352
|w-p-y|	to be beautiful	**|w-p-y|**			ONOM	352
|w-r-d|	to go down, descend	**|w-r-d| (2)**	CTX			353
|w-r-ḳ|	to be green, make green, plant	**|w-r-ḳ|**		LL		354
|w-r-w|	to send, deliver	**|w-r-w/y|**		LL		356
|w-s-n|	to feel sick (?)	**|w-s-n|**		LL		358
|w-s-r| (A)	to put pressure; teach, instruct	**|w-s-r|**	CTX			358
|w-S-r| (B)	to release, dismiss	**|w-s^{1}-r|**	CTX	LL	ONOM	360
|w/y-ṣ-ʔ|	to go out, appear	**|w-ṣ́-ʔ|**	CTX		ONOM	361
|w-ṣ-y|	to be joined (together), destine; to entrust	**|w-ṣ-y|**	CTX			359
|w-s^{1}-n|	to sleep	**|w-s^{1}-n|**	CTX		ONOM	359
|w-ṣ́-ʔ|	to go out, appear	**|w-ṣ́-ʔ|**	CTX	LL	ONOM	361
|w-ṣ́-ʕ|	to spread, put down	**|w-ṣ́-ʕ|**		LL		362
|w-t-ʔ|	to search, find	**|w-t-H|**			ONOM	362

|w-t-n| See *|n/w/y-D-n|*						
|w-t-r|	to be / show oneself excellent	**|w-t-r| (2)**	CTX			363
|w-θ-b|	to sit (down), stay	**|w-θ-b|**			ONOM	365
|w-θ-r|	to organize, insruct	**|w-θ-r|**		LL		366
|w-z-n|	to weigh	**|w-z-n|**	CTX			366

y

|y-ʔ-y|	to be right, fitting	**|y-ʔ-y|**			ONOM	369
|y-ʕ-l|	to accomplish, effect	**|w-ʕ-l| (2)**			ONOM	338
|y-ʕ-r|	to be frightened	**|w-ʕ-r| (1)**	CTX			338
|y-b-b|	to shout, whinge	**|y-b-b|**			ONOM	370
|y-b-l|	to carry, bring, take, supply	**|w-b-l| (1)**	CTX		ONOM	340
|y-b-m|	to consummate the marriage with a brother-in-law (?)	**|w-b-m|**	CTX			341
|y-d-ʕ| (A)	to know, to recognise, distinguish	**|w-d-ʕ|**	CTX		ONOM	342
|y-d-ʕ| (B)	to sweat	**|w-ð-ʕ|**	CTX			345
|y-d-y| (A)	to throw, expel	**|w-d-y| (1)**	CTX			344
|y-d-y| (B)	to praise, thank	**|w-d-y| (2)**			ONOM	345
|y-d-y| (C)	scratch, rip (out).	**|w-ð-y|**	CTX			345
|y-h-b|	to give	**|w-h-b|**			ONOM	346
|y-h-y|	to wane	**|w-h-y|**	CTX			346
|y-k-l|	to endure	**|y-k-l|**			ONOM	372
|y-ḳ-h|	to obey	**|w-ḳ-h|**			ONOM	349
|y-ḳ-ɣ|	to be alert, pay attention	**|y-ḳ-θ̣|**	CTX			372
|y-ḳ-r|	to be heavy, precious	**|w-ḳ-r|**			ONOM	349
|y-ḳ-s¹|	to catch birds	**|y-ḳ-s¹|**			ONOM	372
|y-ḳ-y|	to protect	**|w-ḳ-y|**	CTX		ONOM	350
|y-l-d|	to bear, sire	**|w-l-d|**	CTX			350
|y-m-n-n|	to take with the right	**|y-m-n|**	CTX			373
|y-n-ḳ|	to suck; to suckle, nurse	**|y-n-ḳ|**	CTX			374
|y-n-y|	to be lowered in value, reduced	**|w-n-y|**	CTX			351
|y-p-ʕ|	to go up, arise; to grow; to shine	**|y-p-ʕ|**	CTX		ONOM	374
|y-p-ḳ|	to issue, send on (?)	**|y-p-ḳ|**	CTX			375

<table>
<tr><td>|y-r-ʔ|</td><td>to fear</td><td>|w-r-ʔ|</td><td>CTX</td><td>ONOM</td><td>352</td></tr>
<tr><td>|y-r-d|</td><td>to go down, descend</td><td>|w-r-d| (2)</td><td>CTX</td><td>ONOM</td><td>353</td></tr>
<tr><td>|y-r-θ|</td><td>to inherit, possess; to take possession</td><td>|w-r-θ| (1)</td><td>CTX</td><td></td><td>355</td></tr>
<tr><td>|y-r-y|</td><td>to throw, fire, shoot arrows</td><td>|w-r-w/y|</td><td>CTX</td><td>ONOM</td><td>356</td></tr>
<tr><td>|y-S-r|</td><td>to be just, straight</td><td>|y-s¹-r|</td><td>CTX</td><td>ONOM</td><td>377</td></tr>
<tr><td>|y-ṣ-ʔ|
See |w-ṣ-ʔ|, |y-ṣ-ʔ|</td><td></td><td></td><td></td><td></td><td></td></tr>
<tr><td>|y-ṣ-b|</td><td>to put, set; to load (a bow)</td><td>|w-ṣ-b|</td><td>CTX</td><td>ONOM</td><td>358</td></tr>
<tr><td>|y-ṣ-ḳ|</td><td>to pour (out); to smelt, cast</td><td>|y-ṣ-ḳ|</td><td>CTX</td><td></td><td>376</td></tr>
<tr><td>|y-ṣ-m|</td><td>to curse</td><td>|w-ṣ-m|</td><td>CTX</td><td></td><td>358</td></tr>
<tr><td>|y-ṣ́-ʔ|</td><td>to go out, appear</td><td>|w-ṣ́-ʔ|</td><td></td><td>ONOM</td><td>361</td></tr>
<tr><td>|y-t-n|
See |n/w/y-D-n|</td><td></td><td></td><td></td><td></td><td></td></tr>
<tr><td>|y-t-r|</td><td>to be / show oneself excellent</td><td>|w-t-r| (2)</td><td></td><td>ONOM</td><td>363</td></tr>
<tr><td>|y-θ-ʕ|</td><td>to help, save</td><td>|y-θ-ʕ|</td><td></td><td>ONOM</td><td>379</td></tr>
<tr><td>|y-θ-b|</td><td>to sit (down), stay</td><td>|w-θ-b|</td><td>CTX</td><td>ONOM</td><td>365</td></tr>
<tr><td>|y-θ-n|</td><td>to be(come) old</td><td>|y-θ-n|</td><td>CTX</td><td></td><td>379</td></tr>
<tr><td>|y-z-n|</td><td>to weigh, pay out (?)</td><td>|w-z-n|</td><td>CTX</td><td></td><td>367</td></tr>
</table>

z

<table>
<tr><td>|z-b-r|</td><td>to prune</td><td>|z-b/m-r|</td><td>CTX</td><td></td><td>382</td></tr>
<tr><td>|z-γ-w|</td><td>to low, bellow</td><td>|z-γ-w|</td><td>CTX</td><td></td><td>382</td></tr>
<tr><td>|z-m-m|</td><td>to muzzle, fasten</td><td>|z-m-m|</td><td></td><td>ONOM</td><td>383</td></tr>
<tr><td>|z-n-ḳ|</td><td>to leap</td><td>|z-n-ḳ|</td><td></td><td>ONOM</td><td>384</td></tr>
<tr><td>|z-w-n|</td><td>to nourish</td><td>|z-w-n|</td><td></td><td>ONOM</td><td>385</td></tr>
<tr><td>|z-w-r|</td><td>to divert, go</td><td>|z-w-r|</td><td>CTX</td><td></td><td>385</td></tr>
<tr><td>|z-w-z|</td><td>to move</td><td>|z-w-z|</td><td></td><td>ONOM</td><td>386</td></tr>
<tr><td>|z-y-d|</td><td>to boil, yearn for</td><td>|z-y-d|</td><td>CTX</td><td>ONOM</td><td>386</td></tr>
</table>

B. Nominal bases, syllabic notations

<table>
<tr><th></th><th></th><th>Etymon</th><th>CTX</th><th>LL</th><th>ONOM</th><th>page</th></tr>
<tr><td>=V</td><td></td><td></td><td></td><td></td><td></td><td></td></tr>
<tr><td>=āy, =īy</td><td>(is really, indeed!)</td><td>|y| (2)</td><td></td><td>LL</td><td>ONOM</td><td>369</td></tr>
<tr><td>=ī, =ya</td><td>my, mine, (...) me</td><td>|y| (1)</td><td>CTX</td><td></td><td>ONOM</td><td>368</td></tr>
</table>

=īy See *=āy*, *=īy*						
=īya	(is really, indeed!)	**|y| (2)**				369

ʔ - ḳ

ʔābes^{1}tu See *ʔābis^{1}tu*, *ʔābes^{1}tu*, *yābis^{1}ta*						
ʔābis^{1}tu, ʔābes^{1}tu, yābis^{1}ta	hardtack, biscuit (?)	**|y-b-s^{1}|**	CTX			370
ʔaħad	one	**|w-ħ-d|**		LL		346
ʔamrad	very bold, audacious	**|m-r-d|**			ONOM	47
ʔamSay	the evening before (?)	**|m-s^{1}-y|**	CTX			57
ʔanbūbt, ʔunbūbt	kind of tubular hairpin	**|n-b-b|**	CTX			73
ʔanḳafḳaft	a wooden object carried on a chariot (?)	**|n-ḳ-p|**	CTX			94
ʔarbaʕt	square (?)	**|r-b-ʕ|**	CTX			152
ʔarðāl	men of low condition	**|r-ð-l|**		LL		156
ʔargab	most frightening (?)	**|r-g-b|**	CTX		ONOM	156
ʔasar	obliged to pay a tax	**|w-s-r|**	CTX			358
ʔaSaryān	coat of armour	**|S-r-(y-)n|**	CTX			208
ʔaSḳur	the very high one; DN	**|S-ḳ-r|**			ONOM	194
ʔaθaθu(wā)t	a type of pancake	**|θ-θ-y|**		LL		329
ʔaθba (A)	chair, throne	**|w-θ-b|**	CTX			365
ʔaθba (B)	shelter, hut, residence	**|w-θ-b|**	CTX			365
ʔaθḳaliy	very heavy (?)	**|θ-ḳ-l|**			ONOM	321
ʔid	hand	**|y-d|**			ONOM	374
ʔiSxat See *Saxat*, *ʔiSxat*						
ʔiSkin	addition	**|s^{1}-k-n|**			ONOM	243
ʔis^{1}ħar	black	**|s^{1}-ħ-r| (2)**			ONOM	238
ʔiθbīr	a fine flour	**|θ-b-r|**	CTX	LL		317
ʔiθkimt	shoulder	**|θ-k-m|**		LL		319
ʔiθkittān	the one with misshapen shoulder	**|θ-k-m|**		LL		319

<table>
<tr><td>ʔiθrūt</td><td>abundance (?)</td><td>|θ-r-y| (1)</td><td></td><td></td><td>ONOM</td><td>328</td></tr>
<tr><td>ʔubalaya
See yubila, ʔubalaya</td><td></td><td></td><td></td><td></td><td></td><td></td></tr>
<tr><td>ʔumbūb</td><td>a kind of flute</td><td>|n-b-b|</td><td>CTX</td><td></td><td></td><td>73</td></tr>
<tr><td>ʔurāθ</td><td>house, estate</td><td>|w-r-θ| (1)</td><td></td><td>LL</td><td></td><td>355</td></tr>
<tr><td>ʔus(a)m</td><td>exquisite ornament</td><td>|w-s-m|</td><td>CTX</td><td></td><td></td><td>358</td></tr>
<tr><td>ʔus^{1}dupp</td><td>plaque</td><td>|s^{1}-d-p|</td><td></td><td></td><td></td><td>235</td></tr>
<tr><td>ʔuṭupl</td><td>a serge</td><td>|ṭ-B-l|</td><td>CTX</td><td></td><td></td><td>307</td></tr>
<tr><td>ʕidān</td><td>fixed date, time limit</td><td>|w-ʕ-d|</td><td>CTX</td><td></td><td></td><td>338</td></tr>
<tr><td>bad</td><td>through (into / from) the hands of</td><td>|b|,
|y-d|</td><td>CTX</td><td></td><td>ONOM</td><td>I:103
371</td></tr>
<tr><td>bibilt</td><td>(improper) conduct or tendency</td><td>|w-b-l| (1)</td><td>CTX</td><td></td><td></td><td>341</td></tr>
<tr><td>daʕ, daʕat, diʕat</td><td>knowledge, friendship</td><td>|w-d-ʕ|</td><td></td><td>LL</td><td>ONOM</td><td>343</td></tr>
<tr><td>daʕat
See daʕ, daʕat, diʕat</td><td></td><td></td><td></td><td></td><td></td><td></td></tr>
<tr><td>daʕūt</td><td>knowledge, friendship</td><td>|w-d-ʕ|</td><td></td><td></td><td>ONOM</td><td>343</td></tr>
<tr><td>dawd</td><td>beloved</td><td>|w-d-d|</td><td></td><td>LL</td><td>ONOM</td><td>344</td></tr>
<tr><td>diʕat
See daʕ, daʕat, diʕat</td><td></td><td></td><td></td><td></td><td></td><td></td></tr>
<tr><td>duyt</td><td>blood money, indemnity</td><td>|w-d-y| (3)</td><td>CTX</td><td></td><td></td><td>344</td></tr>
<tr><td>ðābil</td><td>bearer, porter</td><td>|S-b-l</td><td></td><td>LL</td><td></td><td>185</td></tr>
<tr><td>ðuʕt</td><td>sweat</td><td>|w-ð-ʕ|</td><td></td><td>LL</td><td></td><td>345</td></tr>
<tr><td>gan(i)s^{2}a</td><td>violence, injustice (?)</td><td>|n-g-s^{2}|</td><td>CTX</td><td></td><td></td><td>82</td></tr>
<tr><td>γuwr</td><td>rock, mountain</td><td>|θ̣-w-r|</td><td></td><td></td><td>ONOM</td><td>335</td></tr>
<tr><td>ħaħħam</td><td>craving</td><td>|w-ħ-m|</td><td></td><td></td><td>ONOM</td><td>347</td></tr>
<tr><td>xamiSSāt</td><td>five Sūt-measures</td><td>|S-ʔ|</td><td>CTX</td><td></td><td></td><td>182</td></tr>
</table>

l

<table>
<tr><td>la (A), li (A), lu (A)</td><td>to, for</td><td>|l| (1)</td><td></td><td>LL</td><td>ONOM</td><td>2</td></tr>
<tr><td>la (B), li (B),</td><td>yes, truly, indeed; let it be, let me, you,</td><td>|l| (3)</td><td>CTX</td><td>LL</td><td>ONOM</td><td>3</td></tr>
</table>

lu (B), lū	him; may					
la (C)	oh! (?)	**|l| (3)**			ONOM	3
lā	no, not	**|l| (2)**	CTX	LL	ONOM	2
laʔay	suckling (?)	**|l-ʔ-y/w| (2)**			ONOM	7
laʔiy	powerful	**|l-ʔ-w/y| (1)**			ONOM	6
laʔum	low, mean (?)	**|l-ʔ-m| (2)**			ONOM	5
labʔ, labw	lion; DN	**|l-b-ʔ|**	CTX	LL	ONOM	7
labʔa, labwa	lioness; DN	**|l-b-ʔ|**			ONOM	8
laban See *labn* (A), *laban*						
labaya	lioness	**|l-b-ʔ|**	CTX			8
labbān	brickmaker	**|l-b-n| (2)**	CTX			9
labbin	pallid, albino (?)	**|l-b-n| (1)**			ONOM	9
labīs^{1}a	cuirass, leather armour	**|l-b-s^1|**	CTX			10
labitt	brick	**|l-b-n| (2)**	CTX			10
labn (A), laban	white; a lunar deity	**|l-b-n| (1)**		LL	ONOM	9
labn (B)	a kind of incense burner (?)	**|l-b-n| (1)**	CTX			9
labw See *labʔ, labw*						
labwa See *labʔa, labwa*						
lād	child	**|w-l-d|**			ONOM	350
laħ	young shoot	**|l-ħ-ħ|**		LL	ONOM	11
laħam	suitable, fitting (?)	**|l-ħ-m| (3)**		LL		12
laħim	squeezed, put close together	**|l-ħ-m| (3)**		LL		12
laħiy	deceitful	**|l-ħ-y| (2)**	CTX			13
laxr	ewe (?)	**|r-x-l|**			ONOM	161
laxxāS	whisperer, chatterer	**|l-x-s^1|**		LL	ONOM	13
lala(ʔ) See *lall, lala(ʔ), lali(ʔ)*						
lali(ʔ) See *lall, lala(ʔ), lali(ʔ)*						
lall,	suckling (lamb	**|l-l-ʔ|**			ONOM	14

lala(ʔ), lali(ʔ)	or kid)					
lama	why? (?)	**|l| (1)**	CTX			2
lamatt See *lamn, lamatt*						
lami	why? (?)	**|l| (1)**			ONOM	2
lamn, lamatt	ant	**|n-m-l| (1)**		LL		95
las^{1}ān	tongue	**|l-s^{1}-n|**	CTX	LL		17
laṭap	gentle, kind, fine	**|l-ṭ-p|**			ONOM	17
laṭup	gentle, kind, fine	**|l-ṭ-p|**			ONOM	17
lāwiy	one who encircles	**|l-w-y|**			ONOM	19
lawuy	companion, one who surrounds	**|l-w-y|**		LL	ONOM	19
lawθ	brave, lion (?)	**|l-w/y-θ|**			ONOM	18
lēH	plaque	**|l-w-ħ|**	CTX			18
lēl	night	**|l-y-l(-y)|**	CTX		ONOM	20
li (A) See *la* (A), *li* (A), *lu* (A)						
li (B) See *la* (B), *li* (B), *lu* (B), *lū*						
liʔm, līm	people, tribe; DN	**|l-ʔ-m| (1)**	CTX	LL	ONOM	4
liʔy	power	**|l-ʔ-w/y| (1)**			ONOM	6
liʔyan	head of large cattle	**|l-ʔ-y| (3)**		LL		7
liʔyatt	cow	**|l-ʔ-y| (3)**		LL		7
libatt, libitt	brick	**|l-b-n| (2)**		LL		10
libb	heart	**|l-b-b|**			ONOM	8
libitt See *libatt, libitt*						
liḳṭ	harvesting, gathering	**|l-ḳ-ṭ|**		LL		14
liliS	dought (?)	**|l-w-S|**		LL		18
lill	light, weak	**|l-l-l|**	CTX			15
līm See *liʔm, līm*						
liSān	tongue	**|l-s^{1}-n|**		LL		17

lōdan	laudanum resin	**|l-D-n|**	CTX			11
lu (A) See *la* (A), *li* (A), *lu* (A)						
lu (B) See *la* (B), *li* (B), *lu* (B), *lū*						
lū See *la* (B), *li* (B), *lu* (B), *lū*						
luʔm	people, tribe	**|l-ʔ-m| (1)**			ONOM	5
luʔy	bull (?)	**|l-ʔ-y| (3)**			ONOM	7
lūr	nail	**|l-w-r|**	CTX	LL		18
lūz	almond-tree	**|l-w-z|**		LL	ONOM	19
m						
=ma	optional prosodic reinforcer	**|m| (1)**	CTX	LL	ONOM	23
maʔd	(in) abundance	**|m-ʔ-d|**	CTX	LL	ONOM	28
maʔid	abundant, great; 100.000	**|m-ʔ-d|**	CTX	LL	ONOM	28
maʔit	irrigated land, fertile land	**|m-ʔ| (1)**	CTX			27
maʔw, māw, māy	water, liquid, juice	**|m-ʔ| (1)**	CTX	LL	ONOM	27
maʕʕalt	bolt	**|n-ʕ-l|**		LL		69
maʕd	hardness, firmness	**|m-ʕ-d|**			ONOM	29
mabbaʕ	source, spring	**|n-b-ʕ|**		LL		73
mad	stick (?)	**|m-D(-w)|**		LL		30
madar	field	**|m-d-r|**	CTX			30
maddat	measurement	**|m-d-d| (1)**	CTX			30
madid	a vessel	**|m-d-d| (1)**	CTX			29
maðarāna	a weapon (?)	**|m-S-r| (1)**	CTX			53
mah	what, how?	**|m| (2)**		LL	ONOM	24
mahar, mahir, mehir, mihr	warrior; skilled, trained personal	**|m-h-r| (1)**	CTX		ONOM	32
mahhal	resting place (?)	**|n-h-l| (2)**		LL		84
mahir See *mahar*, *mahir*, *mehir*, *mihr*						

maħħāl	dancer	**|m-ħ-l|**		LL		33
maxārt	wooden front part (?)	**|m-x-r|**		LL		34
maxxār See *māxir, maxxār*						
maxir	basket, box	**|m-x-r|**	CTX			34
māxir, **maxxār**	recipient, buyer; opponent, rival	**|m-x-r|**	CTX	LL	ONOM	34
maxirat	bag	**|m-x-r|**	CTX			34
māxiṣ See *māxiṣ́, māxiṣ*						
māxiṣ́, **māxiṣ**	weaver	**|m-x-ṣ́|**	CTX			35
makānn	gift, present	**|m-g-n|**	CTX		ONOM	31
makannūt	gift, present	**|m-g-n|**	CTX			31
mākir	merchant	**|m-k-r|**	CTX			36
māḳ	slack, frailty (?)	**|m-w-ḳ|**		LL		62
maḳīḳ	soft, moist soil	**|m-w-g|**	CTX			61
maḳḳab	a tool (hammer, punch, pick ?)	**|n-ḳ-b|**	CTX	LL	ONOM	91
maḳḳad	grazing tax	**|n-ḳ-d|**	CTX			92
maḳḳaħ	tong(s)	**|l-ḳ-ħ|**	CTX			13
maḳḳart	chisel	**|n-ḳ-r|**		LL		95
maḳḳib	a tool (hammer, punch, pick ?)	**|n-ḳ-b|**	CTX			92
maḳḳīl	rod, branch, staff	**|m-ḳ-l|**	CTX			36
malāk See *malk* (B), *malāk*						
mālak	messenger (?)	**|l-ʔ-k|**	CTX			4
malbas^{1}	cloak	**|l-b-s^{1}|**	CTX			10
malbatt	brick mould	**|l-b-n| (2)**		LL		10
mald(iy)	newly born (stock)	**|w-l-d|**	CTX			351
maliʔ	full	**|m-l-ʔ|**		LL		37
malīħ See *milħ, malīħ*						
mal(i)k	ruler, king; dead king(s); DN	**|m-l-k|**	CTX	LL	ONOM	41
mālik	councellor	**|m-l-k|**	CTX			42
malika, **malikat**, **malikt**	queen, princess; DN	**|m-l-k|**			ONOM	42
malikat See *malika,*						

malikat, *malikt*						
malikt See *malika*, *malikat*, *malikt*						
malīt	artificial terrace(?)	**|m-l-ʔ|**	CTX			37
malk (A)	ruler; (the) king; DN	**|m-l-k|**	CTX	LL	ONOM	39
malk(B), **malāk**,	ruling, guideline, decision, advice	**|m-l-k|**	CTX		ONOM	40
malkat	queen	**|m-l-k|**	CTX			42
mallāx	sailor	**|m-l-x| (2)**		LL		38
mallak	king-size (ration)	**|m-l-k|**	CTX			42
malsam	running, course	**|l-s-m|**		LL		16
malsamūt	running, course	**|l-s-m|**		LL		16
maluyanita	a vessel	**|m-l-ʔ|**	CTX			37
mamṣar	knife, sword	**|m-S-r| (1)**	CTX			53
manʕat	fortress (?)	**|m-n-ʕ|**	CTX			43
mandatt	tax, gift(s)	**|n/w/y-D-n|**	CTX			79
manħat	gift, tribute	**|m-n-ħ|**	CTX			44
manīx, **menīx**, **minīx**	calm, resting place	**|n-w-x|**			ONOM	112
maninn	a necklace	**|m-n(-n)| (2)**	CTX			44
maniy	(the) beloved; DN	**|m-n-w/y| (2)**			ONOM	45
manman	anyone, someone	**|m| (2)**			ONOM	25
man(n) (A)	who?	**|m| (2)**	CTX	LL	ONOM	25
man(n) (B)	what?	**|m| (2)**	CTX			25
man(n) (C)	how many?	**|m| (2)**	CTX			25
man(n) (D)	someone, anyone(?)	**|m| (2)**	CTX			25
mannumma	whoever	**|m| (2)**	CTX			26
manṣart	guard, garrison	**|n-θ̣-r|**	CTX			110
manṣiḳta See *māṣiḳta*, *manṣiḳta*						
mantin, **mattin**	gift	**|n/w/y-D-n|**			ONOM	79
manū	mina	**|m-n-w/y| (1)**	CTX			45
manzal, **mazzal**	pouring vessel	**|n-z-l|**		LL	ONOM	116
mapḳad	inspection, review	**|p-ḳ-d|**	CTX			126
mapras	a cutting or splitting tool	**|p-r-s| (3)**				136
mappax	bellows	**|n-p-x|**		LL		97

mār See *mar?, mār*						
maraS See *marS, maraS*						
maraṣ̌, maruṣ̌	worried, angry; the angry one (also as DN)	**|m-r-ṣ̌|**			ONOM	51
marat	kind of chain (?)	**|m-r(-r)| (3)**	CTX			50
marōma/ēma	height(s)	**|r-w/y-m|**			ONOM	177
marʔ, mār	(the) master; DN	**|m-r-ʔ| (1)**			ONOM	46
marʔiy	a regal garment(?)	**|m-r-ʔ| (1)**	CTX			46
marʕayt	pasture land	**|r-ʕ-y| (1)**		LL		151
marbad	bedspread, counterpane	**|r-b-d|**	CTX			153
marbaḳat See *marbiḳat, marbaḳat, narbiḳat, narbaḳat*						
marbiḳat, marbaḳat, narbiḳat, narbaḳat	a necklace (?)	**|r-b-ḳ|**	CTX			154
marbiṣ̌	resting place, bed	**|r-b-ṣ̌|**		LL		154
mard	bold, audacious	**|m-r-d|**				47
mardad, mardat, mardet	rug, tapestry	**|m-r-d-D|**	CTX			47
mardadoɣl	rug maker	**|m-r-d-D|**	CTX			47
mardam	a kind of walking stick (?)	**|r-d-m| (1)**			ONOM	155
mardamān	a kind of walking stick (?)	**|r-d-m| (1)**	CTX			155
mardat See *mardad, mardat, mardet*						
mardet See *mardad, mardat, mardet*						
mardimt	path (?)	**|r-d-m| (1)**		LL		155
marxaS (A),	a stone	**|m-r-x-S|**	CTX			47

marxuS	(alabastron)					
marxaS (B), **marxiS (A)**	a dagger, slice	**|m-r-x-S|**	CTX			48
marxaSt, **marxiS (B)**	an utensil; spade	**|m-r-x-S|**	CTX	LL		48
marxiS (A) See *marxaS* (B), *marxiS* (A)						
marxiS (B) See *marxaSt*, *marxiS* (B)						
marxuS See *marxaS* (A), *marxuS*						
marīʔ	fattened, fatling, dense	**|m-r-ʔ| (2)**	CTX		ONOM	46
markabt	chariot; corps or rang of charioteer(s)	**|r-k-b|**	CTX			164
marḳ	broth	**|m-r-ḳ| (1)**		LL		48
marmax(x)	a fruit tree	**|m-r-m-x(-x)|**	CTX			48
marmarr	very strong	**|m-r(-r)| (2)**	CTX	LL		50
marpiḳt	support, tray	**|r-p-ḳ|**	CTX			171
marr (A)	strong, valiant, hero	**|m-r(-r)| (2)**			ONOM	49
marr (B)	a trade	**|m-r-r| (4)**	CTX			50
marS, **maraS**	lace, string	**|m-r-s¹|**	CTX			50
marṣ́iy	love, choice	**|r-ṣ́-y|**	CTX			174
maruʔ	a military position (involving horses)	**|m-r-ʔ| (1)**	CTX		ONOM	46
maruṣ́ See *maraṣ́*, *maruṣ́*						
marwaḳat	a (small) pot (?)	**|r-y-ḳ|**	CTX			179
maryann	knight titular of a war-chariot	**|m-r-y-n|**	CTX		ONOM	52
marza/iħ	cultic association, (cultic) banquet	**|m-r-z-ħ|**	CTX		ONOM	51
marziħ See *marza/iħ*						
maSadd	(pulling) pole	**|S-d-d|**	CTX			187
maSʔal	oracle(?)	**|s¹-ʔ-l|**	CTX			230
maSGaSat	battle mace (?)	**|S-G-S|**			ONOM	190
masgin	pick, pickaxe	**|s-g-n| (1)**		LL		190

maSH	a kind of bead or ring	**|m-S-H|**	CTX			53
maSHart	a priestess	**|S-H-r|**	CTX			191
maSHaṭ	a cloth item	**|S-H-ṭ|**	CTX			191
maSħ	anointed	**|m-s^1-ħ|**			ONOM	55
maSxalt	a vessel with lip or spout	**|S-l-x|**	CTX			195
masxarūt	putting / pushing aside	**|s-x-r|**	CTX			192
maSxaṭ	butchers knife	**|s^1-x-ṭ|**	CTX			240
maSīħ	anointed	**|m-s^1-ħ|**			ONOM	55
maSiym	granary, storage place	**|s^2-y-m|**	CTX			282
maSkabt	shelter for the night	**|s^1-k-b|**	CTX			241
maSkan (A)	shackle, rein; addition	**|s^1-k-n|**	CTX	LL		243
maSkan (B)	dwelling place	**|s^1-k-n|**	CTX			243
maSkan (C)	dweller	**|s^1-k-n|**	CTX			243
maSkar, **miSkir**	wage(s), pay	**|s^2-k-r| (2)**			ONOM	274
maSkirt	a drink vessel	**|s^1-k-r| (2)**	CTX			244
maSḳart	an agricultural implement	**|s^1-ḳ-r|**				245
maSlaħ	a garment	**|s^2-l-ħ|**	CTX			275
maSmiʕ	hearing	**|s^1-m-ʕ|**			ONOM	252
maSnuʔ	enemy(?)	**|s^2-n-ʔ|**		LL		276
maSpar, **maSpir**	sending (?)	**|S-p-r| (1)**			ONOM	204
maSpir See *maSpar*, *maSpir*						
maS(S)	corvée worker	**|m-S(-S)| (2)**	CTX			54
maSSaʕ	remoteness	**|n-S-ʕ/x|**	CTX			101
maSSaḳ	kissing, kiss	**|n-s^1-ḳ| (1)**	CTX			104
maSSilāt	a tapestry or embroidered shawl (?)	**|m-s^1-l| (2)**	CTX			56
maSSur, **waSSur**	set free	**|w-s^1-r|**			ONOM	360
maStap	(ceremonial) bandage, *pallium* (?)	**|s^1-t-p|**	CTX			264
maSwat, **maSuwt**	a type of tree or wood	**|m-S-w|**	CTX	LL		54
maSyit	halt, support	**|s^1-y-t|**			ONOM	269
maṣɣarat	youth, childhood	**|ṣ-ɣ-r|**		LL		215
māṣiḳta, **manṣiḳta**	a (large) vessel	**|y-ṣ-ḳ|**	CTX			376
maṣṭapin	watering hole	**|ṣ-p-n| (2)**		LL		221

maṣill	cymbalist	**|ṣ-l-l| (2)**	CTX			217
mas^{1}ʔab	watering place	**|s^1-ʔ-b|**			ONOM	229
mas^{1}ʔirt	kneading trough (?)	**|S-ʔ-r|**	CTX			183
mas^{1}ħīta	trap, snare	**|s^1-ħ-t|, |s^1-w/y-ħ|**	CTX			239
mas^{1}x	a bead (?)	**|m-s^1-x| (2)**	CTX			55
mas^{1}xaṭ	a kind of (axe-shaped?) sail	**|s^1-x-ṭ|**	CTX			240
mas^{1}ix	amphora	**|m-s^1-x| (1)**	CTX			55
mas^{1}kant See *mas^{1}katt, mas^{1}kant*						
mas^{1}katt, mas^{1}kant	dwelling place, (store)house	**|s^1-k-n|**	CTX		ONOM	243
mas^{1}kēn	social designation	**|s^1-k-H-n|**	CTX			241
mas^{1}ḳ	office of cupbearer	**|s^1-ḳ-y|**		LL		246
mas^{1}nāl	sleeping couch	**|n-y-l|**	CTX			116
mas^{1}ōṭa	small galley propelled by oars	**|s^1-w-ṭ|**	CTX			266
mas^{1}ṭir	office, chancellery	**|s^1-ṭ-r|**	CTX			265
maṣ̂biʔt	troops, army	**|ṣ̂-b-ʔ|**	CTX	LL		284
māt	land, country	**|m-ʔ-t| (1)**	CTX		ONOM	28
matāʕ	salvation, rescue	**|m-t-ʕ|**			ONOM	58
mataħ	unit of measurement: length, stretch	**|m-t-ħ|**	CTX			58
mātan, mētan, mattan	gift	**|n/w/y-D-n|**			ONOM	79
matn	tendon	**|m-t-n| (1)**		LL		59
mati	when?	**|m| (2)**	CTX		ONOM	26
mātiʕ	helper, saviour	**|m-t-ʕ|**	CTX		ONOM	58
mattan See *mātan, mētan,*						
mattin See *mantin, mattin*						
maṭar	rain; DN	**|m-ṭ–r|**			ONOM	60
maṭħatta	mortar, quern	**|ṭ-ħ-n|**	CTX			308
maṭniʔ	provision(s), supplies	**|ṭ-n-ʔ|**	CTX			309
maṭray	kind of (tanned) strap, girth or welt	**|ṭ-r-y| (1)**	CTX			311
maṭarayt	a container	**|ṭ-r-y| (1)**	CTX			311

	made from goatskin					
maṭṭal	inspection (?)	**|n-ṭ-l|**		LL		108
maṭṭiy	sort of weapon	**|n-ṭ-y|**		LL		109
maθʕart	a priestess (kind of waitress?)	**|θ-ʕ-r|**	CTX			316
maθall	conduit, pipe, tube	**|θ-l-l|**	CTX			322
maθḳal	weight	**|θ-ḳ-l|**	CTX			321
maθθiyann	a garment, kind of shawl, sash	**|m-θ-y|**	CTX			60
maθ̣iy	successful	**|m-θ̣-ʔ/y|**			ONOM	61
maθnay	secondly (?)	**|θ-n|**	CTX			325
maθ̣θ̣ar	watchman, guard	**|n-θ̣-r|**	CTX		ONOM	110
maθ̣θ̣art	guard, watch, garrison	**|n-θ̣-r|**	CTX	LL		110
maθ̣θ̣ur	watchman, guard	**|n-θ̣-r|**			ONOM	110
māw See *maʔw*, *māw*, *māy*						
mawbaʔt	back	**|w-b-ʔ|**		LL		341
mawbal (A)	flood	**|w-b-l| (1)**		LL		341
mawbal (B)	produce, load (?)	**|w-b-l| (1)**	CTX			341
mawbal (C) See *mawbil*, *mawbal* (C)						
mawbil, mawbal (C)	neck(-sinew)	**|w-b-l| (1)**		LL		341
mawdad	beloved	**|w-d-d|**			ONOM	344
mawhaba	gift	**|w-h-b|**			ONOM	346
mawḳir	dearness	**|w-ḳ-r|**			ONOM	350
mawḳuwuy	kind of band or collar for yokes	**|w-ḳ-y|**		LL		350
mawn	supply, stock	**|m-w-n| (1)**	CTX			61
mawraʔ (A)	fright, fear (?)	**|w-r-ʔ|**	CTX			352
mawraʔ (B)	a garment (apron?)	**|w-r-ʔ|**	CTX			352
mawSar	release, dismissal	**|w-s¹-r|**		LL	ONOM	360
mawṣaʔ	export, produce	**|w-ṣ-ʔ|**	CTX			362
mawṣiʔ	appearance	**|w-ṣ-ʔ|**			ONOM	362
mawt, mōt	death	**|m-w-t|**	CTX			63
māy See *maʔw*, *māw*, *māy*						

may(a)rīn	plow without seeder	**|n-y-r|**		LL		116
mayḳarat	dear, precious, esteemed	**|w-ḳ-r|**			ONOM	350
maySar	justice	**|y-s^1-r|**		LL	ONOM	378
mays^{1}ar	justice	**|y-s^1-r|**			ONOM	378
mays^{1}ur	justice	**|y-s^1-r|**			ONOM	378
maytir	excellence	**|w-t-r| (2)**			ONOM	364
maytmiy	orphaned	**|y-t-m|**			ONOM	378
mayyal	(resting) place, space; treasury	**|n-y-l|**	CTX			116
mazniyat	fornication	**|z-n-y|**			ONOM	384
mazr	yarn, cord, felt (?)	**|m-z-r|**	CTX			64
mazraḳ, mazriḳ	a long wooden device (for hoisting water?)	**|z-r-ḳ|**		LL		385
mazriḳ See *mazraḳ, mazriḳ*						
mazwur	wound (?)	**|z-w-r|**			ONOM	386
mazzal See *manzal, mazzal*						
mazzāl	courier, messenger	**|m-z-l|**	CTX			64
mazzār	spinner, maker of yarn, cord, felt (?)	**|m-z-r|**	CTX			64
=me, =mi	optional prosodic reinforcer	**|m| (1)**	CTX		ONOM	23
mēbiS	dryness, drought (?)	**|y-b-s^1|**			ONOM	370
mehir See *mahar, mahir, mehir, mihr*						
menʕim	loveliness, delightfulness, grace	**|n-ʕ-m|**			ONOM	71
mendib	generous gift	**|n-d-b|**			ONOM	76
menħiy	direction, way (?)	**|n-ħ-w/y|**			ONOM	88
menīx See *manīx, menīx, minīx*						
menīr	candelabrum (?)	**|n-w-r|**			ONOM	115
menḳum	avenged,	**|n-ḳ-m|**			ONOM	94

	saved (?)					
meny	(the) love; DN (?)	**|m-n-w/y| (2)**			ONOM	45
mēpiʕ	splendour	**|y-p-ʕ|**			ONOM	375
merʕuy	supervisor of the royal pasturage	**|r-ʕ-y| (1)**	CTX		ONOM	151
merīθu	steep, mixed drink	**|m-r-S|**	CTX			50
meSkin	firmness (?)	**|s^1-k-n|**			ONOM	243
meSlim	friendliness	**|s-l-m| (1)**			ONOM	197
mes^{1}aru	wetland (?)	**|θ-r-y| (2)**			ONOM	328
mētan See *mātan*, *mētan*, *mattan*						
mētara	cordage	**|w-t-r| (1)**	CTX			363
metmiħ	surprise (?)	**|t-m-h|**			ONOM	297
mēdiʕ	knowledge	**|w-d-ʕ|**			ONOM	343
mēθiʕ	help	**|y-θ-ʕ|**			ONOM	379
=mi See *=me*, *=mi*						
miʔat	hundred	**|m-ʔ| (2)**	CTX			27
miʔt	hundred	**|m-ʔ| (2)**				27
mihr See *mahar*, *mahir*, *mehir*, *mihr*						
mixiṣ	a striking instrument	**|m-x-ṣ|**	CTX			35
mik	a special quality of linen; byssus ?	**|m-k|**	CTX			35
mikiyt	seductive woman	**|m-k-w/y|**	CTX			36
miḳiṭ	the Fall (DN)	**|m-ḳ-ṭ|**			ONOM	37
milħ, malīħ	salt / salty (land)	**|m-l-ħ|**			ONOM	38
milikt	ruling, guideline, decision, advice	**|m-l-k|**			ONOM	42
milk (A)	ruling, guideline, decision, advice	**|m-l-k|**	CTX		ONOM	40
milk (B)	ruler; (the) king; DN	**|m-l-k|**	CTX	LL		41
min (A)	who?	**|m| (2)**	CTX			26
min (B)	what?, why?	**|m| (2)**	CTX		ONOM	26
min (C)	whatever,	**|m| (2)**	CTX			26

	everything, anything					
min (D)	in, at, on	**|m-n-w/y| (1)**	CTX			45
mināt	portion, member	**|m-n-w/y| (1)**			ONOM	45
minīx See *manīx, menīx, minīx*						
minmiy(at)	everything, assets	**|m| (2)**	CTX		ONOM	26
minū	from	**|m-n-w/y| (1)**	CTX			45
mīnumma	whatever, everything, anything	**|m| (2)**	CTX	LL		26
mirʔūt	seeing (?)	**|r-ʔ-y|**	CTX			150
miSkiħ	find, finding	**|s^{1}-k-ħ|**			ONOM	241
miSkir See *maSkar, miSkir*						
miSlam	shown friendly, reconciled (?)	**|s-l-m| (1)**			ONOM	197
miSSaʔ	predilection	**|n-s^{2}-ʔ|**			ONOM	106
mīSy	night	**|m-s^{1}-y|**		LL		56
mis^{1}ḳ	cup (?)	**|s^{1}-ḳ-y|**	CTX			246
mit	man, husband, hero; DN	**|m-t|**			ONOM	57
miθil	mirror	**|m-θ-l|**	CTX			60
miθḳul	weighed out (?)	**|θ-ḳ-l|**	CTX			321
miy	who?	**|m| (2)**	CTX		ONOM	26
miyt	dead, mortal	**|m-w-t|**	CTX			63
mōʕid	assembly	**|w-ʕ-d|**	CTX			338
mōliħ	salt worker	**|m-l-ħ|**	CTX			38
mōθab (A)	residence; seat	**|w-θ-b|**		LL		365
mōθab (B), mūθub	cushion	**|w-θ-b|**	CTX			365
mudan	an animal (tiger / cheetah ?)	**|m-n-d-n|**		LL		43
muðtabbil	servant (?)	**|S-b-l|**		LL		185
muhr	foal, colt	**|m-h-r| (3)**			ONOM	33
muhrat, muhrut	young female animal	**|m-h-r| (3)**			ONOM	32
muhrut See *muhrat, muhrut*						
muxx	top, skull	**|m-x-x|**		LL		33
muxxuw	ecstatic	**|m-x-w|**			ONOM	35
muḳḳ	slow, slack	**|m-w-ḳ|**			ONOM	61
mulabbiSt	female housekeeper, attendant	**|l-b-s^{1}|**	CTX			10

mulk	government, royal authority	**|m-l-k|**	CTX			41
mullukt	enthronement	**|m-l-k|**	CTX			42
muluk	(defunct) member of the royal family; DN	**|m-l-k|**			ONOM	42
mumm	cry (of joy)	**|m-m-m| (2)**		LL		43
mumrāt	rebellion	**|m-r-y|**		LL		52
mumtalk, muttalk	judicious	**|m-l-k|**	CTX			42
mun	caterpillar	**|m-n(-n)| (1)**		LL		44
munabbiʔ	he who invokes, laments	**|n-b-ʔ|**	CTX			73
mupaxxir	who gathers	**|p-x-r| (2)**			ONOM	126
mupattiħ	opener	**|p-t-ħ|**			ONOM	142
murʔ (A)	a kind of cavalier or knight	**|m-r-ʔ| (1)**	CTX			46
murʔ (B)	a container for (fat) ointments	**|m-r-ʔ| (2)**	CTX			46
murd	resistence	**|m-r-d|**			ONOM	47
murħ	lance, spear	**|r-m-ħ|**	CTX			166
murr	bitter(ness); myrrh	**|m-r(-r)| (2)**	CTX	LL		49
muSaʔʔilt	who asks carefully, desires, begs (fem.)	**|s^1-ʔ-l|**	CTX			230
muSāħ	anointed	**|m-s^1-ħ|**			ONOM	55
muSaḳḳiy	(man) that waters (the field)	**|s^1-ḳ-y|**	CTX			246
muSallim	conciliator	**|s-l-m| (1)**			ONOM	197
muSarrik	most open-handed	**|s^2-r-k| (1)**			ONOM	277
muSāṭ	comb	**|m-S-ṭ|**		LL		54
mūsdōt	foundations	**|w-s-d|**			ONOM	357
muStayt	drink, libation	**|s^1-t-y| (1)**		LL		264
muSṭ	comb	**|m-S-ṭ|**	CTX			54
muSṭāt	comb	**|m-S-ṭ|**	CTX			54
mūSy	night	**|m-s^1-y|**	CTX	LL	ONOM	56
mus^1ēniḳtāt	wet nurses	**|y-n-ḳ|**	CTX			374
mut	man, husband, hero; DN	**|m-t|**				57
muttaggiS	wandering (?)	**|n-g-s^1|**			ONOM	82
muttalk See *mumtalk, muttalk*						
muttat	gift	**|n/w/y-D-n|**			ONOM	79
mūθaḳ	reliability	**|w-θ-ḳ|**		LL		366

mūθub See *mōθab* (B), *mūθub*						
muwabbil	(standard) bearer (a priest class?)	**|w-b-l| (1)**	CTX		ONOM	341
muwallidt	midwife	**|w-l-d|**	CTX	LL		351
muwāt	dying(?)	**|m-t|**			ONOM	63
muwdaʕ	knowing, wise, experienced	**|w-d-ʕ|**			ONOM	343
muwdiy	class or corporation (knowing, wise, experienced)	**|w-d-ʕ|**	CTX			343

n

=na (A), =ni (A)	highlighting and euphonic enclitic (≈ yea)	**|n| (1)**	CTX		ONOM	67
=na (B), =nā	our	**|n| (2)**			ONOM	67
nāʔ, niāʔa	our, belonging to us	**|n| (2)**	CTX		ONOM	68
naʔd	exalted	**|n-ʔ-d| (2)**			ONOM	69
naʕam	pleasure, fortune, prosperity, grace				ONOM	70
naʕim	pleasant; the Gracious One (DN)	**|n-ʕ-m|**	CTX		ONOM	70
naʕm	pleasure, fortune, prosperity, grace	**|n-ʕ-m|**	CTX		ONOM	69
naʕmūt	fortune, goodness, grace	**|n-ʕ-m|**			ONOM	70
naʕr	servant; soldier	**|n-ʕ-r| (1)**	CTX	LL	ONOM	72
nab	louse	**|n-b| (1)**		LL		71
nabāʔ	announce, new(s) (?)	**|n-b-ʔ|**			ONOM	74
nabāS	red(-dyed) wool	**|n-B-S|**	CTX			75
nabbāl	the archer; DN	**|n-b-l| (2)**			ONOM	74
nabiʔ	called	**|n-b-ʔ|**			ONOM	72
nābiʔ	who names, calls, invokes	**|n-b-ʔ|**	CTX		ONOM	73
nābiṭ	who shines, appears, looks at	**|n-b-ṭ|**			ONOM	75

naBk	fountain, spring, well	**|n-b-k|**	CTX	LL	ONOM	74
nabl	fire-arrow, flame	**|n-b-l| (2)**			ONOM	74
nablat	excellent, noble	**|n-b-l| (3)**			ONOM	74
nabṭ	splendour	**|n-b-ṭ|**	CTX			75
nabuṭ	brillant, splendorous	**|n-b-ṭ|**			ONOM	75
nad	stela	**|n-d|**		LL		75
nadab	willing, eager to give	**|n-d-b|**			ONOM	76
nadall, nadull	part of harness, halter (?)	**|m-d-l(-l)|**	CTX			30
nādid	wandering labourer, vagrant	**|n-d-d| (1)**		LL		76
nādin	giver, donor	**|n/w/y-D-n|**			ONOM	78
nadūb	generously given	**|n-d-b|**			ONOM	76
nadull See *nadall, nadull*						
nagah	brightness, dawn	**|n-g-h|**			ONOM	81
nagāz	fulfillment (?)	**|n-g-z|**			ONOM	83
nagb (A)	pile, heap, storage	**|n-g-b| (1)**		LL		80
nagb (B)	dryness, dry country	**|n-g-b| (2)**			ONOM	81
nagbat	(food) supply, stock	**|n-g-b| (1)**	CTX			81
nagih	shining	**|n-g-h|**			ONOM	82
nāgir	herald	**|n-g-r|**			ONOM	82
nagiS	ruler, chief	**|n-g-s²|**			ONOM	82
nāgiS	approaching (?)	**|n-g-s¹|**			ONOM	82
nāɣir	watchman, guard	**|n-θ̣-r|**	CTX			110
nah(a)r (A)	river; DN	**|n-h-r| (1)**	CTX			84
nahar (B)	who runs away, fugitive	**|n-h-r| (1)**	CTX			84
nahid	watchful, careful	**|n-h-d|**	CTX			83
nahīr	glorious, shining	**|n-h-r| (2)**	CTX			85
naHiS	lion (?)	**|n-H-S|**		LL		85
nahl	rest, sleep (?)	**|n-h-l| (2)**	CTX			84
naHuB(at)	pendant or necklace (?)	**|n-H-B|**	CTX	LL		83
naḫilt	patrimonial estate	**|n-ḫ-l|**	CTX			86
naḫiS	living, alive	**|n-ḫ-S|**		LL	ONOM	87
naḫlat	inheritance,	**|n-ḫ-l|**	CTX			86

	inalienable possession					
naḫs^{1}	copper, bronze (?)	**|n-ḫ-s^{1}| (2)**	CTX			87
naḫy	direction, way	**|n-ḫ-w/y|**	CTX			88
nāx	reassuring, calm granting, mercy showing; DN	**|n-w-x|**			ONOM	112
nax(a)l	torrent, water course	**|n-x-l|**	CTX		ONOM	88
naxar	snorting	**|n-x-r|**			ONOM	88
nakar See *nakr, nakar*						
nakir	stranger, someone / something strange	**|n-k-r|**			ONOM	90
nakkul	artful, sophisticated	**|n-k-l| (2)**			ONOM	89
nakl	artful, sophisticated	**|n-k-l| (2)**			ONOM	89
nakr, nakar	stranger, someone / something strange	**|n-k-r|**			ONOM	90
nāḳid	stock-breeder, herdsman	**|n-ḳ-d|**		LL	ONOM	92
nāḳim	avenger, saviour	**|n-ḳ-m|**			ONOM	94
naḳir	engraved	**|n-ḳ-r|**	CTX			94
naḳḳab	a tool (hammer, punch, pick ?)	**|n-ḳ-b|**	CTX			92
nalbatt	frame (for gems)	**|l-b-n| (2)**	CTX			10
namal	ant	**|n-m-l| (1)**			ONOM	95
namār	dawn	**|n-w-r|**			ONOM	114
namas^{1}, namis^{1}	ichneumon, mongoose (?)	**|n-m-s^{1}| (1)**			ONOM	96
namiy (A) See *nawiy, namiy* (A)						
namiy (B)	steppe-dweller	**|n-w-y|**	CTX			116
naml	ants, ant hill	**|n-m-l| (1)**	CTX			95
namlakt	realm, territory	**|m-l-k|**	CTX			42
namlaṭ	refuge, shelter	**|m-l-ṭ|**			ONOM	43
namr (A)	leopard	**|n-m-r| (1)**		LL		96
namr (B)	shining	**|n-w-r|**			ONOM	114
namrat See *nawrat, namrat*						
namurr	shining	**|n-w-r|**			ONOM	114

namur(r)at	splendour; bright, shining (a stone)	**|n-w-r|**	CTX			114
nāp	exalting (?)	**|n-w-p|**			ONOM	113
nap(a)S, nap(i)S	throat; breath; life	**|n-p-S|**			ONOM	98
nap(i)S See *nap(a)S, nap(i)S*						
napiSat	throat; breath; life	**|n-p-S|**			ONOM	99
napx	shining, gleaming (stone)	**|n-p-x|**	CTX			97
naplaSt	a kind of payment	**|p-l-s|**	CTX			129
napsuxt	sudden attack, counteraction (?)	**|p-s-x|**	CTX			138
napṭar	exchange, ransom (?)	**|p-ṭ-r|**	CTX			142
napṭart	desertion	**|p-ṭ-r|**	CTX			142
narbaḳat See *marbiḳat, marbaḳat, narbiḳat, narbaḳat*						
narbiḳat See *marbiḳat, marbaḳat, narbiḳat, narbaḳat*						
naSaʕt	removal	**|n-S-ʕ/x|**		LL		100
naSiG	woven	**|n-S-G|**	CTX			100
nāSiʔ	one who raises, accepts; chief, leader; ND	**|n-s^2-ʔ|**		LL	ONOM	106
nasīk	cast metal object, ingot (?)	**|n-s-k|**	CTX			101
nāsik	caster, metalsmith; chief	**|n-s-k|**	CTX		ONOM	101
nasḳ	ascent (?)	**|n-s-ḳ|**			ONOM	101
naSr	eagle, vulture	**|n-s^1-r| (1)**			ONOM	105
nass	wretched	**|n-s-s|**			ONOM	101
naSūʔ	raised, accepted	**|n-s^2-ʔ|**			ONOM	106
nāṣ	plumage	**|n-w-ṣ|**		LL		115
naṣab	erect, put / set upright	**|n-ṣ-b|**			ONOM	102
naṣb (A)	support	**|n-ṣ-b|**			ONOM	102
naṣb (B)	reserve, setting	**|n-ṣ-b|**	CTX		ONOM	102

	apart (?)					
nāṣib	keeper, one who is paying attention	**|n-ṣ-b|**		LL		102
naṣṣ	a wild bird (?)	**|n-ṣ-ṣ|**			ONOM	104
naṣub	erect, put / set upright	**|n-ṣ-b|**			ONOM	103
nas^{1}pat	blown, blowing (?; fem.)	**|n-s^{1}-B| (1)**			ONOM	104
natib	swollen (?)	**|n-t-b| (2)**			ONOM	107
natūn	given	**|n/w/y-D-n|**			ONOM	78
naṭap	drop (of stacte)	**|n-ṭ-p|**			ONOM	108
nāṭil	elegy singer	**|n-ṭ-l|**	CTX	LL		108
naṭl	lamentation	**|n-ṭ-l|**		LL		108
naθk	bite	**|n-θ-k|**	CTX			109
nāθ̣ir	watchman, guard	**|n-θ̣-r|**			ONOM	110
naθ̣r, nuθ̣r	custody, protection	**|n-θ̣-r|**	CTX		ONOM	110
nawar	shining, light, lamp	**|n-w-r|**			ONOM	114
nawil	affection, devotion	**|n-w-l|**		LL		112
nawiy, namiy (A)	pasturage; steppe, encampment; ND	**|n-w-y|**	CTX	LL	ONOM	115
nawrat, namrat	shining, light, lamp	**|n-w-r|**			ONOM	115
=nay(n), =ney(n), =nē(n)	of both of us; both of us	**|n| (2)**	CTX		ONOM	68
neHS	lion (?)	**|n-H-S|**			ONOM	85
neḥar	smiting, smiter; DN	**|n-ḥ-r|**			ONOM	86
neḥ(i)S	alive, the living one	**|n-ḥ-S|**			ONOM	87
=nē(n) See *=nay(n), =ney(n), =nē(n)*						
nepar	workhouse, prison	**|n-p-r| (2)**	CTX			98
nēr, nīr, niwr	light, fire, lamp; DN	**|n-w-r|**	CTX		ONOM	114
=ney(n) See *=nay(n), =ney(n), =nē(n)*						
=ni (A)						

See *=na* (A), *=ni* (A)						
=ni (B)	me, to me (?)	**|n| (2)**			ONOM	67
=ni (C)	our	**|n| (2)**			ONOM	67
niāSi	to us	**|n| (2)**	CTX			68
niāti	our; to us	**|n| (2)**	CTX			68
niāʔa See *nāʔ*, *niāʔa*						
niāʔūti	our	**|n| (2)**	CTX			68
niʔt	axe, hatchet	**|n-ʔ|**	CTX			68
niʕm	pleasure, fortune, prosperity, grace; DN	**|n-ʕ-m|**			ONOM	70
nibʔ	nominal value	**|n-b-ʔ|**	CTX			72
nibʕ	watered field (?)	**|n-b-ʕ|**	CTX			73
nidāħ	kind of weapon	**|n-d-ħ|**	CTX			77
nidint, niditt	gift, dowry	**|n/w/y-D-n|**	CTX		ONOM	78
niditt See *nidint*, *niditt*						
nidn	gift	**|n/w/y-D-n|**			ONOM	78
nigʕ	customary pastoral route	**|n-g-ʕ| (2)**	CTX			80
niGdat	progeny, clan (?)	**|n-G-d|**			ONOM	81
nigh	brightness, dawn (?)	**|n-g-h|**			ONOM	81
niɣr	custody, protection	**|n-θ̣-r|**		LL		110
nih(i)l	a kind of sheep	**|n-h-l| (1)**	CTX			83
niħlat	property handed over	**|n-ħ-l|**				86
nīx, nūx	rest, calm	**|n-w-x|**			ONOM	112
nikar	stranger, someone / something strange	**|n-k-r|**	CTX		ONOM	90
nikipt	an edible(?) plant and its oil	**|n-G-p|**	CTX			82
nik(k)al	DN	**|n-k-l| (1)**			ONOM	89
niḳāḳ	cleft (lip / palate) (?)	**|n-ḳ-ḳ|**			ONOM	92
niḳāl	supply,	**|n-ḳ-l|**	CTX		ONOM	93

	contribution(?)					
niḳitt	retaliation	**|n-ḳ-m|**	CTX			94
niḳm	vengeance, salvation; DN	**|n-ḳ-m|**	CTX		ONOM	93
nimīr	light, pale (oil)	**|n-w-r|**	CTX			114
nip(i)S	throat (?)	**|n-p-S|**	CTX			98
nipīt	sieve, sifter	**|n-p-y| (1)**		LL		99
nipṣ	clearance (?)	**|n-p-ṣ| (1)**	CTX			99
nīr See *nēr*, *nīr*, *niwr*						
niSdupp	plaque	**|s¹-d-p|**	CTX			235
niSG	a kind of hank (?)	**|n-S-G|**	CTX			100
niSḳ	kissing	**|n-s¹-ḳ| (1)**		LL		104
nissat	weakness, indisposition	**|n-s-s|**	CTX			101
niṣb	support	**|n-ṣ-b|**			ONOM	103
niṣīm	thin layer, sheet, plate	**|n-ṣ̂-m|**	CTX			107
niwar, **nimar**, **nimer**, **niwer**, **niwir**	shining, light, lamp	**|n-w-r|**	CTX		ONOM	115
niwr See *nēr*, *nīr*, *niwr*						
nizam, **nizim**	desire (?)	**|n-z-m|**			ONOM	117
nizim See *nizam*, *nizim*						
nizl	first quality oil	**|n-z-l|**		LL		116
nōma See *nūma*, *nōma*						
=nu	our; us	**|n| (2)**	CTX		ONOM	67
nuʕām	pleasant, lovely, delightful	**|n-ʕ-m|**			ONOM	70
nuʕm	pleasure, fortune, prosperity, grace; DN	**|n-ʕ-m|**			ONOM	70
nubāṭ	the brillant, splendorous one	**|n-b-ṭ|**			ONOM	75
nubbūṭ	watched attentively, observed	**|n-b-ṭ|**			ONOM	75

nūbiʔān	an insect (bee ?)	**|n-b| (2)**		LL		71
nubt	bee	**|n-b| (2)**			ONOM	71
nūd	nodded, someone given the nod, granted mercy	**|n-w-d|**			ONOM	111
nuHB	pendant (stone) (?)	**|n-H-B|**	CTX	LL	ONOM	83
nuḥus^{1}t	copper, bronze	**|n-ḥ-s^1| (2)**	CTX			87
nūx See *nīx*, *nūx*						
nukar See *nukr*, *nukar*						
nukr, **nukar**	curiosity, something strange	**|n-k-r|**	CTX		ONOM	90
nūma, **nōma**	sleep	**|n-w-m|**	CTX			113
numaḳ	embellished(?)	**|n-m-ḳ|**			ONOM	95
nūp, **nūpat**	rise, elevation (?)	**|n-w-p|**			ONOM	113
nūpat See *nūp*, *nūpat*						
nuppilān	caterpillar (?)	**|n-B-l| (1)**		LL		74
nupS	throat; breath; life	**|n-p-S|**			ONOM	99
nupuSt	throat; breath; life	**|n-p-S|**		LL		99
nūr, **nuwr**	light, fire, lamp; DN	**|n-w-r|**	CTX		ONOM	114
nurmān	bead (in the shape of a pomegranate)	**|l-r-m-n|**	CTX			16
nūr(u)t	light, lamp	**|n-w-r|**			ONOM	114
nuSaʕt	tear, rip	**|n-S-ʕ/x|**	CTX			101
nuṣab	erect, put / set upright	**|n-ṣ-b|**			ONOM	103
nus^1(s^1)up	blowing, blown (?)	**|n-s^1-B| (1)**			ONOM	104
nutk	a glass paste	**|n-t-k|**	CTX			107
nuṭ(ṭ)up	drop (of stacte)	**|n-ṭ-p|**			ONOM	108
nūθab	cushion	**|w-θ-b|**	CTX			365
nuθ̣ār	custody, protection (?)	**|n-θ̣-r|**			ONOM	110
nuθ̣r See *naθr*, *nuθr*						

nuwāp	elevated, exalted	**|n-w-p|**			ONOM	113
nuwr See *nūr, nuwr*						

p

paʔ(a)d offered	offered	**|p-ʔ-d|**	CTX			119
paʔal See *paʔl, paʔal*						
paʔl, paʔal	a kind of flour	**|p-ʔ-l|**	CTX			120
paʔrat	mouse	**|p-ʔ-r|**		LL		120
paʔS, pāS	axe	**|p-ʔ-S|**	CTX	LL		120
paʕrit	scolding (?)	**|p-ʕ-r|**		LL		121
pad(d)an	road (through a plain) (?)	**|p-d-n|**			ONOM	122
pad(d)in	road (through a plain) (?)	**|p-d-n|**		LL		122
pādim	stutter(ing), stammer(ing)	**|p-d-m|**		LL		122
pādiy	redeemer, ransomer	**|p-d-y|**			ONOM	123
pagraʔ	body, corpse (as a funerary offering)	**|p-g-r|**	CTX			123
pagr	body, corpse (as a funerary offering)	**|p-g-r|**	CTX		ONOM	123
paγaddarr See *paγandarr, paγaddarr*						
paγandarr, paγaddarr	a blanket or cloak	**|p-γ-(n-)d-r|**	CTX			124
paxd	fear, fright	**|p-x-d| (2)**	CTX			125
paxxar	potter	**|p-x-r| (1)**			ONOM	125
paxxur	reunited	**|p-x-r| (2)**			ONOM	126
paxr	assembly (?)	**|p-x-r| (2)**		LL		125
paxūr	assembly / gathered (?)	**|p-x-r| (2)**			ONOM	126
pāḳid	carer	**|p-ḳ-d|**			ONOM	126
palakk	spindle	**|p-l-G-G|**		LL		128
palaṭ	vivid, lasting, prevailing	**|p-l-ṭ|**			ONOM	130
palid	a cloth or garment	**|p-l-d|**	CTX			127
pālil (A)	guide, leader	**|p-l-l/y| (2)**		LL		129

pālil (B)	kind of protective fabric, sac	**|p-l-l/y| (2)**	CTX			129
pall	invocation	**|p-l-l/y| (2)**	CTX			128
palS	watched over, esteemed, cherished	**|p-l-s|**			ONOM	129
palūS	watched over, esteemed	**|p-l-s|**			ONOM	129
panw/y	front; (pl.) face	**|p-n|**	CTX	LL	ONOM	130
pany See *panw/y*						
pār	an equid, wild ass	**|p-r-ʔ| (1)**	CTX		ONOM	131
parʔ	an equid, wild ass	**|p-r-ʔ| (1)**			ONOM	131
parāʔ	an equid	**|p-r-ʔ| (1)**			ONOM	131
paraʔur	an homosexual	**|p-r-ʔ-r|**	CTX			132
paras	laceration (?)	**|p-r-s| (3)**	CTX			136
parīs	a dry measure	**|p-r-s| (2)**	CTX			135
park	false(hood), wrong(fulness)	**|p-r-k|**		LL		133
parr, part, parrat	weaned, weanling	**|p-r-r| (1)**	CTX			134
parrat See *parr, part, parrat*						
parS	spreading (of the wings?)	**|p-r-s²|**		LL		137
part See *parr, part, parrat*						
pāS See *paʔS, pāS*						
paSaħ	tranquil	**|p-s¹-ħ|**			ONOM	139
pasīlān	a peculiar pot shape	**|p-s-l|**	CTX			138
pas¹ṭ	stretching, extension (?)	**|p-s¹-ṭ|**			ONOM	140
patat	hunk, chunk (of bread)	**|p-t-t|**		LL		141
pataḳħ	open	**|p-ḳ-ħ|**			ONOM	127
pātiħ	kind of chest with lock	**|p-t-ħ|**	CTX			141
patīl	bandages	**|p-D-l|**	CTX			121
paṭar	released	**|p-ṭ-r|**			ONOM	142

pāṭir	redeemer; deserter, off-duty soldier	**|p-ṭ-r|**	CTX		ONOM	142
paṭr	release	**|p-ṭ-r|**			ONOM	142
paṭur	redeemed (?)	**|p-ṭ-r|**			ONOM	142
paw	here	**|p-w| (2)**	CTX			144
pazir	sheltered, placed under cover (?)	**|p-z-r|**	CTX		ONOM	146
pazr (A)	shelter, protection	**|p-z-r|**			ONOM	146
pazr (B)	hub (?)	**|p-z-r|**	CTX			146
perd	mount	**|p-r-d| (1)**			ONOM	132
pī See *pu(w)*, *pū*, *pi(y)*, *pī*						
piʔat	edge, border, temple	**|p-ʔ|**	CTX	LL		119
piʔd	mercy, kindness	**|p-ʔ-d|**			ONOM	120
piʔt	edge, border, temple	**|p-ʔ|**		LL		119
pidīt	ransom (?)	**|p-d-y|**			ONOM	123
pigm	section	**|p-g-m|**	CTX			123
piḳdāt	care, allocation	**|p-ḳ-d|**			ONOM	126
pilakk	spindle	**|p-l-G-G|**		LL		128
pilakkuγul	spinner	**|p-l-G-G|**	CTX			128
pilaḳḳ	spindle	**|p-l-G-G|**		LL		127
pilx	fear	**|p-l-x|**			ONOM	128
pilS, pulS	(merciful) look	**|p-l-s|**			ONOM	129
pilSūt	esteem	**|p-l-s|**			ONOM	130
pinn	button, stud (ornament)	**|p-n-n|**	CTX			131
pīr	elephant	**|p-r|**		LL		131
pirx	blossom, sprout, shoot	**|p-r-x|**	CTX			133
pirikk	a symbol or (movable?) cultic installation	**|p-r-k-k|**	CTX			134
pirs (A)	division, section (of troops, workers)	**|p-r-s| (3)**	CTX			136
pirs (B)	a piece of fabric, cut	**|p-r-s| (3)**	CTX			136
pirsēn	weaned animal	**|p-r-s| (3)**	CTX			136
pirz	champion, warrior	**|p-r-z|**		LL		138
pitaħt	opening	**|p-t-ħ|**	CTX			141
pitH	spacer bead in a	**|p-t-ħ|**	CTX			140

	necklace					
pitħ	opening	**|p-t-ħ|**	CTX		ONOM	141
piṭr	release	**|p-ṭ-r|**		LL		142
piθθ	ointment	**|p-θ-θ|**		LL		143
piθθat	ointment spoon	**|p-θ-θ|**	CTX			143
pi(y) See *pu*(*w*), *pū*, *pi*(*y*), *pī*						
pū See *pu*(*w*), *pū*, *pi*(*y*), *pī*						
puʕl	labour deed, work	**|p-ʕ-l|**			ONOM	121
pugart	a funerary rite (?)	**|p-g-r|**	CTX			124
puγ(i)y	boy	**|p-γ-y|**			ONOM	124
puħal	ram / stallion	**|p-ħ-l|**	CTX			124
pūħil	ram / stallion	**|p-ħ-l|**	CTX			124
puxxur	reunited	**|p-x-r| (2)**			ONOM	126
puxr	assembly, cluster, faction	**|p-x-r| (2)**		LL		125
pūl	bean	**|p-w-l|**	CTX			145
pullaṭ	rescue, deliverance (?)	**|p-l-ṭ|**			ONOM	130
pulS See *pilS*, *pulS*						
purāsa	decision (?)	**|p-r-s| (3)**			ONOM	136
purγaθ	flea	**|p-r-γ-θ|**		LL		133
purγuθ	flea	**|p-r-γ-θ|**		LL	ONOM	133
purrus	determined, decided	**|p-r-s| (3)**			ONOM	136
purs	weaning	**|p-r-s| (3)**	CTX			136
purulin	seer, diviner	**|p-r-l-n|**	CTX	LL		134
purūwat	harvesting	**|p-r(-w/y)| (1)**	CTX			137
puSḳ	hardship, need, necessity	**|p-s^1-ḳ|**	CTX		ONOM	139
pusm	a garment (veil ?) or a part thereof (sleeve(s)) (?)	**|p-s-m|**		LL		138
pus^{1}s^{1}uṭ	discomfort (?)	**|p-s^1-ṭ|**		LL		140
puṭr	release	**|p-ṭ-r|**			ONOM	142
pu(w), pū, pi(y), pī	mouth, word	**|p(-w/y)| (1)**	CTX	LL	ONOM	143

puwwat	madder	**|p-w(-t)|**	CTX			145
puzar	sheltered, kept safe	**|p-z-r|**			ONOM	146
puzr	shelter, protection	**|p-z-r|**			ONOM	146

r

rāʔim	lover	**|r-ʔ-m| (2)**			ONOM	149
raʔs^1 See *rāS*, *raʔs^1*						
raʕ	friend, companion	**|r-ʕ|**		LL	ONOM	150
rāʕiy	shepherd	**|r-ʕ-y| (1)**			ONOM	150
rabay	big	**|r-b-b| (1), |r-b-y|**			ONOM	152
rabb	great, large	**|r-b-b| (1), |r-b-y|**	CTX		ONOM	152
rabbat	ten thousand, myriad	**|r-b-b| (1), |r-b-y|**	CTX			153
rabbut	bigness, highness	**|r-b-b| (1), |r-b-y|**			ONOM	153
rabika	a fine bread or pastry	**|r-b-k|**	CTX			154
rabīt (A)	great lady, queen	**|r-b-b| (1), |r-b-y|**	CTX			153
rabīt (B)	capital city	**|r-b-b| (1), |r-b-y|**	CTX			153
rābiṣ	commissioner	**|r-b-ṣ̂|**	CTX			154
raḥāb	wide, broad, open space	**|r-ḥ-b|**			ONOM	158
raḥaba	a vessel	**|r-ḥ-b|**	CTX			158
raḥaḳ	distant	**|r-ḥ-ḳ|**			ONOM	159
raḥ(a)ṣ, riḥṣ	help	**|r-ḥ-ṣ|**		LL	ONOM	160
raḥas^1	pan baked bread (?)	**|r-ḥ-s^1|**	CTX			161
raḥaṣ̂	washed, overflowed (?)	**|r-ḥ-ṣ̂|**			ONOM	161
rāḥat	hand; kind of handle or grip	**|r-ḥ|**	CTX	LL		158
raḥīb	extended, expanded	**|r-ḥ-b|**			ONOM	158
raḥim	merciful	**|r-ḥ-m|**			ONOM	160
rāḥiṣ	helper	**|r-ḥ-ṣ**			ONOM	161
raḥḳ, reḥḳ	distant	**|r-ḥ-ḳ|**			ONOM	159
raḥm	pity, mercy	**|r-ḥ-m|**			ONOM	160
raḥmān	the merciful one	**|r-ḥ-m|**			ONOM	160

rahṭ	a vessel	**|r-h-ṭ|**	CTX			157
rāxiy	inseminating	**|r-x-y|**		LL		162
rakab	control, command, success	**|r-k-b|**			ONOM	163
rakabt	chariot	**|r-k-b|**	CTX			163
rakbūt	corps or rang of riders	**|r-k-b|**	CTX			163
rākib	a type of levee	**|r-k-b|**	CTX			163
rakub	successful	**|r-k-b|**			ONOM	163
rakS	knotting, closing / knotted, closed (?)	**|r-k-S|**	CTX			164
rakūs¹u	equipment, gear	**|r-k-s¹|**	CTX			165
raḳaḳ	thin cake, waffle	**|r-ḳ-ḳ| (1)**		LL		166
rāḳiħ	oil-perfumer	**|r-ḳ-ħ|**		LL		166
raḳḳ	thin, fine	**|r-ḳ-ḳ| (1)**		LL		165
raḳḳat (A)	a type of bread	**|r-ḳ-ḳ| (1)**	CTX			166
raḳḳat (B)	a fine textile	**|r-ḳ-ḳ| (1)**	CTX			166
raḳḳat (C)	a part of the head (?)	**|r-ḳ-ḳ| (1)**	CTX			166
raḳḳat (D)	meadow, swamp, marsh	**|r-ḳ-ḳ| (2)**	CTX	LL		166
rām	high, sublime, exalted; a kind of monument, DN	**|r-w/y-m|**		LL	ONOM	176
ramaS, ramiS	being on the move in a particular manner (?)	**|r-m-S|**			ONOM	167
ramik	bathed, washed	**|r-m-k|**			ONOM	167
ramiS See *ramaS, ramiS*						
rapaḳt	support	**|r-p-ḳ|**		LL		170
rapʔ	purification (?)	**|r-p-ʔ|**		LL		168
rāpiʔ	healer (ancestral hero; DN)	**|r-p-ʔ|**			ONOM	169
rāpid	raider	**|r-p-d| (1)**	CTX			170
rapis¹	wide, extended, generous	**|r-p-s¹|**			ONOM	171
raps¹	wide, extended (?)	**|r-p-s¹|**			ONOM	171
rapūʔ	healed	**|r-p-ʔ|**			ONOM	169
rāS, raʔs¹	head, chief; detachment	**|r-ʔ-s¹|**	CTX		ONOM	149
raSap	flame, blaze; DN	**|r-S-p|**		LL	ONOM	172
raSip						

See *riSp*, *ruSp*, *raSip*, *rSap*						
raṣiy	content, satisfied	**|r-ṣ-y|**			ONOM	174
raṭibt	fresh, juicy	**|r-ṭ-b|**	CTX			174
rāwiθ̣	runner	**|r-w-θ̣|**			ONOM	177
rayb	compensation; plea	**|r-y-b|**			ONOM	178
raybat	compensation; plea	**|r-y-b|**			ONOM	179
raybūt	compensation; plea	**|r-y-b|**			ONOM	179
rayyāṣ	trainer, tamer (?)	**|r-w/y-ṣ|**	CTX			177
rāzimt, **rāzitt**	wailing woman	**|r-z-m|**	CTX			180
rāzitt See *rāzimt*, *rāzitt*						
reʕ	friend, companion	**|r-ʕ|**			ONOM	150
reħḳ See *raħḳ*, *reħḳ*						
reħm, **riħm**	womb	**|r-ħ-m|**		LL		160
riʔm (A)	wild bull, buffalo	**|r-ʔ-m| (1)**		LL	ONOM	148
riʔm (B)	love	**|r-ʔ-m| (2)**			ONOM	149
riʔnt (A)	wild cow	**|r-ʔ-m| (1)**			ONOM	148
riʔnt (B)	love	**|r-ʔ-m| (2)**			ONOM	149
riʔs[1] See *rīS*, *riʔs*[1]						
ribab	ten thousand, myriad	**|r-b-b| (1)**, **|r-b-y|**	CTX			152
ribbat	ten thousand, myriad	**|r-b-b| (1)**, **|r-b-y|**	CTX			153
rīd, **ridy**	amount due	**|r-d-y|**		LL		156
ridy See *rīd*, *ridy*						
rigatt	claim, request	**|r-g-m|**		LL		157
rigl	foot, leg	**|r-g-l|**		LL	ONOM	156
rigm	yell, roar (?)	**|r-g-m|**		LL	ONOM	157
riħbān	wide, spacious	**|r-ħ-b|**		LL		159
riħm See *reħm*, *riħm*						

riḥṣ See *raḥ(a)ṣ*, *riḥṣ*						
riḥṣ̂	washing, flood(ing)	**|r-ḥ-ṣ̂|**			ONOM	161
rixṣ	conference, chatting	**|r-x-ṣ|**	CTX			162
rikab	upper grindstone	**|r-k-b|**		LL		163
rikS	bundle, knot; agreement	**|r-k-S|**	CTX			164
riḳāta	compartments or hollow spaces	**|r-y-ḳ|**	CTX			179
riḳaḥt	spiced, oily ointment	**|r-ḳ-ḥ|**		LL		165
rīm	high, sublime, exalted; DN	**|r-w/y-m|**			ONOM	176
rimmat	a bead (shaped as a maggot ?)	**|r-m-m| (1)**	CTX			167
rimS	moving, setting in motion in a particular manner (?)	**|r-m-S|**			ONOM	167
riʔp	healing, salvation	**|r-p-ʔ|**			ONOM	168
ripʔūt	care, medication	**|r-p-ʔ|**	CTX			170
ripād	support, pedestal	**|r-p-d| (2)**		LL		170
ripiḳt	support	**|r-p-ḳ|**		LL		170
rips[1]	wide, extended	**|r-p-s[1]|**	CTX			171
rīS, **riʔs[1]**	head, chief	**|r-ʔ-s[1]|**		LL	ONOM	149
riSp, **ruSp**, **raSip**, **rSap**	flame, blaze; DN	**|r-S-p|**			ONOM	172
riṣaʕ	point, tip	**|r-ṣ-ʕ|**	CTX			173
riṭb	(sprouting) precious stone trim	**|r-ṭ-b|**		LL		174
riwḥ	odour, fragrance	**|r-w-ḥ|**			ONOM	175
riyb	compensation; plea	**|r-y-b|**			ONOM	178
riybān	strife, plea	**|r-y-b|**		LL		179
riybat	compensation; plea	**|r-y-b|**			ONOM	179
rōpiʔ	healer (ancestral hero; DN)	**|r-p-ʔ|**			ONOM	169
rōs[1]	head; summit	**|r-ʔ-s[1]|**	CTX		ONOM	149

<table>
<tr><td>rSap
See riSp, ruSp, raSip, rSap</td><td></td><td></td><td></td><td></td><td></td><td></td></tr>
<tr><td>rubay</td><td>prince</td><td>|r-b-b| (1), |r-b-y|</td><td></td><td>LL</td><td></td><td>153</td></tr>
<tr><td>rubḳ</td><td>rein, bridle</td><td>|r-b-ḳ|</td><td>CTX</td><td></td><td></td><td>154</td></tr>
<tr><td>ruħāSt
See ruħSat, ruħāSt</td><td></td><td></td><td></td><td></td><td></td><td></td></tr>
<tr><td>ruħb</td><td>width</td><td>|r-ħ-b|</td><td></td><td></td><td>ONOM</td><td>158</td></tr>
<tr><td>ruħḳ</td><td>distant</td><td>|r-ħ-ḳ|</td><td></td><td></td><td>ONOM</td><td>159</td></tr>
<tr><td>ruħSat, ruħāSt</td><td>libation</td><td>|r-ħ-s^{2}|</td><td></td><td>LL</td><td></td><td>161</td></tr>
<tr><td>ruħṣ</td><td>help</td><td>|r-ħ-ṣ|</td><td></td><td></td><td>ONOM</td><td>161</td></tr>
<tr><td>rukab</td><td>successful</td><td>|r-k-b|</td><td></td><td></td><td>ONOM</td><td>163</td></tr>
<tr><td>rukub</td><td>a vehicle with wheels</td><td>|r-k-b|</td><td>CTX</td><td></td><td></td><td>163</td></tr>
<tr><td>ruḳḳ</td><td>sheet of metal</td><td>|r-ḳ-ḳ| (1)</td><td>CTX</td><td></td><td></td><td>166</td></tr>
<tr><td>ruḳḳān</td><td>thin cake, waffle</td><td>|r-ḳ-ḳ| (1)</td><td>CTX</td><td></td><td></td><td>166</td></tr>
<tr><td>ruSp
See riSp, ruSp, raSip, rSap</td><td></td><td></td><td></td><td></td><td></td><td></td></tr>
<tr><td>ruSt</td><td>an ornament</td><td>|r-S-t|</td><td>CTX</td><td></td><td></td><td>172</td></tr>
<tr><td>rutuḳt</td><td>binding, clamping, holding together</td><td>|r-t-ḳ|</td><td>CTX</td><td></td><td></td><td>174</td></tr>
<tr><td>ruwħ</td><td>wind</td><td>|r-w-ħ|</td><td></td><td></td><td>ONOM</td><td>175</td></tr>
</table>

s (and S)

<table>
<tr><td>Saʔʔult</td><td>carefully requested, desired (fem.)</td><td>|s^{1}-ʔ-l|</td><td></td><td>LL</td><td>ONOM</td><td>230</td></tr>
<tr><td>Saʔal</td><td>asked for, requested</td><td>|s^{1}-ʔ-l|</td><td></td><td></td><td>ONOM</td><td>229</td></tr>
<tr><td>Sāʔil</td><td>diviner</td><td>|s^{1}-ʔ-l|</td><td></td><td></td><td>ONOM</td><td>229</td></tr>
<tr><td>Sāʔilt</td><td>woman diviner</td><td>|s^{1}-ʔ-l|</td><td></td><td>LL</td><td></td><td>230</td></tr>
<tr><td>Saʔl</td><td>claim, request, demand</td><td>|s^{1}-ʔ-l|</td><td></td><td></td><td>ONOM</td><td>231</td></tr>
<tr><td>Saʔn</td><td>sandal</td><td>|S-ʔ-n| (2)</td><td></td><td>LL</td><td></td><td>183</td></tr>
<tr><td>Saʔul</td><td>asked for, requested</td><td>|s^{1}-ʔ-l|</td><td></td><td></td><td>ONOM</td><td>229</td></tr>
<tr><td>Saʔūm</td><td>bought (?)</td><td>|s^{1}-ʔ-m|</td><td></td><td></td><td>ONOM</td><td>230</td></tr>
<tr><td>Saʕaḳāta, Saʕaḳōta</td><td>cries, calls</td><td>|S-ʕ-ḳ|</td><td>CTX</td><td></td><td></td><td>184</td></tr>
</table>

Saʕaḳōta See *Saʕaḳāta, Saʕaḳōta*						
Saʕart	wool	**|s^{2}-ʕ-r| (1)**	CTX			271
Saʕd	protective deity, luck; DN	**|s^{1}-ʕ-d|**			ONOM	231
Saʕirāy	hairy (mouse / rat)	**|s^{2}-ʕ-r| (1)**		LL		271
Saʕl	fire, blaze	**|s^{2}-ʕ-l|**		LL		270
Saʕr	wind, breath	**|s^{2}-ʕ-r| (3)**	CTX		ONOM	271
Saʕrat, Seʕrat	hair, pelt	**|s^{2}-ʕ-r| (1)**		LL	ONOM	271
Sabaʕ	seven	**|s^{1}-b-ʕ|**			ONOM	232
Sabaʕt	septenary(?)	**|s^{1}-b-ʕ|**			CTX	232
Sababt	brightness, dawn	**|S-b-b| (1)**		LL		184
Sabalt	ear	**|s^{1}-b-l|**		LL		233
sabayt	brewing (supplies)	**|s-b-y|**		LL		186
Sabbab	brightness, dawn	**|S-b-b| (1)**		LL		184
Sabiʕ	satisfied (?)	**|s^{2}-b-ʕ|**	CTX		ONOM	272
Sabiḥ	praiseworthy	**|s^{1}-b-ħ|**			ONOM	233
Sabil, Sabul	princely	**|S-b-l|**			ONOM	185
sābiyt	female brewer, alehouse keeper	**|s-b-y|**		LL		186
Sabl	work team	**|S-b-l|**	CTX			185
Sabul See *Sabil, Sabul*						
Sadaw/y	open field, field, steppe, mountain; DN	**|s^{2}-d-w|**	CTX	LL	ONOM	272
Saday See *Sadaw/y*						
Sadd	raid	**|S-d-d|**	CTX			187
Saddat	raid, expedition	**|S-d-d|**	CTX			187
Sad(d)in(n)	a shirt or chemise	**|S-d-n| (1)**	CTX			187
Sādid	raiding party	**|S-d-d|**	CTX			187
Saðb, Siðb	a milkweed	**|S-ð-b|**		LL		187
SaGar, SiGar	ritual closing (of doors)	**|s-G-r|**	CTX			189
SaGariy	a metal object (container ?)	**|s^{1}-G-r| (1)**	CTX			236
SaGb(iy)	a special troop (patrol ?)	**|S-G-b|**	CTX			188
Saggaʔ	sanctuary	**|S-g-g-ʔ|**	CTX			188
SaGir	sluice	**|s-G-r|**		LL		189

SāGir	who closes, controls	**|s-G-r|**	CTX			189
SaGirat	sluice	**|s-G-r|**		LL		190
SaGiS	dead	**|S-G-S|**			ONOM	190
Sā/ēGiS	killer	**|S-G-S|**			ONOM	190
Sagīt	roaming people	**|s^1-g-y|**	CTX			237
SaGul(a)t	acquisition, treasure, private property	**|s-G-l|**		LL		189
SaGuS	afflicted (?)	**|S-G-S|**			ONOM	190
Saħ(a)r, Seħ(e)r	dawn	**|s^1-ħ-r| (1)**		LL		238
Saħat	pitfall, trap	**|s^1-ħ-t|, |s^1-w/y-ħ|**	CTX			239
Saħir	black, scorched (barley)	**|s^1-ħ-r| (2)**		LL		238
sāħirat	witch	**|s-ħ-r|**			ONOM	191
Saxat, ʔiSxat	armpit	**|s^1-x-w/y|**		LL		240
sāxil	who pierces	**|s-x-l|**		LL		192
Sāxil	strainer	**|s^1-x-l|**	CTX			239
sāxirt	female peddler; DN	**|s-x-r|**	CTX			192
Saxuppat, Suxuppat	a complement for foot-wear (gaiter ?)	**|S-x-p|**	CTX			192
saxūr	requested, sought (?)	**|s-x-r|**			ONOM	192
Saxurrat	clay vessel	**|S-x-r-r|**	CTX			192
Saxwat	pendant	**|s^1-x-w|**	CTX	LL		240
Sakan	appointed, established	**|s^1-k-n|**			ONOM	243
Sakār	a kind of beer (?)	**|s^1-k-r| (2)**		LL		244
Sakb	resting (?)	**|s^1-k-b|**			ONOM	241
Sakin	appointed, established	**|s^1-k-n|**			ONOM	243
Sākin	provisor; prefect, governor	**|s^1-k-n|**	CTX		ONOM	243
Sakir	favoured, rewarded	**|s^2-k-r| (2)**			ONOM	274
sakk	a kind of close, dense fabric	**|s-k-k| (1)**	CTX			193
Sakk	calm, quietness	**|s^1-k-k| (1)**			ONOM	241
sakkakk	private, secretary's office	**|s-k-k| (1)**	CTX			193
Sakkār	one who favours, rewards (?)	**|s^2-k-r| (2)**			ONOM	274
Sakn (A)	appointed,	**|s^1-k-n|**			ONOM	242

	established					
Sakn (B)	camp	**|s^1-k-n|**	CTX			242
Sakuħ	found, met	**|s^1-k-ħ|**			ONOM	241
Sakun	appointed, established	**|s^1-k-n|**			ONOM	243
Sakūr	favoured, rewarded	**|s^2-k-r| (2)**			ONOM	274
Sakurr	lance	**|s^1-k-r| (1)**	CTX			244
Saḳat	libation	**|s^1-ḳ-y|**	CTX			246
Sāḳir	a craftsman who drills, perforates, pierces (?)	**|s^1-ḳ-r|**				245
Sāḳit	irrigation channel	**|s^1-ḳ-y|**	CTX			246
Sāḳiy	waterer, irrigator; an official (?)	**|s^1-ḳ-y|**	CTX		ONOM	245
Saḳḳa	a cloth or fabric, sack	**|S-ḳ-ḳ|**	CTX			194
Saḳṭ	calm, stillness (?)	**|s^1-D-G|, |s^1-G-D|**			ONOM	235
Salaħpuy	turtle	**|s^1-l-ħ-p-w/y|**		LL		247
Salāx, Sulūx	a long-fleeced garment	**|S-l-m-x|**	CTX			201
Salaxxiy, Suluxxiy	ritually sprinkled animal; garment made from this wool	**|S-l-x|**	CTX			199
Salam	friendly; DN	**|s-l-m| (1)**			ONOM	196
Salām (A)	peace, greetings	**|s-l-m| (1)**	CTX			196
Salām (B)	well-being, health	**|s^1-l-m|**			ONOM	248
Sāliħ	who grants, sends	**|s^1-l-ħ| (1)**			ONOM	246
Salim (A)	friendly; DN Dusk	**|s-l-m| (1)**		LL	ONOM	197
Salim (B)	capitulation, surrender	**|s-l-m| (1)**	CTX			197
Salim (C)	whole, sound	**|s^1-l-m|**			ONOM	248
Salal, Salil, Sullal, Sullul	captive (?)	**|θ-l-l|**			ONOM	322
Salil See *Salal, Salil, Sullal, Sullul*						
Salm (A)	peace	**|s-l-m| (1)**	CTX			196

Salm (B)	well-being, health	**|s^1-l-m|**		LL		248
Salmata	supplies	**|s^1-l-m|**	CTX			248
Salt, **sulta**	finely ground wheat flour	**|s-l-t|**	CTX			198
Salṭ	triumphant	**|s^1-l-ṭ|**			ONOM	249
Saluḫ	sent, granted	**|s^1-l-ḫ| (1)**			ONOM	246
SaLu(y)	a lower status or menial occupation (in the textile craft) (?)	**|S-L(-y)|**		LL		198
Sam	name, posterity, community; DN	**|s^1-m| (1)**			ONOM	249
Sām	red, carnelian	**|S-y-m|**		LL	ONOM	210
Samʔāl, **Samʔīl**, **Simʔāl**	the north, left side	**|s^2-m-ʔ-l|**			ONOM	276
Samʔīl, See *Samʔāl*, *Samʔīl*, *Simʔāl*						
Samʕ	hearing, testimony (?)	**|s^1-m-ʕ|**			ONOM	252
Samaʕ	who has been heard	**|s^1-m-ʕ|**			ONOM	252
Sam(a)k	support	**|s-m-k|**			ONOM	199
Samakt	prostitute	**|s^1-m-x| (2)**		LL		253
Samam, **Samim**, **Samum**	damaged	**|s^1-m-m|**			ONOM	254
Samar	the boisterous, furious one; DN	**|s^1-m-r|**			ONOM	255
Samay, **s^1amayūma**	heavens, sky	**|s^1-m-w/y|**	CTX	LL	ONOM	256
Sāmiʕ	who hears; listener	**|s^1-m-ʕ|**			ONOM	252
samīx	unskilled agricultural labourer	**|s-m-x|**	CTX			198
Samim See *Samam*, *Samim*, *Samum*						
Samīn	fat, fatty (?)	**|s^1-m-n|**			ONOM	254
Samm, **Simm**	damage	**|s^1-m-m|**			ONOM	253
Sammanūt, **Sammunūt**	fat	**|s^1-m-n|**			ONOM	254
Sammun	fat, fatty	**|s^1-m-n|**			ONOM	254
Sammunūt						

<table>
<tr><td>See Sammanūt, Sammunūt</td><td></td><td></td><td></td><td></td><td></td><td></td></tr>
<tr><td>Samn</td><td>oil</td><td>|s^1-m-n|</td><td></td><td>LL</td><td></td><td>254</td></tr>
<tr><td>Samrat, Samrūt</td><td>a kind of spear</td><td>|S-m-r| (1)</td><td>CTX</td><td></td><td></td><td>199</td></tr>
<tr><td>Samrūt
See Samrat, Samrūt</td><td></td><td></td><td></td><td></td><td></td><td></td></tr>
<tr><td>Sams^1</td><td>the Sun, DN</td><td>|S-m-s^1|</td><td></td><td></td><td>ONOM</td><td>200</td></tr>
<tr><td>Sāmt</td><td>red(ness); sunset</td><td>|S-y-m|</td><td>CTX</td><td>LL</td><td></td><td>211</td></tr>
<tr><td>Samux</td><td>stately, luxuriant</td><td>|s^1-m-x| (2)</td><td></td><td></td><td>ONOM</td><td>254</td></tr>
<tr><td>Samūk</td><td>supporting (?)</td><td>|s-m-k|</td><td></td><td></td><td>ONOM</td><td>199</td></tr>
<tr><td>Sanakrat</td><td>recognised (?)</td><td>|n-k-r|</td><td></td><td></td><td>ONOM</td><td>90</td></tr>
<tr><td>Samum
See Samam, Samim, Samum</td><td></td><td></td><td></td><td></td><td></td><td></td></tr>
<tr><td>Sanayt</td><td>an oil-bearing aromatic plant</td><td>|s^1-n-y| (1)</td><td></td><td>LL</td><td></td><td>257</td></tr>
<tr><td>Saniḳ</td><td>approached (?)</td><td>|s-n-ḳ|</td><td></td><td></td><td>ONOM</td><td>201</td></tr>
<tr><td>Sannāʔ</td><td>one who hates</td><td>|s^2-n-ʔ|</td><td>CTX</td><td></td><td></td><td>276</td></tr>
<tr><td>SannuS</td><td>kind of filling</td><td>|S-n-s^1|</td><td>CTX</td><td></td><td></td><td>201</td></tr>
<tr><td>Sapaḳ</td><td>who is given abundantly</td><td>|s^2-p-ḳ|</td><td></td><td></td><td>ONOM</td><td>277</td></tr>
<tr><td>Sapar</td><td>beautiful, pleasing</td><td>|s^1-p-r|</td><td></td><td></td><td>ONOM</td><td>259</td></tr>
<tr><td>saparr, siparr</td><td>bronze covered chariot (?)</td><td>|s-p-r| (2)</td><td>CTX</td><td></td><td></td><td>205</td></tr>
<tr><td>Sap(a)t</td><td>lip, rim (?)</td><td>|s^2-p|</td><td>CTX</td><td>LL</td><td>ONOM</td><td>276</td></tr>
<tr><td>Sapħ</td><td>scion, heir</td><td>|S-p-ħ|</td><td></td><td></td><td>ONOM</td><td>202</td></tr>
<tr><td>Sāpiḳ</td><td>who gives abundantly (?)</td><td>|s^2-p-ḳ|</td><td></td><td></td><td>ONOM</td><td>277</td></tr>
<tr><td>Sapilt</td><td>lowly people</td><td>|s^1-p-l|</td><td>CTX</td><td></td><td></td><td>258</td></tr>
<tr><td>Sapir</td><td>beautiful, pleasing</td><td>|s^1-p-r|</td><td></td><td></td><td>ONOM</td><td>259</td></tr>
<tr><td>sapl</td><td>platter, bowl, cauldron</td><td>|s-p-l|</td><td>CTX</td><td></td><td></td><td>202</td></tr>
<tr><td>Sapl</td><td>low (place); (lowly) people</td><td>|s^1-p-l|</td><td>CTX</td><td></td><td></td><td>258</td></tr>
<tr><td>sapp (A)</td><td>a type of bowl</td><td>|s-p-p| (1)</td><td>CTX</td><td></td><td></td><td>203</td></tr>
<tr><td>sapp (B)</td><td>lance (as emblem ?)</td><td>|s-p-p| (2)</td><td>CTX</td><td></td><td></td><td>203</td></tr>
<tr><td>sapp (C)</td><td>rod</td><td>|s-p-p| (2)</td><td>CTX</td><td></td><td></td><td>203</td></tr>
<tr><td>Sapr</td><td>fairness, beauty</td><td>|s^1-p-r|</td><td></td><td></td><td>ONOM</td><td>258</td></tr>
<tr><td>Saps^1</td><td>the Sun, DN</td><td>|S-m-s^1|</td><td></td><td></td><td>ONOM</td><td>200</td></tr>
<tr><td>Sapt</td><td>bowl (?)</td><td>|s-p-p| (1)</td><td>CTX</td><td></td><td></td><td>203</td></tr>
<tr><td>Sapur</td><td>sent</td><td>|S-p-r| (1)</td><td></td><td></td><td>ONOM</td><td>204</td></tr>
</table>

Sarart	lean, tilt, inclination	**|s^1-r-r| (3)**		LL		261
Saray	saved, protected	**|s^2-r-y|**			ONOM	279
Sarayt	salvation	**|s^2-r-y|**			ONOM	279
sard	load	**|s-r-d| (2)**	CTX			205
Sarx	proud (?)	**|s^2-r-x|**			ONOM	277
Sarxull (A)	a piece of jewellery	**|s^1-r-x-l|**	CTX			260
Sarxull (B)	a bronze item	**|s^1-r-x-l|**	CTX			262
Sarik	donated, given ex voto (?)	**|s^2-r-k| (1)**			ONOM	277
Sāriθt	female brewer	**|s-r-θ|**		LL		207
Sarim See *Sarm, Sarim*						
Sari/ur	leaned, bent	**|s^1-r-r| (3)**	CTX			261
Sarm, Sarim	cut off, portion (?)	**|S-r-m|**			ONOM	205
Sarmīn, Sirmīn	cypress	**|S-r-m-n|**	CTX			206
sarpat	lotus	**|s-r-p-D|**	CTX			206
Sarpat	burnt sacrifice	**|s^2-r-p|**	CTX			277
sarr	stubborn; malicious	**|s-r-r| (1)**		LL	OMOM	207
Sarr (A)	grain heap	**|S-r(-r)| (4)**				207
Sarr (B), s^1arr	king, prince; DN	**|s^2-r-r-|**	CTX	LL	ONOM	278
Sarrāk	pedlar, transporter (?)	**|s^2-r-k| (1)**	CTX			277
Sarrāḳ	refugee, asylum seeker (?)	**|s^1-r-γ|**	CTX			260
Sarrām	cutter, carver (?)	**|S-r-m|**			ONOM	206
sarrān	stubborn; malicious	**|s-r-r| (1)**			ONOM	207
sarrār	stubborn; malicious; out of control	**|s-r-r| (1)**	CTX		ONOM	207
sarrat	ignominy	**|s-r-r| (1)**			ONOM	207
Sarrat	queen	**|s^2-r-r-|**			ONOM	278
Sarratūtt, s^1arratūtt	dignity of a queen	**|s^2-r-r-|**	CTX			278
Sarrūt	sovereignty, power (?)	**|s^2-r-r-|**			ONOM	278
SarSar	saw	**|n-s^2-r|**		LL		107
Sarur See *Sari/ur*						
sās	moth	**|s-s|**		LL	ONOM	208
sass	base (of the mace) (?)	**|S-s-s|**	CTX			208

Sasay	calling	**|s^1-s-y| (1)**			ONOM	262
SaSSamān	ant	**|s^1-m-s^1-m| (1)**			ONOM	255
sas(u)gaL	a kind of swift (?)	**|s-n-n|**		LL		201
Sataḳl	the carried one	**|s^1-ḳ-l|**			ONOM	244
Sata/ipt, **Sitipt**	allocation of garment(s) (?)	**|s^1-t-p|**	CTX	LL		263
Satil	bud, shoot	**|s^1-t-l|**		LL		263
Satipt See *Sata/ipt, Sitipt*						
satūr	covered, protected	**|s-t-r| (1)**			ONOM	209
Saṭip See *Saṭp, Saṭip*						
Sāṭir	registrar (?)	**|s^1-ṭ-r|**			ONOM	265
Saṭiy	bent, curved (?)	**|s^2-ṭ-y|**			ONOM	280
Saṭp, **Saṭip**	rescued, saved	**|s^1-ṭ-p|**			ONOM	264
Saṭṭār	scribe (?)	**|s^1-ṭ-r|**			ONOM	265
Saṭūp	rescued, saved	**|s^1-ṭ-p|**			ONOM	264
Sawp	fine flour	**|s^1-w/y-p|**		LL		265
Sawpān	a wide vessel (for flour ?)	**|s^1-w/y-p|**	CTX			265
sawpuy	late barley (?)	**|s-w-p|**		LL		209
Sawṭ, **Siyṭ**	cisterne, pond	**|s^1-w/y-ṭ|**		LL		267
Sawuy	barren plain, flat wasteland	**|s^1-w-y| (1)**	CTX			267
Say	small livestock beast (?)	**|s^2-w|**			ONOM	280
Sayʕat	roasted barley (?)	**|S-y-ʕ|**		LL		210
Saybat	grey or white fabric	**|s^2-y-b|**	CTX			281
Saym	destiny	**|s^2-y-m|**			ONOM	282
Sayp	foot	**|S-y-p|**	CTX		ONOM	211
Seʕrat See *Saʕrat, Seʕrat*						
Seʕrt	hair	**|s^2-ʕ-r| (1)**	CTX			270
Sebit	(a kind of) lyre, harp	**|S-b-t|**	CTX			186
Sebuʕt	the seventh day of the month	**|s^1-b-ʕ|**	CTX			232
SēGiS See *Sā/ēGiS*						
Seħ(e)r See *Saħ(a)r, Seħ(e)r*						

Seħlat See *Saħlat, Seħlat*						
Sēr, **Sīr (C)**	song	**|s^1-y-r| (1)**	CTX		ONOM	268
se/ird	olive orchard	**|s-r-d| (1)**	CTX		ONOM	205
Serm See *Sirm, Serm*						
Siʔm	price	**|s^1-ʔ-m|**	CTX			230
Siʔr	flesh, entrails	**|s^1-ʔ-r| (2)**	CTX	LL		231
Sibbār	a larger (horned?) animal	**|s^1-p(-p)-r|**		LL		258
Sibl	principality, highness (?)	**|S-b-l|**			ONOM	185
sid(a)r	a plant	**|s-d-r|**		LL		187
Sidilt	pendant	**|s^1-d-l|**	CTX			235
Sidipt	a veil or covering (?)	**|s^1-d-p|**		LL		235
Siðb See *Saðb, Siðb*						
sigad	adoration	**|s-g-d|**			ONOM	188
sigann See *sikkan, sigann*						
sigar	fort; magazine (?)	**|s-G-r|**	CTX			189
SiGar See *SaGar, SiGar*						
SiGGat	trimmings, a kind of lace	**|s^1-k-k| (2)**	CTX			242
SiG(i)l, **SiGilt**	acquisition, treasure, private property	**|s-G-l|**	CTX		ONOM	188
SiGilt See *SiG(i)l, SiGilt*						
SiGirrat, **SiGurrit**	a fastening, hook, buckle (?)	**|s-G-r|**	CTX			190
SiGr	sluice	**|s-G-r|**		LL		189
SiGurrit See *SiGirrat, SiGurrit*						
SiguS(S)	a type of barley	**|s^1-g-s^1|**		LL		237
sikar	tower gate (?)	**|s-G-r|**	CTX			189

sikk	secret affaire	**|s-k-k| (1)**	CTX			193
sikkan, sigann	(inscribed?) stela, standing stone	**|s-k-k| (2)**	CTX	LL	ONOM	193
Sikkat	string of beads	**|s^{1}-k-k| (2)**	CTX			241
sikkur	clasp	**|s-G-r|**	CTX			189
Sik(i)n (A)	appointed, established	**|s^{1}-k-n|**	CTX			242
Sik(i)n (B)	food allocation	**|s^{1}-k-n|**		LL		242
Sikr	wage(s), pay	**|s^{2}-k-r| (2)**			ONOM	274
Siḳl	taking, portion (?)	**|s^{1}-ḳ-l|**			ONOM	244
Siḳr	piercing time, dawn	**|s^{1}-ḳ-r|**	CTX	LL		245
Siḳūt	drinking trough	**|s^{1}-ḳ-y|**	CTX			246
silʕ	cliff, rock (?)	**|s-l-ʕ|**	CTX		ONOM	195
Silaħ	sword; DN (?)	**|s^{1}-ħ-l| (2), |s^{1}-l-ħ|**			ONOM	238
Silām	friendly	**|s-l-m| (1)**			ONOM	196
Silimmiy	fulfilling, observance	**|s^{1}-l-m|**	CTX			248
Silḳ	decision	**|s^{1}-l-ḳ|**	CTX			247
Sim	name, posterity, community; DN	**|s^{1}-m| (1)**			ONOM	250
Sīm	red wine	**|S-y-m|**	CTX			210
Simʔāl See *Samʔāl, Samʔīl, Simʔāl*						
Simx	splendour, radiance	**|s^{1}-m-x| (2)**			ONOM	253
simin	right time, fitting time; DN	**|w-s-m|**			ONOM	357
Simḳat	action, performance (?)	**|s-n-ḳ|**	CTX			201
Simm See *Samm, Simm*						
simmidat	a kind of flour	**|s-m-d| (1)**	CTX			198
SimmiSt	secret	**|S-m-S|**	CTX			201
Sīmt	carnelian	**|S-y-m|**		LL		211
Sin (A)	to, toward, for, through, by	**|s^{1}-n| (1)**	CTX			256
Sin (B)	oracle	**|w-s^{1}-n|**	CTX			359
Sinar	cat (?)	**|S-n-r|, |S-r-n| (1)**			ONOM	201
Sinat	sleep	**|w-s^{1}-n|**			ONOM	359
Sīn(iy)	a crescent-shaped jewel	**|s-y-n|**	CTX			211
Sinn, Sinnat	tooth, point	**|s^{1}-n-n|**		LL		257

Sinnat See *Sinn, Sinnat*						
Sipar	regulation(s), instruction(s) (?)	**|S-p-r| (1)**		LL		204
sipx	new alluvial land (?)	**|s-p-x|**	CTX			202
Sipk (A)	a general term for cereal(s)	**|s^{1}-p-k|**	CTX			257
Sipk (B)	a kind of holdall	**|s^{1}-p-k|**	CTX			258
Sipk (C)	in loose quantity, in bulk	**|s^{1}-p-k|**	CTX			258
Sipḳ	abundance	**|s^{2}-p-ḳ|**			ONOM	277
Sipirt	allocation, forfeit	**|S-p-r| (1)**				204
sipl	large drinking bowl, crater	**|s-p-l|**	CTX			203
Sipl	lower part, lowliness	**|s^{1}-p-l|**		LL		258
Sip(p)arr	a wild animal	**|S-p-p-r|**		LL		203
Sipr	fairness, beauty	**|s^{1}-p-r|**			ONOM	258
Sipt	incantation, spell	**|w-s^{1}-p|**	CTX			359
sīr	a tax revenue	**|w-s-r|**	CTX			358
Sīr (A)	cooking pot, cauldron	**|S-y-r| (1)**	CTX			211
Sīr (B)	sending	**|s^{1}-r-w/y|**	CTX			262
Sīr (C) See *Sēr, Sīr* (C)						
Sirat	chapel, shrine	**|s^{1}-r-t|**		LL		262
sird See *se/ird*						
Sirenn	protective padding	**|S-r-(y-)n|**	CTX			208
Sirm, Serm	cut, cutting off (?)	**|S-r-m|**	CTX			205
Sirmīn See *Sarmīn, Sirmīn*						
SirS	root, foundation	**|s^{2}-r-s^{1}|**		LL		279
Siryān	coat of armour	**|S-r-(y-)n|**	CTX			208
SiSaxal(l)	horseman, courier (?)	**|s-w-s-w|**	CTX			210
SiSSikt	a thin cord	**|S-S-S-k|**	CTX			208
sīs(w)	horse (?)	**|s-w-s-w|**	CTX			209
Sitipt See *Sata/ipt, Sitipt*						
sitr	shelter, cover	**|s-t-r| (1)**			ONOM	209

sitt	exquisite ornament, decoration	**|w-s-m|**	CTX			357
Sitt (A)	dye-stuff; stamp; paint, colour	**|w-s^1-m|**		LL		359
Sitt (B)	sleep	**|w-s^1-n|**	CTX	LL		359
Siyb, **Siybt**, **Siybat**	old age / man / woman	**|s^2-y-b|**		LL	ONOM	281
Siybat See *Siyb*, *Siybt*, *Siybat*						
Siybt See *Siyb*, *Siybt*, *Siybat*						
Siyḳ	summit, top	**|s^2-y-ḳ|**				282
Siym, **Siym(a)t**	destiny	**|s^2-y-m|**			ONOM	282
Siym(a)t See *Siym*, *Siym(a)t*						
Siyt (A)	established	**|s^1-y-t|**			ONOM	268
Siyt (B)	remnant	**|s^1-y-t|**		LL		269
Siyṭ See *Sawṭ*, *Siyṭ*						
Sōkin	provisor; prefect, governor	**|s^1-k-n|**	CTX			243
sol^{e}lā	siege-mound	**|s-l-l|**	CTX			196
sōpir	scribe	**|S-p-r| (1)**	CTX		ONOM	204
Suʔʔul	carefully requested	**|s^1-ʔ-l|**			ONOM	230
suʔn	hem, trimming	**|s-ʔ-n| (1)**	CTX			182
Suʕḳ	cry, outcry	**|S-ʕ-ḳ|**			ONOM	183
Subāħ, **Subūħ**	praise	**|s^1-b-ħ|**		LL		233
Subāl	exalted, prince	**|S-b-l|**			ONOM	184
Subar	handle (of a tool)	**|s^1-b-r| (2)**	CTX			233
Sub(a)t See *θub(a)t*, *Sub(a)t*						
Sub(b)ul	excellency	**|S-b-l|**	CTX			184
Subīl	(little) prince	**|S-b-l|**			ONOM	185
Subūħ See *Subāħ*, *Subūħ*						

Sudan, Sudun(n)iyat	collar	**|S-D-n| (2)**	CTC			187
Sugāg	the big one, sheikh	**|S-g-g|**	CTX		ONOM	188
Sugāgūt	post as sheikh	**|S-g-g|**	CTX			188
Sudun(n)iyat See *Sudan, Sudun(n)iyat*						
suGir	bolt	**|s-G-r|**	CTX		ONOM	190
sugun	an ornament (handle?)	**|s-g-n| (2)**	CTX			189
suGur	bolt	**|s-G-r|**		LL		190
Suxar	gang leader, recruiter	**|s-x-r|**		LL		192
Suxarr See *Suxurr, Suxarr*						
Suxuppat See *Saxuppat, Suxuppat*						
Suxurr, Suxarr	(qualifying a) clay vessel	**|S-x-r-r|**	CTX			192
Sukaħ	found, met	**|s^{1}-k-ħ|**			ONOM	241
sukk	coverlet, cloak	**|s-k-k| (1)**	CTX			193
sukkuk	deaf	**|s-k-k| (1)**	CTX			193
Sukkur	very much favoured, rewarded (?)	**|s^{2}-k-r| (2)**			ONOM	274
Sukull	a weapon (?)	**|S-k-l|**		LL		194
Suḳr	a tool	**|s^{1}-ḳ-r|**	CTX			245
Sulāħ	sent, granted	**|s^{1}-l-ħ| (1)**			ONOM	246
Sulām	friendly	**|s-l-m| (1)**			ONOM	197
Sulīm	(little) friend (?)	**|s-l-m| (1)**			ONOM	197
Sullal See *Salal, Salil, Sullal, Sullul*						
Sulluħ	sent, messenger	**|s^{1}-l-ħ| (1)**			ONOM	246
Sullul See *Salal, Salil, Sullal, Sullul*						
Sullum	reconciled	**|s-l-m| (1)**			ONOM	197
SulluS	plated three times (?)	**|s^{2}-l-θ|**	CTX			275
Sulmān (A)	(little) friend	**|s-l-m| (1)**			ONOM	197
Sulmān (B)	well-being, health	**|s^{1}-l-m|**	CTX			248

Sulmān (C)	present, gift	**|s¹-l-m|**	CTX			248
sulta See *Salt, sulta*						
Suluħt	sending, shipment	**|s¹-l-ħ| (1)**	CTX			246
Sulūx See *Salāx, Sulūx*						
Suluxxiy See *Salaxxiy, Suluxxiy*						
Sulum	well-being, health	**|s¹-l-m|**			ONOM	248
Sulumm	a kind of scabbard (?)	**|s¹-l-m|**	CTX			248
Sum	name, posterity, community; DN	**|s¹-m| (1)**	CTX	LL	ONOM	250
Sumāx	stately, luxuriant	**|s¹-m-x| (2)**			ONOM	253
Sumx	splendour, radiance	**|s¹-m-x| (2)**			ONOM	253
Sumk	support	**|s-m-k|**			ONOM	199
Summa	if	**|s¹-m| (2)**	CTX			251
Sum(m)att, Sum(m)utt	halter, tether	**|s¹-m-(m-)n|**	CTX	LL		254
Summux	most stately, luxuriant	**|s¹-m-x| (2)**			ONOM	253
Summun	the fat one	**|s¹-m-n|**			ONOM	254
SummuS	hidden, secret	**|S-m-S|**	CTX			200
Sum(m)utt See *Sum(m)att, Sum(m)utt*						
supāħ	scattered bread (?, as offering)	**|S-p-ħ|**	CTX			202
supp	a type of glass	**|s-p-p| (1)**	CTX			203
Suppur	very pleasing	**|s¹-p-r|**			ONOM	259
Surān	cat	**|S-n-r|, |S-r-n| (1)**			ONOM	201
SurHat	plough	**|s¹-r-H|**		LL		260
Surk	profit sharing(?)	**|s²-r-k| (2)**	CTX			277
Sur(r)	a piece of jewellery	**|s¹-r(-r)| (5)**	CTX			261
SurS	root, foundation	**|s²-r-s¹|**			ONOM	279
Surθ	a metal vessel	**|s-r-θ|**	CTX			207
SuS	liquorice	**|s¹-s¹|**	CTX			262
susapinnūt	function of best man	**|S-S-B-n|**	CTX			208
sūs(w)	horse	**|s-w-s-w|**	CTX	LL	ONOM	210
Sūt	measure of capacity	**|S-ʔ|**		LL		181

Sutuḳḳ	a chapel	**|s^1-t-G(-G)|**		LL		263
Suyīn	the moon(-god)	**|s-y-n|**		LL	ONOM	211
Suwr, θuwr	bull; DN	**|θ-w-r|**		LL	ONOM	330

Ṣ

ṣāʕ	plate, bassin	**|ṣ-w-ʕ|**	CTX			225
ṣāʕt	a vessel	**|ṣ-w-ʕ|**	CTX			225
ṣāʕy	a type of plate	**|ṣ-w-ʕ|**	CTX			225
ṣabaγbaγa	dunking, soaking	**|ṣ-b-γ|**	CTX			213
ṣabar, ṣibar	aloe (?)	**|ṣ-b-r| (2)**			ONOM	214
ṣabay	desired	**|ṣ-b-y|**			ONOM	214
ṣabr	squinting, muttering	**ṣ-b-r| (1)**			ONOM	213
ṣabrān	the squinting / muttering one	**ṣ-b-r| (1)**			ONOM	213
ṣabur	squinting, muttering	**ṣ-b-r| (1)**			ONOM	213
ṣaby	beauty, desire	**|ṣ-b-y|**			ONOM	214
ṣadaḳ	just, right	**|ṣ-d-ḳ|**			ONOM	214
ṣaduḳ	just, right, just case; DN	**|ṣ-d-ḳ|**	CTX		ONOM	215
ṣaγ(i)r	small	**|ṣ-γ-r|**			ONOM	215
ṣaγirt	a kind of crop (?)	**|ṣ-γ-r|**	CTX			216
ṣaγur	servant, (shepherd-)boy	**|ṣ-γ-r|**		LL		215
ṣaħr, ṣiħr	steppe, open country	**|ṣ-ħ-r|**	CTX	LL		216
ṣaḳḳāl	polisher	**|ṣ-ḳ-l|**			ONOM	215
ṣalaḳ	fissured (?)	**|ṣ-l-ḳ|**			ONOM	217
ṣalil	pure (?)	**|ṣ-l-l| (1)**			ONOM	217
ṣallaħt, ṣillaħt	jar; bowl	**|ṣ-l-ħ|, |ṣ-ħ-l|**	CTX			217
ṣamad, ṣamid	bound	**|ṣ́-m-d|**	CTX			286
ṣamaxa See *ṣamħa, ṣamaxa*						
ṣamħa, ṣamaxa	produce, croops (?)	**|ṣ-m-ħ|**	CTX			218
ṣamid See *ṣamad, ṣamid*						
ṣammūḳ	raisin	**|ṣ-m-ḳ|**	CTX			218
ṣanna	bristling of hair	**|ṣ-n-n-| (2)**	CTX			220
ṣanīʕ	strength, strong	**|ṣ-n-ʕ|**		LL	ONOM	219

ṣanipt	border, fringe	**|ṣ-n-p|**	CTX			219
ṣanṣar See *ṣarṣar, ṣaṣṣar, ṣanṣar*						
ṣapaħa	plank, panel	**|ṣ-p-ħ|**	CTX			220
ṣapān	northwind	**ṣ-p-n| (1)**	CTX		ONOM	220
ṣapōn	North (TN / DN)	**ṣ-p-n| (1)**			ONOM	221
ṣapputt, ṣupputt, ṣuppatt	a kind of bread	**|ṣ-p-d|**	CTX			220
ṣapṣap	willow	**|ṣ-p-ṣ-p|**			ONOM	221
ṣarH	snake	**|ṣ-r-H|**		LL		222
ṣarħ	tower, lofty building, upper chamber	**|ṣ-r-ħ| (1)**	CTX	LL		223
ṣāriH	snake charmer	**|ṣ-r-H|**		LL		222
ṣārir	the flashing one; DN	**|ṣ-r-r| (3)**			ONOM	224
ṣarr	flash(ing)	**|ṣ-r-r| (3)**			ONOM	224
ṣarṣar, ṣaṣṣar, ṣanṣar	cricket	**|ṣ-r-ṣ-r|**	CTX	LL	ONOM	224
ṣaṣṣar See *ṣarṣar, ṣaṣṣar, ṣanṣar*						
ṣaw/yd	round(s) (?)	**|ṣ-w/y-d|**	CTX			225
ṣayaħ	outcry, loud cry	**|ṣ-w/y-ħ|**		LL		226
ṣayd See *ṣaw/yd*						
ṣāyid	hunter, vagrant	**|ṣ-w/y-d|**			ONOM	225
ṣayyād	hunter	**|ṣ-w/y-d|**			ONOM	225
ṣert	female snake	**|ṣ-r-H|**		LL		222
ṣiʕl	reproach	**|ṣ-ʕ-l|**	CTX			213
ṣibar See *ṣabar, ṣibar*						
ṣibīɣ	soaked cloth, poultice	**|ṣ-b-ɣ|**	CTX			213
ṣiby	beauty, desire	**|ṣ-b-y|**			ONOM	214
ṣidḳ	justice, legitimacy; DN	**|ṣ-d-ḳ|**			ONOM	214
ṣiɣara	youthfulness (?)	**|ṣ-ɣ-r|**			ONOM	216
ṣiɣ(i)ru	child	**|ṣ-ɣ-r|**			ONOM	215
ṣiħr See *ṣaħr, ṣiħr*						
ṣiɣṣiɣt	cast figurine	**|ṣ-w-ɣ|**	CTX			225

	(jewel)					
ṣillaħt See *ṣallaħt, ṣillaħt*						
ṣily	curse, spell	**|ṣ-l-w/y|**		LL		218
ṣimirt (A)	top, weatlth; the highest utmost good (?)	**|ṣ-m-r|**			ONOM	219
ṣimirt (B)	morbid boldness (?)	**|ṣ-m-r|**	CTX			219
ṣin(n)ar	fast-flowing stream (?)	**|ṣ-n-r|**			ONOM	220
ṣinnat	(large) shield	**|ṣ-n-n| (1), |ṣ-w-n|**	CTX			219
ṣinnōra See *ṣirrōra, ṣinnōra*						
ṣipayt	platting	**|ṣ-p-y| (1)**	CTX			221
ṣipħ	flat field	**|ṣ-p-ħ|**	CTX			220
ṣip(p)ār, ṣip(p)ōra	bird (?)	**|ṣ-p-r|**			ONOM	221
ṣip(p)ōra See *ṣip(p)ār, ṣip(p)ōra*						
ṣipy	platting	**|ṣ-p-y| (1)**	CTX			221
ṣir(a)x	lamentation	**|ṣ-r-x|**	CTX			223
ṣirH	snake	**|ṣ-r-H|**	CTX	LL		222
ṣirimt	effort, zeal	**|ṣ-r-m|**	CTX			223
ṣirrōra, ṣinnōra	cricket (?)	**|ṣ-r-ṣ-r|**			ONOM	224
ṣirr	flash(ing)	**|ṣ-r-r| (3)**			ONOM	224
ṣirm	effort, zeal	**|ṣ-r-m|**	CTX			223
ṣirp (A)	bright dye, brilliant fabric	**|ṣ-r-p|**	CTX			223
ṣirp (B)	a glazed earthenware (?)	**|ṣ-r-p|**	CTX			223
ṣiyħ	shouting, crying	**|ṣ-w/y-ħ|**			ONOM	226
ṣuby	beauty, desire	**|ṣ-b-y|**			ONOM	214
ṣubyān	the gorgeous, desired one	**|ṣ-b-y|**			ONOM	214
ṣuγar	junior servant, employee	**|ṣ-γ-r|**	CTX	LL		215
ṣuγur	youth	**|ṣ-γ-r|**			ONOM	216
ṣuγwat	pendent	**|ṣ-γ-w|**	CTX			216
ṣulṣul	an insect	**|ṣ-l-l| (2)**		LL		217
ṣuppatt See *ṣapputt, ṣupputt, ṣuppatt*						
ṣupputt						

See *ṣapputt, ṣupputt, ṣuppatt*						
ṣurp (A)	refined silver	**|ṣ-r-p|**	CTX			223
ṣurp (B)	reddish glowing (?)	**|ṣ-r-p|**			ONOM	223
ṣurpān	refined silver	**|ṣ-r-p|**	CTX			224
ṣurr	flash(ing)	**|ṣ-r-r| (3)**			ONOM	224
ṣuṣṣup(a)t	a metallic sheet or plate	**|ṣ-p-y| (1)**	CTX			221
ṣuwl	depth, abyss; DN ?	**|ṣ-w-l| (1)**			ONOM	226

s^{1} (š)

s^{1}aʔīt	a liquid measure	**|S-ʔ|**	CTX			182
s^{1}aʕar	market price	**|s^{1}-ʕ-r|**	CTX			231
s^{1}abal, s^{1}ubl	spikes (of fruit trees), shoots	**|s^{1}-b-l|**	CTX		ONOM	233
s^{1}abbuṭ	staff	**|s^{1}-b-ṭ|**		LL		234
s^{1}adan	hematite (?)	**|s^{1}-d-n|**		LL		235
s^{1}agara	a body of water; ditch, dyke (?)	**|s^{1}-g-r| (2)**	CTX			237
s^{1}aggar	offspring; DN	**|s^{1}-g-r| (2)**	CTX			237
s^{1}agm	uproar, thunder	**|s^{1}-G-m|**	CTX			236
s^{1}aḫaḳ	dust cloud; pulverized grain	**|s^{1}-ḫ-ḳ|**	CTX			237
s^{1}aḫr, s^{1}iḫr	dawn; DN	**|s^{1}-ḫ-r| (1)**	CTX		ONOM	238
s^{1}akbarakba	upper and lower millstones	**|r-k-b|, |s^{1}-k-b|**	CTX			165 241
s^{1}āḳīt	female cupbearer	**|s^{1}-ḳ-y|**	CTX			246
s^{1}aḳōn	watering place (?)	**|s^{1}-ḳ-y|**	CTX			245
s^{1}aluḫata	stalk, bunches (?)	**|s^{1}-l-ḫ| (1)**	CTX			246
s^{1}alummat	a type of metal jewellery	**|s^{1}-l-m-m|**	CTX			249
s^{1}amān	fatty (?)	**|s^{1}-m-n|**			ONOM	256
s^{1}amaSkil	a type of onion	**|s^{1}-m-S-k-l|**		LL		255
s^{1}amayūma See *Samay, s^{1}amayūma*						
s^{1}amna	oil (?)	**|s^{1}-m-n|**			ONOM	254
s^{1}ams^{1}a	the Sun, DN	**|S-m-s^{1}|**			ONOM	200
s^{1}amun	an oily dish	**|s^{1}-m-n|**	CTX			254
s^{1}amutt, s^{1}umutt	reddish shade	**|S-y-m|**	CTX			210
s^{1}an(a)t	year	**|s^{1}-n| (2)**	CTX	LL		256

s^{1}apħ	scion, heir	**|S-p-ħ|**		LL		203
s^{1}aps^{1}	the Sun; DN	**|S-m-s^{1}|**		LL	ONOM	200
s^{1}ār (A)	hostile; enemy	**|s^{1}-w-r| (1)**	CTX			266
s^{1}ār (B)	wall; a kind of building (caravansery ?)	**|s^{1}-w-r| (2)**	CTX			266
s^{1}ār (C)	singer	**|s^{1}-y-r| (1)**	CTX			268
s^{1}arpas^{1}s^{1}	a drape, chair-cover (?)	**|s-r-p-D|**	CTX			206
s^{1}arr See *Sarr* (B), *s^{1}arr*						
s^{1}arratūtt See *Sarratūtt*, *s^{1}arratūtt*						
s^{1}arrumma, s^{1}urrumma	indeed, certainly, forthwith (?)	**|s^{1}-r-r| (2)**	CTX			260
s^{1}as^{1}s^{1}ar	chain	**|s^{1}-r-s^{1}-r| (1)**			ONOM	261
s^{1}as^{1}s^{1}inn	a gem	**|s^{1}-s^{1}-n-n|**	CTX			263
s^{1}awala	trapper (the horse's skirt)	**|s^{1}-w-l|**	CTX			265
s^{1}awas^{1}ata	governing (?)	**|s^{1}-w-s^{1}|**	CTX			266
s^{1}ebʕi	seven	**|s^{1}-b-ʕ|**	CTX			234
s^{1}erdan	appellative / GN	**|s^{1}-r-d-n|**	CTX		ONOM	259
s^{1}erHat	furrow	**|s^{1}-r-H|**		LL		260
s^{1}e/irwanas^{1}e	a variety of gold (?)	**|s^{1}-r-w-n-s^{1}|**	CTX			262
s^{1}es^{1}mit(t)	a stone	**|s^{1}-s^{1}-m-t(-t)|**	CTX			263
s^{1}etayt	a garment	**|s^{1}-t-y| (2)**	CTX			264
s^{1}iʔr	flesh, entrails	**|s^{1}-ʔ-r| (2)**		LL		231
s^{1}iʕr	barley (?)	**|s^{2}-ʕ-r| (2)**		LL		271
s^{1}ibʕitān	seven times	**|s^{1}-b-ʕ|**	CTX			234
s^{1}ibṭ	staff; rod	**|s^{1}-b-ṭ|**	CTX			234
s^{1}idd	a measure of area	**|s^{1}-d-d|**	CTX			234
s^{1}ihar	a crescent shaped sickle (?)	**|s^{2}-h-r|**	CTX			273
s^{1}iħr See *s^{1}aħr*, *s^{1}iħr*						
s^{1}ixr	(leather) brace, strap	**|s^{1}-x-r|**	CTX			240
s^{1}ikrinn	beer vat (?)	**|s^{1}-k-r| (2)**	CTX			244
s^{1}ilina	an ornament	**|s^{1}-l-n|**	CTX			249
s^{1}ipr, s^{1}upr	fairness, beauty	**|s^{1}-p-r|**			ONOM	258
s^{1}īr	song	**|s^{1}-y-r| (1)**		LL		268
s^{1}irar	the firm one	**|s^{1}-r-r| (2)**			ONOM	260
s^{1}irwanas^{1}e See						

s^2 (ś)

ṣ́

ṣ́aʔn, ṣ́ān	small cattle, sheep	|ṣ́-ʔ-n|		LL		283
ṣ́abaʕ	a rapacious animal	|ṣ́-b-ʕ|		LL		284
ṣ́ābiʔ, ṣ́ābiy	warrior(s), troop(s), army	|ṣ́-b-ʔ|	CTX		ONOM	283
ṣ́ābiy See *ṣ́ābiʔ, ṣ́ābiy*						
ṣ́abṭ	captured, taken (?)	|ṣ́-b-ṭ|			ONOM	284
ṣ́amr	wool; a variety of sheep(?)	|ṣ́-m-r|	CTX		ONOM	286
ṣ́ān See *ṣ́aʔn, ṣ́ān*						
ṣ́aras¹, ṣ́aras¹t, ṣ́aris¹t	point, moon's horn(s); splintering; chipping of a tooth	|ṣ́-r-s¹|		LL		287
ṣ́aras¹t See *ṣ́aras¹, ṣ́aras¹t, ṣ́aris¹t*						
ṣ́arbat	a species of tree (poplar / willow?)	|ṣ́-r-b|		LL	ONOM	287
ṣ́aris¹t See *ṣ́aras¹, ṣ́aras¹t, ṣ́aris¹t*						
ṣ́āriṭān	little farter	|ṣ́-r-ṭ|			ONOM	287
ṣ́arrār	rival; spouse other than the first one (?)	|ṣ́-r-r|	CTX			287
ṣ́iʔ (A)	exit, issue, statement	|w-ṣ́-ʔ|	CTX			362
ṣ́iʔ (B)	offspring	|w-ṣ́-ʔ|			ONOM	362
ṣ́ibar	clan, community	|ṣ́-b-r|			ONOM	284
ṣ́ibiṭṭ	seizure (?)	|ṣ́-b-ṭ|			ONOM	285
ṣ́iḥḳ	laughter	|ṣ́-ḥ-ḳ|			ONOM	285
ṣ́ilaʕat	plank	|ṣ́-l-ʕ|	CTX			285
ṣ́ippar	plaited wool	|ṣ́-p-r|	CTX			286
ṣ́irʕu	hornets	|ṣ́-r-ʕ|			ONOM	286
ṣ́iyḳ	the narrow one (said of a small	|ṣ́-w/y-ḳ|	CTX			288

	barge?)					
ṣōn	small cattle, sheep	**|ṣ-ʔ-n|**	CTX			283
ṣurw	(aromatic) resin, balsam	**|ṣ-r-w|**	CTX			288

t

tāʔir See *tawir*, *tāʔir*, *tār*						
taʔm, tuʔam	twin	**|t-ʔ-m|**			ONOM	290
tabarr, tubarr	a red dye; reddish dyed fabric	**|t-b-r-r|**	CTX			292
taditt	gift	**|t-d-n|**	CTX			292
taγapθ	a type of (felt-)rug	**|t-γ-p-θ|**	CTX			292
taγapθuγul	weaver of *t.*-rugs	**|t-γ-p-θ|**	CTX			292
tahāmat	primordial ocean, abyss	**|t-h-m|**		LL		292
taHāy	food	**|t-H-y|**	CTX			293
taHyūt	food	**|t-H-y|**	CTX			293
taħt	underneath, below; instead of	**|t-ħ-t|**	CTX		ONOM	293
takilt, tikilt	purple (wool)	**|t-k-l| (2)**	CTX			300
takkalt	jewel, necklace	**|n-k-l| (2)**	CTX			89
taḳḳan	perfect, straight	**t-k/ḳ-n|**			ONOM	294
taḳḳāt	an ornament or bead	**|n-ḳ-y| (1)**	CTX			95
taḳn	good order	**t-k/ḳ-n|**			ONOM	294
talʔiy	victor	**|l-ʔ-w/y| (1)**			ONOM	7
talama	furrow	**|t-l-m| (1)**	CTX			296
talgim	harness(ing) (?)	**|l-g-m|**		LL		11
tālil	auxiliary	**|t-l-l| (1)**	CTX			295
talīm	nice, lovable (brother); own (?)	**|t-l-m| (2)**		LL	ONOM	296
talṭas^1	sharpness (?)	**|l-t-s^1|**			ONOM	17
tamar	date palm; DN	**|t-m-r| (1)**		LL	ONOM	298
tamāmiyt	asseveration	**|t-m-ʔ|**	CTX			296
tamgur, tumgur	granary	**|m-g-r|**		LL		31
tamxīr	presentation, offering	**|m-x-r|**			ONOM	34
tamk	fixed abode,	**|t-m-k|**	CTX			297

	residence (?)					
tamm	complete, full	**|t-m-m|**			ONOM	298
tamriḳ	crossing, passing (?)	**|m-r-ḳ| (2)**		LL		48
tamrir	bitter (cosmetic oil)	**|m-r(-r)| (2)**	CTX			50
tamtuḳ	sweetness	**|m-t-ḳ|**		LL		59
tamθāl	(fabric) similar (to linen)	**|m-θ-l|**	CTX			60
tanaħħiSt, tinaħħiSt	living, mankind	**|n-ħ-S|**	CTX	LL		87
tandiyat	(golden) application (?)	**|n-d-y|**	CTX			79
tanduy, taddiʔ	fabric with (golden) applications (?)	**|n-d-y|**	CTX			79
tannūra	oven	**|t-n-r|**	CTX			298
tapdēt	exchange	**|p-d-y|**	CTX			123
tappuħ	apple	**|t-p-ħ|**	CTX		ONOM	299
taptayd, taptīd	putting away, making disappear	**|p-w/y-d| (2), |p-d-d|**		LL		144
taptīd See *taptayd, taptīd*						
tār See *tawir, tāʔir, tār*						
tarbaṣ	stable, yard	**|r-b-ṣ|**	CTX			154
tarbīy	promotion (?)	**|r-b-b| (1), |r-b-y|**	CTX			153
tarbīyt	offspring	**|r-b-b| (1), |r-b-y|**	CTX			153
tarDan(n), tarDenn, terDenn, tur(a)Dan(n)	second in rank; younger brother, son	**|t-r-D-n|**	CTX	LL	ONOM	300
tarDenn See *tarDan(n), tarDenn, terDenn, tur(a)Dan(n)*						
tarDennūt	position of a *t.*	**|t-r-D-n|**	CTX			300
tarx (A)	dowry, bride price	**|t-r-x| (1)**	CTX			300
tarx (B)	beer mug	**|t-r-x| (2)**	CTX			300
tāriʔ	keeper, attendant	**|t-r-ʔ|**	CTX		ONOM	299

tāriʔt	female keeper, attendant	**|t-r-ʔ|**		LL		299
tarimt, taritt	cone (of conifer)	**|t-r-m|**		LL		300
tārir	a profession or social class	**|t-r-r| (2)**	CTX			301
taritt See *tarimt, taritt*						
tarmikt	purification, pruning (?)	**|r-m-k|**	CTX			167
tarn	mast (of a ship)	**|t-r-n| (1**	CTX			301
tarna, tarnann	a small capacity measure	**|t-r-n| (2)**	CTX			301
tarnann See *tarna, tarnann*						
tarpīd	support, pedestal (?)	**|r-p-d| (2)**	CTX			170
tarṣ	stretched out, over	**|t-r-ṣ|**			ONOM	302
tarṣ́iyat	pleasure	**|r-ṣ́-y|**	CTX			174
tartappid	trek(?)	**|r-p-d| (1)**		LL		170
tartappiḳ	supporting	**|r-p-ḳ|**		LL		170
tartaθtiy	owed amount	**|r-S-y|**	CTX			174
tarw	(foreign) horde (?)	**|t-r-w|**	CTX			302
taryib	compensation	**|r-y-b|**				179
tarzuHm	hunger, starvation (?)	**|r-z-H|**		LL		180
taSmaʕ	attention, acceptance	**|s^{1}-m-ʕ|**	CTX			252
taSSar	share, part set aside	**|n-s^{1}-r| (2)**	CTX			105
taṣrāħ	warmer (of the horses)	**|ṣ-r-ħ| (2)**	CTX			222
taṣṣib	installation, camp	**|n-ṣ-b|**		LL		103
tas^{1}īʕat See *tas^{1}īʕt, tas^{1}īʕat*						
tas^{1}īʕt, tas^{1}īʕat	a ninth	**|t-s^{1}-ʕ|**	CTX			303
tas^{1}it	goblet	**|s^{1}-t-y| (1)**	CTX			264
tas^{1}rit	beginning, inauguration	**|s^{1}-r-r| (4)**		LL		261
tatāp, tutāp	beer mash	**|t-t-p|**		LL		303
tattam(m)iS	moving around a lot (?)	**|n-m-s^{1}| (2)**		LL		96
taw(i)l	spell, charm (?)	**|t-w-l|**		LL		303

tawir, tāʔir, tār	relenting, merciful (?)	**|t-w-r|**			ONOM	304
tawlaʕt	worm	**|t-w-l-ʕ|**		LL		303
tawladt	first offspring of animals	**|w-l-d|**	CTX			351
tawr, tuwr	return	**|t-w-r|**		LL		304
tawsam	exquisite ornament, decoration	**|w-s-m|**	CTX			358
tawtar	wealth	**|w-t-r| (2)**	CTX			364
tēmāy	overseas (?)	**|t-h-m|**	CTX			293
temr	a ritual or cultic meal (?)	**|t-m-r| (2)**	CTX			298
tēmt	stretch of water, sea, lake	**|t-h-m|**	CTX			292
terDenn See *tarDan*(*n*), *tarDenn*, *terDenn*, *tur*(*a*)*Dan*(*n*)						
tes^{1}pēl	exchange	**|s^{1}-p-H-l|**	CTX			257
ti/eʔ See *tiʔn*, *ti/eʔ*						
tiʔitt	fig (tree)	**|t-ʔ-n|**		LL		290
tiʔn, ti/eʔ	fig	**|t-ʔ-n|**	CTX	LL		290
tiʔnat	fig	**|t-ʔ-n|**		LL		290
tibʕ	rising, lifting	**|t-b-ʕ|**	CTX			290
tibn	straw	**|t-b-n|**		LL		291
tihām(a)t	sea	**|t-h-m|**	CTX	LL		293
tikilt See *takilt*, *tikilt*						
tikkat	neck-line	**|t-k-k| (1)**	CTX			293
tiḳin	a kind of necklace	**t-k/ḳ-n|**	CTX			294
tilʔā	victory	**|l-ʔ-w/y| (1)**			ONOM	7
tilḫamt	tangle	**|l-ḫ-m| (3)**	CTX	LL		12
till (A)	bull; DN (?)	**|t-l-l| (2)**		LL		295
till (B)	mound, heap	**|t-l-l| (3)**	CTX			296
tillay See *tily*, *tillay*						
tily, tillay	a kind of appendage, strap (?)	**|t-l-l/y|**	CTX			296
timert	buried deposit	**|t-m-r| (2)**	CTX			298

tinduH	lyre (?)	**|t-n-d-H|**		LL		298
tīr See *tiwr, tīr*						
tiriS	must	**|(w/y)-r-θ|**	CTX			356
tirt	excess, increase, abundance	**|w-t-r| (2)**	CTX	LL		364
tīSān	a caprid (moufflon?)	**|t-y-s^1|**	CTX			305
tiSkan	established (?)	**|s^1-k-n|**			ONOM	243
tiSn	a container	**|t-S-n|**	CTX			303
tis^{1}ʕ	nine	**|t-s^1-ʕ|**			ONOM	303
tiwr, tīr	returned (?)	**|t-w-r|**			ONOM	304
ti/uwtattir	excess, increase, abundance	**|w-t-r| (2)**	CTX			364
tiyat	a plant or vegetable substance	**|t-y-t|**	CTX			305
tiyriy	throwing (?)	**|w-r-w/y|**		LL		356
tōkiy	inner	**|t-w-k|**			ONOM	303
tolaʕa	dressed in crimson; worm	**|t-w-l-ʕ|**			ONOM	304
tuʔam See *taʔm, tuʔam*						
tuʔimt	twin vessel	**|t-ʔ-m|**	CTX			290
tubarr See *tabarr, tubarr*						
tuggur	a kind of auxiliar structure or building	**|w-g-r|**	CTX			346
tukk	labour camp, workshop	**|t-k-k| (2)**	CTX			294
tukl	safe repository, storehouse (?)	**|t-k-l| (1)**	CTX			294
tuḳ(ḳ)up	prevailing (?)	**|θ-ḳ-p|**			ONOM	321
tulʕuy	breast-shaped	**|t-l-ʕ|**	CTX			295
tumag	a kind of flour (?)	**|t-m-g|**	CTX			297
tumāl	the previous day, yesterday	**|t-m-l|**	CTX			297
tuman	a beam (?)	**|t-m-n|**		LL		298
tunnan	dragon, snake; DN	**|t-n-n-n|**		LL		298
tuppuħ	apple	**|t-p-ħ|**		LL		299
tuppur	a bronze (sewing ?) tool	**|t-p-r|**	CTX			299
tupSikkān	earth-moving troops	**|S-p-S-k|**	CTX			205

tur(a)Dan(n) *See tarDan(n), tarDenn, terDenn, tur(a)Dan(n)*						
turis[1]	harvest	**|t-r-S|**	CTX			301
turSumm	a type of wine (must, wine-dregs, plonk?)	**|t-r-S-m|**	CTX			302
turṣ	alteration, remodelling, enlargement (?)	**|t-r-ṣ|**		LL		302
tūrt	circuit (?)	**|t-w-r|**	CTX			305
turunn	a setting for jewellery	**|t-r-n| (3)**	CTX			301
tuSuʔ	ennead	**|t-s¹-ʕ|**			ONOM	303
tuṣtanniʕ	exerting, enduring	**|ṣ-n-ʕ|**		LL		219
tutāp See *tatāp, tutāp*						
tuttallik	exertion of kingship	**|m-l-k|**		LL		42
tuttaSSil	to act as messenger (?)	**|l-s-m|**		LL		16
tuttur	an elem. in jewellery	**|t-r-t-r|**	CTX			302
tuwr See *tawr, tuwr*						
tuwṣ̌at	offspring	**|w-ṣ̌-ʔ|**			ONOM	362
tuwtabbil(t)	supply, sustenance, maintenance	**|w-b-l| (1)**	CTX			341
tuwtattir See *ti/uwtattir*						
tuwtir, **tuwtur**	abundance, surplus	**|w-t-r| (2)**		LL		364
tuwtur See *tuwtir, tuwtur*						

ṭ

ṭaʕn	injured, hurt(?)	**|ṭ-ʕ-n|**	CTX			306
ṭabīx	an ornamental dagger (?)	**|ṭ-b-x|**	CTX			307
ṭābix	slaughterer, butcher	**|ṭ-b-x|**			ONOM	307
ṭabixūt	slaughter, butchering	**|ṭ-b-x|**	CTX			307

ṭaxd	abundance (?)	**|ṭ-x-d|**			ONOM	308
ṭall, **ṭill**	dripping, filtering; dew, (light) rain	**|ṭ-l-l|**		LL	ONOM	309
ṭamr	tumulus; earth hole, crack(?)	**|ṭ-m-r|**	CTX			309
ṭannāp	dirty	**|ṭ-n-p|**		LL		309
ṭapar	wooden board	**|ṭ-p-r|**		LL		310
ṭard	sending, present	**|ṭ-r-d|**			ONOM	310
ṭārid	he who sends	**|ṭ-r-d|**			ONOM	310
ṭarūd	sent	**|ṭ-r-d|**			ONOM	310
ṭawb, **ṭayb**	good, friendly	**|ṭ-w/y-b|**	CTX	LL	ONOM	311
ṭayb See *ṭawb*, *ṭayb*						
ṭēxiyt	delegation, embassy	**|ṭ-x-w|**	CTX			308
ṭerd	deportation, persecution; DN	**|ṭ-r-d|**			ONOM	310
ṭill See *ṭall*, *ṭill*						
ṭiṭṭ	a sort of malt	**|ṭ-y-n|**		LL		313
ṭōb	merry, pleasant (?)	**|ṭ-w/y-b|**			ONOM	312
ṭubix, **ṭubux**	slaughtering, sacrifice	**|ṭ-b-x|**	CTX		ONOM	307
ṭubḳ	covering, shielding	**|ṭ-b-ḳ|**			ONOM	307
ṭubux See *ṭubix*, *ṭubux*						
ṭuhur	pure	**|ṭ-h-r|**		LL		307
ṭupl	slander(ing)	**|ṭ-p-l|**	CTX			310
ṭupult	abuse	**|ṭ-p-l|**	CTX			310
ṭuwb	goodness, well-being	**|ṭ-w/y-b|**			ONOM	312
ṭuwbāt, **ṭuwbūt**, **ṭuwbuwat**	goodness	**|ṭ-w/y-b|**		LL	ONOM	312
ṭuwbūt See *ṭuwbāt*, *ṭuwbūt*, *ṭuwbuwat*						
ṭuwbuwat See *ṭuwbāt*, *ṭuwbūt*, *ṭuwbuwat*						

θ (ṯ)

θaʔ	ewe	**|θ-ʔ|**		LL		314
θāʔig	screaming	**|θ-ʔ-g|**			ONOM	315
θaʕal	fox	**|θ-ʕ-l(-b)|**			ONOM	315
θaʕara	calculation; scheme	**|θ-ʕ-r|**	CTX			316
θāʕiy	an official; supervisor, examiner of the exta (?)	**|θ-ʕ-y|**			ONOM	316
θaʕitt	a container and measure of capacity	**|θ-ʕ-D| (2)**	CTX			315
θaʕlab	fox	**|θ-ʕ-l(-b)|**			ONOM	316
θaγγār	porter, gatekeeper	**|θ-γ-r| (1)**		LL		324
θaγr	gate; DN	**|θ-γ-r| (1)**	CTX		ONOM	318
θaħlat, θeħlat	a vegetable (cress?)	**|θ-ħ-l|**	CTX			318
θākim	he who carries on the shoulders; DN	**|θ-k-m|**			ONOM	319
θakūm	carried on the shoulders	**|θ-k-m|**			ONOM	319
θaḳ	reliability	**|w-θ-ḳ|**		LL		366
θaḳabān	the little ash tree (?)	**|S-ḳ-b|**			ONOM	194
θāḳil	beam	**|θ-ḳ-l|**		LL		321
θaḳul	weighed, measured	**|θ-ḳ-l|**		LL		321
θalg	snow(-white ?)	**|θ-l-g|**	CTX		ONOM	321
θālil	plunderer	**|θ-l-l|**			ONOM	322
θalk	snow	**|θ-l-g|**	CTX			321
θall	captive	**|θ-l-l|**	CTX			322
θallat	booty	**|θ-l-l|**		LL		322
θallur	plum(?)	**|θ-l-l-r|**		LL		322
θalθ	copper, bronze (?)	**|θ-l-θ|**	CTX			323
θamānay	eight (?)	**|θ-m-n-y|**			ONOM	323
θamr	crop(s), fruit(s)	**|θ-m-r|**	CTX		ONOM	324
θaniy	second	**|θ-n|**	CTX		ONOM	324
θanānu	chariot soldier; archer	**|θ-n-n|**	CTX			325
θanan(n)uγ(γ)	a class (archer?)	**|θ-n-n|**	CTX			325
θanannūt	function of the *θ.*-class	**|θ-n-n|**				325
θannān	a class-designation (archer?)	**|θ-n-n|**	CTX			325
θapaṭ	judged, passed,	**|θ-p-ṭ|**			ONOM	327

	proved					
θāpiṭ	judge, ruler	**|θ-p-ṭ|**	CTX		ONOM	327
θāpiṭūt	governorship	**|θ-p-ṭ|**	CTX			327
θapuṭ	process	**|θ-p-ṭ|**	CTX			327
θariy	wealthy	**|θ-r-y| (1)**			ONOM	329
θarmil	a noble material	**|θ-r-m-l|**			ONOM	328
θarrāk	openhanded	**|θ-r-k|**			ONOM	327
θāt	ewe	**|θ-ʔ|**	CTX			315
θaθθa	sixth(?)	**|s¹-d-θ|**			ONOM	238
θawb	attending to, devoted towards	**|θ-w-b|**			ONOM	330
θeʕlib	fox	**|θ-ʕ-l(-b)|**			ONOM	316
θeħlat See *θaħlat, θeħlat*						
θerr	baby, infant	**|θ-r-r|**			ONOM	328
θertann	a kind of bailiff / sheriff (?)	**|θ-r-t-n-n|**			ONOM	328
θiʔat	ewe	**|θ-ʔ|**	CTX			315
θiduri	girl	**|θ-d-r|**		LL		317
θiḳ	trust (?)	**|w-θ-ḳ|**			ONOM	366
θinaγili	of secondary quality	**|θ-n|**	CTX			325
θipṭ	justice, verdict	**|θ-p-ṭ|**	CTX		ONOM	326
θirk	a taxe	**|θ-r-k|**	CTX			327
θuʕal	fox	**|θ-ʕ-l(-b)|**			ONOM	316
θuʕalt	vixen; DN	**|θ-ʕ-l(-b)|**			ONOM	316
θub(a)t, Sub(a)t	(family) seat, residence	**|w-θ-b|**		LL	ONOM	365
θuγr	victory (?)	**|θ-γ-r| (2)**			ONOM	318
θuḳd	almond	**|θ-ḳ-d| (2)**	CTX			320
θuḳult	weight	**|θ-ḳ-l|**			ONOM	321
θulħān	table	**|θ-l-ħ-n|**			ONOM	322
θurme(h), θurum	cut off, portion (?)	**|S-r-m|**	CTX		ONOM	206
θutum(m)	an administrative official	**|s¹-t-m|**	CTX			263
θuwʕ	hero, noble; DN	**|θ-w-ʕ|**			ONOM	329
θuwb	return	**|θ-w-b|**	CTX			330
θuwr See *Suwr, θuwr*						

θ̣ (ẓ)

θ̣abayt	gazelle	**|θ̣-b-y|**	LL			332
θ̣abiy, θ̣abiyat	gazelle	**|θ̣-b-y|**			ONOM	332
θ̣abiyat See *θ̣abiy, θ̣abiyat*						

θ̣ahr	back	**|θ̣-h-r|**		LL	ONOM	333
θ̣alil	shady, umbrageous (?)	**|θ̣-l-l-|**			ONOM	333
θ̣alm	black, dark, gloomy	**|θ̣-l-m|**			ONOM	334
θ̣amiʔ	thirsty	**|θ̣-m-ʔ|**	CTX		ONOM	334
θ̣arir	sharp blade	**|θ̣-r-r|**		LL		335
θ̣ēmēn	the little fastener (?)	**|ṣ-w-m|**			ONOM	226
θ̣ill	shade, protection; DN	**|θ̣-l-l-|**			ONOM	333
θ̣uhr	back	**|θ̣-h-r|**	CTX			333
θ̣upr	nail, claw, hoof	**|θ̣-p-r|**	CTX		ONOM	334
θ̣urrān	flint	**|θ̣-r-r|**		LL		335
θ̣uwr	rock, mountain	**|θ̣-w-r|**			ONOM	335

w

wa	and (also); namely, or (else)	**|w|**	CTX			337
waʔr	way(s), instruction(s); journey	**|w-ʔ-r|**	CTX	LL		337
waʕr	rugged, coarse	**|w-ʕ-r| (2)**			ONOM	339
waʕil	mountain goat	**|w-ʕ-l| (1)**		LL		338
waʕy	remembrance, awareness (?)	**|w-ʕ-y|**			ONOM	339
wabar	guest-friend	**|w-b-r|**			ONOM	342
wabbāl	porter, runner	**|w-b-l| (1)**		LL		340
wābil	holder, support	**|w-b-l| (1)**	CTX			340
wadiʕ	available, present, complete	**|w-d-ʕ|**	CTX	LL		343
wadiy	praised, acknowledged (?)	**|w-d-y| (2)**		LL		345
w/yagāʕ	negligence	**|w-g-ʕ|**	CTX			345
wahb	gift	**|w-h-b|**			ONOM	346
waħ(a)d	single (person); unique	**|w-ħ-d|**	CTX		ONOM	347
waxim	unhealthy	**|w-x-m|**			ONOM	348
wāxiz	stinging, pricking	**|w-x-z|**			ONOM	348
wakāyt	orphanhood	**|w-k-y|**		LL		348
wakil	person in charge, overseer	**|w-k-l|**	CTX		ONOM	348
wallādt	midwife	**|w-l-d|**		LL		351
wapiy	beautiful	**|w-p-y|**		LL		352
wappād	envoy	**|w-p-d|**		LL		351
wappuy	made beautiful	**|w-p-y|**		LL		352
waray	cloud heavy with rain	**|w-r-y| (1)**		LL		356
ward	servant	**|w-r-d| (1)**			ONOM	353

wardat	girl	**|w-r-d| (1)**		LL	ONOM	353
wariʔt	fear	**|w-r-ʔ|**	CTX			352
warik	side, hip	**|w-r-k|**		LL		354
waraḳ, waruḳ, wurḳ	verdant, greenish (a gem)	**|w-r-ḳ|**	CTX	LL	ONOM	354
warrāθ / yarrāθ	heir	**|w-r-θ| (1)**	CTX			355
waruḳ See *waraḳ, waruḳ, wurḳ*						
waruθ	unclean	**|w-r-θ| (2)**		LL		356
waSir See *(w)aSr, waSir*						
(w)aSr, waSir	submissive	**|w-s^{1}-r|**			ONOM	360
waSSur See *maSSur, waSSur*						
waSt	at; from; after	**|w-s^{1}-ṭ|**	CTX			360
waStay	at, with; from, since	**|w-s^{1}-ṭ|**	CTX		ONOM	360
waStayma	if indeed	**|w-s^{1}-ṭ|**	CTX			360
waStumma	if indeed	**|w-s^{1}-ṭ|**	CTX			360
wāṣir	potter	**|w-ṣ-r|**		LL	ONOM	359
waṣ̌aʕ	lowliness (?)	**|w-ṣ̌-ʕ|**			ONOM	362
watar	excellent, outstanding	**|w-t-r| (2)**	CTX		ONOM	363
watār	abundance	**|w-t-r| (2)**	CTX			363
watax(xa)m See *watxam, watax(xa)m*						
watxam, watax(xa)m	dirty, rotten (liar?)	**|w-x-m|**		LL		348
watin	given	**|n/w/y-D-n|**			ONOM	79
watir	excellent, outstanding	**|w-t-r| (2)**			ONOM	364
w/yatt	dove	**|y-w-n|**		LL		380
wattār	substitute	**|w-t-r| (2)**	CTX			364
wattur	superior	**|w-t-r| (2)**			ONOM	364
waθab	dweller (?)	**|w-θ-b|**	CTX			365
(w)aθ(i)ḳ	firm, secured (?)	**|w-θ-ḳ|**			ONOM	366
wawn, wawnat	dove (?)	**|y-w-n|**	CTX		ONOM	380
wawnat See *wawn, wawnat*						
wayn	wine (?)	**|w-y-n|**			ONOM	366

wazār	decorating	**|w-z-r|**	CTX			367
wazzān	weigher	**|w-z-n|**		LL		367
werḳ	pale; garden, orchard	**|w-r-ḳ|**	CTX	LL	ONOM	354
werḳān	garden, orchard	**|w-r-ḳ|**			ONOM	355
(w)irrat	a weight (strong weight?)	**|w-r-r|**	CTX			355
wirs	a greenish-yellow dye or plant	**|w-r-s| (1)**	CTX			355
wirS, wurS	flow, gush, spurt	**|(w/y)-r-θ|**		LL		356
wiṣṣaʕ	couch (?)	**|w-ṣ-ʕ|**	CTX			362
wuḳḳur	dear, precious, esteemed	**|w-ḳ-r|**			ONOM	349
wurdūt	vassalage, (political) servitude	**|w-r-d| (1)**	CTX			353
(w)uruSS	head-rest	**|w-r-S| (2)**	CTX			355
wuSbub	temporary guest	**|w-θ-b|**	CTX			365
wussum	especially suitable, worthy, nice	**|w-s-m|**			ONOM	357
wuθr	(unresolved) question(s)	**|w-θ-r|**	CTX			366

y

=ya See =*ī*, *=ya*						
ya(ʔ)	(is) mine	**|y| (1)**			ONOM	369
yaʕ(a)b	ample, wide	**|w-ʕ-b|**			ONOM	337
yaʕart	roughness, coarseness	**|w-ʕ-r| (2)**			ONOM	339
yaʕ(i)l	mountain goat	**|w-ʕ-l| (1)**			ONOM	338
yabam	brother-in-law	**|w-b-m|**	CTX		ONOM	341
yabaS	dry; Dry Land (TN)	**|y-b-s^{1}|**			ONOM	370
yabil	ram	**|y-b-l|**		LL		370
yābil	porter, bearer	**|w-b-l| (1)**			ONOM	340
yābilt	irrigation ditch	**|w-b-l| (1)**	CTX			340
yabiS, yabis^{1}	dry	**|y-b-s^{1}|**	CTX	LL	ONOM	370
yābis^{1}ta See *ʔābis^{1}tu*, *ʔābes^{1}tu*, *yābis^{1}ta*						
yabuS	dry	**|y-b-s^{1}|**			ONOM	370
yad	hand, power, portion	**|y-d|**			ONOM	370
yadīd	beloved	**|w-d-d|**			ONOM	344
yadūʕ	known, familiar	**|w-d-ʕ|**			ONOM	343

yadūd	beloved	**|w-d-d|**			ONOM	344
yagāʕ See *w/yagāʕ*						
yagāʕt	sorrow(s)	**|w-g-ʕ|**	CTX			345
yaħad, **yaħid**, **yiħad**	unique	**|w-ħ-d|**			ONOM	347
yaħatt	uniqueness, singularity	**|w-ħ-d|**			ONOM	347
yaħdōn	alone	**|w-ħ-d|**	CTX			347
yaħid See *yaħad*, *yaħid*, *yiħad*						
yaħudiy	simple (-minded?)	**|w-ħ-d|**	CTX			347
yaḳar	dear, precious, esteemed	**|w-ḳ-r|**			ONOM	349
yaḳarah, **yaḳart**	dear, precious, esteemed	**|w-ḳ-r|**			ONOM	350
yaḳart See *yaḳarah*, *yaḳart*						
yaḳir, **yaḳḳir**	(most) dear, precious	**|w-ḳ-r|**			ONOM	349
yāḳis^{1}	fowler, bird catcher	**|y-ḳ-s^{1}|**	CTX			372
yaḳḳir See *yaḳir*, *yaḳḳir*						
yaḳḳur See *yaḳur*, *yaḳḳur*						
yaḳr	dear, precious,	**|w-ḳ-r|**			ONOM	349
yaḳrān	dear, precious	**|w-ḳ-r|**			ONOM	350
yaḳrīt	dear, precious,	**|w-ḳ-r|**			ONOM	350
yaḳur, **yaḳḳur**	(most) dear, precious	**|w-ḳ-r|**			ONOM	349
yald	child	**|w-l-d**		LL		350
yamin, **ya/imitt**	right (side, arm); the South	**|y-m-n|**		LL	ONOM	373
yamitt See *yamin*, *ya/imitt*						
yamm	(primeval) stream; sea, lake; DN	**|y-m-m|**	CTX	LL	ONOM	372
yamāmah	(a kind of) dove	**|y-w-n|**			ONOM	380
yapaʕ	radiant	**|y-p-ʕ|**			ONOM	375
yapiʕ	radiant	**|y-p-ʕ|**			ONOM	375
yapiy	beautiful; nice thing, beauty	**|w-p-y|**	CTX		ONOM	352

<table>
<tr><td>yapuʕ</td><td>radiant</td><td>|y-p-ʕ|</td><td></td><td></td><td>ONOM</td><td>375</td></tr>
<tr><td>yarax
See yar(i)x, yarax</td><td></td><td></td><td></td><td></td><td></td><td></td></tr>
<tr><td>yarbuʕ</td><td>a rodent</td><td>|y-r-b-ʕ|</td><td></td><td>LL</td><td></td><td>376</td></tr>
<tr><td>yardān</td><td>watercourse; DN</td><td>|w-r-d| (2)</td><td>CTX</td><td></td><td></td><td>353</td></tr>
<tr><td>yar(i)x, yarax</td><td>(new) moon, DN</td><td>|w-r-x|</td><td></td><td></td><td>ONOM</td><td>353</td></tr>
<tr><td>yariḳ</td><td>green, verdant</td><td>|w-r-ḳ|</td><td></td><td></td><td>ONOM</td><td>354</td></tr>
<tr><td>yarḳ</td><td>garden, orchard</td><td>|w-r-ḳ|</td><td></td><td></td><td>ONOM</td><td>354</td></tr>
<tr><td>yarḳān</td><td>garden, orchard</td><td>|w-r-ḳ|</td><td>CTX</td><td></td><td>ONOM</td><td>354</td></tr>
<tr><td>yāriθ</td><td>heir</td><td>|w-r-θ| (1)</td><td></td><td></td><td>ONOM</td><td>355</td></tr>
<tr><td>yarrāθ
See warrāθ / yarrāθ</td><td></td><td></td><td></td><td></td><td></td><td></td></tr>
<tr><td>yarθ</td><td>inheritance, possession</td><td>|w-r-θ| (1)</td><td></td><td></td><td>ONOM</td><td>355</td></tr>
<tr><td>yaSar, yaSarah</td><td>just, straight upright</td><td>|y-s^{1}-r|</td><td></td><td></td><td>ONOM</td><td>377</td></tr>
<tr><td>yaSarah
See yaSar, yaSarah</td><td></td><td></td><td></td><td></td><td></td><td></td></tr>
<tr><td>yaSart</td><td>justice, uprightness</td><td>|y-s^{1}-r|</td><td></td><td></td><td>ONOM</td><td>377</td></tr>
<tr><td>yaSīB</td><td>battering ram</td><td>|s^{1}-w/y-p|</td><td>CTX</td><td></td><td></td><td>266</td></tr>
<tr><td>yaSuB(uy)</td><td>a stone (jasper ?)</td><td>|y-S-B(-y)|</td><td>CTX</td><td></td><td></td><td>376</td></tr>
<tr><td>yaSur</td><td>just, upright</td><td>|y-s^{1}-r|</td><td></td><td></td><td>ONOM</td><td>377</td></tr>
<tr><td>yaṣib</td><td>firm, steadfast</td><td>|w-ṣ-b|</td><td></td><td></td><td>ONOM</td><td>358</td></tr>
<tr><td>yāṣiḥ</td><td>bleacher</td><td>|w-ṣ́-ħ|</td><td>CTX</td><td></td><td></td><td>362</td></tr>
<tr><td>yāṣir</td><td>potter</td><td>|w-ṣ-r|</td><td>CTX</td><td></td><td></td><td>359</td></tr>
<tr><td>yaṣūb</td><td>firmly set, made firm</td><td>|w-ṣ-b|</td><td></td><td></td><td>ONOM</td><td>358</td></tr>
<tr><td>yatām, yatūm, yitūm</td><td>orphan</td><td>|y-t-m|</td><td></td><td></td><td>ONOM</td><td>378</td></tr>
<tr><td>yatapʕ</td><td>shiny</td><td>|y-p-ʕ|</td><td></td><td></td><td>ONOM</td><td>375</td></tr>
<tr><td>yatar</td><td>excellent, outstanding</td><td>|w-t-r| (2)</td><td></td><td></td><td>ONOM</td><td>363</td></tr>
<tr><td>yataSr</td><td>justly treated</td><td>|y-s^{1}-r|</td><td></td><td></td><td>ONOM</td><td>378</td></tr>
<tr><td>yataθʕ</td><td>helped</td><td>|y-θ-ʕ|</td><td></td><td></td><td>ONOM</td><td>379</td></tr>
<tr><td>yatin</td><td>given</td><td>|n/w/y-D-n|</td><td></td><td></td><td>ONOM</td><td>79</td></tr>
<tr><td>yatir</td><td>excellent, outstanding</td><td>|w-t-r| (2)</td><td></td><td></td><td>ONOM</td><td>364</td></tr>
<tr><td>yatt
See w/yatt</td><td></td><td></td><td></td><td></td><td></td><td></td></tr>
<tr><td>yatūm
See yatām, yatūm, yitūm</td><td></td><td></td><td></td><td></td><td></td><td></td></tr>
</table>

<table>
<tr><td>yatun</td><td>given</td><td>|n/w/y-D-n|</td><td></td><td></td><td>ONOM</td><td>79</td></tr>
<tr><td>yaθʕ, yaθʕat, yiθʕ, yiθʕah, yiθʕat</td><td>help, salvation</td><td>|y-θ-ʕ|</td><td></td><td></td><td>ONOM</td><td>379</td></tr>
<tr><td>yaθʕat
See yaθʕ, yaθʕat, yiθʕ, yiθʕah, yiθʕat</td><td></td><td></td><td></td><td></td><td></td><td></td></tr>
<tr><td>yaθab</td><td>dweller</td><td>|w-θ-b|</td><td></td><td></td><td>ONOM</td><td>365</td></tr>
<tr><td>yaθan</td><td>old</td><td>|y-θ-n|</td><td></td><td></td><td>ONOM</td><td>379</td></tr>
<tr><td>yaθiʕ, yaθiʕah, yiθiʕ</td><td>helpful, saviour</td><td>|y-θ-ʕ|</td><td></td><td></td><td>ONOM</td><td>379</td></tr>
<tr><td>yaθiʕah
See yaθiʕ, yaθiʕah, yiθiʕ</td><td></td><td></td><td></td><td></td><td></td><td></td></tr>
<tr><td>yaθuʕ, yaθuʕah, yaθuʕat, yiθuʕ</td><td>helpful, saviour</td><td>|y-θ-ʕ|</td><td></td><td></td><td>ONOM</td><td>379</td></tr>
<tr><td>yaθuʕah
See yaθuʕ, yaθuʕah, yaθuʕat, yiθuʕ</td><td></td><td></td><td></td><td></td><td></td><td></td></tr>
<tr><td>yaθuʕat
See yaθuʕ, yaθuʕah, yaθuʕat, yiθuʕ</td><td></td><td></td><td></td><td></td><td></td><td></td></tr>
<tr><td>yaθun</td><td>old</td><td>|y-θ-n|</td><td></td><td></td><td>ONOM</td><td>379</td></tr>
<tr><td>yawm</td><td>day; DN</td><td>|y-w-m|</td><td>CTX</td><td>LL</td><td>ONOM</td><td>379</td></tr>
<tr><td>yaydāʕ, yaydāʕt</td><td>knowledge, friendship; DN</td><td>|w-d-ʕ|</td><td></td><td></td><td>ONOM</td><td>343</td></tr>
<tr><td>yēn</td><td>wine; vineyard</td><td>|w-y-n|</td><td>CTX</td><td>LL</td><td>ONOM</td><td>366</td></tr>
<tr><td>yid, yidat</td><td>hand, arm, power; rental</td><td>|y-d|</td><td>CTX</td><td>LL</td><td>ONOM</td><td>371</td></tr>
<tr><td>yiħad
See yaħad, yaħid, yiħad</td><td></td><td></td><td></td><td></td><td></td><td></td></tr>
<tr><td>yimitt
See yamin, ya/imitt</td><td></td><td></td><td></td><td></td><td></td><td></td></tr>
</table>

<table>
<tr><td>yimnay</td><td>pertaining to the right, southerner</td><td>|y-m-n|</td><td></td><td></td><td>ONOM</td><td>373</td></tr>
<tr><td>yipʕ</td><td>splendour</td><td></td><td></td><td></td><td>ONOM</td><td>374</td></tr>
<tr><td>yipʕūt</td><td>splendour</td><td>|y-p-ʕ|</td><td></td><td></td><td>ONOM</td><td>375</td></tr>
<tr><td>yipaʕ</td><td>radiant</td><td>|y-p-ʕ|</td><td></td><td></td><td>ONOM</td><td>375</td></tr>
<tr><td>yipuʕ</td><td>radiant; DN</td><td>|y-p-ʕ|</td><td></td><td></td><td>ONOM</td><td>375</td></tr>
<tr><td>yiSar, yiSart</td><td>just; DN; favourable (prayer)</td><td>|y-s^1-r|</td><td>CTX</td><td>LL</td><td>ONOM</td><td>377</td></tr>
<tr><td>yiSart
See yiSar, yiSart</td><td></td><td></td><td></td><td></td><td></td><td></td></tr>
<tr><td>yiSr</td><td>just, straight; DN</td><td>|y-s^1-r|</td><td></td><td></td><td>ONOM</td><td>377</td></tr>
<tr><td>yiSrut</td><td>just</td><td>|y-s^1-r|</td><td></td><td></td><td>ONOM</td><td>377</td></tr>
<tr><td>yitar</td><td>excellent, outstanding</td><td>|w-t-r| (2)</td><td></td><td></td><td>ONOM</td><td>364</td></tr>
<tr><td>yitūm
See yatām, yatūm, yitūm</td><td></td><td></td><td></td><td></td><td></td><td></td></tr>
<tr><td>yiθʕ
See yaθʕ, yaθʕat, yiθʕ, yiθʕah, yiθʕat</td><td></td><td></td><td></td><td></td><td></td><td></td></tr>
<tr><td>yiθʕah
See yaθʕ, yaθʕat, yiθʕ, yiθʕah, yiθʕat</td><td></td><td></td><td></td><td></td><td></td><td></td></tr>
<tr><td>yiθʕat
See yaθʕ, yaθʕat, yiθʕ, yiθʕah, yiθʕat</td><td></td><td></td><td></td><td></td><td></td><td></td></tr>
<tr><td>yiθiʕ
See yaθiʕ, yaθiʕah, yiθiʕ</td><td></td><td></td><td></td><td></td><td></td><td></td></tr>
<tr><td>yiθuʕ
See yaθuʕ, yaθuʕah, yaθuʕat, yiθuʕ</td><td></td><td></td><td></td><td></td><td></td><td></td></tr>
<tr><td>yōbil</td><td>porter, bearer</td><td>|w-b-l| (1)</td><td>CTX</td><td></td><td></td><td>340</td></tr>
<tr><td>yōd</td><td>hand (stele) (?)</td><td>|y-d|</td><td></td><td></td><td>ONOM</td><td>371</td></tr>
<tr><td>yōdiʕa</td><td>skilled, learned</td><td>|w-d-ʕ|</td><td>CTX</td><td></td><td>ONOM</td><td>343</td></tr>
</table>

yōm	day; DN	**|y-w-m|**	CTX	LL		380
yomm	sea, lake	**|y-m-m|**			ONOM	373
yuʕr	difficult, rugged (place)	**|w-ʕ-r| (2)**		LL		339
yubila, ʔubalaya	stream	**|w-b-l| (1)**			ONOM	340
yudād	darling	**|w-d-d|**			ONOM	344
yunnuḳ	suckled	**|y-n-ḳ|**	CTX			374

z

zaʔaBt	incision, engraving (on a jewel)	**|z-ʔ-B|**	CTX			381
zabab	a rat	**|z-b-b|**		LL		381
zabin	bought (?)	**|z-b-n|**			ONOM	382
zabug	lizard (?)	**|z-b-g|**	CTX			382
zahw	splendour	**|z-h-w|**			ONOM	383
zakigay	toothache	**|z-G-g|**	CTX			382
zakukiyt	glaze, glass	**|z-k-k|**	CTX			383
zakzakiy	crystal-clear	**|z-k-k|**			ONOM	383
zaḳt	stung (?)	**|z-ḳ-t|**			ONOM	383
zalzala	switch; stick; branch (?)	**|z-l-l|**	CTX			383
zammār	singer	**|z-m-r| (1)**	CTX			384
zammirt	female singer	**|z-m-r| (1)**	CTX			384
zāniy(a)t	prostitute	**|z-n-y|**	CTX	LL	ONOM	384
zāwir	who turns on / against somebody	**|z-w-r|**	CTX			385
zayn	attired (?)	**|z-y-n|**			ONOM	386
zaynūt	attire, ornament (?)	**|z-y-n|**			ONOM	386
zayyār	stranger	**|z-w-r|**	CTX			385
zētu	olive, olive tree, olive oil	**|z-y-t|**	CTX			387
zibbīr	thyme	**|z-b-b-r|**			ONOM	382
ziḳḳ	a skin (for wine)	**|z-ḳ-ḳ|**	CTX	LL		383
zil	a vessel used as measure	**|n-z-l|**	CTX	LL		117
zīn	rain	**|z-n-n|**	CTX			384
ziriḳ	a kind of (wooden?) bucket	**|z-r-ḳ|**			ONOM	385
zirḳ	sprinkling (of a sacrificial sheep)	**|z-r-ḳ|**	CTX			384
ziwr (A)	braid; ball, plait of wool	**|z-w-r|**	CTX			385
ziwr (B)	a close-woven textile	**|z-w-r|**	CTX			385
ziwrt	a woollen fabric; a turban (?)	**|z-w-r|**	CTX			385
ziyḳ	waft, breath	**|z-y-ḳ|**	CTX		ONOM	386

<table>
<tr><td>ziym</td><td>bearing, appearance; DN</td><td>|z-y-m|</td><td></td><td></td><td>ONOM</td><td>386</td></tr>
<tr><td>zumbar</td><td>hornet</td><td>|z-m-b-r|</td><td></td><td>LL</td><td></td><td>386</td></tr>
<tr><td>zurz</td><td>(double) packsack</td><td>|z-r-z|</td><td>CTX</td><td></td><td></td><td>385</td></tr>
</table>

C. Nominal bases, alphabetic tradition

<table>
<tr><th></th><th></th><th>Etymon</th><th>CTX</th><th>ONOM</th><th>page</th></tr>
<tr><td colspan="6">ả/ỉ/ủ - ḳ</td></tr>
<tr><td>ảħd (A)</td><td>one, oneself; together with</td><td>|w-ħ-d|</td><td>CTX</td><td></td><td>346</td></tr>
<tr><td>ảħd (B)</td><td>solitary, single</td><td>|w-ħ-d|</td><td>CTX</td><td></td><td>346</td></tr>
<tr><td>ảħdh, yħdh</td><td>together</td><td>|w-ħ-d|</td><td>CTX</td><td></td><td>347</td></tr>
<tr><td>ảliy(n)</td><td>the most powerful</td><td>|l-ʔ-w/y| (A)</td><td>CTX</td><td></td><td>6</td></tr>
<tr><td>ảlit</td><td>the most powerful (fem.)</td><td>|l-ʔ-w/y| (A)</td><td></td><td>ONOM</td><td>7</td></tr>
<tr><td>ảnxr</td><td>a marine animal (‘dolphin’ ?)</td><td>|n-x-r|</td><td>CTX</td><td></td><td>88</td></tr>
<tr><td>ảns^1</td><td>muscle, tendon</td><td>|n-s^1-y| (1)</td><td>CTX</td><td></td><td>105</td></tr>
<tr><td>ảrbʕ</td><td>four</td><td>|r-b-ʕ|</td><td>CTX</td><td></td><td>152</td></tr>
<tr><td>ảrbʕm</td><td>forty</td><td>|r-b-ʕ|</td><td>CTX</td><td></td><td>152</td></tr>
<tr><td>ảrbʕtm</td><td>four times, fourfold</td><td>|r-b-ʕ|</td><td>CTX</td><td></td><td>152</td></tr>
<tr><td>ảrbx</td><td>four year old (animal) (?)</td><td>|r-b-ʕ|</td><td>CTX</td><td></td><td>152</td></tr>
<tr><td>ảrbʕ</td><td>four</td><td>|r-b-ʕ|</td><td>CTX</td><td></td><td>152</td></tr>
<tr><td>ảs^{1}bħ</td><td>most praiseworthy</td><td>|s^1-b-ħ|</td><td></td><td>ONOM</td><td>233</td></tr>
<tr><td>ảzmr</td><td>foliage, branches</td><td>|z-b/m-r|</td><td>CTX</td><td></td><td>382</td></tr>
<tr><td>(ỉ)blbl</td><td>messenger, bearer (?)</td><td>|w-b-l| (1)</td><td>CTX</td><td></td><td>340</td></tr>
<tr><td>ỉlḳṣ</td><td>exquisite (?)</td><td>|l-ḳ-ṭ|</td><td>CTX</td><td></td><td>14</td></tr>
<tr><td>ỉpdrð</td><td>a unit of measure</td><td>|p-D-r| (2)</td><td>CTX</td><td></td><td>122</td></tr>
<tr><td>ỉrbṣ</td><td>repose, resting place (?)</td><td>|r-b-ṣ|</td><td></td><td>ONOM</td><td>154</td></tr>
<tr><td>ỉtml</td><td>the previous day, yesterday</td><td>|t-m-l|</td><td>CTX</td><td></td><td>297</td></tr>
<tr><td>ỉtnn</td><td>present</td><td>|n/w/y-D-n|</td><td>CTX</td><td></td><td>79</td></tr>
<tr><td>ủlθ</td><td>a tool for moulding or mixing clay</td><td>|l-w-S|</td><td>CTX</td><td></td><td>18</td></tr>
<tr><td>ủθxt</td><td>incense burner; DN</td><td>|θ-x|</td><td>CTX</td><td></td><td>319</td></tr>
<tr><td>ủzʕr</td><td>the smallest, youngest</td><td>|z-ʕ-r|</td><td>CTX</td><td></td><td>381</td></tr>
<tr><td>ʕdt (A)</td><td>assembly;</td><td>|w-ʕ-d|</td><td>CTX</td><td></td><td>338</td></tr>
</table>

<table>
<tr><td></td><td>confluence;
flooding</td><td></td><td></td><td></td><td></td></tr>
<tr><td>ʕdt (B)</td><td>date, moment</td><td>|ʕ-w-d| (1)</td><td>CTX</td><td></td><td>I:96</td></tr>
<tr><td>ʕθḳb,
θḳb</td><td>a species of tree,
ash tree (?)</td><td>|S-ḳ-b|</td><td>CTX</td><td>ONOM</td><td>194</td></tr>
<tr><td>bʕl (A)</td><td>labourer,
craftsman</td><td>|p-ʕ-l|</td><td>CTX</td><td></td><td>121</td></tr>
<tr><td>bʕl (B)</td><td>lord; DN</td><td>|b-ʕ-l| (2)</td><td>CTX</td><td>ONOM</td><td>I:108</td></tr>
<tr><td>bd (A)</td><td>through (into /
from) the hands of</td><td>|b|, |y-d|</td><td>CTX</td><td>ONOM</td><td>I:103
371</td></tr>
<tr><td>bd (B)</td><td>separation</td><td>|b-d-d|</td><td>CTX</td><td></td><td>I:109</td></tr>
<tr><td>bd (C)</td><td>a kind of ad-lib
song (?)</td><td>|b-d-y(?)|</td><td>CTX</td><td></td><td>I:111</td></tr>
<tr><td>blmt</td><td>immortality</td><td>|b-l-y| (2)
|m-w-t|</td><td>CTX</td><td></td><td>I:119
63</td></tr>
<tr><td>bṭr</td><td>emancipated, free,
deserted (?)</td><td>|p-ṭ-r|</td><td>CTX</td><td></td><td>142</td></tr>
<tr><td>dʕt (A)</td><td>knowledge,
friendship</td><td>|w-d-ʕ|</td><td>CTX</td><td></td><td>343</td></tr>
<tr><td>dʕt (B)</td><td>sweat</td><td>|w-ð-ʕ|</td><td>CTX</td><td></td><td>345</td></tr>
<tr><td>dnt [A]</td><td>plight, distress (?)</td><td>|d-n-n| (1)</td><td>CTX</td><td></td><td>I:149</td></tr>
<tr><td>dnt (B)</td><td>lechery,
fornication</td><td>|z-n-y|</td><td>CTX</td><td></td><td>384</td></tr>
<tr><td>ðd (A)</td><td>breast, bosom</td><td>|S-d/ð|</td><td>CTX</td><td></td><td>186</td></tr>
<tr><td>ðd (B)</td><td>?</td><td>|ð-d| (?)</td><td>CTX</td><td></td><td>I:160</td></tr>
<tr><td>ðd (C)</td><td>herd</td><td>|ð-w-d|</td><td>CTX</td><td></td><td>I:168</td></tr>
<tr><td>ðr,
θr (A)</td><td>prince, sovereign;
DN</td><td>|s^2-r-r-|</td><td></td><td>ONOM</td><td>278</td></tr>
<tr><td>γr (A)</td><td>mountain; DN</td><td>|θ̣-w-r|</td><td>CTX</td><td>ONOM</td><td>335</td></tr>
<tr><td>γr (B)</td><td>kind of low
ground (?)</td><td>|γ-w-r| (2)</td><td>CTX</td><td></td><td>I:206</td></tr>
<tr><td>γr (C)</td><td>skin</td><td>|γ-w-r| (1)</td><td>CTX</td><td></td><td>I:206</td></tr>
<tr><td>γr (D)</td><td>an installation for
the funerary cult</td><td>|θ̣-w-r|</td><td>CTX</td><td></td><td>335</td></tr>
<tr><td>γrt</td><td>rock (?)</td><td>|θ̣-w-r|</td><td>CTX</td><td>ONOM</td><td>335</td></tr>
</table>

l

<table>
<tr><td>l (A)</td><td>to, for; from</td><td>|l| (1)</td><td>CTX</td><td></td><td>2</td></tr>
<tr><td>l (B)</td><td>no, not</td><td>|l| (2)</td><td>CTX</td><td></td><td>2</td></tr>
<tr><td>l (C)</td><td>yes, truly, indeed</td><td>|l| (3)</td><td>CTX</td><td></td><td>4</td></tr>
<tr><td>l (D)</td><td>oh!</td><td>|l| (3)</td><td>CTX</td><td></td><td>4</td></tr>
<tr><td>lả</td><td>power, strength</td><td>|l-ʔ-w/y| (1)</td><td>CTX</td><td></td><td>6</td></tr>
<tr><td>lản</td><td>power, strength</td><td>l-ʔ-w/y| (1)</td><td>CTX</td><td></td><td>6</td></tr>
<tr><td>lỉm</td><td>people, tribe</td><td>|l-ʔ-m| (1)</td><td>CTX</td><td>ONOM</td><td>5</td></tr>
<tr><td>lỉy</td><td>powerful</td><td>|l-ʔ-w/y| (A)</td><td>CTX</td><td></td><td>6</td></tr>
<tr><td>lb</td><td>heart</td><td>|l-b-b|</td><td>CTX</td><td></td><td>8</td></tr>
<tr><td>lbỉt</td><td>lioness; DN</td><td>|l-b-ʔ|</td><td></td><td>ONOM</td><td>8</td></tr>
<tr><td>lbủ</td><td>lion; DN</td><td>|l-b-ʔ|</td><td>CTX</td><td>ONOM</td><td>8</td></tr>
<tr><td>lbn</td><td>white</td><td>|l-b-n| (1)</td><td>CTX</td><td>ONOM</td><td>9</td></tr>
</table>

lbnt	brick	**|l-b-n| (2)**	CTX		10
lbs¹	clothing; sails	**|l-b-s¹|**	CTX		10
lg	measure of capacity for liquids, jar	**|l-g-g|**	CTX	ONOM	11
lħ (A)	cheek, jaw	**|l-ħ-y| (1)**	CTX		13
lħ (B)	missive, message	**|l-w-ħ|**	CTX		18
lħm	grain; bread; food, meat	**|l-ħ-m| (1)**	CTX		12
lħr	ewe (?)	**|r-x-l|**		ONOM	161
lxs¹t	chatter, whisper, murmur	**|l-x-s¹|**	CTX		13
ll	night, nightfall	**|l-y-l(-y)|**	CTX		20
llỉt	young sheep or kid	**|l-l-ʔ|**	CTX		14
llủ	suckling (lamb or kid)	**|l-l-ʔ|**	CTX		14
llx	an element of the shabrack (?)	**|l-l-x|**	CTX		15
lm	why?	**|l| (1), |m| (2)**	CTX		2, 24
lmd	trained, pupil, apprentice	**|l-m-d|**	CTX		15
lmdt	female apprentice	**|l-m-d|**	CTX		15
lps¹	cloak, outer garment	**|l-b-s¹|**	CTX		10
lrmn	pomegranate	**|l-r-m-n|**	CTX		15
lsm	swift, steed (horses)	**|l-s-m|**	CTX		16
lsmt	haste, alacrity	**|l-s-m|**	CTX		16
lṣb	brow (?)	**|l-ṣ-b|**	CTX		16
ls¹n	tongue	**|l-s¹-n|**	CTX		17
ltħ	a dry measure	**|l-t-H|**	CTX	ONOM	17
ltn	the wound, coiled one	**|l-w-y|**		ONOM	19
lṭpn	gentle, kind, fine	**|l-ṭ-p|**		ONOM	17
lθ̣t	scorn (?)	**|l-y-θ̣|**	CTX		20
lwn(y)	follower, mate (?)	**|l-w-y|**	CTX		19
lyt	retinue (?)	**|l-w-y|**	CTX		19

m

=m	optional prosodic reinforcer	**|m| (1)**	CTX	ONOM	24
mảdt	great quantity, a crowd	**|m-ʔ-d|**	CTX		28
mỉ/ủd	abundance	**|m-ʔ-d|**	CTX		28
mỉt	hundred	**|m-ʔ| (2)**	CTX		27
mỉyt	irrigated land, fertile land	**|m-ʔ| (1)**	CTX		27
mủd					

See *mìlùd*

<table>
<tr><td>mʕ</td><td>please!</td><td>|m-ʕ|</td><td>CTX</td><td></td><td>29</td></tr>
<tr><td>mʕmʕ</td><td>intest. disease (?)</td><td>|m-ʕ-y| (2)</td><td>CTX</td><td></td><td>29</td></tr>
<tr><td>mʕd</td><td>convention, assembly</td><td>|w-ʕ-d|</td><td>CTX</td><td></td><td>338</td></tr>
<tr><td>mʕt</td><td>kernel (?)</td><td>|m-ʕ-y| (1)</td><td>CTX</td><td></td><td>29</td></tr>
<tr><td>mbk</td><td>fountain, spring, well</td><td>|n-b-k|</td><td>CTX</td><td></td><td>74</td></tr>
<tr><td>md (A)</td><td>cape, covering</td><td>|m-d(-d/w)| (2)</td><td>CTX</td><td></td><td>30</td></tr>
<tr><td>md (B)</td><td>a corporation (knowing, wise)</td><td>|w-d-ʕ|</td><td>CTX</td><td></td><td>343</td></tr>
<tr><td>md (C)</td><td>duration; during</td><td>|m-d-d| (1)</td><td>CTX</td><td></td><td>29</td></tr>
<tr><td>mdʕ (A)</td><td>why?</td><td>|m| (2), |w-d-ʕ|</td><td>CTX</td><td></td><td>24
344</td></tr>
<tr><td>mdʕ (B)</td><td>(royal) family</td><td>|w-d-ʕ|</td><td>CTX</td><td></td><td>343</td></tr>
<tr><td>mdd</td><td>beloved, friend</td><td>|w-d-d|</td><td>CTX</td><td>ONOM</td><td>343</td></tr>
<tr><td>mddt (A)</td><td>beloved</td><td>|w-d-d|</td><td>CTX</td><td></td><td>344</td></tr>
<tr><td>mddt (B)</td><td>dispenser, distributor</td><td>|m-d-d| (1)</td><td>CTX</td><td></td><td>30</td></tr>
<tr><td>mdl</td><td>a part of harness, halter (?)</td><td>|m-d-l(-l)|</td><td>CTX</td><td></td><td>30</td></tr>
<tr><td>mdpt</td><td>type of carder (?)</td><td>|n-d-p|</td><td>CTX</td><td></td><td>79</td></tr>
<tr><td>mðlγ</td><td>watering can (?)</td><td>|S-l-x|</td><td>CTX</td><td></td><td>195</td></tr>
<tr><td>mðnt</td><td>sandal (?)</td><td>|S-ʔ-n| (2)</td><td>CTX</td><td></td><td>183</td></tr>
<tr><td>mðr</td><td>vow</td><td>|n-ð-r|</td><td>CTX</td><td></td><td>80</td></tr>
<tr><td>mðrɣl</td><td>watchman, guard</td><td>|n-θ̣-r|</td><td>CTX</td><td></td><td>110</td></tr>
<tr><td>mðrn</td><td>(broad)sword</td><td>|m-S-r| (1)</td><td>CTX</td><td></td><td>53</td></tr>
<tr><td>mgn (A)</td><td>gift, present</td><td>|m-g-n|</td><td>CTX</td><td>ONOM</td><td>31</td></tr>
<tr><td>mgn (B)</td><td>protective tool</td><td>|g-n-n| (2)</td><td>CTX</td><td></td><td>I:185</td></tr>
<tr><td>mɣmɣ</td><td>a medicinal plant</td><td>|m-ɣ-m-ɣ|</td><td>CTX</td><td></td><td>31</td></tr>
<tr><td>m(h)</td><td>what?; anything</td><td>|m| (2)</td><td>CTX</td><td></td><td>24</td></tr>
<tr><td>mhk(m)</td><td>anything; nothing</td><td>|m| (2)</td><td>CTX</td><td></td><td>24</td></tr>
<tr><td>mhr (A)</td><td>soldier, warrior</td><td>|m-h-r| (1)</td><td>CTX</td><td>ONOM</td><td>32</td></tr>
<tr><td>mhr (B)</td><td>warrior strength</td><td>|m-h-r| (1)</td><td>CTX</td><td></td><td>32</td></tr>
<tr><td>mhr (C)</td><td>dowry, bride-price</td><td>|m-h-r| (2)</td><td>CTX</td><td></td><td>32</td></tr>
<tr><td>mx</td><td>marrow, brains</td><td>|m-x-x|</td><td>CTX</td><td></td><td>33</td></tr>
<tr><td>mxr (A)</td><td>price</td><td>|m-x-r|</td><td>CTX</td><td></td><td>34</td></tr>
<tr><td>mxr (B)</td><td>tax collector</td><td>|m-x-r|</td><td>CTX</td><td></td><td>34</td></tr>
<tr><td>mxṣ (A)</td><td>weaver</td><td>|m-x-ṣ́|</td><td>CTX</td><td></td><td>35</td></tr>
<tr><td>mxṣ (B)</td><td>a striking instrument</td><td>|m-x-ṣ́|</td><td>CTX</td><td></td><td>35</td></tr>
<tr><td>mk (A)</td><td>bog</td><td>|m-k(-k)|</td><td>CTX</td><td></td><td>35</td></tr>
<tr><td>mk (B)</td><td>behold! (?)</td><td>|m| (2),
|k| (1)</td><td>CTX</td><td></td><td>25
I:292</td></tr>
<tr><td>mkr (A)</td><td>merchant, runner</td><td>|m-k-r|</td><td>CTX</td><td></td><td>36</td></tr>
<tr><td>mkr (B)</td><td>sale, trade good</td><td>|m-k-r|</td><td>CTX</td><td></td><td>36</td></tr>
<tr><td>mkt</td><td>immolation, offering (?)</td><td>|n-k-t|</td><td>CTX</td><td></td><td>91</td></tr>
<tr><td>mḳb, mḳp</td><td>a tool (hammer, punch, pick ?)</td><td>|n-ḳ-b|</td><td>CTX</td><td></td><td>92</td></tr>
</table>

mḳd (A)	grazing tax	**|n-ḳ-d|**	CTX		92
mḳħ	tong(s)	**|l-ḳ-ħ|**	CTX		13
mḳp See *mḳb*, *mḳp*					
mlảk	messenger		CTX		4
mlảkt	message	**|l-ʔ-k|**	CTX		4
mlảt	fullness	**|m-l-ʔ|**	CTX		37
mlỉt	fullness, plenty	**|m-l-ʔ|**	CTX		37
mlủ	fill, full measure	**|m-l-ʔ|**	CTX		37
mlbs^1	cloak, cape	**|l-b-s^1|**	CTX		10
mld	newly born	**|w-l-d|**		ONOM	351
mlg	trousseau, dowry	**|m-l-g|**		ONOM	38
mlħt	salt	**|m-l-ħ|**	CTX		38
mlxs^1	snake charmer	**|l-x-s^1|**	CTX		13
mlk (A)	king; dead king(s); DN	**|m-l-k|**	CTX	ONOM	42
mlk (B)	ruling, decision	**|m-l-k|**		ONOM	42
mlk (C)	kingdom	**|m-l-k|**	CTX		42
mlkt	queen	**|m-l-k|**	CTX		42
mll	waste, scraps (?)	**|m-l-l|**	CTX		43
mlsm	chariot runner	**|l-s-m|**	CTX		16
mltħ	a measure of capacity and area	**|l-t-H|**	CTX		17
mm	winter (?)	**|m-m-m| (1)**	CTX		43
mmʕ	gore, innards	**|m-ʕ-y| (2)**	CTX		29
mmskn	earthenware bowl	**|m-s-k|**	CTX		53
mmṭr	portico, porch (?)	**|m-ṭ–r|**	CTX		60
mn (A)	what?	**|m| (2)**	CTX		25
mn (B)	who(so)ever (?)	**|m| (2)**			25
mn (C)	mina	**|m-n-w/y| (1)**	CTX		45
mn (D)	species (of animal)	**|m-y-n|**	CTX		62
mndʕ	perhaps	**|m| (2), |w-d-ʕ|**	CTX		25 343
mndɣ	a type of flour	**|m-n-d|**	CTX		43
mnħ	delivery, tribute	**|m-n-ħ|**	CTX		44
mnħt	tribute	**|m-n-ħ|**	CTX		44
mnħy	offering	**|m-n-ħ|**	CTX		44
mnx	resting place	**|n-w-x|**	CTX		112
mnk (A)	whoever, anyone	**|k| (1),** **|m| (2)**	CTX		I:292 25
mnk (B)	whatever, anything	**|k| (1),** **|m| (2)**	CTX		I:292 25
mnḳt	acquittal, exoneration (?)	**|n-ḳ-y| (1)**	CTX		95
mnm (A)	any(body), whoever	**|m| (2)**	CTX		25
mnm (B)	any(thing), whatever	**|m| (2)**	CTX		25

mnmn	anyone, someone	**|m| (2)**	CTX		25
mnrt	candelabrum	**|n-w-r|**	CTX		115
mnt (A)	portion, ration; piece, member	**|m-n-w/y| (1)**	CTX		45
mnt (B)	enumeration, spell	**|m-n-w/y| (1)**	CTX		45
mpx	(bellows of the) forge	**|n-p-x|**	CTX		97
mpxrt	assembly, gathering	**|p-x-r| (2)**	CTX		126
mptħ	key	**|p-t-ħ|**	CTX		142
mr (A)	son	**|m-r-ʔ| (1)**	CTX		46
mr (B)	bitter; strong	**|m-r(-r)| (2)**	CTX	ONOM	49
mr (C)	myrrh; bitterness	**|m-r(-r)| (2)**	CTX		49
mr (D)	young of an animal, cub (?)	**|m-h-r| (3)**	CTX		33
mrů (A)	cavalier or knight	**|m-r-ʔ| (1)**	CTX		46
mrů (B)	fattened, fatling	**|m-r-ʔ| (2)**	CTX		46
mrů (C)	animal fattener	**|m-r-ʔ| (2)**	CTX		46
mrʕ	pasture land	**|r-ʕ-y| (1)**	CTX	ONOM	151
mrbʕ	measure of capacity, quart	**|r-b-ʕ|**	CTX		152
mrbʕt	the fourth (wife)	**|r-b-ʕ|**	CTX		152
mrbd	bedspread, counterpane	**|r-b-d|**	CTX		153
mrdt	rug, tapestry	**|m-r-d-D|**	CTX		47
mrγθ	suckling, unweaned (lamb)	**|r-γ-θ|**	CTX		157
mrγt	scum, dregs (?)	**|r-γ-w|**	CTX		157
mrħ	lance, spear	**|r-m-ħ|**	CTX		166
mrħḳ	distance	**|r-ħ-ḳ|**	CTX		159
mrħḳt	distance, far away (place)	**|r-ħ-ḳ|**	CTX		159
mrkbt	(war-) chariot	**|r-k-b|**	CTX		163
mrḳd	an instrument (castanet ?)	**|r-ḳ-d|**	CTX		165
mrm, **mrym**	height	**|r-w/y-m|**	CTX		177
mrrt	myrrh; bile (?)	**|m-r(-r)| (2)**	CTX	ONOM	49
mrṣ	illness	**|m-r-ṣ́|**	CTX		51
mrθ (A)	steep, mixed drink	**|m-r-S|**	CTX		50
mrθ (B)	estate (?)	**|w-r-θ| (1)**	CTX	ONOM	356
mrym See *mrm, mrym*					
mryn	knight titular of a war-chariot	**|m-r-y-n|**	CTX	ONOM	52
mrzʕy	divine or cultic title	**|m-r-z-ħ|**	CTX		52
mrzħ	cultic association,	**|m-r-z-ħ|**	CTX		51

	(cultic) banquet				
msdt	foundation(s)	**|w-s-d|**	CTX		357
msgr	closed building	**|s-G-r|**	CTX		191
msk	mixture, mixed wine	**|m-s-k|**	CTX		53
mskt	mixture, emulsion	**|m-s-k|**	CTX		53
mslmt	ascent, slope (?)	**|s-l-m| (2)**	CTX		198
mspr (A)	reciter	**|S-p-r| (1)**	CTX		204
mspr (B)	recitation, story, tale	**|S-p-r| (1)**	CTX		204
msrr	entrails, viscera (?)	**|s-r-r| (2)**	CTX		207
mss	sap, juice (?)	**|m-S-S/w/y| (1)**	CTX		53
mswn	a high official, expert (?)	**|m-S-S-w|**	CTX		54
mṣb (A)	beam, pointer	**|n-ṣ-b|**	CTX		102
mṣb (B)	deposit, reserve	**|n-ṣ-b|**	CTX		102
mṣbṭ	a tool or part of one (handle ?)	**|Ṣ-b-ṭ|**	CTX		285
mṣd (A)	large fortified tower (?)	**|m-ṣ-d|**	CTX	ONOM	54
mṣd (B)	(feast of) game	**|ṣ-w/y-d|**	CTX		225
mṣḳt	trouble	**|Ṣ-w/y-ḳ|**	CTX		288
mṣl	cymbalist	**|ṣ-l-l| (2)**	CTX		217
mṣlt (A)	cymbal(s)	**|ṣ-l-l| (2)**	CTX		217
mṣlt (B)	clang	**|ṣ-l-l| (2)**	CTX		217
mṣmt	treaty, agreement	**|Ṣ-m-d|**	CTX		286
mṣpr	who arranges, reinforces (?)	**|Ṣ-p-r|**	CTX		286
mṣpt	crow's nest	**|ṣ-p-y| (2)**	CTX		222
mṣr	sob	**|n-ṣ-r|**	CTX		103
mṣrrt	bundle, parcel (?)	**|ṣ-r-r| (1), |ṣ-w-r|**	CTX		225
mṣṣ	one who sucks	**|m-ṣ-ṣ|**	CTX		55
ms^{1}bʕ	the seventh	**|s^1-b-ʕ|**	CTX		232
ms^{1}ħt	anointing	**|m-s^1-ħ|**	CTX		55
ms^{1}xṭ	a kind of axe or cleaver	**|s^1-x-ṭ|**	CTX		240
ms^{1}kb(t)	place of rest, bed	**|s^1-k-b|**	CTX		241
ms^{1}knt	residence, mansion	**|s^1-k-n|**	CTX		243
ms^{1}krt (A)	skin (?).	**|s^1-k-r| (2)**	CTX		244
ms^{1}krt (B)	wage(s)	**|s^2-k-r| (2)**	CTX		274
ms^{1}ḳ	cup	**|s^1-ḳ-y|**	CTX		246
ms^{1}lħ	battering-ram (?)	**|s^1-l-ħ| (1)**	CTX		246
ms^{1}lt (A)	garment or harness	**|m-s^1-l| (2)**	CTX		56
ms^{1}lt (B)	a (sharp / sharpening) tool	**|s^1-ħ-l| (2), |s^1-l-ħ|**	CTX		238
ms^{1}mʕt	(body)guard	**|s^1-m-ʕ|**	CTX		252

ms^{1}ms^1	marsh(?)	**|m-S-S/w/y| (1)**	CTX		53
ms^{1}mṭr	rainmaker; DN	**|m-ṭ–r|**	CTX		60
ms^{1}nḳt	she who breast-feeds	**|y-n-ḳ|**	CTX		374
ms^{1}p, ms^{1}py	elevated (place) (?)	**|s^1-p-y|**	CTX	ONOM	259
ms^{1}py See *ms^{1}p, ms^{1}py*					
ms^{1}r (A)	song	**|s^1-y-r| (1)**	CTX		268
ms^{1}r (B)	justice	**|y-s^1-r|**	CTX	ONOM	378
ms^{1}rr	pointer (of the balance), pivot (?)	**|s^1-r-r| (2)**	CTX		260
ms^{1}spdt	wailing woman	**|s-p-d|**	CTX		202
ms^{1}ṣů	one who leads out	**|w-ṣ-ʔ|**	CTX		362
ms^{1}ṣṣ	one who drives out, scares off	**|n-ṣ-ṣ|**	CTX		104
ms^{1}t	banquet (?)	**|s^1-t-y| (1)**	CTX		264
ms^{1}tt	drink, libation	**|s^1-t-y| (1)**	CTX		266
mt (A)	man, husband, hero	**|m-t|**	CTX	ONOM	58
mt (B)	dead; mortal	**|m-w-t|**	CTX		63
mt (C)	death	**|m-w-t|**	CTX		63
mtħ	unit of measurement; length, stretch	**|m-t-ħ|**	CTX		59
mṭx	gift, offering	**|ṭ-x-w|**	CTX		308
mtk	libation	**|n-t-k|**	CTX		108
mtḳ	sweet	**|m-t-ḳ|**	CTX		59
mtḳt	cake (?)	**|m-t-ḳ|**	CTX		59
mtn (A)	tendon, loin	**|m-t-n| (1)**	CTX		59
mtn (B)	gift	**|n/w/y-D-n|**	CTX	ONOM	79
mtnt	loin	**|m-t-n| (1)**	CTX		59
mtr	in addition	**|w-t-r| (2)**	CTX		365
mtrn	surplus	**|w-t-r| (2)**	CTX		364
mtrxt	consort, wife	**|t-r-x| (1)**	CTX		300
mṭ	rod, riding crop	**|m-D(-w)|**	CTX		30
mṭʕt	plantation	**|n-ṭ-ʕ|**	CTX		108
mṭnt	clay container (?)	**|ṭ-y-n|**	CTX		313
mṭr	rain	**|m-ṭ–r|**	CTX		60
mṭrt	rain	**|m-ṭ–r|**	CTX		60
mṭt	bed	**|n-ṭ-y|**	CTX		109
mθ	infant, baby boy	**|m-θ|**	CTX	ONOM	60
mθb (A)	seat, throne	**|w-θ-b|**	CTX		365
mθb (B)	residence, shelter	**|w-θ-b|**	CTX		365
mθdθ	the sixth	**|s^1-d-θ|**	CTX		236
mθlθ (A)	a third	**|s^2-l-θ|**	CTX		275
mθlθ (B)	the third (one)	**|s^2-l-θ|**	CTX		275
mθ̣mů	thirsty	**|θ̣-m-ʔ|**	CTX		334
mθn	repetition	**|θ-n|**	CTX		325

mθpd	layer, stratum	**|θ-p-d|**	CTX		326
mθpṭ, mθpθ̣	command, oracle	**|θ-p-ṭ|**	CTX	ONOM	327
mθpθ̣ See *mθpṭ, mθpθ̣*					
mθt	young lady	**|m-θ|**	CTX		60
mθṭ	oar (?)	**|s¹-w-ṭ|**	CTX		266
mθyn	shawl, sash	**|m-θ-y|**	CTX		60
mθ̣r	rain	**|m-ṭ–r|**	CTX		60
my (A)	who?	**|m| (2)**	CTX	ONOM	26
my (B)	what?	**|m| (2)**	CTX		26
my (C)	water, liquid, juice	**|m-ʔ| (1)**	CTX		27
mzn	weight, scales	**|w-z-n|**	CTX		367

n

=n (A)	highlighting and euphonic enclitic (≈ yea)	**|n| (1)**	CTX		67
=n (B), =ny=	our; us	**|n| (2)**	CTX	ONOM	68
=n(y)	my; me	**|n| (2)**	CTX	ONOM	67
=ny	of both of us; both of us	**|n| (2)**	CTX	ONOM	68
nåt	a type of sacrifice	**|n-ʔ(-t)|**	CTX		69
nît	axe, hatchet	**|n-ʔ|**	CTX		68
nʕm (A)	pleasant, gracious	**|n-ʕ-m|**	CTX	ONOM	70
nʕm (B)	pleasure, fortune, grace; DN	**|n-ʕ-m|**	CTX	ONOM	70
nʕmn	handsome, pleasant, gracious	**|n-ʕ-m|**	CTX		70
nʕmt	fortune, grace	**|n-ʕ-m|**	CTX		71
nʕmy	fortune, grace	**|n-ʕ-m|**	CTX		71
nʕr (A)	boy; servant	**|n-ʕ-r| (1)**	CTX	ONOM	71
nʕr (B)	a type of flour or grain	**|n-ʕ-r| (3)**	CTX		71
nʕrt	girl, maidservant	**|n-ʕ-r| (1)**	CTX		71
nbk, npk	fountain, spring, well	**|n-b-k|**	CTX	ONOM	74
nblů	fire-arrow, flame	**|n-b-l| (2)**	CTX		74
nbs¹t	living being(s), animal(s)	**|n-p-S|**	CTX		99
nbt	honey	**|n-b| (2)**	CTX		71
ndr	vow	**|n-ð-r|**	CTX		80
ngb	victualling	**|n-g-b| (1)**	CTX		81
ngr	herald	**|n-g-r|**	CTX		82

ngrt	herald	**|n-g-r|**	CTX		82
nɣr	watchman, guard	**|n-θ̣-r|**	CTX		110
nhḳt	braying	**|n-h-ḳ|**	CTX		83
nhmmt	drowsiness, fainting fit	**|n-w-m|**	CTX		113
nhr	river; DN	**|n-h-r| (1)**	CTX	ONOM	84
nħ	a type of oil / fat (?)	**|n-ħ(-ħ)|**	CTX		86
nħl	feudatory, sharecropper	**|n-ħ-l|**	CTX		86
nħlt	property; inheritance	**|n-ħ-l|**	CTX		86
nħs^{1}	serpent, snake	**|n-ħ-s^{1}| (1)**	CTX		87
nxl	torrent, water course	**|n-x-l|**	CTX	ONOM	88
nxt	divan	**|n-w-x|**	CTX		112
nkl	DN	**|n-k-l| (1)**		ONOM	89
nkr	stranger	**|n-k-r|**	CTX		90
nks^{1}y	accounting, account(s)	**|n-k-S| (1)**	CTX		91
nkt	immolation, victim	**|n-k-t|**	CTX		91
nky	beaten, distressed (?)	**|n-k-y|**	CTX		91
nḳbn	animal harness, caparison (?)	**|n-ḳ-p|**	CTX		94
nḳd	head shepherd, chief shepherd	**|n-ḳ-d|**	CTX		92
nḳḳ	cleft (lip / palate) (?)	**|n-ḳ-ḳ|**		ONOM	92
nḳl	supply, contribution (?)	**|n-ḳ-l|**	CTX	ONOM	93
nḳm	vengeance	**|n-ḳ-m|**		ONOM	94
nḳpt, **nḳpnt**	turn, (yearly) cycle	**|n-ḳ-p|**	CTX		94
nḳpnt See *nḳpt*, *nḳpnt*					
nḳṭ	chief shepherd (?)	**|n-ḳ-d|**		ONOM	92
nmḳ	embellished (?)	**|n-m-ḳ|**		ONOM	95
nmrt	splendour	**|n-w-r|**	CTX		115
nms^{1}	ichneumon, mongoose (?)	**|n-m-s^{1}| (1)**		ONOM	96
nnů	a medicinal plant	**|n-n-ʔ|**	CTX		96
np	peak	**|n-w-p|**	CTX		113
npk See *nbk*, *npk*					
npr	flyer, bird	**|n-p-r| (1)**	CTX	ONOM	97
npṣ	item, piece	**|n-p-ṣ| (1)**	CTX		99
nps^{1} (A)	throat; breath; life	**|n-p-S|**	CTX		98

nps^1 (B)	red(-dyed) wool	**|n-B-S|**	CTX		75
nps^{1}n	place of / for 'souls' (?)	**|n-p-S|**	CTX		99
npt	sieve, sifter	**|n-p-y| (1)**	CTX		99
npy	purification, expurgation	**|n-p-y| (1)**	CTX		99
npyn	tunic	**|n-p-y| (2)**	CTX		99
nr	light, fire, lamp	**|n-w-r|**	CTX	ONOM	114
nrt (A)	light, lamp	**|n-w-r|**	CTX		114
nrt (B)	ploughed land	**|n-y-r|**	CTX		116
nsk	caster, forger of metals	**|n-s-k|**	CTX	ONOM	101
nskt	casting, cast metal or object; offering	**|n-s-k|**	CTX		101
nṣ	bird, wild bird	**|n-ṣ-ṣ|**	CTX	ONOM	104
nṣbt	display, support (?)	**|n-ṣ-b|**	CTX		103
nṣħ	victory	**|n-ṣ-ħ (1)|**	CTX		103
nṣp	a weight (half a shekel / weak shekel)	**|n-ṣ-p|**	CTX		103
ns^{1}b	a piece of meat	**|n-s^1-b| (2)**	CTX		104
ns^{1}g	cloth, fabric	**|n-S-G|**	CTX		100
ns^{1}lm	guarantee, pledge (?)	**|s^1-l-m|**	CTX		248
ns^{1}r	eagle, falcon	**|n-s^1-r| (1)**	CTX		105
ntb	path	**|n-t-b| (1)**	CTX		107
ntbt	path, (right of) way	**|n-t-b| (1)**	CTX		107
ntk	a glass paste	**|n-t-k|**	CTX		107
ntn	emission (of voice), lament	**|n/w/y-D-n|**	CTX		78
nθk (A)	biter	**|n-θ-k|**			109
nθk (B)	bite; interest	**|n-θ-k|**	CTX		109
nθḳ	a missile (dart) (?)	**|n-θ-ḳ|**	CTX		109
nyr	luminary	**|n-w-r|**	CTX		114
nzl	kind of offering	**|n-z-l|**	CTX		116

p

p (A)	and; thus	**|p| (1)**	CTX		119
p (B)	mouth, voice	**|p(-w/y)|**	CTX	ONOM	144
p (C)	here	**|p-w|**	CTX		144
pålt	cracked land	**|p-ʔ-l|**	CTX		120
påmt	time	**|p-ʕ-m|**	CTX		121
påt, pît	edge, border, temple	**|p-ʔ|**	CTX	ONOM	118
pîd	heart; goodness	**|p-ʔ-d|**	CTX		120
pîl	a kind of flour (?)	**|p-ʔ-l|**	CTX		119
pît					

See *pảt*, *pỉt*					
pʕl	labour deed, work	**|p-ʕ-l|**	CTX		121
pʕn	foot	**|p-ʕ-m|**	CTX		121
pd	lock (of hair)	**|p-w-d| (1)**	CTX		144
pdd	worn out (?)	**|p-w/y-d| (2), |p-d-d|**	CTX		144
pdr (A)	town, city	**|p-D-r| (1)**	CTX		122
pdr (B)	bull, DN	**|p-D-r| (2)**	CTX	ONOM	122
pð	gold	**|p-ð-ð|**	CTX		123
pgů	qualifying a garment	**|p-g-ʔ|**	CTX		123
pglt	unclean offering	**|p-g-l|**	CTX		123
pgm	harm (?)	**|p-g-m|**	CTX		123
pgr	body, corpse	**|p-g-r|**	CTX		124
pγ(n)dr	a blanket or cloak	**|p-γ-(n-)d-r|**	CTX		124
pγt	girl, princess	**|p-γ-y|**	CTX	ONOM	124
pγy	boy	**|p-γ-y|**	CTX	ONOM	124
pħl	jackass	**|p-ħ-l|**	CTX		124
pħlt	mare	**|p-ħ-l|**	CTX		124
pħm	ember; reddish, ruby (purple)	**|p-ħ-m|**	CTX		124
pxd	yearling lamb	**|p-x-d| (1)**	CTX		125
pxr (A)	potter	**|p-x-r| (1)**	CTX		125
pxr (B)	assembly	**|p-x-r| (2)**	CTX		125
pxyr	whole, totality	**|p-x-r| (2)**	CTX		126
pḳr	manumited, enfranchised (?)	**|p-ḳ-r|**		ONOM	127
pld	a cloth or garment	**|p-l-d|**	CTX		127
plg	stream, brook	**|p-l-g|**	CTX		127
plk	spindle	**|p-l-G-G|**	CTX		127
plθt	humiliation	**|p-l-θ|**	CTX		130
pn	don’t!; stop it!	**|p-n-w/y|**	CTX		131
pnm	face, countenance	**|p-n|**	CTX		131
pnt	knuckle, joint, vertebra	**|p-n-n|**	CTX		131
pr (A)	young bull, bullock	**|p-r-r| (1)**	CTX	ONOM	134
pr (B)	fruit	**|p-r(-w/y)| (1)**	CTX		137
prů	an equid, mule	**|p-r-ʔ| (1)**		ONOM	131
prʕ (A)	first fruit, early fruit	**|p-r-ʕ| (1)**	CTX		132
prʕ (B)	first	**|p-r-ʕ| (1)**	CTX		132
prʕt	height, peak	**|p-r-ʕ| (1)**	CTX		132
prd	mule	**|p-r-d| (1)**	CTX	ONOM	132
prγθ	flea	**|p-r-γ-θ|**		ONOM	133
prx	blossom, sprout, shoot	**|p-r-x|**	CTX	ONOM	133
prḳt	a kind of cloth or fabric	**|p-r-ḳ| (1)**	CTX		134

<table>
<tr><td>prln</td><td>seer, diviner</td><td>|p-r(-l-n)|</td><td>CTX</td><td></td><td>134</td></tr>
<tr><td>prs (A)</td><td>a part of a chariot</td><td>|p-r-s| (1)</td><td>CTX</td><td></td><td>135</td></tr>
<tr><td>prs (B),
prS</td><td>a dry measure</td><td>|p-r-s| (2)</td><td>CTX</td><td></td><td>135</td></tr>
<tr><td>prS
See prs (B), prS</td><td></td><td></td><td></td><td></td><td></td></tr>
<tr><td>prst</td><td>a bowl (?)</td><td>|p-r-s-y|</td><td>CTX</td><td></td><td>137</td></tr>
<tr><td>prṣ</td><td>breach, opening</td><td>|p-r-ṣ|</td><td>CTX</td><td></td><td>137</td></tr>
<tr><td>prt</td><td>heifer</td><td>|p-r-r| (1)</td><td>CTX</td><td>ONOM</td><td>135</td></tr>
<tr><td>prṭl</td><td>a kind of turban</td><td>|p-D-l|</td><td>CTX</td><td></td><td>121</td></tr>
<tr><td>prθt</td><td>a portion (of meat) (?)</td><td>|p-r-θ|</td><td>CTX</td><td></td><td>137</td></tr>
<tr><td>prz</td><td>decision, verdict (?)</td><td>|p-r-s| (3)</td><td>CTX</td><td></td><td>136</td></tr>
<tr><td>psħn</td><td>lame, limp</td><td>|p-s-ħ|</td><td></td><td>ONOM</td><td>138</td></tr>
<tr><td>psl</td><td>engraver</td><td>|p-s-l|</td><td>CTX</td><td></td><td>138</td></tr>
<tr><td>pslt</td><td>sculpture</td><td>|p-s-l|</td><td>CTX</td><td></td><td>138</td></tr>
<tr><td>psm</td><td>a garment or a part thereof (?)</td><td>|p-s-m|</td><td>CTX</td><td></td><td>139</td></tr>
<tr><td>ps^{1}ʕ</td><td>rebellion, transgression</td><td>|p-s^1-ʕ|</td><td>CTX</td><td></td><td>139</td></tr>
<tr><td>ptħ</td><td>entrance, door</td><td>|p-t-ħ|</td><td>CTX</td><td></td><td>141</td></tr>
<tr><td>pṭr</td><td>breach, aperture</td><td>|p-ṭ-r|</td><td>CTX</td><td></td><td>142</td></tr>
<tr><td>pθt (A)</td><td>flax; linen (fabric)</td><td>|p-θ|</td><td>CTX</td><td></td><td>143</td></tr>
<tr><td>pθt (B)</td><td>ointment box</td><td>|p-θ-θ|</td><td>CTX</td><td></td><td>143</td></tr>
<tr><td>pθ̣γ</td><td>lacerator</td><td>|p-θ̣-ɣ|</td><td>CTX</td><td></td><td>143</td></tr>
<tr><td>pwt</td><td>madder</td><td>|p-w(-t)|</td><td>CTX</td><td></td><td>145</td></tr>
</table>

r

<table>
<tr><td>rỉb</td><td>compensation; plea</td><td>|r-y-b|</td><td>CTX</td><td></td><td>179</td></tr>
<tr><td>rỉdn</td><td>a large cup / DN (?)</td><td>|r-ʔ-d|</td><td>CTX</td><td></td><td>148</td></tr>
<tr><td>rỉmt</td><td>bull-headed harp</td><td>|r-ʔ-m| (1)</td><td>CTX</td><td></td><td>148</td></tr>
<tr><td>rỉs^1</td><td>head, chief, top, first(fruit)</td><td>|r-ʔ-s^1|</td><td>CTX</td><td>ONOM</td><td>149</td></tr>
<tr><td>rỉs^{1}yt</td><td>beginning, primordial time</td><td>|r-ʔ-s^1|</td><td>CTX</td><td></td><td>149</td></tr>
<tr><td>rủm</td><td>wild bull, buffalo</td><td>|r-ʔ-m| (1)</td><td>CTX</td><td></td><td>148</td></tr>
<tr><td>rủs^1</td><td>disease of the head (?)</td><td>|r-ʔ-s^1|</td><td>CTX</td><td></td><td>149</td></tr>
<tr><td>rʕ</td><td>friend, companion</td><td>|r-ʕ|</td><td>CTX</td><td>ONOM</td><td>150</td></tr>
<tr><td>rʕy</td><td>shepherd</td><td>|r-ʕ-y| (1)</td><td>CTX</td><td>ONOM</td><td>150</td></tr>
<tr><td>rʕt</td><td>terrific shouting</td><td>|r-w-ʕ|</td><td>CTX</td><td></td><td>174</td></tr>
<tr><td>rb (A),
rp</td><td>great, large; chief, grandee</td><td>|r-b-b| (1),
|r-b-y|</td><td>CTX</td><td>ONOM</td><td>152</td></tr>
<tr><td>rb (B),
rbb</td><td>type of dew, drizzle</td><td>|r-b-b| (1),
|r-b-y|</td><td>CTX</td><td></td><td>152</td></tr>
</table>

rbʕ	fourth	**|r-b-ʕ|**	CTX		151
rbʕt	a fourth, quarter	**|r-b-ʕ|**	CTX		151
rbbt See *rbt* (B), *rbbt*					
rbṣ	'the lurker', an inspector	**|r-b-ṣ|**	CTX		154
rbt (B), rbbt	myriad	**|r-b-b| (1), |r-b-y|**	CTX		153
rbt (C)	kind of fisherman's net (?)	**|r-b-b| (2)**	CTX		153
rgbt	respect, fear	**|r-g-b|**	CTX		156
rγbn	hunger	**|r-γ-b|**	CTX		157
rħ (A)	millstone	**|r-ħ-y|**	CTX		161
rħ (B), rx	wind	**|r-w-ħ|**	CTX		175
rħ (C)	aroma, perfume	**|r-w-ħ|**	CTX		175
rħb (A)	wide	**|r-ħ-b|**	CTX	ONOM	158
rħb (B)	width	**|r-ħ-b|**	CTX		158
rħbt	amphora, jar	**|r-ħ-b|**	CTX		158
rħḳ	distant	**|r-ħ-ḳ|**	CTX		159
rħm	womb; nubile girl, damsel	**|r-ħ-m|**	CTX	ONOM	160
rħt	palm of the hand	**|r-ħ|**	CTX		158
rx See *rħ* (B), *rx*					
rxnt	sweetness, tenderness (?)	**|r-x-w|**	CTX		162
rkb (A)	upper grindstone	**|r-k-b|**	CTX		163
rkb (B)	charioteer	**|r-k-b|**	CTX		163
rkb (C)	(an element of the) harness	**|r-k-b|**	CTX		163
rks	belt	**|r-k-S|**	CTX		164
rḳ (A)	fine, thin	**|r-ḳ-ḳ| (1)**	CTX		166
rḳ (B)	sheet	**|r-ḳ-ḳ| (1)**	CTX		166
rḳħ (A)	perfume, ointment	**|r-ḳ-ħ|**			165
rḳħ (B)	perfumer, druggist	**|r-ḳ-ħ|**	CTX		165
rḳt	temple	**|r-ḳ-ḳ| (1)**	CTX		166
rm (A)	high, exalted	**|r-w/y-m|**	CTX	ONOM	177
rm (B)	rising, height (?)	**|r-w/y-m|**	CTX		177
rmṣ	embers, hot stones	**|r-m-ṣ|**	CTX		168
rmθt	a vessel (?)	**|r-m-θ|**	CTX		168
rp See *rb* (A), *rp*					
rpů	healer (ancestral hero; DN)	**|r-p-ʔ|**	CTX	ONOM	170
rps¹	wide, generous; open country	**|r-p-s¹|**	CTX	ONOM	171

rs^1ʕ	bad person	**|r-s^1-ʕ|**	CTX			172
rs^1p	flame, blaze; DN	**|r-S-p|**		LL	ONOM	172
rṯ	(seamless) tunic, veil	**|r-y-ṯ|**	CTX			180
rθ(n)	dirt	**|r-w-θ|**	CTX			177
rθt	net	**|r-S-y|**	CTX			173

s

sỉd	chief butler	**|s-H-d|**	CTX			191
sỉn	hem, trimming	**|s-ʔ-n| (1)**	CTX			183
sỉp	who chews, grinds (?)	**|s-ʔ-p|**			ONOM	183
sbbyn	black cumin	**|S-b-b-y-n|**	CTX			184
sbl, Sbl	prince (?)	**|S-b-l|**			ONOM	185
sbrdn	lancer, spear-bearer / maker (?)	**|s-p-r| (2)**	CTX			204
sbsg, spsg, SpSg	a glaze	**|S-B-S-G|**	CTX			186
sd	council (?)	**|s-w-d|**	CTX			209
sdn	a horse-cloth	**|S-d-n| (1)**	CTX			187
sglt	acquisition, treasure	**|s-G-l|**	CTX			189
sgr (A)	enclosure (?)	**|s-G-r|**	CTX			190
sgr (B)	sewn or decorated in a certain way	**|s-G-r|**	CTX			190
sgrt	room, chamber	**|s-G-r|**	CTX			190
sγr, Sγr	servant, (shepherd-)boy	**|ṣ-γ-r|**	CTX			217
sxl	grinder, polisher, engraver (?)	**|s-x-l|**	CTX			192
sk (A)	coverlet, cloak; lid(?)	**|s-k-k| (1)**	CTX			193
sk (B)	den, cove	**|s-k-k| (1)**	CTX			193
skn (A)	dangerous moment	**|s-k-n| (1)**	CTX			194
skn (B)	stela	**|s-k-k| (2)**	CTX			194
skn (C), Skn	provisor; prefect, governor	**|s^1-k-n|**	CTX			243
sknt	form	**|s^1-k-n|**	CTX			243
skr	bolt	**|s-G-r|**	CTX			190
slʕ	cliff, rock (?)	**|s-l-ʕ|**	CTX			195
slx	a certain material for sacrifice (?)	**|S-l-x|**	CTX			195
slm	staircase (?)	**|s-l-m| (2)**	CTX			197
sm	perfume	**|s-m-m|**	CTX			199
smd	bead, pearl (necklace)	**|s-m-d| (2)**	CTX			198
smkt	height, ceiling	**|s-m-k|**	CTX			199

sn	the moon(-god)	**|s-y-n|**	CTX		211
snnt	swallow	**|s-n-n|**	CTX		201
snr, **Snr**	cat (?)	**|S-n-r|**, **|S-r-n| (1)**		ONOM	201
sp	bowl	**|s-p-p| (1)**	CTX		203
spl	platter, tray	**|s-p-l|**	CTX		203
spr (A)	scribe	**|S-p-r| (1)**	CTX		204
spr (B)	tablet, writing, letter	**|S-p-r| (1)**	CTX		204
spr (C)	number, inventory	**|S-p-r| (1)**	CTX		204
spr(D)	bronze	**|s-p-r| (2)**	CTX		204
sprt	instruction, prescription	**|S-p-r| (1)**	CTX		204
spsg See *sbsg*, *spsg*, *SpSg*					
srd	olive orchard (?)	**|s-r-d| (1)**		ONOM	205
srdnn	type of projectile or missile	**|s-r-d-n-n|**	CTX		205
srn	prince (?)	**|S-r-n| (2)**	CTX		206
srr	sunset (?)	**|s-r-r| (2)**		ONOM	207
ssn	date-palm branch	**|s-n-s-n|**			201
ssw, **SSw**	horse	**|s-w-s-w|**	CTX	ONOM	210
sswt	mare (?)	**|s-w-s-w|**	CTX		210

S (ś)

Sbl See *sbl*, *Sbl*					
Sγr See **sγr**, **Sγr**					
Skn See *skn* (C), *Skn*					
Snr See *snr*, *Snr*					
SpSg See *sbsg*, *spsg*, *SpSg*					
SSw See *ssw*, *SSw*					
Sst	baseboard, floor (of a chariot)	**|S-s-s|**	CTX		209

ṣ

ṣỉn	small cattle, sheep	**|ṣ́-ʔ-n|**	CTX	ONOM	283
ṣʕ	plate, bassin	**|ṣ-w-ʕ|**	CTX		225
ṣʕṣ	terror, agitation (?)	**|ṣ-ʕ-ṣ|**	CTX		213
ṣbủ (A)	troops, army	**|ṣ́-b-ʔ|**	CTX		284
ṣbủ (B)	ducking, setting	**|ṣ́-b-ʔ|**	CTX		284
ṣbr	field rich in thyme	**|z-b-b-r|**	CTX		382
ṣbrt	clan, community	**|ṣ́-b-r|**	CTX		284
ṣd (A)	hunt, game	**|ṣ-w/y-d|**	CTX		225
ṣd (B)	roamer, vagrant (?)	**|ṣ-w/y-d|**			225
ṣdḳ (A)	justice, legitimacy; DN	**|ṣ-d-ḳ|**	CTX	ONOM	215
ṣdḳ (B)	lawful, righteous; DN	**|ṣ-d-ḳ|**	CTX	ONOM	215
ṣdt	roaming, hunting party (?)	**|ṣ-w/y-d|**	CTX		225
ṣγr	small, of tender years, young	**|ṣ-γ-r|**	CTX	ONOM	216
ṣγrt (A)	girl, youngest, small, of tender years	**|ṣ-γ-r|**	CTX		216
ṣγrt (B)	babyhood, tender years, infancy (?)	**|ṣ-γ-r|**	CTX		216
ṣḥḳ	laughter	**|ṣ́-ḥ-ḳ|**	CTX		285
ṣḳ	distressed (?)	**|ṣ́-w/y-ḳ|**	CTX		288
ṣlʕ	rib, chops	**|ṣ́-l-ʕ|**	CTX		285
ṣlm	image, statue (?)	**|ṣ-l-m|**	CTX		217
ṣlt	prayer	**|ṣ-l-w/y|**	CTX		218
ṣly	prayer, spell (?)	**|ṣ-l-w/y|**	CTX		218
ṣmd	pair, team; ‘yoke’	**|ṣ́-m-d|**	CTX		286
ṣmḳ	raisin	**|ṣ-m-ḳ|**	CTX		218
ṣml	dried out (barley) draff (?)	**|ṣ-m-l|**	CTX		218
ṣmrt	weatlth; the highest, utmost good (?)	**|ṣ-m-r|**		ONOM	219
ṣmt	disappearance, destruction	**|ṣ-m-t| (1)**	CTX		219
ṣn	protection, shelter (?)	**|ṣ-n-n| (1), |ṣ-w-n|**		ONOM	219
ṣnr	fast-flowing stream (?)	**|ṣ-n-r|**		ONOM	220
ṣp (A)	embroidered garment	**|ṣ-p-y| (1)**	CTX		221
ṣp (B)	look, glance	**|ṣ-p-y| (2)**	CTX		222
ṣp (C)	white ewe	**|ṣ-p-p|**	CTX		221
ṣpn	the mountain dwelling of Baʕl;	**ṣ-p-n| (1)**		ONOM	221

	DN				
ṣrdt	a large group (of servants) (?)	**|ṣ-r-d|**	CTX		222
ṣrp	reddish dye	**|ṣ-r-p|**	CTX		223
ṣrr	corn (ear with its husk ?)	**|ṣ-r-r| (4)**	CTX		224
ṣrrt	height(s)	**|ṣ-r-r| (2), |ṣ-y-r|**	CTX		224
ṣrry	height(s)	**|ṣ-r-r| (2), |ṣ-y-r|**	CTX		224
ṣrt	enmity, enemy	**|ṣ́-r-r|**	CTX		287
ṣrṭn	little farter	**|ṣ́-r-ṭ|**		ONOM	287
ṣt	a garment (?)	**|w-ṣ́-ʔ|**	CTX		362

s^1 (š)

s^1=	he of	**|s^1|**		ONOM	228
s^1	ram; sheep	**|s^2-w|**	CTX		280
s^{1}ảb, s^{1}ỉb, s^{1}ỉbt	water bearer, water carrier	**|s^1-ʔ-b|**	CTX		229
s^{1}ảl	claim, demand	**|s^1-ʔ-l|**	CTX		230
s^{1}ỉb See *s^{1}ảb, s^{1}ỉb, s^{1}ỉbt*					
s^{1}ỉbt See *s^{1}ảb, s^{1}ỉb, s^{1}ỉbt*					
s^{1}ỉl	interrogator, diviner	**|s^1-ʔ-l|**	CTX	ONOM	230
s^{1}ỉn	sandal(s); rim(?)	**|S-ʔ-n| (2)**			183
s^{1}ỉr (A)	flesh	**|s^1-ʔ-r| (2)**	CTX		231
s^{1}ỉr (B)	unit of area measure	**|s^1-ʔ-r| (3)**	CTX		231
s^{1}ỉy	murderer	**|s^1-ʔ-y|**	CTX		231
s^{1}ủrt	a weapon (?)	**|S-(w-)r|**	CTX		209
s^{1}ʕr	hair, pelisse	**|s^2-ʕ-r| (1)**	CTX		270
s^{1}ʕrm	barley	**|s^2-ʕ-r| (2)**	CTX		271
s^{1}ʕrt	wool, woollen textile	**|s^2-ʕ-r| (1)**	CTX		271
s^{1}b	old man, elderly man	**|s^2-y-b|**	CTX		281
s^{1}bʕ (A)	seven	**|s^1-b-ʕ|**	CTX		232
s^{1}bʕ (B)	seventh	**|s^1-b-ʕ|**	CTX		232
s^{1}bʕ(ỉ)d	seven times	**|ʔ-ð|, |s^1-b-ʕ|**	CTX		I:11 232
s^{1}bʕm	seventy	**|s^1-b-ʕ|**	CTX		232
s^{1}bb	spark, flame; DN (?)	**|S-b-b| (1)**		ONOM	184

s^{1}bħ See *s^{1}pħ*, *s^{1}bħ*, *θpħ*						
s^{1}blt	ear, spike	**|s^{1}-b-l|**	CTX			233
s^{1}bm	muzzle (?)	**|s^{2}-b-m|**	CTX			272
s^{1}br	stick, staff	**|s^{1}-b-r| (1)**	CTX			233
s^{1}bt	greyness, old age	**|s^{2}-y-b|**	CTX			281
s^{1}by	captive	**|s^{1}-b-y| (2)**	CTX			234
s^{1}d (A)	open field, field, steppe, mountain; DN	**|s^{2}-d-w|**	CTX		ONOM	273
s^{1}d (B)	a measure of area	**|s^{1}-d-d|**	CTX			234
s^{1}d (C)	demon; DN	**|s^{1}-ʕ-d|**	CTX			231
s^{1}dmt	terrace	**|s^{1}-d-m|**	CTX			235
s^{1}dy	land labourer, mountain-dweller (?)	**|s^{2}-d-w|**	CTX			273
s^{1}gr	offspring of cattle; DN	**|s^{1}-g-r| (2)**	CTX			237
s^{1}ħlmmt	Mortality	**|m-w-t|,**			ONOM	64
	Shore (?)	**|s^{1}-ħ-l| (1)**				238
s^{1}ħlt	cress seeds (?)	**|θ-ħ-l|**	CTX			318
s^{1}ħr	dawn; DN	**|s^{1}-ħ-r| (1)**	CTX		ONOM	238
s^{1}ħt	shrub, bush	**|s^{2}-ħ-t|**	CTX			274
s^{1}xp	weakness, thinness / colostrum (?)	**|s^{1}-x-p|**	CTX			239
s^{1}xṭ	butcher, slaughterer	**|s^{1}-x-ṭ|**	CTX			240
s^{1}km	one who brays	**|s^{1}-G-m|**	CTX			236
s^{1}kr	a kind of container	**|s^{1}-G-r| (1)**	CTX			236
s^{1}krn	intoxication	**|s^{1}-k-r| (2)**	CTX			244
s^{1}ḳ	thigh, leg	**|s^{1}-w-ḳ| (1)**	CTX			265
s^{1}ḳy	cupbearer, wine waiter (?)	**|s^{1}-ḳ-y|**	CTX			246
s^{1}lħ	sword; DN (?)	**|s^{1}-ħ-l| (2), |s^{1}-l-ħ|**			ONOM	238
s^{1}lħmt	provisions, victuals	**|l-ħ-m| (1)**	CTX			12
s^{1}lm (A)	friendly; DN Dusk	**|s-l-m| (1)**	CTX	LL	ONOM	197
s^{1}lm (B)	well-being, health	**|s^{1}-l-m|**				248
s^{1}lm (C)	a type of sacrifice	**|s^{1}-l-m|**	CTX			248
s^{1}lm (D)	pure	**|s^{1}-l-m|**	CTX			248
s^{1}lmn	(little) friend	**|s-l-m| (1)**			ONOM	198
s^{1}lmt (A)	well-being, health	**|s^{1}-l-m|**	CTX			248
s^{1}lmt (B)	compensation	**|s^{1}-l-m|**	CTX			248
s^{1}lyṭ	tyrant, powerful	**|s^{1}-l-ṭ|**	CTX			249
s^{1}m	name, posterity,	**|s^{1}-m| (1)**	CTX			251

	community, DN				
s^{1}mål	left (hand, side)	**|s^2-m-ʔ-l|**	CTX		276
s^{1}mʕ	auditor	**|s^1-m-ʕ|**	CTX		252
s^{1}mħ	stately, luxuriant (?)	**|s^1-m-x| (2)**		ONOM	253
s^{1}mxt	joy	**|s^1-m-x| (1)**	CTX		253
s^{1}ml	commercial agent, assistant (?)	**|s^1-m-l-l|**	CTX	ONOM	253
s^{1}mm	heavens, sky	**|s^1-m-w/y|**	CTX	ONOM	256
s^{1}mn (A)	oil, fat, butter	**|s^1-m-n|**	CTX	ONOM	254
s^{1}mn (B)	fat, fatling	**|s^1-m-n|**	CTX		254
s^{1}mrr (A)	expulsion, repelling (?)	**|m-r(-r)| (1)**	CTX		48
s^{1}mrr (B)	poisoning, poison (?)	**|m-r(-r)| (2)**	CTX		50
s^{1}mt (A)	fat, grease	**|s^1-m-n|**	CTX		255
s^{1}mt (B)	reddish shade	**|S-y-m|**	CTX		210
s^{1}mtr	cutting	**|m-t-r|**	CTX	ONOM	59
s^{1}n	tooth; ivory	**|s^1-n-n|**	CTX		257
s^{1}nů	enemy	**|s^2-n-ʔ|**	CTX		276
s^{1}nm	DN	**|s^1-n-m|**		ONOM	256
s^{1}npt	the raising (a type of offering)	**|n-w-p|**	CTX		113
s^{1}nt (A)	year	**|s^1-n| (2)**	CTX		256
s^{1}nt (B)	sleep	**|w-s^1-n|**	CTX		359
s^{1}p	tableland, dune (?)	**|s^1-p-y|**	CTX		259
s^{1}pħ, s^{1}bħ, θpħ	family, stock	**|S-p-ħ|**	CTX		202
s^{1}pr	horn(ed animal) (?)	**|s^1-p(-p)-r|**	CTX		258
s^{1}ps^1	sun; the Sun (DN and royal title)	**|S-m-s^1|**	CTX	ONOM	200
s^{1}pt	lip	**|s^2-p|**	CTX		276
s^{1}r (A)	navel	**|s^1-r-r| (1)**	CTX		260
s^{1}r (B)	prince, sovereign; DN	**|s^2-r-r-|**	CTX	ONOM	278
s^{1}r (C)	song	**|s^1-y-r| (1)**	CTX		268
s^{1}r (D)	musician, singer	**|s^1-y-r| (1)**	CTX		268
s^{1}r (E)	violence, vehemence (?)	**|s^1-w-r| (1)**	CTX		266
s^{1}rʕ	storm, gale (?)	**|s^2-ʕ-r| (3)**	CTX		271
s^{1}rp	burnt sacrifice	**|s^2-r-p|**	CTX		277
s^{1}rr	enemy	**|s^1-w-r| (1)**	CTX		266
s^{1}rs^1	root, offspring	**|s^2-r-s^1|**	CTX	ONOM	279
s^{1}rt	dart-thrower squad (?)	**|s^1-r-w/y|**	CTX		262
s^{1}s^{1}lmt	supplementary delivery or ration	**|s^1-l-m|**	CTX		248
s^{1}s^{1}mn	sesame / linseed(s)	**|s^1-m-s^1-m| (2)**	CTX		255

s^{1}s^{1}r	reddish colouring agent, (?) minium	**|s^1-r-s^1-r| (1)**	CTX		261
s^{1}s^{1}rt	chain	**|s^1-r-s^1-r| (1)**	CTX		261
s^{1}t (A)	base, foot	**|s^1-t|**	CTX		263
s^{1}t (B)	measure of capacity	**|S-ʔ|**	CTX		182
s^{1}t (C)	dame, lady	**|s^1-y-d|**	CTX		267
s^{1}tt	spun, woven (wool)	**|s^1-t-y| (2)**	CTX		264

t

tảr	glory, splendour (?)	**|t-ʔ-r|**	CTX		290
tʕdt	embassy, accreditatio	**|w-ʕ-d|**	CTX		338
tbk	a kind of leather	**|t-b-k| (2)**	CTX		291
tbl	blacksmith, smelter (of metal)	**|t-b-l|**	CTX		291
tbθx	bed	**|p-s^1-ħ|**	CTX		139
tbtx	skewer, skewered meat (?)	**|p-t-x|**	CTX		141
tγpθ	a type of (felt-)rug	**|t-γ-p-θ|**	CTX		292
thm	primordial ocean, abyss, DN	**|t-h-m|**	CTX		292
thmt	primordial ocean, abyss	**|t-h-m|**	CTX		292
thw	steppe, desert	**|t-h-w|**	CTX		293
tħt	under, beneath; underneath	**|t-ħ-t|**	CTX		293
tħtn	lower	**|t-ħ-t|**	CTX		293
tħty	lower	**|t-ħ-t|**	CTX		293
tk	centre, middle	**|t-w-k|**	CTX		303
tkyγ	a type of harness or trappings	**|t-k-k| (1)**	CTX		294
tkn	inspector, measurer (?)	**|t-k/ḳ-n|**	CTX		294
tky	inner	**|t-w-k|**	CTX		303
tḳʕt	she who applauds; DN (?)	**|t-ḳ-ʕ|**		ONOM	295
tḳn	perfect, straight	**t-k/ḳ-n|**		ONOM	294
tl (A)	holder, strap; weapon	**|t-l-l/y|**	CTX		296
tl (B)	hill	**|t-l-l| (3)**	CTX		297
tlỉyt	victory	**|l-ʔ-w/y| (A)**	CTX		7
tlʕ	nipple, pectoral(s)	**|t-l-ʕ|**	CTX		295
tlm (A)	furrow (?)	**|t-l-m| (1)**	CTX		296
tlm (B)	nice, lovable (brother); own (?)	**|t-l-m| (2)**		ONOM	296
tlmd	trained, one being tamed	**|l-m-d|**	CTX		15

tm	complete, full	**|t-m-m|**	CTX	ONOM	297
tmn, tmnt	frame, form	**|m-w/y-n| (2)**	CTX	ONOM	62
tmnt See *tmn, tmnt*					
tmr	date palm	**|t-m-r| (1)**	CTX	ONOM	298
tmtxṣ	fight	**|m-x-ṣ|**	CTX		35
tmtt	team, crew	**|m-t|**	CTX		58
tmθl	equal amount, equivalent	**|m-θ-l|**	CTX		60
tnḳt (A)	scream (?)	**|n-w-ḳ|**	CTX		112
tnḳt (B)	lactation, nursing (?)	**|y-n-ḳ|**	CTX		374
tnmy	overflow (?)	**|n-m-y|**	CTX		96
tnn	dragon; DN	**|t-n-n-n|**	CTX	ONOM	298
tp (A)	drum, tambourine	**|t-p-p|**	CTX		299
tp (B)	beauty; countenance	**|w-p-y|**	CTX		352
tpħ	apple	**|t-p-ħ|**	CTX	ONOM	299
tps^{1}lt	oppression (?)	**|p-s^1-l|**	CTX		139
tr (A)	steering pole (chariot); log (?)	**|t-w-r|**	CTX		304
tr (B)	turtle dove	**|t-r(-r)| (3)**	CTX		301
trbṣ(t)	yard, stable; reserve	**|r-b-ṣ|**	CTX		155
trbyt	profit, interest	**|r-b-b| (1), |r-b-y|**	CTX		153
trdn, trtn	second in rank; younger	**|t-r-D-n|**	CTX		300
trħ	flask	**|t-r-ħ|**	CTX		300
trx	newlywed, groom	**|t-r-x| (1)**	CTX		300
trxt	dowry, bride price	**|t-r-x| (1)**	CTX		300
trḳ	a container (?)	**|r-ḳ-ḳ| (1)**	CTX		166
trmt	offering	**|r-w/y-m|**	CTX		177
trn	mast (of a ship)	**|t-r-n| (1)**	CTX		301
trr	a profession or social class	**|t-r-r| (2)**	CTX		301
trtn See *trdn, trtn*					
trθ	new wine; DN	**|(w/y)-r-θ|**	CTX		356
trθ̣θ̣	light march, speed (?)	**|r-w-θ̣|**	CTX		177
tsm	beauty	**|w-s-m|**	CTX		358
ts^{1}ʕ	nine	**|t-s^1-ʕ|**	CTX		303
ts^{1}ʕm	ninety	**|t-s^1-ʕ|**	CTX		303
ts^{1}lm	due, final payment	**|s^1-l-m|**	CTX		248
ts^{1}t	wish; proposal (?)	**|s^1-y-t|**	CTX		269
ts^{1}yt	roar, shouting (?)	**|s^1-w-y| (2)**	CTX		267

tθnt	a container	**|t-S-n|**	CTX		303
tyt	a plant / vegetable substance	**|t-y-t|**	CTX		305
tzγ	offering (table)	**|t-S|**	CTX		302
tznt	provisions	**|z-w-n|**	CTX		385

ṭ

ṭb	good, sweet, pleasant	**|ṭ-w/y-b|**	CTX		312
ṭbx	sacrificer	**|ṭ-b-x|**	CTX		307
ṭbn	sweetness	**|ṭ-w/y-b|**	CTX		312
ṭbt	well-being	**|ṭ-w/y-b|**	CTX		312
ṭhr, θ̣hr	pure, sparkling	**|ṭ-h-r|**	CTX		307
ṭħl	spleen	**|ṭ-ħ-l|**	CTX		308
ṭl	dew, (light) rain	**|ṭ-l-l|**	CTX	ONOM	309
ṭmθ	(menstrual) blood	**|ṭ-m-θ|**	CTX		309
ṭry	fresh, tender	**|ṭ-r-y| (2)**	CTX		311
ṭt	mud	**|ṭ-y-n|**	CTX		313

θ (t̲)

θår	protection (?)	**|θ-ʔ-r|**	CTX		315
θåt	ewe	**|θ-ʔ|**	CTX		315
θǐgt	neighing	**|θ-ʔ-g|**	CTX		315
θǐṭ	mud	**|θ-ʔ-ṭ|**	CTX		315
θʕ (A)	search, supervision, examination of the exta (?)	**|θ-ʕ-y|**	CTX		316
θʕ (B)	hero, noble (as title); DN	**|θ-w-ʕ|**	CTX		329
θʕl	fox	**|θ-ʕ-l(-b)|**		ONOM	316
θʕlb	fox	**|θ-ʕ-l(-b)|**		ONOM	316
θʕt	a container and measure of capacity	**|θ-ʕ-D| (2)**	CTX		315
θʕy	supervisor, examiner of the exta (?)	**|θ-ʕ-y|**	CTX	ONOM	317
θb	repetition, intercalary month	**|θ-w-b|**	CTX		330
θbr	opening	**|θ-b-r|**	CTX		317
θbrn	opening	**|θ-b-r|**	CTX		317
θbt	(family) seat, sitting (down)	**|w-θ-b|**	CTX		366
θd	breast, bosom, chest, teat, udder	**|S-d/ð|**	CTX		186
θdr	waitress, girl	**|θ-d-r|**	CTX		317

<table>
<tr><td>θdθ</td><td>sixth</td><td>|s^1-d-θ|</td><td>CTX</td><td></td><td>238</td></tr>
<tr><td>θγr (A)</td><td>gate, door</td><td>|θ-γ-r| (1)</td><td>CTX</td><td></td><td>318</td></tr>
<tr><td>θγr (B)</td><td>gatekeeper</td><td>|θ-γ-r| (1)</td><td>CTX</td><td>ONOM</td><td>318</td></tr>
<tr><td>θh</td><td>neighbour, neighbourhood (?)</td><td>|θ-h|</td><td>CTX</td><td></td><td>318</td></tr>
<tr><td>θkl</td><td>sterility, loss of children</td><td>|θ-k-l|</td><td>CTX</td><td></td><td>319</td></tr>
<tr><td>θkm</td><td>shoulder, top</td><td>|θ-k-m|</td><td>CTX</td><td></td><td>319</td></tr>
<tr><td>θkmt</td><td>she who carries on her shoulders, who shoulders</td><td>|θ-k-m|</td><td>CTX</td><td></td><td>319</td></tr>
<tr><td>θkt</td><td>adornment, jewellery (?)</td><td>|s^1-k-n|</td><td>CTX</td><td></td><td>244</td></tr>
<tr><td>θḳ</td><td>a cloth or fabric, sack</td><td>|S-ḳ-ḳ|</td><td>CTX</td><td></td><td>194</td></tr>
<tr><td>θḳb
See ʕθḳb, θḳb</td><td></td><td></td><td></td><td></td><td></td></tr>
<tr><td>θḳd</td><td>almond</td><td>|θ-ḳ-d| (2)</td><td>CTX</td><td>ONOM</td><td>320</td></tr>
<tr><td>θḳl</td><td>shekel</td><td>|θ-ḳ-l|</td><td>CTX</td><td>ONOM</td><td>321</td></tr>
<tr><td>θlb</td><td>flute</td><td>|θ-l-b|</td><td>CTX</td><td></td><td>321</td></tr>
<tr><td>θlħn</td><td>table</td><td>|θ-l-ħ-n|</td><td>CTX</td><td>ONOM</td><td>322</td></tr>
<tr><td>θlln</td><td>captive (?)</td><td>|θ-l-l|</td><td></td><td>ONOM</td><td>322</td></tr>
<tr><td>θllt</td><td>booty (?)</td><td>|θ-l-l|</td><td>CTX</td><td></td><td>322</td></tr>
<tr><td>θltx</td><td>arrow(head)</td><td>|θ-l-t-x|</td><td></td><td>ONOM</td><td>322</td></tr>
<tr><td>θlṭ</td><td>tyrant, powerful</td><td>|s^1-l-ṭ|</td><td></td><td>ONOM</td><td>249</td></tr>
<tr><td>θlθ (A)</td><td>three; set of three</td><td>|s^2-l-θ|</td><td>CTX</td><td></td><td>275</td></tr>
<tr><td>θlθ (B)</td><td>third</td><td>|s^2-l-θ|</td><td>CTX</td><td></td><td>275</td></tr>
<tr><td>θlθ (C)</td><td>third man</td><td>|s^2-l-θ|</td><td>CTX</td><td></td><td>275</td></tr>
<tr><td>θlθ (D)</td><td>triple, three times</td><td>|s^2-l-θ|</td><td>CTX</td><td></td><td>275</td></tr>
<tr><td>θlθ (E)</td><td>copper, bronze(-bolt)</td><td>|θ-l-θ|</td><td>CTX</td><td></td><td>323</td></tr>
<tr><td>θlθỉd</td><td>three times</td><td>|=(ỉ)d|,
|s^2-l-θ|</td><td>CTX</td><td></td><td>I:11
275</td></tr>
<tr><td>θlθm</td><td>thirty</td><td>|s^2-l-θ|</td><td>CTX</td><td></td><td>275</td></tr>
<tr><td>θm</td><td>there; then</td><td>|θ-m-m| (1)</td><td>CTX</td><td></td><td>323</td></tr>
<tr><td>θmdl</td><td>gapping (?)</td><td>|θ-d-l|</td><td>CTX</td><td></td><td>317</td></tr>
<tr><td>θmn (A)</td><td>eight</td><td>|θ-m-n-y|</td><td>CTX</td><td></td><td>323</td></tr>
<tr><td>θmn (B)</td><td>eighth</td><td>|θ-m-n-y|</td><td>CTX</td><td></td><td>323</td></tr>
<tr><td>θmnỉd</td><td>eight times</td><td>|=(ỉ)d|,
|θ-m-n-y|</td><td>CTX</td><td></td><td>I:11
323</td></tr>
<tr><td>θmnym</td><td>eighty</td><td>|θ-m-n-y|</td><td>CTX</td><td></td><td>323</td></tr>
<tr><td>θmr (A)</td><td>fennel (?)</td><td>|S-m-r| (3)</td><td>CTX</td><td></td><td>199</td></tr>
<tr><td>θmr (B)</td><td>crop(s), fruit(s)</td><td>|θ-m-r|</td><td></td><td>ONOM</td><td>324</td></tr>
<tr><td>θn (A)</td><td>two</td><td>|θ-n|</td><td>CTX</td><td></td><td>324</td></tr>
<tr><td>θn (B)</td><td>second, vice-</td><td>|θ-n|</td><td>CTX</td><td>ONOM</td><td>324</td></tr>
<tr><td>θn (C)</td><td>crimson, scarlet</td><td>|θ-n-y|</td><td>CTX</td><td>ONOM</td><td>325</td></tr>
<tr><td>θnỉd</td><td>twice</td><td>|=(ỉ)d|,
|θ-n|</td><td>CTX</td><td></td><td>I:11
325</td></tr>
<tr><td>θnγly</td><td>deputy, second</td><td>|θ-n|</td><td>CTX</td><td></td><td>325</td></tr>
</table>

θnn	a class-designation (archer?)	**|θ-n-n|**	CTX		325
θnt	urine	**|θ-y-n|**	CTX		331
θpħ See *s^1pħ*, *s^1bħ*, *θpħ*					
θprt	a woman's intimate garment	**|θ-p-r|**	CTX		326
θpṭ (A)	lawsuit, judgement	**|θ-p-ṭ|**	CTX	ONOM	327
θpṭ (B), **θpθ̣**	judge, ruler	**|θ-p-ṭ|**	CTX		327
θpθ̣ See *θpṭ* (B), *θpθ̣*					
θr (A) See *ðr*, *θr* (A)					
θr (B)	bull; DN	**|θ-w-r|**	CTX	ONOM	331
θr (C)	a vegetable product (?)	**|θ-r| (1)**	CTX		327
θr (D)	a bird(?)	**|θ-r| (2)**	CTX		327
θrml	a noble material	**|θ-r-m-l|**	CTX		328
θrmn (A)	royal	**|s^2-r-r|**	CTX		278
θrmn (B)	cypress (?)	**|S-r-m-n|**		ONOM	206
θrmt	meat, victuals	**|S-r-m|**	CTX		206
θrn	a vegetable product (?)	**|θ-r-n|**	CTX		328
θrrt See *θrry* (A), *θrrt*					
θrry (A), **θrrt**	powerful (?)	**|s^2-r-r-|**	CTX	ONOM	278
θrry (B)	baby, infant	**|θ-r-r|**		ONOM	328
θrt	abundance	**|θ-r-y| (1)**	CTX		328
θrtn	a kind of bailiff / sheriff (?)	**|θ-r-t-n-n|**	CTX		328
θryn	(suit of) armour, protective padding	**|S-r-(y-)n|**	CTX	ONOM	208
θtḳt	she who splits (?)	**|θ-t-ḳ|**		ONOM	329
θṭ	a piece of cloth or a garment	**|θ-n-ṭ|**	CTX		325
θθ	six	**|s^1-d-θ|**	CTX		236
θθm	sixty	**|s^1-d-θ|**	CTX		236

θ̣ (ẓ)

θ̣ů	secretion, excrement	**|θ̣-y|**	CTX		335

θ̣by	gazelle	**|θ̣-b-y|**	CTX		332
θ̣br	clan, community (?)	**|ṣ-b-r|**		ONOM	284
θ̣hr See *ṭhr*, *θ̣hr*					
θ̣l	shade, reflection sheen, spirit	**|θ̣-l-l|**	CTX	ONOM	333
θ̣lmt	darkness	**|θ̣-l-m|**	CTX		334
θ̣m	fasting	**|ṣ-w-m|**	CTX		226
θ̣mn	fastener (?)	**|ṣ-w-m|**		ONOM	226
θ̣pr	(sharp) claw(ed)	**|θ̣-p-r|**	CTX	ONOM	334
θ̣r	back	**|θ̣-h-r|**	CTX	ONOM	334
θ̣rw	(aromatic) resin, balsam	**|ṣ-r-w|**	CTX		288

w

w	and (also); namely, or (else)	**|w|**	CTX		337
wry	a type of boat	**|w-r-y| (2)**	CTX		356

y

=y (A)	my, mine, (...) me	**|y| (1)**	CTX		369
=y (B)	(is really, indeed!)	**|y| (2)**	CTX	ONOM	369
y	oh!, woe!	**|y| (3)**	CTX		369
yʕb	ample, wide	**|w-ʕ-b|**		ONOM	337
yʕl	mountain goat	**|w-ʕ-l| (1)**	CTX	ONOM	338
yʕr [A]	razor	**|ʕ-r|(?)**	CTX		I:86
yʕr (B)	wood, thicket; rugged, coarse	**|w-ʕ-r| (2)**	CTX	ONOM	339
yʕrt	wood, thicket	**|w-ʕ-r| (2)**		ONOM	339
ybl (A)	produce	**|w-b-l| (1)**	CTX		340
ybl (B)	rod	**|w-b-l| (1)**	CTX		340
yblt	flowing current, stream	**|w-b-l| (1)**	CTX		240
ybm	brother-in-law	**|w-b-m|**	CTX		341
ybmt	widow sister-in-law, nubile widow	**|w-b-m|**	CTX		341
yd (A)	hand, power, portion	**|y-d|**	CTX	ONOM	371
yd (B)	love	**|w-d-d|**	CTX		344
ydd	the loved one	**|w-d-d|**	CTX	ONOM	344
ydt	she who casts out, expels	**|w-d-y| (1)**	CTX		344
ydy (A)	one who casts out, expels	**|w-d-y| (1)**	CTX		344
ydy (B)	banishment	**|w-d-y| (1)**	CTX		344
ydyt	untilled, barren	**|w-d-y| (1)**	CTX		344

ygb	a commodity	**|y-G-B|**	CTX		371
yγl	poor, barren land	**|w-γ-l|**	CTX		346
yħd	solitary, single	**|w-ħ-d|**	CTX		347
yħdh See *àħdh, yħdh*					
yḳr	(most) dear, esteemed	**|w-ḳ-r|**		ONOM	349
yḳs¹ (A)	fowler, bird-catcher	**|y-ḳ-s¹|**	CTX	ONOM	372
yḳs¹ (B)	game (?)	**|y-ḳ-s¹|**	CTX		372
yld	son; young (animal)	**|w-l-d|**	CTX		353
yly	comrade, companion	**|w-l-y|**	CTX	ONOM	353
ym (A)	(primeval) sea; DN	**|y-m-m|**	CTX	ONOM	373
ym (B)	day	**|y-w-m|**	CTX		380
ymn	right (side, hand)	**|y-m-n|**	CTX		373
yn	wine	**|w-y-n|**	CTX	ONOM	366
ynḳ	who sucks, suckling	**|y-n-ḳ|**	CTX		374
ynt	dove	**|y-w-n|**	CTX		380
yp	beauty, dignity	**|w-p-y|**	CTX	ONOM	352
ypħ	witness	**|y-p-ħ|**	CTX		375
ypt	cow, yearling calf	**|y-p-n|**	CTX	ONOM	376
yr	early rain	**|w-r-y| (1)**	CTX		356
yrdt	step, stair	**|w-r-d| (2)**	CTX		353
yrx	(new) moon, DN; month	**|w-r-x|**	CTX	ONOM	353
yrk	body back part, flank; side	**|w-r-k|**	CTX		354
yrkt	support, thigh (?)	**|w-r-k|**	CTX		354
yrḳ	greenish yellow (gold)	**|w-r-ḳ|**	CTX		354
yrḳn	garden, orchard	**|w-r-ḳ|**		ONOM	355
yrθ	heir	**|w-r-θ| (1)**	CTX	ONOM	355
yryt	coral (?)	**|y-r-yǂ**	CTX		376
ysd, ySd	base	**|w-s-d|**		ONOM	357
ySd See *ysd, ySd*					
ysm (A)	handsome, pleasant	**|w-s-m|**	CTX		357
ysm (B)	elegance (?)	**|w-s-m|**	CTX		357
ysmsm	most handsome	**|w-s-m|**	CTX		357
ysmsmt	exceptional handsomeness	**|w-s-m|**	CTX		357
ysmt	handsomeness, beauty	**|w-s-m|**	CTX		357
yṣů	exit, departure	**|w-ṣ-ʔ|**	CTX		362

yṣḥ	bleacher	**|w-ṣ̌-ḥ|**	CTX		362
yṣr	potter	**|w-ṣ-r|**	CTX	ONOM	359
ys¹r	justice, uprightness	**|y-s¹-r|**	CTX	ONOM	377
ytm	orphan	**|y-t-m|**	CTX		378
ytmt	orphan girl	**|y-t-m|**	CTX		378
ytn	a group or social class	**|n/w/y-D-n|**	CTX		79
ytnt	gift, offering	**|n/w/y-D-n|**	CTX		79
ytr	excellent, outstanding	**|w-t-r| (2)**		ONOM	364
yθb	assistant	**|w-θ-b|**	CTX		365
yθbt	residence, dwelling	**|w-θ-b|**	CTX		365
yθn	old, rancid	**|y-θ-n|**	CTX		379
yw	Sea (?), DN	**|y-m-m|**		ONOM	373

z

zbl (A)	prince	**|S-b-l|**	CTX		185
zbl (B)	principality	**|S-b-l|**	CTX		185
zbl (C)	one carried, an invalid person	**|S-b-l|**	CTX		185
zbln	sickness, illness	**|S-b-l|**	CTX		185
zd	breast, chest	**|S-d/ð|**	CTX		187
zγt	howl, bark	**|z-γ-w|**	CTX		382
zn	provider, supplies official	**|z-w-n|**	CTX		385
znt	sustenance, provision(s)	**|z-w-n|**	CTX		385
ztr	cippus, votive stela	**|S-t-r| (2)**	CTX		209
zt	olive, olive tree(s)	**|z-y-t|**	CTX		387